1,000,000 Books

are available to read at

www.ForgottenBooks.com

Read online
Download PDF
Purchase in print

ISBN 978-0-331-49512-6
PIBN 11085062

This book is a reproduction of an important historical work. Forgotten Books uses
state-of-the-art technology to digitally reconstruct the work, preserving the original format
whilst repairing imperfections present in the aged copy. In rare cases, an imperfection in
the original, such as a blemish or missing page, may be replicated in our edition. We do,
however, repair the vast majority of imperfections successfully; any imperfections that
remain are intentionally left to preserve the state of such historical works.

Forgotten Books is a registered trademark of FB &c Ltd.
Copyright © 2018 FB &c Ltd.
FB &c Ltd, Dalton House, 60 Windsor Avenue, London, SW19 2RR.
Company number 08720141. Registered in England and Wales.

For support please visit www.forgottenbooks.com

1 MONTH OF
FREE
READING

at
www.ForgottenBooks.com

By purchasing this book you are
eligible for one month membership to
ForgottenBooks.com, giving you
unlimited access to our entire
collection of over 1,000,000 titles via
our web site and mobile apps.

To claim your free month visit:
www.forgottenbooks.com/free1085062

* Offer is valid for 45 days from date of purchase. Terms and conditions apply.

English
Français
Deutsche
Italiano
Español
Português

www.forgottenbooks.com

Mythology Photography **Fiction**
Fishing Christianity **Art** Cooking
Essays Buddhism Freemasonry
Medicine **Biology** Music **Ancient
Egypt** Evolution Carpentry Physics
Dance Geology **Mathematics** Fitness
Shakespeare **Folklore** Yoga Marketing
Confidence Immortality Biographies
Poetry **Psychology** Witchcraft
Electronics Chemistry History **Law**
Accounting **Philosophy** Anthropology
Alchemy Drama Quantum Mechanics
Atheism Sexual Health **Ancient History**
Entrepreneurship Languages Sport
Paleontology Needlework Islam
Metaphysics Investment Archaeology
Parenting Statistics Criminology
Motivational

60th Cong 1st Sess H. Doc. r. 43, 5312

DECISIONS

OF THE

COMMISSIONER OF PATENTS

IN

PATENT

AND

TRADE-MARK AND LABEL CASES

COMPILED FROM VOLS. 126, 127, 128, 129, 130, AND 131 OF THE
OFFICIAL GAZETTE OF THE UNITED STATES
PATENT OFFICE DURING THE YEAR

. 1907

WASHINGTON
GOVERNMENT PRINTING OFFICE
1908

COMMISSIONERS OF THE UNITED STATES PATENT OFFICE
DURING THE YEAR 1907,

HON. F. I. ALLEN,
TO MAY 31, 1907.

HON. E. B. MOORE,
FROM JUNE 1, 1907.

ASSISTANT COMMISSIONERS,

HON. E. B. MOORE,
TO MAY 31, 1907.

HON. C. C. BILLINGS,
FROM JUNE 1, 1907.

II

LETTER OF TRANSMITTAL.

DEPARTMENT OF THE INTERIOR,
Washington, January 8, 1908.

The SPEAKER OF THE UNITED STATES HOUSE OF REPRESENTATIVES.

SIR: The act of Congress entitled "An act providing for the public printing and binding and the distribution of public documents," approved January 12, 1895 (28 Stat., 620), provides, among other things, that—

SEC. 73. * * * Seventh. Annual volumes of the decisions of the Commissioner of Patents and of the United States courts in patent cases, not exceeding one thousand five hundred in number, of which the usual number shall be printed, and for this purpose a copy of each shall be transmitted to Congress promptly when prepared.

In compliance with the requirements of the statute, I have the honor to inclose herewith copy of a letter from the Commissioner of Patents, dated the 7th instant, forwarding the decisions of the Commissioner of Patents and of the United States courts in patent cases for the year 1907.

Very respectfully,   JAMES RUDOLPH GARFIELD,
Secretary.

III

204466

TABLE OF CONTENTS.

DECISIONS OF THE COMMISSIONER OF PATENTS.

A.

O.

P.

R.

S.

DECISIONS OF THE UNITED STATES COURTS.

DECISIONS

OF THE

COMMISSIONER OF PATENTS

FOR

THE YEAR 1907.

Ex parte Klepetko.

Decided November 26, 1906.

(126 O. G., 387.)

AMENDMENT—ENTRY OF AFTER REJECTION UNDER RULE 132.

Where following the termination of an interference and the rejection of the defeated party's claims he filed an amendment canceling the rejected claims and adding new claims, which amendment was refused admission by the Examiner on the ground that the prosecution before the Primary Examiner was closed by reason of the fact that the application had been appealed to the Examiners-in-Chief, allowed, and passed to issue prior to the declaration of the interference, *Held* that the rejection of the claims involved in the interference under Rule 132 is a new ground of rejection and that the rules and statute give applicant the right to amend in an endeavor to overcome said ground of rejection.

ON PETITION.

ROASTING-FURNACE.

Mr. Emil Starek for the applicant.

ALLEN, *Commissioner:*

This is a petition from the action of the Examiner refusing to enter an amendment.

It appears that this application was appealed to the Examiners-in-Chief, who allowed the claims appealed, and the application was then passed to issue. The application, however, was subsequently withdrawn from issue and placed in interference. Said interference was decided adversely to petitioner, and he was informed that his claims 11 and 12 involved in the interference stood finally rejected under Rule 132. Petitioner thereupon filed an amendment on July 5, 1906, canceling the above-mentioned claims and adding four additional claims. The Examiner refused to admit this amendment, whereupon applicant took this petition.

The Examiner states that he refused to enter the amendment for the reason that the prosecution before the Primary Examiner was closed by the appeal to the Examiners-in-Chief and by the allowance of the application. He takes the position that the withdrawal of the application from issue was " for the purpose of declaring an interference only," and that while the further prosecution of the case is not closed by the interference, neither is it reopened thereby.

The position of the Examiner is considered untenable. In my decisions in the cases of *ex parte Harvey* (C. D., 1903, 21; 102 O. G., 621) and *ex parte Greuter* (C. D., 1905, 167; 116 O. G., 596) I held that an applicant is entitled to amend after the termination of the interference in an effort to secure allowable claims. The decision in *ex parte Harvey, supra*, states:

> It is true that Rule 132 provides that the Examiner shall inform the defeated party in an interference that his claims involved in the interference "stand finally rejected." This proceeding does not, however, close the consideration of the whole case, as in the case of a second and final rejection in view of the same references under Rule 133. Rule 132 merely provides for the final rejection of the claim involved. That claim must, if it is insisted upon by the applicant, stand as finally rejected; but in view of the fact that but one action has been taken against it it may be amended in order to avoid the "reason for rejection," or, what is the same thing, it may be canceled and a new and different claim presented in lieu thereof. Rule 96 specifically provides that after an interference has been decided the application may be held for revision and restriction. If by the provisions of this rule the Examiner is given jurisdiction to enter and consider amendments filed after the determination of an interference proceeding when he specifically reserves the same, there is no good reason why he should not have such jurisdiction whether he specifically reserves it under Rule 96 or not.

The Examiner, however, attempts to make a distinction between the above-cited cases and the present one, where an appeal was taken and an allowance of the application secured prior to the declaration of the interference. The above decisions make no such distinction. In the present case, following the termination of the interference, certain previously-allowed claims were rejected because applicant was not the first inventor thereof, as disclosed by the interference proceeding. Such rejection is based upon a new ground and is a new reason for rejection, in view of which applicant has the right to amend under Rules 65 and 68 and section 4903 of the Revised Statutes.

In the case of *ex parte Thurman* (C. D., 1904, 317; 111 O. G., 1625) the Examiner refused to admit an amendment after the termination of an interference on the ground—

> that the prosecution of the case was closed when the interference was declared, as it was then in all other respects ready for allowance.

In that case there was stated the following principle, which is applicable in the present case:

> The Examiner refers to the well-settled principle that there must be at some time an end to the prosecution of an application, and he is of the opinion that the prosecution of an application is closed when it has been placed in condition for allowance prior to the declaration of an interference, and it should therefore be treated as though it were in condition for appeal or had been formally passed to issue.
>
> An application which is in condition for appeal or which has been formally allowed and passed to issue has had the benefit of the careful consideration of the applicant, and his amendments have been filed at his own pleasure within the one-year limit of time prescribed by section 4894 of the Revised Statutes in which to prosecute the application. Therefore when a case is prosecuted to a final rejection or to a formal allowance some restriction must of necessity be placed upon the right of further amendment; but a different principle applies to a case such as this one where an interference has been declared, whether the case is then believed to be ready for allowance or whether it has been held to be subject to revision and restriction after the determination of the interference. In cases where the applicant has put his case in condition for allowance prior to the declaration of an interference he has usually done so within a fixed time set by the Office. As new light is often thrown upon an invention while involved in an interference, it would be unjust to an applicant to hold that no further amendments could be presented and considered after the termination of the proceeding. The application is then within the jurisdiction of the Examiner, and there is no rule which prohibits the formal entry and consideration of an amendment after the proceeding has terminated. It is the province and aim of this Office to grant to an applicant a patent which will fully cover his invention, and all proper amendments should be considered and acted upon which are not prohibited by the rules.

In the present case permission was given to withdraw the application from issue for the consideration of a possible new ground of rejection—to wit, the prior invention of the opponent to the interference proceeding. Such ground having been found to exist and the claims of the issue having been rejected thereon under Rule 132, the rules and the statute heretofore noted give applicant the right to amend in an endeavor to avoid such reference. Said rules, for the reasons stated, are considered applicable to this application rather than Rule 142.

The Examiner calls attention to the fact that applicant attempted to insert the claims of the present amendment at the time he made claims suggested to him for the interference proceeding and that their admission was then denied on petition to the Commissioner. The ground of this refusal, however, was that " the declaration of the interference should not be delayed to await the consideration of claims not to be included as issues." This ground is not applicable at the present time.

The petition that the amendment be entered and considered is granted.

DENSTEN *v.* BURNHAM.

Decided November 26, 1906.

(126 O. G., 388.)

TRADE-MARK INTERFERENCE—FAILURE TO TAKE DEPOSITION IN ACCORDANCE WITH
   NOTICE—SUBSEQUENT DEPOSITION—SUPPRESSION.
      Where a party to an interference gives notice to the opposing party of
      his intention to take testimony at a certain time and place, but fails to
      appear at the time and place stated, and no notice is given of his inability
      to take testimony in accordance with the notice, testimony taken under a
      subsequent notice will not be considered if proper objection is made by the
      opposing party unless it appears that the opposing party was not injured
      by the failure to act upon the original notice or that there were good rea-
      sons for such failure to act then and for the failure to duly notify the op-
      posing party of the postponement.

ON APPEAL.

TRADE-MARK FOR MEDICINE.

Dr. J. C. Densten pro se.
Messrs. Ellis Spear & Co., for Burnham.

ALLEN, *Commissioner:*

This is an appeal by Burnham from a decision of the Examiner
of Interferences refusing to suppress Densten's deposition.

The record shows that a notice was served on Burnham and his
attorney, who reside at Auburn, Me., stating that testimony on behalf
of Densten would be taken at a specified place in Scranton, Pa., on
July 2, 1906, at nine o'clock a. m. Burnham and his attorney appeared at the time and place designated. Although Scranton is the
residence of Densten, neither Densten nor his attorney appeared at
the place designated up to twelve o'clock of the day named, at which
time Burnham and his attorney left.

On August 7, 1906, the deposition was taken, the suppression of
which is now asked. Although the record contains no proof of the
service of a notice that such deposition would be taken, it appears
from the deposition itself that the attorney for Burnham was notified
and that he appeared and cross-examined the witness, noting an objection, however, to the irregularity of the proceeding. This objection was followed up by bringing this motion to suppress said deposition.

The recognition of a right in a party to take such action as has been
taken in this case may work much mischief. When a proper notice
of taking testimony is given to an opposing party, a failure to attend
at the time and place stated acts as a waiver of the right to cross-
examine. The party whom notice is given must therefore comply
strictly with its terms in order to preserve this invaluable right. If

it be contended that a party has the right to set a second time and place for the taking of testimony after having failed to appear in accordance with a previous notice given by him, no reason is apparent why he could not give a third notice and continue giving notices as often as he desired within the limit set for the taking of testimony. This might not be such an important consideration were the proceeding one in which the parties were likely to be residing in the same locality; but in interference proceedings parties are likely to reside in widely-separated parts of the country. Under these circumstances a party must bear the expense of a long journey or place the case in the hands of persons unfamiliar with the particular case and possibly unfamiliar with interference proceedings, which often results disastrously. Thus in order to preserve his rights a party might be compelled to keep his counsel in constant attendance within the limit set for the taking of testimony in accordance with the notices successively given by his adversary.

I am of the opinion that a party who fails to take his testimony in accordance with the notice of the taking of testimony which he has given to his opponents should not be permitted to present and have considered testimony taken under a subsequent notice when objection is made by the opponents unless it appears that the opponents were not injured by the failure to act upon the original notice or that there were good reasons for such failure to act then and for the failure to duly notify the parties of the postponement.

In the present case no excuse whatever has been offered by the appellee for the failure to take his testimony in accordance with the first notice or for the failure to give the appellant such notice of the fact that the testimony would not be taken at that time as might have saved him the expense and loss of time incident to the journey taken by him and his attorney pursuant to the first notice. The deposition in question should be suppressed.

The decision of the Examiner of Interferences is reversed.

BEALL, JR., *v.* LYON.

Decided December 18, 1906.

(126 O. G., 388.)

INTERFERENCE—PRELIMINARY STATEMENT—AMENDMENT—CARRYING BACK OF OPPONENT'S DATE.

A party will not be permitted to amend his preliminary statement to carry back his date of disclosure to cover the date proved by his opponent in a prior interference with a third party where the amended date is earlier than that set up in a preliminary statement filed three years before in an interference between him and said third party and where the affidavit in support of the motion indicates an uncertainty whether the alleged disclosure took place prior to the date originally given.

APPEAL ON MOTION.

Messrs. John B. Thomas & Co., and *Mr. W. S. Duvall* for Beall, Jr.
Mr. Franklin H. Hough and *Messrs. Smith & Frazier* for Lyon.

ALLEN, *Commissioner:*

This case comes before me on appeal from the decision of the Examiner of Interferences denying Lyon's motion for leave to file an amended preliminary statement.

Beall, Jr., in his preliminary statement alleged conception and disclosure on August 1, 1902. Lyon in his original statement alleged conception on July 27, 1902, and disclosure on or about August 16, 1902. He now desires to amend his statement by alleging disclosure between July 27 and August 16, 1902.

The application upon which Lyon's patent involved in this interference was granted was previously in interference with an application of one Shuman, and an interference was also declared between applications of the same parties for the process disclosed in the apparatus applications. Shuman was defeated and purchased Lyon's applications, subsequently assigning them, together with the patent granted on his own application, to the Simplex Concrete Piling Company. Shuman then became involved in an interference with Beall, Jr., and judgment was rendered against Shuman by the Patent Office and by the court of appeals. The party in interest opposed to Beall, Jr., in the case now at bar is the Simplex Concrete Piling Company, assignee of Lyon's patent, which company was also the party in interest opposed to him in the Beall, Jr.-Shuman interference. Lyon in his interference with Shuman filed preliminary statements in which he alleged conception and disclosure of the invention in issue on August 16, 1902. In the Beall, Jr.-Shuman interference Beall, Jr., introduced testimony to the effect that he conceived and disclosed the invention about August 6, 1902, and the evidence was held sufficient to establish that he made the invention at about that time. Lyon, knowing this fact, did not in his original statement in the present interference adhere to the date of conception alleged by him in his prior interference with Shuman, which date was subsequent to that established by Beall, Jr., but alleged conception on July 27, 1902, a few days earlier than the date established by Beall, Jr., in the Beall, Jr.-Shuman interference. Lyon did not, however, allege disclosure of the invention until August 16, 1902. This being subsequent to the date credited to Beall, Jr., in the prior interference, it would apparently be impossible on the state of facts established in the Beall, Jr.-Shuman interference for Lyon to prevail in the case at bar unless he were permitted to file an amended statement setting forth an earlier date of disclosure.

It is alleged in affidavits filed by Lyon in support of his motion that on August 18, 1906, the day after times were set for taking testimony, a conference was held by Lyon and his attorneys and that Lyon then and there recalled sending a letter to one Kort Berle while the latter was at Spray Beach, N. J., in the summer of 1902. Lyon states that on August 20, 1906, Berle told him that the invention here in issue was described in the letter referred to. Berle states that he received this letter while at Spray Beach in August and September, 1902, but that he has been unable to find the letter and cannot recall its date. He does not state what part of the months of August and September he was at Spray Beach.

Lyon in his affidavit in support of his motion also states that he has endeavored to learn from the office records of one James L. Parsons the date of a certain experiment with wooden piles at the "Stoneleigh Court" apartment-house in this city, but that he has been unable as yet to ascertain the date. He believes, however, that the experiment took place between July 27 and August 16, 1902, and says that he disclosed the invention in issue during that period.

It seems fair to assume that Lyon's memory relative to occurrences in the summer of 1902 was more accurate and reliable in the summer of 1903, when he executed his preliminary statement in the Lyon-Shuman interference, than it is now, four years after the occurrences took place. The fact that Lyon states in his affidavit that he *believes* the Parsons experiment was made between July 27, 1902, and August 16, 1902, and that he is *positive* he disclosed the invention to others between the dates mentioned indicates that he is uncertain whether the experiment and his disclosure of the invention to others took place at the same time or at different times. The fact, moreover, that Lyon is now attempting to fix the date of the Parsons experiment would be no reason for permitting him to amend his statement even if the date of the experiment were connected with his date of disclosure. Amendments to preliminary statements are not permitted on the mere possibility that something may some time be discovered to justify such amendment. The same criticism applies to the letter written to Kort Berle. There is nothing in the record to indicate that this letter was written prior to August 16, 1902, the date of disclosure originally alleged by Lyon, Berle merely stating that he received it while at Spray Beach in August and September, 1902. The letter may have been written in the latter part of August or in September. The fact that a letter of unknown date may be found at some future time and may confirm Berle's recollection that such a letter was written and contained a description of the invention in issue affords no ground whatever for permitting Lyon to amend his preliminary statement.

The decision of the Examiner of Interferences is affirmed.

NAULTY *v.* CUTLER.

Decided December 21, 1906.

(126 O. G., 389.)

1. INTERFERENCE—MOTION FOR REHEARING—JURISDICTION TO DETERMINE AFTER LIMIT OF APPEAL.

The question of the Examiner's retaining jurisdiction to determine, after the expiration of the limit of appeal, a motion for rehearing brought before the expiration of the limit of appeal is a different matter from that of the termination of the limit of appeal. No good reason appears for holding that a tribunal may not properly render a decision on a motion for rehearing brought before the expiration of the limit of appeal, even though the date of the decision is after the limit of appeal has expired.

2. SAME—SAME—DOES NOT EXTEND LIMIT OF APPEAL.

The filing of the motion for rehearing does not extend the limit of appeal, and in case the motion is denied the moving party will have lost its right of appeal unless he has taken the precaution to file his appeal within the limit originally set or has obtained an extension of the limit of appeal.

3. SAME—SAME—QUESTION OF APPEAL.

The rule that there is no appeal from a decision denying a rehearing does not cover the case where the holding is want of jurisdiction to entertain the motion.

4. SAME—SAME—DATE OF FILING.

Where a motion was filed by N. on the last day of the limit of appeal and on the same day notice by registered letter was mailed to C.'s attorney and C. makes no contention that said notice was not received in ample time to prepare for the hearing, *Held* that N. is entitled to the date of the receipt of his motion in this Office as its date of filing.

5. SAME—SAME—PRACTICE.

It is not the practice to require service of requests or motions for rehearing upon the opposite party (*Townsend* v. *Copeland* v. *Robinson*, C. D., 1906, 379; 124 O. G., 1845) or to set such motions for hearing unless examination of the motion and of the record shows that a rehearing ought to be granted. (*Adams* v. *Murphy*, C. D., 1900, 100; 91 O. G., 2373.)

6. SAME—SAME—JURISDICTION NOT AFFECTED BY APPEAL.

Where a motion is filed for rehearing of the Examiner's decision and also an appeal from said decision, *Held* that the filing of the appeal does not oust the Examiner of jurisdiction to entertain the motion.

APPEAL AND PETITION.

MAIL-CHUTE.

Mr. Chas. J. Stockman for Naulty.
Mr. Frederick F. Church for Cutler.

ALLEN, *Commissioner:*

This case comes up on an appeal and a petition by Naulty from the action of the Primary Examiner holding that he was without jurisdiction to hear and decide Naulty's motion for a rehearing.

On September 7, 1906, the Primary Examiner denied a motion by Naulty to dissolve the interference and set September 27, 1906, as the limit of appeal from his decision. On September 27 Naulty filed a motion, noticed for hearing on October 3, 1906, for a rehearing by the Examiner of his decision. The Examiner on October 1, 1906, notified Naulty that a hearing on his motion for a rehearing was set for October 11, 1906. On October 15, 1906, the Primary Examiner dismissed the motion for a rehearing on the ground that he was without jurisdiction to rehear the case and held that his jurisdiction terminated with the limit of appeal. The Examiner was mistaken in this conclusion. Naulty obtained no extension of the limit of appeal or stay of the running of the limit of appeal and filed no motion for that purpose. Rule 123 and the decisions in *Carmichael* v. *Fox*, (C. D., 1903, 177; 104 O. G., 1656,) *Cole* v. *Zarbock* v. *Greene*, (C. D., 1905, 194: 116 O. G., 1451,) and *Felsing* v. *Nelson* (C. D., 1906, 185; 122 O. G., 1722) provide that the filing of a motion for rehearing does not operate to stay the running of the limit of appeal. Otherwise it would be within the power of a party to obtain at will an extension of the limit of appeal by merely filing such a motion.

The question of the Examiner's retaining jurisdiction to determine, after the expiration of the limit of appeal, a motion for rehearing brought before the expiration of the limit of appeal is a different matter from that of the termination of the limit of appeal. No good reason appears for holding that a tribunal may not properly render a decision on a motion for rehearing brought before the expiration of the limit of appeal, even though the date of the decision is after the limit of appeal has expired. It is often inconvenient or impossible to hear and properly dispose of a motion for rehearing within the limit of appeal, or even of a motion for extension of the limit of appeal, where the party has filed his motion within the limit. Such a practice is not believed to be inconsistent with the rules and decisions. The filing of the motion for rehearing does not extend the limit of appeal, and in case the motion is denied the moving party will have lost his right of appeal unless he has taken the precaution to file his appeal within the limit originally set or has obtained an extension of the limit of appeal.

The Examiner based his decision that he was without jurisdiction to determine the motion, in part at least, upon the ground that the motion had not been noticed for hearing within the limit of appeal, citing the case of *Meyrose* v. *Jahn*, (C. D., 1891, 145; 56 O. G., 1447.) In that case it was held that motions after judgment should be noticed for hearing within the time set for appeal, as otherwise the tribunal rendering judgment would not have jurisdiction at the time of hearing. This holding was based on Rule 114, which as then in force and as amended on April 18, 1888, contained a provision that—

The filing of such a motion, noticed for hearing within the limit of appeal, will operate to stay the running of the time so limited until the final determination of the motion.

Rule 114 was amended on March 13, 1903, by the omission of this provision, and the practice under *Meyrose* v. *Jahn, supra,* has been modified by my decision in *Kneedler* v. *Shephard*, (C. D., 1903, 180; 104 O. G., 1895,) so that motions under said rule need not be noticed for hearing within the term allowed for filing motions.

That it is the present practice to decide such motions after the expiration of the limit of appeal appears from the following cases. In *Wilderman* v. *Simm* (C. D., 1904, 76; 109 O. G., 275) the action of the Examiner of Interferences was held proper in a case where, on December 10, 1903, he granted a motion of Simm's filed December 8, 1903, for an extension of the limit of appeal, although the limit of appeal expired on December 9, 1903. In that case it was stated:

Simm's motion having been brought before the limit of appeal as originally set had expired, the Examiner of Interferences had jurisdiction to grant the extension asked for.

In the case of *Cole* v. *Zarbock* v. *Greene* (C. D., 1905, 194; 116 O. G., 1451) the Examiner denied Zarbock's motion to dissolve and set March 7, 1905, as the limit of appeal. A motion for a rehearing filed March 3, 1905, was entertained and denied by the Examiner on March 9, 1905, two days after the expiration of the limit of appeal.

The contention of Cutler that there is no appeal from a decision denying a motion for a rehearing is sound. (*Macey* v. *Laning* v. *Casler*, C. D., 1902, 399; 101 O. G., 1608; *Carmichael* v. *Fox*, C. D., 1903, 177; 104 O. G., 1656; *Cole* v. *Zarbock* v. *Greene*, C. D., 1905, 194; 116 O. G., 1451; *Hewitt* v. *Thomas* v. *Kruh* v. *Weintraub*, C. D., 1906, 165; 122 O. G., 1045.) In the present case, however, the motion for a rehearing was not denied, but dismissed for want of jurisdiction. Naulty's appeal and petition are from the holding of the Examiner that he is without jurisdiction to entertain the motion.

Although the holding in this decision is that the Examiner has jurisdiction to entertain Naulty's motion, he also has the power, when the case is returned to him, to deny the motion for rehearing if he is of the opinion that the reasons advanced do not warrant granting a rehearing. From such a decision no appeal will lie.

Cutler also contends that the motion of Naulty for a rehearing was not filed within the limit of appeal. The record shows that Naulty's motion paper was filed in this Office on the last day of the limit of appeal and that on the afternoon of the same day notice by registered letter was mailed to Cutler's attorney at Rochester, N. Y. Cutler makes no contention that this notice was not received by him in ample time to prepare for the hearing. Under these circumstances Naulty is considered entitled to the date of the receipt of his motion in this Office as its date of filing. To hold that acknowledgment of receipt of service must accompany the motion would often prevent the filing of motions within the limit of appeal and would work great hardship, especially where the party served resides at a great distance or in a foreign country.

Furthermore, it is not the practice to require service of requests or motions for rehearing upon the opposite party. (*Townsend* v. *Copeland* v. *Robinson*, C. D., 1906, 379; 124 O. G., 1845.) Such motions are not ordinarily set for hearing unless examination of the motion and of the record shows that a rehearing ought to be granted. (*Adams* v. *Murphy*, C. D., 1900, 100; 91 O. G., 2373.) In case the motion for rehearing is granted, a date for the rehearing is fixed and all the parties are notified by this Office.

The record shows that on the day he filed his motion for a rehearing, September 27, 1906, Naulty also filed an appeal from the Examiner's decision, and that on October 9, 1906, after receiving notice that his motion would be heard on October 11, 1906, he withdrew said appeal. Cutler's contention that the filing of this appeal ousted the Examiner of jurisdiction to entertain the motion for a rehearing is contrary to the practice of this Office. In the case of *Greuter* v. *Mathieu*, (C. D., 1904, 380; 112 O. G., 254,) where motion was made before the Examiner of Interferences to reopen the interference, it was stated:

* * * as the motion to reopen was brought on the last day within which Greuter had to file his appeal to the Examiners-in-Chief he should, out of an abundance of caution, have filed his appeal the same day on which he made the motion to reopen the interference.

The decision of the Examiner holding that he is without jurisdiction to consider Naulty's motion for a rehearing *is reversed.*

WOODS *v.* POOR.

Decided October 8, 1906.

(126 O. G., 391.)

1. INTERFERENCE—PRIORITY—DILIGENCE.

Where P. conceived the invention in the early part of November, 1903, and filed his application December 11, 1903, and W. conceived the invention on September 16, 1903, but did not reduce it to practice prior to the filing of his application on January 27, 1904, *Held* that W. was lacking in diligence in the absence of a sufficient excuse for the delay.

2. SAME—SAME—SAME—ENDEAVOR TO IMPROVE DEVICE.

The claim of an inventor, advanced as an excuse for his delay in reducing to practice, that he was endeavoring to improve upon his conception is not supported by testimony showing merely that conversations were held looking to the improvement thereof where it does not appear that any changes were actually made or that any material changes were even suggested.

3. SAME—SAME—SAME—CLAIM OF POVERTY NOT PROVED.

A claim of an inventor that he was financially unable to reduce his invention to practice after paying the necessary expenses of his business is not proved where the evidence does not show what the necessary expenses of the business were and where there is no evidence of the inventor's resources except his own statement that he had only a given amount of cash on hand.

4. SAME—ORIGINALITY.

An allegation of derivation of an invention by one party from another is not proved by a mere showing that opportunity for such derivation existed.

APPEAL from Examiners-in-Chief.

SIDE BEARING FOR CARS.

Messrs. Bond, Adams, Pickard & Jackson and *Messrs. Meyers, Cushman & Rea* for Woods.

Mr. Thomas F. Sheridan for Poor.

MOORE, *Acting Commissioner:*

This is an appeal by Woods from a decision of the Examiners-in-Chief affirming the decision of the Examiner of Interferences and awarding priority of invention to Poor on the following issue:

1. A side bearing for railway-cars comprising a casing or shell which has openings in its top and bottom and a roller in said shell adapted for rolling contact through said openings with bearing-surfaces; said casing or shell being provided with tracks located in position to support the roller when the latter is below and free from the upper bearing-surface and the said roller having free movement in the shell both endwise of the latter and vertically with respect to said tracks.

2. A side bearing for railway-cars comprising a casing or shell which has openings in its top and bottom and a roller in said shell adapted for rolling con-

tact through said openings with bearing-surfaces and provided with trunnions at its ends; said casing or shell having inwardly-extending flanges forming tracks which are located in position to engage the said trunnions when the roller is below and free from the upper bearing-surface, and the said roller having free movement in the shell both endwise of the latter and vertically with respect to the said track.

3. In a device of the class described, the combination with a suitable roller, having oppositely-extending gudgeons, of a box open at the top to receive the roller and having a longitudinally-slotted bottom through which the roller projects, there being inwardly-extending side flanges on the box, to limit the downward movement of the roller, and a cover for the box, separately formed and adapted to furnish an upper tread for the roller.

The Examiner of Interferences and the Examiners-in-Chief both found that Woods was the first to conceive, but the last to reduce to practice, and that he was not exercising diligence when Poor entered the field.

The correctness of the decisions of the lower tribunals with respect · to the facts does not seem to be seriously disputed; but it is strenuously contended by appellant that their conclusion upon the question of diligence is unjust and inequitable and contrary to the principles announced in prior decisions upon this point. Although the question is not entirely free from doubt, I am of the opinion that the conclusions reached below are correct.

Poor's application was filed December 11, 1903. Woods's application was filed January 27, 1904.

Woods conceived the invention in issue on September 16, 1903, but did not reduce it to practice prior to the filing of his application. Poor conceived the invention in the early part of November, 1903, and claims no reduction to practice prior to the filing of his application. In order that Woods shall prevail, it is necessary for him to show that he was exercising diligence just prior to the time when Poor entered the field and up to the time of filing his application.

At the time Woods conceived the invention he was vice-president and general manager of the Kindl Car Truck Company, which was engaged in the business of exploiting truck-frames for freight-cars. He was the inventor, jointly with Samuel W. McMunn, the president of the company, of a roller side bearing for car-trucks protected by Letters Patent No. 703,148, upon which the invention in issue was designed as an improvement. This patented device was exploited by Woods and McMunn up to the time when Woods left the employ of the company on October 10, 1903. It appears that a disagreement with respect to a division of profits from the sale of these devices led Woods to sever his connection with the company. After resigning his position Woods went into the railway supply business himself, continuing the exploitation of the patented side bearings.

It appears from the testimony that about the middle of December, 1903, Woods heard through his father that Poor, the opposing party, who was connected with the Kindl Car Truck Company, had filed or was about to file an application for patent on an improved roller side bearing (Woods, X-Q. 79) and that he also heard that the final fee on such application had been paid. Upon receipt of this information he took immediate steps to file his application and diligently continued his efforts until the same was filed.

The testimony shows that Woods did little, if anything, toward reducing his invention to practice prior to the time when he called on his attorney with a view to filing his application. It appears that immediately after conceiving the invention and disclosing it to one John Jacob, who was an employee of the Kindl Car Truck Company, Woods had a number of conversations with Jacob, who was working under his direction, relative to the practicability of the invention. In discussing the invention with Jacob " large sketches, full size or greater " were made upon a blackboard in Wood's office. (Woods, Q. 29.) It seems that these sketches remained on the blackboard for at least a number of days, and perhaps, for two or three weeks, but that they were erased prior to Wood's resignation on October 10, 1903. (Jacob, X-Q. 94.) Jacob made objections to the construction of the device, and one of the principal excuses which Woods offers for his delay in filing the application is that he was endeavoring to overcome these objections, which he regarded as well founded. Testimony with respect to conversations held by him with Jacob is given to support his claim that he was diligently endeavoring to perfect his device; but it appears that no changes were ever made, and it does not appear that any material changes were even suggested. The claim of an endeavor to further improve the details of a device is one that could well be made by every inventor seeking to excuse his delay, and for this reason testimony on this point is regarded as of little weight unless it is shown that material changes were actually made.

Evidence of the circumstances surrounding Woods after his resignation is also offered as an excuse for this delay in reducing the invention to practice. According to his own testimony his bank account amounted only to about twelve hundred and fifty dollars, and all of this and more was necessary to start his business and pay running expenses. Could his uncorroborated statement be taken as sufficient proof on this point the evidence would still be insufficient, as there is no proof that he had no other resources; nor is there any evidence of the amount of money required to run his business. This evidence is not sufficient to show that he was financially unable either to file an application or to make a full-sized device. It would seem that the cost to him of making such a device would not be great, especially as he was manufacturing or having manufactured for him similar devices. Nor can the fact that the inventor was very busy in getting his new business started excuse the absence of practically all effort for a period of three months where the rights of other parties intervene.

On behalf of appellant attention is directed to the decision *O'Connell* v. *Schmidt*, (C. D., 1906, 662; 122 O. G., 2065,) recently rendered by the Court of Appeals of the District of Columbia, which, it is claimed, is a departure from previous adjudications in the line of more liberality on the question of diligence toward the party who was the first to conceive; but the circumstances in that case are materially different from the circumstances presented here in several respects, but one of which need be mentioned. In that case the party who was required to show diligence had made a model showing every feature of the invention so complete that had it been tested it would have amounted to a reduction to practice, and this model was completed before the opposing party had entered the field. In this case Woods did nothing prior to Poor's entry into the field except make sketches of the invention. This is believed to be a very material distinction in the circumstances present in the two cases and it is thought to be sufficient to warrant a different conclusion from that reached in the case cited.

When this interference was declared it involved a third party, Edward A. Bern, who was connected with the Kindl Car Truck Company. The opposing party was also connected with the same company, and both of these parties had access to Woods's office at the time the sketches illustrating the invention were on the blackboard. It is suggested by appellant that when these sketches were on the blackboard they were seen by some of the officers or employees of the company, who thereupon entered into a conspiracy with McMunn and others to deprive him of his invention. This suggestion may be dismissed with the comment that the proofs utterly fail to substantiate the same.

The decision of the Examiners-in-Chief is affirmed.

NORMAND v. KRIMMELBEIN.

Decided November 13, 1906.

(126 O. G., 757.)

1. INTERFERENCE—APPEAL AFTER EXPIRATION OF LIMIT OF APPEAL.

A motion to extend the limit of appeal to include an appeal filed about three weeks after the expiration of the limit of appeal, supported by affidavits tending to excuse the delay, granted, where it appeared that the granting of the motion was not opposed and that the appeal might be heard with an appeal filed by the opposing party, to whom no delay would therefore result.

2. SAME—SAME—MOTION CONSIDERED BY COMMISSIONER IN PERSON.

It is the practice for the Commissioner to consider in person a motion to extend the limit of appeal to include an appeal to the Examiners-in-Chief filed after the expiration of the limit of appeal rather than to restore jurisdiction to the Examiner of Interferences for this purpose.

ON MOTION.

QUICK-ACTION AUTOMATIC RELEASE MECHANISM FOR AIR-BRAKES.

Mr. Joseph E. Normand pro se.
Mr. Edward A. Wright and *Mr. J. Snowden Bell* for Krimmelbein.

ALLEN, *Commissioner:*

Krimmelbein moves that the limit of appeal from the decision of the Examiner of Interferences which expired September 17, 1906, be extended to include his appeal to the Examiners-in-Chief filed on October 25, 1906. From the affidavits filed it appears that the delay in filing the appeal was due to the loss or miscarriage in the mails of a letter and to the mistaken understanding of counsel for Krimmelbein, two of whom are of record, that the appeal had been filed by reason of the receipt of official notice fixing the date of hearing of an appeal to the Examiners-in-Chief, but which did not indicate that it was the appeal of the opposite party, Normand.

The granting of the motion is not opposed. Krimmelbein requests that his appeal be set for hearing on the date—December 13, 1906—fixed for the hearing of Normand's appeal from the portion of the decision of the Examiner of Interferences adverse to him. The delay in filing the appeal cannot, therefore, work any hardship on Normand. Under these circumstances the limit of appeal is extended to include Krimmelbein's appeal, and the Examiners-in-Chief are authorized to entertain the same.

Krimmelbein's accompanying motion to restore the jurisdiction of the Examiner of Interferences for the purpose of considering the appeal calls for no consideration, since it is the practice, as appears in the case of *Brissenden* v. *Roesch*, (C. D., 1905, 440; 118 O. G., 2253,) for the Commissioner to consider in person the motion to extend the limit of appeal to include an appeal filed after the limit of appeal has expired.

The motion is granted to the extent indicated.

OUTCAULT *v.* THE NEW YORK HERALD COMPANY.

Decided November 17, 1906.

(126 O. G., 757.)

TRADE-MARK INTERFERENCE—MOTION TO SUSPEND PROCEEDINGS—APPEAL.

The decision of the Examiner of Interferences refusing to suspend proceedings pending a determination of contempt proceedings brought in a United States circuit court for failure of witnesses to appear and testify in response to subpoena will not be disturbed where it does not appear that great hardship will otherwise ensue.

APPEAL from Examiner of Interferences.

TRADE-MARK FOR COMIC SECTIONS OF NEWSPAPERS.

Messrs. Mason, Fenwick & Lawrence for Outcault.
Mr. William A. Megrath for The New York Herald Company.

ALLEN, *Commissioner:*

This case comes up on appeal from the decision of the Examiner of Interferences denying Outcault's motion for a suspension of proceedings pending a decision of Judge Lacomb, of the Circuit Court of the United States for the Southern District of New York, and on a motion by The New York Herald Company that the above appeal of Outcault be dismissed.

It appears that contempt proceedings were instituted by Outcault against The New York Herald Company and others for failing to appear and testify as witnesses for appellant in response to subpoena and that the matter is awaiting the decision of the court.

The record shows that Outcault was granted several extensions of his time for taking testimony and that the times last set by the Examiner of Interferences are as follows:

Outcault's testimony to begin October 15, 1906, and to close October 22, 1906.
The New York Herald Co.'s time for taking testimony to begin October 23, and to close November 23, 1906.
Outcault's rebuttal testimony to close December 8, 1906.
Final hearing January 8, 1907, at 11 a. m., as before set.

A motion by Outcault for a further extension of the times set for taking testimony was denied by the Examiner of Interferences on October 29, 1906. Outcault thereupon filed a motion for suspension of proceedings pending the decision of the court mentioned above, and upon its denial by the Examiner of Interferences filed this appeal.

The effect of granting this appeal would be an indefinite postponement of the further taking of testimony. It is the practice, as stated in *Goodfellow* v. *Jolly* (C. D., 1905, 105; 115 O. G., 1064) and *Chris-*

tensen v. *McKenzie*, (C. D., 1905, 238; 117 O. G., 277,) in appeals of this nature to reverse the decisions of the Examiner of Interferences only—

in extreme cases, and then only when it appears that great hardship will ensue unless his decision be reversed.

It is not clear that this appeal presents such a case or that the matter pending in the United States Circuit Court for the Southern District of New York warrants further postponement at this time of the regular proceedings in this case. The Examiner of Interferences has stated that in case the decision of the court is not rendered prior to the date now set for final hearing the final hearing will be postponed.

The decision of the Examiner of Interferences *is accordingly affirmed*, but without prejudice to appellant's bringing, when the court's decision is rendered, such motions as may be necessary to carry into effect the decision of the said court.

EX PARTE CRAIN.

Decided November 26, 1906.

(126 O. G., 758.)

1. DIVISION—SHOULD BE SETTLED BY APPEAL TO EXAMINERS-IN-CHIEF BEFORE ACTION ON PATENTABILITY OF CLAIMS.

Where the Examiner based his requirement for division upon proper grounds, the question of whether the Examiner is right in his requirement is a matter for consideration on appeal by the Examiners-in-Chief before action is made upon the patentability of the claims.

2. SAME—PRACTICE.

The fact that as an aid to applicant in electing how he will divide the Examiner cited patents showing the prior art and volunteered the opinion that the claims are for aggregations does not change the practice and does not warrant the assumption that the Examiner's action amounts to a refusal to examine the case on the ground that the claims cover aggregations.

ON PETITION.

CARRIAGE-MACHINE.

Messrs. Wilkinson & Fisher for the applicant.

ALLEN, *Commissioner:*

This is a petition that the Examiner in charge of this application be directed to make an examination and act upon the claims upon their merits.

The Examiner has made a requirement of division and has refused to act on the merits of the claims prior to compliance with said requirement. The Examiner states that claim 1 covers a general combination machine and is examinable in class 144, subclass 1; that claim

2 is for a wheelwright-machine and belongs in class 157, subclass 1; that claims 3 and 5 are for a lathe appliance, which comes in class 142, subclass 55, and that claim 4 may be retained with either claim 1 or claim 2. He required division between these three groups of claims on the ground that each covers subject-matter which has acquired a distinct status in the arts and industries and in the Office classification.

Petitioner admits that under the present practice the question of division is appealable to the Examiners-in-Chief and not directly to the Commissioner; but he contends that the Examiner's actions—

really amount to a refusal to examine the case, on the ground that the claims are aggregations—

and that they are—

equivalent to the requirement of division of some of the claims, and not merely a requirement of division between different claims.

Petitioner's contentions are believed to be unwarranted. The Examiner has based his requirement for division upon proper grounds. These grounds, noted above, are the usual grounds upon which division is required. Whether the Examiner is right in his conclusion that they are applicable to the claims of the present case is a matter for consideration on appeal to the Examiners-in-Chief. Although it is true that the Examiner has volunteered the statement that the claims cover aggregations and not proper combinations, this does not appear to be the ground upon which the requirement of division is based. On the contrary, in his action of August 8, 1906, the Examiner states that although—

applicant's attention has been called to the fact that his claims confuse independent matters, the requirement of division has not been based upon this fact.

It is further noted that each action of the Examiner has been a requirement of division and not an action rejecting claims, although as an aid to applicant in electing how he will divide the Examiner has cited patents showing the prior art, as well as volunteered the opinion that the claims are for aggregation. The record of this case is not found to justify the assumption of petitioner that the Examiner has—

refused an examination on the real ground of aggregation, veiling this under a requirement of division.

Concerning petitioner's contention that the requirement of division is in, effect, a requirement that applicant be required to divide his claims, the Examiner states that—

there has been no requirement of division which necessitates the division of a claim.

If the claims in each group in fact cover subject-matter which has acquired a distinct status in the arts and industries and in the Office classification, the requirement of division on this ground appears to be a proper one, and there is thought to be no necessary inconsistency in this requirement and in the holding at the same time that the claims cover aggregations. Moreover, such requirement, under the well-established Office practice, should precede any action on the merits of the claims. (Rule 42; *ex parte Pickles*, C. D., 1904, 126; 109 O. G., 1888; *ex parte Snyder*, C. D., 1904, 242; 110 O. G., 2236.)

The petition is denied.

HERR *v.* HERR, GROVES, AND FOREMAN *v.* DODDS.

Decided August 11, 1906.

(126 O. G., 758.)

INTERFERENCE—ACCESS TO APPLICATION OF FORMER OPPONENT.

Where the joint applicants H., G., and F. filed a concession in favor of the sole applicant H. and judgment was thereupon entered against the joint applicants, *Held* that the application of H., G., and F. is no longer involved in the interference proceedings, and the fact that it was formerly so involved is no reason for permitting D., another party to said interference, to obtain a copy of it at this time.

ON PETITION.

DUMPING-CAR.

Mr. A. J. O'Brien and *Messrs. Spear, Middleton, Donaldson & Spear* for Herr and for Herr, Groves, and Foreman.

Messrs. Offield, Towle & Linthicum for Dodds.

MOORE, *Acting Commissioner:*

This is a petition by Dodds that he be permitted to inspect and obtain copies of the application and preliminary statement of the joint applicants Herr, Groves, and Foreman, formerly involved in this interference, or that it be ordered that Herr shall not be permitted to rely upon the application of Herr, Groves, and Foreman for any purpose in connection with said interference.

It appears that the interference was originally declared between the joint application of Herr, Groves, and Foreman and the application of Dodds. Before preliminary statements were filed an application was filed by Herr as the sole inventor of the subject-matter of the interference, which application was added to the interference. The joint applicants Herr, Groves, and Foreman then filed a concession of priority of invention in favor of Herr, and judgment was thereupon rendered against said joint applicants.

The application of Herr, Groves, and Foreman is no longer involved in the interference proceeding, and the fact that it was formerly involved in said interference is no reason for permitting Dodds to obtain a copy of it at this time. No reference is made to the joint application of Herr, Groves, and Foreman in the application of Herr or in his preliminary statement. The interference having been concluded, so far as the application of Herr, Groves, and Foreman is concerned, Dodds now stands upon the same footing as any member of the general public with respect to obtaining access to said application. (*Ex parte Warner*, C. D., 1901, 97; 96 O. G., 1238; *in re Mygatt*, C. D., 1905, 110; 115 O. G., 1066.)

The reasons stated above for refusing Dodds access to the application of Herr, Groves, and Foreman would also apply to their preliminary statement, provided they had filed one, which, however, does not appear to be the case. Dodds contends that he should be permitted access to the application of Herr, Groves, and Foreman for the reason that he anticipates that Herr intends to rely upon said application, and he requests in the latter part of his petition as an alternative remedy that it be ordered that Herr be prohibited from relying upon said application in the interference. This contention is hypothetical. There is nothing to indicate that Herr intends to rely upon the application of Herr, Groves, and Foreman. Furthermore, it does not appear how Herr can obtain any benefit from the joint application unless it be by introducing it in evidence, when it will then be open to the inspection of Dodds.

The petition is denied.

GREENAWALT *v.* MARK.

Decided November 17, 1906.

(126 O. G., 1063.)

1. INTERFERENCE—PRIORITY—BASED ON OPERATIVENESS OF DEVICE.

    Where the Examiner of Interferences awarded priority of invention to one party on the ground that the application of his opponent fails to show an operative device, *Held* that the operativeness of an applicant's device affects his right to make the claim and that the action of the Examiner of Interferences was in accord with the rules and decisions.

2. SAME—SAME—DECISION OF EXAMINER OF INTERFERENCES.

    The decision of the Examiner of Interferences is not a rejection of the claims under section 4903, Revised Statutes, although it may form a basis for such rejection by the Primary Examiner under Rule 132.

ON PETITION.

ROASTING-FURNACE.

Mr. A. J. O'Brien and *Messrs. Spear, Middleton, Donaldson & Spear* for Greenawalt.

Mr. C. C. Bulkley and *Mr. Eugene A. Byrnes* for Mark.

ALLEN, *Commissioner:*

This is a petition by Mark that—

the Commissioner direct the Examiner of Interferences to vacate the judgment of priority entered by said Examiner.

It appears that the Examiner of Interferences awarded priority of the interference *Greenawalt* v. *Mark*, No. 25,291, on August 23, 1906, to Greenawalt on the ground that the application of Mark fails to show an operative device. Petitioner contends that the Examiner of Interferences in basing an award of priority upon this ground instead of calling it to the attention of the Commissioner under Rule 126 has violated said rule and also section 4903 of the Revised Statutes.

The action of the Examiner of Interferences is in accord with present Rule 130 and with the decision of the Court of Appeals of the District of Columbia in *Podlesak and Podlesak* v. *McInnerney*, (C. D., 1906, 558; 120 O. G., 2127,) which held that the right of a party to make a claim may be considered as a basis for awarding priority of invention. The operativeness of an applicant's device affects his right to make the claims.

The decision of the Examiner of Interferences is not a rejection of the claims under section 4903, Revised Statutes, although it may form a basis for such rejection by the Primary Examiner under Rule 132. It is not, therefore, contrary to the provisions of said statute. (*Ex parte Lyon*, C. D., 1906, 422; 124 O. G., 2905.)

The petition is denied.

BIGBIE BROTHERS & COMPANY *v.* BLUTHENTHAL & BICKART *v.* THE J. & H. BUTLER COMPANY.

Decided November 26, 1906.

(126 O. G., 1063.)

1. TRADE-MARKS—INTERFERENCE—PRIORITY—OWNERSHIP OF MARK.

Where the claim of Bigbie Brothers & Company to ownership of the mark of the issue through transfer from Joseph Lawson & Son in 1887 is questioned, but neither of the other parties to the interference claims title from the Lawsons, *Held* that said other parties' claims to registration are defeated by the use of the mark in issue by Bigbie Brothers & Company in 1887 and subsequently, irrespective of whether Bigbie Brothers & Company's use was based upon ownership, and that Lawson's right to the mark after the transfer in 1887 is only of consequence, therefore, in determining whether Bigbie Brothers & Company shall be denied registration, notwithstanding their position as the first to adopt and use the mark among those before the Office seeking registration.

2. SAME—TO ACQUIRE RIGHTS NAME MUST BE PHYSICALLY APPLIED TO GOODS.

The mere adoption of a name for its goods does not vest in the company trade-mark rights. To acquire such rights, the name must be physically applied to the goods in trade, as by brands or labels on the packages sold.

3. SAME—RIGHTS ACQUIRED ONLY BY PRESENCE OF MARK UPON GOODS AFTER PASSING FROM HANDS OF ORIGINATOR.

There is no liability to confusion of the origin of goods which are sold only on the premises of the originator. The utility of a trade-mark does not come into existence until the goods have passed from the hands of the originator, and it is only by the presence of the mark upon the goods after they have so passed that rights to the same as a trade-mark are believed to become established.

APPEAL from Examiner of Interferences.

TRADE-MARK FOR WHISKY.

Messrs. Mason, Fenwick & Lawrence for Bigbie Brothers & Co.
Mr. Joseph L. Atkins for Bluthenthal & Bickart.
Mr. Arthur E. Wallace for The J. & G. Butler Co.

ALLEN, *Commissioner:*

This case is before me upon appeals by Bluthenthal & Bickart and The J. & G. Butler Company from the decision of the Examiner of Interferences awarding priority of adoption and use of the trade-mark "Velvet" or "Old Velvet" for whisky to Bigbie Brothers & Company.

The Examiner of Interferences found Bigbie Brothers & Company entitled to a date of adoption and use as early as the year 1868. He found that Bluthenthal & Bickart have continuously used the mark since 1888, and that The J. & G. Butler Company and their predecessors have used it since 1882. Bluthenthal & Bickart do not claim any earlier date than 1888, but contend that neither of the other parties to the interference has succeeded in proving a date earlier than this. The J. & G. Butler Company contends that it is entitled to the year 1851 as its date of adoption and use.

I agree with the conclusion of the Examiner of Interferences that Bigbie Brothers & Company are entitled to prevail; but in reaching this conclusion I have taken a somewhat different view of the evidence from that taken by him. It is believed that The J. & G. Butler Company has failed to establish any earlier date than 1890 for the adoption and continuous use of the mark. As Bluthenthal & Bickart do not claim a date prior to 1888, continuous use by Bigbie Brothers & Company from 1887, when they went into the whisky business, would negative the claims of Bluthenthal & Bickart and The J. & G.

Butler Company to registration and would entitle Bigbie Brothers & Company to register, unless it appear that the ownership of the mark at the time of its supposed adoption by Bigbie Brothers & Company in 1887 was in and continued in others not parties to this proceeding. It is believed that continuous use of the mark by Bigbie Brothers & Company since 1887 is established, and that the contentions of Bluthenthal & Bickart of ownership of the mark then and thereafter by one Lawson are not established.

It is settled by the testimony of Bluthenthal & Bickart's witness Withers that Bigbie Brothers & Company bought out Joseph Lawson & Son's wholesale and retail whisky business and started in business as their successors upon May 1, 1887. (Qs. 8, 27, and 28.) Bigbie, testifying for Bigbie Brothers & Company, states that all the whiskies, brands, labels, and stencils of Joseph Lawson were transferred to Bigbie Brothers & Company on that date, (Q. 11,) as well as the formula for making "Old Velvet whisky." (Q. 19.) It appears that whisky was shipped in a barrel bearing the brand "Old Velvet" by predecessors of Joseph Lawson & Son in 1872 or 1873. (Bigbie, Q. 21; Thurman, Q. 10; Humbles, Qs. 23, 24.) There were a few barrels of "Old Velvet" whisky in the stock which Bigbie Brothers & Company obtained from Lawson (Bigbie, Q. 18) and also an "Old Velvet Rye Whisky" stencil, Bigbie Brothers & Company's Exhibit E, (Bigbie, Q. 14,) which has been used by Bigbie Brothers & Company for branding their half barrels and kegs. (Bigbie, Qs. 15, 17.) Bigbie states that Bigbie Brothers & Company have used the brand "Old Velvet" on whisky continuously since May 1, 1887, (Q. 28,) and that they made sales and shipments of whisky so branded in 1887 and continuously thereafter up to the present time. (Qs. 34–37.) He gives the names of parties to whom such sales were made and the towns in which they resided. (Qs. 38–41.)

Bigbie Brothers & Company used Lawson's labels until they could get their own, which were not received until October. (Bigbie, Q. 43.) Bigbie Brothers & Company's Exhibit G contains a bill for labels bearing the date October 15, 1887, and containing an item of "2,000 Old Velvet Whisky Labels, lith'd." "Old Velvet" labels of Bigbie Brothers & Company are in evidence as Bigbie Brothers & Company's Exhibits L and M. Bigbie states that after buying out Joseph Lawson they bottled and barreled "Old Velvet" whisky, applying the labels "Bigbie Bros. & Co., Successors to Jos. Lawson & Son, Old Velvet Whiskey" to the bottles and a similar stamp on the barrels. (Qs. 43–49.) Bigbie also identifies a print (Exhibit K) as one made from a stencil which his firm has used since the fall of 1887, (Qs. 70–72,) and states that prior to the use of this stencil and since the first of May, 1887, they branded barrels with the "Old Velvet" stencil which they got from Lawson. (Qs. 73 and 74.)

Bigbie's testimony is supported to some extent by that of Bigbie Bros. & Co.'s witnesses, Broyles, Frye, and Humbles, to the effect that whisky was sold under the brands and labels "Old Velvet" by the various predecessors in business of Bigbie Brothers & Company, as well as by Bigbie Brothers & Company. (Bigbie Bros. & Co.'s record, pp. 14–16; pp. 35, 36, Qs. 2–10; pp. 42, 43, Qs. 22–34.) The evidence is regarded as ample to establish use of the words "Old Velvet" by Bigbie Brothers & Company as a trade-mark for whisky in the year 1887 and continuously thereafter.

It appears that Lawson entered the liquor business in Roanoke, Va., after selling out his business in Lynchburg to Bigbie Brothers & Company in 1887 and that he opened business again in Lynchburg in 1889. It does not appear that whisky was sold in the Roanoke business prior to 1889; but Bluthenthal & Bickart's witness Withers states that "Old Velvet" was among his brands in both the Roanoke and Lynchburg houses subsequent to May 1, 1889. (Qs. 39, 40.) Bluthenthal & Bickart urge that Bigbie Brothers & Company have not, in view of this evidence, established such transfer of business from Joseph Lawson & Son to them as would carry the rights in the trademark "Old Velvet." Bigbie Brothers & Company's Exhibit B purports to be the agreement between Joseph Lawson & Son and Bigbie Brothers & Company upon which the transfer of business on May 1, 1887, was effected. This exhibit was objected to by Bluthenthal & Bickart on the ground that it was not properly proved. The objection was well taken, and the paper is therefore not in evidence as proof of anything for either party. Bigbie, however, testifies that an agreement in accordance with the terms of this exhibit was consummated May 1, 1887. (Bigbie Bros. & Co.'s record, p. 52, Qs. 9–12.) That Bigbie Brothers & Company purchased the stock of Joseph Lawson & Son and rented his place of business upon that date is established by Bluthenthal & Bickart's witness Withers. (Qs. 27, 28.) That Bigbie Brothers & Company regarded themselves as the successors in business of Joseph Lawson & Son subsequent to that purchase appears from the conduct of Bigbie Brothers & Company immediately upon their entrance into business in the matter of brands and labels, as shown by the testimony of Bigbie, to which reference has already been made. It is not testified by any witness that Joseph Lawson & Son did not make such transfer of business to Bigbie Brothers & Company as would carry the right to the trade-mark "Old Velvet." Neither Bluthenthal & Bickart nor The J. & G. Butler Company claim title from the Lawsons, and it is believed that their claims to registration are defeated by the use of the mark in issue by Bigbie Brothers & Company in 1887 and subsequently, irrespective of whether Bigbie Brothers & Company's use was based upon ownership.

Lawson's right to the mark after the transfer in 1887 is only of consequence, therefore, in determining whether Bigbie Brothers & Company shall be denied registration, notwithstanding their position as the first to adopt and use the mark among those before the Office seeking registration thereon. It is believed that they should not be denied registration under such circumstances unless the ownership by outsiders is proved. Such proof is wanting in this case. The proper inference from all the evidence is believed, on the contrary, to be that the whisky business of Joseph Lawson & Son, including the trade-mark rights in the words "Old Velvet," passed to Bigbie Brothers & Company in 1887 and that the subsequent use of this mark by Lawson_was probably an infringement of their ownership thereof.

Bluthenthal & Bickart contend that Bigbie Brothers & Company have been guilty of laches in the enforcement of their rights; but the evidence cited in support of this contention is entirely insufficient to support the rejection of Bigbie Brothers & Company's application on that ground.

That The J. & G. Butler Company is entitled to no earlier date of adoption and use of the words "Velvet" or "Old Velvet" as a trademark for whisky than 1890 is believed to be clear. The only witnesses who testify definitely to the use of brands or labels in commerce are Fred W. Butler and George S. Butler. Fred W. Butler proves the Butler exhibit "Later Formula Book" and the formula entitled therein "Velvet Rye" as written by him on December 20, 1883. (Qs. 8 and 9.) He also testifies to continuous sale, handling, or preparation of "Old Velvet" rye whisky by the company since 1882, (Q. 12;) but the mere adoption of a name for its goods did not vest in the company trade-mark rights. To acquire such rights, the name must be physically applied to the goods in trade, as by brands or labels on the packages sold. As to the application of the mark to the goods Fred W. Butler was asked and answered as follows:

Q. 15. I hand you three labels which are marked, respectively, "Butler Exhibit, 1871 Label," "Butler Exhibit, 1890 Label" and "Butler Exhibit, Present Label," and ask you if you are familiar with these labels and if you can do so, tell us when and how they are used or have been used?

(Objection by counsel for Bluthenthal & Bickart, on the ground that the question is rendered indefinite and obscure by presenting three different labels to the witness at the same time and that the question is grossly leading in respect to the dates which have been applied to the several labels as descriptive of them respectively.)

(Same objection by counsel for Bigbie Bros. & Co. and further objected to if it seeks to obtain from the witness testimony as to facts outside of his pernal knowledge.)

A. Yes, I can. This label, marked "1871 Label," was used, I am told by embers of the firm at that time, from 1871 and know them to be used until

1890. From 1890 until 1900 we used the "1890 Label." From 1900 until the present time we use the "Present Label."

It appears to have been upon this answer that the Examiner of Interferences gave The J. & G. Butler Company the date 1882. when Fred W. Butler entered the business, as its date of adoption of the mark. It is very possible, however, that the witness had no personal knowledge of the use of the labels to which he refers when he entered the business or until shortly before the year 1890. He does not state that he did, and it is not believed that this crucial point, which if true could have been stated and should have been stated by the witness, should be inferred from the statements made. In failing to produce more definite evidence of an earlier date than 1890 for the use of the mark as a trade-mark in the business The J. & G. Butler Company clearly failed to prove its case.

George S. Butler became connected with the company in 1894 or 1895 (Q. 4) and does not claim any knowledge of the business, except by hearsay, prior to 1888, when he was about the store more or less as a fourteen-year-old school-boy. (X-Qs. 42–44.) He offered no admissible statements of the application of the mark in trade prior to 1890. The witness Riley fixes nothing concerning the trade-mark in issue. Samuel H. Davis bought "Old Velvet" whisky from the Butlers in 1851; but he does not establish that the name was applied as a trade-mark. His nearest approach is in answer to question 20; but this unsupported reference to the indication of the brand on a card attached to a jug is regarded as entirely insufficient to prove that the title was so habitually attached to the goods sold as to have become a trade-mark. Marion Davis, referring to the year 1861, or thereabout, states that his father bought "Old Velvet" whisky from J. & G. Butler in jugs which were not labeled, as he remembers. (Qs. 16–18.) He states that whisky was kept in the store in barrels and that the kind of whisky was indicated on the barrel in chalk. No sale of labeled or branded barrels or packages appears. Fuller's testimony covers the period from 1862 to 1890 more or less fully, but is defective in the matter of sales of marked packages. He states that there was only one barrel marked "Velvet Rye" in the store. (X-Q. 33.)

The indication of a name in chalk upon a single barrel from which whisky is sold is not believed to establish a trade-mark right, though continued through a long period of years. There is no liability to confusion of the origin of goods which are sold only upon the premises of the originator. The utility of a trade-mark does not come into existence until the goods have passed from the hands of the originator, and it is only by the presence of the mark upon the goods after they have so passed that rights to the same as a trade-mark are believed to become established.

In *Columbia Mill Co.* v. *Alcorn* (C. D., 1893, 672; 65 O. G., 1916; 150 U. S., 460, 463) Justice Jackson said of a trade-mark:

> It must be designed, as its primary object and purpose, to indicate the owner or producer of the commodity and to distinguish it from like articles manufactured by others.

In *McLean* v. *Fleming* (C. D., 1878, 262; 13 O. G., 913; 96 U. S., 245, 254) Justice Clifford stated:

> Stamps or trade-marks of the kind are employed to point out the origin, ownership, or place of manufacture or sale of the article to which it is affixed, or to give notice to the public who is the producer or where it may be purchased.

In *Dennison Mfg. Co·* v. *Thomas Mfg. Co.* (94 F. R., 651, 656) it was said:

> The function of a trade-mark is to indicate to the public the origin, manufacture or ownership of articles to which it is applied, and thereby secure to its owner all benefit resulting from his identification by the public with the articles bearing it.

In *Larrabee* v. *Lewis* (67 Ga., 561) it was said:

> A trade-mark is defined to be the name, symbol, figure, letter, form, or device, used by a manufacturer or merchant to designate the goods he manufactures or sells, to distinguish from those manufactured or sold by another, to the end that they may be known *in the market* as his, and to secure such profits as result from a reputation for superior skill, industry, or enterprise. (Italics mine.)

The only use of the words " Old Velvet " by the Butlers, so far as proved, seems to have been merely as a name for a certain kind of whisky—a mere matter of convenience in the store or of advertisement. This name does not appear to have served, to have been intended to serve, or to have been so used that it might serve as a means of distinguishing in the market the goods of the Butlers from those of others.

The decision of the Examiner of Interferences awarding priority of adoption and use of the trade-mark in issue to Bigbie Brothers & Company *is affirmed.*

BEHREND *v.* LAMME.

Decided November 26, 1906.

(126 O. G., 1065.)

INTERFERENCE—SHIFTING CLAIMS FROM ONE APPLICATION TO ANOTHER—TRANSMISSION AT REQUEST OF PRIMARY EXAMINER.

> Where a party having two applications involved in companion interferences presents amendments canceling the interfering claims from one application and adding them to the other for the purpose of withdrawing one application from interference and concealing its subject-matter, *Held* that the request of the Primary Examiner that the interference be trans-

mitted to him for the purpose of considering these amendments should be granted, as the other party will not be seriously inconvenienced by the slight delay caused by taking the desired action.

ON PETITION.

DYNAMO-ELECTRIC MACHINE.

Mr. Charles E. Lord and *Mr. Thomas Howe* for Behrend.
Mr. Wesley G. Carr for Lamme.

ALLEN, *Commissioner:*

This is a petition by Behrend from the refusal of the Examiner of Interferences to grant the Primary Examiner's request that the interference papers be transmitted to him for the purpose of considering certain amendments.

It appears from the record that this interference is one of a series of three involving related subject-matter. The preliminary statements have not been opened and the parties have not had access to their opponent's applications. Behrend has two applications, one involved in this interference and the other in interferences No. 26,071 and No. 26,072. In all of the interferences Behrend's opponent is the Westinghouse Electric & Manufacturing Company, as assignee of the applications involved. Behrend has filed amendments canceling from his application involved in this interference the claims in issue and inserting those claims in his other application. His purpose in doing so is to withdraw one of the applications from the interference proceedings, thus withholding it from the view of his opponents. If Behrend's application contains matter which he desires to keep secret, there appears to be no reason why he should not be permitted to do so in the manner suggested.

While, as stated by the Examiner of Interferences, Behrend did not file the amendments referred to above as promptly as he might have done, it is not thought that this is a sufficient reason for refusing to enter them, especially as it does not appear that the other party to the interference will be seriously inconvenienced by the slight delay that will be caused by taking the desired action.

The petition is granted.

EX PARTE HEYLMAN.

Decided November 26, 1906.

(126 O. G., 1066.)

APPLICATION—DESCRIPTION—LAUDATORY STATEMENTS.

An applicant should under no circumstances be allowed in his specification to make derogatory statements as to the inventions of others; but within reasonable limits he may in pointing out the advantages of his invention indicate also what he regards as the defects or deficiencies common to structures representing the unimproved art, and the fact that in making this distinction he states that his device is superior to preceding forms in certain respects wherein it differs from them is not a matter of importance. (Citing *ex parte Shaw*, C. D., 1890, 31; 50 O. G., 1129; *ex parte Schoshusen*, C. D., 1905, 214; 116 O. G., 2008.)

ON PETITION.

CULTIVATOR.

Mr. George Wetmore Colles for the applicant.

ALLEN, *Commissioner:*

This is a petition from the requirement of the Primary Examiner that certain passages in the specification be canceled or revised. The Examiner is of the opinion that the passages referred to consist of laudatory statements of the character condemned in certain decisions, which he cites. The matter objected to is as follows:

While former cultivators have been provided with a joint permitting of these movements, the joint or articulation herein shown is of a novel and improved form and constitutes an important element of my invention. * * *

The form of articulation thus described offers advantages over the form previously used, both in the ease of construction and of adjustment, and in the manner of removing and replacing the same, because the gang can be disconnected by withdrawing either the bolt 96 or the bolt 102, and withdrawn from the machine without disturbing any other parts of the apparatus. * * *

This construction is superior to old forms not only in the fact that a lateral movement of the treadle is produced by a vertical movement of the foot, which is easiest for the operator to exert, but also in the fact that the link 117 is independent of the axle-arm 28, consequently is removed from the axle-arm along with the shovel-gang by removing the bolt 96; and when the position of the piece 90 is movably adjusted upon the sleeves 82, the link 117 does not require separate adjustment, as is the case in a former construction.

The rule to be followed in determining the limit to which an applicant may go in comparing his invention with the prior art was well stated in the case of *ex parte Shaw*, (C. D., 1890, 31; 50 O. G., 1129,) from which the following passage is quoted:

I am very clear that under no circumstances whatever should applicants be allowed in their specifications to make derogatory statements as to the inventions of others; but, on the other hand, I am equally convinced that the Office cannot assume the duty of determining when language of general criticism may be employed, as in the present case. It may be difficult to draw the line; but the line must be drawn; and it must be held that within reasonable limits an applicant may, in pointing out the advantages of his invention, point out also what he regards as the defects or deficiencies common to the structures representing the unimproved art.

The language used by the applicant to which exception has been taken does not seem to exceed the bounds of propriety either in the way of hostile criticism of the inventions of others or objectionable praise of his own device. Rule 36 of the Rules of Practice requires that the specification must distinguish between what is old and is claimed as new. The fact that the applicant in making this distinction states that his device is superior to preceding forms in certain respects wherein it differs from them is not a matter of importance. It is probable that in all cases applicants regard their inventions as having some points of superiority over prior devices.

The language objected to in this case seems to distinguish between what is new and what is old, as required by the rule, and, as stated in *ex parte Schoshusen*, (C. D., 1905, 214; 116 O. G., 2008,) should be distinguished from statements which are mere laudatory and are inserted for advertising purposes.

The petition is granted.

Ex parte Leich.

Decided November 26, 1906.

(126 O. G., 1066.)

1. ABANDONED APPLICATION—SUFFICIENCY OF AMENDMENT.

   Where the first amendment made by applicant five days before the expiration of the year from the Examiner's first action rejecting all the claims consisted of a few corrections to the specification, an argument as to the patentability of the claims, and the addition of a new claim, and the Examiner in admitting this amendment and rejecting the claims warned applicant that it was not such an action as the condition of the case required and that the added claim was so broad as to be met in nearly all selective signaling systems, and where, following this, applicant filed an amendment two days before the expiration of a year from the last action of the Examiner in which he amended all of the claims except the broad claim added by the previous amendment, which claim he neither canceled nor amended nor presented any reasons why he considered it allowable, *Held* that the latter amendment was not entirely responsive to the Examiner's rejection and was not sufficient to save the application from abandonment.

2. SAME—REPEATED DELAYS—RIGHTS STRICTLY CONSTRUED.

   Where an applicant attempts to excuse the delay in the prosecution of his case on the ground that its subject-matter is dominated by certain claims in a copending application and that he considered it advisable to press the broad application to allowance before letting this application go to issue, *Held* that the conduct of applicant in the prosecution of his case has not been such as to entitle him to leniency in the application of the rule that amendments must be such as the condition of the case requires and that in electing to prosecute his application in this manner he must assume all risk as to the sufficiency of his actions.

On Petition.

SELECTIVE SIGNALING SYSTEM.

Messrs. Bulkley & Durand for the applicant.

Allen, *Commissioner:*

This is a petition from the action of the Primary Examiner holding this application to be abandoned.

The record of this application shows that applicant's first amendment was filed April 10, 1905, five days before the expiration of the year from the Examiner's first action rejecting all the claims. This amendment made a few corrections in the specification, argued the patentability of the claims over the references, and added a new claim. This amendment was admitted by the Examiner; but in his letter rejecting all of the claims he warned applicant that his amendment was not such an action as the condition of the case required and that the added claim was so broad as to be met in nearly all of the many selective signaling systems. It thus appears that the Examiner is of the opinion that this claim was inserted merely to prevent him from finally rejecting the claims in his next action, and thereby closing the prosecution of the case before him.

The Examiner's action of May 2, 1905, following this amendment, rejected all the claims. On April 30, 1906, two days before the expiration of a year from the Examiner's action, applicant filed an amendment in which all of the claims were amended except the broad claim added by the previous amendment. This claim 11 was neither amended nor canceled by applicant, nor did he present any reasons why he considered it allowable. The Examiner held this amendment not to be such an amendment as the case required and that the case was abandoned. Following this action of the Examiner, applicant filed an amendment on June 7, 1906, canceling claim 11, which amendment the Examiner refused to enter and repeated his action holding the case abandoned. Applicant thereupon brought this petition.

Accompanying the brief in behalf of applicant is the affidavit of one of his attorneys that—

* * * in the preparation of the amendment dated April 28, 1906, it was applicant's intention to cancel claim 11, as this claim was clearly met by the references; that the failure to do so was a mere clerical error, and an oversight in the preparation of the said amendment.

The amendment of April 30, 1906, was clearly not entirely responsive to the Examiner's rejection, since no action whatever was taken as to claim 11. (*Ex parte Schmitt and Tanody*, C. D., 1906, 102; 121 O. G., 688.)

Applicant's conduct in the prosecution of the case has not been such as to entitle him to leniency in the application of the rule that the amendment must be such as the condition of the case requires. (*Ex parte Ries*, C. D., 1904, 501; 113 O. G., 1147; *ex parte Naef*, C. D., 1905, 137; 115 O. G., 2135.)

Petitioner attempts to excuse the delay in the prosecution of his case on the ground that the subject-matter of this application is dominated by certain claims in a copending application and that he has " considered it advisable to press the broad application to allowance before letting this application go to issue." In electing to prosecute his application in this manner, however, the applicant must assume all risk as to the sufficiency of his action. (*Ex parte Morrison*, C. D., 1902, 226; 99 O. G., 2969.)

Under the circumstances of this case it is held that applicant's amendment is not sufficient to save the case from abandonment.

The petition is denied.

Ex parte Hiett.

Decided November 16, 1906.

(126 O. G., 1067.)

REISSUE—LONG-DELAY IN FILING APPLICATION EXCUSED.

H. filed an application on September 16, 1896, upon which a patent was granted on April 20, 1897. In 1898 H. instructed his attorneys to prepare a reissue application, but before such application was filed F. obtained a patent dated July 4, 1899, on an application filed May 31, 1898, covering mechanism of the character covered by H.'s patent. In looking over the record of the F. patent H. found an affidavit filed to overcome the rejection of his claims, the oath stating that the invention had been made " many months prior to September 16, 1896," the filing date of H.'s application. In view of this affidavit H. considered it useless to apply for a reissue. In a suit brought in 1904 by the assignee of the F. patent against the assignee of the H. patent it was brought out that the machine to which the affidavit referred as having been made " many months " before H. filed his application had, in fact, been made in 1889 or 1890, and the court held that said machine was either inoperative and impracticable or abandoned by laches. *Held* that under the circumstances a reissue applied for promptly after the decision of the court should not be refused on the ground of delay in applying therefor.

APPEAL from Examiners-in-Chief.

CALCULATING-MACHINE.

Mr. Thomas F. Sheridan for the applicant.

MOORE, *Acting Commissioner:*

This case comes before me on appeal from the decision of the Examiners-in-Chief affirming the rejection by the Primary Examiner, on the ground of laches, of claims 55, 56, and 57 of Hiett's application for a reissue patent.

Hiett filed his original application September 16, 1896, and his patent was granted April 20, 1897. On May 31, 1898, Dorr E. Felt applied for a patent on mechanism of the character covered by the Hiett patent, and in order to overcome the rejection of his claims he filed an affidavit containing allegations of fact which, if true, were a sufficient compliance with Rule 75 of the Rules of Practice. In this affidavit Felt stated that he made the invention covered by the rejected claims—

many months prior to September 16, 1896, which is the filing application date of Patent No. 580,863, to D. J. K. T. Hiett.

Felt's patent was granted July 4, 1899.

In his affidavit accompanying his reissue application Hiett alleges that in the year 1898 he instructed his attorneys to prepare an application for reissue and that during the investigation necessary for this action the Felt patent was issued. Hiett states that the record of this patent was then examined and that in view of the fact that Felt had, as stated in his affidavit, made the invention " many months prior to September 16, 1896," he, Hiett, realized that it would be useless for him to apply for a reissue.

It appears that on April 18, 1904, the Comptograph Company, assignee of Felt's patent, filed a bill in equity against the Universal Adding Machine Company, assignee of Hiett's patent, for infringement of claims 1, 2, and 4 of the Felt patent, which are identical with claims 55, 56, and 57 of Hiett's reissue application. In the final adjudication of this case by the Circuit Court of Appeals for the Seventh Circuit it was found that the machine which Felt in his patent application made oath that he constructed many months prior to September 16, 1896, was, in fact, made many years prior to that date— namely, in the year 1889 or 1890. The court further found upon the evidence that this machine was either inoperative and impracticable or, if operative and practical, it was abandoned and lost through the eight years of inaction that followed its construction. In accordance with these findings the decree of the circuit court was reversed, with instructions to enter a decree dismissing the bill for want of equity. Promptly thereafter Hiett filed his application for reissue, upon which this appeal is based.

It is contended on behalf of Hiett that he is not chargeable with laches on account of accepting Felt's sworn statement as true; that Felt in alleging that he made the invention many months prior to September 16, 1896, conveyed a false impression and prevented either the Patent Office or Hiett from entertaining the idea that his machine was built eight or nine years prior to the filing of his application and from raising the question of abandonment upon which the Circuit Court of Appeals based its decision. This contention is considered sound, and there appears to be no good reason for charging Hiett with laches for attaching the same significance to Felt's affidavit that was given to it by this Office at the time of granting Felt's patent. The expression "many months" naturally excluded the idea that Felt had made the machine eight or nine years prior to the filing of his application and had since abandoned it. As soon as the true state of facts was revealed by the proceedings in the infringement suit provoked by Hiett's assignees he promptly filed his reissue application. To hold that his inaction prior to that time worked a forfeiture of his right to a reissue patent would have the effect of enabling Felt to profit by the misleading statement made in his affidavit. Under these circumstances the precise length of the delay in applying for a reissue is thought to have no bearing on the rights of the reissue applicant.

So far as known no case has ever arisen involving a state of facts identical with that existing in the present case. In the cases of *Dunbar* v. *Eastern Elevating Company* (C. D., 1896, 478; 76 O. G., 788; 75 Fed. Rep., 570) and *Thomson-Houston Electric Company* v. *Black River Traction Company* (135 Fed. Rep., 759) the facts were somewhat similar, and in both cases the reissued patents were held valid.

The decision of the Examiners-In-Chief is reversed.

TOWNSEND *v.* COPELAND *v.* ROBINSON.

Decided January 11, 1907.

(126 O. G., 1355.)

1. INTERFERENCE—CLAIMS PRESENTED UNDER RULE 109—PRACTICE.

   The reasons which led to the change in Rule 124, set forth in *Newcomb* v. *Thomson*, (C. D., 1906, 232; 122 O. G., 3012,) apply with nearly the same force to motions under Rule 109. The purpose of Rule 109 is to avoid a second interference. If a party wishes to appeal from an adverse decision on the merits of his claims presented under Rule 109, he should be permitted to do so to the full extent provided by law in order that the necessity for a subsequent *ex parte* appeal and the possibility of a second interference may be avoided.

2. SAME—SAME—SAME.

   The practice concerning motions to add claims under Rule 109 should follow the procedure set forth in Rule 124 relative to motions for dissolution. The amendment accompanying the motion made under Rule 109 should be entered in the application, and if the Examiner holds that the claims are not allowable to the party bringing the motion he will reject the claims. Following Rule 124, the Examiner will also set a time for reconsideration, and if after reconsideration he adheres to his original decision he will finally reject the claims and fix a limit of appeal.

APPEAL ON MOTION.

ON PETITION.

BICYCLE.

Mr. T. Hart Anderson and *Mr. Melville Church for* Townsend.
Mr. Gales P. Moore for Copeland.
Mr. William Robinson pro se.

ALLEN, *Commissioner:*

This case comes up on appeals by Townsend and Copeland from the decision of the Primary Examiner denying their motions to amend their applications under Rule 109, also on petitions by the same parties that—

* * * the Primary Examiner's action refusing to permit your petitioner to amend his application and to include his amended claims in the interference, be revised and reversed, or that the Examiner be directed to reconsider his action and if, on such reconsideration, he is still of the opinion that your petitioner's motion should be denied, that he be directed to set a limit of appeal in order that your petitioner's right of appeal to the Board of Examiners-in-Chief may be perfected.

Motions by Townsend and Copeland to amend their applications under Rule 109 so as to include as additional counts of the interference twelve claims made by Robinson were denied by the Primary Examiner on the ground that said claims are not patentable to either Towensend or Copeland in view of Robinson's patent, No. 723,408. Townsend and Copeland thereupon requested a reconsideration of the Examiner's action. This request was denied by the Primary Examiner, who held that the rules do not provide for a reconsideration of motions brought under Rule 109 and that the reconsideration provided for in Rule 124 applies only to motions for dissolution.

It is well established that no appeal lies to the Commissioner in the first instance from the action of the Primary Examiner denying motions on grounds involving the merits of the claims. The appeal and so much of the petition as asks that the decision of the Examiner be revised and reversed are accordingly dismissed.

It remains to consider that portion of the petition which asks that the Primary Examiner be directed to reconsider his actions and, if of the same opinion, to set a limit of appeal in order that appeal may be taken to the Board of Examiners-in-Chief.

That the denial of a motion under Rule 109 on grounds involving the merits of the claims is appealable in the first instance to the Examiners-in-Chief is well settled. (*Berry* v. *Fitzsimmons*, C. D., 1902, 153; 99 O. G., 862; *Hillard* v. *Fisher*, C. D., 1902, 448; 101 O. G., 2290; *Hillard* v. *Eckert*, C. D., 1902, 413; 101 O. G., 1831; *O'Connor* v. *Vanderbilt*, C. D., 1903, 68; 102 O. G., 1782.) The only question for determination is the procedure to be followed in taking the appeal to the Examiners-in-Chief.

Formerly in case of motions under Rule 109, as well as in motions for dissolution, if the matter was an appealable one the case was in condition for appeal after the first decision of the Examiner. A different course of procedure was established by Rule 124 as amended June 12, 1906, (122 O. G., 2690,) in the case of motions for dissolution. The petition presents the question whether this course of procedure is also applicable to motions under Rule 109. The reasons` which led to the change in Rule 124, set forth in my decision in the case of *Newcomb* v. *Thomson*, (C. D., 1906, 232; 122 O. G., 3012,) apply with nearly the same force to motions under Rule 109. As stated in the case of *ex parte Sutton, Steele, and Steele*, (C. D., 1906, 111; 121 O. G., 1012,) the purpose of Rule 109 is to avoid a second interference. If the claims presented under Rule 109 are to become the issue of an interference proceeding, they should be included in the pending interference and not in a second interference subsequently declared. If a party wishes to appeal from an adverse decision on the merits of his claims presented under Rule 109, he should be permitted to do so to the full éxtent provided by law in order that the necessity for a subsequent *ex parte* appeal and the possibility of a second interference may be avoided.

No difficulty is anticipated in applying the procedure of Rule 124 to motions under Rule 109. In the case of motions for dissolution the claims are already in the applications. Under Rule 109 the claims are presented by a proposed amendment which accompanies the motion, and the practice will require the entry first of the amendment in the application. The rejection of the claims and subsequent procedure will then follow the practice indicated in Rule 124. If the Examiner holds that the claims are not allowable to the party bringing the motion, under the former practice the amendment was refused admission, while under the practice announced in this decision the amendment will be entered and the claims rejected. In neither case would the claims be added as counts to the interference unless the decision of the Examiner is reversed on appeal. The practice indicated above is not believed to be inconsistent with the present wording of Rule 109. The rule states that—

on the admission of such amendment the intervention shall be included in the interference.

The entry and rejection of claims is not such admission of the amendment as the rule contemplates in order that the claims may be added to the interference.

The Examiner is directed to enter the amendments of Copeland and Townsend in their applications and, in view of his decision of record, to reject the claims, also to set a time for reconsideration, and **if after** reconsideration he adheres to his original decision, to finally reject the claims and fix a limit of appeal in accordance with the provisions of Rule 124.

The petition is granted to the extent indicated.

MacMulkin v. Bollée.

Decided November 3, 1906.

(126 O. G., 1356.)

1. INTERFERENCE—PRIORITY—INSUFFICIENCY OF DISCLOSURE IN APPLICATION.

Where M., a patentee, who is a junior party in an interference, did not take testimony, but relied upon the insufficiency of the disclosure of B.'s application, which was pending at the time M.'s application was filed, and his patent issued, and it subsequently appears that B.'s original application did, in fact, disclose the invention in issue, *Held* that priority of invention should be awarded to B., the senior party.

2. SAME—SAME—SAME.

Where in his original drawing B. showed a valve controlling communication between several chambers and a passage leading to the cylinder of an engine and in his specification referred to the chambers as "carbureters" supplying sprayers with mixtures varying in proportion of hydrocarbon contained in the several chambers, *Held* that the use of the word "carbureter" was a sufficient disclosure of the idea of providing "hydrocarbon-inlets" in which air and hydrocarbon were to be supplied separately to each of the passages controlled by the valve, as called for by the issue.

3. SAME—DECLARATION—SUGGESTION OF CLAIMS NEGATIVES PRESUMPTION OF
    NEW MATTER IN SUBSTITUTE SPECIFICATION.

Where the Examiner stated in a letter to B. suggesting the claims in interference that the interference was not declared during the pendency of M.'s application for the reason that B.'s original specification so obscurely presented his invention that it could not be understood at that time, *Held* that the Examiner's action in admitting a substitute specification and drawing was, in effect, a ruling on his part that the substitute specification and drawing did not contain new matter.

APPEAL from Examiners-in-Chief.

CARBURETER.

Messrs. Howson & Howson for MacMulkin.
Mr. Wm. E. Boulter for Bollée.

MOORE, *Acting Commissioner:*

‥is case comes before me on appeal from the decision of the Ex-
    ‥s-in-Chief reversing the decision of the Examiner of Interfer-
    ‥nd awarding priority of invention to the senior party, Bollée.
    ‥ invention in issue is an improvement in carbureters for inter-
    ‥ombustion engines. The object of the invention is to provide
    ‥ns for varying the quantity of explosive mixture supplied to the
    ‥nder without altering the proportion of air to gas in the mixture.
    ‥s object is accomplished by providing a plurality of carbureters.

together with a valve, by means of which one or more of the carbureters can be placed in communication with the cylinder. The subject-matter in issue is defined in the following counts:

1. A vaporizer for liquid hydrocarbons, comprising a number of hydrocarbon-inlets, a separate air-inlet to each hydrocarbon-inlet, a common outlet-pipe and means for cutting off one or more of the pairs of hydrocarbon-inlets and air-inlets simultaneously, as described.

2. A vaporizer for liquid hydrocarbons, comprising a number of inlets for hydrocarbon and means at all times to supply a constant flow to each inlet, an air-supply to each said inlet, an outlet for the vaporized mixture and a throttle-valve between the individual inlets and the outlet adapted to cut off or open more or fewer of the combined air and hydrocarbon inlets, substantially as described.

3. A vaporizer for liquid hydrocarbons, comprising an outlet-pipe, a throttle-valve opening thereto, a body part containing a plurality of chambers, a separate passage from each chamber to the throttle-valve and an air-supply and a hydrocarbon-supply to each chamber, the throttle-valve being adapted to cut off more or fewer of the chambers from the outlet-pipe, substantially as described.

MacMulkin, the junior party, has taken no testimony, but contends that the invention in issue was not disclosed in Bollée's application as originally filed and that no amendment embodying the invention was filed until subsequently to the filing of MacMulkin's application. Bollée's application was filed August 3, 1903. On September 3, 1903, the Examiner stated that the invention was not sufficiently explained or illustrated and declined to act on the merits of the claims. MacMulkin filed his application December 3, 1903, and his patent was granted May 10, 1904. On July 14, 1904, Bollée filed a substitute specification, and on August 22, 1904, he filed a substitute drawing. The Examiner on October 1, 1904, directed Bollée's attention to MacMulkin's patent and suggested to him for the purpose of declaring an interference the claims now in issue. The Examiner informed Bollée in the letter suggesting these claims that interference proceedings were not instituted at the time MacMulkin's application was pending, for the reason that Bollée's original specification so obscurely presented his invention that it could not be understood therefrom. The Examiner's action in admitting the substitute specification and drawing was, in effect, a ruling on his part that the substitute specification and drawing did not contain new matter and that there was a foundation in Bollée's original application for the claims which he suggested to him. The Examiner of Interferences, however, ruled to the contrary; but the Examiners-in-Chief found that the invention was disclosed in Bollée's original application and accordingly awarded priority of invention to him. I am of the opinion that the conclusions reached by the Examiners-in-Chief were correct.

In the drawing of his original application Bollée showed a valve controlling communication between several chambers, which he termed "carbureters," and a passage leading to the cylinder of the engine. The primary purpose of a carbureter for an internal-combustion engine is to form a mixture of air with hydrocarbon. There can be no question, therefore, that the mere use of the term "carbureter" was a sufficient disclosure of the idea of providing " hydrocarbon-inlets," as specified in the issue. It is contended by MacMulkin that from all that appears in Bollée's application he might have intended to supply carbureted air from a reservoir, or if he intended to use an oil-supply he might have used a common mixer leading to the various passages controlled by the valve. Bollée, however, in his original specification stated that he proposed to use a number of carbureters, and he referred to the several chambers controlled by the valve as " carbureters." He furthermore stated that practically perfect results could be secured by the use of two carbureters. In this connection the following passage occurs on page 3 of his original specification:

The size of two carbureters is calculated so that at low speeds the proper mixture is supplied by the small carbureter alone, while at high speeds it is insured by the two carbureters acting together, the carburation in the small one becoming too rich while in the large one it is a little too poor.

In claim 2 as originally filed Bollée also referred to the use of several carbureters supplying mixtures containing different proportions of air and hydrocarbon.

The language referred to conclusively shows that Bollée did not intend to supply carbureted air from a reservoir or to use a common mixer communicating with the several passages controlled by the valve. If he had done either of these things, he would not have had, as he states, a mixture from one carbureter too rich in hydrocarbon and from another too poor in hydrocarbon, but would have had a mixture of the same strength coming from all of the openings controlled by the valve. Furthermore, the mere fact that he described the use of several carbureters negatives MacMulkin's contention that from all that appears in the specification Bollée might have intended to supply carbureted air from a reservoir or might have used a common mixer. If he had proceeded in either of these ways, he would not have had a plurality of carbureters, as described in his original specification, but would have had a single carbureter.

Bollée's original specification not only shows that he intended each of the passages governed by the valve to be provided with an air-inlet and a hydrocarbon-inlet, as specified in the issue, but that he intended to use a hydrocarbon-inlet of the specific character shown in his amended drawings—i. e., a " sprayer "—for in lines 17 to 26 of page 3 he referred to the escape of the liquid fuel from the sprayer.

I am of the opinion that it would be impossible for any one skilled in the art to read Bollée's original specification in connection with the drawing accompanying it without perceiving that air and hydrocarbon were to be supplied separately to each of the passages controlled by the valve. In the original specification a plurality of carbureters is referred to, and the drawing shows a plurality of chambers referred to as "carbureters." The specification refers to the use of sprayers and contains a statement to the effect that the several chambers or carbureters supply mixtures varying in the proportion of hydrocarbon contained therein. Such a result could be secured only by providing each of the chambers controlled by the valve with means for supplying air and hydrocarbon. In other words, each chamber must be what Bollée called it in the original specification—a "carbureter" containing the elements common to the carbureters which were old and well known long before the filing of either of the applications involved in this interference.

The decision of the Examiners-in-Chief is affirmed.

EX PARTE HIPP.

Decided December 6, 1906.

(126 O. G., 2189.)

OATH—BEFORE NOTARIES PUBLIC—APPLICATION OF ACT OF JUNE 29, 1906.

The act of June 29, 1906, amending section 558 of the code of the District of Columbia relative to the powers of notaries public, is of local application only.

ON PETITION.

FISH-HOOK.

Messers. Paul & Paul for the applicant.

ALLEN, *Commissioner:*

This a petition that the Primary Examiner be directed to withdraw his requirement for a new oath.

The oath of the inventor forming part of the application was sworn to before Richard Paul, a member of the firm of Paul & Paul, the inventor's attorneys of record. Under the provisions of the act of June 29, 1906, amending section 558 of the code of the District of Columbia, the Examiner held that Paul was disqualified from administering the oath in this case by reason of the fact that he is the applicant's attorney of record.

The provision of the act of June 29, 1906, relied upon by the Examiner reads as follows:

And provided further, that no notary public shall be authorized to take acknowledgments, administer oaths, certify papers, or perform any official acts in connection with matters in which he is employed as counsel, attorney, or agent or in which he may be in any way interested before any of the Departments aforesaid.

In an opinion rendered on October 12, 1906, the Assistant Attorney-General for the Interior Department made the following statement:

It cannot be properly inferred that Congress intended by this provision in an act having local application only, to amend the general laws (section 4892, Revised Statutes) prescribing the officers before whom applicants for patents may make the oath required.

In view of the construction placed upon the statute in the opinion referred to the petition is granted.

CLEMENT v. BROWNE v. STROUD.

Decided January 10, 1907.

(126 O. G., 2189.)

1. INTERFERENCE—DISSOLUTION—INOPERATIVENESS—MOTION TO TAKE TESTIMONY.
   In presenting a motion to dissolve based upon alleged inoperativeness there is no necessity for a showing on the part of the moving party that his own structure is not inoperative, since dissolution will be necessary whether one or both of the structures is inoperative; but such showing is necessary to support a motion before the Examiner of Interferences for permission to take testimony on the question of operativeness.

2. SAME—SAME—SAME—AFFIDAVITS IN SUPPORT OF MOTION TO TAKE TESTIMONY.
   Where affidavits are presented in support of a motion to take testimony on the question of the operativeness of the opposing party's device, they will not be transmitted to the Primary Examiner to consider the sufficiency thereof, as they are not pertinent to the motion to dissolve, but only to the motion to take testimony, which is a matter for the consideration of the Examiner of Interferences.

ON MOTION.

TELEPHONY.

Mr. Edward E. Clement pro se.

Mr. Charles Neave and *Messrs. Mauro, Cameron, Lewis & Massie* for Browne.

Mr. George L. Cragg and *Messrs. Bacon & Milans* for Stroud.

ALLEN, *Commissioner:*

This case comes up on motion by Stroud that the interference be transmitted to the Primary Examiner with instructions to fix a date for hearing the parties on the following questions:

The sufficiency of the showing made by Browne to warrant his motion to take testimony relative to the inoperativeness of Stroud system, and

2. Whether the showing of inoperativeness made by Browne is as fully applicable to his own device as to that of Stroud.

The third ground involves the questions referred to in the second ground mentioned above.

The record shows that Browne filed a motion to dissolve the interference on the ground that Stroud's application does not disclose an operative telephone system. This motion was denied by the Primary Examiner. Thereupon Browne moved before the Examiner of Interferences for permission to take testimony relative to the question of the operativeness of the system disclosed in Stroud's application. The Examiner of Interferences granted the motion; but upon appeal it was held that as Browne had failed to show that the arguments and statements of facts directed against the operativeness of Stroud's device did not apply to the system shown in his own application the motion should not have been granted, and the case was remanded to the Examiner of Interferences for the purpose of permitting Browne to cure the defect referred to. Browne has now filed additional affidavits for this purpose, and it is the object of the motion now under consideration to have this additional showing considered by the Primary Examiner. There is nothing in Rule 130 or in the decisions relative to the practice to be followed in cases of this kind warranting such action. In presenting a motion to dissolve based upon alleged inoperativeness there is no necessity for a showing on the part of the moving party that his own structure is not inoperative. Dissolution will be necessary whether one or both of the structures is inoperative. It is only on motion before the Examiner of Interferences for permission to take testimony that the necessity arises for a showing that the alleged ground of inoperativeness does not apply to the structure of the moving party, and the necessity for such showing at that time arises from the fact that an attack upon the operativeness of the devices disclosed by both parties does not relate to the question of priority of invention. In the present case all matters necessary to the determination of Browne's motion to dissolve have already been before the Primary Examiner, and no reason is apparent for remanding the interference to him again for the consideration of the additional affidavits filed by Browne, as these affidavits have been filed solely for the purpose of showing that the questions raised by his motion relate to priority of invention, a matter not within the jurisdiction of the Primary Examiner.

The motion is denied.

THE UNITED STATES PLAYING CARD COMPANY *v.* C. M. CLARK
PUBLISHING COMPANY.

Decided January 10, 1907.

(126 O. G., 2190.)

1. TRADE-MARK INTERFERENCE—MARK USED TO INDICATE GRADE INSTEAD OF
ORIGIN OF GOODS NOT A TRADE-MARK.

The price-lists and sample pack of cards indicate that the company
adopted the mark to designate a certain grade or style of cards which they
offered for sale at a specified price and to distinguish this variety of cards
from numerous other styles made and sold by said company. There is no
evidence that the mark was used to indicate the origin or manufacture
of the cards; but, on the contrary, a fanciful figure labeled "Trade-Mark"
appears to be for the purpose of indicating the origin of the goods and to
constitute properly the trade-mark of the company. *Held* that the mark
in controversy was used by said company as a grade, quality, or style
mark, and not as a technical trade-mark.

2. SAME—GRADE-MARK NOT A VALID TRADE-MARK.

Where a mark is adopted and used primarily to indicate style, grade, or
quality of goods, and not for the purpose of indicating origin or manufacture of the goods, *Held* that it does not constitute a valid trade-mark.

APPEAL from Examiner of Interferences.

TRADE-MARK FOR PLAYING-CARDS.

Messrs. Briesen & Knauth for The United States Playing Card
Company.

Mr. A. H. Spencer and *Mr. F. A. Spencer* for C. M. Clark Publishing Company.

ALLEN, *Commissioner:*

This is an appeal by C. M. Clark Publishing Company from the
decision of the Examiner of Interferences awarding priority of adoption and use to The United States Playing Card Company of the
word " Stage " as a trade-mark for playing-cards.

The senior party, C. M. Clark Publishing Company, has a registration of the mark issued November 29, 1904, on an application filed
October 20, 1904. It took no testimony and stands on its record date.

The United States Playing Card Company took the testimony of
three witnesses and has filed several exhibits in evidence. This evidence is not contradicted and must be held to establish that The
United States Playing Card Company adopted and used the word
" Stage " in connection with a certain style of playing-cards as early
as 1897.

The decision in this case turns on whether the evidence is held to
show that The United States Playing Card Company adopted and
used the mark as a trade-mark or merely as a style or grade mark.

The decision of the Examiner of Interferences that The United States Playing Card Company adopted and used the mark as a trade-mark as early as 1897 is believed to be in error.

Exhibits 1 to 19 are the semiannual price-lists of The United States Playing Card Company and cover the period from January 1, 1897, to January 1, 1906. On the first page of each of these circulars is a mark apparently consisting of the ace of spades bearing a conventional figure of Columbia, together with the label " Trade Mark." At the bottom of page 1 of Exhibits 1, 2, and 3 is the statement:

" Bicycle " and other brands of " U. S." and " National " Playing Cards (nearly 1,000 different kinds) received the " Highest Awards " at the World's Fair, Chicago. The highest official mark of distinction ever bestowed upon playing cards in America.

The other pages of the price-lists quote the prices of a large number of different styles, brands, or grades of cards. Under " Class D " of the " Wholesale Price List ' U. S.' Playing Cards " is the statement:

No.   Per gross.

65x. The Stage Playing Cards, gold edges------------------------------ $72. 00
  Professional stars, actors and actresses of the stage.
  The most attractive edition of playing cards ever issued. New and beautiful court card designs, showing portraits of world-renowned celebrities of the stage. Handsome backs in gold and colors; finest linen stock; double enameled and highly finished, and put up in handsome embossed cases.

The price-lists contain no reference to the use of the words " The Stage " or " The Stage Playing Cards " as a trade-mark.

Exhibit 20 consists of a pack of cards having the inscription—

No. 65x. The Stage Playing Cards. Gold Edges.
  Copyrighted, 1896, by The U. S. Playing Card Co., Cincinnati, U. S. A.

on the face of the box, while the ace-of-spades card in the pack has the same figure, labeled " Trade Mark," as the price-lists mentioned above. The significance of the word " Stage " appears to lie in the fact that the aces and court cards are decorated with the portraits of actors and actresses.

The price-lists and the sample pack of cards indicate that The United States Playing Card Company adopted the term including the word " Stage " to indicate a certain grade or style of cards which they offered for sale at the price specified. It distinguishes this variety of cards from the numerous other styles made and sold by the company, but it nowhere appears that it was used to indicate the origin or manufacture of the cards. On the contrary, the fanciful figure labeled " Trade Mark," noted above, appears to be for purpose of indicating the origin of the goods and to constitute properly the trade-mark of the company.

Concerning the testimony the witness Ansley states that he is the superintendent of the stationery department of the American N Company, and in answer to the leading question—

Q. 9. Have you ever handled any of the U. S. Playing Card Company's cards which were marked with a trade-mark "Stage?"

he says:

I have. I have a pack here.

This pack is then offered in evidence as "Exhibit No. 20." It is evident that this witness does not mean by this answer that the mark was used otherwise than is indicated on the pack itself.

The witness Crusius refers to "these 'stage' cards," but makes no mention of the use of the mark specifically as a trade-mark.

McCutcheon, the secretary and manager of The United States Playing Card Company, testifies:

The word "Stage" was adopted as a trade-mark in 1896 by the United States Playing Card Company, and has been used continuously since that time by said company; and at all times since there have been for sale at the New York office cards marked as shown by Exhibit 20; we have published in price-lists and catalogues and offered for sale, cards marked "Stage." A copyright was applied for by the company under my instructions through Briesen & Knauth, in 1896. Shortly after this copyright was issued, the cards were put upon the market and sold both in this country and foreign countries. It will be noted that all the price-lists produced by Mr. Ansley, marked from 1 to 19, contain advertisements of our trade-mark "Stage." (Q. 3.)

While this witness refers to the use of the mark as a trade-mark, he does not state that it was used to indicate the origin of the cards or otherwise than to indicate a certain kind of cards.

The principle that where a mark is adopted and used primarily to indicate style, grade, or quality of goods it is not a valid trade-mark is well settled by the following decisions of the United States Supreme Court: *Canal Company* v. *Clark*, (1 O. G., 279; 13 Wall., 311;) *Manufacturing Company* v. *Trainer*, (C. D., 1880, 464; 17 O. G., 1217; 101 U. S., 51;) *Lawrence Manufacturing Company* v. *Tennessee Manufacturing Company*, (C. D., 1891, 415; 55 O. G., 1528; 138 U. S., 537;) *Columbia Mill Company* v. *Alcorn*, (C. D., 1893, 672; 65 O. G., 1916; 150 U. S., 460.)

Chief Justice Fuller in *Lawrence Manufacturing Company* v. *Tennessee Manufacturing Company, supra*, said:

Nothing is better settled than that an exclusive right to the use of words, letters, or symbols, to indicate merely the quality of the goods to which they ⁻fixed, cannot be acquired. And while if the primary object of the mark dicate origin or ownership, the mere fact that the article has obtained ide sale that it has also become indicative of quality, is not of itself to debar the owner from protection, and make it the common property ade, (*Burton* v. *Stratton*, 12 Fed. Rep., 696,) yet if the device or symbol ↓ adopted for the purpose of indicating origin, manufacture, or owner- ut was placed upon the article to denote class, grade, style, or quality, it ↓ be upheld as technically a trade-mark.

In *Columbia Mill Company* v. *Alcorn*, *supra*, the Court stated:

These cases establish the following propositions: (1) That to acquire the right to the exclusive use of a name, device, or symbol, as a trade-mark, it must appear that it was adopted for the purpose of identifying the origin or ownership of the article to which it is attached, or that such trade-mark must point distinctively, either by itself or by association, to the origin, manufacture, or ownership of the article on which it is stamped. It must be designed, as its primary object and purpose, to indicate the owner or producer of the commodity and to distinguish it from like articles manufactured by others. (2) That if the device, mark, or symbol was adopted or placed upon the article for the purpose of identifying its class, grade, style, or quality, or for any purpose other than a reference to or indication of its ownership, it cannot be sustained as a valid trade-mark.

The evidence is found to show that The United States Playing Card Company adopted and used a mark the prominent feature of which is the word " stage " in 1897 as a grade, quality, or style mark for playing-cards, but fails to show that it adopted and used it as a trade-mark to indicate origin or manufacture of the goods prior to the filing date of the senior party.

The decision of the Examiner of Interferences is reversed.

WERT *v*. BORST AND GROSCOP.

Decided November 17, 1906.

(126 O. G., 2191.)

INTERFERENCE—APPEAL—DISCLAIMER BY APPELLEE—APPEAL DISMISSED.

Where appeal is taken from a decision of the Examiners-in-Chief on the question of priority and the appellee files a motion to dismiss the appeal, accompanied by a disclaimer of the invention in issue signed by the appellant, *Held* that the disclaimer will be considered a concurrence in the motion of the appellee to dismiss the appeal.

APPEAL from Examiners-in-Chief.

CEMENT-BLOCK MACHINE.

Messrs. C. A. Snow & Co. for Wert.
Mr. Edward N. Pagelsen for Borst and Groscop.

MOORE, *Acting Commissioner:*

This case comes before me on appeal by Wert from the decision of the Examiners-in-Chief affirming the decision of the Examiner of Interferences awarding priority of invention to Borst and Groscop and also on motion by Borst and Groscop that the appeal be dismissed. The motion to dismiss is based upon a duly-executed disclaimer of the invention by Wert, which disclaimer accompanies the motion. Under the rules the disclaimer cannot be given effect as such, for the reason that parties are not permitted to terminate an interference by disclaimer after the preliminary statements have been opened and approved. The filing of the disclaimer in this case, however, clearly indicates Wert's concurrence in the motion to dismiss his appeal and his consent that the judgment of priority of invention rendered against him by the Examiners-in-Chief shall become final.

The appeal is therefore dismissed.

CLEMENT *v.* BROWNE *v.* STROUD.

Decided January 10, 1907.

(126 O. G., 2589.)

1. INTERFERENCE—MOTION TO TAKE TESTIMONY ON OPERATIVENESS—GOOD FAITH.
   It must appear from the showing accompanying a motion to take testimony on the question of operativeness that the moving party is acting in good faith and that the matters alleged in support of the motion are such as to justify the setting of times for taking testimony.

2. SAME—SAME—HEARING ON SUFFICIENCY OF SHOWING—COUNTER AFFIDAVITS.
   Motions to take testimony on the question of the operativeness of an opposing party's device will generally be disposed of on the showing made by the moving party, and when the moving party files affidavits in support of his motion the Office will hear the opposing party on the sufficiency of the showing; but counter affidavits should not be admitted.

ON PETITION.

TELEPHONY.

Mr. Edward E. Clement pro se.

Mr. Chas. Neave and *Messrs. Mauro, Cameron, Lewis & Massie* for Browne.

Mr. George L. Cragg and *Messrs. Bacon & Milans* for Stroud.

ALLEN, *Commissioner:*

This is a petition by Stroud that he be given twenty days in which to reply to certain affidavits filed on behalf of Browne in connection with the latter's motion for permission to take testimony relative to the operativeness of the structure disclosed in Stroud's application involved in this interference. It was not apparent from the showing originally made in support of Browne's motion that his reasons for considering Stroud's structure inoperative would not apply to the device disclosed in his own application, as required by the decision rendered in this case on May 21, 1906, (C. D., 1906, 226; 122 O. G., 2688.) Upon appeal from this action of the Examiner of Interferences granting Browne's motion it was held that this requirement could not be dispensed with, and the case was remanded to the Examiner of Interferences for the purpose of permitting Browne to remedy the defect in the showing accompanying his motion. Browne has now filed affidavits for this purpose, and the present petition by Stroud is that a time be assigned for a reply to these affidavits.

It must appear from the showing accompanying motions of the kind under consideration that the moving party is acting in good faith and that the matters alleged in support of the motion are such as to justify the setting of times for taking testimony. No good reason is apparent for permitting the opposing party to file counter affidavits or to make any reply other than by brief or argument. As stated in the decision in *Lowry and Cowley* v. *Spoon*, (C. D., 1906, 381; 124 O. G., 1846,) it was not intended that the question of operativeness should be exhaustively considered on motions for leave to take testimony relative to that question. To permit the opposing party to file counter affidavits would result in a complete trial of the case on *ex parte* affidavits as a condition precedent to the taking of testimony. Such a course of procedure would result in unnecessary expense and delay. The purpose of requiring a preliminary showing is to prevent the expense and delay of taking testimony in those cases where the question of operativeness can be determined from inspection of the applications or patents in interference, and this purpose will be best accomplished by deciding motions of this character on the showing made by the moving party. While counter affidavits should not be considered in the present case, Stroud should be heard upon the sufficiency of the supplemental showing made by Browne. It does not appear that so long a period as twenty days should be required to prepare for the hearing in question. The Examiner of Interferences, however, will assign such date for hearing as in his opinion may be proper.

The petition is granted to the extent indicated.

WEINTRAUB *v.* HEWITT AND ROGERS.

Decided January 11, 1907.

(126 O. G., 2589.)

1. TESTIMONY UNDER RULE 130—RIGHT TO MAKE CLAIMS.

The question whether certain elements of the issue are not present in one party's structure, but can only be read into such issue by applying limitations which do not operate in the manner defined in the claims, is one of fact, upon which the opposing party may be permitted to present testimony.

2. SAME—IDENTITY OF INVENTION.

There appears to be no warrant for the taking of testimony relative to the identity of the inventions of the parties to an interference. If the inventions are not identical, it must follow either that one of the parties has no right to make the claims in issue or that the claims are indefinite and ambiguous and do not with sufficient exactness define the invention of either party. This is not a question of priority of invention.

30997—H. Doc. 470, 60-1——4

APPEALS ON MOTION.

GAS OR VAPOR ELECTRIC APPARATUS.

Mr. Albert G. Davis for Weintraub.
Mr. Charles A. Terry for Hewitt and Rogers.

ALLEN, *Commissioner:*

This case comes before me on appeal by Weintraub from the decision of the Examiner of Interferences denying his motion for leave to take testimony relative to the identity of the inventions of the parties to this interference and on appeal by Hewitt and Rogers from the decision of the Examiner of Interferences granting a motion by Weintraub for permission to take testimony for the purpose of showing that Hewitt and Rogers have no right to make the claims corresponding to certain counts of the issue.

An examination of the record in connection with the briefs and arguments of the parties indicates that the motions were correctly disposed of by the Examiner of Interferences.

Counsel for Hewitt and Rogers contends that Weintraub's arguments in connection with his motion to dissolve are inconsistent with his present attitude and that Weintraub is therefore estopped from now alleging that Hewitt and Rogers have no right to make the claims. I am of the opinion that a party should be permitted to contend both that the issue has a different meaning in the different applications and that his opponent has no right to make the claims and that there is therefore nothing in the record to prevent Weintraub from now contending that Hewitt and Rogers have no right to make the claims in issue.

Weintraub contends that certain elements of the issue are not present in Hewitt and Rogers' structure and that the claims can be read upon Hewitt and Rogers' structure only by applying the limitations of the claims to parts of Hewitt and Rogers' structure which do not operate in the manner defined in the claims. This is a question of fact, and Weintraub should be permitted to take testimony relative thereto. Nothing is found in the record, however, to warrant the taking of testimony on the question raised by Weintraub in his motion relative to the identity of the inventions of the parties to the interference. If the inventions of the parties are not identical, it must follow either that one of the parties has no right to make the claims in issue or that the claims are indefinite and ambiguous and do not with sufficient exactness define the invention of either party. The Examiner of Interferences has properly granted Weintraub's motion relative to Hewitt and Rogers' right to make the claims, thus enabling him to present testimony relative to this phase of the question raised by his other motion. The record contains nothing to indicate that the claim as applied to the structure of either or both of the parties is indefinite or ambiguous or that it can be read with different meanings upon the structures of the two parties. The question raised by such a showing, if made, would not be one of priority of invention of the subject-matter defined by the issue, but would amount to a contention that the issue did not properly define an invention made by either of the parties. I am of the opinion that the character of the showing and the nature of the question raised justified the decision of the Examiner of Interferences denying Weintraub's motion for leave to take testimony relative to the identity of the inventions of the adverse parties, for the reason that this motion raises no question not involved in the motion relative to Hewitt and Rogers' right to make the claims in issue, except the question of identity of meaning of the issue when applied to the structures of the respective parties.

The decisions of the Examiner of Interferences are affirmed.

Ex parte Fleming.

Decided January 19, 1907.

(126 O. G., 2590.)

1. Petition—Amendment Under Rule 78.

    A petition for the entry of an amendment presented under Rule 78 after the allowance of the application will be denied where the amendment includes claims which the Examiner in his report upon the petition states are not patentable.

2. Amendment Under Rule 78—Discretion of Examiner.

    The entry of claims under Rule 78 is not a matter of right, but a privilege allowed applicants where claims are found allowable by the Examiner upon such consideration of the case as he may deem proper. The Examiner will not be directed to consider the question of patentability of claims presented after his report upon petition.

On Petition.

ROLLER-BEARING.

Messrs. Hazard & Harpham and *Messrs. Davis & Davis* for the applicant.

Allen, *Commissioner:*

This is a petition for the entry of an amendment presented under Rule 78 after allowance of the application.

The amendment includes claims which the Examiner in his report upon the petition states are not patentable. The Examiner having reported that the claims are not patentable, the petition must be denied. A review of the Examiner's position upon patentability can not be undertaken upon petition for the entry of claims after allowance.

It is understood that the Examiner has refused to consider a proposed amendment and argument filed after the entry of his report upon the petition and that an order is desired directing consideration of these matters. Entry of claims under Rule 78 is not a matter of right, but a privilege accorded applicants where the claims are found allowable by the Examiner upon such consideration of the case as he may deem proper. He should not be forced to consider the question of patentability upon a petition of this kind. The time for amendment in this case as a matter of right has expired. No hardship or irreparable injury results from the refusal to enter the claims, as the applicant may secure consideration of the same as a matter of right by forfeiture and renewal of his application or by abandoning the same in favor of a continuing application.

The petition is denied.

THE CASEY-SWASEY COMPANY *v.* ROSENFIELD BROTHERS & COMPANY.

Decided October 15, 1906.

(126 O. G., 2590.)

1. TRADE-MARK INTERFERENCE—NOT RES ADJUDICATA.

The appellants took no testimony, but contend that the rights of the respective parties are *res adjudicata* by reason of a decision of the appellate court of Kentucky. This decision, however, is not of record in this case. The judgment of the court was neither pleaded nor proved, and no certified copy of the decision has been placed in evidence A different record from that filed in this proceeding was before the court.

2. SAME—TWO INTERFERING MARKS NOT ENTITLED TO REGISTRATION.

Where appellants do not claim to be the first to adopt and use the mark, but contend that they have as good a right to the mark as their opponent and that the mark should be registered to both parties or refused to both, *Held* that this contention is inconsistent with the provisions of section 7 of the act of February 20, 1905.

ON APPEAL.

TRADE-MARK FOR WHISKY.

Mr. A. L. Jackson for The Casey-Swasey Company.
Mr. A. E. Wallace for Rosenfield Brothers & Company.

MOORE, *Assistant Commissioner:*

This is an appeal from the decision of the Examiner of Interferences awarding priority of adoption and use to The Casey-Swasey Company of the words "Kentucky Comfort" as a trade-mark for whisky.

The Examiner of Interferences held that the testimony in behalf of The Casey-Swasey Company established that the mark in issue was adopted by The Casey-Swasey Company not later than 1893 and has been in continuous use since its adoption by this firm and its successors and that as this date is prior to any date that can be awarded Rosenfield Brothers & Company The Casey-Swasey Company must prevail. This finding of the Examiner of Interferences is believed to be correct.

The senior party, Rosenfield Brothers & Company, took no testimony and did not contest the interference before the lower tribunal. On the appeal, however, they filed a brief in which they contend that the rights of the respective parties to the proceeding are *res adjudicata* by reason of a decision of the appellate court of Kentucky, which they state is reported in 104 Kentucky Reports, page 616. This decision, however, is not a matter of record in this case. The judgment of the court was neither pleaded nor proved, and no certified copy of this decision has been placed in evidence. A different record from that filed in this proceeding was before the court.

According to appellants' own statement as to the nature of the court's decision, moreover, it does not appear that the decision of the Examiner of Interferences should be reversed. They do not claim to be the first to adopt and use the mark, but they contend that they have as good a right to the mark as The Casey-Swasey Company and that the mark should be registered to both parties or refused to both. They state:

It is thought by this appellant that the decision of the Kentucky court of appeals holding both parties entitled to use the mark, authorizes the honorable Commissioner of Patents, under section 7, of act of February 20, 1905, to order its registration for both parties so as to enable them to enforce their respective rights as against any one else who may attempt, at any time, to use the mark on the same class of goods, but it is insisted that if registration is refused to one party, it should be refused to both under the same section of law.

Section 7 of the act of February 20, 1905, however, provides for an interference proceeding in case applications are filed for the same or interfering marks, and states:

The Commissioner * * * may refuse to register both of two interfering marks, or may register the mark, as a trade-mark, for the person first to adopt or use the mark, if otherwise entitled to register the same. * * *

The decision of the Examiner of Interferences is found to be in accord with the evidence of record and *is therefore affirmed.*

MIEL *v.* YOUNG.

Decided October 29, 1906.

(126 O. G., 2591.)

1. INTERFERENCE—RIGHT TO MAKE CLAIM.

A party cannot be deprived of the right to make a claim by reason of the fact that his structure performs some function in addition to what is called for by the claim.

2. SAME—SAME—LIMITATION OF CLAIM BY CONSTRUCTION CONDEMNED.

A claim made by a patentee involved in interference with an applicant which refers broadly to reinforcing means should not be limited by construction to reinforcing means operating in a specified way where there is nothing in the record to show that such a limitation is necessary to render the claim patentable over the prior art, and where it is not clear that the reinforcing means disclosed by the applicant does not operate in the same way as that disclosed by the patentee.

3. SAME—SAME—ONE PARTY A PATENTEE—CONSTRUCTION OF CLAIM.

The fact that one of the parties to an interference has obtained a patent should have no bearing on the interpretation of a claim in issue in determining the right of an applicant to make such claim. If the terms of the claim do not in their ordinary meaning define the invention of the patentee as he wishes to have it defined, he may, as intimated in *Andrews* v. *Nilson*, (C. D., 1906, 717; 123 O. G., 1667,) apply for a reissue.

APPEAL from Examiners-in-Chief.

STONE-SAW.

Messrs. Bartlett, Brownell & Mitchell for Miel.
Mr. F. G. Dieterich and *Messrs. F. G. Dieterich & Company* for Young.

MOORE, *Assistant Commissioner:*

This is an appeal from the decision of the Examiners-in-Chief reversing the decision of the Examiner of Interferences and awarding priority of invention to Miel.

Miel is a patentee. His application was filed and his patent issued during the pendency of Young's application. Upon the issuance of Miel's patent Young presented in his application a claim corresponding in terms to claim 1 of the patent. This claim, which is the issue of the interference, reads as follows:

In a stone-saw, the combination of a saw-beam, a series of long bearing-blades carried thereby, and removable means for reinforcing the lower ends of the blades during the initial part of a cutting operation.

Miel filed no preliminary statement, and, being the junior party, an order to show cause why judgment should not be rendered against him was issued. Miel thereupon moved that the interference be dissolved on the ground that there was no interference in fact and that Young had no right to make the claim in issue. The motion was denied on both grounds. Miel appealed to the Commissioner from that part of the Examiner's decision relative to the question of interference in fact; but it was held that there was no reason 'he contention that the claims had different meanings in the ap-
ns of the respective parties. The Examiner of Interferences
on rendered judgment against Miel, and the latter appealed
Examiners-in-Chief. He based his appeal on the contention

that Young had no right to make the claim in issue and that the claim had different meanings in the cases of the respective parties. Before discussing the question at issue between the parties it will be necessary to consider the structure disclosed in their applications.

The invention in issue relates to means for supporting the blades of stone-saws. These saws consist of a number of strips of steel projecting perpendicularly from a saw-beam. The blades in some cases are several feet in length. The sawing is effected by the ends of the blades forcing an abrasive material against the stone. Owing to the great length of the blades they have a tendency to vibrate; but after they have entered the stone they are prevented by the sides of the kerf from vibrating laterally.

To prevent vibration, Miel shows rigid blocks between the blades, the blocks being notched at the ends to receive the edges of the blades. The blocks are suspended from the saw-beam by screw-threaded bars and may be shifted in position by means of nuts on the rods. As the sawing progresses it is necessary either to remove or raise the blocks, as their thickness is greater than the width of the kerf formed by the saw. In his specification Miel says that he may taper the blades, and thus draw the blocks up to the narrower portion of the space between the blades, where they will press upon the edges of the blades and rigidly unite them.

Young unites the blades of his saw by thin strips of metal having hooked ends which pass through apertures in the blades. The apertures are perpendicular to the faces of the blades with the exception of a slight inclined portion at one end. The hooks on the supporting members correspond in form with the apertures. The outer supporting members of the end blades are threaded and provided with a nut, by means of which all of the supporting members may be put under tension. The supporting-strips are thin and are so arranged that they can enter the kerf formed by the saw.

Miel contends that the supporting member shown by Young is not removable. Upon this point the Examiners-in-Chief state that it is clear that the reinforcing devices of Young—

are not the readily-removable reinforcing means of the issue, and that they are not intended to be removed after the initial cut has been made by the saw-blades, and furthermore are not, because of the fact that they are riveted in place, adapted to be removed after the initial part of the cutting operation has been completed.

In his specification Young states that the slots in the blades are slightly beveled to receive the upset or rivet-over portion of the inserted strip end. This language has reference to the inclined portion of the aperture in the blade referred to above. From the use of the terms "upset or rivet-over" Miel argues that the connection is a permanent one and that the means for reinforcing the lower ends of the blades are not, as specified in the claim, " removable." Young, however, in his specification states that—

the blade members are each provided with several of the slots 13 so that as the blades wear down the strip-stays 12 may be moved to the next slot higher.

The drawing of Young's application shows that the strips are not riveted to the blades in the sense in which the term " rivet " is ordinarily used. The ends of the strips are not spread or upset to form a head; but the hooked end of the strip is merely sprung into the correspondingly-shaped slot in the blade. The resiliency of the metal would doubtless be sufficient to permit the springs to be forced into the slots and out again. As no permanent connection or riveting in the ordinary sense of the term is shown and as Young specifically states that the strips can be moved from one position to another, it cannot be held that he has no right to make the claim in issue. The fact that Young's reinforcing device may not be as readily removable as Miel's and that it is not designed to be removed after the initial part of the cutting operation is completed has no bearing upon Young's right to make the claim. This claim merely specifies that the device shall be removable and is in no way limited to the manner or time of such removal. The fact that Young's reinforcing means may be used not only during the initial part of the cutting operation, but throughout the entire operation, does not deprive him of the right to a claim to " means for reinforcing the lower ends of the blades during the initial part of the cutting process." A party cannot be deprived of the right to make a claim by reason of the fact that his structure does not only what the claim calls for, but something else in addition.

The Examiners-in-Chief state in their decision that as the claim was originally made by Miel its meaning must be determined from an examination of his patent. Proceeding upon this theory, they have laid stress upon the fact that Miel's device is intended to be removed after the initial part of the cutting operation is completed. The claim, however, is silent as to whether the reinforcing means shall be removed after the completion of the initial cutting operation, merely specifying that it shall be present at that time. Furthermore, Young, if he so desired, might remove his reinforcing means at this juncture instead of permitting them to enter the kerf formed by the saw.

The Examiners-in-Chief in support of their ruling that Young has no right to make the claim also state that Miel's device is designed to prevent the blades from chattering or wabbling laterally, while Young's structure is for the purpose of enabling the blades of saw " to stand the strain of their work "—that is, to support the longitudinally. There is no limitation to this effect in the claim, which refers broadly to reinforcing means, and there is nothing in the record to show that such a limitation is necessary to render the claim patentable over the prior art. Furthermore, it is not altogether clear that the blades would not be supported laterally by Young's device as fully as by Miel's. This point, however, is not important, as the claim contains no limitation to the manner in which the blades are supported. Under somewhat similar circumstances the following language was used in the case of *Podlesak and Podlesak* v. *McInnerney*, (C. D., 1906, 268; 123 O. G., 1989:)

No better method of construing claims is perceived than to give them in each case the broadest interpretation which they will support without straining the language in which they are couched. This method would seemingly give more uniform and satisfactory results than are obtained by methods largely in vogue—such, for example, as that of importing limitations from the specification according to the exigencies of the particular situation in which the claim may stand at a given moment.

The fact that Miel is a patentee should have no bearing upon the interpretation of the claim in issue. If the terms of his claim do not in their ordinary and natural meaning define his invention as he wishes to have it defined, he may, as intimated in *Andrews* v. *Nilson*, (C. D., 1906, 717; 123 O. G., 1667,) apply for a reissue. In that case the Court said:

The reasonable presumption is that an inventor intends to protect his invention broadly, and consequently the courts have often said that the scope of a claim should not be restricted beyond the fair and ordinary meaning of the words, save for the purpose of saving it. * * *

The senior party who has a patent may not be heard to ask that his claim be rewritten so that he may prevail in an interference. He would be in somewhat better position had his patent not been issued, or had he surrendered it for reissue.

I am of the opinion that Young has fully disclosed the invention defined by the terms of the interference issue and when those terms are taken in their ordinary and commonly-accepted meaning and that no reason exists for reading into the issue limitations which are not contained therein, but are found only in the specification of Miel's patent.

The decision of the Examiners-in-Chief is reversed.

BROWNE *v.* STROUD.

Decided February 1, 1907.

(126 O. G., 3041.)

SERVICE—PETITIONS AND MOTIONS.

All petitions and motions in *inter partes* cases must be accompanied by proof of service or by copies to be forwarded by the Office.

ON PROTEST.

TELEPHONY.

Mr. Charles Neave and *Messrs. Mauro, Cameron, Lewis & Massie* for Browne.

Mr. George L. Cragg and *Messrs. Bacon & Milans* for Stroud.

ALLEN, *Commissioner:*

This is a protest by Browne against the action of Stroud filing a petition in the above-entitled interference without service upon Browne and against the action of the Office entertaining such petition and disposing of the same upon its merits.

It does not appear that protestant has any objection to make to the decision which has been rendered upon the petition. This protest might, therefore, be dismissed without further consideration. It appears, however, that some uncertainty exists as to the proper practice to be followed in the matter of service of petitions in *inter partes* cases, and advantage will therefore be taken of this opportunity to set forth a definite practice to be followed in this Office in such cases.

Hereafter all petitions and motions in *inter partes* cases must be accompanied by proper evidence of service upon the various parties or with copies to be forwarded by the Office to such parties. Upon failure to comply with the above requirement the petition or motion will not be set down for hearing or receive consideration upon its merits. Exception will be made, however, in the case of a request for rehearing, which request will be considered *ex parte.*

The protest is dismissed.

EX PARTE HESS.

Decided February 1, 1907.

(126 O. G., 3041.)

ABANDONMENT OF APPLICATION—EXCUSE FOR DELAY.

> Confusion upon the attorney's docket by reason of Office action suggesting claims for interference is not acceptable as a showing of unavoidable delay in responding to the prior Office action.

ON PETITION.

BALL-BEARING.

Mr. Fenelon B. Brock for the applicant.

ALLEN, *Commissioner:*

This is a petition that the application be held not abandoned notwithstanding delay by the applicant for more than a year in replying to the last action by the Office upon the merits of the application.

The Office action upon the merits is dated December 1, 1905. On April 16, 1906, the Examiner suggested claims for the purpose of interference proceedings. No reply was made by the applicant to either action until December 24, 1906, when this petition and the accompanying amendment in response to the rejection of December 1, 1905, were filed. The reason for the delay seems to have been confusion upon the attorney's docket of the dates of the Office actions December 1, 1905, and April 16, 1906, the attorney assuming that he had a year from the latter date for his action.

This reason would apply to any case in which the Examiner suggests claims after an action upon the merits which has not been replied to by the applicant. Such suggestion of claims is of common occurrence, and it must be held to be the duty of applicants and their attorneys to take precautions against confusion of the dates of the two Office letters. It would seem that effective precautions might readily be devised. Under these circumstances the delay cannot be held to have been unavoidable.

The petition is denied.

COREY *v.* EISEMAN AND MISAR.

Decided December 15, 1906.

(126 O. G., 3421.)

TESTIMONY—USE IN SECOND INTERFERENCE—RULE 157.

> Where C. was denied the privilege of introducing testimony taken in his behalf in a prior interference between the same parties in view of the opposition of E. and M. on the ground that they were not represented at the taking of C.'s testimony, a motion by E. and M. to introduce testimony taken in their behalf in the same interference should not be granted merely because C. was represented at the examination of their witnesses.

APPEAL ON MOTION.

AIR-BRAKE CONTROLLER.

Mr. Albert G. Davis for Corey.
Mr. Charles E. Smith for Eiseman and Misar.

ALLEN, *Commissioner:*

This is an appeal by Eiseman and Misar from the decision of the Examiner of Interferences denying their motion that testimony taken in their behalf in a prior interference between the same parties and the same applications be admitted in this interference under the provisions of Rule 157.

A similar motion brought by Corey was denied by the Examiner of Interferences. The denial of that motion was based on the fact that Eiseman and Misar were not represented at the taking of Corey's testimony. In his motion, however, Corey offered to Eiseman and Misar the privilege of cross-examining the witnesses whose testimony he wished to introduce. Eiseman and Misar's motion now under consideration stands upon practically the same basis as Corey's previous motion, except for the fact that Corey was represented at the examination of Eiseman and Misar's witnesses. Eiseman and Misar offer in their motion to permit Corey to further cross-examine the witnesses, if he desires to do so. Inasmuch as Eiseman and Misar opposed the grant of Corey's motion, it does not seem that they are in a good position to ask that their motion be granted. The mere fact that Corey was represented at the examination of Eiseman and Misar's witnesses in the prior interference is not considered sufficient to justify favorable action upon the present motion in the face of Eiseman and Misar's opposition to such action upon Corey's motion.

The decision of the Examiner of Interferences is affirmed.

Ex parte Röchling.

Decided December 18, 1906.

(126 O. G., 3421.)

Issue—Withdrawal from.

Applications will not be withdrawn from issue merely for the purpose of granting the applicant more time than is permitted by the statute for the payment of the final fee.

On Petition.

MACHINE FOR MAKING MOLDS FOR FOUNDING, WITH DIRECT AIR-PRESSURE.

Mr. Frank V. Briesen for the applicant.

ALLEN, *Commissioner:*

This is a petition that the above-entitled application be withdrawn from issue and reallowed upon the filing of a certified copy of letters testamentary.

It is alleged in the petition that the applicant died recently, that the application was allowed on May 9, 1906, and that as the executrix resides in Germany it will be impossible to file copies of letters testamentary prior to November 9, when the six months allowed by law for the payment of the final fee expire.

The withdrawal of the application from issue is not desired for the purpose of taking any action therein, but merely to secure more time than permitted by the statute for the payment of the final fee. It is not thought that applications should be withdrawn from issue for this purpose, especially in view of the fact that provision has been made in the law for the renewal of applications upon which the final fee has not been paid within the time prescribed for that purpose.

Petition denied.

IN RE SETTER.

Decided December 26, 1906.

(126 O. G., 3421.)

PUBLIC USE—PROCEEDINGS INSTITUTED WHERE APPLICANT CLAIMS ISSUE OF INTERFERENCE IN WHICH HE IS NOT AT PRESENT INVOLVED.

Where in response to an order to show cause why public-use proceedings should not be instituted against his application an applicant states that an interference is in progress involving the same subject-matter and it appears that his application was not added to the interference by reason of the progress in that interference already made when his application was filed, *Held* that public-use proceedings should be instituted, as a finding of public use applicable to this application would cause all proceedings upon the applications in interference and this application to terminate with the interference now pending.

IN THE MATTER of the protest of certain parties against the issue of a patent to Michael Setter and the request that public-use proceedings be instituted.

Messrs. Bulkley & Durand for Setter.
Mr. Charles A. Brown for Stromberg-Carlson Telephone Mfg. Co., protestant.
Mr. Curtis B. Camp for Kellogg Switchboard & Supply Co., protestant.

MOORE, *Acting Commissioner:*

Upon August 4, 1906, an order was issued in this case calling upon the applicant Setter to show cause why public-use proceedings should not be instituted against his application. In response thereto it has been set up that an interference is in progress in the Office involving the same subject-matter which is alleged to have been in public use, and it is urged that public-use proceedings should not be instituted until Setter shall have had an opportunity to contest with the parties to the interference or with the party who shall prevail therein the question of priority of invention. It is understood that an attempt was made to have the Setter application included in the interference, but that the same failed by reason of the progress which had already been made in that proceeding when this application was filed.

If the public-use proceeding is instituted now, the same may be carried on simultaneously with the interference proceeding, and it may well be that the question of public use will have been finally disposed of by the time that the interference is concluded. Indeed, it is possible that a finding of public use applicable to the Setter application will cause all proceedings upon the applications in the interference and in Setter's application to terminate with the interference now pending. On the other hand, postponement of the investigation of public use will naturally lead to a new interference, after the present interference shall have been disposed of, between the successful party therein and Setter, with the possibility of public-use proceedings after the termination of such second interference.   It is true that investigation of public use at the present time resulting in a finding against Setter will preclude a contest in the Patent Office between Setter and the prevailing party to the interference upon priority and may result in the grant of a patent to one who is not the prior inventor.   This fact is not believed to be controlling, however, in the present case.   The interest of the public and, in general, of parties in an early termination of proceedings in the Patent Office and an early issue of a patent, if one is to be granted, outweigh other considerations under the circumstances of the present case and call for the investigation of the question of public use without further delay.   In reaching this conclusion it has not been necessary to consider those matters submitted by the protestants to the consideration of which objection was made by the applicant.   It is not deemed expedient or proper to comply with the request of the protestants that certain limitations be imposed in this order upon the scope of the investigation and upon the effect of the evidence which may be adduced, and such request *is therefore denied.*

It is directed that public-use proceedings be instituted without unnecessary delay.

DUKESMITH *v.* CORRINGTON *v.* TURNER.

Decided January 10, 1907.

(126 O. G., 3422.)

INTERFERENCE—MOTION TO DISSOLVE—NO APPEAL FROM HOLDING THAT COUNTS HAVE IDENTICAL MEANING.

From the decision of the Examiner holding that there is interference in fact or that the counts of the issue have the same meaning in the cases of the different parties no appeal is permitted under the provisions of Rule 124.

APPEAL ON MOTION.

FLUID-PRESSURE BRAKE.

Messrs. Kay, Totten & Winter for Dukesmith.
Mr. Murray Corrington pro se.
Mr. Edward A. Wright for Turner.

ALLEN, *Commissioner:*

This is an appeal by Dukesmith from the decision of the Primary Examiner denying his motion to dissolve the above-entitled interference on the ground of " no interference in fact."

From the decision of the Examiner holding that there is interference in fact or that the counts of the issue have the same meaning in the cases of the different parties no appeal is permitted under the provision of Rule 124, (amended June 12, 1906,) which reads:

No appeal will be permitted from a decision rendered upon motion for dissolution affirming the patentability of a claim or the applicant's right to make the same or the identity of meaning of counts in the cases of different parties.

The appeal is accordingly dismissed.

THE ALBERT DICKINSON COMPANY *v.* CONKLIN.

Decided January 11, 1907.

(126 O. G., 3422.)

1. TRADE-MARK OPPOSITION—AMENDMENT BASED ON NEW GROUNDS NOT PERMISSIBLE.

Where the notice of opposition alleged that "the trade-mark consists merely of the word 'King,' without any distinctive features, is merely the name of an individual, and its registration as a trade-mark is prohibited by the clause (*b*) of section 5 of the Trade-Mark Act of February 20, 1905," and the opponent desires to amend by adding that the mark is not registrable because it is a geographical name or term, *Held* that the broad reference to clause *b* of section 5 of the act merely conveys the idea that in this part of the act is to be found the prohibition against the registration of names of individuals, that the proposed amendment is based on new ground, and is not proper subject-matter for an amendment filed after the expiration of the thirty days prescribed in the statute.

2. SAME—GENERAL REFERENCE NOT SUFFICIENT.

It is not a sufficient ground for a notice of opposition to make a general reference to the Trade-Mark Act or to some part thereof.

APPEAL from Examiner of Interferences.

TRADE-MARK FOR GRASS-SEED.

Messrs. Munday, Evarts, Adcock & Clarke and *Mr. H. N. Low* for The Albert Dickinson Company.
Messrs. Munn & Co. for Conklin.

ALLEN, *Commissioner:*

This is an appeal by the opponent, The Albert Dickinson Company, from the decision of the Examiner of Interferences denying a motion for leave to amend the notice of opposition.

The first paragraph of the notice of opposition reads as follows:

The said trade-mark consists merely of the word "King," without any distinctive features, is merely the name of an individual, and its registration as a trade-mark is prohibited by the clause (*b*) of section 5 of the Trade-Mark Act of February 20, 1905.

The opponent now desires to add the following phrase to his notice of opposition:

That the registry of the alleged trade-mark sought to be registered would be illegal because the word "King" is merely a geographical name or term, and shall not be registered under the terms of the act of 1905.

It is contended that there is sufficient foundation for this amendment in the first paragraph of the original notice which is quoted above. I am of the opinion, however, that the Examiner of Interferences was correct in holding that there is nothing in the paragraph referred to to indicate that the opponent desired to raise any ground of opposition other than that the word "King" is non-registrable for the reason that it is the name of an individual.

The broad reference to clause *b* of section 5 of the act of February 20, 1905, merely conveys the idea that in this part of the act is to be found the prohibition against the registration of names of individuals. It is not a sufficient ground for a notice of opposition to make a general reference to the Trade-Mark Act or to some part thereof, even if that reference were not, as in the present case, coupled with other words indicating a ground different from that which is subsequently raised. I am of the opinion that the proposed amendment to the notice of opposition is based upon a new ground and is not therefore proper subject-matter for an amendment filed after the expiration of the thirty days permitted in the statute.

The decision of the Examiner of Interferences is affirmed.

IN RE J. G. B. SIEGERT & HIJOS.

Decided January 11, 1907.

(126 O. G., 3423.)

TRADE-MARKS—PUBLICATION IN OFFICIAL GAZETTE.

A trade-mark will not be republished merely for the purpose of extending the period of thirty days provided by statute for the filing of oppositions.

ON PETITION.

Mr. Charles S. Jones for the petitioner.

ALLEN, *Commissioner:*

This is a petition that the trade-mark of Miguel Bethencourt, published in the OFFICIAL GAZETTE of September 25, 1906, be republished in order that the petitioner may have time in which to execute and forward to this Office a notice of opposition.

It is alleged by the petitioner's attorney that the petitioner, Dr. J. G. B. Siegert & Hijos, resides in the island of Trinidad, and the period of thirty days from the date of publication is not sufficient for the preparation of the opposition papers and their transmission to and from the island of Trinidad. In order to secure additional time for this purpose, the petitioner desires to have the trade-mark republished, which w,ould have the effect of extending for another thirty days the period in which notices of opposition may be filed. In support of this request attention is directed to the provision of section 6 of the act of February 20, 1905, that—

the Commissioner shall cause the mark to be published at least once in the OFFICIAL GAZETTE of the Patent Office.

It is contended that the use of the words "at least once" indicates that where it becomes necessary under peculiar conditions, such as exist in this case, the mark may be republished. The language quoted indicates, as contended, that in certain cases the mark may be republished. The fact, however, that in the same section of the statute it is provided that notices of opposition shall be filed within thirty days of the date of publication indicates that the authority to republish a mark was not granted for the purpose of enabling the Commissioner of Patents to prolong the period during which notices of opposition might be filed. If the period of thirty days had been considered insufficient for the purpose indicated, Congress would undoubtedly have fixed a longer period or would have expressly empowered the Commissioner to grant an extension thereof. It is to be observed, moreover, that the petitioner is not dependent solely upon opposition proceedings for the adjudication of his rights, but may file an application for registration and secure an interference or may institute cancelation proceedings after the registration of Bethencourt's mark.

The petition is denied.

HANAN AND GATES *v.* MARSHALL.

Decided January 11, 1907.

(126 O. G., 3423.)

APPEAL—NON-APPEALABLE QUESTION—APPEAL DISMISSED.
Where a ruling is made that an appeal from the Examiner of Interferences will not be entertained by the Commissioner on a given question, an appeal on that question will not be considered even though filed prior to the rendition of the decision.

APPEAL ON MOTION.

FOLDING-MÁCHINE.

Mr. Nelson W. Howard and *Mr. A. D. Salinger* for Hanan and Gates. (*Messrs. Dodge & Sons* of counsel.)

Messrs. Southgate & Southgate and *Messrs. Davis & Davis* for Marshall.

ALLEN, *Commissioner:*

This is an appeal by Marshall from the decision of the Examiner of Interferences granting Hanan and Gates's motion that times be set for taking testimony.

It appears from the record that Hanan and Gates made a motion to dissolve on the ground that there is no interference in fact between Marshall and the other parties, that Marshall has no right to make the claims, and that the counts are unpatentable if construed broadly enough to include Marshall. Since the filing of Marshall's appeal it has been decided that appeals will not be entertained from the decisions of the Examiner of Interferences on motions for permission to take testimony relative to questions of the kind raised in this case. (*Lowry and Cowley* v. *Spoon*, C. D., 1906, 381; 124 O. G., 1846.) The fact that the present appeal was filed prior to the rendering of the decision referred to is not considered a sufficient reason for departing from the rule announced in that decision.

The appeal is dismissed.

EX PARTE BENECKE.

Decided January 11, 1907.

(126 O. G., 3423.)

APPLICATION OATH—SECTION 4892, REVISED STATUTES, CONSTRUED.

Where an applicant is not a citizen of any country and so alleges in his oath, *Held* to be a proper compliance with the requirements of section 4892, Revised Statutes, and that this section should not be construed as requiring citizenship of some country as a condition precedent to the grant of a patent.

ON PETITION.

ELECTRICAL MEASURING INSTRUMENT.

Messrs. Fischer & Sanders and *Messrs. Bacon & Milans* for the applicant.

ALLEN, *Commissioner:*

This is a petition from the refusal of the Primary Examiner to accept the oath forming part of the application. It appears from the record that in the oath originally filed with the application papers no allegation was made with reference to the applicant's citizenship, the omission being due, according to applicant's statement, to the fact that owing to his prolonged absence from his native country, Germany, he has, under the laws of that country, forfeited his status as a German subject and has never become a citizen of the United

States, where he has lived since his departure from Germany. Upon petition from the Examiner's objection to the original oath it was held that section 4892 of the Revised Statutes had not been complied with and that the Office had no authority to waive the requirement of that section of the statute that applicants for patents shall state of what country they are citizens. Subsequently to the rendering of this decision the applicant filed a new oath, in which he states that he is not a citizen of any country. From the Examiner's objection to this oath the present petition was taken.

Section 4886 of the Revised Statutes provides that *any* person having made an invention as therein set forth may obtain a patent therefor. Reading this section in connection with section 4892, I am of the opinion that the latter section should not be construed as requiring citizenship of some country as a condition precedent to the grant of a patent. The original oath was defective for the reason that it contained no allegation whatever regarding citizenship. The oath now on file sets forth the true state of facts relative to the question of citizenship and should be accepted as a compliance with the statute.

The petition is granted.

Ex parte E. C. Atkins & Company.

Decided January 17, 1907.

(126 O. G., 3424.)

1. TRADE-MARKS—ACT OF MAY 4, 1906, CONSTRUED.

Section 1 of the act of May 4, 1906, amending section 1 of the Trade-Mark Act of February 20, 1906, by inserting after the words "a description of the trade-mark itself" the words "only when needed to express colors not shown in the drawing," is construed to mean that the drawing should be relied upon to disclose the mark and that a description of the mark should be permitted "only when needed to express colors not shown in the drawing."

2. SAME—SAME.

The purpose of the amendment contained in section 1 of the act of May 4, 1906, is to make the registration definite by limiting it to the disclosure in the drawing, leaving the question of what is an immaterial variation in the mark to the courts.

3. SAME—SAME—APPLIES TO APPLICATIONS PENDING AT DATE IT BECAME EFFECTIVE.

The fact that the application was filed under the former statute does not excuse the applicant from complying with the amended statute, since the latter makes no exception of applications pending at the date it became effective.

ON PETITION.

TRADE-MARK FOR SAWS.

Messrs. Bradford & Hood for the applicants.

ALLEN, *Commissioner:*

This is a petition from the action of the Examiner requiring the cancelation from the application of the description of the mark and from his requirement that the class of merchandise shall conform to the classification established under the act approved May 4, 1906.

The record shows that petitioners' trade-mark was published in the OFFICIAL GAZETTE of May 15, 1906, and that the thirty days allowed for filing oppositions expired on June 14, 1906. If the mark had then been immediately passed for registration, it would have been registered on July 10, 1906. Since the mark could not be registered before July 1, 1906, the date on which the act approved May 4, 1906, took effect, applicants were required to amend their application to conform to the provisions of said act by changing the class of merchandise to read:

Class 20, Cutlery not included in Class 61, and edge-tools—

and by substituting for the description of the mark, which reads—

has adopted for its use a trade-mark, of which the following is a description: The trade mark consists of a symbol composed of the letters "A A A"—

the statement —

has adopted for its use the trade-mark shown in the accompanying drawings.

Petitioners at the hearing indicated their willingness to comply with the first of the above requirements and filed an amendment substituting the title of the class suggested for that originally given.

The second requirement of the Examiner was based on the act approved May 4, 1906, which amended section 1 of the act of February 20, 1905, by inserting after the words—

a description of the trade mark itself

the words

only when needed to express colors not shown in the drawing.

Petitioners contend

* * * that it is quite as clear that the language " only when needed to express colors not shown in the drawing " is of the legislative intent, *permissive* and not mandatory. In other words the law means the same as though it read

a description of the trade mark itself shall not shall be required only when needed to express colors not shown in the drawing.

In this connection petitioners are believed to be in error. It is not thought that it was the intention of Congress in amending the statute to leave it optional with the applicant whether his application should contain a description of the trade-mark. On the contrary, I believe it was the intention that the drawing should be relied upon to disclose the mark and that a description of the mark should be permitted " only when needed to express colors not shown in the drawing." The language of the amended section appears to be clear and definite, while applicants' interpretation requires a strained construction.

It is understood that the purpose of this amendment is to make the registration definite by limiting it to the disclosure in the drawing, leaving the question of what is an immaterial variation in the mark to the courts. It thus appears that the object of the amended statute is to prevent just such an apparently indefinite extension of the scope of the registered mark by a generic description as the petitioners contend for. In view of this interpretation of the statute there is no error in the requirement of the Examiner. The fact that the application was filed under the former statute does not excuse petitioners from complying with the amended statute. On account of the thirty days allowed by section 6 of the act of February 20, 1906, for the filing of notices of opposition after publication in the OFFICIAL GAZETTE it was impossible to register petitioners' mark until after the statute went into effect on July 1, 1906, and the amended statute makes no exception of applications pending at the date it became effective.

The petition is denied.

A. A. ROSENBUSH & COMPANY *v.* THE ROSE SHOE MANUFACTURING COMPANY.

Decided May 26, 1906.

(127 O. G., 391.)

TRADE-MARK INTERFERENCE—PRIORITY—CREDIBILITY OF TESTIMONY.

Where the testimony presented in behalf of both the opposing parties is subject to uncertainty, the testimony of Rosenbush concerning the adoption of the mark in 1895 or 1896, which is supported by the testimony of his former partner, Levie, is entitled to as great weight as the testimony of a single disinterested witness testifying from his unaided memory concerning the adoption of the mark by The Rose Shoe Manufacturing Company nearly eight years after the event.

ON APPEAL.

TRADE-MARK FOR BOOTS AND SHOES.

Messrs. Noyes & Harriman and *Mr. Howard A. Coombs* for A. A. Rosenbush & Company.

Mr. C. T. Belt for The Rose Shoe Manufacturing Company.

ALLEN, *Commissioner:*

This is an appeal by A. A. Rosenbush & Company from the decision of the Examiner of Interferences awarding priority of adoption and use of the trade-mark in issue to The Rose Shoe Manufacturing Company.

The issue is the word " Rose " as a trade-mark for shoes. The Rose Shoe Manufacturing Company registered this mark on July 21, 1905. The application of A. A. Rosenbush & Company was filed on July 22, 1905. The date of adoption and use alleged in the statement of The Rose Shoe Manufacturing Company is 1900. The statement of A. A. Rosenbush & Company alleges adoption and use in 1891. The Examiner of Interferences found that The Rose Shoe Manufacturing Company have established adoption and use in and from the spring of 1898 at least and that A. A. Rosenbush & Company have established adoption and use in and from the spring of 1899 and no earlier. He therefore decided the case in favor of The Rose Shoe Manufacturing Company.

The Rose Shoe Manufacturing Company took depositions of seven persons. The depositions of Bartold and Muckle are of no assistance in determining when the mark was adopted and used. Nissen refers to the date 1892; but it is not clear that he meant to testify to use of the trade-mark " Rose " at that time. (Record of The Rose Shoe Manufacturing Company, p. 15, Qs. 13–17.) His answer to question 19 indicates that the first use of the mark within his knowledge was not long prior to 1900. Leckinger testifies that he has bought shoes from The Rose Shoe Manufacturing Company and from their predecessor for the past nineteen years. When asked what trade-mark was associated with these shoes, he answered " Rose." (Pp. 8–9, Qs. 6–8, 13, 14, and 16.) I cannot gather from the testimony that this witness meant to state that the trade-mark " Rose " was used in 1886 or at any other definite date subsequent thereto. The testimony of Levis is likewise unsatisfactory. He has made boxes and printed labels for The Rose Shoe Manufacturing Company since 1896. (Pp. 7 and 8, Qs. 4, 6, and 10.) He was asked what the firm-name was in 1896 and after answering was asked and answered :

Q. 8. I hand you three (3) cartons bearing the word "Rose" and ask you if these are some of the boxes you have made and labels you have printed as referred to in your preceding answer? (Cartons referred to produced in evidence and marked " Exhibit A.")

A. They are.

Q. 9. Have you continuously made these boxes and printed these labels?

A. I have.

Q. 10. Since when?

A. I have made the box for the " Rose " shoes since 1896.

The witness may have intended to testify that boxes bearing the de-mark " Rose " were made in 1896; but it is not at all certain that such is the case. The propositions are wholly statements by counsel, and it is not clear as to just what the witness was assenting. The testimony of all of these witnesses is insufficient to fix any date early enough to avail in this proceeding. This is especially true in view of the fact that the dates which The Rose Shoe Manufacturing Company seeks to establish are long prior to the date set up in the statement of their registration. As was pointed out by the Examiner of Interferences on the authority of *The Gem Cutlery Company* v. *Leach* (C. D., 1905, 58; 114 O. G., 2089,) a trade-mark applicant may prove an earlier date of adoption and use than that alleged in his statement; but to avail him such proof must be clear and convincing.

The testimony of Rooker and Prusick is more satisfactory. The former testifies that the mark was used by The Rose Shoe Manufacturing Company and its predecessors from before early in 1899, when a change was made in the name of the company. The latter, who is a shoe dealer, asserts that he has bought shoes from The Rose Shoe Manufacturing Company and their predecessors continuously since May, 1898, bearing the trade-mark "Rose." (P. 25, Qs. 7–13.) It is not apparent how he fixes the date; but he is a disinterested witness, and his testimony, so far as appears, is worthy of belief. It is not important whether the date fixed is correct within several months, and there are no unquestioned facts or circumstances which justify disregard of what he says. It is concluded, therefore, that the Examiner of Interferences correctly held that The Rose Shoe Manufacturing Company is entitled to a date of adoption and use as early as 1898; but it is further concluded that this company is not entitled to any earlier date.

The case of A. A. Rosenbush & Company as to a date prior to April or May, 1898, rests on the testimony of Rosenbush and Levie. Rosenbush testified in part as follows:

Q. 5. When did you go into business on your own account?

A. On August 1st, 1894. I went into partnership in the wholesale boot and shoe business in Chicago, firm-name being Goldsmith, Rosenbush & Levie.

Q. 6. What were the names of your partners?

A. Samuel Goldsmith and Jerome M. Levie.

Q. 8. How long did this partnership continue?

A. This partnership continued until December 15, 1898.

Q. 10. When you started in business in 1894 did you immediately begin to sell shoes?

A. Yes, sir.

Q. 11. What trade-marks, if any, did you use upon the shoes sold by your concern?

A. We used the word "Rose."

Q. 14. Now, will you state as nearly as possible to date when you first sold shoes bearing this "Rose" trade-mark?

A. The spring of 1895.

Q. 15. You are unable to fix the date any nearer at the present time?

A. Yes, sir.

Q. 18. How much did you use this trade-mark while your concern was doing business at Chicago?

A. We used it continuously from spring of '95 to the spring of '98.

Q. 19. State when, as nearly as you can remember, the last shipment of shoes was made bearing this trade-mark by the concern of which you were a member?

A. About November of 1898.

Levie testifies in part as follows:

Q. 7. What was the business of Goldsmith, Rosenbush & Levie?

A. Jobbing shoes.

Q. 8. How long did this partnership continue?

A. About four and one-half years.

Q. 9. You commenced then, in August, 1894?

A. Yes.

Q. 11. State whether or not Goldsmith, Rosenbush & Levie used any trade-marks upon the shoes sold by them?

A. Some.

Q. 12. What trade-mark did they use?

A. Well, we used the name "Waddell" used the name "Rose" and several others.

Q. 14. When did you first start to use the name "Rose" on the shoes sold by this firm?

A. Can't tell exactly—haven't any data to go by. It was between 1894 and 1898.

Q. 15. Could you tell whether it was nearer 1894 than 1898?

A. Well, yes, it was about a year or a year and a half after we started in business.

Both Rosenbush and Levie give the names of a number of dealers to whom their firm sold shoes bearing the trade-mark in issue. It appears that the firm of Goldsmith, Rosenbush & Levie went out of business in December of 1898. It is regarded as satisfactorily established that A. A. Rosenbush & Company are the successors of that firm and that they acquired whatever rights the prior firm may have had in the trade-mark in issue. I regard the testimony of Rosenbush and Levie as sufficient to establish adoption of the mark in issue by the predecessor of A. A. Rosenbush & Company prior to April, 1898, the earliest date which the evidence will support for The Rose Shoe Manufacturing Company.

It is true of the testimony of Rosenbush and Levie, as it is of that of Rooker and Prusick, that the witnesses are testifying long after the event and that the dates are not fixed by one scrap of physical evidence, and it is also true in each case that one of the two witnesses is interested. Yet with Rosenbush and Levie, as has been stated of Prusick, I find no good reason to doubt their veracity or believe that they were mistaken as to the dates and facts which they allege. The

Examiner of Interferences rejected their testimony for the following reasons:

> The fact that Rosenbush does not remember whether or not any of the shoes purchased from Goldsmith, Rosenbush & Levie and sold after he had removed to Boston bore the trade-mark "Rose," when taken in connection with Levie's testimony on cross-examination, that many marks were adopted by this firm and abandoned (Levie, X-Q. 2), and the inconsistent statements of Rosenbush and Levie as to the date of adoption of the trade-mark "Rose," and their contradictory statements as to the kind of shoes upon which this trade-mark was used, renders the testimony insufficient to satisfactorily establish its use prior to its adoption by the firm of A. A. Rosenbush & Co., as will hereinafter appear.

Whether the shoes shipped to Boston bore the trade-mark in issue seems to me to be of no consequence here, nor do I find in the professed inability of Rosenbush to remember the fact an indication that his memory is unreliable as to the facts which he does profess to remember, and the same reasoning applies to Levie's admission that several marks were abandoned It does not, in my opinion, materially weaken his assertion that the use of the mark "Rose" was continuous. The slight discrepancy as to the kinds of shoes upon which the marks were used is also regarded as inconsequential. The fact is not relevant, and Levie practically admitted an uncertainty as to the same, which does not appear to be remarkable. The difference in the dates of adoption fixed by the two witnesses is more serious. Nevertheless, their testimony taken as a whole convinces me that in all probability the firm of Goldsmith, Rosenbush & Levie adopted the mark some time in the years 1895 or 1896, and in any event prior to The Rose Shoe Manufacturing Company's date of April or May of 1898. I am particularly well satisfied in basing my decision on the probable use of the mark by Goldsmith, Rosenbush & Levie in 1895 or 1896 by reason of the fact that The Rose Shoe Manufacturing Company's date of April or May, 1898, is subject to uncertainty to at least the same extent, being fixed by a single witness testifying nearly eight years after the event and, so far as appears, from his unaided memory.

The decision of the Examiner of Interferences is *reversed*, and priority of adoption and use *is awarded* to A. A. Rosenbush & Company.

FUNKE *v.* BALDWIN.

Decided January 10, 1907.

(127 O. G., 392.)

1. TRADE-MARKS—CANCELATION OF REGISTRATION—SECTION 13 OF ACT OF 1905 CONSTRUED.

Section 13 of the act of 1905, providing for the cancelation of trade-mark registrations, applies only to those registrations made under that act.

2. SAME—SAME—SAME—NOT APPLICABLE TO REGISTRATIONS UNDER ACTS OF 1881
   AND 1882.

> By section 30 of the act of 1905 all legislation inconsistent with the provisions of the act of 1905 is repealed except the Trade-Mark Acts of 1881 and 1882 in their application to registrations made thereunder. The acts of 1881 and 1882 are to stand, so far as registrations made thereunder are concerned, whether consistent with the act of 1905 or otherwise.

APPEAL from Examiner of Interferences.

TRADE-MARK FOR LAMPS.

Mr. Grafton L. McGill for Funke.
Messrs. Kerr, Paige & Cooper for Baldwin.

ALLEN, *Commissioner:*

This in an appeal from a decision of the Examiner of Interferences denying an application for cancelation of the registration of a trade-mark.

The registration is one under the Trade-Mark Act of 1881. The application for cancelation is made under section 13 of the Trade-Mark Act of February 20, 1905. The Examiner of Interferences refused cancelation on the ground that the provisions for cancelation of registration found in the act of 1905 do not apply to registrations under the act of 1881 and that the Office is without other authority to cancel the registration of a trade-mark.

The conclusion of the Examiner of Interferences is believed to be correct.

The issue of a certificate of registration under the act of 1905 for a definite period is by the act made subject to the possibility that the Commissioner of Patents may cancel the registration before the expiration of this period. Such a cancelation will undoubtedly completely destroy all effect of the registration. The right to sue and *prima facie* evidence of ownership which the registration represented will no longer exist. Certificates of registration under the act of 1881 were issued for a period which when those certificates were issued was not terminable by any act of the Commissioner of Patents. He might reregister the same mark to another party and issue a new certificate thereon, but the old registration and certificate would remain in force, representing the same right to sue and the same *prima facie* evidence of ownership as when first issued. Neither were registrations under the act of 1881 terminated by adverse decisions in the courts upon the supposed trade-mark rights which they represented. The right to sue and to assert as *prima facie* evidence of ownership remained inherent in the registration until the end of the period for which it was issued, notwithstanding and such decisions which might be rendered.

The question which is now presented is whether section 13 of the act of 1905, providing in general terms for the cancelation of trademark registrations, authorizes in the case of registration under the act of 1881 curtailment of the period for which the earlier act provided that such registrations should represent a right to sue and should be *prima facie* evidence of ownership of a trade-mark.

The answer to this question is believed to be found in section 30 of the act of 1905, providing as follows:

> Sec. 30. That this act shall be in force and take effect April first, nineteen hundred and five. All acts and parts of acts inconsistent with this act are hereby repealed except so far as the same may apply to certificates of registration issued under the act of Congress approved March third, eighteen hundred and eighty-one, entitled "An act to authorize the registration of trade-marks and protect the same," or under the act approved August fifth, eighteen hundred and eighty-two, entitled "An act relating to the registration of trade-marks."

All legislation inconsistent with the provisions of the act of 1905 is repealed except the Trade-Mark Acts of 1881 and 1882 in their application to registrations made thereunder. The acts of 1881 and 1882 are to stand, so far as registrations made thereunder are concerned, whether consistent with the act of 1905 or otherwise. The intention of Congress as gathered from this is that as to registrations under the act of 1881 the provisions and conditions of those acts only are to apply and that the act of 1905, except as it duplicates the provisions of the earlier acts, applies only to registrations which shall be made under it. It is concluded, therefore, that section 13 of the act of 1905, providing for the cancelation of trade-mark registrations, applies only to those registrations made under that act.

Of the many arguments advanced by the appellant it is only necessary to refer here to that alleging an express distinction in the present trade-mark statute of those sections which apply only to registrations under it, leaving the remaining sections, including section 13 upon cancelation, applicable to all registrations. The phrase "trade-marks registered under this act" appears in sections 17, 18, 19, and 20 of the act of 1905, and from this the appellant infers that the remaining sections are applicable to registrations under either act. This inference, however, is believed to be unwarranted, for the reason that the phrase in question appears to be used merely to distinguish those suits brought upon registrations under the statute from those which may be brought upon State registrations or upon common-law rights.

The decision of the Examiner of Interferences denying the application of Funke for the cancelation of trade-mark registration of Baldwin, No. 39,885, of March 3, 1903, *is affirmed.*

Ex parte Barrett and Alter.

Decided January 15, 1907.

(127 O. G., 847.)

1. APPLICATION, JOINT—PROSECUTION OF BY ONE APPLICANT WHERE COAPPLICANT REFUSES TO ACT.

    Where one of two joint inventors seeks to cause the abandonment of their application by preventing amendment thereof, claiming that he is a sole inventor, and also files a written abandonment of the application, *Held* that permission will be given to the coinventor to prosecute the application through an attorney of his own selection.

2. ATTORNEYS—APPOINTMENT OF BY ONE OF TWO JOINT APPLICANTS.

    Where the attorneys for joint applicants are prevented from amending the application by one of the joint inventors, who in order to cause the case to become abandoned also refuses to permit them to give an associate power of attorney to an attorney of the other joint applicant's selection, *Held* that an attorney appointed by the coinventor will be permitted to prosecute the application.

3. ABANDONMENT OF APPLICATION—MUST BE SIGNED BY ALL JOINT INVENTORS.

    Where one coapplicant does not join in the written abandonment of an application, it can be given no effect.

On Motion.

CONVERTIBLE CUSHIONED AND NON-CUSHIONED SEAT.

Messrs. Poole & Brown for the applicants.

Allen, *Commissioner:*

This case comes before me on motion by Lute S. Alter, one of the joint applicants, that he be permitted, through his attorney, John H. McElroy, to amend the joint application above entitled. The motion is accompanied by a proposed amendment filed on October 31, 1906.

It appears from the record that the last official action was made on November 11, 1905. No action has been taken by the applicant since that time except the filing of the proposed amendment referred to above. If this amendment was not a proper action under the law, the application must be considered as having become abandoned on November 11, 1906. At the time of executing their application the joint inventors appointed the members of the firm of Poole & Brown their attorneys. In an affidavit in support of the motion Alter states that he has learned that Barrett is now exploiting another form of the invention described in the joint application and has expressed his intention of abandoning the joint invention and the application therefor. Alter has sold part of his interest in the invention to McElroy and has appointed him his attorney. In an affidavit by McElroy it is stated that Barrett has refused to join with Alter in giving him, McElroy, a power of attorney to prosecute the application and has refused to authorize the original attorneys, Poole & Brown, to give McElroy an associate power of attorney. McElroy also states that Poole & Brown refused to give him an associate power, for the reason that they were not authorized to do so by Barrett, and that Poole & Brown were unable to amend the application by reason of the fact that Barrett had possession of their copy of the application papers.

In an affidavit in opposition to the motion Barrett states that the invention disclosed in the application is not a joint invention, but is his sole invention, Alter having no interest or participation therein other than an agreement on his part to furnish funds to procure a patent. Inasmuch as in the oath accompanying the application both parties stated that they were joint inventors, it would be unjust in the absence of other evidence to base any action adverse to Alter's interest upon Barrett's subsequent affidavit to the contrary. A somewhat similar state of facts was presented in the case of *ex parte Benjamin and Bailey*, (C. D., 1892, 85; 59 O. G., 298,) in which a power of attorney given by one of the joint inventors and an assignee of the joint inventors was accepted.

Barrett has filed a written abandonment of the application; but as his coapplicant, Alter, does not join in the abandonment it can be given no effect.

The motion is granted.

Ex parte Brooks.

Decided January 15, 1907.

(127 O. G., 847.)

1. ABANDONMENT OF APPLICATION—WITHDRAWAL FROM ISSUE—FAILURE TO TAKE ACTION.

Where an application is withdrawn from issue at the request of the applicant to await the allowance of a related application and no action is taken therein until after the expiration of the statutory period allowed for taking action, which dates from the notice of allowance, the application is abandoned in the absence of special circumstances excusing the delay.

2. WITHDRAWAL FROM ISSUE DOES NOT EXTEND STATUTORY PERIOD FOR ACTION.

Rule 166 was intended to indicate to applicants that the withdrawal of an application from issue at their request would not operate to extend the period within which the statute requires that applications be prosecuted.

ON PETITION.

TYPE-WRITING MACHINE.

Messrs. Gifford & Bull for the applicant.

ALLEN, *Commissioner:*

This case came before me for consideration of a petition that the application be passed to issue.

It appears from the record that the application was passed to issue on July 12, 1897. On January 12, 1898, the applicant made the following request:

In view of the pendency of a parent application for Letters Patent of applicant Serial No. 509,086, involving an invention related to that covered in this case, we respectfully request, in view of the decision of the Supreme Court of the United States in *Miller* v. *Eagle M'f'g Co.*, that this case be withdrawn from the issue files pending the amendment and allowance of said other parent application.

In accordance with this request the application was on January 13, 1898, withdrawn from issue, and no action has been taken by the applicant since that date except the filing on October 10, 1906, of the petition now under consideration. Rule 166, in force at the time the application was withdrawn from issue and continuously since that time provides that whenever the Commissioner shall direct the withdrawal of an application from issue on request of an applicant such withdrawal shall not operate to stay the period of one year running against the application, which begins to attach from the date of the notice of allowance. The application now under consideration was filed prior to January 1, 1898, and hence the applicant was entitled to a period of two years within which to respond to official actions. It appears, therefore, that in the absence of some special circumstances justifying the applicant's delay of eight years the application is abandoned.

The applicant's reasons for desiring to withdraw the application from issue in 1898 are not clear. In the case of *ex parte Drawbaugh*, decided in 1893, (C. D., 1893, 85; 64 O. G., 155,) it was held that there was no good ground for the practice then prevailing of requiring that divisional applications should issue simultaneously. There was nothing therefore in the mere fact that this application was a division of a prior application to necessitate or justify withholding it from issue until the issuance of the prior application or any other division thereof. In his request for withdrawal of the application from issue the applicant did not explain his grounds nor state what bearing the decision in *Miller* v. *Eagle Manufacturing Company* had upon his request. It is not apparent that it had any bearing whatever. However this may be, the Office granted his request and withdrew the application from issue. Withdrawing the case from issue could work no injury to the public or to other inventors, for the reason that under Rule 166, referred to above, the application would become abandoned two years after it had been passed to issue whether withdrawn from issue or left in issue and permitted to become forfeited. It is clear that Rule 166 was intended to indicate to applicants that the withdrawal of an application from issue would not operate to extend the period within which the statute requires that applications be prosecuted.

· If it appeared that a valid patent could not have been issued upon this application at the time of its withdrawal from issue or at any time since until the present, there might be reason for holding the applicant's action justified and for finding that the application was not, in fact, abandoned; but there is nothing whatever in the record to show that the applicant contends that such is the case, and no ground for such a contention is apparent. It must be held, therefore, that this application became abandoned on July 12, 1899, two years after it was passed to issue.

The petition is denied.

EX PARTE BETTENDORF.

Decided March 1, 1907.

(127 O. G., 848.)

DESIGNS—PATENTABILITY—NEW APPEARANCE MUST BE ORNAMENTAL.

> A design patent for an article will be granted only when there can be found in such article a new appearance created by inventive process which serves the purpose of embellishment. It is not enough that the design should possess features of utilitarian attractiveness which would commend it to persons familiar with the art because of its functional value; it must possess an inherent beauty.

APPEAL from Examiners-in-Chief.

DESIGN FOR A SIDE FRAME FOR CAR-TRUCKS.

Mr. Frank D. Thomason for the applicant.

ALLEN, *Commissioner:*

This is an appeal from the decision of the Examiners-in-Chief affirming the decision of the Examiner of Designs in the rejection of a design for side frames of car-trucks.

The Examiner found the design claimed devoid of patentable novelty in view of the following references: Smyser, October 24, 1899, No. 635,357; Symons, October 16, 1900, No. 659,903; Woods, August 7, 1900, No. 655,386.

Upon appeal the Examiners-in-Chief held that the design was not found in or suggested by the references and reversed the decision of the Examiner of Designs. Soon after this decision the Examiners-in-Chief of their own motion reheard the case and, arriving at the conclusion that the design was not ornamental, reversed their first decision and affirmed the decision of the Examiner of Designs.

It is from the later decision of the Examiners-in-Chief that this appeal is taken, and inasmuch as they did not reverse their earlier finding that the design was not anticipated by the references the sole question to be determined is whether the design claimed is an ornamental design which required the exercise of the inventive faculties in its construction.

The decision of the Examiners-in-Chief is, in my opinion, correct.

The changes which distinguish the appellant's design for side frames of car-trucks from those of the prior art as summarized in his brief are as follows:

(a) The homogenity and continuity of the design from one end of the side frame to the other including the journal-boxes.

(b) The relatively great height of the center of length of the side frame as compared to that of the ends thereof where said ends merge into the journal-boxes, which convey the impression of lightness and speed.

(c) The tapering of the upper arch and the lower arch from the journal-boxes to the common-guides, which help give the center of length of the side frame the appearance of power and strength.

(d) The relatively greater height of the journal-boxes than the ends of the side frame merging into the same, giving the side frame a festoon-like appearance hung from the centers of the wheels.

(e) The slanting appearance of the column-guides.

(f) The making of the web of the body of the side frame in the same plane and the distribution of flanges upon this web to produce a pleasing effect and appearance of advanced and depressed surfaces.

An analysis of these alleged changes discloses the fact that each is based upon well-recognized principles of machine design whose advantages are within the knowledge of skilled draftsmen and designers of machinery. (a) relates to integrability of structure. (b) and (c) disclose the standard form used to obtain greatest strength with the least material. (d) provides for lowering the support for the car-body to give it greater stability. (e) refers to the means for providing a broad seat for the springs supporting the car-body. (f) is for the ordinary means of laterally strengthening a webbed beam. Each of these alleged changes is clearly for a utilitarian effect. It is, however, contended that by combining these features Bettendorf has produced a design which would appeal to men who are connected with railroads. This fact was recognized by the Examiners-in-Chief in their decision upon rehearing, and the distinction between the attractiveness to the eye of persons familiar with side frames of cars of a device embodying well-recognized mechanical principles and an ornamental device is clearly stated in the following extract from their decision:

We are of opinion that its attractiveness to such men lies wholly in the apprehension of its utility, in its superior adaptation of its shapes to utilitarian ends. They see that the design is compact lengthwise by reason of the location of the journal-boxes against the end of the frame. They see that it is lowered by making the inverted-arch tires farther down from the bearings than the upper tires are distant from those bearings. So made the side bar is not only lower but is stronger. They see that a minimum of weight is attained by skeletonizing the side bar by two openings near its ends and they see that in doing that the old upper truss and lower truss and the old guides are made with edge flanges which, as is well known, add strength to them. They also see here and there cross-webs, which,.they well know, also add to the strength of the parts on which they are made and with which their ends are connected. All this makes the design attractive to them as practical men in the art.

But we are of opinion that this utilitarian attractiveness is far from ornamentation. We find nothing beautiful or esthetic in the structure.

This statement of the Examiners-in-Chief is entirely in accordance with my views. It is not enough that the design should comprise features which would commend it to persons familiar with the art because of its functional value; it must possess an inherent beauty.

The principle stated in my decision in *ex parte Knothe* (C. D., 1903, 42; 102 O. G., 1294) and reiterated in *ex parte Nickel and Crane* (C. D., 1904, 135; 109 O. G., 2441) applies to this case.

A new and ornamental design will be found in an article of manufacture when there can be found in such article a new appearance created by inventive process and serving the purpose of embellishment. Such new appearance may be superficially applied or it may rest more or less deeply in the structure of the parts, but it must be a creation of inventive genius, accomplishing the purpose of ornament and not used for its functional value. It will be found, weighed, and valued by the test of ornament. It will not be found in those articles whose visible forms are only modeled to develop function.

I find nothing in the appearance of the design claimed by the appellant which commends itself to the eye or even suggests the beautiful.

The decision of the Examiners-in-Chief is affirmed.

KUGELE *v.* BLAIR.

Decided January 26, 1907

(127 O. G., 1253.)

INTERFERENCE—ACCESS TO OPPONENT'S APPLICATION PART OF WHICH IS CONCEALED UNDER RULE 105.

Where the interfering subject-matter of the application of one of the parties to an interference is disclosed to the other by means of a certified copy, as provided by Rule 105, an auxiliary invention which has been described and claimed by the former, but which might be omitted without destroying the operativeness of the invention in issue, will not be disclosed where the latter has presented no claim which includes this invention either broadly or specifically.

APPEAL ON MOTION.

LAMP.

Mr. Nicholas M. Goodlett, Jr., for Kugele.
Messrs. Warfield & Duell for Blair.

ALLEN, *Commissioner:*

This is an appeal by Kugele from a decision of the Primary Examiner denying a motion to furnish him with copies of certain portions of Blair's application, which have been concealed in accordance with the provisions of Rule 105.

It appears that the Office inadvertently furnished Kugele with a copy of Blair's original drawing, and it is urged by Kugele that the elements which are shown in Blair's original drawing, but omitted from the certified copy furnished him, are a part of an integral indivisible invention which he is entitled to inspect in order to determine the propriety of certain actions which he is entitled to take under Rules 109 and 122.

The Primary Examiner has held that the matter omitted from the certified copy of Blair's application comprises a " distinctively divisible and independent invention," which Blair is entitled to conceal from his opponent. I am of the opinion that this conclusion is correct.

The subject-matter of Blair's application which has been disclosed to Kugele includes all the elements of the issue of this interference. The matter which is withheld comprises features which are auxiliary to the invention in issue, but might be omitted without destroying the operativeness of the main invention.

Where one of the parties to an interference shows, describes, and claims an auxiliary invention which is not essential to the operativeness of the invention in issue and the other party has presented no claim which includes this auxiliary invention either broadly or specifically, there appears to be no reason why it should be disclosed to him.

The decision of the Primary Examiner is affirmed.

IN RE HUNTER.

Decided February 28, 1907.

(127 O. G., 1253.)

TRADE-MARKS—ASSIGNMENT—MUST BE ACKNOWLEDGED TO BE RECORDABLE—SECTION 10 OF TRADE-MARK ACT OF FEBRUARY 20, 1905, CONSTRUED.

In order that an assignment of a trade-mark may be recordable in this Office, section 10 of the Trade-Mark Act of February 20, 1905, clearly provides that the assignment must not only be by an instrument in writing, but that it must be acknowledged according to the laws of the country or State in which the same is executed. If the laws of the country or State do not require assignments of trade-marks to be acknowledged or are silent on this point, it is believed to be necessary in order to comply with the section mentioned that there be an acknowledgement such as the laws of the country or State provide for other instruments in writing or legal documents of similar character.

ON PETITION.

Messrs. Wilkinson & Fisher for the petitioner.

ALLEN, *Commissioner:*

This is a petition from the refusal of the Chief of the Assignment Division to record a certain assignment.

Petitioner has filed for record in this Office an assignment of Trade-Mark No. 23,817, registered November 14, 1895, from Wailes Dove and Company, Limited, (the old company,) and Frank Herbert Hunter to Wailes Dove & Co., Limited, (the new company,) all of Newcastle-upon-Tyne, Northumberland, England. The assignment is not acknowledged, and for this reason the Chief of the Assignment Division refused to record it.

Section 10 of the Trade-Mark Act of February 20, 1905, which provides for the recording in this Office of trade-mark assignments, is as follows:

SEC. 10. That every registered trade-mark, and every mark for the registration of which application has been made, together with the application for registration of the same, shall.be assignable in connection with the good-will of the business in which the mark is used. Such assignment must be by an instrument in writing and duly acknowledged according to the laws of the country or State in which the same is executed; any such assignment shall be void as against any subsequent purchaser for a valuable consideration, without notice, unless it is recorded in the Patent Office within three months from date thereof. The Commissioner shall keep a record of such assignments.

It appears from this section that in order to be recordable in this Office the—

assignment must be by an instrument in writing and duly acknowledged according to the laws of the country or State in which the same is executed.

According to the *American and English Encyclopædia of Law:*

Acknowledgment is the act of one who has executed a deed, in going before some competent officer or court and declaring it to be his act or deed.

The object of acknowledgment is twofold: first, to entitle a deed to be recorded: and, second, to make it competent evidence without further proof of its execution.

Petitioner states that the assignment is in full compliance with both the common and statute law of England and is sufficient to pass title, and he contends that it is therefore a full compliance with the statute quoted above. In this contention petitioner is clearly in error.

It may not be necessary that the assignment should be acknowledged in order to pass title in England, as stated by petitioner; but in order to be recordable in this Office the act clearly provides that the assignment must not only be by an instrument in writing, but that it must be acknowledged according to the laws of the country or State in which the same is executed. If the laws of the country or State do not require assignments of trade-marks to be acknowledged or are silent on this point, it is believed to be necessary in order to comply with the section mentioned that there be an acknowledgment such as the laws of the country or State provide for other instruments in writing or legal documents of similar character. Inasmuch as the assignment in question contains no acknowledgment whatever, it clearly does not comply with said act.

The petition is denied.

EX PARTE MIDGLEY.

Decided January 10, 1907.

(127 O. G., 1577.)

1. ABANDONMENT OF APPLICATION—WHEN HOLDING IS PROPER.

Where twenty-seven claims were rejected on August 9, 1905, and on June 9, 1906, the applicant amended two of the rejected claims and added two new claims, but made no allusion to the remaining twenty-five rejected claims, and the Examiner on August 14, 1906, on taking up the case in the regular course of his work, notified applicant that his case was abandoned, *Held* that the Examiner's action is entirely in accord with sound reason and well-established practice and is the only proper action which could have been given under the circumstances.

2. SAME—UNRESPONSIVE ACTION NOT ENTITLED TO CONSIDERATION.

Petitioner's contention that his unresponsive amendment filed within the year is entitled to consideration and action upon its merits is clearly unfounded, since the statutes provide for no piecemeal consideration and the rules prohibit the same.

3. SAME—APPLICANT RESPONSIBLE FOR FAILURE TO COMPLY WITH RULES.

The fact that the Examiner in the regular course of business did not reach applicant's case and give him notice of the insufficiency of his action until after the year allowed for action had expired does not relieve applicant of the necessity of taking responsive action within the year required by the rules or shift the responsibility for failure to comply with the rules to the Patent Office.

4. SAME—APPLICATION ABANDONED WHERE DELAY WAS NOT UNAVOIDABLE.

Where the delay has not been terminated by the filing of an action fully responsive to the last rejection and where no good reason appears why such an action should not have been filed within the year allowed therefor, *Held* that the delay was not unavoidable and that the application is abandoned.

ON PETITION.

WIRELESS-TELEGRAPH SYSTEM.

Mr. Cornelius D. Ehret for the applicant.

ALLEN, *Commissioner:*

This is a petition that the Examiner's action holding the case abandoned be set aside as improper and that the application be revived and given status as a pending application.

It appears from the statement of the Examiner upon the petition that twenty-seven claims in this application were rejected on August 9, 1905; that on June 9, 1906, the applicant amended two of the rejected claims and added two new claims, but made no allusion to the remaining twenty-five rejected claims, and that upon August 14, 1906, the Examiner, taking up the case in the regular course of his work, held that it was abandoned.

There is no error in the Examiner's action. It is entirely in accord with sound reason and well-established practice and is the only proper action which could have been given under the circumstances. Rule 69 provides that in order to be entitled to reconsideration the applicant must distinctly and specifically point out the supposed errors in the Examiner's action. The applicant has made no attempt to comply with this rule. Rule 171 provides that prosecution of an application to save it from abandonment must include such proper action as the condition of the case may require. These rules for the conduct of proceedings in the Patent Office, made with the approval of the Secretary of the Interior and not inconsistent with law, have all the force and effect of statutes. (Sec. 483, Rev. Stats.) No proper action in accordance therewith having been taken within the year following the official action of August 9, 1905, the application is clearly abandoned under section 4894, Revised Statutes. The petitioner's contention that his amendment of June 9, 1906, is entitled under the statutes to consideration and action upon its merits is clearly unfounded. The statutes provide for no piecemeal consideration, and the rules referred to prohibit the same. Nor is this position a merely technical one, as is contended by the petitioner. The same reasons upon which the requirement for action by the applicant within a year following the Office action is based require that his action shall be fully responsive to the Office action. There appears to have been no reason why the applicant in this case should not have furnished the Examiner, as required by the rules, with his reasons for persisting in the twenty-five rejected claims. There was certainly no reason why the Examiner should have reconsidered his rejection of such claims without a statement of such reasons from the applicant, and, in fact, such reconsideration would have been improper. (*Ex parte*

Alton, C. D., 1904, 541; 113 O. G., 1968.) Action by the Examiner without reconsideration of the rejection of the twenty-five unamended claims leading to a finding that the case was otherwise ready for allowance would have resulted in an extension of the period for prosecution by the applicant of another year for no other purpose than the filing of his reasons for persisting in these claims, which reasons could and should have been filed in the preceding year.

The petitioner contends that the Examiner's failure to act upon the case and give notice of the insufficiency of the applicant's action for something over two months from the date of the applicant's action and until after the year allowed for action had expired is responsible in some way not made clear for the petitioner's failure to file proper action within the proper time. The Examiner states that the case was acted upon by him in the regular course of business. Does the pressure of work in the Patent Office, resulting in a delay in action of two months or more, relieve applicants of the necessity of taking responsive action within a year, as required by the rules? Or should the Examiners single out those cases in which the action taken is not fully responsive and give notice thereof at once in advance of action upon other cases? The answer to each of these questions obviously is no. The requirement of the practice for responsive actions is clearly set forth in the rules and in many published decisions. (*Ex parte Vaughen*, C. D., 1901, 161; 97 O. G., 957; *ex parte Kuper*, C. D., 1901, 258; 97 O. G., 2981; *ex parte Whiting*, C. D., 1902, 72; 98 O. G., 1969; *ex parte Alton*, C. D., 1904, 541; 113 O. G., 1968; *ex parte Linde*, C. D., 1905, 118; 115 O. G., 1329; *ex parte Buschbenz*, C. D., 1905, 248; 117 O. G., 600; *ex parte Schmidt and Tandly*, C. D., 1908, 102; 121 O. G., 688.) To comply with this requirement, the exercise of merely ordinary care is in general necessary. It is not alleged that more than that would have been required in this case. Clearly the responsibility for failure to comply rests in general upon the applicant or his representatives and cannot be shifted to the Patent Office. This case appears to be no exception to this rule.

The application is clearly abandoned unless the delay in prosecuting the same has been unavoidable. The delay cannot be held to have been unavoidable, however, first, because it has not as yet been terminated by the filing of an action fully responsive to the rejection of August 9, 1905, and, second, because no good reason appears why such an action should not have been filed within the year originally allowed therefor.

The petition is denied.

ADKINS AND LEWIS *v.* SEEBERGER.

Decided January 17, 1907.

(127 O. G., 1578.)

1. INTERFERENCE—MOTION FOR DISSOLUTION—EXTENSION OF LIMIT OF APPEAL.

The limit of appeal will not be extended to permit an appeal upon motion to transmit a motion for dissolution where the transmission of said motion would merely result in a reconsideration by the Primary Examiner under the head of irregularity in declaring the interference of the facts he has already considered under the right to make the claims.

2. SAME—SAME—SAME.

A long and unexcused delay in filing an appeal conftitutes a sufficient reason for denying an extension of the limit of appeal. (*Hewitt* v. *Steinmetz*, C. D., 1906, 174; 122 O. G., 1395.)

3. SAME—SAME—EXERCISE OF SUPERVISORY AUTHORITY OF COMMISSIONER.

Where the question presented upon a motion for dissolution can be raised, under Rule 130, at final hearing before the Examiner of Interferences and upon appeals from such decision, there is no occasion for the exercise of the supervisory authority of the Commissioner.

ON PETITION.

ESCALATOR.

Messrs. Duncan & Duncan for Adkins and Lewis.
Messrs. Coburn & McRoberts for Seeberger.

ALLEN, *Commissioner:*

This is a petition either (1) that the limit of appeal from the decision of the Examiner of Interferences refusing to transmit the interference upon the ground of irregularity be extended and the accompanying appeal from said decision be entertained or (2) that the question of irregularity in the declaration of the interference be considered by the Commissioner under his supervisory authority.

The motion to dissolve alleged irregularity in declaring the interference and that Seeberger has no right to make the claims of the issue. The contention that Seeberger is estopped from making the claims by reason of his failure to insert them in his application under Rule 109 during a prior interference is urged in support of both grounds of the motion. The Examiner of Interferences transmitted the second ground and refused to transmit the first ground of this motion, setting a limit of appeal that expired June 7, 1906.

The Primary Examiner held that Seeberger has a right to make the claims, whereupon Adkins and Lewis on October 23, 1906, brought the present petition. No excuse whatever is made for the long delay in filing the appeal, and this alone is sufficient reason for denying the petition. (*Hewitt* v. *Steinmetz*, C. D., 1906, 174; 122 O. G., 1395.) Moreover, if the appeal should be granted and the motion to dissolve again transmitted it would merely result in a reconsideration by the Primary Examiner under the head of irregularity of the very facts that he has already considered under the right to make the claims. That these facts were properly considered under the ground of the right to make the claims has not been questioned. The conduct of the petitioners in prosecuting that ground of their motion indicates that they are of the opinion that they were properly raised under said ground.

No occasion appears for the exercise of supervisory authority. Under present Rule 130 petitioners can raise the question of their opponent's right to the claims at the final hearing before the Examiner of Interferences and upon appeals from such decision.

The petition is denied.

EX PARTE FOWLER, JR.

Decided January 17, 1907.

(127 O. G., 1578.)

1. ABANDONED APPLICATION—WHAT IS RESPONSIVE ACTION.

On October 16, 1905, the Examiner finally rejected certain claims. The applicant on June 6, 1906, filed an amendment substituting new claims for those rejected, which amendment was refused entry by the Examiner in view of the final rejection. On September 24, 1906, applicant filed a request for reconsideration of the final rejection and refusal of his amendment, accompanied by a statement of reasons why he considered said actions improper. In reply he was notified by the Examiner on November 3, 1906, that his application was abandoned, and on November 6, 1906, he took this petition. *Held* that if the final rejection of October 16, 1905, was proper, the condition of the case called for either a cancelation of the rejected claims or an appeal to the Examiners-in-Chief, and since such action was not taken within the year the case is abandoned; but in case the final rejection was irregular or premature, then the actions of June 6 and September 24 were such as the condition of the case required, and the application is not abandoned.

2. FINAL REJECTION—WHEN UNWARRANTED.

Where appellant's letter stated that the prior Office action was not understood, requested that the pertinency of the references be pointed out as a guide to applicant in the further prosecution of the case, and expressly stated that it was not intended as a request for reconsideration, *Held* that the action of the Examiner in treating this letter as calling for a reconsideration and in finally rejecting the claims was unwarranted.

3. SAME—WHEN PREMATURE.

Where in the Office action prior to the final rejection a claim was criticised, but its rejection was inadvertently omitted, *Held* that the final rejection was premature.

On Petition

WEIGHING AND VENDING MACHINE.

Mr. Jonathan O. Fowler, Jr., pro se.

ALLEN, *Commissioner:*

This is a petition from the actions of the Primary Examiner finally rejecting the case, refusing to enter and consider an amendment, and holding the application abandoned.

After numerous actions during the prosecution of this application the Primary Examiner on October 16, 1905, finally rejected certain claims. In response to this action the applicant on June 6, 1906, presented a proposed amendment. On June 25, 1906, the Primary Examiner informed applicant that the proposed amendment would not be entered or considered in the case. Under date of September 24, 1906, applicant replied by a further argument and request for reconsideration of the final action and refusal of the amendment. He was notified by the Primary Examiner on November 3, 1906, that as he had not made a responsive action within a year from the final rejection his application was abandoned. From this action the present petition was filed on November 6, 1906.

If the final rejection of October 16, 1905, was proper, the condition of the case called for either a cancelation of the rejected claims or an appeal to the Examiners-in-Chief, and since such action was not taken within the year it would follow that the action of the Examiner holding the case abandoned is correct. Petitioner, however, claims that the final rejection was irregular and premature and desires to further prosecute the application before the Primary Examiner. Following the final rejection of October 16, 1905, Fowler filed on June 6, 1906, an amendment consisting of thirty-two claims and a cancelation of the former claims. This amendment was refused entry by the Primary Examiner on June 26, 1906, in view of the final rejection of October 16, 1905. On September 24, 1906, applicant filed a request for reconsideration of the Office actions of October 16, 1905, and June 25, 1906, accompanied by a statement of reasons why he considered said actions improper. Such request for a second action was necessary under the provisions of Rule 145 to entitle applicant to raise the question of the propriety of the final rejection by petition. In case it is found that the final rejection was irregular or premature, then the request for reconsideration of September 24, 1906, was such an action as the condition of the case required, and since it was taken within the year after the final rejection it must follow that the case is not abandoned. (*Ex parte Thayer,* C. D., 1906, 189; 122 O. G., 1724.)

Petitioner contends that the Office action of July 8, 1905, which the Examiner states was intended as a rejection of all of the fifty-eight claims of the case, does not contain a rejection of claims 35, 47, 48, 49, and 50, also that his letter of July 14, 1905, in response thereto was not a request for reconsideration, and that the Examiner should not, therefore, have made his next action a final rejection.

In his letter of July 14, 1905, applicant stated that a part of the prior Office action rejecting certain claims is not understood. He then discussed the structures intended to be covered by said claims and concluded with the statement:

Applicant begs to have it distinctly understood that this communication is in no sense to be regarded as a re-presentation of the claims for action, but simply as a request that the pertinence of the references to the various claims may be clearly explained, under Rule 66, as a means of aiding applicant to judge of the propriety of further prosecuting or altering the said claims.

In order to avoid any mistake, applicant desires to state more specifically that what he wishes is to have each part, or coöperating parts, of the Stallwerck structure pointed out and designated by its appropriate reference-symbol which is the equivalent of each of the various elements of the claims and particularly the equivalent of one of the eight elements of the combination of parts contained in claim 1 and recited above.

The same information is also desired in regard to the Ubrig machine, and also in regard to the Page, Wallace, Muller and Milo machines or structures that disclose the said combination of parts.

This letter requested that the pertinency of the references be pointed out as a guide to applicant in the further prosecution of the case and expressly stated that it was not intended as a request for reconsideration. The Examiner, however, treated this letter as calling for a reconsideration, and in his letter of final rejection stated that the " references have been explained and their pertinency pointed out many times." The record shows that on three occasions applicant was notified that upon the correction of slight informalities the case would be passed to issue. In his reply to this petition the Examiner states that the final rejection was intended to cover all the claims in the case. These facts indicate some basis for applicant's claim that the position of the Office with respect to the references was not entirely understood.

In view of all the circumstances the final rejection is believed to have been unwarranted. (*Ex parte Miller*, C. D., 1903, 147; 104 O. G., 309.)

Concerning the claims which petitioner contends were not rejected in the Office letter of July 8, 1905, said letter states:

In claim 35 it is not clear what limitation is covered by the negative expression in the last line of said claim.

Claims 47, 48, 49 and 50, cover merely a " plurality " of devices for actuating the goods-delivery mechanism, and are regarded as presenting nothing patentable over the construction shown by the patent to Ubrig of record.

Although the word " reject " is not used, the language clearly indicates that claims 47 to 50 were intended to be rejected and must have been so understood. This is not the case, however, with respect to claim 35, which is merely criticised. The Examiner admits that the rejection of claim 35 was " inadvertently omitted from the Office letter," but claims that it is not materially different from claims 34 and 36 and that applicant should have understood that " it was clearly the intention of the Examiner to reject it along with the rest." In his brief, which has been sworn to, petitioner says:

That believing claim 35 to be allowable from the fact that the same had not been rejected, the final rejection of the application was a surprise to your petitioner against which he was not able to guard or protect himself.

Since claim 35 had not been previously rejected, the final rejection is held to have been premature.

Having found that the final rejection was irregular and premature, it is directed that it be set aside and that the amendment filed June 6, 1906, be entered and considered. For reasons stated above it follows that if this amendment is a proper response to the Office action of July 8, 1905, the application is not abandoned.

The petition is granted to the extent indicated.

BAY STATE BELTING COMPANY *v.* KELTON-BRUCE MANUFACTURING COMPANY.

Decided January 18, 1907.

(127 O. G., 1580.)

1. INTERFERENCE—TESTIMONY—CONTROL OF WITNESSES.

The Patent Office has no power to compel the attendance of witnesses or to enforce the production of evidence of any kind. (*Lindstrom v. Lipschutz*, C. D., 1906, 39; 120 O. G., 904; *Kelly et al. v. Park et al.*, C. D., 1897, 182; 81 O. G., 1931.)

2. SAME—SAME—BOOKS USED TO REFRESH MEMORY NEED NOT BE OFFERED IN EVIDENCE.

Books produced at the examination of a witness for the purpose of refreshing his memory need not be offered in evidence. (*Laas and Sponenburg v. Scott*, C. D., 1906, 621; 122 O. G., 352; *McCormick v. Cleal*, C. D., 1898, 492; 83 O. G., 1514.)

3. SAME—SAME—SUPPRESSION—REFUSAL TO PLACE BOOKS IN EVIDENCE.

Where certain books were referred to by a witness for the purpose of refreshing his recollection, and opposing counsel, who was given an opportunity to examine them, did not interpose any objection to the books or cross-examine the witness relative to the entries, *Held* that a subsequent refusal to produce the books for inspection or to offer them in evidence does not warrant the suppression of any part of the deposition of the witness who referred to said books.

APPEAL from Examiner of Interferences.

TRADE-MARK FOR BELT AND LACE LEATHER.

Mr. George N. Goddard for Bay State Belting Company.
Messrs. Pennie & Goldsborough for Kelton-Bruce Manufacturing
Company.

ALLEN, *Commissioner:*

This is an appeal from the decision of the Examiner of Interferences
denying the motion of the applicant, the Kelton-Bruce Manufacturing
Company, that the opponent, the Bay State Belting Company, be required to produce for inspection and to offer in evidence certain books
of the last-named company referred to by one of their witnesses,
George B. Rowbotham, or in lieu thereof that certain questions and
answers be stricken from the record.

The decision of the Examiner of Interferences denying the motion
that the Bay State Belting Company be required to produce the books
referred to and to offer them in evidence was clearly correct. The
Patent Office has no power under the law to compel the attendance of
witnesses or to enforce the production of evidence of any kind.
(*Lindstrom* v. *Lipschutz*, C. D., 1906, 39; 120 O. G., 904; *Kelly et al.*
v. *Park et al.*, C. D., 1897, 182; 81 O. G., 1931.)

The decision of the Examiner of Interferences refusing to strike
parts of Rowbotham's deposition from the record was also correct.
It appears from the record that the books referred to by the witness
for the purpose of refreshing his recollection were produced during
his examination and that counsel for the applicant was given an
opportunity to inspect the items referred to by the witness. Applicant's counsel did not at the time the books were produced make any
attempt to inspect them other than to refer to the items mentioned
by the witness, nor did he cross-examine the witness relative to the
contents of the books. Several days after the examination of this
witness had been concluded the applicant's counsel entered upon the
record a request that the books referred to be produced for inspection
and offered in evidence. Upon opposing counsel's refusal to comply
with this request counsel for the applicant gave notice of his intention
to bring the motion now under consideration. It is well settled that
books produced at the examination of a witness for the purpose of
refreshing his memory need not be offered in evidence. (*Laas and
Sponenburg* v. *Scott*, C. D., 1906, 621; 122 O. G., 352; *McCormick* v.
Cleal, C. D., 1898, 492; 83 O. G., 1514.) The failure of applicant's
counsel to interpose any objection to the books or to cross-examine the
witness relative to the entries therein when they were presented
to him for inspection warrants the presumption that he was at that

time satisfied with the authenticity of the books and their contents. No reason therefore appears for striking out any part of Rowbotham's deposition.

The decision of the Examiner of Interferences is affirmed.

Ex parte Bullock.

Decided February 7, 1907.

(127 O. G., 1580.)

1. Claims—Independent Inventions—Practice.

Where claims presented by amendment are held by the Examiner to be for an independent invention from that presented in the other claims, *Held* that the question of whether the claims are in fact for an independent invention must be settled before applicant can demand an action upon their merits. If for an independent invention, applicant is estopped from prosecuting said claims on their merits in this application, and they should be canceled. This question is the same as that ordinarily presented in a requirement for division, with the exception that in originally presenting and prosecuting claims to one invention only applicant has already made his election and has now no choice as to which set of claims he will cancel. (*Ex parte Selle*, C. D., 1904, 221; 110 O. G., 1728; *ex parte Tuttle*, C. D., 1904, 537; 113 O. G., 1967.)

2. Same—Indefinite and Functional.

Where the claim is not for a combination of which the "means" for the purpose mentioned is an element, but is merely for means as an element and covers all possible means for accomplishing a certain function regardless of structure, *Held* that the claim is indefinite and functional.

On Petition.

CLOTHES-DRYING DEVICE.

Mr. F. G. Dieterich and *Messrs. Fred G. Dieterich & Company* for the applicant.

Allen, *Commissioner:*

This is a petition from the refusal of the Examiner to forward an appeal to the Examiners-in-Chief.

The claims originally presented were all rejected as covering aggregations. Present claims 9 and 10 presented in applicant's second amendment were held in the following action of the Examiner to be for an independent invention, and the remaining claims were rejected as covering aggregations. Claim 9 was also objected to as indefinite. Upon a repetition of this action applicant filed an appeal to the Examiners-in-Chief upon all of these points. The Examiner refused to forward this appeal, for the reason that the case is not in condition for such an appeal until the formal objection to claim 9 is cured and until the question of whether claims 9 and 10 cover an independent invention is finally determined and an examination made as to their novelty, if it is held on appeal that they may be prosecuted in this case.

The question whether claims 9 and 10 are for an independent invention from that presented in the other claims must be settled before applicant can demand an action upon their merits. If for an independent invention, applicant is estopped from prosecuting said claims on their merits in this application, and they should be canceled. This question is the same as that ordinarily presented in a requirement for division, with the exception that in originally presenting and prosecuting claims to the invention of claims 1 to 8 only applicant has already made his election and has now no choice as to which set of claims he will cancel. (*Ex parte Selle*, C. D., 1904, 221; 110 O. G., 1728; *ex parte Tuttle*, C. D., 1904, 537; 113 O. G., 1967.)

Claim 9 reads as follows:

9. In a device of the class described, means for transferring clothes-carrying rods from one position and depositing them on a suitable support, substantially as shown and described.

The claim is clearly indefinite and functional. No structure by which the function stated is accomplished is set forth in the claim. The claim is not for a combination of which the " means " for the purpose mentioned is an element, but is merely for means as an element and covers all possible means for accomplishing a certain function regardless of structure. (*Ex parte Kotler*, C. D., 1901, 62; 95 O. G., 2684.)

The Examiner was right in refusing to forward applicant's appeal in its present form. The case is in condition for appeal merely on the question whether the claims cover more than one invention, and the appeal should be limited to this question.

The petition is denied.

Ex parte M. Zimmermann Company.

Decided January 12, 1907.

(127 O. G., 1991.)

Trade-Marks—Practice Regarding Expression of Color.

Where in an application for registration of a trade-mark colors are indicated in the drawing by conventional lining in accordance with the chart for draftsmen on page 87 of the Rules of Practice in the United States Patent Office, *Held* that if color forms a material feature of the mark the colors should be described in order to comply fully with section 1 of the act of May 4, 1906, while if color is not an essential feature a new drawing omitting the conventional lining used to express color should be filed.

ON PETITION.

TRADE-MARK FOR CURED MEATS.

Mr. Titian W. Johnson, for the applicant.

ALLEN, *Commissioner:*

This is a petition from the following requirement of the Examiner of Trade-Marks:

> The mark is shown in the drawing as in particular colors. Therefore the colors of the mark should be described.

The labels filed with the application show the letter " Z " in red on a field of dark blue surrounded by an annular band of lighter blue. These colors are indicated in the drawing of the application by lining it in accordance with the chart for draftsmen on page 87 of the Rules of Practice in the United States Patent Office.

So far as the drawing is concerned, it would appear that applicant intends to make color an essential feature of its mark. This appears to be admitted by the applicant, for it states in its petition:

> Because the mark has been shown or shaded in the drawing to indicate certain colors as shown by the "draftsman's chart," in a case of this sort can only show that the draftsman has followed his subject closely, and to those familiar with the "chart" it would probably appear, if they thought of it at all, that the " Z " was printed in red, but it does not necessarily follow, or follow at all, that the color is a part or essential to applicant's mark, unless he so expresses it in his statement, and relies upon the color to form a part thereof.

While to one familiar with the draftsman's chart the lining of the mark would indicate the color scheme, to one not thus familiar it would not express color. Therefore if color forms a material feature of the mark the colors should be described in order to comply fully with section 1 of the act of May 4, 1906, which requires—

> a description of the trade-mark itself, only when needed to express colors not shown in the drawing.

In its petition, however, applicant disclaims color as an essential feature of the mark. It states:

> In this case colors are shown or indicated, but as above suggested they are not important to applicant or depended upon by applicant to form an essential feature of his trade-mark. In this case colors are not needed or depended upon, and no expression of colors should, in opinion of counsel, appear in the statement.

If such is the case, it is obvious that in order to avoid confusion and ambiguity color should not be indicated in the drawing.

If petitioner regards color as a feature of its mark, it should be described; if not, a new drawing should be filed omitting the conventional lining used to express color.

The petition is denied.

BARBER *v.* WOOD.

Decided January 26, 1907.

(127 O. G., 1991.)

1. INTERFERENCE—MOTION TO TAKE TESTIMONY TO SHOW INOPERATIVENESS—NOT APPEALABLE.

Where a motion for permission to take testimony for the purpose of showing that the opponent's device is inoperative, pending the determination of a motion to dissolve the interference, was denied by the Examiner of Interferences on the ground that the rules do not provide for the taking of testimony in interference cases prior to the determination of a motion to dissolve, *Held* that no appeal lies from the decision of the Examiner of Interferences on the question of taking testimony to show inoperativeness and that no occasion is presented for the exercise of the supervisory authority of the Commissioner.

2. SAME—INOPERATIVENESS OF OPPONENT'S DEVICE—PRACTICE.

Under Rule 130 where the operativeness of an opponent's device or his right to make the claim is material to the right of a party to a patent said party may urge the matter at final hearing before the Examiner of Interferences as a basis for his award of priority; but as a condition precedent to such right, the party must first present the matter upon a motion for dissolution, or show good reason why such motion was not made and prosecuted.

ON PETITION.

SHEET-DELIVERY MECHANISM.

Messrs. Brown & Seward and *Mr. Walter F. Rogers* for Barber.
Messrs. Southgate & Southgate for Wood.

ALLEN, *Commissioner:*

This is a petition by Barber that under the exercise of my supervisory authority the Examiner of Interferences be directed to retain the custody of this case and that petitioner may be permitted to take testimony upon the question of inoperativeness and of public use.

On June 30, 1906, in response to an order to show cause why judgment on the record should not be entered against him, Barber brought a motion to dissolve this interference on several grounds, including inoperativeness and public use of Wood's device, all of which were transmitted to the Primary Examiner by the Examiner of Interferences except that of public use. An appeal was taken from the refusal to transmit this ground.

On July 25, 1906, Barber made a motion before the Examiner of Interferences for an order permitting him to take testimony in support of the ground of his preceding motion that the Wood invention is in certain respects inoperative and also to establish public use and abandonment by Wood.

The portion of the motion relating to the taking of testimony on the question of public use was dismissed by the Examiner of Interferences on the ground that only the Commissioner has authority to institute public-use proceedings. Petitioner has not made such a showing as would warrant the institution of public-use proceedings. (*Siebert* v. *Bloomberg*, C. D., 1906, 325; 124 O. G., 628.)

Concerning the taking of testimony on the question of inoperativeness, the motion was denied without prejudice, on the ground that the rules do not provide for the taking of testimony in interference cases prior to the determination of a motion to dissolve. In *Lowry and Cowley* v. *Spoon* (C. D., 1906, 381; 124 O. G., 1846) it was held that no appeal would lie from the decision of the Examiner of Interferences on the question of taking testimony to show inoperativeness. Barber, however, asks that I exercise my supervisory authority and reverse the decision of the Examiner of Interferences.

It is noted that the Examiner of Interferences has not finally determined whether Barber should be permitted to take the desired testimony for use at final hearing, but has merely held that he should not do so until the motion to dissolve now before the Primary Examiner is decided.

I find no occasion for the exercise of supervisory authority in this case.

Under Rule 130 where the operativeness of an opponent's device or his right to make the claim is material to the right of a party to a patent said party may urge the matter at final hearing before the Examiner of Interferences as a basis for his award of priority; but as a condition precedent to such right the party must first present the matter upon a motion for dissolution or show good reason why such motion was not made and prosecuted. Petitioner apparently wishes to have waived this preliminary presentation of the matter by motion to dissolve. I do not find that the circumstances of the case warrant a waiver of this preliminary requirement or that petitioner will suffer any injustice by following the usual course of procedure. As stated in *Clement* v. *Browne* v. *Stroud*, (C. D., 1906, 461; 125 O. G. 992:)

It is for the guidance and assistance of the other tribunals of the Office that Rule 130 provides that a motion to dissolve shall be a condition precedent to urging before the Examiner of Interferences that an opponent's claim is unpatentable.

The consideration of the grounds of the motion to dissolve upon the papers of record may dispose of the interference without the delay and expense incident to the taking of testimony. From the denial of the motion to dissolve upon the grounds urged there is no appeal from the decision of the Primary Examiner, (Rule 124,) while if the motion prevails upon the matter of record the time that would be consumed by taking testimony is saved. After the present

seems to be uselessly complex and burdensome in its application to such cases as the present one. The order issued in the present case was an intentional departure from that practice.

Under *Snider* v. *Bunnell, supra*, this case would have been sent to the Examiner after the recommendation by the Examiners-in-Chief to consider the matters to which attention had been called and to render a decision thereon. In the event of conflict between his conclusions and those of the Examiners-in-Chief the case would then be forwarded to the Commissioner for another decision. Two decisions would thus be rendered by the Office upon the merits of the petitioner's application for patent, in addition to the opinion expressed by the Examiners-in-Chief, without appeal or other action upon the part of the petitioner. If the decision of the Commissioner should be adverse to the applicant, the case would still be in no condition for appeal to the court of appeals, but would have to be returned to the Primary Examiner for the institution of a new course of appeals and *pro forma* decisions by the Primary Examiner and the Examiners-in-Chief before that end could be attained. It is designed by the practice instituted in the present case to avoid these complications, in those cases where the recommendation of the Examiners-in-Chief covers matters considered and passed upon by the Primary Examiner in an *inter partes* decision, by substituting at the outset the entry of a rejection *pro forma* by the Primary Examiner, putting the case at once in condition for a course of appeal which may be carried to the court of appeals if the application is otherwise in condition therefor.

It is not to be presumed that the Examiners-in-Chief would form an opinion adverse to a party's interest and call attention to the same upon the record without careful consideration in those cases where the grounds of their opinion had already been considered by the Primary Examiner and held insufficient to warrant such adverse opinion. When they express such an opinion under these circumstances, the same is clearly of sufficient force to bind the Primary Examiner and sustain his *pro forma* rejection of claims until the opinion is withdrawn by the Examiners-in-Chief themselves or overruled by the Commissioner or court of appeals in the regular course of appeal.

The decision upon priority in the present case having become final through the failure of Holz to appeal, there is no reason for further *inter partes* consideration of the applications. The entry by the Primary Examiner of a rejection in the application of Hewitt based upon the opinion expressed by the Examiners-in-Chief seems to open to Hewitt a way of securing final determination of the question of patentability attended with less complication, labor, and delay than is in general incident to the practice heretofore followed in *Snider* v.

Bunnell, supra. However this may be, the fact that the opinion of the Primary Examiner upon the question raised is of record in the case renders further consideration thereof by him unnecessary, and the fact that of the conflicting opinions of the different tribunals the later opinion comes from the higher tribunal after consideration of the position taken by the lower renders further consideration by any tribunal of the Office of the question superfluous until presented by a statutory appeal.

The petition is denied.

DIXON AND MARSH *v.* GRAVES AND WHITTEMORE.

Decided March 5, 1907.

(127 O. G., 1993.)

1. INTERFERENCE—TESTIMONY TO SHOW ISSUE UNPATENTABLE TO EITHER PARTY IRRELEVANT TO QUESTION OF PRIORITY.

Where during the time assigned him for the purpose of taking testimony upon the question of priority of invention one party took merely the testimony of an expert for the purpose of showing that the issue is not patentable to either party over the prior art, *Held* that the decision of the Examiner of Interferences was proper in granting a motion to strike said testimony from the record on the ground that it is irrelevant to the question of priority.

2. SAME—UNPATENTABILITY OF ISSUE TO ALL PARTIES—PROPERLY RAISED BY MOTION TO DISSOLVE UNDER RULE 122.

Where it is contended that the non-patentability of the issue to either party to the interference may be urged at final hearing, *Held* that during the preliminary stages of the interference and before the parties have been put to the trouble and expense of taking testimony on the question of priority either party may raise the question of the patentability of the issue by motion to dissolve the interference under Rule 122. Contestants are thus given an opportunity to have determined the question of whether the Office was right in declaring the interference and whether the proceeding should continue before testimony as to priority is taken. It is essential to the orderly proceeding of the interference that the question of patentability be finally settled at this time, and for this purpose the rules provide for an appeal from the rejection of claims based on the decision on the motion to the full extent permitted by law.

3. SAME—SAME—CANNOT BE RAISED UNDER RULE 130.

Where it is contended by one party to an interference that he has a right to urge the unpatentability of the issues to either party at the final hearing under Rule 130 and to take testimony in support thereof, *Held* that the contention is erroneous and that this rule permits a party to urge the non-patentability of a claim to his opponent as a basis for the decision upon priority of invention only when it is materal to his own right to a patent.

4. SAME—LIMITED TO QUESTION OF PRIORITY OF INVENTION.

The United States Supreme Court in the case of *ex rel. George A. Lowry* v. *Frederick I. Allen, Commissioner of Patents*, (C. D., 1906, 765; 125 O. G., 2305,) held that section 4904 of the Revised Statutes limits the declaration of interferences to the question of priority of invention. Should a party be permitted to urge that the claims of the issue are patentable to neither party in the interference, a decision that the issue is not patentable would not result in a decision of priority of invention in favor of either party or in the issue of a patent to one of the parties. In the cases contemplated by Rule 130, however, a decision that the issue is not patentable to one party would necessarily result in a decision of priority in favor of the other party.

APPEAL ON MOTION.

METHOD OF SHAPING GLASS.

Messrs. Bakewell & Byrnes and *Mr. H. S. Shepard* for Dixon and Marsh.

Mr. James Whittemore and *Messrs. Bacon & Milans* for Graves and Whittemore.

MOORE, *Acting Commissioner:*

This is an appeal by Dixon and Marsh from the decision of the Examiner of Interferences granting a motion brought by Graves and Whittemore to strike from the record the deposition of Daniel C. Ripley taken on behalf of Dixon and Marsh.

The Examiner of Interferences granted the motion on the ground that the testimony of Ripley is in the nature of an expert deposition intended to show that the claims corresponding to the counts of the issue are not patentable to either party and that it is irrelevant to the question of priority of invention. I am of the opinion that the Examiner of Interferences is correct in his conclusion.

It is admitted by Dixon and Marsh that the deposition of Ripley is in the nature of an expert opinion directed entirely to the question of the patentability of the issue over the prior art, and they contend that they have a right to urge the unpatentability of the issues to either party at the final hearing and to present evidence of this character in support thereof for consideration at said final hearing in the interference proceding under Rule 130.

Appellants are in error in this contention. An interference is a proceeding instituted for the purpose of determining the question of priority of invention. Before the interference is declared the issue must be found patentable. During the preliminary stages of the interference and before the parties have been put to the trouble and expense of taking testimony on the question of priority either party may raise the question of the patentability of the issue by motion to dissolve the interference under Rule 122. Contestants are thus given an opportunity to have determined the question of whether the Office was right in declaring the interference and whether the proceeding should continue before testimony as to priority is taken. It is essential to the orderly proceeding of the interference that the question of patentability be finally settled at this time, and for this purpose the rules provide for an appeal from the rejection of claims based on the decision on the motion to the full extent permitted by law. Neither the rules nor the practice as announced in the cases of *Sobey* v. *Holsclaw* (C. D., 1905, 523; 119 O. G., 1922) and *Potter* v. *McIntosh*, (C. D., 1906, 56; 120 O. G., 1823,) recently affirmed by the Court of Appeals of the District of Columbia in *Sobey* v. *Holsclaw* (*post*, 465; 126 O. G., 3041) and *Potter* v. *McIntosh*, (decided December 14, 1906, *post*, 505; 127 O. G., 1995;) provide for raising the question of the patentability of the issue at all parties as a matter of right at the final hearing or on appeal from the decision on priority.

The contention of appellants that this case comes under the provisions of Rule 130 is erroneous. Rule 130 reads:

Where the patentability of a claim to an opponent is material to the right of a party to a patent, said party may urge the non-patentability of the claim to his opponent at final hearing before the Examiner of Interferences as a basis for the decision upon priority of invention, and upon appeals from such decision. A party shall not be entitled to take such step, however, unless he has duly presented and prosecuted a motion under Rule 122 for dissolution upon the ground in question, or shows good reason why such a motion was not presented and prosecuted.

This rule permits a party to urge the non-patentability of a claim to his opponent as a basis for the decision upon priority of invention only when it is material to his own right to a patent. The principle upon which this rule is based is announced in the decision of the Court of Appeals of the District of Columbia in the case of *Podlesak and Podlesak* v. *McInnerney*, (C. D., 1906, 558; 120 O. G., 2127,) as follows:

The question of the right of a party to make a claim goes to the very foundation of an interference for if the party has not such right the interference falls. If it be incorrectly held that such party has a right to make the claim priority may be awarded to him and his adversary be deprived of a substantial right in that he is not given a claim where he necessarily is the prior inventor, his adversary never having made the invention. Manifestly that question should not be finally determined by the Primary Examiner who originally declared the interference. We therefore take jurisdiction to determine that question in this case as an ancillary question to be considered in awarding priority of invention.

In the case under consideration Dixon and Marsh brought a motion to dissolve the interference on the ground of non-patentability of the issue to either party. The Primary Examiner held that the issue is patentable and denied the motion. To now permit appellants to take testimony concerning patentability of the issue and to contest it at final hearing would, in effect, nullify the provision of Rule 124, which reads:

No appeal will be permitted from a decision rendered upon motion for dissolution affirming the patentability of a claim or the applicant's right to make the same or the identity of meaning of counts in the cases of different parties.

The authority of this Office, with the approval of the Secretary of the Interior, to promulgate Rule 124 has been recently upheld in the decision of the United States Supreme Court in the case of *The United States, ex rel. George A. Lowry,* v. *Frederick I. Allen, Commissioner of Patents* (C. D., 1906, 765; 125 O. G., 2365.) Moreover, this decision states, concerning the purpose of an interference:

It certainly could not have been the intention to destroy all distinctions in procedure. But we are not left to inference. The statute is explicit. It limits the declaration of interferences to the question of priority of invention. Section 4904 provides that in case of conflict of an application for a patent with a pending application or with an unexpired patent (as in the case at bar,) the Commissioner shall give notice thereof—
"and shall direct the Primary Examiner to proceed to determine the question of *priority of invention.*" (Italics ours.)
And it is provided that the Commissioner shall issue a patent to the party adjudged the prior inventor, unless the adverse party appeals from the decision of the Primary Examiner or Examiners-in-Chief, as the case may be.

Should a party be permitted to urge that the claims of the issue are patentable to neither party in the interference, a decision that the issue is not patentable would not result in a decision of priority of invention in favor of either party or in the issue of a patent to one of the parties. In the cases contemplated by Rule 130, however, a decision that the issue is not patentable to one party would necessarily result in a decision of priority in favor of the other party. (*Greenawalt* v. *Mark, ante,* 21; 126 O. G., 1063.)

Since the rules and decisions do not permit the non-patentability of the issue to all the parties to be urged at final hearing on the question of priority, it is unnecessary to consider the further contention of appellants that they have a right to take testimony in the interference proceeding in support of their claim that the issues are not patentable. It may be stated, however, that the practice of not permitting the introduction of such testimony is well established and should be adhered to, for reasons stated in the following decisions: *Huber* v. *Aiken,* (C. D., 1899, 166; 88 O. G., 1525,) *Stroud* v. *Miller,* (C. D., 1902, 423; 101 O. G., 2075,) and *Parkes* v. *Lewis,* (C. D., 1906, 2; 120 O. G., 323.)

The decision of the Examiner of Interferences is affirmed.

DIXON v. McELROY.

Decided January 11, 1907.

(127 O. G., 2393.)

INTERFERENCE—PRELIMINARY STATEMENT—AMENDMENT OF.

> Where D. was notified that his preliminary statement was indefinite and should be amended, but no amendment was made, and the present motion was not brought until eight months later and after testimony had been taken by D., and was inspired by a statement placed on the record by his opponent, *Held* that the motion was properly denied in the absence of a showing in excuse for the long delay in bringing the motion or the failure to respond to the requirement for a more definite statement or of a satisfactory showing of accident or mistake or of newly-discovered evidence.

APPEAL ON MOTION.

STEAM-JACKET.

Messrs. Warfield & Duell for Dixon.
Mr. Robert M. Pierson for McElroy.

ALLEN, *Commissioner:*

This is an appeal by Dixon from the decision of the Examiner of Interferences denying his motion to amend his preliminary statement.

Dixon alleged conception, drawings, disclosure, and reduction to practice " prior to November 30, 1900," in his original preliminary statement. He now desires by amending his preliminary statement to carry back his date of conception, drawings, and disclosure to February, 18, 1892, and his reduction to practice to " the years 1892, 1903, and 1894."

The Examiner of Interferences upon the receipt of Dixon's original preliminary statement notified him on February 2, 1906, that the words " prior to " were indefinite and fixed no date and informed him that an amended preliminary statement " stating the first dates upon which Dixon relies " must be filed by February 19, 1906, or he would be restricted to the date named in the original statement. No amended statement, however, was filed by Dixon in response to this notice. The present motion was brought October 31, 1906, over eight months later and after testimony had been taken by Dixon.

It appears from the brief filed in behalf of Dixon that his attempt to amend his preliminary statement at this time is inspired by the following statement placed on the record during the taking of testimony by counsel for McElroy:

> Notice is here given by counsel for McElroy that the testimony of witnesses for Dixon including those who have already testified, in so far as such testimony bears upon the statutory bar of public use, will be offered in evidence

for McElroy in this or a proper proceeding, and counsel for Dixon is offered the opportunity to cross-examine his own witnesses or rebut their testimony so far as it relates to public use.

Dixon contends that the amendment should be permitted in view of this statement on the record, as without the amendment he cannot have the benefit of the early dates in the interference proceeding, while testimony concerning them might be effective for McElroy in case a public-use proceeding should be instituted.

This contention is hypothetical and is entitled to little weight. No showing is made in excuse for the long delay in bringing the motion or the failure to respond to the requirement of the Examiner for a more definite statement. No showing is made of accident or mistake or of newly-discovered evidence. Such a showing of a satisfactory character is uniformly required as a basis for the granting of a motion to amend the preliminary statement.

For the reasons stated the decision of the Examiner of Interferences is affirmed.

KARPENSTEIN *v.* HERTZBERG.

Decided January 17, 1907.

(127 O. G., 2393.)

INTERFERENCE—PRELIMINARY STATEMENT—AMENDMENT OF.
    The question of amending the preliminary statement is a matter largely within the discretion of the Examiner of Interferences. Unless it be shown that such discretion has been abused his decision will not be disturbed.

APPEAL ON MOTION.

MASSAGE APPARATUS.

Mr. James H. Westcott for Karpenstein.
Messrs. Griffin, Bernard & Cavanagh and *Messrs. Griffin & Bernard* for Hertzberg.

ALLEN, *Commissioner:*

This is an appeal by Hertzberg from the decision of the Examiner of Interferences granting Karpenstein's motion to amend his preliminary statement.

Karpenstein's amended statement carries back his date of reduction to practice from February 1, 1903, to July 1, 1902. Hertzberg's alleged date of reduction to practice is December 2, 1902.

Notice of the motion was given prior to the taking of testimony, and a stipulation was entered into that said amendment should be ~ued at final hearing.

Karpenstein claims that he was not advised of the true meaning of the term " reduction to practice " and that he understood it to mean " a device that was commercially practical and which could be put upon the market and sold at a profit." The Examiner of Interferences found the testimony in behalf of Karpenstein to be consistent with the allegations of the amended statement, and he was of the opinion that—

This seems to be one of those cases of honest mistake in making the preliminary statement where the rule against amendment should not be enforced with such strictness as to deprive an inventor on technical grounds of the right to prove his true dates. ·

The question of amending the preliminary statement is a matter largely within the discretion of the Examiner of Interferences. Unless it be shown that such discretion has been abused his decision will not be disturbed. I find no such abuse of discretion in this case.

The decision of the Examiner of Interferences is affirmed.

Ex parte Pietro.

Decided February 12, 1907.

(127 O. G., 2394.)

1. TRADE-MARKS—REGISTRATION BY FOREIGNERS—MUST CORRESPOND WITH FOREIGN REGISTRATION.

The only mark which a foreign applicant is entitled to register in this country is the mark which he has registered in the country in which he is located. Such mark is presumably that set forth and shown in the foreign registration, and the Office must so assume until furnished with proofs to the contrary.

2. SAME—SAME—SAME—DRAWING.

Where a foreigner applies for registration in this country, his registration in the country in which he is located will be presumed to set forth and show his trade-mark, and in the absence of proof to the contrary the drawing of his application for registration in this country will be required to conform to such foreign registration.

ON PETITION.

TRADE-MARK FOR STOMACH-TONIC.

Messrs. Wilkinson & Fisher for the applicant.

ALLEN, *Commissioner:*

This is a petition from the action of the Examiner of Trade-Marks requiring a new drawing.

The applicant is a subject of the King of Italy, residing in that country. He has furnished the Office with a certified copy of his registration there, as required by Rule 17. The Italian registration comprises applicant's entire label. The drawing of the application in this country comprises a signature and fanciful device taken from the label, but fails to include a large amount of printed matter found on the latter. The applicant contends that the portions of the label omitted from the drawing are not portions of the trade-mark. The Examiner requires that they be shown in the application without regard to their actual relation to the mark in order that the registration in this country may conform to that secured abroad.

Section 4 of the Trade-Mark Act of 1905 provides:

Sec. 4. That an application for registration of a trade-mark filed in this country by any person who has previously regularly filed in any foreign country which, by treaty, convention, or law, affords similar privileges to citizens of the United States an application for registration of the same trade-mark shall be accorded the same force and effect as would be accorded to the same application if filed in this country on the date on which application for registration of the same trade-mark was first filed in such foreign country: *Provided,* That such application is filed in this country within four months from the date on which the application was first filed in such foreign country: *And provided,* That certificate of registration shall not be issued for any mark for registration of which application has been filed by an applicant located in a foreign country until such mark has been actually registered by the applicant in the country in which he is located.

Under this section of the statute the only mark which the applicant is entitled to register in this country is the mark which he has registered in Italy. The mark registered in Italy is presumably that set forth and shown in the Italian registration, and the Office must so assume until furnished with proofs to the contrary. There appears to be no evidence in this case that the Italian registration is a registration of a trade-mark right in that country in the mark shown upon the drawing of this application. There was therefore no error in the Examiner's action requiring modification of the same to conform to the registration abroad.

Petition denied.

EX PARTE HOEY.

Decided March 27, 1906.

(127 O. G., 2815.)

PATENTABILITY—NON-INVENTION—CHANGE OF LOCATION.

The change of location of projections on the seat portion of a bed-couch *Held* to relate to mechanical skill.

APPEAL from Examiners-in-Chief.

BED-COUCH.

Mr. Geo. H. Strong and Mr. T. W. Fowler for the applicant.

ALLEN, *Commissioner:*

This is an appeal from the decision of the Examiners-in-Chief affirming the action of the Primary Examiner rejecting the following claims:

10. The combination in a bed-couch of a containing box or case, a seat hinged to the top of the box between the front and rear edges thereof, said seat having rearward projections extending from its under side and beyond and below the hinges, and within the box, a back pivotally connected with the seat and a foldable leg connected with the back and with said seat projections.

13. In a bed-couch, the combination of a hollow base, a seat hinged to the base and having rearward projections within the base and below and beyond its hinges, a back turnably connected with the seat and braces connecting the back with said seat projections and tiltable in unison with, and normally holding the back at right angles to the seat.

17. The combination in a bed-couch of a containing box or base, a seat hinged to the top of the box, between the front and rear, said seat having side bars extending back of and below the hinges and within the box and a suitable stop between the side bars and the base to keep the seat from tilting farther back than is desirable.

18. In a couch, the combination of a hollow base, a seat hinged thereto between the front and rear thereof and having projections extending behind its hinges, a back hinged to the seat, hinged legs carried by the back, braces hinged to the legs and to said rearward projections on the seat, said legs and braces coöperating with the back to hold the back and seat at right angles to one another, and means to prevent the accidental disarrangement of said braces and legs relative to said back and thereby allow the back and seat to open out, when the seat is opened to give access to the box.

21. In a couch, the combination of a box, a seat hinged thereto forward of the back edge of the box and forming a cover therefor, rearward projections on the back of the seat, a back hinged to the seat, legs hinged to the back, braces hinged to the legs and to said rearward projections, said legs foldable against the back with the pivots of the braces and legs in front of the lines through the pivots of the legs to the back and the braces to the projections to hold the back at right angles to the seat, and said seat and back adapted to be turned in unison on the seat-hinges to give access to the box, means for holding the seat in lifted position, and means to prevent the legs and braces falling down accidentally when the seat is in such lifted position.

The reference relied upon is patent to Bühner, April 9, 1901, No. 671,906.

Claims 10 and 13 distinguish from the device of Bühner only by providing that the projections from the back of the seat shall extend from the lower side thereof below the hinges and within the box or base. These distinctions do not involve invention, but are mere matters of mechanical skill.

Claim 17 contains an additional distinction in the limitation to the stops 11 of the applicant's drawing. Bühner sets forth in his specification the same result that is secured by the use of these stops. This feature of the applicant's device in view of the Bühner disclosure likewise involves mere mechanical skill and not invention.

Claims 18 and 21 have been refused on the ground that they involve an unwarranted departure from the invention claimed in the original patent. These claims include means for preventing accidental disarrangement of the legs relative to the back when the seat is raised. This result is to be secured through engagement of the links 5 with the bottoms of the slots 10 upon motion of the legs 6 tending to displace them from their position against the back C. The Examiners-in-Chief correctly stated that no such construction was shown or described in the original construction. The rejection of claims 18 and 21 was proper.

The decision of the Examiners-in-Chief holding that claims 10, 13, 17, 18, and 21 are not allowable *is affirmed.*

Ex parte Trebon.

Decided February 1, 1907.

(127 O. G., 2815.)

1. ABANDONMENT—FAILURE OF APPLICANT TO AUTHORIZE ATTORNEY TO TAKE ACTION DOES NOT EXCUSE.

   The failure of the attorney to act within the statutory period is not excused by the allegation that he did not act earlier because not authorized by the applicant to do so, where it does not appear that he could not have been earlier authorized to proceed.

2. SAME—UNAVOIDABLE DELAY.

   The delay of more than one year in responding to the Office action is not unavoidable in those cases where action might have been taken had reasonable efforts been exercised to that end at any time within the period following the Office action.

3. SAME—SAME—INTENTION OF APPLICANT.

   Applications are abandoned without regard to what the intentions of the applicant may have been in case of delay for more than one year in responding to the Office action unless the delay was unavoidable.

ON PETITION.

MANURE-DROPPER.

Mr. Joseph L. Atkins for the applicant.

ALLEN, *Commissioner:*

This is a renewal of a petition that an application be held not abandoned by reason of delay for more than a year from the date of the Office action in responding thereto.

It is urged in support of the renewed petition that the applicant had no intention of abandoning the application, and the affidavit of the attorney is filed alleging that he did not act earlier because not authorized by the applicant to do so.

Reference to section 4894 of the Revised Statutes will show that applications are abandoned without regard to what the intention of the applicant may have been in case of delay for more than one year in responding to the Office action unless the delay was unavoidable. The delay is not unavoidable in those cases where action might have been taken had reasonable efforts been exercised to that end at any time within the period following the Office action. The only showing, therefore, offered in this case why action was not earlier taken is the affidavit of the attorney that he was not earlier authorized to take the same. It does not appear that he could not have been earlier authorized to proceed. Abandonment cannot be avoided merely by an allegation that the applicant was responsible for the attorney's inaction. In such cases it must be shown that the applicant's failure to proceed with the case earlier was unavoidable.

The renewed petition is denied.

BASTIAN *v.* CHAMP.

Decided February 8, 1907.

(127 O. G., 2816.)

1. INTERFERENCE—MOTION TO DISSOLVE—REJECTION OF CLAIMS—REQUEST FOR FURTHER EXPLANATION.

Where in acting upon a motion to dissolve the interference the Primary Examiner held the counts of the issue unpatentable and upon reconsideration finally rejected the claims, *Held* that if petitioner did not understand the position of the Examiner or desired a more specific statement of his position concerning the references he should have made his request before the dates set for reconsideration and closing of the case before the Examiner. While the Examiner should indicate the grounds for his rejection as fully as in the ordinary *ex parte* consideration of a case, the applicant can request as a matter of right a more complete explanation only while the case is still pending before the Examiner.

2. SAME—SAME—SAME—PRACTICE.

Where the Examiner rejected the claims constituting the issue in his decision dissolving the interference and not in the application files, *Held* the proper practice under Rule 124 is for the Examiner to indicate his findings regarding the claims in his decision on the motion in the interference file and at the same time to make the rejection of the claims affected in the application files. In making such rejection, if desired, reference may be made as a basis therefor to the findings in the decision on the motion. The purpose of this practice is to enable applicants to appeal to the full extent provided by statute and, if an appeal is desired, to require the appeal to be taken at once.

ON PETITION.

BOTTLE-FILLING MACHINE.

Mr. William O. Belt and *Messrs. Bacon & Milans* for Bastian.
Mr. Thomas B. Hall for Champ.

ALLEN, *Commissioner:*

This is a petition by Champ that the Examiner be directed—

to prepare a new action in which he shall specifically cite and apply each and all the references upon which he bases his rejection of the several counts of the above interference.

In his decision upon a motion for dissolution the Examiner held the counts of the issue unpatentable and upon reconsideration finally rejected the claims. Upon the last day of the limit of appeal petitioner filed, in addition to this petition, an appeal to the Examiners-in-Chief and a motion for a rehearing before the Primary Examiner. The Examiner dismissed the motion for rehearing, and the appeal is still pending.

If petitioner did not understand the position of the Examiner or desired a more specific statement of his position concerning the references, he should have made his request before the dates set for reconsideration and closing of the case before the Examiner. No such request is of record, and petitioner does not now contend that he does not understand the position taken by the Examiner. The motion to dissolve specifically sets up the grounds upon which it is based, and it appears that the matter has been fully argued *inter partes* before the Examiner.

While the Examiner should indicate the grounds for his rejection as fully as in the ordinary *ex parte* consideration of a case, the applicant can request as a matter of right a more complete explanation only while the case is still pending before the Examiner. It is believed that the case should not be remanded to the Primary Examiner at this stage of the proceeding for a more specific statement of his reasons for rejection, but that petitioner should pursue his appeal to the Examiners-in-Chief.

It is noted that the Examiner has rejected the claims constituting the issue in his decision dissolving the interference, and not in the application files. The proper practice under Rule 124, however, is for the Examiner to indicate his findings regarding the claims in his decision on the motion in the interference file and at the same time to make the rejection of the claims affected in the application files. In making such rejection, if desired, reference may be made as a basis therefor to the findings in the decision on the motion. The purpose of this practice is to enable applicants to appeal to the full extent provided by statute and, if an appeal is desired, to require the appeal to be taken at once.

The petition is denied.

Ex parte Continental Car and Equipment Company.

(127 O. G., 2816.)

Decided March 19, 1907.

1. Trade-Marks—Geographical—"Continental."

The word "Continental" as applied to dump, flat, logging, and ballast push and mine cars is primarily geographical and not registrable.

2. Same—Registrability Depends Upon Predominance of Arbitrary Feature.

The registrability of a trade-mark depends upon the predominance of the arbitrary features to give character to the mark. It cannot be based upon features incapable of exclusive appropriation merely because they are embellished by arbitrary features which are in themselves insignificant.

3. Same—Same—"Continental" Not Made Registrable by Surrounding Same with Diamond-Shaped Figure.

The geographical word "Continental" being the predominant feature of the mark by which the goods would become known, a diamond-shaped figure surrounding the same instead of being a further distinguishing feature of the mark serves merely as a frame to give prominence to the inclosed symbol of ownership.

On Appeal.

TRADE-MARK FOR DUMP, FLAT, LOGGING, AND MINE CARS.

Messrs. Robinson, Martin & Jones for the appellant.

Allen, *Commissioner:*

This is an appeal from the action of the Examiner of Trade-Marks refusing to register the word "Continental" within a diamond-shaped figure as a trade-mark for dump, flat, logging, cane-ballast, push, and mine cars. This mark is presented for registration as a technical trade-mark.

In the decision in the *Continental Insurance Company* v. *Continental Fire Association* (101 Fed. Rep., 255) the Court said:

We think that the word "Continental," a geographical adjective, meaning pertaining to or relating to a continent, is a word in common use, more or less descriptive of extent, region, and character, and like the words "Columbian," "International," "East Indian," and some other geographical adjectives, it cannot be exclusively appropriated as a trade-mark or trade-name.

It is therefore clear that registration of this word alone as a trade-mark is prohibited by section 5 of the act of 1905, which provides that no mark which consists of—

merely a geographical name or term shall be registered under the terms of this act.

The diamond-shaped figure is not in itself claimed by the appellant to be the arbitrary symbol of ownership. It is, however, urged that this figure which incloses the word "Continental" is a part of the mark and that—

proposed trade-marks are to be considered as a whole and not with reference to what may be regarded as their distinguishing feature.

Section 5 of the act of 1905 provides:

That no mark by which the goods of the owner of the mark may be distinguished from other goods of the same class shall be refused registration
as a trade-mark on account of the nature of such mark unless such mark—

comprises certain stated properties. By virtue of this section it is
necessary that a technical trade-mark in order to be registrable must
consist of an arbitrary symbol which is capable of exclusive ownership, and while registration of such a trade-mark will not be refused
because the mark contains other features not in themselves capable
of exclusive appropriation its registrability depends upon the predominance of the arbitrary features to give character to the mark.
It cannot be based upon features incapable of exclusive appropriation merely because they may be embellished by arbitrary features
which are in themselves insignificant.

In the decision in *ex parte Hopkins*, (C. D., 1906, 452; 125 O. G.,
670,) which has recently been affirmed by the Court of Appeals of
the District of Columbia, it was held that a " fantastic winged
figure " which was associated with the words ' Oriental Cream ' as
a trade-mark for a skin-lotion was " relatively so small as to leave
the words ' Oriental Cream ' the predominating features of the
mark," and the trade-mark refused registration because of its geographical and descriptive character.

In *ex parte Weil* (C. D., 1898, 612; 83 O. G., 1802) Commissioner
Duell in considering the registrability of the word "Yucatan " within
a square figure, after holding this word to be merely a geographical
term, said:

As " Yucatan " taken by itself is not registrable, I do not think it is made
so by placing it within a square figure.

The function of a trade-mark is to designate the origin of the merchandise to which it is applied, and the significant features of trade-
marks are those which by word or picture symbolize the name by
which the manufacturer's goods are known. In this case the word
" Continental " is undoubtedly the predominant feature by which
the goods would become known, and the diamond-shaped figure surrounding the same, instead of being a further distinguishing feature
of the mark, serves merely as a frame to give prominence to the
inclosed symbol of ownership.

The decision of the Examiner of Trade-Marks is affirmed.

THE UNITED STATES GRAPHITE COMPANY *v.* BOMHARD.

Decided January 10, 1907.

(127 O. G., 3215.)

TRADE-MARK INTERFERENCE—MOTION TO DISSOLVE—INTERFERENCE IN FACT.

The marks of the parties consist, respectively, of the words "Raven" and "Crow" accompanied in each case by representation of a blackbird perched on a branch of a tree. *Held,* there is no interference between the words "Raven" and "Crow," and although there is a certain similarity in the representations of the birds, taking the marks as a whole, there is no such resemblance as would be likely to cause confusion or mistake in the mind of the public or deceive purchasers.

ON APPEAL.

TRADE-MARK FOR STOVE-POLISH.

Mr. George B. Willcox for The United States Graphite Company.
Mr. George W. Colles for Bomhard.

ALLEN, *Commissioner:*

This is an appeal by the United States Graphite Company from the decision of the Examiner of Trade-Marks refusing to dissolve the interference on the ground of non-interference in fact.

The mark of the United States Graphite Company consists of the word "Raven" and a representation of a bird purporting to be a raven perched on a branch of a tree.

Bomhard's mark comprises the word "Crow" and a representation of a bird purporting to be a crow perched upon a branch.

Both parties use the mark in connection with the same class of goods—namely, stove-polish.

This case is quite similar to that of *Gaines & Co.* v. *Knecht & Son,* (C. D., 1906, 690; 123 O. G., 657,) in which the Court of Appeals of the District of Columbia held that there is no such similarity as would lead to confusion between a mark consisting of the words "Old Crow" and the picture of a crow and a mark composed of the words "Raven Valley" accompanied by a pictorial representation of three ravens in the bare limbs of a tree; also to the case of *W. A. Gaines & Co.* v. *Carlton Importation Company,* (C. D., 1906, 731; 123 O. G., 1994,) where in holding that a mark consisting of the words "Old J" and "Old Jay Rye," together with the representation of a jay-bird perched on the branch of a tree, is not anticipated by a mark composed of the words "Old Crow" and a picture of a crow the Court of Appeals of the District of Columbia stated:

We entirely agree with the Commissioner, and adopt the reasons therefor given in his decision as follows:

"Both marks include the word 'old' and both include the representation of a bird, but there the similarity ends. The jay as disclosed in the application and in the specimens accompanying it is entirely different in appearance from a crow and could by no possibility be mistaken therefor. The name 'Jay' is entirely different in sound from 'crow,' and suggests a different idea. If there is to be any confusion between the marks, it must be because of the association of the word 'old' with the name of bird. I am satisfied, however, that this one point of similarity is not sufficient to confuse the public nor to mislead purchasers exercising ordinary care."

In the present case there is clearly no interference between the words " Raven " and " Crow." As to the representations of the birds there is a certain similarity, in that both represent black birds. The positions of the birds, however, are different, and it cannot be said that the pictures are any more prominent in the trade-marks than the words. Taking the marks as a whole, there is not believed to be such resemblance as would be likely to cause confusion or mistake in the mind of the public or deceive purchasers.

The decision of the Examiner of Trade-Marks is reversed.

BEALL, JR., *v.* LYON.

Decided February 28, 1907.

(127 O. G., 3215.)

INTERFERENCE—TESTIMONY—USE IN SUBSEQUENT INTERFERENCE.

> Where the real parties in interest in a pending interference are the same as in a prior interference and the inventions involved are substantially the same, permission may be obtained, under the provisions of Rule 157, to use in the pending interference the testimony taken in the former interference.

APPEAL ON MOTION.

APPARATUS FOR USE IN MAKING CONCRETE PILES.

Messrs. John B. Thomas & Co. and *Mr. W. S. Duvall* for Beall, Jr. *Mr. Franklin H. Hough* and *Messrs. Smith & Frazier* for Lyon.

ALLEN, *Commissioner:*

This is an appeal by Lyon from the decision of the Examiner of Interferences granting the motion of Beall, Jr., for permission, under the provisions of Rule 157, to use in this interference the depositions of certain named witnesses taken in the interferences of *Beall, Jr.,* v. *Shuman*, Nos. 22,932 and 23,933.

Lyon contends that Rule 157, under the authority of which the Examiner of Interferences granted the motion—

> is invalid if it be construed as justifying the use in this interference of depositions of witnesses taken in another interference, unless those witnesses are either dead, insane, or otherwise incapable of appearing as witnesses in the case.

For reasons stated in my decision in *Kenny and Thordarson* v. *O'Connell* v. *Baird* v. *Schmidt* (C. D., 1905, 257; 117 O. G., 1163) this contention is believed to be in error. The records of this Office show, and it is admitted by Lyon, (p. 5 of brief,) that prior to the *Beall, Jr.,* v. *Shuman* interference, noted above, Shuman had acquired a right to the Lyon inventions and later conveyed them to the Simplex Concrete Piling Company. The records of this Office also show that the Shuman patents involved in said *Beall, Jr.,* v. *Shuman* interferences are assigned to the Simplex Concrete Piling Company and were assigned to said company prior to the declaration of those interferences, also that the Lyon patents involved in this interference are now likewise assigned to the said Simplex Concrete Piling Company.

The Simplex Concrete Piling Company therefore appears as the real party in interference in both sets of interferences. The invention involved in the two series of interferences are substantially the same. These reasons are believed to warrant the introduction of the evidence in question.

The decision of the Examiner of Interferences is affirmed.

Ex parte Lincoln.

Decided February 13, 1907.

(127 O. G., 3216.)

1. EXAMINATION OF APPLICATION—CITATION OF REFERENCES.

> Where several claims are rejected, it should appear in the Examiner's letter whether all the references are cited against each claim or whether they are cited distributively against the various claims. In the latter event it should be made clear in connection with each claim which references are relied upon in the rejection thereof.

2. SAME—COMBINATION OF REFERENCES.

> Where references cited are to be taken jointly, the theory upon which they are combined must be pointed out. The Examiner need not, however, ordinarily apply the references to the claim element for element, the specification and drawings of the references being ordinarily sufficient to indicate their application to the claims.

3. SAME—EXPLANATION OF REFERENCES.

> If any doubt exists as to the interpretation placed by the Examiner upon a feature of the drawing or portion of the specification, he will furnish an explanation in response to a specific request making clear the uncertainty existing in the mind of the applicant.

ON PETITION.

ARC-LAMP.

Mr. Albert Lynn Lawrence for the applicant.

ALLEN, *Commissioner:*

This is a petition that the final rejection entered in this case be withdrawn and that the Examiner be instructed to specifically apply the references which have been cited.

The first and second actions on this case do not make clear upon what theory the claims are rejected. It is simply stated that the claims are rejected on the many references cited. Where several claims are rejected, it should appear in the Examiner's letter whether all the references are cited against each claim or whether they are cited distributively against the various claims. In the latter event it should be made clear in connection with each claim which references are relied upon in the rejection thereof. Furthermore, where several references are cited against a claim it should be made clear whether each reference is regarded as sufficient in itself to defeat the claim or whether the references are to be taken jointly. If to be taken jointly, the theory upon which they are combined must be pointed out. The applicant and others who may have to interpret the Examiner's action should not be left to surmise to determine what was in the Examiner's mind in the respects hereinabove referred to. The common impression, however, that the Examiner should ordinarily apply the references to the claims element for element is unwarranted. The specifications and drawings of the references are ordinarily to be had by the applicant or his attorney, who must determine for themselves what the references disclose and whether they justify the action based by the Examiner upon them. Of course where there is any doubt as to the interpretation placed by the Examiner upon a feature of a drawing or portion of a specification the Examiner will furnish an explanation in response to a specific request making clear the uncertainty existing in the mind of the applicant.

The first and second actions of the Examiner were not clear; but in the subsequent action, dated November 25, 1905, the Examiner applied one of the references to the applicant's device, stating that the explanation furnished might be taken as a sample of the applicability of the remaining references. This letter may be fairly taken to mean that each claim is met in each of the references and to be a sufficient statement of the Examiner's position in view of the general character of the applicant's requests for explanation thereof. That the present attorney did not get a copy of this action until after the final rejection of October 9, 1906, appears to have been due to no fault of the Office, the Examiner having mailed a second copy thereof to the applicant at the address given by him upon July 2, 1906. Upon August 29, 1906, the applicant filed an action calling attention to his previous arguments traversing the sufficiency of the references and stating—

specific application of the particular references to the claims or reconsideration for the reasons previously set forth at length are now requested.

The Examiner complied with the latter of these alternative requests and finally rejected the claims. The final rejection seems to have been in order, and no good reason is seen why it should be set aside.

Petition denied.

MARTIN *v.* MULLIN.

Decided April 2, 1907.

(127 O. G., 3216.)

1. INTERFERENCE—MOTION FOR DISSOLUTION—DENIAL BY A PARTY OF HIS OWN RIGHT TO MAKE CLAIM—TRANSMISSION.

   A motion for dissolution based upon the ground that the moving party has no right to make the claim to the subject-matter in issue should not be transmitted to the Primary Examiner.

2. SAME—CONCESSION OF PRIORITY NOT NECESSARILY ACQUIESCENCE IN IDENTITY OF CLAIMS.

   An award of priority may mean either that one of two inventors of the same thing is subsequent in date to another or that one party is the only inventor of the issue, because the other never invented the same at all, and there seems to be no reason why this should not be as true where the award is based upon concession as where it is based upon testimony.

APPEAL ON MOTION.

CABLE-GRIP.

Mr. Vernon M. Dorsey for Martin.
Messrs. Griffin & Bernhard for Mullin.

ALLEN, *Commissioner:*

This is an appeal by Martin from the decision of the Examiner of Interferences refusing to transmit his motion for dissolution, so far as the same relates to his own right to lay claim to the subject-matter in issue.

The Examiner of Interferences refused to transmit the motion on the authority of my decision in the case of *Miller* v. *Perham* (C. D., 1906, 157; 121 O. G., 2667,) holding that a party will not be permitted to urge his own lack of right to make claims upon motion for dissolution of interference and pointing out that a contest as to priority upon claims adopted by a party under misapprehension as to his right to make them may be avoided by concession of priority with respect thereto. The appellant seeks to have the practice set forth in that decision modified. His reason is that the award of priority by the Patent Office, based upon a concession, may be given effect by the courts as a determination by the Patent Office of identity of the appellant's device with that of his opponent. He also fears that a concession of priority will be interpreted by the courts as an acquiescence upon his part in such determination.

Nothing is found in the above reasons justifying modification of the practice followed in *Miller* v. *Perham, supra.*

That concession of priority is not necessarily acquiescence in the finding of identity which is involved in the declaration of interference is believed to be readily capable of demonstration. An award of priority is the usual form of judgment in the Patent Office and upon appeal therefrom to the court of appeals of this district in those cases where it is found that one party was not an inventor of the subject-matter in issue, whether the finding be based upon the proved derivation of the invention from his opponent or upon the failure of his exhibits to disclose the invention in issue. An award of priority is also proper, under Rule 130 of the Rules of Practice of the Office, where it is shown at the final hearing of an interference that the application of a party relied upon as evidence of invention at the date thereof does not warrant the claim in issue. An award of priority, therefore, may mean either that one of two inventors of the same thing is subsequent in date to another or that one party is the only inventor of the issue, because the other party has never invented the same at all, and there seems to be no reason why this should not be as true where the award is based upon concession as where it is based upon testimony. It does not seem that there should be any difficulty in presenting these facts to the courts or in showing that in view thereof the mere fact of concession of priority does not necessarily involve acquiescence in the finding of the Patent Office upon identity.

That the courts may, nevertheless, give weight to the finding of the Office that the parties disclosed the same invention is no reason why the Office should reconsider the conclusion. If the courts give no more weight to the Office decision than the circumstances under which it is rendered justify, there would seem to be no just cause of complaint. The appellant seems to fear, however, that the courts may give the Office finding upon identity more weight than should be given to an *ex parte* conclusion unattended either by an opportunity for argument, a demand for reconsideration, or an appeal. The facts attending the adoption of claims by parties upon suggestion under Rule 96 and the practice in the Patent Office subsequent to the adoption of the suggested claims in the matter of the adopter's right to make the same being presented to the court, it is not to be presumed that the court will render an improper decision because of a concession of priority. Moreover, the place to guard against decisions by the courts which are not warranted by the facts and circumstances would seem to be in the courts. The possibility that such a decision might by inadvertence be rendered affords no reason for conducting proceedings in the Patent Office merely to determine the right of a party to assert claims to a patent when no one but him denies that he has that right.

The decision of the Examiner of Interferences is affirmed.

DAGGETT v. KAUFMANN.

Decided March 22, 1907.

(127 O. G., 3641.)

1. INTERFERENCE—MOTION FOR DISSOLUTION—INTERFERENCE IN FACT.

If there is no interference in fact, it is either because one of the parties has no right to make the claims or because the claims have different meanings in the applications of the different parties. The parties will not be heard to deny their own right to make the claims. (*Miller* v. *Perham*, C. D., 1906, 157; 121 O. G., 2667.)

2. SAME—SAME—APPEAL—RIGHT OF OPPONENT TO MAKE CLAIM.

There is no appeal from the decision of the Primary Examiner affirming the opponent's right to make the claims of the identity of meaning of the claims in their respective applications.

3. SAME—SAME—EXERCISE OF SUPERVISORY AUTHORITY OF COMMISSIONER.

Where at the hearing upon a motion for dissolution attention is directed to a patent which is in a remote art and it appears that the Examiner has held the claims in issue patentable thereover, no such unusual circumstances as will justify the exercise of supervisory authority exist.

APPEAL ON MOTION.

MANTLE.

Mr. A. B. Stoughton for Daggett.
Mr. Joseph L. Levy for Kaufmann.

ALLEN, *Commissioner:*

This is an appeal by Kaufmann from the decision of the Primary Examiner denying his motion for dissolution of the interference.

The appeal alleges error in the Examiner's conclusions that the declaration was regular and that there is interference in fact. Appellant also called attention at the hearing to a prior patent alleging anticipation of the claims in issue thereby.

It was conceded at the hearing that the alleged irregularity raises no other questions than those of patentability and interference in fact. The distinctions between the several grounds of dissolution which are enumerated in Rule 122 have been frequently pointed out and should be observed. The Primary Examiner did not err in denying the motion so far as the same relates to the regularity of the declaration, and his decision to that extent is affirmed.

If there is no interference in fact, it is either because one of the parties has no right to make the claims or because the claims have different meanings in the applications of the different parties. The parties will not be heard to deny their own right to make the claims. (*Miller* v. *Perham*, C. D., 1906, 157; 121 O. G., 2667.) There is no appeal from the decision of the Primary Examiner affirming the opponent's right to make the claims or the identity of meaning of the claims in their respective applications. (Rule 124.) The appeal, so far as it presents the question of interference in fact, is dismissed.

The patent to which attention was called is in a remote art, and the Examiner, it is understood, has held the claims in issue patentable thereover. No such unusual circumstances as will justify the exercise of supervisory authority exist.

The request for consideration of the question of patentability is denied.

Ex parte The Yale & Towne Manufacturing Company.

Decided April 5, 1907.

(127 O. G., 3641.)

1. TRADE-MARKS—NAME OF PATENTED ARTICLE—REGISTRABLE UNDER TEN-YEAR PROVISO OF SECTION 5 OF ACT OF 1905—" YALE " FOR LOCKS AND LATCHES.
   Held that the word " Yale " is registrable as a trade-mark for locks and latches under the ten-year proviso of section 5 of the act of 1905, although it is the name of a patented article.

2. SAME—SAME—EXCLUSIVE USE.
   The function of the name of a patented article is twofold: (1) It designates or identifies the thing patented, and (2) it indicates the original source of manufacture of the article. Where a word or name which has been applied to a patented article has in addition to its descriptive significance also become indicative of the origin of the article, a limited right remains in the original maker after the expiration of the patent to exclude others from such unqualified use of the word or name as would deceive a careful public into the belief that their articles are those of the original maker. This right to exclude, it is believed, satisfies the requirement of " exclusive use " stated in the ten-year proviso of the act of February 20, 1905.

ON APPEAL.

TRADE-MARK FOR LOCKS AND KEYS.

Mr. Henry A. Seymour for the applicant.

ALLEN, *Commissioner.*

This is an appeal from the action of the Examiner of Trade-Marks refusing to register the word " Yale " as a trade-mark for locks and latches.

Registration was refused upon the ground that " Yale " as applied to locks is the name of a patented article, the patents upon which have expired, as was held in the decision of Commissioner Butterworth in *ex parte Yale & Towne Manufacturing Company*, (C. D., 1897, 786; 81 O. G., 801.)

This application for registration is presented in accordance with the ten-year proviso of the Trade-Mark Act, being accompanied by an affidavit alleging actual and exclusive use of the trade-mark by the applicant for ten years next preceding the passage of the act of February 20, 1905.

The Examiner of Trade-Marks has held that the word " Yale," having become the identifying or generic name of a patented article, is public property and incapable of appropriation by any one and that therefore the applicant has not had the right to exclude others from the use of this mark for ten years next preceding the passage of the act of February 20, 1905, which was held in my decision in *ex parte Cahn, Belt & Company* (C. D., 1905, 422; 118 O. G., 1936) to be a prerequisite to registration under the ten-year proviso of this act. In my opinion the position taken by the Examiner of Trade-Marks is untenable in the present case.

Upon close scrutiny of the decisions upon the subject it appears that an exclusive right in the name of a patented article upon the part of the manufacturer who first adopted it is not wholly precluded by the expiration of the patents upon such article. The function of the name is such cases is twofold: First, it designates or identifies the thing patented, and, second, it indicates the sources of manufacture of that article. Upon the expiration of the patent the right to use the word or name as the means of designating or identifying the article passes irretrievably to the public; but by reason of the second significance of the mark a member of the public who chooses to manufacture the article and designate it by the name it has acquired must so distinguish his use of that name that it will not indicate to the public that the article is the product of the original maker.

This fact was recognized in the leading case of *Singer Manufacturing Company* v. *June Manufacturing Company*, (C. D., 1896, 687; 75 O. G., 1703; 163 U. S., 169) in which the Supreme Court of the United States, while holding that the name " Singer " for sewing-machines had become public property by reason of having become the generic name of an article, the patents upon which had expired, nevertheless perpetually enjoined the defendant from—

marking upon sewing-machines or upon any plate or device connected therewith or attached thereto the word "Singer," or words or letters equivalent thereto, without unmistakably specifying in connection therewith that such machines are the product of the defendant or other manufacturer, and therefore not the product of the Singer Manufacturing Company.

In that case the Court said:

It is obvious that if the name dedicated to the public, either as a consequence of the monopoly or by the voluntary act of the party, has a twofold significance, one generic and the other pointing to the origin of manufacture and the name is availed of by another without clearly indicating that the machine, upon which the name is marked, is made by him, then the right to use the name because of its generic signification, would imply a power to destroy any good-will which belong to the original maker. It would import, not only this, but also the unrestrained right to deceive and defraud the public by so using the name as to delude them into believing that the machine made by one person was made by another.

To say that a person who has manufactured machines under a patented monopoly can acquire no good-will, by the excellence of his work, or the development of his business, during the patent, would be to seriously ignore rights of private property, and would be against public policy, since it would deprive the one enjoying the patent of all incentive to make a machine of a good quality, because at its termination all the reputation or good-will resulting from meritorious work would be subject to appropriation by every one. On the other hand, to compel the one who uses the name after the expiration of the patent, to indicate that the articles are made by himself, in no way impairs the right of use, but simply regulates and prevents wrong to individuals and injury to the public.

In the case of *Singer Manufacturing Company* v. *Hipple* (109 Fed. Rep., 152) the Court, in referring to the decision of the Supreme Court in *Singer Manufacturing Company* v. *June Manufacturing Company*, *supra*, said:

In short the principle of that decision is not that the first user of a mark indicative of origin forfeits his exclusive right thereto for that purpose by allowing it to be applied for the additional purpose of designating the thing itself, but that this monopoly of it for the one purpose cannot be so inforced as to nullify the general right to apply it for the other.

In the case of *Centaur Company* v. *Killenberger* (87 Fed. Rep., 725) the Court said:

The right to manufacture " Castoria " according to Pitcher's patented process or formula may be free to the world, also the right to sell the manufactured article by the name " Castoria;" but, in putting it upon the market, the new manufacturer must clearly identify his goods, and not engage in unfair competition, nor do anything which will tend to deceive the public, and induce them to take his goods under the belief that they are those which it has theretofore been accustomed to purchase under the same name.

It is therefore clear that where a word or name which has been applied to a patented article has also become indicative of the origin of that article a limited right remains in the original maker after the expiration of the patent to exclude others from such unqualified use of the word or name as would deceive a careful public into the belief that their articles are those of the original maker. This right to exclude, it is believed, satisfies the requirement of " exclusive use " stated in the ten-year proviso of the act of February 20, 1905.

It is believed that the same reasons and principles apply in many cases of geographical and descriptive terms and names of individuals. Here, as in the case of the name of a patented article, the first adopter may often have the right to exclude others from using the exact term or mark, although no technical trade-mark right could exist. (*Elgin National Watch Company* v. *Illinois Watch Case Company*, C. D., 1901, 273; 94 O. G., 755; 179 U. S., 665; *Walter Baker & Company* v. *Baker*, C. D., 1897, 797; 78 O. G., 1427; 77 Fed. Rep., 884; *Shaver et al.* v. *Heller & Merz Company*, C. D., 1901, 424; 96 O. G., 2229; 108 Fed. Rep., 821; *Genesee Salt Company* v. *Burnap*, 73 Fed. Rep., 818; *American Waltham Watch Company* v. *Sandman*, 96 Fed. Rep., 330.)

The affidavit filed by the applicant in the present case affirms the exclusive use required by the statute as a basis for registration under the ten-year proviso. In view of the authorities and conclusions hereinabove discussed no reason is found for believing that there was not such exclusive use. It is therefore held that the applicant should be permitted to register the mark for which he has made application for registration.

The decision of the Examiner of Trade-Marks is reversed.

Ex parte Cross.

Decided January 19, 1907

(128 O. G., 455.)

Trade-Marks—" Olivoint " Anticipated by "Oliveine."

"Olivoint" used as a trade-mark for ointment for skin affections so closely resembles the mark "Oliveine" registered as a trade-mark for ointments and salves as to be likely to cause confusion or mistake in the mind of the public or to deceive purchasers.

On Appeal.

TRADE-MARK FOR OINTMENTS FOR ALL SKIN AFFECTIONS.

Mr. Francis M. Wright and *Messrs. Byrnes & Townsend* for the applicant.

Allen, *Commissioner*:

This is an appeal from the action of the Examiner of Trade-Marks refusing to register the word " Olivoint " as a trade-mark for ointments for all skin affections.

The Examiner's action is based on the ground that the mark so closely resembles the trade-mark " Oliveine," registered to Caldwell,

No. 14,043, February 1, 1887, for ointments and salves, as to be likely to cause confusion or mistake in the mind of the public or to deceive purchasers.

The decision of the Examiner is believed to be correct. The mark appears to be in the same class as those mentioned in my decisions in *ex parte Holbert,* (C. D., 1905, 139; 115 O. G., 2136,) where the word "Optine" was refused registration by reason of its resemblance to the registered mark "Optal," and in *ex parte The Dr. Parker Medicine Company,* (C. D., 1903, 378; 106 O. G., 1779,) where the word "Liveroid" was refused on the registered marks "Liveraid" and "Liverine."

The decision of the Examiner of Trade-Marks is affirmed.

IN RE WILDER.

Decided March 14, 1907.

(128 O. G., 455.)

REJECTION OF CLAIMS—CANNOT BE BASED UPON EVIDENCE TAKEN IN SECOND INTERFERENCE WHICH HAS BEEN HELD TO BE RES ADJUDICATA.

Where in a second interference the question of priority was held to be *res adjudicata* and a decision rendered in favor of Blackford, Blackford's claims corresponding to the issue of the interference cannot be rejected upon the ground that they are anticipated by an exhibit introduced into the second interference by Wilder. Inasmuch as the second interference should not have been declared, the testimony taken therein is of no force and is to be given no effect for any purpose whatever.

IN THE MATTER of the protest of William H. Wilder against the issue of a patent to A. J. Blackford.

ALLEN, *Commissioner:*

This is a protest by Wilder against the issue of a patent to Blackford upon an invention involved in the interference *Blackford* v. *Wilder,* No. 22,702, which was recently decided in favor of Blackford by the Court of Appeals of the District of Columbia, as *res adjudicata,* (*post,* 491; 127 O. G., 1255.)

Wilder contends that Blackford's claims corresponding to the issue of the interference should be rejected on the ground that they are anticipated by an exhibit introduced into the interference by Wilder.

It does not appear that the Office can find from the testimony taken in the second interference anticipation of the claims of Blackford without finding prior possession of the invention by Wilder; but this is exactly what the Office is prevented from doing by the decision of the court in the second interference. The decision of the court is understood to amount to this: that the second interference should not have been declared and that the testimony taken therein is of no force and is to be given no effect for any purpose whatever.

The question presented by the protest is somewhat analogous to the question which arises in those cases where the first to reduce to practice is held to be estopped from asserting his right to a patent by reason of delay in applying therefor or in disclosing the same to the public. (*Mason* v. *Hepburn*, C. D., 1898, 510; 84 O. G., 147; *Mower* v. *Duell, Commissioner of Patents*, C. D., 1899, 395; 88 O. G., 191; *Thomson* v. *Weston*, C. D., 1902, 521; 99 O. G., 864.) If the contentions of the protestant here were sound, the subsequent inventor in those cases should be denied a patent upon the ground of anticipation by the prior reduction to practice of his opponent. It is not understood, however, that such was the intention of the court in those cases, and such has not been the practice.

Protest dismissed.

HARNISCH *v.* GUENIFFET, BENOIT, AND NICAULT.

Decided March 25, 1907.

(128 O. G., 455.)

1. INTERFERENCE—MOTION TO DISSOLVE—TRANSMISSION OF.

> Where on appeal from the decision of the Primary Examiner dissolving an interference the Examiners-in-Chief affirmed the decision of the Examiner as to claims 2, 3, and 4 and reversed it as to claim 1, and thereupon one party filed an amendment to his case, while the other party brought a motion to dissolve, *Held* that the decision of the Examiner of Interferences refusing to transmit the motion to dissolve to the Primary Examiner is correct, since the motion is based on the proposed amendment and presupposes its entry.

2. SAME—AMENDMENT—ENTRY OF.

> Where during the interference proceeding one of the parties filed an amendment canceling the claims rejected under Rule 124 and substituted a substitute specification and drawing, *Held* that the amendment is not of the character permitted under the rules during the interference proceeding and that the special circumstances are not such as to warrant its admission.

APPEAL ON MOTION.

CIGARETTE-TUBE.

Messrs. Philipp, Sawyer, Rice & Kennedy for Harnisch.
Messrs. Fraser & Usina for Gueniffet, Benoit, and Nicault.

ALLEN, *Commissioner:*

This case is before me, first, on an appeal by Harnisch from the refusal of the Examiner of Interferences to transmit his motion to dissolve this interference, and, second, on his petition that the Examiner of Interferences be directed to transmit the case to the Primary Examiner for the consideration of an amendment filed by his opponents, as well as the above-mentioned motion to dissolve.

It appears that upon a prior motion by Harnisch the Primary Examiner dissolved the interference on the ground that the claims forming the issue were not patentable to Gueniffet, Benoit, and Nicault, and he rejected the claims under the provisions of Rule 124. On appeal the Examiners-in-Chief affirmed the decision of the Primary Examiner as to claims 2, 3, and 4 and reversed it as to claim 1. No appeal was taken from their decision; but Gueniffet, Benoit, and Nicault filed an amendment consisting of a substitute specification and drawing and canceled the rejected claims 2, 3, and 4, but made no change in claim 1. Harnisch thereupon filed his present motion to dissolve. The Examiner of Interferences refused to transmit this motion on the ground that it is based on the amendment and presupposes its entry in the case. He held that since said amendment had not been entered and could not be entered under the rules without special order of the Commissioner there is no proper foundation for the motion.

The decision of the Examiner of Interferences is clearly correct and is accordingly affirmed. Rule 109 provides that amendment will not be permitted during an interference proceeding without the consent of the Commissioner except as provided in said Rule 109 and in Rules 106 and 107. The proposed amendment does not come under either of these exceptions.

It remains to consider whether the special circumstances of this case are such as to make it an exception to the above rules and to warrant granting the petition to admit the amendment. The Examiner-in-Chief rejected claims 2, 3, and 4 on the ground that their subject-matter is not disclosed in a prior application of which the application in interference purports to be a division and that they are consequently barred by certain specified patents. The amendment appears to have been filed for the purpose of canceling these claims and of eliminating from the specification the subject-matter held not to be disclosed in the parent case. There appears, however, to be no good reason why this amendment should be entered or considered prior to the termination of the interference. Concerning claim 1, the Examiners-in-Chief held that it is broader than the other claims, that its subject-matter is disclosed in the earlier application, and so far as disclosure is concerned it might have been made in the first case. The Primary Examiner held that Gueniffet, Benoit, and Nicault had a right to make the claim in the present application. The interference stands dissolved as to claims 2, 3, and 4. No additional claims are presented in the proposed amendment, and no amendment is necessary to the proper determination of the question of priority in the interference. It is not the practice to suspend an interference proceeding to permit of the cancelation of the claims where an interference is dissolved as to some of the counts, and no reason appears for departing from the usual practice in this case. After the termination of the interference the application will be held for such revision and restriction as may be necessary. (Rule 96.)

In my decision in *Sanders* v. *Hawthorne* v. *Hoyt* (C. D., 1906, 467; 125 O. G., 1347) reasons are set forth why in amending Rule 124 to provide for the rejection and appeal of such claims involved in an interference as have been made the object of an adverse decision upon their merits without awaiting the termination of the interference it was not deemed advisable to provide for amendment of the case during the interference.

There are additional reasons why the proposed amendment should not be admitted during the interference proceeding. Harnisch has filed a motion to dissolve, referred to above, which he desires transmitted if his petition to have the amendment entered is granted. One of the grounds of the motion is that there has been such irregularity in disclosing the interference as will preclude a proper determination of the question of priority, such irregularity consisting in permitting the entry of the amendment, and thus making a substantially new application for Gueniffet, Benoit, and Nicault during the pendency of the interference. In other words, he petitions to have the amendment entered and then file a motion to have the interference dissolved on account of the entry of said amendment. In any event the entry of the amendment will further delay the interference proceeding. This delay is entirely unnecessary, since the status of claim 1 with respect to the present specification is clearly fixed by the decision of the Examiners-in-Chief. No injury or hardship, so far as appears, can result from continuing the interference with the application in its present condition.

There is no necessity for considering that portion of the petition relating to the transmission of the motion to dissolve based upon the amendment in view of the holding that the amendment is not admissible during the interference proceeding.

The petition is denied.

CUSHMAN *v.* EDWARDS.

Decided April 4, 1907.

(128 O. G., 456.)

INTERFERENCE—MOTION FOR DISSOLUTION—DIFFERENCE IN MEANING OF CLAIMS.

The provision in Rule 122 for dissolution upon the ground of difference in the meaning of claims was placed there to cover a clean-cut class of cases which theoretical considerations show may arise, but which, in fact, are of very rare occurrence. To justify transmission of a motion brought upon this ground, facts must be alleged indicating something more than a possible lack of right upon the part of one or the other of the parties to use the language of the claim in issue.

APPEAL ON MOTION.

DYNAMO-ELECTRIC MACHINE.

Messrs. Roberts & Mitchell and *Messrs. Meyers, Cushman & Rea* for Cushman.

Messrs. Foster & Freeman and *Messrs. Harper & Allen* for Edwards.

ALLEN, *Commissioner:*

This is an appeal by Cushman from the decision of the Examiner of Interferences refusing to transmit a supplemental motion for dissolution of the interference on the ground that the claims corresponding to the counts of the issue have different meanings in the cases of the different parties.

. Motions to dissolve the interference have been transmitted alleging non-patentability of the issue and lack of right upon the part of Edwards to make claims corresponding to the counts of the issue. The present motion was denied transmission on the ground that it is not accompanied by a sufficient statement of facts supporting the allegations of differences in the meanings of the claims in the different cases. The provision in Rule 122 for dissolution upon the ground of difference in the meaning of claims was placed there to cover a clean-cut class of cases which theoretical considerations show may arise, but which, in fact, are of very rare occurrence. To justify transmission of a motion brought upon this ground, facts must be alleged indicating something more than a possible lack of right upon the part of one or the other of the parties to use the language of the claim in issue. The lack of right to make claims, so far as this question is properly reviewable on motion, may be raised by a motion entitled in appropriate terms. To permit the same question to be raised in a motion entitled as one upon another ground would result in useless multiplication of records and in confusion of issues. Nothing is alleged in this case in support of the motion which has been denied transmission which may not be fully accounted for by lack of right of one or the other of the parties to make the claims or which indicates that any other reason exists for dissolving the interference. Under these circumstances the refusal to transmit the motion was right.

The decision of the Examiner of Interferences is affirmed.

PYM v. HADAWAY.

Decided April 8, 1907.

(128 O. G., 457.)

INTERFERENCE—MOTION—APPEAL.

Where a motion for permission to take testimony in opposition to an opponent's right to make the claims in issue for use at final hearing under the provisions of Rule 130 is denied by the Examiner of Interferences, *Held* that an appeal will be permitted from his adverse decision. (Practice announced in *Lowry and Cowley* v. *Spoon*, C. D., 1906, 381 ; 124 O. G., 1846, and *Hanan and Gates* v. *Marshall, ante,* 65 ; 126 O. G., 3423, modified.)

MOTION to dismiss.

TACK-PULLER AND NAIL-DRIVER.

Messrs. Parker & Burton and *Mr. Geo. H. Maxwell* for Pym.

Mr. Benjamin Phillips and *Messrs. Phillips, Van Everen & Fish* for Hadaway.

ALLEN, *Commissioner:*

This is a motion by Hadaway to dismiss the appeal by Pym taken from the decision of the Examiner of Interferences denying Pym's motion for an order authorizing him to take testimony in opposition to Hadaway's right to make the claims in issue.

The motion to dismiss is based upon statements in the cases of *Lowry and Cowley* v. *Spoon* (C. D., 1906, 381; 124 O. G., 1846) and *Hanan and Gates* v. *Marshall* (*ante*, 65; 126 O. G., 3423) that no appeals will be permitted from decisions of the Examiner of Interferences upon the matter of taking testimony upon an opponent's right to make claims. The statements in these decisions upon this question are, however, broader than was necessitated by the circumstances of the cases. In each of them the Examiner of Interferences authorized the taking of testimony. An error in his decision would not prevent the correct determination of the questions in issue in the interference. When permission to take testimony is denied, however, the decision may operate to control the final decision upon the merits of the controversy between the parties. In such cases it is believed that an appeal would be permitted. The appeal of Pym will be set down for hearing.

The motion to dismiss Pym's appeal is denied.

EX PARTE GRANT.

Decided December 11, 1906.

(128 O. G., 885.)

1. ABANDONED APPLICATION—BY FAILURE TO TAKE RESPONSIVE ACTION.

Where the action taken near the close of the year was not a proper action, *Held* that the applicant has a perfect right to delay action until the close of the year allowed by law therefor, but in doing so he assues the risk of any mistake in the character of the action.

2. SAME—SAME.

Since earlier action by applicant would have permitted correction of the mistake within the year and since it does not appear that earlier action could not have been taken, the failure to duly prosecute the application cannot be regarded as unavoidable, and it is therefore abandoned under the statute.

ON PETITION.

PRINTING DEVICE.

Mr. William M. Monroe and *Messrs. Hall & Heylmun* for the applicant.

ALLEN, *Commissioner:*

This is a petition from the action of the Examiner holding the application to be abandoned by reason of the unresponsive character of the only action filed by the applicant within the year following the last Office action.

The failure to take proper action within the year following the Office action seems to have been due to the postponement of the attempted response until near the close of that period. The applicant has a perfect right to delay action until the close of the year allowed by law therefor, but in doing so he assumes the risk of such a mistake as occurred in this case. Since earlier action by the applicant would have permitted correction of the mistake within the year and since it does not appear that earlier action could not have been taken, the failure to duly prosecute this case cannot be regarded as unavoidable and the same is therefore abandoned under the statute.

The petition is denied.

EX PARTE THE DE LONG HOOK & EYE COMPANY.

Decided January 19, 1907.

(128 O. G., 885.)

1. TRADE-MARKS—"RUST? NEVER!" FOR HOOKS AND EYES—DESCRIPTIVE—NOT REGISTRABLE.

The phrase "Rust? Never!" is clearly the predominant feature of the mark presented for registration and indicates that the hooks and eyes are so treated that they will never rust and that therefore "rust" will never be transmitted to the goods to which they are applied.

2. SAME—SAME—SAME—RED RECTANGULAR BACKGROUND NOT A DISTINCTIVE FEATURE.

The fact that the words "Rust? Never!" appear upon a red rectangular background does not confer registrability upon the mark. It is not an unusual configuration which would impress itself upon the memory of the purchaser, but merely serves to throw the words "Rust? Never!" into bold relief.

ON APPEAL.

TRADE-MARK FOR HOOKS AND EYES.

Mr. W. C. Strawbridge for the applicant.

ALLEN, *Commissioner:*

This is an appeal from the decision of the Examiner of Trade-Marks refusing to register a trade-mark which comprises the words "Rust? Never!" on a red rectangular background for hooks and eyes.

The words "Rust? Never!" are clearly the predominant feature of the mark presented for registration and indicate that the hooks and eyes are so treated that they will never rust and that therefore "rust" will never be transmitted to the goods to which they are applied.

The combination "Rust? Never!" is analogous to the marks "No-rip" and "Felt-less" for harness sweat pads, which were held to be descriptive, and therefore not registrable. (*Ex parte The Crescent Manufacturing Company*, C. D., 1901, 160; 97 O. G., 750; *ex parte McClain*, C. D., 1902, 185; 99 O. G., 2101.)

It is urged that the mark offered for registration presents, as a whole, a distinctive appearance to the eye, and therefore constitutes a valid trade-mark. This contention is not believed to be well founded. The red rectangular background is not an unusual configuration which would impress itself upon the memory of a purchaser, but merely serves to throw the words "Rust? Never!" into bold relief.

The decision of the Examiner of Trade-Marks is affirmed.

EX PARTE STRAUSS.

Decided April 4, 1907.

(128 O. G., 885.)

LABEL.—THE WORDS "RED CROSS" REFUSED REGISTRATION IN VIEW OF THE ACT OF JANUARY 5, 1905.

The words "Red Cross," whether construed as "the sign of the Red Cross" expressed in language or as the alternative of the sign "Red Cross," clearly come within the spirit and intent of the provisions of section 4 of the act entitled "An act to incorporate the American National Red Cross," approved January 5, 1905, prohibiting the use of "such sign or any insignia colored in imitation thereof for the purposes of trade or as an advertisement to induce the sale of any article whatsoever."

as waived and a decision will be rendered upon an appeal in which
the new reference, as well as the references previously cited, will be
considered. If the applicant does not desire to amend, a rehearing of
the appeal will be granted for argument upon the new reference upon
request therefor.

EX PARTE FAULKNER.

Decided April 19, 1907.

(128 O. G., 886.)

1. SUPPOSED FORMAL OBJECTIONS DISCOVERED BY ISSUE AND GAZETTE DIVISION—
   DECISION OF EXAMINER CONTROLLING.
   When, in the revision of the application in the Issue and Gazette Division,
   supposed formal objections are discovered, the Examiner's attention should
   be called thereto; but the Examiner's decision, indorsed upon the reference-
   slip, that a supposed objection is not in fact one or that correction is not
   necessary, should settle the matter for this Office.

2. NAME OF APPLICANT—"RAY" FULL CHRISTIAN NAME—NO AFFIDAVIT NECES-
   SARY.
   The name "Ray" is commonly used as a full Christian name and no
   affidavit should be required in connection therewith.

ON PETITION.

COAL-CABINET.

Messrs. C. A. Snow & Co. for the applicant.

ALLEN, *Commissioner:*

This is a petition from the action of the Primary Examiner requiring an affidavit that *Ray* is the full first name of the applicant.

The Examiner has made an elaborate report upon the petition in
which he urges that the requirement was unnecessary. It appears
that he passed the case to issue without requiring such an affidavit,
but that the case was returned to him from the Issue and Gazette
Division with a request that he require one. The Examiner thereupon made the requirement, although it appears that he believed the
same to be improper.

I am of the opinion that under such circumstances there is no occasion for the entry of the requirement by the Examiner. When, in
the revision of the application in the Issue and Gazette Division,
supposed formal objections are discovered, the Examiner's attention
should be called thereto; but the Examiner's decision, indorsed upon
the reference-slip, that a supposed objection is not in fact one or
that correction is not necessary, should settle the matter for this
Office. The responsibility in such cases rests with the Examiner,

and no reason is known why his conclusion should not be binding upon the Chief of the Issue and Gazette Division. This petition might well be dismissed, with instructions to follow the practice herein announced. It may be stated, however, that in view of the facts set forth in the Examiner's statement showing common acceptance of " Ray " as a full Christian name no affidavit should be required in connection therewith.

Petition granted.

EX PARTE PITTSBURGH VALVE, FOUNDRY AND CONSTRUCTION COMPANY.

Decided April 27, 1907.

(128 O. G., 887.)

1. TRADE-MARKS—"ATWOOD" ASSOCIATED WITH AN ARROW-HEAD AND THE LETTER "A"—NOT REGISTRABLE.

Where the name "Atwood" is the predominating feature of the mark and it appears from applicant's specimens to be applied to the goods merely as raised capital letters in the casting bearing the mark, the association with the name of the fanciful symbol is not considered sufficient to render the mark registrable as a whole.

2. SAME—DESCRIPTIVE.

A statement which does not purport to be a description of the mark, but indirectly states the nature of the principal feature of applicant's mark, was properly objected to by the Examiner of Trade-Marks.

3. SAME—DATE OF ADOPTION.

The date of adoption and use of applicant's mark means the whole mark presented for registration, and it is not apparent that any useful purpose can be subserved by a statement as to the date of use of the various features of the mark.

ON APPEAL.

TRADE-MARK FOR VALVES, PIPE-FITTINGS, AND CASTINGS.

Mr. F. N. Barber for the applicant.

ALLEN, *Commissioner:*

This is an appeal from the action of the Examiner of Trade-Marks in refusing to register the mark as presented and in requiring that the statement be revised to omit the partial description of the mark contained therein.

The mark presented for registration consists of the word "Atwood " associated with an arrow-head and the letter "A."

The Examiner regarded the latter portion of the mark as a fanciful and arbitrary symbol and proper subject-matter for registration. He refused registration of the mark as a whole on the ground that the term "Atwood " is the name of an individual and is not associated with a portrait of the individual or printed in a particular or distinctive manner, and therefore is not registrable as a technical trade-mark under the provisions of section 5 of the act of February 20, 1905, which states—

That no mark which consists merely in the name of an individual, firm, cor-poration, or association, not written, printed, impressed, or woven in some particular or distinctive manner or in association with a portrait of the indi-vidual, * * * shall be registered under the terms of this act.

This conclusion of the Examiner is considered sound. The name "Atwood" is the predominating feature of the mark, and it appears from applicant's specimens to be applied to the goods merely as raised capital letters in the casting bearing the mark. The association with the name of the fanciful symbol is not considered sufficient to render the mark registrable as a whole. In this respect the mark is similar to that involved *in re Ferdinand T. Hopkins*, decided by the Court of Appeals of the District of Columbia February 5, 1907, (*post*, 549; 128 O. G., 890.) In that case the court did not consider the mark consisting of the words "Oriental Cream, assiciated with an eagle holding a scroll in its beak" as registrable, notwithstanding the geo-graphical term was associated with a "fantastic winged figure."

The descriptive statement objected to by the Examiner reads as follows:

The trade-mark was first used by said corporation on December 15, 1906, and has been continuously used in the business of said corporation since December 15, 1906, and all of said trade-mark except the word "Atwood" has been con-tinuously used in the business of said corporation since April 15, 1904.

Section 1 of the act approved May 4, 1906, provides—

That the owner of a trade-mark * * * may obtain registration for such trade-mark by complying with the following requirements: * * * a descrip-tion of the trade-mark itself, only when needed to express colors not shown in the drawing.

In my decision in *ex parte E. C. Atkins Company*, (*ante*, 67; 126 O. G., 3424,) affirmed by the court of appeals on April 9, 1907, this section of the act was construed to mean that the drawing should be relied upon to disclose the mark and that a description should be per-mitted only when needed to express color not shown in the drawing. Although the above-mentioned statement does not purport to be a description of the mark, it indirectly states the nature of the principal feature of applicant's mark. Attempts to evade the express terms of the act by indirect descriptions should not be encouraged. Inasmuch as the date of adoption and use of applicant's mark means the whole mark presented for registration, it is not apparent that any useful purpose can be subserved by a statement as to the date of use of the various features of the mark.

The decision of the Examiner is affirmed.

Ex parte The De Long Hook & Eye Company.

Decided January 19, 1907.

(128 O. G., 1291.)

TRADE-MARKS—"DULL BLACK" FOR HOOKS AND EYES—DESCRIPTIVE—NOT REGISTRABLE.

The words "Dull Black" as applied to hooks and eyes are obviously descriptive of the color of these articles and therefore not registrable.

ON APPEAL.

TRADE-MARK FOR HOOKS AND EYES.

Mr. W. C. Strawbridge for the applicant.

ALLEN, *Commissioner:*

This is an appeal from the decision of the Examiner of Trade-Marks refusing to register the words "Dull Black," appearing upon a red oblong background, as a trade-mark for hooks and eyes.

The words "Dull Black" are the distinctive feature of the mark by which the goods would be known, the red oblong background serving merely to bring the words "Dull Black" into prominence.

"Dull Black" as applied to hooks and eyes is obviously descriptive, and therefore not registrable. Any manufacturer of hooks and eyes has the right to enamel his articles any color he may choose and to describe the color so applied. This being a common right, no manufacturer can exclusively hold the right to any particular color against others. (*Ex parte Olive Wheel Company*, C. D., 1898, 629; 84 O. G., 1871; *ex parte Pearson Tobacco Company*, C. D., 1898, 613; 85 O. G., 287.)

The decision of the Examiner of Trade-Marks is affirmed.

Ex parte Duryea.

Decided February 1, 1907.

(128 O. G., 1291.)

ABANDONED APPLICATION—DELAY NOT UNAVOIDABLE.

Where it is alleged that the case was inadvertently crossed off the attorney's docket, and therefore overlooked until after the period for action had expired, but it does not appear that there was any intention to respond to the last Office action until near the close of the year allowed therefor or that action could not have been taken in the earlier part of this period had it been so desired, *Held* that the delay was not unavoidable and the case is abandoned.

ON PETITION.

DOUBLE-ACTING GAS OR VAPOR ENGINE.

Mr. James R. Townsend for the applicant.

ALLEN, *Commissioner:*

This is a petition that the application be regarded as a pending case, notwithstanding a delay of more than a year in replying to the last Office action.

It is set forth in the affidavit accompanying the petition that the case was inadvertently crossed off the attorney's docket, and therefore overlooked until after the period for action had expired. It appears, however, that the attorney had instructions before July, 1905, to take the action finally taken if necessary, but delayed taking the same after the Office action of October 26, 1905, repeating the Office action of July 26, 1904, for further consultation with the applicant. It does not appear that there was any intention to respond to the Office action of October 26, 1905, until near the close of the year allowed therefor or that action could not have been taken in the earlier part of this period had it been so desired. Under these circumstances the delay cannot be held to have been unavoidable and the case is abandoned.

Petition denied.

IN RE BOOTH BROTHERS.

Decided February 25, 1907.

(128 O. G., 1291.)

1. PUBLIC USE—PRIMA FACIE CASE—SHOWING REQUIRED.

Where the single affidavit upon which the protest rests sets forth the conclusions of the affiant that the machine alleged to have been in public use corresponded to a certain claim of the application instead of giving a description of the machine itself, *Held* that the showing made is entirely insufficient to justify the institution of a public-use proceeding.

2. SAME—SAME—SAME.

In a public-use protest the facts should be set forth as fully as possible, so that the Office may pass upon the identity of the machine used with that claimed by the applicant and upon the success of its operation in determining whether proceedings shall be instituted. Corroborating affidavits should also be filed if other witnesses are to be relied upon. Altogether, the protestants should present their *prima facie* case as well as may be done by affidavits so as to give the applicant opportunity to intelligently oppose the institution of the proceeding and the consequent delay in the prosecution of his application.

Messrs. Bacon & Milans for the protestants.

ALLEN, *Commissioner:*

This is a protest against the issue of a patent upon a certain alleged invention alleging the bar of two years' public use or sale.

The protest was once dismissed because unaccompanied by an offer to produce witnesses and bear expenses. It has been reconsidered, however, in connection with the offer contained in the attorney's letter of February 15, 1907, to produce witnesses and bear the expenses of taking their testimony.

It is found that the showing made is entirely insufficient to justify the institution of a proceeding which may involve considerable delay and some expense to the successful party in the interference. The single affidavit upon which the protest rests sets forth the conclusions of the affiant that the machine alleged to have been in public use corresponded to a certain claim of the Hadaway application instead of giving a description of the machine itself. The facts should be set forth as fully as possible, so that the Office may pass upon the identity of the machine used with that claimed by the applicant and upon the success of its operation in determining whether proceedings shall be instituted. Corroborating affidavits should also be filed if other witnesses are to be relied upon. Altogether, the protestants should present their *prima facie* case as well as may be done by affidavits so as to give the applicant opportunity to intelligently oppose the institution of the proceeding and the consequent delay in the prosecution of his application.

The protest is again dismissed.

McCANNA *v.* MORRIS.

Decided April 4, 1907.

(128 O. G., 1292.)

INTERFERENCE—MOTION TO DISSOLVE—DEFINITENESS.

A motion to dissolve on the ground of non-patentability which states that a given count "does not involve patentable invention over each of the following Letters Patent" after which certain patents are specified is not open to the objection of indefiniteness.

APPEAL ON MOTION.

LUBRICATOR.

Messrs. Coburn & McRoberts for McCanna.
Mr. Jesse B. Fay for Morris.

ALLEN, *Commissioner:*

This is an appeal by Morris from a decision of the Examiner of Interferences transmitting a motion to dissolve the interference.

Appellant assigns as reasons for appeal three errors in the decision of the Examiner of Interferences, the first two of which relate to the delay in presenting the motion to dissolve, the third relating to alleged indefiniteness of the motion.

No reason is seen for disturbing the decision of the Examiner of Interferences on the sufficiency of the showing in excuse for the delay.

It is urged that the motion is indefinite, because it does not specify with sufficient particularity the reasons or grounds for the allegation of non-patentability of the issue. In connection with count 1 the motion states that this count " does not involve patentable invention over each of the following Letters Patent " after which certain patents are specified. Appellant calls attention to this part of the motion and contends that it does not comply with the requirements of *Heyne et al.* v. *De Vilbiss*, (C. D., 1906, 450; 125 O. G., 669.) In this decision, referring to the citation of a number of references, it was said:

If the moving party is of the opinion that each of the references is a substantial anticipation of each of the claims, it should be so stated.

The part of the motion to which attention is directed satisfies this requirement and seems not to be violative of any other requirement of that decision.

The decision of the Examiner of Interferences is affirmed.

EX PARTE GOLDEN & CO.

Decided April 26, 1907.

(128 O. G., 1292.)

1. TRADE-MARKS—ANTICIPATION—CONSIDERATION OF THE MARK AS A WHOLE.

The right to registration of a mark in view of earlier registrations must be determined from consideration of the entire mark shown upon the application drawing. It is the mark shown which is registered and not any supposed distinguishing feature thereof. However, in determining the substantial identity or non-identity of two marks it is obviously necessary to consider the comparative prominence in each mark of those features which it has in common with the other mark and those features in which it differs therefrom.

2. SAME—SAME—SAME—ELK'S HEAD, ETC.

Where in an interference involving marks having elks' heads prominently displayed thereon the decision was adverse to the appellant, *Held* that registration of the appellant's mark, which comprises the picture of an elk's head standing out prominently thereon and having in addition thereto the inscription "Elk Grove Creamery, Manufacturers of finest pasteurized Elgin Butter" presented in various styles of lettering and set off in circles and scrolls with other minor ornamentation, should be refused.

ON APPEAL.

TRADE-MARK FOR BUTTER.

Mr. E. G. Siggers and *Mr. J. H. Siggers* for the applicants.

ALLEN, *Commissioner:*

This is an appeal from the action of the Examiner of Trade-Marks refusing trade-mark registration upon the above-entitled application.

This application was recently involved in an interference proceeding which terminated in a decision that neither party thereto was entitled to any exclusive right in the mark in issue or to the registration thereof. (*Golden & Company v. Heitz & Company*, C. D., 1906, 453; 125 O. G., 989.) It is not understood that the applicants question here the correctness of that decision, and it is clear that they have no right to do so. Their contention, as understood, is that they are entitled to register the mark shown in their application, notwithstanding the prior adoption of marks by others and the rights of others to use marks established in the interference, and this by reason of the differences between the applicant's mark and those marks which were first adopted by others or which others have acquired the right to use. It is this question that will be considered.

Reference may be made first, however, to the exception taken by the applicants to the Examiner's selection of a portion of their mark as the distinguishing feature in the rejection thereof on the interference record and to their contention that the registrability of the mark must be determined from consideration thereof as an entirety. The applicants are right in their contention that the right to registration must be determined from consideration of the entire mark shown upon the application drawing. It is the mark shown which is registered and not any supposed distinguishing feature thereof. Nevertheless the difference between the applicants and the Examiner upon this point appears to be a mere matter of expression and point of view and not one of substance. In determining the substantial identity or non-identity of two marks it is obviously necessary to consider the comparative prominence in each mark of those features which it has in common with the other mark and those features in which it differs therefrom. Such consideration is of the mark as a whole and is presumably all that is meant by the Examiner of Trade-Marks in his reference to distinguishing characteristics.

Considering the applicants' mark as a whole, it is found that the same has the picture of an elk's head standing out prominently thereon and in addition thereto the following inscription:

> ELK GROVE CREAMERY
> MANUFACTURERS OF
> FINEST
> PASTEURIZED
> ELGIN BUTTER.

This inscription is presented in various styles of lettering and set off in circles and scrolls with other minor ornamentation.

The marks of Compton Brothers and of Heitz & Company, upon which the interference proceeding was decided adversely to the applicants, have elks' heads prominently displayed thereon. It is believed that the mark of the applicants taken in its entirety so nearly resembles the marks of Compton Brothers and Heitz & Company established in the interference, similarly considered, as to be likely to cause confusion or mistake in the mind of the public or to deceive purchasers. Under such circumstances registration must be refused under section 5 of the Trade-Mark Act.

The action of the Examiner of Trade-Marks refusing registration is affirmed.

PIONEER SUSPENDER COMPANY *v.* LEWIS OPPENHEIMER'S SONS.

Decided April 27, 1907.

(128 O. G., 1293.)

1. TRADE-MARKS—REGISTRATION FOR CARTONS—INVALID.

Where a mark is registered for cartons, but the actual trade which the mark represents is in merchandise contained in the cartons, *Held* that the registration is invalid.

2. SAME—MARK NOT USED ON GOODS—CANCELATION.

Where certain words were registered as a trade-mark for merchandise of certain characteristics and the words as used by the registrant in trade represented goods of different characteristics, *Held* that the registration should be canceled.

3. SAME—SAME—SAME—SECTION 13 ACT OF 1905 CONSTRUED.

Held that the right to use referred to in the first ground of cancelation set forth in section 13 of the Trade-Mark Act means a right of exclusive use and that the use referred to in the second ground is a use of the mark as a trade-mark for the goods mentioned in the registration.

ON APPEAL.

TRADE-MARK FOR PAPER BOXES.

Mr. Melville Church and *Mr. John P. Croasdale* for Pioneer Suspender Company.

Messrs. Wiedersheim & Fairbanks for Lewis Oppenheimer's Sons.

ALLEN, *Commissioner:*

This is an appeal by Lewis Oppenheimer's Sons from the decision of the Examiner of Interferences sustaining the application for the cancelation of their trade-mark registration 47,163, brought by the Pioneer Suspender Company.

The registration of the Lewis Oppenheimer's Sons is of the words " Combination Sets " for paper boxes. It is stated in the registrants' brief (p. 1) that—

The trade-mark in question is "Combination Set" as applied to boxes. The proofs establish that Lewis Oppenheimer's Sons first, so far as the record goes, used the words "Combination Set" or "Combination Sets" in connection with boxes which were put out to the trade containing suspenders, garters, and arm-bands. So far as the record shows and as Oppenheimers believe, they also first advertised these words and made them valuable, both in connection with the boxes themselves and with the boxes as containing the contents mentioned.

Lewis Oppenheimer's Sons have sold boxes independently of the contents though always with the expectation or intention that suspenders, garters, and arm-bands were to be placed in the boxes. The number of such empty boxes was very small. (Stipulation paragraph 4A.)

It was testified on behalf of the Pioneer Suspender Company that this company has been selling since August, 1905, a combination of suspenders, garters, and arm-bands, and that one of its customers was Marshall E. Smith & Brother, and the following letter to the latter firm was introduced in evidence:

Lewis Oppenheimer's Sons,
" Eagle Make " Suspenders, Garters and Belts,
627 Market St. and 618 Commerce street.

New York,
 Chicago,
  Pittsburg,
   St. Louis.

PHILADELPHIA, December 15, 1905.

Messrs. MARSHALL E. SMITH & BRO.,
 No. 25 S. Eighth St., Philadelphia, Pa.

GENTLEMEN: It has come to our notice that you are offering for sale garters, arm-bands and suspenders packing in a single box, as Combination Sets. We beg to inform you that this is a registered trade-mark of ours, and would ask you to kindly not offer these goods under this name.

 Respectfully yours,

LEWIS OPPENHEIMER'S SONS.

Dic. No. 1.

It is clear from the above admissions, testimony, and exhibit that the registration should be canceled. The trade-mark right of the registrants, if any might be predicated upon their use of the words " Combination Sets," was in connection with the sets of suspenders, garters, and arm-bands and not in connection with paper boxes. The registration of the term as a mark for boxes looks very much like an attempt to escape the objection of descriptiveness which is inevitably suggested when the words are considered in connection with the goods for which they were evidently in fact adopted.

The registrants contend that none of the conditions under which cancelation is authorized by the statute are present in this case. Cancelation is authorized by section 13 of the Trade-Mark Act if it appear upon application therefor by any person deeming himself injured by the registration—

(1) That the registrant was not entitled to the use of the mark at the date of his application for registration thereof, or

(2) That the mark was not used by the registrant, or

(3) That it has been abandoned.

It is believed that cancelation is authorized in this case under both the first and second of these conditions. The right to use, referred to in the first of the above conditions, is believed to mean a right of exclusive use. The use referred to in the second condition is clearly a use of the mark as a trade-mark for the goods mentioned in the registration.

The decision of the Examiner of Interferences is believed to be right and is affirmed.

BEECH HILL DISTILLING COMPANY *v.* BROWN-FORMAN COMPANY.

Decided February 6, 1907.

(128 O. G., 1293.)

1. TRADE-MARKS—"TEN-YEAR" PROVISO—EXCLUSIVE USE BUT NOT NECESSARILY SOLE USE REQUIRED.

The word "Exclusive" in the ten-year proviso of section 5 of the Trade-Mark Act is believed to necessarily imply the right to exclude. Provided there is a clear right to exclude, however, it is not thought that there must necessarily have been sole use; otherwise use by another, no matter how fraudulent or trivial, would defeat the right to registration under this provision of the statute.

2. SAME—SAME—SAME.

Where it appears that each party to this interference independently originated the mark and neither party had knowledge of the use of the mark by the other party until nearly two years after the Beech Hill Distilling Company began using the mark and that then the Brown-Forman Company made no objection, but acquiesced in the use of the mark by the former company, *Held* that these circumstances do not show such exclusive use on the part of the Brown-Forman Company as to entitle it to register the mark in issue under the ten-year proviso of section 5 of the Trade-Mark Act.

ON PRIORITY.

Messrs. Mason, Fenwick & Lawrence for Beech Hill Distilling Company.

Mr. Arthur E. Wallace for Brown-Forman Company.

MOORE, *Assistant Commissioner:*

This is an appeal by Brown-Forman Company from the decision of the Examiner of Interferences that it is not entitled to register the trade-mark forming the issue of this interference. Said issue consists of the words " Old Tueker " or " J. C. Tucker " as a trade-mark for whisky.

The mark of the Beech Hill Distilling Company, the junior party, is presented for registration as a technical trade-mark. The words " Old Tucker," arranged in a fanciful scroll, are presented by Brown-Forman Company for registration as a non-technical trade-mark under the ten-year proviso of section 5 of the act of February 20, 1905.

The Examiner of Interferences found that the trade-mark was adopted and used by the Beech Hill Distilling Company as early as January 15, 1902, and that its use since that date has been continuous. He also found that the trade-mark was adopted and has been continuously used by Brown-Forman and Company and their successor, the Brown-Forman Company, since at least as early as October 21, 1895; also that the Brown-Forman Company had knowledge and acquiesced in the use of the mark " J. C. Tucker " by the Beech Hill Distilling Company since December 1, 1903. The Examiner of Interferences held that these findings warranted the conclusion, under the authority of section 7 of the Trade-Mark Act, that neither party is entitled to register the mark—the Brown-Forman Company because it has not had the exclusive use of the trade-mark in issue for ten years next preceding the passage of the Trade-Mark Act of 1905 and the Beech Hill Distilling Company for the reason that it was not the first to adopt and use the mark.

The Beech Hill Distilling Company took no appeal from this decision, and on December 17, 1906, filed a formal withdrawal of its application involved in this interference.

The Brown-Forman Company, however, appealed from said decision. I am of the opinion that the Examiner of Interferences was right in refusing its application for registration.

The only question involved in the case is whether the evidence shows that the Brown-Forman Company had the exclusive use of the mark for ten years next preceding the passage of the Trade-Mark Act of February 20, 1905.

There is no dispute in this case on the question of priority of adoption and use. The Beech Hill Company does not claim to have

used the mark prior to January, 1902. The Examiner of Interferences found that the Brown-Forman Company and its predecessor
had used the mark " since at least as early as October 21, 1895." He
apparently fixed on this date because the witness Anawalt states
that he has been connected with said companies since October 21, 1895,
and that the mark has been in use by them since that date, but how
long prior to said date he does not know. (Q. 7.) This date is early
enough to prove prior use by the Brown-Forman Company, but it
does not show use for ten years prior to the statute of February 20,
1905. In my opinion, however, the testimony of Brown, the orders
for Tucker Rye, (Exhibits G, H, and I,) and the testimony of Barret
to the printing of " Old Tucker Rye labels " for the Brown-Forman
Company in 1892 show the adoption and use by this company of the
mark in 1892.

It remains to consider whether this use was such exclusive use
within the meaning of the statute as to entitle the Brown-Forman
Company to registration.

The word " Exclusive " is believed to necessarily imply the right
to exclude. As stated in the decision in *ex parte Cahn, Belt & Company.* (C. D., 1905, 422; 118 O. G., 1936:)

The word "exclusive" in the above-quoted proviso is particularly significant.
It necessarily implies the right of the applicant to exclude others from using the
mark during the period mentioned, and not merely that he was the *sole* user
during that period. He might be the only actual user and at the same time
might have no right to prevent others from entering the field and using the
mark, and in such case he would not have "exclusive" use.

Providing there is a clear right to exclude, it is not thought that
there must necessarily have been sole use. Otherwise use by another,
no matter how fraudulent or trival, would defeat the right to registration under this provision of the statute.

Brown, the president of the Brown-Forman Company, testifies that
he first learned of the use of the trade-mark "J. C. Tucker " by the
Beech Hill Distilling Company on December 1, 1903. (X-Q. 25.)
He states that he wrote to this company about the matter and had a
reply to the effect that some one in its employ was named "J. C.
Tucker, that he has no recollection of replying thereto, nor does he
find any indication of having done so in the records of his office.
(Q. 14, X-Q. 31.) He admits on cross-examination that since De-
cember, 1903, he has " made no further objection to the Beech Hill
Distilling Company to the use by them of their brand J. C. Tucker "
(X-Q. 34) and that as president of the Brown-Forman Company
he would be the proper one to make objection. (X-Q. 35.)

Ullman, of the Beech Hill Distilling Company, testifies that in
1902 he was the sole owner of the Beech Hill Distilling Company

and that he originated the brand "J. C. Tucker." (Q. 7.) He further states on cross-examination concerning the Brown-Forman Company:

Q. 3. How long have you known of their use of the brand "Old Tucker?"

A. I think it is about two years.

Q. 4. Did you not know or hear of their using their name "Old Tucker" as a trade-mark for whiskies prior to the date of your adoption of the "J. C. Tucker" brand?

A. No, sir.

The evidence shows that the Beech Hill Distilling Company commenced to use the "J. C. Tucker" mark in January, 1902. So far as the evidence discloses it appears that each party to this interference independently originated the mark and that neither party had knowledge of the use of the mark by the other party until December, 1903, nearly two years after the Beech Hill Distilling Company began using the mark. It also appears that following the letter of inquiry of December, 1903, the Brown-Forman Company has made no objection to the use of the mark by the Beech Hill Distilling Company, but, on the contrary, has acquiesced in such use. These circumstances do not, in my opinion, show such exclusive use on the part of the Brown-Forman Company as to entitle it to register the mark in issue under the ten-year proviso of section 5 of the Trade-Mark Act.

The decision of the Examiner of Interferences is affirmed.

Ex parte Crescent Typewriter Supply Company.

Decided March 11, 1907.

(128 O. G., 1295.)

1. TRADE-MARKS—GEOGRAPHICAL—"ORIENT."

The word "Orient" as applied to ink-ribbons and carbon-paper is primarily geographical in significance, and therefore not registrable.

2. SAME—SAME—ASSOCIATION WITH ARBITRARY SYMBOL—"ORIENT" WITHIN A WREATH.

The fact that the geographical word "Orient" is printed in a certain manner and inclosed within a wreath does not make the word registrable as a trade-mark.

ON APPEAL.

TRADE-MARK FOR INK-RIBBONS AND CARBON-PAPER.

Mr. Guy Cunningham for the applicant.

MOORE, *Assistant Commissioner:*

This is an appeal from the action of the Examiner of Trade-Marks refusing to register a mark comprising the word "Orient" inclosed in a wreath as a trade-mark for ink-ribbons and carbon-paper upon the ground that the predominating feature "Orient" is merely geographical in significance.

The objection of the Examiner of Trade-Marks is, in my opinion, well founded.

The word "Orient" as applied to ink-ribbons and carbon-paper clearly signifies ribbons or paper treated with an ink made in the Orient, such as "India" ink, and for the reasons stated in the decision in *ex parte Hopkins*, (C. D., 1906, 452; 125 O. G., 670,) which has recently been affirmed by the Court of Appeals of the District of Columbia, it is held that the word "Orient" is merely geographical in significance, and therefore not registrable as a trade-mark.

It is, however, contended that the mark presented does not include the word "Orient," but merely the letters "OR" and "NT" placed at the side of "E" and "I" in monogram. This contention is clearly refuted by the fact that the applicant described the trade-mark in the statement forming part of his original application as follows:

The trade-mark consists of the word "Orient" inclosed in a wreath, the letters "e" and "i" of the word "Orient" being printed as a monogram.

The fact that the applicant has arranged the letters which spell the word "Orient" in a certain manner does not alter the significance of the word or render it capable of exclusive appropriation, nor does the fact that it is associated with a wreath, which is in itself an arbitrary feature, confer registrability upon this term. In their decision in *ex parte Hopkins*, *supra*, the court disregarded an arbitrary "fantastic winged figure" which was associated with the words "Oriental Cream" and denied the registrability of the mark in view of the descriptive character of the predominating words.

In *ex parte Weil* (C. D., 1898, 612; 83 O. G., 1802) Commissioner Duell, holding "Yucatan" to be a merely geographical term, said:

As "Yucatan" taken by itself is not registrable, I do not think it is made so by placing it within a square figure.

In this case the wreath does not, in my opinion, form a distinguishing feature of the mark, but serves merely to embellish the inclosed name "Orient," by which the merchandise will undoubtedly be known.

The decision of the Examiner of Trade-Marks is affirmed.

Ex parte Knapp and Cade.

Decided May 3, 1907.

(128 O. G., 1687.)

Amendment After Final Rejection—Explanation by Examiner Prior to Final Rejection.

Where after a rejection by the Primary Examiner an applicant requests a reconsideration and files an argument fully presenting the case upon the merits and the Examiner in view thereof finally rejects the claims, he cannot submit new claims and have them entered and considered thereafter upon the allegation that the letter asking for reconsideration was in fact a request for an explanation of the Examiner's position.

REQUEST for reconsideration.

ELECTRIC-CURRENT REGULATOR.

Mr. Robert D. Kinney for the applicants.

ALLEN, *Commissioner:*

This case is before me upon request for reconsideration of a petition taken from the action of the Examiner adhering to a final rejection and refusing to admit amendments presented thereafter.

The petition has been reconsidered without discovery of any merit therein. A request for explanation of the Examiner's position should be full and specific and should not be confused with the argument upon the merits of the action. No such request was made. The case, on the contrary, was fully presented to the Examiner by the applicants' action of May 5, 1906, for his reconsideration, and such reconsideration was in fact requested by the applicants. That a final rejection might result should have been contemplated by the applicants, and the newly-offered claims should have been earlier presented. Applicants should fully present their cases upon each action. There is nothing in the letter of final rejection to excuse the presentation of the new claims at this time, nor can the alleged insufficiency of the Examiner's prior actions afford such excuse, as the explanation of the Examiner's position, which the applicants contend to be necessary, has not yet been furnished.

As a matter of fact, the Examiner's actions appear to be as complete as need be. The real disagreement between the Examiner and the applicants is one of merits, which should be settled by appeal to the Examiners-in-Chief upon the finally-rejected claims, if the applicants still regard the rejection as improper.

The petition is again denied.

WORCESTER BREWING CORPORATION *v.* RUETER & COMPANY.

Decided May 4, 1907.

(128 C. G., 1687.)

1. TRADE-MARKS—TEN-YEAR PROVISO—EXCLUSIVE USE DOES NOT NECESSARILY REQUIRE SOLE USE.

The word "exclusive" in the ten-year proviso is believed to necessarily imply the right to exclude. But provided there is a clear right to exclude it is not thought that there must necessarily have been sole use. Otherwise use by another, no matter how fraudulent or trivial, would defeat the right to registration under this proviso of the act.

2. SAME—SAME—SAME.

Where it appears that the opposer at the time of its adoption of the mark was aware of the fact that it had been used for a long time as a trade-mark by the applicant and that said applicant had built up a large business thereon and it further appears that the applicant has not acquiesced in the use of the mark by the opposer and that it has been guilty of no laches in asserting its rights, *Held* that the applicant has established a case of "exclusive use" within the meaning of the last proviso of section 5 and is entitled to register its mark.

3. SAME—SAME—DESCRIPTIVE MARK.

The fact that a mark is descriptive is not in itself a bar to its registration under the ten-year proviso. (Citing the decision of the Court of Appeals of the District of Columbia *in re Cahn, Belt & Company,* C. D., 1906, 627; 122 O. G., 354.)

4. SAME—SAME—SAME—RIGHT TO EXCLUDE.

It has been repeatedly held by the courts that where a party was the first to apply a certain mark to a particular class of goods and by long and extensive use the mark has become indicative of the origin of the goods he may acquire a property right in the mark, even though it be a descriptive or geographical term, which the courts will uphold by requiring others who use the mark to so qualify it as to distinguish their goods from those of the original user.

ON APPEAL.

TRADE-MARK FOR ALE.

Messrs. Southgate & Southgate for Worcester Brewing Corporation.

Mr. George H. Maxwell for Rueter & Company.

ALLEN, *Commissioner:*

This is an appeal by the Worcester Brewing Corporation from the decision of the Examiner of Interferences dismissing its opposition and holding that Rueter & Company has a right to register the word "Sterling" as a trade-mark for ale.

The application of Rueter & Company contains all the allegations required for the registration of its mark as a technical trade-mark, and in addition the declaration contains the allegation, required of applicants under the ten-year proviso of section 5 of the Trade-Mark Act of February 20, 1905—

That the trade-mark has been in actual use as a trade-mark of applicant and its predecessors for ten years next preceding the passage of the act of February 20, 1905, and that to the best of his knowledge and belief such use has been exclusive.

The Examiner of Interferences held that Rueter & Company has the right to register its mark both as a technical trade-mark and also under the ten-year proviso.

The question of the registrability of the mark under the ten-year proviso of the Trade-Mark Act will be first considered. The testimony in this case clearly shows that the applicant has actually, extensively, and continuously used the mark in issue for more than ten years next preceding the passage of the act of February 20, 1905; but the Worcester Brewing Corporation contends that, (p. 36 of brief)—

Of course, Rueter & Company have no right under the ten-year clause because the use by the Worcester Brewing Corporation of the words "Worcester Sterling" as a trade-mark for ale at any time prior to April 1, 1905, would prevent any use by Rueter & Company of the word "Sterling" for being an exclusive use of such words as a trade-mark for the ten years next preceding the passage of the act.

This contention of the Worcester Brewing Corporation is believed to be erroneous. In the case of *ex parte Cahn, Belt & Company* (C. D., 1905, 422; 118 O. G., 1936) I stated concerning the ten-year proviso:

The word "exclusive" in the above-quoted proviso is particularly significant. It necessarily implies the right of the applicant to exclude others from using the mark during the period mentioned, and not merely that he was the *sole* user during that period. He might be the only actual user and at the same time might have no right to prevent others from entering the field and using the mark, and in such case he would not have "exclusive" use.

The word "exclusive" is believed to necessarily imply the right to exclude. But provided there is a clear right to exclude it is not thought that there must necessarily have been sole use. Otherwise use by another, no matter how fraudulent or trivial, would defeat the right to registration under this proviso of the act.

The testimony of Finnigan and Maynard, the only witnesses testifying on behalf of the Worcester Brewing Corporation, shows that Finnigan is president, a director, and the principal owner of the Worcester Brewing Corporation and that he was instrumental in organizing said corporation in 1899, that for a number of years prior thereto he was the exclusive agent in Worcester for the Rueter & Company "Sterling Ale," and that such agency terminated in the summer of 1900. Thereafter he marketed the products of the Worcester Brewing Corporation, including its "Worcester Sterling Ale." Maynard, the secretary and treasurer of the Worcester Brewing Corporation, admitted on cross-examination (X-Q. 182) that so far as he remembers no advertising of the "Worcester Sterling Ale" was done by the Worcester Brewing Corporation at least up to May, 1904. The evidence also shows that the right of the opposer to use the mark in issue was challenged and that suit was brought in the courts of the State of Massachusetts as soon as Rueter & Company became aware of the use of the mark by the Worcester Brewing Corporation. (Rueter's testimony, answer 52.) The above suit at the time of the final hearing in this opposition proceeding was still pending before the courts of Massachusetts. It thus appears that the Worcester Brewing Corporation at the time of its adoption of the mark was aware of the fact that "Sterling" had been used for a long time as a trade-mark by the applicant and that Rueter & Company had extensively advertised and built up a large business in "Sterling Ale." It further appears that Rueter & Company has not acquiesced in the use of the mark by the Worcester Brewing Corporation and that it has been guilty of no laches in asserting its rights. Under these circumstances the applicant is believed to have established a case of "exclusive use" within the meaning of the last proviso of section 5 and is entitled to register its mark thereunder.

The Worcester Brewing Corporation contends that the word "Sterling" is not registrable because it is descriptive of the goods to which it is applied. It is unnecessary to determine whether the mark is descriptive in considering its registrability under the ten-year proviso, since the fact that a mark is descriptive is not in itself a bar to its registration under said proviso. The Court of Appeals of the District of Columbia *in re Cahn, Belt & Company* (C. D., 1906, 627; 122 O. G., 354) stated:

It is clear that these changes were made for the purpose of permitting the registration of marks which were not trade-marks but which had been actually used as trade-marks by the applicants or their predecessors from whom they derived title, and in which the user had acquired property rights for more than ten years next preceding the passage of the act.

It has been repeatedly held by the courts that where a party was the first to apply a certain mark to a particular class of goods and by long and extensive use the mark has become indicative of the origin of the goods he may acquire a property right in the mark, even though it be a descriptive or geographical term, which the courts will uphold by requiring others who use the mark to so qualify it as to distinguish their goods from those of the original user. In *ex parte The Yale & Towne Manufacturing Company* (*ante*, 122; 127 O. G., 3641) I stated:

It is believed that the same reasons and principles apply in many cases of geographical and descriptive terms and names of individuals. Here, as in the case of the name of a patented article, the first adopter may often have the right to exclude others from using the exact term or mark, although no technical trade-mark right could exist. (*Elgin National Watch Company v. Illinois Watch Case Company*, C. D., 1901, 273; 94 O. G., 755, 179 U. S., 665; *Walter Baker & Company, v. Baker*, C. D., 1897, 797; 78 O. G., 1427; 77 Fed. Rep., 884; *Sharer et al. v. Heller & Merz Company*, C. D., 1901, 424; 96 O. G., 2229; 108 Fed. Rep., 821; *Genesee Salt Company v. Burnap*, 73 Fed. Rep., 818; *American Waltham Watch Company v. Sandman*, 96 Fed. Rep., 330.)

The opposer also contends that Rueter & Company is not entitled to register the word "Sterling" because it used the mark as a grade mark rather than to indicate the origin of the goods. The evidence, on the contrary, is believed to show that the mark as used by Rueter

& Company was intended to indicate and does indicate primarily to the purchasing public that "Sterling Ale" is the product of Rueter & Company and that any indication it may possess as to the grade or quality of the ale is secondary and subordinate. This contention cannot be sustained. *Columbia Mill Company* v. *Alcorn*, C. D., 1893, 672; 65 O. G., 1916; 150 U. S., 460.

It does not appear that the official sign of Rueter & Company and its registration certificate in the State of Massachusetts, under which the Worcester Brewing Corporation claims that applicant is estopped from asserting that the word "Sterling" constitutes an essential feature of its trade-mark, have any connection with the mark of the application. On the contrary, they evidently relate to a different and distinct sign or mark.

Having found that Rueter & Company are entitled to register the word "Sterling" under the ten-year proviso of the Trade-Mark Act, it is unnecessary to consider whether the mark is also registrable as a technical trade-mark. But one application for registration of the mark is before me, and upon that application Rueter & Company is adjudged entitled to registration.

The decision of the Examiner of Interferences is affirmed.

HEWITT *v.* WEINTRAUB *v.* HEWITT AND ROGERS.

Decided April 26, 1907.

(128 O. G., 1689.)

INTERFERENCE—TESTIMONY—RIGHT TO MAKE CLAIMS—PRIORITY.

> In an interference proceeding where, in addition to the taking of testimony as to who was the first inventor, permission was obtained to take testimony concerning the right of one of the parties to make the claims for use at the first hearing on priority under Rule 130, *Held* that the rule contemplates but one contest, and that leading to an award of priority, and not two distinct contests and two separate proceedings. The taking of testimony on the question of priority should not therefore be suspended until the question of the right to make the claims has been determined.

APPEAL ON MOTION.

GAS OR VAPOR ELECTRIC APPARATUS.

Mr. Charles A. Terry for Hewitt and Hewitt and Rogers. (*Mr. George H. Stockbridge* of counsel.)

Mr. Albert G. Davis for Weintraub. (*Mr. Alexander D. Lunt* of counsel.)

MOORE, *Assistant Commissioner:*

This is an appeal by Huett from the decision of the Examiner of Interferences denying his petition that the taking of testimony for

Hewitt upon the question of priority be suspended until the question of the right of the senior party, Hewitt and Rogers, to make claims corresponding to the counts of the issue has been determined.

Weintraub's preliminary statement failed to overcome the record date of Hewitt and Rogers. In response to an order to show cause why judgment should not be rendered against him Weintraub moved to dissolve the interference on the ground that Hewitt and Rogers had no right to make claims corresponding to the counts of the issue. This motion was denied; but Weintraub obtained permission to take testimony to show that Hewitt and Rogers had no right to make the claims for use at the final hearing on priority under Rule 130. Times were therefore set by the Examiner of Interferences for the taking of testimony by all parties.

In case Hewitt's petition was granted the first contest would be between Weintraub and the senior party, Hewitt and Rogers. Then the winning party would have to contest priority with the junior party, Hewitt. The judgments in each contest would be by award of priority and in each there would be the statutory right of appeal. Hewitt contends that there are two distinct contests and should therefore be two separate proceedings. This contention is erroneous. If, under Rule 130, Weintraub can establish that Rogers and Hewitt have no right to make the claims, the judgment will be an award of priority in his favor as against the senior party. The rule contemplates but one contest, and that leading to an award of priority. To make the question the subject-matter of two contests, each resulting in an award of priority with the right of appeal to the Court of Appeals of the District of Columbia, would be piecemeal action and unnecessarily prolong the contest.

The decision of the Examiner of Interferences is affirmed.

MUNSTER *v.* ASHWORTH.

Decided July 23, 1906.

(128 O. G., 2085.)

1. INTERFERENCE—EVIDENCE—CONSIDERATION OF DEPOSITION—FAILURE TO AFFORD OPPORTUNITY FOR CROSS-EXAMINATION.

   Where the direct examination of a witness is completed and after answering certain questions upon cross-examination he is withdrawn from the stand on account of sickness and his counsel refuses to take any steps to produce him again, in order that the cross-examination may be completed, on the ground that he had been sick for over a year, had undergone several operations, and that there was no probability that he would be able to testify at any definite time in the future, if at all, *Held* that in so far as the answers given on direct examination were not tested by cross-examination the deposition should not be considered.

2. SAME—DEPOSITIONS—NOTICE OF TAKING—NOTICE WAIVED.

Where a record as made up by the officer before whom testimony is taken in an interference proceeding shows that counsel for one of the parties desired to examine certain witnesses as to whom no notice had been given by opposing counsel and the latter stated that while he had no objection to their direct examination he did not care to cross-examine and thereupon went away, *Held* that the depositions of such witnesses will not upon motion be stricken out because of lack of notice, notwithstanding an affidavit by counsel stating that he had refused to take the testimony of such witnesses.

APPEAL from Examiners-in-Chief.

COÖPERATING DOORS.

Mr. Robert Klotz and *Mr. J. W. Beckstrom* for Munster.
Mr. Charles W. La Porte for Ashworth.

ALLEN, *Commissioner:*

This is an appeal by Ashworth from a decision of the Examiners-in-Chief reversing the decision of the Examiner of Interferences and awarding priority of invention to Munster.

The issue is stated in three counts, which are as follows:

1. The combination, with a door-opening, of a swinging door and a pair of slide-doors arranged to close said opening and connections between all of said doors whereby same are caused to open and close simultaneously.
2. The combination, with a door-opening, of an angularly-movable door and a pair of slide-doors for closing said opening, and means between all of said doors for opening and closing them together.
3. The combination with a single door-opening, of a swinging door, a pair of superposed sliding doors movable toward and from each other, a lever, means for moving said sliding doors in opposite directions by said lever and means for actuating said lever by said swinging door.

Ashworth's application was filed March 21, 1904, and Munster's application was filed on May 27, 1904. The burden is upon Munster to establish his case by a preponderance of evidence.

Munster alleges conception, disclosure, and the making of sketches and a model about September 1, 1902, and reduction to practice on May 1, 1903. Ashworth claims conception on January 1, 1903, disclosure in April, 1903, the making of drawings and a model in February and March, respectively, of 1904, and no reduction to practice other than his constructive reduction to practice of March 21, 1904.

Both parties took testimony. The Examiner of Interferences found that Munster failed to establish either a conception or reduction to practice prior to Ashworth's date of filing and awarded priority to Ashworth. On the other hand, the Examiners-in-Chief found that Munster's record established both a conception and reduction to practice prior to the filing of Ashworth's application and reversed the decision of the Examiner of Interferences. I am of the opinion that the evidence shows Munster to have been the first to conceive, but the last to reduce to practice, and that he was lacking in diligence.

Ashworth has raised the question whether the testimony of Munster or any of his witnesses can be considered in the disposition of this case. It appears that in taking the testimony on behalf of Munster the inventor was produced as a witness and his testimony-in-chief was taken, and witness was then tendered to the opposite party for cross-examination, and he was cross-examined at some length. Before the cross-examination was completed a recess was taken.

The witness and counsel for the opposing parties having met pursuant to the adjournment, the witness declared that he was too ill to proceed with the cross-examination and went home to go to bed. Thereupon, it appears from the record, counsel for Ashworth stated that he was willing that cross-examination should be suspended and asked counsel for Munster to have the time for the taking of testimony extended and to give him due notice thereof. Counsel for Munster refused to make any attempt to produce the witness again for cross-examination, on the ground that the witness had been sick for over a year, had undergone three operations, and that there was no probability of witness being able to testify at any definite time or of his ever being able to testify. Counsel for Munster has made no attempt to reproduce him in order that the cross-examination may be completed. It is now urged on behalf of Ashworth, as it was urged before the Examiner of Interferences and the Examiners-in-Chief, that the deposition of Munster can be given no consideration, as he did not submit himself to complete cross-examination.

In so far as the answers given on direct examination were not tested by cross-examination, it is believed that the point is well taken. That the direct testimony of a witness cannot be considered where there has been no opportunity to cross-examine seems to be well settled. (*The People v. Cole*, 43 N. Y., 508; *Heath v. Waters*, 40 Mich., 457; *Clements v. Benjamin*, 12 Johns, 299; *Wigmore on Evidence*, Vol. II, sec. 1390.) In a few cases where the direct examination has been completed and cross-examination has been prevented by circumstances beyond the control of the witness or the party in whose behalf he testified the testimony has been admitted. (*Arundel v. Arundel*, 1 Chand., Wis., 90; *Forrest v. Kissam*, 7 Hill, N. Y., 463) But the circumstances present in this case are not so extraordinary as to constitute an exception to the general rule. While the record indicates that the witness was too ill to undergo further cross-examination at that time, there seems to be no justification for the refusal of his counsel to make every reasonable effort to produce the witness for further cross-examination at some future time, even at the expense of some delay in the final disposition of the case. For these reasons those parts of Munster's deposition relating to conception and reduction to practice of the invention will not be considered.

The question is also presented whether or not the testimony of the other witnesses produced on behalf of Munster is entitled to consideration, it being urged by appellant that it is not, on the ground of lack of proper notice of the taking of such testimony. It appears that the notice of taking testimony stated simply that at a certain time and place—

I shall proceed to take Munster's testimony.

At the time and place stated counsel for the opposing parties met and proceeded to take the testimony of Munster. Prior to the completion of his testimony the proceedings were interrupted, as above pointed out. With regard to subsequent proceedings the record as made by the officer taking the deposition states as follows:

Counsel for A. P. Munster then offered to very briefly examine the other witnesses present and turn them over to counsel for Ashworth for cross-examination. Counsel for Ashworth announced that while he had no objection to the direct examination of other witnesses present, he would not care to cross-examine them and went away.

Thereupon the testimony of three other witnesses was taken—Nicholas M. Munster, son of the inventor and an assignee of a part interest in the invention, Bernard Heinig, also assignee of a part interest in the invention, and Robert Klotz, Munster's attorney of record. Attorney for Ashworth had left, and hence these witnesses were not cross-examined. Prior to final hearing Ashworth gave notice that at the final hearing he would move that the testimony of all of these witnesses be stricken out. This notice was accompanied by an affidavit of counsel for Ashworth stating that he had refused to take the testimony of these witnesses under the circumstances and went away. From a comparison of this statement with the statement on the record of the officer taking the deposition quoted above it is at once apparent that they do not agree. Under these circumstances the statement in the record will be accepted as correct. The statement made by an officer charged with the duty of correctly recording the testimony of a witness and such events as counsel may desire to have recorded cannot be overcome by the oath of a single witness. Moreover, an affidavit filed by counsel for Munster in opposition to the affidavit of Ashworth denies the accuracy of such affidavit and avers the facts to be as stated in the record. The statement by counsel for Ashworth that he had no objection to the direct examination of these witnesses and that " he would not care to cross-examine them " must be considered as an express waiver of notice and of the right to cross-examine, and for this reason the depositions of the witnesses will be received and given full weight.

With the inventor's testimony out of consideration Munster's conception and reduction to practice must be established, if at all, by the testimony of his son and Bernard Heinig.

A single model has been introduced in evidence on behalf of Munster which is relied upon to establish conception. An examination of this model discloses the fact that it embodies all the elements of the issue. The testimony shows that Munster made this model and that it was in existence at least as early as September or October, 1902. Without a discussion of the testimony in detail it may be said that it is believed to show a conception of the invention of Munster in September or October, 1902.

The testimony tending to establish an actual reduction to practice by Munster is as follows:

By Nicholas M. Munster:

Q. 12. A. P. Munster's preliminary statement says that he built some 33 doors for Armour and Co., in 1903; is this model exactly like those doors?

A. Yes, sir.

Q. 13. When were these doors put up, if you know?

A. He began to build them in May, 1903.

Q. 14. About when were they completed, to your knowledge?

A. Some time in October, 1903.

*   *   *   *   *   *   *

Q. 41. Did you show him this model that you have brought here and offered in evidence, which you say is exactly like the doors put up at Armour & Co.'s plant in October, 1903?

A. Yes, sir.

By Bernard Heinig:

Q. 16. Have you seen the doors put up at Armour & Co.'s plant?

A. Yes.

Q. 17. When did you first see those doors?

A. When I went down to label them.

Q. 18. What do you mean by "label them."

A. I mean, I put "Patent applied for" upon the doors.

Q. 19. How many doors did you label?

A. Thirty-three.

Q. 20. About what time did you go down to label those 33 doors?

A. After the application for patent was made out.

Q. 21. Had you seen the doors before that time?

A. No, I hadn't seen them before, but I heard they had been there about a year.

The deficiencies in this testimony are apparent. Question 12 propounded to Nicholas M. Munster assumes the truth of the preliminary statement regarding the building of thirty-three doors for Armour & Company and asks if those doors were exactly like the model. He ~d that they were; but the form of the question is grossly lead-nds to lessen its weight. The succeeding questions proceed ie assumption and ask when those thirty-three doors were completed, to which answer is made that his father began to make the doors in May, 1903, and that they were completed some time in October, 1903. It does not appear anywhere in the testimony that Nicholas M. Munster ever saw any of these thirty-three doors, and for this reason his statement that they were like the model can be given little weight. The testimony of Heinig appears to add nothing of consequence on the question of reduction to practice. While he states that he saw thirty-three doors at Armour & Company's plant and labeled them " Patent applied for," this took place after Munster's application was made out in the latter part of May, 1904. He makes no statement regarding the construction of these doors. He does not know when they were built or anything about them, except that he " heard they had been there about a year." This hearsay testimony can be given no weight.

The testimony is deficient in another respect. It fails to show that the doors put up at Armour's plant, assuming it to be proved that they were constructed as claimed, were ever operated or subjected to any tests to show that they were capable of successful operation. Neither of the witnesses saw these doors at any time previous to the date of execution of Munster's application, and while Heinig saw them about this time he makes no statement relative to their construction or condition. It is therefore concluded that the testimony fails to show a reduction to practice by Munster prior to the filing of his application. Munster was therefore the last to reduce to practice.

Ashworth does not claim to have conceived the invention prior to January, 1903. For the purpose of this decision we may accept this date as his date of conception. Munster's evidence having established a date of conception as early as September or October, 1902, he is thus the first to conceive and the last to reduce to practice. In order for him to prevail, he must therefore show that he was exercising diligence when Ashworth entered the field and up to the time of the filing of his application.

The evidence does not show that anything whatever was done by Munster after October, 1903, up to the filing of his application in May, 1904, and there appears to be no excuse for the inaction. In answer to question 15 Heinig states the delay was caused by Munster's desire to—

demonstrate the utility of the invention in actual service * * * and in the meantime he also became sick.

With regard to appellee's sickness it appears that he did not become sick before March, 1904, which was four or five months after the thirty-three doors were alleged to have been completed. With regard to demonstrating the utility of the invention it is to be said that the record does not show that the doors were ever actually subjected to any tests. For these reasons the excuses for the delay are insufficient, and it must be found that Munster was lacking in diligence in reducing his invention to practice.

The conclusion is that Munster's evidence does not sustain his claim to prior reduction to practice, that while he was·the first to conceive he was the last to reduce to practice, and that he was lacking in diligence.

The decision of the Examiners-in-Chief is reversed, and priority of invention is awarded to Ashworth.

DUNBAR *v.* SCHELLENGER.

Decided May 17, 1907.

(128 O. G., 2087.)

FILING OF BILL IN EQUITY BY DEFEATED PARTY TO INTERFERENCE WILL NOT STAY ISSUE OF PATENT TO SUCCESSFUL PARTY.

The filing of a bill in equity under section 4915, Revised Statutes, by the defeated party to an interference will not operate to stay the issue of a patent to the successful party, nor will it justify the Commissioner of Patents in withholding it until the equity proceeding is terminated. (citing case of *Sargent*, C. D., 1877, 125; 12 O. G., 475, and *Wells* v. *Boyle*, C. D. 1888, 36; 43 O. G., 753.)

ON PETITION.

TELEPHONE SYSTEM.

Messrs. Jones & Addington and *Mr. Robert L. Ames* for Dunbar. *Mr. Charles A. Brown* for Schellenger.

MOORE, *Acting Commissioner:*

This is a petition by Francis W. Dunbar and his assignee, the Kellogg Switchboard & Supply Company, that the application of Schellenger be withheld from issue until a bill in equity pending in the United States Circuit Court for the Western District of New York has been heard, determined, and disposed of.

The applications of Dunbar and Schellenger have been in interference, in which contest Schellenger was successful both in the Patent Office and on appeal to the Court of Appeals of the District of Columbia. Dunbar then filed the bill in equity noted above, under the provisions of section 4915, Revised Statutes, for the purpose of having the court pass upon his right to receive a patent. He requests that in the meantime no patent be granted on the application of Schellenger.

The question raised in this petition was considered by the Secre- of the Interior on appeal from the decision of the Commissioner of Patents in the case of *Sargent*, (C. D., 1877, 125; 12 O. G., 475.) In ordering the issue of the patent in that case the Secretary said:

If the decision made in your Office is erroneous, Mr. Burge has his remedy in the court, but pending that inquiry executive action cannot be stayed. Due regard must always be given to the rights of all parties in interest in any proceeding, but if, after a fair consideration of all the questions affecting them, you are compelled, in obedience to law and the facts presented, to decide in favor of one and against the other, so that your judicial functions are exhausted, it is neither equitable nor just that the party who has established his right to the claim in controversy, should be delayed in the enjoyment of it, so far as it depends upon your action, because it is possible that another tribunal, not appellate, may determine the same question otherwise.

If the filing a bill in equity by parties asserting adverse claims, to retry questions already decided by your Office, could be permitted to stay final action on your part, very few patents for really valuable inventions would, in my opinion, hereafter be issued, and the injurious results which would necessarily follow would be beyond calculation.

This ruling of the Secretary of the Interior has since been followed by this Office, as appears from the decision of the Commissioner of Patents in *Wells* v. *Boyle*, (C. D., 1888, 36; 43 O. G., 753,) and it is still considered controlling. The act of February 9, 1893, establishing the Court of Appeals of the District of Columbia and providing for an appeal to said court from the decision of the Commissioner of Patents in interference cases did not change the provisions of section 4915 with respect to bills in equity. The ruling made in the above decisions are therefore applicable, notwithstanding the act of 1893, and the provision for a review by said court of the Commissioner's decision as to the award of priority is all the more reason why the issue of a patent to the successful party should not be withheld after the court's decision.

In view of the ruling of the Secretary noted above and for reasons similar to those stated to the decision of the Commissioner, *supra*, the petition *is denied*.

MAGIC CURLER COMPANY *v.* PORTER.

Decided May 23, 1907.

(128 O. G., 2088.)

1. TRADE-MARKS—CANCELATION—REGISTRANT'S RIGHT TO THE USE OF THE MARK.
   The right registered is a supposed right to exclusive use. The evident intention of Congress was to permit any person deeming himself to be injured by a registration to question the validity in the Patent Office and to

obtain cancelation thereof if the registrant had no trade-mark right therein at the time of his application for registration, or if, having had such a right at that time, he has subsequently lost the same.

2. SAME—SAME—NEED NOT SHOW WHY OPPOSITION WAS NOT FILED.

The applicant for cancelation need not show why an opposition was not filed. The question as to the registrability of a mark is not *res adjudicata* by reason of its registration.

3. SAME—SAME—ALLEGATION OF CONTINUOUS USE.

The allegation of continuous use of the mark by the applicant for cancelation is immaterial, as the applicant is not seeking registration and may establish a case for cancelation without such use.

ON APPEAL.

HAIR-WAVER.

Messrs. Wiedersheim & Fairbanks for Magic Curler Company.
Messrs. Louis Bagger & Co. for Porter.

MOORE, *Acting Commissioner:*

This is an appeal by the Magic Curler Company from the decision of the Examiner of Interferences dismissing its application for cancelation of the trade-mark registration of Charles F. Porter.

The Magic Curler Company has applied for cancelation upon the ground that the registered mark is the name of an individual whose consent to registration has not been given and that the mark is descriptive and that the Magic Curler Company and its predecessors had been using the registered mark in business prior to the alleged adoption thereof by the registrant and have not abandoned it. The Examiner of Interferences held, upon motion by the registrant, treated as a demurrer to the application for cancelation; that none of these allegations, if proved, would affect the registrant's right to the use of the mark. He did not consider the use alleged by the Magic Curler Company to be used as a trade-mark and held that the case does not therefore fall within the provisions of section 13 of the Trade-Mark Act for the cancelation of registrations through proceedings in the Patent Office.

Section 13 is as follows:

That whenever any person shall deem himself injured by the registration of a trade-mark in the Patent Office he may at any time apply to the Commissioner of Patents to cancel the registration thereof. The Commissioner shall refer such application to the Examiner in charge of interferences, who is empowered to hear and determine this question and who shall give notice thereof to the registrant. If it appear after a hearing before the Examiner that the registrant was not entitled to the use of the mark at the date of application for registration thereof, or that the mark is not used by the trant, or has been abandoned, and the Examiner shall so decide, the Commissioner shall cancel the registration. Appeal may be taken to the Commissioner in person from the decision of Examiner of Interferences.

The question is, Does the provision of this section for cancelation, when—

the registrant was not entitled to the use of the mark at the date of his application for registration thereon—

authorize cancelation generally where it appears that the registrant was not entitled to the registration obtained, or whether cancelation under this provision is limited to those cases where a trade-mark right resided in another party? This question was decided by the Commissioner in *Pioneer Suspender Company* v. *Lewis Oppenheimer's Sons*, (*ante*, 144; 128 O. G., 1293,) where it was held that the right to use referred to in this section means a right to exclusive use. There seems to be no reason why the consideration of the right to registration upon an application for cancelation should be restricted to a determination of the registrant's right to use the mark. The right registered is a supposed right to exclusive use. The evident intention of Congress was to permit any person deeming himself injured by a registration to question the validity thereof in the Patent Office and to obtain cancelation thereof if the registrant had no trade-mark right therein at the time of his application for registration, or if, having had such a right at that time, he has subsequently lost the same. There is more reason why a party who has himself no trade-mark right, but who is harassed in his business through an improper registration, should be permitted to overthrow that registration than there is for according this relief to one who is the possessor of a trade-mark right. The latter party may obtain relief against injury through the invalid registration by interference proceedings, registration to himself, and suit thereon. The former party, though liable to the same injury, has not the same opportunity for combating it. In the face of these reasons the meaning which the statute appears to have when construed strictly in accordance with the exact definitions of the words used is believed to be accidental and not controlling.

As the conclusion reached herein is contrary to that reached by the Examiner of Interferences on the point upon which the case turned before him, his conclusions unfavorable to the appellee on other points have been reviewed and the appellee's arguments thereon considered. The conclusion that the applicant for cancelation need not show why an opposition was not filed and that the registrability of the mark is not *res adjudicata* by reason of the registration are considered to be right. The matter of allegations by the applicant of continuous use is immaterial, as the applicant is not seeking registration and may establish a case for cancelation without such use.

The decision of the Examiner of Interferences is reversed.

RICHARDS *v.* BURKHOLDER.

Decided October 12, 1906.

(128 O. G., 2529.)

INTERFERENCE—REDUCTION TO PRACTICE—SIMPLE DEVICE—ORIGINAL DEVICE NOT
PRODUCED.

. Where the device in issue is said to belong to that class of simple devices
the mere production of which without test is regarded as an actual reduction to practice, but the device originally made was not produced in evidence, and the testimony tending to establish the identity of a later device,
which was introduced in evidence, with the original device is so general as
to leave it uncertain whether this later device is of the same strength, size,
shape, and proportion as the original, *Held* that actual reduction to practice
is not proved.

APPEAL from Examiners-in-Chief.

DOOR-HANGER.

Messrs. Bond, Adams, Pickard & Jackson for Richards.
Messrs. Offield, Towle & Linthicum for Burkholder.

MOORE, *Assistant Commissioner:*

This is an appeal by Richards from a decision of the Examiners-in-
Chief affirming the decision of the Examiner of Interferences and
awarding priority of invention to Burkholder on the following issue:

1. In a device of the class described, the combination with a hollow track
opened in the rear for the reception of supporting-brackets, of supporting-
brackets having spring-heads adapted to fit the inner contour of said hollow
track, substantially as described.

2. In a device of the class described, the combination with a hollow track
opened in the rear for the reception of supporting-brackets, of a supporting-
bracket made of a single piece of metal and having a spring-head adapted to
fit the inner contour of said hollow track, substantially as described.

3. The combination with a hollow track having a longitudinal opening in one
side, of a supporting-bracket having portions doubled to form a head sprung into
said hollow track and arms extending transversely through said opening in said
track, substantially as described.

4. A supporting-bracket for a hollow slotted track, comprising spring-arms
having attaching ends, and a connection between their opposite ends adapted
to allow normal expansion of said arms, and forming a head to fit with the
track, substantially as described.

The interference was declared between Richards's application, filed
November 10, 1904, and a patent granted to Burkholder, dated October 4, 1904, on an application filed October 21, 1903. Under these
circumstances it is necessary for Richards to establish beyond a reasonable doubt a prior reduction to practice or a prior conception
coupled with diligence. Both of the lower tribunals held that he
'd failed to sustain this burden.

The issue relates to a track for sliding doors, consisting of a tube slotted in the rear and a supporting-bracket having a spring-head fitting the inner contour of the tube and adapted to slide therein.

I fully concur in the reasoning and in the conclusions reached by the Examiners-in-Chief, and it is deemed unnecessary to discuss the testimony further, except to state the view which I take of the evidence relating to the two devices on which appellant relies for a reduction to practice.

It is claimed that a full-sized device embodying the invention was made in 1902 and placed on a shavings-shed which stood in the factory-yard, where it remained in satisfactory operation for at least a number of months. Richards testified that this device consisted of several brackets and about four or six feet of tubular slotted track involving the construction in issue, upon which a door of the ordinary size was hung.

D. W. Simpson, the president of the company which employed Richards at the time the invention was made, Le Roy Simpson, who was also an officer of the company, and George Wheeler, an employee closely associated with Richards, all claim to have seen this device on the shavings-shed; but their testimony is so conflicting as to attendant circumstances as to leave the question in much doubt. Richards states that this door was placed on the shed "regardless of closing openings." (Richards, X-Q. 200.) Le Roy Simpson claims that it closed a small opening. (Le Roy Simpson, Q. 11.) Wheeler claims to have seen it at one time, some time after July 1902, but knows very little about it. (Wheeler, Q. 25.) D. W. Simpson states that he saw this test on the shavings-shed; but upon being asked how the brackets were fitted to the track he said they were riveted thereto. In a later answer (Q. 25) he corrects this statement by saying that he understood the question to be how the first brackets (meaning the brackets first put on the market) were fitted to the tubular track. There seems to be no ambiguity about the question; but the explanation might be accepted were it not for the fact that another witness, Tolman, who moved the shavings-shed in 1903, testified that the only track which he saw on the shed at that time was riveted to its sustaining-brackets. (Tolman, Q. 47.) Moreover, this witness states that there was no opening adjacent the track, (Q. 45,) and on this point his testimony is in agreement with that of the inventor, but opposed to that of Le Roy Simpson.

It is also claimed that the evidence shows a successful test of the invention by means of a device set up in Richards's workroom. Richards testified (Q. 16) that he put up in his room a full-sized piece of track about three feet long with brackets to fit the inside of the track, hung a small door about twelve by twenty-four inches (X-Q

67) thereon, and attached a set of weights to the door. This device, he states, remained for some time, and was seen by Wheeler and D. W. Simpson. Wheeler testified (Q. 30) that he saw in Richards's room a small model consisting of a small piece of track mounted on a board, having a hanger to fit the track. He described the construction of the device no further than to say that the hanger had a block about a foot and a half long attached to it. (Qs. 30–32.) With respect to this device D. W. Simpson says:

> I first saw a mounted model in Mr. Richards's room composed of a small door about two feet wide and about a foot and a half long. The testing of the hanger and track occurred some time later. * * * This test, to which I refer, was made by attaching a door on the side of a building. (Q. 18.)

Not only does this testimony leave the question of the precise construction of the track and bracket used in this device in doubt, but it utterly fails to prove that the device was subjected to the tests necessary to constitute a reduction to practice.

It is further claimed by appellant that the testimony clearly proves that one or more brackets like " Richards's Exhibit Richards's Bracket " were actually constructed not later than the summer of 1902, and it is contended that even though it be conceded that there is not sufficient proof of an actual test of the invention the device belongs to that class of simple devices the mere making of which is sufficient to give to the inventor the benefit of an actual reduction to practice. This contention is unsound. In the first place, the original device is not produced in evidence, and the witnesses do not specifically describe the structure which they claim to have seen in 1902. The general character of their testimony is illustrated by the following questions and answers:

> Q. 7. Please look at the bracket I now hand you, marked " Richards's Exhibit Richards's Bracket," and state when you first saw a bracket of that shape and construction.
>
> A. About September 3, 1902. (Richards's Record, p. 37.)
>
> Q. 18. Did you see such bracket and track in any other place than on that shavings-shed at the time you returned from Europe, if so, please state where?
>
> A. I saw them in Mr. Richards's department; he had a number of hand-made samples around the bench, hand-made brackets. (Richards's Record, p. 38.)
>
> Q. 8. Please look at the bracket I now hand you marked " Richards's Exhibit Richards's Bracket," and state when you first saw a bracket of that form and construction, and the circumstances under which you saw it.
>
> A. I saw this style of bracket first as I recollect it, in the spring, early spring of 1903, this form of bracket, however, was shown to me by Mr. Richards being made of tin. It was shown to me in his workroom. (Richards's Record, p. 57.)
>
> > Q. 17. You have testified that you first saw a bracket of this form made of when did you first see one made of iron or steel?
> >
> > A few days later. (Richards's Record, p. 58.)

This testimony is too general in character to be accepted as proof beyond a reasonable doubt that a bracket of the same strength, size, shape, and proportion as the exhibit in evidence was made at the time stated. In the second place, it is doubtful whether or not the construction in issue belongs to that class of simple devices which require no actual test to determine their fitness to withstand commercial use. This doubt is increased by the fact that the inventor himself and the officers of the company which employed him, who had had long experience with devices of this character, deemed it necessary to test the device before placing the same on the market or applying for a patent thereon. The testimony of all the witnesses clearly shows that the device alleged to have been placed on the shavings-shed was placed there solely for the purpose of testing it and that the device alleged to have been set up in Richards's room was set up for the same purpose.

The decision of the Examiners-in-Chief is affirmed.

Ex parte Sacks.

Decided February 6, 1907.

(128 O. G., 2530.)

TRADE-MARKS—THE WORD " UNION " GEOGRAPHICAL AND DESCRIPTIVE.

>   The word " Union " refused registration as a trade-mark for heel-plates for boots and shoes on the ground that it is a geographical term, also for the reason that it is commonly used as a descriptive term to designate the goods made by members of a trade-union.

ON APPEAL.

TRADE-MARK FOR BOOTS AND SHOES.

Mr. W. P. Preble, Jr., for the applicant.

ALLEN, *Commissioner:*

This is an appeal from the action of the Examiner of Trade-Marks refusing to register the word " Union " as a trade-mark for heel-plates for boots and shoes.

The Examiner refused registration on the ground that the mark is geographical in character or indicates that the goods are union-made.

The action of the Examiner is believed to be correct.

The first definition of " Union " given in *The Century Cyclopedia of Names* is " The United States of America." The registration of appellant's mark is refused in view of the above definition, and of section 5 of the Trade-Mark Act of February 20, 1905, which provides that no mark consisting merely of " a geographical name or term, shall be registered under the terms of this act," and of the decisions of the courts holding such terms as " Columbia," (*Columbia Mill Company* v. *Alcorn*, C. D., 1893, 672; 65 O. G., 1916; 150 U. S., 460.) " Old Country " and " Our Country," (*Wrisley Company* v. *Iowa Soap Company*, 122 Fed. Rep., 796,) and " Continental " (*Continental Insurance Company* v. *Continental Fire Association*, 101 Fed. Rep., 255) to be geographical and not capable of appropriation as trade-marks.

In *Columbia Mill Company* v. *Alcorn*, *supra*, the United States Supreme Court said:

> The appellant was no more entitled to the exclusive use of the word " Columbia " as a trade-mark than he would have been to the use of the word "America," or " United States," or " Minnesota," or " Minneapolis." These merely geographical names cannot be appropriated and made the subject of an exclusive property.

The word " Union " should also be refused registration on the ground that the word is descriptive of a characteristic of the goods. The words " Union " or " Union Made " are commonly applied to goods to indicate that they are made by members of the trade-union to distinguish them from goods made by non-union workmen. As applied to heel-plates the inference would be that they are made by union labor.

That it is the practice of this Office to refuse to register the word " Union " as a trade-mark appears from the cases of *ex parte The Union Metallic Cartridge Company* (70 MS. Dec., 400) and *Martin H. Taylor*, (71 MS. Doc., 480,) where the word " Union " was refused registration as a trade-mark for cartridges and cartridge-belts and for smoking and chewing tobacco, respectively.

The decision of the Examiner of Trade-Marks is affirmed.

THE ELLISON-HARVEY CO. *v.* MONARCH.

Decided March 19, 1907.

(128 O. G., 2530.)

TRADE-MARKS—INTERFERENCE IN FACT—BULL'S HEAD AND ENTIRE BULL.

Where the registrant's mark comprised the picture of the head of a bull and the words " Doherty's Short Horn " and the applicant's mark presented for registration consisted only of a full-length picture of a bull, although the words " Old Durham Rye " appear on the label, *Held* that inasmuch as it is probable that the goods of both parties would be known as " bull " whisky interference in fact exists. (*Coleman* v. *Crump*, 70 N. Y., 573, 580, cited.)

N APPEAL.

TRADE-MARK FOR WHISKY.

Mr. Howard A. Coombs for The Ellison-Harvey Co.
Mr. Arthur E. Wallace for Richard Monarch.

ALLEN, *Commissioner:*

This is an appeal by The Ellison-Harvey Co. from the decision of the Examiner of Trade-Marks denying its motion to dissolve the interference on the ground of non-interference in fact.

Richard Monarch has registered as a trade-mark for whisky the picture of the head of a bull and the words " Doherty's Short Horn."

The Ellison-Harvey Co. shows as its trade-mark for the same goods the full-length representation of a bull.

The Examiner of Trade-Marks held that the distinguishing feature of each mark is the representation of the bull and that it is immaterial whether merely the head of the bull is shown or the full length of the bull. In my opinion the decision of the Examiner of Trade-Marks is correct.

Appellant's label contains in addition to the picture of an entire bull the words " Old Durham Rye " and other reading matter. It contends that—

goods of this character are always known by their name, and a purchaser desiring "Doherty's Short Horn" would not be misled into buying "Old Durham."

Appellant, however, has applied for the registration of a mark consisting merely of the full-length picture of a bull. Whether this picture is intended to represent a Durham bull or a short-horn bull does not appear from the mark, and it is doubtful whether an expert could tell from the representation.

In *Coleman* v. *Crump* (70 N. Y., 573, 580) an injunction was granted restraining defendant from infringing plaintiff's trade-mark consisting of the figure of a bull's head for mustard, whereby this article was known as " bull-head mustard," although there were certain points of difference between the bulls' heads used by the respective parties. In this case the court said:

Slight variations in the figure of the head, by which an expert might detect a resemblance to an animal of a different descent or breed in the simulated trade-mark from that which might be supposed to have been in the eye of the artist in designing the original, cannot avail the defense. There is a general resemblance in all the bull's heads printed and made exhibits in this action. Any difference is colorable, and would not prevent the ordinary purchaser from being deceived.

(See also *Johnson & Johnson* v. *Bauer & Black*, 82 Fed. Rep., 662, and cases therein cited.)

The fact that one mark shows merely the head of a bull while the other shows the entire bull is not thought to be material or to be a distinction which the purchasing public would appreciate. (*Corbin & Son Co.* v. *Miller, Kohlhepp, Giese & Co.,* C. D., 1902, 49; 98 O. G., 1485.) It seems probable that the goods of both parties would be known as " bull " whisky. It is believed that the use of the two marks upon the same class of goods would be likely to cause confusion in the trade and deceive purchasers.

The decision of the Examiner of Trade-Marks is affirmed.

EX PARTE L. & A. SCHARFF.

Decided April 13, 1907.

(128 O. G., 2531.)

1. TRADE-MARKS—" SPRING HILL " ANTICIPATED BY " SPRING VALLEY."

   Held that the words " Spring Hill " as a trade-mark for whisky so nearly resembles a prior registered mark which is described as a " crescent " or " new moon " and the words " Spring Valley " as to cause confusion in trade.

2. SAME—ANTICIPATION OF " TEN-YEAR " MARKS.

   The allegation of ten years' exclusive use next preceding the passage of the act of February 20, 1905, does not confer registrability upon the mark if it so nearly resembles a registered or known trade-mark owned and in use by another upon merchandise of the same descriptive properties as to be likely to cause confusion in trade.

ON APPEAL.

TRADE-MARK FOR WHISKY.

Messrs. Mason, Fenwick & Lawrence, for the applicants.

ALLEN, *Commissioner:*

This is an appeal from the action of the Examiner of Trade-Marks refusing to register the words " Spring Hill " as a trade-mark for whisky in view of a prior registration by E. Walters, June 25, 1872, No. 873, of a trade-mark the essential features of which are described as " the crescent " or " new moon " and the words " Spring Valley."

The trade-mark of the applicants is presented for registration under the ten-year proviso of the act of 1905. The allegation of ten years' exclusive use next preceding the passage of that act does not, however, confer registrability upon the mark if it so nearly resembles a registered or known trade-mark owned and in use by another and appropriated to merchandise of the same descriptive properties as to be likely to cause confusion in the mind of the public. As stated in my decision in the *International Silver Company* v. *William A. Rogers, Limited,* (C. D., 1906, 301; 124 O. G., 318:)

When the differences between marks are insignificant, trifling, or not readily stinguishable, the marks are the same for all practical purposes, and it is not reasonable to believe that the intent of the law is to register on the ground of exclusive use where practically the same mark has been used by others.

In the present case the initial word of each mark, which by virtue of its position is the most prominent feature thereof, is the same, and it is believed that the words " Hill " and " Valley " in the respective marks do not so clearly distinguish the marks that a purchaser using ordinary care would not be likely to mistake one for the other.   The fact that the representation of a crescent appears in the registered mark is immaterial, since the name " Spring Valley " is the predominating feature by which the goods would be known.

The decision of the Examiner of Trade-Marks is affirmed.

Ex parte Dodge Manufacturing Company.

Decided April 18, 1907.

(128 O. G., 2531.)

TRADE-MARKS—REPRESENTATION OF MERCHANDISE WITH MERE NAME OF AN INDIVIDUAL APPEARING THEREON—NOT REGISTRABLE.

When the trade-mark shown in the drawing comprises the representation of an ingot of bearing metal of a particular form with the name " Dodge " cast thereon and similar bars of metal are shown in prior registrations, *Held* that since the applicant can have no trade-mark in the form or appearance of the merchandise or in the mere name of an individual appearing thereon the mark is not registrable.

ON APPEAL.

TRADE-MARK FOR BABBITT OR BEARING METAL.

Mr. George E. Waldo and *Messrs. Davis & Davis* for the applicant.

ALLEN, *Commissioner:*

This is an appeal from the action of the Examiner of Trade-Marks refusing to register a trade-mark.

The mark as shown upon the applicant's drawing consists of the name " Dodge" cast upon a bar of metal of a particular form.   The Examiner calls attention to the registration of Hagenfield, No. 14,232, April 5, 1887, which shows a bar of metal of similar form to that of the applicant.   Another bar of this form is shown by the registration of the New York Smelting and Refining Company, No. 23,057, May 16, 1893.   The Examiner states in his statement upon the appeal in part as follows:

The mark claimed is the name of an individual and it is submitted that the impressing of the letters of the name on the blocks of an ingot of bearing metal in the common way in which marks are impressed on blocks of bearing metal is not a particular or distinctive display of the mark.   It is believed that the mark should not be registered as a technical trade-mark. In this connection it is noted that the name is the trade-mark and not the block of metal bearing the name. In other words, if the block of metal, which forms no part of the trade-mark, were removed from the drawing merely the name of an individual in an ordinary style of lettering would remain.

The position taken by the Examiner is correct. That the applicant can have no trade-mark in the form or appearance of the merchandise is well settled. Nothing more than this is presented for registration in this case but the name of the individual.

The action of the Examiner refusing registration is affirmed.

BARBER *v.* WOOD.

Decided January 26, 1907.

(128 O. G. 2835.)

INTERFERENCE—MOTION TO DISSOLVE—TRANSMISSION—GROUND OF PUBLIC USE.
  Public use is considered in the practice of this Office as a separate question requiring an investigation independent of the question of priority of invention involved in an interference proceedng. A motion for dissolution based upon the ground of public use should not therefore be transmitted.

APPEAL ON MOTION.

SHEET-DELIVERY MECHANISM.

Messrs. Brown & Seward and *Mr. Walter F. Rogers* for Barber.
Messrs. Southgate & Southgate for Wood.

MOORE, *Assistant Commissioner:*

This is an appeal by Barber from the decision of the Examiner of Interferences refusing to transmit his motion to dissolve so far as based on the ground of public use.

On June 30, 1906, Barber brought a motion to dissolve this interference on several of the grounds mentioned in Rule 122, also on the ground that the invention of the issue had been in public use for more than two years prior to the filing of Wood's application involved in the interference. This motion was transmitted to the Primary Examiner by the Examiner of Interferences upon all the grounds alleged except that of public use.

Public use is considered in the practice of this Office as a separate question, requiring an investigation independent of the question of priority of invention involved in an interference proceeding. (*Davis* v. *Swift*, C. D., 1901, 134; 96 O. G., 2409; *Shrum* v. *Baumgarten*, C. D., 1903, 150; 104 O. G., 577.) No testimony has been taken, and there is nothing in the case upon which the Primary Examiner at the present time can intelligently consider the bar of public use. No error is found in the refusal to transmit this ground.

Other questions are raised in appellant's brief; but they do not properly relate to the question appealed, but rather to matter embraced in appellant's petition, subsequently filed, and will be considered in disposing of said petition.

The decision of the Examiner of Interferences is affirmed.

KEITH, ERICKSON, AND ERICKSON *v.* LUNDQUIST.

Decided March 6, 1907.

(128 O. G., 2835.)

INTERFERENCE—MOTION TO TAKE TESTIMONY ABROAD—SUFFICIENCY OF SHOWING—APPEAL.

The sufficiency of a showing in support of a motion to take testimony abroad is a matter which should be left largely to the discretion of the Examiner of Interferences, and his decision granting such a motion should not be reviewed except where clear error is made to appear.

APPEAL ON MOTION.

AUTOMATIC EXCHANGE.

Mr. A. Miller Belfield for Keith, Erickson, and Erickson.
Mr. Casper L. Redfield for Lundquist.

MOORE, *Assistant Commissioner:*

This case comes up on an appeal by Lundquist from a decision of the Examiner of Interferences granting the motion of Keith, Erickson, and Erickson to take testimony abroad.

The substance of the assignments of errors is that the Examiner of Interferences erred in holding that the competency of the proposed testimony should not be decided on motion and in failing to hold the showing in support of the motion insufficient.

With respect to the first alleged error it is believed that it was not the intention of the Examiner of Interferences to decide that the competency of the proposed testimony should not be considered on motion. On the other hand, the decision indicates that he considered the proposed testimony and found that it appeared to be competent, but concluded that the question whether it was, in fact, competent should not be finally decided. The decision in this respect is believed to be correct and in accordance with Rule 158 (2).

With respect to the sufficiency of the showing in support of the motion it is believed that this is a matter which should be left largely to the discretion of the Examiner of Interferences and that his decision granting a motion to take testimony abroad should not be reviewed except where clear error is made to appear. In this case it is not made to appear that the Examiner of Interferences has waived any requirement of the rules or that error has been made in the interpretation thereof.

The decision of the Examiner of Interferences is affirmed.

TURNER *v.* MACLOSKIE.

Decided May 18, 1907.

(128 O. G., 2835.)

INTERFERENCE—MOTION FOR DISSOLUTION BASED UPON CONTINGENCY—NOT TRANSMITTED.

A motion by one party to an interference to dissolve the interference as to certain counts in case certain other counts are found to be unpatentable in view of the same references upon a motion to dissolve brought by his opponent should not be transmitted.

APPEAL ON MOTION.

AIR-BRAKE.

Mr. E. A. Wright for Turner.
Mr. Albert G. Davis for Macloskie.

MOORE, *Acting Commissioner:*

This is an appeal by Macloskie from the decision of the Examiner of Interferences refusing to transmit his motion.

Macloskie moved to dissolve on the ground that counts 1, 2, and 3 are unpatentable in view of certain patents cited in case counts 4, 5, 6, 7, and 8 are found unpatentable in view of the same patents on Turner's motion to dissolve. Macloskie states that he regards counts 1, 2, and 3 as patentable over the references cited and brought his motion merely because of Turner's motion to dissolve as to the other counts now pending before the Primary Examiner. His contention is that the patents cited are as pertinent to the one set of claims as to the other and that if the Examiner dissolves the interference as to counts 4, 5, 6, 7, and 8 on said references he should do the same with respect to counts 1, 2, and 3.

Macloskie's motion is objectionable in form in that it is based on a contingency and requires that the patentability of counts 4, 5, 6, 7, and 8 be first considered. The Examiner of Interferences properly refused to transmit the motion for this reason and also because Macloskie's motion was brought long after the limit allowed for filing such motions.

The transmission of Macloskie's motion is not believed necessary in order that his interests may be properly safeguarded. If his contention is true that the references are as applicable to one set of claims as to the other, it is to be presumed that the Examiner will take notice of the fact in considering Turner's motion to dissolve, and if in his opinion they are pertinent he will request jurisdiction under Rule 128 for the purpose of considering the patentability of counts 1, 2, and 3.

The decision of the Examiner of Interferences is affirmed.

EX PARTE MILLETT AND REED.

Decided May 23, 1907.

(128 O. G., 2836.)

RES ADJUDICATA—PRACTICE—REJECTION.

Where an application is filed the specification and claims of which the Examiner holds to be substantially the same as those of a prior application of the same party the claims of which have been declared unpatentable by the Commissioner and the courts, *Held* that the application should be examined and the claims rejected on the ground that the question of their patentability is *res adjudicata*.

ON PETITION.

PRESSURE-GAGE.

Mr. Ralph W. Foster for the applicants.

MOORE, *Acting Commissioner:*

This is a petition that the Examiner be directed to examine the application as to its merits.

The character of the present application is stated by the Examiner as follows:

The above-named application is the last of a continuous series of four applications each based upon the same subject-matter as the others and each, after the original, purporting to be a continuation of its immediate predecessor and, consequently, of the original. That each before the present one was such a continuation has not been questioned. The specification of this last application has been rewritten so as to present in a somewhat different manner from the preceding ones, the alleged difficulties that have been overcome by the applicants in making their assumed invention. * * * It is, therefore, submitted that this application is what it purports to be, a continuation of the prior ones.

The claims of the last of this series of applications prior to the present application were held to be unpatentable by the various tribunals of the Office and by the Court of Appeals of the District of Columbia. Applicants also attempted unsuccessfully to obtain the issue of a patent thereon through a bill in equity under the provisions of section 4915 of the Revised Statutes. Then the applicants filed a petition before the Commissioner of Patents to reopen their case for further prosecution under Rule 142. Said petition having been denied, applicants filed the present application on February 11, 1907.

The Primary Examiner declined to examine this latter application as to its merits unless directed to do so by the Commissioner, upon the ground that to do so would virtually nullify the Commissioner's decision refusing to reopen the prior application under Rule 142.

This rule is not considered applicable to the present case. Applicants have filed a new application with the specification and claims differing in certain respects from those of the prior application. The Examiner regards these differences as unessential. The question of whether the changes are, in fact, immaterial or whether the present application is properly a continuation of the prior application is not up for consideration upon this petition. The single question presented is what disposition should be made of the application by the Examiner under the circumstances stated and in view of the holding of the Examiner.

The Court of Appeals of the District of Columbia has held in the cases of *Barratt* (C. D., 1899, 320; 87 O. G., 1075) and *Fay* (C. D., 1900, 232; 90 O. G., 1157) that the doctrine of *res adjudicata* may be applied in the discretion of the Commissioner to new applications of the character that the Examiner finds to exist in the present case.

In his statement the Examiner says:

It is submitted that the subject-matter of the present claims has been already adjudicated upon not only by the highest tribunals of the Office but by the courts as well.

In view of this opinion the Examiner should reject the claims on the ground of *res adjudicata* in accordance with the practice set forth in *ex parte Kenney*, (C. D., 1905, 441; 118 O. G., 2253.) In this case the Commissioner stated:

It is therefore clear that this Office is justified in refusing to consider successive applications for the same subject-matter. In other words, it is not required to reëxamine the question of patentability, but may take it as settled by the first adjudication. It is not understood, however, that the ruling of the court means that the existence of the second application may be ignored. It is on file and must be disposed of in some way. It is obviously necessary to make some examination of it before it can be determined that it presents the same questions as were adjudicated in the first case. When that determination is reached, however, the Office may refuse to examine the case further and may refuse to allow it because of the previous adjudication. Such refusal to allow must be regarded as a rejection, and therefore the Examiner should state clearly and definitely that the claims are rejected.

It is believed that the applicant is entitled to a review of the Examiner's ruling by the several appellate tribunals. That review, like the Examiner's action, will be confined to the question whether the matter is *res adjudicata* and will not extend to a reconsideration of the question whether the claims cover patentable subject-matter.

Although the letter of the Examiner refusing to examine the application as to its merits for the reasons stated by him might be construed as equivalent to a rejection of the same, it is thought that the action should be in the form of a rejection on the ground that the question of the patentability of the claims is *res adjudicata* by reason of the adjudication in the prior application. (*Commissioner of Patents* v. *Whiteley*, 71 U. S. Sup. Ct., 522; *ex parte Nichols*, C. D., 1870, 71; *ex parte Le Van*, C. D., 1872, 40; 1 O. G., 226; *ex parte Arkell*, C. D., 1877, 73; 11 O. G., 1111. Having entered such an action in the case, the Examiner need not further examine the merits of the claims unless convinced that there is error in his finding or unless it is reversed on appeal.

The petition is granted to the extent indicated.

Bastian *v.* Champ.

Decided May 24, 1907.

(128 O. G., 2837.)

1. Interference—Motion to Amend Issue—Transmission of.

   Where a certified copy of a part of an application was filed under Rule 105, but later the entire case was thrown open to inspection by order of the Commissioner, *Held* to excuse delay in bringing a motion to amend under Rule 109 as to claims which were not in certified copy.

2. Same—Same—Practice.

   Where a sufficient excuse is offered for the delay in bringing a motion to amend as to certain claims thereof, *Held* that the entire motion should be transmitted, as no additional delay will be occasioned.

Appeal on Motion.

BOTTLE-FILLING MACHINE.

Mr. William O. Belt and *Messrs. Bacon & Milans* for Bastian.
Mr. Jesse B. Fay for Champ.

Moore, *Acting Commissioner:*

This is an appeal by Champ from the decision of the Examiner of Interferences transmitting Bastian's motion as a whole to amend his application by inserting six claims for the purpose of having them added as counts to the issue of the interference.

The motion is based on Rule 109 as to two of the claims and on the practice set forth in *Churchyard* v. *Douglas* v. *Cutler* (C. D., 1903, 389; 106 O. G., 2016) as to the remaining claims.

A certified copy under Rule 105 of a portion of Champ's application was originally included in the interference as declared in May, 1906; but the entire application of Champ was thrown open to the inspection of Bastian on March 19, 1907, as the result of an order of the Commissioner. The present motion was filed March 23, 1907.

It is conceded by Champ that the above facts excuse the delay in bringing the portion of the motion based on Rule 109; but he appeals from the transmission of the remainder of the motion on the ground that no satisfactory excuse has been made for the delay in filing the same. The question of the transmission of a motion filed outside of the usual time rests largely within the discretion of the Examiner of Interferences. (*Winter* v. *Slick* v. *Vollkommer*, C. D., 1901, 210; 97 O. G., 1837; *Harrison* v. *Shoemaker*, C. D., 1904, 129; 109 O. G., 2170.) The action of the Examiner is not found to involve an abuse of discretion, and it will not, therefore, be disturbed. In view of the transmission of the portion of the motion based on Rule 109 the transmission of the remainder of the motion will not occasion additional delay.

The decision of the Examiner of Interferences is affirmed.

In re Battle Creek Sanitarium Company, Limited.

Decided April 17, 1907.

(128 O. G., 2837.)

1. TRADE-MARK OPPOSITION—ALLEGATION OF USE OF MARK.

   An alleged use of the mark sought to be registered by the opposer as a part of its name and in its advertising is not a trade-mark use, and therefore forms no basis for refusing registration to the applicant.

2. SAME—AMENDMENT.

   Amendment to an opposition subsequent to the expiration of thirty days after publication will not be permitted where it would result in presenting a new ground in an opposition which is otherwise invalid.

ON APPEAL.

TRADE-MARK FOR BAKERY PRODUCTS, ETC.

Messrs. Chappel & Earl for the Battle Creek Sanitarium Company.

Mr. Fritz von Briesen for Fuller.

ALLEN, *Commissioner:*

This is an appeal by the Battle Creek Sanitarium Company, Limited, from the decision of the Examiner of Interferences sustaining the demurrer of Frank Fuller to its notice of opposition to the registration of a trade-mark.

Frank Fuller is an applicant for the registration of a trade-mark. The Battle Creek Sanitarium Company, Limited, have filed a notice of opposition to such registration. The opposition is based upon alleged use of the mark sought to be registered by the opposer as a part of its name and in its advertising. The applicant by demurrer has denied the sufficiency of such use to negative his right to registration, and his demurrer has been sustained on this ground by the Examiner of Interferences.

I am of the opinion that the position taken by the Examiner of Interferences is right. The use of a term by the opposer in advertising or as part of a corporate name is not a trade-mark use and would not form a ground for suit by the applicant upon his registration should it be granted. Section 16 of the Trade-Mark Act limits the right to sue upon the registration to those cases where the mark or an imitation thereof has been affixed by the defendant to the merchandise. The allegations of the notice of opposition in this case, if proved, would therefore form no basis for refusing registration to the applicant, and, so far as may be determined from such allegations, the registration of the mark of the applicant cannot result in legal injury to the opposer.

The opposer asks leave to amend its notice of opposition to set up use of the mark by it upon merchandise. This would be to lay a ground for opposition where at present there is none and bring the real notice of opposition after the statutory time for bringing such notices has expired. It is believed that amendment should not be permitted in such cases, and permission to do so in this case is denied.

The decision of the Examiner of Interferences sustaining the demurrer dismissing the opposition and adjudging that Frank Fuller is entitled to the registration of the mark for which he has made application *is affirmed.*

THE PETERS CARTRIDGE COMPANY *v.* THE WINCHESTER REPEATING ARMS COMPANY.

Decided June 3, 1907.

(128 O. G., 3287.)

TRADE-MARK OPPOSITION—" SELF LOADING " AS APPLIED TO CARTRIDGES A DESCRIPTIVE TERM.

  Where an applicant desires to register the words "Self Loading" as a trade-mark for cartridges adopted for use on a rifle placed upon the market by applicant and called a "self-loading" rifle from the fact that the gun reloads itself, *Held* that the words as applied to the cartridges state the purpose for which they are made and sold, that the reasons for the prohibition of the statute to the registration of marks which consist merely of descriptive matters are applicable to this case, and that the mark is, in fact, nothing more than a descriptive term.

ON APPEAL.

Messrs. Seymour & Earle for the applicant.
Messrs. Brown, Darby & Hopkins for The Peters Cartridge Company.

MOORE, *Commissioner:*

This is an appeal by The Winchester Repeating Arms Company from the decision of the Examiner of Interferences sustaining the opposition to its registration brought by The Peters Cartridge Company.

The applicant seeks to register the words " Self Loading " as a trade-mark for cartridges. The opposer contends that these words should not be registered, on the ground that they are descriptive. It appears that the applicant has placed upon the market a rifle which is called a " self-loading " rifle, which words are descriptive of the performance of the gun in reloading itself. The trade-mark registration sought here is intended to cover the use of these words in connection with cartridges adapted for use with that rifle. These words when so applied obviously tell to those in the trade and those using such goods the purpose for which they are made and sold. They convey this information in a simple and direct manner by the use of ordinary words. The reasons for the prohibition of the statute to the registration of marks which consist merely of descriptive matter are all applicable to this case, and it is believed that the mark is, in fact, nothing more than a clearly descriptive term. *The Circular Loom Case* (*post*, 452; 127 O. G., 393, court of appeals,) is entirely pertinent. The mark in that case told nothing about the goods except that they were made upon a particular kind of a machine. The statement of the kind of a machine with which the goods are to be used in this case is descriptive in the same manner, and as much so.

Appellant's contention that the opposer has not made out a case of probable injury is immaterial. The statute prohibits registration of a mark which consists merely of a descriptive term. The Examiner of Interferences has found that the applicant's mark is such a term, and I am of the opinion that this conclusion is right. No registration can be had upon the appellant's application, therefore, unless this conclusion is reversed upon appeal.

The decision of the Examiner of Interferences adjudging that the applicant is not entitled to registration *is affirmed.*

Ex parte Doebler.

APPLICATION FOR PATENT.

Decided June 12, 1907.

(128 O. G., 3287.)

INTERFERENCE—SUGGESTION OF CLAIMS UNDER RULE 96—PRACTICE—INVENTOR AND ASSIGNEES PERSONALLY NOTIFIED.

In all cases where claims are suggested for the purpose of interference under the provisions of Rule 96 copies of the letter containing the suggested claims will be sent to the applicant and to the assignees, if the invention is assigned, as well as to the attorney of record.

ON REFERENCE.

DRILL-CHUCK.

Mr. Harrie E. Hart for the applicant.

MOORE, *Commissioner:*

This case has been referred to me by the Examiner for instructions as to whether personal notice should be given to the applicant, as well as to his attorney of record, of certain claims which are to be suggested to him under the provisions of Rule 96.

It appears from a communication in this case from the attorney of record that he has received letters in two other cases in which he is attorney for the inventors in which the same claims are suggested. He states that these three applications are the property of a single corporation and that he wishes to be advised whether there is a fourth party to the prospective interference, so that he—

may arrange the three applications in order not to conflict with one another.

While there appears to be no reason to doubt the statement of the attorney that these three applications are owned by the same corporation, there are no assignments of record in this Office in two of said applications.

Rule 97 provides that—

Whenever it shall be found that two or more parties whose interests are in conflict are represented by the same attorney, the Examiner will notify each of said principal parties, and also the attorney of the fact.

The reasons upon which this rule is based equally warrant the notification of the principal parties of claims which are suggested in applications of different inventors who are represented by the same attorney.

In view of the fact that under the provisions of Rule 96 the failure or refusal to make claims which are suggested for the purpose of interference within the time specified acts as a disclaimer of the invention covered by such claims it is believed that notification of suggested claims should be given to all parties of interest of record in the application.

Rule 107 provides that—

An applicant involved in an interference may, with the written consent of the assignee, when there has been an assignment, before the date fixed for the filing of his preliminary statement (see Rule 110,) in order to avoid the continuance of the interference, disclaim under his own signature, attested by two witnesses, the invention of the particular matter in issue, and upon such disclaimer and the cancelation of any claims involving such interfering matter judgment shall be rendered against him, and a copy of the disclaimer shall be embodied in and form part of his specification. (See Rule 182.)

While it is not deemed expedient to require the same formality of disclaimer to avoid an interference in respect to suggested claims as to claims already incorporated in a party's application or to require an applicant to personally sign an amendment incorporating suggested claims into his application it is believed that in all cases the applicant and his assignees, if the invention is assigned, should be personally notified of suggested claims. The Examiner will therefore send copies of the letter suggesting claims to the applicant and to the assignees, as well as to the attorney of record in each case, and this practice will be followed in all cases where claims are suggested for the purpose of interference under the provisions of Rule 96.

O'BRIEN *v.* GALE, SR., *v.* MILLER *v.* ZIMMER *v.* CALDERWOOD.

Decided June 17, 1907.

(128 O. G., 3288.)

1. INTERFERENCE—MOTIONS FOR DISSOLUTION—SETTING LIMIT OF APPEAL—PRACTICE.

Where the decision of the Examiner upon motions for dissolution includes an adverse decision upon the merits of a party's case which is subject to reconsideration under the provisions of Rule 124, no limit of appeal should be set in any of the motions until the decision is rendered upon the rehearing.

2. SAME—SAME—HEARING OF APPEALS BY COMMISSIONER.

Where appeals are taken from the decision of the Examiner upon motions for dissolution both to the Commissioner and to the Examiners-in-Chief, action upon the appeal to the Commissioner will be suspended until after the decision of the Examiners-in-Chief is rendered, in order that all appeals upon the motions may be considered at the same time. Where the Examiner upon the rehearing entirely dissolves the interference the question of irregularity in declaration of the interference, becomes a moot question and will not be entertained unless the decision dissolving the interference is reversed on appeal.

APPEAL ON MOTION.

CURRENT-CONTROLLING APPARATUS.

Mr. Robert Watson for O'Brien.
Messrs. Brown & Darby and *Mr. C. M. Nissen* for Gale, Sr.
Messrs. Jones & Addington and *Mr. E. B. H. Tower, Jr.*, for Miller.
Mr. Albert G. Davis for Zimmer. (*Mr. Robert H. Read* and *Mr.*
Frank J. Seabolt of counsel.)
Mr. G. F. De Wein for Calderwood.

MOORE, *Commissioner:*

This is an appeal by O'Brien from the decision of the Primary
Examiner denying his motion to dissolve the interference on the
ground of informality in declaring the same.

The record shows that O'Brien's motion to dissolve the interference
is based on each of the grounds specified in Rule 122. A decision on
this motion, as well as on motions to dissolve by Zimmer and Miller,
two other parties to this interference, was rendered by the Primary
Examiner on April 4, 1907. The motion by O'Brien to dissolve was
denied; but the other motions to dissolve were granted in part, and
the interference, at least as to the party Calderwood, was dissolved
on grounds relating to the merits. In the decision on each motion
April 25, 1907, was fixed by the Examiner as the limit of appeal. On
April 13 the Primary Examiner set May 1, 1907, as the date for rehearing the motions of Zimmer and Miller, in conformity to the provisions of Rule 124, and set aside the limit of appeal previously fixed
from the decisions on these motions. O'Brien, however, filed this
appeal to the Commissioner from the refusal of the Examiner to dissolve the interference on the ground of informality in its déclaration,
which appeal also came on for hearing on May 1, 1907. Final decisions following the rehearing on the motions of Zimmer and Miller
have not as yet been rendered by the Primary Examiner.

While the Examiner did not set aside the limit of appeal, April
25, 1907, fixed in his decision on O'Brien's motion, and O'Brien,
therefore, had to take his appeal to the Commissioner within the
time fixed in order to save his right of appeal, it is thought that the
Primary Examiner should have also set aside the limit of appeal on
O'Brien's motion, so that all the appeals could go forward at the
same time. It is considered the proper practice where a time is fixed
for reconsideration under Rule 124 to set no limit of appeal on any
of the motions for dissolution until the decision is rendered on the
rehearing. Otherwise the appeals will be taken piecemeal, although
ordinarily no material advance can be made in the interference until
all the motions for dissolution have been finally disposed of by the
Primary Examiner.

In the present case while O'Brien's motion is not set for rehearing the decision already rendered by the Primary Examiner on his motion may be affected by the final decision of the said Examiner on the other motions. Furthermore, Miller has also alleged in his motion to dissolve irregularity in the declaration of the interference, and it is possible an appeal may be taken to the Commissioner from the Examiner's decision on this ground of Miller's motion. Obviously the appeals on this ground should be considered together, and not piecemeal. Again, in case the Primary Examiner on the rehearing should entirely dissolve the interference the question appealed would become a moot question. Under the practice announced in *Story* v. *Criswell,* (C. D., 1902, 262; 100 O. G., 683,) *Fickinger and Blake* v. *Hulett* (C. D., 1904, 360; 111 O. G., 2492,) and *Newell* v. *Hubbard* (C. D., 1905, 128; 115 O. G., 1847) an appeal on the question of irregularity in the declaration of the interference will not be entertained and determined unless a decision dissolving the interference is reversed on appeal.

For the reason stated above action on this appeal is suspended until the question of dissolution of the interference on grounds relating to the merits is determined. In case the Examiners-in-Chief should sustain a decision of the Primary Examiner dissolving the interference and an appeal be taken to this tribunal both appeals on the question of dissolution will be considered at the same time.

IN RE COMMERCIAL MICA COMPANY.

Decided March 30, 1907.

(129 O. G., 479.)

1. COPIES OF ABANDONED APPLICATION—APPLICATION REFERRED TO IN PATENT.
   A reference in a patent to an application is not sufficient to justify allowing copies of the application to be made where the reference is not of such a nature as to indicate that it was relied on for any purpose in the proceeding eventuating in the patent.

2. SAME—SAME—CERTIFICATE OF COURT.
   Petition to have such copies made denied in the absence of a certificate of the court before whom the suit is pending.

3. SAME—SAME—NOTICE TO APPLICANT OR ASSIGNEE.
   Where an application has been abandoned a long time, notice of the petition to inspect should be given to the owner of the invention, whether applicant or assignee.

Mr. Walter Groesbeck for the Commercial Mica Company.
Mr. E. P. Thompson for Dyer.

MOORE, *Acting Commissioner:*

This is a petition by the Commercial Mica Company for permission to inspect and be furnished with copies of the abandoned application Serial No. 435,217 of Arthur H. S. Dyer.

The petition is denied for the following reasons.

First. The reference by Dyer in his Patent No. 483,646 to his application is not of such a nature as to indicate that it was relied upon for any purpose in the proceeding eventuating in the patent or to indicate a waiver by Dyer of his right of secrecy concerning said application.

Second. The petition is not accompanied, as required in such cases, by the certificate of the court before whom suit is pending. (*Ex parte Heard*, C. D., 1905, 66; 114 O. G., 2381; *ex parte Brown*, C. D., 1905, 75; 115 O. G., 248.)

Third. No service was made upon the assignee of the abandoned application. Where the application has been abandoned for a long time, service upon the attorney of record is not deemed sufficient. It does not appear that said attorney is at present in any way connected with the assignee or that the notice to the attorney ever reached the assignee. In a case of this kind it is thought that service should be made upon the owner of the invention, whether applicant or assignee, for the same reason that Rule 103 requires in case of a patent notices of interference to be forwarded to the patentee and assignee, as well as to the attorney of record. Whether the owner of the invention of the abandoned application enters objection is a material factor in considering the petition.

The petition is denied without prejudice.

BOMHARD *v*. THE UNITED STATES GRAPHITE COMPANY.

Decided April 9, 1907.

(129 O. G., 479.)

1. TRADE-MARKS—OPPOSITION—HEARINGS—MOTION TO POSTPONE.

A hearing will not be postponed because hearings before two tribunals of the Office were set for the same hour. The hearing before one tribunal can be easily arranged to follow the termination of the hearing before the other.

2. SAME—SAME—ISSUING ORDER TO SHOW CAUSE—PRACTICE.

Order to show cause properly issued without setting the case down for a hearing.

3. SAME—SAME—SAME—REFUSED TO EXTEND TIME FOR.

A decision of the Examiner of Interferences denying a motion to extend time to show cause will not be reversed in the absence of a clear showing of abuse of discretion.

APPEAL ON MOTION.

ON PETITION.

ON MOTION.

TRADE-MARK FOR STOVE-POLISH.

Mr. George W. Colles for Bomhard.
Mr. George B. Willcox for The United States Graphite Company.

MOORE, *Assistant Commissioner:*

This case comes before me upon an appeal by Bomhard from the decision of the Examiner of Interferences denying his motion for an extension of time in which to show cause why his opposition should not be dismissed: upon a petition by Bomhard to set aside the decision of the Examiner of Interferences dismissing the opposition and to reinstate the opposition proceedings; also, on a motion by Bomhard to postpone the hearings on the above matters.

Considering, first, the motion to postpone the hearings before the Commissioner, all of the above matters were set down for hearing on March 28, 1907, at ten a. m. In support of his motion Bomhard states that a motion before the Examiner of Interferences was also set for hearing on the same day and at the same hour, that hearings before two different tribunals could not be heard at the same time, and that the notice setting the hearings is therefore irregular and void. This showing is entirely inadequate as a basis for granting the motion. Where a hearing is set for a certain hour, it merely means that the matter will be heard at that time or as soon thereafter as it may be reached on the docket. It is not an uncommon practice in this Office for matters to be set for hearings before various tribunals at the same time. Many attorneys from a distance desire such an arrangement so that several matters may be disposed of on the same trip. In such a case it is easily arranged to have the hearing before one tribunal follow the termination of the hearing before another tribunal.

Bomhard has made no showing of circumstances which rendered it impossible for him to attend the hearing at the time fixed or to prepare his case properly for hearing at that time. Bomhard's opponent found the time ample for him to be represented at the hearing and to file a brief. This motion is denied.

Bomhard contends that the action of the Examiner of Interferences in issuing the order to show cause why the opposition should not be dismissed upon the *ex parte* request of the applicant for registration and without any formal motion or opportunity for him to be heard was irregular. This contention is without merit. The order of the Examiner of Interferences of August 10, 1906, merely suspended proceedings in the opposition cause until the final determination of the pending interference No. 26,203 between the same parties. Said interference having been finally disposed of by the decision of the Commissioner on January 10, 1907, it was the duty of the Examiner of Interferences to take up the opposition proceedings again without waiting for the parties to bring the matter to his attention.

The practice concerning an order to show cause is indicated in the Commissioner's decision in *McHarg* v. *Schmidt and Mayland*, (C. D., 1903, 378; 106 O. G., 1780,) which states:

> If there were good reasons why judgment should not have been rendered against McHarg on the question of priority under Rule 119, he should have brought them forward in answer to the order to show cause. If he was dissatisfied with the judgment which was rendered, his remedy was by an appeal from the judgment. He cannot have that judgment reviewed on appeal from the order to show cause.

No error is found in this action of the Examiner of Interferences, and the petition *is therefore denied.*

It remains to consider Bomhard's appeal from the decision of the Examiner of Interferences denying his motion for an extension of time in which to show cause why his opposition should not be dismissed. Appellant contends that the Examiner erred in setting an unreasonably short time in which to make said showing. Although the order to show cause was issued on February 1, 1907, appellant has not as yet filed his showing. His failure to take action within the time set appears to have been merely a matter of business convenience.

I find no abuse of discretion on the part of the Examiner of Interferences in refusing the extension of time.

The decision of the Examiner of Interferences refusing an extension of time *is therefore affirmed.* As heretofore stated, Bomhard's *motion and petition are denied.*

PYM *v.* HADAWAY.

Decided May 1¼, 1907.

(129 O. G., 480.)

INTERFERENCE—RIGHT TO MAKE CLAIM—TESTIMONY UNDER RULE 130—PRIMA FACIE SHOWING OF AGGREGATION—EXPERT AFFIDAVITS NOT ACCEPTED.

Where motion is made for leave to take testimony under the provisions of Rule 130 to establish that the claim as applied to one party's structure is a true combination, while as applied to the other party's structure is merely for an aggregation, affidavits in support of such motion which consist wholly of the opinion of expert patent lawyers as to the legal effect of the claims will not be received.

APPEAL ON MOTION.

TACK-PULLER AND NAIL-DRIVER.

Messrs. Parker & Burton and *Mr. George H. Maxwell* for Pym.
Mr. Benjamin Phillips and *Messrs. Phillips, Van Everen & Fish* for Hadaway.

MOORE, *Acting Commissioner:*

This is an appeal from the decision of the Examiner of Interferences denying a motion by Pym to set aside his decision of priority rendered under the provision of Rule 114 and to issue an order setting times for Pym to take testimony relative to Hadaway's right to make the claims an issue. He desires to prove a certain commonly-used hand method of removing lasting-tacks and driving stay-tacks and also to establish by expert testimony that in view of this hand method the mechanism shown in Hadaway's application is in fact and in law an aggregation of old devices so far as the issue of this interference is concerned.

The motion is supported by certain affidavits of Clark, Arnold, Everson, and Cushman, which the Examiner of Interferences found to be insufficient to establish a *prima facie* case which would warrant the issuance of an order for the taking of testimony to show that the Hadaway application discloses only an aggregation of elements or devices.

In a decision of the Commissioner in this case rendered September 18, 1906, it is said that—

In the cases of *Lowry and Cowley* v. *Spoon* (C. D., 1906, 224; 122 O. G., 2087) and *Brown* v. *Stroud* (C. D., 1906, 226; 122 O. G., 2688) it was decided that where a party makes a reasonable showing before the Examiner of Interferences of inoperativeness of his opponent's device and that showing does not extend to his own structure he may be permitted to take testimony, provided that the proposed testimony is of a character to justify such action. No reason appears for making any distinction between a case where a party alleges that his opponent's device is inoperative and one where it is contended that the opponent has no right to make the claim in issue.

The Commissioner, however, held that such testimony should be permitted only under the provisions of Rule 130 after a motion for dissolution based upon this ground had been prosecuted before the Primary Examiner. The record shows that such a motion by Pym was duly considered by the Primary Examiner, who held—

that Hadaway discloses a machine in which the elements combined in the sense of a patentable combination to the accomplishment of a step in the manufacture of shoes never performed by a machine prior to the dates of the applications of Pym and Hadaway in this interference, so far as this record shows.

The question presented upon this appeal is whether there is a sufficient showing presented in support of the motion to warrant the taking of testimony to establish facts which would justify a contrary conclusion to that expressed by the Examiner. The affidavits of

Clark, Arnold, and Everson relate merely to the use of a hand-tool for withdrawing lasting-tacks and driving stay-tacks where necessary, which has been employed for many years.

The only apparent bearing that testimony concerning this alleged fact may have upon the issue is to show that the operations of pulling the lasting-tacks and driving the stay-tacks are separate operations, and it would seem that any objection of this character which would operate against Hadaway's claims would apply with equal force to the same claims of Pym's application.

The affidavit of the expert Cushman sets forth no facts which do not appear upon the face of the applications of the opposing parties. It is mainly a statement of reasons why in the opinion of the affiant Hadaway's claims cover aggregations of old devices and not true combinations. Whether a claim covers an aggregation or a combination of elements is a question of law which the tribunals of this Office are specially qualified to determine. The Office cannot delegate the interpretation of the legal character of the claims of an application to experts employed by the opposing parties. It is believed that testimony consisting wholly of the opinion of expert patent lawyers as to the legal effect of claims should not be received. The purpose of allowing a party to present testimony in support of his denial of his opponent's right to make the claims in issue is solely to permit the presentation of facts bearing upon this question which are not accessible to the officials of this Office. The determination of the legal bearing of such facts rests upon the officials of this Office.

I do not find in the affidavits in support of Pym's invention any *prima facie* showing of facts adverse to the right of Hadaway to make the claims in issue and not applicable to the claims made by Pym which would warrant the production of testimony upon this question.

The decision of the Examiner of Interferences is affirmed.

Ex parte WALKER.

Decided May 18, 1907.

(129 O. G., 481.)

FINAL REJECTION—PREMATURE.

In response to an action by an applicant canceling two rejected claims and substituting claims therefor, accompanied by an argument setting forth how the substitute claims distinguished from the references, the Examiner rejected the substitute claims, stating that "there is no invention in applicant's device over the art cited." Thereupon the applicant asked for an explanation of the grounds of rejection, distinctly stating that he was not asking for a reconsideration, in response to which the Examiner explained the references and finally rejected the claims. *Held* that the final rejection was premature. While the Examiner contended that the substitue claims were substantially the same as previous claims with respect to which the references had been explained, the Examiner did not finally reject the claims on the first action nor did he refuse the request for explanation on the ground that the pertinency of the references had been previously explained.

ON PETITION.

COMBINATION OFFICE APPLIANCE.

Mr. David N. Harper and *Mr. George E. Kirk* for the applicant.

MOORE, *Acting Commissioner:*

This is a petition that the Examiner be directed that the final rejection of April 16, 1907, was premature and that the amendment of April 22, 1907, should be entered and considered on its merits.

On April 1, 1907, applicant canceled the rejected claims, presented two substitute claims, and pointed out wherein he regarded these claims as avoiding the references. In his action on this amendment the Examiner rejected the claims on the reference of record and stated that—

In the opinion of the examiner there is no invention in applicant's device over the art cited.

In response to this action applicant requested the Examiner to point out the pertinency of the reference and explain the ground of rejection, and he expressly stated that his letter was not a request for reconsideration. He referred to his argument filed with the claims in his former action setting forth the alleged novelty over the reference. In reply the Examiner explained the pertinency of the reference and finally rejected the claims. Applicant claims that the final rejection was premature and filed an amendment, which the Examiner refused to enter.

The Examiner contends that the substitute claims are substantially the same as the former claims with respect to which the pertinency of the reference had been explained; but it is noted that he did not finally reject the new claims in the first action thereon. In his action of April 16, 1907, the Examiner did not refuse the request on the ground that the pertinency of the reference had been explained; but by coupling his explanation with a final rejection he rendered the information of no avail to the applicant except through petition. The letter of the applicant is of the character referred to in *ex parte Wainwright*, (C. D., 1906, 495; 125 O. G., 2047,) *ex parte Fowler, Jr.*, (*ante*, 88; 127 O. G., 1578,) and *ex parte Lincoln*, (*ante*, 117; 127 O. G., 3216,) rather than that mentioned in the case of *ex parte Almy* (C. D., 1905, 125; 115 O. G., 1584,) cited by the Examiner, and the Examiner should not have finally rejected the claims in his response thereto. Applicant is prosecuting the case with great diligence, and although the Examiner has stated that in his opinion there is no novelty in the device it is possible that applicant wishes to amend his claims in order to distinguish more clearly from the reference or to present them in better form on appeal.

The final rejection is thought to have been premature, and *the petition is accordingly granted.*

IN RE THE NATIONAL RAILWAY MATERIALS COMPANY.

Decided May 23, 1907.

(129 O. G., 481.)

1. INTERFERENCE—INTERVENTION BY EXCLUSIVE LICENSEE.

   An exclusive licensee of an invention will not be permitted to intervene in the prosecution of an interference so long as the interference is being prosecuted in good faith by his licensor.

2. SAME—SAME—ACCESS TO RECORDS.

   Where it appears that the inventor has entered the employment of a company which is the assignee of his opponent in an interference proceeding, the exclusive licensee of said inventor will, upon request, be furnished with copies of all notices in the interference and papers accompanying the same, including the preliminary statements, when approved, and the notices for taking testimony, and will also be permitted to be present at all proceedings in the interference.

ON PETITION.

Messrs. Chamberlin & Wilkinson for Smith.
Mr. Russell M. Everett and *Messrs. Bacon & Milans* for Allen.
Messrs. Davis & Davis for the petitioner.

MOORE, *Acting Commissioner:*

This is a petition by The National Railway Materials Company for leave to intervene and contest the interference *Smith v. Allen* in behalf of John H. Allen's application.

It appears from an affidavit by Hall, the president of The National Railway Materials Company, that Allen gave to this company an exclusive license to manufacture and sell railway offset joints in accordance with the invention set forth in his application involved in this interference. A paper purporting to be a copy of the license accompanies the petition, and its authenticity is not denied by Allen. By the terms of this agreement the licensee is empowered—

* * * to the exclusion of all others to manufacture and sell within the United States railway joints embodying the said invention of the party of the first part (Allen) and to receive all the profits and advantages of such manufacture and sale, as hereinafter named to the end of the term of the patent for which Letters Patent will be granted.

The license also contains the following provision:

V. It is understood and agreed between the parties hereto that the party of the first part is to thoroughly protect party of the second part in all rights to the patent herein mentioned against any action in law or interference on the part of others by giving testimony favorable to the party of the second part and such assistance as the case may require.

It appears that because of a default in payment of certain royalties Allen has notified his licensee that this license stands revoked. The Office cannot undertake to determine the rights of parties under their contracts, and inasmuch as the mere non-payment of royalties when due is insufficient in the absence of an express agreement to cause the annulment of the license (*New York Phonograph Co.* v. *Edison et al.*, 136 Fed. Rep., 600; *Wagner Typewriter Co.* v. *Watkins*, 84 Fed. Rep., 62; *Consolidated Middlings Purifier Co.* v. *Wolf et al.*, C. D., 1886, 461; 37 O. G., 567; 28 Fed. Rep., 814) the validity of this license, the terms of which are not denied, will not now be questioned.

It is alleged that since granting this license Allen has become an employee of the Quincy Manchester Sargent Company, a competitor of the petitioner company, which also employs the opposing party, Smith, and it is stated that in the affiant's belief this interference proceeding has been resorted to by Allen and Smith in an effort to deprive Allen's licensee of its rights under the agreement with Allen, above referred to.

Hall further avers that Allen, under the coercion of his employer, the Quincy Manchester Sargent Company, has declined to permit his licensee, The National Railway Materials Company, to prosecute this interference or to be represented therein by counsel.

It has been the uniform practice of this Office to decline to permit any person other than the assignee of the entire interest of an invention to prosecute an application or an interference to the exclusion of the applicant. (*Reiner* v. *Macphail*, C. D., 1899, 196; 89 O. G., 521; *ex parte McTammany*, C. D., 1900, 168; 93 O. G., 751; *ex parte Sandstrom*, C. D., 1904, 486; 113 O. G., 850; *ex parte Hertford*, C. D., 1904, 487; 113 O. G., 851;) but the equitable assignees have been permitted to inspect and to obtain copies of the applications of their assignors. There appears to be no reason for departing from this practice in the present instance. The records show that preliminary statements have been filed by both parties within the period allowed by this Office, and the proceedings have, to the present time, progressed in a regular manner. I am of the opinion, therefore, that under the circumstances of this case The National Railway Materials Company should not be permitted to intervene in the prosecution of the interference, but that it is entitled to be kept fully informed of the status of the interference. In the case of *Reiner* v. *Macphail*, *supra,* the equitable owner of an application was permitted access to the records of the interference where the assignor had refused to defend the interference. The reasons for permitting Allen's licensee to be kept fully informed of the status of the present interference appears to be equally well founded.

This petition is opposed by Allen upon the ground that a licensee is not an equitable owner of the application and is therefore not entitled to be heard. While a licensee is not permitted to prosecute a suit in equity in his own name against a third party for infringement, it is well settled that a licensee of an exclusive right may join the patentee as a co-complainant whether the patentee is willing or unwilling. (*Birdsell* v. *Shaliol,* C. D., 1885, 126; 30 O. G., 261; 112 U. S., 485; *Littlefield* v. *Perry,* 7 O. G., 964; 21 Wall., 205; *Paper Bag Machine Cases,* C. D. 1882, 197; 21 O. G., 1275; 105 U. S., 766; *Brush Electric Company* v. *California Electric Light Company,* 52 Fed. Rep., 945; *Excelsior Wooden Pipe Company* v. *City of Seattle,* 117 Fed. Rep., 140.) It is therefore believed that a licensee having an exclusive right has such an equitable interest in the application of his licensor as entitles him to knowledge of the steps taken in the prosecution of an interference, especially where it appears that the licensor by reason of his position is likely not to make a *bona fide* contest of the interference.

In view of the facts stated it is directed that the attorneys for The National Railway Materials Company be furnished, upon their request, copies of all notices in the interference and papers accompanying the same, including the preliminary statements, when approved, and the notices for taking testimony, and that they be permitted to be present at all proceedings in the interference. If in the future conduct of the interference any evidence of collusion shall appear, leave is given to renew this petition.

In view of the fact that Allen has already filed his preliminary statement the petitioner's request that the times for filing preliminary statements be extended thirty days is denied.

The petition is granted to the extent indicated.

Ex parte Floyd.

APPLICATION FOR PATENT.

Decided June 8, 1907.

(129 O. G., 482.)

JURISDICTION OF EXAMINERS-IN-CHIEF.

> Cases are considered to be "pending before" the Examiners-in-Chief for the purpose of entertaining a motion for rehearing (Rule 142) until the expiration of the statutory period or specified limit of appeal or until such appeal shall have been taken.

On Request.

SPRING-PLANK SEAT FOR CAR-TRUCKS.

Messrs. Offield, Towle & Linthicum for the applicant.

BILLINGS, *Assistant Commissioner:*

This is a request by the Board of Examiners-in-Chief that jurisdiction of this case be restored to them for the purpose of including in a recommendation heretofore made a certain proposed claim.

This request is approved.

Hereafter cases will be considered to be " pending before " the Examiners-in-Chief for the purpose of entertaining a motion for rehearing (Rule 142) until the expiration of the statutory or specified limit of appeal or until such appeal shall have been taken.

THE PERFECT SAFETY PAPER COMPANY *v.* GEORGE LA MONTE & SON.

Decided May 24, 1907.

(129 O. G., 869.)

TRADE-MARKS—OPPOSITION—QUALIFIED WITHDRAWAL OF APPLICATION NOT ACCEPTED.

Where in an opposition proceeding the applicant for registration files a withdrawal of its application which purports to merely withdraw or abandon the present application and does not abandon its claim to the trademark involved or to the right to registration of the mark, it will not be accepted. The applicant will not be permitted by such a withdrawal to escape judgment in an opposition proceeding and at the same time reserve the determination of the questions involved for whatsoever time it may feel inclined to raise the same

APPEAL ON MOTION.

TRADE-MARK FOR WRITING AND PRINTING PAPER.

Messrs. Dyrenforth, Dyrenforth, Lee & Wiles for The Perfect Safety Paper Co.

Messrs. Kenyon & Kenyon for George La Monte & Son.

MOORE, *Acting Commissioner:*

This is an appeal by the applicants from the decision of the Examiner of Interferences sustaining the opposition.

The decision of the Examiner of Interferences sets forth the facts of the case as follows:

This is a motion by George La Monte & Son that the above-entitled cause be dismissed, for the reason that the applicant, George La Monte & Son, has filed formal notice of withdrawal or abandonment of the application herein involved. In the letter of abandonment of the application the following statement appears:

"The applicant states, however, that it merely withdraws or abandons the present application, and does not abandon its claim to the said trade-mark here involved, or to the right of registration of said mark."

The opposer objects to any action taken in this case which would preclude its opposition from taking effect, should renewed application be made for registration of the mark under the general provisions of the law, either by amendment of the present application or by the filing of a new application.

It is believed that the facts set forth justify the action taken. Any other course would permit any applicant in an opposition proceeding to escape judgment in due course and at the same time reserve the determination of the questions involved for whatsoever time he may feel inclined to raise the same. There seems to be no good reason why such a course should be permitted.

The decision of the Examiner of Interferences is affirmed.

BECKER *v.* OTIS.

PATENT INTERFERENCE.

Decided June 11, 1907.

(129 O. G., 1267.)

INTERFERENCE—MOTION TO TRANSMIT MOTION TO AMEND—DELAY.

Where the Primary Examiner refused to dissolve an interference on the ground that the senior party had no right to make the claims, but the Examiner of Interferences under Rule 130 decided that he had no right to make the claims, *Held* that this state of facts was sufficient to excuse delay in bringing a motion to amend the 'issue under the practice announced in *Churchward* v. *Douglas* v. *Cutler*, (C. D., 1903, 389; 106 O. G., 2016,) especially in view of the recent decisions of the court of appeals in *Blackford* v. *Wilder* (*post*, 491; 127 O. G., 1255) and *Horine* v. *Wende* (*post*, 615; 129 O. G., 2858.)

APPEAL ON MOTION.

DUMP-CAR.

Mr. Henry A. Seymour for Becker.

Mr. Thomas F. Sheridan for Otis. (*Mr. George L. Wilkinson* and *Mr. Walter A. Scott* of counsel.)

MOORE, *Commissioner:*

This is an appeal by Otis from the decision of the Examiner of Interferences refusing to transmit to the Primary Examiner a motion to add certain counts to the issue on the ground that no showing was made why the claims were not earlier presented.

The record shows that the interference was declared in May, 1906. The dates set up in Becker's preliminary statement failed to overcome the filing date of the Otis application, and Becker was ordered

of C. D. De Koning Tilly. Subsequently Tilly filed application Serial No. 25,859, which was added to the interference. The mark of the Holland Medicine Company consists of the portrait of Claes Tilly in an oval frame, under which is the name " Claes Tilly " and the figures " 1696." The mark of the earlier application of Tilly is composite in nature and shows, among other features, portraits of seven individuals, including that of Claes Tilly, also the figures "1696." The later application of Tilly consists merely of the portrait of Claes Tilly in an oval frame. The motion does not seek to dissolve the interference as to the application of the Holland Medicine Company and the later application of Tilly.

The Examiner of Trade-Marks held that the marks of the application of the Holland Medicine Company and the earlier application of Tilly so closely resemble each other by reason of the common features of the Claes Tilly portrait and the figures " 1696 " as to be likely to cause the public to mistake one mark for the other and to permit the goods of one applicant to be palmed off for the goods of the other.

I am of the opinion that the decision of the Examiner of Trade-Marks is correct and that the prominence of the portrait and the figures " 1696," constituting the main features of the Holland Medicine Company's mark, in the composite mark of the earlier Tilly application is likely to cause confusion and to enable the goods of one concern to be substituted for those of the other. The question, however, is not free from doubt, but is one upon which the testimony in the interference may throw additional light. Moreover, the interference must at any event be continued as to the application of the Holland Medicine Company and the later application of Tilly. Should the evidence taken in the interference proceeding establish, in the opinion of the Examiner of Interferences, the fact that no interference exists or that there has been irregularity in declaring the same, he may direct attention to the fact under Rule 48.

The decision of the Examiner of Trade-Marks is affirmed.

PEAK *v.* BRUSH.

PATENT INTERFERENCE.

Decided July 5, 1907.

(129 O. G., 1268.)

INTERFERENCE—TESTIMONY—PRINTING.

The fact that only one party has taken testimony constitutes no sufficient reason for excusing him from printing the same.

ON PETITION.

GUN.

Mr. J. L. Atkins for Peak.
Mr. N. S. Wright and *Mr. G. C. Shoemaker* for Brush.

BILLINGS, *Assistant Commissioner:*

This is a petition by Peak, the junior party to the above-entitled interference, that he be excused from printing his testimony. The grounds of the petition are that Peak is the junior party by less than a month, and consequently was obliged to take testimony. The senior party took no testimony.

Peak's counsel wishes to conduct the case with as little expense as possible to his client.

The rules regarding the printing of testimony are clear and specific, and in the interests of good practice they must be enforced. The rules only provide for excusing a party from printing his testimony where that party makes a satisfactory showing of poverty. There is no such allegation in this case. While the Office would like to take any action consistent with good practice to relieve applicants from expense, it is very clear that to make an exception to this rule would be equivalent to abrogating the same. It is essential for obvious reasons that parties be required to print their testimony unless they are in fact too poor to do so.

The practice of the Office will not admit of the grant of this petition. *It is therefore denied.*

HORNE *v.* SOMERS & COMPANY.

Decided November 27, 1906.

(129 O. G., 1609.)

1. TRADE-MARKS—INTERFERENCE—PRACTICE.
   The question of interference in fact will not be considered upon an appeal on priority.

2. SAME—SAME—USE OF MARK IN INTERSTATE COMMERCE.
   Continuous use of mark in interstate commerce not necessary to entitle applicant to register the mark.

3. SAME—SAME—INTERFERENCE BETWEEN APPLICANT AND REGISTRANT.
   The fact that one of the parties is a registrant does not necessarily create a bar to the other party's obtaining registration.

APPEAL from Examiner of Interferences.

TRADE-MARK FOR RYE WHISKY.

Mr. Arthur O. Wallace and *Messrs. Mason, Fenwick & Lawrence* for Horne.
Mr. R. H. McNeill and *Mr. W. E. Nattress* for Somers & Co.

MOORE, *Assistant Commissioner:*

This is an appeal by Somers & Company from the decision of the Examiner of Interferences awarding priority of adoption and use to Horne of the words "Poplar Log" or "Old Poplar Log" as a trademark for whisky.

The Examiner of Interferences in awarding priority to Horne held that the testimony shows that Horne adopted the mark in issue for whisky prior to 1884, the earliest date of adoption alleged by Somers & Company, and that Horne has used it continuously from the date of its adoption to the present time as a trade-mark for whisky.

No error is found in the conclusions of the Examiner of Interferences.

Somers & Company contend that because they use the mark on corn whisky, while Horne uses it on rye whisky, there is no interference in fact. If Somers & Company desired to raise this question, they should have done so by motion to dissolve prior to the taking of testimony, as provided in Rule 49 of the rules of the Patent Office relating to trade-marks. For reasons similar to those stated in *Potter* v. *McIntosh* (C. D., 1906, 183; 122 O. G., 1721) and *Sobey* v. *Holsclaw* (C. D., 1905, 523; 119 O. G., 1922) this question will not be considered upon this appeal on priority. It is noted, however, that the application of Somers & Company is for the use of the mark on whisky, and not merely on corn whisky.

Somers & Company also contend that Horne has not shown the necessary use in interstate commerce to entitle him to register the mark. Somers & Company, however, admit (pp. 4 and 5 of brief) that Horne proved specific sales of whisky bearing the mark of the issue outside of the State of Tennessee by Newman, Horne's agent, while on a trip to New York City in 1903. Additional sales made outside of the State are also established by Horne, notably to Cain in North Carolina and to George of Cartersville, Ga., in the year 1874.

It is not understood that the statute requires that the use in interstate commerce should have been continuous to entitle the applicant to register the mark. In the case of *Sleepy Eye Milling Company* v. *C. F. Blanke Tea and Coffee Company* (C. D., 1898, 662; 85 O. G., 1905) this Office held:

The only other point to which I deem it necessary to refer as having any bearing on the question of priority is the one urged by counsel for registrant— that applicant has shown no use of the mark in commerce with foreign nations or Indian tribes. The testimony, however, I deem sufficient to show use in foreign commerce, and the affidavit forming a part of the application has been accepted by the Office as a compliance with the requirement of the law as to use in foreign commerce. The time when the mark was used in foreign commerce by the Sleepy Eye Milling Company is of no moment so long as that use occurred before the application for registration was filed. The Sleepy Eye

Milling Company having a valid trade-mark at common law cannot be deprived of it by the fact that one later to adopt and use the mark in State or interstate commerce was earlier to use it in foreign commerce.

This decision was under the statute of 1881, but is applicable to the registration of trade-marks used in interstate commerce which the act of February 20, 1905, includes, together with trade-marks used in commerce with foreign nations and with Indian tribes, as entitled to registration.

The fact that Horne is an applicant, while Somers & Company obtained a registration of the mark on December 30, 1902, does not, as contended by Somers & Company, necessarily create a bar under section 5 of the Trade-Mark Act against Horne's obtaining a registration of the mark. Section 7 of the act provides that the Commissioner may declare an interference in such cases as may—

register the mark, as a trade-mark, for the person first to adopt and use the mark.

The Examiner of Interferences has carefully and fairly analyzed the testimony on behalf of Horne. A review of this testimony here is unnecessary. It is believed to establish that Horne adopted the mark prior to the date claimed by Somers & Company, that his use of the mark has been continuous, and that it has been used in interstate commerce.

The decision of the Examiner of Interferences is affirmed.

DE FERRANTI *v.* LINDMARK.

PATENT INTERFERENCE.

Decided March 19, 1907.

(129 O. G., 1610.)

APPLICATION DATE—FOREIGN APPLICATION—SECTION 4887 OF THE REVISED STATUTES CONSTRUED.

Under the second clause of section 4887 of the Revised Statutes as amended March 3, 1903, an application for patent in the United States is not entitled to the date of an application filed by the applicant in a foreign country prior to March 3, 1903, although the United States application was filed after this date.

APPEAL from Examiners-in-Chief.

STEAM-TURBINE.

Messrs. Spear, Middleton, Donaldson & Spear for De Ferranti.
Mr. Park Benjamin and *Messrs. Wilkinson & Fisher* for Lindmark.

MOORE, *Assistant Commissioner:*

This is an appeal by De Ferranti from the decision of the Examiners-in-Chief affirming the decision of the Examiner of Interferences awarding priority of invention to Lindmark.

An application for patent for an invention or discovery or for a design filed in this country by any person who has previously regularly filed an application for a patent for the same invention, discovery, or design in a foreign country which, by treaty, convention, or law, affords similar privileges to citizens of the United States shall have the same force and effect as the same application would have if filed in this country on the date on which the application for patent for the same invention, discovery, or design was first filed in such foreign country, provided the application in this country is filed within twelve months in cases within the provisions of section forty-eight hundred and eighty-six of the Revised Statutes, and within four months in cases of designs, from the earliest date on which any such foreign application was filed. But no patent shall be granted on an application for patent for an invention or discovery or a design which had been patented or described in a printed publication in this or any foreign country more than two years before the date of the actual filing of the application in this country, or which had been in public use or on sale in this country for more than two years prior to such filing.

The statute does not state in express terms whether it is retrospective in its effect. Unless it clearly appears to have been the intention of the enacting body that the statute is to be given a retroactive effect it is a well-settled rule that the law is not to be construed retrospectively, and this is especially true where such a construction will affect vested rights. The Supreme Court of the United States in *Heong* v. *United States* (112 U. S., 536, 559) said it is the settled doctrine of this Court that—

words in a statute ought not to have a retrospective operation unless they are so clear, strong and imperative that no other meaning can be annexed to them, or unless the intention of the legislature cannot be otherwise satisfied.

The present Commissioner of Patents in the cases of *Stiff* v. *Galbraith* and *Brown* v. *Lindmark, supra,* held that the act of March 3, 1903, was not intended to have and did not have a retroactive effect. In the former decision the Commissioner said:

It is to be noted that the second clause of the law refers only to the filing of an application and its effect, and by similar reasoning it would seem that it applies only to applications filed under the amended law. It appears, furthermore, that to apply it to cases filed before the passage of the amendment might disturb vested rights. It might render invalid patents which were valid before the passage of the amendment. It does not merely make competent evidence that which was not evidence before, as contended by Galbraith, but confers upon the applicant a distinct right which he did not have before. It does not enable the applicant to prove what he has done by evidence of different character, but attaches a different legal effect to the act itself. Prior to the amendment of the law the filing of a foreign application or other acts performed abroad were not acts within the meaning of the law, (*Rousseau* v. *Brown*, C. D., 1122,) whereas under the amended law the filing of a application within twelve months before the application here is an act conferring upon the applicant a distinct right. It appears, clause of section 4887, Revised Statutes, was not to be given a retroactive effect.

In both of the above-cited cases the United States applications were filed prior to March 3, 1903. The present case differs therefrom in that De Ferranti's domestic application was filed subsequently to March 3, 1903, and his foreign application prior thereto. The reasons upon which the conclusions were based in the above decisions appear to be equally applicable to the present case. To give the United States application filed subsequently to the date of the act the benefit of the foreign application filed prior to the act would make the act retroactive and might disturb vested rights and render invalid patents which were valid before the act, in the same manner as would the extension of the provisions of that act to applications filed in the United States prior to the date of the act.

In the present case, under the statutes in force prior to March 3, 1903, Lindmark had an undoubted right to a patent at the time he filed his United States application on January 16, 1903; but if the act of March 3, 1903, is given the construction contended for by De Ferranti this right was taken from him by the passage of this act. Furthermore, had Lindmark's patent issued prior to March 3, 1903, his patent, which was valid at the date of its issue, would be rendered invalid by the act. Such a construction would make the act retrospective under the following definition given by the Supreme Court of the United States in *Sturges* v. *Carter*, (114 U. S., 519:)

Upon principle, every statute which takes away or impairs vested rights acquired under existing laws, or creates a new obligation, imposes a new duty, or attaches a new disability, in respect to transactions or considerations already past, must be deemed retrospective.

Again, the application of De Ferranti can be given the benefit of his foreign application only by construing the act retroactively. Prior to the act of March 3, 1903, the filing of a foreign application was not an act of invention. That statute makes the filing of a foreign application followed within twelve months by an application in this country an act of invention and confers a distinct right upon the applicant. The filing of the foreign application and the filing of the domestic application are related and continuous acts, and both must be performed to secure the benefit of the act of March 3, 1903. The filing of the two applications constitutes the " act of invention " in the United States as of the date of the foreign application. Where the domestic application was filed subsequently to March 3, 1903, and the foreign application prior thereto, it is, therefore, only by giving the act a retroactive effect that the foreign application can inure to the benefit of the domestic application.

Since, as stated above, the act cannot be construed retrospectively and since Lindmark was the first to file his application in the United States, he is entitled to the award of priority.

The decision of the Examiners-in-Chief is affirmed.

In re The Bullock Electric Manufacturing Company.

Decided March 30, 1907.

(129 O. G., 1611.)

1. ABANDONED APPLICATIONS—PETITION TO INSPECT.
   A petition to inspect an abandoned application will be denied where the reference to the abandoned application in applicant's patent is not of such a nature as to indicate that it was relied upon for any purpose in the proceeding eventuating in the patent or to indicate a waiver by the patentee of the right of secrecy concerning said application.

2. SAME—SAME—PRACTICE.
   Such petitions should be accompanied by a certificate of the court before whom a suit is pending.

3. SAME—SAME—SERVICE.
   Where an application has been abandoned a long time, service of petition to inspect upon the attorney of record is not sufficient, but service should be made upon the owner of the invention, whether applicant or assignee.

ON PETITION.

Mr. Charles E. Lord for The Bullock Electric Manufacturing Company.

Mr. E. P. Thompson for Dyer.

MOORE, *Acting Commissioner:*

This is a petition by The Bullock Electric Manufacturing Company for permission to inspect and to be furnished with copies of an abandoned application of Arthur H. S. Dyer.

The petition is denied for the following reasons:

First. The reference by Dyer in his Patent No. 483,646 to his application is not of such a nature as to indicate that it was relied upon for any purpose in the proceeding eventuating in the patent or to indicate a waiver by Dyer of his right of secrecy concerning said application.

Second. The petition is not accompanied, as required in such cases, by the certificate of the court before whom a suit is pending. (*Ex parte Heard*, C. D., 1905, 66; 114 O. G., 2381; *ex parte Brown*, C. D., 1905, 71; 115 O. G., 248.) Furthermore, it does not appear that petitioner has such an interest as entitles him to have access to said application. Petitioner does not allege that suit has been instituted, but merely that he has been threatened with suit on the Dyer patent.

Third. No service was made upon the assignee of the abandoned application. Where the application has been abandoned for a long time, service upon the attorney of record is not deemed sufficient. It does not appear that said attorney is at present in any way connected with the assignee or that the notice to the attorney ever reached the was analogous to the invention at issue. The Examiner responded by finally rejecting the claims.

It does not appear that the Examiner has answered the contention of the applicant as to the reasons why he regards the patent cited as belonging to the same art so as to justify its citation in this case. It is quite clear that if an appeal should be taken from the final rejection it would be necessary for the Examiner to touch upon this subject. It is believed that the Examiner should do so before an appeal is made necessary.

The petition is granted.

PYM *v.* HADAWAY.

PATENT INTERFERENCE.

Decided June 14, 1907.

(129 O. G., 2073.)

1. INTERFERENCE—LIMIT OF APPEAL.

Where a judgment on the record is rendered and a limit of appeal set, the running thereof is not stayed by filing a petition to set the case down for hearing under Rule 130.

2. SAME—PRACTICE—RULE 130.

A refusal to reopen a case to permit Examiner of Interferences to consider a petition and set case down for hearing under Rule 130 proper where it appears from a consideration of the record that the question sought to be raised is not one of priority.

3. SAME—SAME—SAME.

A party is deprived of no rights by a refusal to set for hearing under Rule 130 a case where the objections urged against one party's case apply equally well to that of the other.

PETITION for rehearing.

TACK-PULLER AND NAIL-DRIVER.

Messrs. Parker & Burton and *Mr. Geo. H. Maxwell* for Pym.

Mr. Benjamin Phillips and *Messrs. Phillips, Van Everen & Fish* for Hadaway.

MOORE, *Commissioner:*

This is a petition by Pym for a rehearing of his petition that jurisdiction be restored to the Examiner of Interferences for the purpose of fixing a day certain for "final hearing" (Rule 130) in the above-entitled interference and for a rehearing in the matter of the appeal from the decision of the Examiner of Interferences holding that he was without authority to set the case down for final hearing except upon jurisdiction for that purpose being restored by the Commissioner.

The petition was decided by the Assistant Commissioner; but in view of the fact that in that decision he construed my decision of May 14, 1907, I have considered the petition for rehearing..

Taking up the second part of the petition first, the record shows that when the preliminary statements were opened it was found that Pym had failed to overcome the *prima facie* case made out by the record. Therefore a motion was made to dissolve the interference, which was finally transmitted as to certain grounds thereof. After this motion was transmitted Pym moved that he be given permission to take testimony to establish certain facts set forth in one of the grounds of the motion for dissolution. The Commissioner refused to allow testimony to be taken for this purpose, and the motion to dissolve was, after due proceedings had, denied by the Primary Examiner. The Examiner of Interferences therefore, in acordance with the usual practice, rendered a decision in favor of Hadaway. This decision was rendered December 19, 1906, and the limit of appeal set to expire January 8, 1907.

On January 2, 1907, Pym filed a motion that the decision of December 19, 1906, be set aside and that he be authorized to take testimony to show, first, how the result attained by the machines of Pym and Hadaway was attained prior to the Hadaway invention; second, that the mechanism shown in the Hadaway application is in law and in fact an aggregation of old elements so far as this interference is concerned; third, that the invention shown in the application of Pym is, on the other hand, for a legitimate combination. This motion was not accompanied by a motion to stay the running of the limit of appeal or to extend the same.

On February 15, 1907, the motion was denied by the Examiner of Interferences, and his decision was affirmed on appeal. Pym then brought a motion that the case be set down for final hearing in accordance with the requirements of Rule 130. This motion was dismissed by the Examiner of Interferences on the ground that he had no jurisdiction in the case, the limit of appeal from the judgment of December 19, 1906, having expired.

This decision was right. It is the well-settled practice of the Office that the bringing of motions or taking petitions to the Commissioner will not stay the running of the limit of appeal from a decision on priority. The Examiner of Interferences could not set the case down for final hearing without setting aside the decision of December 19, 1906, in favor of Hadaway, and this he had no authority to do, the case being no longer within his jurisdiction.

It is contended by counsel for Pym that the Examiner of Interferences was in error in rendering the decision of December 19, 1906, in view of Pym's motion of June 21, 1906, to take testimony and the statement in the Commissioner's decision affirming the decision of the Examiner of Interferences dismissing this motion, that—

If Pym desires to take testimony relative to the matter above referred to he should proceed in accordance with Rule 130 and the decisions above referred to, first prosecuting his motion to dissolve before the Primary Examiner and subsequently if necessary, bringing his motion before the Examiner of Interferences for leave to take testimony.

This contention is not well taken. The motion to dissolve was brought by Pym in response to the order of March 16, 1906, to show cause why judgment on the record should not be rendered against him. This motion having been denied by the Primary Examiner, there was nothing to show why judgment should not be rendered in accordance with the regular established practice.

As to the first part of the present petition it was found upon taking up the petition to restore the jurisdiction of the Examiner of Interferences that the question which it was desired to argue was not one of priority, and therefore not one coming within the provisions of Rule 130. This had been pointed out in my decision dated May 14, 1907, (*ante*, 189; 129 O. G., 480,) as follows:

* * * It would seem that any objection of this character which would operate against Hadaway's claims would apply with equal force to the same claims of Pym's application.

* * * * * * *

I do not find in the affidavits in support of Pym's invention any *prima facie* showing of facts adverse to the right of Hadaway to make the claims in issue and not applicable to the claims made by Pym which would warrant the production of testimony upon this question.

Rule 130 was intended to cover those cases where it was contended that one party had a right to make the claims, but the other did not, and that therefore the latter was not entitled to the date of filing of his application as a date of conception and constructive reduction to practice of the invention in issue. Manifestly, to bring a case within this rule the criticism applied to one case must not apply equally as well to the other, for then neither party would be entitled to the claims in issue and the question of priority would be a moot one.

It is contended that the decision refusing to restore jurisdiction to the Examiner of Interferences has deprived Pym of his right to have the question which he desires to argue passed upon by the Court of Appeals of the District of Columbia.

This contention is not sound. Not every case, as pointed out above, comes within the provisions of Rule 130, and until it has been shown that it does come within the provisions of this rule a party has no right to argue the question of the non-patentability of the claims in issue to his opponent before the Examiner of Interferences. The case would have been in the same state as at present if the Examiner of Interferences had refused to set the case down for final hearing on the ground that it did not come within the provisions of Rule 130 and an appeal had been taken from that refusal. Manifestly, in that case it could not be said that in affirming such a decision the Commissioner had deprived the party of any rights to which he was entitled under the rules.

The petition for rehearing is denied.

Clausen *v.* Dunbar *v.* Schellenger.

Decided May 15, 1907.

(129 O. G., 2499.)

1. Interference—Reopening—Delay in Bringing Motion—Originality.

   Where after judgment had been rendered against C., a junior party, for failure to take testimony and later in another interference S. admitted a disclosure of the issue of this interference to him by C., but C. waited over a year after obtaining knowledge of this fact before bringing a motion to reopen, *Held* that the long delay indicates that the motion was not brought in good faith, but merely for the purpose of delay, and the motion to reopen denied.

2. Same—Same—Evidence of Originality Long After Final Judgment Not Received.

   Where judgment was rendered against C. by default and long afterward it appeared from testimony in a different interference that C. disclosed the invention to S., the successful party, *Held* that C., having failed to contest the question of originality or to move promptly to have the case reopened for the introduction of newly-discovered evidence as to this fact, has no greater right to contest the patentability of the issue to S. than any other member of the public and that right of S. to make the claim is not a matter for *inter partes* consideration.

On Motion.

TELEPHONE SYSTEM.

Messrs. Jones & Addington and *Mr. Robert L. Ames* for Dunbar.
Mr. Charles A. Brown for Schellenger.
Mr. C. C. Bulkley for Clausen.

Moore, *Acting Commissioner:*

This is a motion by Clausen, who was formerly the junior party to this interference, No. 22,795, that jurisdiction be restored to the Examiner of Interferences to consider a motion to reopen the case for the purpose of enabling Clausen to present certain alleged newly-discovered evidence—

showing, or tending to show, that the said Clausen is the first inventor of some or all of the subject-matter of said interference.

The record shows that Clausen presented before the Commissioner a motion to reopen the interfernece based upon this ground which was dismissed in a decision rendered April 15, 1907, upon the ground of informality, since motions to reopen should be heard and determined in the first instance by the Examiner of Interferences, and no motion to restore his jurisdiction for this purpose was presented. In that decision the Commissioner said:

It may be stated, however, that even though a motion to restore jurisdiction had been brought, it would not have been granted under the present circumstancs because the motion to reopen is not in proper form. It does not point out with sufficient clearness the character or scope of the evidence to be adduced and no attempt is made to account for the long delay in bringing the motion. Moreover, the fact that no excuse is offered for the delay, taken in connection with the circumstances that the reasons now given for failing to prosecute the interference at the proper time differ widely from the reasons given in the letter of March 14, 1904, indicate that the motion is not brought in good faith but rather for the purpose of delay.

The questions to be considered upon the present motion are whether the motion to reopen is in proper form and whether it is brought in good faith and not for the purpose of delay. (*Newell* v. *Clifford* v. *Rose*, C. D., 1906, 164; 122 O. G., 730.)

The alleged newly-discovered evidence comprises a deposition made between July 5 and July 18, 1905, by Schellenger, the successful party in this interference, in another interference, *Clausen* v. *Dean*, No. 23,797. It is alleged that this deposition contains admissions by Schellenger that Clausen disclosed to him a sketch showing the invention in issue. It is also desired to produce other evidence, the nature of which does not appear, to show that he was the first inventor of some of the counts of the issue.

The record shows that Clausen did not take testimony during the time set for that purpose, but filed a letter upon March 14, 1904, denying the patentability of the issue and refusing to prosecute the interference for this reason. Subsequently on April 5, 1904, judgment was rendered against him by the Examiner of Interferences, and no appeal from that decision was taken. Testimony was taken by Dunbar and Schellenger and judgment of priority rendered by the Examiner of Interferences. Appeals were prosecuted through the successive tribunals of the Office and the Court of Appeals of the District of Columbia, and final judgment was rendered in favor of Schellenger.

In July, 1905, when Schellenger's deposition containing the alleged newly-discovered evidence was taken, this case was pending before the Board of Examiners-in-Chief on appeal from the decision of the Examiner of Interferences. Clausen, however, did not endeavor to have the case reopened until more than a year later, September 12,

1906, when the case was pending before the Court of Appeals of the District of Columbia.

It is well settled that motions to reopen an interference for the purpose of introducing newly-discovered evidence should be presented promptly after the discovery of such evidence. It is, however, urged by Clausen that a motion to reopen could not be entertained by the Examiner of Interferences until a final determination of the question of priority by a final appellate tribunal. For the reasons stated in my decision in *Clement* v. *Richards* v. *Meissner* (C. D., 1904, 321; 111 O. G., 1627) it is competent for the Commissioner to entertain a motion to restore jurisdiction to the Examiner of Interferences to hear and determine a motion to reopen while the case is pending before any of the appellate tribunals of this Office. This contention is therefore without foundation. No other excuse for the delay in bringing the present motion is found.

It does not appear from the facts stated in the affidavits in support of this motion that the evidence now sought to be introduced could not have been acquired if Clausen had chosen to take testimony during the time originally set. In view of his failure to show his inability to secure this evidence while a party to the interference, the fact that Clausen not only failed to prosecute the interference, but specifically declined to do so and acquiesced in the judgment rendered against him, and further waited more than a year after having obtained knowledge of the very facts he now wishes to introduce as new evidence, and until the final adjudication of the interference in favor of Schellenger, before making any effort to have the case reopened, is believed to show that the motion is not brought in good faith, but merely for the purpose of delay. It was urged in behalf of Clausen at the hearing that in view of the fact that the present practice in interference proceedings allows a party to an interference to contest his opponent's right to the claim in issue, providing the objections do not apply to his own claim, Clausen should not have been dropped from the interference and that he is now entitled to contest Schellenger's right to make the claim. This contention is not believed to be well founded. Clausen did not choose to contest the right of Schellenger to the claims in issue either by the production of testimony or by argument at the final hearing of the case. The decision of priority adversely to him therefore finally disposed of his claim to the invention in issue, and he was properly excluded from the further prosecution of the interference.

It is also urged that in the testimony presented in the interference of *Clausen* v. *Dean* the Office has evidence that Schellenger has not the right to the claims in issue in this interference in view of his admission that Clausen disclosed a drawing to him showing the invention covered by some, if not all, of the counts of the issue, and Clausen contends that it is incumbent upon the Office to issue a patent to the first inventor and that therefore this interference should be reopened for the purpose of receiving evidence relative to his right to the claims in issue.

Clausen has been given every opportunity to establish the superiority of his claim to the invention in issue and in view of the judgment rendered against him upon his default has no greater right to contest the patentability of the issue to Schellenger than any other member of the public. Schellenger's right to make the claim is not therefore a matter for *inter partes* consideration, and there is no reason for reopening this interference for the purpose of such consideration.

The motion is denied.

Ex parte Smith & Hemenway Company.

APPLICATION FOR REGISTRATION OF TRADE-MARK.

Decided June 26, 1907.

(129 O. G., 2500.)

1. TRADE-MARKS—ANCHOR AND CROWN WITH LETTERS "S" AND "H" ANTICIPATED BY ANCHOR AND STAR.

The mark comprising the representation of an anchor surmounted by a crown with the letters "S" and "H" near the opposite sides of the shank of the anchor *Held* to be anticipated by the representation of an anchor with an arrow and a star superimposed upon the shank of the anchor.

2. SAME—REGISTRATION UNDER ACT OF 1881 NOT CONCLUSIVE OF DISSIMILARITY OF MARKS.

The fact of registration under the act of 1881 should weigh in favor of the applicant for registration where the near resemblance of the applicant's mark with that of a prior registration is doubtful, but does not warrant registration of the mark under the act of 1905 where the similarity of the marks is clearly apparent.

ON APPEAL.

TRADE-MARK FOR KNIVES, CUTTING-PLIERS, ETC.

Mr. E. B. Stocking, for the applicant.

MOORE, *Commissioner:*

This is an appeal from the action of the Examiner of Trade-Marks refusing to register a trade-mark which comprises the representation of an anchor surmounted by a crown with the letters "S" and "H" near the opposite sides of the shank of the anchor in view of a prior registration to Jacoby & Wester, No. 20,953, April 5, 1892, of a trade-mark, the essential features of which are described as the—

representation of an anchor and a transverse arrow and a star superimposed upon the shank of the anchor—

for merchandise of the same descriptive character.

It appears that the mark of the applicant was registered under the act of 1881, and it is urged that in view of this fact registration should not now be refused. While the fact of registration under the act of 1881 should weigh in favor of the applicant for registration in cases where the near resemblance of the applicant's mark with that of a prior registration is doubtful, it does not warrant the registration of the mark under the act of 1905 where the similarity of the marks is clearly apparent.

It is contended in the present case that the registered trade-mark—

* * * rests for its distinction upon the association of an arrow and star with an anchor which is a different essential composition from the letters "S" and "II" with the crown which in the applicant's mark are associated with a different type of anchor, and that the marks as a whole are clearly independent of each other.

This contention is not believed to be well founded. The predominant feature of each mark which would impress the eye of the purchaser is the anchor, and doubtless the goods of each party is known as the "anchor" brand. I am therefore of the opinion that the applicant's mark so nearly resembles the mark of the registrant as to cause confusion in the mind of the purchasing public.

In the case of *Bass, Ratcliff & Gretton* v. *Christian Feigenspan* (96 Fed. Rep., 206) a trade-mark which consisted of a red equilateral triangular figure was held to be infringed by a nearly-equilateral red triangle bearing the letters "C" and "F" in monogram and having a gold border and certain scroll ornamentation in each corner. In the case of *Hutchinson et al.* v. *Blumberg* (C. D., 1892, 652; 61 O. G., 1017; 51 Fed. Rep., 829) a trade-mark consisting of the word "Star" and a symbol of a six-point star was held to be infringed by a five-point star and crescent.

The similarity between the applicant's mark and that of the registrant is in my opinion quite as great as the similarity between the conflicting marks in the cases above cited. It is therefore held that registration of the applicant's mark was properly refused, notwithstanding the fact that this mark was registered by the applicant under the provisions of the act of 1881.

The decision of the Examiner of Trade-Marks is affirmed.

SERRELL *v.* DONNELLY.

PATENT INTERFERENCE.

Decided July 6, 1907.

(120 O. G., 2501.)

1. INTERFERENCE—RECOMMENDATION OF EXAMINERS-IN-CHIEF UNDER RULE 126—
   NOT DECIDED BY COMMISSIONER WITHOUT REMANDING TO PRIMARY EX-
   AMINER.

   The recommendation of the Examiners-in-Chief that the issue is not patentable is not a final decision of this question by them, and as the statutes
   provide for appeals to the Court of Appeals of the District of Columbia
   only after successive appeals have been taken to the Examiners-in-Chief
   and the Commissioner from a second rejection of the Primary Examiner the
   question of patentability will not be reviewed by the Commissioner until
   it has been finally passed upon by the lower tribunals.

2. SAME—SAME—ACTION BY PRIMARY EXAMINER—PRACTICE.

   Where a case is remanded to the Primary Examiner by the Commissioner
   upon reference by the Examiners-in-Chief under Rule 126, the Primary
   Examiner will enter a *pro forma* rejection of the claims. (*Holz v. Hewitt,
   ante,* 98; 127 O. G., 1992.) He may, however, in such action include any
   recommendation he may deem proper in order that the Examiners-in-Chief
   may have the benefit of his expert knowledge of the art if the case comes
   before them on appeal.

APPEAL from Examiners-in-Chief.

ON PETITION.

STEAM-HEATING APPARATUS.

Mr. Ernest H. Hunter for Serrell.

Messrs. Gifford & Bull and *Messrs. Foster, Freeman & Watson* for
Donnelly.

MOORE, *Commissioner:*

This case is before me on an appeal by Serrell from the decision of
the Examiners-in-Chief upon the question of priority of invention
and also upon a petition by Serrell that the case be remanded to the
Primary Examiner in accordance with a recommendation of the
Examiners-in-Chief in connection with their decision upon the question of priority that in their opinion the issue is unpatentable.

It is urged in behalf of Donnelly that the case should not be transmitted to the Primary Examiner, but that the patentability of the
issue should be determined by the Commissioner in connection with
his decision on the question of priority, under the provision of Rule
126, that—

If the case shall not be so remanded the Primary Examiner will, after judgment, consider any matter affecting the rights of either party to a patent which

may have been called to his attention unless the same shall have been previously disposed of by the Commissioner.

It is contended that this last clause of Rule 126 contemplates that the Commissioner may dispose of the question raised by the recommendation of the Examiners-in-Chief without remanding the case to the Primary Examiner and that the circumstances of the present case warrant such action.

The recommendation of the Examiners-in-Chief that in their opinion a claim is unpatentable is made upon their own initiative and is not a final decision upon this question by them. It is not, therefore, believed to be advisable for the Commissioner to review the question of patentability of such claims until this question has been finally decided by the lower tribunals after opportunity has been given to the applicants to present arguments to overcome such objections.

Sections 4903, 4909, 4910, and 4911 of the Revised Statutes and section 9 of the act of March 3, 1897, provide for appeal to the Court of Appeals of the District of Columbia from the rejection of claims only after successive appeals have been taken from a second rejection of the claims by the Primary Examiner to the Examiners-in-Chief and to the Commissioner. If, therefore, the Commissioner should now review the recommendation of the Examiners-in-Chief and hold the claims to be unpatentable, the cases of the parties would be in no condition for appeal to the Court of Appeals of the District of Columbia upon the question of patentability, but would have to be returned to the Primary Examiner for the institution of a new course of appeals and *pro forma* decisions by the Primary Examiner and Examiners-in-Chief before that end could be attained.

For the Commissioner now to review the recommendation of the Examiners-in-Chief would be, in effect, to invoke the supervisory authority of the Commissioner to decide a question in an irregular manner, although the specific procedure for the determination of this question is provided for by the rules and has long been followed by the Office. The supervisory authority of the Commissioner will be exercised only where a manifest error has been committed. In the present case the Examiners-in-Chief clearly acted within their authority, and there is no reason for departing from the regular procedure in this case.

The case is hereby remanded to the Primary Examiner, and he is directed to reject the claims which are in the opinion of the Examiners-in-Chief unpatentable, in accordance with the practice announced in *Holz* v. *Hewitt*, (*ante*, 98; 127 O. G., 1992.) The Examiner may in such action include any recommendation he may deem proper in order that the Examiners-in-Chief may have the benefit of his expert knowledge of the art if the applicant, persisting in the rejected claims, appeals to the Examiners-in-Chief.

Decision upon the question of priority is suspended pending the final determination of the question of the patentability of the issue.

The petition is granted.

WICKERS AND FURLONG *v.* WEINWURM.

Decided June 28, 1907.

(120 O. G., 2501.)

INTERFERENCE—EXTENSION OF TIME FOR TAKING TESTIMONY—PRACTICE.

It is well settled that no appeal lies from the decision of the Examiner of Interferences on motion to extend the time for taking testimony, and the sufficiency of the showing made in support of the motion will not be considered by the Commissioner on petition except in cases where it appears that there has been a clear abuse of discretion operating to the injury of one of the parties.

ON PETITION.

METHOD OF PRODUCING ADJUSTED PRINTING-PLATES.

Mr. John T. Canavan and *Messrs. Griffin & Bernhard* for Wickers and Furlong.

Mr. Walter F. Rogers for Weinwurm.

BILLINGS, *Assistant Commissioner:*

This is a petition by Wickers and Furlong that the decision of the Examiner of Interferences dated May 31, 1907, granting two months' extension of time for taking testimony to Weinwurm, be set aside. Under the practice which is now well settled there is no appeal from the decision of the Examiner of Interferences on such motions. The decision can only be modified by the exercise of the supervisory authority of the Commissioner. This authority will not be exercised except in cases where it appears that there has been a clear abuse of discretion operating to the injury of one of the parties.

It is urged in behalf of Wickers and Furlong that the showing made by Weinwurm, upon which the Examiner of Interferences granted the motion, does not measure up to the requirements of such showing as laid down in the rules. It is believed that the showing does meet the requirements. This being the case, the sufficiency of the same is within the discretion of the Examiner of Interferences. His decision cannot be set aside or modified merely because upon a review thereof a tribunal in authority might have acted differently in the first instance. To take such action would be tantamount to the allowance of appeals in all such cases.

The petition is denied.

ILLINOIS HYDRAULIC CEMENT MANUFACTURING COMPANY *v.* UTICA HYDRAULIC CEMENT COMPANY.

Decided April 23, 1907.

(129 O. G., 2502.)

1. TRADE-MARKS—SHOWING REQUIRED OF APPLICANT FOR CANCELATION.

Where the Examiner of Interferences required the applicant for cancelation of a registered mark to file in duplicate affidavits showing the facts upon which it relied in its application for cancelation before further action would be taken, *Held* the action of the Examiner of Interferences is deemed reasonable and proper in requiring an applicant for the cancelation of a registered mark to make such a showing of facts as would establish, if proved, that the registrant was not entitled to the use of the mark at the date of his application for registration thereof or that the mark is not used by the registrant or has been abandoned. (Sec. 13 of Trade-Mark Act of February 20, 1905.)

2. SAME—SAME—PRIMA FACIE CASE NECESSARY.

Where application is made for the cancelation of a registration, *Held* that unless a *prima facie* case is made out, such as is required for the institution of a public-use proceeding in case of application for patent, it is not thought that the registrant should now be called upon to defend its right or forfeit its registration upon its failure to do so.

3. SAME—SAME—SAME.

Where the application for cancelation is in the form of an affidavit sworn to by the president of the company filing the application and contains positive allegations of facts which, if true, constitute proper ground for cancelation of the registration under the statute, *Held* that a *prima facie* case is made out such as will warrant instituting the cancelation proceeding and requiring the registrant to file its plea, answer, or demurrer.

ON PETITION.

TRADE-MARK FOR HYDRAULIC CEMENT.

Mr. John H. Whipple for Illinois Hydraulic Cement Manufacturing Company.

Messrs. Mason, Fenwick & Lawrence for Utica Hydraulic Cement Company.

ALLEN, *Commissioner:*

This is a petition by the Illinois Hydraulic Cement Manufacturing Company that—

* * * the Examiner in charge of Interferences be advised that the requirement to file the affidavits as made by him in the letters of November 15 and December 1, 1906, be not insisted upon, and directed to disregard said order of dismissal and proceed to give notice to the registrant and to hear and determine the merits of the question.

On November 7, 1906, the Illinois Hydraulic Cement Manufacturing Company filed an application for the cancelation of Trade-

Mark No. 54,487, registered June 26, 1906, by the Utica Hydraulic Cement Company. The Examiner of Interferences on November 15, 1906, required the applicant for cancelation to file in duplicate affidavits showing the facts upon which it relied in its application for cancelation before further action would bε taken. Not having complied with the requirement, the Examiner of Interferences on December 18, 1906, notified the applicant that its application for cancelation would be dismissed unless it showed cause on or before December 28, 1906, why such action should not be taken. No showing having been made which the Examiner of Interferences deemed sufficient, he dismissed the application for cancelation on January 17, 1907, without notifying the registrant of the filing of said application.

The action of the Examiner of Interferences is deemed reasonable and proper in requiring an applicant for the cancelation of a registered mark to make such a showing of facts as would establish, if proved, that the registrant was not entitled to the use of the mark at the date of his application for registration thereof or that the mark is not used by the registrant or has been abandoned. (Sec. 13 of Trade-Mark Act of February 20, 1905.)

The mark of the Utica Hydraulic Cement Company was published in the OFFICIAL GAZETTE on May 8, 1906, and under section 6 of the Trade-Mark Act applicant had a right to oppose the same within thirty days after the publication. It did not, however, oppose the registration of said mark, and the certificate of registration was issued to the Utica Hydraulic Cement Company on June 26, 1906. Section 16 of the Trade-Mark Act of February 20, 1905, makes this registration *prima facie* evidence of ownership. Unless a *prima facie* case is made out, such as is required for the institution of a public-use proceeding in case of application for patent, is it not thought that the registrant should now be called upon to defend its right or forfeit its registration upon its failure to do so. The Examiner of Interferences, however, is believed to be in error in holding that such a showing has not been made in this case. The application for the cancelation of the registration is in the form of an affidavit sworn to by C. B. Lihme as president of the Illinois Hydraulic Cement Manufacturing Company. It contains the positive allegation that this applicant has used continuously since 1901 the word " Utica " by affixing it to the sacks and barrels containing the cement made by it at its factory in the village of Utica " for the purpose of naming and describing such cement, its character or quality and the place of its manufacture;" also that the word " Utica " was not in the actual and exclusive use as a trade-mark of the registrant for ten years next preceding the passage of the act of February 20, 1905. Inasmuch as the registration appears to have been granted under the ten-year proviso of section 5 of the act of February 20, 1905, a *prima facie* case is believed to be made out such as will warrant instituting the cancelation proceeding and requiring the registrant to file its plea, answer, or demurrer.

The petition is granted.

Ex parte Shaw.

APPLICATION FOR REISSUE OF PATENT.

Decided June 6, 1907.

(129 O. G., 2857.)

RECOMMENDATIONS UNDER RULE 139—ACTION OF PRIMARY EXAMINER—PRACTICE.

The recommendation of the Examiners-in-Chief under Rule 139 that in their opinion claims are not patentable is binding upon the Primary Examiner, and he should enter a *pro forma* rejection of such claims upon the grounds stated by the Examiners-in-Chief. If the Examiner is of the opinion that the claims should be rejected for any other reasons, they should also be stated in his letter of rejection.

APPEAL from Examiners-in-Chief.

FLUID-PRESSURE FEED FOR ROCK-DRILLS.

Messrs. Mason, Fenwick & Lawrence for the applicant.

MOORE, *Commissioner:*

This case is before me upon appeal from the decision of the Examiners-in-Chief.

The Examiners-in-Chief reversed the action of the Examiner as to appealed claims 1, 2, 3, and 4, but in their decision stated:

We are, however, of the opinion that the first four claims should be rejected upon the grounds, first, that there is obviously no invention in equipping any drill with a brace-bar extending from its rear end to any proximate fixed object, and, second, that they include an invention which was not covered by the original patent. (*Corbin Cabinet Lock Co.* v. *Eagle Lock Co.*, C. D., 1893, 612; 65 O. G., 1066; *Parker & Whipple Co.* v. *Yale Lock Co. et al.*, C. D., 1887, 584; 41 O. G., 811; 123 U. S., 99.)

No recommendation accompanied this statement of the Examiners-in-Chief; but inasmuch as it sets forth new reasons for the rejection the case is hereby remanded to the Examiner under the provisions of Rule 139. It is believed that the practice in cases remanded to the Primary Examiner under Rule 139 should follow that announced in the decision in *Holz* v. *Hewitt*, (*ante*, 98; 127 O. G., 1992,) in which it was held that where a case is remanded to the examiner under Rule 126 the Examiner should enter a *pro forma* rejection of the claims in ler that the case would be put in condition for a course of appeals which might be carried to the Court of Appeals of the District of Columbia. In that case Commissioner Allen said:

It is not to be presumed that the Examiner-in-Chief would form an opinion adverse to a party's interest and call attention to the same upon the record without careful consideration in those cases where the grounds of their opinion had already been considered by the Primary Examiner and held insufficient to warrant such adverse opinion. When they express such an opinion under these circumstances, the same is clearly of sufficient force to bind the Primary Examiner and sustain his *pro forma* rejection of claims until the opinion is withdrawn by the Examiners-in-Chief themselves or overruled by the Commissioner or court of appeals in the regular course of appeal.

The recommendations of the Examiners-in-Chief in cases remanded to the Primary Examiner under the provisions of Rule 139 are as binding upon him as those in cases remanded under Rule 126. The Examiner is therefore directed to enter a rejection *pro forma* of claims 1 to 4 upon the grounds stated in the decision of the Examiners-in-Chief. If in his opinion these claims should be rejected for any other reasons which have not been considered by the Examiners-in-Chief, such reasons should also be stated in his letter of rejection. Upon final rejection of these claims appeal will lie to the Examiners-in-Chief. Action upon the appeal now before me *is suspended* pending the determination of the lower tribunals of the patentability of claims 1 to 4.

Ex parte Actien-Gesellschaft für Anilin-Fabrikation.

APPLICATION FOR REGISTRATION OF TRADE-MARK.

Decided June 22, 1907.

(129 O. G., 2857.)

TRADE-MARKS—FOREIGN APPLICANT—REQUIREMENTS FOR REGISTRATION BY "TEN-YEAR" PROVISO.

The requirement that a foreigner who applies for registration shall show either that the mark has been registered in the country where he resides or is located or that he has a manufacturing establishment within the territory of the United States is applicable to those cases where registration is sought under the "ten-year" proviso as well as where the mark is a technical trade-mark.

ON APPEAL.

TRADE-MARK FOR SUBSTANTIVE COLORS.

Messrs. O. E. Duffy & Son for the applicant.

BILLINGS, *Assistant Commissioner:*

This is an appeal from the Examiner of Trade-Marks and purports to be from the requirement that applicant file a certified copy of its registration in Germany. In fact, it is an appeal from the action of the Examiner of Trade-Marks refusing to register a mark on the ground that applicant has not complied with the requirements of the statute.

It appears that applicant is a corporation organized under the laws of Germany and located at Berlin and that registration was refused because applicant neither stated in its declaration that its mark was registered in Germany in accordance with the requirements of section 2 of the Trade-Mark Act of February 20, 1905, nor that it had a manufacturing establishment within the territory of the United States, as provided in section 3 of the act of May 4, 1906. The requirement that a certified copy of the German registration be filed was in accordance with Rule 17 of the Trade-Mark Rules and the decision in *ex parte Beckett*, (C. D., 1905, 464; 119 O. G., 340.)

It is stated in the brief filed on behalf of applicant that it cannot file a certified copy of a German registration of its mark, since the mark has never been registered in Germany. It is contended, however, that since this application is filed under the " ten-year " clause of section 5 of the act of 1905 such German registration is not necessary in order to obtain registration in this country.

Section 2 of the act of February 20, 1905, provides as follows:

If the applicant resides or is located in a foreign country, the statement required shall, in addition to the foregoing, set forth that the trade-mark has been registered by the applicant, or that an application for the registration thereof has been filed by him in the foreign country in which he resides or is located * * *

Section 4 provides—

That certificate of registration shall not be issued for any mark for registration of which application has been filed by an applicant located in a foreign country until such mark has been actually registered by the applicant in the country in which he is located.

The " ten-year " proviso of section 5 is as follows:

That nothing herein shall prevent the registration of any mark by the applicant or his predecessors, or by those from whom title to the mark is derived, in commerce with foreign nations or among the several States, or with Indian tribes, which was in actual and exclusive use as a trade-mark of the applicant or his predecessors from whom he derived title for ten years next preceding the passage of this act.

This proviso manifestly refers to the grounds given in section 5 for refusing the registration of a mark and does not relate back to the requirements of the preceding sections.

The reason for the requirement that a certified copy of applicant's foreign registration be filed is not that the Office may have evidence that applicant is the owner of the mark in question, but that the Office may have evidence that the applicant has complied with the requirement of section 4 above cited.

The decision of the Examiner of Trade-Marks is affirmed.

KUTTROFF *v.* CASSELLA COLOR COMPANY.

OPPOSITION.

Decided July 1, 1907.

(129 O. G., 3159.)

1. TRADE-MARKS—OPPOSITION—IDENTITY OF MARKS.

    Held that the mark "Alizarine Black 4 B" of the applicant so nearly resembles the mark "Alizarine Black 4" of the opposer and the words "Alizarine Black 3 B" used by the Farbenfabriken of Elberfeld Company as to cause confusion in trade and is therefore not registrable under the ten-year proviso of section 5 of the act of 1905.

2. SAME—SAME—TESTIMONY SHOWING USE BY THIRD PARTIES CONSIDERED.

    The stipulated use of the mark "Alizarine Black 3 B." by parties other than those directly involved in this proceeding is admissible to show that the applicant did not have exclusive use of the mark for ten years next preceding the passage of the act of February 20, 1905.

3. SAME—SAME—DESCRIPTIVE USE OF MARK BY OTHER PARTIES.

    Where the use by others of the mark sought to be registered has been as a descriptive use rather than a continued trade-mark use, but it appears that the mark was "used in the usual and regular order of business on the tins or kegs or whatever containers contained the colors," *Held* that such use was similar to a trade-mark use and would render the users liable under section 16 of the trade-mark act to be held as infringers if the applicant's mark should be registered, and that since such use if subsequent to applicant's would infringe, when prior thereto it is good cause for refusing registration.

APPEAL from Examiner of Interferences.

TRADE-MARK FOR DYESTUFFS.

Mr. Anthony Gref and *Messrs. Foster, Freeman & Watson* for Kuttroff.

Mr. J. D. Caplinger for Cassella Color Company.

MOORE, *Commissioner:*

This is an appeal by the Cassella Color Company from the decision of the Examiner of Interferences holding that it is not entitled to register the words "Alizarine Black 4 B" as a trade mark for dyestuffs.

No testimony was taken by the applicant. A stipulation was filed that two or more competent witnesses, if called on behalf of Adolph Kuttroff, the opposer, would testify to certain facts.

The Examiner of Interferences found that—

It is held that the mark "Alizarine Black 4 B" of applicat so nearly resembles the mark "Alizarine Black 4" of opponent and the words "Alizarine Black 3 B" of the Farbenfabriken of Elberfeld Company as to cause confusion

infringers if applicant's mark should be registered. Since such use if subsequent to applicant's would infringe, when prior thereto it is good cause for refusing registration.

The third ground of the decision of the Examiner of Interferences for holding applicant not entitled to register its mark—namely, " that the name ' Alizarine Black 4 B ' is a grade mark"—is believed to be unwarranted. In the absence of proof concerning the character of the use of the mark by applicant it cannot be told whether the mark was used to indicate the grade or the origin of the goods.

The decision of the Examiner of Interferences *is affirmed* upon the first two grounds noted by him for sustaining the opposition.

EX PARTE NESTLÉ AND ANGLO-SWISS CONDENSED MILK COMPANY.

APPLICATION FOR REGISTRATION OF TRADE-MARK.

Decided July 17, 1907.

(129 O. G., 3160.)

1. TRADE-MARKS—CLASSIFICATION—DIVISION.

The scope of the classes of merchandise established under section 2 of the act of May 4, 1906, is peculiarly within the knowledge of the Examiner of Trade-Marks, and his conclusions upon questions of classification will not be disturbed except in cases of obvious error.

2. SAME—SAME—DIVISION.

Where it appears from the labels submitted as specimens that "coffee with milk " is intended for use in making beverages only and that " cocoa with milk " and "chocolate with milk " are adapted to be used in making "chocolate creams," "blanc-mange," and for "other culinary purposes," *Held* that the requirement that the former be classified in Class 46, Coffee, tea, and substitutes, and the latter in Class 47, Confectionery, in order to preserve the established lines of classes is well founded.

ON APPEAL.

TRADE-MARK FOR INFANTS' FOOD, COFFEE WITH MILK, CHOCOLATE WITH MILK, COCOA WITH MILK.

Mr. James Hamilton for the applicant.

MOORE, *Commissioner:*

This is an appeal from the action of the Examiner requiring division of the application for registration of a certain trade-mark for coffee with milk, chocolate with milk, cocoa with milk, in Class 46, " Coffee, tea, and substitutes."

The Examiner holds that " coffee with milk " is properly classifiable in Class 46, but that " chocolate with milk " and " cocoa with milk " are not properly classifiable in that class, and that all such preparations as the latter are classified in Class 47, Confectionery.

It is contended by the appellant that the goods upon which his mark is used are " chocolate and cocoa condensed with milk for exclusive use as table beverages," that they are put on the market in liquid form, and should therefore be included in Class 46.

The Examiner in his statement relative to the merchandise included in Class 46, " Coffee, tea, and substitutes," holds that the term " substitutes " does not, however, include all beverages, but is intended to include what are commonly known as " coffee substitutes " and " coffee surrogates "—that is, preparations for making beverages in imitation of coffee. Preparations for making beverages in imitation of tea are also included under the term " substitutes." He further states that—

Chocolate and cocoa are used for other purposes than for making beverages. The specimen labels filled by the applicant show that the particular preparations may be used for making chocolate creams, blanc-mange, and other culinary products, and all chocolate and cocoa and preparations thereof have been classified in Class 47, Confectionery, for the reason that they are essentially confectionery and that their use in the manufacture of beverages is only one of the uses to which they may be put.

The scope of the classes of merchandise established under section 2 of the act of May 4, 1906, is peculiarly within the knowledge of the Examiner of Trade-Marks, and his conclusions upon questions of classification will not be disturbed except in cases of obvious error.

In the present case the labels filed as specimens indicate that the " coffee and milk " preparation is intended for use only in making beverages, while the cocoa and chocolate preparations are said to be " excellent for chocolate creams, blanc-mange, and other culinary uses." It is therefore believed that the action of the Examiner in requiring division in order to preserve the established lines of classes above indicated is well founded.

The decision of the Examiner of Trade-Marks is affirmed.

EX PARTE SYLVESTERSEN.

APPLICATION FOR PATENT.

Decided July 18, 1907.

(129 O. G., 3160.)

DRAWINGS—AMENDMENTS OF—SUFFICIENCY OF DISCLOSURE IN SPECIFICATION AND CLAIMS.

Where in the original specification one member is said to be secured to a part " by means of a bolt or pivot " and in an original claim the member is referred to as being " connected adjustably " with such part, but no means for permitting such adjustment is shown in the drawing, *Held* that amendment to the drawing should be permitted to show suitable means for performing the function claimed, if supported by a supplemental oath.

ON PETITION.

PLOW.

Messrs. C. A. Snow & Co. for the applicant.

MOORE, *Commissioner:*

This is a petition from the action of the Examiner refusing to permit certain amendments to the drawing.

The invention relates to a plow for turning back into ditches the furrow slice or material excavated therefrom in the process of making the ditch. It comprises, in addition to the usual plow, a supplemental cutting member attached to the rear leg of a bifurcated landside-arch. In his specification the applicant states that this cutting member is secured to the rear leg of the landside-arch " by means of a bolt or pivot." Braces are shown extending from rigid members of the plow to the rear end of the cutting-blade 20; but the means for connecting such braces to the cutting-blade is not shown in the drawing or disclosed in the specification. In original claim 5, however, the cutting member is referred to as " connected adjustably with the rear leg of said arch." The Examiner holds that since no means is shown or described for adjusting the cutting member 20 to different positions it is to be presumed that the cutter is fixed by a bolt to the rear leg of the arch, and that if the applicant had contemplated adjusting the bar on the pivot he would have described some mechanism whereby such adjustment could be accomplished, and that therefore an amendment to the drawing to show a means for adjusting the cutting-blade 20 is not warranted by the original disclosure.

The position of the Examiner, in my opinion, is untenable. The statement in the original specification that the cutter 20 is secured to the leg of the landside by a pivot or bolt, when taken in connection with the statement in claim 5 that the cutter is adjustable, is believed to constitute a sufficient disclosure of the adjustable feature of this invention to warrant amendment to the drawing showing an ordinary means for adjusting said cutter. As stated in my decision in *ex parte Wareham,* (C. D., 1901, 204; 97 O. G., 1600:)

Under the practice laid down in *ex parte Snyder* (C. D., 1882, 22; 22 O. G., 1975) an applicant may be permitted to add to his drawing—
" to supply suitable connections * * * or other manifest defects or omissions in features essential to the operation of the invention or to the completeness of the disclosure."

In view of the fact that the applicant in his original application claimed the means for effecting the function of adjusting the cutter and disclosed a pivot about which such adjustment might be made, amendment to the drawing should be permitted to show suitable means for performing the function claimed. The proposed amendment should, however, be supported by proper supplemental oath under Rule 48.

The petition is granted.

EICHELBERGER AND HIBNER *v.* DILLON.

PATENT INTERFERENCE.

Decided August 13, 1907.

(129 O. G., 3161.)

1. INTERFERENCE—MOTION FOR DISSOLUTION—CLAIMS MADE UNDER PROTEST—
   INFORMALITY IN DECLARATION.

   Where suggested claims were made by the joint applicants under protest,
   with a statement that they did not think they had a right to make the
   same, giving their reasons therefor, *Held* that the declaration of interference did not constitute informality within the contemplation of the rules
   and that the transmission of a motion for dissolution based upon this
   ground was properly refused.

2. SAME—SAME—SAME—MOVING PARTY'S RIGHT TO MAKE CLAIMS.

   Where claims have been suggested to an applicant and he made the same
   under protest, with a statement that he does not believe he has a right to
   make them, and where after inspecting the other party's application he still
   contends that he has no right to make these claims, *Held* that he should
   be permitted to argue the question before the Primary Examiner, and the
   motion to dissolve should therefore be transmitted. (*Miller* v. *Perham,*
   C. D., 1906, 157; 121 O. G., 2667, modified.)

APPEAL ON MOTION.

BOILER-FLUE CLEANER.

Messrs. H. C. Evert & Co. for Eichelberger and Hibner.
Mr. Frederick G. Fischer and *Messrs. Collamer & Co.* for Dillon.

BILLINGS, *Acting Commissioner:*

This is an appeal by Eichelberger and Hibner from the decision of
the Examiner of Interferences refusing to transmit their motion to
dissolve as to the first, second, and fourth grounds and the first part
of the third ground thereof.

The motion to dissolve was based on four grounds:

1st. Informality in the declaration of the interference.

2d. Non-patentability of the issue.

3d. Lack of right on the part of Eichelberger and Hibner to make
the claims and lack of right on the part of Dillon to make the claims.

4th. That the claims have different meanings in the two applications.

An examination of the motion shows that the alleged informality
consists in the fact that the interference was declared, although when
the applicants made the claims which were suggested to them they
did so under protest and with a statement that they did not think
they had a right to make the same, giving their reasons therefor.
This was not such an informality in the declaration of interference as
contemplated in the rules, for after the applicant had filed an amendment containing claims which had previously been made by another

applicant the proper course for the Examiner was to declare the interference.

In support of the second ground fifteen patents were cited. It was not stated whether each of these references was relied on to anticipate each claim, or, if they were to be combined, in what manner this was to be done. This ground of the motion does not therefore conform to the practice as laid down in the decision *Heyne, Hayward, and McCarthy v. De Vilbiss, Jr.*, (C. D., 1906, 450; 125 O. G., 669,) and transmission thereof was properly denied.

The reasons given in support of the fourth ground are general and do not point out the specific portion of the claims which are alleged to have different meanings in the two applications, and this ground of the motion is therefore too indefinite to be transmitted.

In the third ground of the motion the contention is made that the moving party has no right to make claims corresponding to some of the counts of the issue. This part of the motion was refused primarily in accordance with the practice laid down in *Miller v. Perhan*, (C. D., 1906, 157; 121 O. G., 2667.) It appears, however, from the record that after the Examiner had suggested these claims to the appellant under provisions of Rule 96 the appellant filed an amendment containing these claims, accompanying the same with a statement that the claims were filed under protest, for the reason that he did not believe they could be rightfully based on the structure disclosed by him. Specific reasons were given for this belief.

Where claims have been suggested to an applicant and he makes the same under protest, accompanying the protest with a statement that he does not believe he has a right to make them, giving his reasons for that statement, and where after inspecting the other party's application he still contends that he has no right to make these claims, he should be permitted to argue the question before the Primary Examiner. The practice announced in *Miller v. Perhan, supra*, is modified to this extent.

The decision of the Examiner of Interferences refusing to grant the motion as to the first, second, and fourth grounds thereof *is affirmed*. His decision refusing to transmit the first part of the third ground *is reversed*.

Ex parte The Sauers Milling Company.

Decided April 23, 1907.

(129 O. G., 3161.)

TRADE-MARKS—"INFALLIBLE"—DESCRIPTIVE—NOT REGISTRABLE.
   Held that the word "Infallible" as applied to flour is descriptive or indicative of the quality of the flour, and therefore not registrable.

ON APPEAL.

Mr. Bruce S. Elliott and *Messrs. Meyers, Cushman & Rea* for the applicant.

ALLEN, *Commissioner:*

This is an appeal from the action of the Examiner of Trade-Marks refusing to register the word " Infallible " as a trade-mark for wheat-flour on the ground that the word describes the character or quality of the goods.

Appellant contends that—

The word "Infallible" as used by the appellant, is used in a purely arbitrary way and comes within the rulings which your Honor and the courts have frequently and almost uniformly made that the word sought to be registered or under consideration was merely suggestive of a possible result.

The mark is not regarded as arbitrary and fanciful or as merely suggestive, as contended by appellant.

The *Century Dictionary* defines " infallible " as " unfailing in character or effect; exempt from uncertainty or liability to failure; absolutely trustworthy," and it refers to the quotation, " He * * * mended china with an infallible cement," as an example of its proper use. Given its customary meaning, the word " Infallible " as applied to flour is considered as descriptive or indicative of the quality of the flour and to mean that the flour never fails to make good bread or other food product. Since the word " infallible " is in common use as descriptive of character or indicative of quality, it is not open to appropriation by any one member of the public in connection with a particular kind of merchandise.

The decision of the Examiner is affirmed.

ANHEUSER-BUSCH BREWING ASSOCIATION *v.* D. G. YUENGLING & SON *v.* KOEHLER *v.* HABICH & COMPANY *v.* PETER STUMPF BREWING COMPANY *v.* RUPPERT.

TRADE-MARK INTERFERENCE.

Decided May 28, 1907.

(129 O. G., 3501.)

1. TRADE-MARKS—IDENTITY OF MERCHANDISE—BEER NOT INCLUDED IN " WINES AND LIQUORS."

Where the merchandise upon which a trade-mark is used is stated in the registration of such mark to be " wines and liquors," it is doubtful whether the registrant meant by this statement that his mark had been used upon beer, and in the absence of more convincing evidence that it ~as used upon beer, and not merely upon wines and distillates, the registration should not be held to anticipate an application for the registration of a similar mark for beer.

2. SAME—PUBLIC MARK—EAGLE.

The action of the Office in issuing a number of registrations of trademarks which include the representation of an eagle for beer does not indicate that the Office has recognized the representation of an eagle for beer as common property.

3. SAME—ESTOPPEL BY PRIOR REGISTRATIONS.

Where an applicant for the registration of the representation of an eagle as a trade-mark has several prior registrations of a trade-mark which includes the capital letter "A" entwined with the figure of an eagle, *Held* that he is not estopped by his prior registrations from obtaining registration upon his present application.

4. SAME—INTERFERENCE IN FACT—CASES OF DOUBT.

In case of doubt upon the question of interference of marks the determination thereof should be postponed until final hearing in order to get the benefit of any testimony that may be taken on the subject.

APPEALS ON MOTION.

TRADE-MARK FOR BEER.

Mr. George H. Knight and *Messrs. Knight Brothers* for Anheuser-Busch Brewing Association.

Messrs. Redding, Kiddle & Greeley and *Mr. Titian W. Johnson* for D. G. Yuengling & Son.

Messrs. Burger & Baird for Koehler.

Messrs. Crosby & Gregory for Habich & Company.

Mr. Julien Gunn for Peter Stumpf Brewing Company.

Mr. Joseph L. Atkins for Ruppert.

MOORE, *Acting Commissioner:*

This case comes up upon appeals by (1) the Peter Stumpf Brewing Company, (2) the Anheuser-Busch Brewing Association, and (3) Jacob Ruppert from the decision of the Examiner of Trade-Marks upon Ruppert's motion for dissolution.

This interference as redeclared involved nine applications and registrations, as follows: (1) Ruppert application No. 5,958; (2) Ruppert application No. 16,336; (3) Ruppert registration No. 10,004; (4) Anheuser-Busch Brewing Association application No. 9,759; (5) Yuengling & Son application No. 19,586; (6) Yuengling & Son registration No. 30,707; (7) Koehler registration No. 27,691; (8) Habich & Company registration No. 25,124; (9) Stumpf Brewing Company registration No. 23,522.

The Examiner of Trade-Marks dissolved the interference as to Ruppert's application No. 5,958, the Anheuser-Busch application, and Habich & Company's registration. The dissolution as to Ruppert's application No. 5,958 was based upon the ground that the mark shown therein is not registrable. Ruppert has taken no appeal from the decision upon this point. In fact, he has expressed his concurrence therein, so that this application need not be further considered.

The dissolution as to the Anheuser-Busch Brewing Association application No. 9,759 was based upon the grounds, first, that the registration to E. Simpson & Company, No. 620, dated January 2, 1872, anticipates the earliest date of use claimed by the Anheuser-Busch Brewing Association; second, that the mark shown in the Anheuser-Busch Brewing Association application is nothing more than an eagle, which has become a public mark for beer, and, third, that many earlier registrations to this party, all including certain other features associated with the eagle, now shown alone, establish an estoppel upon this party precluding its registration of this mark. The Anheuser-Busch Brewing Association has appealed from the Examiner's decision upon these questions.

The dissolution as to Habich & Company's registration was based upon the ground that the mark there shown is not so similar to the marks of the remaining parties as to be liable to cause confusion in trade or to deceive purchasers. This conclusion is traversed by the Anheuser-Busch Brewing Association in the sixteenth ground of its appeal. The remaining parties have acquiesced therein.

In addition to the appeals of Ruppert and the Anheuser-Busch Brewing Association there is one taken by the Peter Stumpf Brewing Company.

(1) It does not appear that the appeal of the Peter Stumpf Brewing Company is founded upon the denial of any motion brought by that company or upon the grant of a motion brought by any of its opponents. It has no right of appeal under such circumstances, and the appeal taken is therefore dismissed.

(2) The first question raised by the appeal of the Anheuser-Busch Brewing Association is whether this association is shown by the registration of E. Simpson & Company, No. 620, dated January 2, 1872, to have been anticipated in its adoption of an eagle as a trade-mark for beer. This registration states that the mark shown had been used for ten years for wines and liquors. It is very doubtful whether the registrant meant by this statement that his mark had been used upon beer. In the absence of more convincing evidence that it was used upon beer and not merely upon wines and distillates, the registration should not be held an anticipation here unless beer, and wines and distillates are to be considered goods of the same descriptive properties. I am of the opinion that they are not to be so considered. They represent different manufacturing interests and, to a large extent, ferent retail business. They are made by distinctly different proc-

esses and have widely different physical characteristics. It is held that the Examiner was in error in his conclusion that the Anheuser-Busch Brewing Association's application should be refused upon this reference.

The second question raised by the Anheuser-Busch Brewing Association's appeal is whether the eagle for beer is a public mark. The Examiner's conclusion that it is rests upon a large number of registrations for beer in which an eagle appears as a part of the mark. He states that these registrations show that this Office has recognized the eagle for beer as common property. Each of the registrations referred to is subsequent in date to the date of the use claimed by the Anheuser-Busch Brewing Association. It is not understood how the action of the Office issuing any number of registrations, which issues the present applicant had no duty and probably no opportunity to oppose, could take away rights which this party may have acquired by prior adoption and use of its mark. It is held that the Examiner erred in finding that registration by the Anheuser-Busch Brewing Association is barred on this ground.

The third question presented by the Anheuser-Busch Brewing Association's appeal, that of estoppel, rests upon the action of this party in making application for and obtaining several registrations under the acts of 1870, 1881, and 1905 of marks including an eagle, which marks, like those upon labels furnished with the present application, include the capital letter " A " entwined with the figure of the eagle. Why an estoppel should arise from these registrations is difficult to perceive. It was the practice of the Office at one time to require the mark registered to include all the consequential features of the mark used by the labels furnished with the registration. This practice was overturned by the court of appeals in the case of the *Standard Underground Cable Company*, (C. D., 1906, 687; 123 O. G., 656,) wherein the Court held that the applicant was free to elect how much of the mark used should be shown upon the drawing of his registration. The Anheuser-Busch Brewing Association's application seems to be strictly in accordance with this decision. No reason is seen why this applicant's prior registrations in conformity to an earlier practice should preclude him from registration now in the manner made possible by the decision in the *Standard Underground Cable Company* case, *supra*.

If the inclusion of features of a mark in a registration corresponded to the limitation of the claim of a patent, doubtless the Anheuser-Busch Brewing Association would now be estopped from registering a mere eagle on the ground of dedication and abandonment. There is, however, no such analogy. In a trade-mark case the mark is ordinarily registered as used, and such a registration is undoubtedly intended to afford a basis for suit against the subsequent adopter of any mark causing confusion therewith and mistake in trade, no matter how much of the registered mark may have been omitted in the creation of the mark which is confused therewith. It is held that the Anheuser-Busch Brewing Association is not estopped from obtaining registration upon its present application by its previous registrations.

The fourth question raised by the Anheuser-Busch Brewing Association's appeal is whether there is interference between the Anheuser-Busch Brewing Association's mark and that of the Habich & Company's registration. It is believed that the conclusion of the Examiner of Trade-Marks upon this question was right. The mark and that of the appellant are not so similar, in my opinion, as to cause confusion in trade or deceive purchasers. It is recognized that in case of doubt upon a question of interference of marks the determination thereof should be postponed until final hearing in order to get the benefit of any testimony that may be taken on the subject. No doubt is entertained, however, as to the non-interference of the Habich & Company's registration with the registrations and applications of the remaining parties.

(3) The appeal of Jacob Ruppert is from the refusal of the Examiner of Trade-Marks to dissolve the interference between his application No. 16,336 and registration No. 10,004 and the applications and registrations of the remaining parties. There is, in my opinion, no chance of confusion between the mark of registration No. 10,004 and the remaining marks, and the interference should be dissolved as to this registration. It is believed that the interference should proceed upon the remaining cases—namely, the application of Ruppert, No. 16,336, the Anheuser-Busch Brewing Association application, the D. G. Yuengling & Son application, the D. G. Yuengling & Son registration, the registration of Koehler, and that of the Peter Stumpf Brewing Company. The eagle is so prominent in each of these marks as to make confusion and deception a probable consequence of their concurrent use by different parties. The parties should be given an opportunity to produce evidence regarding actual conflict.

The decision of the Examiner of Trade-Marks dissolving the application of the Anheuser-Busch Brewing Association from the interference and refusing to dissolve out the registration of Jacob Ruppert, No. 10,004, *is reversed* and *is affirmed* upon the dissolution as to the Habich & Company's registration and the refusal to dissolve as to the remaining registrations and applications.

Ex parte Meinhardt.

APPLICATION FOR PATENT.

Decided July 25, 1907.

(129 O. G., 3503.)

PATENTABILITY—SYSTEM FOR SPACING FREE-HAND LETTERS—NOT AN ART, MACHINE, MANUFACTURE, OR COMPOSITION OF MATTER.

A " system " which consists in the adoption of a certain scale for the height of letters and then determining in terms of this scale the proper width of the letters and the spaces between consecutive letters, *Held* to be neither an art, machine, manufacture, or composition of matter, and therefore not patentable. although the system as such is apparently new and useful.

APPEAL from Examiners-in-Chief.

SYSTEM FOR SPACING FREE-HAND LETTERS.

Mr. Thomas F. Meinhardt pro se.

BILLINGS, *Assistant Commissioner:*

This is an appeal from the decision of the Examiners-in-Chief affirming the decision of the Primary Examiner rejecting the following claims:

1. A system for spacing free-hand letters, consisting of a complete spacing-guide which is composed from a mechanical scale of sixteen units, dividing the desired height of a letter into four equal parts, and constituting the bottom guide-line, the 4th, 8th, 12th and 16th units as the five principal guide-lines, which facilitates the construction of the letter in correct optical proportion, as described.

2. A system for spacing free-hand letters, consisting of a mechanical scale of sixteen units and a complete spacing-guide which indicates in horizontal direction the exact number of units of the said mechanical scale required for the variable areas of the letters to be formed, in comparative optical relation to any other letters with which they may be grouped, also the exact number of units of the said mechanical scale required for the variable spaces between separate letters in any desired combination.

The Examiners-in-Chief rejected the claims on the ground that the system set forth therein is not a subject-matter which is patentable under the statute, although the system as such is apparently new and useful.

As stated by the Examiners-in-Chief, the statute, section 4886, provides that patents may be obtained for any new and useful art, machine, manufacture, or composition of matter or any new and useful improvement thereof, and as it is apparent that the system is neither a machine, manufacture, nor a composition of matter. if patentable at all it must be as an " art," or, as it is usually termed, a " process."

Robinson in his work on patents, section 159, thus defines an art:

An art or operation is an act or a series of acts performed by some physical agent upon some physical object and producing in such object some change either of character or condition.

In *In re Weston* (C. D., 1901, 290; 94 O. G., 1786) the Court of Appeals of the District of Columbia in discussing the question of process claims came to the conclusion, from a consideration of the decisions on the subject, that there are two classes of processes which if new and useful are patentable: first, those which involve a chemical or other elemental action, and, second, those which are of a mechanical nature and which, although perhaps best illustrated by mechanism, are not absolutely dependent on a machine.

Appellant's system consists in the adoption of a certain scale for the height of his letters and then determining in terms of this scale the proper width of the letters and the spaces between consecutive letters.

It is evident that such a system conforms to neither of the above quoted definitions of a patentable " art " or " process."

It would seem rather to be such a plan as is referred to by Robinson in his work on patents, section 166, as follows:

Hence a plan or theory of action which, if carried into practice, could produce no physical results proceeding directly from the operation of the theory or plan itself, is not an art within the meaning of the patent law, however greatly it may promote the comfort or the welfare of mankind. It is, indeed, a means and may accomplish an important end, but it lies outside the domain of the industrial arts; and its inventor, if he is entitled to protection from any source, must seek it from the Copyright and not the patent law.

Appellant's device being neither an art, machine, manufacture, nor composition of matter must be held to be not patentable.

The decision of the Examiners-in-Chief is affirmed

Ex parte Meinhardt.

APPLICATION FOR PATENT.

Decided August 5, 1907.

(129 O. G., 3503.)

PATENTABILITY—SYSTEM FOR SPACING FREE-HAND LETTERS—REHEARING.

While it is conceivable that some person after long and arduous study might discover a new method for solving certain mathematical problems which was much simpler and shorter than any known method, such method would not be a proper subject for patent. So, in the present case, applicant's plan for spacing free-hand letters, no matter what its merit, does not come within the classes for which protection can be secured under the patent laws.

ON PETITION.

Mr. Thomas F. Meinhardt pro se.

BILLINGS, *Acting Commissioner:*

This is a petition for a rehearing of the appeal from the decision of the Examiners-in-Chief affirming the action of the Primary Examiner rejecting the claims.

On July 18, 1907, a decision was rendered affirming the decision of the Examiners-in-Chief.

The arguments advanced by applicant have been carefully considered. They go to show that applicant's discovery is a meritorious and useful one; but that such is the case has not been disputed. It cannot be held, however, that this plan for spacing letters is a patentable invention within the meaning of the statute.

It is conceivable that some person after long and arduous study might discover a new method for solving certain mathematical problems which was much simpler and shorter than any known method; but such method would not be a proper subject for a patent. So, in the present case, applicant's plan, no matter what its merit, does not come within the classes for which protection can be secured under the patent laws.

This conclusion is, however, not necessarily a final determination of applicant's right to a patent, for the law provides that if a party is dissatisfied with a decision of the Commissioner of Patents he may take an appeal to the Court of Appeals of the District of Columbia. (Rules 148–149.)

The petition for rehearing is denied.

EX PARTE GREEN.

Decided March 11, 1907.

(130 O. G., 209.)

1. FINAL REJECTION—·FORMAL OBJECTION DOES NOT RENDER PREMATURE.

　　Where the Examiner points out certain formal objections in his letter finally rejecting the claims of an application, *Held* that the final rejection is not thereby rendered premature.

2. ABANDONMENT—CLAIMS PRESENTED AFTER FINAL REJECTION UNACCOMPANIED BY SHOWING DOES NOT AVOID.

　　Where after final rejection the applicant presents an amendment curing informalities and containing claims which differ substantially from those finally rejected, but does not make a showing of good and sufficient reasons why the amendment was not earlier presented, *Held* that the amendment is inadmissible, although it would have been proper to cure the informalities by proper amendment, and that such action does not relieve the application from its condition as subject to appeal or save it from abandonment.

ON PETITION.

METHOD FOR EXTRACTING, CONVEYING, STERILIZING, AND MOISTENING DIRT.

Mr. Nicholas Du Bois for the applicant.

MOORE, *Acting Commissioner:*

This petition requests that the Examiner be advised that—

* * * your petitioner's proposed amendments dated March 17, 1906, and April 20, 1906, respectively be admitted and considered without withdrawing the application from the condition of appeal, and that he be directed to incorporate said proposed amendment, to the end that the claims may, upon appeal to the Board of Examiners-in-Chief, be in condition for intelligent action on the merits by that tribunal.

Following several actions in the case, all the claims were rejected on December 20, 1905. On January 8, 1906, applicant amended by canceling claims 1 and 2 and substituting two new claims therefor. Concerning these claims, applicant stated in his amendment:

The foregoing claims 1 and 2 are in substance the same as the claims on which the Examiner's action was based.

In his action of February 24, 1906, the Examiner criticised and finally rejected the claims as follows:

The parenthetical clause in claims 1 and 2 should be canceled, because it is not clear and because it sets out nothing positively. The expression "moist suction" is meaningless.

The claims are again rejected on the references and reasons of record, and as the claims have not been amended in matter of substance, this action is made final.

Appeal lies to the Examiners-in-Chief.

Petitioner contends that—

* * * in view of the new objection raised by the Examiner the final rejection at this time was premature.

The claims, as applicant admits, had not been amended in matter of substance. No new grounds of rejection were cited by the Examiner. The final rejection was therefore not premature. The fact that certain formal objections were made did not prevent the final rejection from being proper.

The circumstances in this case are similar to those in the case of *ex parte Severy*, (C. D., 1901, 244; 97 O. G., 2745,) in which it was stated:

The petitioner contends that the requirement for a showing does not apply, since in his opinion the application was not in condition for appeal. He calls attention to the rule which requires that all formal matters be settled before appeal is taken and argues that since such matters had not been settled when the letter referred to was written the consideration of the merits of the case could not properly be closed by the Examiner.

All of the rules must be construed together, and when so construed the Examiner clearly has authority to finally reject the claims before all formal matters e settled, and such final rejection has as much force as if there were no controversy as to formal matters. It is merely necessary that the formal matters be disposed of before an appeal is forwarded. This subordination of formal defects to matters of merits is for the purpose of facilitating the prosecution of the case upon its merits and is believed to be founded upon good reason and to work to the interest of parties having business before the Office. The question of main interest is the merits, and the postponement of formal matters is for the purpose of preventing delay in reaching a conclusion upon that question. To permit the postponement of such matters to result in delays in settling questions of merits would be to defeat the very purpose for which the rule was adopted.

The Examiner holds that the claims which applicant seeks to have admitted differ substantially from the finally-rejected claims. This is admitted by applicant, for in the proposed amendment containing said claims he says:

> The claims now submitted are in substance different from the canceled claims in that they clearly recite that the suction is induced by an agent not in contact with the article being operated upon and that the dirt is extracted by the suction of air free from moisture likely to be injured by wetting the article to which it is applied.

Applicant did not make a showing duly verified of good and sufficient reasons why the amendments were not earlier presented, as required by Rule 68. Without such a showing the amendments submitted were not admissible, although it would have been proper to cure the informalities by proper amendment. (*Ex parte Paige*, C. D., 1904, 59; 108 O. G., 1587.) Such an amendment, however, under the provisions of Rule 68 would not relieve the application from its condition as subject to appeal or save it from abandonment.

The final rejection of February 24, 1906, having been proper, a responsive action thereto such as would save the case from abandonment would have been an appeal to the Examiners-in-Chief. Inasmuch as no such action has been taken within the year provided by statute, the application is abandoned. (*Ex parte Thayer*, C. D., 1906, 189; 122 O. G., 1724.)

The petition is denied.

Ex parte The Rat Biscuit Company.

APPLICATION FOR REGISTRATION OF TRADE-MARK.

Decided August 3, 1907.

(130 O. G., 300.)

TRADE-MARKS—"RAT BIS-KIT" FOR POISONOUS COMPOUND FOR RATS AND MICE—DESCRIPTIVE—NOT REGISTRABLE.

The words "Rat Bis-Kit" indicate a product to be eaten by rats, which would be understood by the public to contain a rat-poison. *Held*, therefore, to be descriptive and not registrable as a trade-mark for a poisonous compound for rats and mice.

ON APPEAL.

TRADE-MARK FOR POISONS FOR ANIMALS.

Mr. H. A. Toulmin for the applicant.

BILLINGS, *Assistant Commissioner:*

This is an appeal by The Rat Biscuit Company from the decision of the Examiner of Trade-Marks refusing to register the words "Rat Bis-Kit" as a trade-mark for poisonous compound for rats and mice.

Registration was refused on the ground that the mark is descriptive of the character or quality of the goods.

Section 5 of the Trade-Mark Act of February 20, 1905, provides that no mark shall be registered which consists—

merely in words or devices which are descriptive of the goods with which they are used or of the character or quality of such goods.

The words are not descriptive of the goods, but are descriptive of the character and use thereof. The word "Bis-Kit," which is merely a misspelling of the word "biscuit," indicates that the compound is something to be eaten and the word "Rat" that it is to be eaten by rats. As it is not customary to feed rats, it will be understood by every one that the compound is a rat-poison put up in the form of a biscuit, which might be of rectangular form, like the well-known "Uneeda" biscuit.

In the case of *Barrett Chemical Co. v. Stern,* (176 N. Y., 27; 68 N. E. Rep. 65,) where the word "Roachsault," used on a compound for destroying insects, was held to be descriptive, and therefore not a valid trade-mark, the Court of Appeals of New York said:

The word "roach" can be used as descriptive of the common insect whose life is sought to be destroyed by the use of the article and so the word "salt" may be used since it is a word in common use to describe chemical preparations and an article for the preparation of food. The two words may be written and used as one word to describe a salt to be used for the purpose of destroying roaches. * * * The case in its legal aspect is the same as if each party had labeled his goods "Roach Poison" instead of "Roach Salt."

The principles thus announced by the court are applicable to the facts in this case.

The decision of the Examiner of Trade-Marks is affirmed.

GOURD *v.* CHARLES JACQUIN ET CIE., INC.

OPPOSITION.

Decided June 29, 1907.

(130 O. G., 655.)

1. TRADE-MARK OPPOSITION—SIMILARITY OF MARKS INCLUDING COMMON FEATURE.
   Held that the mark of the appellant, which consists of the representation of a cross having rays radiating from its upper portion, associated with the

title-phrase "Liqueur de St. Dominic," and the name "Charles Jacquin et Cie" appearing above and below the title-phrase, the whole inclosed in a circular border of dots and crosses arranged alternately, does not so nearly resemble the mark of the opponent, which comprises the words "Veritable Benedictine," "D. O. M.," and the representation of a "cross," as to cause confusion in the mind of the public, where crosses of various types have been used upon liqueurs and cordials by many other dealers.

2. SAME—SAME—UNFAIR COMPETITION IN TRADE NOT CONSIDERED.

The question of unfair competition in trade cannot be. considered in an opposition proceeding.

3. SAME—LIMITATION BY REGISTRATION.

Where it is stated in the certificate of registration that the essential features of the trade-mark are the words "Veritable Benedictine," "D. O. M.," and a "cross," *Held* that the registrant having limited himself in the registration to a mark containing these features is not entitled broadly to the use of a cross so as to exclude others from the use of the same regardless of the similarity of the marks. (Citing *Richter v. Reynolds et al.,* C. D., 1894, 260; 67 O. G., 404; 59 Fed. Rep., 577.)

ON APPEAL.

TRADE-MARK FOR CORDIAL.

Mr. A. Parker-Smith for Gourd.

Messrs. Straley & Hasbrouck for Charles Jacquin et Cie., Inc.

MOORE, *Commissioner:*

This is an appeal from the decision of the Examiner of Interferences dismissing the opposition of Henry E. Gourd to the registration by Charles Jacquin et Cie. of a trade-mark for cordial, consisting of the representation of a cross having rays radiating from the upper portion, associated with the title-phrase "Liqueur de St. Dominic," and the name "Charles Jacquin et Cie" appearing above and below said title-phrase, the whole inclosed by a circular border of dots and crosses arranged alternately.

The grounds of opposition on which the appeal is based may be summarized as follows:

1. That Henry E. Gourd is the agent in the United States for the sale of a cordial known as "Benedictine," which is manufactured by the Societe Anonyme de la Distillerie de la Liqueur Benedictine de L'Abbaye de Fecamp as successor to A. Legrand. that this company has used as its trade-mark the representation of a Latin cross, and that the trade-mark sought to be registered so nearly resembles that of the opposer as to cause confusion in the mind of the public.

2. That the trade-mark sought to be registered is anticipated by trade-mark registration No. 10,410 to Legrand.

The answer of the applicant comprises a formal denial of the allegations of the notice of opposition and the additional defense that the Latin cross has been so generally used in the past by other firms in connection with their trade-marks for cordials that it has become public property and that if the opposer ever had the right to use a Latin cross the same has been lost by reason of his acquiescence in the general use of the same by other manufacturers and dealers in wines and cordials.

Some months after the notice of opposition was filed Gourd filed a motion that he be allowed to amend his notice of opposition by including certain registrations of Legrand which it was alleged anticipated the mark of the applicant.

This motion was denied by the Examiner of Interferences on the ground that the reasons given why these registrations were not included in the original notice of opposition were insufficient to warrant their admission.

It is not necessary to consider whether this was a proper ground for denying the motion, for clearly these registrations furnish new grounds of opposition and as such could not be filed after the expiration of the thirty days allowed by the statute for filing notices of opposition.

As pointed out by the Examiner of Interferences, the question of unfair competition in trade cannot be considered in a proceeding of this kind. The question to be here determined is whether the mark of applicant so nearly resembles a mark used by the opposer as to cause confusion in the mind of the public and deceive purchasers and, if so, whether the opposer has the exclusive right to use this mark.

It was found by the Examiner of Interferences that Charles Jacquin et Cie. had used its mark since 1896, that the Societe Anonyme de la Distillerie de la Liqueur Benedictine de L'Abbaye de Fecamp, which for brevity will be referred to as the " Societe," had used for many years prior to this date a mark one of the features of which is a Latin cross. He held further, however, that the mark used by the opposer does not so closely resemble that of the applicant as to cause confusion in the mind of the public or deceive purchasers and that the opposer has not the exclusive right to the use of a Latin cross broadly as a trade-mark for cordials.

The testimony has been discussed fully by the Examiner of Interferences, and his conclusions as to the use of their marks by the respective parties is correct.

From an inspection of the mark of the applicant and of that which Gourd testifies has been used by the opposer I am of the opinion that these marks are not so alike as to cause confusion in the mind of the public.

There remains to be considered, therefore, only the question whether " Societe " acquired broadly such a right to the use of a Latin s by reason of using it as one feature of its mark as to exclude rs from the use thereof.

The record shows the use of crosses of various types on various kinds of liqueurs and cordials by others than the " Societe." It does not appear that any attempt has been made to stop such use. According to the testimony of Gourd various suits have been brought by the " Societe" against alleged infringers but all these suits turned on the question of unfair competition in trade. On cross-examination on the point Gourd testified as follows:

X-Q. 56. And was the sole issue in all these procedings and in all the others which you have not named, merely the shape of the bottle?

A. The issue rested upon the shape of the bottle, the labels, caps, seals and the general appearance of the bottle.

X-Q. 57. Then do I understand you correctly that each one of these suits was for unfair competition of trade?

A. In a general way they were, as they were instituted against counterfeiters or imitators of the Benedictine package.

It would appear from these facts that the " Societe" did not consider that it was entitled broadly to the use of the representation of a cross as a trade-mark for cordial.

In only one of the certificates of registration of Legrand introduced in evidence is it stated that the cross is an essential feature of the mark, and in that one the essential features of the mark are said to be the words, letters, and symbol " Veritable Benedictine," " D. O. M.," and a " cross."

The question of the effect of such a limited registration arose in the case of *Richter* v. *Anchor Remedy Company*, (52 Fed. Rep., 455,) where it was held that a registrant who had in his registration stated that the essential feature of his mark was the representation of a red anchor on an oval space or field was not entitled to the use of an anchor broadly. The decision was affirmed on appeal, (*Richter* v. *Reynolds et al.*, C. D., 1894, 260; 67 O. G., 404; 59 Fed. Rep., 577,) where the Court said:

* * * As late as July 7, 1885, he registered as his trade-mark an accurately and distinctively defined design, the " essential feature of which " (as he then declared) " is the representation of a red anchor in the oval space." As evidence tending to show what was really claimed or had been intended to be appropriated the court below was clearly right in taking this into consideration, and, in our opinion, it was right, also, in concluding therefrom that the complainant's intention was to confine his claim of trade-mark to the specific device designated and described, and which he further declared to be the one which he had " adopted."

Under the doctrine laid down in these decisions it is held that having limited himself in his registration as pointed out above Legrand and his successors in business are not entitled broadly to the use of a Latin cross as a trade-mark for cordials and to exclude others from the use of the same regardless of the similarity of the marks.

The decision of the Examiner of Interferences is affirmed.

CUTLER *v.* CARICHOFF.

Decided July 31, 1907.

(130 O. G., 656.)

1. INTERFERENCE—MOTION TO TRANSMIT A MOTION TO DISSOLVE—DELAY IN BRINGING.

Where the reasons which are alleged to excuse delay in bringing a motion appear clearly from the record, it is only necessary for the moving party to call attention thereto.

2. SAME—SAME—SAME.

The fact that similar motions have been brought in companion interferences constitutes no sufficient excuse for delay in bringing a motion to dissolve.

APPEAL ON MOTION.

MOTOR-CONTROL SYSTEM.

Messrs. Jones & Addington and *Mr. E. B. H. Tower, Jr.,* for Cutler.

Mr. Albert G. Davis for Carichoff. (*Mr. Arthur A. Buck* and *Mr. Howard M. Morse* of counsel.)

BILLINGS, *Assistant Commissioner:*

This is an appeal by Cutler from the decision of the Examiner of Interferences refusing to transmit a motion to dissolve the above-entitled interference. The motion was filed more than six months from the expiration of the time within which it should have been brought. The Examiner of Interferences refused to transmit the motion because the moving party did not accompany his motion with a sufficient showing of the reasons for delay. It is contended by the appellant that the reasons are to be found in the record and that it is not necessary in such cases to again set forth these reasons in the affidavit. It is believed that in many instances the reasons for delay do appear clearly from the record, and when such is the case it is only necessary for the moving party to call attention to these reasons in order to justify the transmission of the interference. The reasons, however, appearing in the record in this case, which reasons are specified in the affidavit filed by counsel accompanying the motion, are not thought to justify the long delay. The hearings on the motions in the companion interferences have already been had before the Primary Examiner, and the transmission of this motion would entail more expense upon the appellee. There is no reason why this motion could not have been brought when the other motions were brought, for it is alleged, and not denied, that the questions involved before the Examiner in the companion interferences are practically the same. Counsel for appellee well states in his brief that—

It should be noted also that the refusal to transmit this motion imposes no hardship whatever upon Cutler since the ground set up in it is substantially the same as that alleged in the motions filed by him in the companion interferences upon which he has already had a chance to argue, and if the Primary Examiner should grant these motions he could, and of course would, if he thought it necessary, request jurisdiction of the present interference in order that he might take action therein consistent with his decisions in the companion interferences.

On the other hand, should the Primary Examiner deny the motions which are now before him it would clearly be a hardship on the appellee to transmit the present motion.

The decision of the Examiner of Interferences is affirmed.

THE DREVET MANUFACTURING COMPANY *v.* THE LIQUOZONE COMPANY.

Decided January 21, 1907.

(130 O. G., 977.)

1. TRADE-MARKS—OPPOSITION—PRACTICE.

Where no pleading was filed in response to a notice of opposition and no action taken in response to an order to show cause why the opposition should not be sustained, *Held* that a judgment sustaining such notice of opposition was proper.

2. SAME—SAME—ALLEGATION OF ADOPTION AND USE.

An allegation in a notice of opposition that the opposer adopted " Glycozone" as a trade-mark for a remedy for the treatment of germicidal diseases and that its use was begun prior to the use of the trade-mark "Liquozone" and that it is still sold to a large extent is a sufficient allegation of ownership and continuous use.

3. SAME—SAME—SIMILARITY OF MARKS.

Where two marks which are not identical in appearance are similar in sound and it is alleged that such similarity has caused confusion in trade and the applicant does not see fit to put the opposer to proof of the allegation, the contention as to similarity should be sustained.

ON APPEAL.

TRADE-MARK FOR GERMICIDAL REMEDIES.

Messrs. Mason, Fenwick & Lawrence for The Drevet Manufacturing Company.

Messrs. Rector & Hibben and *Messrs. Bacon & Milans* for The Liquozone Company.

MOORE, *Assistant Commissioner:*

This is an appeal by The Liquozone Company from the decision of the Examiner of Interferences sustaining a notice of opposition of The Drevet Manufacturing Company.

The record shows that the Examiner of Interferences overruled a demurrer to the notice of opposition and set times for the filing of a plea or answer. No pleading was filed, and at the expiration of the time allowed an order was issued to show cause within thirty days why the notice of opposition should not be sustained. No further action was taken by the applicant, and at the end of the thirty days judgment was rendered sustaining the notice of opposition.

The above procedure is in accordance with the practice of the United States courts of equity leading to a decree *pro confesso*. By analogy to the practice of the courts the question to be determined upon this appeal is whether the allegations of the notice of opposition are sufficiently distinct and positive when taken as true to warrant the decision refusing registration of the trade-mark in issue. (*Ohio Central Railroad Company* v. *Central Trust Company of New York*, 133 U. S., 83.)

The trade-mark presented for registration by The Liquozone Company is the word " Liquozone " for a germicidal medicine.

The grounds of opposition are stated as follows:

The Drevet Manufacturing Co. are the manufacturers and sole proprietors of Glycozone, a germicidal remedy which is a thoroughly scientific and legitimate preparation for the treatment of germicidal diseases.

Glycozone was on the market for a number of years prior to the introduction of Liquozone on the market, and is still sold to a large extent. Liquozone being so similar in sound to Glycozone when properly pronounced, has caused confusion and unfair competition in trade, and also deception; parties calling for Glycozone being furnished with Liquozone in numerous instances.

It is urged by the applicant that the notice of opposition fails to allege that the opponent ever used the word " Glycozone " as a trademark or that the use of the word "Glycozone " was continuous from a date prior to the date of adoption of the trade-mark " Liquozone " by the applicant. It is also urged that the words " Glycozone " and " Liquozone " are not so similar as to cause confusion in the mind of the public.

These contentions are not well founded. The statements in the notice of opposition that The Drevet Manufacturing Company is the manufacturer and sole proprietor of the remedy " Glycozone " for the treatment of germicidal diseases, that its use was begun prior to the use of the trade-mark " Liquozone " by the applicant, and that it is still sold to a large extent, when given an ordinary meaning are clearly sufficient allegations of ownership and of continuous use of this trade-mark by the opponent.

The words " Liquozone " and " Glycozone " are not identical in appearance. They, however, contain a common final syllable, " ozone," signifying an oxidizing agent, and are susceptible of substantially the same pronunciation. The notice of opposition alleges that the similarity in sound has caused confusion in trade. The appellant has not seen fit to put the opponent to proof of this allegation or to take testimony in contradiction of the same. Under these circumstances the contention of the opponent that "Liquozone" so closely resembles "Glycozone" as to bar registration of the former word should be sustained.

The decision of the Examiner of Interferences is affirmed.

BROWN v. INWOOD AND LAVENBERG.

Decided May 17, 1907.

(130 O. G., 978.)

1. INTERFERENCE—MOTION FOR DISSOLUTION—TRANSMISSION—APPLICATION OF REFERENCES.

Where a motion for dissolution refers to the prior art cited in the records of the applications and gives no information as to what patents are to be urged against the respective counts or how they are to be used or combined to anticipate invention stated in said counts, *Held* that the motion is too indefinite and transmission of the same was properly refused.

2. SAME—MOTION TO AMEND—QUESTION OF NEW MATTER—TRANSMISSION.

The contention that the motion to amend contains new matter relates to the merits and is a matter for the consideration of the Primary Examiner and not the Examiner of Interferences. The motion was therefore properly transmitted.

APPEAL ON MOTION.

MEANS FOR MAKING BOX-BLANKS.

Messrs. Bulkley & Durand and *Messrs. Davis & Davis* for Brown.
Messrs. Dyrenforth, Dyrenforth & Lee for Inwood and Lavenberg.

MOORE, *Acting Commissioner:*

This case is before me on appeals by Brown (1) from the decision of the Examiner of Interferences refusing to transmit the first ground of his motion to dissolve and (2) from the decision of the Examiner of Interferences transmitting the motion of Inwood and Lavenberg to amend their application under Rule 109.

Under his first appeal Brown contends that—

* * * the Examiner of Interferences erred in ignoring the fact that the two counts in question were alleged to be not patentable "in view of the prior art, particularly as disclosed in the records of the applications herein involved;" and for the further reason that the Examiner of Interferences erred in passing upon the pertinency and relevancy of the Walker patent set up in the motion as an anticipation of the counts in question.

The ground of the motion based upon the prior art is entirely too indefinite to satisfy the requirements of the present practice concerning motions to dissolve. It gives the opponent no information as to what patents are to be urged against the respective counts or how appellant proposes to use or combine the patents to anticipate the invention of said counts.

Concerning the patent to Walker, the motion does not state that it alone is relied upon to anticipate the counts, but rather that it is to be used in connection with the machine by which it is alleged the box of the Walker patent was made. The nature of this machine or where it may be found is not disclosed in the motion. The Examiner of Interferences refused to transmit this ground of the motion on account of its indefiniteness, and not for the reason that the patent cited is not pertinent.

This ground of the motion was properly refused transmission by the Examiner of Interferences.

The second appeal of Brown alleges that the motion of his opponents to amend should not have been transmitted, for the reason that the amendment seeks to introduce new matter into the application. This, however, relates to the merits and is clearly a matter for the consideration of the Primary Examiner and not the Examiner of Interferences. No error is found in the decision of the Examiner of Interferences transmitting this motion.

Both decisions of the Examiner of Interferences are affirmed.

LUTHY & COMPANY *v.* PEORIA DRILL & SEEDER COMPANY.

INTERFERENCE.

Decided June 19, 1907.

(130 O. G., 978.)

1. TRADE-MARK INTERFERENCE—USE OF MARK.
   A mere casual use of a mark is insufficient to establish a right to protection in the use thereof.

2. SAME—SAME.
   Slight and immaterial changes in an article to which a trade-mark is applied do not render the use of said mark fraudulent.

ON APPEAL.

TRADE-MARK FOR SEEDING-MACHINES.

Mr. L. M. Thurlow and *Mr. Wallace Greene* for Luthy & Company.
Mr. W. V. Tufft and *Mr. E. M. Giles* for Peoria Drill & Seeder Company.

MOORE, *Commissioner:*

This is an appeal by the Peoria Drill & Seeder Company from a decision of the Examiner of Interferences awarding priority of adoption and use of the trade-mark "Mogul" for seeding-machines to Luthy & Company.

The Peoria Drill & Seeder Company, a corporation organized and existing under the laws of Illinois, is the successor in business of

Selby, Starr & Company, whose business, including its good-will and trade-marks, it acquired on January 2, 1905.

Appellant is engaged in manufacturing farm machinery, as was its predecessor, while Luthy & Company are engaged in jobbing such machinery. In November, 1904, Luthy & Company entered into a contract with Selby, Starr & Company whereby the latter agreed to sell and the former agreed to buy certain machines, including " Force Feed End Gate Seeders (Double)." This seeder is a broadcast seeder for grain adapted to be supported by the end-gate of a wagon, the mechanism of the seeder being driven by gearing leading to one of the rear wagon-wheels. It was to this type of seeder that the trade-mark was applied, and it does not appear that it was applied to any other type of seeder. This machine is referred to in the record as the " double-fan end-gate seeder " or " double-fan seeder."

On January 7, 1905, the Peoria Drill & Seeder Company addressed a letter to Luthy & Company, which was, in part, as follows:

We desire that you let us know what name you desire to have stencilled on the hoppers of the double-fan seeders for which you recently arranged with our Mr. Pattison for the sale, so that we can get stencils ready and have name on the printed matter.

On January 10, 1905, Luthy & Company sent a reply, in which they said:

You may stencil our double-fan seeders "Mogul, Luthy & Co., Peoria, Illinois;" as this is the name we have decided to use on our double-fan seeders.

On behalf of the Peoria Drill & Seeder Company it is claimed that in a conversation previously held between Pattison, the secretary and general manager of the Peoria Drill & Seeder Company, and Voorhees, the manager of Luthy & Company, Pattison suggested a number of names to Voorhees for use on the double-fan seeder, which included the name " Mogul." This is denied by Voorhees, and the testimony of this witness and of others in the employ of Luthy & Company is submitted to prove that the name was selected by them independently from a list of names prepared by Flenner, the assistant manager of Luthy & Company, and submitted to Voorhees. The testimony on this point was fully discussed by the Examiner of Interferences, and it is deemed unnecessary to again discuss it in detail, it being sufficient to say that the evidence seems to warrant the conclusion that the name " Mogul " was adopted by Luthy & Company on January 10, 1905, independently of any suggestions received from the officers of the Peoria Drill & Seeder Company. The evidence further shows that Luthy & Company have continuously used the mark since its adoption on double-fan seeders.

In the declaration of the application filed by appellant it is stated that the mark in issue was adopted January 1, 1905; but evidence is presented tending to show that it was adopted for this machine as early as August, 1904. It is claimed that in the summer and fall of 1904 from ten to sixteen double-fan end-gate machines like the one furnished to Luthy & Company were made and stenciled "Mogul," one of which was sent to the Des Moines fair in August, 1904, some of the remainder being kept at the factory and others being sent to various jobbing firms in the Middle West, among which firms were the Eastern Moline Plow Company, of Indianapolis, Ind., and Liniger & Metcalf, of Omaha, Nebr. It is satisfactorily shown by the evidence that a machine of the double-fan type like that furnished to Luthy & Company was made and exhibited at the Des Moines fair in August, 1904, as claimed, and that this machine was stenciled "Mogul." It is also shown by the evidence that prior to the making of the machine the parties interested in its manufacture had suggested the use of the mark "Mogul" therefor; but the evidence is deemed insufficient to show that this mark was placed on any machine sold or sent out as a sample prior to January 10, 1905, except that exhibited at the Des Moines fair. In answer to cross-question 209 Pattison states that he does not know of any seeder sold and delivered prior to January 10, 1905. As to the sample machines, while both Roby and Pattison say that some were sent out prior to January 10, 1905, and that they were stenciled "Mogul," Roby does not appear to have any positive knowledge, but apparently merely assumes that they were stenciled "Mogul," because he thought that all the sample machines that were sent out were so stenciled.

While I am not convinced by the evidence that any seeder marked "Mogul" of the kind under discussion was ever put out by the Peoria Drill & Seeder Company or its predecessors prior to January 10, 1905, other than the machine exhibited at the Des Moines fair, I do not deem this material to a disposition of this case. It may be assumed for the purposes of this case that sample machines so marked were placed with prospective customers prior to January 10, 1905; but the law requires more than a mere casual use of a mark to establish right to protection in the use thereof. There must be evidence of adoption and use under such "circumstances, as to publicity and length of use, as to show an intention to adopt it as a trade-mark for a specific article." (*Kohler Manufacturing Company* v. *Beshore,* C. D., 1894, 277; 67 O. G., 678; 59 Fed. Rep., 572, 576; *Menendez* v. *Holt,* C. D., 1889, 344; 46 O. G., 971; 128 U. S., 514.) It is believed that the evidence fails to show adoption and use of this mark by appellant or its predecessors for the purpose of identifying the seeder to which it was applied as its product for the following reasons:

At the time the contract of November 24, 1904, was made Selby, Starr & Company said nothing whatever about the adoption of the word "Mogul" for the double seeder. The contract described the seeder as a "Force Feed End Gate Seeder (Double);" but it was not referred to by the name alleged to have been adopted for it, although several of the other items of the contract were referred to by their trade-mark names. Although Pattison claimed to have suggested the word " Mogul " to Voorhees in a conversation held about January 5 or 6, 1905, he did not tell Voorhees that his company had decided to use this name on the double-fan seeder. (P. D. & S. Company record, p. 42 X-Q. 183.) On January 7 the letter above referred to was written asking what name Luthy & Company had decided to use on the seeder, in response to which Luthy & Company wrote that they had decided to use " Mogul," to which no protest whatever was made. On the other hand, the seeders delivered to Luthy & Company subsequently were so stenciled, and Luthy & Company were never advised by the Peoria Drill & Seeder Company that it had adopted this mark or intended to use the same until the fall of 1905, when Luthy & Company failed to renew their contract. Moreover, the contract provided that the right was reserved to the Peoria Drill & Seeder Company to sell other parties under a different brand. Therefore when Luthy & Company selected the brand " Mogul " appellant was not at liberty to use that mark according to the terms of the contract, at least in Luthy & Company's territory, and it appears that it did not use it on machines sold within or outside of such territory until Luthy & Company failed to renew their contract in the fall of 1905. There is some evidence tending to show the use of the mark by appellant concurrently with Luthy & Company during the season of 1905; but I am of the opinion that the record fails to establish the use thereof prior to the fall of 1905, except as above stated in the summer and fall of 1904. In this connection it is significant to note that a circular which was put out by the Peoria Drill & Seeder Company dated October 23, 1905, referred to a number of prominent dealers who sold Mogul seeders the previous season, (season of 1905,) each of whom it appears was a customer of Luthy & Company, and not of the Peoria Drill & Seeder Company. It is significant that this circular did not contain the names of one or more customers of the Peoria Drill & Seeder Company if it had made the sales as alleged. This evidence indicates that appellant did not sell seeders marked " Mogul " to any one except Luthy & Company. The record also shows that appellant sold some of these double-fan seeders under the name " Duplex." (P. D. & S. Company record, p. 27, Q. 56.) These circumstances indicate that appellant never had a fixed intention to use the mark " Mogul " to designate the origin of the double-fan seeder of the construction exhibited at the Des Moines fair in August, 1904, and that the use of the mark in the summer or fall of 1904 was a mere casual one, insufficient to secure an exclusive right thereto.

Evidence was presented on behalf of the Peoria Drill & Seeder Company to show that the seeders manufactured for Luthy & Company by J. A. Engel & Company for the season of 1906, which were placed upon the market as " Mogul " seeders, differed in construction from those furnished by appellant, and it is contended that the use of the mark on such changed construction was fraudulent. While it appears that the constructions were not precisely the same, the differences were slight and immaterial to the present controversy in view of the fact that the mark was adopted and used by Luthy & Company to indicate the goods of their selection and not of their manufacture. (*Menendez* v. *Holt, supra.*)

The decision of the Examiner of Interferences awarding priority of adoption and use to Luthy & Company *is affirmed.*

LATSHAW *v.* DUFF *v.* KAPLAN.

PATENT INTERFERENCE.

Decided September 5, 1907.

(130 O. G., 980.)

1. INTERFERENCE—REOPENING.

   An interference will not be reopened for the purpose of introducing newly-discovered evidence where it does not appear that the evidence could not have been discovered at the time of taking testimony.

2. SAME—APPEAL—REHEARING.

   An appeal from the Examiners-in-Chief will not be reheard for the purpose of considering a patent of one of the parties to the interference which is not in evidence.

ON PETITION.

PULLEY.

Messrs. Kay, Totten & Winter for Latshaw.
Messrs. Bakewell & Byrnes for Duff.
Messrs. Kay, Totten & Winter for Kaplan.

MOORE, *Commissioner:*

This is a petition by Duff that the case be reopened to permit him to offer in evidence a patent granted to him on April 4, 1905, No. 786,274, and that his appeal from the decision of the Examiners-in-Chief be reheard in view of said patent.

This petition is supported by the affidavit of George H. Parmelee, of counsel for Duff, who alleges that this patent was not called to his attention nor to that of any member of the firm of Bakewell & Byrnes, attorneys of record, until after the decision of the Examiners-in-Chief.

It appears that the decision largely turned on which of the parties to the interference first suggested the use of a solid arm for a split pulley and that the patent in question shows such an arm in a split gear-wheel. The application on which this patent was granted was filed August 25, 1904, and it is contended that as this date is prior to any date which Latshaw claims for conception of the invention in issue it proves conclusively that Duff was the first inventor.

The fact that a patent was issued to Duff is not conclusive proof that he was the inventor of the invention shown therein, and it would be manifestly improper to admit the patent in evidence without allowing Latshaw an opportunity to take testimony with respect thereto.

It is well settled that in order to reopen a case for the purpose of taking additional testimony it must be shown that such evidence could not have been sooner discovered. Such is not the case here. Frequent reference is made in the record to a gear-wheel which Duff made, and in answer to cross-question 216 Duff stated that an application for patent on this construction had been filed.

The fact that Duff did not appreciate that this patent might have a bearing on the case, and therefore did not call the attention of the attorneys to it, amounts to an error in judgment, and, as pointed out by Commissioner Mitchell in *Lorraine* v. *Thurmond*, (C. D., 1890, 140; 52 O. G., 1949,) such an error affords no ground for reopening a case.

Since the patent referred to is not in evidence and cannot at this stage of the proceedings be put in evidence for the reasons above stated. there is no reason why the appeal should be reheard.

The petition is denied.

EX PARTE McKEE.

APPLICATION FOR PATENT.

Decided September 5, 1907.

.(130 O. G., 980.)

ABANDONMENT AND REVIVAL—UNAVOIDABLE DELAY.

The fact that the Office did not suggest claims from a copending application does not render applicant's delay in prosecuting his case unavoidable.

ON PETITION.

TIE-PLATE.

Messrs. Christy & Christy and *Mr. D. S. Wolcott* for the applicant.

MOORE, *Commissioner:*

This is a renewal petition that this case, which became abandoned for lack of prosecution, be revived.

It appears that the claims of this application were rejected on references and that no response was made to this action within a year therefrom. It is alleged that subsequently to the filing of this application an application was filed by one De Remer for substantially the same invention, which application was passed to issue without suggesting the claims thereof to the petitioner, and the patent to De Remer was issued on May 14, 1907. This fact, however, in no way renders applicant's delay in prosecuting his case unavoidable. It may be that had such claims been suggested this case would have been further prosecuted; but the fact that they were not so suggested constitutes no excuse for applicant's inaction.

It is also alleged that the delay was unavoidable, because applicant became convinced that the position of the Examiner in rejecting said claims could not be changed and that he was unavoidably delayed in consulting with his attorney. It is not stated, however, how this consultation was prevented, nor does it appear why the attorney could not have asked for a reconsideration of the action of the Examiner and endeavored to show why the claims were not met in the references.

The petition is denied.

THE THOMSON WOOD FINISHING COMPANY *v.* RINALD BROTHERS.

TRADE-MARK INTERFERENCE.

Decided June 14, 1907.

(130 O. G., 980.)

TRADE-MARK INTERFERENCE—ABANDONMENT.
   A declaration of abandonment filed for the purpose of terminating an interference must be unconditional and unequivocal. (*Gabrielson* v. *Felbel*, C. D., 1906, 108; 121 O. G., 601.)

ON PETITION.

TRADE-MARK FOR PAINTS.

Messrs. Wiedersheim & Fairbanks and *Messrs. Howson & Howson* for The Thomson Wood Finishing Company.
Mr. T. W. Johnson and *Mr. Horace Pettit* for Rinald Brothers.

BILLINGS, *Assistant Commissioner:*

This is a petition that jurisdiction be restored to the Examiner of Interferences for the purpose of considering the following motion:

* * * that the judgment entered in this case on May 11th, 1907, be modified by the addition thereto of the words "and it is held that Rinald Brothers are 't entitled to register the word 'Porceline" or the word 'Porcelain' as a trade-rk for paints, enamels, or varnish-paints;

, if it be held that this modification is not proper, that a date be for a hearing on the proofs taken.

It appears that on May 9, 1906, Rinald Brothers filed an abandonment of the word "Porceline" as a trade-mark for paints. This abandonment was accompanied by a statement that they had no intention of abandoning the trade-mark " Porcelain."

On this abandonment the Examiner of Interferences on May 11, 1907, rendered judgment of priority of adoption and use of the mark in issue in favor of The Thomson Wood Finishing Company.

This statement of abandonment was not so unequivocal and unconditional as required by the rules. (*Gabrielson* v. *Felbel*, C. D., 1906, 108; 121 O. G., 691.)   The case is therefore remanded to the Examiner of Interferences with directions to vacate the judgment of May 11, 1907, and resume proceedings.

The petition is granted to the extent indicated.

EX PARTE NIEDENFÜHR.

APPLICATION FOR PATENT.

Decided August 1, 1907.

(130 O. G., 981.)

EXECUTORS AND ADMINISTRATORS OF FOREIGN INVENTORS—GERMANY—PROOF OF AUTHORIZATION.

Where it appears that the applicant, who was a subject of the Emperor of Germany and resided in Germany, is dead and application is made by Mrs. Niedenführ, his alleged administratrix, to prosecute the application, *Held* that in addition to a properly-authenticated certificate of inheritance there should be filed either a certificate of a German court of record that Mrs. Niedenführ is entitled to administer the estate, such certificate being properly proved by the certificate of a consular or diplomatic officer, or else a formal statement to that effect from the German Embassy or the German consulate.

ON PETITION.

PROCESS FOR THE MANUFACTURE OF SULFURIC ACID.

Messrs. Wright, Brown, Quinby & May and *Mr. A. W. Harrison* for Mrs. Olga Niedenführ, administratrix of estate of H. H. Niedenführ.

BILLINGS, *Assistant Commissioner:*

This is a petition that an amendment filed March 8, 1907, by Olga Niedenführ, as administratrix of Heinrich Hugo Niedenführ, the applicant, be entered.

It appears that the applicant was a resident of Germany and died on April 21, 1906. On March 8, 1907, an amendment was filed in response to the Office action of March 8, 1906, signed by Olga Niedenführ, as administratrix of the applicant. This amendment was accompanied by a certificate of inheritance, showing that there were two heirs of the applicant, Olga Niedenführ, his widow, and Henriette

Niedenführ, his mother, and an agreement showing that Henriette Niedenführ had sold her share of the estate to Olga Niedenführ.

These papers were certified to by a notary, whose authority was certified to by the consul-general at Berlin. A letter was also filed from an attorney in Berlin stating that under the German law Olga Niedenführ, as sole heir, was entitled to administer the estate, and that the certificate of inheritance was properly certified to by a notary was sufficient proof of her authority, and that, further, it was impossible to file copies of letters testamentary, as required by Rule 25, as the German law did not provide for such.

The Examiner held that since the amendment was not accompanied by a certified copy of letters of administration in favor of Mrs. Olga Niedenführ she had no authority to make an amendment to the case and that it was abandoned.

Subsequently there were filed a power of attorney from Mrs. Niedenführ to Messrs. Wright, Brown, Quinby & May and a letter from the acting German consul at Baltimore to A. W. Harrison, who represents Wright, Brown, Quinby & May, in answer to a request made of the German embassy as to the law as to the appointment of administrators. In this letter it is stated that the German law makes no provisions for the grant of letters of administration, but the assets and liabilities pass directly to the heirs to whom the court issues a certificate of inheritance.

In *ex parte Huch* (80 MS. Dec., 147, 16 *Gourick's Digest*, 75-77), the widow of a foreign inventor filed a certified copy of the will, together with a certificate of a judge of the Royal Prussian Court at Hanover, Germany, setting forth the death of the inventor and stating that his widow was authorized under the law of Germany to administer upon the estate, and it was held that this was sufficient to comply with the requirements of section 4896 of the Revised Statutes. In the present case the certificate of inheritance and the agreement of sale properly certified have been filed; but the only statement that Mrs. Niedenführ is entitled under the German law to administer the estate and that the papers on file are sufficient evidence under the German law of such authority is contained in the letter above referred to from the acting German consul at Baltimore, which, it is to be noted, is a personal letter written to counsel in this case.

In order to complete the records, there should be filed either a certificate of a German court of record that Mrs. Niedenführ is entitled to administer the estate, such certificate being properly proved by the certificate of a consular or diplomatic officer, or else a formal statement to that effect from the German embassy or the German consulate at Baltimore.

The petition *is denied without prejudice* to its renewal upon the filing of the court certificate or the formal statement of the German law.

SANDAGE v. DEAN v. WRIGHT v. McKENZIE.

PATENT INTERFERFNCE.

Decided August 3, 1907.

(130 O. G., 981.)

1. **INTERFERENCE—TESTIMONY—SURREBUTTAL.**
   Where an inventor testifying in rebuttal on behalf of his opponent denies that he is the inventor of a part of the invention in issue, his testimony constitutes such legal surprise as will entitle his assignee, who is prosecuting the invention, to take surrebuttal testimony.

2. **SAME—SAME—SAME.**
   Where the instances alleged to show that the inventor has testified falsely amount to no more than a difference of opinion between the witness and the affiant, a motion to take surrebutal testimony should be denied.

APPEAL ON MOTION.

VOTING-MACHINE.

Messrs Minturn & Woerner for Sandage.
Messrs. Peirce & Fisher for Dean.
Mr. Francis M. Wright pro se.
Messrs. Wilkinson & Fisher for McKenzie.

BILLINGS, *Assistant Commissioner:*

This case comes up on an appeal by Sandage from a decision of the Examiner of Interferences granting a motion by McKenzie for leave to take surrebuttal testimony and a cross-appeal by McKenzie from so much of the decision as limits the scope of this testimony.

It appears that the interference is being prosecuted by McKenzie's assignee, The U. S. Standard Voting Machine Co. McKenzie was not called as a witness by his assignee, but was called in rebuttal by Sandage.

It is alleged that many of the statements made by McKenzie are untrue, and it is desired to take surrebuttal to show this.

The Examiner of Interferences held that McKenzie's assignee should be permitted to take surrebuttal testimony with respect to what is known as the " spear-head," but that the showing made as to the rest of the testimony did not justify taking surrebuttal with respect thereto.

The " spear-head " construction is shown in McKenzie's drawing and is included in each of the counts as " laterally-movable wedge-shaped plates." This being true, McKenzie's assignee could have no reason to anticipate that McKenzie would deny that he was the inventor thereof. Having made such a denial, his assignee is clearly

entitled to take surrebuttal on this point. If the statement of Mc-
Kenzie that he was not the inventor of the device shown in his application was allowed to go uncontroverted, the Office would be justified in refusing to grant a patent on such an application based
on McKenzie's inventorship, and this statement having been made
during the taking of Sandage's rebuttal McKenzie's assignee would
have no opportunity to deny it unless the motion to take surrebuttal
should be granted.

As to the rest of McKenzie's testimony, it appears, as noted in the
decision of the Examiner of Interferences, that many of the instances
pointed out in the affidavit of Keiper, filed in support of the motion
as showing that McKenzie had testified falsely, amount merely to
differences of opinion between McKenzie and Keiper. Evidently
this is no ground for taking surrebuttal testimony.

As to McKenzie's statement that he never saw certain drawings, it
appears that McKenzie testified that he never saw these drawings
before the applications of which they form a part were filed. The
fact that McKenzie signed the drawings of one of his applications,
as alleged, does not in any way show that he was testifying falsely
when he denied having seen the drawings of other applications.

No error is found in the decision of the Examiner of Interferences,
and it *is accordingly affirmed.*

Ex parte Ravelli.

APPLICATION FOR PATENT.

Decided August 8, 1907.

(130 O. G., 982.)

1. APPLICATION—PERIOD OF ONE YEAR AFTER FILING OF APPLICATION IN FOREIGN
COUNTRY NOT EXTENDED.

Where the applicant filed an application in a foreign country on May 7,
1906, and a patent was granted thereon, an application filed in this country
after May 7, 1907, cannot be received. Applications which the law requires to be filed in this Office within a certain time cannot be held to be
so filed by reason of the fact that they are in the hands of the postal authorities.

2. SAME—SAME—REVISED STATUTES 4894 INAPPLICABLE.

Section 4894 of the Revised Statutes only applies to applications which
already have a status in this Office and is not applicable to cases in which
an application is filed in this Office more than one year from the date upon
which the applicant filed an application in a foreign country and upon
which he has received a patent.

ON PETITION.

APPARATUS FOR UTILIZING THE POWER OF THE SEA-WAVES.

Alfred Müller for the applicant.

BILLINGS, *Acting Commissioner:*

This is a petition that the provisions of section 4887 of the Revised Statutes be waived in respect to the above-entitled application and that the same be accepted as having been filed within the period of twelve months provided for by such section.

It appears from the applicant's oath that he acknowledges the filing of an application for patent on the same invention on the 7th day of May, 1906, in Italy, and it is admitted that this patent has been granted. The application for patent was filed in this Office on May 31, 1907. The applicant states that the application would have been filed in this Office within the year, which expired May 7, 1907, if it had not been for the delay of the postal authorities in delivering to counsel in New York city packages containing the application papers, for they show by postmarks that they arrived in New York on May 5.

It has been repeatedly held, however, that applications which the law requires to be filed in this Office within a certain time cannot be held to be so filed by reason of the fact that they are in the hands of the postal authorities.

It is urged by the petitioner that section 4894, which provides that an application may be revived upon a showing satisfactory to the Commissioner that delay in the prosecution of the application within one year was unavoidable, should be made applicable to this case. That section of the statute only applies to applications which already have a status in this Office. It is clear that it is not applicable to such cases as this, where an application is filed in this Office more than one year from the date upon which the applicant has filed an application in a foreign country upon which he has already received a patent.

It is clear that the Commissioner has no authority under the statutes to grant this petition, and it *is therefore denied.*

POE *v.* SCHARF.

Decided May 17, 1907.

(130 O. G., 1309.)

INTERFERENCE—PRIORITY—DILIGENCE.

Where Poe, who was the first to conceive, but the last to constructively reduce to practice, was diligent at the time Scharf entered the field and the delay of three months between this time and the filing of his application is due to no inaction on the part of Poe, but to the fact that the attorney for his assignee, who was particularly skilled in the art and prepared all its patent applications, was delayed by other work which had accumulated because of his sickness, and the testimony shows that there was no intentional delay upon his part in the preparation of Poe's application, *Held* that Poe was not lacking in diligence.

APPEAL from Examiners-in-Chief.

LINOTYPE MACHINES.

Mr. Philip T. Dodge and *Mr. R. F. Rogers* for Poe.
Messrs. Redding, Kiddle & Greeley for Scharf.

MOORE, *Acting Commissioner:*

This is an appeal from the decision of the Examiners-in-Chief reversing the decision of the Examiner of Interferences in awarding priority of invention to Poe.

The issue of the interference as originally declared contained fifteen counts; but upon reference to the Primary Examiner on the recommendation of the Examiner of Interferences under Rule 126 it has been dissolved as to counts 1, 2, 4, and 7. The question of priority of invention as to counts 3, 5, 6, and 8 to 15, inclusive, remains to be considered.

The following claims serve to illustrate the character of the invention:

8. In a linotype machine, the combination with an assembler and means to discharge the assembled line from the assembler, of means to turn the assembler, the means for discharging the line being under the control of the means for turning the assembler.

11. In a linotype-machine, the combination with an assembler and means to discharge the assembled line therefrom, of a single lever adapted to lock the assembler in either of its positions, to turn the assembler and to control the discharge of the line therefrom.

15. In a linotype-machine, the combination of an assembler having sliding parts, a lever to turn the assembler from its receiving to its discharging position and vice versa, an actuating-bar, said sliding parts including a spring-pawl and a latch normally holding the pawl away from the actuating-bar, means to release the pawl from the latch so that it may engage the bar, and means to disengage the pawl from the bar again, both of which means are operated through the lever.

Both inventors are residents of Canada, and the effective date of conception of each is the date of his introduction of the invention into this country. Neither party claims an actual reduction to practice of the invention, but relies upon the date of filing of his application as his date of constructive reduction to practice.

It is undisputed that Scharf introduced his invention into this country by a communication to his attorneys which was received by them November 4, 1904. His application was filed December 19, 1904.

The Examiner of Interferences and the Examiners-in-Chief found that Poe introduced his invention into this country by a description of the invention accompanied by blue-prints which were sent to Dodge, the president of The Mergenthaler Linotype Company, in May, 1904. The sufficiency of the disclosure of the invention by means of the description and blue-prints was disputed before the lower tribunals, but was not contested at the hearing upon this appeal. It is not disputed, however, that the invention was fully disclosed by Poe to Dodge and to a draftsman, Kittredge, and pencil drawings made illustrating the invention in October, 1904, which is prior to Scharf's available date of conception. The sole questions to be determined are, therefore, whether Poe was active when Scharf entered the field November 4, 1904, and diligent in his endeavor to constructively reduce the invention to practice during the interval between that date and the date upon which he filed his application, February 4, 1905. The conclusion of the Examiners-in-Chief that Poe was diligent during this period differs from that reached by the Examiner of Interferences. The testimony shows that upon October 13, 1904, Poe visited New York and upon October 19 had an interview with Dodge, at which it was arranged that he should be given the services of a draftsman to make patent drawings, and that he should remain in New York and superintend the making of these drawings. Kittredge, the draftsman who was employed, finished the drawings, which are a part of Poe's application, in pencil on or before October 26, 1904, and upon October 29 Poe returned to Montreal. Kittredge completed the drawings in ink and turned them over to Dodge November 8, 1904. It is therefore clear that Poe was active at the time Scharf entered the field.

On November 12 Dodge wrote to Poe requesting a brief memorandum to guide him in preparing the application, and upon November 16 wrote again, acknowledging its receipt.

December 14 Dodge wrote to Poe, stating:

I hope to send you the application papers to-morrow. I have been called away repeatedly and overwhelmed with work, hence the delay.

The application papers were sent to Poe January 10, 1905, and were accompanied by a letter from Dodge, stating:

I am sending you herewith the long-delayed application papers. I rather fear that I have overlooked some of your points, or that I have not properly amplified them. I wish you would slash into the specification and into the claims, which were necessarily prepared in haste, and make any improvements you see fit.

On January 16 Poe returned the application papers to Dodge with certain suggestions, and upon January 25 Dodge sent the application in proper form for execution to Poe. The record shows that the papers were executed January 30 and the application filed February 4, 1905.

Poe's invention is assigned to The Mergenthaler Linotype Company, of which Dodge is president, and it appears that because of his familiarity with linotype-machines Dodge prepares all the applications for patent filed by this company. Dodge states that the delay in filing Poe's application was due to pressure of other work which came upon him by reason of his position and which had accumulated because of his severe sickness in April, June, and July, 1904.

It is shown by Scharf (stipulation, p. 16, Scharf's record) that during the period from November 2, 1904, to February 4, 1905, Dodge filed thirty-three applications for patent, and it is contended that the delay in filing Poe's application was merely for the purpose of business convenience. It is further urged that the preparation of Poe's application might have been delegated to others, since the invention is not in itself particularly complicated, and that therefore the reasons for delay in filing were not of such a compelling nature as should excuse the lack of diligence in constructively reducing the invention to practice.

While these contentions are not without force, it is believed that there was no such lack of diligence as should cause the forfeiture of Poe's rights. It is undisputed that Poe was first to conceive, and his personal efforts to have the application filed are beyond criticism. The delay of three months in filing the application after the drawings had been placed in the hands of the assignee is not, in my opinion, unreasonable in view of the circumstances above referred to. Where the preparation of a large number of applications in a particular art is customarily placed in the hands of one person who is most highly skilled in that art, it is easily understood how the preparation of one may be temporarily postponed, and Dodge's letter of December 14 indicates that this is what occurred in the present case. Dodge's letters of December 14, 1904, and January 10, 1905, clearly show that there was no intent to abandon the invention and no intentional delay in preparing Poe's application.

In the recent case of *Woods* v. *Poor*, (*post*, 651; 130 O. G., 1313;) decided by the Court of Appeals of the District of Columbia April 2, 1907, the facts were analogous to those in the present case and the period of delay was almost the same. Woods conceived the invention in September, 1903, and filed his application January 27, 1904. Poor conceived his invention about November, 1, 1903, and filed his application December 17, 1903. It was shown that in October or November, 1903, Woods embarked in business for himself, but did nothing in respect to his invention but discuss the invention with an employee with a view to overcoming certain supposed defects. In that case the Court said:

Taking into consideration the nature of the invention, the circumstances surrounding him at the time, the comparatively short time between his date of conception and the date Poor entered the field, his promptness in filing his application thereafter, and the fact that the reduction to practice was constructive and not actual in each case, we conclude that Woods has shown that degree of diligence which the law requires and that he is justly entitled to the fruits of his discovery.

In the present case the reduction to practice of each party was constructive. Poe was active at the time Scharf entered the field. It is clearly shown that there was no intentional delay upon the part of the assignee in filing Poe's application. The period of delay was not long, and the circumstances causing the postponement of the preparation of the application were reasonable. I find, therefore, no reason why Poe should be deprived of the benefits of his invention or his rights subordinated to those of Scharf.

The decision of the Examiners-in-Chief is affirmed.

Ex parte International Corset Company.

APPLICATION FOR REGISTRATION OF TRADE-MARK.

Decided June 24, 1907.

(130 O. G., 1310.)

1. TRADE-MARKS—ANTICIPATION.

    "La Camille" for corsets *Held* to be anticipated by "Camille Royal Combination" for feminine apparel.

2. SAME—IDENTITY OF MERCHANDISE—FEMININE APPAREL—CORSETS.

    Held that the term "feminine apparel" stated as the particular description of the goods to which the registrant's mark is applied is comprehensive enough to include "corsets."

ON APPEAL.

TRADE-MARK FOR CORSETS.

Messrs. Poole & Brown for the applicant.

MOORE, *Commissioner:*

This is an appeal from the action of the Examiner of Trade-Marks refusing to register the words "La Camille" as a trade-mark for corsets in view of the registration by C. Caen, November 11, 1890, No. 18,603, of the words "Camille Royal Combination" for feminine apparel.

It is contended by the appellant that his mark does not so nearly resemble that of the registrant as to cause confusion in the mind of the public and that corsets do not fall within the class of goods covered by the registration.

In my opinion neither of these contentions is well founded. The salient feature of each mark by which the goods would be identified is clearly the word "Camile," and the use of these marks upon goods of the same descriptive properties would be likely to cause confusion in trade.

The class of goods to which the registered trade-mark is appropriated is set forth in the statement of the registration as " garments " and the particular description of goods comprised in such class upon which the mark is used as " feminine apparel." It is apparent that the registrant by using the broad term " feminine apparel " intended to cover all body-garments worn by women and girls.

The facts in this case are closely analogous to those in *ex parte A. Stein & Company*, (C. D., 1898, 635; 85 O. G., 147,) in which registration of a trade-mark for garters, which closely resembled a registered trade-mark for " wearing-apparel for men and boys," was refused. In that decision Commissioner Duell said:

It is apparent that the registrant intended to cover the class of wearing-apparel used by men and boys. In view of the decisions, both of the courts and of the Office, I am of the opinion that where an applicant intends to cover a class broadly it is unnecessary to mention every particular description of goods comprised in such class. (*Smith et al.* v. *Reynolds & Jacobs*, 3 O. G., 214; *ex parte Boehm & Co.*, C. D., 1875, 103; 8 O. G., 319.) Under these decisions I think that the registrant would be protected by the courts in the use of the trade-mark when applied to garters. I think, therefore, that the applicants are anticipated by the present registration. (*Ex parte Manny & Co.*, 17 MS. Dec., 455.)

It may be that the registered mark is not in use or that its owner has not used it and does not care to use it in connection with such articles as garters. I think it would be proper for the Office to register the mark if applicants should file a written statement from the registrant evidencing his consent.

The term " feminine apparel " is clearly comprehensive enough to include corsets, and unless evidence is presented showing that the registrant's mark is not used upon corsets it is believed that registration of the applicant's mark should be refused.

The decision of the Examiner of Trade-Marks is affirmed.

WENDE *v.* HORINE.

PATENT INTERFERENCE.

Decided September 6, 1907.

(130 O. G., 1311.)

1. INTERFERENCE—REOPENING—PRACTICE.

The Court of Appeals of the District of Columbia having held that a second interference involving claims differing merely in scope from those involved in the first interference should not have been declared, the latter will not be reopened for the purpose of allowing the issue of the second interference to be contested therein.

2. SAME—SAME—SAME.

The fact that a proceeding by bill in equity under section 4915 Revised Statutes might prove slow and expensive should not outweigh the necessity for proper and orderly procedure in an interference.

ON PETITION.

MANIFOLDING APPARATUS.

Mr. George E. Waldo for Wende.
Messrs. Bond, Adams, Pickard & Jackson for Horine.

MOORE, *Commissioner:*

This is a petition by Wende that the Commissioner, under the exercise of his supervisory power, reinstate the interference *Wende v. Horine*, No. 20,587, and remand the same to the Primary Examiner with instructions to amend or re-form the issue of the interference by adding thereto certain counts of the issue of a second interference, No. 24,488, between the same parties.

The interference No. 20,587, which petitioner desires to have reinstated, was determined by the decision of the Commissioner awarding priority in favor of Horine on January 2, 1904, and this decision became final through the failure of Wende to take an appeal. Horine subsequently took out his patent, whereupon Wende copied certain claims, and a second interference, No. 24,488, was declared between the same cases, but upon counts differing somewhat in scope. In the second interference Wende prevailed upon certain counts before the various tribunals of the Patent Office, but upon appeal to the Court of Appeals of the District of Columbia that court held (*post*, 615; 129 O. G., 2858) that the case came within the rules laid down in *Blackford* v. *Wilder* (*post*, 491; 127 O. G., 1255) and that Wende by acquiescing in the decision in the first interference was estopped from again litigating in a second interference the same subject-matter upon claims differing merely in scope. Wende now seeks to reopen the first interference in order that he may contest therein the subject-matter of the second interference.

It is contended by Horine that the Commissioner is without authority to grant petitioner's request. It is unnecessary to discuss this contention, since even if possessed of the authority I do not consider that the circumstances of the present case would justify the exercise of that authority. The first interference was finally determined over three years ago. To excuse the long delay of Wende in bringing his motion or petition would require a most extraordinary showing. Instead of bringing his motion promptly Wende chose to pursue another course, which the court held was an improper one. He now wishes to retrace his steps and pursue the other course. This is clearly not such a showing of extraordinary circumstances or unavoidable delay as would justify reopening the interference.

Another reason why the interference should not be reopened is that Wende claims to have a remedy by bill in equity under section 4915, Revised Statutes; but he states that he anticipates such remedy would prove slow and expensive. Even if the latter remedy is subject to the disadvantages mentioned this should not outweigh the necessity for proper and orderly procedure in the case. Wende has had his day in court so far as the interferences mentioned are concerned, and where Congress has provided still another remedy his proper course is to seek relief in that way. Moreover, Horine has his patent, so that the only question to be determined, if the interference should be reinstated, would be Wende's right to a patent, and as to this he admits he has an adequate remedy by bill in equity.

The petition is denied.

EX PARTE THE RAINIER COMPANY.

APPLICATION FOR REGISTRATION OF TRADE-MARK.

Decided June 21, 1907.

(130 O. G., 1311.)

1. TRADE-MARKS—" RAINIER "—SURNAME.

The primary significance of the word " Rainier " which forms part of applicant's name is that of the name of an individual, and it is therefore not registrable as a trade-mark.

2. SAME—SAME—NOT WRITTEN IN FANCIFUL MANNER.

The word " Rainier " written in large script letters, with a flourish extending from the letter " R " beneath certain letters of the word, *Held* not to be such a distinctive display of the name as required by the act of 1905 to confer registrability upon the mere name of an individual.

ON APPEAL.

TRADE-MARK FOR MOTOR-CARS, &C.

Mr. H. A. West for the appellant.

BILLINGS, *Assistant Commissioner:*

This is an appeal from the action of the Examiner of Trade-Marks refusing to register the word " Rainier " as a trade-mark for automobiles.

Registration was refused on the ground that the word " Rainier " is geographical and on the further ground that it is the mere name an individual not written in a particular or distinctive manner.

That the word " Rainier " is the name of an individual is not controverted by the applicant; but it is contended, first, that it is not merely the name of an individual, and, second, that if it is merely the name of an individual it is written, printed, or impressed in a peculiar and distinctive manner, and therefore registrable.

This first contention is based on the ground that besides being the name of an individual Rainier is the name of a mountain in Washington. This use of the word is, however, not its principal use, and its primary significance is as the name of an individual, as is shown by the fact that the word constitutes the distinguishing feature of applicant's name, which is apparently derived from the name of an individual. It is held, therefore, that within the meaning of the Trade-Mark Act this name is merely that of an individual.

The word is written in large script letters with a flourish extending from the letter " R " beneath certain letters of the word.

This is not such a distinctive display of the name as required by the Trade-Mark Act. A similar question came up in *ex parte United States Brewing Company*, (C. D., 1906, 437; 125 O. G., 352,) and it was held by the Commissioner that a family name printed in script on a diagonal line, the letters being shaded so as to appear in perspective and with a paraph under the word, was not such a distinctive display as to justify registration.

The decision of the Examiner of Trade-Marks is affirmed.

SMITH *v.* FOX.

Decided July 18, 1907.

(130 O. G., 1312.)

INTERFERENCE—MOTION TO TRANSMIT A MOTION TO DISSOLVE—DELAY IN BRINGING.
  Where the hearing on a motion to transmit a motion to dissolve is extended by stipulation of the parties and, before the hearing an amended motion is filed stating the grounds of the first motion more specifically, *Held* that the motion, if in proper form, should have been transmitted even if the first motion was not sufficiently specific.

APPEAL ON MOTION.

STEAM-TURBINE.

Messrs. Goepel & Goepel for Smith.
Mr. Albert G. Davis for Fox.

BILLINGS, *Assistant Commissioner:*
This is an appeal by Smith from the decision of the Examiner of Interferences refusing to transmit an amended motion to dissolve the above-entitled interference.

to 9 in view of certain prior patents. The Examiner held that the allegation made in the motion was indefinite. It is stated in the motion that each of the counts from 1 to 9, inclusive, is unpatentable in view of the eight cited patents, and it is said:

Each of the counts is also met in each of the above patents, singly or in combination.

This statement is clearly alternative, and therefore the motion in this particular instead of being clear and specific, which was the end desired to be accomplished by inaugurating the present practice, is vague and indefinite.

The decision of the Examiner of Interferences is affirmed.

Ex parte Walters.

Decided January 19, 1907.

(130 O. G., 1483.)

Anticipation—Patent—Failure of Specification to State Character of Material.

Where the specification of a patent cited as an anticipation does not state of what material the article is composed, it cannot ordinarily be assumed . to be of any particular material.

Appeal from Examiners-in-Chief

BANDAGE.

Messrs Wiedersheim & Fairbanks for the applicant.

Moore, *Assistant Commissioner:*

This is an appeal from a decision of the Examiners-in-Chief refusing the allowance of the following claims:

1. A bandage having its inner or contact face composed wholly of soft rubber, and having means associated therewith for adjustment upon the anatomy of the wearer.

2. A bandage composed of soft rubber, and having a flap for bridging the ends of the bandage thus to present a continuous structure, the flap being also of soft rubber.

3. A bandage composed of soft rubber and having its terminals reinforced, adjusting means associated with the reinforced portion, and a soft-rubber flap bridging the gap between the terminals.

4. A bandage composed of soft rubber, and having its terminals reinforced and provided with lacing-eyes, and a flap secured to the inner side of one end of the bandage and bridging the gap between the terminals.

5. A bandage composed of soft rubber and having a flap for bridging its ends ᵐn positioned upon the wearer. the flap in conjunction with the body of the lage forming a continuous and unbroken sweating zone.

A bandage composed of soft rubber and having its terminals reinforced . provided with lacing-eyes, and a flap secured to the inner side of one end the bandage and bridging the gap between the terminals, the back of the ᵃandage being wider than the front.

The references are Rowley, July 27, 1875, No. 165,955; Wilson, November 12, 1901, No. 686,498; Barnett, August 12, 1902, No. 706,715; Ewing, April 21, 1903, No. 725,688.

The object of the invention is stated to be—

* * * to retain the natural heat of the body or part to which the bandage is applied and to stimulate circulation, thereby preventing and curing inflammatory and muscular rheumatism, reducing objectionable adipose tissue and preventing formation thereof; to obviate the necessity of employment of supporting-straps to hold the device in position upon the wearer; to dispense with the employment of fabric in the making up of the bandage and also of bones, stays and other additions which would render it uncomfortable in use; and generally to improve bandages of this character.

The most pertinent references are the patents to Ewing and Barnett. The patent to Ewing discloses a bandage composed of textile fabric and soft rubber, the soft rubber forming a continuous lining adapted to lie next to the body of the wearer, lacing-eyes to secure the ends of the bandage together, and a flap to bridge the gap between the ends of the bandage when laced together. Although the specification does not specify of what material this flap is made, it is represented in the drawings in the same way as another part which is said to be composed of drilling—a textile material. It is thought, therefore, that this flap cannot be assumed to be of soft rubber.

The patent to Barnett discloses a bandage made of " a single sheet of rubber or gutta-percha." As the properties of gutta-percha are very different from soft rubber, it can scarcely be concluded that the "sheet of rubber " described by this patentee is the *soft* rubber of appellant. This bandage is primarily intended to fit the abdomen, and in order to give it the proper form the sheet is gored at points, the edges of the gores are secured together, and strips of rubber secured over the joints. These strips present an irregular surface, which tends to chafe the skin.

Appellant uses soft rubber instead of the gutta-percha or equivalent of the Barnett patent, and she does away with the textile backing of the Ewing patent except for a fabric strip to strengthen the eyelets; but what seems more important, she uses a flap of soft rubber and so disposes it as to make, with the main portion of the bandage, a continuous " sweating " zone. The structure as a whole appears to present a slight improvement over the prior art sufficient to sustain claims 2 and 3, which include the bandage composed of soft rubber and the soft-rubber flap. Claims 1, 4, 5, and 6 do not properly bring out the distinctions of appellant's construction over the prior art and should not be allowed.

The decision of the Examiners-in-Chief *is affirmed* as to claims 1, 4, 5, and 6, and *reversed* as to claims 2 and 3.

EX PARTE STREATOR METAL STAMPING COMPANY,

APPLICATION FOR REGISTRATION OF TRADE-MARK.

Decided September 10, 1907.

(130 O. G., 1483.)

TRADE-MARKS—RED CROSS ACT.

A mark an essential feature of which is a cross printed in red properly refused registration under the act of January 5, 1905, since such a cross is a colorable imitation of the cross of the American National Red Cross.

ON APPEAL.

TRADE-MARK FOR CARPET-SWEEPERS.

Messrs. Parker & Carter for the applicant.

MOORE, *Commissioner:*

This is an appeal by the Streator Metal Stamping Company from a decision of the Examiner of Trade-Marks refusing to register as a trade-mark for carpet-sweepers a mark the essential feature of which is a red cross.

Registration was refused under authority of the act of Congress approved January 5, 1905, entitled "An Act to Incorporate the American National Red Cross." Section 4 of this act provides in part as follows:

Nor shall it be lawful for any person or corporation, other than the Red Cross of America, not now lawfully entitled to use the sign of the red cross hereafter to use such sign or any insignia colored in imitation thereof for the purposes of trade or as an advertisement to induce the sale of any article whatsoever.

The applicant does not claim to have adopted its mark prior to the passage of this act, but contends that the act should be construed narrowly, and that as the cross of its mark is not exactly the same as the red cross of the Red Cross Society the mark should be registered.

Applicant's mark comprises the representation of a cross inclosed in a circle which cuts the arms of the cross. Both circle and cross are described as printed in red and are so shown in the specimens on file. The cross of the Red Cross Society has rectangular arms.

The difference between the two crosses is not, however, sufficient to entitle the applicant to register its mark. The cross printed in red is certainly a colorable imitation of the red cross of the American National Red Cross, whether it be an exact copy of that cross or differs slightly therefrom.

It is also contended that the act referred to is unconstitutional; but it is deemed unnecessary to discuss that matter. The question of the constitutionality of an act of Congress is one which this Office cannot pass upon, but which must be left to the courts to decide. .

The decision of the Examiner of Trade-Marks is affirmed.

PLANTEN *v.* CANTON PHARMACY COMPANY.

TRADE-MARK INTERFERENCE.

Decided September 19, 1907.

(130 O. G., 1484.)

1. TRADE-MARKS—MOTIONS FOR DISSOLUTION—INTERFERENCE IN FACT—MARKS SHOWN IN DRAWINGS ALONE CONSIDERED.

In determining the question of interference in fact between two trade-marks which are presented for registration only the marks disclosed in the applications of the respective parties are to be considered.

2. SAME—SAME—SAME.

Held that interference in fact exists between the words "Black Caps" written in script on a black rectangular background and a mark comprising the words "Black Capsules" printed in Roman letters on a similar background.

APPEAL ON MOTION.

TRADE-MARK FOR PHARMACEUTICAL PREPARATIONS.

Mr. James L. Ewin for Planten.
Mr. A. S. Pattison for Canton Pharmacy Company.

MOORE, *Commissioner:*

This is an appeal from the decision of the Examiner of Trade-Marks refusing a motion of the Canton Pharmacy Company to dissolve this interference on the ground that there is no interference in fact between the trade-marks disclosed in the applications of the respective parties.

The trade-mark of the Canton Pharmacy Company consists of the words "Black Caps" written in script upon a black rectangular background. The trade-mark disclosed in the application of John Rutgert Planten consists of the words "Black Capsules" in Roman type on a black rectangular background.

The specimens filed by Planten disclose a black rectangular background having thereupon the words "Planten's C & C or Black Capsules."

It is contended upon behalf of the appellant that it is necessary to consider the entire mark used by Planten upon the goods as his trade-mark and not merely that which is shown in the drawing forming a part of his application. It is urged that the marks when thus considered are sufficiently distinguished to avoid confusion in the mind of the public.

This contention is untenable. The court of appeals *in re Standard Underground Cable Company* (C. D., 1906, 687; 123 O. G., 656) refused to restrict an applicant to the registration of a device including all the matter shown in his specimens and held that the applicant had the right to designate the part of the mark shown which he considered his trade-mark.

In that decision the Court said:

> The act is silent as to the use to which the specimens are to be put. The drawing is manifestly to be furnished for photolithographic purposes. It may be that the specimens may be required for the purpose of showing that the mark has actually been used, how affixed to the goods, and that the claimed mark actually appears upon the specimens furnished. It does not seem to us that it is to be presumed that the specimens are to be furnished in order that the Commissioner of Patents may pass upon the question as to how much of the matter which appears upon the specimens constitutes the mark. * * *
>
> We repeat that we do not think that Congress intended to confer upon the Commissioner of Patents authority to say to an applicant how much or how little of the embellishments appearing, in connection with what may be called the essential feature of a trade-mark. form an actual part of the trade-mark. Rather do we think that this right of selection and designation rests with the applicant. No general rule can possibly be applied, and where this is the case, it is unwise to attempt to exercise a power not expressly vested in an executive officer.

Planten has in his application for registration averred that he is the owner of the trade-mark shown in his drawing, and this, in view of the decision of the court above cited, is all that can be considered in determining whether or not there is interference in fact. The similarity in appearance and in the significance of these marks is in my opinion such as would be likely to cause confusion in the mind of the public and to deceive purchasers.

The decision of the Examiner of Trade-Marks refusing to dissolve the interference is right and *is affirmed.*

SUGDEN AND PIDGIN *v.* LAGANKE AND SMITH *v.* MARSHALL.

PATENT INTERFERENCE.

Decided June 13, 1907.

(130 O. G., 1484.)

INTERFERENCE—MOTION TO DISSOLVE—TRANSMISSION.

A motion to dissolve on the ground of irregularity in the declaration of the interference properly refused transmission where the alleged irregularity is that the issue of the present interference is substantially the same as that of a former interference which the Primary Examiner dissolved.

APPEAL ON MOTION.

Messrs. Wright, Brown, Quinby & May, for Sugden and Pidgin.
Mr. E. G. Siggers for Laganke and Smith.
Messrs. Bates, Fouts & Hull for Marshall.

BILLINGS, *Assistant Commissioner:*

This is an appeal by Laganke and Smith from a decision of the Examiner of Interferences in part denying their motion to transmit a motion to dissolve the above-entitled interference.

The Examiner of Interferences refused to transmit that part of the motion which alleged that there had been an irregularity in the declaration of the interference such as to preclude the proper determination of the question of priority of invention. The ground of irregularity as contemplated by the rule relates to some formal error in the declaration of the interference and does not contemplate those errors which necessarily arise because there has been an alleged mistake in considering questions relating to the merits.

As stated in the decision of the Examiner of Interferences, the alleged irregularity consists in the fact—

* * * that the declaration of this interference is on substantially the same issue as that of a former interference which the Examiner dissolved on the ground that the combination of a book type-writer and an adding-machine was not patentable, the issue of the present interference differing only from the first by the inclusion of the ordinary features of a book type-writer, which in no way affect the combination.

The Examiner of Interferences was right in holding that this objection forms no basis for a motion to dissolve on the ground of irregularity, since it relates to the patentability of the issue.

The decision of the Examiner of Interferences is affirmed.

EX PARTE COLLINS.

APPLICATION FOR REGISTRATION OF TRADE-MARK.

Decided July 22, 1907.

(130 O. G., 1485.)

1. TRADE-MARKS—ANTICIPATION—EXPIRED REGISTRATION.

An expired registration is still evidence to some extent of the existence of a mark, and the Office is not justified in permitting registration of the same mark or a similar mark by another until he has in some way overcome the registration:

2. SAME—SAME—SAME—FOREIGN APPLICANT.

Inasmuch as the act of 1881 did not require that applicants residing in a foreign country obtain registration in that country as a prerequisite to registration in this country and since the laws of Great Britain, where the applicant resides, provides for re-registration of marks, *Held*, that in the absence of proof the expiration of the trade-mark, registration under section 5 of the act of 1881 will not be presumed merely because more than fourteen years, the period of registration in Great Britain, has elapsed since registration in this country.

ON APPEAL.

TRADE-MARK FOR PORTLAND CEMENT.

Mr. Richard H. Manning for the applicant.

BILLINGS, *Assistant Commissioner:*

This is an appeal from the decision of the Examiner of Trade-Marks refusing to register as a trade-mark for cement a mark consisting of three pyramids with their bases united and the word " Pyramid " appearing therebelow.

Registration was refused on the prior registrations of Knight, Bevan & Sturge, No. 11,787, December 16, 1884, and No. 13,782, November 2, 1886. In the former of these the representation of a pyramid is claimed as a mark for cement; in the latter the word " Pyramid."

Applicant does not contend that the mark shown in these registrations is not so nearly like his as to cause confusion in trade and deceive the public, but contends that under section 5 of the act of 1881 these registrations expired in 1898 and in 1900, respectively, and therefore are not available as references.

It appears that Knight, Bevan & Sturge are or were at the time the marks were registered residents of Great Britain, doing business in the city of London. Section 5 of the act of 1881 is as follows:

Section 5. That a certificate of registry shall remain in force for thirty years from its date, except in cases where the trade-mark is claimed for and applied to articles not manufactured in this country, and in which it receives protection under the laws of a foreign country for a shorter period, in which case it shall cease to have any force in this country by virtue of this act at the time that such trade-mark ceases to be exclusive property elsewhere. At any time during the six months prior to the expiration of thirty years, such registration may be renewed on the same terms and for a like period.

The original registration of a trade-mark in Great Britain is for a period of fourteen years. Applicant therefore contends that the registrations are of no force and effect. It does not appear, however, that the trade-marks in question were registered in Great Britain at the time they were registered here, such prior registrations not being required by the act of 1881 as a prerequisite to the registration in this country. Furthermore, the laws of Great Britain provide for the re-registration of a mark, and it does not appear that the marks in estion have not been re-registered.

Moreover, if the registrations of Knight, Bevan & Sturge have expired they would still be evidence to some extent of the existence of a mark substantially the same as that of applicant, and for the reasons pointed out in *ex parte The Star Distillery Company* (C. D., 1905, 493; 119 O. G., 964) and *Schneider v. The Union Distilling Company*, (C. D., 1906, 129; 121 O. G., 1676,) with reference to the marks registered under the invalid act of 1870, the Office would not be justified in registering applicant's mark until he has in some way overcome these registrations.

The decision of the Examiner of Trade-Marks is affirmed.

MARTIN *v.* GOODRUM *v.* DYSON *v.* LATTIG AND GOODRUM.

PATENT INTERFERENCE.

Decided July 31, 1907.

(130 O. G., 1480.)

MOTION TO DISSOLVE—NON-PATENTABILITY—REFERENCE FAILING TO ANTEDATE ALLEGATIONS OF PRELIMINARY STATEMENT—TRANSMISSION.

Although the date of a reference relied upon in a motion to dissolve alleging anticipation of the issue is later than the date of conception set up in the preliminary statement of the opposing party, the motion may nevertheless be transmitted in order that the Primary Examiner may consider the pertinency of the reference and permit the filing of an affidavit alleging the facts required by Rule 75 outside of those contained in such preliminary statement.

APPEAL ON MOTION.

TELEPHONE SYSTEM.

Messrs. Bulkley & Dyrand for Martin.
Messrs. Church & Rich for Goodrum.
Mr. Thos. H. Ferguson for Dyson.
Messrs. Church & Rich for Lattig and Goodrum.

BILLINGS, *Assistant Commissioner:*

This is an appeal by Martin from the decision of the Examiner of Interferences transmitting Dyson's motion to dissolve the interference.

It is alleged in behalf of Martin that that portion of the motion which sets forth an alleged bar to the grant of a patent to him should not have been transmitted, because the reference cited in the motion is on its face not a reference for his application. Martin alleges in his preliminary statement a date of conception prior to the filing date of the application upon which the patent cited as a reference was granted. The proofs to be submitted by Martin if effective to warrant a decision in his favor in the interference would also be effective to overcome the reference cited. In such cases the interfer-

ence should continue without requiring a party to set forth his case
by means of the *ex parte* affidavits provided for in Rule 75. The appellee however, contends that the appellant should be required at
least to file an affidavit setting forth the other facts required to be
alleged by Rule 75 before Martin should have standing in this interference. It is believed that this contention has sufficient force to
warrant the transmission of the motion to the Primary Examiner
to consider the pertinency of the reference cited and to permit the
filing of an affidavit by Martin alleging the facts required by Rule
75, should he be able to do so, in addition to those which he has
already set forth in his preliminary statement.

The decision of the Examiner of Interferences is affirmed.

In re U. S. Standard Voting Machine Company.

Decided August 10, 1907.

(130 O. G., 1486.)

COPIES OF AFFIDAVIT FILED UNDER RULE 75—CERTIFICATE OF COURT REQUIRED.

    The Patent Office will not, upon the request of the defeated party of an
interference proceeding, furnish copies of an affidavit filed *ex parte* by his
opponent under Rule 75 to overcome a reference against claims not involved
in the interference merely upon a showing that petitioner has brought a
suit in equity under Sec. 4915 Rev. Stats. to determine priority of
invention and desires a copy of such affidavit for use in such suit. Under
such circumstances a copy will be furnished only upon a certificate of the
court that such affidavit would constitute material and proper evidence in
such suit.

ON PETITION.

Mr. Melville Church for the U. S. Standard Voting Machine Company.

Mr. William A. Megrath for James C. Garrett.

BILLINGS, *Acting Commissioner:*

This is a petition by the U. S. Standard Voting Machine Company
that it be permitted to have a certified copy of an affidavit (paper
No. 49) filed under Rule 75 by Garrett in his application No. 552,153.
The U. S. Standard Voting Machine Company is the assignee of the
application of Davis, No. 727,200, formerly involved with said application of Garrett in interference No. 22,102, *Davis v. Garrett.*

Petitioner and its assignor have made repeated but unsuccessful
efforts extending over a number of years, not only in the Patent
Office, but before the Secretary of the Interior and the courts, to
obtain access to said affidavit.

Petitioner represents that after the adverse decision in the interference by the Court of Appeals of the District of Columbia a suit in equity was brought in the United States Circuit Court for the District of New Jersey under section 4915, Revised Statutes, for the purpose of having the said Davis adjudged entitled to a patent for the invention constituting the issue of said interference and that petitioner deems said affidavit material evidence in its behalf.

The record shows that the said affidavit was filed by Garrett prior to the declaration of the interference for the purpose of overcoming the Davis patent, No. 526,668, issued on an application filed June 13, 1894, and cited as a reference against his claims 39, 40, 41, and 270. It should be noted that these claims were not involved in the interference, nor are they involved in the present court proceeding.

Petitioner claims that it is advised and believes that in said affidavit Garrett states that he actually constructed a machine embodying the subject-matter of said claims prior to June, 1894, and that if such is the case it contradicts his testimony given in the interference proceedings that he never constructed a machine prior to December, 1894. Petitioner states that he therefore desires a copy of said affidavit for the purpose of attacking Garrett's credibility as a witness in the pending court proceeding.

In this contention petitioner starts out with a false premise. It is not necessary that Garrett should have actually constructed a machine prior to June, 1894, in order to overcome the Garrett patent under Rule 75. As stated in *ex parte Gasser*, (C. D., 1880, 94; 17 O. G., 507:)

The applicant, therefore, must state on oath facts showing either that a reduction to practice had been made before the filing of the application on which the patent was granted, or that the invention had been conceived before that time and by due diligence connected with a subsequent reduction to practice.

See also *ex parte Donovan*, (C. D., 1890, 109; 52 O. G., 309.)

In view of petitioner's repeated efforts to obtain access to this affidavit it is believed to be not improper to state that said affidavit has been inspected and is not found to disclose the inconsistency alleged by petitioner.

Petitioner bases his right to a certified copy of said affidavit on section 892 of the Revised Statutes.

On an appeal by Davis to the Secretary of the Interior from a former denial by the Commissioner of a petition for said affidavit the Acting Secretary of the Interior held, (*Davis v. Garrett*, C. D., 1904, 578; 112 O. G., 1211:)

Upon the merits of the matter presented, it is not open to question, and is admitted, that the Commissioner of Patents is not bound to submit for either public or private inspection many papers filed in his Office in support of applications for patents. This is in accord with a manifest public policy, declared by the rules governing procedure in that Office and recognized by the courts, and, in my judgment, no good reason is shown and none exists why a party to an interference proceeding should be permitted to examine papers relating to claims not involved in the interference, even though the party in whose interest the papers were filed happens to be a party to such proceeding.

In *Electric Light Company* v. *Commissioner of Patents* (C. D., 1891, 271; 54 O. G., 267;) and *Bulkley* v. *Butterworth*, (C. D., 1897, 685; 81 O. G., 505;) where it was attempted by mandamus proceedings to compel the Commissioner of Patents to furnish copies of applications, the court held that section 892 does not require or authorize the Commissioner to furnish such copies. In the latter case the Court said:

No person is required to submit his private papers to others or produce them in court on the demand of a party to a suit on his allegation or claim that they are material evidence for such party, but only in obedience to the mandate of the court in which such suit is pending, and it is only reasonable that when a public officer has under his control a paper or document in its nature private, or such as the public generally is not entitled to have access to as a public record, he should not be compellable to produce it or deliver copies of it until he has some information from the court in which the case is pending that it is required as evidence. The certificate or order which the regulation in question provides for is the equivalent of a subpoena *duces tecum*, and the statute in question was enacted to avoid the necessity of using such process to obtain papers required as evidence from the Executive Departments of the Government. The court in which a suit is pending and not the Department officer is the appropriate tribunal to determine whether a given paper should be produced as evidence, and it is not to be doubted that the respondent upon such certificate from the Circuit Court of the United States for the Northern District of California would furnish the copies requested.

The affidavit of Garrett in question does not relate to the claim forming the issue, and its relevancy to the suit in question is not apparent. Under these circumstances it is not believed that this Office would be warranted in permitting petitioner to have access to said affidavit or in furnishing it with a certified copy thereof without a certificate of the court before which the suit is pending that said affidavit would constitute material and proper evidence in said suit. (*In re Heard*, C. D., 1905, 66; 114 O. G., 2381; *in re Benedict and Morsell*, C. D., 1905, 176; 116 O. G., 874.)

The petition is denied.

STONE *v.* FESSENDEN.

PATENT INTERFERENCE.

Decided August 15, 1907.

(130 O. G., 1487.)

INTERFERENCE—ACCESS TO RECORDS OF ANOTHER INTERFERENCE.

Where S. requested copies of the decision of the Examiner upon a motion for dissolution in another interference to which F. was a party and which

Is referred to in F.'s record, *Held* that since S. was not a party to the other interference and the claims forming the issue of that interference are not made by S. he should be denied access to the record of that interference, even though the issue thereof is based upon the same structure as that upon which the claims in the present interference are drawn.

ON PETITION.

Messers. Browne & Woodworth and *Messrs. Foster, Freeman, Watson, & Coit* for Stone.

Mr. Francis W. H. Clay for Fessenden.

BILLINGS, *Acting Commissioner:*

This is a petition by Stone that he be permitted to obtain copies of certain papers containing actions upon the merits of certain claims of Fessenden not included in the issue of this interference. The papers which Stone requests copies of comprise a decision of the Primary Examiner upon a motion for dissolution in another interference, *Vreeland* v. *Fessenden* v. *Schloemilch*, to which Stone is not a party, the decision of the Board of Examiners-in-Chief upon appeal by Vreeland from the decision of the Examiner upon the motion for dissolution, and a subsequent action of the Examiner in that interference relative to Fessenden's claims. It is contended by Stone that he is entitled to access to all the data of actions upon claims relating to the invention in issue and that the claims forming the issue of the other interference do not relate to a divisible invention from that involved in the present interference. Stone now has access to the specifications and all the claims of Fessenden's application and is therefore in possession of sufficient information to enable him to determine the propriety of any action which he is entitled to take in this interference. No reason therefore appears why he should be permitted access to records of an interference in which he is not involved. The fact that the claims of the other interference are based upon the same structure as that upon which the claims involved in this interference are drawn is not thought to be material so long as these claims are not made by Stone.

In Stone's request for access to these papers he states that he does not ask to see the data relating to the applications of Vreeland and Schloemilch in the other interferences, but only to the subject-matter relating to the Fessenden application. It would be impracticable in many cases, as in the present, for the Office to furnish extracts of decisions upon motion for dissolution in other cases, since in such decisions the merits of each party's application is discussed with more or less particularity in connection with the applications of the other parties and disclosure would be made to the moving party of subject-matter of applications which are not concerned in the present interference.

It is believed that the Office would not be justified in permitting Stone to have copies of the papers requested in view of the facts above stated.

The petition is denied.

EX PARTE FIELD.

Decided December 13, 1906.

(130 O. G., 1687.)

INTERFERENCE—SUSPENSION—POSTPONEMENT OF TIME FOR OPENING PRELIMINARY STATEMENTS.

> An interference relating to a machine will not be suspended and the time for opening the preliminary statements postponed in order that one of the parties may take out a patent upon an application covering a closely related process not involved in the interference before the existence of such application is discovered by his opponent through access to the machine application which contains a cross-reference thereto.

ON PETITION.

METHOD OF ACTING UPON WARP-THREADS.

Messrs. Emery & Booth for the applicant. (*Messrs. Dodge & Sons* of counsel.)

MOORE, *Assistant Commissioner:*

This is a petition for suspension of interference proceedings and postponement of the time for opening the preliminary statements therein in order that the petitioner may take out a patent upon an application not involved in the interference before the existence of such application is discovered by his opponent through access to the application in interference which contains a cross-reference to the application which it is desired to issue.

On November 1, 1906, the Examiner made the following action in the case which is not involved in the interference:

> The amended method claims are considered to be allowable, but this application must be withheld from issue pending a decision on the question of priority of invention of the subject-matter of such apparatus claims of the original application as are involved in the issues of the interference proceedings now under way.

The applicant brought a petition from this action, which was recently granted. Prior to the grant of said petition the present petition for suspension of proceedings in interference was brought.

It seems clear that this Office should no more suspend an interference proceeding for a party in order that an application of his not involved therein may be issued as a patent before his opponents obtain knowledge thereof than it should withhold his application from issue for the sole purpose of permitting such knowledge to be obtained. The Office is not interested in pursuing one of these courses rather than the other, and there seems to be no point to the statement in the brief last filed that the Office in refusing to grant the requested suspension of the interference is taking an advantage in the matter. Nor does it appear that in withholding the application from issue pending the determination of the question whether issue should be suspended until the interference is concluded the Office has been guilty of any wrong to the applicant, as charged in said brief. The applicant has no right at any time in the matter of an application for patent to any other status than that which has resulted through the regular course of the prosecution of his application. He is not injured in any legal sense by any delay in the issue of his application incident to the proper determination by the Patent Office of the propriety of issuing the same. In this case the Examiner was of the opinion that the application should be withheld from issue pending the determination of the question of priority in the interference proceedings. There are some reasons which may be urged in support of this position, and the language of Rule 106 might well have been taken to authorize the same. Being of this opinion, the Examiner properly withheld the case, and the fact that his judgment has been reversed upon appeal affords the petitioner no good reason to complain of the delay incident to obtaining such reversal.

The petitioner states that refusal to suspend the interference, resulting in the disclosure to his opponents of the existence of the application not involved therein, gives them information to which they have no right in law or in equity. I find in this, however, no reason why the suspension should be granted. It does not appear that the petitioner has any right in law or equity to have this information kept from his opponents. A disclosure of such information under the circumstances of this case is fully contemplated by the very decision upon which the petitioner has relied in his contention for the early issue of his application. In the decision *ex parte Atwood*, (C. D., 1888, 74; 44 O. G., 341,) referring to the application involved in interference and to the application not involved, but which had been held up by the Examiner in view of the interference, Commissioner Hall stated:

Not only this, but in the present application I understand there is a cross-reference to the apparatus application, and I infer that there is a similar cross-reference in the latter. If there is not there should be, and it should still be introduced. This gives the other party to the interference notice of the existence of the present application for the process, and if he does not choose to promptly file his application for such process (if he claims to be the inventor of it,) and thus bring himself into interference with it, he ought not to be allowed by indirection to do what he refuses to do directly—tie up the present application and delay issuance upon an imaginary or supposititious interference not contemplated and not provided for in the rules.

No good reason is found in the matters which have been called to my attention for suspending proceedings in the interference. It seems clear that this Office should not take action in a proceeding for no other purpose than to insure to a party a business advantage which he might otherwise fail to secure.

The petition is denied.

EX PARTE WILLIAMS.

Decided December 15, 1906.

(130 O. G., 1688.)

PATENTABILITY—CHANGES INVOLVING MECHANICAL SKILL ONLY—NO INVENTION.
  Where the device shown in the application differs from that of a prior patent merely in the shape of the grooves in which a sealing mixture is to be placed, *Held* that it would be a mere matter of mechanical skill to adapt the shape of the groove to the nature of the sealing material to be used.

APPEAL from Examiners-in-Chief.

BURIAL-CASE.

Messrs. Robinson, Martin & Jones for the applicant.

MOORE, *Assistant Commissioner:*

This is an appeal from the decision of the Examiners-in-Chief affirming the Primary Examiner's rejection of the following claim:

An outside burial-case consisting of a cement body of suitable form and size to receive a casket having an open top with a shoulder and an upwardly-standing flange outside of the shoulder around the upper edge of the wall, the flange having an inwardly-facing groove, a cement cover adapted to close the top of the case and rest on the shoulder and having around its edge an outwardly-facing groove, the groove of the cover and the groove of the flange together forming an upright elliptical space, and the cover and flange arranged to provide an open joint to receive in connection with said elliptical space a liquid cement, substantially as set forth.

The claim was rejected on the ground that the structure specified therein is anticipated in the patent to Zarling, No. 712,030, granted October 28, 1902. In the patentee's structure the grooves in the cover and the wall of the case are rectangular in cross-section, while in the applicant's structure the grooves are of curved outline in cross-section, forming, as stated in the claim, an elliptical space when the cover is in place.

It is contended on behalf of the applicant that the construction shown by the patentee could not be better devised to facilitate the formation of cracks and defects in the joint-filling and that the form of the grooves is such that when the joint filling or sealing material is poured in air will be trapped and prevent the grooves from being properly filled. These defects, it is contended, are overcome in the joint shown in the application and defined in the appealed claim.

It is not apparent that the sealing material which the patentee states is to be poured into the groove or the liquid cement mentioned in the claim would not properly fill the groove shown in the patent or that air would be trapped in the groove. It would seem, on the contrary, that a liquid of a consistency to permit its being poured into the comparatively narrow channels shown in the patent and in the appellant's application would fill the rectangular space of the patentee's structure as completely as the elliptical space to which the appealed claim is limited. Moreover, even if it were satisfactorily established that the patentee's structure is defective for the reasons referred to by the appellant nothing more than ordinary mechanical skill would be required to adapt the shape of the sealing-grooves to the nature of the sealing material used in closing the casket.

The decision of the Examiners-in-Chief is affirmed.

Ex parte Smith.

APPLICATION FOR DESIGN PATENT.

Decided September 5, 1907.

(130 O. G., 1688.)

DESIGN—FONT OF TYPE—PATENTABILITY.

Where, as in the art of printing, the field of inventive design is limited to modifications of detail in predetermined forms of letters, and an inventor has succeeded in producing a new font having clearly distinguishing characteristics running through the whole, and the esthetic value of his production is confirmed by an extensive demand for the same, it is believed that he should be granted the right to a lawful monopoly of the results of his labor for the limited time provided by the design statutes.

APPEAL from Examiners-in-Chief.

DESIGN FOR A FONT OF TYPE.

Mr. Ernest W. Bradford for the applicant.

MOORE, *Commissioner:*

This is an appeal from the decision of the Examiners-in-Chief affirming the action of the Examiner of Designs and refusing a patent upon a design for a font of type in view of the design patent to Capitain, No. 36,461, July 21, 1903. The Examiners-in-Chief agree with the Examiner of Designs that the peculiarities of the individual letters of the appellant's font do not bear such relation to the font as a whole as to render it patentable and that the differences in the appellant's font over that of the patent are not such as involved the exercise of the inventive faculties.

The fonts of type disclosed in both the application and the patent are of the bold characters used in advertising and comprise, in general, the " Roman " form of letters.

In the font disclosed in the patent the letters are composed wholly of heavy lines, which, while varying somewhat in breadth in different parts of the letters, when observed in a line of type give an impression of bold uniformity of heavy lines. In the font shown by the appellant the letters, which include a plurality of straight lines, comprise certain heavy lines and other thin lines, which the appellant well states—

gives the letter an open and easily-read character while at the same time, because of the thick lines, it has a heavy appearance.

The letters embodying curved lines are similarly distinguished and where joined to straight lines form well-defined angles instead of being provided with fillets. The serifs in the appellant's font are formed of much thinner lines than those of the patented font. The union between the main parts of the letters and their serifs is also distinguished by sharply-defined angles. Where fillets are employed, as in the letters E, F, L, T, and Z, they are formed of straight lines terminating short of the points of the letters, while the fillets of the corresponding letters of the patented font merge into the curved or rounded points of the letters. By reason of these features the " counters " or open spaces within appellant's letters are made more prominent, giving the letters an open appearance when assembled in words. This characteristic is common to all the letters of the alphabet, both in the capitals and the small or lower-case letters, and is the real distinguishing feature of the appellant's font. I do not agree with the opinion of the lower tribunals that the peculiarities of the individual letters of the appellant's font do not bear a definite relation to the whole.

It remains to be considered whether the differences between the appellant's font and that of the reference involved invention and not merely the exercise of mechanical skill and whether the design is ornamental in character.

The " Roman " form of type is used both by the appellant and by the patentee. The question of invention is therefore limited to whether the variation in the details of the letters is such as involved the exercise of anything more than mechanical skill.

The style of letter designed by the patentee is uniform in character, but has an individuality which has been recognized to involve patentability. The appellant's font by reason of the open character of the letters, produced more or less by changes in detail, has an individuality which clearly distinguishes it from that of the reference. No confusion would, in my opinion, be likely to exist between these fonts when used upon the printed page, whether found side by side or in separate places.

It is believed that more than ordinary skill of a designer was required to produce the font of type presented by the applicant, which differs not merely in individual letters but as an entirety from the font disclosed in the reference.

The esthetic value of a new font of type is in a great measure dependent upon the harmonious effect produced upon the eye of the observer by the predominant characteristics of the font.   In the decision *in re Schraubstadter* (C. D., 1906, 541; 120 O. G., 1167) the Court of Appeals of the District of Columbia said that—

The eye to which the design is to appeal is that of the ordinary man and not the eye of the artist.

In the art of printing, and especially the advertising branch of that art, the measure of the artistic value may often be determined by the extent of use of the font, for if the font does not as a whole commend itself to the purchaser the demand therefor will fail.   In the present case there is no doubt that the appellant's font of type is ornamental in appearance, and the fact that it has gone into very extensive use, as shown by affidavits on record in this case, confirms, in my mind, the artistic value of the design.

Where, as in the art of printing, the field of inventive design is limited to modifications of details in predetermined forms of letters and an inventor has succeeded in producing a new font having clearly distinguishing characteristics running through the whole and the esthetic value of his production is confirmed by an extensive demand for the same, it is believed that he should be granted the right to a lawful monopoly of the results of his labors for the limited time provided by the design statutes.

The decision of the Examiners-in-Chief is reversed.

Ex parte Meyer.

APPLICATION FOR PATENT.

Decided September 17, 1907.

(130 O. G., 1689.)

WITHDRAWAL OF APPLICATION FROM ISSUE.

An application will not be withdrawn from issue for the purpose of permitting the applicant to adopt claims of a patent where it appears that the question of interference between the applications of the respective parties was considered by the Examiner before the cases were allowed.

ON PETITION.

Messrs. Barthel & Barthel for the applicant.

MOORE, *Commissioner:*

This is a petition that the application be withdrawn from issue.

As the ground for the petition it is stated that a patent to Parker, No. 855,198, was issued May 28, 1907, on an application copending with this application, that the Parker patent contains claims dominating and conflicting with applicant's invention and the claims drawn thereon, and that applicant was given no chance to contest the same.

The petition is not accompanied by an amendment containing the claims of the Parker patent which it is stated applicant has a right to make. This of itself is sufficient ground for denying the petition.

In his statement the Examiner says that the question of interference between this application and the Parker application was carefully considered, and it was decided there were no conflicting claims. It is not the practice of the Office to withdraw a case from issue unless the Office has made an obvious mistake, except in a case where irremediable injury would occur.

In this case applicant is not without his remedy, for he can allow the case to become forfeited, renew the same, and present the claims of the Parker patent which he thinks he is entitled to make.

The petition is denied.

JOSLEYN *r.* HULSE.

PATENT INTERFERENCE.

Decided June 20, 1907.

(130 O. G., 1689.)

1. INTERFERENCE—MOTION FOR DISSOLUTION—TRANSMISSION OF.

Where a motion to dissolve, on the ground that the adverse party had no right to make the claims and that his application did not show an operative device, was brought nearly two months after the expiration of the thirty days, *Held* that the fact that attorneys were busy with other matters and that it was necessary to make certain models constitutes no sufficient excuse for the delay, especially as no showing was made why it was necessary to make so many models or to take so long a time to complete them.

2. SAME—SAME—SAME.

The pendency of a motion under Rule 109 is no excuse for the delay in ʳing a motion to dissolve.

L ON MOTION.

TYPE-WRITING MACHINE.

Mr. Jacob Felbel for Josleyn.
Messrs. Knight Bros. for Hulse.

BILLINGS, *Assistant Commissioner:*

This is an appeal by Josleyn from a decision of the Examiner of Interferences refusing to transmit to the Primary Examiner a motion to dissolve on the ground that Hulse has no right to make the claims.

The Examiner of Interferences refused to transmit the motion on the ground that it was brought long after the expiration of the thirty days allowed for bringing such motions and that no sufficient excuse had been given for such delay.

The reason alleged why Hulse has no right to make the claims is that his application does not disclose an operative device.

Motions on the ground of inoperativeness are not favored, and it is incumbent upon a party bringing such a motion to do so promptly.

It appears that nearly two months elapsed between the expiration of the thirty days and the bringing of the motion to dissolve.

In explanation of this delay it is stated in affidavits accompanying the motion that it was found necessary to make certain models and that the attorneys for Josleyn were exceedingly busy with this matter and with other matters.

It is well settled, as pointed out by the Examiner of Interferences, that the mere fact that the attorneys were busy with other matters will not excuse delay. Furthermore, it does not appear why, if it was necessary to test the question of inoperativeness by making models, it was necessary to make so many of them or why it should have taken so long a time to complete them. The models exhibited at the hearing were small and apparently could have been made in a short time by a mechanic skilled in the art.

The fact that there is now pending before the Primary Examiner a motion to amend under Rule 109 is no excuse for the delay in bringing the present motion. (*Townsend* v. *Copeland* v. *Robinson*, C. D., 1906, 356; 124 O. G., 1210.)

Moreover, if this motion should be transmitted merely because of the pendancy of another motion a third motion might be brought before the Primary Examiner had decided this one and its transmission urged on the same ground. Such practice would tend to cause endless delays.

The decision of the Examiner of Interferences is affirmed.

DYSON *v.* LAND *v.* DUNBAR *v.* BROWNE.

PATENT INTERFERENCE.

Decided August 17, 1907.

(130 O. G., 1690.)

1. INTERFERENCE—MOTION TO SUPPRESS TESTIMONY—CONSIDERATION POSTPONED UNTIL FINAL HEARING.

Where a consideration of a motion to suppress testimony would involve a consideration of a large portion of the record, a decision upon the motion will be postponed until final hearing.

2. SAME—SAME—QUESTION OF RIGHT TO TAKE SURREBUTTAL TESTIMONY.

The right to take surrebuttal testimony is not merely dependent upon the propriety of opponent's testimony and is therefore not affected by a refusal to consider a motion to suppress prior to final hearing.

APPEAL ON MOTION.

TELEPHONE SYSTEM.

Mr. George L. Cragg for Dyson.
Mr. Thomas S. Ferguson for Land.
Messrs. Bacon & Milans for Dunbar.
Mr. Charles Neave and *Messrs. Mauro, Cameron, Lewis & Massie* for Browne.

BILLINGS, *Acting Commissioner:*

This is an appeal by Browne from the decision of the Examiner of Interferences dismissing his motion to strike out certain portions of the deposition of Harry G. Webster, a witness testifying in behalf of Dyson. The record shows that the motion as brought before the Examiner of Interferences also requested the suppression of parts of the testimony of Dyson and of Land, together with certain exhibits of the latter. The present appeal is confined to the action of the Examiner of Interferences in dismissing the motion to suppress the deposition of Webster. The Examiner of Interferences in his decision dismissing the motion held that the consideration of this motion would involve a review of a large portion of the records of the case and dismissed the motion without prejudice to the right of Browne to renew the same at the final hearing. The action of the Examiner of Interferences is in accordance with the well-established practice of the Office (*Talbott* v. *Monell*, C. D., 1902, 216; 99 O. G., 2965; *Hall* v. *Alvord*, C. D., 1902, 418; 101 O. G., 1833; *Royce* v. *Kempshall*, C. D., 1905, 461; 119 O. G., 338) and should not be disturbed unless an obvious error has been committed. It may be observed that in the cases cited by Browne in support of his contention motion to suppress testimony should be decided prior to the ring the testimony which it was found necessary to suppress was apparent without reviewing a large part of the record of the case in which it was involved.

It is alleged in the motion and also in the affidavit of McKnight, of counsel for Browne, that the deposition of Webster comprises expert testimony and information evidence. It is, however, apparent from statements in McKnight's affidavit that the testimony of Webster refers to testimony of Browne, Morowck, McDonough, and other witnesses and also to certain exhibits presented by Browne. It is therefore apparent that the consideration of Browne's motion would involve the consideration of a large portion of the record, which would necessarily be reviewed upon the final hearing of the case.

It is urged by Browne that the decision should be rendered upon the question of the suppression of Webster's testimony prior to the final hearing in order that he may know whether to bring the motion for permission to take surrebuttal testimony. As well stated by the Examiner of Interferences:

> The right to take surrebuttal testimony is not merely dependent upon the propriety of opponent's testimony. If the opponent's testimony is improper it will not be considered and surrebuttal is unnecessary. If it is proper the right to take surrebuttal founded upon this alleged impropriety falls. It is clear that the surprise which will authorize surrebuttal testimony must reside in something else than the fact that the opponent has offered inadmissible evidence.

It is not therefore apparent that the refusal to consider the motion to suppress testimony at this time will impose any hardship upon Browne.

The decision of the Examiner of Interferences is affirmed.

UNDERWOOD TYPEWRITER COMPANY *v.* A. B. DICK COMPANY.

OPPOSITION.

Decided August 27, 1907.

(130 O. G., 1680.)

1. OPPOSITION—TESTIMONY—SUPPRESSION.
    Rebuttal testimony taken for the purpose of establishing facts not alleged in the notice of opposition or which should have been offered as part of the testimony-in-chief is improper rebuttal, and a motion to suppress the same will be granted.

2. SAME—SAME—PRINTED RECORD.
    Where the motion to suppress was granted after the testimony was printed, it will be a sufficient compliance with the ruling in *Marconi v. Shoemaker v. Fessenden* (C. D., 1906, 149; 121 O. G., 2664) for the docket clerk to indicate in the usual manner in the printed record the matter which has been expunged.

APPEAL ON MOTION.

Messrs. Mason, Fenwick & Lawrence for Underwood Typewriter Company.

Mr. S. O. Edmonds for A. B. Dick Company.

BILLINGS, *Acting Commissioner:*

This is an appeal by the Underwood Typewriter Company from the decision of the Examiner of Interferences holding that certain testimony taken by said company in rebuttal was not proper rebuttal testimony and that it should for that reason be expunged from the record.

An examination of the record shows that in the notice of opposition it was alleged that the A. B. Dick Company was not entitled to register the word " Mimeograph " as a trade-mark for duplicating-machines on the ground that that word was the name of a patented article, the patent having expired. In the rebuttal witnesses are called for the purpose of showing that the word " mimeograph " was generally used in the trade to identify any one of a number of duplicating-machines for doing similar work. It is very clear that this testimony is taken for the purpose of establishing facts not alleged in the notice of opposition, for the notice of opposition alleges that the word particularly identifies the machine of a certain patent.

On the other hand, if the notice of opposition could be construed broadly enough to warrant the presentation of such testimony, which has been taken in rebuttal and which has been objected to by the A. B. Dick Company, it is very clear that this testimony should have been made a part of the testimony-in-chief.

Viewed in either light the testimony objected to is improper rebuttal testimony, and the Examiner of Interferences was right in granting the motion.

It is set forth in the appeal that the Examiner of Interferences did not indicate in what manner the testimony should have been expunged. This has been clearly indicated by the Commissioner in the case of *Marconi v. Shoemaker v. Fessenden*, (C. D., 1906, 149; 121 O. G., 2664.) The facts in this case, however, differ from those in the Marconi case, in that the motion to strike out was not brought until after the testimony of the Underwood Typewriter Company had been printed. While the excuse for the delay in bringing the motion is regarded as sufficient, yet in view of the fact that the motion was not brought until after the testimony had been printed it will be a sufficient compliance with the ruling in this case for the docket clerk to indicate in the usual manner in the printed record the testimony which has been expunged.

The decision of the Examiner of Interferences is affirmed.

GORDON v. WENTWORTH.

Decided March 22, 1907.

(130 O. G., 2065.)

1. INTERFERENCE—PRIORITY—REDUCTION TO PRACTICE—TEST.

As a general rule, before a machine can be considered as a reduction to practice it must be subjected to a test, and the test must demonstrate the fitness of the machine for a useful purpose.

2. SAME—SAME—SAME—EVIDENCE OF SUCCESSFUL TEST.

The mere general statements of witnesses that a device operated successfully, unsupported by the production of the articles upon which the machine operated at the time, must be regarded as meager evidence of a successful test.

3. SAME—SAME—SAME—SAME—SUCCESSFUL OPERATION OF DEVICE AT TRIAL.

If a machine may be successfully operated at the time testimony is taken, this fact, taken in connection with statements of witnesses that it operated successfully when first constructed, may be considered sufficient evidence of a successful test where it appears that the device has not been changed in the meantime.

4. SAME—SAME—SAME—EVIDENCE THAT DEVICE WAS UNSUCCESSFUL.

Where after an alleged successful test a device is thrown aside and apparently forgotten until knowledge is gained of a rival's successful invention, notwithstanding an apparent demand for such a device, *Held* that such conduct carries a strong presumption that the device was regarded only as an unsuccessful experiment.

APPEAL from Examiners-in-Chief.

HEEL-SEAT-FORMING MACHINE.

Messrs. Phillips, Van Everen & Fish for Gordon.
Messrs. Wood & Wood for Wentworth.

MOORE, *Assistant Commissioner:*

This is an appeal by Gordon from a decision of the Examiners-in-Chief affirming the decision of the Examiner of Interferences awarding priority of invention to Wentworth.

The issue is as follows:

1. A machine for beating out shoe-uppers, having, in combination, two series of rotating beaters arranged to act simultaneously upon the lower edge of a shoe-upper at opposite sides of the shoe and beat out the lower edge of the upper upon the insole at opposite sides of the shoe and arranged to exert a shoe-upper at opposite sides of the shoe and beat out the lower edge of the upper upon 'the insole, and means for actuating said beaters, substantially as described.

2. A machine for beating out shoe-uppers, having, in combination, two series of rotating beaters acting simultaneously to beat out the lower edge of a shoe-upper upon the insole at opposite sides of the shoe and to draw the upper over the edge of the insole toward the medial line of the insole, and means for actuating said beaters.

3. A machine for beating out shoe-uppers, having, in combination, two series of rotating beaters acting simultaneously to beat out the lower edge of a shoe-upper upon the insole at opposite sides of the shoe and arranged to exert a wiping action on the upper from the edge of the sole toward the medial line of the sole, and means for actuating said beaters.

The invention relates to the manufacture of shoes, and more especially to a machine for pressing down or beating out the lower edge of the upper about the heel in order to fold this portion of the upper over the inner sole before the outer sole and heel are applied. The purpose is to make the upper conform to the last and to furnish a smooth seat upon which the heel portion of the sole may rest.

Wentworth's application was filed December 8, 1904. Gordon's application was filed March 23, 1905.

Gordon claims to have reduced the invention to practice in 1902, while Wentworth does not claim to have conceived the invention prior to 1904. The lower tribunals found that Gordon built a machine in 1902 which appears to contain the elements of the issue; but they held that it did not constitute a reduction to practice, because the proofs failed to show that it was a successful machine. I am of the opinion that the conclusions reached below were correct.

It is clear that Gordon was the first to conceive the invention. It is equally clear that he was not exercising diligence when Wentworth entered the field. Hence the only question which need be considered is whether the Gordon machine of 1902 constituted a reduction to practice.

The evidence shows that this machine, which is in evidence and known as "Gordon's Exhibit, Gordon Machine," was made prior to August, 1902, and tried on twenty-four pairs of dummy-shoes at the Albany-street factory, Boston, of the United Shoe Machinery Company. It was then sent, in August, 1902, to Snow's shoe factory, at Brockton, Mass., where it was operated for half a day. Shortly after this it was returned to the Albany-street factory, where it remained unused until May, 1903, when, at the instance of the inventor, it was sent to a training-school at Lynn, Mass., maintained by the United Shoe Machinery Company, where men were taught the use of the lasting-machines of the company for the purpose of taking positions with shoe manufacturers as operators on lasting-machines. It appears that the machine remained here for above five or six weeks, during which time it was operated more or less, after which it was returned to the Albany-street factory, where it remained until the filing of Gordon's application. This, briefly stated, is a history of this exhibit machine which is now claimed as a reduction to practice.

As a general rule, before a machine can be considered as a reduction to practice it must be subjected to a test, and the test must demonstrate the fitness of the machine for a useful purpose. The evidence seems to show clearly that the "Gordon Exhibit, Gordon Machine" was operated at Snow's factory, Brockton, Mass., in August, 1902, and at the Lynn school about May, 1903, and the question to be determined is the measure of success which attended these trials. The evidence to be considered on this point consists of the testimony of the witnesses as to the character of the work done by the machine at the time the test took place, the character of the work done by the machine at the time the testimony was taken, and the presumptions arising from the conduct of the inventor and his assignee.

There is no direct evidence tending to show the character of the work done by the machine in 1902 and 1903 except the conclusions of the witnesses that it operated successfully and performed the functions for which it was designed. In the absence of more specific testimony or the production of some of the articles on which the machine operated at that time these conclusions of the witnesses must be regarded as meager evidence of a successful test. During the taking of the testimony the exhibit machine was operated in the presence of counsel of both parties and the results of such operation are shown in a number of exhibit shoes introduced into evidence by both parties. If these exhibits show that the machine may be successfully operated now, it would seem a sufficient confirmation of the opinions of the witnesses who saw the original test, and who state that it was successful, it appearing that the machine has not been changed in the meantime.

A mere inspection of these exhibits is not sufficient to enable a determination to be made as to the successful operation of the machine. Whether a given heel-seat is a good heel-seat or a heel-seat which will satisfy the requirements of the trade is a technical matter which can be properly passed upon only by those skilled in the manufacture of shoes, and for this reason I shall be guided by the expert testimony introduced on this point. The testimony is quite contradictory and unsatisfactory. Certain exhibits were made with the "Gordon Exhibit, Gordon Machine" by one of the appellant's witnesses. Two other exhibits were made by one of appellee's witnesses. Appellant claims that the operator for appellee tried to get as poor results as possible, while appellee claims that appellant's operator did not operate the machine the way it was designed to be operated. Appellant's witnesses state that the exhibits produced are as good as the average work done in factories to-day, while appellee's witnesses state that a machine which would not produce better work would be absolutely useless. Under those circumstances seemingly unimportant details brought out by the witnesses must be given greater weight than would be the case were the testimony more in harmony.

The allegation of appellee that the machine was not operated in the way it was intended to be operated is supported by the testimony. The two rotating hammers which operate to beat out the upper are designed first to operate on the center portion of the upper at the back, at which time the hammers lie side by side, after which by pushing the heel of the shoe farther into the machine the hammers spread apart and simultaneously operate on opposite sides of the heel portion. In connection with Gordon's Exhibit Shoes Nos. 1, 2, 3, and 4, which Gordon's witness Gifford subjected to the Gordon Exhibit, Gordon Machine, and which exhibits are relied upon to show that the machine will make a satisfactory heel-seat, Gifford was asked:

X-Q. 20. When this exhibit is thus first presented to the Gordon machine, you first present one of these upstanding edges upon one side of the center tack to the hammers, and then present the upstanding edge on the other side to the hammers, do you not, or, at least, you did so yesterday?

A. Yes, sir; this is the way I operated the machine yesterday.

It is not clear that a machine operated in the way which this witness operated it would be a satisfactory machine, and these tests do not satisfactorily prove that the machine would produce a satisfactory product when operated in the way it was designed to operate.

Moreover, even if these exhibit shoes had been produced by the machine when operated in the way it was designed to operate it would not avail appellant, because the testimony of his own witnesses leaves in doubt the question whether the results produced are satisfactory. Of the experts called by Gordon, Tarr states that Exhibits Nos. 1 and 2 are very fair heel-seats, that No. 3 is a good heel-seat, and that No. 4 is an excellent heel-seat. (Record, p. 246.) Arnold states on direct examination (Record, p. 251) that Exhibit No. 1 is a " good " heel-seat, that No. 2 is a " pretty good " heel-seat, that No. 3 is a " good average " heel-seat, and that No. 4 is an " extra good heel-seat, as good, if not better, than the average run in the common factory to-day." If an " extra good " heel-seat is only as good as the average heel-seat used by manufacturers, it would seem that heel-seats which are denominated " good," " pretty good," and a " good average heel-seat " were not as good as average heel-seats, and for this reason would not be satisfactory.

It appears, further, from the testimony that the machine will not operate on the larger sizes of shoes made in the ordinary factory. This objection is met by appellant by the argument that it could be made to operate on all sizes and shapes of shoes by making the device larger and that in any event if the machine operated successfully on certain sizes of shoes that is sufficient to constitute a reduction to practice. It is not clear that a machine which could operate only on certain sizes and shapes of shoes would be entitled to be considered as reduction to practice. In this connection it is important to note the testimony of Fredericks, who was the foreman of the Lynn school, where Gordon's machine was operated to a greater extent than anywhere else. In testifying for Gordon on his direct examination he states:

Q. 11. Did you experiment with the machine in 1903 upon the regular work of that school, and, if so, what was the result of the experiments?

A. We could run it satisfactorily on the small sizes of shoes, and do the work even better than we were doing it by hand, and our cases run from 6 to 11 generally and the machine would not take a shoe and do a satisfactory job on it of a larger size than 8, and in doing that we couldn't run the machine to advantage, for the reason that in carrying the shoes back and forth, part of the case by machine and part doing by hand, it confused the help and the cases were mixed up continually all the time.

Nor is it clear that by the mere enlargement of the parts of the machine it could be made to operate on all sizes or shapes of lasts, because the hammers are mounted to move about a fixed axis. For this reason it would seem that if the hammers were so made as to be in proper position to operate with a wide last they would not sustain precisely the same relation to the shoe when operating in connection with a narrow last. In these cases the hammers sustain different relations to the articles operated upon, and it is a question of doubt whether the results would be the same, and this doubt could only be removed by building a machine with the proposed changes, which was not done.

There is another circumstance which throws doubt on the question of the success of the Gordon machine. Gordon testified that his purpose was to provide a mechanism which would do the work that had theretofore been done by hand. It appears from the testimony of expert Arnold, testifying in behalf of Gordon, (Record, p. 253, X-Q. 25,) that in the hand operation the operator hammers the sides of the last adjacent the sole as well as the turned-over edge of the counter and upper. The Gordon machine operates only on the turned-over edge. It therefore appears that the machine performs only a part of the hand operation to take the place of which it was designed. The testimony tends to indicate that this is one of the features which causes the product to fall short of commercial requirements and renders the machine impractical. This circumstance is not of itself sufficient to show that the machine was not a success; but it is one of the circumstances which tends to show that it did not accomplish what it was intended to accomplish or any other result which tended to materially improve the art.

But the product of the inventor and the assignee furnishes the strongest evidence that the utility of the machine was not made apparent by the trial at Snow's factory in August, 1902, as is now claimed, or by the later trials at the Lynn school in 1903. After the test at Snow's factory the machine was returned to the Albany-street factory of the assignee company, the United Shoe Machinery Company. Here it remained unused for months, until at the inventor's solicitation it was sent to the Lynn school for further trial. While it is now claimed that the trials at Snow's factory fully demonstrated the success of the machine, the inventor was not satisfied to go ahead and make the changes which he thought were necessary without a further trial, and it was for this purpose, the inventor states, (Record, pp. 38, 39, X-Q. 104,) that he asked to have the machine sent to the Lynn school. But the contemplated changes were never made, and the inventor lost sight of the machine entirely from the spring of 1903 to the time this proceeding was instituted. It appears that the United Shoe Machinery Company lost their interest in this machine immediately after the trial at Snow's factory in August, 1902, and it was only revived by knowledge obtained about two years later through their Cincinnati representative that Wentworth had in operation a successful machine for accomplishing similar results. The testimony shows that a machine which would accomplish the results which it is now claimed the Gordon machine did and will accomplish was urgently demanded by the trade. The inactivity of the inventor's assignee in the face of this demand tends strongly to show that the Gordon machine was not a reduction to practice, but only an abandoned experiment. On behalf of appellant it is claimed that this conduct is satisfactorily explained by the testimony showing that about the time Gordon completed his machine another inventor employed by the United Shoe Machinery Company was working on a machine designed to accomplish the same purpose and something in addition thereto and that it was customary where they had two or more machines for accomplishing the same purpose to withhold them all until it could be determined whether one or all should be adopted for use on the market. The other machine is referred to in the record as the McFeeley machine. A number of the McFeeley machines were made and put in the hands of manufacturers, and it is claimed that this machine was still in the experimental stage when they heard of Wentworth's device and that it was in the experimental stage as late as the taking of testimony in this case in January, 1906. It is rather remarkable that the utility of the Gordon machine was demonstrated after a half-day's use, while to show the utility of a similar device it required the building of several machines and their trial for more than a year. Moreover, it seems improbable that a machine whose successful operation had been satisfactorily demonstrated should be thrown aside for about three years in order to experiment with a machine designed to accomplish substantially the same results when all the time a machine of that character was urgently in demand. The explanation given for the delay in placing appellant's device on the market or in filing an application is regarded as of no substantial merit. The conduct of the inventor and his assignee is alone sufficient to warrant the conclusion that the Gordon machine was only an abandoned experiment. But aside from this consideration it is believed that the testimony fails to overcome the burden imposed upon appellant of proving that the Gordon machine constituted in law a reduction to practice.

The decision of the Examiners-in-Chief awarding priority of invention to Wentworth *is affirmed.*

PARKER *v.* CORKHILL.

PATENT INTERFERENCE.

Decided September 26, 1907.

(130 O. G., 2067.)

1. INTERFERENCE—REOPENING.

A motion to reopen a case for the purpose of allowing a party to print testimony taken by his opponent will be denied where such motion was brought after the decision of the Examiner of Interferences was rendered and no satisfactory reason for such delay is given.

2. SAME—SAME—PIECEMEAL CONDUCT OF CASE.

A piecemeal conduct of a case cannot be allowed. Where a contestant elects to stand upon the record as presented at final hearing he is bound by the decision rendered thereon.

APPEAL ON MOTION.

BOX-MAKING MACHINE.

Messrs Hazard & Harpham and *Mr. Wallace Greene* for *Parker.*
Mr. David A. Gourick for Corkhill.

MOORE, *Commissioner:*

This is an appeal by Parker from the decision of the Examiner of Interferences denying his motion that the case be reopened and that he be permitted to print the testimony filed in behalf of his opponent Corkhill.

The record shows that final hearing in the case was had before the Examiner of Interferences on March 20, 1907, and his decision was rendered April 9, 1907. Parker's motion that the interference be reopened and that he be permitted to print the testimony filed by Corkhill was not made until May 21, 1907, which is over a month after the decision of the Examiner of Interferences was rendered. Parker was aware at the time of the final hearing that Corkhill's testimony had not been printed; but no steps were taken by· him to have the same printed in order that it might be considered until after the adverse decision as to his rights had been rendered by the Examiner of Interferences.

No satisfactory account for the delay in presenting this motion has been made. A party cannot be permitted to try his case piecemeal. Having elected to stand upon the record as presented, Parker is bound by the decision in the interference upon the facts presented at the final hearing in the case.

The decision of the Examiner of Interferences is affirmed.

Ex parte F. Blumenthal & Co.

APPLICATION FOR REGISTRATION OF TRADE-MARK.

Decided August 7, 1907.

(130 O. G., 2068.)

1. TRADE-MARKS—" GOLDEN BROWN COLOR " DESCRIPTIVE.
    The words " Golden Brown Color No. 21 " refused registration as a trademark for leather, since the words " Golden Brown Color " are descriptive of the character or quality of the goods.
2. SAME—DESCRIPTIVE WORDS ASSOCIATED WITH ARBITRARY SYMBOLS.
    Descriptive words are no less so because associated with some arbitrary symbol.
3. SAME—DESCRIPTIVE WORDS ARRANGED IN AN ARBITRARY MANNER.
    Combining descriptive words in an arbitrary manner does not render a mark registrable.

ON APPEAL.

TRADE-MARK FOR LEATHER.

Messrs. Bartlett, Brownell & Mitchell for the applicant.

BILLINGS, *Assistant Commissioner:*

This is an appeal from a decision of the Examiner of Trade-Marks refusing to register as a trade-mark for leather " Golden Brown Color No. 21."

The ground upon which the registration was refused is that the words " Golden Brown Color " indicate the color of the goods and are therefore descriptive of the character or quality of the goods.

Applicant, while admitting that these words are descriptive, contends that they are not " merely " descriptive, since they are connected with the term " No. 21."

This contention is thought to be not well taken. As pointed out in *ex parte Jewell and Vinson,* (C. D., 1903, 348; 106 O. G., 1242,) where registration of the words "Ox Blood" combined with a pictorial representation of the horns of an ox as a trade-mark for paints was refused, descriptive words are no less descriptive because associated with some arbitrary symbol.

The words are combined in a peculiar way; but this does not confer registrability on the mark. The Trade-Mark Act provides that the name of an individual may be registered as a trade-mark if written, printed, impressed, or woven in a particular or distinctive manner; but no such provision is made with respect to descriptive words or devices.

The decision of the Examiner of Trade-Marks is affirmed.

BRAUNSTEIN *v.* HOLMES.

Decided March 21, 1907.

(130 O. G., 2371.)

INTERFERENCE—PRIORITY—ORIGINALITY.

Where an invention is reduced to practice by B. while working as an assistant of H. and in pursuance of a general plan arranged by H. and his associate officers with a view to the attainment of the result actually accomplished by such invention, the presumption is that the reduction to practice is a result of H.'s disclosures to B., and in order for the matter to prevail on the question of priority he must affirmatively show that he was an independent inventor.

APPEAL from Examiners-in-Chief.

EXPLOSIVE AND PROCESS OF MAKING SAME.

Messrs. Howson & Howson for Braunstein.
Messrs. Harding & Harding for Holmes.

MOORE, *Assistant Commissioner:*

This is an appeal by Braunstein from a decision of the Examiners-in-Chief affirming the decision of the Examiner of Interferences and awarding priority of invention to Holmes on the following issue:

An explosive consisting of a mixture of nitro-starch and ammonium oxalate.

Prior to the invention in controversy it was known that "nitro-starch" was a powerful explosive; but it was not used commercially, owing to the fact that it was unstable—that is, that at ordinary temperatures it decomposed and exploded. It was discovered by one of the parties to this proceeding that the difficulty could be overcome by mixing the compound with ammonium oxalate.

Each contestant claims to have made the invention while employed in the eastern laboratory of the E. I. du Pont de Nemours

Powder Company. Holmes, the senior applicant, entered the employ of the company about June 1, 1903, while Braunstein entered their employ about October 1, 1902. Braunstein claims to have conceived the invention prior to Holmes's employment by the company, while Holmes claims that the invention was the outcome of a series of experiments planned by him and executed in part by Braunstein as his assistant. Upon these contentions the subordinate tribunals found in favor of Holmes.

The evidence clearly shows, and it seems to be undisputed, that Braunstein performed the physical acts constituting the actual reduction to practice which both claim. The precise relation existing between the parties at the time of this reduction to practice is a closely-contested question. It is deemed unnecessary to discuss in detail the testimony which has been adduced on this point. The evidence seems to show clearly that shortly after Holmes entered the employ of the company in June, 1903, he was assigned to make a research on what is referred to in the record as the " nitro-starch problem." A number of reports were introduced into evidence which show in connection with the other evidence that he was investigating this problem during the months of June, July, and August, 1903. His work broadened out as he proceeded, and it was determined by the officers of the company that one of the laboratory employees should be assigned to assist him, and Braunstein was chosen for this purpose, beginning his work in this capacity about September 1, 1903. The testimony of Reese and Emery, who were the director and assistant director, respectively, of the laboratory, and of Murrill, who appears to have been in charge of the laboratory in the absence of Reese and Emery, and the testimony of other employees of the laboratory, all tending to show that Braunstein was working as Holmes's assistant, is deemed sufficient to overcome the testimony of Braunstein that he was working independently of Holmes, and of Heard, a coemployee, to the effect that he never knew that Braunstein was working as Holmes's assistant and that he never heard Holmes give Braunstein any instructions. Moreover, Dawson, a stenographer called as a witness by Braunstein, who wrote out the earlier reports made by Holmes and Braunstein, admitted that Holmes sometimes revised the reports of Braunstein. That Braunstein was working as Holmes's assistant at the time the invention was reduced to practice is believed to be clearly established.

The evidence further shows that prior to the assignment of Braunstein as Holmes's assistant a general plan had been laid out by Holmes for the investigation of a series of ammonium compounds with respect to their " stabilizing " effect on nitro-starch. These compounds included ammonium oxalate, which is the specific ammonium compound mentioned in the issue. This plan was laid before the officers of the eastern laboratory and approved by them, and about September 1, 1903, Braunstein was assigned to Holmes to assist in carrying out this investigation.

Under these circumstances the burden is upon Braunstein to show that he communicated the invention to Holmes or that it was in his possession prior to his association with Holmes.

The evidence adduced on these points consists of the testimony of Braunstein, Heard, and Souder. Braunstein testified that as early as June, 1903, he made tests of several nitro-starch powders, one containing carbonate of ammonia and another ammonium oxalate. He further testified that he again took up the problem in July, 1903, making up at this time several nitro-starch powders containing ammonium carbonate. The testimony of Souder, with whom Braunstein was boarding, is to the effect that about June, 1903, Braunstein told him that he was working on an article known as nitro-starch in an endeavor to make it stable and that he was quite assured that he had discovered the right process. Heard testified that about the 1st of May, 1903, Braunstein spoke to him about a stable nitro-starch powder and that some time later Braunstein spoke to him concerning the same problem and stated that he had tried ammonium carbonate as a stabilizing agent. The testimony of Souder is of practically no weight, as he mentions no specific materials, and that of Heard is insufficient, as he does not fix the date of the alleged disclosure with sufficient certainty, and he does not mention ammonium oxalate, which is the specific material called for by the issue. As to the July experiments there appears to be no testimony whatever to corroborate that of the inventor.

Braunstein further testified that he disclosed the invention to Holmes; but this is flatly denied by the latter, and there is no other evidence sufficient to prove Braunstein's claims in this regard. Moreover, the alleged disclosure took place subsequently to Braunstein's assignment as Holmes's assistant and subsequently, therefore, to the time when it had been determined by Holmes and the officers of the laboratory to try a number of ammonium compounds as stabilizers, including the specific material specified in the issue.

Braunstein has failed to discharge the burden imposed upon him by reason of his later filing date and his relation to the senior party when the invention was reduced to practice, and Holmes is therefore entitled to the award of priority.

The decision of the Examiners-in-Chief is affirmed.

FORDYCE *v.* STOETZEL.

Decided March 22, 1907.

(130 O. G., 2372.)

INTERFERENCE—PRIORITY—DILIGENCE—WORK ON AUXILIARY INVENTION.

Work on an auxiliary invention which the inventor regarded as necessary to the commercial success of his invention cannot be regarded as constituting diligence where the evidence does not satisfactorily show the nature of the experiments or when they were made.

APPEAL from Examiners-in-Chief.

PNEUMATIC-TUBE SYSTEM.

Mr. J. Stuart Rusk and *Mr. Edwin C. Gilman* for Fordyce.
Messrs. Poole & Brown and *Mr. Harry P. Simonton* for Stoetzel.

MOORE, *Assistant Commissioner:*

This is an appeal by Fordyce from the decision of the Examiners-in-Chief affirming the decision of the Examiner of Interferences and awarding priority of invention to Stoetzel.

The issue is set forth in seventeen counts, but one of which need be stated to indicate the character of the invention.

1. In an apparatus of the character described, a transit-tube through which carriers are transmitted, an air-valve controlling the passage of air through said tube and normally closed, an exhaust-tube, mechanism under the control of said exhaust-tube for operating said valve and mechanism operated by the insertion of a carrier into said tube for opening said air-valve and allowing a passage of air through said tube for driving carriers.

This interference is between an application of Stoetzel and a patent inadvertently granted Fordyce during the pendency of Stoetzel's application. Stoetzel's application disclosing the invention in issue was filed April 25, 1904. Fordyce filed his application August 25, 1904. The burden, therefore, is upon Fordyce to establish priority of invention by a preponderance of evidence. (*Furman* v. *Dean*, C. D., 1905, 582; 114 O. G., 1552.)

The invention in controversy relates to improvements in pneumatic-despatch systems for retail and department stores, in which the air in the transit-tube is exhausted and the carrier impelled to its destination by the air which enters the tube behind the carrier.

In some of the systems in use the transit-tubes are open at the receiving end and a partial vacuum maintained therein by a pump or blower which draws a continuous current of air through the transit-tube. This causes considerable waste of power, since the blower is operated continuously whether carriers are being transmitted or the system is idle. In the invention in issue a normally closed valve is provided between the exhausting mechanism and the

transit-tubes which upon the introduction of a carrier is automatically opened by a supplemental pneumatic system to allow the exhaust to become effective in the despatch-tube only during the transmission of the carrier.   In order to provide for the maximum saving
of power, it is desirable to have in connection with this conveyer
system an automatically-regulable suction device which will develop
more or less power, according to the demand upon the system by the
number of carriers in use.

Stoetzel alleges in his preliminary statement that he conceived the
invention in issue on or about June 15, 1902, and that he reduced it
to practice in December, 1902.   His application for patent was filed
April 25, 1904.

Fordyce alleges conception March 21, 1895, and reduction to practice in March, 1901.   The application upon which Fordyce's patent
was granted was filed August 25, 1904.

The testimony presented in behalf of Fordyce shows, and it is
not disputed, that in the spring of 1901 Fordyce equipped a single
line of pneumatic-despatch tubing with a system of valves such as
are defined by the issue, and his claim to priority rests upon the sufficiency of the evidence to establish the fact of reduction to practice
in this device or diligence in reducing the invention to practice after
Stoetzel's filing date, since no intermediate reduction to practice is
alleged.

The Examiners-in-Chief and the Examiner of Interferences held
that the device constructed by Fordyce in 1901 was merely experimental in character and did not constitute a reduction to practice of
the invention.   They also held that Fordyce was not diligent in
reducing the invention to practice when Stoetzel entered the field,
reduced the invention to practice, and filed his application.

In my opinion the conclusions of the lower tribunals are correct.

The device which was made by Fordyce in the spring of 1901
embodied the invention in substantially the form shown in the drawings of his application.   The automatic valves were applied to a
despatch-tube which was used for testing and experimental purposes
in the shops of the Bostedo Pneumatic Tube Company, where Fordyce was employed, and the system tested for a short time, after
which it was dismantled.   (Fordyce, Q. 51.)   According to the testimony of Fordyce and of Chase, who was also in the employ of the
Bostedo Pneumatic Tube Company in 1901, the test of this device
satisfactorily demonstrated that it would save power.   Fordyce was
of the opinion, however, that in order that this device should be
made commercially successful it would be necessary to have a coöperating speed-regulator for the blower, so that the exhaust could be
varied in proportion to the number of carriers being transmitted.
He therefore laid aside transmitting mechanism until he could

develop a suitable speed-regulator. This was not accomplished until subsequent to the date upon which he filed his application. (Fordyce, X-Qs. 36 and 51.)

It is contended by Fordyce that the device made by him in the spring of 1901 constituted a reduction to practice and that inasmuch as in his own opinion the cylinder and piston mechanism for controlling the valve was not adapted to commercial use with any known type of blower or compressor (X-Qs. 105–106) he was justified in delaying the·filing of an application for patent during the progress of experiments to perfect. a suitable power-controlling device for the blower.

The argument advanced by Fordyce in excuse of the delay in filing his application is refuted by the fact that when his application was finally filed the problem of the speed-regulator for the blower remained unsolved by him.

The admissions of Fordyce that the 1901 device was merely an experimental apparatus and was not adapted to be placed upon the market (Q. 59; also Chase, Q. 54) when taken in connection with the delay of nearly three and one-half years in constructing a practically operative system or filing an application clearly warrants the conclusion that the device did not constitute a reduction to practice of the invention.

The testimony relating to Fordyces's investigations in respect to a suitable regulator for the blower does not satisfactorily establish diligence in the endeavor to perfect his invention into a commercial form. He offers the testimony of two electrical experts, Markle and Parker, to show that variable-speed electrical motors had not been satisfactorily developed in 1901 and to indicate the necessity of original research upon variable-speed regulators. Fordyce states that he performed a large number of experiments relating to speed-regulators of various types and finally succeeded in constructing a satisfactory device in the fall of 1904. It is stipulated that if Frederick A. Spear, the general agent of the Lamson Consolidated Store Service Company, with which Fordyce has been connected since 1903, were called as a witness he would testify that " Fordyce made numerous experiments regarding devices to control blowers for pneumatic-despatch-tube systems." Chase describes a single experiment in 1901 with coned pulleys (Q. 60) and states that Fordyce made other experiments at various times. Fordyce also tells of observing certain experiments made by others upon variable-speed regulators. There is, however, no satisfactory evidence to the nature of the experiments performed by Fordyce, and it does not appear when the alleged .experiments were made. During the interval between the spring of 1901 and August, 1904, no experiments appear to have been made which included the invention in issue. The automatic valve-operating mechanism "was stored on the shelves in the factory of the Bostedo Company," (Chase, Q. 50,) and the tubing was frequently used by Fordyce in the development of other inventions. (Fordyce, X-Q. 66.) The record, moreover, shows that during this period Fordyce filed six applications for patent upon these other inventions.

This testimony is clearly insufficient to show that Fordyce was diligently endeavoring to reduce the invention to practice at the time Stoetzel filed his application April 25, 1904, or at any time prior to his own filing date, August 25, 1904. His lack of diligence cannot be excused because of his inability to procure a supposedly necessary auxiliary invention which had not been developed and which might never have been produced. In view of these facts Stoetzel is clearly entitled to the award of priority of invention.

If, however, it could be conceded that Fordyce's experiment in 1901 constituted a reduction to practice, the testimony, in my opinion, shows that the invention was concealed in the shops of the Bostedo Pneumatic Tube Company for such a period of time as would subordinate his rights to those of Stoetzel, who installed and successfully operated several systems embodying this invention prior to the date upon which Fordyce filed his application. (*Mason* v. *Hepburn*, C. D., 1898, 510; 84 O. G., 147; *Warner* v. *Smith*, C. D., 1898, 517; 84 O. G., 311; *Fefel* v. *Stocker*, C. D., 1901, 269; 94 O. G., 433.)

The decision of the Examiners-in-Chief is affirmed.

KENTUCKY DISTILLERIES AND WAREHOUSE COMPANY *v.* P. DEMPSEY & COMPANY.

OPPOSITION.

Decided September 26, 1907.

(130 O. G., 2373.)

1. TRADE-MARK OPPOSITION—REGISTRATION OF A NON-TECHNICAL MARK MAY BE OPPOSED BY OWNER OF A SIMILAR NON-TECHNICAL MARK.

Where an applicant seeks to register a mark under the ten-year proviso of section 5 of the act of 1905 and the registration of that mark is opposed by a party who claims ownership of a mark consisting of a surname or a geographical term which resembles the applicant's mark, *Held* that the notice of opposition will not be dismissed upon the ground that the opposer's mark is not a proper trade-mark.

2. SAME—PROOF OF CONFUSION IN TRADE.

Where the opposer alleged in his notice of opposition that confusion in trade had occurred, but introduced no testimony that such confusion had taken place, and where the marks are not so nearly alike that in the absence of proof as to actual confusion it can be held that confusion would be likely to occur, the applicant's mark will not be refused.

3. SAME—SAME—DOUBTFUL SIMILARITY—"MAYFIELD," "MAYFAIR."

> *Held* that the marks "Mayfield" and "Mayfair" are not so nearly alike that in the absence of proof as to actual confusion it can be held that confusion would be so likely to occur as to justify refusing to register the applicant's mark.

APPEAL from Examiner of Interferences.

TRADE-MARK FOR WHISKY.

Mr. James L. Hopkins for Kentucky Distilleries and Warehouse Company.

Mr. James H. Churchill for P. Dempsey & Company.

MOORE, *Commissioner:*

This is an appeal from a decision of the Examiner of Interferences dismissing the opposition and holding that the applicant is entitled to register the mark for which application has been made.

The mark of the applicant is "Mayfair," while that of the opponent is "Mayfield."

The opposition is brought on the ground that the Kentucky Distilleries and Warehouse Company is the sole and exclusive owner of the word "Mayfield" as a trade-name for whisky and that the word "Mayfair" similarly used is calculated to deceive the public into the belief that the goods bearing the trade-mark are those of the opponent and that the public has been so deceived.

It appears from the record that the applicant adopted its mark about 1885 and that the opponent and its predecessors in business have used the word "Mayfield" continuously since about 1872.

It is contended by appellant that the opposition should be dismissed for the reason that "Mayfield" is not a proper trade-mark, being both a surname and a geographical name.

The contention is thought to be not well taken. Applicant seeks to register its mark under the ten-year clause of the Trade-Mark Act of 1905—that is to say, it alleges that it has had exclusive use of its mark for ten years next preceding the passage of the act. Manifestly, if some one else had prior to the time when applicant adopted its mark adopted and used continuously since such adoption a mark which was either the same as applicant's or so nearly the same as to cause confusion in trade and deceive the public, applicant's use was not exclusive.

If, therefore, the testimony shows that the marks are so similar that confusion in trade has taken place or if it is evident from an inspection of the marks that confusion in trade will be likely to occur. (*Wolf Bros. & Co. v. Hamilton Brown Shoe Co.*, C. D., 1906, 445; 125 O. G., 667.) the opposition should be sustained.

Although opponent alleged in his notice of opposition that confusion in trade had occurred, he introduced no testimony to show that such confusion had taken place. It is contended by counsel for opponent that on cross-examination certain of applicant's witnesses admit that there has actually been confusion in the use of the two marks; but the testimony upon careful examination does not bear out the contention.

The testimony of Hunt, a liquor dealer, on this point is as follows:

Cross-int. 25. Did, you ever hear or know of any confusion arising from a similarity between the names "Mayfield" and "Mayfair?"

(Objected to as not proper cross-examination.)

A. I did hear that there was some controversy about it.

In answer to recross-question 19, Cox, a salesman for P. Dempsey & Co., states that on one occasion some one asked him if the whisky he was selling was anything like that sold by Peter Moran for forty cents a pint, and that he afterward found that Moran was selling Mayfield whisky. It appears from Cox's answer to cross-question 20 that this question was asked as a joke; but even if this were not true such a chance question asked of a salesman would not establish such confusion in trade as to justify holding that the applicant was not entitled to register his mark.

It would seem to have been a comparatively easy matter to have established that confusion had arisen between the marks if such had been the case. The marks are not so nearly alike that in the absence of proof as to actual confusion it can be held that confusion would be so likely to occur as to justify refusing to register applicant's mark. It is true that the first syllable of the two words "Mayfield" and "Mayfair" are the same; but this is also true of the words "Cuticura" and "Cuticle," the former of which was held, in *Potter Drug and Chemical Co.* v. *Pasfield Soap Co.*, (106 F. R., 914,) not to be infringed by the latter.

The decision of the Examiner of Interferences is affirmed.

DIXON AND MARSH *v.* GRAVES AND WHITTEMORE.

PATENT INTERFERENCE.

Decided October 14, 1907.

(130 O. G., 2374.)

INTERFERENCE—CONSIDERATION OF PATENTABILITY ON APPEAL ON PRIORITY— SUPERVISORY AUTHORITY.

The question of the patentability of issue will be considered on appeal on priority only under the supervisory authority of the Commissioner for the purpose of correcting a manifest error.

APPEAL from Examiners-in-Chief.

METHOD OF SHAPING GLASS.

Messrs. Bakewell & Byrnes and *Mr. H. S. Shepard* for Dixon and Marsh.

Mr. James Whittemore and *Messrs. Bacon & Milans* for Graves and Whittemore.

MOORE, *Commissioner:*

This is an appeal by Dixon and Marsh from a decision of the Examiners-in-Chief affirming the decision of the Examiner of Interferences awarding priority of invention to Graves and Whittemore.

Graves and Whittemore are the senior parties. The only testimony taken by the junior parties was that of an expert, tending to show that the issue is not patentable, which testimony was upon motion suppressed, and priority of invention was awarded to Graves and Whittemore on the record dates.

The sole contention on this appeal is that the issue is not patentable to either party. This question has been before the Primary Examiner, both *ex parte* and *inter partes,* and in each case he has held the issue to be patentable. Both the Examiner of Interferences and the Examiners-in-Chief upon appeal on priority have refused to recommend, under Rule 126, that the claims be rejected as being without patentable novelty. Under these circumstances the question presented will be considered only under my supervisory authority for the purpose of correcting a manifest error. No such error is apparent here, and priority of invention is therefore awarded to Graves and Whittemore.

The decision of the Examiners-in-Chief is affirmed.

FELBEL *v.* FOX.

PATENT INTERFERENCE.

Decided October 11, 1907.

(130 O. G., 2375.)

1. INTERFERENCE—JUDGMENT ON RECORD—ORDER TO SHOW CAUSE—SUFFICIENCY OF SHOWING.

Where in response to an order to the junior party to show cause why judgment of priority should not be rendered against him because his alleged date of conception was subsequent to the filing date of the senior party the junior party files a statement alleging that certain of the counts are specific to his structure and that the subject-matter covered thereby was not shown or described by the senior party, *Held* to be insufficient, as the question sought to be raised was one which should have been raised by a motion to dissolve rather than by the mere filing of a statement.

2. SAME—DELAY IN FILING MOTION—CHARACTER OF SHOWING REQUIRED.

A mere unverified statement accompanying a motion filed one day late stating that the motion could not be brought sooner on account of other work is insufficient. A showing in excuse for delay should be under oath, and it should state facts from which the Office may judge whether or not the delay was excusable.

3. PRACTICE—ADHERENCE TO RULES NECESSARY.

While it is not the desire of the Office to be too technical, it is better to insist upon a reasonable and just compliance with the rules of the Office, though it may work a hardship in an individual case, than to adopt a course that would result practically in abrogating the rules, with consequent confusion. (*Keller* v. *Wethey* v. *Roberts*, C. D., 1897, 157; 81 O. G., 331; *Estes* v. *Gause*, C. D., 1899, 164; 88 O. G., 1336.)

ON PETITION.

TYPE-WRITING MACHINE.

Mr. Jacob Felbel pro se.
Messrs. Chappell & Earl for Fox.

BILLINGS, *Assistant Commissioner:*

This is a petition by Felbel that the judgment of priority of invention in favor of Fox rendered by the Examiner of Interferences be set aside and an *inter partes* hearing upon the merits of Felbel's showing be granted.

The records of this interference show that on July 5, 1907, the Examiner of Interferences gave notice that judgment on the record would be rendered against Felbel unless he should on or before August 5, 1907, show good and sufficient cause why such action should not be taken. The ground of the notice was that the date of conception alleged by Felbel of the invention in issue was subsequent to the filing date of the senior party. This notice was given under the provisions of Rule 114, which is as follows:

114. If the junior party to an interference, or if any party thereto other than the senior party, fails to file a statement, or if his statement fails to overcome the *prima facie* case made by the respective dates of application, such party will be notified by the Examiner of Interferences that judgment upon the record will be rendered against him at the expiration of thirty days, unless cause is shown why such action should not be taken. Within this period any of the motions permitted by the rules may be brought. Motions brought after judgment on the record has been rendered will not be entertained unless sufficient reasons appear for the delay.

One day after the time set by the Examiner of Interferences within which cause should be shown Felbel filed a statement of reasons why in his opinion judgment should not be rendered against him as to certain counts of the issue, the reasons being that the claims corresponding to these counts were specific to Felbel's invention and were not shown and described in Fox's application. The Examiner held the showing to be insufficient under the order to show cause and rendered judgment of priority of invention in favor of Fox, the senior party, The Examiner of Interferences held that the showing made by Felbel in order to be heard by the proper tribunal of the Office was such as should have been made in a motion to dissolve the interference.

Felbel contends—

That Rule 114, relating to the showing of cause why judgment should not be rendered, does not specify that such showing must be made by way of "motion to dissolve," or even by motion.

This Office has found by experience that in order to properly transact business the questions which are sought to be raised by applicants appearing before it must be presented according to certain procedure. To permit applicants to raise questions in the Office by merely filing papers setting forth those questions and without regard to the procedure which is well established and settled by a long line of decisions would result in endless confusion, both to the parties practicing before the Office and to the officials whose duty it is to pass upon these questions. While *ex parte* petitions are sometimes considered in an *inter partes* case, to do so is the exception and not the rule. Where, as in this case, the junior party fails to overcome the filing date of the senior party, it follows as a matter of course that judgment must be rendered against the junior party unless he can show to the satisfaction of the Office some valid reason why the judgment should not be entered. In the present case applicant was given thirty days within which to present these reasons. Rule 114 states:

Within this period any of the motions permitted by the rules may be brought.

This provision of the rule permits the junior party to present to the Office any reason which in his opinion requires that judgment be not rendered. It is well settled that these reasons should be brought in the form of a motion. The applicant has stated in his brief several of the motions which might be brought, as follows:

To amend his preliminary statement; to dissolve the interference for any cause; to amend his application; to shift the burden of proof; to stay proceedings; to permit an assignee to intervene and prosecute.

Every one of these questions should be raised by a motion. Each of them may be heard and determined by the Examiner of Interferences, except questions relating to the dissolution of the interference. Felbel, however, did not bring any of the above-mentioned motions, nor did he raise any of the above-mentioned questions, except that which should, if raised at all, be presented in a motion to dissolve. This latter question, it is well settled, must be heard and determined by the Primary Examiner. As said by the Examiner of Interferences, Felbel contends—

* * * that Fox is not entitled to make claims corresponding to certain counts of the issue. Such a question can only be raised on motion to dissolve.

Inasmuch as it is very clear that the question raised by Felbel is one which if granted would result in the dissolution of the interference, it becomes necessary to consider Rule 122, which provides for motions to dissolve an interference.   This rule provides, in part:

> Such motions, and all motions of a similar character, should be accompanied by a motion to transmit the same to the Primary Examiner, and such motion to transmit should be noticed for hearing upon a day certain before the Examiner of Interferences.

It is well settled, also, that where motions are made they should be accompanied by proof of service upon the opposing party.   Felbel merely stated that he sent a copy of his statement to the opposing party; but this is not proof of service as required by the rule.   Rule 153 states, in part:

> In contested cases reasonable notice of all motions, and copies of motion papers and affidavits, must be served, as provided in Rule 154 (2).   Proof of such service must be made before the motion will be entertained by the Office.

Rule 154 (2) states specifically how service may be made.   The statement filed by Felbel in this case, was filed late, and it was accompanied by a mere *ex parte* unverified statement that—

> Owing to unavoidable delay in securing copies of Fox's file, and the necessity for acting in other interferences and on pending cases within prescribed times, it has been impossible to make this showing previously.

It is well settled by the practice of this Office that when motions or other papers are filed late they must be accompanied by a verified showing of facts upon which the Office may base conclusions as to the sufficiency of the reasons alleged for the delay.   With the exception of the fact that the statement filed by Felbel in answer to the order to show cause was specific he has complied with none of the formal requirements so well established by the practice which are necessary in order to insure consideration of the question raised.   While it is not the desire of the Office to be too technical, yet applicants must be required to follow the simple and well-known procedure laid down in the rules and in a long line of decisions.   As so well stated by former Commissioners, it is better to insist upon a reasonable and just compliance with the rules of the Office, though it may work a hardship in an individual case, than to adopt a course that would result practically in abrogating the rules, with consequent confusion.   (*Keller* v. *Wethey* v. *Roberts*, C. D., 1897, 157; 81 O. G., 331; *Estes* v. *Gause*, C. D., 1899, 164; 88 O. G., 1336.)

The decision of the Examiner of Interferences was right, and the petition *is denied.*

Ex parte Isaacs & Speed.

APPLICATION FOR PATENT.

Decided June 20, 1907.

(130 O. G., 2717.)

PATENTABIITY—PRIOR PATENT OF APPLICANT DISCLOSING BUT NOT CLAIMING
INVENTION.

A patent disclosing a process and apparatus and claiming only the process is no bar to the allowance of an application covering the apparatus filed by the same party within two years after the grant of the patent. (*Ex parte Mullen & Mullen*, C. D., 1890, 9; 50 O. G., 837.)

APPEAL from Examiners-in-Chief.

HELICALLY-CORRUGATED PIPE.

Mr. William F. Booth and *Messrs. Bacon & Milans* for the applicants.

MOORE, *Acting Commissioner:*

This is an appeal from the decision of the Examiners-in-Chief affirming the action of the Examiner rejecting the following claims:

1. A fluid-pipe line composed of sections each section being formed with end couplings, and having a helically-directed cross-sectionally-convex elevation on its inner wall terminating short of its end couplings.

2. In an apparatus for the method stated and in combination with means for supplying the lighter and heavier fluids to a pipe-line, the pipe-line having a helically-directed cross-sectionally concavo-convex impression in its walls, the convexity being presented inwardly to form an elevation on the interior of the pipe-line.

3. In an apparatus for the method stated and in combination, a pipe-line having a helically-directed cross-sectionally concavo-convex impression in its walls, the convexity being presented inwardly to form an elevation on the interior of the pipe-line, means for supplying lighter and heavier fluids to the pipe-line including connected pipes, and a screw-threaded connection between said means and the pipe-line, the impression in the walls of the pipe-line terminating short of said connection.

The references are Haas, August 17, 1886, No. 347,594; Morrison, December 18, 1894, No. 531,000; Whitney, May 29, 1900, No. 650,575; Isaacs & Speed, May 10, 1904, No. 759,374.

The Examiner rejected the claims upon the patent to Isaacs & Speed in view of the patent to Morrison, holding that the adoption of corrugations of the latter in lieu of the helical obstructions shown in the patent to Isaacs & Speed would not involve invention. He also cited the patents to Haas and Whitney as showing the prior art in respect to corrugated tubes.

The Examiners-in-Chief properly held the earlier patent to Isaacs & Speed, which is for a process and was granted less than two years prior to the filing date of this application, to be too late to constitute a disclosure which would defeat the present application, for the reasons fully stated in *ex parte Mullen & Mullen* (C. D., 1890, 9; 50 O. G., 837) and the decisions cited therein. They, however, held the state of the art to be sufficient to anticipate the appealed claims. I do not entirely agree with the conclusions of the Examiners-in-Chief.

Claim 1 comprises nothing more than a pipe-line composed of sections of pipe of the form disclosed in the patent to Whitney, connected by ordinary end couplings, and was correctly held to be unpatentable.

Claims 2 and 3, however, in my opinion comprise new structural combinations adapted to effect a result which is not suggested in any of the references other than the earlier patent to the. applicants, which is not a valid reference. These claims call for means for supplying lighter and heavier fluids to a pipe-line having helical corrugations. The helical corrugations of the sections of pipe cause the denser fluid to form around and incase the lighter fluid thereby intervening between the latter and the pipe-walls and reducing the friction, which impedes the progress of the lighter fluid.

In the patent to Morrison the corrugations of the outer cylinder by contacting with the inner cylinder form merely a spiral conduit of substantially rectangular cross-section, which is not adapted to produce the same function as the structure called for by the claims. The patents to Whitney and Haas, while showing corrugated pipes, contain no suggestion of the function which is performed by the structure set forth in the applicants' claims. This case is analogous to the case of *Potts* v. *Creager*, (C. D., 1895, 143; 70 O. G., 494,) in which the Supreme Court of the United States said:

As a result of the authorities upon this subject, it may be said that, if the new use be so nearly analogous to the former one, that the applicability of the device to its new use would occur to a person of ordinary mechanical skill, it is only a case of double use, but if the relations between them be remote, and especially if the use of the old device produce a new result, it *may* at least involve an exercise of the inventive faculty. Much, however, must still depend upon the nature of the changes required to adapt the device to its new use.

The same court reiterated this statement in the later case of *Hobbs* v. *Beach*, (C. D., 1901, 311; 94 O. G., 2357.)

In the present case the provision of means for supplying both lighter and heavier fluids to the pipe-line comprises a change which adapts the old corrugated form of pipe to its new use, and this in my opinion involved sufficient exercise of the inventive faculty to warrant the allowance of claims 2 and 3.

The decision of the Examiners-in-Chief is *affirmed* as to count 1 and is *reversed* as to counts 2 and 3.

PROUTT *v.* JOHNSTON AND JOHNSTON.

PATENT INTERFERENCE.

Decided June 24, 1907.

(130 O. G., 2718.)

FINAL JUDGMENT BY PATENT OFFICE—APPEAL TO COURT PENDING.

Judgment in an interference proceeding will not be made final by the Patent Office after the filing of a notice of appeal to the Court of Appeals of the District of Columbia and pending such appeal, on the ground that such notice was filed one day outside the forty-day period set by the Rules of that court for filing notice of appeal, it being regarded as within the discretion of the court to waive a strict adherence to the rule and to entertain the appeal notwithstanding the delay in filing the notice.

ON MOTION.

ELECTRIC-CIRCUIT CUT-OUT.

Messrs. Knight Brothers for Proutt.
Messrs. Munn & Company for Johnston and Johnston.

MOORE, *Commissioner:*

This is a motion by Johnston and Johnston that judgment in this interference be made final and the interference determined upon the ground that Proutt failed to file an appeal to the Court of Appeals of the District of Columbia within forty days after the decision of the Commissioner adversely to him upon the question of priority of invention.

The record shows that the decision of the Commissioner was rendered April 11, 1907, and that notice to the Commissioner of appeal to the Court of Appeals of the District of Columbia was filed May 29, 1907, which is one day outside of the forty days allowed by Rule 21 of the rules of the Court of Appeals of the District of Columbia and Rule 149 of the Rules of Practice of the Patent Office. It is contended that there is no regular notice of appeal in the present case which the Court of Appeals of the District of Columbia can possibly entertain.

The time within which an appellant is required to give notice to the Commissioner of Patents and to the Court of Appeals of the District of Columbia is fixed by a rule of that court and not by statute. It is therefore within the discretion of that court whether or not a strict adherence to the letter of that rule will be insisted on. While in the cases cited by the petitioner the court of appeals has refused to entertain appeals where notice has been given to the Commissioner a considerable time after the expiration of the forty days and has also indicated that strict adherence to the rule would be insisted on, it has not held that no excuse for failure to give notice within forty days will be considered or accepted. *In re Bryant* *(C. D., 1896, 648; 9 App. D. C., 447)* the Court said.

The second section of Rule 20 provides that appeals from decisions of the Commissioner of Patents "shall be taken within forty days from the date of the ruling or order appealed from, and not afterwards;" and the present appeal has been taken in plain disregard of that rule. Not even an excuse is sought to be given for the delay. Now, while some rules of the court, from their peculiar nature and application, may have in them an inherent element of elasticity that would justify their modification from time to time in special cases, rules of court are intended to be a law for the court itself, as well as for parties and counsel, until they are changed in pursuance of the same power under which they have been promulgated; and to no rule is rigid adherence required more than to those which prescribe the time within which appeals are to be taken, and which in their nature, as long as they are in force, are intended to have the effect of statute.

Before these rules were promulgated there was much controversy in regard to the time to be allowed for the taking of appeals from the Commissioner of Patents, and this rule was made for the express purpose of setting the controversy at rest. We do not feel that we are at liberty ourselves to disregard the rule or to permit it to be disregarded by parties to proceedings in the Patent Office.

We come to this conclusion more readily in the present case for the reason that even upon a consideration of the merits of the case we see no sufficient reason to disturb the decision of the Commissioner of Patents.

In view of the fact that appeals of which notice has not been given to the Commissioner of Patents within forty days of the date of his decision have not been dismissed by the court of appeals *pro forma*, it is not believed that further action should be taken by this Office in the present case upon the assumption that the court would not in any event consider the appeal.

Furthermore, it does not appear that any great hardship will be imposed upon Johnston and Johnston by the postponement of action upon this case pending the decision of the court upon the question presented, since they are already in possession of a patent upon the subject-matter in issue, and the rejection of Proutt's claims in view of the decision upon priority cannot affect their rights.

The motion is denied.

LIPSCHUTZ *v.* FLOYD.

PATENT INTERFERENCE.

Decided September 12, 1907.

(130 O. G., 2718)

INTERFERENCE—PRACTICE UNDER RULE 124—SUPERVISORY AUTHORITY OF COMMISSIONER.

No appeal lies from a favorable decision on the right to make the claims or the identity of meaning of the counts in the cases of different parties, and such a decision will be reviewed on petition in the exercise of the Commissioner's supervisory authority only to correct some palpable error in the decision which is clear and evident on its face.

APPEAL AND PETITION.

CAR-TRUCK SIDE FRAME.

Mr. Charles G. Hawley for Lipschutz.
Messrs. Offield, Towle & Linthicum for Floyd.

MOORE, *Commissioner:*

This case comes up on an appeal by Lipschutz from the action of the Primary Examiner holding that Floyd has a right to make a claim in the terms of count 1 and that said count has the same meaning when read upon the disclosure of both parties, and a petition that in the exercise of my supervisory authority I dissolve the interference on the ground that there is no interference in fact. Floyd has filed a motion to dismiss both the appeal and the petition.

As to the appeal, Rule 124 specifically provides that no appeal will be permitted from a decision affirming the applicant's right to make a claim or the identity of meaning of counts in the cases of different parties.

The appeal is therefore dismissed.

As to the petition, it is well settled that the supervisory authority of the Commissioner will be exercised only in exceptional cases and then only to correct some palpable error in the decision of the Examiner which is clear and evident on its face. No such case exists here. The questions which applicant seeks to have reviewed were considered by the Examiner in his decision. Applicant under the guise of a petition merely seeks to have the same points reviewed that he attempts to have reviewed on appeal.

The petition is dismissed.

BORG *v.* STRAUSS.

PATENT INTERFERENCE.

Decided October 7, 1907.

(130 O. G., 2719.)

1. INTERFERENCE—PRELIMINARY STATEMENT—SECOND PROPOSED AMENDMENT—SHOWING REQUIRED.

Where after decision upon a motion for dissolution a party moves to amend his preliminary statement and it is held that the showing in support thereof is insufficient to warrant such amendment, a second motion to amend will not be granted where no good reason appears why the showing then made could not have been presented in connection with the first motion. Parties cannot be permitted to try their cases piecemeal and experimentally.

2. SAME—SAME—SAME—SAME.

Amendments to preliminary statements are to be permitted after a party has had an opportunity to inspect his opponent's case only in cases where *bona fide* mistakes of fact have been made and a full and clear showing is made that there was no negligence in discovering the true facts.

APPEAL ON MOTION.
ON PETITION.

BRIDGE.

Mr. George E. Waldo for Borg.
Messrs. Parker & Carter for Strauss.

MOORE, *Commissioner:*

This case is before me on appeal by Borg from the decision of the Examiner of Interferences denying a second motion by him to amend his preliminary statement and also upon petition by Borg that the decision of the Examiner of Interferences denying said motion be set aside and that the Examiner be instructed to decide the motion on its merits upon full consideration of affidavits presented by him.

The record shows that after the preliminary statements in this case had been approved Borg moved to dissolve the interference upon the ground, *inter alia*, that Strauss had no right to make the claims.

This motion having been denied by the Primary Examiner, Borg presented a motion for leave to file an amended preliminary statement setting back his dates of conception and reduction to practice of the invention. The Examiner of Interferences denied this motion on the ground that the alleged mistake in Borg's original statement was one of law and not of fact and that there was no showing of such care and diligence in the preparation of that statement as would warrant an amended preliminary statement.

Appeal was taken from this decision of the Examiner of Interferences; but prior to the hearing on appeal Borg presented additional affidavits in support of his motion to amend and moved that the motion to amend be remanded to the Examiner of Interferences for reconsideration in connection with said affidavits. The Assistant Commissioner denied the motion to remand on the ground that the showing in excuse of the failure to present these affidavits in conjunction with the original motion to amend was insufficient. Subsequently the decision of the Examiner of Interferences upon the motion to amend was affirmed in my decision rendered June 28, 1907, the additional affidavits filed by Borg not being considered.

On August 2, 1907, Borg again moved to amend his preliminary statement in view of the affidavits above referred to, together with an affidavit by his attorney showing why the original motion to amend did not include a full showing of the facts now presented. In this affidavit the attorney for Borg states:

That the failure of said Borg to make a fuller and more complete showing at the time he presented his original motion to amend was for the reason that affiant advised him (Borg) that in his (affiant's) opinion the showing would be sufficient. * * * Furthermore, relying on the case of *Fowler* v. *Boyce* v. *Temple and Goodrum*, (C. D., 1904, 22; 108 O. G., 561,) attorney for Borg advised said Borg that in case the showing on the first motion was not sufficient he could bring a second motion to amend on additional showing and that therefore it was advisable to disclose no more of his case than was necessary to secure the amendment asked.

In the case referred to the second motion by Fowler to amend his preliminary statement was denied for the reason that this party did not exercise reasonable care in the preparation of his original statement. This case does not in any way support the contention of Borg. On the contrary, it clearly indicates that the Office will not consider additional showing made upon a second motion where such showing might as well have been made in the first instance.

The affidavit of Borg's attorney clearly shows that there was no good reason why the entire showing now relied upon in support of the motion to amend could not have been presented when the motion was first made. Parties cannot be permitted to try their cases piecemeal and experimentally. Amendments to preliminary statements are to be permitted after a party has had an opportunity to inspect his opponent's case only in cases where *bona fide* mistakes of fact have been made and a full and clear showing is made that there was no negligence in discovering the true facts.

The decision of the Examiner of Interferences in this case is right and *is affirmed*, and the petition *is denied*.

EMMET *v.* FULLAGAR.

PATENT INTERFERENCE.

Decided October 9, 1907.

(130 O. G., 2719.)

INTERFERENCE—MOTION TO DISSOLVE—OATH TO REISSUE APPLICATION INSUFFICIENT.

A motion to dissolve an interference involving a reissue application, alleging that the oath accompanying the application was insufficient to warrant the grant of a reissued patent, should be transmitted to the Primary Examiner.

APPEAL ON MOTION.

Mr. A. G. Davis and *Messrs. Dyer & Dyer* for Emmet.
Mr. Thos. F. Sheridan for Fullagar.

MOORE, *Commissioner:*

This is an appeal by Fullagar from a decision of the Examiner of Interferences granting Emmet's motion to transmit to the Primary Examiner a motion to dissolve the interference.

The motion to dissolve is divided into two sections, one relating to Fullagar's reissue application filed October 31, 1906, and the other to Fullagar's reissue application filed January 7, 1907, each of which is involved in this interference. Only one ground is urged for dissolving the interference—namely, that Fullagar is not entitled to claim the subject-matter of the issue in these reissue applications. It is contended on behalf of Fullagar that the motion to transmit should have been denied, for the reason that none of the facts alleged are such as would justify the granting of the motion to dissolve. More specifically, it is urged that the questions raised do not affect the question of priority, since it is merely alleged that Fullagar is not entitled to receive a patent on either of his reissue applications and that therefore should a decision in Emmet's favor be rendered a patent would be issued to Emmet without his first establishing that he is the prior inventor.

The questions raised are all such as could have been considered in the *ex parte* prosecution of Fullagar's applications and which, if finally decided adversely to him, would have resulted in the rejection of his claims. In such an event it would have been manifestly improper for the Primary Examiner to have declared the interference. The mere fact that two parties claim the same invention is not sufficient to justify the declaration of an interference, but it must appear that each one is entitled to claim it. If for any reason one of the parties is barred from claiming the invention, then he has no more interest in the other party's claim thereto than has any other member of the public.

In *Felbel* v. *Aguilar* (C. D., 1906, 113; 121 O. G., 1012) and in *Felsing* v. *Nelson* (C. D., 1906, 118; 121 O. G., 1347) a motion to dissolve based on grounds similar to those of Emmet's motion and to which the same objections that are raised by Fullagar to that motion would have applied was transmitted and considered. It is contended by Fullagar that in *Wert* v. *Borst and Groscop* (C. D., 1906, 198; 122 O. G., 2062) a contrary holding was made, and that being later that decision is controlling. It appears, however, that in that case a motion to dissolve was brought after final hearing on the question of priority on the ground that the testimony showed such a case of intervening rights as would bar a reissue to Borst and Groscop. This motion was denied transmission on the ground that—

* * * where the evidence relating to priority of invention is before the Office and the question of a statutory bar is raised which applies to but one of two applications involved in the inference and which requires for its determination consideration of evidence, and possibly further taking of testimony, such determination should be postponed until priority of invention has been settled, at least so far as the same can be settled in this Office.

This decision followed the well-established practice that an interference will not be dissolved on grounds arising out of testimony taken on the question of priority. (*Paget* v. *Bugg*, C. D., 1899, 214; 89 O. G., 1342.)

The facts in the present case are different, since the grounds alleged in support of the motion to dissolve do not arise out of testimony which has been taken, but relate merely to Fullagar's right to the claims in issue as made out by his application papers.

The decision of the Examiner of Interferences is affirmed.

BRANTINGHAM *v.* DRAVER AND DRAVER.

PATENT INTERFERENCE.

Decided October 16, 1907.

(130 O. G., 2720.)

INTERFERENCE—MOTION TO DISSOLVE—DELAY IN BRINGING—EXCUSE.

The fact that numerous appeals and petitions have been taken to have transmitted a motion to dissolve which was not in proper form constitutes no excuse for the delay in bringing the motion in proper form.

APPEAL ON MOTION.

CONTROL DEVICE FOR SIFTERS.

Mr. George E. Kirk for Brantingham.
Messrs. Williamson & Merchant and *Messrs. Pennie & Goldsborough* for Draver and Draver.

BILLINGS, *Assistant Commissioner:*

This is an appeal from a decision of the Examiner of Interferences refusing to transmit a motion to dissolve.

The motion to transmit was denied on the ground that the motion to dissolve was brought long after the time allowed by the rules for bringing such motions.

It appears that on May 31, 1907, Brantingham brought a motion to dissolve on the grounds of irregularity in declaring the interference, non-patentability of the issue, lack of right of Draver and Draver to make the claims, and non-interference in fact. This motion was transmitted as to the third ground, but refused transmission as to the other three grounds. The reason given in support of the ground of non-interference in fact was that the device shown in the application of Draver and Draver is inoperative and that therefore the issue is not patentable to Draver and Draver and that they have no right to make the claims.

The Examiner of Interferences refused to transmit the motion as to this ground for the reason that—

It deals with matters which should have been alleged under the other grounds of the motion.

From this decision a petition was taken which was treated as an appeal and the decision affirmed in a decision rendered June 27, 1907, in which the following statement was made:

The other ground as to which the motion was refused transmission was that of non-interference in fact. This ground is based on the allegation that Draver and Draver have no right to make the claims since the device shown by them is inoperative. As pointed out in *Lizotte* v. *Neuberth*, (C. D., 1906, 370; 124 O. G., 1842,) the facts alleged to show no right to make the claims can have no bearing on the question of non-interference in fact and this part of the motion was properly refused transmission.

A petition was then brought asking that the Examiner of Interferences be directed to transmit the motion to dissolve as to patentability and right to make the claims. This petition was denied on the ground that it was well settled that non-interference in fact exists only where the same claims mean one thing in one application and another in the other application, and that the question of operativeness of the Draver and Draver device can therefore have no possible bearing on the question of non-interference in fact.

The present motion alleges that Draver and Draver have no right to make the claims corresponding to the counts of the issue. The reasons alleged in support of this motion are the same as those set up in the original motion under the head of non-interference in fact. While the motion is in proper form, it is brought long after the period allowed by the rules for bringing such motion, and the Examiner of Interferences was clearly right in holding that no sufficient excuse had been given for the delay.

The practice as to the transmission of motions to dissolve is well settled, and where a motion is brought which in accordance with the practice cannot be transmitted it is no excuse for the delay in bringing the motion in proper form that numerous appeals and petitions have been taken in an attempt to have the original motion transmitted.

The decision of the Examiner of Interferences is affirmed.

EILERMAN *et al.* v. McELROY.

PATENT INTERFERENCE.

Decided October 23, 1907.

(130 O. G. 2721.)

1. INTERFERENCE—MOTION FOR DISSOLUTION—TRANSMISSION—RIGHT TO MAKE CLAIM AND DIFFERENCE IN MEANING OF CLAIMS.

Where in a motion for dissolution the right of the adverse party to make the claims in issue is denied and it is also alleged that the claims when read upon the structures disclosed by the respective parties have different meanings, reasons relied upon in support of such contentions being clearly pointed out, *Held* that the motion to dissolve should be transmitted as to both grounds (*Cushman v. Edwards, ante*, 120: 128 O. G. 458, modified.)

2. SAME—DISSOLUTION—CLAIMS HAVING DIFFERENT MEANINGS IN OPPOSING PARTIES' APPLICATION—PRACTICE.

Where it is found upon motion for dissolution that the claims in issue have different meanings in the cases of the respective parties, the Examiner should require one or both of the applicants to so modify the claims as to avoid a conflict in the terms employed to define the respective inventions.

APPEAL ON MOTION.

VOTING-MACHINE.

Messrs. Bradford & Hood for Eilerman *et al.*
Mr. John H. McElroy, pro se.

BILLINGS, *Assistant Commissioner:*

This case is before me on appeals by Eilerman *et al.* from two decisions of the Examiner of Interferences refusing to transmit their motions to dissolve as to certain grounds stated therein. The first motion to dissolve was filed within the time allowed by Rule 122 and alleged the following grounds:

1. That McElroy had no right to make the claims.

2. That there is no interference in fact.

3. That the claims have different meanings in the cases of the respective parties.

This motion was transmitted by the Examiner of Interferences as to that part alleging that McElroy had no right to make the claims and was denied transmission as to the remaining grounds, for the reason that no other showing was made in respect to these grounds than that relied upon in connection with the denial of McElroy's right to make the claims. The decision of the Examiner of Interferences in refusing to transmit the first motion as to these grounds was clearly right and is affirmed.

Subsequently Eilerman *et al.* presented a motion to transmit the second motion to dissolve, stating more fully the grounds upon which the second and third parts of the original motion were based. The Examiner of Interferences considered the showing in excuse of the delay in presenting this motion to be sufficient, but denied transmission of the motion as to the first ground, for the reason that the question of interference in fact is no longer a part of the grounds enumerated in Rule 122. It appears that this conclusion is now acquiesced in by the appellant. He also refused to transmit the motion as to the second ground, because it was not accompanied by a statement of reasons in support thereof, as required by the decision of *Cushman* v. *Edwards*, (*ante*, 129: 128 O. G., 456.)

The invention in issue is an improvement in voting-machines, and it appears from the statement of grounds in the second motion for dissolution that the claim as read upon McElroy's device refers to the actuation of certain mechanisms in such a manner that it will be fully operated only when the voter leaves the booth, while as disclosed in the application of Eilerman *et al.* the actuation of corresponding mechanism occurs while the voter remains within the booth. It is therefore urged by Eilerman *et al.* that if the Primary Examiner should hold that the language of the issue sufficiently defines McElroy's invention, then the claims in issue when read upon the different structures must have a different meaning in the respective applications and the interference should be dissolved for that reason.

If the motion for dissolution is transmitted only as to the denial of the right of one of the parties to make the claims, such party's case is alone considered in respect to the applicability of the language to the structure disclosed in that application. In cases of this character it is, however, necessary that the terms of the issue should be considered in the light of each party's application, and it is for this reason that it is urged that the present motion should be transmitted.

The action of the Examiner of Interferences in refusing to transmit the second motion for dissolution was in accordance with the decision of *Cushman* v. *Edwards*, *supra*, in which it is pointed out that—

The provision in Rule 122 for dissolution upon the ground of difference in the meaning of claims was placed there to cover a clean-cut class of cases which theoretical considerations show may arise, but which, in fact, are of very rare occurrence. To justify transmission of a motion brought upon this ground, facts must be alleged indicating something more than a possible lack of right upon the part of one or the other of the parties to use the language of the claim in issue.

It is believed that this principle is not applicable to all cases. Interferences are necessarily between inventions. Claims are verbal ... employed to express the extent of the applicant's alleged invention, and when broad terms are employed they may cover structures which ... widely different in detail and which do not produce the same ... results in substantially the same manner. The real ... words of the claim may not be apparent when viewed ... ght of the disclosure of one party. It is believed.

therefore, that the best practical results will be obtained by permitting a party when moving to dissolve an interference not only to raise the question of the right of the other party to make the claims of the issue, but also the question of the meaning of the claims when applied to the respective structures involved. The reasons relied upon in support of these contentions must, of course, be clearly stated in the motion in accordance with the well-settled practice. The motion should in such cases be transmitted in order that the Primary Examiner may consider the applicability of the terms of the claims to the devices of the respective parties in connection with his consideration of the right of one of the parties to make the claims in issue in order that he may more correctly reach a determination of the real question at issue—viz., whether the interference should be dissolved.

Where it is found that the claims have different meanings in the cases of the respective parties, the Examiner should require one or both of the applicants to so modify the claims as to avoid conflict, in accordance with the holding in the decision of the Court of Appeals of the District of Columbia in *Podlesak and Podlesak* v. *McInnerney*, (C. D., 1906, 558; 120 O. G., 2127,) which is as follows:

> We think neither party is entitled to a claim, for the feature here in controversy, which shall dominate the other. It would seem that the claims presented by both, and made the issue of this interference, should be so reformed that each should have a specific claim provided each can draw a claim that avoids the reference. We do not mean to hold that appellant's claim, which has been held patentable, is not patentable as read in the light of their specification. If, as we think, the claim read in the light of their specification means one thing, and the same claim read in the light of appellee's specification means another the same phraseology should not be employed.

For the reasons above stated it is believed that the showing made by Eilerman *et al.* in connection with the ground alleging different meanings of the claims in the applications of the respective parties is sufficient to warrant the transmission of the second motion as to this ground.

The decision of the Examiner of Interferences is reversed to this extent.

AUXER *v.* PEIRCE, JR.

Decided May 15, 1907.

(131 O. G., 359.)

INTERFERENCE—MOTION TO DISSOLVE—DELAY IN BRINGING EXCUSED.

A delay of seven days in filing an amended motion to dissolve, curing objections relating to indefiniteness of the allegations of a prior motion, may be excused where it appears that the first motion attempted in good faith to comply with the practice of the Office.

APPEAL ON MOTION.

CABLE-HANGER.

Messrs. Thurston & Woodward for Auxer.
Messrs. Owen & Owen and *Messrs. Church & Church* for Peirce, Jr.

MOORE, *Acting Commissioner:*

This is an appeal by Auxer from the decision of the Examiner of Interferences refusing to transmit his motions to dissolve the interference.

Auxer's motion for dissolution filed February 25, 1907, in response to an order to show cause why judgment on the record should not be rendered against him, alleged the non-patentability of each count of the issue in view of a large number of domestic and foreign patents cited. This motion was brought within the proper time, but was properly refused transmission by the Examiner of Interferences on the ground that the motion is indefinite in that it fails to specify what particular patents are to be urged against the respective counts or are to be combined together to show anticipation.

Seven days from the date of the above decision of the Examiner of Interferences Auxer filed an amended motion to dissolve. The form of this motion was not objected to by the Examiner of Interferences; but he refused transmission on the ground that it was—

filed late and is accompanied by no reasons to show why a specific motion was not filed in the first place.

The motion is accompanied by the affidavit of counsel that it is filed in good faith and not for the purpose of delay and that the former motion to dissolve was thought at the time it was filed to set forth with sufficient particularity the grounds for dissolution in view of the simple nature of the invention involved.

Allowing for the time required for transmission in the mails, this motion was filed promptly after the decision of the Examiner of Interferences refusing to transmit the prior motion. Reference to the former motion shows that appellant considered the patents cited by him as divisible into two groups, and he stated how he proposes to combine the two groups to anticipate the counts; but he failed to specify which patents constitute the respective groups. The simple character of the invention is admitted by the opponent. In view of this attempt to apply the references, the promptness with which the second motion was filed, and the fact that refusal of the motion will be fatal to appellant's case, it is thought the last motion to dissolve should be transmitted to the Primary Examiner.

The decision of the Examiner of Interferences *is reversed* as to the amended motion and *is affirmed* as to the prior motion.

COLLOM *v.* THURMAN.

PATENT INTERFERENCE.

Decided June 21, 1907.

(131 O. G., 359.)

INTERFERENCE—CONSTRUCTION OF ISSUE—EQUIVALENTS.

Where the claim in issue calls for a " plurality of blast nozzles," a device which has an " oscillating blast-nozzle " cannot be considered as a reduction to practice on the ground that it is an equivalent. In the consideration of an interference the Patent Office is no more competent than the courts to say that an element which an applicant has placed in his claims is an immaterial one. (*Streat* v. *Freckleton,* C. D., 1899, 85 ; 87 O. G., 695.)

APPEAL from Examiners-in-Chief.

PNEUMATIC RENOVATOR.

Mr. H. S. Bailey and *Messrs. Byrnes & Townsend* for Collom.
Messrs. Higdon & Longan and *Mr. John S. Barker* for Thurman.

MOORE, *Commissioner:*

This is an appeal by Collom from a decision of the Examiners-in-Chief affirming a decision of the Examiner of Interferences and awarding priority of invention to Thurman upon the following issue:

1. In a pneumatic renovator, the combination with a casing, of a plurality of blast-nozzles carried by said casing, and an extensible handle connected with said casing and provided with an air-supply conduit, said handle having two members, one longitudinally movable relative to the other and said handle comprising a valve situated outside said casing, said valve being governed by the longitudinal movement of one of said members.

2. In a pneumatic renovator, the combination with a casing, of a plurality of blast-nozzles carried by said casing, and a telescopic handle connected with said casing and provided with an air-supply conduit, said handle having two members, one telescoping the other and said handle comprising a valve situated outside said casing, said valve being governed by the telescopic movement of one of said members.

3. In a pneumatic renovator, the combination with a casing, of a plurality of blast-nozzles carried by said casing, a hollow member having ports communicating with said nozzles, and a second hollow member sliding in said first-named member and provided with ports adapted to successively register with the ports in said first-named member.

4. In a carpet-renovator, a casing having blast-nozzles and air-passages leading to said nozzles, a handle formed of two members, one of which is movable relative to the other, and an air-valve controlling said passages and actuated by said movable member.

5. In a carpet-renovator, a casing having blast-nozzles and air-passages leading to said nozzles, a handle formed of two members, one of which is movable relative to the other, an air-valve controlling said passages and actuated by

said movable member, and means for limiting the operative stroke of said movable member.

6. In a carpet-renovator, a casing having blast-nozzles and air-passages leading to said nozzles, a handle formed of two members, one of which is movable relative to the other, an air-valve controlling said passages and actuated by said movable member, and abutments for limiting the reciprocatory movement of said movable member and valve.

7. In a carpet-renovator, a casing having blast-nozzles, a handle consisting of two members, one of which is reciprocally mounted within the other, said renovator having an inlet-port and air-passages extending from said port to said blast-nozzles, and a valve connected to the reciprocatory member of said handle and arranged to control said air-passages.

Thurman has taken no testimony and is therefore restricted to his record date, November 5, 1904. Collom in his preliminary statement alleged conception, disclosure, and the making of drawings about May 19, 1902, the making of a model about February 14, 1903, and a reduction to practice on December 20, 1904.

The Examiner of Interferences held that Collom had not proved reduction to practice prior to Thurman's filing date, that the testimony tending to show conception by Collom prior to that date was not satisfactory, but that if it be held to so establish conception Collom was not diligent in reducing the invention to practice just prior to Thurman's record date and subsequent thereto. The Examiners-in-Chief held that Collom had proved no date sufficiently early to overcome Thurman's filing date.

Collom has introduced in evidence as " Exhibit No. 3 " and " Exhibit No. 5 " two machines which are alleged to embody the invention in issue.

Exhibit No. 3 comprises a casing having therein an oscillatory drum provided with a single slot from which the blast of air is projected upon the carpet in alternate directions as the drum is oscillated in consonance with the backward-and-forward movement of the renovator. Branch pipes lead from the main air-supply pipe to each end of this drum, a flexible branch pipe connecting the main air-supply pipe to the outer member of the handle of the renovator. Manifestly the exhibit is not an embodiment of the invention set forth in counts 1, 2, and 3 of the issue, each of which includes as an element " a plurality of blast-nozzles carried by said casing," nor of counts 4, 5, 6, and 7, each of which includes as an element " a casing having blast-nozzles and air-passages leading to said nozzles."

It is urged that this exhibit should be considered a reduction to practice because the oscillating blast-nozzle is the equivalent of two nozzles facing in opposite directions; but in the consideration of an interference the Office is no more competent than the courts to say that an element which an applicant has placed in his claims is an immaterial one. (*Streat* v. *Freckleton*, C. D., 1899, 85; 87 O. G., 695.)

In view of the holding that this exhibit does not embody the invention in issue it is unnecessary to consider the testimony as to the time when it was made and tested.

Exhibit No. 5 is the renovator shown in Collom's application in interference and embodies the invention in issue.

Collom testifies that work on this machine was begun about November 30, 1904, and that the machine was completed and put in operation before Christmas of that year. (Qs. 180–182.)

The only other witness who testified with any definiteness as to the date when work on this machine was started and when the machine was completed is Nock, in whose shop it was constructed.

Tabor and Crawford each testifies that he was familiar with the machine and its operation: but neither fixes the time when he first saw it used. Each of them testified that he could fix this time by reference to certain books. (Tabor, Q. 24; Crawford, Q. 15;) but these books were not produced, nor did either witness testify to having looked up the entries therein to which he had referred.

Nock testifies that he commenced work on "Exhibit No. 5" October 1, 1904, and that it was completed not later than December 7, 1904. (Qs. 20–21.) He does not say how he fixes these dates. No bill for this work is produced, and he makes no reference to an entry in his books, although it is apparent from his answer to question 6, when testifying as to "Exhibit No. 3," that he had books to which reference could have been made.

This testimony is clearly insufficient to establish that work was commenced on "Exhibit No. 5" earlier than November 30, 1904, which according to Collom's preliminary statement and his testimony is the time when he began work on this machine.

It is therefore not necessary to consider the testimony offered to establish conception and disclosure by Collom prior to Thurman's record date. If this testimony is not sufficient to establish such conception, then Collom was the last to conceive and the last to reduce to practice. If it is sufficient, then Collom, while the first to conceive, was the last to reduce to practice, and there is no testimony to show that he was diligent at the time Thurman filed his application nor at any time subsequent thereto until he commenced work on "Exhibit No. 5." In neither case can Collom prevail.

The decision of the Examiners-in-Chief awarding priority of invention to Thurman *is affirmed.*

CROUSE-HINDS COMPANY *v.* APPLETON ELECTRIC COMPANY.

OPPOSITION.

Decided September 25, 1907.

(131 O. G., 360.)

1. TRADE-MARKS—OPPOSITION—DISSIMILARITY OF MARKS—DEMURRER.
   Held that trade-marks for electric-wiring purpose consisting of the words "Wirelets" and "Condulets" are not so similar in appearance as to deceive a purchaser using reasonable care and diligence in the selection of the goods and that a demurrer to the notice of opposition was properly sustained.

2. SAME—SAME—SAME—UNFAIR COMPETITION IN TRADE NOT CONSIDERED.
   The question of unfair competition in trade cannot be considered in an opposition proceeding.

APPEAL from Examiner of Interferences.

OUTLET BUSHING FOR ELECTRIC-WIRING PURPOSES.

Mr. Arthur E. Parsons for Crouse-Hinds Company.
Mr. Luther L. Miller for Appleton Electric Company.

MOORE, *Commissioner:*

This is an appeal from the decision of the Examiner of Interferences sustaining the demurrer of the Appleton Electric Company and dismissing the notice of opposition filed by the Crouse-Hinds Company on the ground that the trade-mark of the applicant does not so nearly resemble the trade-mark of the opposer as to cause confusion in the mind of the public or as to deceive purchasers. The trade-mark sought to be registered by the applicant is the word "Wirelets" for outlet-bushings for electric-wiring purposes. The trade-mark of the opposer is the word "Condulets." These trade-marks are applied in the same manner to goods which are substantially identical in construction. It is urged that the trade-marks have the same suggestive meanings, "wire-outlets" and "conduit-outlets" each signifying an outlet for electrical conductors, and that the manner in which the marks are applied to articles of the same construction is calculated to cause confusion in the mind of the public. In the notice of opposition it is alleged that actual confusion in trade has been caused by the similarity of these marks. It is therefore contended that the demurrer should have been overruled and the applicant required to answer the notice of opposition, so the opposer might present testimony relative to this confusion in trade.

The questions whether the goods of the opposing parties are identical and whether the marks are applied to such goods in the same manner by the opposing parties relate to unfair competition in trade, and it is not a matter which can be settled in opposition proceedings.

The similarity of appearance in the words "Wirelets" and "Condulets" is not in my opinion such as would deceive an ordinary purchaser using reasonable care and diligence in the selection of the goods. In the case of *Hall and Ruckel* v. *Ingram* (*post*, 441; 126 O. G., 759) the Court of Appeals of the District of Columbia said:

> Two trade-marks are substantially the same if the resemblance would deceive an ordinary purchaser giving such attention as he usually gives in making a purchase and to cause him to purchase one article mistaking it for the other. (See *Gorham Company* v. *White*, 2 O. G., 592; 14 Wall., 511; *McLean* v. *Fleming*, C. D., 1878, 262; 13 O. G., 913; 96 U. S., 256; *Gaines* v. *Carlton Importation Company*, C. D., 1906, 731; 123 O. G., 1994; 27 App. D. C., 574; *Buchanan-Anderson-Nelson Company* v. *Breen & Kennedy*, C. D., 1906, 750; 124 O. G., 322; 27 App. D. C., 574.)

While in the present case the marks may possibly be considered as remotely having the same suggestion, it is not believed that this is sufficient in view of the difference in appearance and sound of the respective words to cause an ordinary purchaser to mistake the goods of one manufacturer for those of the other.

The decision of the Examiner of Interferences is affirmed.

LEWIS AND BROS. COMPANY *v.* PHOENIX PAINT AND VARNISH COMPANY.

TRADE-MARK INTERFERENCE.

Decided August 3, 1907.

(131 O. G., 361.)

1. TRADE-MARK INTERFERENCE—RE-FORMATION OF ISSUE.
    Where the issue of a trade-mark interference is declared to be for "mixed paints" it should not be re-formed so as to read "ready-mixed paints" when one of the parties does not use the words "ready-mixed paints" to define the goods upon which the mark is used.

2. SAME—SAME CLASS OF GOODS—CONSIDERED AT FINAL HEARING.
    The question whether the goods to which a mark forming the issue of an interference has been applied by the respective parties are of the same descriptive properties is a question which may be decided by the Examiner of Interferences at final hearing.

APPEAL from Examiner of Interferences.

TRADE-MARK FOR PAINTS.

Mr. Francis M. Phelps for Lewis and Bros. Company.
Mr. T. W. Johnson for Phoenix Paint and Varnish Company.

BILLINGS, *Acting Commissioner.*

This is an appeal by the Phoenix Paint and Varnish Company from the decision of the Examiner of Interferences dismissing its motion to re-form the issue without prejudice to the moving party to urge the subject-matter thereof at final hearing.

The issue of the above interference is the word "Phoenix" for mixed paints. The testimony has been taken. It is now desired by the Phoenix Paint and Varnish Company to change the issue from "mixed paints" to "ready-mixed paints." It appears from the record that the issue was made "mixed paints" by the Examiner of Trade-Marks upon consideration of the definitions of the goods respectively used by the parties to this interference. In support of the motion it is urged that the testimony taken in the interference shows "mixed paints" and "ready-mixed paints" to be goods of distinctively different characteristics. An inspection of the respective files, however, shows that while the Phoenix Paint and Varnish Company claims the use of the mark as applied to "ready-mixed paints and stains, japans and varnishes" the John T. Lewis and Bros. Company claim the use of the mark applied to "mixed paints, white zinc and pigments other than white lead used for paints, in Class 16, Paints and painters' materials." It is therefore seen that John T. Lewis and Bros. Company do not use the words "ready mixed paints" to define the goods upon which their trade-mark is used. Obviously it would not be proper to change the issue so as to specifically exclude the goods now claimed by John T. Lewis and Bros. Company. It is believed that the issue as it now stands clearly defines those goods used by both parties which have common characteristics.

It is to be noted that the Examiner of Interferences has jurisdiction to decide at final hearing the question raised upon this motion—namely, whether "mixed paints" and "ready mixed paints" are goods of different descriptive properties, for the trade-mark statute provides for the determination of the question of the "right of registration to such trade-mark." The trade-mark statute gives a much larger jurisdiction than the patent statute, which merely provides for the determination of the question of priority.

The decision of the Examiner of Interferences is affirmed.

Ex parte Herbst.

APPLICATION FOR PATENT.

Decided October 16, 1907.

(131 O. G., 361.)

REJECTION—EXPLANATION OF GROUNDS OF REJECTION BY EXAMINERS.

Where in answer to a rejection by the Examiner giving a fair statement of his reasons for rejection the applicant responds by fully stating what he considered to be disclosed in the references, what he considered to be covered by the rejected claims, and why such claims were not anticipated and requests a further statement from the Examiner as to the bearing of the references upon the broadest claim presented, the Examiner should not finally reject merely upon the reasons formerly stated, but he should make a further statement of the reasons of rejection in the light of applicant's argument.

ON PETITION.

APPARATUS FOR COOLING SYRUP-CANS OF SODA-FOUNTAINS.

Mr. E. G. Siggers and *Mr. H. F. Riley* for the applicant.

BILLINGS, *Assistant Commissioner:*

This is a petition that the final rejection entered in the case be withdrawn and the references cited be more fully explained.

The record shows that the Examiner rejected certain claims in this application on certain specified patents, and he gave a fair statement of his reasons for the rejection. The applicant responded by filing a paper in which he quite fully stated what he considered to be disclosed in the references and what he considered to be covered by the claims which were rejected, and he pointed out why, in his opinion, the references did not meet the claims. He also asked for a further statement from the Examiner as to the bearing of the references upon the broadest claim presented. The Examiner responded by stating that the reasons for rejection were so fully stated in the first Office letter that any additional statement was unnecessary, and he finally rejected the claims. In the present condition of the case there is nothing for the applicant to do but to appeal to the Examiners-in-Chief.

While it is not incumbent upon the Office to answer all the arguments presented by counsel in the prosecution of his case, yet the prosecution of the case should be so conducted as to permit a fair chance for the amendment of the claims after the decision of the Office is made clear. In this particular case it is believed that the applicant was entitled to a further statement of the reasons for rejection in the light of his argument, so that he might amend or request a reconsideration in view of further argument.

The petition is granted.

PAPENDELL *v.* BUNNELL *v.* REIZENSTEIN *v.* GAISMAN *v.* GILLETTE.

PATENT INTERFERENCE.

Decided October 29, 1907.

(131 O. G., 362.)

1. INTERFERENCE—MOTION TO DISSOLVE—GROUND OF NON-PATENTABILITY BASED ON ART TO BE SUBSEQUENTLY CITED—TRANSMISSION.

Held that a motion to dissolve an interference on the ground that the claims in issue are not patentable in view of certain patents and others which "will be cited more than five days before the hearing" should not be transmitted. Rule 122 requires that the motion for dissolution must "contain a full statement of grounds relied upon."

2. SAME—MOTION TO DISSOLVE BROUGHT IN ANSWER TO ORDER TO SHOW CAUSE UNDER RULE 114 MAY BE TRANSMITTED.

The fact that a record judgment may be rendered against a junior party under the provisions of Rule 114 does not preclude him from presenting motions for dissolution.

APPEAL ON MOTION.

SAFETY-RAZOR.

Messrs. Redding, Kiddle & Greeley for Papendell.

Messrs. Redding, Kiddle & Greeley and *Mr. A. P. Greeley* for Bunnell.

Messrs. Wiedersheim & Fairbanks for Reizenstein.

Mr. T. F. Bourne for Gaisman.

. *Mr. E. D. Chadwick* and *Messrs. Bacon & Milans* for Gillette.

BILLINGS, *Assistant Commissioner:*

This case is before me upon appeals by Bunnell from the decision of the Examiner of Interferences denying the transmission of his motion for dissolution; by Reizenstein from the denial of the transmission of one motion for dissolution and also from the denial of the transmission in part of a second motion for dissolution, and by Gillette from the decision of the Examiner of Interferences transmitting Reizenstein's second motion in part.

The transmission of the motion for dissolution by Bunnell was denied upon the ground that the allegations upon which the motion was based were not sufficiently specific. The grounds alleged in that motion were irregularity in declaration of the interference, that the counts have different meanings in the cases of the different parties, and that the issue of the interference was not patentable—

* * * in view of the prior state of the art, part of which is set forth in United States Letters Patent No. 375,592, dated December 27, 1887, and granted to A. S. Aloe. Further matter showing the state of the art will be cited more than five days before the hearing on this motion as soon as found.

No sufficient reasons were alleged in support of the first and second grounds of this motion, and its transmission was properly denied as to these grounds. In respect to the third ground of the motion it is to be noted that but one patent is cited. There is a reservation that other art will be cited in connection with this ground of the motion before the hearing upon the same by the Primary Examiner. This portion of the motion is also informal. It has been held that where but a single reference is cited against a claim the motion may be transmitted. (*McCanna v. Morris, ante,* 141; 128 O. G., 1292.) In this case, however, the reference cited does not appear to be relied upon as wholly anticipating the issue, inasmuch as it is stated to be a part only of the art relied upon, and no other reference is cited, but the matter left open for further citation. The statement of reasons for the ground of the motion is wholly insufficient.

It is contended by Bunnell that under long standing practice he should be permitted to give notice of other references five days before the hearing of the motion. The reasons for this practice, which was followed in the past, but which has not been permitted for some time, do not now exist. Since the date of the decisions under which an applicant was permitted to give notice five days before the date of hearing of additional reasons for dissolving the interferences Rule 122 has been amended and the time within which motions may be brought in interference cases extended from twenty days to thirty days. It has also been amended to require that a motion for dissolution must contain "a full statement of the grounds relied upon." The rule further provides that such motions—   .

should if possible be made not later than the thirtieth day after the statements of the parties have been received and approved.

It is therefore open to the applicant, if he is unable to make a sufficiently exhaustive search of the art within the thirty days provided for by the rule, to present the motion for dissolution after the expiration of the thirty days, accompanied by a sufficient showing of compelling reasons why he was unable to present such motion at an earlier date. (*Sturgis* v. *Hopewell*, C. D., 1904. 82; 109 O. G., 1067; *McKee* v. *Baker*, C. D., 1906, 22: 120 O. G., 657; *Steinmetz* v. *Thomas*, C. D., 1905, 507; 119 O. G., 1260.)

The decision of the Examiner of Interferences in refusing to transmit Bunnell's motion as to all grounds was right and is affirmed.

Reizenstein in his first motion for dissolution alleged that each count of the issue is an aggregation—   .

* * * according to the interpretation of the claims set forth in the decisions of *Reckendorfer* v. *Faber* (C. D., 1876, 430; 10 O. G., 71; 92 U. S., 347) and the decisions cited in and based upon this decision.

2d. That each of the counts of the interference has a different meaning when based upon the construction illustrated and described by the different parties hereto.

3d. That each issue of the interference is not patentable in view of certain prior patents.

Two patents were cited in support of the third ground of the motion, over each of which it is alleged "no invention is shown." The motion also states:

* * * and certain other Letters Patent and a state of art not herein cited but which will be cited and notice thereof, as well as reasons therefor, served upon the parties hereto more than five days before the hearing of this motion.

The first ground of this motion is insufficiently stated, for the reason that it is not pointed out in what respect the claims of the issue comprise aggregations and not combinations. The second ground is insufficiently stated, since the differences in the meanings of the claims are not pointed out. The third ground in so far as it relates to the cited patents is believed to be sufficient and should have been transmitted for the reasons stated in *McCanna* v. *Morris, supra.*

The decision of the Examiner of Interferences is affirmed as to the first and second grounds and is reversed as to the third, it being understood that subsequently-cited art should not be considered by the Primary Examiner in consideration of this motion for the reasons above stated.

In respect to Reizenstein's second motion it appears that the third ground thereof, which is substantially the same as the corresponding ground of the first motion, was transmitted, and in view of the conclusion above reached it is unnecessary to discuss this ground of the motion.

The first ground of Reizenstein's second motion comprises merely an elaboration of the first ground of his original motion, and this was denied transmission by the Examiner of Interferences because in his opinion no reason appeared why this ground might not have been made specific in the first instance.

The record shows that the second motion by Reizenstein was filed five days after the decision upon his first motion was rendered and is supported by an affidavit by counsel in the case setting forth facts in excuse of the delay and further stating that the reasons set forth in connection with the first ground of the first motion were believed to be sufficient, for the reason that in the *Reckendorfer* v. *Faber* decision the analogy to the present case was believed to be apparent, since—

* * * each of the counts of the present interference claims the combination of a razor with a handle; the party Reizenstein relied upon the seeming evident applicability of the rubber and its handle as aggregations to the razor and its handle in the present instance as like aggregations.

In view of the fact that Reizenstein moved promptly to make his motion in respect to this ground more specific when informed that the original ground was not presented with sufficient particularity, it is believed that the motion should have been transmitted as to this ground, especially in view of the fact that the showing in support of the second motion was considered by the Examiner of Interferences sufficient to warrant its transmission as to the third ground.

No attempt has been made to set forth the second ground of the motion with more particularity, and this ground of the motion was properly denied transmission.

The decision of the Examiner of Interferences is reversed as to the first ground of Reizenstein's second motion and is affirmed as to the second ground. Since it has been held that the original motion should have been transmitted as to the third ground, it is not necessary to consider that branch of the motion in connection with this appeal.

It is contended in behalf of Gillette that motions to dissolve an interference upon the ground that the issue is not patentable should not be transmitted where such motions are brought by junior parties in response to an order to show cause under Rule 114. It is urged that the junior party against whom a record judgment will be rendered is in no better position to contest the question of patentability of the issue to the senior party than any other member of the general public and that he should not therefore be heard to deny the patentability of the same. This contention is believed to be untenable. Judgment of priority will not be rendered in any case except upon a patentable invention. Until the interference has been finally determined the parties involved in such interference clearly have the right to invoke all of the provisions of the rules which may be applicable to the case, and since Rule 122 includes a provision that motions for dissolution may be presented upon the ground that the issue is not patentable any party to an interference has a right under proper conditions to present a motion upon this ground within the time limit prescribed by the rule.

To summarize: The decision of the Examiner of Interferences in refusing to transmit Bunnell's motion *is affirmed*. The motions of Reizenstein *should be transmitted* in so far as relates to the denial of the patentability of the claims in issue upon the ground of aggregation and in view of the two references cited in the third part of these motions.

JUNGE *v.* HARRINGTON.

Decided February 4, 1907.

(131 O. G., 691.)

1. INTERFERENCE—CONSTRUCTION OF THE ISSUE.
   While applications are pending in this Office the claims thereof will be construed as broadly as the ordinary meaning of the language employed will permit.

2. SAME—SAME.
   The party who first presents claims should not later be heard to urge limitations upon the terms thereof which might readily have been expressed therein had it been intended that they should be so restricted.

APPEAL from Examiners-in-Chief.

Mr. Edward A. Lawrence for Junge.
Messrs. Poole & Brown for Harrington.

MOORE, *Assistant Commissioner:*

This is an appeal from the decision of the Examiners-in-Chief affirming the decision of the Examiner of Interferences and awarding priority of invention to Junge upon the following issue:

1. In a furnace in which the fuel is caused to travel within the combustion-chamber, the combination of a fuel-support, a fuel-retarding device, means for adjusting said retarding device, to vary the distance between it and said fuel-support, and for securing it in its adjusted position.

2. In a furnace in which the fuel is caused to travel within the combustion-chamber, the combination of a fuel-support, a hollow fuel-retarding device, means for circulating a cooling agent through said retarding device, means for adjusting said retarding device to vary the distance between it and said fuel-support, and for securing it in its adjusted position.

3. In a furnace in which the fuel is caused to travel within the combustion-chamber, the combination of a fuel-support, a hollow fuel-retarding device provided with journals arranged at one side of its axial line, means for circulating a cooling agent through said retarding device, said cooling agent being introduced through one of said journals, and means for adjusting said retarding device to vary the distance between it and said fuel-support, and for securing it in its adjusted position.

Harrington, the senior party, has taken no testimony and relies upon his record date, September 28, 1904, as his date of conception and constructive reduction to practice. Junge alleges in his preliminary statement that he conceived the invention in May, 1903, disclosed it to others in June, 1903, and reduced it to practice in February, 1904.

Junge shows in the drawings of his application involved in this interference two specific forms of apparatus embodying his invention. Figures 12 and 13 show a vertically-sliding retarding device provided with a conduit for a cooling medium located over the rear end of a traveling grate. The retarding device is supported by one arm of a bell-crank lever and is adapted to be maintained in adjusted positions by a segment-and-pawl-controlled lever connected with the other member of the bell-crank lever.

Figs. 1 and 2 illustrate a pivoted water-cooled retarding device similarly located and adapted to be held in adjusted position by lugs or projections on a rod connected with an arm upon the retarding device.

The testimony shows, and it is not disputed, that a retarding device like that shown in Figs. 12 and 13 of his apparatus was installed by Junge in a furnace at the plant of Edward E. Rieck Company in February, 1904, and that retarding devices like that illustrated in

Figs. 1 and 2 were placed in furnaces in the same place in March and June, 1904, and successfully operated. Inasmuch as these dates are all prior to Harrington's date of conception, the sole question to be determined is whether either of these devices constituted a reduction to practice of the invention by Junge.

It is contended in behalf of Harrington that the counts of the issue must be given a limited construction in view of the prior art as illustrated by patents to McKenzie, No. 679,240, and Coxe, No. 510,569. It is urged that in view of these patents the "means for adjusting said retarding device to vary the distance between it and said fuel-support" must be construed to include positive means for retaining it in its adjusted position and not merely means for raising and supporting the retarding device at different elevations.

The Examiner of Interferences and the Examiners-in-Chief concurred in finding that this limitation should not be read into the claims in issue and, further, that even if the claims were construed to have this limitation the devices installed by Junge in the Edward E. Rieck's furnaces constituted reduction to practice of the invention.

The conclusions of the lower tribunals as to both points are in my opinion correct.

In addition to the reasons given by the Examiners-in-Chief for refusing to place a limited construction upon the issue it is noted that the record shows that the claims in issue were first presented by Harrington. He should not now be heard to urge limitations upon the terms of such claims which might readily have been expressed therein had it been intended that they should be so restricted. In general while applications are pending in this Office the claims thereof will be construed as broadly as the ordinary meaning of the language employed will permit, for reasons stated in my decisions in *ex parte Cutler*, (C. D., 1906, 247; 123 O. G., 655,) *Briggs* v. *Lillie* v. *Cooke* v. *Jones and Taylor*, (C. D., 1905, 168; 116 O. G., 871,) *Podlesak and Podlesak* v. *McInnerney*, (C. D., 1906, 265; 123 O. G., 1989,) and *Lovejoy* v. *Cady*, (C. D., 1906, 245; 123 O. G., 654.)

The testimony clearly shows that the retarding devices installed by Junge in the furnaces of the Edward E. Rieck Company each had " means for adjusting the retarding device " and that the pivoted devices put in operation in March and June, 1904, contained all the features called for by the terms of the issue.

These devices not only embodied the subject-matter of the issue when broadly construed, but also when read with the limitations sought to be imposed by Harrington. It is clear from the testimony of Junge (Q. 49) and Daniels (Q. 44) that the operating-lever for the sliding retarding device installed in February, 1904, was provided 'th a latch adapted to engage in any one of a series of notches in a drant for the purpose of adjusting the height of the retaining device above the grate, and therefore constituted a reduction to practice of counts 1 and 2 of the issue. In the pivoted retarding devices of March and June, 1904, the " reach-rod " for tilting the retarding device was provided with a series of notches adapted to engage a fixed lug on the boiler for the purpose of providing any desired adjustment in the elevation of the retarding device over the grate. (Junge, Q. 74; Daniels, Q. 62; Slean, X-Q. 36.)

It appears that the original " reach-rod " used with the pivoted retarding devices was broken and when a new rod was substituted but three notches were placed upon it—one for holding it at its lowest point, another for holding it at its highest point, and an intermediate notch holding it near its highest point. It is urged by Harrington that this fact indicates that there was no intent to provide means for adjusting the working height of the retarding device above the grate. Daniels (RD. Q. 28) and Junge (X-Q. 111) testify that it was found that with the uniform character of fuel being used the intermediate adjustments of the retarding device were unnecessary at the time the new lever was substituted. These notches could, moreover, be easily added at any time. In view of the fact that the device as originally constructed and used embodied all the features of the invention the subsequent omission of some of the intermediate notches based upon the knowledge of the requirements of the furnace does not cast doubt upon the original intent to provide for various adjustments.

The evidence clearly warrants the conclusion that Junge reduced the invention stated in all the counts of the issue to practice in the pivoted type of retarding device installed in March, 1904, which is prior to the date of conception accorded to Harrington by the filing of his application September 28, 1904.

The decision of the Examiners-in-Chief is affirmed.

EX PARTE THE SAMUEL WINSLOW SKATE MFG. CO.

APPLICATION FOR REGISTRATION OF LABEL.

Decided June 5, 1907.

(131 O. G., 692.)

LABEL—REGISTRABILITY.
   The use of a paraph under certain words of a label which is otherwise devoid of artistic merit is not sufficient to render the label registrable.

ON APPEAL.

Mr. Hartley H. Bartlett for the applicant.

MOORE, *Commissioner:*

This is an appeal from the action of the Examiner refusing to register a label intended to be used upon skates and entitled " Winslow's Skates The Best Ice and Roller Skates."

Registration was refused by the Examiner for the reason that the label is not an artistic production.

The letter " s " at the end of the words " Winslow's " and " Skates " has a continuation forming a paraph or underscoring of the words. Neither this feature nor the form of the letters used is novel or involves more than the skill of the printer. The production of the label is believed to involve no originality or creative power of the mind and in my opinion the Examiner's action was correct in refusing registration on the ground that the label is not an artistic production. (*Ex parte Baldwin*, C. D., 1902, 54; 98 O. G., 1706; *ex parte Houghton*, C. D., 1902, 176; 99 O. G., 1623; *ex parte The Clark Cast Steel Cement Company*, C. D., 1902, 223; 99 O. G., 2968; *ex parte Booth*, C. D., 1902, 351; 101 O. G., 219; *ex parte Ambròsia Chocolate Company*, C. D., 1906, 231; 122 O. G., 3011.)

The decision of the Examiner is affirmed.

PYM *v.* HADAWAY.

PATENT INTERFERENCE.

Decided July 11, 1907.

(131 O. G., 692.)

1. INTERFERENCE—RULE 130.

   Rule 130 does not confer upon a party the absolute right to contest his opponent's right to a claim, but allows him to do so only when the objections urged against his opponent's right to make the claim do not apply with equal force to his own case.

2. SAME—LIMIT OF APPEAL FROM DECISION ON PRIORITY.

   The bringing of motions or the taking of petitions to the Commissioner will not stay the running of the limit of appeal from a decision on priority.

ON MOTION.

TACK-PULLER AND NAIL-DRIVER.

Messrs. Parker & Burton and *Mr. George H. Maxwell* for Pym. *Mr. Benj. Phillips* and *Messrs. Phillips, Van Everen & Fish* for Hadaway.

MOORE, *Commissioner:*

This is a motion by Pym that the limit of appeal from the decision of the Examiner of Interferences rendered December 19, 1906, which expired January 8, 1907, be extended to include an appeal to the Board of Examiners-in-Chief filed June 24, 1907.

The record shows that in response to an order to show cause why judgment should not be rendered against him under Rule 114 Pym brought a motion to dissolve, alleging all the grounds for dissolution provided by Rule 122. Pym's motion to dissolve was finally denied by the Commissioner and judgment rendered against him under the provisions of Rule 114 for failure of the allegations of his preliminary statement to overcome Hadaway's record date. Thereafter Pym brought motions to set aside said judgment and for leave to take testimony to show that Hadaway had no right to make the claims in issue, contending that the claims as read upon Hadaway's structure comprised merely an aggregation, while as read upon Pym's structure formed true combinations. This motion having been finally decided adversely to Pym by the Commissioner on appeal, Pym brought a motion that jurisdiction be restored to the Examiner of Interferences in order that he might contest the question of Hadaway's right to make the claim in issue under the provisions of Rule 130. This motion was denied by the Assistant Commissioner in a decision rendered June 6, 1907, upon the ground that the matters desired to be urged before the Examiner of Interferences related to the non-patentability of the issue with respect to both parties, which is not a question of priority that can properly be raised under Rule 130.

It is contended in behalf of Pym that his failure to file an appeal from the final decision of the Examiner of Interferences was because he understood that the clause of Rule 130 which provides that—

where the patentability of a claim to an opponent is *material* to the right of a party to a patent, said party may urge the non-patentability of the claim to his opponent at final hearing before the Examiner of Interferences as a basis for the decision upon priority of invention and upon appeals from such decision—

conferred upon him an absolute right to be heard upon the question of Hadaway's right to make the claims and that he therefore believed he had no reason to file an appeal to the Examiners-in-Chief until after the decision of the Commissioner finally denying him this right under the circumstances of this case.

This contention is believed to be untenable. The decision of the Primary Examiner affirming Hadaway's right to make the claims and holding that the objections urged against Hadaway's right to make the claims applied with equal force to Pym's case, which was rendered December 15, 1906, and from which there was no appeal, gave Pym sufficient notice that the grounds upon which he desired to contest Hadaway's right to make the claims were not material to the question of priority and could not be urged at the final hearing und Rule 130. Appeal from the final decision of the Examiner of Inte ferences should therefore have been taken within the limit of appeal. It is well settled that the bringing of motions or the taking of petitions to the Commissioner will not stay the running of the limit of appeal from a decision on priority. The presentation of motions by Pym in the endeavor to obtain a decision by the Examiner of Interferences upon a question which could not properly be urged before him does not therefore constitute a sufficient excuse for the delay in taking an appeal from the final decision of the Examiner of Interferences.

The motion is denied.

EHRET *v.* STAR BREWERY COMPANY.

TRADE-MARK INTERFERENCE.

Decided October 12, 1907.

(131 O. G., 693.)

1. TRADE-MARKS—ABANDONMENT—SUBSEQUENT RIGHTS OF OTHERS.

   If the word "Star" or the representation of a star as a trade-mark for beer has become public property, an applicant is not entitled to the registration of a mark for the same class of goods consisting of two superimposed equilateral triangles forming a six-pointed star, with a monogram of the letters "G. E." in the center thereof, unless his mark differs from a mere star to such an extent that the simultaneous use of the same would not be likely to cause confusion in the mind of the public.

2. SAME—IDENTITY.

   A mark consisting of a six-pointed star having in the center thereof a monogram of the letters "G. E." *Held* to so nearly resemble a mark in prior use by another, consisting of a six-pointed star surrounded by two concentric circles, between which are the words "The Celebrated Star Lager Beer," as to be likely to cause confusion in the mind of the public.

ON APPEAL.

TRADE-MARK FOR LAGER-BEER.

Messrs. Goepel & Goepel for Ehret.

Mr. Wallace A. Bartlett and *Mr. Fenelon B. Brock* for Star Brewery Company.

MOORE, *Commissioner:*

This is an appeal from a decision of the Examiner of Interferences awarding to the Star Brewery Company priority of adoption and use of "the representation of a star" as a trade-mark for lager-beer.

The mark shown in Ehret's application consists of two superimposed equilateral triangles forming a six-pointed star, with a monogram of the letters "G. E." in the center thereof. The mark shown in the certificate of registration of the Star Brewery Company is a six-pointed star surrounded by two concentric circles, between which are the words "The Celebrated Star Lager Beer." The essential feature of the registered mark is stated to be the word "Star" or the representation of a star.

The Star Brewery Company's registration is dated December 5, 1893, and it is alleged therein that the registrant is the successor to Hartmann Bros., by whom this mark was registered February 27, 1877, Serial No. 4,402.

Ehret's mark was registered June 9, 1896, Serial No. 28,360. He applied for registration under the act of 1905 on April 19, 1905, Serial No. 2,273, and it is this application that is involved in the present interference.

Ehret took no testimony-in-chief. The Star Brewery Company took testimony which it was alleged was not for the purpose of establishing a date of adoption and use, but merely for the purpose of perpetuating the testimony of certain witnesses who were growing old. Ehret then took rebuttal testimony. This testimony does not purport to rebut any testimony taken by the Star Brewery Company, but was taken for the purpose of showing that the mark as actually used by that company consisted of a star with either an inner or an outer circle, or both, and that persons other than the present contestants had for many years used trade-marks for beer in which a star was a prominent feature.

The Examiner of Interferences held that as the Star Brewery Company was a registrant the only question to be decided was Ehret's right to register his mark, that it was immaterial whether the Star Brewery Company used circles with the star or not, as they were mere embellishments, that as the Star Brewery Company was a registrant the use of a star as a trade-mark by other brewers was immaterial, and that as Ehret had taken no testimony to show adoption and use prior to the date of registration of the Star Brewery Company priority of adoption and use must be awarded to the latter.

Section 7 of the act of 1905 provides in part as follows:

That in every case of interference or opposition to registration he (the Commissioner) shall direct the Examiner in charge of interferences to determine the right of registration to such a trade-mark.

Since the Star Brewery Company is a registrant, it is evident that the only question to be determined in this proceeding is the right of Ehret to register his mark. Since Ehret took no testimony to establish a date of adoption and use, but relied on his registration of June 9, 1896, as *prima facie* evidence of ownership as of that date, the Examiner of Interferences was clearly right in deciding priority of adoption and use in favor of the Star Brewery Company, since it's registration is dated December 5, 1893.

It is contended by Ehret, however, that the evidence which he presented in rebuttal shows that the Star Brewery Company never held the exclusive right to the use of a star as a trade-mark for beer, as the mark which it actually used was a star and a circle. It is further contended that this evidence shows that for a number of years many brewers have used trade-marks an essential feature of which was a star and that as the Star Brewery Company made no effort to stop such use it has by its laches lost any right that it might have had to claim the exclusive use of a star broadly.

It is not seen that these contentions, even if well taken, affect Ehret's right to register. If a star as a trade-mark for beer has by reason of the laches of the Star Brewery Company become public property, then Ehret is not entitled to the exclusive use of such a mark nor to register the same. Not being entitled to register a mere star, Ehret could not register the mark shown in his application unless this mark differs from a mere star to such an extent that the simultaneous use of the same would not be likely to cause confusion in the mind of the public.

In *ex parte Flint and Walling Mfg. Co.*, (C. D., 1898, 636; 85 O. G., 148) a trade-mark consisting of a pictorial symbol of a star with a windmill in the center was refused registration in view of a registered mark the essential features of which were the letters " U S " and the word-symbol " Star " or the representation of a star. In *ex parte Swan and Finch Co.* (C. D., 1902, 260; 100 O. G., 682) a trade-mark described as a red star was refused registration in view of a prior mark consisting of a star inclosing the letter " G." In *Galena Oil Co.* v. *W. P. Fuller & Co.* (C. D., 1902, 404; 101 O. G., 1611) it was held that a five-pointed star is the equivalent of a six-pointed star as a trade-mark. In *Hutchinson* v. *Blumberg* (C. D., 1892, 652; 61 O. G., 1017) it was held that a trade-mark consisting of the word " Star " and the symbol of a star was infringed by the use of a star and a crescent, even though in the one case the star was five-pointed and in the other six-pointed and the stars were printed in different colors.

In view of these decisions it is held that Ehret is not entitled to registration, whether the Star Brewery Company is entitled to the exclusive use of a mere star or such a mark is public property.

As to Ehret's contention that the mark actually used by the Star Brewery Company consisted of a star and a circle, it is apparent from a consideration of all the record that such a mark has been used by the company since a date prior to the date of Ehret's registration. Since this is true and since, in view of the decisions above cited, Ehret's mark must be held to so nearly resemble this composite mark as to be likely to cause confusion, Ehret must be denied registration under that portion of section 5 of the act of 1905 which provides that a trade-mark which so nearly resembles a known trade-mark owned and in use by another and appropriated to merchandise of the same descriptive properties as to be likely to cause confusion in the mind of the public shall not be registered.

The decision of the Examiner' of Interferences is affirmed.

Ex parte Granger & Company.

APPLICATION FOR REGISTRATION OF TRADE-MARK.

Decided August 21, 1907.

(131 O. G., 694.)

TRADE-MARKS—ANTICIPATION.

> *Held* that the trade-mark " Royal Blend." for coffee is anticipated by a registered mark comprising a Maltese cross surmounted by a crown and bearing the word " Royal." *Held* also that the word " Blend " for coffee is merely descriptive of the merchandise, and its presence as part of the mark does not confer any arbitrary or distinguishing significance upon the mark sought to be registered.

On Appeal.

TRADE-MARK FOR COFFEE.

Mr. George C. Shoemaker for the applicant.

Billings, *Acting Commissioner:*

This is an appeal from the action of the Examiner of Trade-Marks refusing the registration of the mark " Royal Blend " for coffee upon the ground that the term " Blend " is descriptive of the character of the goods and the word " Royal " is anticipated in each of the following registered trade-marks for coffee:

McEwan, 16,160, January 8, 1889; Chase & Sanborn, 17,743, April 8, 1890; Washburn, 27,596, January 7, 1896; Wolfe, McMillan & Co., 32,260, December 20, 1898.

The term " Blend " is clearly descriptive as indicating a coffee comprising a mixture of two or more coffees of different characteristics and does not, therefore, confer any arbitrary or distinguishing feature upon the trade-mark claimed by the applicant.

Each of the trade-marks cited includes the word " Royal " as an essential feature, and the use of this word by the applicant would apparently indicate that the coffee produced or sold by it comprised a blend which included coffee that had become known as " Royal."

In the registration of Wolfe, McMillan & Co., the essential features of the trade-mark are said to consist " in a descriptive representation of the Maltese cross having radiating streamers between its arms and surmounted by a representation of a crown having trefoil points and bearing the word ' Royal.' " The name by which the coffee bearing this trade-mark would be known is " Royal," and it is clear that the use of the mark " Royal Blend " by the applicant would cause confusion in the mind of the public and tend to deceive purchasers who were familiar with the coffee of the registrant Wolfe, McMillan & Co.

Similar considerations indicate the confusion which would be likely to exist between the applicant's mark and each of the other registrations above referred to.

The decision of the Examiner of Trade-Marks is affirmed.

DAVIS *v.* KENNARD.

PATENT INTERFERENCE.

Decided October 22, 1907.

(131 O. G., 695.)

INTERFERENCE—PRELIMINARY STATEMENT—AMENDMENT—CARRYING BACK DATE OF REDUCTION TO PRACTICE.

The junior party to an interference permitted to amend his preliminary statement by carrying the date of the production of two full-sized devices from a date subsequent to the opponent's filing date, on which the opponent alone relies for reduction to practice, to a date prior thereto, where the motion to amend was brought only thirteen days after the filing of the original statement and before any testimony was taken and where it appears from affidavits filed that prior to the execution of his first preliminary statement he examined such records and consulted with such persons as would in his opinion enable him to secure all the necessary facts.

APPEAL ON MOTION.

BUILDING CONSTRUCTION.

Mr. Ernest W. Marshall and *Messrs. Bradford & Hood* for Davis. *Messrs. Smith & Frazier* for Kennard.

BILLINGS, *Assistant Commissioner:*

This is an appeal by Davis from the decision of the Acting Examiner of Interferences denying his motion for leave to amend his preliminary statement.

The preliminary statement of Davis was filed July 23, 1907. His motion to amend his preliminary statement was filed thirteen days later, on August 5, 1907. The only change appellant desires to make in his preliminary statement is the insertion of the allegation that in July, 1905, he produced two full-sized complete usable building-blocks embodying the essential features of all the counts of the interference. Kennard alleges no reduction to practice, save a constructive reduction to practice by the filing of his application February 19,

1906. If the amendment of the preliminary statement of Davis is permitted, it may have the effect of enabling him to carry his reduction to practice from a subsequent date to a date prior to Kennard's filing date.

It appears from the affidavits in support of the motion that Davis executed and delivered his original preliminary statement to his attorney on July 22, 1907, and that said attorney left the same night for Washington, where the preliminary statement was filed on July 23, 1907.

The affidavits of Davis and his wife are to the effect that during the night of July 22, after the preliminary statement had left his possession, Davis told his wife of the preliminary statement he had executed and reviewed with her the history of the invention; that she then recalled that her husband had made a journey to Indianapolis in July, 1905, and after his return told her he had constructed two full-sized hollow building-blocks; that she had forgotten this fact until her memory was refreshed by this conversation, and that Davis had also forgotten about these facts, but recalled them distinctly upon his memory being thus refreshed.

This showing concerning the business trip to Indianapolis and the work of Davis on vitrified hollow tiles is corroborated by the affidavit of the stenographer of Davis. It also appears that Davis communicated these facts to his attorney upon his next interview with him during the following week and that the motion to amend followed promptly.

The motion was denied by the Acting Examiner of Interferences on the ground that Davis had not shown that the facts discovered on July 22 could not have been discovered before the execution of his preliminary statement by careful and diligent search or consultation with persons likely to be familiar therewith.

Davis in his affidavit does state that he made careful examination of such records as were in his possession or accessible to him, that he consulted with the persons whom he thought likely to have any knowledge of the development of his invention, and that he wrote to persons with whom he could not personally consult. This showing is criticised by the Acting Examiner of Interferences on the ground that the names of the parties he claims to have consulted are not given; also for the reason that it does not appear that he had consulted with his wife or stenographer prior to July 22 or that if he had done so he could not have discovered the facts prior to the execution of his original preliminary statement.

While the showing would have been more complete if this matter had been set forth in the affidavits, it is believed to be sufficient under the circumstances of this case. (*Whitney* v. *Gibson*, C. D., 1899, 54 ; 86

O. G., 1983.)   The motion to amend was brought with great promptness and prior to the taking of any testimony, so that Kennard's interests will not be injured except by the proven facts.   To deny the motion may result in the issue of an invalid patent to one who is not the prior inventor.   This case is similar to that of *Silver* v. *Eustis*, (C. D., 1902, 91; 98 O. G., 2361,) in which it was held:

> In the present case Eustis states in his affidavit that he had forgotten the date of his earliest conception and reduction to practice.   The affidavits of Kellogg and Chamberlain corroborate that of Eustis, so that if the facts alleged are true they prove that Eustis conceived the invention, disclosed it to others, and reduced to practice at a time prior to that set forth in his original statement. Should the Office refuse to permit the amendment to the statement, it might result in the allowance of a patent to one who is not the prior inventor.   Justice demands that the possibility of such a result be removed so far as it can be done without injury to others.   In this case Silver will not be injured except as the true state of facts will injure him.   He will not be misled, nor will the expenses of the proceeding be increased.

The decision of the Acting Examiner of Interferences is reversed.

EX PARTE WENTZEL.

APPLICATION FOR PATENT.

Decided November 5, 1907.

(131 O. G., 941.)

1. ABANDONMENT OF APPLICATION—FINAL ACTION ON FORM AND MERITS—APPEAL ON MERITS TOO LATE.

Where the Examiner finally rejected the claims of an application and also made final certain objections to such claims on July 3, 1906, and a petition upon the formal matters was taken on August 2, 1906, which was decided by the Commissioner on August 27, 1906, an appeal to the Examiners-in-Chief filed August 24, 1907, is filed without the period of one year allowed for prosecution, which dates from the final rejection and not from the decision of the Commissioner on the petition.

2. SAME—DELAY SLIGHT—UNAVOIDABLE.

Where delay beyond the year allowed for action is slight and the application prior to such delay had been prosecuted vigorously and in good faith and the applicant had reason to suppose that his action was filed in time, the delay may be regarded as unavoidable.

ON PETITION.

EDGE-BLACKING MACHINE.

Messrs. Crosby & Gregory for the applicant.

MOORE, *Commissioner:*

This is a petition from the action of the Primary Examiner refusing to forward an appeal to the Examiners-in-Chief on the ground that the application is abandoned.

On July 3, 1906, the Examiner finally rejected certain claims and also made his formal objections to certain claims final. Applicant took a petition on August 2, 1906, to the Commissioner from the Examiner's ruling on the formal matters, which petition was granted in a decision of the Commissioner dated August 27, 1906. No further action was taken until August 24, 1907, when applicant filed an appeal to the Examiners-in-Chief upon the finally-rejected claims.

This appeal the Examiner refused to forward on the ground that through appellant's failure to file it within one year from the final rejection of July 3, 1906, the case had become abandoned.

Petitioner contends that the petition of August 2, 1906, was a proper action in the case, that under Rule 134 it was necessary to settle all preliminary questions before an appeal could be taken on the merits, and that he was entitled to one year from the Commissioner's decision of August 27, 1906, upon the petition in which to file his appeal. In support of this contention he cites the case of *ex parte Thomas*, (C. D., 1906, 312; 124 O. G., 623,) where appeal to the Examiners-in-Chief was permitted more than a year after the final rejection of the claims. In that case, however, certain formal objections were raised for the first time when the claims were placed under final rejection. Subsequently the applicant made an action directed to said informalities, concerning which the Commissioner said:

This action was responsive to the requirements of the case, and manifestly the applicant is entitled to a year from the Examiner's action of April 6, 1905, repeating certain of the objections, in which to take a petition or to cure the said objections. In the absence of any rule or practice to the contrary the applicant should likewise be allowed this year in which to take his appeal to the Examiners-in-Chief or to cancel the rejected claims and put his case in condition for allowance.

That decision merely held that applicant was entitled to a year from the final action of the Examiner upon the informalities in which " to take a petition or to cure said informalities " and in which to take his appeal to the Examiners-in-Chief. It did not hold that applicant has a year from the decision on the petition in which to appeal, nor does it support petitioner's contention to this effect.

In the present case the final action on both the informalities and the merits were made in the same Office letter. Consequently even under the above decision the applicant would be entitled to but one year from the date of said letter in which to take his appeal.

In *ex parte Walton* (C. D., 1906, 28; 120 O. G., 659) it was held an amendment curing formal defects filed after final rejection of the claims will not save the case from becoming abandoned where appeal is not taken within a year from the final rejection.

TRADE-MARK FOR LEATHER BOOTS AND SHOES.

Mr. H. E. Dunlap for the applicant.

BILLINGS, *Assistant Commissioner:*

This is a petition that the Examiner of Trade-Marks be directed to clearly point out the distinction which he makes between the mark sought to be registered and the registered trade-marks No. 61,951 and No. 61,930.

It appears from the record that the Examiner refused to register the applicant's trade-mark on the ground that the distinguishing feature thereof, the word " Dresden," is a mere geographical term. The applicant, while admitting that the word " Dresden " in and of itself is geographical, contends that the background upon which the word is printed forms an essentially distinguishing feature of the trade-mark, and therefore urges that the mark as a whole should be registered. The Examiner adhered to his first ruling and cited in support thereof the decisions of the courts and of the Commissioner controlling such cases.

It is not believed that the Examiner should be required to give his reasons why certain marks are registered. The decisions rendered by the courts and by the Commissioner, which are published in the OFFICIAL GAZETTE, announce the principles which control the registration of trade-marks. A mark which is sought to be registered is either passed upon favorably or adversely by the Examiner of Trade-Marks in accordance with his construction of the principles announced in the decisions published. If there be error in the decision of the Examiner refusing to register a trade-mark, the applicant has his remedy by appeal.

While it is proper for an applicant to cite previous registrations in his argument for the purpose of showing that his mark also should be registered, it is not believed to be necessary to good practice to require the Examiner to explain the reasons why these marks were registered. In this particular case, however, the Examiner has in his statement given his reasons why in his opinion trade-marks Nos. 61,951 and 61,930 were registered, which reasons are quite clearly distinguishable from the reasons given by him for refusing the registration of this case.

The petition would have been denied ; but inasmuch as the Examiner has given his reasons for the registration of these marks in his answer the *petition is dismissed.*

Ex parte Danford.

APPLICATION FOR PATENT.

Decided October 3, 1907.

(131 O. G., 942.)

EXAMINATION OF APPLICATIONS—SUFFICIENCY OF DISCLOSURE—PRACTICE.

> Where no reason is given for the use of certain ingredients of the article of manufacture which are set forth in the specification and the Examiner is of the opinion that such ingredients have a deleterious effect or no effect at all, he should not refuse to act upon the merits of the case, but should reject the claim for this reason.

ON PETITION.

ARTIFICIAL STONE.

Messrs. Munn & Co. for the applicant.

BILLINGS, *Assistant Commissioner:*

This is a petition from the action of the Primary Examiner refusing to examine the case on its merits on the ground that no explanation has been given of the reason for using the ingredients set forth in the specification.

It would appear from the statement of the Primary Examiner that his ground for refusing to act on the case is that the composition which applicant uses either has no effect at all or a deleterious one. This is a question of the merits, and the claim should have been rejected on this ground in order that applicant, if he so desires, might take an appeal to the Examiners-in-Chief.

The petition is granted to the extent indicated.

Hopkins *v.* Newman.

Decided April 6, 1907.

(131 O. G., 1161.)

1. INTERFERENCE—RIGHT TO MAKE CLAIMS—RES ADJUDICATA.

> Where the Examiner, on a motion to dissolve, holds that a party has a right to make the claims in issue and upon petition to the Commissioner by the opposing party asking him, under his supervisory authority, to review the favorable decision of the Examiner the Commissioner refuses to pass upon the question, it cannot be successfully urged that the question of the right of such party to make the claims is *res adjudicata.*

2. SAME—PRIORITY—SECOND INTERFERENCE—RES ADJUDICATA.

> As to claims involved in a second interference between the same parties ·h could have been made in the first interference. *Held* that a final de-
> In the first interference on the question of priority renders that
>)n *res adjudicata.*

8. AMENDMENT—NEW MATTER—RIGHT TO MAKE CLAIMS.

Where the original specification of an application relating to combined type-writing and adding machines did not describe the adding-machine, but stated that the invention was illustrated "in connection with an adding-machine of the class known as 'registering-accountants'" and only the case and a few minor elements thereof were shown in the drawings, *Held* that an amendment of the application reciting a patent disclosing the construction referred to by the words "registering-accountants" did not constitute a departure from the original disclosure, in view of evidence showing that such term referred to a construction well known in the market embodying the construction of the patent and that such construction was the only one on the market which had the distinctive appearance illustrated in the original drawing. *Held*, further, that such party had a right to make claims to a combination including specific elements of such adding-machine.

APPEAL from Examiners-in-Chief.

ADDING AND WRITING MACHINE.

Mr. John D. Rippey and *Mr. George R. Hamlin* for Hopkins.
Messrs. Rector & Hibben for Newman.

MOORE, *Assistant Commissioner:*

This is an appeal by Hopkins from the decision of the Examiners-in-Chief affirming the decision of the Examiner of Interferences and awarding priority of invention to Newman. The issue is stated in thirteen counts, of which the following are sufficient to illustrate the character of the invention:

1. In an adding-machine, a platen, type-carriers, type mounted in frames on the carriers, devices for operating the carriers adjacent to the platen, hammers for driving the type against the platen to print numbers, and mechanism operable to accumulate the numbers so printed, in combination with mechanism operable to print any desired words on the platen in alinement with the printed numbers.

3. In an adding and writing machine, a platen, type-writing mechanism operable to print any desired words thereon, devices carrying movable type for printing numbers, means for moving said devices adjacent to the said platen, hammers mounted in position to drive the type against the platen, and means for striking the hammers against the type when the type has been positioned for printing.

9. In an adding and writing machine, the combination with the word-printing mechanism having a platen arranged to carry paper, of devices carrying type independent of the word-printing mechanism, means for moving said devices toward the platen as required for printing numbers thereon, means for printing the number by use of the type after said devices have been so moved, and a totalizer operable to add the numbers as printed.

13. In a machine of the character described, word-printing mechanism having a platen arranged to carry paper, adding mechanism, type-carriers separate from the word-printing mechanism, a series of relatively movable type carried by each of said type-carriers adjacent to the platen aforesaid, means for driving the type so alined against the said platen to print numbers, and means for operating the adding mechanism to add the numbers so printed.

The invention in issue consists in the combination of a type-writer and an adding-machine in which a single platen or roller is adapted to coöperate with the printing mechanisms of both the type-writer and the adding-machine in such a manner as to provide for the writing of items and amounts in alinement and for the automatic totalizing of the latter.   In accomplishing this result Hopkins has superposed the type-writing mechanism upon the adding-machine.   Newman accomplishes the same purpose by placing the type-writer and adding-machine side by side and providing suitable means for conducting the platen from a position where it coöperates with the printing mechanism of the type-writer to a position where it coöperates with the printing mechanism of the adding-machine.

In a prior interference between the same parties involving the same applications Hopkins failed to file a preliminary statement, and Newman, who was first to file his application, was awarded priority of invention upon the following issue:

1. The combination with a type-writing mechanism, and an adding mechanism, of a paper-carriage, a roller or platen thereon arranged to feed a sheet of paper to both mechanisms, and means for rotating the roller operated by a part of the adding mechanism.

2. The combination with a type-writing mechanism, and an adding mechanism, of a paper-carriage, a roller or platen thereon arranged to feed a sheet of paper to both mechanisms and means for rotating the roller operated by a part of the adding mechanism or manually as desired.

3. The combination with a type-writing mechanism, and an adding mechanism, of a paper-carriage, a roller or platen thereon arranged to feed a sheet of paper to both mechanisms, manually-operated mechanism for rotating the roller, and automatic means for rotating the roller at the end of each line of printing.

The issue of this interference differs from that of the former interference in that it includes certain specific elements of the printing and adding mechanism of the adding-machine which were old in the art prior to the date of invention alleged by either party.   These elements are not shown in detail in the drawing of Newman's application or specifically described in his specification.

Newman has presented no testimony relative to his date of conception and relies upon the date of filing of his application, February 7, 1901, for his constructive reduction to practice.   Hopkins alleges in his preliminary statement that he conceived the invention in September, 1897, and reduced the same to practice in June, 1902.   In addition to the testimony bearing upon his dates of conception and reduction to practice Hopkins contests the right of Newman to make the claims forming the issue of this interference upon the grounds that Newman's application now contains no sufficient disclosure of the elements of the adding-machine specified in the claims in issue, such as " means for striking the hammers against the type," " devices for drawing the hammers away from the type after operation," " a totalizer operable to add the numbers as printed," etc., and that his original application contained no basis for the assumption that these elements formed part of his invention which would warrant the addition of a specific disclosure of these elements to his application or their inclusion in his claims.

The Examiner of Interferences and the Examiners-in-Chief concurred in finding that Hopkins had failed to prove priority of invention, that Newman has the right to make the claims in issue, and that the question of priority as to the present issue is *res adjadicata* in view of the decision in the prior interference upon a broad issue which differs from the present issue only by the omission of old and well-known elements. In my opinion the conclusions of the lower tribunals are correct.

Hopkins's application involved in this interference is assigned to the Addograph Manufacturing Company. It appears that Hopkins is now hostile to his assignee, and it is sought to establish Hopkins's conception of the invention by the testimony of one Bullock, to whom, it is alleged, Hopkins disclosed his invention in 1897. Bullock's testimony concerning this alleged disclosure indicates that Hopkins had an idea of what he wished to accomplish at that time, but that there was no such communication of the idea to Bullock as would enable one skilled in the art to embody the invention in physical form, which is essential to an effective disclosure under the patent laws. (*Sendelbach* v. *Gillette*, C. D., 1904, 597; 109 O. G., 276.) If, however, it could be conceded that Hopkins conceived the invention in 1897, as alleged, he was clearly lacking in diligence in reducing it to practice until after Newman's application was filed. If, therefore, Newman's application comprised a disclosure of the invention in issue at the time it was filed. it constitutes a constructive reduction to practice of the invention by Newman. and he is entitled to the award of priority of invention.

It appears from the history of the cases of the parties involved in this interference that ten of the claims forming the issue of this interference were in Hopkins's application at the time of the earlier interference. After the conclusion of that interference the remaining three claims of the issue were added by Hopkins. The Examiner rejected all of the claims now in controversy upon the ground that they were readable upon the structure disclosed in Newman's application, but subsequently withdrew his rejection and suggested these claims to Newman for the purpose of interference. After the declaration of the present interference both parties moved for dissolution— Newman upon the ground that Hopkins has no right to make the claims, in view of the decision in the prior interference, and Hopkins upon the ground that there was irregularity in the declaration of the

interference and that Newman had no right to make the claims, because his application as originally filed did not disclose the elements
of the printing mechanism of the adding-machine recited in the
claims in issue. The Examiner denied both motions. Upon appeal
the Commissioner affirmed the decision of the Primary Examiner as
to the appealable grounds of the decision and also dismissed a petition by Hopkins that the Commissioner use his supervisory authority
and set aside the decision of the Examiner affirming Newman's right
to make the claims. In respect to the right of Newman to make the
claims the Commissioner said:

> I fail to find any clear unmistakable error in the Examiner's conclusion that
> Newman has the right to make the claims in issue. The correctness of the
> Examiner's conclusion that Newman's application as filed, contained sufficient
> foundation for the amendments to which Hopkins objects as new matter
> therein, is a question upon which there is room for honest difference of opinion
> among those competent to judge. Since this is the case, and the question is
> one upon which Hopkins has no right of appeal, the Examiner's conclusion
> will be accepted here without further consideration.

It is contended in behalf of Newman that the question of Newman's right to make the claims is *res adjudicata* in view of the decisions upon Hopkins's motion to dissolve and petition above referred to.
This contention is not sound. In his decision upon Hopkins's petition the Commissioner did not decide the question of Newman's
right to make the claims, but merely refused to exercise his supervisory authority and review the decision of the Examiner upon this
question.

The right of a party to contest his opponent's right to make the
claim in issue as a basis for an award of priority is specifically provided for by Rule 130, which is in accordance with the holding of
the court of appeals in the decision in *Podlesak and Podlesak* v. *Mc-
Innerney* (C. D., 1906, 558; 120 O. G., 2127) and in *Kilbourn* v.
Hirner, (*post*, 552; 128 O. G., 1689,) and *in re Wickers and Furlong*, (*post*, 587; 129 O. G., 869,) both of which were decided by that
court February 5, 1907. The testimony presented by the respective
parties relative to Newman's right to make the claims were therefore
properly considered by the lower tribunals in connection with the
disclosure in Newman's original application.

Newman illustrates in his drawing a type-writing machine and an
adding-machine placed side by side with suitable means for adapting
a single platen to coöperate with the printing mechanism of each machine. The printing mechanism of the type-writer is shown and
described, as is also the mechanism for actuating and controlling the
movement of the platen; but only the case and a few minor elements
of the adding-machine are shown in the drawing, and the computing

and writing mechanism thereof is not described. The statement of invention in Newman's original application is, in part, as follows:

My invention relates to combined type-writing and adding machines and has for its object to provide type-writing mechanism and improved means for combining the same with adding mechanism.

In the present embodiment of my invention I have illustrated it in connection with an adding-machine of the class known as " registering-accountants " and a special object of the present invention is to provide means whereby type-writing mechanism may be combined with such an adding-machine.

As is well known to those skilled in the art, adding-machines of the class mentioned are provided with keyboards and in their operation they print the several numbers to be added as well as the sum of said numbers.

The Examiner in his first action requested Newman to " state the name of the patentee of the adding-machine," and Newman in response amended his specification upon April 29, 1901, to state that his improved type-writing mechanism is illustrated—

in connection with an adding-machine of the class known as " registering-accountants " such as those machines patented to W. S. Burroughs, No. 504,963, dated September 12, 1893.

This patent and the Burroughs patents to which it refers illustrate and describe the specific features of the adding and printing mechanism stated in the claims in issue in this interference, and the question of Newman's right to make these claims depends upon whether his designation of the adding-machine by reference to it as the " registering-accountant " and illustration of its external form is a sufficient disclosure of the invention to warrant the amendment of April 29, 1901, and the subsequent amendment presenting the claims in issue.

The specification of a patent is addressed to persons skilled in the art, and a disclosure therein which is sufficient to enable such persons to make and use the same constitutes a compliance with the requirements of section 4888 of the Revised Statutes. Newman's original specification when supplemented with the disclosure of the Burroughs patent 504,963, referred to in Newman's amendment of April 24, 1904, clearly constitutes such a disclosure of the invention in issue. It is, however, contended by Hopkins that there was no sufficient identification in Newman's original specification of the device shown in Burroughs's patent and that the name " registering-accountant " is merely a transitory name which might not be perpetuated to inform the public in the future of the character of adding and recording machine involved in Newman's device. The evidence, in my opinion, clearly refutes these contentions. The testimony of Boyer, the president of the Burroughs Adding Machine Company, who is called as a witness by Newman, and of Dorman and Perkins, who are called as expert witnesses in behalf of Hopkins, shows conclusively that the "registering-accountant" was a well-known machine upon the market in 1901, that it embodied the structure disclosed in the Burroughs patent above referred to, and that it was the only adding-machine then on the market whose case had the distinctive appearance illustrated in Newman's drawings. It is conceded by Dorman and Perkins that the type-writing mechanism and carriage shown in Newman's application could be applied to the Burroughs "registering-accountant." In view of these facts it is believed that Newman's original specification and drawing sufficiently identify the adding-machine with which his mechanism was adapted to coöperate as that embodied in the well-known machine illustrated in Burroughs's patent and known to the public as the "registering-accountant" to enable a person skilled in the art to produce the invention in controversy and to warrant the amendment of April 24, 1901, by which a description of this machine is made a part of Newman's specification. Such a disclosure was found by the Court of Appeals of the District of Columbia to be sufficient to warrant a party to make claims embracing old elements not shown or specifically described in the recent case of *Kilbourn* v. *Hirner, supra*.

It is urged that Newman's present drawing is insufficient to comply with the requirements of Rule 50 and that the oath does not cover the claims of the issue, which were presented by an attorney nearly four years after the application was filed. These contentions are without force. Whether a further drawing is necessary in Newman's application or a supplemental oath should be required are *ex parte* questions which are not involved in this proceeding. The sworn preliminary statement of Newman is sufficient to support the claims in issue for the purpose of this interference, since it is found that their subject-matter is disclosed in his original application and comprehended in the statement of invention therein.

It is also urged that intervening rights have accrued which estop Newman from now making the claims in issue. In the decisions cited in support of this contention the facts differed from those in this case in that the later amendments comprised new matter or claims covering a broader invention or a different species of invention than that embraced in the original application. In such cases it has been held that claims presented at a late date which would dominate inventions made by others in a field which was unoccupied at the time such inventions were made should not be permitted. In the present case the claims in issue are based upon the structure originally disclosed, but are narrower in scope than those originally presented. The invention was embraced in the claims of the original application, and therefore no rights have become vested in later inventors which estop Newman from making these claims. (*McBerty* v. *Cook.* C. D., 1900, 248; 90 O. G., 2295.)

The claims now in controversy might have been made by Newman at the time the earlier interference between these applications was declared. Such of these claims as were in Hopkins's application at that time should have been made part of the issue of that interference, and in view of the holding of the Court of Appeals of the District of Columbia in the recent case of *Blackford* v. *Wilder* (*post*, 491; 127 O. G., 1255) the question of priority as to the claims now before me is *res adjudicata* by reason of the decision in the earlier interference.

In *Blackford* v. *Wilder*, *supra*, Blackford was awarded priority as to certain specific claims. Subsequently broader claims based upon the same structure were presented by Wilder and a second interference instituted. The Court said in their decision that Wilder—

> Having had the right to make the broader claims in the earlier stages of the proceedings in the Patent Office, as well as the opportunity, in the first proceeding, to introduce all of his evidence relating to the contruction and operation of his Exhibit E structure, his right, in both respects, terminated with that litigation.
>
> Whether the former decision was right or wrong, or was induced by the want of the particular evidence that was offered in the present case, is not the question. However that might be it was final and put an end to the litigation in the first interference. It must be held, therefore, as conclusive of every question that not only was, but also might have been presented and determined in that case.

Having determined that Newman has by virtue of the disclosure in his original application the right to make the claims now in issue, he is entitled to the award of priority not only in view of Hopkins's failure to establish priority of invention, but also by reason of this question being *res adjudicata*.

The decision of the Examiners-in-Chief is affirmed.

EX PARTE SAUNDERS, JR.

APPLICATION FOR DESIGN PATENT.

Decided October 28, 1907.

(131 O. G., 1164.)

APPLICATION—AMENDMENT FROM DESIGN TO MECHANICAL CASE.

Where an applicant in presenting his own case requested in his petition the grant of a design patent upon a letter-scale, but his specification, claim, and oath were of the form prescribed for mechanical application, and it appears from the actions by the applicant in the case that it was his intention to obtain protection for an article of manufacture, *Held* that he should be permitted to amend the case to accord with the form prescribed for mechanical applications.

ON PETITION.

Mr. Daniel G. Saunders, Jr., pro se.

MOORE, *Commissioner:*

This is a petition that this application, which as originally presented requested the grant of a patent for a design, be allowed to be amended as a mechanical case and examined as an application for a machine patent.

It appears from the record that the applicant originally presented a petition praying that Letters Patent be granted to him for a term of seven years for the new and original design for letter-scales set forth in the annexed specification. A fee of fifteen dollars was paid upon the filing of this application. The preamble of the specification alleged that the applicant had invented a new, original, ornamental, and useful design for letter-scales as a new article of manufacture. The specification clearly described the construction of the device and concluded with a claim for an article of manufacture, setting forth the specific features of the device. The oath accompanying the original application was in the form prescribed for mechanical appliances.

On examination of the case the Examiner of Designs required the applicant to amend the application to agree with the practice in design cases and also required him to file a new oath in the terms prescribed by the statute for design applications. He further required that the applicant file an exhibit showing the design of a letter-scale.

The applicant in presenting an amendment in accordance with the Examiner's requirement stated that he was—

* * * in doubt whether the exhibit shall be a working model of the device, or a drawing showing the weight-indicating pointer and full details of the process of weighing.

The model which was filed clearly showed that the invention consists of improvements in machines and was not an ornamental design for an article of manufacture. The applicant's claim was therefore rejected as not covering the proper subject-matter for design. Thereupon this petition that the case be amended in such a manner as to form a mechanical application was presented.

It is clear from the above-stated facts that from the first the intention of applicant, who is prosecuting his own case, was to obtain protection upon the article of manufacture and that his failure to present a proper application in the first instance was due to his unfamiliarity with the patent law. In view of these circumstances it is believed that the amendment should be permitted and that the oath originally filed in the application should be accepted in connection with the amendment of the petition and specification and that the case should be examined as for a mechanical application for patent.

The petition is granted.

Ex parte Utica Drop Forge and Tool Co.

APPLICATION FOR REGISTRATION OF TRADE-MARK.

Decided August 9, 1907.

(131 O. G., 1164.)

Trade-Marks—Requirement that Class of Merchandise be Limited is in Effect a Rejection.

Where the Examiner required that the particular description of his merchandise stated by the applicant as falling in Class 23 be limited to "Pliers without a cutting edge" or that the class stated be changed to Class 20 and the particular description of goods made to read "Nippers and pliers provided with a cutting edge," *Held*, that this action is in effect a refusal to register the mark, and the applicant's remedy is by appeal and not by petition.

On petition.

TRADE-MARK FOR NIPPERS AND PLIERS.

Messrs. Robinson, Martin & Jones for the applicant.

Billings, *Acting Commissioner:*

This is a petition from the action of the Examiner of Trade-Marks requiring that the particular description of goods be made definite.

It appears that the Examiner has required that the words " without a cutting edge " be added after " Pliers " if the class of merchandise be stated as Class 23 or that the class be changed to Class 20 and the particular description of goods be made to read " Nippers and pliers provided with a cutting edge."

This action of the Examiner is in effect a refusal to register the mark, and the applicant's remedy is therefore by an appeal and not by petition.

It does not appear from the record whether the Examiner regards the mark as registrable except for this requirement. The Examiner should therefore, if he has any other reasons for refusing registration, state them, in order that, if applicant sees fit to appeal, he may bring up the entire case.

The petition is dismissed.

Standard Import Co., Ltd., *v.* New Orleans Import Co., Ltd.

TRADE-MARK INTERFERENCE.

Decided October 31, 1907.

(131 O. G., 1164.)

1. Interference—Reopening to Take Testimony to Strengthen Case.

A practice which would allow a contestant to experimentally conduct his case to a probable failure and then permit him after consultation and with competent assistance to further make endeavors to show what he could and should have earlier shown with such assistance would be contrary to all well-established rules and legal principles.

2. SAME—SAME—MOTION BROUGHT BEFORE FINAL HEARING.

The fact that a motion to reopen an interference to take additional evidence was brought before final hearing is no reason why it should be granted.

APPEAL ON MOTIONS.

TEA.

Mr. J. J. Sheehy for Standard Import Co., Ltd.
Messrs. Goepel & Goepel for New Orleans Import Co., Ltd.

BILLINGS, *Assistant Commissioner:*

This case comes up on appeal from the decisions of the Examiner of Interferences of July 24 and August 15, 1907, denying two motions of the New Orleans Import Co. that the case be reopened in order that further testimony be taken.

In the first of these motions it was asked that the case be reopened in order to take testimony to contradict the testimony of a certain witness and that testimony might be taken as to sales by the New Orleans Import Co. of tea bearing the trade-mark in issue.

The second motion asked, first, that the testimony of two witnesses, Winn and McClure, might be taken to rebut certain statements of the Standard Import Co.'s witness Harris, and, second, that the testimony of the witness Bailey be taken for the purpose of allowing him to correct an error in his deposition. No appeal is taken from the decision refusing permission to take the testimony of Winn and McClure.

The first of these motions was denied on the ground that it was indefinite, since the names of the witnesses whose testimony it was desired to take were not given and on the further ground that the evidence was not newly discovered and that the motion was not brought with diligence.

The second motion was denied as to the second part thereof on the ground that it had not been shown that the testimony of Bailey was material and that the moving party had not been diligent in bringing his motion.

The appellant argues that the cases of *Robinson v. Copeland* (C. D., 1903, 471; 107 O. G., 1376) and *Estes v. Gause*, (C. D., 1899, 64; 88 O. G., 1336,) cited by the Examiner of Interferences, are not pertinent, since the motions in this case were brought before final hearing, not afterward, as in those decisions. It is also argued that there is no evidence in the case to establis' l use of the mark by either party and that the testimony d uld b mitted in the interest of truth and justice.

The pertinency of the latter ar
evidence in the case is a nullity t

New Orleans Import Co., since it was the first to file an application for registration.

The mere fact that the motion was brought before final hearing is no reason why it should be granted. for. as pointed out in *Donnellan* v. *Berry* (37 MS., 386.) quoted with approval in *Sutter* v. *McDonnell* v. *Jolly* v. *Neff*, (C. D., 1902. 49; 98 O. G., 1484)—

A practice which would allow a contestant to experimentally conduct his own case to a probable failure and then permit him. after consultation and with competent assistance. to make further endeavors to show what he could and should have earlier shown with such assistance, would be contrary to all well-established rules and legal principles.

In each of these cases the motion to reopen was brought before final hearing.

The record clearly shows that the motions to reopen were not brought with due diligence. and, as pointed out by the Examiner of Interferences, it has not been shown that the testimony of Bailey is material.

The decision is affirmed.

Ex parte Plumb.

APPLICATION FOR PATENT.

Decided November 4. 1907.

(131 O. G., 1165.)

CLAIMS—FUNCTIONAL—OPEN TO OBJECTION.

Claims which fail to include sufficient mechanical elements to effect the function expressed in the claims are open to objection. and from objection on such ground petition may be taken to the Commissioner.

ON PETITION.

DISINFECTING ATTACHMENT FOR CARPET-SWEEPERS.

Messrs. Raymond & Barnett for the applicant.

BILLINGS, *Assistant Commissioner:*

This is a petition that the Examiner be directed to forward an appeal to the Examiners-in-Chief.

It appears that on May 21, 1907. the Examiner objected to claims 2, 4, 5, and 6 as being functional and indefinite and rejected claims 1 and 3 on references. This action was made final on May 25, 1907.

On July 12, 1907, the applicant filed an appeal from this decision which the Examiner refused to forward, holding that the objection to the form of claims 2, 4, 5, and 6 should be disposed of prior appeal and that this question was one which went to the Comm on petition. This action was repeated on September 9, 1907 the same time the objection of vagueness and indefiniteness to apply to claim 1 also.

It was from this action that the present petition was taken, the appellant contending that the Examiner's action was in reality a rejection of the claims as being too broad and that the question is properly reviewable by the Examiners-in-Chief on appeal.

The distinction between claims which should be objected to as functional and claims which should be rejected on the ground that the statement of function contained therein is insufficient to distinguish them from the prior art is well stated in *ex parte McMullen* (C. D., 1898, 119; 84 O. G., 507) as follows:

Functional claims—that is, claims for a function merely or which fail to include sufficient mechanical elements to effect the function expressed in the claim—are open to objection, and from objection made upon such ground petition may be taken to the Commissioner.

On the other hand, claims which while including sufficient mechanical elements to effect a function stated therein, depend upon that statement of function to distinguish them from what is old in the prior art are not to be objected to as functional, but are open to rejection if in the opinion of the Examiner the statement of function is insufficient, the question being a question of merits and not of form.

It has also been pointed out in *ex parte Holder* (C. D., 1903, 442; 107 O. G., 833) that where the claim distinctly specifies a certain structure which is adapted to perform a particular function there is no objection to setting out in the claim also the function which the structure is adapted to perform.

The Examiner's objection to claims 1, 5, and 6 is well taken, for these claims do not include sufficient mechanical elements to effect the functions expressed therein.

Claims 2 and 4 appear to be unobjectionable in form, except that the brush is not positively included as an element in claim 2. If the Examiner knows of references which anticipate these claims, he should cite the same.

As the appeal cannot be forwarded till the objection to the form of claims 1, 5, and 6 have been overcome, the petition cannot be granted, but the case is remanded to the Examiner for action in conformance with this decision.

The petition is denied.

ALBERS BROS. MILLING COMPANY *v.* FORREST.

TRADE-MARK INTERFERENCE.

Decided July 8, 1907.

(131 O. G., 1419.)

INTERFERENCE—PRINTING TESTIMONY.

The fact that the senior party took no testimony is not a sufficient reason waiving the requirements of Rule 162.

PETITION.

Mr. Chas. J. Schnabel and *Mr. John Imirie* for Albers Bros. Milling Company.

Mr. A. O. Behel for Forrest.

MOORE, *Commissioner:*

This is a petition that the requirement of the printing of testimony in this case be waived.

The senior party took no testimony and, according to the statement of the petitioner, was not represented at the taking of testimony by the junior party. It is urged that the petitioner should not be put to the expense of printing testimony when the opposing party did not actively defend his case, and the petitioner now offers to print the record should the other party, Forrest, appeal.

Rule 162 was clearly not intended to permit the filing of type-written copies of the record in place of printed copies under such circumstances as appear in this case. Exemption from printing is to be permitted only where by reason of poverty an inventor is, in fact, unable to bear the cost of printing the testimony.

The reasons for requiring printed copies of testimony apply as forcibly to records presented before the Office as to those presented before the courts, and it is not believed that the additional burden should be placed upon any of the tribunals of this Office of considering type-written instead of printed copies of testimony. In respect to the offer of the petitioner to print the testimony if appeal is taken it may be said that such agreements cannot be enforced by the Commissioner and should not therefore be considered.

The petition is denied.

HESS *v.* JOERISSEN *v.* FELBEL.

INTERFERENCE.

Decided July 19, 1907.

(131 O. G., 1419.)

APPEAL ON PRIORITY—PATENTABILITY OF THE ISSUE.

The question of the patentability of the issue will not be considered on an appeal on priority except under such special circumstances as would warrant the exercise of the supervisory authority of the Commissioner.

APPEAL from Examiners-in-Chief.

30997—H. Doc. 470, 60-1——24

Messrs. Baldwin & Wight for Hess.
Messrs. Knight Bros. for Joerissen.
Mr. Jacob Felbel pro se.

MOORE, *Commissioner:*

This is an appeal by Hess from the decision of the Examiners-in-Chief affirming the decision of the Examiner of Interferences that he is not the prior inventor of the invention in issue.

In his preliminary statement Hess alleged a date of conception subsequent to the filing date of the senior party. In response to an order of the Examiner of Interferences to show cause why judgment should not be rendered against him on the record Hess moved to dissolve the interference, alleging the non-patentability of the issue to all parties. This motion was denied by the Primary Examiner, and the Examiner of Interferences thereupon rendered judgment against Hess.

On appeal to the Examiners-in-Chief Hess urged the non-patentability of the issue to all parties; but they declined to make a recommendation under Rule 126.

Hess has again urged the non-patentability of the single claim of the issue upon this appeal and requests consideration under the exercise of my supervisory authority. The question raised in this case is similar to those considered in the Commissioner's decisions in *Sobey v. Holsclaw* (C. D., 1905, 523; 119 O. G., 1922) and *Potter v. McIntosh,* (C. D., 1906, 56; 120 O. G., 1823,) which decisions were affirmed by the Court of Appeals of the District of Columbia in *Sobey v. Holsclaw* (*post,* 465; 126 O. G., 3041) and *Potter v. McIntosh,* (*post,* 505; 127 O. G., 1995.) In these decisions it was stated that under the circumstances here presented only the question of priority was raised and that the question of patentability would not be considered and that there was no occasion for the exercise of supervisory authority. This practice is believed to be a proper one, and no special circumstances are presented in this case which would warrant a deviation therefrom.

The decision of the Examiners-in-Chief is affirmed.

SILVER LAKE COMPANY *v.* SAMSON CORDAGE WORKS.

OPPOSITION.

Decided October 15, 1907.

(131 O. G., 1420.)

1. TRADE-MARKS—THE WORDS "SPOT CORD" AND A CORD HAVING SPOTS THEREON NOT ALTERNATIVES.

  The words "Spot Cord" as a trade-mark for braided sash-cord *Held not in conflict* with the use of spots on a cord, the latter being a mere sym-

· bol which may be translated into words other than the words " spot cord." Spots on a cord and the words " Spot Cord " are not true alternatives.

2. SAME—THE WORDS " SPOT CORD " NOT INDEFINITE.

The words "Spot Cord" not being the mere equivalent or alternative, in a trade-mark sense, of a cord having spots thereon, such words will not be refused registration on the ground that a mark consisting of spots on a cord is too indefinite to form trade-mark subject-matter.

APPEAL from Examiner of Interferences.

TRADE-MARK FOR BRAIDED SASH-CORD.

Messrs. Macleod, Calver, Copeland & Dike for Silver Lake Company.

Messrs. Clarke, Raymond & Coale for Samson Cordage Works.

MOORE, *Commissioner:*

This is an appeal by the Silver Lake Company from a decision of the Examiner of Interferences dismissing its notice of opposition to the registration by the Samson Cordage Works of the words " Spot Cord " as a trade-mark for braided sash-cord.

Appellant asks that registration be refused to applicant on the ground that the mark described in such application conflicts with a mark to which it has a prior right. Appellant's rights are founded upon evidence showing that prior to the adoption of its trade-mark by applicant and prior to its manufacture of the article to which the mark is applied appellant manufactured and sold braided cords of various sizes and for various purposes having colored spots thereon. Appellant therefore urges that it acquired an exclusive right to the use of spots on braided cord as a mark of origin or ownership, that the words " Spot Cord " have the same significance as appellant's mark, and that it would therefore be damaged by the registration.

It may be observed that the testimony taken on behalf of appellant does not show that it ever used or intended to use the spots on its braided cord as a mark of origin or ownership or that the trade ever relied on such marks as an indication that the goods bearing them were made by appellant. It would therefore seem that the opposition might be dismissed on the ground that appellant has not shown the possession of any right which would be in any way interfered with by granting registration to the applicant. However, I prefer to place my decision of this case on the ground that, assuming appellant to have a right to the use of spots on a braided cord as a mark of origin or ownership, there is no conflict between such mark and the words " Spot Cord," for which applicant seeks registration. In the first place applicant's mark consists of words which may be spoken and which at the same time give a distinct impression to the eye, while the opposer's mark consists merely of a symbol which is liable to be translated into words differently by different individuals. It has been held, both by the Patent Office and by the courts, that many words and symbols are full equivalents—as, for example, the word *star* and the representation of a star or the word *squirrel* and the representation of a squirrel—and in such. cases the registration of one of these would bar the registration of the other for the same class of goods.   But in the examples given the symbol immediately suggests the word which it represents and no other, and vice versa. Such is not the case here.   The appearance of opposer's product does not suggest the words " Spot Cord " any more than it suggests the words *fancy cord*.   In this connection it is interesting to note that in the taking of testimony by appellant the cord was referred to as " fancy cord. "   The testimony of G. H. Shapley, the treasurer of appellant, (X-Q. 50, S. L. C. Rec., p. 33,) indicates that the cord was ordered by the term " fancy cord " or by submitting samples.   If the words " Spot Cord " or *spotted cord* constituted a natural expression of the mental impression created by appellant's symbol, the trade would undoubtedly have used such terms; but if such is the fact the record fails to show it.   As it does not appear from the record that applicant's product has become known as " spot cord " and as there is no reason to apprehend that it will become so known, I conclude that the registration of applicant's mark will not tend to cause confusion between the goods of the parties to this proceeding.

It is urged by appellant that registration should be refused in view of the decision of the Circuit Court of Appeals for the Eighth Circuit, reported in 134 Fed. Rep., 571, in which it was held that a mark for wire rope consisting of a colored strand twisted in the rope and not restricted to any particular color is too indefinite to constitute a valid trade-mark.   This decision has been affirmed by the United States Supreme Court, their decision being reported in 201 U. S., 166. Since I do not regard applicant's mark as the mere equivalent of a cord having spots thereon, the decision referred to is not considered material to the disposition of this case.

The decision of the Examiner of Interferences dismissing the opposition and granting registration to the applicant *is affirmed*.

EX PARTE WESTINGHOUSE.

APPLICATION FOR PATENT.

Decided October 29, 1907.

(131 O. G., 1420.)

ABANDONMENT OF APPLICATION—SUFFICIENCY OF ACTION.

   Where on December 29, 1905, an Examiner rejected certain claims and made a formal objection to another claim. to which the applicant made a sufficient response on January 27, 1906, with the exception that he failed *to mention* the informal claim. and the Examiner in his next action on

February 16, 1906, reiterated the formal objection, but did not state that the applicant's action by reason of failure to mention the informal claim was unresponsive and did not make such objection final, *Held* that an amendment curing the informality filed January 18, 1907, is filed in proper time, the renewal of the objection by the Examiner without objection to the insufficiency of the applicant's action of January 27, 1906, constituting a waiver of the question of incompleteness of such action.

APPEAL from Examiners-in-Chief.

ELASTIC-FLUID TURBINE.

Mr. J. S. Green and *Mr. Melville Church* for the applicant.

MOORE, *Commissioner:*

This is an appeal from the decision of the Examiners-in-Chief affirming a decision of the Primary Examiner holding that the application is abandoned because of " lack of proper prosecution."

As originally filed the application contained thirteen claims, of which the thirteenth read as follows:

A turbine, substantially as herein shown and described.

On December 29, 1905, the Examiner rejected claims 2, 3, and 4 upon a French patent, and with reference to claim 13 said:

Claim 13 is informal, being merely a reference to the specification.

On January 27, 1906, applicant authorized and requested the cancelation of claims 2, 3, and 4, but made no reference to claim 13. The Examiner apparently treated this action as a request for reconsideration of his action on claim 13 and on February 16, 1906, replied to applicant's letter of January 27, 1906, as follows:

Claim 10 is informal, being merely a reference to the specification.

The claims having been renumbered, claim 10 of this letter is original claim 13.

On January 18, 1907, applicant authorized and requested the cancelation of claim 10 and added three new claims. This amendment was not entered, the Examiner holding that the application was abandoned, since no action was taken with reference to original claim 13 within one year from the Office action of December 29, 1905. It is from this holding that the appeal was taken to the Examiners-in-Chief.

It would have been perfectly proper for the Examiner to have made his action of February 16, 1906, final, for it was a repetition of his action of December 29, 1905. However, this was not done, nor was any reference made to the fact that applicant's action of January 27, 1906, was not completely responsive to the Office action of December 29, 1905.

In view of the character of the Office action of February 16, 1906, it must be *held that the* Examiner thereby waived the question of the incompleteness of applicant's action of January 27, 1906, and that applicant was, under the statute, entitled to a year from February 16, 1906, within which to amend his application. Such an amendment having been filed on January 18, 1907, the case cannot be held to have been abandoned.

The decision of the Examiners-in-Chief is reversed.

EX PARTE LASANCE.

APPLICATION FOR PATENT.

Decided November 15, 1907.

(131 O. G., 1421.)

FINAL REJECTION—WHEN WARRANTED.

Where substitute claims were rejected upon the same references as the prior claims and it was stated that the " claims are substantially like those previously rejected on the same references, being, if anything, a little broader." *Held* that a final rejection was proper.

ON PETITION.

DOVETAILING-MACHINE.

Messrs. Heidman & Street for the applicant.

MOORE, *Commissioner:*

This is a petition that the Examiner be instructed that the final rejection of February 11, 1907, was premature and that the amendment filed February 23, 1907, should be entered and considered.

In his sixth action, dated February 11, 1907, the Examiner rejected substitute claims 1 and 5 upon the same references as the prior claims and stated:

As these claims are substantially like those previously rejected on the same references—being, if anything, a little broader.—this action is made final.

Petitioner contends that as the Examiner admits that the substitute claims are " a little broader " they are not the same as those previously rejected and that a final rejection was therefore improper.

It is not necessary that the claims should be identical to warrant a final rejection. If the claims have not been materially amended, but are substantially the same, a final rejection is proper. (*Ex parte Cox*, C. D., 1906, 167; 122 O. G., 1045.) Slightly broadening the claims in no way avoids the references. An amendment which merely broadens the scope of the claims is not apparently an attempt to avoid the references and must be construed as either a desire on the part of applicant to present broader claims on appeal or an attempt to merely avoid a final rejection. If such an amendment was considered sufficient to prevent a final rejection, it would be impossible for the Primary Examiner to ever bring the prosecution of the case before him to a close.

The petition is denied.

THE W. BINGHAM COMPANY v. G. W. BRADLEY'S SONS.

TRADE-MARK INTERFERENCE.

Decided November 9, 1907.

(131 O. G., 1421.)

1. TRADE-MARKS—INTERFERENCE IN FACT—ARROW PIERCING LETTER "B" AND LETTERS "X L C R" PIERCED BY ARROW INCLOSED IN DIAMOND-SHAPED BORDER.

Held that a trade-mark comprising the letters "X L C R" pierced by an arrow, the whole being inclosed in a diamond-shaped figure, does not so nearly resemble a trade-mark for the same merchandise which comprises the letter "B" pierced by an arrow as to cause confusion in the mind of the public.

2. SAME—SAME—FORMER DECISION DISTINGUISHED.

Where the words are alike in appearance or where the common features of a mark are of sufficient prominence as to cause the merchandise of both parties to become known by a common name, the interference should be continued in order that the Office may have the benefit of testimony showing whether confusion in trade has actually occurred; but where there is so marked a difference in appearance and significance of the marks when considered as a whole that no likelihood of confusion in trade is apparent the interference should be dissolved.

ON APPEAL.

TRADE-MARK FOR HARDWARE.

Mr. T. W. Johnson for The W. Bingham Company.
Messrs. Munn & Co. for G. W. Bradley's Sons.

BILLINGS, *Assistant Commissioner:*

This in an appeal from the decision of the Examiner of Trade-Marks dissolving an interference. The trade-mark of G. W. Bradley's Sons consists of the letter "B" pierced by an arrow. The trade-mark of The W. Bingham Company as originally filed comprised the letters "X L C R" pierced by an arrow. Subsequently to the declaration of interference, upon his request, jurisdiction was given to the Examiner of Trade-Marks for the purpose of re-forming the issue of interference, and The W. Bingham Company was permitted to amend its drawing to show the entire mark disclosed in the specimens originally filed. The mark thus displayed comprises the letters "X L C R " pierced by an arrow, the whole being inclosed in a diamond-shaped figure bounded by two parallel lines. The Examiner of Trade-Marks then held in his decision on the motion for dissolution that there was no such close resemblance between the marks of the two applications which would be likely to cause confusion in trade, and dissolved the interference. It is contended upon behalf of G. W. Bradley's Sons that the representation of an arrow is the salient feature of the mark and that confusion in trade would be likely to follow from the concurrent use of the marks of the respective applicants upon goods of the same descriptive properties. This contention is believed to be untenable. In determining the question of interference in fact between the trade-marks it is necessary to consider the appearance of the mark as a whole and to determine whether the predominating features of the mark are substantially identical in appearance, significance, and sound. In the present case the mark of G. W. Bradley's Sons consists of an arrow crossing the letter " B," and it is doubtful if the mark would be known as the " arrow " brand in view of the prominence of the letter " B." The mark of The W. Bingham Company, on the other hand, consists of a composite mark, the most striking features of which are the letters " X L C R," which is merely a misspelling of the word " Excelsior." This, it is believed, far overshadows the significance of the arrow, and by reason of its location within the diamond-shaped frame gives the mark an entirely different appearance from that of G. W. Bradley's Sons. It is likely that the goods of The W. Bingham Company would be known as the " Excelsior " brand, and not as the " arrow " brand. There is, therefore, not only a difference in appearance of the marks, but also a difference in significance.

In each of the cases cited in support of the contention of G. W. Bradley's Sons that the interference should be continued it appears that either the trade-marks of the respective parties had become known by a common name or, as in the case of *ex parte Smith & Heminway*, (*ante*, 215; 129 O. G., 2500,) that the common feature of the mark is of so great prominence as to overshadow other features of the mark. In such cases the interference should be continued in order that the Office may have the benefit of testimony showing whether confusion in trade has actually occurred; but where, as in the present case, there is so marked a difference in appearance and significance of the marks when considered as a whole that no likelihood of confusion in trade is apparent it is believed that the interference should be dissolved.

The decision of the Examiner of Trade-Marks is affirmed.

GOLD *v.* GOLD.

PATENT INTERFERENCE.

Decided November 7, 1907.

(131 O. G., 1442.)

INTERFERENCE—INDEFINITE MOTION—AMENDED MOTION—TRANSMISSION.

It is well settled that piecemeal action cannot be permitted; but where a party acting in good faith files a motion which is held to be indefinite and an amended motion curing the informalities is promptly filed within the limit of appeal set from the previous decision the amended motion should be transmitted.

APPEAL ON MOTION.

STEAM-HEATING SYSTEM.

Messrs. Raymond & Barnett and *Messrs. H. C. Evert & Co.* for E. H. Gold.

Messrs. Arthur C. Fraser & Usina for E. E. Gold.

BILLINGS, *Assistant Commissioner:*

This case is before me on two appeals by E. H. Gold from decision of the Examiner of Interferences.

The first appeal is from the decision granting E. E. Gold's motion for transmission and denying the transmittal of E. H. Gold's motion. The second appeal is from the decision of the Examiner of Interferences refusing to consider the amended motion of E. H. Gold.

It appears from the record of this interference that under date of August 2, 1907, times were set for taking testimony. The limit for filing motions for dissolution was set to expire September 3, 1907. There was subsequently a motion filed in behalf of E. H. Gold to extend the time within which motions might be filed, and this motion was accompanied by the affidavit of Percival H. Truman, an employee of counsel for E. H. Gold, which affidavit was executed August 7. In this affidavit it was stated that his employer was ill, was absent from the city at that time because of this illness, that he would not return to the city for some time, and that in the opinion of the affiant a motion for dissolution should be filed; that in view of the fact that his employer was counsel in this case and had charge of this interference and others relating thereto, it would be practically impossible for a motion to be filed within the time specified. This motion was of course denied under the prevailing practice, for the reason that it was not positively known that a motion would be filed; but in the decision denying the extension it was stated that the reasons given in support of that motion would be considered in connection with any showing that might be made later should a motion for dissolution be filed. It appears that eleven days after the expiration of the time E. H. Gold filed a motion, accompanying the same with a showing why the motion was filed late. This showing was also to be taken in connection with the showing previously made with the motion for an extension of time. The Examiner of Interferences held that the motion was informal in some respects, while formal in others, but refused to transmit any part of the motion, on the ground that the showing for the delay was not sufficient. In this latter holding it is believed that the Examiner of Interferences was in error. The showing accompanying the motion for dissolution, when taken in connection with the previous showing accompanying the motion for an extension of time, is regarded as sufficient to excuse the short delay of eleven days. Subsequently counsel for E. H. Gold filed an amended motion for dissolution which clearly corrected the informalities in the first motion and gave more specific statements of reasons in excuse of the delay. The second motion was filed within the limit of appeal and on the same day that an appeal was filed from the decision on the first motion. The Examiner of Interferences dismissed the second motion because an appeal had also been filed from the previous decision. It is well settled that the practice which has been characterized as piecemeal cannot be permitted. Where, however, the record indicates good faith in interference cases and where the Office holds that a motion is not sufficiently specific to warrant transmittal and the applicant promptly files a specific motion within the limit of appeal set from the previous decision and it is found that the second motion is sufficiently definite to meet all requirements, it is believed that less delay will be experienced and less harm done to any parties in the case by transmitting the second motion than by denying the transmission thereof. In such cases the amended motion should be transmitted, provided, of course, that the excuse for the delay in filing the first motion, should it be filed late, is regarded as satisfactory.

There is no error found in transmitting the motion filed by E. E. Gold for dissolution.

The decision of the Examiner of Interferences transmitting the motion of E. E. Gold *is affirmed*, and his decision refusing to transmit E. H. Gold's amended motion *is reversed*.

BROWN *v.* INWOOD AND LAVENBERG.

PATENT INTERFERENCE.

Decided November 13, 1907.

(131 O. G., 1423.)

INTERFERENCE—MOTION TO DISSOLVE—AFFIDAVITS.

When a party may not appeal from a decision on a motion to dissolve, he may not appeal from a determination upon the admissibility of affidavits filed with that motion.

ON PETITION.

MEANS FOR MAKING BOX-BLANKS.

Messrs. Bulkley & Durand and *Messrs. Davis & Davis* for Brown.
Messrs. Dyrenforth, Dyrenforth & Lee for Inwood and Lavenberg.

BILLINGS, *Assistant Commissioner:*

This case comes up on petition by Brown from the action of the Primary Examiner in refusing to consider an affidavit of William P. Healy filed in support of a motion to dissolve.

It appears that Brown brought a motion to dissolve on the ground that the device of Inwood and Lavenberg is inoperative, and therefore they have no right to make the claims corresponding to the issue of the interference.

The Primary Examiner denied this motion and refused to consider in connection therewith the affidavit above referred to, on the ground that certain testimony taken in an equity suit in which Brown's assignee and the parties Inwood and Lavenberg were involved and which is quoted in the affidavit was not supported by a certificate from the clerk of the court or other proper evidence as to its authenticity.

It is pointed out in *Browne* v. *Stroud* (C. D., 1906, 226; 122 O. G., 2688) that the consideration of affidavits upon a motion to dissolve is not a right which parties are entitled to demand, and in that case, where, as in this, no appeal lay from the decision of the Primary Examiner, it is stated:

When, as is the position of the petitioner here, a party may not appeal from the decision on the motion, he may not appeal from a determination upon the admissibility of affidavits. The determination in such cases will only be reviewed upon a petition making out an apparent case of abuse of discretion.

No such abuse of discretion has been shown in this case.

The petition is denied.

GUENIFFET, BENOIT, AND NICAULT *v.* WICTORSOHN.

Decided May 15, 1907.

(131 O. G., 1685.)

1. INTERFERENCE—PRIORITY—FOREIGN PATENT AS BAR NOT CONSIDERED.

Where the proofs of the junior party to an interference are insufficient to overcome the date of a foreign patent granted to the senior party, the question whether a foreign patent granted to such senior party stands as a bar to the allowance of his United States application will be left for *ex parte* consideration after the termination of the interference.

2. SAME—SAME—CONCEPTION—KNOWLEDGE IN THIS COUNTRY BY FOREIGN INVENTOR.

Mere knowledge of an invention in this country by a foreign inventor or his agent *Held* not equivalent to a conception of the invention in this country.

APPEAL from Examiners-in-Chief.

MACHINE FOR MAKING MOUTHPIECES.

Messrs. A. C. Fraser & Usina for Gueniffet, Benoit, and Nicault.
Messrs. Philipp, Sawyer, Rice & Kennedy for Wictorsohn.

MOORE, *Assistant Commissioner:*

This is an appeal by Gueniffet, Benoit, and Nicault from a decision of the Examiners-in-Chief affirming a decision by the Examiner of Interferences and awarding priority of invention to Wictorsohn.

The issue is as follows:

1. The combination of means for fringing one end of mouthpieces and bending tongues of said fringe, with means for rolling up said mouthpieces with the bent tongues extending inwardly.

2. The combination of means for feeding wrapper-tubes with rolled mouth-pieces therein with a concave guide and a cylinder coacting therewith to slightly unroll the mouthpieces.

3. In combination in a cigarette-machine, means for feeding the mouthpiece-paper, means for fringing the same and means for rolling the fringed papers.

4. Means for forming mouthpieces for cigarettes, said means including in combination a hollow casing, a rod arranged to turn in the interior of said casing, and an eccentric portion on said rod forming a nipper for gripping the paper against the inner periphery of the casing by the turning movement of said rod.

5. In a machine for making mouthpieces for cigarettes, the combination of means for producing teeth or serrations at one edge of a piece of paper, and for bending up said teeth, and means for rolling said paper to form a mouth-piece with said teeth projecting into its interior.

The invention relates to automatic mechanism adapted to form from a strip of paper a tubular mouthpiece for a cigarette, across the opening near one end of which extends a series of radial tongues cut from an edge of the strip, whereby the tobacco of the cigarette is prevented from passing into the smoker's mouth.

The parties to the interference are each citizens and residents of foreign countries, and the invention in each case was made abroad.

Wictorsohn filed his application on January 9, 1901. Gueniffet, Benoit, and Nicault filed theirs on May 9, 1901. The parties have each secured foreign patents for the invention in controversy, the earliest granted to Wictorsohn being the French patent, No. 301,190, dated September 25, 1900, granted on an application filed June 13, 1900, and the earliest granted to Gueniffet, Benoit, and Nicault being a French patent, dated January 26, 1901, on an application filed October 27, 1900. Wictorsohn also filed an application for the same invention in Austria on June 5, 1900, upon which a patent was granted on December 27, 1901.

The lower tribunals awarded priority of invention to Wictorsohn on the ground that Gueniffet, Benoit, and Nicault's proofs failed to *overcome the* date of Wictorsohn's French patent.

One of the main questions urged on appeal rélates to the status of Wictorsohn's application in view of the grant of his Austrian patent. It is to be observed that the application was filed here more than seven months after the filing of the Austrian application, upon which a patent was granted December 27, 1901. According to the provisions of section 4887, Revised Statutes, in force at the time this Austrian application was filed and the patent was granted thereon, said patent stood as an absolute bar to the grant of a valid patent on the United States application. However, on March 3, 1903, this statute was amended by extending the period of seven months to twelve months. Upon this state of facts appellant strenuously urges that Wictorsohn's application was either (1) unaffected by the amendment of the law, and was therefore permanently barred from eventuating in a patent, or (2) was revived after having been abandoned, the law not having been amended until more than a year after the existence of the bar created by the grant of the Austrian patent.

In the view which I take of the case, however, it is unnecessary to decide these questions in order to dispose of the question of priority of invention. It is believed that appellants' proofs fail to overcome the date of Wictorsohn's French patent, and as appellants cannot prevail whether their contentions are found to be correct or not the question of the appellee's right to a patent should be left for *ex parte* consideration after the termination of this proceeding.

It is claimed on behalf of appellants that the invention was introduced into this country by Julius N. Jaros, their agent, on September 17, 1900, eight days prior to the date of appellee's French patent, as shown by the testimony of Julius N. Jaros, corroborated as to what he saw in Paris by the testimony of Julien Gueniffet, one of the inventors, and as to what he did and communicated here by the testimony of his brother, Alfred L. Jaros.

It appears that Julius N. Jaros was in Paris from May to September, 1900, and during this time visited the Decouple works a number of times, where appellees were employed, who showed him a machine embodying the issue in controversy. He states that he saw it in operation and that the mechanism was fully explained to him. It further appears that he left Paris for New York, arriving on September 17, 1900, bringing with him a number of cigarettes which had been made with appellee's machine. It appears that after his arrival he said nothing about this machine or the product manufactured by it to any one prior to December, 1900, when he had a conversation with his brother, Alfred L. Jaros. It is unnecessary to consider what was disclosed to the latter at this time, as it is subsequent to the date of Wictorsohn's French patent. Alfred L. Jaros testified that his brother wrote him from Paris in May and June regarding the machine in question; but it does not appear that the mechanism was

Rules 122 and 114 provide that the question of the patentability of the issue may be raised at the outset of the interference proceeding as one of the questions involved in determining whether the interference should have been declared. Whether an affirmative determination of this question will be followed by an immediate award of priority or by judgment only after the taking of testimony appears to be immaterial to the right of any interferant to raise this question *inter partes.* The time provided for raising these questions is during the thirty days following the approval of the preliminary statements and the throwing open of each party's application to his opponent. Motions raising these questions cannot be intelligently made earlier in the proceeding, and the fact that the preliminary statement also discloses a basis for an immediate award of priority should not militate against this right, for unless the issue is patentable no judgment of priority should be rendered.

Moreover, it is by no means certain that such a judgment would expedite the issue of the patent, inasmuch as the defeated party may appeal from such judgment through the various Patent Office tribunals to the Court of Appeals of the District of Columbia. Appellant asserts that the public is protected against the issue of a patent with improper claims, since the Examiner of Interferences or the Examiners-in-Chief on appeal may call the Commissioner's attention to any statutory bar. That such a procedure would effect a material saving in time or expense over the present practice is seriously doubted.

Colman further objects to the consideration under the above ground of the motion, prior to the determination of a motion to shift the burden of proof, of certain patents issued subsequently to the filing date of Colman's original application, of which the present application has been held a continuation by the Examiner. Action on the motion to shift the burden of proof, however, in accordance with the usual practice has been postponed until the determination of the motion to dissolve. To permit this ground of the motion to dissolve to go over until after the decision on the motion to shift the burden of proof would result in piecemeal prosecution of the motion for dissolution. It is within the province of the Primary Examiner to consider the prior applications of Colman to determine whether they disclose the invention of the issue for the purpose of ascertaining whether the issue is patentable to Colman. Moreover, if the patents fail to show that the issue is unpatentable to Colman they may show it unpatentable to Field and that the interference should be dissolved without a decision on priority.

Colman also appeals from the transmission of the fourth ground the motion in so far as it alleges informality in the declaration of *interference* based upon indefiniteness and vagueness in the language of certain counts of the issue. Vagueness and indefiniteness of the issue have uniformly been held a proper question to raise under informality or irregularity in the declaration of the interference, and it is thought properly so held. (*Woodward* v. *Newton*, C. D., 1899, 13; 86 O. G., 490; *Goodwin* v. *Smith*, C. D., 1906, 257; 123 O. G., 998; *Anderson* v. *Vrooman*, C. D., 1906, 295; 123 O. G., 2975.)

As stated in *Dinkel* v. *D'Olier*, (C. D., 1904, 572; 113 O. G., 2507:)

It is the policy of the Office to avoid all contentions as to the scope of the issues, and when counts are so vague and indefinite that it is practically impossible to determine their scope such an irregularity has become apparent in the declaration of the interference as to preclude a proper determination of the question of priority.

The decision of the Examiner of Interferences is affirmed.

'EX PARTE HELBIG. :

APPLICATION FOR PATENT.

Decided November 20, 1907.

(131 O. G., 1687.)

1. EXAMINERS-IN-CHIEF—DECISION BY TWO MEMBERS.

A decision by two of the Examiners-in-Chief is a decision of the Examiners-in-Chief.

2. SAME—SAME—REHEARING.

A rehearing of an appeal to the Examiners-in-Chief is not necessary merely because one of the Examiners-in-Chief was not present. If the two members are present, the decision is valid. If they disagree, the case may be set for rehearing, as provided in Order No. 1664, (121 O. G., 1983.)

ON PETITION.

MILL FOR GRINDING AND SEPARATING CEMENT PRODUCTS.

Mr. John H. Whipple for the applicant.

MOORE, *Commissioner:*

This is a petition that a decision made by two of the Examiners-in-Chief (the third member not sitting) be held—

* * * without authority of law and of no effect applicant not having waived his right to the hearing and determination of his appeal which the law gives him—

and that the Examiners-in-Chief be directed to rehear the case.

Section 476 of the Revised Statutes provides that there shall be in the Patent Office three Examiners-in-Chief, and section 482, Revised Statutes, prescribes their duties. The statutes, however, are silent as to what number of the Examiners-in-Chief shall constitute a quorum. In the absence of such a provision it is the practice of this Office to follow the general rule of judicial bodies stated in *Am. and Eng. Enc. of Law*, (vol. 23, p. 590,) as follows:

A majority of the justices constituting a court are a quorum; and the act or decision of a majority of such quorum is the act or decision of the court.

Said practice is set forth in the following provision of Commissioner's Order No. 1664, (121 O. G., 1983:)

During the absence of one member of the Board of Examiners-in-Chief the other two members may hear and determine cases and are not required to continue them at the mere request of the parties. Where the two members hearing the case are unable to agree, they may set the case down for rehearing before three members either before or after announcing judgment.

Where, as in the present case, the decision is concurred in by two of the Examiners-in-Chief, the presence or absence of the third member obviously cannot affect the conclusion, as the most that he could do would be to file a dissenting opinion. If the case is heard by only two members and they disagree, the above order provides that " they may set the case down for rehearing before three members;" otherwise the divided opinion must be treated as an affirmance of the decision below. (*Adams* v. *Murphy*, C. D., 1900, 86; 91 O. G., 2207; *Potter* v. *McIntosh*, C. D., 1906, 56; 120 O. G., 1823.)

If petitioner is dissatisfied with the conclusion reached in the decision of the Examiners-in-Chief, his remedy is by appeal to the Commissioner under section 4910 of the Revised Statutes.

A decision by two of the Examiners-in-Chief is believed to properly constitute a decision of the Examiners-in-Chief, and the *petition is accordingly denied.*

L. W. LEVY & CO. *v.* URI.

TRADE-MARK INTERFERENCE.

Decided November 5, 1907.

(131 O. G., 1687.)

1. TRADE-MARKS—" BROOKWOOD "—NOT GEOGRAPHICAL.
   The mark " Brookwood " for whisky *Held* not geographical.

2. SAME—APPLICATION—ALLEGATION UNDER TEN-YEAR PROVISO—TECHNICAL MARK.
   Where the declaration of an application for the registration of a trademark contains the allegations requisite to obtain registration of the mark as a technical mark, it may be registered as such, notwithstanding the fact that other allegations are made sufficient to obtain registration under the ten-year proviso of the Trade-Mark Act, such additional allegations being in the nature of mere surplusage.

3. SAME—ASSIGNMENT OF BUSINESS AND TRADE-MARK AFTER FILING OF APPLICATION.

The assignment of the business with which a trade-mark is used, together with the trade-mark and good-will of the business after the filing of an application for the registration of such mark, does not work an abandonment of the application, but necessitates suitable action under section 10 of the Trade-Mark Act in order that registration may be issued to the assignee.

4. SAME—MISREPRESENTATION ON LABELS—REGISTRATION NOT REFUSED.

The use of the words "Pure Old Rye Whisky" on labels containing the trade-mark "Brookwood" adopted and used for whisky composed of rye and other whiskies *Held* not such deception as would warrant the refusal of registration, there apparently being no actual intent to deceive.

APPEAL from Examiner of Interferences.

TRADE-MARK FOR WHISKY.

Mr. Willis L. Gibson, Mr. Arthur P. Greeley, and *Mr. Francis B. James* for L. W. Levy & Co.

Mr. Arthur E. Wallace for Uri.

MOORE, *Commissioner:*

This is an appeal by Levy & Co. from a decision of the Examiner of Interferences awarding priority of adoption and use to N. M. Uri and holding that the successor of the latter was entitled to register the word " Brookwood " for whisky.

It is clear from the record that the Examiner of Interferences was correct in holding that N. M. Uri was the first to adopt and use the mark, and this holding does not appear to be questioned by appellant. A number of other objections are urged, however, as grounds for refusing registration to appellee. These objections are, first, that the mark is geographical; second, that appellee has not had ten years' exclusive use thereof; third, that appellee has no title to the mark, and, fourth, that registration should be refused to appellee on the ground that by means of statements on his labels he has been guilty of misrepresentation.

In support of appellant's first objection, that the mark is geographical, the only argument advanced is that the Examiner of Trade-Marks raised this objection in the prosecution of appellee's application, in response to which appellee canceled the original declaration and substituted a declaration bringing the mark within the ten-year proviso. The Examiner also made the same objection to appellant's mark, but it was not insisted upon and evidently was withdrawn. If the mark is not geographical in one case it is not in the other. No other reason being given why the mark is regarded as geographical, and as I see no reason why it should be so regarded, it is held that the mark in question is a technical mark.

Since the declaration of N. M. Uri contains the allegations requisite to obtain registration of his mark as a technical mark, it may be registered as such, notwithstanding the fact that other allegations, sufficient to obtain registration under the ten-year proviso, are made, these additional allegations being in the nature of surplusage. Appellee's mark being registrable as a technical mark, it is unnecessary to show that he has had exclusive use of the mark for ten years' next preceding the passage of the act of February 20, 1905. This disposes of the second objection raised by appellant.

Upon the question of title to the mark, it appears that N. M. Uri was the owner of the mark at the time the application was filed, but that subsequently the entire business, including the trade-mark, was assigned to N. M. Uri & Company, a corporation. As held by the Examiner of Interferences, such transfer of the trade-mark right does not work an abandonment of the application, but necessitates suitable action under section 10 of the Trade-Mark Act of February 20, 1905, in order that the registration may be issued to the assignee. It is therefore held that the application of N. M. Uri is a proper basis for an award of priority of adoption and use.

The principal objection urged by appellant is that N. M. Uri or N. M. Uri & Company are not entitled to registration because the labels on which the trade-mark was displayed were deceptive.

It seems to be well settled that the courts will refuse injunctive relief to a complainant who in his labels or advertisements has been guilty of misrepresentation, although there is nothing misleading about the mark itself; but in the application of this doctrine a liberal attitude is generally assumed upon the question of what is and what is not a misrepresentation. It has also been held that injunctive relief will not be refused to one who has built up his business in part on misrepresentations where such misrepresentations have been discontinued. (*Moxie Nerve Food Company of New England* v. *Modox Co. et al.*, 153 F. R., 487.) It has been further held by the Court of Appeals of the District of Columbia in the case of *The Schuster Co.* v. *Muller* (*post*, 455; 126 O. G., 2191) that collateral misrepresentations furnish a sufficient ground for refusing registration. The question presented is therefore one which may be considered in this case.

There is nothing misleading in itself in the mark in controversy; but it appears from the record of appellee th.... is used mixture of rye and Bourbon whiskies with s.... and ing materials, while the labels represent " Br.... a " Pure Old Rye Whisky." Strictly speaki.... is a whisky made from rye grai.... the .... internal-revenue laws a rye whi.... .... *is predominantly rye or has a ry....* *in the trade; but* appellant co....

resented his whisky as a rye whisky, but as a " pure " rye whisky, and hence has clearly been guilty of deception. If a strictly pure rye whisky were a very desirable article which the public or a large number of individuals using whisky were anxious to secure, the contention might be of some weight; but as far as I have been able to ascertain a pure rye whisky is not agreeable to the taste of most users, and but a small amount of it is sold compared with the sale of what has been known as a blended whisky. This tends to indicate that appellee used the word " pure " on his labels to convey the impression that " Brookwood " whisky was a *pure* whisky, rather than a strictly rye whisky, as no advantage would seem to be gained by creating the latter impression. For these reasons I am convinced that appellee did not use his labels with an actual intent to deceive. In any event I am of the opinion that the deception is not sufficient to warrant the refusal of registration.

The decision of the Examiner of Interferences is affirmed.

L. W. LEVY & COMPANY *v.* URI.

TRADE-MARK INTERFERENCE.

Decided November 25, 1907.

(131 O. G., 1689.)

1. TRADE-MARKS—INTERFERENCE—SUBSTITUTION OF ASSIGNEE.

> Where an application for registration of a trade-mark which is involved in an interference has been assigned and the assignment recorded in the Patent Office contains a request that the certificate of registration be issued to the assignee, *Held* that the assignee may be substituted for the nominal applicant in the interference proceedings.

2. SAME—SAME—SAME.

> *Held* that the technical relation of plaintiff and defendant does not exist in trade-mark interference proceedings and that the substitution for the applicant of the party to whom the certificate of registration may be issued if the final decision in the interference should be adverse to the opposing party should not be refused even if the courts do not allow the substitution by a defendant of a party defendant.

ON MOTION.

TRADE-MARK FOR WHISKY.

Mr. W. L. Gibson, *Mr. A. P. Greeley*, and *Mr. F. B. James* for L. W. Levy & Company.

Mr. Arthur E. Wallace for Uri.

MOORE, *Commissioner:*

This case comes up on a renewal of the motion of Nathan M. Uri that N. M. Uri & Company, a corporation, be substituted for Nathan M. Uri in the above-entitled interference.

In my decision of November 14, 1907, I stated that the substitution might be permitted if a request for the recording of the assignment which acompanied the former motion were made and the fee for the recording of the assignment were tendered. These conditions have been complied with.

L. W. Levy & Company have renewed their protest to the grant of the motion, on the ground that the case is now in the jurisdiction of the Court of Appeals of the District of Columbia, due to a notice of appeal from my decision of November 5, 1907, having been filed, and also on the ground that Nathan M. Uri is the defendant in the proceeding and that there is no court practice which allows a defendant to substitute a party defendant in a proceeding.

As stated in my decision of November 14, 1907, I am of the opinion that I have jurisdiction to take the requested action, at least until the appeal is perfected.

It is evident that the substitution should not be allowed at this time if the rights of L. W. Levy & Company would be prejudiced by such action; but it is not seen that they would in any way be affected thereby. Section 10 of the Trade-Mark Act of 1905 provides that a mark for the registration of which application has been made and the application for the registration of the same shall be assignable in connection with the good-will of the business in which the mark is used, and section 11 provides that the certificate of registration may be issued to the assignee of the applicant if the assignment be entered of record in the Patent Office. These conditions have been complied with, and if it shall be found that Nathan M. Uri was entitled to registration when he filed his application then a certificate of registration could properly be issued to the assignee. The technical relation of plaintiff and defendant does not exist between these parties, and it is not believed, therefore, that the mere substitution for the applicant of the party to whom this certificate of registration may be issued, should the final decision be adverse to L. W. Levy & Company, should be refused even if the courts do not allow the substitution by a defendant of a party defendant.

It is contended by counsel for L. W. Levy & Company that they should have an opportunity to raise the question of the existence of the alleged corporation or the validity of the transfer from Nathan M. Uri thereto, which they were not enabled to do in this proceeding.

If this contention were well founded, it would necessitate the republication of the mark with a renewed opportunity for opposition or the requirement that an application be filed in the name of N. M. Uri & Company, a corporation, which mark would of course have to be published. It is not believed that under the statute any such proceeding is necessary. The question involved in this interference *is the right of* the respective parties to registration at the time their applications were filed. As stated above, if such question be finally determined in favor of Nathan M. Uri a certificate of registration can be issued upon his application, though in view of the assignment such certificate will be issued to N. M. Uri & Company, a corporation.

Furthermore, after the certificate of registration shall have been issued L. W. Levy & Company can file an application for the cancelation of the same if they deem that this transfer was such as to render the registration invalid.

The motion is granted.

MILLER *v.* WALLACE.

PATENT INTERFERENCE.

Decided November 15, 1907.

(131 O. G., 1689.)

INTERFERENCE—PRELIMINARY STATEMENT—AMENDMENT—MISTAKE OF LAW.

An amendment to a preliminary statement will not be permitted upon the allegation of the moving party that at the time of the declaration of the interference he supposed that the issue was restricted to the machine shown in the application, but that he later learned that the Examiner construed it so broadly as to read on a prior application, where it did not appear that the Examiner had construed the issue except by declaring the interference, and that the Examiner had held, on a motion to shift the burden of proof, that the issue was not readable upon the earlier application. In any event the mistake was one of law and affords no ground for amendment.

APPEAL ON MOTIONS.

BUTTON-MACHINE.

Messrs. Alexander & Dowell for Miller.

Mr. H. M. Richards and *Messrs. Offield, Towle & Linthicum* for Wallace.

BILLINGS, *Assistant Commissioner:*

This case comes up on appeal by Miller from two decisions of the Examiner of Interferences.

It appears that on September 26, 1907, Miller filed a series of motions, viz: (1) that he be permitted to file an amended preliminary statement; (2) that the burden of proof be shifted to Wallace, the senior party; (3) that he be granted a reasonable time to present a motion to dissolve the interference or that an accompanying motion be transmitted to the Primary Examiner.

The Examiner of Interferences denied these motions and set a limit of his appeal from his decision. Subsequent to the taking of his appeal from this decision Miller brought an amended motion to dissolve, which was denied transmission on the ground that it was not accompanied by a showing of satisfactory reasons for delay in filing the same.

The Examiner of Interferences properly refused to extend the time for filing a motion to dissolve, (*Egly* v. *Schulze*, C. D., 1905, 237; 117 O. G., 276,) and, as no reasons were given in support of the three grounds of dissolution alleged his action in refusing to transmit the motion to dissolve was correct.

From his decision in refusing to shift the burden of proof no appeal lies. (*Raulet and Nicholson* v. *Adams*, C. D., 1905, 55; 114 O. G., 1827.)

In support of his motion to amend his preliminary statement Miller alleges that at the time of the declaration of the interference he supposed that the issue was restricted to the machine shown in his application involved in this interference and that he made his preliminary statement with reference to that machine, but that he later learned that the Examiner had so broadly construed the issue that it was readable on the construction of his prior application which had been involved in an interference with the application of Wallace.

It does not appear in what way the Examiner has construed the issue except by the declaration of the interference. It is to be noted in this connection that the Examiner of Interferences in denying the motion to shift the burden of proof has held that the issue is not readable on Miller's earlier application.

Without passing on this question applicant's mistake as to the scope of the issue is a mistake of law and affords no ground for granting the motion to amend the preliminary statement.

The second motion to dissolve was not accompanied by a showing of satisfactory reasons for the delay in bringing the same within the time set for bringing such motions, and it was properly refused transmission on that ground.

The decisions of the Examiner of Interferences are affirmed.

MARCONI *v.* SHOEMAKER.

PATENT INTERFERENCE.

Decided October 4, 1907.

(131 O. G., 1939.)

1. APPLICATION—COMPLETION—DRAWINGS SIGNED BY ATTORNEY WITHOUT FULL POWER.

Where all papers necessary for a complete application are filed on October 30, 1902, but the drawings were signed by substitute attorneys who had not full power, and on November 28, 1902, full power is given to such attorneys, upon whose request the date of the application is changed to November 28, 1902, *Held* that the application is entitled to the date of October 30, 1902, as a constructive reduction to practice, the informality being one which could be cured, and was in fact cured, by subsequent ratification by the persons delegating the power.

2. INTERFERENCE—PRIORITY—CONSTRUCTIVE REDUCTION TO PRACTICE OVERCOME BY PUBLICATION.

A published description of an invention by the inventor describing the invention in such full and intelligible manner as to enable persons skilled in the art to understand the operation of the invention and to carry it into practical use is sufficient to overcome the filing date of the application of the opposing party.

3. SAME—ACTUAL REDUCTION TO PRACTICE—EVIDENCE OF SUCCESS OF TESTS.

In view of the failure of the inventor to testify as to the character or results of tests of a magneto receiver for wireless telegraphy and the testimony of a witness who assisted in the tests that the signals were faint, the unsupported statement of an electrical engineer who tested the device that his operator received intelligible messages is not sufficient to establish the operativeness of the device, especially where it does not appear with what certainty or rapidity the signals or messages were received.

4. SAME—SAME—SAME—CONSTRUCTION OF ANOTHER DEVICE.

The construction of another device to obviate defects in a prior device tends to show that the first device was unsatisfactory.

5. SAME—SAME—SAME—SAME.

Where it is claimed that the form of device described and illustrated in the application produced the most satisfactory results, and it appears that a device of this construction was built and tested and afterward several modifications of such device were made and tried without success, and that a prior construction was finally reverted to, and that a number of devices of the latter construction were built for use in preference to the former, the presumption is warranted, in the absence of testimony establishing a satisfactory test, that such device was not successful.

6. SAME—SAME—SAME—EX PARTE TEST DURING REBUTTAL TESTIMONY.

A test by a party during the taking of rebuttal testimony out of the presence of the opposing party or his agent is entitled to no consideration as proof of the operativeness of the device several years previous under different conditions.

7. SAME—CONCEALMENT OR SUPPRESSION AFTER REDUCTION TO PRACTICE.

Where a party constructed a device in October, 1900, but allowed it to remain entirely within the knowledge of the inventor and his co-employees until knowledge was obtained of the invention of the opposing party when the application in interference was filed showing a different form, apparently suggested by such knowledge, *Held* that such party's rights were forfeited by concealment.

APPEAL from Examiners-in-Chief.

SIGNALING BY ELECTROMAGNETIC WAVES.

Messrs. Betts, Betts, Sheffield & Betts and *Mr. Thos. E. Robertson* for Marconi.

Mr. Philip Farnsworth and *Messrs. Foster, Freeman & Watson* for Shoemaker.

MOORE, *Commissioner:*

This is an appeal by Shoemaker from the decision of the Examiners-in-Chief affirming the decision of the Examiner of Interferences and awarding priority of invention to Marconi upon an issue the following count of which sufficiently illustrates the nature of the invention:

1. The method of detecting electrical oscillations which consists in receiving said oscillations by means of a coil maintained in a magnetic field, which field is continually varied independently of the oscillations, substantially as described.

The invention in issue relates to magnetic detectors or receivers for wireless telegraphy. This invention is based upon the principle that a rod of magnetic material placed in the vicinity of a conductor leading to the aerial and ground of a wireless-telegraph station while not sensibly affected by high frequency electrical oscillation under ordinary circumstances becomes sensitive to them when placed in a varying magnetic field. In utilizing this principle each of the inventors, as disclosed in his application, has inclosed the armature of a magnet in a coil one end of which is connected to the aerial and the other to the ground. Another coil surrounding the armature is connected with a telephone-receiver. The magnet and armature are movable relative to one another, thus varying the magnetic field. By reason of this construction the variations in the current induced by the sudden varying magnetizations of the core are caused to vibrate the diaphragm of the telephone, and thus produce audible signals.

This interference as originally declared involved three parties—Marconi, Shoemaker, and Fessenden. The Examiner of Interferences awarded priority of invention to Marconi.

Fessenden having taken no appeal from that decision is no longer a party to this case.

Shoemaker's application involved in this interference, Serial No. 138,228, filed January 8, 1903, is a division of an earlier application, Serial No. 130,492, filed November 8, 1902.

Marconi's application Serial No. 141,339, which embodies the claims in issue, was filed February 2, 1903, and is a division of an earlier application Serial No. 132,974, which bears the filing date of November 28, 1902.

It appears from the record that the petition, specification, oath, and drawing of application Serial No. 132,974 were filed on October 30, 1902, and that the case was originally given the Serial No. 129,395, and the filing date of October 30, 1902, and was forwarded to the Primary Examiner. When the Primary Examiner took up the case for examination, he discovered that the attorneys who signed the drawings had not been given a full power of attorney in the case and expressed a doubt that the case should receive the status of a complete application.

It appears that Marconi originally gave a power of attorney to the the firm of Baldwin, Davidson & Wight, with full power of substitution and revocation. A paper was filed in conjunction with the application papers in which Baldwin, Davidson & Wight purported to " consent " to the substitution of the firm of Betts, Betts, Sheffield & Betts in their place and stead as attorneys for Marconi. The drawings were signed by the latter firm. Subsequently, on November 28, 1902, a formal paper was filed by Baldwin, Davidson & Wight, substituting Betts, Betts, Sheffield & Betts as attorneys, and a request was also filed by the latter that the case be given a new date of filing and serial number. This request was complied with and the case given the Serial No. 132,974 and date of November 28, 1902.

After the declaration of this interference, in view of the fact that Shoemaker's parent application was filed November 8, 1902, Marconi brought a motion before the Primary Examiner that he be given the date October 30, 1902, upon which he originally filed the papers of his application, as his date of constructive reduction to practice of the invention and that the burden of proof thereupon be shifted to Shoemaker. The Primary Examiner denied this motion. The same question was presented before the Examiner of Interferences at the final hearing of the case, and he held that inasmuch as Marconi had, through his attorneys, requested in the *ex parte* prosecution of his case that the case be given a new serial number he should not in an *inter partes* proceeding ask that this action be set aside.

This point was not decided by the Examiners-in-Chief; but in my opinion it is material to a complete determination of the question of priority and will therefore be considered.

The question to be determined is whether Marconi's application as filed on October 30, 1902, was an application upon which a valid patent could have been granted. If so, the refiling of the application constituted merely a substitution for the original application, and under the well-settled practice of the Office Marconi is entitled to the date upon which he filed his original application. (*Silverman* v. *Hendrickson*, C. D., 1902, 527; 99 O. G., 1171; *Lotterhand* v. *Hanson*, C. D., 1904, 646; 110 O. G., 861; *Duryea and White* v. *Rice*, *post*, 443; 126 O. G., 1357.)

The record shows that the present application has the identical disclosure which was filed October 30. The only thing lacking was the authorization of the act of the substitute attorneys in signing the drawing. This informality is one which could be remedied by the ratification of the act either by the principal attorneys or by the inventor himself. Both have been done. The filing of a formal substitute power of attorney by Baldwin & Wight clearly validated all acts done by Betts, Betts, Sheffield & Betts under the power given by the paper consenting to their substitution. Upon June 15, 1904, Marconi over his own signature ratified the acts of Betts, Betts, Sheffield & Betts. In view of these facts it is clear that a valid patent might have issued on Marconi's original application, and it is not believed that he should be deprived of the benefit of his earlier date of filing merely because he, of his own volition, requested that his case be given a new serial number and filing date. It is therefore held that Marconi should have been given the date of October 30, 1902, as the date of his constructive reduction to practice of the invention and the burden of proof shifted to Shoemaker.

Shoemaker alleges in his preliminary statement that he conceived the invention August 15, 1900, that he reduced the same to practice September 3, 1900, and that he used apparatus embodying the invention for the reception of wireless messages in long-distance signaling on or about June 1, 1901, and subsequently thereto.

Marconi in his preliminary statement alleges conception on December 10, 1901, disclosure to others in the United States in January, 1902, and the publication of a full disclosure of the invention in the *Electrical World and Engineer* at New York city July 12, 1902. He also refers to various patents taken out by him in foreign countries, the earliest one of which to be published in his Brazilian patent, dated August 19, 1902. He also refers to a British application filed May 5, 1902.

The Examiner of Interferences and the Examiners-in-Chief concurred in finding that Marconi's invention was fully disclosed in an article published in the United States in the *New York Electrical World and Engineer* on July 12, 1902, and also in the Brazilian patent to Marconi, published August 19, 1902, and constituted constructive reduction to practice. He held that Shoemaker had established conception of the invention as early as November, 1900, but that he had failed to establish a reduction to practice of the invention prior to the date upon which he filed his application and that he was lacking in diligence at and subsequent to the time Marconi entered the field and reduced the invention to practice. He also held that if Shoemaker could be accorded a reduction to practice in 1900, as alleged, he had forfeited his right by concealment of the invention under the principle stated in *Matthes v. Burt*, (C. D., 1905, 574; 114 O. G., 764.)

The Examiners-in-Chief agreed with the conclusions of the Examiner of Interferences, but in addition thereto expressed the opinion that it was doubtful whether Shoemaker ever had, prior to Marconi's disclosure, a definite conception of the principle upon which his apparatus operated, if it operated at all.

Marconi contends that he is entitled to the date of filing of his British application, May 5, 1902, as his date of constructive reduction to practice of the invention, under the provisions of the International Convention for the Protection of Industrial Property and of the act of March 3, 1903. For the reasons stated in *Stiff* v. *Galbraith* (C. D., 1903, 515; 107 O. G., 2532) I am of the opinion that the second clause of section 4887 of the Revised Statutes, as amended March 2, 1903, was not intended to have, and should not be given, a retroactive effect. The date of filing of Marconi's British application is not therefore available to him as his date of constructive reduction to practice of this invention.

The disclosure of the invention in the articles published in the *Electrical World and Engineer* of New York on July 12, 1902, was a reproduction of a part of an article by Marçoni read before the Royal Institute of Great Britain in England on June 13, 1902. Copies of the *Electrical World and Engineer* of July 12, 1902, and of the published proceedings of the Royal Institution for June 13, 1902, are in evidence. Each· comprises a description of the form of apparatus described in Figures 3 and 4 of Marconi's parent application Serial No. 132,974, together with a full description of the theory of its operation. Reference is also made to the successful use of this apparatus in the reception of wireless messages over distances of 30 and 152 miles.

The disclosure in the *Electrical World and Engineer* is clearly sufficient to enable any person skilled in the art to construct and use the invention described therein.

The Brazilian patent to Marconi, published August 19, 1902, a certified copy of which is in evidence, likewise contains a full and complete disclosure of the invention in issue.

It is contended by Shoemaker that these publications have not the force of constructive reduction to practice of the invention and that the publication of the invention by Marconi prior to Shoemaker's filing date is insufficient to overcome Shoemaker's filing date.

This contention is believed to be untenable. Under section 4886 of the Revised Statutes the disclosure of an invention in any prior printed publication in this or in any foreign country is an absolute bar to the granting of a patent to one who subsequently makes that invention. It is well settled, however, that in order to constitute such a bar the earlier printed and published description must exhibit the invention in such full and intelligible manner as to enable persons skilled in the art to which the invention relates to understand the operation of the invention and to carry it into practical use. (*Seymour* v. *Osborne*, 11 Wall., 516; *Cohen* v. *United States Corset Co.*, C. D., 1877, 205; 11 O. G., 457; 93 U. S., 366,370; *Downton* v. *Yeager Milling Co.*, C. D., 1883, 434; 25 O. G., 697; 108 U. S., 466,

471; *Eames* v. *Andrews*, C. D., 1887, 378; 39 O. G., 1319; 122 U. S., 40, 66.) When, therefore, a publication is sufficient to constitute a bar against all later inventors, it should manifestly be accepted as eslishing the rights of the one who made that disclosure and who with reasonable promptness filed his application for patent in the United States. As was well stated by Commissioner Mitchell in the case of *Deprez and Carpentier* v. *Bernstein* v. *Hunter* v. *Gaulard and Gibbs* (C. D., 1891, 53; 54 O. G., 1711:)

> If a patent or printed publication, foreign or domestic, were evidence of conception only, the law would extend to it that tolerance and generosity which are extended to private drawings and descriptions representing the inceptive ftages of an invention. It is because a patent or printed publication is evidence, when it is evidence at all, of a perfected invention, that it is required to speak in unequivocal language and fully, clearly, and exactly describe the invention against which it is urged, whether as a bar to a patent granted or as a basis for a patent asked.

Shoemaker claims to have conceived the invention in August, 1900, and to have disclosed it to others by means of sketches at that time. He also claims to have had certain apparatus constructed to embody his invention at various times during the latter part of the year 1900 and in the year 1901. Several of these sketches and devices are offered in evidence. The testimony relative to the dates upon which these sketches and devices were made has been fully discussed by the Examiner of Interferences and there appears to be no doubt that the true dates are ascribed to them.

The first of these exhibits which needs to be considered for the purpose of this case is a device which was made in October, 1900, marked "Exhibit No. 5," "Device No. 2," and a sketch and description of this apparatus dated November 2, 1900.   (Exhibit No. 6.)

The device comprises a core of iron or steel wires surrounded by two coils of wire, one of which is adapted to be connected to the ground and to the aerial of a wireless station, the other coil being adapted to be connected to a telephone-receiver. A magnet having down-turned ends is rotatably supported over the cores in such a manner that the poles of the magnet alternately pass in close proximity to the ends of the core. This device corresponds closely in construction with the structure shown in Figs. 1 and 2 of Marconi's application.

In his description of the operation of this device in "Exhibit No. 6" Shoemaker states:

> The object of the magnet is to magnetize the core as the high-frequency oscillations demagnetize them. There are other methods by which I can magnetize the core as by passing an alternating current of very low frequency through one of the coils on the core. The frequency must be low enough so as not to
> ᵗe signals in the telephone-receiver which is connected to the secondary
> 7 and 8.

When the magnet is revolved and signals are sent the high-frequency oscillations set up in the primary, Ariel A and Ground G, demagnetize the core 5 as it is passing through vering (varying) magnetic state and the change of magnetic lines being very rapid a click is heard on the telephone which corresponds to the signal sent and the telephone responds to the period at which the transmitting-coil is run.

The signals received are very faint and I have not been able yet to use a relay instead of the telephone and receive the signal on a Sounder.

It is contended by Marconi that Shoemaker did not, prior to the date of filing of his application, nor even at that time, have a conception of the true principles upon which the invention in issue is dependent. It is not denied by Shoemaker that the vibration of the diaphragm of the telephone-receiver in magnetic detectors of the character in controversy is dependent upon variations in the magnetic hysteresis in a varying magnetic field due to the influence of the received oscillations. Marconi therefore urges that because Shoemaker, as shown by his testimony, and that of his associate, Midgley, believed that the effect of the received oscillations was a demagnetizing effect he constructed his apparatus accordingly and endeavored to remagnetize the core as fast as the received oscillations demagnetized it, and that such a construction was not adapted to utilize hysteresis effects, although such effects might be produced in the apparatus as constructed. He further contends that Shoemaker's apparatus is constructed to provide for the rotation of the magnet at such speed as would prevent the desirable hysteresis effects, and is therefore inoperative.

This contention is not without force, and in the light of Shoemaker's unsuccessful endeavors to obtain a satisfactory operation of this apparatus, as will hereinafter appear, I am constrained to agree with the statement of the Examiners-in-Chief that—

It may well be doubted whether Shoemaker ever had, prior to Marconi's disclosure, a definite conception of the principle upon which the apparatus operated, if it operated at all.

In view, however, of the fact that the issue of this interference is not specifically limited to effects caused by magnetic hysteresis, but relates broadly to the method of detecting electrical oscillations by receiving such oscillations by means of a coil maintained in a continually varying or moving magnetic field, it is believed that any doubt as to the sufficiency of Shoemaker's conception of the invention should be waived in his favor. I therefore agree with the conclusion of the Examiner of Interferences that Shoemaker is entitled to a date of conception not later than November 2, 1900, which is the date appearing upon his " Exhibit No. 6," above quoted.

Shoemaker's efforts toward reducing the invention in issue to practice are represented by four devices, which are in evidence.

The first " Exhibit No. 2," which was constructed in September, 1900, consists of a core formed of a number of wires which is surrounded by a primary and a secondary coil. The varying magnetic field was provided in this device by passing a magnet, held in the hand, across the end of the core.

The second device was " Exhibit No. 5," above referred to, which was constructed in October, 1900, and is described in " Exhibit No. 6," dated November 2, 1900.

The third device, " Exhibit No. 7," constructed in December, 1900, consists of a ring of iron wire over which two coils are wound, one to be connected to the aerial and the ground and the other to be connected to the telephone-receiver to detect the changes in the core, caused by the electrical oscillations, and also to be used to vary the magnetism in the core by passing an alternating current of low frequency through this coil, as suggested in " Exhibit No. 6," above quoted.

The fourth and last device, " Exhibit No. 8," is similar to " Exhibit No. 5," except that instead of a U-shaped magnet a ring so magnetized as to have its poles at the ends of a diameter is used, the core and surrounding coils lying in the plane of ring. This device was made in the latter part of 1901.

The testimony relative to the operation of these devices is unsatisfactory. Shoemaker and Midgley, the mechanic who constructed these devices, testify that they were able to receive signals on " Exhibit No. 2: " that more satisfactory signals were received on " Exhibit No. 5 " at the time it was made: that " Exhibit No. 7 " was less efficient than " Exhibit No. 5," and that " Exhibit No. 8 " gave more distinct responses to the electrical oscillations than " Exhibit No. 5." There is, however, no satisfactory testimony that any of these exhibits were actually used to receive telegraphic messages or that any of them were adapted for practical use under normal conditions. The history of the construction and use of these devices, moreover, leads to the conclusion that all were unsatisfactory, and that until Shoemaker had been made aware of Marconi's successful use of similar apparatus he deemed this invention of little importance.

The statement in " Exhibit No. 6," above quoted, that " the signals received are very faint." which is borne out by the testimony of Midgley (Q. 43) and of Gehring, (Q. 2, p. 218, Shoemaker's record,) who was Shoemaker's employer, clearly indicates that at the time " Exhibit No. 5 " was constructed it was not satisfactory, and this is emphasized by the fact soon afterward, in December, 1900, an entirely different form of apparatus, " Exhibit No. 7," was constructed. Upon the failure of the latter to give better results Shoemaker returned to " Exhibit No. 5," and in June, 1901, tested the same at a wireless station at Brielle, N. J., which was in communication with a similar station at Galilee, N. J.

Midgley testifies (p. 65, Shoemaker's record,) that these experiments extended over a period of five or six weeks. He does not, however, state whether complete messages were received or what proportion of the signals could be detected.

Gehring testifies that during these tests he listened for the signals from the Galilee station, but that " the signals came just as faint as before." He further states that Mr. Pickard, an electrical engineer, also tested it at that time, and that

" He (Pickard) kind of discouraged me saying that it was not as good as his carbon receiver."

Pickard, who is called as a witness by Shoemaker, testifies (Q. 3) that he tested this device during June and July, 1901, and also in the fall of 1901, and says in respect thereto that:

Because of its simplicity of construction and reliability of operation, we realized from the first that it was a promising line of investigation, and I personally gave much time to its investigation and experiment. Although from the first the magnetic detector showed itself to be sufficiently sensitive for commercial work, yet there were several objectionable features. Prominent among these objectionable features was the great variation in the magnitude of the response at certain points in the rotation of the magnet. This variation in response had the effect of creating two dead points, or points of very faint response, in each cycle or rotation of the permanent magnet.

Upon cross-examination he was asked:

X-Q. 7. Do you wish to be understood as testifying that " Shoemaker Exhibit No. 5," " Shoemaker Device No. 2," was, in June and July, 1901, in such a state of completion that satisfactory commercial messages could be transmitted from a transmitting circuit and received by it?

and replied:

A. I do not wish to be understood that the device was entirely satisfactory. In my previous testimony I have stated that this particular form of magnetic detector had the objectionable feature of varying the intensity of the response according to the relative positions of the rotating magnet and the core. It was, however, a sensitive instrument and with the addition of a suitable motor to maintain the rotation of the magnet, could have been used for commercial work.

It appears, however, from cross-question 12 that when provided with a suitable motor it was still subject to the objectionable features above referred to.

Pickard states (X-Qs. 8, 9) that during these tests intelligible messages were received by his operator, Rodebaugh, while he, Pickard, who is not a Morse operator, listened in a second receiver. Rodebaugh is not called as a witness, and Pickard's statement stands uncorroborated.

In view of the failure of Shoemaker to testify as to the character or results of these tests and the testimony of Gehring that the signals were as faint as when he first used the device in November, 1900, Pickard's unsupported statement that his operator received intelligible messages is clearly insufficient to establish the operativeness of the device, especially since it does not appear with what certainty or rapidity the signals or messages were received.

That this device was not satisfactory is further evidenced by the fact that in December, 1901, the device having an annular form of magnet, " Exhibit No. 8," was constructed in the endeavor to obviate the dead-points in the rotation of the magnet referred to by Pickard in his testimony above quoted.

It was urged at the hearing, and is commented upon at length in Shoemaker's brief, that the testimony establishes the successful operation of the device " Exhibit No. 8 " and, further, that its operativeness is not disputed by Marconi or the expert witnesses called in his behalf.

A careful scrutiny of the testimony presented by Shoemaker fails to disclose any sufficient evidence of the successful use of this device. Midgley says the results obtained with " Exhibit No. 8," " were rather more satisfactory than were the results with Shoemaker ' Exhibit No. 5,' ' Device No. 2 ' we being able to get more even signals with this device than with ' Exhibit No. 5,' ' Device No. 2,' " (X-Q. 143:) but the testimony shows that several modifications of device No. 8 were tried without success and that the original construction as shown in " Exhibit No. 5 " was finally reverted to. It further appears from Midgley's testimony that in the summer of 1903 Shoemaker had a number of devices constructed for use at Annapolis on the principles and lines of " Exhibit No. 5," " this device being much easier to construct than ' Exhibit No. 8 ' * * * which was a slight improvement on Shoemaker ' Exhibit No. 5.' " (Midgley, X-Q. 144.)

It is a significant fact that although the device " Exhibit No. 8 " is the only one of those offered in evidence which is illustrated in the drawings of Shoemaker's application and is the form of the invention in which it is alleged the most satisfactory results were obtained, no sufficient testimony is adduced to establish any specific satisfactory test of the device, and the further fact that it was, after its alleged successful operation, discarded in favor of the less efficient form " Exhibit No. 5," clearly warrants the inference that it was unsuccessful.

There is some testimony concerning a test made by Pickard during the taking of Shoemaker's rebuttal testimony; but Marconi was not represented at this test. An *ex parte* test of this character is entitled to no consideration and, furthermore, constitutes no proof, even if successful, of the operativeness of the apparatus when tested under *different* conditions several years previous. As pointed out by the

Examiner of Interferences, it is also doubtful whether at this test more than a small fraction of the predetermined signals sent were received.

The character of the present invention is such that the operativeness of the apparatus for performing the method claimed is not obvious. It clearly belongs to that class of inventions which requires actual use or thorough tests to demonstrate its practicability, and in the absence of satisfactory proof of actual use or successful tests it must be held that the devices offered in evidence by Shoemaker were merely experimental in character and that none of them constitute a reduction to practice of the invention in issue. (*Dashiell* v. *Tasker*, C. D., 1903, 551; 103 O. G., 2174; *Macdonald* v. *Edison*, C. D., 1903, 622; 105 O. G., 1263; *McKenzie* v. *Cummings*, C. D., 1904, 683; 112 O. G., 1481; *Gallagher* v. *Hien*, C. D., 1905, 624; 115 O. G., 1330; *Ocumpaugh* v. *Norton*, C. D., 1905, 632; 115 O. G., 1850.)

Shoemaker is therefore entitled to no earlier date of reduction to practice than the date upon which he filed his application, November 8, 1902.

It remains to be seen whether Shoemaker was active at the time Marconi entered the field and exercised due diligence thereafter in reducing the invention to practice.

Midgley states that Shoemaker and himself experimented with "Exhibits No. 5" and "No. 8" up to the latter part of the year 1903, but makes no specific statement as to any work or test between February, 1902, and November 8, 1902, the date upon which Shoemaker filed his application. Gehring does not refer to any work done after April, 1902. Pickard says that during the summer and fall of 1902 he made several visits to Shoemaker's laboratory and was shown certain models of magnetic detectors embodying alterations in dimensions and material; but he does not describe the devices he saw, nor are the dates of these visits specified. Shoemaker merely states that he conducted tests with "Exhibit No. 8" during April, May, and the summer months of 1902. It does not appear what such tests comprised, nor when nor where they were made.

During the period intervening between October, 1900, when Shoemaker's "Exhibit No. 5" was constructed, and the date upon which he filed his application for patent upon this invention Shoemaker filed applications for a large number of patents in wireless telegraphy, (Shoemaker's record, pp. 36–39,) and it is apparent from Gehring's statements (Q. 2) that no application for patent upon the invention in issue was made during this time because it was not considered to be satisfactorily developed. It also appears that an application for patent was finally made because of the knowledge of Marconi's published disclosure of the invention in the *Electrical World and Engineer.*

In view of the facts above stated it is clear that Shoemaker was lacking in diligence and cannot prevail.

It is alleged that Shoemaker's invention was disclosed to Marconi through Gehring. This allegation is denied by Marconi. The testimony relative to the interview between Gehring and Marconi is fully discussed by the Examiner of Interferences in his decision and need not be repeated. I agree with his conclusion that the testimony fails to establish this disclosure.

The lower tribunals have each held that if it could be admitted that Shoemaker reduced his invention to practice in the device "Exhibit No. 5," which was made in October, 1900, he is guilty of concealment under the doctrine stated in *Matthes* v. *Burt*, (C. D., 1905, 574; 114 O. G., 764,) and with this conclusion I also concur. So far as can be gathered from the testimony, Shoemaker's invention was seen only by co-employees of the company with which he was connected. It appears that his device "Exhibit No. 5" was as complete in October, 1900, as at any time thereafter, but that it remained within the knowledge of these few until Shoemaker was stimulated by knowledge of Marconi's publication to make application for a patent. (Gehring, Q. 2, p. 221, Shoemaker's record.) In this connection it is to be observed that Shoemaker discloses in his applications only the form of the invention embodied in his later "Exhibit No. 8" and mechanism corresponding to an apparatus described in Marconi's publication, which, so far as appears from the testimony, was not thought of by Shoemaker prior to the date of that publication.

For the reasons stated I fully concur with the conclusions of the lower tribunals that Marconi is the prior inventor of the subject-matter in issue.

The decision of the Examiners-in-Chief is affirmed.

WEIDMANN *v.* KNUP.

Decided January 22, 1907.

(131 O. G., 2143.)

1. INTERFERENCE—ORIGINALITY—FAILURE TO ASSERT CLAIM TO INVENTION.

Where W. stated in the presence of K. and a witness that he proposed to file an application for patent for an invention which each now claims to have made and K. at that time made no protest, but a few days later went to W. and asked to have his name in the patent, *Held* that as it appeared that W. was at the head of the business and was a man of violent temper and that K. made it a practice not to dispute W. in the presence of others, and in view of the fact that K. was an intelligent man at the head of a *large department,* his request to have his name in the patent indicated that *he regarded himself* at that time to be the inventor of the process in issue.

2. SAME—SAME—SILENCE AFTER FILING APPLICATION.

A failure to assert the origination of an invention by a subordinate officer against the claims of his superior cannot be regarded as acquiescence in the superior officer's claims to the invention where prior to that time the subordinate officer had filed an application for such invention.

APPEAL from Examiners-in-Chief.

DYEING.

Mr. R. G. Dyrenforth for Weidmann.
Mr. Otto Munk and *Mr. William F. Hall* for Knup.

MOORE, *Assistant Commissioner:*

This is an appeal by Weidmann from a decision of the Examiners-in-Chief affirming the decision of the Examiner of Interferences and awarding priority of invention to Knup, the senior party.

The issue is stated in two counts, which read as follows:

1. The process of dyeing tin-weighted silk a uniform blue black, which consists in weighting the silk with tin, then subjecting it to a bath of black iron, and finally treating it with suitable vegetable extracts or dyes.

2. The process of dyeing silk blue black, obtaining a product of any desired weght, which consists in weighting the silk with tin, subjecting it in sequence to an acidulated bath, a black-iron bath, a black-iron gambier-bath, containing matter for coloring according to the shade desired, and, then, to the dye-bath, substantially as described.

The issue relates to dyeing silk, and particularly to the process of dyeing silk a blue black, which has been previously treated with a solution of tin to increase its weight. The invention consists in the application to silks which have been weighted with tin of a process which had been previously considered applicable only to unweighted silks.

Weidmann alleges conception and disclosure in the early part of the fall of 1903 and reduction to practice in the early part of the winter of 1903-4. Knup alleges conception and reduction to practice on November 13, 1903, and disclosure on December 9, 1903.

The controversy between the parties is one of originality rather than priority of invention, each alleging disclosure to the other.

Knup's application was filed December 28, 1903, and Weidmann's application, which eventuated in his Patent No. 780,924, here involved, was filed January 7, 1904. Weidmann's patent was inadvertently granted, and hence the possession thereof gives him no advantage, the burden of proof resting upon him by virtue of Knup's earlier filing date.

The Examiner of Interferences found in favor of Knup, and his conclusion was sustained by all of the members of the Board of Examiners-in-Chief, one of the members, however, writing a separate opinion, stating reasons for his conclusion, which differed in some respects from the majority opinion. In view of the facts that the burden of proof is upon Weidmann and that three separate opinions have been written below, each finding in favor of Knup, the conclusions of the lower tribunals will not be disturbed unless error is made to appear clearly.

At the time the invention was made both parties were connected with the Weidmann Silk Dyeing Company, Weidmann being the president of the company and Knup the foreman of the black-dyeing department. Knup left the employ of the company in January, 1904.

The evidence submitted on behalf of Weidmann clearly shows that the process of the issue was successfully carried out on December 11 and December 12, 1903, by Knup or by the workmen in his department under his supervision, two samples being produced, which are in evidence and known as " Weidmann's Exhibit No. 1 " and " Weidmann's Exhibit No. 2." Weidmann claims that these samples were produced by Knup under his (Weidmann's) directions, while Knup claims that although Weidmann told him to make these samples he did so only after Knup had told him of his previous successful practice of the process in connection with an order received some time in November, 1903, from one of their regular customers. The controversy therefore turns on the question whether Weidmann told Knup how to produce these samples at the time in question or whether the process was disclosed to Knup by Weidmann at some previous time.

The lower tribunals found that Weidmann's proofs failed to show that he disclosed the invention to Knup or to any one else prior to December 14, 1903. In accordance with the well-established practice this conclusion of fact will not be disturbed unless it is clearly against the weight of evidence. (*Flora* v. *Powrie*, C. D., 1904, 636; 109 O. G., 2443.) The evidence on this point has been carefully examined, but no reason is found for coming to a different conclusion. Since Knup is proved to have been in possession of the invention on December 11, 1903, and since he is *prima facie* an original inventor, he must prevail unless his own record or the circumstances surrounding the parties clearly indicate the contrary.

Appellant assigns as an error of the Examiners-in-Chief their failure to give proper weight to the silence of Knup in the presence of an assertion by Weidmann of ownership of the invention and his intention to take out a patent therefor and to Knup's failure to assert claim to the invention until he had made arrangements to leave the Weidmann Silk Dyeing Company; but the claim on behalf of appellant that Knup laid no claim to the invention in the face of Weidmann's assertion that he was the inventor thereof is not borne out by the evidence. It appears that in a conversation between Weidmann, August Hunziker, and Knup about December 14, 1903, Weidmann stated that he intended to take out a patent for the invention in controversy, and Knup at this time made no protest or claim to the invention; but it further appears from the testimony of both Weidmann and Knup that a few days after this occurrence Knup went to Weidmann and asked to have his name in the patent. On behalf of Weidmann it is claimed that Knup made this request not because he had any part in the inventive act, but because he was the head of the black-dyeing department and performed the physical acts of the reduction to practice or directed their performance. On behalf of Knup it is claimed that he wanted his name in the patent because he was the inventor of the process. It is scarcely probable that a man of the intelligence of Knup, who was an expert chemist and at the head of a department employing three hundred or four hundred men and drawing a salary of $5,000 per year, would ask his employer to put his name in a patent to be granted for an invention made solely by the employer and with which he had nothing to do except to perform the physical acts necessary to its reduction to practice under his employer's direction. These circumstances are believed to be a sufficient basis for the conclusion that Knup's request to have his name in the patent was an assertion that he claimed the invention as his own. Knup's explanation of the reason for failing to assert his rights in the presence of Weidmann and Hunziker on the occasion of the conversation about December 14, 1903, appears to be reasonable. It appears from the evidence that Weidmann has a violent temper, and Knup states that he made it a practice not to dispute Mr. Weidmann on any matter in the presence of others. For this reason he awaited a more opportune time to assert his claims, in the meantime talking the matter over with his wife to determine the best way to proceed under the circumstances. It does not appear that at the time this conversation took place between Weidmann, Knup, and Hunziker, Knup had any fixed intention to resign his position. This is the only time that Weidmann asserted his intention, in the presence of Knup and others, to take out a patent for the invention in controversy up to the time of the filing of Knup's application, after which, it is believed, mere silence on the part of Knup would not create a presumption against him. Under all the circumstances Knup's explanation seems reasonable, and it is deemed sufficient to negative any presumption arising from his failure to assert his rights at the time in question.

It is contended by appellant that the Examiners-in-Chief erred in the conclusions which they drew from the evidence submitted to show Knup's use of the process in issue in connection with certain samples alleged to have been made by Knup on an order from Givernaud Brothers in November, 1903. It is evident from the opinion of the Examiners-in-Chief that they fully considered the evidence relating to this transaction, and they found as a fact that Knup reduced the invention to practice at the time this order was filled in November, 1903. No reason is seen for disturbing this conclusion, which seems to be in accordance with the evidence. Moreover, there is no evidence to overcome the *prima facie* reduction to practice by Knup on December 11, 1903.

It is further contended by appellant that the Examiners-in-Chief erred in giving undue weight to the fact that Knup preceded Weidmann only by ten days in the filing of an application. The rule is well established that the junior party must establish his case by a fair preponderance of evidence in order to prevail, and this rule seems to have been followed in this case.

No error is found in the conclusion reached by the Examiners-in-Chief, and their decision awarding priority of invention to Knup *is affirmed.*

Ex parte Keil.

APPLICATION FOR PATENT.

Decided November 25, 1907.

(131 O. G., 2144.)

DRAWINGS—ELIMINATION OF UNNECESSARY ILLUSTRATIONS.

Held that the requirement by the Examiner that unnecessary **figures** be canceled and that the remaining figures be reduced to a **reasonable** scale and placed on a single sheet was right.

ON PETITION.

LOCK.

Mr. J. Odell Fowler for the applicant.

MOORE, *Commissioner:*

This is a petition from the requirement of the Examiner that applicant reduce the number of sheets of drawings in this case.

It appears that the application as originally filed contained five sheets of drawings. The applicant has canceled three of these in response to the Examiner's requirement. The Examiner now requires that all the figures of the drawings be placed on one sheet.

From an inspection of the drawings it is not seen that the large perspective view of Figure 2 is necessary to a complete illustration of the invention. The invention disclosed in the application consists in making the opening in the escutcheons larger than the knob-spindle, and while this is shown in dotted lines in Fig. 2 it could be so shown in original Fig. 7, or that figure could be modified so as to show a section through one of the escutcheons in the plane of *knob-spindle*, which would show the opening larger laterally than the spindle, as it is shown larger vertically in original Fig. 8. However, if applicant desires to retain a perspective view the same could be placed on a sheet with the other figures by making it of reasonable size and omitting the knobs of original Figs. 7 and 8.

The petition is denied.

Ex parte Alart and McGuire.

APPLICATION FOR REGISTRATION OF TRADE-MARK.

Decided December 12, 1907.

(131 O. G., 2145.)

1. TRADE-MARKS—DECEPTIVE.

A mark containing the legend " Guaranteed under the Food and Drugs Act of June 30, 1906," *Held* deceptive, since the registration of such a mark would lead the public to believe that the Government had guaranteed the purity of the article upon which the mark was used.

2. SAME—PUBLIC POLICY.

It is believed to be against public policy to register a mark which indicates or suggests that the Government has given its official approval of the character or quality of the merchandise to which such mark is affixed.

ON APPEAL.

TRADE-MARK FOR PICKLES, ETC.

Messrs. Arthur C. Fraser & Usina for the applicant.

MOORE, *Commissioner:*

This is an appeal from the decision of the Examiner of Trade-Marks refusing to register a trade-mark consisting of a red seal bearing an arbitrary device and also containing the legend " Guaranteed under the Food and Drugs Act, June 30, 1906, Serial Number 1,281."

The ground upon which registration was refused is that—

* * * registration of the mark in its present form would lead to confusion and convey the idea that the guaranty clause is protected by the registration of the mark claimed. This is contrary to the reason and spirit of the law and it is believed to be contrary to public policy to grant a registration to any person which includes the specific form of notice which the Government permits manufacturers to use in giving the notice of guaranty under the Food and Drugs Act of June 30, 1906.

It is contended by the appellant that under section 5 of the Trade-Mark Act of 1905 registration of an arbitrary trade-mark permits the inclusion of matter not registrable *per se* and that registration of a mark which includes a descriptive phrase written in a particular manner should be permitted in order that the benefit of this arrangement may be obtained in any suit of unfair competition in trade in which such arrangement might be simulated in the mark of the adverse party. It appears from this contention that the guaranty clause is intended to be an integral part of the trade-mark sought to be registered.

It is well settled that no property can be claimed in a trade-mark so constructed or worded as to contain a false or misleading representation. In the case of *The Schuster Co.* v. *Muller* (*post*, 455; 126 O. G., 2192) the Court of Appeals said:

Recent salutary laws restrain manufacturers and dealers from imposing upon the public preparations injurious to health. The courts grow increasingly careful and cautious in restraining false representations as to the public in vending such preparations. Where any symbol or label claimed as a trade-mark is so worded as to contain a distinct assertion which is false, no property right can be claimed nor can the right to the exclusive use of it be maintained by a court of equity. Courts of equity will not interfere by injunction where there is any lack of proof in the applicant's case or any misrepresentation in his trade-mark or label, nor will the courts uphold in any one a privilege of deceiving the public. An exclusive privilege to deceive the public is not one that a court of equity can sanction nor one which the Commissioner of Patents should aid. While there is a right of property in a trade-mark in connection with a vendible commodity it is essential that the vender should not in his trade-mark or in the printing connected therewith, or in the business use of the trade-mark, himself be guilty of any false or misleading representations. It is settled that where the owner of such a trade-mark applies for an injunction to restrain another, his petition will be denied. (See *Worden* v. *California Fig Syrup Co.*, 187 U. S., 516; *California Fig Syrup Co.* v *Stearns & Co.*, 73 Fed. Rep., 812; *Leathercloth Co.* v. *American Leathercloth Co.*, 4 De Gex, J. & S., 137; *Eleven House of Lords Cas.*, 523; *Fetridge* v. *Wells*, 4 Abbott N. Y., 144; *Manhattan Medicine Co.* v. *Wood*, C. D., 1883, 268; 23 O. G., 1925; 108 U. S., 218; *Siegert et al.* v. *Gandolfi et al*, 139 Fed. Rep., 917.)

Rule 19 of the Trade-Mark Rules provides that no deceptive mark shall be registered, and the provisions of this rule have been rigidly enforced by this Office.

While the guaranty clause included in the applicants' trade-mark is in the terms prescribed by the Secretaries of the Treasury, Agriculture, and Commerce and Labor, under the authority vested in them by the Food and Drugs Act, its use as an integral part of a trade-mark is unwarranted in view of the rulings of the Department of Agriculture.

At the time the Food and Drugs Act first became effective various manufacturers, either intentionally or inadvertently, so included the guaranty clause with other printed matter upon their labels as to make it appear that the Government had guaranteed the purity of the articles upon which these labels were affixed. This having been called to the attention of the Secretary of Agriculture, the following order was issued by him:

No other word should go upon this legend or accompany it in any way. Particular attention is called to the fact that nothing should be placed upon the label, or in any printed matter accompanying it, indicating that the guaranty is made by the Department of Agriculture. The appearance of the serial number with the phrase above mentioned upon a label does not exempt it from inspection nor its guarantor from prosecution in case the article in question be found in any way to violate the Food and Drugs Act of June 30, 1906.

It is believed that if the trade-mark now presented for registration should be registered in its present form and if the applicant should place in connection therewith the words " Registered in the U. S. Patent Office," as he is required to do by section 28 of the Trade-Mark Act of 1905, and as the specimen labels filed with his brief show he has done, the public would be led to believe that the Government had, by registering this trade-mark, guaranteed the purity of the article upon which it was used. Registration of the mark is therefore refused upon the ground that the mark is deceptive in its nature.

It is also believed that registration of the mark here presented should be refused upon the ground that its registration is contrary to public policy. The Court of Appeals of the District of Columbia *in re Cahn, Belt & Co.* (C. D., 1906, 627; 122 O. G., 354) cited with approval several decisions of the Commissioner of Patents which refused registration of national flags and coats-of-arms of States upon the ground that the registration of such marks was contrary to public policy. (*Ex parte Schmachtenburg Bros.*, 51 MS. Dec., 204; *New Prague Flouring Mill Co.*, 62 MS. Dec., 437; *ex parte Penny*, 67 MS. Dec., 136; *ex parte Standard Fashion Co.*, C. D., 1899, 187; 89 O. G., 189; *ex parte Ball*, C. D., 1902, 102; 98 O. G., 2366; *ex parte Brandsville Fruit Farm Company*, C. D., 1903, 103; 103 O. G., 660.) It is believed that for equally cogent reasons public policy demands the refusal of registration of any trade-mark which indicates or suggests that the Government has given its official approval of the character or quality of the merchandise to which such mark is affixed.

The decision of the Examiner of Trade-Marks is affirmed.

BAY STATE BELTING COMPANY *v.* KELTON-BRUCE MANUFACTURING COMPANY.

OPPOSITION.

Decided August 29, 1907.

(131 O. G., 2146.)

1. TRADE-MARKS—MARK MUST BE AFFIXED TO THE GOODS.
    In order that a party may acquire a trade-mark right, it must be shown that he affixed the mark to the goods.
2. SAME—EVIDENCE—COMPETENCY OF WITNESS.
    The fact that the witnesses testifying in behalf of a corporation were officers of the corporation furnishes no sufficient reason for disregarding their depositions.

ON APPEAL.

TRADE-MARK FOR BELT AND LACE LEATHER.

Mr. George N. Goddard for the opposer.
Messrs. Pennie & Goldsborough for the applicant.

BILLINGS, *Acting Commissioner:*

This is an appeal from the decision of the Examiner of. Interferences sustaining the opposition of the Bay State Belting Company and holding that the Kelton-Bruce Manufacturing Company is not entitled to register the words " Indian Tanned " as a trade-mark for belt and lace leather.

The Examiner of Interferences found that the testimony fails to establish the use of the mark in question as a trade-mark by the Kelton-Bruce Company or its predecessors prior to 1892. He found that the Bay State Belting Company adopted in 1885 a mark of which the words " Indian Tanned " formed a prominent part and has continuously used the mark. The Examiner of Interferences thereupon held that the Kelton-Bruce Company has no right to register the mark of its application as a trade-mark.

The testimony of both Rowbotham and Carter is to the effect that they assisted in the organization of the Bay State Belting Company in 1884 and have ever since been officers of the company. Both witnesses testify that the Bay State Belting Company began in March, 1885, to mark its sides of lace-leather with the figure of an Indian and the words " Indian Tanned," the work being that shown in the Bay State Belting Company's certificate of registration No. 23,185, issued on June 6, 1893. They testify that the mark has been used continuously by said company and that the leather was sold under the name " Indian Tanned." A bill for a stencil, dated March 24. 1885, was introduced in evidence which these witnesses state was for a stencil bearing the mark above. The stencil was not introduced in evidence: but the witnesses state that it was worn out long ago and has been supplanted by a rubber stamp.

Rowbotham testified to sales of lace-leather by the company marked " Indian Tanned," some of them to customers outside the State of Massachusetts. He produced the books at the examination for the inspection of applicant's counsel containing entries of such sales.

The testimony in behalf of the Bay State Belting Company is believed to satisfactorily establish its continuous use of the mark since 1885.

Although the testimony in behalf of the Kelton-Bruce Manufacturing Company shows that its predecessor, the Kelton & Bruce Company, sold lace-leather under the name of " Indian Tanned " from the time of the organization of the company in 18__ ___ _quently used these words on their bill-heads and in ___ there is no testimony as to the actual use of the mark on the goods prior to 1892. This is admitted by counsel for the Kelton-Bruce Manufacturing Company in the following statement, (p. 6 of brief:)

The remark of the Examiner of Interferences that there is no proof in the record of actual marking of the goods by Kelton & Bruce prior to 1892 is well founded only if it be taken to mean actual testimony to that effect. It was impossible for us to find any employee of Kelton & Bruce who could have had any knowledge of such marking, but the witnesses Pennoyer and Nichols testified that when they first entered the employ of Kelton & Bruce in 1892 and 1893, respectively, the goods were being marked. The only proof of marking prior to that date is the natural inference from the fact that the words were being used on all the stationery of Kelton & Bruce, and from the fact that the goods were being sold and were known to the trade as "Indian Tanned" leather.

Under section 16 of the act of 1905 in order that a party may be found guilty of infringing a registered trade-mark it must be established that he has affixed the mark "to merchandise," and it is equally true that in order to acquire a trade-mark right the mark must be affixed to the goods. A mere possibility or presumption that the mark was so affixed is not sufficient to establish the existence of the right.

It is contended by the Kelton-Bruce Manufacturing Company that the unsupported testimony of Rowbotham and Carter does not amount to proof, because they are officials of the Bay State Belting Company, and therefore interested parties. The mere fact, however, that they are interested parties is no reason for disregarding their depositions where their testimony was not discredited or impeached on cross-examination, nor is it true that their testimony is entirely unsupported, as appears from the brief analysis of the evidence heretofore made.

The evidence is found to establish the conclusions reached by the Examiner of Interferences, and his decision is accordingly *affirmed.*

DEITSCH BROTHERS *v.* LOONEN.

CANCELATION PROCEEDING.

Decided December 17, 1907.

(131 O. G., 2146.)

1. TRADE-MARKS—CANCELATION—MOTION TO SUPPRESS TESTIMONY—OBJECTION INDEFINITE.

An objection that "the proceedings about to be taken are contrary to the statutes and the rules in these cases made and provided" *Held* too indefinite to warrant suppressing testimony where no other notice of the real ground of objection was given prior to the hearing on the motion.

2. SAME—SAME—TESTIMONY—PRINTING EXHIBITS.

The printing or reproduction of paper exhibits will not be required, since if the case should be appealed to the Court of Appeals of the District of Columbia these exhibits can be sent to the court as physical exhibits.

3. SAME—SAME—MOTIONS—APPEAL.

An appeal from a decision of the Examiner of Interferences to which no limit of appeal was set will not be dismissed because the appellant did not first ask leave of the Commissioner to file such appeal.

4. SAME—MOTION TO SUPPRESS EVIDENCE OR TO PRINT EXHIBITS—APPEAL.

Appeals will not hereafter be allowed from a decision of the Examiner of Interferences denying a motion to strike out testimony or a motion to require the printing of exhibits prior to the appeal from the decision on the merits rendered after final hearing.

APPEAL from Examiner of Interferences.

TRADE-MARK FOR TOOTH-BRUSHES.

Mr. Joseph L. Levy and *Mr. Howard A. Coombs* for Deitsch Brothers.

Messrs. Goepel & Goepel for Loonen.

BILLINGS, *Assistant Commissioner:*

This case comes up on appeal by Deitsch Brothers from a decision of the Examiner of Interferences denying a motion (1) to suppress the entire deposition of certain witnesses for Loonen; (2) to require Loonen to print or reproduce as part of his printed record all the exhibits offered in his behalf capable of printing or reproduction; (3) to stay proceedings pending the determination of the motion. Loonen has filed a motion to dismiss the appeal.

It appears that the Examiner of Interferences denied the motion of Deitsch Brothers, but did not set a limit of appeal from his decision. Loonen's motion to dismiss is based on this fact. He contends that, no limit of appeal having been set, Deitsch Brothers should have applied to the Commissioner for leave to take an appeal or for an order restoring the jurisdiction to the Examiner of Interferences, so that he could hear argument as to whether he would permit an appeal.

This appeal being in proper form, it is believed that it would be highly technical to dismiss it for the reason urged by Loonen. For this reason the motion to dismiss must be denied.

In view of the fact that it has heretofore been the practice to entertain appeals from decisions of the Examiner of Interferences on a motion to suppress testimony and to require exhibits to be printed the present appeal will be considered.

The motion to suppress the testimony was, as appeared from a brief filed at the hearing, based on the ground that the notice of taking testimony did not give the names of the witnesses, as required by Rule 154.

The record shows that counsel for Deitsch Brothers attended the examination of the witnesses and objected on the ground that the—

proceedings now to be taken on behalf of the party Loonen are contrary to the statutes and the rules in these cases made and provided.

It does not appear from this general objection what the real ground of objection was, and the motion to strike out does not state therein the specific objection. The decision of the Examiner of Interferences was clearly right, since it was not made to appear that the moving party was injured or inconvenienced by the failure to give the names of the witnesses and, as pointed out above, due notice of thé objection was not given. (Rule 159.)

The second part of the motion asks that Loonen be required to print or reproduce his exhibits. No reason is seen for making such a requirement. It is true that the rules of the Court of Appeals of the District of Columbia require that the transcript of the record shall be printed; but these exhibits can go to the court as physical exhibits and need not be included in the transcript. Counsel for Deitsch Brothers in his affidavit filed in support of his motion states that owing to the nature of these exhibits it would be exceeding expensive to reproduce them. This same question was before Commissioner Duell in *Freeman* v. *Bernstein*, and in a decision reported in C. D., 1898, 39; 83 O. G., 155, he refused to require that the paper exhibits be printed.

It is believed that it will be in the interest of good practice and will work no hardship to the parties if hereafter no appeal be allowed from a decision of the Examiner of Interferences denying a motion to suppress testimony or a motion to require the other party to print exhibits prior to the appeal from his decision on priority rendered after final hearing. The question of the correctness of his decision on the motion can of course be raised on such appeal.

The setting of times for hearings of necessity rests in the discretion of the Examiner of Interferences, and his decision on this question will be reviewed only in a case where the circumstances are such as to call for the exercise of the supervisory authority of the Commisisoner.

The decision of the Examiner of Interferences denying the motion of Deitsch Brothers *is affirmed*, and the motion of Loonen to dismiss the appeal of Deitsch Brothers *is denied*.

HALLWOOD *v.* CARROLL.

PATENT INTERFERENCE.

Decided August 1, 1907.

(131 O. G., 2417.)

1. INTERFERENCE—PRIORITY—SECOND INTERFERENCE—RES ADJUDICATA.

Where in the first interference between the same parties C. formally abandoned the invention specifically stated in the issue, *Held* that in a second interference the issue of which is based upon the same disclosure as that upon which the issue of the first interference was based judgment must be rendered against C. upon the ground that the matter is *res adjudicata.*

2. SAME—SAME—SAME—SAME.

The fact that no testimony was taken in the first interference does not avoid the application of the doctrine of *res adjudicata* to the second interference, even though the issue of the latter includes details not expressly recited in the first interference, [citing *Blackford* v. *Wilder, post,* 491; 127 O. G., 1255, and *Wende* v. *Horine, post,* 615; 129 O. G., 2858.)

APPEAL from Examiners-in-Chief.

CASH-REGISTER.

Mr. Chester C. Shepherd and *Mr. S. E. Fouts* for Hallwood.
Mr. Wm. H. Muzzy and *Mr. F. P. Davis* for Carroll.

MOORE, *Commissioner:*

This is an appeal from the decision of the Examiners-in-Chief reversing the decision of the Examiner of Interferences and awarding priority of invention to Hallwood.

The issue is stated in seven counts, of which the following count will serve as an illustration:

1. In a cash-register, the combination with a register, comprising a plurality of wheels having ratchet-teeth formed on their peripheries, of operating-pawls engaging said ratchet-teeth, locking devices for said pawls normally locking the same to the wheels, and operating mechanism for effecting retraction of the pawls over the ratchet-teeth and subsequent advance of the pawls to turn the wheels, and means connected to said operating mechanism and arranged to engage the locking devices for withdrawing them from the pawls upon the initial movement of said operating mechanism with provisions for reëngaging the locking devices with the pawls for the advance movement of the same.

The invention involved in this interference relates to means for preventing " overthrow " of the adding-wheels of a cash-register, due ordinarily to the slamming of the drawer. This is accomplished by providing locking devices for the pawls which actuate the registering-wheels so constructed as to remain in locked position during the closing of the drawer and until the initial movement in the next opening of the drawer.

This is the second interference between the same applications, the issue of the prior interference, No. 21,803, being as follows:

In a cash-register, the combination with registering devices, of a series of operating-pawls, means for locking said pawls in engagement with said registering devices, a movable frame arranged to govern said means, a spring for holding said frame in one position, and mechanism for moving said frame against the tension of the spring.

The record of the earlier interference shows that after the preliminary statements were approved motions for dissolution were brought by both parties, Hallwood's motion relating to irregularity in the declaration of the interference and Carroll's alleging all the grounds provided for by Rule 122. The motions to dissolve were denied, and times were set for taking testimony.

Shortly before the date set for Hallwood, the junior party, to begin taking his testimony-in-chief Carroll filed a written declaration of abandonment of the invention, as provided for by Rule 125. Judgment was thereupon rendered in favor of Hallwood.

Subsequently Carroll presented an amendment containing the claims forming the issue of this interference. The Examiner finally rejected these claims upon the ground that they "read directly on the apparatus of Hallwood, with which this case has been in interference." Upon appeal by Carroll the Examiners-in-Chief reversed the decision of the Primary Examiner. The present interference was then declared.

After the preliminary statements in this interference were approved Hallwood filed a motion for dissolution, alleging all the grounds provided for by Rule 122. In his decision upon this motion the Primary Examiner held that Carroll had no right to make the claims in issue in view of the decision in the prior interference, stating, in part:

It is true that the present issues are in some respects narrower than the issue of the first interference and in other respects broader, but they all read on the disclosures of both parties, are directed to the same subject-matter, and when construed in view of the disclosures, there is no structural line of division between the thing covered by the issue of the first interference and the thing covered by the issues of the present interference.

The Examiners-in-Chief upon appeal from this decision again . reversed the Primary Examiner, holding that there was a clear and definite structural line of division between the thing covered by the issue of the first interference and the thing covered by the issue of the present interference. In view of this favorable decision upon Carroll's right to make the claims proceedings in the interference were resumed and testimony was taken by both parties. The Examiner of Interferences held in his decision upon the question of priority that Carroll had a right to make the claims in issue and that the testimony showed that Carroll was first to conceive and reduce to practice the invention stated in counts 1, 4, 5, 6, and 7, and that as to counts 2 and 3 Hallwood, though first to conceive, was last to reduce to practice and was lacking in diligence at the time Carroll entered the field and subsequently thereto. He therefore awarded priority of invention to Carroll upon all the counts of the issue.

Hallwood then appealed to the Examiners-in-Chief, again urging that the question of priority was *res adjudicata* in view of the decision upon the prior interference.

The Examiners-in-Chief in their decision upon this appeal reversed the decision of the Examiner of Interferences and awarded priority of invention to Hallwood, in view of the principle announced in the then recent decision of the Court of Appeals of the District of Columbia in *Blackford* v. *Wilder*, (*post*, 491; 127 O. G., 1255,) in which the Court said:

To sum up—the parties are the same. The applications are the same and disclose the invention of each issue. The constructions relied on, respectively, as evidencing conception and reduction to practice of the invention of both issues are the same. The fundamental facts of both cases are the same. Applying the well-settled principle of estoppel by judgment, before stated, it follows inevitably that the final decision in the first interference is conclusive, unless it can be made to appear that the question upon which the determination of the second case rests is one that neither was, nor could have been presented and determined in the first case.

The Examiners-in-Chief held that notwithstanding their former conclusion that there was a " structural line of division between the thing covered by the issue of the first interference and the thing covered by the issue of the present interference " the claims now involved between the same parties " are claims for the same general structure that was covered by the issue of the prior interference and might have been presented in the first instance if Carroll or Hallwood had so desired."

It is contended on behalf of Carroll that the issue of the original interference was suggested from his case to Hallwood and that inasmuch as Hallwood had no claims corresponding to the counts of the present issue he could not amend within the provisions of Rule 109. It is further urged that at the time the first interference was declared the practice stated in the decision of Commissioner Allen in *Churchward* v. *Douglas* v. *Cutler*, (C. D., 1903, 389; 106 O. G., 2016,) permitting the addition of new claims made by both parties, had not been instituted and that the parties could not therefore amend their cases to include claims covering all the subject-matter common to the two applications. This contention is not well founded. The first interference was declared May 13, 1902. Prior to this date, on April 15,

1902, a decision by Commissioner Allen was published in the case of *Reece* v. *Fenwick*, (C. D., 1902, 145; 99 O. G., 669,) in which a motion presented by both parties was granted permitting the entry by the Primary Examiner of certain claims in each party's application and directing the Primary Examiner to re-form the issue to include such claims in case he found the proposed claims allowable to the parties. In his decision upon that motion the Commissioner said:

It is the general policy of the Office to have all questions which may be brought in issue between the parties settled in one interference, and it would seem to be to the interest of the parties and of the Office to have the question whether the proposed claims may constitute an issue in this case settled at this time rather than at the conclusion of the interference.

It is therefore clear that under the practice of this Office existing at that time claims might have been introduced to cover all the interfering subject-matter.

Aside from this consideration, however, the court of appeals in the case of *Blackford* v. *Wilder, supra,* and in the more recent case of *Horine* v. *Wende,* (*post,* 615; 129 O. G., 2858,) did not excuse the failure to contest all the subject-matter common to the interfering applications, upon the ground that the rules of this Office did not provide a means for introducing claims to common subject-matter not included in the interference as at first declared.

It is further contended that the claims of the present issue do not differ merely in scope from the issue of the prior interference, but that they comprehend a separable invention. This contention is clearly untenable. The claims forming the issue of this interference, as well as those which formed the issue of the prior interference, are predicated upon the same mechanical constructions. The following principle, stated in the decision of the Commissioner in the case of *Corry and Barker* v. *Trout* v. *McDermott,* (C. D., 1904, 144; 110 O. G., 306,) which was quoted with approval by the Court of Appeals of the District of Columbia in *Horine* v. *Wende, supra,* is clearly applicable to this case:

The Office is justified in taking the decision as to priority of invention as *prima facie* evidence that the successful party was the first inventor not merely of the particular issue in controversy, but of the invention common to the two cases, whether more broadly or more specifically stated. The burden is upon the defeated party to show special circumstances of the particular case which make it improper to apply the decision to the other claims presented. It is not sufficient that the claims differ and that it is theoretically possible for one party to be prior inventor as to the first and the other party prior inventor as to the second, for this would apply in all cases where the claims are not identical.

The special circumstances relied upon by Carroll to avoid the effect of the decision of the earlier interference as an estoppel to his right to the claims in issue in this interference are clearly insufficient for that purpose.

It is contended that the abandonment of the invention filed by Carroll in the earlier interference was restricted to the one definite invention set forth in the issue of that interference and that it was not a general concession of priority of invention. By the terms of that instrument Carroll formally abandoned "the invention which is the subject-matter of said interference and is defined in the issue thereof, which is as follows: " reciting the issue in that interference.

The claim which formed the issue of the prior interference is based upon the same disclosure as that upon which the claims of the present issue are based, and since Carroll abandoned the invention covered by the issue of the first interference he is clearly estopped from prosecuting other claims based upon the identical structure.

It is also urged that in view of the fact that no testimony was taken in the earlier interference the doctrine of *res adjudicata* should not be applied to the claims which are now presented and which it is claimed were capable of embodiment in a different machine from that which constituted a reduction to practice of the issue of the first interference. This contention is untenable. As stated in *Horine* v. *Wende, supra:*

The judgment or decree in the former case is not conclusive in the later one as to matters which might have been decided, but only to those which were in fact decided. (*Cromwell* v. *Sac. Co.*, 94 U. S., 351, 353; *Last Chance Mining Co.* v. *Tyler Mining Co.*, 157 U. S., 683, 687.) The issue of the estoppel is that there has been a judicial determination of the fact and this includes every fact put in issue and necessary to the judgment or decree, whether expressly recited therein or not.

To determine, then, what has been adjudicated in the former litigation on which the claim of estoppel is founded, resort is had to the material facts alleged with certainty in the declaration or bill on which the plaintiff's right to recover is founded, and a general judgment thereon is conclusive of such facts. Hence a final judgment by default or upon demurrer is as efficacious as one rendered after a contest between the parties.

The fact judicially determined in the earlier interference between the present contestants comprised the same invention based upon the same disclosure as that upon which the present issue is predicated, and the judgment by the Examiner of Interferences in that case was conclusive of the question of priority of that invention whether the details thereof were expressly recited or not.

I find no error in the decision of the Examiners-in-Chief, and it is accordingly *affirmed.*

JOHNSTON *v.* EREKSON AND CARLSON *v.* BARNARD.

PATENT INTERFERENCE.

Decided November 22, 1907.

(131 O. G., 2419.)

PRELIMINARY STATEMENT—MOTION TO AMEND.

A motion to amend a preliminary statement cannot be granted where it has not been shown that proper care was exercised in the preparation of the original statement and no explanation is given of how the original mistake occurred or why it was not sooner discovered.

APPEAL ON MOTION.

FISH-SCREEN.

Mr. John A. Saul for Johnston.

Mr. W. N. Moore for Erekson and Carlson.

Messrs. C. A. Snow & Co. for Barnard.

MOORE, *Commissioner:*

This is an appeal by Johnston from the decision of the Examiner of Interferences denying his motion for permission to amend his preliminary statement.

In his original statement Johnston alleged conception in January, 1905, and disclosure in June, 1906. By his proposed amendment he desires to allege disclosure in January, 1905, and thereby carry his date back of the dates of disclosure alleged by his opponents. The affidavits of Johnston and his attorney, filed in support of the motion to amend, are very brief and general in their statements. Johnston merely states that a mistake was made in not alleging the earlier date and that it was caused by his misinterpreting the word " disclosure " to mean the time when he first showed to others the completed model. His attorney states that his communication with Johnston was through a local attorney who is a regular practitioner and not skilled in patent practice and that " it appears that Johnston is totally ignorant of the meaning of the word disclosure." It is not shown that proper care was exercised in drafting the original statement. There is no explanation of how this alleged mistake was discovered and why it was not discovered sooner.

The preliminary statements were approved and times for taking testimony were set on May 31, 1907; but the motion to amend was not filed until October 16, 1907, and after the testimony of one of Johnston's opponents had been taken and filed.

The showing is deemed insufficient to warrant the amendment for reasons indicated above and more fully set forth in *Bliss* v. *Creveling,* (C. D., 1904, 381; 112 O. G., 449;) *Fowler* v. *Boyce* v. *Temple and Goodrum,* (C. D., 1904, 22; 108 O. G., 561;) *Neth and Tamplin* v. *Ohmer,* (C. D., 1905, 177; 116 O. G., 874.)

The decision of the Examiner of Interferences is affirmed.

EX PARTE UNDERWOOD TYPEWRITER COMPANY.

APPLICATION FOR REGISTRATION OF TRADE-MARK.

Decided November 27, 1907.

(131 O. G., 2419.)

TRADE-MARKS—PART OF A MACHINE NOT REGISTRABLE ON A TRADE-MARK.

It being well settled that the form of part of a machine is not proper subject-matter for a trade-mark, the form of the face-plate of a type-writing machine is not registrable, since it is necessary to give a finished appearance to the machine.

ON APPEAL.

TRADE-MARK FOR TYPE-WRITERS.

Mr. Fred B. Fetherstonhaugh for the applicant.

MOORE, *Commissioner:*

This is an appeal from a decision of the Examiner of Trade-Marks refusing to register the form of a face-plate used on what is known as the " Underwood " type-writing machine as a trade-mark for type-writers.

The drawing filed as a part of the application consists of the outline of a rectangular figure having a length about twice its height, the greater portion of the upper side of which is cut out in the form of a curve. It is not a representation similar to this which appellant claims as a trade-mark; but he claims the thing itself—*i. e.*, the front face-plate, which is used on the " Underwood " type-writing machine.

The Examiner refused registration on the ground that under well-established law, as set forth in numerous decisions of the courts, the form of an article or a part of an article or machine is not proper subject-matter for a trade-mark. Appellant does not deny that this is the law; but he contends that this case does not fall within this doctrine, for the reason that the plate which he seeks to register is not really a part of the machine, as it can be removed without changing the shape of the machine or interfering with its operation or with the supporting structure. While it is true that this plate performs none of the mechanical functions of the machine, it is, nevertheless, a part of the machine as actually made and is regarded almost as essential as the frame itself, so far as the production of a commercial article is concerned. This plate is necessary to give a finished appearance to the machine, and it would not be salable without it. This being so, if the trade-mark here claimed were valid appellant would be enabled to prevent the manufacture of the Underwood machine as it is constructed to-day after all the patents covering its structure had expired, since no salable machine could be produced without infringing the trade-mark. This is obviously contrary to the spirit of the law, which contemplates the freedom of the public to make a patented structure after the patent thereon shall have expired.

The decision of the Examiner is affirmed.

Ex parte C. H. Alden Company.

APPLICATION FOR REGISTRATION OF TRADE-MARK.

Decided November 11, 1907.

(131 O. G., 2419.)

1. TRADE-MARKS—REGISTRATION—"THE ALDEN SHOE"—NAME OF INDIVIDUAL.

   A trade-mark consisting of the words "The Alden Shoe," of which the word "Alden" is printed in letters of such relative sizes as to form an ellipse, inclosed within a circle around which is printed the words "Mannish Shoes" at the top and "For Boys" at the bottom, these phrases being separated on either side by two stars, *Held* not entitled to registration, on the ground that "Alden" is the name of an individual and that the other features are descriptive.

2. SAME—SAME—NAME OF INDIVIDUAL—DISTINCTIVE PRINTING.

   The use of the letters forming the name of an individual of different sizes increasing from each end toward the center, forming in outline an ellipse, *Held* not such a distinctive manner of printing as to warrant registration, since the name is still the predominating feature.

ON APPEAL.

TRADE-MARK FOR LEATHER BOOTS AND SHOES.

Mr. T. Hart Anderson for the applicant.

BILLINGS, *Assistant Commissioner:*

This is an appeal from the decision of the Examiner of Trade-Marks refusing registration of a trade-mark for shoes comprising the words "The Alden Shoe" inclosed within a circle, the words "Mannish Shoes" being printed around the top and "For Boys" printed around the bottom of the circle, these phrases being separated on either side by two stars.

Registration of this mark is refused on the ground that the controlling feature of the mark is the word "Alden," and that being the mere name of an individual, not written or printed in a distinctive manner, is prohibited registration under section 5 of the Trade-Mark Act of 1905, which provides in part that—

* * * no mark which consists merely in the name of an individual, firm, corporation, or association, not written, printed, impressed, or woven in some particular or distinctive manner or in association with a portrait of the individual, or merely in words or devices which are descriptive of the goods with which they are used, or of the character or quality of such goods, or merely a geographical name or term, shall be registered under the terms of this act.

It is contended by the applicant that the trade-mark is registrable under the provisions of this section, for the reason, first, that said trade-mark is not "merely the name of an individual or of the applicant," and, second, that it is not "merely words or devices which are descriptive of the goods on which the said trade-mark is used."

The words " Mannish Shoes for Boys " are clearly descriptive of the character of the goods. The circle inclosing the words " The Alden Shoe " and the stars appearing on either side of the circle are merely ornamental devices, which do not confer any arbitrary signification on the trade-mark. The salient feature of the mark by which the merchandise of the applicant would undoubtedly become known is the phrase " The Alden Shoe." Of these words " The Shoe " is descriptive and " Alden " is the name of an individual. In the present case it is the surname of the president of the applicant company. The letters of the word " Alden," as appears from the specimens and the drawing forming part of the application, are of a different size, so that the word " Alden " has the general form of an ellipse. The real question to be determined in this case is whether the word " Alden " is printed in such a distinctive manner as to warrant registration under the provisions of section 5 of the act of 1905, above noted. It is believed that the controlling principle underlying the requirement of the statute that a mere name unless written or printed in a distinctive manner may not be registered is that the distinctive manner in which the name is displayed must be of a character as to give such a distinct impression to the eye of the ordinary observer as to outweigh the significance of the mere name.

As stated in the decision in *ex parte Mark Cross* (C. D., 1903, 23; 102 O. G., 622.) in which the word " Cross " written in the same manner was considered—

The peculiarities must dominate the mere name and reduce it to a position of relative obscurity. This result has not been accomplished in the case under consideration. In this case only a slight peculiarity of form of expression of the mere name has been obtained by the use of a common expedient of the type-setter, and it must be held that for determination of the identity of this mark it remains practically the mere name " Cross."

In the present case the manner in which the word " Alden " is written is not so dissimilar from that in which another person by the name of " Alden " might employ his name in ordinary block type as to avoid confusion in the mind of the public. It is therefore held that the predominating feature of this mark by which the goods would be known is not displayed in such a distinctive manner as to warrant the registration of the mark under section 5 of the act of 1905. The mere inclusion of descriptive words written in a certain manner does not confer registrability upon the mark, and the ornamental devices are not of sufficient prominence to create an arbitrary symbol or to warrant the registration of the mark as a whole.

The decision of the Examiner of Trade-Marks is affirmed.

SMITH v. INGRAM.

PATENT INTERFERENCE.

Decided December 4, 1907.

(131 O. G., 2420.)

1. INTERFERENCE—MOTION TO AMEND PRELIMINARY STATEMENT.

Where it appears that at the time of making his preliminary statement a party did not read the counts of the issue, that the alleged mistake therein was not discovered till testimony was taken, and the motion to amend was not brought for more than two months thereafter, *Held* that neither proper care in preparing the statement nor diligence in investigating the matter and discovering the mistake was shown.

2. SAME—SAME—POSTPONING DECISION AND FINAL HEARING.

Whether a decision on a motion to amend a preliminary statement should be rendered before or at final hearing is a matter within the discretion of the Examiner of Interferences.

APPEAL ON MOTION.

ADDING-MACHINE.

Mr. E. G. Siggers for Smith.
Mr. Jacob Felbel for Ingram.

BILLINGS, *Assistant Commissioner:*

This case comes up on two appeals by Smith, first, from the decision of the Examiner of Interferences denying his motion to amend his preliminary statement, and, second, from the decision of the Examiner of Interferences denying his motion for postponement of the consideration of the motion to amend until final hearing.

Smith's original preliminary statement, filed May 29, 1906, alleged disclosure and reduction to practice in September, 1904. The dates alleged by his opponent are March, 1903, for conception, and July, 1903, for reduction to practice. Smith by his amendment desires to allege, as to counts 1, 3, 4, 6, 7, and 8, disclosure in December, 1902, and reduction to practice in January, 1903, and to thereby carry his dates, except for the invention of counts 2 and 5, back of those of his opponent.

It appears that the original interference was dissolved in part and redeclared with added counts and that Smith filed a second preliminary statement containing the same allegations as the first. Smith took his testimony in June and July, 1907, but did not file his motion to amend his preliminary statement until September 25, 1907, though he did give notice of his intention to file such motion to amend during the taking of testimony. In support of his motion Smith relies upon the testimony taken in the interference and on the affidavit of his attorney. According to the showing made therein the Examiner of Interferences found that Smith was careless and negligent in the preparation of his preliminary statement and denied his motion to amend upon this ground.

As an excuse for the alleged error in the original statement, it is asserted that Smith was sick at the time it was prepared and upon being advised that the interference related to the "comb-plate or actuator master-wheel guide-plate," assumed that it related merely to a certain machine; that he did not read the counts of the interference and did not know that the issue was broad enough to include earlier machines. It does not appear, however, that Smith's sickness was responsible for the alleged error in the statement, for he did not after his recovery read over the counts of the issue, and certainly it does not excuse the mistake in the second preliminary statement. The second preliminary statement related to the counts added to the interference, and Smith was under obligation to prepare this statement concerning the invention of these counts with the same care he should have exercised with respect to the counts of the original interference. It is claimed that the error in the statement was discovered by Smith in May, 1907, at about the time his attorney visited the factory for the purpose of preparing the evidence to be offered in his behalf. This was not until a year after the execution of his original preliminary statement and some months after the execution of the second statement. No excuse is offered for the failure to sooner discover the error. It appears that both Smith and Laganke, the superintendent of the factory, were conversant all this time with the earlier machines claimed to embody the invention of the issue, but failed to recognize that they might embody the issue. This fact Smith claims to have perceived at once when he on this occasion read over for the first time the counts of the interference. Apparently it would have been equally clear at any previous time since the declaration of the interference if he had taken the trouble to examine the issue.

Appellant is held not to have exercised proper care in preparing his statement, nor diligence in investigating the matter and discovering the alleged mistake. No error is found in the decision of the Examiner of Interferences denying the motion on this ground.

The second motion, requesting that consideration of the subject-matter of the first motion be postponed until final hearing, raises a matter that is properly within the discretion of the Examiner of Interferences. Where testimony taken must be considered in determining a motion to amend a preliminary statement, it is within his discretion to consider such testimony for the purpose of deciding the motion prior to final hearing. When in his opinion the conditions of the case justify an early adjudication of the questions raised, his decision should not be delayed.

For the reasons stated the decision of the Examiner of Interferences upon both motions *is affirmed.*

DANQUARD *v.* COURVILLE.

PATENT INTERFERENCE.

Decided December 7, 1907.

(131 O. G., 2421.)

1. INTERFERENCE—MOTION TO DISSOLVE—INFORMALITY IN DECLARATION.

    A motion to dissolve on the ground of informality in declaring the interference was properly refused transmission where it appears that the alleged informality relates to the right of the parties to make the claim.

2. SAME—SAME—MOVING PARTY'S RIGHT TO MAKE THE CLAIM.

    Where both parties are applicants and under the head of informality in declaring the interference it is alleged in a motion to dissolve that the claims do not apply to the structures of either party, *Held* that this is not such an admission as to justify a decision on priority adverse to the moving party. (The case of *Lipe v. Miller* C. D., 1904, 114; 109 O. G., 1608 distinguished.)

APPEAL ON MOTION.

REGULATOR FOR PNEUMATICALLY-OPERATED MUSICAL INSTRUMENTS.

Messrs. Southgate & Southgate for Danquard.
Messrs. Whittemore, Hulbert & Whittemore and *Messrs. Bacon & Milans* for Courville.

BILLINGS, *Assistant Commissioner:*

    This is an appeal by Courville from the decision of the Examiner of Interferences transmitting Danquard's motion to dissolve as to the grounds that the issue is not patentable and that the applicant Courville had no right to make the claims.

    The record shows that the Examiner of Interferences refused to transmit the first ground of Danquard's motion, which alleges that there has been an informality in the declaring of the interference, for the reason that the grounds of the issue are incorrectly drawn and that they do not apply to the structure of either party. This ground was refused transmission by the Examiner of Interferences, for the reason that the facts stated in support thereof relate to the right of the parties to make the claim and are not properly transmissible under the head of informality in the declaration of an interference.

    It is not denied by the appellant that the grounds of the motion which were transmitted are sufficiently explicit; but it is contended that the reasons set forth in the first grounds of Danquard's motion which was not transmitted constitute an admission by him that the issue is not patentable to him; that in view of this admission the motion to transmit should have been denied and priority of invention awarded to Courville. This contention is not well founded. As stated in the case of *Goodwin* v. *Smith*, (C. D., 1906, 257; 123 O. G., 998)—

> There is no reason, as was pointed out in *Miller* v. *Perham*, (C. D., 1906, 157; 121 O. G., 2067,) why the Office, having once decided that a party is entitled to make certain claims, should reconsider the question on that party's own motion.

The alleged ground of irregularity in the declaration stated in Danquard's motion is therefore not one which could be properly transmitted. Furthermore, this ground of the motion does not merely deny the right of Danquard to claim the invention in issue and is not therefore an admission upon which a decision of priority could be rendered in favor of his opponent.

The appellant has cited the decision of *Lipe* v. *Miller*, (C. D., 1904, 114; 109 O. G., 1608,) in which it was held that where an applicant alleges that the issue is not patentable to him when in interference with a patent the motion should not be transmitted, but the interference summarily dissolved. The conditions of that case were radically different from those in the present case. In the case of *Lipe* v. *Miller* the sole question to be determined was the right of the applicant to make the claim in issue. This claim had already been granted to the patentee.   In the present case neither party has been granted a patent; but the Office has already held that each of the applicants is entitled to make claims in the terms of the issue. No reason, therefore, appears which would warrant the summary dissolution of the interference or a decision of priority in favor of Courville.

The decision of the Examiner of Interferences is affirmed.

EX PARTE SHAVER.

APPLICATION FOR PATENT.

Decided December 9, 1907.

(131 O. G., 2422.)

APPLICATION—SWORN TO IN BLANK—STRIKING FROM FILES—RULE 31.

Where an inventor assigns an invention and subsequently alleges that the application papers were executed in blank and petitions that the application be stricken from the files, *Held* that because of the assignment he is estopped from denying the validity of the executed papers, especially when the application has been on file nearly a year.

ON PETITION.

SOAP-DISPENSING MACHINE.

Messrs. Sturtevant & Mason for the petitioner.

BILLINGS, *Assistant Commissioner;*

This is a petition by the applicant that the above-entitled application be stricken from the files in accordance with the provisions of Rule 31, since it was signed and sworn to in blank and without actual inspection of the petition and specification.

The specification is dated October 29, 1906, and the jurat to the oath and the assignment are dated October 29, 1906, and November 5, 1906, respectively. In affidavits accompanying the petition applicant states that he signed these papers in blank prior to severing his connection with the Hygienic Soap Granulator Company, the assignee of this application, in September, 1906, and that since that time he has signed no papers for this company. There are also filed affidavits corroborating applicant's statement that he severed his connection with the assignee company in September, 1906.

The showing made is not deemed sufficient to justify striking the case from the files. A petition of this kind would be looked upon with disfavor even if it had been filed promptly; but it appears from the records of this Office that the applicant took no steps to find out if the application had been filed in his name for nearly a year after the time when he alleges that he severed his connection with the assignee company. If a patent had been granted on this application, applicant would have been estopped from denying its validity. (*Force* v. *Sawyer-Boss Mfg. Co. et al.*, 111 F. R., 902; *Siemens-Halske Electric Co.* v. *Duncan Electric Mfg. Co. et al.*, 142 F. R., 157; *Mathews Gravity Carrier Co.* v. *Lister et al.*, 154 F. R., 490.) It is believed that in this case, by a parity of reasoning, he should be estopped from denying that the application which he has assigned was properly executed. It is not shown that the assignment was made without consideration or, if consideration was given, as stated in the assignment, that it has been returned. The fact that no affidavits have been filed on behalf of the assignee controverting the allegations in the applicant's affidavits does not affect the operation of the estoppel.

The petition is denied.

DECISIONS

OF THE

SECRETARY OF THE INTERIOR,

1907.

DUKESMITH *v.* CORRINGTON *v.* TURNER.

(126 O. G., 3425.)

INTERFERENCE—DEFECTIVE APPLICATION OATH—APPEAL TO SECRETARY.

> The decision of the Commissioner of Patents ruling that defects in the application oath of one of the parties, if there were such, might be corrected after the termination of the interference is judicial or quasi-judicial in character and subject only to review by the courts, and the Secretary of the Interior has no appellate or supervisory control of the matter.

Messrs. Kay, Totten & Winter for Dukesmith.
Mr. Murray Corrington pro se.
Mr. Edmund A. Wright for Turner.

DEPARTMENT OF THE INTERIOR,
OFFICE OF THE ASSISTANT ATTORNEY-GENERAL,
Washington, February 14, 1907.

THE SECRETARY OF THE INTERIOR.

SIR: By your reference I am asked for opinion upon the petition of Murray Corrington in the nature of a proffered appeal to the Secretary of the Interior from the action of the Commissioner of Patents, denying Corrington's motion that one Turner be required to file a supplementary oath, and denying his further motion to dissolve an interference as to Turner upon their respective applications for Letters Patent for an invention.

The motion to dissolve the interference was made upon the ground of irregularity and insufficiency of Turner's oath in that proceeding, and the Commissioner of Patents, having previously ruled that defects in Turner's oath, if there were such, might be corrected after the termination of the interference proceedings, refused to entertain the motion.

I am of opinion that the questions presented are judicial or quasi-judicial in character, within the jurisdiction of the Commissioner

Patents, subject only to review by the courts; that the Secretary of the Interior has no appellate or supervisory control of this matter, and advise you that the petition should not be entertained. (See *Poole* v. *Avery*, and cases therein cited, C. D., 1899, 255; 87 O. G., 357; 14 Opinions of Assistant Attorney-General, 177.)

Very respectfully,

(Signed)   FRANK L. CAMPBELL,
Assistant Attorney-General.

Approved February 14, 1907.
(Signed)   E. A. HITCHCOCK,
Secretary.

IN RE BLOCH.

(128 O. G., 457.)

ATTORNEYS—UNITED STATES COMMISSIONERS INELIGIBLE TO ACT AS ATTORNEYS BEFORE THE PATENT OFFICE.

Held that under section 1782 of the Revised Statutes a person holding the office of United States commissioner is ineligible to practice as an attorney representing applicants for patents before the United States Patent Office.

DEPARTMENT OF THE INTERIOR,
OFFICE OF THE ASSISTANT ATTORNEY-GENERAL,
Washington, April 23, 1907.

THE SECRETARY OF THE INTERIOR.

SIR: I am in receipt through your reference of the 26th ultimo, with request for an opinion thereon, of a letter from the Commissioner of Patents, dated the 13th ultimo, in which, after referring to the application of one Lester W. Bloch, United States commissioner, of Albany, N. Y., and to section 1782 of the Revised Statutes, he says:

The question presented is: Does the inhibition of the statute referred to apply so as to make this applicant ineligible to practice as an attorney representing applicants for patent before the United States Patent Office?

Section 1782 reads as follows:

No Senator, Representative, or Delegate, after his election and during his continuance in office, and no head of a department, or other officer or clerk in the employ of the Government, shall receive or agree to receive any compensation whatever, directly or indirectly, for any services rendered, or to be rendered, to any person, either by himself or another, in relation to any proceeding, contract, claim, controversy, charge, accusation, arrest, or other matter or thing in which the United States is a party, or directly or indirectly interested, before any department, court-martial, bureau, officer, or any civil, military, or naval commission whatever. Every person offending against this section shall be deemed guilty of a misdemeanor, and shall be imprisoned not more than two years, and fined not more than ten thousand dollars, and shall moreover, by conviction therefor, be rendered forever thereafter incapable of holding any office of honor, trust, or profit under the Government of the United States.

Section 5498 prohibits under like penalty "every officer of the United States, or person holding any place of trust or profit from discharging any official function under or in connection with any executive department of the Government of the United States or under the Senate or House of Representatives," from acting as an agent or attorney in prosecuting any claim against the United States, etc.

September 15, 1880, this Department considered and rejected the application of one Ewell Dick, a United States commissioner, to be admitted to practice before it, holding that his office brought him within the inhibition of the section last referred to. July 29, 1885, (4 L. D., 55,) the Department adhered to said holding in denying the application of Neil Dumont, a United States commissioner, to practice as agent or attorney before this Department.

Section 5498 is limited in its restriction to the prosecution of a claim against the United States, and while an application for a patent for an invention may not be considered as a claim against the United States these decisions would clearly bring a United States commissioner within the phrase "officer of the United States" as used in said section 5498, and in my opinion he is clearly within the phrase "officer or clerk in the employ of the Government," as used in section 1782. This section prohibits and renders highly penal the reception or agreement to receive by officers or clerks in the employ of the Government, compensation for services to any person, in relation to any matter or thing before any department, court-martial, bureau, officer, or any civil, military, or naval commission whatever. A patent upon an invention guarantees to the patentee protection in the enjoyment of the matters patented for a stated period, and, surely, the granting of such a right or privilege is a matter in which the United States, representing the people, is directly or indirectly interested, and it is my opinion that said section renders a person holding the office of United States commissioner ineligible to practice as an attorney representing applicants for patent before the United States Patent Office.

The papers are herewith.

Very respectfully,

(Signed) GEORGE W. WOODRUFF,
Assistant Attorney-General.

Approved: April 23, 1907.

(Signed)

JAMES RUDOLPH GARFIELD, *Secretary.*

IN RE ADAMS.

(129 O. G., 1612.)

DEPARTMENT OF THE INTERIOR,
Washington, June 19, 1907.

ASSIGNEE OF ENTIRE INTEREST—RIGHT TO PROSECUTE APPLICATION TO EXCLUSION
OF INVENTOR.

 Rules 5 and 20, which provide that the assignee of the entire interest of
an invention may prosecute the application for patent to the exclusion of
the inventor, *Held* to be valid.

THE COMMISSIONER OF PATENTS.

 SIR: I have considered the petition of Arthur J. Adams, proffered
as an appeal and request for supervisory action in the matter of the
action of the Patent Office denying him the right to prosecute in person or by attorney of his own selection application for Letters Patent
for an invention entitled " Improvements in Perambulators or Go-
Carts."

 It appears that Adams had executed an assignment of this invention and also a power of attorney to prosecute it, when he filed another
application for an invention entitled " Improvements in Baby-Car-
riages," which your Office reports contained five broad claims embracing subject-matter common to both applications. Subsequently he
assigned this latter application, and filed a paper in the Patent Office
attempting to revoke the power of attorney given in the first application, appointing a firm of attorneys to prosecute his second application
and containing an amendment canceling the broad claims of the first
application which were common to the second one.

 This paper was refused consideration by the chief clerk of the Patent Office, and Adams proffered an appeal here, but the appeal was
dismissed upon the ground that in any state of the case an appeal did
not lie to the Secretary of the Interior from the action of such officer.
The petitioner then took his appeal to the Commissioner of Patents,
who concurred in and approved the action of the chief clerk, and
Adams again invokes the supervisory power of the Secretary of the
Interior.

 The contention of Adams is, in substance, that he has the right to
prosecute his assigned application himself, or through his attorney,
to the exclusion of his assignee of the entire interest, and to revoke
such assignee's power of attorney. Viewed in the light of the entire
record it looks like an effort to repudiate and avoid his contract by
circumlocution, and does not present a case which appeals to the con-
science of a supervising officer. Moreover, the action of the Commissioner of Patents is within both the letter and spirit of Rules 5 and
20 governing Patent Office procedure, which provide that—

 5. The assignee of the entire interest of an invention is entitled to hold correspondence with the Office to the exclusion of the inventor.

and the latter part of Rule 20, which provides that—

20. * * * the assignee of the entire interest may be represented by an attorney of his own selection.

But it is contended by the petitioner that these rules are without authority of law. To this it will be enough to say that so long as these rules remain in force, they will be given effect and a collateral attack on them will not be considered. If it is thought that their operation is unjust or inequitable, the matter can be brought to the attention of the Commissioner of Patents and the Secretary of the Interior in a direct proceeding. Upon a cursory examination they do not appear to be without authority of law, and if their operation does this petitioner an injustice, he has adequate remedy in the courts.

This case on its merits presents nothing within the supervisory powers of the Secretary of the Interior, and the petition is denied.

The papers belonging to the files of your Office are herewith returned.

Very respectfully, GEORGE W. WOODRUFF,
Acting Secretary.

OPINION

OF THE

ATTORNEY-GENERAL,

1907.

NOTARIES PUBLIC—AMENDED LAW.

(127 O. G., 3642.)

AMENDED SECTION 558 OF THE CODE OF THE DISTRICT OF COLUMBIA CONSTRUED.
  Held that the " proviso "—
  "And provided further, That no notary public shall be authorized to take acknowledgments, administer oaths, certify papers, or perform any official acts in connection with matters in which he is employed as counsel, attorney, or agent in which he may be in any way interested before any of the Departments aforesaid,"
  in the recent act of Congress amending section 558 of the code of the District of Columbia applies to all notaries who may practice before the Departments and not merely to notaries of the District of Columbia.

DEPARTMENT OF JUSTICE,
Washington, April 18, 1907.

The SECRETARY OF THE INTERIOR.

SIR: I duly received your request for my opinion whether the " proviso " in the recent act of Congress amending section 558 of the code of the District of Columbia applies to local notaries only or to notaries throughout the country. Briefs on both sides of the question and an opinion of the Assistant Attorney-General for your Department accompanying your letter have been carefully considered by me.

Section 558 before amendment was as follows:

Notaries. The President shall also have power to appoint such number of notaries public, residents of said District, as, in his discretion, the business of the District may require.

The amendatory act, complete, is as follows:

An act to amend section five hundred and fifty-eight of the code of law for the District of Columbia.

Be it enacted by the Senate and House of Representatives of the United States of America in Congress assembled, that section five hundred and fifty-eight of the code of law for the District of Columbia, relating to notaries public, be amended by adding at the end of said section the following: "Provided, That the appointment of any person as such notary public, or the acceptance of his commission as such, or the performance of the duties thereunder, shall not disqualify or prevent such person from representing clients before any of the Departments of the United States Government in the District of Columbia or elsewhere, provided such person so appointed as a notary public who appears to practice or represent clients before any such Department is not otherwise engaged in Government employ, and shall be admitted by the heads of such Departments to practice therein in accordance with the rules and regulations prescribed for other persons or attorneys who are admitted to practice therein: And provided further, That no notary public shall be authorized to take acknowledgments, administer oaths, certify papers, or perform any official acts in connection with matters in which he is employed as counsel, attorney, or agent in which he may be in any way interested before any of the Departments aforesaid."

Do the words " no notary " in the last sentence mean *no notary of the District of Columbia,* or is the prohibition general? This question is not altogether free from difficulty.

It appears probable that this second proviso was added to the bill to meet an objection raised by the Secretary of the Treasury and the Comptroller, which is thus stated by the latter officer:

Persons who are notaries public and not Government employees may, in the business represented by them as attorneys before the Departments, act as notaries, *c. g.*, have executed before them affidavits and powers of attorney, in cases in which they are acting as attorneys in claims before the Departments. Such practice, in my opinion, would open the doors to fraud and deceit.

I do not see that any sufficient reason exists for limiting the prohibition contained in this proviso to notaries public of the District of Columbia: the practice it was intended to prevent is no less objectionable on the part of other notaries than on theirs. Doubtless the law was originally intended to remove a legal disability which affected only notaries of the District. But it must be remembered that the one legislative body, by one method of law making at one and the same sitting, enacts laws for at least three different classes of business in the District. It makes laws to be applied by the Executive Department, situated in the District, to the whole country; it makes laws to regulate the practice and management of those Executive Departments themselves and it is the legislature of the District considered as a quasi-Territory. There is no constitutional or other legal obstacle to the embodiment of laws of all three kinds in one act.

Such being the case, when debate or committee deliberation may suggest a wise and needed rule of law, so busy a body as the Congress may be unwilling to postpone its enactment merely to effect a logical separation of subjects among these three classes. The Senate added this final proviso to the bill after it had passed the House.

The amendatory law not only deals with notaries of the District, but also with the practice and management of the Executive Departments; and with the relations of notaries to that practice.

The attention of the Congress being thus directed to the subject of departmental practice, it seems, to my mind, reasonable to believe that when it said "no notary public" shall act as such in cases in which he is attorney before any of the Departments, it meant what it said; that is to say, it intended to embrace all the notaries who could practice before those Departments.

The fact that the enactment took the form of a proviso in an act relating in other respects to notaries of the District is unquestionably entitled to weight; but it is not decisive. Had Congress intended to restrict the operation of the proviso to notaries of that District, it could have inserted the word "such" or some equivalent qualifying expression, as it actually did in the body of the act: not having done this, I feel bound to assume it acted advisedly and intended to say what it said in fact. Therefore, although there may be room for a reasonable divergence of views in the premises, I am, on the whole, of the opinion that the proviso applies to all notaries who may practice before the Departments.

Respectfully,

(Signed)   CHARLES J: BONAPARTE,
                          Attorney-General.

DECISIONS

OF THE

UNITED STATES COURTS

IN

PATENT CASES,

1907.

[Court of Appeals of the District of Columbia.]

HALL AND RUCKEL *v.* INGRAM.

Decided December 4, 1906.

(126 O. G., 759.)

TRADE-MARKS—OPPOSITION—DISSIMILARITY OF MARKS—DEMURRER.

Held that trade-marks consisting of the words "Zodenta" and "Sozodont" are quite dissimilar and that "Zodenta" is not calculated to mislead or deceive the average purchaser who may seek to buy "Sozodont." The resemblance is not such as to preclude a proper determination of the question upon demurrer.

Mr. C. T. Milans and *Mr. S. O. Edmunds* for the appellants.
Mr. L. S. Bacon and *Mr. J. H. Milans* for the appellee.

McComas, *J.*:

This is an appeal from a decision of the Commissioner of Patents (C. D., 1906, 278; 123 O. G., 2312) sustaining a demurrer filed by the appellee to the appellant's notice of opposition to the appellee's application for registration of the trade-mark "Zodenta," for use on a dentifrice, the appellee claiming to have continuously used this trade-mark on a dentifrice since 1891. Within due time, under section six of the statute of February 20, 1905, the appellant filed notice of opposition to the registration of "Zodenta."

The grounds for opposition were: that the word "Sozodont" has been used continuously by the appellants and their predecessors in

441

business as a trade-mark for dentifrices since 1863; that appellants are the sole and rightful proprietors of this mark and that the mark "Zodenta" so nearly resembles the word "Sozodont" as used by the appellants—

as to be calculated to mislead, deceive and confuse and to result in interference and conflict in trade.

The appellee demurred to the opposition. After hearing, the Examiner of Interferences sustained the demurrer, holding that the words in question—

do not so nearly resemble each other as to cause confusion in the mind of the public or deceive purchasers using ordinary care in the selection of the goods.

The Commissioner affirmed the Examiner's decision from which the present appeal was taken.

We are not impressed by the argument that "Sozodont" is a derivative from the two Greek words mentioned and "Zodenta" from combining the Greek and Latin words named. These fanciful etymologies are not apt to occur to the mind of the public nor to deceive purchasers. It is admitted upon this demurrer that during fifteen years the appellee had used the word "Zodenta" as his trade-mark. The two words differ so much in appearance and in sound that ordinary purchasers buying with ordinary caution are not likely to be misled. It is unnecessary to review the authorities. Two trademarks are substantially the same if the resemblance would deceive an ordinary purchaser giving such attention as he usually gives in making a purchase and to cause him to purchase one article mistaking it for the other. (See *Gorham Company* v. *White*, 2 O. G., 592; 14 Wall., 511; *McLean* v. *Fleming*, C. D., 1878, 262; 13 O. G., 913; 96 U. S., 256; *Gaines* v. *Carlton Importation Company*, C. D., 1906, 731; 123 O. G., 1994; 27 App. D. C., 574; *Buchanan-Anderson-Nelson Company* v. *Breen and Kennedy*, C. D., 1906, 750; 124 O. G., 322; 27 App. D. C., 574.) In considering the similarity between "Anderson" and "Henderson" Chief Justice Shepard remarked:

The single question for our determination is whether the resemblance between the two marks as used is calculated to deceive and mislead the public into purchasing Breen and Kennedy's whisky under the belief that it is the whisky of The Buchanan-Anderson-Nelson Co.

It is claimed by the appellants that the two trade-marks here considered by close resemblance are calculated to mislead and deceive and it is further claimed that such an issue should not be decided upon a demurrer. It is said that a demurrer precludes the aid of evidence which might so inform the Office as to make it possible for the Office to intelligently decide this question. We think the Commissioner capable of deciding the resemblance or the difference between these words by the spelling, the appearance and the sound correctly. In the case last cited, as in this, the question arose upon a demurrer to the opposition sustained by the Commissioner of Patents. The Federal cases cited by the appellant on this point apply with great force where novelty or invention is involved and where the court may desire proof to be taken to better instruct the court. Witnesses were not needed to enable the Examiner and Commissioner of Patents to decide that " Zodenta " and " Sozodont " are quite dissimilar and that " Zodenta " is not calculated to mislead or deceive the average purchaser who may seek to buy " Sozodont."

The decision of the Commissioner of Patents *is affirmed* and it is further ordered that this decision be certified to the Commissioner of Patents as provided by law.

[Court of Appeals of the District of Columbia.]

DURYEA AND WHITE *v.* RICE, JR.

Decided December 4, 1906.

(126 O. G., 1357.)

1. INTERFERENCE—PRIORITY—APPEAL TO COURT—OPERATIVENESS.

The Court of Appeals of the District of Columbia will not consider the operativeness of a device disclosed by one of the interfering parties as incident to the main question of priority where that question has been settled in favor of such party by the Patent Office in accordance with the practice of that Office.

2. SAME—SAME—CONSTRUCTIVE REDUCTION TO PRACTICE—DIVISIONAL APPLICATION ENTITLED TO DATE OF ORIGINAL.

An application was filed on June 8, 1895, covering an igniter and an engine. The claims of the engine were erroneously rejected, were canceled, the application was allowed, and subsequently became forfeited. On July 16, 1898, the application was renewed, and additional claims to the engine were included. Division was required between the claims to the igniter and the engine. On March 28, 1899, applicant canceled the claims to the engine, and on April 25, 1899, the Office acted on the remaining claims to the igniter. Subsequently applicant reinstated the claims to the engine, and the Office again permitted him to elect which of the inventions he would prosecute in the application, but afterward informed him that he was bound by the previous cancelation of the claims to the engine, and applicant thereupon, on October 30, 1900, canceled the engine claims, and after several communications between the Office and applicant the application matured into a patent, dated January 12, 1904. On April 16, 1903, applicant filed a divisional application covering the engine. *Held* that the divisional application is entitled to the date of the original application of June 8, 1895, as a constructive reduction to practice.

3. CONTINUING APPLICATION—DIVISIONAL APPLICATION COPENDING WITH ORIGINAL.

A divisional application filed while the original application is pending in the Office covering matter carved out of the original is a continuation of the latter and is entitled to its date as a constructive reduction to practice, even though such divisional application was filed more than two years after an action by the Office on claims which applicant elected to retain in response to a requirement of division.

Mr. F. M. Phelps and *Mr. Frederick S. Lyon* for the appellants.
Mr. Fred. E. Tasker and *Mr. John A. Saul* for the appellee.

SHEPARD, *J.:*

This is an interference proceeding between rival applicants for the invention of an improved gas-engine, the issue in which has been defined in twenty-two counts, as follows:

1. A plurality of compressing-chambers and separate explosion-chambers, free connected piston-heads in the explosion-chambers, and means for supplying explosive charges from the compressing to the explosion chambers and firing the same to propel said piston-heads reciprocally in both directions.

2. A plurality of compressing and explosion chambers, free piston-heads therein, positively connected for mutual reciprocation, means for supplying explosive charges to the compressing-chamber, transferring the charge to the explosion-chamber and firing the same therein to propel the piston-heads reciprocally in both directions.

3. A plurality of explosion-chambers each having inlet and exhaust ports, free piston-heads in said chambers positively connected for mutual reciprocation to open and close said ports, and to supply explosive charges to said chambers through said inlet-ports, means for firing said charges and a free power-transmitting element actuated by the piston-heads.

4. Separate charge compressing and explosion chambers in pairs, free piston-heads, one for each pair, means positively connecting the piston-heads for mutual reciprocation, a free power-transmitting element connected with the piston-head, and means for causing the compression and explosion of a charge by and against each piston-head at each complete reciprocation.

5. The combination with separate charge compressing and explosion chambers arranged in pairs, of free piston-heads, one for each pair, means positively connecting said piston-heads and means for causing the compression and explosion of a charge by and against each piston-head at each complete reciprocation.

6. In an explosion-engine, a body provided with separate charge compressing and explosion chambers, a free piston between said chambers, and a free power-transmitting element connected with the piston.

7. A body having separate charge compressing and explosion chambers in pairs, supply-ports, each connecting a compression-chamber with an explosion-chamber, an inlet for each compression-chamber and an exhaust-port for each explosion-chamber; free piston-heads for said pairs respectively, positively connected for mutual reciprocation, each closing the supply and exhaust ports of its explosion-chamber during compression and explosion; means for causing explosions for propelling the piston-heads respectively, and a free power-transmitting element connected with the piston-head.

8. A body provided with a plurality of separate charge-compressing chambers and explosive-chambers respectively, free piston-heads therein, positively con-

nected for mutual reciprocations, and free power-transmitting element connected with the piston-heads.

9. A body provided with a plurality of alined separate charge-compressing chambers and explosion-chambers respectively, axially-alined free piston-heads in said chambers, positively connected for mutual reciprocation, and a free power-transmitting element connected with the piston-heads and arranged in axial alinement with the chambers.

10. A body provided with a plurality of alined separate charge-compressing chambers and explosion-chambers respectively and a bearing; free piston-heads in the chambers, an axially-movable element in the bearing and means for positively connecting the element with the piston-heads.

11. Separate charge compressing and explosion chambers, piston-heads therefor, positively connected for mutual reciprocation and having variable termination of stroke at both ends; means for supplying explosive charges to said explosion-chambers through said compression-chambers, and means for firing the charges in each explosion-chamber when the piston-head therefor is within the zone of its stroke termination.

12. A plurality of axially-alined close-ended separate charge compressing and explosion chambers in pairs, a free piston-head for each pair, a connector positively connected with said piston-heads, and a free power-transmitting element connected with the connector.

13. Explosion-chambers, means for supplying unignited explosive charges of gas or vapor to and firing the same in said chambers, free piston-heads in said chambers rigidly connected for mutual reciprocation, a free power-transmitting element connected with said piston-heads and a guide for said element.

14. A casing, a cylinder, a piston therein, a second cylinder, a piston therein, a piston-rod connecting said pistons, means for holding a tool connected to said piston-rod, means to cause an explosion of gases against first one and then another of said pistons to reciprocate the same, said cylinders being connected to said casing, said casing being slidably mounted in a frame, and means to slide said casing along said frame.

15. A plurality of cylinders, each of said cylinders containing a piston, said pistons being connected, means for connecting a drill or other tool to said pistons, means for causing an explosion of gases against first one of said pistons and then against another of said pistons to reciprocate the same, a casing, said cylinders being mounted in said casing, a frame, said casing being slidably mounted in said frame, and means to move said casing along said frame.

16. A plurality of cylinders, each of said cylinders containing a piston, said pistons being connected, means for connecting a drill or other tool to said pistons, means for causing an explosion of gases against first one of said pistons and then against another of said pistons, means for cushioning said pistons throughout the length of their stroke, a casing, said cylinders being mounted in said casing, a frame, said casing being slidably mounted in said frame, and means to move said casing along said frame.

17. Two pistons connected by a piston-rod and arranged in their respective cylinders, means for connecting a drill or tool to said piston-rod, means to cause an electric spark and explode a gas alternately against each piston at the end of each stroke, a casing, said cylinders being mounted in said casing, a frame, said casing being slidably mounted in said frame, and means to move said casing along said frame.

18. A plurality of oppositely-arranged cylinders, a piston in each cylinder, said pistons being connected, a charge-receiving chamber in each cylinder, each piston sliding in one of said charge-receiving chambers, an explosion-chamber

opposite each charge-receiving chamber, but separated therefrom by a piston, means for causing an electric spark alternately in each explosion-chamber to explode a gas therein to propel the adjacent piston, a casing, said cylinders being mounted in said casing, a frame, said casing being slidably mounted in said frame, and means to move said casing along said frame.

19. A rear-compression internal-combustion motor having a double-acting un-ignited charge-compressing free piston, and a free power-transmitting element connected therewith.

20. A motor having a self-balanced piston situated between chambers for con-fined compressed explosive charges of gas or vapor, and power-transmitting means connected with such piston.

21. Explosion-chambers, means for supplying unignited explosive charges of gas or vapor to and firing the same in said chambers, free piston-heads in said chambers positively connected for mutual reciprocation, an axially-moving free power-transmitting element connected with said piston-heads and a guide for said element.

22. Explosion-chambers, means for supplying unignited explosive charges of gas or vapor to and firing the same in said chambers, free piston-heads to said chambers rigidly connected for mutual reciprocation, a free power-transmitting element connecting with said piston-heads and a guide for said element.

The interfering applications bear the following filing dates: Duryea and White, March 27, 1902; Rice, April 16, 1903. It appears, however, that Rice had filed his original application for the invention on June 8, 1895, of which this is a division; and this having been re-garded as a continuation of the former, he was considered the senior party. For the reason that the preliminary statement of Duryea and White had failed to overcome the *prima facie* case of Rice made by the filing of said two applications, the Primary Examiner cited them to show cause on or before October 10, 1904, why a decision against them should not be rendered on the record. They did not amend their statement, and in reply to the rule to show cause filed a motion to dis-solve the interference on the following grounds: 1. That no inter-ference in fact exists: 2. That there has been irregularity in declar-ing the interference: 3. That Rice has no right to make the claims in issue: 4. That the structure disclosed by Rice is inoperative. It was also moved that Rice be declared the junior party and the burden of proof shifted to him.

This motion was referred to the Primary Examiner who overruled it on all points in an elaborate decision. An appeal therefrom was taken to the Examiners-in-Chief who dismissed the same on the ground that they had no jurisdiction thereof. This action of the Examiners-in-Chief was in turn affirmed on appeal to the Commis-sioner.

They then renewed their motion to shift the burden of proof, before the Examiner of Interferences, who denied the same, and on the same day, July 8, 1905, awarded priority to Rice, no attempt hav-ing been made by Duryea and White to amend their preliminary statement. Appeal from this decision was taken to the Examiners-in-Chief who affirmed it, holding that Rice was entitled to the filing date of his original application and was therefore the senior party. Under authority conferred by Rule 126 they examined a number of affidavits presented by Duryea and White, and one by Rice, relating to the operativeness of Rice's device; and coming to the conclusion that it was not operative, they called the attention of the Commissioner to the fact as provided in said rule. Pending appeal to the Commissioner from their decision affirming the award of priority to Rice, the latter referred the question of operativeness back to the Primary Examiner for reëxamination and decision. The latter, with a number of expert affidavits before him, reviewed the alleged grounds of inoperativeness at length, and again decided that the device was an operative one. Duryea and White then petitioned the Commissioner to refer the case to the Examiners-in-Chief for rehearing, and were, denied. The Commissioner then affirmed the decision of the Examiners-in-Chief awarding priority to Rice. From that decision this appeal was taken.

But two questions for determination are presented by the elaborate statement of the reasons of appeal: 1. Is the device described in Rice's application an operative one? 2. Is Rice the senior party in interference; or, in other words, is he entitled to date back to the filing of his original application on June 8, 1895?

The question of the operativeness of the device described in the application of the senior party to an interference has been presented to this court twice in different appeals in the same case. (*Dodge* v. *Fowler*, C. D., 1898, 320; 82 O. G., 595; 11 App. D. C., 592; *Fowler* v. *Dodge*, C. D., 1899, 316; 87 O. G., 895; 14 App. D. C., 477.) In the first of those appeals, the Commissioner awarded priority to Fowler, and that decision was reversed on the ground that Fowler, though the first to conceive the invention, had failed to exercise due diligence in the matter of reduction to practice prior to the time that Dodge entered the Office. Dodge was given the benefit of the application as a constructive reduction to practice, but as the Commissioner had incidentally expressed the opinion that Dodge's disclosed device was inoperative, the opinion of the Court concluded with these words:

We do not desire it to be understood by our decision that Dodge is entitled to a patent for his alleged invention. What we decide is simply that, assuming that Fowler and Dodge have made the same invention independently of each other and that Dodge has been the first to reduce it to constructive reduction to practice by his first application for a patent, we think the question of due diligence should be settled in his favor as against Fowler. From the statements of the Commissioner and the Board of Examiners the inference to be drawn would seem to be that Dodge's device is found to be wanting in patentability and therefore that the declaration of interference was based upon mistake or inadvertence. It is true that no motion was made on behalf of Fowler to dissolve the interference; but if under the law and the rules of the Patent Office it is not improper after adjudication of priority of invention to refuse a patent to the successful party in the interference proceedings upon grounds that have first been developed in those proceedings or upon grounds manifested at any time after the declaration of interference, we are not to be understood by this decision as precluding such action by the Office. (C. D., 1808, 320; 82 O. G., 595.)

Upon the return of the case to the Patent Office a motion was made by Fowler to dissolve the interference on the ground that Dodge's device was inoperative. The Commissioner referred the question to the determination of the expert Primary Examiner in the department to which the art belonged, who decided that the device was operative. This decision was treated by the Commissioner as finally settling the question of operativeness in Dodge's favor, and in obedience to the determination of the court on the first appeal, he awarded priority to Dodge. On Fowler's appeal therefrom the question of operativeness was again raised. In its consideration we then said:

Under the special circumstances of this case we will assume that the appeal fully brings before us for determination the whole question of the operativeness of the Dodge device and its patentability. (C. D., 1899, 316; 87 O. G., 805.)

Patentability it is obvious had reference solely to the matter of operativeness. The decision was then affirmed.

Whether a device is operative is a question that necessarily presents itself in every application for a patent referred, in due course of proceeding under the rules of the Office, to the expert Examiner of the class to which the alleged invention belongs. For that reason he is required to be skilled in the particular art. The decision of this Examiner in respect of operativeness and other questions affecting patentability, if favorable to the applicant, is subject to the supervising power of the Commissioner only. It is only where the application is rejected for any reason, that an appeal regularly lies to this court in the last resort.

When an application has been allowed as patentable, and an interference declared, each party may raise the question of the operativeness of his opponent's device by a motion to dissolve the interference as was done in this case. The question goes again to the Primary Examiner for his reconsideration, but no appeal from his decision, at the time it was rendered in this case, lay to the Examiners-in-Chief. The Commissioner alone could review it. The Examiners-in-Chief have the power, under Rule 126, to report to the Commissioner in the course of their decision in an interference case, that the device of either party is, in their opinion, inoperative, or unpatentable for any other reason. The Commissioner may then, and his general practice has been to, refer the question back to the Primary Examiner for further inquiry and determination. As the statement of the case shows, that practice was followed in this proceeding.

In adopting the conclusion of the Primary Examiner in respect of the operativeness of Dodge's device in *Fowler* v. *Dodge, supra*, the question was merely assumed as being before the court by reason of the peculiar conditions of the case.

As the question of the operativeness of one of the devices of the application now in interference is directly presented to us as an incident of the main question, of priority, we hold that it is not one for our consideration. It is, as we have before indicated, a preliminary question determinable, in the first instance, in the case of every application for a patent; and when determined in favor of the applicant is not appealable. When determined in his favor, and an interference is declared thereon with another similarly-allowed application, the same rule applies. Priority of invention is the issue to be determined in an interference proceeding the final decision of which is appealable to this court. The question of operativeness having been settled in accordance with the practice of the Patent Office, cannot again be raised as incidental to the issue of priority, and brought up therewith for review.

This brings us to the consideration of the remaining question: Is Rice entitled to date back to June 8, 1895, when his original application was filed, and thereby become the senior party to the interference? If so entitled, the decision in his favor must be affirmed on the record.

Duryea and White filed no preliminary statement; and are, therefore, confined by the record to the filing of their application, on March 27, 1902. It is stated by the Primary Examiner in his decision upon the motion of Duryea and White to dissolve the interference, and shift the burden of proof, that Rice's original application contained claims to both an igniter and an engine; and that—

the disclosure therein is identical, so far as the issue is concerned, with that of the pending case.

Neither of these statements has been controverted. We adopt the following extract from his decision as stating correctly the proceedings had in regard to that application, and the conclusions deducible therefrom:

Rice's original application was filed June 8, 1895, No. 552,163, and contained claims both to the engine and to the igniter, a fact at that time not regarded as necessitating division. The engine claims were rejected erroneously, it must be held in view of the subsequent decision by the Examiners-in-Chief on the appeal taken by Duryea and White, allowing certain claims now in issue. After prosecution in the usual course, Rice's application was passed for issue June 18, 1897; was allowed to forfeit, and was renewed July 16, 1898, with additional claims to the engine, which as is not denied, it was entirely within the applicant's legal right to present. These additional claims were overlooked by the

Office, and the case passed for issue, July 22, 1898, but almost at once, July 27, 1898, withdrawn, and the engine claims were then rejected on references after several actions. On Dec. 30, 1898, the engine claims were rejected and for the first time division was required between them and claims to the igniter. In responding to this action on March 28, 1899, Rice canceled the engine claims, not it is to be observed as anticipated, but in response to the requirement of division; and upon the case so limited, the Office took action April 25, 1899. It was by acceptance of this action only that Rice completed his election of the igniter, and not as stated by Duryea and White, by his cancelation on March 28, 1899. (*Ex parte Preston*, C. D., 1880, 125; 17 O. G., 853; *Johnston*, C. D., 1887, 64; 40 O. G., 574; *Zabel*, C. D., 1888, 35; 43 O. G., 627; *Maxim*, C. D., 1888, 27; 43 O. G., 506.) At any time up to April 25, 1899, Rice could have reinstated his claims to the engine as a matter of course, and for prosecution by appeal if necessary; after that date he could not do so, unless perhaps by a clear showing of mistake in the cancelation, or by such acquiescence of the Office as actually occurred. He did in fact again present claims to the engine in his amendment of Sept. 28, 1899, responding to the Office action of April 25, 1899. In the Office action (of Nov. 2, 1899) upon the amendment of Sept. 28, 1899, Rice was erroneously informed that he might elect whichever invention he chose, and it was not until Oct. 25, 1900, in the Office letter replying to his amendment of Oct. 12, 1900, that he was informed to the contrary. Upon being so informed, he promptly complied with the Examiner's ruling, viz: Oct. 31, 1900, by canceling the engine claims. It is to be observed that this action by Rice was less than two years from the date of the Office action of April 25, 1899; so that even if he be held to have been concluded by his election in accepting the action of that date, he nevertheless took such proper action as the case required within two years from the date of the last Office action thereon. In other words, he prosecuted his case in good faith by doing all that the law and the rules required up to Oct. 30, 1900, and in view of the Office actions, it was on that date only that he was finally concluded by his election from reinserting claims to the engine. Duryea and White are therefore wholly in error, as well as obscure, in their statement that "since Dec. 30, 1898, John V. Rice has had no right to include in his original or renewed application any claim to the engine structure," since on Dec. 30, 1898, the original application was no longer in being, having been superseded by the renewal, and as to the latter no final election took effect until Oct. 30, 1900.

Although Rice's action of Oct. 30, 1900, canceled the claims to the igniter, certain formal defects remained uncured and being noted in the Office letters of Oct. 31, 1902, and May 13, 1903, were disposed of by amendments April 30, and May 18, 1903, putting the case in condition for allowance, and it matured into the Patent No. 749,324, above referred to.

There is nothing in the foregoing recital tending to show an abandonment of the claim of invention of the engine of the issue, disclosed in Rice's original application.

When the claims therefor were rejected, for the reasons given, he had his election to insist thereon and appeal from a second rejection, or to accept the action of the Patent Office, take his patent for the igniter, and then file another application for a patent for the invention of the engine. Electing to pursue the latter course, he filed the new application, which is substantially a division of the former application, on which the interference was declared with Duryea and

White, and while that original application was still depending in the Office awaiting final action. There is no express limitation in respect of the time within which a divisional application shall be filed in order to relate to, and constitute a continuation of the original application. The rule that seems to prevail in the Patent office is, that to maintain this continuity, it must be filed while the original is depending in the Office. When filed within that time, it has been repeatedly held by different Commissioners of Patents, that the second application stands in lieu of the first to the extent of the matter subtracted from the other. (*Forbes* v. *Thompson*, C. D., 1890, 61; 51 O. G., 297, and cases cited; *Forbes* v. *Thompson*, C. D., 1890, 185; 53 O. G., 2042; *Bundy* v. *Rumbarger*, C. D., 1900, 143; 92 O. G., 2002; *Hopfelt* v. *Read*, C. D., 1903, 319; 106 O. G., 767.) In the decision last cited, Mr. Commissioner Allen, after stating the rule that a complete application warranting the issue of a patent, and unabandoned, is in law a constructive reduction to practice, said:

This is so when two applications are pending contemporaneously and the first is not abandoned, whether the claims are presented in the original application itself or in a later application filed as a division or a continuation of the original application, as in the second place the application dates back to the earlier one. It is only necessary that the description in both applications shall be sufficient to support the claims. The fact that the Office practice may prohibit the prosecution and allowance of the claims in an earlier application does not prevent the applicant from availing himself of the earlier date of filing as his date of constructive reduction to practice when he files a later application containing the same description and the claims based upon the same.

This Court has heretofore held that where an application has been forfeited for failure to pay the fee on allowance of the claims, and the applicant had filed a new application within the prescribed period permitted in such cases, he was entitled to the benefit of his original application as a constructive reduction to practice of the invention set forth therein and afterward embodied in the second application. (*Cain* v. *Park*, C. D., 1899, 278; 86 O. G., 797; 14 App. D. C., 42, 46.)

For a stronger reason, we think that a divisional application, filed while the original application is depending in the Office, must be held a continuation of the latter, and, therefore, to relate back to its filing date.

The situation is not governed by section 4894, Revised Statutes, as contended on behalf of the appellants. That section requires that all applications for patents shall be completed within two years after filing—

and in default, or upon failure of the applicant to prosecute the same within two years after any action therein, of which notice shall have been given to the applicant, they shall be regarded as abandoned by the parties thereto, unless it be shown to the satisfaction of the Commissioner of Patents that such delay was unavoidable.

The section has been held to apply to a case where more than two years had been permitted to elapse between the final rejection of the application and the date of filing a bill in equity to compel issue under section 4915, Revised Statutes. (*Gandy* v. *Marble*, C. D., 1887, 413; 39 O. G., 1423; 122 U. S., 432, 440.)

Let it be granted that the section applies, likewise, in a case where the divisional application shall have been filed after the lapse of two years from the time of final action in the Office upon the original; still the facts of this case do not warrant its application. Two years did not elapse after such final action on the original application before the divisional application was filed. Until all the objections to the final application had been met and overcome, and the same had been finally allowed for patent, Rice was not put finally upon his election to accept the action necessitating the division of his application. When the time arrived for him to take final action, he filed the divisional application with the required diligence, and thereby preserved the continuity of the first for his protection as the inventor of the engine of the issue.

We are of the opinion that the decision appealed from was right, and it will be affirmed. It is so ordered, and the clerk will certify this decision to the Commissioner of Patents as the statute provides. *Affirmed.*

[Court of Appeals of the District of Columbia.]

In re American Circular Loom Company.

Decided December 4, 1906.

(126 O. G., 2191.)

1. TRADE-MARKS—REGISTRATION—SYMBOLS INDICATING MERELY QUALITY NOT REGISTRABLE.

A trade-mark consisting of " flakes of mica impressed or otherwise applied to the external surface of an insulating-tube or tubular coverings for electric wires " was properly refused registration, for the reason that the registration would operate, so far as it could have any effect, to give the applicant a monopoly of conduits or tubular coverings of flake-mica composition. The office of a trade-mark in a legal sense is to point out distinctly the origin or ownership of the article to which it is affixed, or, in other words, to give notice who was the producer. Words, letters, or symbols which indicate merely the quality of the goods to which they are affixed cannot be appropriated as trade-marks. (*Canal Co.* v. *Clark*, 1 O. G., 279; 13 Wall., 311, 322; *Lawrence Mfg. Co.* v. *Tennessee Mfg. Co.*, C. D., 1891, 415; 55 O. G., 1528; 138 U. S., 537, 547.)

2. SAME—SAME—COLOR THE ESSENTIAL FEATURE.

If the sole purpose of the use of the flakes of mica is to obtain protection " for the distinctive appearance obtained by placing bright scales on a dark background," registration was properly denied, on the ground that it was an ingenious attempt to obtain a trade-mark of which color, unconnected with some symbol or design, is the essential feature. (*Leschen Rope Co.* v. *Broderick*, 201 U. S., 166, 171.)

Mr. Wm. S. Hodges, Mr. Everett N. Curtis, and *Mr. Charles F. Perkins* for the appellant.

Mr. Fairfax Bayard for the Commissioner of Patents.

SHEPARD, J.:

The American Circular Loom Company appeals from the refusal of registration of a trade-mark for insulating-tubes or tubular coverings for electric wires, (C. D., 1906, 192; 122 O. G., 1725,) described as follows:

The trade-mark is shown in the accompanying drawing and consists of flakes of mica impressed in or otherwise applied to the external surface of an insulating-tube or tubular coverings for electric wires.

The articles of manufacture, as shown by specimen tube-sections submitted to the Office Examiner, consist of a fiber spiral, a covering of fiber and tape, a protective cotton tube, and an outer covering of the insulating-tube. The applicant states that the trade-mark is usually applied by—

pressing small flakes of mica against the surface of an insulating-tube or tubular covering while the said surface is in a somewhat soft and yielding condition, the flakes being partially embedded in and caused to adhere to the surface of the tube.

The trade-mark is represented also as—

displayed on the goods by attaching thereto a tag having thereon a printed representation of sparkling flakes or scales or a picture of a section of tubing.

Registration was refused by the Examiner on the ground that it—

is not a distinctive mark, indicative of origin and ownership, but a mere representation of the goods—

that is to say, of their character or quality.

Mica is itself an insulating material or substance, and the specimen sections of the tubes appear to the ordinary observer to have a thin covering of it, sparkling more at some points than at others. The trade-mark drawing or print shows something like a similar mica covering with a number of larger sparkling spots distinct from each other.

Regarding this as intended to represent, in probably an exaggerated form, what is shown on the tubes themselves, we agree with the Examiner, that permission to register this trade-mark would be, so far as registration could have any effect, to give the applicant a monopoly of conduits or tubular coverings of flake-mica composition. The office of a trade-mark in a legal sense is to point out distinctly the origin or ownership of the article to which it is affixed; or in other words to give notice who was the producer. Words, letters, or symbols which indicate merely the quality of the goods to which they are affixed cannot be appropriated as trade-marks. (*Canal Co.* v. *Clark*, 1 O. G., 279; 13 Wall., 311, 322; *Lawrence Mfg. Co.* v. *Tennessee Mfg. Co.,*

C. D., 1891, 415; 55 O. G., 1528; 138 U. S., 537, 547.)   This doctrine, in our opinion, was correctly applied to the conditions of this case by the Commissioner in the following words:

Custom and reason require that a trade-mark shall have an existence so distinct from the goods to which it is applied that it will be readily recognized by the public and by purchasers as an arbitrary symbol adopted to authenticate origin.   The surface effect which the applicant calls his trade-mark is not so clearly distinct from the article upon which it appears as to be readily recognized as an arbitrary symbol for this purpose, and in my opinion it would not be so recognized by those not specifically informed.

It is earnestly contended for the appellant that mica is not in fact used, or intended to be represented as used to form any part of the insulating-covering of the tubes, and that the sole purpose of its use, illustrated by the drawing, is to seek protection—

for the distinctive appearance obtained by placing bright scales on a dark background.

Viewed in this light alone, we are of the opinion that registration was properly denied, for it is nothing more, substantially, than an ingenious attempt to obtain a trade-mark of which color, unconnected with some symbol or design, is the essential feature.   (*Leschen Rope Co.* v. *Broderick*, 201 U. S., 166, 171.)   The trade-mark was claimed in that case by a rope manufacturer, and consisted of a red or other distinctively colored streak applied, or woven into a wire rope.   It was also stated that the color of the streak might be varied at will so long as it is distinctive from the color of the body of the rope, though it was usually applied by painting one strand of the rope red.   In delivering the opinion of the Court, Mr. Justice Brown said:

Certainly a trade-mark could not be claimed of a rope, the entire surface of which was colored; and if color be made the essential feature, it should be so defined or connected with some symbol or design, that other manufacturers may know what they may safely do.

After discussing and pointing out the great breadth of the trade-mark as described, it was further said:

Whether mere color can constitute a valid trade-mark may admit of doubt. Doubtless it may be, if it be impressed in a particular design, as a circle, square, triangle, a cross, or a star.   But the authorities do not go farther than this.   In the case of Handon's trade-mark, (37 Ch. Div., 112.) in which a trade-mark was claimed for a red, white and blue label, in imitation of the French tricolor, for French coffee, it was held not entitled to registration under the English statute which requires a trade-mark to be distinctive in order to be valid.   The court remarked as follows: " It is the plain intention of the act that, where the distinction of a mark depends upon color, that it will not do.   You may register a mark which is otherwise distinctive, in color, and that gives you the right to use it in any color you like; but you cannot register a mark of which the only distinction is the use of a color, because practically under the terms of the act, that would give you a monopoly of all the colors of the rainbow."

The English case cited and quoted above arose under an act which provided for the registration of a trade-mark in color. (See also, *Putnam Nail Co.* v. *Dulany*, 140 Pa. St., 205; *Von Mumm* v. *Kirk*, C. D., 1890, 243; 50 O. G., 1134; 40 Fed. Rep., 589.)

For the reasons given the decision will be affirmed.

The clerk is directed also to certify this decision to the Commissioner of Patents as the law provides. *Affirmed.*

[Court of Appeals of the District of Columbia.]

THE SCHUSTER CO. *v.* MULLER.

Decided December 4, 1906.

(126 O. G., 2192.)

1. TRADE-MARKS—PRIORITY—GOODS OF THE SAME DESCRIPTIVE PROPERTIES.

> In determining the question of priority of adoption and use of a trade-mark for bitters made from certain roots and barks and bottled, evidence of the use of such mark on a package containing a mixture of ground roots and bark with directions how to make the bitters by steeping them in Holland gin may be properly considered, the goods being of the same descriptive properties.

2. SAME—DECEPTIVE MARKS.

> Where any symbol or label claimed as a trade-mark is so worded as to contain a distinct assertion which is false, no property right can be claimed, nor can the right to the exclusive use of it be maintained by a court of equity. Courts of equity will not interfere by injunction where there is any lack of proof in the applicant's case or any misrepresentation in his trade-mark or label, nor will the courts uphold in any one a privilege of deceiving the public. An exclusive privilege to deceive the public is not one that a court of equity can sanction nor one which the Commissioner of Patents should aid.

3. SAME—SAME—EVIDENCE OF DECEPTION INSUFFICENT.

> Evidence submitted by a party to a trade-mark interference tending to show that the mark as used by the opposing party was deceptive considered and *Held* insufficient to establish the fact.

Mr. A. E. Wallace for the appellant.
Mr. F. M. Phelps for the appellee.

McComas, *J.:*

This appeal is from a decision of the Commissioner of Patents (C. D., 1906, 252; 123 O. G., 996;) concerning a trade-mark for bitters. Wm. H. Muller filed his application October 5, 1905, and therein claimed to have continuously used the word " Bismarck " as his trade-mark for bitters since January, 1892. On May 25, 1905, the Schuster Company filed its application for a trade-mark consisting of the word " Bismarck " and the picture of Bismarck inclosed in a circle, which trade-mark for bitters it claimed to have continuously used since the year 1895.

The question is, priority of adoption and use of the word " Bismarck " as a trade-mark for bitters. The Schuster Company as a corporation succeeded to a copartnership of the same name in 1900 and to the title of the firm to all trade-marks. The firm conducted the business from 1890 until 1900. The company is a wholesale dealer in wines and liquors.

Edward L. Schuster, its vice-president, testified that the firm adopted the mark, he should judge, about 1892 and it was used while the firm still sold its goods at retail, and his company he thinks has been engaged in the wholesale business since 1898. The only book entry he produced was the entry of a sale on March 17, 1899, of one gallon of " Bismarck Pepsin Bitters " to a clergyman, although he said the company had been selling to the trade, of late years, about two thousand cases annually; he knew that the firm had sold goods under this trade-mark seven or eight years previous to the time, 1898, when the company engaged in the wholesale business. Upon cross-examination he said he could not accurately fix the date, it might have been six, or seven, or eight, or nine years prior to the entry into the wholesale business. The firm kept no cash-books, no entry of sales while in the retail business.

Charles F. Schuster, aged twenty-nine years, secretary of the company, testified that for eleven years he had been connected with the business of the company; since he was eighteen, he had been engaged with it in a business capacity; previous to that, while going to school, he had assisted in the retail sales after school hours, and he knew that the firm had used this trade-mark for a good many years prior to his connection with the company. This witness had signed the application fixing the date of use as 1895 and he said he had fixed the date without any research, because he remembered that the firm sold the goods under this trade-mark at that time. Upon cross-examination he said that as far as he can remember the firm used the trade-mark about sixteen years back while he was going to school, but he could not produce any records to confirm his memory. The vice-president, he said, had fixed the date for this application.

The third and last witness was Jacob Schuster, aged twenty-one years, who for four years has been compounder for The Schuster Company, and during all that time this trade-mark had been used. He was positive of its use in 1899 when the witness was fourteen years old, for then he had started to assist in the business after school hours.

The Schuster Company in its application claimed continuous use since 1895, while Muller, the appellee, claimed continuous use since 1892. When The Schuster Company endeavored to prove adoption and use of the trade-mark, prior to January, 1892, all three witnesses were members of the Schuster family and officers of the company, and king together their statements, their best recollection appears to be that the trade-mark was used six or seven, or eight, or nine years prior to 1898, when the retail business and the wholesale business commenced. In January, 1892, one of these witnesses was a boy of fourteen, another a child of eight years of age, and the only record of sale produced was of a sale of a gallon of bitters in March, 1899. All of these witnesses are parties in interest.

Muller, the other applicant, in his own behalf testified that he adopted this mark in December, 1891. He registered it in the trade-mark record in January, 1892, and in that month commenced selling a mixture of ground roots and barks to be used in making bitters, each package being inclosed in a wrapper, bearing the words " Bismarck Bitters " and other printed matter, including directions for making the bitters by steeping the contents in Holland gin. In 1894, he commenced selling the bitters in liquid form, each bottle having a label bearing the identical label accompanying the application for registration. A package of the mixture of roots and barks, and a bottle of the bitters each bearing the label " Bismarck Bitters " were introduced in evidence. He also introduced his ledger, which shows sales of " Bismarck Bitters " during 1892, 1893, 1894, 1895.

One Kennedy, of the firm of Charles N. Crittenton and Company, testified that the firm books show that his firm purchased " Bismarck Bitters " from Muller, first on May 14, 1892, and at other times during that year and the two following years and regularly since 1894. He produced his firm's catalogue, listing Muller's " Bismarck Bitters " in the issues for the years 1893 and 1894, and he identified the bottle bearing the label " Bismarck Bitters."

Gazley, a printer, testified that on January 5, 1892, he had printed the identical wrapper with the mark " Bismarck Bitters," and also circulars containing it and again had printed circulars on January 13, 1892, and had printed the like in each of the next succeeding years. He identified the label as one he had printed on the package of ground roots and barks in 1892.

Lowenherz, an advertising agent, employed by Muller, testified that he had caused advertisements of the " Bismarck Bitters " to be published in the German *Morgen Journal* from April 18, 1892, up to October of that year, and he identified clippings as such printed advertisements and he also identified like advertisements in the *Evening Sun*, probably in 1892 or 1893, in *Frank Leslies* in 1892, and in the *Evening World* as early as June, 1894. Refreshed by the advertisements he had clipped from the newspapers and placed in his scrap-book, the witness testified from personal recollection. This evidence on the part of Muller, who produced in addition to his own recollection his ledger and also the important testimony of three di' interested witnesses, clearly establishes that as early as January, 189 Muller adopted the trade-mark in issue and has used it continuous since that time. The mixture of ground roots and bark having on the wrapper of the package containing the mixture, directions how to make the bitters by steeping the contents in Holland gin, was properly considered by the Commissioner to be goods of the same descriptive property as bitters made from these roots and barks and bottled. We have stated in detail the testimony produced in support of each application and it so clearly preponderates in favor of the prior adoption and use of this trade-mark by Muller, the appellee, that it needs no further discussion. The Schuster Company have failed to establish by clear and convincing proof that they were using the mark prior to January 5, 1892, and, as we have said, the proof is convincing that ever since that date, when Muller adopted it, he has been continuously using this trade-mark for bitters.

The appellant evidently appreciating the weakness of its testimony, introduced testimony the object of which was to show that the printed matter on the label of Muller is deceptive.

The Examiner of Interferences decided that the testimony does not show such deception and the Commissioner of Patents concluded that the contention of The Schuster Company that the bitters of Muller are without effect upon the kidneys and are not proper medicine for children should not deprive Muller of the trade-mark, because the truth of these contentions is not satisfactorily established. Recent salutary laws restrain manufacturers and dealers from imposing upon the public, preparations injurious to health. The courts grow increasingly careful and cautious in restraining false representations to the public in vending such preparations. Where any symbol or label claimed as a trade-mark is so worded as to contain a distinct assertion which is false, no property right can be claimed nor can the right to the exclusive use of it be maintained by a court of equity. Courts of equity will not interfere by injunction where there is any lack of proof in the applicant's case or any misrepresentation in his trade-mark or label, nor will the courts uphold in any one a privilege of deceiving the public. An exclusive privilege to deceive the public is not one that a court of equity can sanction nor one which the Commissioner of Patents should aid. While there is a right of property in a trade-mark in connection with a vendible commodity it is essential that the vender should not in his trade-mark or in the printing connected therewith, or in the business use of the trade-mark, himself be guilty of any false or misleading representations. It is settled that where the owner of such a trade-mark applies for an injunction to restrain another, his petition will be denied. (See *Worden* v. *California Fig Syrup Co.*, 187 U. S., 516; *California Fig Syrup Co.* v. *Stearns & Co.*, 73 Fed. Rep., 812; *Leathercloth Co.* v. *American Leathercloth Co.*, 4 De Gex, J. & S., 7; *Eleven House of Lords Cas.*, 523; *Fetridge* v. *Wells*, 4 Abbott,

N. Y., 144; *Manhattan Medicine Co.* v. *Wood*, C. D., 1883, 268; 23 O. G., 1925; 108 U. S., 218; *Siegert et al.* v. *Gandolfi et al.*, 139 Fed. Rep., 917.)

These considerations require us to carefully scrutinize the testimony of the two witnesses produced by the appellant upon the point of deceptive use of this trade-mark by Muller.

John G. Spenzer, a chemist in Cleveland, Ohio, of twenty years' experience, testified that he had analyzed a bottle of Muller's " Bismarck Bitters " and found that it contained cardamom, calamus, galangal, aloes, capsicum, coriander, rhubarb, sugar, alcohol and water. The alcohol was forty-two and five-tenths per cent. This bottle was not purchased directly from Muller, the manufacturer. The Schuster Company notified the witness that the package would arrive from New York and he received it by express from Hageman's pharmacy in that city with the seal unbroken. Counsel after cross-examination appear to be satisfied that the bottle and the contents were the same Muller usually sold under this trade-mark. Dr. J. B. McGee, a physician of Cleveland, Ohio, was asked respecting the contents of the bottle as stated by the preceding witness and to tell whether or not in his opinion (following the language on the printed label on the bottle under the words " Bismarck Bitters ") a cordial-glassful of bitters taken once or twice a day from a bottle containing the contents just read to the witness, is a tonic preparation, or a small wineglassful before breakfast or at bedtime is a health-preserving preparation, and for children in proportion, beneficial or otherwise for regulating the bowels, eliminating tendency to catarrh of the stomach and liver and diseases of the kidney; and Doctor McGee testified that the bitters would be stomachic and the action good in dyspepsia; that the only agents mentioned therein that would have any special effect upon the liver are aloes and rhubarb and that he did not recall any ingredient that has any action upon the kidneys. As he recalled it, the physician pronounced it a very good bitter. He would not use the preparation as a routine remedy for children for he would have no alcohol. The physician stated that possibly twenty per cent. of alcohol was necessary to preserve the bitters, and any percentage beyond that would be a stimulant and that this bitter tonic appeared to contain the ordinary ingredients of bitters.

Upon this testimony we cannot say that the Commissioner of Patents erred in determining that the contention of the appellant that the printed matter upon Muller's label is deceptive, was not satisfactorily established. The order of the Commissioner of Patents in so far as it relates to this interference is affirmed and this opinion will be certified to the Commissioner of Patents in accordance with law. *Affirmed.*

[Court of Appeals of the District of Columbia.]

IN RE DUNCAN, PRICHARD, AND MACAULEY.

Decided December 4, 1906.

(126 O. G., 2592.)

CLAIMS—NEW MATTER—"MOUNTED UPON" CONSTRUED.

A claim for a latch mounted upon a mold-blade section of a type-mold, *Held* to cover matter not within the original disclosure, the words "mounted upon" not being properly descriptive of a part which merely rides in or over another in a slot for the purpose.

Mr. J. B. Church and *Mr. Melville Church* for the appellant.
Mr. Fairfax Bayard for the Commisioner of Patents.

SHEPARD, *J.:*

This is an appeal from a decision of the Commissioner of Patents (C. D., 1906, 348; 124 O. G., 1207) refusing the thirty-sixth claim for a patent for improvement in type-casting machines. The claim reads as follows:

36. In a type-mold such as described, provided with a sectional mold-blade and in combination therewith a latch mounted upon one mold-blade section in position to engage a shoulder on the other section when their casting-faces are in alinement, and an actuating connection coupled with one mold-blade section.

The invention of the application is described by the Examiner in the following words:

The invention, generally, relates to type-casting machines wherein it is possible to cast full-body type or short or low quads and spaces, and to this end the mold-blade, as disclosed in each application, is divided longitudinally into sections, an upper and a lower section, the upper section resting upon and capable of movement independent of the lower section. When the mold is employed for casting full-body or character type, the two mold-sections are maintained in a fixed relation to each other so that their casting-faces will be in the same plane, but when short or low quads and spaces are required the sections are uncoupled so as to be capable of independent movement, the one to cut off or close the matrix end of the mold, and the other to measure the width of the mold-cavity below or in rear of the cut-off.

By the Examiner's decision, claims 32, 33, 34 and 35, as well as 36, of the appellants' application were rejected. On appeal to the Examiners-in-Chief, he was reversed as to all but No. 36. Their decision was in turn affirmed by the Commissioner. It appears from the record that there had been several interferences in the Patent Office relating to applications for improvements in type-casting machines, to some of which the appellants were parties. One Eschinger, one of the parties to one of the proceedings, it seems, had a claim substantially the same as No. 36. In those proceedings the Examiner refused to dissolve the interference in which Eschinger was a party. ⟶ the ground that the original disclosure in the appellants' applica- ⟶ did not offer a sufficient basis for the structure as embodied in the ⟶ in interference.

April 21, 1905, by amendment the appellants presented the afore-mentioned claims, 32 to 36 inclusive. The description in their orig-inal application, on which these claims are founded, is the following:

The cross-pin 12 through which motion is transmitted from slide 2 to the mold-blade, in dimensioning the mold, is utilized for effecting this shifting of the sections one upon the other, to which end said cross-pin is rendered movable in its bearings and caused to act upon the upper section 10, to advance and re-tract it as desired. In the present embodiment the cross-pin 12 is longitudinally movable and is formed in cross-section with a straight section 13 riding in a slot 14 in the lower mold-blade section 11, and a flanged or cam section 15 riding in a slot 16 in the upper section 10.

The settled limitation upon the amendment of applications in re-spect of claims is, that there must be a basis for them in the descrip-tion and specifications of the application as originally filed. (*In re Dilg*, C. D., 1905, 620; 115 O. G., 1067; 25 App. D. C., 9.) The bur-den is upon the appellants, therefore, to show that this claim 36, which is the only one now in issue, was within the description afore-said. There was a difference between the decision of the Examiners-in-Chief and the Commissioner as regards the latch mechanism in the mold-board section. He sustained their decision denying the claim, however, making the following statement:

I am not convinced, however, that the latch may be considered as being " mounted upon one mold-blade section," as stated in this claim. The latch or cross-pin is described by applicants as " * * * movable in its bearings and caused to act upon the upper section 10, to advance and retract it as desired. In the present embodiment the cross-pin 12 is longitudinally movable and is formed in cross-section with a straight section 13 riding in a slot 14 in the lower mold-blade section 11."

It seems clear from applicants' disclosure that the bearings for the latch are formed in the arms of the slide 2 and the straight section 13 of the latch merely rides in the slot in the mold-blade. Manifestly, the latch is " mounted upon " the slide and not on the mold-blade, as required by this claim.

The ambiguity in the description in the application as applied to this particular mechanism, is apparently due to the fact that this claim was not in mind when the application was prepared, and has been suggested by the claim of a conflicting application. Without going into the question at length, we think it sufficient to say that we are satisfied with the statement which has been quoted above from the Commissioner's decision. The expression " mounted upon " seems to have an ordinary meaning in machine construction. The thing mounted upon another must be borne or supported by it. Mere riding in or over another in a slot for the purpose, although operating in connection therewith, is not equivalent to being mounted thereon.

Finding no error in the decision rejecting claim 36, it will be af-firmed. It is ordered that the clerk certify this decision to the Com-missioner of Patents, as required by law. *Affirmed.*

[Court of Appeals of the District of Columbia.]

IN RE VOLKMANN AND TRUAX.

Decided December 4, 1906.

(126 O. G., 2503.)

PATENTABILITY—NON-INVENTION—CARRYING FORWARD AN OLD IDEA.

Where the prior art disclosed a train of gearing positively connecting the hour, minute, and second hands of a time mechanism, whereby the rotation of one would cause the proper relative movement of the others, and it also disclosed a winding and setting mechanism controlling the proper relative rotation of the minute and hour hands, it did not amount to invention to insert an additional gear and pinion in the latter mechanism to secure the proper position of the second-hand with relation to the minute and hour hands upon operation of the setting mechanism.

Mr. Perry B. Turpin for the appellant.
Mr. Fairfax Bayard for the Commissioner of Patents.

McComas, *J.:*

This is an appeal from the decision of the Commissioner of Patents (C. D., 1906, 372; 124 O. G., 1843,) refusing to issue a patent to the appellants upon certain alleged improvements in timepieces. The appellants' specification states that the alleged invention relates to watches, clocks and like timepieces and its object is to provide certain new and useful improvements in timepieces whereby the second-hand can be set from the stem and at any point desired and the second-hand agrees at all times with the minute-hand. The appellants have set forth so much of the structure shown and described as in their view constitutes their alleged invention, in seven claims. Each of the three tribunals of the Patent Office have rejected the claims, deciding that none of them involve patentable invention in view of the state of the art. The seven claims are as follows:

1. In a stem-setting timepiece, the combination of a gear-wheel forming a part of a dial-train, minute-hand arbor, a pinion secured on said arbor and meshing with the gear-wheel of the dial-train, an arbor, a pinion loose on the arbor and carrying a gear-wheel, a second pinion on the arbor and carrying a second-hand, an intermediate gear meshing with the first-named pinion of the said arbor and the pinion of the minute-hand arbor, and a loosely-mounted pinion meshing with the gear-wheel carried by the pinion on the second arbor and carrying a gear-wheel meshing with the second-hand pinion.

2. In a stem-setting timepiece, the combination of a gear-wheel carrying a pinion and forming a part of a dial-train, a minute-hand arbor, a pinion secured to the arbor and meshing with the gear-wheel of the dial-train, an hour-hand gear-wheel loose on the minute-hand arbor and meshing with the pinion carried by the gear-wheel of the dial-train, a second arbor, a pinion loose on the arbor and carrying a gear-wheel, a second-hand pinion also on the said second arbor,

an intermediate gear between the pinion of the minute-hand arbor and the pinion of the second arbor carrying the gear-wheel, and a loose pinion meshing with the gear-wheel of the second arbor and carrying a gear-wheel meshing with the second-hand pinion.

3. In a stem-setting timepiece, the combination of the minute-hand arbor, a pinion secured thereto, a gear-wheel loose on the arbor, a gear-wheel meshing with the pinion of the said arbor and forming part of a dial-train, said gear-wheel being provided with a pinion meshing with the gear-wheel of the arbor, a setting mechanism for the said gear-wheel, a pinion carrying a second-hand, and gearing between the said pinion and the pinion on the minute-hand arbor.

4. In a stem-setting timepiece, the combination of a gear-wheel forming a part of a dial-train, a setting mechanism for the said gear-wheel, a minute-hand arbor, a pinion secured on said arbor and meshing with the gear-wheel of the dial-train, an arbor, a pinion loose on the arbor and carrying a gear-wheel, a second pinion on the arbor and carrying a second-hand, an intermediate gear meshing with the first-named pinion of the said arbor and the pinion of the minute-hand arbor, and a loosely-mounted pinion meshing with the gear-wheel carried by the pinion on the second arbor and carrying a gear-wheel meshing with the second-hand pinion.

5. In a stem-setting timepiece, the combination of a gear-wheel carrying a pinion and forming a part of a dial-train, a setting mechanism for the said gear-wheel, a minute-hand arbor, a pinion secured to the arbor and meshing with the gear-wheel of the dial-train, an hour-hand gear-wheel loose on the minute-hand arbor and meshing with the pinion carried by the gear-wheel of the dial-train, a second arbor, a pinion loose on the arbor and carrying a gear-wheel, a second-hand pinion also on the said second arbor, an intermediate gear between the pinion of the minute-hand arbor and the pinion of the second arbor carrying the gear-wheel, and a loose pinion meshing with the gear-wheel of the second arbor and carrying a gear-wheel meshing with the second-hand pinion.

6. In a stem-setting timepiece, the combination of a setting mechanism including a pinion, a gear-wheel forming a part of a dial-train and with which the pinion of the setting mechanism is adapted to mesh, a pinion carried by the gear-wheel, a minute-hand arbor, a pinion secured to the arbor and meshing with the gear-wheel of the dial-train, an hour-hand gear-wheel loose on the minute-hand arbor and meshing with the pinion carried by the gear-wheel of the dial-train, a second arbor, a pinion loose on the arbor and carrying a gear-wheel, a second-hand pinion also on the said second arbor, an intermediate gear between the pinion of the minute-hand arbor and the pinion of the second arbor carrying the gear-wheel, and a loose pinion meshing with the gear-wheel of the second arbor and carrying a gear-wheel meshing with the second-hand pinion.

7. In a stem-setting timepiece, the combination of a setting mechanism including a pinion, and a train of gearing forming a part of a dial-train for operating the minute, hour, and second hands and with the first wheel of which the pinion of the setting mechanism is adapted to mesh, whereby provision is made for causing the second-hand to move at all times in unison with the minute-hand, whether the watch is running or is being set.

Upon this appeal, appellants do not appear to insist upon claims 3 and 7. Concerning claim 7, the Examiners-in-Chief remark that there is no invention in adding a setting mechanism such as shown in the patent to Thommen to the clock mechanism shown in Crook's patent. And the mechanism covered by claim 3 except for the setting mechanism is shown in the Crook patent and it does not appear inventive to apply a setting mechanism to Crook's device.

Four patents were cited as references and the patent of Crook appeared to all the tribunals to be an anticipation of the mechanism defined in appellants' claims for Crook's patent discloses the positive gear connection between the minute-hand and the second-hand.

Now the Crook patent for an electric clock, shows a clock in which the minute, hour and second hands are so connected by a system of gears and pinions, substantially the same system as that of the appellants, as to cause each of the three hands to rotate at the proper speed relatively. To set any one of the hands of the clock is to set each of the other hands. The Thommen patent shows a watch with a stem setting and winding mechanism, for the minute and hour hands substantially the same as that of the appellants. In the case before us, claim 1 covers the train of gearing connecting the second and minute hands, and claim 2 covers the gearing connecting the minute-hand with the hour-hand. By inserting an additional gear and pinion wheel in a train of such wheels arranged to transmit motion the appellant has not achieved invention, and the Commissioner believes that the appellants' device possesses no particular advantage over that of Crook. The remaining claims include in addition to the mechanism covered by claims 3 and 7 the intermediate gear and the pinion and gear wheel as a part of the train of gearing. While the specific detail of the train of gears connecting the pinion of the minute-hand with the second-hand does not appear in the reference cited, the Patent Office tribunals are unanimous in the opinion that it required no more than the skill of a mechanic familiar with clock and watch making to provide the needed pinions and gears of proper size and the necessary number of teeth, arranged in relation to each other, so as to include the mechanism within the desired dimensions. The appellants' application is not limited and may be applied to a clock or to a watch. The opinions cited by appellants' counsel state legal propositions to which we may give our assent. None of them, however, remove the chief difficulty, which is that the particular claims before us fail to disclose invention when compared with the state of the art disclosed by the patents of Crook and Thommen.

The decision of the Commissioner of Patents *is hereby affirmed* and this opinion will be certified to the Commissioner of Patents in accordance with law.

[Court of Appeals of the District of Columbia.]

SOBEY v. HOLSCLAW.

Decided June 6, 1906.

(126 O. G., 3041.)

1. INTERFERENCE — DISSOLUTION — APPEAL FROM AFFIRMATIVE DECISION ON PATENTABILITY.

Neither the rules of the Patent Office nor any section of the Revised Statutes provide for nor permit appeals from a decision rendered upon a motion for dissolution affirming the patentability of the issue. (*Allen v. Lowry*, C. D., 1905, 643; 116 O. G., 2253.)

2. SAME—APPEAL ON PRIORITY—PATENTABILITY OF ISSUE.

Where the patentability of the claims of an interference issue has been favorably passed upon by the Primary Examiner *ex parte* and also *inter partes* upon a motion to dissolve, from whose affirmative decision in the latter case no right of direct appeal is given either by the patent statutes or the rules of the Patent Office, and both the Examiner of Interferences and the Examiners-in-Chief have refused to direct the attention of the Commissioner, under Rule 126, to the fact that the claims were unpatentable, it cannot be successfully maintained that the Commissioner of Patents decided the question of priority without first determining and deciding that the subject-matter was patentable.

3. SAME—SAME—REVIEW BY COMMISSIONER OF DECISION OF EXAMINER ON PATENTABILITY OR RIGHT TO MAKE CLAIMS.

The Primary Examiners, who are given statutory authority to decide questions of patentability, are under the supervision of the Commissioner, and it would seem to be not only his right but his duty to correct any manifest error committed by any of the Primary Examiners relative to the patentability of a supposed invention or of the right of an applicant to claim it whenever such error was called to his attention. To warrant any action on his part in such a case, the error must be so gross that it would be a wrong to the public to permit a patent to issue. It manifestly should not be based upon a mere difference of opinion.

4. SAME—SAME—ADOPTION BY COMMISSIONER OF VIEWS OF SUBORDINATE TRIBUNALS.

Where the question of the patentability of the claims of the issue has been repeatedly raised before the subordinate tribunals of the Patent Office and is again raised upon appeal to the Commissioner on priority, the adoption by the Commissioner of the views of the subordinate tribunals is a sufficient determination by him of the question so far as it is necessary to be determined in an interference proceeding.

5. SAME—SAME—CONSIDERATION OF PATENTABILITY BY COURT.

Where the Primary Examiner has held claims to be patentable and the Examiner of Interferences and the Examiners-in-Chief have omitted or declined to call the attention of the Commissioner to the unpatentability of the issue or where the Commissioner has declined to review the decision of the Primary Examiner after his attention has been called to the alleged unpatentability of the issue, the Court of Appeals of the District of Columbia should hold the question of patentability to be settled, except in an extraordinary case. The statute does not provide for an appeal to the court from a ruling by the Commissioner or of any subordinate tribunals affirming the patentability of a claimed invention. It is only from a decision adverse to the patentability of a claim that an appeal will lie.

6. ISSUES—CONSTRUED IN LIGHT OF APPLICATION FIRST CONTAINING THEM.

Since the claims of an interference issue are to be construed in the light of the application of the party first making them, it would be manifestly improper for the Commissioner of Patents to read into them for any purpose limitations not disclosed in the application of such party.

7. JURISDICTION—COURT OF APPEALS OF DISTRICT OF COLUMBIA—CONTROL OVER PROCEDURE BEFORE COMMISSIONER.

On an appeal from the Commissioner of Patents to the Court of Appeals of the District of Columbia on the question of priority of invention the court has no power to hold that the Commissioner has committed an error for which a case should be reversed because of a claim that he refused to permit counsel to be heard in support of a given contention. The court cannot in such a proceeding control his action in a discretionary matter such as the extent of oral argument he will permit at a hearing of an interference.

8. JURISDICTION OF COMMISSIONER AFTER APPEAL TO COURT ON PRIORITY.

After a decision of the court of appeals on the question of priority the Commissioner of Patents may refuse a patent to the successful interferant.

Mr. George P. Fisher, Jr., Mr. Percy B. Hills, and *Mr. Melville Church* for Sobey.

Mr. E. M. Kitchin and *Mr. E. T. Fenwick* for Holsclaw.

DUELL, *J.:*

This case comes to us upon an appeal from the decision of the Commissioner of Patents (C. D., 1905, 523; 119 O. G., 1922,) awarding priority of invention to Holsclaw of certain improvements in planters which are set forth in the following issues:

1. In a planter, a cultivator and a seed-dropper, and a vertically-movable bar capable of lifting both said cultivator and the said dropper.

2. A seed-planter, comprising a seed-dropping mechanism, a reciprocating standard carrying a furrow-opener in front of the same, means for raising and lowering the said standard and furrow-opener simultaneously, said means also operating to raise the seed-dropping mechanism out of operative position.

3. A seed-planter provided with a reciprocating vertically-adjustable standard, antifriction means for guiding the same in its movement and yet capable of exerting a pull upon the same, and means engaging the standard for raising and lowering it.

4. A seed-planter provided with a vertically-movable seed-dropping mechanism, a chute therefor, a soil-preparing mechanism, a reciprocating standard carrying the same, a draw-bar engaging said standard, and means for adjusting the standard vertically with respect to said draw-bar.

5. A seed-planter provided with a reciprocating vertically-adjustable standard, antifriction means for guiding the same in its movements and means for raising and lowering the said standard.

. A planter comprising a rigid frame, pivoted frames carried thereby, a ler carried by one of said pivoted frames, covering means carried by the r pivoted frame and means for elevating one pivoted frame whereby the pivoted frame carrying the seeder will also be elevated for interrupting the operation of the seeder.

7. In a seeding-machine, the combination of a main frame supported on the carrying-wheels, a supplemental frame pivoted to the main frame and extending rearwardly of such pivotal connection, a furrow-opener, and a seed-box and covering-shovels adapted to be elevated when said supplementary frame is elevated, and a sweep supported in advance of said furrow-opener and in line therewith.

8. In a seed-machine, the combination of a main frame, a supplementary frame pivotally connected therewith, and free to swing vertically therein, a furrow-opener, a seedbox adapted to be moved when the frame is swung upon its pivot, covering-shovels carried by said supplementary frame, and a sweep arranged in advance of the furrow-opener.

The record discloses that Holsclaw, the senior party, filed his application September 10, 1903, while that of Sobey, the junior party, was not filed until June 22, 1904. The issues are claims made by Holsclaw and suggested by the Primary Examiner to Sobey, who filed an amendment to his application incorporating therein the suggested claims as claims 44 to 51 inclusive. In filing this amendment Sobey stated that he did so—

Without prejudice to our right to make motion for dissolution of the interference, when declared, should careful search and study show that the proposed claims (1) are unpatentable for lack of novelty or (2) raise no real conflict, as applied to the rival devices taken in conjunction with other inventions existing prior.

The interference having been declared, and the preliminary statements filed and opened, it was found that Sobey had failed to overcome Holsclaw's record date so that the Examiner of Interferences, in conformity with the rules of the Patent Office thereto pertaining notified the parties that unless Sobey should show good and sufficient cause before a given date judgment on the record would be rendered against him.

Thereupon Sobey moved to dissolve the interference upon the grounds that, no interference in fact existed, irregularity in its declaration which would preclude a proper determination of the question of priority, that the issues were unpatentable, and that Holsclaw had no right to make the claims. The motion was referred to and heard by the Primary Examiner, who filed an opinion specifically passing upon each ground upon which the motion was based. He denied the motion save as to count 5 which he held to be unpatentable in view of a prior patent. From this decision an appeal was taken to the Commissioner of Patents upon grounds stated in the latter's opinion, which also gives his reasons for affirming the decision of the Primary Examiner. The Commissioner said:

The grounds upon which this appeal is taken are that the Examiner erred in holding that there has been no such irregularity in declaring the interference as to preclude the proper determination of the question of priority, and that interference in fact exists between the inventions claimed in the respective applications.

Considering the question of interference in fact, it is found that both inventions relate to improvements in the type of agricultural implements known as planters. The machines disclosed by the respective parties to this interference, though differing in details of construction, are practically identical as to their main features, and they are used to accomplish the same purpose. The inventions defined in the counts of the issue cover the general combinations of elements and are not limited to the specific details which constitute the differences between the machines. The Examiner in his decision has set forth very specifically the structures of the two machines and had also correctly stated the functions which are accomplished in operating the mechanisms claimed. A comparison of the counts of the issue with the disclosures in both applications makes it clear that these counts have the same meaning when applied to each structure, and, consequently, there is an interference in fact. The reasons for this conclusion have been clearly stated by the Examiner in his decision and to state them again would be mere repetition of what has already been well said. No irregularity appears in the declaration of the interference and none has been pointed out by the appellant.

It will be noted that no appeal was taken from the Examiner's decision holding the issues, save the fifth, to be patentable and that Holsclaw had a right to make the claims. Neither the rules of the Patent Office nor any section of the Revised Statutes provide for nor permit such appeals. (*Allen* v. *Lowry*, C. D., 1905, 643; 116 O. G., 2253.)

The interference proceedings were thereupon continued by the Examiner in Interferences who awarded priority of invention of all of the issues, save the one formerly declared unpatentable, to Holsclaw. Thereupon Sobey moved the Examiner of Interferences to vacate the judgment in Holsclaw's favor, to suspend the proceedings and to direct the attention of the Commissioner of Patents to certain reasons why the interference should be dissolved. These reasons again attacked the patentability of the issues. This motion was stated to be made under the authority of Patent Office Rule 126 which in substance provides that the Examiner of Interferences or the Board of Examiners-in-Chief, either before or in their decision on the question of priority, may direct the attention of the Commissioner to any matter not relating to priority which may have come to their notice, and which, in their opinion, establishes the fact that no interference exists, or that there has been irregularity in declaring the same, or which amounts to a statutory bar to the grant of a patent to either of the parties for the claim or claims in interference.

The Interference Examiner in denying the motion said:

The matters now set up as anticipating the issue were not called to the attention of the Examiner of Interferences before the decision on priority and not until the limit of appeal from said decision has nearly expired. The authority of the Examiner to act upon these matters under the rule is therefore doubtful. However, no useful purpose would be accomplished by the grant of the present motion, since Sobey, in order to preserve his rights, must take his appeal on the question of priority to the Board of Examiners-in-Chief. He may, under the rule, direct the attention of the Examiners-in-Chief to the matters alleged to anticipate the issue, thus preventing useless delay.

Appeal was then taken by Sobey to the Examiners-in-Chief from the Interference Examiner's decision awarding priority to Holsclaw. In his reasons of appeal he set forth that the Examiner of Interferences erred in awarding priority to Holsclaw because the issues were unpatentable, and clearly so when construed to cover Sobey's construction. He further urged that the Examiner erred in failing to direct the Commissioner's attention under Rule 126 to the unpatentability of the issues. At the time of taking this appeal he filed a petition asking them before any decision upon the question of priority to call the attention of the Commissioner of Patents to the claimed fact that a statutory bar (unpatentability of the issues) existed to the issue of a patent to either party.

The Examiners-in-Chief after a hearing, rendered a decision holding that they did not have jurisdiction to consider any of the questions raised by the assignment of errors save that of priority. They said that the question of the patentability of the claims was *res adjudicata* for them at the hearing of the question of priority of invention and that the Commissioner had settled the question of interference in fact.

In referring to the petition asking them to direct the attention of the Commissioner to the alleged unpatentability of the issues as provided by Rule 126 they said:

Rule 126 reads:

"Examiner of Interference or the Examiners-in-Chief may, either before or in their decision on the question of priority * * * direct the attention of the Commissioner * * * to any ground for rejection of the claims which are the counts of the issue."

It is not necessary to decide whether the rule authorizes the Examiners-in-Chief to direct the attention of the Commissioner to their opinion on such a matter and to refrain from deciding the question of priority of invention. It is enough to say that it is left to their discretion whether or not they will call the attention of the Commissioner to any such matter, and that their opinion should be certain and beyond doubt in order to enable them to so act.

We have considered the question which we have been petitioned to consider, in view of the patents cited by Sobey to sustain his contention against the claim and of the decision of the Principal Examiner and decline to express the opinion that the counts of the issue are unpatentable.

Appeal was duly taken to the Commissioner of Patents, and at the same time he was petitioned to dissolve the intereference because the issues were anticipated by the patents of the prior art, and because they could only be held patentable by reading into them features of construction not found in Holsclaw's application, but disclosed in Sobey's. In passing it may be said that as the issues are claims originally made by Holsclaw, and therefore, as we have repeatedly held, in such case the issues are to be construed in the light of the application of the party making them, it would be manifestly improper for the Commissioner of Patents to read into them, for any purpose, limitations not disclosed in the application of the party first making the claims. Holsclaw's attorneys moved to dismiss the petition.

The Commissioner affirmed the decision of the Examiners-in-Chief awarding priority of invention of Holsclaw and at the same time dismissed Sobey's petition for reasons stated in his opinion deciding the question of priority.

The Commissioner in reviewing the case said:

It appears that the dates of invention alleged by Sobey in his preliminary statement are insufficient to overcome the case established for Holsclaw by the filing date of his application and that Sobey can therefore make no contest upon the question of priority of invention. That he can make no further contest upon priority is conceded by Sobey, who admittedly took his appeal to the Examiners-in-Chief from the decision of the Examiner of Interferences upon priority of invention and also the present appeal for the sole purpose of attacking the patentability of the issue. The regular procedure for raising the question of patentability by a party in an interference proceeding is by motion under Rules 114 and 122. Such motion was made by Sobey, and his contention that the issues are not patentable was considered thereon by the Primary Examiner in connection with the same references upon which Sobey seeks to present this contention here. The Primary Examiner held upon this *inter partes* consideration, as he had previously held in the *ex parte* prosecution of the applications, that the issues were patentable. Well-established policy, expressed in Rule 124, denies the right of appeal from decisions affirming the patentability of claims. It would seem, in view of this policy and rule and in view of Sobey's preliminary statement, that Sobey's opportunity to contest the right of Holsclaw to a patent upon the claims in issue was at an end when this decision of the Primary Examiner appeared.

However, Rule 126 provides that the Examiners-in-Chief may, either before or in their decision on the question of priority, direct the attention of the Commissioner to any matter not relating to priority which may have come to their notice and which in their opinion amounts to a statutory bar to the grant of a patent to either of the parties of the claims in interference. Sobey petitioned the Examiners-in-Chief to take action under this rule by calling attention to the fact that in their opinion the claims are not patentable. In view of this petition, the Examiners-in-Chief did include in their decision upon priority the following statement:

" We have considered the question which we have been petitioned to consider, in view of the patents cited by Sobey to sustain his contention against the claim and of the decision of the Principal Examiner, and decline to express the opinion that the counts of the issue are unpatentable."

It is clear to my mind that this case is before me upon the single question of the priority of the parties with regard to the subject-matter of the issue and that Sobey having conceded that he is subsequent to Holsclaw in the possession of this matter there is nothing for me o do here but affirm the decision of the Examiners-in-Chief in favor of Holsclaw. It is urged that there can be no roper decision upon priority of invention until the claims in controversy have been determined to be patentable. This contention does not, however, appear to have any application in the present case, for the claims in issue have been regularly determined to be patentable, and the determination was a final one, so far as the necessity for a basis for determination of priority is concerned. (C. D., 1905, 523; 119 O. G., 1922.)

We have thus fully set forth the proceedings in the Patent Office because they show that the questions of patentability of the issues and of the proper construction-to be given them were repeatedly called to the attention of the various tribunals and as fully considered as the rules governing the proceedings in that Office permit. These rules are presumably made to conform to the patent statutes, have been in force for many years, and have been found, in the main, to give satisfactory results. They show that the decision of the Primary Examiner, that the claims which are the issues of an interference are patentable and that all the parties to the interference have a right to make them, is final when rendered after the hearing of a motion to dissolve the interference. Furthermore, the rules provide for the further consideration of the question of patentability.

In the appeal taken to this court from the decision of the Commissioner of Patents awarding priority of invention to Holsclaw it is asserted on behalf of Sobey that the following errors were committed:

1. In deciding priority of invention in favor of Wilford H. Holsclaw;

2. In deciding upon the question of priority of invention without first determining and deciding that the subject-matter of the interference was a patentable subject-matter;

3. In not dissolving the interference (a) because of the lack of patentability in the subject-matter thereof and (b) because no interference in fact exists between the parties;

4. In refusing to consider or decide upon the patentability of the subject-matter of the interference;

5. In refusing to permit counsel for William Sobey to be heard in support of the contention on behalf of Sobey that the subject-matter of the interference is not a patentable subject-matter.

That the first assigned error is not well founded cannot be gainsaid, provided the issues set out a patentable invention and show rival claimants of it. Sobey failed to overcome Holsclaw's record date, and, so failing, no award of priority can be made in his favor.

The second alleged error does not seem to us well founded for the reason that the question of patentability had been affirmatively decided by the officer expressly authorized by law to decide that question, and from whose favorable decision no right of direct appeal is given by the patent statutes or the rules of the Patent Office lawfully promulgated. The Primary Examiners, who are given statutory authority to decide questions of patentability are under the supervision of the Commissioner and it would seem to be not only his right but his duty to correct any manifest error committed by any of the Primary Examiners relative to the patentability of a supposed invention, or of the right of an applicant to claim it whenever such error was called to his attention. To warrant any action on his part in such a case the error must, we think, be so gross that it would be a wrong to the public to permit a patent to issue. It manifestly should not be based upon a mere difference of opinion. The rules of the Patent Office, as we have seen, provide means by which the Examiner of Interferences and the Examiners-in-Chief, can, in an interference proceeding, express their opinion upon the question of the patentability of the issues of an interference and upon kindred questions. In the case at bar not only did the Primary Examiner pass upon the question of patentability and of the right of Holsclaw to make the claims in controversy, *ex parte*, but also in *inter partes* proceedings. Furthermore the Examiner of Interferences and the Examiners-in-Chief had their attention called to these questions, and, in declining to call the attention of the Commissioner of Patents to the alleged unpatentability of the issues, they in effect held them to be patentable. We think all the proceedings to prove that the Commissioner was so far satisfied of the patentability of the issues that he to all intents and purposes did decide that there was a patentable invention involved in the interference. He says:

The claims in issue have been regularly determined to be patentable and the determination was a final one, so far as the necessity for a basis for determination of priority is concerned.

In view of this statement and of the proceedings in the Office, we are not prepared to say that the Commissioner did not to his own satisfaction determine that there was a patentable subject-matter. He adopted the views of the subordinate tribunals of the Office after the question of patentability had been repeatedly raised, and, in so doing, he determined the question of a patentable subject-matter so far as was necessary in this proceeding. These views dispose also of the fourth alleged error. Of the fifth it need only be said that we have no power over the Commissioner in such a proceeding as this to hold that he has committed an error, for which a case should be reversed, because of a claim that he has refused to permit counsel to be heard in support of a given contention. The method of procedure upon a hearing in an interference proceeding is fixed by rules or is within the discretion of the Commissioner, and a review, if any could be had, would be by some proceeding other than by the ordinary appeal. We cannot control his action in a discretionary matter such as the extent of oral argument he will permit at a hearing of an interference: certainly we cannot, on appeal from his decision awarding priority of invention.

This leaves for consideration the question raised by the third assignment of error. We are asked to reverse the Commissioner because he refused to dissolve the interference for the reason that the issues are not patentable and because no interference in fact exists between the parties. In this connection it becomes necessary to consider to what extent we are called upon, or bound, to review the action of the Patent Office tribunals upon these, or analogous findings.

The question presented to us is not a new one. Unsuccessful parties to interferences have urged us to reëxamine about every question that has been litigated in the Patent Office during the course of interference proceedings. It will be sufficient to refer to a few of the cases illustrating the view this court has taken of questions the same, and similar, to those here presented.

In *Hisey* v. *Peters*, (C. D., 1895, 349; 71 O. G., 892; 6 App. D. C., 68,) where it was urged that the interference did not present a patentable invention, Chief Justice Alvey, delivering the opinion of the Court, said:

The question of patentability of the claim for invention was referred to and passed upon by the Primary Examiner in the Patent Office, who is the expert as to the state of the art involved, and it was not until that examination was had and favorably reported that the interference was or could be declared. The appellant making claim for an alleged patentable invention, is not to be heard to urge non-patentability of his claim after it had been placed in interference with another claim. He is effectually estopped on that question by reason of his own affirmative assertion that his claim is patentable, and if his own claim is patentable that with which it would interfere may be equally so, if priority of invention be shown. Moreover, the right of appeal in case of the refusal of a patent upon the ground of non-patentability of the claim and refusal of a patent because of interference with a prior right of invention are distinct rights, and the latter does not involve the former. This is clearly indicated in the Revised Statutes of the United States, section 4911, and in section 9 of the act of Congress of February 9, 1893, providing for the organization of this court.

In *Doyle* v. *McRoberts* (C. D., 1897, 413; 79 O. G., 1029; 10 App. D. C., 445) Mr. Justice Hagner, of the Supreme Court of the District of Columbia, sitting in the place of Chief Justice Alvey and delivering the opinion of the Court, said:

In our opinion it is not competent for this court, in an interference proceeding, to abandon the question of priority and pass upon the patentability of the alleged invention. This was decided as far back as 1875 by the Supreme Court in general term, (*U. S., ex rel. Bigelow,* v. *Thatcher,* 2 MacA., 24,) where the petitioner in interference asked for the vacation of the patent upon the ground that the inventor had abandoned his invention to public use. In *Hisey* v. *Peters* (C. D., 1895, 349; 71 O. G., 892; 6 App. D. C., 70) the identical motion interposed here was made and was overruled upon the ground that the applicant was effectually estopped to dispute the patentability of the invention by reason of his own affirmative assertions that his claim was patentable. (See also *U. S., ex rel. Brodie,* v. *Seymour, Comr.,* C. D., 1897, 372; 79 O. G., 509; 25 Wash. Law Rep., 181.) But it is insisted that under the authority of *Hill* v. *Wooster* (C. D., 1890, 230; 50 O. G., 560; 132 U. S., 694) the Supreme Court has settled the competency of this court to sustain this claim.

That decision has no relevancy to a case like the present.

Section 52 of the Patent Office Act of July, 1870, (R. S., sec. 4915) provides that: "Whenever a patent or application is refused, either by the Commissioner of Patents or by the Supreme Court of the District of Columbia upon appeal from the Commissioner, the applicant may have a remedy by bill in equity, and the court having cognizance thereof, on notice to adverse parties and other due proceedings may adjudge that such applicant is entitled, according to law, to receive a patent for his invention as specified in his claim as the facts in the case may appear and such adjudication, if it be in favor of the right of the applicant shall authorize the Commissioner to issue such patent, etc."

It was in a proceeding under this special statute that the Supreme Court held an equity judge was obliged, under the language of the act, to consider the patentability of the invention covered by the claim, and if he should find it not patentable should deny the application. Such a provision is in entire sympathy with the general principles of equity, which refuses to decree in favor of the most specious of two applicants under a claim of an illicit character.

But the present is not a proceeding in a court of equity; nor is it an application for the issue of a patent under the circumstances recited in the statute.

It is a proceeding as at law and under altogether different conditions, and hence the decision can have no application to the matter before us.

In *Oliver* v. *Felbel*, (C. D., 1902, 565; 100 O. G., 2384; 20 App. D. C., 262) Mr. Justice Morris, speaking for the Court, said:

In the sense of the patent law there can be no interference unless there is patentable invention and there are rival claimants of it. Patentability of the invention or device is a necessary prerequisite to a declaration of interference; and the patentability of an invention, in controversy, except under some extraordinary circumstances, is not an open question before us.

In that case there had been " no final and definite adjudication of patentability." The Examiners-in-Chief were of the opinion that the claim in issue was not patentable. The Commissioner had not acted on the question of patentability thus called to his attention, but had reserved it for the consideration of the Primary Examiner after the question of priority should be finally decided. It was held, that, as the question of patentability had not been finally decided, the cause as presented was in effect a moot cause. Notwithstanding this the court assumed that the question of patentability had been definitely decided and expressed an opinion on the merits.

In *Luger* v. *Browning*, (C. D., 1903, 593; 104 O. G., 1123; 21 App. D. C., 201,) in connection with the appeal from the Commissioner's decision on the question of priority, a motion was made to remand the proceeding to the Commissioner for a final determination of the question of patentability. That motion was denied and the Court distinguished the case from that of *Oliver* v. *Felbel, supra*, saying:

But we have repeatedly held that the question of patentability in general is not open in this court in interference proceedings. And so far as concerns the question of the reservation of the question of patentability of the invention, and the application of the case of *Oliver* v. *Felbel*, we find no such reservation in e present case as there was in that of *Oliver* v. *Felbel*. There the Board of

Examiners had expressed the opinion that the subject-matter in issue was not patentable; and the Commissioner in his decision expressly reserved that question for future consideration by the Primary Examiner when the case should go back to him. No such conditions appear in the present case. In the brief submitted by the appellant before the Commissioner the appellant suggested some new references on the question of the patentability of the invention. The Commissioner, properly, as it would seem, declined to consider them; and directed that the Primary Examiner should consider them, when the appellee's application should come before him again after the conclusion of the interference. We cannot hold that this amounted to a reservation of the question of patentability under the ruling in the case of *Oliver v. Felbel.* The contents of the references are not disclosed; it is not shown that they are material; the Commissioner has expressed no opinion in regard to them; and a mere suggestion by a party in interference to the effect that new references brought forward before the Commissioner for the first time will show want of patentable novelty in the subject-matter of controversy is not the equivalent of a reservation of the question of patentability by the Commissioner. The motion to remand the cause, therefore, for the determination of this question cannot be allowed.

In *Allen* v. *Lowry*, (C. D., 1905, 643; 116 O. G., 2253,) which came before us on appeal from a decision of the Supreme Court of the District of Columbia directing the issue of a writ of mandamus to the Commissioner of Patents commanding him to direct the Examiners-in-Chief to take jurisdiction of an appeal taken by Lowry from a ruling of the Primary Examiner denying Lowry's motion to dissolve an interference on the ground that his adversary had no right to make the claim because his application disclosed an inoperative device, we reversed the court below and held that such a motion was not applicable. We held that whatever right a party to an interference had to contest the right of his adversary to make an interfering claim, such right, if any, was reviewable, if at all, upon the final decision of the question of priority.

In *Podlesak and Podlesak* v. *McInnerney* (C. D., 1906, 558; 120 O. G., 2127) we remanded an interference to the Commissioner of Patents for further consideration of the question of identity of invention. We considered the case as being one out of the ordinary and felt constrained, in view of certain matters called to our attention, and which apparently had not been considered by the Commissioner, to take such action. We said:

We find that the question of appellee's right to make the claim has received the consideration of the Primary Examiner, of the Examiners-in-Chief and of the Commissioner. Where a question such as this has been fully considered by them, and all have concurred in finding a party to an interference has the right to make a claim which is the same as the count of the issue of an interference, their concurrent finding should not be lightly disturbed and will be ordinarily considered by this court as conclusive. In an *ex parte* case the decision of the Primary Examiner that a party has a right to make a claim is final unless for good cause shown the Commissioner, under his supervisory powers, takes jurisdiction to review the question. It is generally left to courts in a suit brought after the issue of the patent, for infringement of a claim thus allowed to determine whether the patentee ever had a right to make the claim. If however an interference, involving such claim, be instituted the rules of the Patent Office provide for an examination by the Primary Examiner of the question of the right of either party to make the claim. If his decision be in the affirmative the rules do not provide for an appeal to the Examiners-in-Chief. In *Allen* v. *United States ex rel. Lowry* (C. D., 1905, 643; 116 O. G., 2253) this court held that where such a decision was rendered by the Primary Examiner on a motion to dissolve no appeal would lie. It was there said that the court had reviewed other ancillary questions when they properly came before it on appeal from final judgments awarding priority of invention. The question of the right of a party to make a claim goes to the very foundation of an interference for if the party has not such right the interference falls. If it be incorrectly held that such party has a right to make the claim priority may be awarded to him and his adversary be deprived of a substantial right in that he is not given a claim where he necessarily is the prior inventor, his adversary never having made the invention. Manifestly that question should not be finally determined by the Primary Examiner who originally declared the interference. We therefore take jurisdiction to determine that question in this case as an ancillary question to be considered in awarding priority of invention. Where however three tribunals of the Patent Office have concurred in answering the question in the affirmative, as they have in this case, we shall follow them unless a manifest error has been committed.

In *Parkes* v. *Lewis*, decided at the present term, we have again held that the question of patentability will not ordinarily be reviewed in this court. In so holding we must not be understood as deciding that there can be an interference without there is a patentable invention, or that, should we be satisfied that there was no patentable invention involved, we should make an award of priority. It would be our manifest duty to remand an interference to the Commissioner of Patents, or at least call his attention to the fact, whenever it is shown that there is a bar to the issue of a patent to both parties to an interference. But where the Primary Examiner has held claims to be patentable, and the Examiner of Interferences and the Examiners-in-Chief have omitted or declined to call the attention of the Commissioner of Patents to the unpatentability of the issue of an interference, or where the Commissioner has declined to review the decision of the Primary Examiner, after his attention has been called to the alleged unpatentability of the issues, we are of the opinion that, except in an extraordinary case, we should hold the question of patentability to be settled. The statute does not provide for an appeal to this court from a ruling by the Commissioner of Patents, or of any of the subordinate tribunals, affirming the patentability of a claimed invention. It is only from a decision adverse to the patentability of a claim that an appeal will lie to this court. (U. S. R. S., sec. 4911; sec. 9 of the act of February 9, 1893, establishing this court.) It is however strenuously urged that the proceeding authorized by section 4915 of the Revised Statutes, which provides for relief by bill in equity where a patent has been finally refused, is sufficiently analogous to an appeal like the present to warrant and even require this court to consider, upon its own motion the question of patentability. We cannot agree with this contention. The proceedings are quite different. One is a proceeding in equity the other at law. The proceeding under section 4915 will only be open to the parties to this interference when a patent shall finally be refused to one of them because he shall fail to prove that his inventive act was earlier than that of his successful adversary, or for any other reason. Then and not till then can he avail himself of the provision of the section, and not till then will the case of *Hill* v. *Wooster* (C. D., 1890, 230; 50 O. G., 560; 132 U. S., 693) be controlling.

In interferences we do not determine whether either party shall receive a patent. The question presented to us is, conceding that there is a patentable invention, which party was the one first to invent or discover the same. When an interference is returned to the Patent Office after we have decided the question of priority it is within the power of the Commissioner of Patents to withhold a patent from the successful interferant. In such case by an orderly system of appeals provided by the statute the action of the Commissioner of Patents may be reviewed on an *ex parte* appeal. It is only on such appeals that we can decide that a patent shall or shall not issue. Appeals frequently come to this court in *ex parte* cases where some claims have been allowed and others refused. The appeal is only before us to consider the correctness of the Commissioner's decision in disallowing the appealed claims. We may doubt the patentability of the allowed claims, but are without power to act. So in interferences we may doubt the patentability of the issues, but we find no provision in the statute warranting us in overruling the deliberate decision of the Patent Office because of any such mere doubt. Authority to grant patents is vested in the Commissioner of Patents. If he errs and grants an invalid patent, his error is corrected by the court whenever the validity of the patent is questioned.

In cases such as the one at bar where the patentability of the claims which are the issues of an interference has been attacked in the Patent Office, and alleged invalidity has been repeatedly called to the attention of its officers authorized and required by the statutes and rules to consider the subject, we think their conclusion should, except perhaps in extraordinary cases, be held controlling upon us in interference cases where we are called upon to determine which of two or more parties first made the invention which they are claiming. Any doubt we may have should be resolved in favor of the correctness of the finding that there is a patentable invention involved in the interference. Especially so when the alleged invalidity is based upon the prior art.

We do not feel warranted in disturbing the rulings of the Commissioner of Patents, and those of the subordinate tribunals, which have considered this case and we therefore affirm the decision of the Commissioner of Patents awarding priority of invention to Holsclaw.

Let this opinion, and the proceedings of the court in the premises, be certified to the Commissioner of Patents according to law. *Affirmed.*

[Court of Appeals of the District of Columbia.]

IN RE MCNEIL AND STURTEVANT.

Decided December 4, 1906.

(126 O. G., 3425.)

1. PATENTABILITY—DOUBLE USE.

  A patent will not be granted upon the discovery of a new and analogous function for an old machine. (*Roberts* v. *Ryer*, C. D., 1876, 439; 10 O. G., 204; 91 U. S., 150; *Ansonia Co.* v. *Electrical Supply Co.*, C. D., 1892, 313; 58 O. G., 1692; 144 U. S., 11; *Potts* v. *Creager*, C. D., 1895, 143; 70 O. G., 494; 155 U. S., 597.)

2. SAME—REVERSAL OF PARTS.

  Claims which comprise merely a reversal of parts disclosed in a prior machine are not patentable.

3. SAME—CONSTRUCTION OF CLAIMS—IMPLYING STRUCTURES NOT IN CLAIMS.

  Where an applicant's claims to a trimmer for sewing-machines make no mention of a presser-foot, a difference in structure embodying a particular form of presser-foot which is not clearly pointed out in the record will not be assumed.

Mr. C. L. Sturtevant and *Mr. E. G. Mason* for the appellant.

Mr. Fairfax Bayard for the Commissioner of Patents.

ROBB, *J.:*

This is an appeal from a decision of the Commissioner of Patents rejecting all the claims, eight in number, of an application for patent.

The second, fifth and eighth claims contain the substance of all, and are as follows:

2. In a sewing-machine, the combination with suitable stitch-forming mechanism, a work-support, mechanism for feeding a plurality of thicknesses of fabric to the stitch-forming mechanism, a trimming mechanism, comprising two members, one operating above the work-support and having its upper surface serving as a support for the upper layer of fabric and to separate the layers of fabric, and having its lower edge coöperating with the other trimming member to sever the lower layer of fabric, said separating member of the trimmer deflecting the severed edge from the body portion of the fabric; substantially as described.

5. In a sewing-machine, the combination with suitable stitch-forming mechanism, a *work-support*, mechanism for feeding a plurality of thicknesses of fabric

to the stitch-forming mechanism, a trimming mechanism located below the work-support, and comprising two members, one of which extends through the work-support and above the same, said member having an upper edge serving as a support for the upper layer of fabric, and having its lower edge coöperating with the other member of the trimming device to sever the lower layer of fabric, the vertical rear portion of said upper member serving to deflect the free severed edge from the stitched portion of the fabrics; substantially as described.

8. In a sewing-machine, the combination with suitable stitch-forming mechanism, a work-support, and mechanism for feeding a plurality of thicknesses of fabric to the stitch-forming mechanism, a trimming mechanism comprising two members, one of which has its upper surface serving as a support for the upper layer of fabric, and to separate the layers of fabric and the other of which coöperates with the first member to sever one of the layers of fabric; substantially as described.

The references forming the basis for the rejection of these claims are: *Borton et al.*, March 28, 1882, No. 255,578; *Willcox*, June 28, 1887, No. 365,716. Other patents are referred to by the Examiner, but it is unnecessary to notice them here.

The subject-matter of appellants' alleged invention consists of a mechanism for stitching together two superposed layers of material and a coacting mechanism for trimming or cutting one of the layers just beyond the seam. This combination, stitching mechanism and trimming mechanism, is not new in the art, but appellants contend that by a readjustment and modification of certain parts they have secured for the upper member of their trimmer, or cutting-blade, a new function, and, therefore, the combination is patentable.

In the Willcox patent there is shown acting in conjunction a stitching mechanism and a trimming mechanism, the difference being that in the Willcox patent the upper member of the cutting or trimming mechanism is stationary, the lower member being pivoted to coöperate therewith, but the upper member although stationary projects forward so that its pointed end penetrates between the superposed layers of fabric, and the member itself is mounted on the work-support, which of necessity brings the cutting edge in the same plane with the work-support as in appellants' machine. In other words, appellants, so far as their claims disclose, have done nothing more than to reverse the parts of the Willcox patent. The similarity between the Borton and Willcox patent and appellants' claims is still more striking. We say appellants' " claims," because their drawings fail to disclose in unbroken lines a complete trimmer. Counsel in the argument at bar, however, contended that the structure of the Borton and Willcox presser-foot was such as to preclude the possibility of the upper cutting member performing the function performed by appellants' upper cutting member. In the Borton and Willcox patent the presser-foot is divided so that one side comes close to the needle-hole while the other is cut away sufficiently to enable the cutting-blade to trim close to the seam. In appellants' machine, counsel stated, the presser-foot is not divided, and this results, it is contended, in giving the upper trimming-blade free scope and enables it to lift and support the upper layer of fabric while the lower is being trimmed, and thereby perform an important function of which the Borton and Willcox machine is not capable. But, this contention rests upon a premise not sustained by the record. Appellants' claims make no mention of a presser-foot, and we are not at liberty to assume a difference in structure when it is not clearly pointed out in the record. So far as this record discloses, a patent is sought on the discovery of a new and analogous function for an old machine. That such a discovery is not patentable has long since been determined: *Roberts* v. *Ryer*, (C. D., 1876, 439; 10 O. G., 204; 91 U. S. 150;) *Ansonia Co.* v *Electrical Supply Co.*, (C. D., 1892, 313; 58 O. G., 1692; 144 U. S., 11;) *Potts* v. *Creager*, (C. D. 1895, 143; 70 O. G., 494; 155 U. S., 597.)

The Examiner, whose decision was in turn sustained by the Examiners-in-Chief, and the Commissioner, has this to say in construing the Borton and Willcox patent:

Of these patents the one to Borton and Willcox (No. 255,578) shows a trimming mechanism which is essentially the same as that of McNeil and Sturtevant. The blade projecting above the bed-plate is immediately in the rear of the needle and so arranged relative to the stitching mechanism as to trim, (in the use described) the fabric parallel to the line of stitching. There appears to be no reason whatever why this machine could not be used to stitch a single-turn hem and trim the free or raw edge parallel to the line of stitching precisely in the same manner as McNeil and Sturtevant's machine. Even if patentees did not have this use in mind at the time the patent was granted, it is a well-settled principle of law that an inventor of a machine or a mechanism is entitled to all the uses to which it may be applied without changing the machine or mechanism itself. Attention is called in this connection to the case of the *Western Electric Co.* v. *Sperry Electric Co. et al.*, (C. D., 1893, 573; 65 O. G., 597,) and to the decision of the present Commissioner in the case of *Blue* v. *Power* v. *Owens*, (C. D., 1902, 425; 101 O G., 2076.) In this latter decision, the Commissioner stated that—

" Where a party obtains a patent on an apparatus, he is entitled to all the analogous uses of which his apparatus is capable. The Office cannot grant a patent on a device to one party for a particular use and then grant a second patent on the same device to a second party who employs it for a different but analogous purpose."

It is contended, however, that—

It is not a question of whether certain limitations should be put into the claims of appellants, but wholly a question of whether the Borton and Willcox patent discloses a structure capable of securing the same functions as appellants'.

The complete answer to this contention, it seems to us, lies in the fact that appellants' claims are for a mechanism, which, so far as *described*, does not differ in essential details from the Borton and

Willcox patent. The Examiner, in treating of this phase of the case, said:

If there is anything in applicants' construction which adapts it to perform a class of work not capable of being performed by the Borton machine it must be due to a difference in structure and certainly no real difference in structure over that shown by Borton is found in these claims.

Finding no error, the decision appealed from will be affirmed, and this opinion and the proceedings in this court will be certified to the Commissioner of Patents as required by law, and it is so ordered. *Affirmed.*

[Court of Appeals of the District of Columbia.]

In re American Circular Loom Company.

Decided December 4, 1906.

(127 O. G., 393.)

1. TRADE-MARKS—" CIRCULAR LOOM "—DESCRIPTIVE.

The words "Circular Loom" refused registration as a trade-mark for "conduits and coverings for electrical conductors consisting of fiber spirals wrapped with fiber and tape, and covered with a protective cotton tube with an outer coating of an insulating compound and mica" on the ground that they are descriptive of the protective cotton tube, which is one of the material parts of the construction. An inspection of the article shows that the cotton tube is woven on a circular loom, which must be known to dealers in the goods, and it may well be inferred that this product of a circular loom is considered a superior quality in the trade.

2. SAME—ARBITRARY WORDS—SECONDARY MEANING.

Sometimes arbitrary words, adopted primarily as a mark to indicate origin or ownership, may through long-continued and wide sale of the particular article come to indicate quality also, and in such event the owner would not be debarred from their protection as a trade-mark. It would have to appear with certainty, however, that at the time of adoption the mark was for the purpose of indicating origin, manufacture, or ownership and not at all as descriptive of grade or quality.

Mr. William S. Hodges, Mr. Everett N. Curtis, and *Mr. Charles F. Perkins* for the American Circular Loom Company.

Mr. Fairfax Bayard for the Commissioner of Patents.

SHEPARD, J.:

The appellant appeals from a decision refusing registration of the words "Circular Loom" as a trade-mark for "conduits and coverings for electrical conductors containing a resilient spiral lining, and an element for closing the openings between the spirals."

The specimen sections of tubes exhibited with the applications show, as stated by the Examiner of Trade-Marks—

conduits and coverings for electrical conductors consisting of fiber spirals wrapped with fiber and tape, and covered with a protective cotton tube with an outer coating of an insulating compound and mica.

The ground of refusal is thus stated:

The protective cotton tube is obviously woven on a circular loom, of the type shown in the patent to C. N. Brown, No. 690,355, December 31, 1901, (see Fig. 10, thereof,) and, therefore, the term "Circular Loom," as applied to the applicant's goods, is believed to be descriptive.

If the term be in fact descriptive, the refusal of registration was undoubtedly right; for as said by Mr. Chief Justice Fuller in *Lawrence M'f'g. Co.* v. *Tennessee M'f'g. Co.*, (C. D., 1891, 415; 55 O. G., 1528; 138 U. S., 547:)

Nothing is better settled than that an exclusive right to the use of words, letters, or symbols, to indicate merely the quality of goods to which they are affixed, cannot be acquired.

See, also, *Brown Chemical Co.* v. *Meyer*, (C. D., 1891, 343; 55 O. G., 287; 139 U. S., 540, 542,) in which it was held that the words "Iron Bitters" were "so far indicative of the ingredients, characteristics and purposes of the plaintiff's preparation," that they could not be appropriated as a trade-mark. In the opinion in that case, Mr. Justice Brown said:

The general proposition is well established that words which are merely descriptive of the character, qualities, or composition of an article, or of the place where it is manufactured or produced, cannot be monopolized as a trademark.

The principle so well established has been embodied in the recent Trade-Mark Act, section 5 of which denies registration to—

words or devices which are descriptive of the goods with which they are used, or of the character or quality of such goods.

It is true that the entire conduit of the applicant is not the product of a circular loom, but a material part of the construction is the protective cotton tube that receives the outer coating, and which, as said by the Examiner, is "obviously woven on a circular loom." What plainly appears on ordinary inspection must, for a stronger reason, be well known to dealers in the goods; and it may well be inferred that this product of a circular loom, namely, a seamless protective cotton tube, is considered a superior quality in the trade. To this extent, the words "Circular Loom" are clearly descriptive of one of the chief ingredients or characteristics of the conduits to which they are applied. Nor is this objection met by the contention of the applicant, that, as shown in the Herrick patent under which its manufacture is carried on, this element may be braided or knitted and not necessarily woven; and even if woven it is not indispensable to employ a circular loom, as a strip woven in a straight loom and folded longitudinally about the tube would accomplish the purpose shown in Fig. 4 of the Herrick patent. The answer is that it is not made in either of these possible forms; and if it were, the words "*Circular Loom*" would amount to a false description.

It is further contended that—

the words "Circular Loom" have never been used by the trade in a strictly descriptive sense, but have always been used in an arbitrary manner, and at the most are merely suggestive of one of the several parts of the appellant's conduit.

It would seem that what is " suggestive " of an ingredient or characteristic of an article of manufacture is also descriptive of the same. Be that as it may, there is nothing beyond this argumentative statement to show that the words were originally adopted, or have ever been understood in a secondary sense as indicative of origin or ownership, and not of quality. They are not merely coined, fancy or arbitrary words that can have no other reasonable effect than to indicate origin or ownership. Sometimes arbitrary words, adopted primarily as a mark to indicate origin or ownership, may, through long-continued and wide sale of the particular article come to indicate quality also, and in such event the owner would not be debarred from their protection as a trade-mark. It would have to appear with certainty, however, that at the time of adoption the mark was for the purpose of indicating origin, manufacture or ownership, and not at all as descriptive of grade or quality. (*Lawrence M'f'g. Co.* v. *Tennessee M'f'g. Co.*, C. D., 1891, 415; 55 O. G., 1528; 138 U. S., 537, 547; *Cellular Clothing Co.* v. *Maxton*, 1899 App. Cas., 326.) In that case, as in the first of the two citations, the question of unfair trade or competition was also involved. It was held that the word " Cellular," being a word descriptive of the article of cloth manufactured, could not be appropriated as a technical trade-mark. It was also contended in that case that by long-continued manufacture and sale of the particular goods the word had come to be generally regarded in a secondary sense as indicating nothing more than origin and manufacture. Considerable evidence was offered on the point, but its sufficiency was denied. Referring to the case of *Reddemay* v. *Benham*, known as " The Camel's Hair Belting Case " (1896 App. Cas., 199,) which all of the judges distinguished from the case at bar, Lord Shand said, (p. 340:)

Of that case I shall only say, that it no doubt shows it is possible where a descriptive name has been used to prove that so general, I should rather say so universal has been the use of it as to give it a secondary meaning and so to confer on the person who has so used it a right to its exclusive use or, at all events, to such a use that others employing it must qualify their use by some distinguishing characteristic. But I confess I have always thought, and I still think, that it would be made almost impossible for any one to obtain the exclusive right to the use of a word or term which is in ordinary use in our language and which is descriptive only—and, indeed, were it not for the decision in Reddemay's case, I should say this would be made altogether impossible.

Lord Davy said, (p. 343:)

A man who takes upon himself to prove that words, which are merely descriptive or expressive of the quality of the goods, have acquired the secondary sense to which I have referred, assumes a much greater burden—and, indeed, a burden which it is not impossible, but at the same time extremely difficult to discharge—a much greater burden than that of a man who undertakes to prove the same thing of a word not significant and not descriptive, but what has been compendiously called a "fancy" word.

See, also, *Bennett* v. *McKinley*, (13 C. C. A., 25, 26; 65 Fed. Rep., 505.)

We consider the question presented here as governed by the foregoing authoritative decisions, and shall not consume time in an attempt to review the multitude of cases cited on the briefs—in many of which analogous words have been upheld as trade-marks, and in many others denied. In very many of them, moreover, the question involved was one of fair trade and not of technical trade-mark. It is only a question of the latter kind that can come before us on appeals from the refusal of registration in the Patent Office. We agree with the tribunals of the Patent Office that the words "Circular Loom," as presented on the application, are descriptive in the sense of the law forbidding registration as a trade-mark.

The decision appealed from will, therefore, be affirmed; and the clerk will certify this decision to the Commissioner of Patents as required by law. *Affirmed.*

[Court of Appeals of the District of Columbia.]

THE ROSE SHOE MANUFACTURING COMPANY *v.* A. A. ROSENBUSH & CO.

Decided December 4, 1906.

(127 O. G., 394.)

1. TRADE-MARKS—PRIORITY.

Where Rosenbush in his application alleges adoption in 1891, but the earliest date mentioned in his testimony is the "spring of 1895," and his testimony is only supported by that of a former partner, who fixes the date as "about a year and a half" after August 1, 1894, when the firm commenced business, *Held* insufficient to prevail over the Rose Shoe Manufacturing Company, which presents the testimony of several credible witnesses who clearly trace the use of the trade-mark by the Rose Shoe Manufacturing Company, and its predecessors in business from the year 1894.

2. SAME—CONTINUOUS USE—PRESUMPTION.

Where several successive firms manufacturing ladies' shoes are shown to have occupied the same factory, it is reasonable to suppose that once having adopted a trade-name, they would continue its use notwithstanding a reorganization of the firm.

Mr. C. E. Foster for The Rose Shoe Manufacturing Company.
Mr. Louis H. Harriman for A. A. Rosenbush & Co.

ROBB, J.:

Hearing on appeal from a decision of the Commissioner of Patents in a trade-mark interference case. (*Ante,* 69; 127 O. G., 391.)

The issue is the word " Rose " as a trade-mark for shoes. The Rose Shoe Manufacturing Company, of Rochester, N. Y., the senior party, and appellant here, registered this mark July 21, 1905, and the application of A. A. Rosenbush & Co., the appellee, was filed July 22, 1905. An interference was duly declared, testimony in the form of depositions taken by both parties, and priority of adoption and use awarded appellant by the Examiner of Interferences. From this decision an appeal was taken to the Commissioner of Patents, who reversed the decision of the Examiner of Interferences, and awarded priority of adoption and use to appellee. The decision of the Commissioner is here challenged.

A. A. Rosenbush, a partner in the firm of A. A. Rosenbush & Co., of Boston, Mass., about August 1, 1894, formed a partnership at Chicago, Ill., with Samuel Goldsmith and Jerome M. Levie, under the firm-name of Goldsmith, Rosenbush & Levie, and engaged in the wholesale boot and shoe business in Chicago. Rosenbush testified that the firm first used the word " Rose " as a trade-mark " in the spring of 1895," and that the word was thereafter continuously used " to the spring of '98." In November, 1898, Rosenbush purchased the stock, fixtures and good-will of the firm and removed to Boston. Shortly thereafter he opened a place of business in Boston, and continued the use of the word " Rose " as a trade-mark down to the time when he sought its registry. His testimony as to the use of the word as a trade-mark in Boston is corroborated by other witnesses, and we find no difficulty on that point. The deposition of his former partner, Levie, was taken in Chicago, and he was asked " Whether or not Goldsmith, Rosenbush & Levie used any trade-marks upon the shoes sold by them? " He answered: " Some." He was then asked what trade-marks they used, and to this he replied: " Well, we used the name ' Waddell,' used the name ' Rose,' and several others." He was asked when the firm first used the name " Rose " as a trade-mark, and he answered: " Can't tell exactly—haven't any data to go by. It was between 1894 and 1898." When asked if he could tell whether it was nearer 1894 than 1898, he said: " Well, yes, it was about a year or a year and a half after we started in business." On cross-examination he was asked: "About how many other trade-marks did you use besides the words ' Rose ' and ' Waddell? ' " and replied: " Not over half a dozen, they changed from time to time. The merchandise would not market, and we would have to change them."

In the above application for registry of A. A. Rosenbush & Co., the truth of the statements therein being sworn to by A. A. Rosenbush, it is stated that—

the trade-mark has been continuously used in our business since the year 1891.

In the application of the appellant it is stated that—

this trade-mark has been continuously used in business by said corporation and in the business of M. J. Whitman Co., from whom title is derived, since the 1st day of March, 1900.

Charles A. Rooker, the secretary and treasurer of the Rose Shoe Manufacturing Company, was asked why he did not give an earlier date, and replied as follows:

I simply gave 1900 from my personal knowledge without any investigation or inquiry among my predecessors, as to the first use of the word "Rose." If I had been asked by my attorney to give an earlier date, I certainly could have done so.

He further testified that the original company was known as S. Raubert & Siebert, and that this company was succeeded by Siebert, Whitman & Bartold, who were in turn succeeded by Siebert, Whitman & Co., and they in turn by M. J. Whitman Co., the immediate predecessor of The Rose Shoe Manufacturing Company. Mr. Rooker was asked whether the trade-mark "Rose" was used on shoes sold by the predecessors of his company, and answered that shoes bearing that trade-mark were manufactured and sold by Siebert, Whitman & Bartold, Siebert, Whitman & Co., M. J. Whitman Co., and The Rose Shoe Manufacturing Company, and that Siebert, Whitman & Bartold manufactured and sold the "Rose" shoe prior to 1899 when the firm changed to Siebert, Whitman & Co.

John A. Levis, a paper-box manufacturer, of Rochester, testified that he had been making boxes and printing cartons bearing the word "Rose" for The Rose Shoe Manufacturing Company and its predecessors since 1896, when the firm-name was Siebert, Whitman & Bartold. Mr. Levis identified three cartons bearing the word "Rose" as having been printed by him for Siebert, Whitman & Bartold.

Philip H. Leckinger, of Rochester, a salesman in the retail shoe store of his father who had been a retail shoe dealer for forty-five years, testified that his father had bought shoes from Raubert & Siebert and all their successors down to The Rose Shoe Manufacturing Company, and that the trade-mark "Rose" was associated with these shoes.

Frank J. Nissen, of Port Clinton, Ohio, succeeded his father in 1901 in the retail boot and shoe business at that place. Mr. Nissen testified that he first bought shoes from the predecessors of the appellant when he started to manage his father's business in 1892, and that he had since continuously bought the " Rose " shoe. Mr. Nissen did not definitely state when the trade-mark " Rose " was first used on the shoes he purchased from the various predecessors of the appellant. He did, however, produce two shoes so marked, which were bought in 1900, and he testified that these were not the earliest shoes so marked which he had purchased.

Ferdinand Bartold testified that he was employed by Raubert & Siebert for five or six years prior to 1894; that in 1894 he became a member of the firm of Siebert, Whitman & Bartold, which firm continued in business for about four years and a half when it was succeeded by Siebert, Whitman & Co., in whose employ and its successors, the M. J. Whitman Co. and The Rose Shoe Manufacturing Company, he continued; and that each of these firms manufactured and sold shoes under the name " Rose." He testified further: .

, Q. By what name were the shoes manufactured by these various concerns known, and particularly Siebert, Whitman & Bartold?

A. The name " Rose."

Q. Was the name used on the shoes?

A. Yes, sir.

Q. I hand you exhibits " B " and " C " and ask you if the marks you find on those shoes are practically the same as originally used?

A. Yes, sir.

Q. Since your first connection with the " Rose " shoe, has the " Rose " shoe to your personal knowledge, been continuously manufactured and sold by the Rose Shoe Company and their predecessors?

A. Yes, sir.

William J. Muckle, president of the Rose Shoe Manufacturing Company, testified that his knowledge of the Company and its predecessors extended over a period of about eighteen years; that he was in the factory, saw the shoes made, and knew that they were manufactured and sold as the " Rose " shoe. He further testified that each of these companies had used the trade-mark " Rose " exclusively; and that over ninety per cent. of the output of the factory contained the word as a trade-mark.

A Mr. Prusick, of Philadelphia, testified to buying the " Rose " shoe from these companies since April or May, 1898, but his testimony is not material here.

Both Mr. Rooker and Mr. Muckle testified that the appellant and its predecessors had built up an extensive interstate and foreign business.

The sole issue is whether the adoption of this trade-mark by the appellant antedates its adoption by the appellee. Although Rosenbush, in his application, claimed 1891 as his date of adoption, the earliest date mentioned in his testimony is " the spring of 1895." His former partner, Levie, as we have seen, finally fixes the date as

" about a year or a year and a half " after August 1, 1894, when the firm commenced business. From this testimony, and from this alone, we must find when appellee first used the word. Appellant, on the other hand, produced several credible witnesses, who clearly traced the use of the word by Siebert, Whitman & Bartold in 1894, and by all their various successors down to and including The Rose Shoe Manufacturing Company. The testimony of Mr. Leckinger is susceptible of no other reasonable construction than that he had been purchasing shoes containing the trade-mark " Rose " from these various companies for about nineteen years. Mr. Leckinger is an entirely disinterested witness, and his testimony must be given the weight to which it is entitled. Mr. Bartold, to be sure, is employed by the appellant, but his testimony being consistent and reasonable is certainly entitled to as much weight as the testimony of one of the parties. His testimony is clear and convincing that the word " Rose " has been used by the various companies since 1894 at least. Having been connected with these firms, either as a partner or as an employee, Mr. Bartold is in a position to intelligently testify concern- ing the subject-matter of this controversy. Mr. Muckle, the president of the company, and presumably a man of intelligence and char- acter, testified, in effect, that the word " Rose " has been used by his company and its predecessors for about eighteen years. His testi- mony is entitled to as much weight as the testimony of the appellee. These various firms occupied the same factory, and each manufac- tured ladies' shoes. It is reasonable to suppose that once having adopted a trade-name, they would continue its use notwithstanding a reorganization of the firm, and, therefore, the testimony of Mr. Bartold, that the name has been in continuous use since 1894, cor- roborated as it is by the testimony of the other witnesses, is not only reasonable but, to our minds, conclusive as to when the mark was first adopted by appellant's predecessors.

A careful analysis of the whole evidence, we think, irresistibly leads to the conclusion that appellant adopted this mark prior to the date of its adoption by appellee even though we accept the uncor- roborated statement of Mr. Rosenbush that his predecessor first used the mark " in the spring of 1895."

It follows that the decision of the Commissioner must be reversed. The clerk of the court will certify this opinion, and the proceedings of this court in the premises, to the Commissioner of Patents, accord- ing to law. *Reversed.*

[Court of Appeals of the District of Columbia.]

BECHMAN v. SOUTHGATE.

Decided December 4, 1906.

(127 O. G., 1254.)

INTERFERENCE—PRIORITY—INTERFERENCE IN FACT—CONCLUSIONS BY PATENT OF-
FICE GENERALLY ACCEPTED BY COURT OF APPEALS.

Ordinarily where the point has been raised whether the application of
one of the parties was broad enough in the terms of its specification and
claims to embrace the invention of the other, and especially where the invention is one of elaborate and complicated mechanism, the decisions of the
expert tribunals of the Patent Office in respect of identity have, for obvious
reasons, been accepted as conclusive.

Mr. A. E. Dowell for the appellant.
Mr. Louis W. Southgate for the appellee.

ROBB, *J.:*

This is an interference proceeding between the above-named applicants for the invention of a traveling-cylinder web-printing press,
comprising three printing-couples, the issue in said proceeding being
expressed in five counts:

1. A printing-press comprising three printing-couples arranged in parallel
planes, each couple consisting of a bed and coacting cylinder, and means for
feeding webs through said couples, to be perfected thereby.

2. A printing-press comprising three stationary type-beds arranged in parallel
planes, and three reciprocating cylinders coacting with the beds; with means
for feeding webs through the press so that they shall be perfected thereby at
each operation of the press.

3. The combination in a web-printing press of three stationary form-beds, a
traveling impression-cylinder coacting with each of said form-beds, a single reciprocating mechanism for actuating all of said cylinders, web-guides a deflector
and web-manipulating mechanisms.

4. The combination of a web-printing press of three stationary form-beds, a
traveling impression form-cylinder coacting with said bed, a reciprocating
mechanism for actuating said impression-cylinders, connections whereby one
of said impression-cylinders may be thrown out of operation and the other two
kept in operation, web-guides and web-manipulating mechanisms.

5. The combination in a web-printing press of three stationary form-beds, a
pair of carriers in which two impression-cylinders are journaled, a reciprocating mechanism for said carriers, a second set of carriers, in which a third impression-cylinder is journaled, means for connecting and disconnecting the two
sets of carriers, and suitable web guides and manipulating mechanisms.

Southgate, the senior applicant, filed his application November 30,
1896; Bechman, the junior applicant, May 21, 1903. An interference
was duly declared, testimony taken, and all the tribunals of the Patent Office concurred in awarding judgment of priority of invention to
the senior applicant, Southgate. Bechman has appealed, but in his

assignment of errors does not challenge the decision of the Commissioner (C. D., 1906, 270; 123 O. G., 2309) on the question of priority of invention; "and to this extent he is to be presumed to have acquiesced in the decision against him." (*Bechman* v. *Wood*, C. D., 1899, 453; 89 O. G., 2459; 15 App. D. C., 487.) Bechman's contentions, as disclosed in his brief, are as follows:

First. That there is no invention common to the machines disclosed in the respective applications.

Second. The first and second issues (claims made by Bechman) are for a specific form of press not disclosed by Southgate; and the third, fourth and fifth issues (claims made by Southgate) are restricted to a construction not disclosed in Bechman's application.

Third. If Southgate has any patentable invention and Bechman has a patentable invention, there is nothing patentably novel in common between these two, and each can legally only procure a patent on his specific machine. Neither is entitled to a claim which will dominate the machine of the other.

His first and second contentions, in substance, challenge the ruling that there is an interference in fact between the two machines.

We have repeatedly held that, except in extreme cases, we will not go behind the declaration of interference in order to determine the question of identity of invention. (*Swihart* v. *Mauldin*, C. D., 1902, 540; 99 O. G., 2322; 19 App. D. C., 573.)

What are the facts in this case? Briefly stated, they are as follows: The Campbell Printing Press & Manufacturing Company, Southgate's original assignee, and the Duplex Printing Press Company, Bechman's assignee, were rival concerns, and from 1892 to 1902 engaged in litigation covering the broad patents on flat-bed web-printing presses of the style here involved. In June, 1902, an agreement was entered into between these rival concerns whereby the Campbell Company, in consideration of being paid a royalty on certain machines, withdrew from the field and assigned all patents and applications for patents included in the agreement to the Duplex Company. The Southgate application now in issue was one of the applications assigned and upon which, if adopted, a royalty was to be paid. Mr. Bechman, the mechanical expert and inventor for the Duplex Company, in the summer of 1902 saw the Southgate application and drawings and also the following memorandum in reference thereto:

Case 104.
Louis W. Southgate. Filed Nov. 30, 1896.
Serial No. 615,928.
This case covers the three-bed multipress for making ten and twelve page products. Good claims have been allowed, but not as broad as they should be. The case will probably have to be taken to the Board of Examiners-in-Chief, and must be appealed before Aug. 13, 1903.

Nothing further appears to have been done by the Duplex Company in respect of this application; hence its prosecution by the Campbell Company. The Bechman application was subsequently filed, and the specifications filed therewith read much like the original Southgate specifications.

The Patent Office, after careful consideration, has found that there is an interference in fact between these applicants. Without discussing the evidence further, we hold that the record does not disclose this to be such a case as would warrant us in disturbing that finding.

The third contention is really a restatement of the first and second. It is fully answered, however, by the decision of this court in *Seeberger* v. *Dodge*, (C. D., 1905, 603; 114 O. G., 2382; 24 App. D. C., 481,) where it is said that—

> Ordinarily, where the point has been raised, whether the application of one of the parties was broad enough in the terms of its specification and claims to embrace the invention of the other, and especially where the invention is one of elaborate and complicated mechanism, the decisions of the expert tribunals of the Patent Office in respect of identity have, for obvious reasons, been accepted as conclusive. (*Stone* v. *Pupin*, C. D., 1902, 550; 100 O. G., 1113; 19 App. D. C., 396, 400; *Schüpphaus* v. *Stevens*, C. D., 1901, 365; 95 O. G., 1452; 17 App. D. C., 548, 555; *Ostergren* v. *Tripler*, C. D., 1901, 350; 95 O. G., 837; 17 App. D. C., 557. 559; *Luger* v. *Browning*, C. D., 1903, 593; 104 O. G., 1123; 21 App. D. C., 201, 204; *Herman* v *Fullman* C. D., 1904, 625; 109 O. G., 1888; 23 App. D. C., 259, 265.)

The decision will be affirmed, and this opinion certified to the Commissioner of Patents, as required by law, and it is so ordered. *Affirmed.*

[Court of Appeals of the District of Columbia.]

BLACKFORD *v.* WILDER.

Decided January 8, 1907.

(127 O. G., 1255.)

1. INTERFERENCE—SECOND INTERFERENCE—RES ADJUDICATA.

Where a second interference is declared between the same applications on an issue relating to the same subject-matter of invention as that of a prior interference, of broader scope than the first issue, and the constructions relied on, respectively, as evidencing conception and reduction to practice of the invention of both issues are the same and the fundamental facts of both cases are the same. *Held* that the final decision in the first interference is conclusive and that the question of priority is *res adjudicata* unless it can be made to appear that the question upon which the determination of the second case rests is one that neither was nor could have been presented and determined in the first case.

2. RES ADJUDICATA—DOCTRINE STATED BY THE SUPREME COURT.

The doctrine of *res adjudicata*, or estoppel by former judgment, has been thus declared by the Supreme Court of the United States:

"When the second suit is upon the same cause of action, and between the same parties as the first, the judgment in the former is conclusive in the latter as to every question which was or might have been presented and determined in the first action; but when the second suit is upon a different cause of action, though between the same parties, the judgment in the former action operates as an estoppel only as to the point or question actually litigated and determined, and not as to other matters which might have been litigated and determined." (*Nesbit* v. *Riverside Independent District*, 144 U. S., 610, 618; *New Orleans* v. *Citizen's Bank*, 167 U. S., 371, 386; *S. P. R. R.* v. *U. S.*, 168 U. S., 1, 48)—

and the doctrine as thus laid down is applicable to adjudications made in the Patent Office.

Mr. A. S. Pattison and *Mr. Philip Mauro* for the appellant.

Mr. James M. Spear and *Mr. C. H. Duell* for the appellee.

SHEPARD, *J.*:

This is the second interference between the same parties declared on the same application.

The issue of the first was defined in four counts as follows:

1. In a burner the combination with a trough and perforated tubes situated thereabove and forming a combustion-chamber, said trough having at its bottom a liquid-containing portion, and an enlarged upper vapor-receiving space, and a vertically-disposed lighting member seated in the liquid-containing portion and extending upward between the walls of the enlarged vapor-receiving portion to form a vapor-space at the side of the lighting member.

2. In a burner the combination of a trough and perforated tubes situated thereabove and forming a combustion-chamber, a lighting member vertically disposed between the upwardly-disposed walls of the trough, said trough having a contracted lower portion in which the lighting member is seated, and a vapor-space above the contracted portion at the side of the vertically-disposed lighting member.

3. In a burner, the combination of a trough and perforated tubes situated thereabove and forming a combustion-chamber, said trough being contracted at its lower portion, and a vertically-disposed lighting member seated in said contracted portion and extending upward between the upwardly-disposed walls and constituting a vapor-space in the upper portion of the trough at the side of the said lighting member.

4. In a burner the combination of a trough and perforated tubes situated thereabove and forming a combustion-chamber, said trough being contracted at its lower portion and being provided with a wick seated in the contracted portion of the trough and extending upwardly between and distant from its upwardly-disposed walls.

The original applications contained numerous claims and were met from time to time with suggestions of amendments, rejections on references, and so forth, in the ordinary course of procedure. The Examiner finally suggested that the broadest allowable subject-matter of the invention, consisted:

In a burner, the combination of a trough and perforated tubes seated thereon forming a combustion-chamber, said trough being contracted at its lower portion and being provided with a wick seated in the contracted portion of the ugh and extending upwardly between and distant from its upwardly-disposed lls.

This suggestion developed into the issue of the interference thereafter declared. The Examiner of Interferences and the majority of the Examiners-in-Chief decided the question of priority in favor of Blackford. The Commissioner made the final award of priority to Wilder. (C. D., 1902, 204; 99 O. G., 2769.) On appeal to this court that decision was reversed, and priority awarded to Blackford. (*Blackford* v. *Wilder*, C. D., 1903, 567; 104 O. G., 578; 21 App. D. C., 1.)

The issue turned, mainly, upon the point whether Wilder's " Exhibit E " showed the invention of the issue and as such had been reduced to practice. This exhibit had passed through the Patent Office and had been produced in this court on the hearing of the appeal. It had no lighting member in it, and attempt was made by Wilder, on a motion for rehearing, to introduce affidavits to show that it had, when presented in the Patent Office and considered by the several tribunals therein, a thin, vertical asbestos lighting member or kindler, answering the requirements of the issue. It appearing to the court from the recitals in the decisions of the Examiners-in-Chief and the Commissioner, that the lighter was not in the exhibit when considered by them, the motion was denied.

In coming to their conclusion, in the first case, the majority of the Examiners-in-Chief were of the opinion that the issue was " very specific;" and there was general concurrence in the fact that the subject-matter of the invention was a narrow one. In view of the preliminary proceedings in the Office, culminating in the communication of the Primary Examiner, before quoted, the conclusion was natural. As recited in the opinion on the former appeal:

In Blackford's answer to some of the objections of the Primary Examiner,
- on May 2, 1898, he asked a reconsideration on the ground of the combination of the V-shaped burner with his new form of wick; and this it was, he claimed, that enabled him to accomplish what former patented devices would not do.

He was finally informed on September 12, 1899, of the view of the Office in respect of patentability, as before stated.

Even in the narrow form, Wilder denied patentability, and moved the Examiners-in-Chief to report to the Commissioner, under Rule 126, that there was no patentable novelty in the issue. The Examiners, believing the issue, as defined, patentable, refused to make the suggestion. One of the Examiners-in-Chief, who dissented from the others as to priority, took a somewhat different view of the extent of the issue. He said:

This issue is broader than it is stated to be by my associates, and it is satisfied by any liquid-holding trough which is not filled by the wick at its upper portion, and which is restricted at its lower portion so as to limit the evaporating-surface of the contained oil to approximately the requirements of combustion. It is immaterial whether or not the evaporation takes place from the surface of the oil or from the surface of the wick, or from both, as long as the surface which sustains the oil is duly limited in its area, and operates to expose to the heat of the flame only a relatively small surface of oil. An examination of the records of both parties shows that this is the breadth of the invention to which the interfering claims were intended to, and do apply. Viewed in this light, said claims and the corresponding counts of the issue are distinctly applicable to Wilder's Exhibit E.

The Commissioner, who reversed the decision of the Examiners-in-Chief, said:

Exhibit E consists of a V-shaped trough essentially like that shown in Blackford's application. If the ordinary lighting member shown in the other exhibits is placed in this trough and the ordinary combustion-tubes are used above, every element of the issue is present. There is no question but that the combustion-tubes were intended to be and were, in fact, used with it; but a question is raised as to the lighting member. There is no lighting member in the exhibit now, and the testimony upon that point is not very full; but it is obvious upon mere inspection that there must have been a lighting member when the device was used, for it well understood by those familiar with this art that a lighting member is necessary to start the operation of a burner of this kind. (C. D., 1902, 204; 99 O. G., 2769.)

The different views upon those points were considered by the court, and that of the majority of the Board of Examiners-in-Chief was adopted. When the final decision was certified to the Commissioner, Wilder presented amended claims not specifically limited to the lighting member and the V-shaped trough of the original interference, but drawn, nevertheless, on his same Exhibit E, and requested an interference thereon with Blackford. Further proceedings resulted in the present interference with an issue defined as follows:

1. In an oil-burner, the combination with an oil-holding trough having a contracted lower part and an enlarged upper part, the lower part of the trough being adapted to contain a body or column of oil when in normal operation and the upper part forming a vaporizing-chamber to vaporize the oil from its free surface and means located in the trough for igniting or starting the vaporization of the oil, of perforated combustion-tubes forming an uninterrupted continuation of the vapor-chamber and adapted to cause the vapors arising from the surface of the oil to burn with a blue flame by admixture with the air.

2. In an oil-burner, the combination with an oil-holding trough, the lower part of the trough being adapted to contain a body or column of oil when in normal operation, and the upper part forming a vaporizing-chamber to vaporize the oil from its free surface and means located in the trough for igniting or starting the vaporization of the oil, of perforated combustion-tubes forming an uninterrupted continuation of the vapor-chamber and adapted to cause the vapors arising from the surface of the oil to burn with a blue flame by admixture with the air.

Blackford moved to dissolve the interference, the chief ground, stated in different forms, being that the subject-matter of the second interference was *res adjudicata;* that is to say, was embraced in, and included by the judgment of this court on the former appeal. This motion was denied by the Primary Examiner to whom it had been referred, in a lengthy decision; and his conclusion was adopted in turn by all of the tribunals of the Patent Office.

It was conceded that the doctrine of *res adjudicata* applies to proceedings in the Patent Office to the same extent as in the courts. The parties being the same, the ground of the decision was, necessarily, that the subject-matter was different; and is thus stated in the Examiner's decision:

The issues of this interference differ from the issues of the former interference in that they are not limited to any specific form of lighting device. Neither are they limited to the lighting member being seated in the contracted portion of the trough, nor are they limited to a lighting member seated in the contracted portion of the trough and extending upwardly so as to allow a vapor-space above the contracted portion of the trough on either or both sides of said lighting member.

The issues of the present interference are further distinguished from the former interference in that they are limited to " perforated combustion-tubes *forming an uninterrupted continuation of the vapor-chamber.*"

The limitation is material and was for the purpose of differentiating the contestant's structure from patent to Stacey, 473,858. Said patent discloses a trough covered by a perforated cap 9 which tends to prevent the vaporization of the oil from its free surface in the manner contemplated by the issues.

Further than this, the second count of the issue is differentiated from the matter of the former interference in that it is not limited to a trough having a lower *contracted portion* which was one of the essential qualifications of the issues in the other interference.

From this it appears that the present issues cover an entirely different structure from the structures which were held to be within the scope of the issues of the former interference and it is believed that they involve separate and distinctive inventive subject-matter.

The conclusion in respect of the patentability of the broader claims of the present issue seems rather inconsistent with the views apparently controlling the earlier proceedings in the Patent Office on each of the applications, as well as with the view of Wilder, himself, who, as has been seen, formerly denied the patentability of the narrower issue of the first interference. The patentability of the present issue, however, is not a question involved in this proceeding. Assuming patentability, therefore, the question to be determined is whether, in view of the former proceedings in the Office culminating in the first declaration of interference between these same applications, and the final decision therein in favor of Blackford, Wilder is now deprived of the right to go back and amend by inserting broader claims dominating those that were by that decision awarded to Blackford? In other words, is Wilder's right to make the amended claims and maintain the present interference thereon concluded by the former adjudication?

The doctrine of *res adjudicata*, or estoppel by former judgment, has been thus declared by the Supreme Court of the United Staes:

When the second suit is upon the same cause of action, and between the same parties as the first, the judgment in the former is conclusive in the latter as to every question which was or might have been presented and determined in the first action; but when the second suit is upon a different cause of action, though between the same parties, the judgment in the former action operates as an estoppel only as to the point or question actually litigated and determined, and not as to other matters which might have been litigated and determined.

(*Nesbit* v. *Riverside Independent District*, 144 U. S., 610, 618; *New Orleans* v. *Citizens Bank*, 167 U. S., 371, 386; *S. P. R. R.* v. *U. S.*, 168 U. S., 1, 48.)

The same rule applies to adjudications made in the Patent Office. (*In re Barratt's* appeal, C. D., 1899, 320; 87 O. G., 1075; 14 App. D. C., 255, 257; *in re Fay*, C. D., 1900, 232; 90 O. G., 1157; 15 App. D. C., 515, 517.) It is also declared in Patent Office Rule 127, that—

a second interference will not be declared upon a new application for the same invention filed by either party.

It is further provided in Rule 132, that whenever an award of priority has been rendered in an interference proceeding by any tribunal, and the limit of appeal therefrom has expired, the Primary Examiner shall advise the defeated party that the claims so involved in the issue stand finally rejected. In interpreting this rule, Mr. Commissioner Mitchell held that the Examiner, after rejecting all claims which are or could be made by the prevailing party, may properly allow to the defeated party such other claims as are held to be patentable and which could not be made by the prevailing party; and that no claim should be allowed to the defeated party which could by any latitude of construction be held to embrace matter common to the structure of both parties to the interference. (C. D., 1891, 141; 56 O. G., 141.)

In *Corry and Barker* v. *Trout*. (C. D., 1904, 144; 110 O. G., 306,) Mr. Commissioner Allen reversed a decision of the Primary Examiner refusing dissolution of a second interference between the same parties. In doing so he said:

The prior interference included the application now involved and the claim in controversy was drawn upon the same structure as that now claimed. Corry and Barker contend that the present issue is not substantially different from that in the first interference, and Trout admits that they differ merely in scope. Trout, however, argues that the present issue being broader than the first can not be regarded as substantially the same and that it can not be assumed that he will be unable to prove priority of invention on this issue merely because he failed on the specific issue.

The declaration of a second interference between the same applications should *be necessary* only in rare cases and under very exceptional circumstances. It *should not ordinarily* be declared upon claims to the same device and differing from the first issue merely in scope. If a mere change in the scope of claims were considered good ground for a second interference, the number of successive interferences between the same parties would be practically unlimited and the interference procedure would become an intolerable burden to applicants. The Office is justified in taking the decision as to priority of invention as *prima facie* evidence that the successful party was the first inventor not merely of the particular issue in controversy, but of the invention common to the two cases, whether more broadly or more specifically stated. The burden is upon the defeated party to show special circumstances of the particular case which make it improper to apply the decision to the other claims presented. It is not sufficient that the claims differ and that it is theoretically possible for one party to be prior inventor as to the first and the other party prior inventor as to the second, for this would apply in all cases where the claims are not identical. To justify a second interference, there must be some exceptional circumstances, such as were present in *Sarfert* v. *Meyer* (76 MS. Dec., 410) where the decision in the first interference was in favor of Sarfert upon the specific issue; but it appeared from the findings of fact that Meyer was the first inventor of the broad invention common to the two cases.

(See also *Phelps* v. *Wormley*, C. D., 1905, 374; 118 O. G., 1069; *ex parte Neiswanger*, C. D., 1890, 37; 50 O. G., 1132.)

The foregoing decision is in substantial accord with the long-established doctrine of the Patent Office, that an interference in fact depends chiefly upon the subject-matter disclosed and not merely upon the language of the respective claims. (*Drawbaugh* v. *Blake*, C. D., 1885, 7; 30 O. G., 259.) In that case Mr. Commissioner Butterworth said:

I have no doubt about the correctness of the rule laid down in *ex parte Upton* (C. D., 1884, 26; 27 O. G., 99.) It is the *substance* of things and not the *shadow* with which we deal.

(*Gray* v. *Robertson*, C. D., 1890, 1; 50 O. G., 165; *Bissell* v. *Robert*, C. D., 1890, 77; 51 O. G., 1618. See also *Miller* v. *Eagle Mfg. Co.*, C. D., 1894, 147; 66 O. G., 845; 151 U. S., 186, 198.)

In that case the question was as to the validity of two patents to the same party. The drawings in each patent were identical, and the specifications in each substantially the same, but the first patent covered both the lifting and depressing actions of the machine, while the second was limited to the lifting effect only. The second patent was held to be void. Mr. Justice Jackson, who delivered the opinion of the Court, said:

The result of the foregoing and other authorities is that no patent can issue for an invention actually covered by a former patent, especially to the same patentee, although the terms of the claims may differ; that the second patent, although containing a broader claim more generical in its character, than the specific claims contained in the prior patent, is also void; but that where the second patent covers matter described in the prior patent, essentially distinct and separable from the invention covered thereby, and claims made thereunder, its validity may be sustained. * * * It is settled also that an inventor may make a new improvement on his own invention of a patentable character, for which he may obtain separate patent, and the cases cited by the appellee come to this point, and to this point only, that a later patent may be granted where the invention is clearly distinct from, and independent of, one previously patented. ·

(*Porter* v. *Louden*, C. D., 1895, 707; 73 O. G., 1551; 7 App. D. C., 64, 69.)

It remains to apply the foregoing principles to the facts of this case which are substantially these: The applications of the two interferences are the same: The issue of each reads on Wilder's original Exhibit E, and Blackford's Exhibit D. It was on Exhibit E, and the evidence relating to its several parts, time of construction and operation that Wilder's right to priority was founded and determined in each case. That exhibit when produced before the Examiners-in-Chief, the Commissioner, and this court, in the hearing of the first interference, did not show the wick of the issue therein involved, and Wilder was denied the right to introduce additional evidence tending to show that the wick was in the device when constructed, and when offered for inspection in the Patent Office. He was confined to the evidence contained in the record. When the decision awarding priority to Blackford was certified to the Commissioner, Wilder presented the broader claims, and secured the declaration of a second interference with Blackford, supporting his claim to priority with his same Exhibit E and some additional evidence tending to show that the wick of the former issue was contained in it when constructed. The decisions of the several tribunals of the Patent Office in favor of Wilder were founded upon this exhibit and evidence as appears from the following extracts:

(1) From decision of Examiner of Interferences:

Wilder's Exhibit E was in the prior case held by the Board of Examiners-in-Chief and by the court of appeals to be a fatal defect. It is now satisfactorily established that this element was present when the device was tested in 1896 and also when it was filed as an exhibit in the first interference. A corresponding part has now been added to this exhibit, and the part which became misplaced has been recovered and filed as a separate exhibit, "Wilder's Lighting Medium, Exhibit E." With the exception of the testimony regarding the lost part of Wilder's Exhibit E, the state of facts in the present interference is almost identical with that prevailing when the case was previously considered by the several appellate tribunals, and for this reason the findings of the court of appeals in the prior case, so far as not affected by the introduction of new evidence, are considered binding in the present case. For the same reason, and for the further reason that Blackford in his brief seeks to derive the benefit of the findings of the court in the first interference, comment has been made in one instance upon the fact that certain of Blackford's testimony in the present case does not harmonize with that in the first interference.

＊　　　＊　　　＊　　　＊　　　＊　　　＊　　　＊

Wilder has proved that the lighting member was present in Exhibit E when tested in 1896, and it appears from the testimony of Harlan P. Wilder (Q. 19) it *combustion*-section of the form specified in the issue was used at that time with Exhibit E, which in other respects embodies the issue of the present interference as fully as it did that of the first interference. Wilder must therefore be credited with the date of Exhibit E as his date of reduction to practice of the invention in issue. Inasmuch as none of the structures which Blackford alleges were made before Wilder's Exhibit E embodied the invention in controversy, Wilder must by reason of the construction and operation of that exhibit be considered the first inventor.

(2) From decision of Examiners-in-Chief:

The issue of the interference being thus a new one, it is clear that the decision of the court of appeals in the former proceeding does not, as contended by counsel for Blackford, render the question of priority *res adjudicata*. The court, however, determined certain questions of fact and their findings as to these matters will of course not be controverted. Thus it was decided that Blackford's Exhibit D embodies the subject-matter of the prior interference and was completed and successfully operated in November, 1896. If, as held by the court of appeals, this exhibit is an oil-bowl it necessarily contains also the issue of the present interference.

We have therefore as a starting-point in the present controversy the established fact that Blackford embodied the invention of the issue in a practical device as early as November, 1896, or prior to the date (April 19, 1897) of Wilder's application, and Wilder in order to prevail must overcome this reduction to practice by showing priority as to both conception and reduction to practice, or, by showing a prior conception and a later reduction to practice coupled with reasonable diligence.

Wilder has offered in evidence an oil-bowl that is known to the record as Exhibit E. This exhibit when associated with perforated combustion-tubes, such as the testimony shows were used in connection with it, clearly embodies the issue of this interference. The exhibit was made and successfully operated in the early part of 1896, or prior to the date of Blackford's Exhibit D, and is a valid reduction to practice antedating the above-mentioned reduction of Blackford. The Examiner of Interferences holds that this Exhibit E was constructed some months prior to June, 1896, and we agree with this conclusion as to the date of its production. This agrees with the finding in the previous interference that the exhibit was made in April, 1896.

It appears that when Exhibit E was considered in the prior interference it was, on account of the absence therefrom of a lighting medium (a wick,) held not to involve the issue of that interference. The Examiners-in-Chief and the court of appeals both concurred in this finding of fact, although while the case was pending before the court of appeals on a motion for rehearing it was shown that the wick with which the exhibit was originally provided had become separated from the exhibit and could not be found. Testimony introduced in the present case, however, shows that the exhibit originally contained a wick similar to the one which now lies within its annular channel and that when it was operated a wick was employed as a starting or lighting member.

It is evident from the foregoing that Wilder by his proof concerning the production and operation of Exhibit E has established a conception and reduction to practice antedating the reduction to practice to which Blackford is entitled by virtue of his Exhibit D.

(3) From decision of Commissioner:

The applications involved in the present interferences were involved in a prior interference No. 20,427, upon a different issue, in which the Court of Appeals of the District of Columbia awarded priority to Blackford. (Blackford v. Wilder,

C. D., 1903, 567; 104 O. G., 578.) In said prior interference the court agreed with the majority of the Examiners-in-Chief in the conclusion that Blackford was the first to reduce to practice the invention of that interference in his Exhibit D in November, 1896. The Examiners-in-Chief and the court of appeals found that Wilder's Exhibit E when the case was before them was incomplete and did not have a " vertically-disposed lighting member." Wilder claimed that Exhibit E when filed in the Patent Office contained a wick, but that it became displaced between the time the case was before the Examiner of Interferences and the time it was considered by the Examiners-in-Chief. He brought a motion before the court of appeals that an investigation be instituted as to the alleged loss and recovery of the missing member of Exhibit E and that a rehearing be granted. In denying this motion the court held (*Blackford* v. *Wilder*, C. D., 1903, 573; 104 O. G., 580) that the matter of the wick should have been settled in the Patent Office before appeal was taken to the court, also that the question of priority turned upon the fact whether Exhibit E contained a lighting member of the specific character called for by the issue at the time of the alleged reduction to practice in 1896, and not at the time it was introduced in evidence, and that the evidence failed to establish satisfactorily this essential fact.

Upon the conclusion of the interference and the resumption of *ex parte* proceedings in the Patent Office, Wilder presented a claim not limited to the specific form of igniting member of the former interference, but which he alleged was based on his Exhibit E, and he requested the institution of an interference proceeding for the purpose of contesting the question of priority of the invention of said claim.

    *   *   *   *   *   *   *

In the former interference the court of appeals based its decision in favor of Blackford on the finding that his Exhibit D was completed and successfully operated in November, 1896. If this exhibit has an oil-bowl and embodied that issue of that interference, it undoubtedly is a reduction to practice of the present invention. Starting with this exhibit, the burden is therefore on Wilder, to establish either a prior reduction to practice or a prior conception, coupled by due diligence, with a subsequent reduction to practice.

The only exhibits alleged to have been made prior to November, 1896, when Exhibit D was completed, and the only ones which require consideration are, for Wilder, Exhibit E, alleged to have been made in April, 1896, and, on the part of Blackford, Exhibits C and A, alleged to have been made in January and February, 1896, respectively.

It has been found in both this and the prior interference that these exhibits were made at these dates, as alleged. The dates of these exhibits are not contested; but the controversy relates to whether these exhibits embody the invention and were successful reductions to practice of the invention on the dates they were made.

    *   *   .   *   *   *   *

It thus appears that the court did not hold that Exhibit E had no igniting member, but that the evidence did not show that it had the one called for by the issue of that interference in April, 1896. It is to be noted that the present issue is broader than the issue of the former interference in respect to the igniting member. While the present issue is satisfied with " means located in the trough for igniting or starting the vaporization of the oil," count 1 of the issue of the former interference called for " a vertically-disposed lighting member *seated in the* liquid-containing portion and extending upward between the walls of the enlarged vapor-receiving portion to form a vapor-space at the side of the lighting-chamber." Counts 2, 3 and 4 of the former issue call for a lighting member of substantially similar character.

The testimony in this interference of Wilder and his corroborating witnesses conclusively establishes that Exhibit E was provided with the igniting member of the issue of this interference when operated in April, 1896.

To sum up—the parties are the same. The applications are the same and disclose the invention of each issue. The constructions relied on, respectively, as evidencing conception and reduction to practice of the invention of both issues are the same. The fundamental facts of both cases are the same. Applying the well-settled principle of estoppel by judgment, before stated, it follows inevitably that the final decision in the first interference is conclusive, unless it can be made to appear that the question upon which the determination of the second case rests is one that neither was, nor could have been presented and determined in the first case.

The contention is that this essential difference between the two cases lies in the fact that the claims of the second interference are broader in scope than those of the first, and cover an essentially separate and distinct invention. We are unable to concur in the decisions of the Patent Office tribunals maintaining this view. As pointed out in the cases heretofore cited, in declaring interferences in the Patent Office, identity of subject-matter is not determinable merely by the language of the claims preferred by the respective applicants. By the several decisions under review on this appeal it is shown that the later claims of Wilder might have been presented in the first instance, if so advised, and Blackford brought into interference with him then as he has been since; for, as they expressly hold, Blackford's Exhibit D, being an oil-bowl, necessarily contained the issue of the second interference. Instead, Wilder preferred to adopt the more specific claims of the first issue drawn as the present ones were upon the structure shown in his Exhibit E, and reading as well on Blackford's Exhibit D. That issue having been decided in favor of Blackford, Wilder has been permitted to make the new claims and has been awarded priority of invention over the claim of Blackford founded on the structures proved in the first case, on additional evidence to that introduced on the first trial tending to show that his Exhibit E did, in fact, have in it the wick of the first issue, notwithstanding that had been one of the questions expressly decided in the former case. Having had the right to make the broader claims in the earlier stages of the proceedings in the Patent Office, as well as the opportunity, in the first proceeding, to introduce all of his evidence relating to the construction and operation of his Exhibit E structure, his right, in both respects, terminated with that litigation.

Whether the former decision was right or wrong, or was induced by the want of the particular evidence that was offered in the present case, is not the question. However that might be it was final and put an end to the litigation in the first interference. It must be held, therefore, as conclusive of every question that not only was, but also might have been presented and determined in that case.

The motion to dissolve the second interference ought to have been sustained, and Wilder's claims finally rejected as provided in Rule 132.

The decision appealed from will therefore be reversed. It is so ordered; and that this decision be certified to the Commissioner of Patents as required by law. *Reversed.*

[Court of Appeals of the District of Columbia.]

KREAG *v.* GEEN.

Decided December 4, 1906.

(127 O. G., 1581.)

ORIGINALITY—EMPLOYER AND EMPLOYEE—IMPROVEMENTS BY EMPLOYEE.

When one conceives the principle or plan of an invention and employs another to perfect the details and realize his conception, though the latter may make valuable improvements therein, such improved result belongs to the employer.

Mr. C. S. Davis and *Mr. H. L. Osgood* for Kreag.
Mr. F. F. Crampton and *Mr. Geo. H. Hamlin* for Geen.

SHEPARD, J.:

The subject-matter of invention in this case is an improvement in brushes used for polishing shoes. Geen holds a patent for the invention issued October 4, 1904, upon an application filed December 3, 1903. Kreag filed an application making the same claims on November 25, 1904. An interference was declared between the two with issue defined as follows:

1. In a brush, a back, a felt pad, and a pad-cover having free side edges and constituting a brushing-surface, said pad being compressed near its ends by fastening devices and the parts between the fasteners of the pad and the proximate ends of the brush still further compressed by the cover fastened to the said ends.

2. In a brush, a back, a felt pad, and a pad-cover constituting a brushing-surface, said pad having fluted edges whereby said edges are made more compressible.

3. In a brush, a back, a plurality of felt pads, and a pad-cover constituting a brushing-surface, said pads having fluted edges whereby said edges are made more compressible.

4. In a brush, a wooden back having the overhanging end extensions, a plurality of felt pads tacked to the back near its ends, a pad-cover consisting of a strip of animal skin with its natural covering, said pads being narrower than the back and narrower than the strip and having fluted edges, and fastening

devices securing the strip to the back under the extensions, said natural covering of the strip of skin extending outside of the back, both at its sides and ends.

The Examiner of Interferences decided in favor of Geen, and was
reversed by the Examiners-in-Chief who awarded priority to Kreag.
This decision was in turn reversed on appeal to the Commissioner,
from whose decision awarding priority (C. D., 1906, 350; 124 O. G.,
1208,) to Geen this appeal has been taken by Kreag.

The decision that the issue is a patentable one, having been made
in the Office and a patent issued thereon to Geen, although it is con-
fessed by the Examiner of Interferences that "the invention is an
exceedingly limited one," is binding upon us on this appeal.   Assuming, as we must, for the purposes of this case, that the original conclusion, arrived at, it appears, with considerable difficulty in the
Office in passing Geen's application to patent, was a sound one, the
single question for our determination is the disputed claim of priority
between the patentee and the later applicant.

The question as presented on the evidence is one of originality
rather than the ordinary one of priority between independent inventors.

Kreag was an officer of the American Chemical Manufacturing and
Mining Company that was engaged in the manufacture of a shoe-
polish called "Shinola."   Geen was his neighbor, and was the manager of a department in the Fred O. Todd Co., whose business was
the manufacture of shoes.   Geen was also a mechanic of some skill,
and said, in giving testimony, that Kreag thought him capable of
producing a brush suitable for paste polish.   As early as November,
1901, Kreag had been looking about for a satisfactory brush for use
with his "Shinola" polish.   He collected a number of brushes in
ordinary use for polishing with paste, and finding none to answer his
purposes, applied to Geen to assist him.   Kreag and Geen differ in
their statements as to communications made by Kreag to the latter,
and there is no independent testimony.   It is clear, however, that
Geen began his labors at the instigation of Kreag.

In this conflict of testimony, the burden being heavily upon Kreag
in the first instance as claiming against a patentee, we must resort to
certain well-established circumstances in the case to ascertain from
them, if possible, the exact relations of the parties, and the extent
of the communication made by Kreag to Geen at the time of enlisting
the latter's services.   Geen admits that Kreag sent and brought him
several old brushes, and most if not all of them were produced by the
parties and made exhibits in the case.   Some of these were felt and
some bristle brushes; some had daubers attached, but the majority
had not.   Two had sheepskin faces for polishers attached to wooden
backs, and in one of them the woolly-skin pad was secured by nails
to an undercut portion of the back.   Kreag also furnished anoth

brush which had the wooden back of the ordinary shoe-brush. A thick felt pad, thicker or more resilient midway between the ends, was nailed to the wooden back, and covered with a strip of cloth for a polishing-surface. It was in a new combination of the materials of these old brushes and their arrangement, making a superior polisher, that invention was found to exist when the patent was issued to Geen.

Kreag undoubtedly employed Geen to make a new brush, and, in addition to the sample brushes, furnished him with the materials used in his experiments. The itemized accounts rendered by Geen and paid by Kreag show this plainly. When the desired brush was produced, Geen made them in large quantities for Kreag who furnished the materials and paid for the work. The relation of employer and employee once established, the law is well settled that when one conceives the principle or plan of an invention, and employs another to perfect the details and realize his conception, though the latter may make valuable improvements therein, such improved results belong to the employer. (*Milton* v. *Kingsley.* C. D., 1896, 420, 426; 75 O. G., 2193, 2195; 7 App. D. C., 531, 537; *Gedge* v. *Cromwell*, C. D., 1902, 514; 98 O. G., 1486; 19 App. D. C., 192; *Miller* v. *Kelley*, C. D., 1901, 405; 96 O. G., 1038; 18 App. D. C., 163; *Gallagher* v. *Hastings*, C. D., 1903, 531; 103 O. G., 1165; 21 App. D. C., 88; *Flather* v. *Weber*, C. D., 1903, 561; 104 O. G., 312; 21 App. D. C., 179.) Applying this principle to the established circumstances of the case, we are forced to the conclusion that Kreag had in mind the general plan of the new brush with resilient felt pads and sheepskin polishing-surface when he employed Geen to undertake the work of construction. Whether he had in mind the fluted edges of the pads, also, is immaterial. With the three brushes, before described, in his possession, and with his mind bent on improvement upon them, we must believe that he had a general conception of the new construction; and that he must necessarily have communicated that conception to Geen, who by his skill as a mechanic was able to produce the desired construction, as well as to improve it. Notwithstanding the improvement upon the combinations of form and materials shown in the old brushes has been declared the exercise of inventive talent, we think that it was undoubtedly within the conception of Kreag in a crude form, at least, and that he disclosed it to Geen. As before declared, it is not within our province, under the limitation of the jurisdiction conferred upon us in such cases as this, to say that the improvement was the result of mere mechanical skill rather than of invention. Whatever it was, we are of the opinion upon consideration of all the facts and circumstances disclosed by the evidence, that Kreag and not Geen is entitled the benefit of it. The decision will therefore be reversed, and this sion will be certified to the Commissioner of Patents. *Reversed.*

[Court of Appeals of the District of Columbia.]

POTTER *v.* McINTOSH.

Decided December 14, 1906.

(127 O. G., 1995.)

INTERFERENCE—APPEAL ON PRIORITY—CONSIDERATION OF PATENTABILITY.

> Where the junior party to an interference concedes that his preliminary
> statement fails to overcome the filing date of the senior party and the pat-
> entability of the issue has been favorably passed upon by the tribunals of
> the Patent Office, before whom the question was brought in accordance with
> the practice of that Office, on appeal to the court of appeals from a judg-
> ment on priority the question of patentability will not be considered where
> it is raised merely for the purpose of preventing the grant of a patent to
> the senior party, except in an extraordinary case.

Mr. A. A. Buck, Mr. G. P. Whittlesey, and *Mr. Albert G. Davis* for
the appellant.

Mr. Charles H. Roberts for the appellee.

McComas, *J.:*

John T. McIntosh, who filed his application June 14, 1902, for a
patent for an automatic safety stop device for electric vehicles was
later placed in interference with other parties with whose devices
three interferences were declared. There were twenty-six counts in
the three interferences, and such proceedings were had that to all of
these except one, the Primary Examiner dissolved the interference.
This single count is in issue here, for the Commissioner of Patents
sustained the Examiner; (C. D., 1906, 56; 120 O. G., 1823;) and this
count is as follows:

An automatic safety stop device, comprising a mechanism in the controller-
arm of an electric motor, synchronously operated with an air-brake valve
through a lever connection, substantially as described and shown.

The interference is between McIntosh and the junior party, William B. Potter, who filed his application August 28, 1902. We refrain
from reciting the preliminary decision of the Examiner of Interferences and the several appeals for rehearing before him and before the
Examiners-in-Chief and the elimination of several interferences because in our opinion it suffices to consider the record and arguments of
counsel in connection with the final rulings of the tribunals of the
Patent Office upon the single issue whereon the Commissioner made
the final decision brought before this court upon this appeal.

After the count just quoted became the remaining count of the issue,
the Examiner of Interferences decided that Potter, the junior party,
had failed, and gave judgment of priority of invention as to this
count in favor of John T. McIntosh, the senior party. Upon appeal,
the Examiners-in-Chief (two of them passing upon the question
raised) held that because McIntosh filed June 14, 1902, and because

Potter, who filed August 28 in that year, does not allege conception of the invention before July preceding, McIntosh was the prior inventor and was entitled to an award of priority.

Counsel for Potter urged that it is essential to an interference proceeding that the issue be patentable and this issue is not patentable, therefore the Examiner of Interferences should be reversed because there being no patentable invention involved, the Examiner was without jurisdiction to render a decision of priority in favor of either party. The Examiners-in-Chief held that their course was to decide the question of priority on the record as made out by the parties and then under Rule 126—

direct the attention of the Commissioner to any matter not relating to priority which may have come to their notice, and which in their opinion amounts to a statutory bar to the grant of a patent to either of the parties for the claim or claims in interference.

And they affirmed the decision of the Examiner of Interferences. One of the two Examiners-in-Chief under this rule called the Commissioner's attention to the opinion of the Examiner-in-Chief that this issue is not patentable in view of several patents cited by him. The other Examiner-in-Chief was of opinion that the application of McIntosh carrying this claim should be allowed. The Commissioner of Patents held that since the Primary Examiner considered the cited patent on motion to dissolve, and reached the conclusion that the issue was patentable over them and the two members of the Board of Examiners-in-Chief differed in opinion upon the question of patentability, this division of opinion in the appellate tribunal amounts to an affirmance of the decision below and therefore no good reason was seen for referring this case to the Primary Examiner for reconsideration of the question of patentability. Thereupon counsel for Potter appealed from the decision of the Examiners-in-Chief awarding priority of invention to McIntosh. The Commissioner held that—

In this case the appellant failed to allege in his preliminary statement dates of invention early enough to overcome the record date of his opponent and brings this appeal for the sole purpose of attacking the patentability of the issue and preventing the grant of a patent to his opponent for the invention defined therein. An appeal of this kind was brought and disposed of in the case of *Sobey* v. *Holsclaw* (C. D., 1905, 523; 119 O. G., 1922.)

It was pointed out there that upon such appeal as the present the case is before me simply upon the question of the priority of the parties with regard to the subject-matter of the issue and that the junior party having conceded in his preliminary statement that he was subsequent to his opponent in the possession of this matter there is nothing for me to do but to affirm the decision of the Examiners-in-Chief in favor of the senior party. I am convinced that Potter should not be heard upon this appeal in opposition to the grant of a patent to McIntosh on the ground that the issue is not patentable. The reasons for this conclusion were set forth fully in *Sobey* v. *Holsclaw, supra,* and need not be repeated here. (C. D., 1906, 56; 120 O. G., 1823.)

The circumstances of the present case do not appear to be distinguished from those of that case, except in regard to the matter of recommendation by the Examiners-in-Chief under Rule 126. In the former case, the Examiners-in-Chief, after considering the arguments upon patentability, refused to include in their decision upon priority, a statement that in their opinion the issue was not patentable; in the present case one Examiner-in-Chief found the issue to be patentable, another found it was not patentable, and they so stated; the third was absent. This distinction between the cases is not one of consequence. The Commissioner added that the Primary Examiner had twice found the issue to be patentable and—

Whatever objections there may be to the policy and rule preventing appeal from decisions affirming patentability or right to make claims, in those cases where affirmance may result in preventing the issue of a patent to a party who, in the event of a contrary decision, might have been entitled thereto, this policy and rule are believed to be in accordance with sound reason and unimpeachable in their application to cases like the present, where the would-be appellant upon patentability has in any event no standing before the Office as a claimant for a patent upon the matter in question. (C. D., 1906, 56; 120 O. G., 1823.)

Upon a petition by Potter for rehearing his counsel urge that the decision of this Court in *Podlesak* v. *McInnerney* (C. D., 1906, 558; 120 O. G., 2127; 26 App. D. C., 399) sufficiently supported his contention, and the Commissioner adhered to his ruling correctly stating—

that the consideration of the questions of right to make the claim in issue and of identity of invention was undertaken by the court because the appellant in that case came before them seeking to have determined his right to a patent to which he was apparently justly entitled if there was error in the decisions below holding that his opponent was entitled to make the claim in issue and that there was interference in fact. In the present case the appellant is admittedly not entitled to a patent on the matter in issue and as was pointed out in my decision in this case, and in the case of *Sobey* v. *Holsclaw*, no good reason appears for hearing at this time the arguments of the appellant upon the patentability of his opponent's claims, or for reviewing the affirmative decision of the Primary Examiner on that question. (C. D., 1906, 183; 122 O. G., 1721.)

We concur in this very satisfactory exposition of the view which this court so recently expressed in *Sobey* v. *Holsclaw*, (*ante*, 465; 126 O. G., 3041.)

All three tribunals of the Patent Office have held that McIntosh was already in the Patent Office with a complete invention before Potter conceived it. Inasmuch as Potter concedes that his preliminary statement has failed to overcome the filing date of the application of McIntosh, the only office of his appeal here is to argue against the patentability of the invention of McIntosh. The appellant here, who admits that he is not the first inventor, has no exclusive personal right in the determination of the patentability, he has no greater interest than other citizens and yet he is here asking us in a case of interference, where the patentability of the invention is a necessary prerequisite to a declaration of interference, and in a class of cases wherein, except under extraordinary circumstances the patentability of an invention is not an open question before us, to review that question and no other. In *Hisey* v. *Peters* (C. D., 1895, 349; 71 O. G., 892; 6 App. D. C., 68) this Court said an appellant who claims an alleged patentable invention is not to be heard to urge non-patentability of his claim after it has been placed in interference with other claims. IIis affirmation that his claim is patentable estops him. In *Sobey* v. *Holsclaw, supra,* Mr. Justice Duell so fully and exhaustively reviewed the decisions conclusive of the present case, in a case substantially like the one now before us that it is unnecessary to repeat the grounds upon which we affirm the Commissioner of Patents in this case. *We adopt the views so well stated by the Commissioner and now affirm his final decision.* The arguments of Potter's counsel have failed to satisfy us that the case before us is one of those extraordinary cases in which this court may be called upon to inquire whether there is a patentable invention involved.

This decision will be certified to the Commissioner of Patents in accordance with the statute.

[Court of Appeals of the District of Columbia.]

LARKIN *v.* RICHARDSON.

Decided December 7, 1906.

(127 O. G., 2394.)

INTERFERENCE—ORIGINALITY—EMPLOYER AND EMPLOYEE—ANCILLARY INVENTION.
   Where a person has discovered an improved principle in a manufacture and employs others in assisting him to carry out that principle, and these in that employment make valuable additions to the preconceived design of the employer, such suggested improvements are in general to be regarded as the property of the party who discovered the original improved principle and may be embodied in his patent as part of his invention. (See *Agawam Co.* v. *Jordan,* 7 Wall., 583, 602; *Gedge* v. *Cromwell,* C. D., 1902, 514; 98 O. G., 1486; 19 App. D. C., 198; *Milton* v. *Kingsley,* C. D., 1896, 420; 75 O. G., 2193; 7 App. D. C., 537.)

Mr. H. N. Low, Mr. Edmond Adcock, and *Mr. L. A. Welles* for Larkin.

Mr. L. S. Bacon, Mr. C. K. Offield, Mr. H. S. Towle, Mr. C. C. Linthicum, and *Mr. Earl D. Babst* for Richardson.

McComas, J.:

   Bernard II. Larkin appealed from a decision of the Commissioner f Patents (C. D., 1906, 209; 122 O. G., 2390.) that John D. Rich n *is the prior inventor of certain improvements in the constr* of sheet-metal display-cans for bakery products. Richardson is the advertising manager of the National Biscuit Company to which he assigned his application. Larkin was at the time to which this interference relates, a district manager of the western factories of the American Can Company, to which company his application was assigned. At the time the testimony was taken he was no longer in the employment of this assignee. The issues of the interference are as follows:

1. A receptacle of the class described, consisting of a sheet-metal can having a cover, and its front wall provided with oblong panel-like openings, the margins of the sheet-metal surrounding said panel-openings being inturned, and sheets of material removably secured behind said openings, the upper sheet constituting a name-plate and the lower being transparent to display the contents in the bottom of said receptacle and held against the inturned margin of the metal surrounding the lower panel, substantially as described.

2. A receptacle of the class described, comprising a sheet-metal can having its front plate or side provided with two oblong panel-openings of substantially equal size and extending substantially across the front of the can, a name-plate fitted behind the upper panel-opening, the margins of the sheet along the lower panel-opening being inturned to provide a narrow ledge or bearing, and a sheet of glass removably secured behind the lower panel-opening in contact with said ledge, substantially as described.

3. A sheet-metal display can or box, comprising in combination a body having three sheet-metal sides, furnished at their upper ends with hollow, triangular strengthening bars or braces, and provided with a hollow, triangular strengthening bar or brace at its front, and a sheet-metal front plate having an upper or sign opening therein, and provided with sheet-metal guides having horizontal and upright flanges soldered to said front plate to form a pocket thereon to receive a removable sign-plate, said front strengthening-bar and said front plate forming a slot between them for removal and insertion of the sign-plate, substantially as specified.

4. A sheet-metal display can or box, comprising in combination a bottom, a body, and a hinged cover, the front of the body having two openings therein, two removable plates for closing said openings, fixed guides for holding one of said plates in place, and fastening means for holding the other removable plate in place, substantially as specified.

5. A sheet-metal display can or box having a bottom, a body and a cover, the sheet-metal front of said body having two openings therein, two removable plates for closing said openings, guides for holding one of said plates in place, and a turn-button guide for holding the other plate in place, substantially as specified.

6. A sheet-metal display can or box having a bottom, a body and a cover, the sheet-metal front of said body having two openings therein, two removable plates for closing said openings, guides for holding one of said plates in place, a turn-button guide for holding the other plate in place, said turn-button guide being mounted on one of the guid̶e̶ ̶f̶o̶r̶ said first-mentioned plate, substantially as specified.

The Patent O̶f̶f̶i̶c̶e̶ ̶d̶e̶ḏermined that the subject-matter of this ̶ ̶ ̶ ̶ ̶ ̶ ̶ ̶ṟunsel for Larkin claim that such̶ ̶ ̶ ̶ ̶ ̶ ̶ition of six features, which̶ ̶ ̶ ̶ ̶ ̶ldditional opening at the upper part of the brass front plate, a removable sign-plate, fixed guides of triangular pieces secured on the inside of the front-plate for holding the removable sign-plate in place behind the upper opening, a removable glass plate behind the lower opening in the front plate. Counsel for Richardson say the gist of the invention consists in the can having two front openings with two removable plates applied thereto, one to display the goods and the other the name of the National Biscuit Company, whose cans of the older style were provided with a single opening covered by a large removable sheet of glass which displayed the contents of the can but which large opening was more expensive, more fragile, and also greatly weakened the can-front. The Board of Examiners-in-Chief, which awarded priority to Larkin, took the former view, while the Examiner of Interferences and the Commissioner of Patents inclined to the latter view, and these awarded priority to Richardson, who was, in the opinion of the Commissioner, " the inventor of the broad idea of the can with the two openings, with removable panels."

In his preliminary statement, Larkin alleged conception, disclosure, and drawings on June 15, 1902, and reduction to practice about June 20, 1902, while Richardson alleged conception and disclosure in May, 1902, drawings, June 1, 1902, and reduction to practice on the first day of July, following. Richardson filed his application on November 1, 1902, and Larkin filed his application January 14, 1904. Each party here claims to have originated the idea in the display-can, and we must determine which of the two suggested the material improvements in the can which constitute the invention.

The officers of the National Biscuit Company wanted a can wherein to pack its various bakery products that should be distinctive in appearance and thus easily identified with its products, and so pleasing as to be acceptable to its customers. Early in 1902, officials of the National Biscuit Company, considered a new style of display-can for their goods. They were dissatisfied with the old can, which had one large opening in the front covered by a glass plate, removably fitted. Above this opening the name of the company appeared in embossed letters. Richardson at the head of the advertising department, actively engaged in the search for a new can, and about the first of May, 1902, he says he had in his own mind completed the can and about the sixth of May, he spoke about it to Fraser and described to him the can. Fraser, a draftsman, was Richardson's chief clerk and assistant, who undertook after his return from a trip to New York to produce for Richardson working drawings. Richardson's instructions to Fraser were to make drawings for cans with two openings, showing the openings in various proportions. Fraser consulted with Richardson from time to time while the drawings were in progress and worked them out to meet his approval, and about June 2, Fraser submitted the drawings, which were satisfactory to Richardson, and Richardson directed Fraser to have such cans made at once. Fraser reported to Richardson that he had placed the order with the American Can Company and had turned over to Wells, the sales agent of that company these sketches and instructed him to send cans so constructed to Richardson's office as soon as possible. Fraser testified that he returned to Chicago June 2, 1902, and made about eight drawings for the can, and he produced from memory four drawings which he said were essentially the same. It is difficult to excavate the actual statements of Fraser, buried as they are under the long leading questions of counsel examining the witness and too often testifying for him. Enough, however, is found to show that Fraser in the presence of Barnard, an officer of the Biscuit Company, in its purchasing department, gave to Wells, the sales agent of the Can Company, the original eight drawings about June 16, or 17, 1902. Wells suggested to Fraser, that he should visit the factory and then gave Fraser a letter of introduction to Larkin, which is dated June 17, 1902. Fraser had his interview with Wells in the purchasing department of the Biscuit Company, and Fraser wrapped up the drawings and Wells took them away with him. Later by telephone, Fraser talked with Wells about the delivery of the sample cans. Wells, however, died before the taking of the testimony. Fraser identified the can with two openings shown him as one similar in construction and appearance to the cans made by the Can Company after his working drawings. Fraser fixes the date of his drawings by another circumstance. Before he talked to Wells, by a letter in evidence to the Burdick Sign Company, dated June 14, 1902, Fraser had ordered four sample enameled signs, ten inches in length, which Richardson's counsel claims was the inside length dimension of the standard size made by the Can Company after Fraser delivered his drawings to Wells.

Fraser says when he gave the drawings to Wells, the explanation and directions given at same time, were given by Fraser alone. Barnard, who was present, says that prior to this interview, Fraser had brought to him a number of sketches for sample-cans, and that because Barnard received from Wells his letter presenting Fraser to Larkin, which letter Barnard sent to Fraser, Barnard can swear positively that the interview between Wells and Fraser was either on June 17 or a day or two before. Barnard's testimony-in-chief is practically the answer "yes" to very long, leading questions of Richardson's counsel. It seems just to say from Barnard's answers upon cross-examination that he substantially confirms Fraser. Barnard now says he saw Fraser's drawings but once, on the occasion when Fraser gave them to Wells, and the eight drawings shown him seemed to be the same drawings that Fraser gave to Wells. Barnard remembers that Fraser told Wells that he wanted him to make the cans in accordance with the drawings of Fraser, and Barnard thinks it was two or three weeks after this interview that the first sample display-can, having two openings in its front, one containing a sign-plate and one a glass plate, was delivered by the Can Company to the Biscuit Company. Evans, an officer of the Biscuit Company, says that just prior to August 1, 1902, he was with others, in a conference in Richardson's office, when they selected a can which was Richardson's original can, containing two openings. He identified this can by his own marks thereon and he fixes the time of the conference because on August 1, 1902, he gave an order for three thousand of these cans to be shipped to Kansas City. In frequent subsequent talks with Wells and Maas, they always referred to this can as the Biscuit Company's can, and the witness produced a circular sent to the managers of various bakery plants dated September 4, 1902, in which Evans notified them that the new can to be known as "501 can" had been adopted for general use. The circular recites the important features of the can described in this issue. Maas testifies that he brought the drawings from Barnard to Wells and Wells sent them to the Maywood factory where Larkin was employed by the Can Company. Maas only remembers one drawing having two openings, the one for the Biscuit Company's name at the top and the other covered by glass to display goods. It was Maas who at Well's instance delivered to Barnard of the Biscuit Company, the can actually made by the Can Company in accordance with this drawing and Maas thinks this occurred about a week after he had given the sample drawing to Wells, and the Richardson exhibit can is to Maas's best knowledge the first sample-can. Upon cross-examination, Maas testified that none of the eight drawings shown to him was the drawing he delivered to Wells. But Maas remembered the drawing marked "B" and finally said that he had seen these drawings in Mr. Wells's office to which they had been sent from the Can Company's factory.

On March 30, 1903, Evans, for the Biscuit Company, wrote to the Can Company to stamp on the backs of all the "501 cans" the words "patent applied for." Whether the cans thereafter were so marked is disputed. It is undisputed that the Can Company made no objection to the request.

Richardson has the burden of proving beyond a reasonable doubt that he was the original inventor of the subject-matter in controversy. Where a person has discovered an improved principle in a manufacture and employs others in assisting him to carry out that principle, and these in that employment make valuable additions to the preconceived design of the employer, such suggested improvements are in general to be regarded as the property of the party who discovered the original improved principle and may be embodied in his patent as part of his invention. (See *Agawam Co.* v. *Jordan,*

7 Wall., 583, 602; *Gedge* v. *Cromwell*, C. D., 1902, 514; 98 O. G., 1486; 19 App. D. C., 198; *Milton* v. *Kingsley*, C. D., 1896, 420; 75 O. G., 2193; 7 App. D. C., 537.)

Whatever weight be given to the argument that the issues contained specific limitations which Richardson did not disclose, Fraser makes clear Richardson's disclosure to him of a two-opening can with the removable plates and that several of the drawings he gave to Wells disclose such a can and that the American Can Company made such a can for the Biscuit Company and the Commissioner says that such can with two openings with plates to be removably secured behind the opening constitute the main and predominating structural features of this invention. The details of the fastening means if they call for anything more than the skill of a mechanic are merely ancillary features suggested by the general plan, and according to the cases last cited, in the absence of specific proof that they were suggested by Richardson, are to be regarded as part of his invention. The circumstances we have mentioned and the testimony to which we have adverted not only overcome the burden upon Richardson but create a strong presumption that in trying to satisfy the desire of his company for a new design for a display-can, Richardson became the real inventor and that Larkin, the employee of the Can Company, called upon to make the can Richardson desired, made his present claim after the Can Company had failed to procure a long-term contract, such as it desired, for the manufacture of the new cans.

Larkin is the junior party who filed more than one year after Richardson had filed, about a year and a half after the Can Company began to furnish the new can to the Biscuit Company and about nine months after Evans, for the Biscuit Company, directed the Can Company to stamp on the can the words " patent applied for." The burden of proof upon the junior party and the still heavier burden upon one employed to carry out the ideas of another, if he would claim originality in the thing produced, must be remembered even though Larkin's testimony may show that he added specific elements in completing the sample-cans. Much must appear in Larkin's behalf if his reduction to practice in this case is not to be deemed a reduction to practice on the part of Richardson which should inure to Richardson's benefit as the person who proposed and outlined the invention. Under all the circumstances Larkin's reduction to practice appears to be the result of Richardson's communication to Larkin's employer. If so, Larkin must prove beyond a reasonable doubt that what he did was his independent invention. Richardson's disclosure was not as ample as it might have been but several of the drawings made by Fraser and delivered through Wells to the Can Company and to Lar-

kin suffice to make out a sufficient disclosure on his part. Larkin's disclosure was not complete. The drawings sent to his company through Fraser and Wells impute notice to Larkin of what they disclose. The letter of Wells to Fraser shows he intended Larkin to have these drawings, and Larkin admits that Wells told him the Biscuit Company wanted to change the style of their packages, though Larkin said they wanted to leave off embossed lettering and lithograph instead and that Larkin suggested another opening for the lettering, to be removable and held by cleats on the inside of the front. Branninger made the first can under his instruction and Larkin had the first sheet-metal can, embodying the invention made about June 27, 1902.

Larkin says the only suggestion he had from Wells was that the Biscuit Company wanted a lithographed front instead of the embossed front and that after he had conceived this invention and had constructed a sample-can, he told Wells there should be a patent applied for and Wells promised to attend to it. It was stipulated that five workmen would testify that they each saw a can constructed like the Larkin exhibit can, which embodies the issues, on the dates named by him, and that they constructed cans like the exhibit can, and other cans like the pattern described by Larkin. It was also agreed that three officers of the Can Company would testify that they had never seen the eight drawings lettered A, B, C, D, E, F, G, H, until a search for them was made after Fraser testified he had delivered them to Wells nor could they after full inquiry find any employee of theirs who had seen Fraser's drawings and that Wells would naturally have shown these drawings to these witnesses if to any one; that the display-can in controversy was commonly called the Biscuit Company's can because it was their custom to name a can as that of the particular customer for whom it was made, and such designation was a matter of convenience and in no manner signified the designer of each particular can. After Fraser had testified concerning his drawings to Richardson, Larkin testified that these lettered drawings were sent to him from Wells just before July 14 and thereupon he had his workmen make cans with the single opening on July 14, the date being fixed by the memoranda of his workmen and between June 30, and July 18, his workmen made eight cans with two openings, in each instance differing somewhat in size; that he had never seen or heard of the drawing referred to by Maas, nor did he know that the lettered drawings were in the possession of the Can Company. It is conceded that the five workmen would testify that they for the first time saw these eight drawings shortly before July 14, and then proceeded to make the display-cans at Larkin stated, and they were sent to the Biscuit Company, and after a search these drawings were found in *the main work* factory on January 30, 1905. It was about June 7,

1902, that Larkin claims the conception of the invention, and on that day the first display-can was made and this was the reduction to practice claimed by both parties. Branninger made this can under instructions from his foreman, Xavier, and from Larkin. Six patterns for the front of the can, between June 30, and July 15, were in evidence as Larkin's patterns and it was testified that the seventh pattern representing the style accepted by the Biscuit Company was delivered to the machinery department of the Can Company as a guide in making dies used in producing cans like the accepted sample. Under all the circumstances we are convinced that the lettered drawings were sent to the Can Company near about the time Fraser gave them to Wells for that purpose and written and oral evidence convince us that Larkin received them before he made the sample-can which contains the two openings clearly shown in the drawings lettered A and B. For while the four drawings produced by Fraser from memory have two openings and Fraser was mistaken in saying that all of the eight original drawings showed two openings; the two drawings " A " and " B " of the series of eight do contain two openings, and Richardson says these two are in accordance with his instructions to Fraser, and he believes they are the original drawings; and that Fraser did show him additional drawings with single openings which did not embody Richardson's idea. Richardson urged and Fraser urged speedy delivery of the sample-can and Fraser by telephone after he had given Wells the drawings, talked with Wells concerning the time of delivery. We are convinced Larkin is mistaken as to the time he received the patterns from Wells. We believe when Wells directed Larkin to construct the cans desired by the Biscuit Company, that Wells gave or sent to Larkin the drawings showing the style of can Richardson asked for. Not only do the circumstances impute notice to the Can Company and Larkin, but these circumstances and the related evidence justify the inference that early in June Larkin actually received the drawings and verbal instructions from Wells, now dead, relating thereto. There is not a scintilla of evidence to support Larkin's recollection that Wells told him that the Biscuit Company only wanted lithographed lettering on the can-front.

We can not agree with counsel for Larkin that the testimony that Larkin's exhibit can produced from the middle of July, 1902, with the particular size and proportion is very significant, since the earlier sample-can made by Richardson embodied the main elements of the issue; size and shape of the opening, are only details. We will not discuss the Smith patent glass-holder, the invention of an employee of the Biscuit Company, as an explanation of the silence of the Can Company when asked to mark the cans " patent applied for." It suffices to say it does not appear that any employee of the Can Company had knowledge of Smith's existence or of his application for this patent. The actual existence of this application at the time unknown to the Can Company, is not a good reason for its silence when requested to mark the cans made for the Biscuit Company "patent applied for." It was then the Can Company should have protested if it believed that the tin package was the invention of their employee Larkin. The details of the fastening means which the Commissioner regards as the skill of the mechanic, or merely ancillary features were not suggested by Larkin to Branninger who made the first can. Inasmuch as Richardson was the inventor of the idea of the can with the two openings with removable panels, and by his draftsman instructed the Can Company to make them, we need not further discuss the lesser details in the can produced. We think this case is well characterized in *Gallagher* v. *Hastings* (C. D., 1903, 531; 103 O. G., 1165; 21 App. D. C., 91.) There Justice Shepard said:

These were not independent inventors, working out the same conception separately and unknown to each other, but each claims the conception, and reduction to practice, of a construction that was set on foot by one, to meet a novel condition, and was manufactured by the other.

The decision of the Commissioner of Patents *is affirmed* and this opinion will be certified to him in accordance with the statute.

[Court of Appeals of the District of Columbia.]

In re Hoey.

Decided December 4, 1906.

(127 O. G., 2817.)

1. PATENTABILITY—NON-INVENTION—CHANGE OF LOCATION.

The change in location of projections on the seat portion of a bed-couch from the upper to the lower side of the seat does not amount to invention. It is possible, but not apparent, that a better balance of the seat and back is secured by changing these projections. It is possible that a more attractive exterior is thereby presented. It is possible that a more salable article is thereby secured; but all this does not prove originality of invention. While courts deal liberally with inventors in sustaining patents having but slight distinctions over prior structures, they do not and ought not to permit the real inventor to be deprived of the fruits of his genius and labor by a mere copyist.

2. REISSUE APPLICATION—NEW MATTER.

Where a patent describes certain parts of a device as having a specified function, a claim in an application for the reissue of such patent which *refers* to such parts as "means" for performing a different function, requiring a relative location of the parts which was not originally disclosed, relates to new matter. The facts that the reissue application was not filed for about two years after the grant of the patent and that the claim was not made for about nine months after the filing of such application strongly indicate that the claim was not suggested by the original disclosure.

Mr. T. Walter Fowler for the appellant.
Mr. Fairfax Bayard for the Commissioner of Patents.

ROBB, *J.*:

Hearing on appeal from a decision of the Commissioner of Patents (*ante*, 108; 127 O. G., 2815) refusing the following claims upon an application for the reissue of a patent:

10. The combination in a bed-couch of a containing box or case, a seat hinged to the top of the box between the front and rear edges thereof, said seat having rearward projections extending from its under side and beyond and below the hinges, and within the box, a back pivotally connected with the seat and a foldable leg connected with the back and with said seat projections.

13. In a bed-couch, the combination of a hollow base, a seat hinged to the base and having rearward projections within the base and below and beyond its hinges, a back turnably connected with the seat and braces connecting the back with said seat projections and tiltable in unison with, and normally holding the back at right angles to the seat.

17. The combination in a bed-couch of a containing box or base, a seat hinged to the top of the box, between the front and rear, said seat having side bars extending back of and below the hinges and within the box and a suitable stop between the side bars and the base to keep the seat from tilting farther back than is desirable.

18. In a couch, the combination of a hollow base, a seat hinged thereto between the front and rear thereof and having projections extending behind its hinges, a back hinged to the seat, hinged legs carried by the back, braces hinged to the legs and to said rearward projections on the seat, said legs and braces coöperating with the back to hold the back and seat at right angles to one another, and means to prevent the accidental disarrangement of said braces and legs relative to said back and thereby allow the back and seat to open out, when the seat is opened to give access to the box.

21. In a couch, the combination of a box, a seat hinged thereto forward of the back edge of the box and forming a cover therefor, rearward projections on the back of the seat, a back hinged to the seat, legs hinged to the back, braces hinged to the legs and to said rearward projections, said legs foldable against the back with the pivots of the braces and legs in front of the lines through the pivots of the legs to the back and the braces to the projections to hold the back at right angles to the seat, and said seat and back adapted to be turned in unison on the seat-hinges to give access to the box, means for holding the seat in lifted position, and means to prevent the legs and braces falling down accidentally when the seat is in such lifted position.

The references, upon which the Primary Examiner and the Examiners-in-Chief rejected the claims, are: Bühner, April 9, 1901, No. 671,906; Weyer, May 9, 1899, No. 624,691; Beloud, July 27, 1897, No. 586,959. The Commissioner, however, in his decision was satisfied to rely solely upon the Bühner patent.

The above claims, as will be seen, have reference to a so-called bed-couch, which, as the term implies, serves the double purpose of a couch and bed. There are many kinds of bed-couches on the market which closely resemble each other in appearance and structure; hence it was necessary for this applicant in his original and in his reissue application to carefully limit and differentiate his claims. This fact, in view of his present contention, is material.

This bed-couch, briefly described, consists of a box which constitutes the base, and a seat portion about three-fourths as wide and hinged in the rear upon the top of the box. The front of the seat portion, being even with the front of the box, of course, leaves an open space of about one-fourth of the width of the box in the rear of the seat. Suspended nearly over this open space and attached as hereafter described is the back of the couch, the framework of both seat and back being upholstered. Firmly fastened to either end of the bottom of this seat are two side arms, which project almost to the back of and, of course, just inside the box where they are pivoted or hinged to braces connected with the lower part of the folding legs to the adjustable back of the couch, the other ends of the legs being in turn pivoted with the upper rear portion of the back. When the back is in a vertical position, its folded legs and the arm-braces pivoted therewith are also nearly vertical, being inclined just enough forward in the center, that is, at the point where they are pivoted, to lock the legs into position in the channel provided therefor, and at the same time lock and brace the back in its vertical position. This back is directly connected with the seat by two braces pivoted or hinged in the center, one end of each being firmly fastened to the inside top end portions of the seat a little forward of the hinges on the bottom of the seat, the other ends of said braces being firmly fastened to each end of the box. The projections or arms on the under side of the seat being within the box, and being connected with the legs of the back by pivoted braces, it follows that, when the back is lowered, or technically speaking, in a horizontal position and the legs down, either the back of the box must be cut away at each end, or slots cut therein, to permit the passage of said braces, one end of each being pivoted to said seat projections or arms just within the box, and the other end of each then extending downward outside of the box to the lower ends of said legs. When the seat is raised, the stationary arms on the bottom necessarily project downward within the box. Small stops are provided on either end within and near the bottom of the box against which the arms strike when the hinged seat is raised sufficiently high to balance the back.

In the Bühner patent we find exactly the same structure except that the projections to the ends of the seat extend from the *upper*

instead of the lower side thereof, and project just beyond the back of instead of to a point just within the box. Projecting just beyond the back of the box, no slots are necessary, as the pivoted braces connecting the projections with the legs of the couch-back do not at any time come in contact with the back of the box. It is claimed that, by changing the seat projections from the *upper* to the *lower* side thereof and within the box, a better balance of the box and seat is secured. Claims 10 and 13 relate to and embody this change. It seems to us clear that these two claims are anticipated by the Bühner construction, and that the change involves nothing more than mere mechanical skill. While it is true that courts deal liberally with inventors, it is equally true that they do not, and ought not, to permit the real inventor to be deprived of the fruits of his genius and labor by a mere copyist. It is possible, but not apparent, that a better balance of the seat and back is secured by changing these projections. It is possible that a more attractive exterior is thereby presented. It is possible that a more salable article is thereby secured, but all this does not prove originality of conception. We must look to the thing itself, examine its structure, and compare the new with the old. When we do this, we are forced to conclude that had any competent mechanic been directed to change the location of these projections or arms so that they would be within instead of without the box, he would speedily have accomplished the result embodied in these two claims.

Claim 17 involves the little stops on either end of and within the box, and so placed that, when the seat is opened sufficiently to balance the back, the projecting arms strike thereon or come in contact therewith. In the Bühner construction the back of the box itself serves the same purpose, or, to use a more apt expression, performs the same function. The lack of originality in these stops is so apparent that we dismiss the claim without further comment.

We next consider claims 18 and 21, which include " means to prevent the accidental disarrangement " of the legs relative to the back when the seat is raised, the " means " being the slots in the back of the box into which the braces hinged to the legs drop when the back is down. It is now contended that the bottoms of these slots form supports or stops for the leg-braces when the seat is raised, and thereby prevent the braces from unlocking or opening out and releasing the back and seat. It is urged that, while this important function was not included in the original application, it was nevertheless suggested by the original specifications and drawings, and that, therefore, it should not now be considered new matter. These two claims were not only in the original application but they were not in the original reissue application. The original patent was granted Novem-

ber 25, 1902, and the original application for reissue containing *seventeen claims* was filed September 1, 1904, and it was not until June 16, 1905, that claims 18 and 21 were filed. If these claims were in fact suggested by the original specifications and drawings, it is a little singular, to say the least, that appellant, a man skilled in the art, should have taken so long to discover the fact. In his original specifications he stated that these slots were made—

in order to allow the braces, which are connected with the rear ends of the side bars, to drop into the inclined position which they occupy when the back and the legs have been opened outwardly

and, when the seat is lifted, to allow the braces—

to drop into the slots * * * until the bottom rail of the back contacts with the upper edge of the box.

Neither this language nor the original drawings, in our opinion, justify the present claim. These slots were evidently originally cut in the back of the box to make room for the braces and not the purpose now claimed. Had they been designed to perform the function now claimed, obviously they would have been cut at a different angle, and the drawings and specifications would have shown contact between the braces and the slots when the seat was opened. The law authorizes a reissue of a patent under certain conditions, but the reissue must be one in fact and not an additional patent on something neither shown or described in the original application. Section 4916, Revised Statutes, so far as applicable, reads:

Whenever any patent is inoperative or invalid, by reason of a defective or insufficient specification, or by reason of the patentee claiming as his own invention or discovery more than he has a right to claim as new, if the error has arisen by inadvertence, accident, or mistake, and without any fraudulent or deceptive intention, the Commissioner shall, on the surrender of such patent and the payment of the duty required by law, cause a new patent for the same invention, and in accordance with the corrected specification, to be issued to the patentee; * * * but no new matter shall be introduced into the specification, nor in case of a machine patent shall the model or drawings be amended, except each by the other; but when there is neither model or drawing, amendments may be made upon proof satisfactory to the Commissioner that such new matter or amendment was a part of the original invention, and was omitted from the specification by inadvertence, accident, or mistake, as aforesaid.

That appellant did not regard the feature embodied in these two claims as part of his original invention, is, to us, clear. The language of the Supreme Court in *Chicago & Northwestern Railway Co.* v. *Sayles* (C. D., 1879, 349; 15 O. G., 243; 97 U. S., 554) is, therefore, applicable:

The law does not permit such enlargement of an original specification, which would interfere with other inventors who have entered the field in the meantime, any more than it does in the case of reissues of patents previously granted. Courts should regard with jealousy and disfavor any attempts to enlarge the .

scope of an application once filed, or of a patent once granted, the effect of which would be to enable the patentee to appropriate other inventions made prior to such alteration, or to appropriate that which has in the meantime gone into public use.

(See also: *in re Dilg*, C. D., 1905, 620; 115 O. G., 1067; 25 App. D. C., 9; *Haskill* v. *Myers*, 81 Fed., 854.)

Finding no error in the record, the decision appealed from will be affirmed, and this opinion and the proceedings in this court will be certified to the Commissioner of Patents as required by law, and it is so ordered. *Affirmed.*

[Court of Appeals of the District of Columbia.]

IN RE HEROULT.

Decided February 5, 1907.

(127 O. G., 3217.)

1. REISSUE—SAME INVENTION—PROCESS AND APPARATUS.

Where an application clearly discloses a process and an apparatus and through inadvertence, accident, or mistake the applicant accepts a patent with a limited claim to the apparatus, although the process is the dominant part of the invention, *Held* that the patent may be reissued to include the process in the absence of intervening rights.

2. SAME—INADVERTENCE, ACCIDENT, OR MISTAKE.

Where a patentee clearly discloses a process and an apparatus for carrying out the process and claims only the apparatus, the failure to claim the process was either intentional or the result of inadvertence, accident, or mistake, for which section 4916, Revised Statutes, furnishes a remedy.

3. SAME—SAME—ACTS OF ATTORNEYS.

Applicants usually act through solicitors or attorneys, and their inadvertence, accident, and mistakes, if such in fact, are remediable under the statute permitting reissue when it is clear that there is no fraudulent or deceptive intent or attempt to destroy an intervening right. (*In re Briede*, C. D., 1906, 677; 123 O. G., 322; 27 App. D. C., 298, 301.)

Mr. Charles H. Duell, Mr. D. A. Usina, Mr. L. S. Bacon, Mr. J. H. Milans, and *Mr. A. C. Fraser* for the appellant.

Mr. Fairfax Bayard for the Commissioner of Patents.

SHEPARD, *J.*:

This is an appeal from the decision of the Commissioner of Patents (C. D., 1906, 374; 124 O. G., 1843) rejecting an application for the reissue of a patent.

The applicant is a citizen of the Republic of France, and a skilled metallurgist. Having invented a new electrical process for obtaining soft metals, consisting of substances which tend to combine with carbon, through the avoidance of the introduction of carbon from the electrode used therein, and a furnace to carry out said process, the applicant obtained a patent therefor in France. Being then in one of the provincial towns, the inventor instructed an attorney in Paris to secure patents for his invention in other countries. Pursuant thereto an application containing the description of the French patent was filed in the United States Patent Office. The patent issued in due course with the following single claim:

5. In an electric furnace, the combination of a crucible adapted to carry a bath of molten material, two electrodes supported above it and connected in series, a conductor in position to effect contact with material contained in the crucible, and a voltmeter in shunt between one of said electrodes and said conductor, said conductor consisting of a rod passing through the refractory material of the crucible and projecting outside and inside of the same whereby the portion of the rod which is melted is replaced by molten material which fills up the space and thus insures good conductivity.

Having discovered that his process was not protected by the patent so obtained, the inventor, something more than two years after his patent issued, filed the present application for reissue, presenting five claims, the fifth one of which is the claim above set out as contained in the patent. The other four claims are the following:

1. In the manufacture of soft metals such as chromium, manganese or iron by means of an electric furnace, the method which consists in playing two separate arcs in series through an insulating layer of slag between the metal on the one hand, and the two carbon electrodes on the other hand.

2. In the manufacture of metals having a strong affinity for carbon, such as chromium, manganese, iron, or the like, by means of an electric furnace with carbon electrodes, the method which consists in submitting the charge to the heat of electric arcs between the electrodes and the metal itself, and regulating the arcs so as to avoid contact of the electrodes with the metal.

3. In the manufacture of metals having a strong affinity for carbon, such as chromium, manganese, iron, or the like, by means of an electric furnace with carbon electrodes, the method which consists in passing the current from one electrode into and through the metal, thence through another electrode, and regulating the position of each electrode separately, so as to avoid contact thereof with the metal.

4. In the manufacture of metals having a strong affinity for carbon, such as chromium, manganese, iron, or the like, by means of an electric furnace with carbon electrodes, the method which consists in maintaining a layer of non-conducting slag between the end of an electrode and the molten metal, so as to avoid the combining of the carbon of the electrode with the metal.

In the affidavit accompanying the application the applicant said that the Letters Patent are inoperative for the reason that the specification thereof is defective and insufficient, and that such defect or insufficiency consists particularly in the failure of the claim to describe applicant's real invention; and deponent further says that the error which renders such patent inoperative arose from inadvertence, accident or mistake, and not in fraudulent or deceptive intention on the part of the deponent.

Under the French system a patent is construed to cover whatever of novelty is described in the specification. The affidavit recites that the applicant was ignorant of the difference between the French patent law and that of the United States, and believed that being the first to disclose the real invention his patent would secure to him whatever was new in the same as described. That visiting the United States and discussing his patent with his present New York attorneys, he learned for the first time of the practical inoperativeness of his patent, and was advised that he might apply for reissue to correct the insufficiency. That he was familiar with the state of the industry in the United States; and that to the best of his knowledge and belief his real invention as now claimed has not been in use therein up to the present time. This statement in respect of his previous knowledge and belief as to the protection of his patent, and of the advice given him by his American counsel, was supported by the affidavit of one of them.

It is apparent that the patent as issued is of little or no practical value; and there is no question but that the process is both novel and valuable. This is shown in recent publications by writers of established standing in Europe and America, to which our attention has been called. These show also that the process has been largely applied by the inventor and his licensees, or assignees. The statement of the invention in the specifications of the French and American patents contains a particular description of the process from which any one skilled in the art could utilize the invention. They also describe the apparatus of the claim of the latter patent, as used in the process. The process is first described, and then it is said: "Such is the principle of the invention which is carried out," in the apparatus immediately after described.

So thoroughly was the process described that the description was copied *verbatim* in the reissue application. In view of the established skill and learning of the applicant, in the art, and from all the facts and circumstances disclosed, we think it apparent that he considered the process as the real or main invention, and that his failure to make specific claims therefor was due to inadvertence, accident, or mistake. It is unnecessary to discuss the facts as to diligence in applying for the reissue, as that has been conceded by the tribunals of the Office. It is sufficient to say that the applicant acted without unnecessary delay; and there was no intervening claim.

The grounds of the Primary Examiner's decision are stated, as follows:

Claims 1 to 4 inclusive are for a process of making metals in an electric furnace, in which the apparatus may differ widely from the specific structure covered by claim 5. The process of these claims was fully disclosed in the original specifications. No anticipatory references are known for these method claims, and it is generally conceded, in the art to which this application relates, that the present applicant is the inventor of the process claimed. The sole ground for rejection from which the appeal is taken is that the method of making metals is a different invention from the furnace which forms the subject-matter of the original claim, and that neither the patent nor the correspondence in the case contains a suggestion that the process of claims 1 to 4 was a part of applicant's invention.

As indicated above we cannot agree that the description of the patent contains no suggestion that the process of claims 1 to 4 was a part of applicant's invention. If, as declared, " the process of these claims was fully disclosed in the original specification," and was novel, they would either have been allowed if set out along with the claim made, or a divisional application required under Rule 41, as then in force. Having disclosed the process, the failure to claim was either intentional, or the result of inadvertence, accident, or mistake for which section 4916 Revised Statutes furnishes a remedy.

The Examiners-in-Chief in affirming that decision on appeal, did so on the ground that a reissue can only be granted for the same issue as the original patent, and say :

The only thing claimed in the original patent was the furnace itself. While the applicant, being a foreigner, may have been mistaken as to the scope of his patent when granted, he was not acting without the advice of competent counsel. It is hardly to be believed that they applied for and took out a patent for the furnace when they intended to apply for a patent for the process.

The question is, however, was this omission to make claims covering the novel process disclosed in the application, the result of inadvertence, mistake, or accident. Applicants usually act through solicitors or attorneys, and their inadvertence, accidents, and mistakes, if such in fact, are remediable under the statute permitting the reissue, when it is clear that there is no fraudulent or deceptive intent, or attempt to destroy an intervening right. (*In re Briede*, C. D., 1906, 677; 123 O. G., 322; 27 App. D. C., 298, 301.)

The Commissioner, who in turn affirmed the decision of the Examiners-in-Chief, stated the grounds of his decision as follows:

These claims have been refused on the ground that they cover a different invention from that of the patent.

It is contended by appellant that a reissue may be granted for subject-matter which was intended to be claimed in the original patent. The intention to claim the process is alleged to be shown in the present case by the fact that the process covered by claims 1, 2, 3, and 4 is described in the patent. It is stated that the applicant, being a foreigner, was of the impression that the description in a patent determined its scope, and that therefore the patent as granted covered the process described. Having discovered that the patent did not cover the process described, patentee now comes asking for a reissued patent with claims to the process.

The question of whether there was an intention to claim the process in the original patent does not appear to have any material bearing on the present case. It is clear that the claim of the patent was for a machine, and it is well established that a patent for a machine will not sustain a reissue for a process. (C. D., 1906, 374; 124 O. G., 1843.)

Assuming, then, that the invention of the process was fully described in the original application; that it was the original intention of the applicant to secure protection for his entire invention through a patent; and that the failure to do so through specific claims was the result of inadvertence, accident, or mistake; is it true that the patent limited in claim to a machine will not sustain a reissue for the process? The Commissioner's conclusion that it will not is rested upon the cases of *James* v. *Campbell*, (C. D., 1882, 67; 21 O. G., 337; 104 U. S., 356;) *Heald* v. *Rice*, (C. D., 1882, 215; 21 O. G., 1443; 104 U. S., 737;) and several others referring to them. We do not understand those decisions as establishing such an invariable rule. In *James* v. *Campbell* the patent, held void on all points involved, was a second reissue in 1870 of a patent granted in 1863. The invention was declared to be a very narrow one, and the two claims of the original patent were for specific machines. The application for the last reissue made many changes in the specifications, materially enlarging them and the apparatus claims, and adding a new claim for the process. The Court expressly declared that an inspection of former patents showed that the process could not be lawfully patented because anticipated. In regard to this process it was also said:

Leaving out of view the history of the art prior to the invention claimed by the patentee, what possible pretense can there be for contending that the general process was part of the invention which formed the subject of the original patent? Suppose it to be true that Norton was the first inventor of this process, was that process the invention which he sought to secure in the original patent? A patent for a process and a patent for an implement or a machine are very different things. (*Powder Co.* v. *Powder Works*, C. D., 1879, 356; 15 O. G., 289; 98 U. S., 126.) Where a new process produces a new substance the invention of the process is the same as the invention of the substance, and a patent for the one may be reissued so as to include both, as was done in the case of Goodyear's vulcanized-rubber patent. But a process and a machine for applying the process are not necessarily one and the same invention. They are generally distinct and different. The process or act of making a postmark and canceling a postage-stamp by a single blow or operation as a subject of invention is a totally different thing in the patent law from a stamp constructed for performing that process. The claim of the process in the present case, however, is not so broad as this. It is for the process or act of stamping letters with a postmark and canceling the postage-stamp at one and the same blow or operation of the instrument *in the manner and by the means described and set forth.* Perhaps this claim amounts to no more than a claim to the exclusive use of the patented instrument or device. If it is anything more, it is for a different invention from that described in the original patent. If it is not for anything more, the question is brought back to the instrument or device itself which forms the subject of the patent, and which has been already considered.

In *Heald* v. *Rice*, the application for the reissued patent contained material changes in the description. These having been stated, the Court said:

It appears, then, from the mere reading of the two specifications that the invention *described in the first is* for the return-flue boiler while that described in the second, abandoning the claim for the boiler itself, is for a particular mode of using it, with straw as a fuel, by means of an attachment to the furnace-door for that purpose. It might well be that Rice was entitled to patents for both separately or to one for both inventions; but it is too plain for argument that they are perfectly distinct. A patent, consequently, originally issued for one cannot lawfully be surrendered as the basis for a reissue for the other. They are as essentially diverse as a patent for a process and one for a compound, as in the case of *Powder Co.* v. *Powder Works* (C. D., 1879, 356; 15 O. G., 289; 98 U. S., 126) where the reissue patent was avoided, although the original application claimed the invention both of the process and the compound. The case comes directly within the principle held in *James* v. *Campbell*, that a patent for a machine cannot be reissued for the purpose of claiming the process of operating that class of machines; because if the claim for the process is anything more than for the use of the particular machine patented, it is for a different invention.

It is to be observed that in *James* v. *Campbell* the Court did not say that a process, and a machine for applying the process, are always distinct and different, but " generally distinct and different."

A rule of the Patent Office has long provided that two or more independent inventions cannot be claimed in one application; and in conformity with the doctrine thought to have been established in the foregoing cases, a specific provision was added thereto, that:

Claims for a machine and the process in the performance of which the machine is used must be presented in separate applications.

Rule 41 (recently amended by striking out the above quoted.) The question has recently been reëxamined by the Supreme Court of the United States, and the power to make a hard and fast rule of the kind denied. (*Steinmetz* v. *Allen*, C. D., 1904, 703; 109 O. G., 549; 192 U. S., 543.) It was said that inventions may be so connected or related, as to constitute substantially one invention.

They may be completely independent. (*Cochrane* v. *Deener*, C. D., 1877, 242; 11 O. G., 687; 94 U. S., 780.) But they may be related. They may approach each other so nearly that it will be difficult to distinguish the process from the function of the apparatus. In such case the apparatus would be the dominant thing. But the dominance may be reversed and the process carry an exclusive right, no matter what apparatus may be devised to perform it. There is an illustration in the *Telephone Cases*, (C. D., 1888, 321; 43 O. G., 377; 126 U. S., 1.)

Stating the claim in that case as referring to the art described, as well as the means of making it useful, the opinion was quoted from as follows:

Other inventors may compete with him for the ways of giving effect to the discovery, but the new art he has found will belong to him during the life of his patent.

* * * The patent for the art does not necessarily involve a patent for the particular means employed for using it. Indeed, the mention of any means in the specification or descriptive portion of the patent is only necessary to show that the art can be used, for it is only the useful arts—arts which may *be used to an* advantage—that can be made the subject of a patent.

Of *James* v. *Campbell* the Court said that—

was a case of reissued patent, and by express provision of the statute as to reissued patents no new matter can be introduced in them. In other words, the reissue is to perfect, not to enlarge, the invention. Whether the principle of the case applies to related as well as to independent inventions is not clear from its language.

After quoting several passages from the opinion in that case, the following language was used:

The case, however, indicates what embarrassment and peril of rights may be caused by a hard and fixed rule regarding the separation of related inventions.

Whatever the doctrine of those earlier cases, a more liberal rule has since prevailed in respect of the right of reissue. (*Eames* v. *Andrews*, C. D., 1887, 378; 39 O. G., 1319; 122 U. S., 40, 59; *Topliff* v. *Topliff*, C. D., 1892, 402; 59 O. G., 1257; 145 U. S., 156, 171; *Hobbs* v. *Beach*, C. D., 1901, 311; 94 O. G., 2357; 180 U. S., 383, 394.)

In *Eames* v. *Andrews* the Court said:

If the amended specification does not enlarge the scope of the patent by extending the claim so as to cover more than was embraced in the original, and thus cause the patent to include an invention not within the original, the rights of the public are not thereby narrowed, and the case is within the remedy intended by the Statute.

Topliff v. *Topliff*, *supra*, is a leading and most instructive case on this point. After reviewing very many of the former decisions, beginning with *Powder Co.* v. *Powder Works*, (C. D., 1879, 356; 15 O. G., 289; 98 U. S., 126,) it was said by Mr. Justice Brown, who delivered the opinion:

From this summary of the authorities it may be regarded as the settled rule of this Court that the power to reissue may be exercised when the patent is inoperative by reason of the fact that the specification as originally drawn was defective or insufficient, or the claims were narrower than the actual invention of the patentee, provided the error has arisen from inadvertence or mistake, and the patentee is guilty of no fraud or deception; but that such reissues are subject to the following qualifications.

After stating these to be, first, that it shall be for the same invention as the original patent, and that diligence must be exercised, and is ordinarily determined by the lapse of two years, he proceeded to say:

To hold that a patent can never be reissued for an enlarged claim would be not only to override the obvious intent of the statute, but would operate in many cases with great hardship upon the patentee. The specification and claims of a patent, particularly if the invention be at all complicated, constitute one of the most difficult legal instruments to draw with accuracy, and in view of the fact that valuable inventions are often placed in the hands of inexperienced persons to prepare such specifications and claims, it is no matter of surprise that the latter frequently fail to describe with requisite certainty the exact invention of the patentee, and err either in claiming that which the patentee had not in fact invented, or in omitting some element which was a valuable or essential part of his actual invention. Under such circumstances, it would be manifestly unjust to deny him the benefit of a reissue to secure to him his actual invention, provided it is evident that there has been a mistake and he has been guilty of no want of reasonable diligence in discovering it, and no third persons have in the meantime acquired the right to manufacture or sell what he had failed to claim. The object of the patent law is to secure to inventors a monopoly of what they have actually invented or discovered, and it ought not to be defeated by a too strict and technical adherence to the letter of the statute, or by the application of artificial rules of interpretation.

The doctrine of that case was applied by this court in the recent case of *in re Briede*, (C. D., 1906, 677; 123 O. G., 322; 27 App. D. C., 298). In this case, as in that, no new matter was contained in the specification, and the applicant applied promptly for reissue. The statement of the invention in the original application, followed without change in the reissue application, shows that the process and the apparatus are connected in their design and operation, and are so related as to entitle the applicant to claims for both within the rule declared in *Steinmetz* v. *Allen, supra*. In the language of that case, the process is " the dominant thing." Consequently, as was said in the case of *in re Briede, supra:*

Had the claim in controversy been submitted while the application for the original patent was pending, we cannot believe that it would have been refused as not being for the same invention as that described and shown. * * * Rather, we think, the Office approached its consideration with the idea that it was an unwarranted attempt to obtain a broadened claim by means of a reissue, and with the mistaken idea that such a reissue was not permissible. The construction placed upon the patent statutes by the courts is favorable toward inventors having meritorious inventions and they do not put upon them harsh or technical interpretations. They do not look with favor upon the refinements of division which lead to many patents being issued for various improvements incorporated in a single device. They are inclined to resolve all doubts as to whether more than one invention is embraced in one patent in favor of the patentee.

Whatever of doubt there may be whether the reissue in this case is for the same invention described in the original patent, and under all the circumstances allowable, should, we think, following the ordinary practice of the Patent Office, be resolved in favor of the inventor of a meritorious invention, especially when it is now too late to file an independent application for a patent for the same. No absolute right of property is conferred by the grant of the patent. The patentee is merely put in position to assert his *prima facie* right in case of infringement, and have the same adjudicated in a court where extrinsic evidence, if important, may be heard: and not confined, as is this court, to a review of the decisions of the Patent Office upon the record is made up therein. (*In re Thomson*, C. D., 1906, 566; 120

O. G., 2756; 26 App. D. C., 426, 429; *Seymour* v. *Osborne*, 11 Wall., 516, 544; *Parker & Whipple Co.* v. *Yale Clock Co.*, C. D., 1887, 584, 41 O. G., 811; 123 U. S., 87, 98.)

Our conclusion is that there was error in refusing the reissue application, and the decision must be reversed. It is so ordered, and that this decision be certified to the Commissioner of Patents. *Reversed.*

[Court of Appeals of the District of Columbia.]

GIBBONS *v.* PELLER.

Decided January 8, 1907.

(127 O. G., 3643.)

INTERFERENCE—ORIGINALITY—DISCLAIMER OF INVENTORSHIP.

A statement by applicant to his assignee that he does not regard himself as the inventor of the subject-matter claimed in such application is not sufficient to warrant an award of priority to an opponent where it appears that such statement was made during a controversy between the parties with regard to the amount of royalty which should be paid to the assignor.

Mr. Robert B. Killgore for Gibbons.
Mr. George D. Seymour for Peller.

McCOMAS, *J.:*

It appears that the application of Stephen P. Gibbons was filed March 21, 1903, that the application of Morris Peller was filed January 8, 1902, and that all the tribunals of the Patent Office have awarded priority of invention to Peller, the senior party. We find no error in the decision of the Commissioner of Patents (C. D., 1906, 314; 124 O. G., 624) upon the issue now before us. The issue of this interference is as follows:

1. In a rustless suspender-buckle, the combination with a frame having an upper and a lower side with an opening between the same, of a lever pivoted to the upper side of the frame in position to have its clamping edge conct with the upper edge or top of the lower side of the frame, and a piece of webbing having its lower reach attached to the lower side of the frame and its upper reach passed from front to rear through the said opening and engaged by the clamping edge of the lever which deflects it over or approximately over the upper edge or top of the lower side of the frame.

2. In a rustless buckle, the combination with a frame having an upper and a lower side with an opening between them, the lower side of the frame being wider than the upper side to form a finger-piece, of a lever pivoted in position to have its clampig edge conct with the upper edge or top of the wider lower side of the frame, of a piece of webbing having its lower reach attached to the lower side of the frame and its upper reach passed from front to rear through the said opening and engaged by the clamping edge of the lever which deflects it over or approximately over

the upper edge or top of the lower side of the frame, whereby the upper reach of the webbing is brought into or approximately into line with the lower reach of the webbing on the back of the buckle when the webbing is under draft as in use.

Of numerous parties once included in this interference only Gibbons and Peller remain. Peller did not testify nor is there any testimony confirming the dates of conception of invention and disclosure alleged by Peller in his preliminary statement. There are circumstances indicating that after Peller had assigned his interest he became indifferent to the rights of his assignee, the Waterbury Buckle Company. Maltby, the secretary of that company, testifies that in the fall of 1901, he corresponded with Peller and talked with him about a " rustless buckle " and that on December 31, 1901, buckles made in accordance with Peller's disclosure were first shipped and that the buckle exhibited to him was substantially the same as those then shipped, and this buckle embodies the issue of this interference. Thus December 31, 1901, is the date of reduction to practice by Peller. Gibbons is the junior party and the burden of proof is upon him and to prevail he must prove a reduction to practice prior to the last-mentioned date or at least to January 8, 1902, when Peller filed his application, or a prior conception followed by due diligence in reduction to practice. Gibbons claimed that he conceived the invention in November, 1900, and that he disclosed it to M. L. and L. Rothschild then. These men were officers of the Connecticut Web Company from which Gibbons, as manager of the Gibbons Manufacturing Company of Baltimore, bought supplies. Each of the tribunals of the Patent Office after reviewing the testimony, conclude that Gibbons failed to make a disclosure to these persons of the specific form of buckle which is here in issue, and it is quite remarkable that although Gibbons alleges that he is the inventor, yet when he testifies after repeated efforts he did not succeed in describing the invention in issue. His testimony is vague and indefinite upon the point and the tribunals of the Patent Office concur that Gibbons had no conception of the invention in issue prior to the time when the first shipment of Peller buckles was made or to the time when Peller filed his application. The testimony of M. L. Rothschild appears to be unreliable and it is not clear that the buckle he claims to have made for Gibbons can aid Gibbons's case for it does not appear to embody the invention in issue.

The Examiners-in-Chief say—

It is to be noted that this issue is specific and carefully drawn as to its language and has only been held to be patentable after much discussion by the Examiner and this Board. Where the invention is so specific any oral testimony must of course correspond in every detail with the requirements of the issue. (See *Blackford* v. *Wilder, ante,* 491; 127 O. G., 1255; 21 App. D. C., 1.)

And as the Commissioner of Patents says, this issue calls for a buckle with a frame having an upper and a lower side with an opening between the same, of a lever pivoted to the upper side of the frame in position to have its clamping edge coact with the upper edge or top of the lower side of the frame, which is not found in this " buckle of original disclosure " produced by M. L. Rothschild. The device in issue has a lever pivoted above the top edge of the lower side of the frame, the lever in the buckle exhibited is pivoted to ears in the same plane as the frame of the buckle and it is the former construction which produces the result of holding the web by deflection rather than by a clamping action. At most this buckle produced by Rothschild as Gibbons's original disclosure, was an experimental model put away in a drawer for years. It was in the nature of an abandoned experiment. Gibbons has given no explanation of his long delay in filing his application, except that he thought the buckle on which he did obtain a patent at home and three patents abroad was a better buckle and he lacked the money to make an earlier application for the invention of the issue. That other invention Gibbons understood although when repeatedly asked he repeatedly proved unable to state intelligently what the construction here in issue is. We agree with the tribunal of the Patent Office that Gibbons's case wholly failed, and here discussion would end were it not that the appellant further urges that the testimony shows that Peller was not the inventor of the buckle shown in his application. Here the appellant relies upon the case of *Oliver* v. *Felbel*, (C. D., 1902, 565; 100 O. G., 2384; 20 App. D. C., 260,) where Oliver, when a witness in his own behalf, swore that he did not claim to be the inventor of the mechanism embracing the particular combination of parts or elements specified in the issue of interference. The circumstances in this case are different. Maltby, the secretary of the Waterbury Buckle Company, did testify that at one time after Peller had assigned his application for a patent to Maltby's company, Peller intimated that he was not the real inventor of the construction shown in his application and now involved in this interference. It appears that Peller's brother had been the mechanic in this instance and the testimony indicates that Rothschild, who with another first made application for this invention, and later testified that it was Gibbons's invention and sought to explain the inconsistency by his former belief that the mechanic who constructed the invention for another was the inventor, had about this time striven to enlist Peller against Peller's assignee, and it appears that Peller was at that time seeking a better agreement for a royalty from the Waterbury Buckle Company.

We do not find that Peller deliberately denied that he was the inventor but we conclude that his acts and declarations and his re-

The sheet-metal cover is countersunk or depressed at its center, so as to be provided with an upright neck or shoulder, which is adapted to fit snugly within the opening of the can-body.   Around this neck the cover is provided with the laterally-extending flange, which should be considerably wider than the flange. After the cover has been pressed into the above-described form its neck and flange are covered with an air-excluding adhesive body, that adheres to the cover and constitutes in effect a packing.   *This coating consists of a layer of rubber cement, which may be applied to the parts with a brush, and a thin layer of asbestos pulp, which forms a film on the surface of the cement. * * ** The rubber in my improved packing forms the air-excluding body proper, while the asbestos forms a coating or skin upon the surface of the same which greatly increases the tightness of the joint.   Thus a packing of superior merit is produced, and, moreover the resistance offered by the ordinary washers to the crimping operation and the consequent frequent imperfections of the seam are entirely avoided.

The application contained but one claim, which is as follows:

The combination of a sheet-metal can with a flanged and countersunk cover and with an adhesive coating secured to the cover, and consisting of rubber cement and an asbestos film, substantially as and for the purpose specified.

More than five years after the date of the original, namely on March 31, 1902, appellant filed his application for a reissue.   Owing to the simplicity of the invention, the exactness with which it is described in the original application, the specific and limited nature of the claim therein, and the long delay attending the filing of this reissue application, we must carefully scrutinize the reasons assigned by the patentee why it should be allowed.   The reissue claims are as follows:

1. A metal can comprising a can-body and cover and joined by a crimped seam having on one side of said parts at the seam portion a permanently fixed composition coating forming the packing means, substantially as described.

2. A metal can for containing food products having a can-body and its cover joined by a crimp-joint composed of overlapped and tightly-closed flanges in combination with a heat-resisting, non-deleterious composition inherently adhesive in application and fixed to the neck of the can at said joint in a dry coating or layer and forming a packing between said flanges, substantially as described.

3. An air and water tight packing for a joint for a sheet-metal can-body and its cover designed for food products, consisting of an inherent adhesive, heat-resisting non-deleterious yielding coating dried on said cover and independent of the can-body, substantially as described.

4. In a joint for a metal can-body and its cover, a fixed coating forming a packing for said joint and plastered on one of said parts, said coating consisting of an adherent and packing layer affixed to the article and an outside non-deleterious and heat-resisting layer or film, substantially as described.

5. The combination of a sheet-metal can with a flanged and countersunk cover and with an adhesive coating secured to the cover, and consisting of rubber cement and an asbestos film, substantially as and for the purpose specified.

6. A sheet-metal can designed for packing food products, comprising a can-body and a cover, said body and cover connected by a lap-joint, in combination with a tight packing for sealing the cover and body independent of the lap-joint, packing consisting of a non-deleterious, heat-resisting, air-excluding and

adhesive plastered compound extending into every portion of the lap-joint and between the inner surface of the can-body and the neck of the cover, substantially as described.

In appellant's affidavit, accompanying his reissue application, he states that the original—

Letters Patent do not protect and cover by their claim the real invention of deponent nor its equivalent, but only a particular form of embodiment thereof, such defect being due to the omission to claim the following essential parts of the invention, namely, a fixed coating forming the packing in combination with the joint of the can and cover; second, the heat-resisting character of the coating, apart from the particular ingredients thereof; third, the non-deleterious character of the coating apart from the particular ingredients thereof; fourth, the feature of having a coating consisting of an adherent medium affixed to a complementary part of the article to be joined and a heat-resisting and non-deleterious film or covering without limitation to the particular ingredients employed; fifth, in combination with the crimped joint of the can and cover, a packing consisting of an adhesive water and air tight, heat-resisting, non-deleterious coating applied to said cover, all of which enumerated parts or features are essential characteristics of the coating described and claimed or necessarily of any coating which is the true equivalent thereof;

that he carefully explained his invention to his attorneys at the time of making the original application, and—

Informed his attorneys that he wanted to have a claim for an adhesive *coating* forming a packing in combination with the flanged and countersunk cover and lapped joint; that he does not believe that said attorneys ever understood the deponent's explanation of the value of his invention and its essential features; that deponent was informed by his attorneys that a claim such as he has above set forth could not be obtained; but that he is informed and believes that said attorneys did attempt to obtain a claim or claims for an adhesive *packing* but not for an adhesive *coating* forming a packing in combination with the flanged and countersunk cover and lapped joint, but that upon the citation of references thereto said attorneys canceled said claim or claims and retained merely the claim now set forth in said Letters Patent; * * * that at the time said Letters Patent were issued and were examined by deponent he discovered that the claim thereof was limited to the combination of a sheet-metal can with a flanged and countersunk cover, and consisting of rubber cement and an asbestos film, substantially as described; that to the best of deponent's knowledge and belief, no cans for food similar to his invention having been ever made prior to said invention, deponent was greatly disappointed that his patent was not issued to a better advantage; whereupon he informed his attorneys that there were other ingredients that could be used instead of rubber cement and asbestos to constitute the affixing and packing medium and the heat-resisting and non-deleterious surface respectively and that therefore the claim was too narrow; whereupon his said attorneys informed deponent that said claim was as broad as could be obtained from the Patent Office in view of the previous state of the art and the objections of the Patent Office; that thereupon, deponent, relying upon the said statement of his attorneys as to the position and objections of the Patent Office, and being entirely ignorant of the remedy of a defective patent by reissue and no mention of such a remedy having been made by his said attorneys took no further steps in the matter but very reluctantly accepted the situation;

that at about the time of the issuance of said patent deponent formed a company known as The Max Ams Machine Company which company was organized for the purpose of making and selling machines for making tin cans for food articles and for making and selling a composition for use in producing the invention set forth in the said Letters Patent, and also for making said invention and that said company did carry on such manufacture and sale;

that appellant was abroad from May until November, 1897, for the purpose of having a surgical operation performed, and from October, 1899, until April, 1900, he was " distressed and worried over the illness and death of his wife;"

that in consequence of these circumstances whereby he was unable to devote much if any time to the business of the said The Max Ams Machine Company, said business did not develop and did not attain much importance; that the said The Max Ams Machine Company's business was and is a side issue with nearly all his time since the issue of said patent to his said main business;

*   *   *   *   *   *   *

that in view of the above circumstances deponent has been obliged to devote nearly all his time since the issue of said patent to his said main business;

that appellant subsequently intrusted the management of said company to his son, who in December, 1901, through other counsel learned " of the proceeding and remedy known as reissue of a defective patent; " that appellant thereupon authorized the filing of this application for reissue; that he believes—

there is great danger that his invention will be appropriated and his rights thereto invaded by parties who may make, use and sell his real invention without embodying it in the particular form set forth in the claim of said Letters Patent; and by substituting for either or both of the ingredients of the coating set forth in said claim other ingredients or for both of said ingredients a single ingredient, thereby avoiding or attempting to avoid said claim while really appropriating the essence of deponent's invention.

All doubt as to the scope and purpose of this reissue application is removed by reading the above affidavit. The patentee therein frankly states that he was greatly disappointed at the time his patent was issued because of the narrow and limited nature of the claim granted him; that he now fears others will take advantage of his failure to obtain a broader claim unless this reissue is allowed.

No good purpose will be subserved by a reiteration of the well-established rules applicable to such a case as this. Suffice it to say that a delay of two years in filing an application for a reissue of a patent with broader claims will usually be treated as an abandonment to the public of everything not claimed in the original. This rule is based upon the analogy between a reissue application and the case of an inventor who fails to apply for a patent of his invention within two years from the date of its public use or sale, which the statute ordains is conclusive evidence of its abandonment. (See *in re Starkey*, C. D., 1903, 607; 104 O. G., 2150; 21 App. D. C., 519, and cases cited therein.)

The facts relied upon by the patentee do not, in our opinion. constitute a sufficient excuse for his lack of diligence. As above stated, his invention is a simple one, and his patent as issued clearly and definitely describes it. The real object, therefore. of this application is to secure something not originally claimed, or, if claimed, not pressed or abandoned. In such a case unusual circumstances must be present, or the delay will be fatal. No such circumstances are shown here. Appellant himself immediately discovered that his patent was " too narrow " and after discussing the subject with his attorneys " took no further steps in the matter but very reluctantly accepted the situation." He now asks relief because he believes his then attorneys were mistaken as to the law. As Mr. Chief Justice Fuller aptly observed in a similar case: " Manifestly this will not do." (*Halliday* v. *Stewart*, 151 U. S., 229.) There is no allegation that his attorney did not act in good faith; on the contrary, it is expressly stated that they informed him " that said claim was as broad as could be obtained from the Patent Office in view of the previous state of the art and the objections of the Patent Office." That other attorneys undertook to appeal from the judgment of the Patent Office in 1896 to its judgment in 1902 certainly does not excuse the intervening delay. If the patentee did not think the attorneys who prosecuted his original application thoroughly understood his invention. and for that reason failed to obtain as broad a claim as might have been obtained, he should have consulted other counsel without delay. It is apparent, however. as he himself says. that this was merely a " side issue " with him. to which he gave little thought or attention until a considerable business had been established. when the importance of his invention and the necessity for giving it wider scope was first pressed upon him. We note his statement that he " knows of no one who is practicing or using said invention without his consent or whose business would be dominated by the reissue of said Letters Patent to protect said invention," but this statement would not justify us in overruling the tribunals of the Patent Office and granting him a patent that might affect the business of those of whom appellant has no present information. Moreover, we believe applications for reissue filed long after the date of the patent. and which have for their object the enlargement of its claims, should be discouraged, and should be countenanced only in exceptional cases.

The decision appealed from will. therefore. be affirmed, and it is so ordered. The clerk of the court will certify this opinion and the proceedings in this court to the Commissioner of Patents, as required by law. *Affirmed.*

[Court of Appeals of the District of Columbia.]

BLISS v. McELROY.

Decided February 5, 1907.

(128 O. G.. 458.)

INTERFERENCES—PRIORITY—DELAY AFTER ALLEGED CONCEPTION AND REDUCTION TO PRACTICE.

Where an inventor after an alleged reduction to practice of his invention lays it aside for five years, during which time he files several domestic and foreign applications and develops another system to accomplish the same purpose which he regards as superior, and fails to file an application until after the grant of a patent to another for the same invention who was proceeding in good faith, he is guilty of inexcusable laches.

Mr. W. C. Jones, Mr. J. R. Edson, and *Mr. R. L. Ames* for Bliss. *Mr. Charles Neave* and *Mr. William Duvall* for McElroy.

ROBB, *J.:*

This is an appeal from the decision of the Commissioner of Patents (C. D., 1906, 222; 122 O. G., 2687,) in an interference proceeding awarding priority of invention to the senior party, McElroy.

The counts of the issue relate to a system for lighting railway-vehicles by electricity, and are as follows:

1. In a system of lighting railway-vehicles electrically the combination with an axle, of a dynamo-electric generator of a capacity greater than the normal lamp-load driven thereby having its field-magnet strength independent of the armature-current, electric lamps and a storage battery connected in multiple with each other to the armature of said generator, a potential-magnet also independent of the armature-current connected in multiple to the said armature and a field-magnet regulator for the generator controlled by the said magnet.

2. In a system for lighting railway-vehicles electrically the combination with an axle, of a generator of a capacity greater than the normal lamp-load driven thereby having its field-magnet independent of the armature-current and energized by a shunt-circuit, electric lamps and a storage battery connected in multiple with each other to the armature of the generator, a potential-magnet also independent of the armature-current connected to the armature in multiple with the said lamps and battery, a circuit-closer in the main circuit between the point of said circuit at which the magnet and the field-magnet are connected on the one hand, and the lamps and battery are connected on the other hand, and an operating connection between the said circuit-closer and the said magnet, whereby the said magnet and the field-magnet will be permanently in circuit, but the lamps and battery will have their circuit connection closed by the said magnet.

3. In a system for lighting railway-vehicles electrically, the combination with a generator driven by the vehicle, of a group of lamps and a storage battery connected thereto in multiple, a regulator for the dynamo, a second regulator in the lamp-circuit, and a magnet measuring the potential applied to the lamps and controlling the said second regulator.

4. In a system for lighting railway-vehicles electrically, the combination with a generator driven by the vehicle, of a storage battery connected thereto, a of lamps connected thereto in multiple with the battery, a resistance in

the lamp branch in series with the lamps, a regulator-magnet between said resistance and the dynamo measuring the storage-battery conditions, a regulator controlled thereby, and supplementary regulating devices controlled by a magnet in the lamp branch measuring the lamp conditions.

5. In a system for lighting railway-vehicles electrically, the combination with a generator of a capacity greater than the normal lamp-load driven by an axle, of lamps and a storage battery, a switch in the main-line circuit between the said lamps and the battery and the generator, three shunt-magnates all independent of the armature-current but connected to the main line between the said switch and the generator, one being the field-magnet, another controlling the field-magnet, and the third controlling the said switch, and two magnets connected to the main line, one being a series magnet controlling the opening of the said switch, and the other being a shunt-magnet for regulating the current delivery to the lamps.

6. In a system for lighting railway-vehicles electrically, the combination with an axle, of a generator of a capacity greater than the normal lamp-load driven thereby at a variable speed, a potential-magnet permanently connected in a shunt-circuit from the armature, lamps and a storage battery having their connection with the said generator controlled by the potential of the system and their disconnection therefrom by the current of the system, a shunt-circuit containing the field-magnet of the generator, a resistance in said circuit, a motor operating the resistance and a director for the said motor controlled by the said potential-magnet so as to be set and maintained for one direction of action of said motor or another as long as the potential of the system is either above or below the point determined by the said magnet.

7. In a system for lighting railway-vehicles electrically, the combination with a generator, of an automatic connection-switch set to connect the generator to the line at a given speed, a storage battery permanently connected to the line while the said switch is closed, electric lamps intermittently connected to the line while the said switch is closed, a magnet measuring the generator potential, a current-changing regulator controlled by the said magnet and adjusting the amount of the battery-current to the counter electromotive force of the battery whenever the lamps are disconnected, and a resistance in the lamp branch determining, together with the said magnet, the potential applied to the lamps whenever both lamps and battery are connected to the generator.

8. In a system for lighting railway-vehicles electrically, the combination with lamps and a storage battery in multiple of a constant-potential dynamo driven by the vehicle at an intermittent and varible speed and having a capacity sufficient to simultaneously operate the lamps and charge the battery and a current-varying regulator for the dynamo adjusting the volume of armature-current to either the lamps along (the battery being charged) to the battery along (the lamps being out of use,) or to lamps and battery together.

The senior party, McElroy, filed his application September 9, 1901, upon which a patent issued February 17, 1903. He has taken no testimony and, therefore, must stand upon his filing date. Bliss filed his application September 10, 1904, which is subsequent to the date of the McElroy patent. As to counts 1 and 8 of the issue, however, Bliss contends that the burden of proof is not so heavily upon him because those counts are a continuation of an application filed by him February 26, 1902, while the McElroy application was still pending in the Patent Office. This contention is contested by McElroy, but

fusal to testify at Maltby's request were part of an effort to secure better terms from his assignee. When Peller executed the application in interference he testified under oath that he was the inventor of the invention of the issue and we do not find evidence sufficient to overcome it. The decision of the Commissioner *is affirmed.* The clerk of this court will certify this opinion and the proceedings in this court to the Commissioner of Patents according to law.

[Court of Appeals of the District of Columbia.]

IN RE AMS.

Decision February 5, 1907.

(127 O. G., 3644.)

1. REISSUE—DELAY OF TWO YEARS—PRESUMPTION OF ABANDONMENT.

Delay of two years in filing an application for a reissue of a patent with broader claims will usually be treated as an abandonment to the public of everything not claimed in the original. This rule is based upon the analogy between a reissue application and the case of an inventor who fails to apply for a patent of his invention within two years from the date of its public use or sale, which the statute ordains is conclusive evidence of its abandonment. (See *in re Starkey,* C. D., 1903, 607; 104 O. G., 2150; 21 App. D. C., 519, and cases cited therein.)

2. SAME—LONG DELAY—FAILURE OF ATTORNEYS TO UNDERSTAND INVENTION.

Where the invention covered by a patent is simple and the patent clearly and definitely describes it, and the patentee immediately upon the issue thereof discovers that the single claim allowed is too narrow and does not properly cover his invention, and upon calling his attorney's attention to this fact they advised him that the claim was as broad as could be obtained, and it does not appear that they acted in bad faith, *Held* that a delay of five years in seeking a reissue cannot be excused upon the plea that the original attorneys did not understand the invention, since under the circumstances it was the duty of the patentee to consult other counsel without delay.

Mr. H. P. Doolittle for the appellant.
Mr. Fairfax Bayard for the Commissioner of Patents.

ROBB, *J.:*

This is an appeal from concurrent decisions of the Patent Office tribunals refusing to reissue a patent. (C. D., 1906, 424; 125 O. G., 347.) The original patent, issued November 3, 1896, relates, quoting from the specification, " to a sheet-metal can designed for packing food products, and more particularly to an improved construction of the seam between the can-body and the cover," and is described in said *specifications* as follows:

The sheet-metal cover is countersunk or depressed at its center, so as to be provided with an upright neck or shoulder, which is adapted to fit snugly within the opening of the can-body. Around this neck the cover is provided with the laterally-extending flange, which should be considerably wider than the flange. After the cover has been pressed into the above-described form its neck and flange are covered with an air-excluding adhesive body, that adheres to the cover and constitutes in effect a packing. *This coating consists of a layer of rubber cement, which may be applied to the parts with a brush, and a thin layer of asbestos pulp, which forms a film on the surface of the cement.* * * * The rubber in my improved packing forms the air-excluding body proper, while the asbestos forms a coating or skin upon the surface of the same which greatly increases the tightness of the joint. Thus a packing of superior merit is produced, and, moreover the resistance offered by the ordinary washers to the crimping operation and the consequent frequent imperfections of the seam are entirely avoided.

The application contained but one claim, which is as follows:

The combination of a sheet-metal can with a flanged and countersunk cover and with an adhesive coating secured to the cover, and consisting of rubber cement and an asbestos film, substantially as and for the purpose specified.

More than five years after the date of the original, namely on March 31, 1902, appellant filed his application for a reissue. Owing to the simplicity of the invention, the exactness with which it is described in the original application, the specific and limited nature of the claim therein, and the long delay attending the filing of this reissue application, we must carefully scrutinize the reasons assigned by the patentee why it should be allowed. The reissue claims are as follows:

1. A metal can comprising a can-body and cover and joined by a crimped seam having on one side of said parts at the seam portion a permanently fixed composition coating forming the packing means, substantially as described.

2. A metal can for containing food products having a can-body and its cover joined by a crimp-joint composed of overlapped and tightly-closed flanges in combination with a heat-resisting, non-deleterious composition inherently adhesive in application and fixed to the neck of the can at said joint in a dry coating or layer and forming a packing between said flanges, substantially as described.

3. An air and water tight packing for a joint for a sheet-metal can-body and its cover designed for food products, consisting of an inherent adhesive, heat-resisting non-deleterious yielding coating dried on said cover and independent of the can-body, substantially as described.

4. In a joint for a metal can-body and its cover, a fixed coating forming a packing for said joint and plastered on one of said parts, said coating consisting of an adherent and packing layer affixed to the article and an outside non-deleterious and heat-resisting layer or film, substantially as described.

5. The combination of a sheet-metal can with a flanged and countersunk cover and with an adhesive coating secured to the cover, and consisting of rubber cement and an asbestos film, substantially as and for the purpose specified.

6. A sheet-metal can designed for packing food products, comprising a can-body and a cover, said body and cover connected by a lap-joint, in combination with a tight packing for sealing the cover and body independent of the lap-joint, said packing consisting of a non-deleterious, heat-resisting, air-excluding and

adhesive plastered compound extending into every portion of the lap-joint and between the inner surface of the can-body and the neck of the cover, substantially as described.

In appellant's affidavit, accompanying his reissue application, he states that the original—

Letters Patent do not protect and cover by their claim the real invention of deponent nor its equivalent, but only a particular form of embodiment thereof, such defect being due to the omission to claim the following essential parts of the invention, namely, a fixed coating forming the packing in combination with the joint of the can and cover; second, the heat-resisting character of the coating, apart from the particular ingredients thereof; third, the non-deleterious character of the coating apart from the particular ingredients thereof; fourth, the feature of having a coating consisting of an adherent medium affixed to a complementary part of the article to be joined and a heat-resisting and non-deleterious film or covering without limitation to the particular ingredients employed; fifth, in combination with the crimped joint of the can and cover, a packing consisting of an adhesive water and air tight, heat-resisting, non-deleterious coating applied to said cover, all of which enumerated parts or features are essential characteristics of the coating described and claimed or necessarily of any coating which is the true equivalent thereof;

that he carefully explained his invention to his attorneys at the time of making the original application, and—

informed his attorneys that he wanted to have a claim for an adhesive *coating* forming a packing in combination with the flanged and countersunk cover and lapped joint; that he does not believe that said attorneys ever understood the deponent's explanation of the value of his invention and its essential features; that deponent was informed by his attorneys that a claim such as he has above set forth could not be obtained; but that he is informed and believes that said attorneys did attempt to obtain a claim or claims for an adhesive *packing* but not for an adhesive *coating* forming a packing in combination with the flanged and countersunk cover and lapped joint, but that upon the citation of references thereto said attorneys canceled said claim or claims and retained merely the claim now set forth in said Letters Patent; * * * that at the time said Letters Patent were issued and were examined by deponent he discovered that the claim thereof was limited to the combination of a sheet-metal can with a flanged and countersunk cover, and consisting of rubber cement and an asbestos film, substantially as described; that to the best of deponent's knowledge and belief, no cans for food similar to his invention having been ever made prior to said invention, deponent was greatly disappointed that his patent was not issued to a better advantage; whereupon he informed his attorneys that there were other ingredients that could be used instead of rubber cement and asbestos to constitute the affixing and packing medium and the heat-resisting and non-deleterious surface respectively and that therefore the claim was too narrow; whereupon his said attorneys informed deponent that said claim was as broad as could be obtained from the Patent Office in view of the previous state of the art and the objections of the Patent Office; that thereupon, deponent, relying upon the said statement of his attorneys as to the position and objections of the Patent Office, and being entirely ignorant of the remedy of a defective patent by reissue and no mention of such a remedy having been made by his said attorneys took no further steps in the matter but very reluctantly accepted the situation;

that at about the time of the issuance of said patent deponent formed a company known as The Max Ams Machine Company which company was organized for the purpose of making and selling machines for making tin cans for food articles and for making and selling a composition for use in producing the invention set forth in the said Letters Patent, and also for making said invention and that said company did carry on such manufacture and sale;

that appellant was abroad from May until November, 1897, for the purpose of having a surgical operation performed, and from October, 1899, until April, 1900, he was " distressed and worried over the illness and death of his wife;"

that in consequence of these circumstances whereby he was unable to devote much if any time to the business of the said The Max Ams Machine Company, said business did not develop and did not attain much importance; that the said The Max Ams Machine Company's business was and is a side issue with nearly all his time since the issue of said patent to his said main business;

    *   *   *   *   *   *   *

that in view of the above circumstances deponent has been obliged to devote nearly all his time since the issue of said patent to his said main business;

that appellant subsequently intrusted the management of said company to his son, who in December, 1901, through other counsel learned " of the proceeding and remedy known as reissue of a defective patent; " that appellant thereupon authorized the filing of this application for reissue; that he believes—

there is great danger that his invention will be appropriated and his rights thereto invaded by parties who may make, use and sell his real invention without embodying it in the particular form set forth in the claim of said Letters Patent; and by substituting for either or both of the ingredients of the coating set forth in said claim other ingredients or for both of said ingredients a single ingredient, thereby avoiding or attempting to avoid said claim while really appropriating the essence of deponent's invention.

All doubt as to the scope and purpose of this reissue application is removed by reading the above affidavit. The patentee therein frankly states that he was greatly disappointed at the time his patent was issued because of the narrow and limited nature of the claim granted him; that he now fears others will take advantage of his failure to obtain a broader claim unless this reissue is allowed.

No good purpose will be subserved by a reiteration of the well-established rules applicable to such a case as this. Suffice it to say that a delay of two years in filing an application for a reissue of a patent with broader claims will usually be treated as an abandonment to the public of everything not claimed in the original. This rule is based upon the analogy between a reissue application and the case of an inventor who fails to apply for a patent of his invention within two years from the date of its public use or sale, which the statute ordains is conclusive evidence of its abandonment. (See *in re Starkey*, C. D., 1903, 607; 104 O. G., 2150; 21 App. D. C., 519, and cases cited therein.)

The facts relied upon by the patentee do not, in our opinion, constitute a sufficient excuse for his lack of diligence. As above stated, his invention is a simple one, and his patent as issued clearly and definitely describes it. The real object, therefore, of this application is to secure something not originally claimed, or, if claimed, not pressed or abandoned. In such a case unusual circumstances must be present, or the delay will be fatal. No such circumstances are shown here. Appellant himself immediately discovered that his patent was "too narrow" and after discussing the subject with his attorneys "took no further steps in the matter but very reluctantly accepted the situation." He now asks relief because he believes his then attorneys were mistaken as to the law. As Mr. Chief Justice Fuller aptly observed in a similar case: "Manifestly this will not do." (*Halliday* v. *Stewart*, 151 U. S., 229.) There is no allegation that his attorney did not act in good faith; on the contrary, it is expressly stated that they informed him "that said claim was as broad as could be obtained from the Patent Office in view of the previous state of the art and the objections of the Patent Office." That other attorneys undertook to appeal from the judgment of the Patent Office in 1896 to its judgment in 1902 certainly does not excuse the intervening delay. If the patentee did not think the attorneys who prosecuted his original application thoroughly understood his invention, and for that reason failed to obtain as broad a claim as might have been obtained, he should have consulted other counsel without delay. It is apparent, however, as he himself says, that this was merely a "side issue" with him, to which he gave little thought or attention until a considerable business had been established, when the importance of his invention and the necessity for giving it wider scope was first pressed upon him. We note his statement that he "knows of no one who is practicing or using said invention without his consent or whose business would be dominated by the reissue of said Letters Patent to protect said invention," but this statement would not justify us in overruling the tribunals of the Patent Office and granting him a patent that might affect the business of those of whom appellant has no present information. Moreover, we believe applications for reissue filed long after the date of the patent, and which have for their object the enlargement of its claims, should be discouraged, and should be countenanced only in exceptional cases.

The decision appealed from will, therefore, be affirmed, and it is so ordered. The clerk of the court will certify this opinion and the proceedings in this court to the Commissioner of Patents, as required by law. *Affirmed.*

[Court of Appeals of the District of Columbia.]

BLISS v. MCELROY.

Decided February 5, 1907.

(128 O. G., 458.)

INTERFERENCES—PRIORITY—DELAY AFTER ALLEGED CONCEPTION AND REDUCTION
TO PRACTICE.

Where an inventor after an alleged reduction to practice of his invention
lays it aside for five years, during which time he files several domestic and
foreign applications and develops another system to accomplish the same
purpose which he regards as superior, and fails to file an application until
after the grant of a patent to another for the same invention who was proceeding in good faith, he is guilty of inexcusable laches.

Mr. W. C. Jones, *Mr. J. R. Edson*, and *Mr. R. L. Ames* for Bliss.
Mr. Charles Neave and *Mr. William Duvall* for McElroy.

ROBB, *J.:*

This is an appeal from the decision of the Commissioner of Patents
(C. D., 1906, 222; 122 O. G., 2687,) in an interference proceeding
awarding priority of invention to the senior party, McElroy.

The counts of the issue relate to a system for lighting railway-
vehicles by electricity, and are as follows:

1. In a system of lighting railway-vehicles electrically the combination with
an axle, of a dynamo-electric generator of a capacity greater than the normal
lamp-load driven thereby having its field-magnet strength independent of the
armature-current, electric lamps and a storage battery connected in multiple
with each other to the armature of said generator, a potential-magnet also independent of the armature-current connected in mutiple to the said armature and
a field-magnet regulator for the generator controlled by the said magnet.

2. In a system for lighting railway-vehicles electrically the combination with
an axle, of a generator of a capacity greater than the normal lamp-load driven
thereby having its field-magnet independent of the armature-current and energized by a shunt-circuit, electric lamps and a storage battery connected in multiple with each other to the armature of the generator, a potential-magnet also
independent of the armature-current connected to the armature in multiple with
the said lamps and battery, a circuit-closer in the main circuit between the
point of said circuit at which the magnet and the field-magnet are connected on
the one hand, and the lamps and battery are connected on the other hand, and
an operating connection between the said circuit-closer and the said magnet,
whereby the said magnet and the field-magnet will be permanently in circuit,
but the lamps and battery will have their circuit connection closed by the said
magnet.

3. In a system for lighting railway-vehicles electrically, the combination with
a generator driven by the vehicle, of a group of lamps and a storage battery
connected thereto in multiple, a regulator for the dynamo, a second regulator
in the lamp-circuit, and a magnet measuring the potential applied to the lamps
and controlling the said second regulator.

4. In a system for lighting railway-vehicles electrically, the combination with
a generator driven by the vehicle, of a storage battery connected thereto, a
[lamps] connected thereto in multiple with the battery, a resistance in

the lamp branch in series with the lamps, a regulator-magnet between said resistance and the dynamo measuring the storage-battery conditions, a regulator controlled thereby, and supplementary regulating devices controlled by a magnet in the lamp branch measuring the lamp conditions.

5. In a system for lighting railway-vehicles electrically, the combination with a generator of a capacity greater than the normal lamp-load driven by an axle, of lamps and a storage battery, a switch in the main-line circuit between the said lamps and the battery and the generator, three shunt-magnates all independent of the armature-current but connected to the main line between the said switch and the generator, one being the field-magnet, another controlling the field-magnet, and the third controlling the said switch, and two magnets connected to the main line, one being a series magnet controlling the opening of the said switch, and the other being a shunt-magnet for regulating the current delivery to the lamps.

6. In a system for lighting railway-vehicles electrically, the combination with an axle, of a generator of a capacity greater than the normal lamp-load driven thereby at a variable speed, a potential-magnet permanently connected in a shunt-circuit from the armature, lamps and a storage battery having their connection with the said generator controlled by the potential of the system and their disconnection therefrom by the current of the system, a shunt-circuit containing the field-magnet of the generator, a resistance in said circuit, a motor operating the resistance and a director for the said motor controlled by the said potential-magnet so as to be set and maintained for one direction of action of said motor or another as long as the potential of the system is either above or below the point determined by the said magnet.

7. In a system for lighting railway-vehicles electrically, the combination with a generator, of an automatic connection-switch set to connect the generator to the line at a given speed, a storage battery permanently connected to the line while the said switch is closed, electric lamps intermittently connected to the line while the said switch is closed, a magnet measuring the generator potential, a current-changing regulator controlled by the said magnet and adjusting the amount of the battery-current to the counter electromotive force of the battery whenever the lamps are disconnected, and a resistance in the lamp branch determining, together with the said magnet, the potential applied to the lamps whenever both lamps and battery are connected to the generator.

8. In a system for lighting railway-vehicles electrically, the combination with lamps and a storage battery in multiple of a constant-potential dynamo driven by the vehicle at an intermittent and varible speed and having a capacity sufficient to simultaneously operate the lamps and charge the battery and a current-varying regulator for the dynamo adjusting the volume of armature-current to either the lamps along (the battery being charged) to the battery along (the lamps being out of use,) or to lamps and battery together.

The senior party, McElroy, filed his application September 9, 1901, upon which a patent issued February 17, 1903. He has taken no testimony and, therefore, must stand upon his filing date. Bliss filed his application September 10, 1904, which is subsequent to the date of the McElroy patent. As to counts 1 and 8 of the issue, however, Bliss contends that the burden of proof is not so heavily upon him because those counts are a continuation of an application filed by him February 26, 1902, while the McElroy application was still pending in the Patent Office. This contention is contested by McElroy, but we incline to accept the view of the Examiner of Interferences, who alone of the Patent Office tribunals passed upon the question, that these counts "appear to be fairly described in the earlier application."

The Examiner of Interferences and the Board of Examiners-in-Chief hold that Bliss has failed to prove reduction to practice prior to McElroy's filing date. The Commissioner, without considering the evidence bearing upon that question, finds that—

his very long delay in asserting claim to the invention discredits his allegations of a successful test of the invention and makes it necessary to resolve against him any doubt in the matter.

Each of the three tribunals of the Patent Office finds that, regardless of the question of reduction to practice, Bliss has forfeited any right he may have had by inactivity and delay. We proceed to a consideration of this question without expressing any opinion as to whether the experiments and tests of Mr. Bliss in 1897 constituted a reduction to practice.

Mr. Bliss is an electrical engineer. From the spring of 1897 down to the time he testified in this proceeding he devoted all his time to the invention of electric-lighting systems for railway-cars. The system involved in this issue was the first to engage his attention. This, he states, he conceived in the early spring of 1897, and immediately proceeded to construct in the cellar of 128 Front street, New York city, where he asembled it for the first time about the middle of June, 1897; that he then devoted several weeks "to testing it under conditions as nearly like those that would obtain upon a railroad-car" as he could reproduce; that some of these tests were made in the presence of three witnesses, one of whom was his brother and the other two close friends, and who all testified in reference thereto. The result of these tests, according to the testimony of Mr. Bliss, convinced him that he was "in possession of a thoroughly practical system." He was not convinced, however, that this system as he had developed it "was the ultimate solution of the problem of axle-lighting." He thus frankly criticises his own invention:

I would state that while this apparatus was exceptionally well built and performed its functions under test in a highly satisfactory manner, a knowledge of railroad conditions led me to analyze and criticise my own work with the object in view of being able to offer to the public a far better system of car-lighting. This apparatus, while nothing like as complicated and trappy as systems of a similar nature found to-day having had an advantage of some eight years in which to have had their crudeness reduced and their operativeness enhanced, was to my mind too delicate, too complicated, too subject to derangement, too costly to maintain, and not quick enough, accurate enough, or reliable enough in its operation to warrant its being foisted upon the public.

Thereupon the apparatus comprising this system "was carefully dismantled, cleaned up, and set temporarily to one side," where it remained so far as the evidence discloses until the application herein was filed. Immediately after dismantling this apparatus Mr. Bliss applied himself to the development of another system. That he worked with great industry and success is evidenced by the fact that his next system called the " bucker " was actually constructed during the months of July, August, and September, 1897, and an application for patent thereon filed October 14, 1897, which was granted March 29, 1898. The bucker system was tested without delay, and early in 1898 permission was obtained to install it on a Pullman car, and it was in fact installed on such car in March of that year. Mr. Bliss was asked why he placed the bucker system on the car instead of his original system, and frankly answered that he did so " because the bucker system overcame all of the difficulties encountered in the other apparatus." Subsequently the Bliss Electric Car Lighting Company was organized, and Mr. Bliss was given a salary of $3,000 per year. The bucker system was developed, and exploited, and installed on cars of different railroads, but absolutely nothing was done with the other system so far as the record discloses. Mr. Bliss was asked by his counsel whether he tried to sell "*these* systems " to the Pennsylvania Railroad Company, or to any other company. To this question Mr. Bliss answered:

I made continual efforts to sell *this* apparatus to other railroads besides the Pennsylvania R. R. Co. and the Pullman Co.

Mr. Bliss further testified that he developed the bucker system in preference to the one in issue because it " appeared to be a structure far less liable to derangement when placed in actual service; " that there was nothing particularly delicate about the bucker system; that " the bucker proposition looked more hopeful from a financial standpoint: " that his father, who had advanced money to the enterprise, " insisted upon driving the bucker invention through to a finish, regardless of anything else."

Mr. Bliss made no attempt to secure a patent on any feature of the invention in issue until after he discovered that a patent involving the invention had issued to one Creveling December 10, 1901, although he had since his conception of this invention obtained several domestic and several foreign patents on other inventions. On February 26, 1902, shortly after his discovery of the Creveling patent and *about five years after he had conceived this invention*, and, as he contends, had reduced the same to practice, he filed the application to which we have heretofore alluded. The application herein was not filed by him until more than a year and a half after a patent had been issued to McElroy, and more than six years and a half after the alleged conception and reduction to practice by Bliss.

Mr. Bliss, in answer to this cumulative and overwhelming evidence *of lack of diligence*, says his means were so limited that he could patent only such inventions as he made public; that the evidence does not affirmatively show abandonment by him, and that he did not in fact intend to abandon his invention; that as to counts 1 and 8 of the issue McElroy had not given " the invention of these counts to the public, either by patent or by public use," when the earlier Bliss application was filed, and that, therefore, the rule announced in *Mason* v. *Hepburn* (C. D., 1898, 510; 84 O. G., 147; 13 App. D. C., 86) is not applicable to these counts.

In *Mason* v. *Hepburn*, Mason delayed the filing of his application about seven years after conception and reduction to practice, while Hepburn's application was filed about nine months, and a patent was issued to him about four months, *prior* to Mason's filing date. In that case as in the instant case the evidence cast no cloud on the good faith of the senior party, and the court observed that his invention was an independent act. After a very thorough and careful analysis of the leading cases applicable to the question involved, the Court said:

Considering, then, this paramount interest of the public in its bearing upon the question as presented here, we think it imperatively demands that a subsequent inventor of a new and useful manufacture or improvement who has diligently pursued his labors to the procurement of a patent in good faith and without any knowledge of the preceding discoveries of another shall, as against that other, who has deliberately concealed the knowledge of his invention from the public, be regarded as the real inventor and as such entitled to his reward.

In *Thomson* v. *Weston* (C. D., 1902, 521; 99 O. G., 864; 19 App. D. C., 373) there was a delay of about four years by Thomson after conception and reduction to practice in filing his application, and Weston's patent antedated by a few months the Thomson application. After referring to the decision in *Mason* v. *Hepburn* (C. D., 1898, 510; 84 O. G., 147; 13 App. D. C., 86) the Court said:

It is true that the time of concealment in this case was something less than four years as against seven years in that. The mere difference in time, however, is not sufficient to affect the application of the principle, for it is as certain in one case as in the other that the application for patent was solely stimulated by the publication of the patent granted to another inventor. No substantial or even plausible excuse for Thomson's inaction is disclosed by the testimony * * * The particular object of the beneficence of the patent law is the individual who first conceives, and with diligence perfects an invention. And where one has completed the act of invention his right to the reward in the form of a patent becomes complete save in two instances that may be satisfactorily shown to exist. First, he loses the right as against the public in general by a public use for the statutory period. Second, by his deliberate concealment or suppression of the knowledge of his invention he subordinates his claim, in accordance with the general policy of the law in the promotion of the public interest, to that of another and *bona fide* inventor who during the period of inaction and concealment shall have given the benefit of the discovery to the public. Viewed in the light of " the true policy and ends of the patent laws," the latter is the first to invent, and therefore entitled to the reward.

There was less delay in *Matthes* v. *Burt* (C. D., 1905, 574; 114 O. G., 764; 24 App. D. C., 265) than in the present case, and in that case the Matthes application was filed while Burt's was still pending in the Patent Office. The invention related to a billiard-ball, and the evidence showed that after Matthes had tested his invention to his own satisfaction and to the satisfaction of his employers, "it was laid aside and the manufacture was continued in the old way." Meanwhile Burt working independently conceived the same invention and promptly proceeded to utilize it and sell the product. He applied for a patent without delay, and shortly thereafter Matthes having learned of Burt's success also filed an application. The court ruled that Matthes in concealing his invention for three and a half years forfeited his rights as against Burt. The Court also said:

That Burt's application had not ripened into a patent before Matthes filed his does not substantially affect the application of the cases of *Mason* v. *Hepburn*, and others *supra*. Whilst the possession of a patent makes. ordinarily, a stronger case in favor of the holder, the doctrine in respect of concealment by one earlier to invent does not necessarily depend upon that fact. In *Warner* v. *Smith*, (C. D., 1898, 517; 84 O. G., 311; 13 App. D. C., 111) in which the reasons for that doctrine are explained at length, the later inventor had not received a patent.

In the present case Bliss concealed his invention for a period of five years after his tests convinced him "that it was the best system in existence in June, 1897." He invented and exploited another system, and did nothing with or about this system until he saw the Creveling patent. Having discovered that Creveling's patent encroached upon his invention he filed an application for so much of the invention as the Creveling patent covered. It was not until he saw the McElroy patent a year and a half later that he filed this application covering all his invention. The following reference to his cross-examination is timely:

Q. You are aware, are you not, that Mr. McElroy has a car-lighting system on the Delaware & Hudson R. R.?

A. Only by hearsay.

Q. Were you aware of it at the time you filed your application in issue?

A. I understood that he was carrying on some kinds of experiments in this line.

The conclusion is irresistible that Mr. Bliss set this system to one side because he believed he could invent a better one. It is equally clear that, having invented what in his opinion was a better system, he permitted this one to remain to one side until others after independent and patient efforts had conceived and developed similar systems. Then to clear the field of troublesome competition he sought a patent. The patent laws were not enacted for any such purpose. They were not enacted to discourage but to stimulate invention, and, as was pointed out in *Mason* v. *Hepburn*, *supra*, the object of the Government in fostering inventions is to benefit the public. The public receives no benefit from an invention that is locked up in a cupboard, or exists only in the brain of the inventor. For this reason it is the policy of the law to encourage activity and diligence and discourage delay.

The reasons for the delay in this case are not sufficient as to any of the counts of the issue, and we, therefore, affirm the decision of the Commissioner, and it is so ordered.

The clerk of the court will certify this opinion and the proceedings in this court to the Commissioner of Patents, as required by law. *Affirmed.*

[Court of Appeals of the District of Columbia.]

In re Hodges.

Decided January 8, 1907.

(128 O. G., 887.)

PATENTABILITY—SUBSTITUTION OF EQUIVALENTS.

Where it is old to heat exhaust-air as it passes from the high-pressure to the low-pressure cylinder of a compound air-engine by means of a liquid substance, and it is also old to use atmospheric air to impart heat to air within a receptacle, it does not amount to invention to substitute the latter heating medium for the former.

Mr. Bayard H. Christy for Hodges.
Mr. Fairfax Bayard for the Commissioner of Patents.

ROBB, J.:

This is an appeal from a decision of the Commissioner of Patents sustaining the decisions of two other tribunals in the Patent Office and rejecting five of appellant's ten claims for patent on interheaters for compound compressed-air engines.

The rejected claims follow:

1. An interheater for a compound compressed-air engine which consists of a receptacle receiving air from the high-pressure cylinder and delivering air to the low-pressure cylinder and provided with an extended surface adapted to absorb heat from the atmosphere at normal temperature and impart heat so absorbed to the compressed air in its flow to the low-pressure cylinder, substantially as described.

2. An interheater for a compound compressed-air locomotive-engine which consists of a receptacle receiving air from the high-pressure cylinder and delivering air to the low-pressure cylinder, the said receptacle provided with an extended heating surface and arranged to receive a flow of atmospheric air at normal temperature over said surface, substantially as described.

3. An interheater for a compound compressed-air locomotive-engine which consists of a receptacle receiving air from the high-pressure cylinder and delivering air to the low-pressure cylinder, the said receptacle provided with an extended heating surface and arranged to receive a flow of atmospheric air at normal temperature over said surface, substantially as described.

4. An interheater for a compound compressed-air engine which consists of a receptacle receiving air from the high-pressure cylinder and delivering air to the low-pressure cylinder and provided with an extended heating surface together with means for causing a flow of atmospheric air at normal temperature over the said surface of said receptacle, substantially as described.

5. An interheater for a compound compressed-air engine which consists of a receptacle for the air in its passage from the high-pressure cylinder to the low-pressure cylinder, provided with an inlet at its lower end and an outlet at its upper end, and having an extended surface exposed to the heating influence of atmospheric air at normal temperature, substantially as described.

A compound compressed-air engine is an engine in which the compressed air is first used in a high-pressure cylinder, that is. in a cylinder of relatively small diameter, and, after driving the piston connected therewith, instead of being permitted to escape is conveyed to a low-pressure cylinder, that is, to a cylinder of larger diameter where it still has sufficient expansive force to drive another piston. This operation may be again repeated in a third cylinder, or the air be permited to escape to the atmosphere. When the compressed air enters the first cylinder, it necessarily partially expands and in expanding becomes much colder, and by becoming colder its expansive power is, of course, correspondingly lessened or diminished. It is manifest, therefore, that any arrangement or device that will operate to warm or heat the air after it leaves one cylinder and before it enters the next will greatly increase its efficiency in the second cylinder. Inasmuch as such compressed air, after being partially expanded in the first cylinder, is frequently colder than atmospheric temperature, appellant has arranged what he calls an " interheater," which in fact is a plurality of longitudinally-extending tubes within and along which the compressed air flows from one cylinder to another, and over which a current of atmospheric air passes. The atmospheric air, being warmer than the compressed air within the tubes, imparts or gives up some of its warmth to the compressed air within, and to that extent increases the efficiency of the compressed air. It is simply a reversal of the old idea of warming atmospheric air by a plurality of tubes called radiators through which steam or hot water passes. In one case the atmospheric air absorbs heat from the substance within the tubes, and in the other case it imparts heat to the tubes and the substance therein.

The following references are cited by the Commissioner as the basis for the rejection of the above claims: British patent. No. 3,056. of 1871, Geisenburger. No. 222,950. December 23, 1879. Reynolds & Haupt, No. 344,006. June 22, 1886, Palmer. No. 655,148. July 31, 1900, Dickerson, No. 745,373, December 1, 1903, Nutty.

Reynolds & Haupt in their specification say:

We employ an engine of the compound type, and though we may or may not heat the air before its introduction to the engine we always heat it a exhaust from the high-pressure cylinder and before its induction to the low-pressure cylinder; and to this end our invention consists in the combination, with a compound engine for the use of compressed air for motive power, of a heater placed between its high and low pressure cylinders and containing heated water or other liquid, through or in contact with which the air passes between its eduction from the one cylinder and its induction into the other.

It will be observed that this patent, like the claim in issue, has reference to an interheater for a compound compressed-air engine, the only real difference being that Hodges uses atmospheric air instead of a liquid substance to impart heat to the compressed air within the interheater. Inasmuch as it is obvious that, under certain conditions, an interheater dependent wholly upon atmospheric air for its successful operation possesses advantages over one requiring some liquid substance, Hodges will be entitled to a patent if it can be successfully demonstrated that he is the originator of the idea embodied in this difference between the two devices. On the other hand, if he is not the originator of the idea of using atmospheric air to impart heat to air within some receptacle for the purpose and with the effect of increasing its expansive force, then obviously he ought not to be given a monopoly on all such devices. We pass, therefore, to the other references to determine this question.

The Dickerson patent, as described by him—

consists in the combination, with a receiver for containing the liquid air, of an air-motor connected therewith through suitable intermediate expansion coils or chambers, and a blower or fan which is driven by the motor and which is arranged to produce a current of air over the expansion-coil, so as to impart to the latter sufficient heat to effect the expansion of the air therein and to be delivered at a reduced temperature into the room or other space which is to be cooled and ventilated. * * * The expansion-coils are located in the conduit, through which air is forced by the blower, so that by the absorption of heat from the latter the air in said coils is raised in temperature and expanded. This expanded air on reaching the reservoir is still further expanded by the absorption of heat from the incoming air and exerts a sufficiently high pressure to run the motor.

Without describing this patent further, we refer to the statement in the brief of counsel for appellant in reference thereto:

Although Dickerson here shows that one body of air may impart heat to another body flowing in a coil, and by thus imparting heat may increase the expansive power of the inclosed body of air, it teaches nothing more which is pertinent to the invention under consideration.

Appellant concedes he did not invent the interheater. He found that in the Reynolds & Haupt patent. His claim is for a device susceptible of using atmospheric air instead of a liquid substance to heat and expand air therein, and in the Dickerson patent we find such a device for such a purpose. We think appellant concedes this in the statement taken from his brief.

30997—H. Doc. 470, 60-1——35

In *Smith* v. *Nichols*, (2 O. G., 649; 21 Wall., 112,) it is said:

A mere carrying forward of new or more extended application of the original thought, a change only in form, proportions, or degree, the substitution of equivalents, doing substantially the same thing in the same way by substantially the same means with better results, is not such invention as will sustain a patent.

The use of atmospheric air as a heating medium is also shown in the Geisenburger patent, and also in the Palmer patent. In the Geisenburger patent the carbonic-acid gas in liquid form passes to the expansion-cylinder through a coil or heater " inclosed in a tank or vessel filled with water or *air*, or any body capable of having the same temperature as the circumambient air."

A careful examination of these cited patents and the drawings and specifications filed therewith convinces us that the Commissioner of Patents was right in disallowing all these claims, and we, therefore, affirm his decision, and direct the clerk to certify the proceedings in this court to him as the law provides. *Affirmed.*

[Court of Appeals of the District of Columbia.]

FEINBERG *v.* COWAN.

Decided February 5, 1907.

(128 O. G., 889.)

INTERFERENCE—PRIORITY—DILIGENCE.

F. conceived the invention in September, 1900, and disclosed it in September, 1903, but did nothing toward reducing it to practice until April, 1904. C. conceived the invention in January, 1904, and reduced it to practice in the following March. The excuse offered by F. for his delay was that he was too busy earning his living to attend to it, and, moreover, he did not have the means to reduce it to practice unless he borrowed the money, which he did not want to do. *Held* that F. was lacking in diligence, it being shown by the evidence that subsequent to his conception he borrowed $3,000 with which to engage in a venturesome undertaking, while a small amount of money would have enabled him to construct the invention.

Mr. Joseph L. Levy and *Mr. A. O. E. Edwards, Jr.*, for Feinberg.
Mr. R. B. Wilson for Cowan.

ROBB, *J.*:

This is an appeal involving three concurrent decisions of the Patent Office ((C. D., 1906, 443; 125 O. G., 667) in an interference proceeding awarding priority of invention to appellee Cowan, the senior *party,* upon an issue expressed in the following counts:

Count 1. In a device of the class described, in combination, a pair of angularly-disposed legs adapted to rest against the outer face of two abutting plates, a member attached to one of said legs and having an inclined extension lying in the angle between said legs, and a clamping-block attached to said extension.

Count 2. A fastening device for connecting plates, comprising a member having angularly-disposed legs, a stud attached to one of said legs, adapted to pass between the edges of said plates and having an inclined threaded extension lying in the angle between said legs, and a clamping member attaching to the same and engaging the faces of said plates.

The invention described in the above counts is a very simple one, and covers a clamp for holding glass plates. Cowan by competent evidence conclusively established conception of the invention about January 1, 1904, and reduction of the same to practice on or about March 25, 1904, at which time he had a full-sized clamp made. The manager of the shop, where Cowan's clamp was made, identified shop orders under date of March 24, 1904, which Cowan gave him for making the clamp, and testified that Cowan also gave him a wooden pattern; that the order and pattern were delivered to a workman who completed the clamp on March 25, 1904; and that this clamp was delivered to Cowan on the day it was made. Witness identified Cowan's exhibit as being the clamp made on said March 25, 1904. Cowan followed this diligence by having other clamps made.

Feinberg testifies that from some time in September, 1900, to November, 1900, he worked selling plate-glass for I. Feinberg, who was a cousin and a plate-glass dealer in New York, and that during the month of September, 1900, he conceived the invention in issue. His testimony concerning conception in 1900 is not corroborated, and is moreover vague and unsatisfactory. On November 30, 1900, he abandoned his position as plate-glass salesman and went to Philadelphia, where with $3,000 he had borrowed for the purpose he opened and managed three different music schools for mandolin, violin, banjo, guitar, and piano teaching. This venture was not a success, and at the end of August, 1903, he returned to New York, and again engaged as a plate-glass salesman for I. Feinberg. About the middle of October, 1903, he engaged in the business, with his cousin Samuel Feinberg, of soliciting orders for glass for buildings. He continued in this last venture until July, 1904. Feinberg testifies that:

In the early part of September, 1903, cousin Ike Feinberg and myself agreed upon terms and I became salesman on the very first day that was on Wednesday after Labor Day, 1903. I bethought myself of my glass-fastener which I thought out before I went in the music business and the very evening when I got home I drafted in my order-book a crude sketch of that clamp, which looked to me like a printed capital F with an elongated incline in a dash together with a triangular inner filler and a thumb-screw and when on the following Saturday I went to Philadelphia, I showed the sketch to my cousin Sam. Feinberg. He however thought it will not hold together.

Feinberg produced his order-book showing this sketch, and his cousin gave corroborative testimony on this point. Nothing, however, was actually done by Feinberg, according to his own testimony, toward reducing his invention to practice until some time in April, 1904, probably late in April, when he engaged a model-maker to make a clamp for him. He introduced in evidence a bill dated June 27, 1904, for making this clamp. The explanation was made that bills were sent out about four weeks after the completion of the work. Accepting this statement as correct, the earliest date of reduction to practice by Feinberg is May 27, 1904. Inasmuch as Cowan reduced his invention to practice on March 25, 1904, it is apparent that, unless Feinberg can satisfactorily explain his failure to reduce his invention to practice prior to that date, Cowan must prevail. The excuse Feinberg gives for his lack of diligence may be found in the following statement:

I was so busy earning my living, in soliciting, hunting up business, taking orders, that I did not have time to attend to the matter in that period, and one of the main reasons why I didn't do anything was that I didn't have any money to do it with, and I did not want to borrow the money to have the samples made.

The reasons are not sufficient to entitle Feinberg to an award of priority. According to his own statement, he conceived this invention in September, 1900, when he was engaged in selling plate-glass. He subsequently borrowed $3,000 to engage in an entirely different line of business, the success of which must have been more uncertain than the success of such a simple and useful device as he claims to have invented. His lack of diligence throughout the three years between his original conception of the invention and his second disclosure to Sam. Feinberg "some time in September, 1903," throws some light on his subsequent conduct, and leads to the conclusion that until late in 1904, he did not regard his invention as of sufficient importance to warrant the expenditure of either time or money. He was willing to borrow $3,000 with which to engage in a new and venturesome business, but delayed the expenditure of the almost nominal sum required to reduce his invention to practice. In view of the very simple nature of his device, the small expense involved in its construction, and the intervention of another party, we do not think his lack of diligence excusable. Manifestly, we cannot now permit him to displace a man who diligently followed conception of the invention with actual reduction to practice prior to the most favorable date of reduction to practice which can be given Feinberg. To do so under the facts disclosed by the record would be to discourage diligence and to encourage delay. Such a decision would tend in the future to subject diligent and honest inventors to needless and expensive litigation, and pave the way for deception and fraud. We therefore affirm the decision of the Commissioner of Patents, and it is so ordered.

The clerk of the court will certify this opinion and the proceedings in this court to the Commissioner of Patents, as required by law. *Affirmed.*

[Court of Appeals of the District of Columbia.]

IN RE HOPKINS.

Decided February 5, 1907.

(128 O. G., 890.)

TRADE-MARKS—"ORIENTAL CREAM" FOR SKIN-LOTION—GEOGRAPHICAL IN SIG-NIFICANCE—NOT REGISTRABLE.

Held that a trade-mark comprising the words "'Oriental Cream,' asso-ciated with an eagle holding a scroll in its beak," is not registrable as a trade-mark for a skin-lotion because of its geographical significance.

Mr. Joseph L. Atkins for Hopkins.
Mr. Fairfax Bayard for the Commissioner of Patents.

SHEPARD, *J.:*

The applicant appeals from a decision of the Commissioner of Pat-ents (C. D., 1906, 452; 125 O. G., 670,) refusing registration of a trade-mark. The original application was accompanied by a label containing in large letters across the top the words " Oriental Cream," under which follow the words, " or Magical Beautifier." It then pro-ceeds to describe the article as the most elegant and delicate prepara-tion for the skin, etc., etc., with other words indicating manufacturer etc. Under the large words at the top, and about the middle of the label is a figure resembling the eagle on the larger silver coins of the United States, which was described as " a fantastic winged figure." By amendment, the trade-mark was described as the words, " ' Ori-ental Cream ' associated with an eagle holding a scroll in its beak."

The refusal to register was on the ground that the term " Ori-ental " is a geographical term and, therefore, prohibited from regis-tration by section 5 of the Trade-Mark Act of February 20, 1905. The Commissioner said:

The Orient is a term used to indicate the East, eastern countries, and speci-fically the regions to the east and southeast of the leading States of Europe. (*Century Dictionary*.) The term " Oriental " is in general use in commerce to indicate goods that are manufactured in this region—as, for example, Oriental rugs. As applied to a cream it would indicate that the cream came from the Orient.

In support of his conclusion he cites cases holding such terms as: " Lackawanna " in connection with coal (*Del. & H. C. Co. v. Clark,*

1 O. G., 279; 13 Wall., 311;) "Columbia" (*Columbia Mill Co.* v. *Alcorn*, C. D., 1893, 672; 65 O. G., 1916; 150 U. S. 460;) "Old Country" and "Our Country" (*Wrisley Co.* v. *Iowa Soap Co.*, 122 Fed. Rep., 796); "East Indian" in connection with "Remedy" (*Connell* v. *Reed*, 128 Mass., 477), to be geographical and not capable of appropriation as trade-marks. See also *Continental Ins. Co.* v. *Continental Fire Association*, 101 Fed. Rep., 225 (word "Continental";) and *Koehler* v. *Sanders*, 122 N. Y., 65, (word "International".)

The contention of the appellant that the words "Oriental Cream" are not descriptive but arbitrary as applied to his product, which is not a cream but a cosmetical lotion of a creamy appearance, is met by a recent decision of this Court in which the question is fully considered. (*In re American Circular Loom Co.*, ante, 481; 127 O. G., 393.)

The decision of the Commissioner of Patents is affirmed; and this decision will be certified to him as required by law. *Affirmed.*

[Court of Appeals of the District of Columbia.]

IN RE NATIONAL PHONOGRAPH COMPANY.

Decided February 18, 1907.

(128 O. G., 1295.)

1. TRADE-MARKS—"STANDARD" DESCRIPTIVE—NOT REGISTRABLE.

   Held that the word "Standard" as applied to phonographs is descriptive and therefore not registrable.

2. SAME—SAME—IMMATERIAL WHETHER TRULY OR FALSELY DESCRIPTIVE.

   The applicant's claim to the use of "Standard" as a trade-mark is in nowise strengthened, because the word is applied only to machines of inferior design which are not in any sense standard. The word cannot be appropriated as a trade-mark whether it is truly descriptive or falsely descriptive.

Mr. Frank L. Dyer for the National Phonograph Company.
Mr. Fairfax Bayard for the Commissioner of Patents.

McCOMAS, *J.:*

The Examiner of Trade-Marks refused to register the word "Standard" as a trade-mark for phonographs upon the ground that the mark is descriptive. The Commissioner of Patents affirmed this decision (C. D., 1906, 410; 124 O. G., 2901,) and the National Phonograph Company thereupon appealed to this court. The appellant claims to have continuously used this word as a trade-mark in its *business of* producing and selling phonographs, since April, 1898.

The act of 1905, chapter 84, section 5, only declared the accepted law of trade-marks when it prohibited the registration of marks which consists—

merely in words or devices which are descriptive of the goods with which they are used, or of the character of such goods.

The general proposition was well established that words merely descriptive of the character, qualities or composition of an article or of the place where it was manufactured or produced, could not be monopolized as a trade-mark. (*Brown Chemical Co.* v. *Meyer*, C. D., 1891, 346; 55 O. G., 287; 139 U. S., 540; *Canal Company* v. *Clark*, 1 O. G., 279; 13 Wall., 311; *Manufacturing Company* v. *Trainer*, C. D., 1880, 464; 17 O. G., 1217; 101 U. S., 51.)

The adjective " Standard " upon varying applications for its registration as a trade-mark, was held not to be a lawful trade-mark by Commissioners Payne, Doolittle, Fisher and by Commissioner Duell, afterward Justice Duell of this court. The exclusive right to the use of such a word as a trade-mark on a particular article cannot be acquired by the first appropriation of it by one person because other persons who may produce and sell a similar article have equal right in describing it to employ any appropriate term, including such word.

No one has the right to appropriate to his exclusive use a sign or symbol' which from the nature of the fact it is used to signify, others may have an equal right to employ for the same reason. It is because of this principle that a trade-mark cannot be acquired by the adoption of a word which is merely descriptive of the quality, ingredients or characteristics of a commodity. (*Manufacturing Co.* v. *Spear*, 2 Sandf., 599; *Medicine Company* v. *Hilton*, 60 Fed. Rep., 756.)

Chief Justice Shepard, speaking for this court, concluded that the words "Circular Loom" were descriptive of one of the characteristics of the article to which they were applied as a trade-mark, in the case, *in re American Circular Loom Company*, ante, 481; 127 O. G., 393; Judge Lurton held that " Standard " is a descriptive word and in the particular case before him, stood for a class of computing-scales and, of course, in that connection, it was aptly descriptive of a standard of weights. (*Computing Scale Co.* v. *Standard Computing Scale Co.*, 118 Fed. Rep., 971.)

In my collocation, "Standard" in its common meanings, signifies authority, a type, excellence, fixed or permanent value, a test or rule, or measure of quality. Other makers of phonographs should not be deprived of its use.

We agree with the Commissioner that the applicant's claim to use "Standard" as a trade-mark is in nowise strengthened because the appellant contends that it only applies the word to machines of inferior design and which are not in any sense standard. The word cannot be used whether it is truly descriptive or falsely descriptive.

It would be unprofitable to discuss the numerous cases cited by the appellant's counsel in which other words were registered as trademarks, since they cannot help us to determine whether "Standard" is a descriptive word. In the instances cited where the words are descriptive, we think such words were improperly held valid as trademarks, and in the cases where they were not descriptive, such instances do not support the applicant's contention here. The argument in *Williams* v. *Mitchell*, (106 Fed. Rep., 168,) that a word may be a descriptive word and yet used in a non-descriptive sense is not convincing, for the Commissioner should prohibit the registration of descriptive words, and the affidavits of the president of the phonograph company and two other persons that the word "Standard" does not indicate to their minds or to the minds of other persons in the phonograph trade a phonograph of any particular type, quality or character is not convincing, if indeed relevant here. The three affiants can testify only concerning the impression the word "standard" makes upon their minds. This applicant has no right to appropriate the word "standard" which others may desire to employ with equal sincerity. The applicant should not have the exclusive right to describe its product as "Standard Phonographs" and another producer should have an equal right to employ the same word to describe its similar product. Many manufacturers would be tempted to use "Standard" to indicate the quality or grade or uniformity of the goods they produce.

The predecessors of the Commissioner of Patents, who regarded the word "Standard" as a descriptive word, do not appear to have erred and we are convinced that the present Commissioner has not committed error in this instance and his decision *is affirmed*. The clerk of this court will certify this opinion and decision to the Commissioner of Patents in accordance with law.

[Court of Appeals of the District of Columbia.]

KILBOURN *v.* HIRNER.

Decided February 5, 1907.

(128 O. G., 1689.)

INTERFERENCE—PRIORITY—SUFFICIENCY OF DISCLOSURE—CONCLUSIVENESS OF PATENT OFFICE DECISIONS.

The decisions of the expert tribunals of the Patent Office on the question of the sufficiency of the disclosure of a party to an interference will be accepted by the court of appeals as conclusive, except in extreme cases where palpable error has been committed (*Seeberger* v. *Dodge*, C. D., 1905, 603; 114 O. G., 2382; 24 App. D. C., 481; *Podlesak* v. *McInnerney*, C. D., 1906, 558; 120 O. G., 2127; 26 App. D. C., 405.)

Mr. J. H. Whitaker and *Mr. Melville Church* for Kilbourn.
Mr. C. L. Sturtevant and *Mr. H. N. Paul* for Hirner.

ROBB, *J.:*

This is an appeal from a decision of the Commissioner of Patents (C. D., 1906, 367; 124 O. G., 1841) in an interference case involving an automatic stocking-knitting machine.

The assignment of error relied upon in argument challenges the ruling that appellee has the right to claim in his application in interference the subject-matter in issue.   The counts of the issue follow:

Count 1. In a circular-knitting machine having independent needles and means for narrowing and widening the back of the knit tube, means for knitting open-work and plain knitting at any point around the said tube and means for changing the open-work on the back of the tube to plain knitting.

Count 2. In a circular-knitting machine having independent needles, cam mechanism to coöperate with all of said needles, to produce tubular work, to coöperate with each needle of a continuous portion of said needles to form narrowed and widened fabric, and to operate certain needles of said portion without causing them to knit, thereby forming drop-stitch work.

Hirner is the senior party, having filed his application July 5, 1901. Kilbourn filed his application December 16, 1902, more than seventeen months later.   An interference was declared November 3, 1903, and then involved, in addition to the applications of the parties hereto, the application of Sylvester J. Kutz filed May 1, 1902, the application of John B. Hipwell filed June 3, 1902, and the application of John C. Duemler filed July 19, 1902.   Kutz, Hipwell and Duemler took no testimony, and, being junior parties, their failure in that respect resulted in their applications being eliminated from further consideration.   Hirner and Kilbourn each proceeded to take testimony on the question of priority.   Subsequently a hearing was had before the Examiner of Interferences, who in a carefully considered opinion awarded judgment of priority to Hirner.   During the argument before the Examiner counsel for Kilbourn for the first time, as far as the record discloses, raised the question whether Hirner's application contains a sufficient basis for the claims in interference.   This question was also carefully considered by the Examiner, and his ruling thereon sustained Hirner.   An appeal was taken to the Examiners-in-Chief, who affirmed the decision appealed from. The case was then taken to the Commissioner, who, without deciding the question of priority, remanded the proceeding to the Primary Examiner, saying:

No motion for dissolution was made by Kilbourn, and no statement upon the record appears to have been made by the Primary Examiner of his reasons for holding that the issues are properly grounded upon Hirner's disclosure. The machines upon which the issue is drawn and those of the prior art are complex and intricate and their operation involved. The Primary Examiner is the technical expert of this Office as to those arts in which he examines. He should through his special experience be peculiarly fitted to determine the meanings of the terms used in the specification of the parties and to determine the relations of their disclosures to prior devices. I am unwilling to pass upon the question of disclosure by Hirner without the benefit of the opinion and the reasons of the Primary Examiner based upon discussion of the question by the parties in case they desire to be heard.

The interference is remanded to the Primary Examiner, who will hear the parties and furnish me with his opinion as to the question raised, together with a statement of the reasons for his conclusion. (C. D., 1906, 161; 122 O. G., 729.)

Thereupon the Primary Examiner heard counsel for both parties, considered the question submitted to him, and furnished the Commissioner with an elaborate opinion, saying in conclusion:

The examiner is of the opinion that Hirner's showing is sufficient to support his right to make the claims made the issue of the interference, and it is so held.

Thereupon the Commissioner rendered a final decision (C. D., 1906, 367; 124 O. G., 1841,) in which he said:

The Primary Examiner heard the parties and has rendered his opinion, which is now before me. He has given a clear and fair discussion of the facts and concluded, as did the Examiners-in-Chief and Examiner of Interferences, that Hirner's disclosure justified the claims in issue.

After careful consideration I am convinced that the unanimous conclusion expressed by the three opinions which have been written upon the sufficiency of Hirner's disclosure is sound.

The reasons that impelled the Commissioner to seek the opinion of the Primary Examiner on the question here involved have heretofore impelled this court to announce the rule that the decisions of the expert tribunals of the Patent Office on such a question will be accepted as conclusive, except in extreme cases where palpable error has been committed. (*Seeberger* v. *Dodge*, C. D., 1905, 603; 114 O. G., 2382; 24 App. D. C., 481; *Podlesak* v. *McInnerney*, C. D., 1906, 558; 120 O. G., 2127; 26 App. D. C., 405.)

We see nothing unusual or extreme in this case unless it be the failure of appellant to discover what he now urges as an obvious and fundamental defect in Hirner's application until more than a year after the declaration of interference. Unless, therefore, a manifest error has been committed, the judgment must be affirmed.

The specific objection to the Hirner application is that it neither shows nor describes narrowing and widening devices for making the heel and toe of the stocking. The record discloses that at the time Hirner made this application he was, and for a long time had been, a prolific inventor as well as a manufacturer of circular-knitting machines. It also discloses that he himself had invented and patented machines containing narrowing and widening devices. It *is apparent*, therefore, that he was highly skilled in the art filed this application. The Examiner of Interferences after quoting from Hirner's application says:

It seems quite apparent from Hirner's specification that the machine described therein is the ordinary stocking-knitting machine in which not only the leg portion but the heel and toe portions of the stocking are made. Of necessity such a machine must comprise narowing and widening mechanism. This, indeed, is well known in the art. To say that a complete stocking is produced upon a knitting-machine means, to one skilled in art, that such a machine contains the ordinary narrowing and wideing mechanism. It is believed that Hirner's specification contains a sufficient basis for the present claims.

The Examiners-in-Chief—

find that Fig. 10 of the application of Hirner discloses device lettered F, and a shape of the upper portion of device E which are provisions for the guidance of pickers for automatically operating the needles to effect narowing and widening. In short this figure of the drawings clearly so shows a part of the machine as to make the machine one having automatic narrowing and widening mechanisms.

Also the entire specification of Hirner is drawn to indicate that all of the operations are automatically performed by the machine, excepting in one instance where it states that the cam N may be operated either automatically or by hand.

Furthermore at the date of Hirner's application, Hirner, an inventor and manufacturer of circular-knitting machines, cannot be presumed to have presented an improvement on merely the very old type of machines wherein the narrowing and widening was done by hand operation of needles and the cylinder but rather on one of the then more modern automatic narrowing and widening machines with which he must have been well acquainted.

The Primary Examiner, to whom the question was then referred, says *inter alia:*

It is fundamental knowledge in this art that the heel, sole, and toe of a stocking knit of solid fabric can be produced only upon a continuous series of needles having no omissions therein.

It is also fundamental knowledge in this art that the heel and toe pockets of a stocking can be made upon a circular machine (the product of which is a " seamless " stocking,) only by widening and narrowing the fabric to form said pockets.

*   *   *   *   *   *   *

The showing comprised in Hirner's Fig. 10 appears to the Examiner to be alone sufficient to entitle Hirner to make in this case claims to the combination of the particular devices clearly shown in the application with " means for narrowing and widening the back of the knit tube " or " cams to coöperate with each needle of a continuous portion of said needles to form narrowed and widened fabric."

The cam shown in Fig 10, apparently an accurate drawing of the inner surface of the cam-cylinder of the actual machine made by Hirner is most distinctive in its design, and would be recognized by any one skilled in this art as belonging to an automatic knitting-machine having narrowing and widening devices. The configuration of the cam D and E, particularly of the upper ardly-sloping surfaces, which are shown as containing recesses, would be useless in any other type of machine. The recesses mentioned are for the purpose of accommodating the narrowing-pickers when in position for action. See in this connection Fig. 2 of Hirner's prior patent No. 471,220, Mar 22, 1892, (Knitting and Netting, Circular Machines, Independent Needles, Fashioning,) and his patent No. 753,260, Mar. 1, 1904, (Circular Machines, Independent Needles,) wherein a cam-cylinder is similarly conventionally shown with the same recesses, and his patent No. 686,070, Nov. 5, 1901, wherein see particularly Fig. 2 and Fig. 13, and the narrowing-pickers E³ shown in said figures.

The Commissioner, as before stated, accepted and approved the finding of the Primary Examiner, saying:

In Hirner's specification as filed, however, reference is made to ordinary stocking-knitters and to a cam which when controlled by proper mechanism may be used as a pull-down cam to lower the needles after knitting a heel or toe pocket, and also to cams which may be used in conjunction with other mechanism at the commencement of the formation of the heel and toe pockets as needle-raising cams. These references, in view of the general use of pickers upon stocking-knitters, would, it is believed, unmistakably inform those skilled in the art that the devices shown by Hirner are to be used in practice with the usual pickers for widening and narrowing.

We have carefully examined and considered this record, and find no sufficient basis therein for disturbing the conclusion thus carefully reached by the successive tribunals of the Patent Office. The parties, Kutz, Hipwell, and Duemler, each senior to Kilbourn, and each presumably skilled in the art, did not question the sufficiency of Hirner's application, and Kilbourn himself failed to discover any defect therein until the testimony had been taken which convinced the Patent Office that Hirner was entitled to a judgment of priority.

Without considering the question further, we affirm the decision of the Commissioner, and it is so ordered.

The clerk of the court will certify this opinion and the proceedings in this court to the Commissioner of Patents, as required by law. *Affirmed.*

[Court of Appeals of the District of Columbia.]

MUNSTER *v.* ASHWORTH.

Decided February 5, 1907.

(128 O. G., 2088.)

1. INTERFERENCE—EVIDENCE—CONSIDERATION OF DEPOSITION—FAILURE TO AFFORD OPPORTUNITY FOR CROSS-EXAMINATION.

Where a witness after testifying on his own behalf and after answering a few questions on cross-examination states that he is unable to withstand the strain of cross-examination and leaves the stand and his counsel refuses to ask for an extension of time for taking testimony in order that the witness may be cross-examined at ~~ time in the future, alleging that *the witness is in such bad physica* ~~ that there is no prospect of his being able to testify within a year, if at all, *Held* that counsel, knowing the condition of the witness, should either have refrained from offering him as a witness in his own behalf or, having done so, should have consented to some reasonable postponement. Under such circumstances the direct examination should have been excluded upon motion.

2. SAME—SAME—AFFIDAVIT ATTACHED TO DEPOSITION.

An affidavit of a physician attached to a deposition, setting forth the physical condition of a witness who has left the stand during cross-examination because of inability to stand the strain of cross-examination, forms no part of such deposition. The affiant should have been called and sworn to testify as a witness.

Mr. Wm. Small for the appellant.
Mr. F. J. Kent and *Mr. Samuel Herrick* for the appellee.

SHEPARD, *J.:*

This is an interference proceeding involving priority of invention of the following issue:

1. The combination, with a door-opening, of a swinging door and a pair of slide-doors arranged to close said opening, and connections between all of said doors whereby same are caused to open and close simultaneously.

2. The combination, with a door-opening, of an angularly-movable door and a pair of slide doors for closing said opening, and means between all of said doors for opening and closing them together.

3. The combination with a single door-opening, of a swinging door, a pair of superposed sliding doors movable toward and from each other, a lever, means for moving said sliding doors in opposite directions by said lever and means for actuating said lever by said swinging door.

The invention of this issue is an arrangement of certain elements which coöperate to close at the same time two openings in a smoke-house or a refrigerator. The larger opening is closed by a swinging door. A smaller opening immediately above is closed by a pair of sliding doors which are caused to move into position by the swinging of the larger door.

Munster, the junior party, claims to have conceived the invention September 1, 1902, and to have reduced it to practice May 1, 1903. His application was filed May 27, 1904. Ashworth, who filed March 21, 1904, claims conception January 1, 1903, the making of a model March 1, 1903, but no actual reduction to practice.

The Examiner of Interferences decided in favor of Ashworth. His decision was reversed on appeal to the Examiners-in-Chief; and they, in turn, were reversed by the Commissioner who awarded priority to Ashworth. From his decision, *ante*, 156; 128 O. G., 2085, Munster has prosecuted this appeal.

The burden was upon Munster, as the later applicant, to show that he conceived the invention before Ashworth, and that he reduced it to actual practice, or was exercising due diligence in prosecuting his invention when Ashworth entered the field.

It seems sufficiently clear that unless he reduced to actual practice, as claimed, he was lacking in the required diligence. His case turns, therefore, upon the proof of reduction to practice.

We confess embarrassment in the determination of this question. The difficulty lies in the meagerness of the testimony and the manner in which it was taken. In the first place, Munster, having testified on his own behalf, was not subjected to cross-examination. He was undoubtedly in bad health, but we are not satisfied that he could not have been cross-examined later. After answering a few questions of opposing counsel, he announced that he was not well and was unable to stand the strain of cross-examination. Counsel for Ashworth expressed willingness to suspend, and asked Munster's counsel to extend the time of taking the testimony. The record shows that Munster's counsel refused—

to delay indefinitely the determination of the issue of this interference, especially in view of the aimless trend of cross-examination.

He further announced that Munster's mental and physical condition is such that he is unable to stand the strain imposed upon him as a witness; that he has been sick for over a year, has spent most of his time in a hospital; has undergone three different operations: has come to the hearing in a plainly-emaciated condition without appreciating what is required of him; and that the prospect of his being able to testify within a year, if at all, is very slight. As these conditions were so well known to his counsel, he should either have refrained from offering him as a witness on his own behalf, or, having done so, should have consented to some reasonable postponement. There was no testimony tending to show that Munster might not be able to appear for cross-examination within some reasonable period. The examination of other witnesses heard at the same time was concluded on June 14, 1905. An affidavit of a physician is attached to the record of the deposition as made July 20, 1905, to the effect that he had treated Munster from time to time for a year last past: that three different surgical operations had been performed on him to remove gall-stones; that he has not been for many months past in a condition to withstand the strain imposed upon a witness; and that his present condition does not hold out any hope that he will be able to resume active mental and physical labors for perhaps years to come, if at all. An affidavit of this kind forms no part of the deposition. The affiant should have been called and sworn to testify as a witness. Under the circumstances, the direct examination ought to have been excluded on motion, and is entitled to no weight. That his testimony, if considered, is entitled to little or no weight is shown in the direct examination of his son Nicholas Munster who testified on the same day. The question of appellant's counsel, and witness's answer thereto are as follows:

Q. 28. In your father's testimony he appears to have dates badly mixed. How did you manage to get the data for the preliminary statement, and how does it happen that your father to-day seems utterly unable to remember what he has heretofore done? A. When the preliminary statement was made up I was at home with my father, he was rested and mentally collected. We went over the matter together at that time, and I assisted him to refresh his memory. To-day the trip weakened and confused him, apparently, so that his mind is in a muddle.

The notice to take testimony for Munster at that time recites the name of Munster only as the witness to be examined. After Munster retired, three other witnesses were produced. The record recites that Ashworth's counsel stated that he had no objection to the examination of the other witnesses and did not care to cross-examine them; and then left. Ashworth moved to suppress these depositions because taken without notice, and filed an affidavit of his counsel denying the correctness of the recital that he had waived objections to the examination of witnesses not named in the notice. This motion was overruled. The testimony was therefore considered as properly in the case. It is to be observed of this testimony that the important facts were stated in answer to leading questions propounded to the witnesses. The following question to Nicholas Munster is an example:

Q. 36. Are you positive that your father conceived the invention set forth in this declaration of interference on or about the 1st day of September, 1902, according to the preliminary statement, which you helped your father prepare? A. Yes, sir.

(See also question 12 and answer hereafter.)

Questions asked this witness, who is also one of the assignees of his father's invention, relating to the construction of doors in accordance with the model of his father, together with his answers, are as follows:

Q. 12. A. P. Munster's preliminary statement says that he built some 33 doors for Armour and Co. in 1903; is this model exactly like those doors? A. Yes, sir.

Q. 13. When were these doors put up, if you know? A. He began to build them in May, 1903.

Q. 14. About when were they completed, to your knowledge? A. Some time in October, 1903.

The witness did not describe the construction of the doors, or undertake to say where or how they had been made. To the question asking if they were exactly like the model, he simply answered yes.

The next witness, Heinig, is also an assignee of Munster's invention. He said that he first heard of the invention in September, 1902, at which time Munster's son, Nicholas, showed him a partly-completed model. He did not see this model in a completed state until the application for patent had been made. As regards the completion of this model, Heinig differs from Nicholas Munster who said it was completed in September, 1902. Heinig also testified that he was not interested in the invention prior to the time of filing the application for patent, and gives that as his reason for not having then seen the doors of which he had heard of the construction. He said that after the application had been filed he went to Armour's plant in Chicago, where Munster and his witnesses lived, and labeled thirty-three doors " Patent applied for." He was not asked to describe the construction of these doors, or their mode of operation. He says he had heard that they had been used there about a year; and all that he did was to " label them." The testimony of the remaining witness, Klotz, who was Munster's attorney, had no relation to this question; it was introduced for an entirely different purpose.

Assuming that thirty-three doors were erected in the Armour plant of a construction designed by Munster, the testimony does not show, save by inference derived in part from hearsay, that these doors were constructed from the completed model of Munster, and embodied the elements of the issue. It does not appear how they worked. If these doors were constructed by Munster for the Armour Company in accordance with the requirements of the issue, and then used by them as answering the purpose, we cannot understand why some member, or competent employee of that company was not called to testify. The plant was situated in Chicago, and such witness or witnesses could have proved the necessary facts, if they existed, beyond the shadow of a doubt. Yet none were called, and no reason was suggested for the omission. In this connection it is pertinent to call attention to the fact that in the cross-examination of Ashworth he was asked if he had seen or heard of the doors put by Munster in the Armour plant. His answer was that he had heard of them after the declaration of interference, and had visited the plant for the purpose of seeing them; but that after being shown through the visitors' department he had asked if he could see the smoke-house where they had rails running through an opening in the smoke-house door, and that his request had been politely denied. He also said that he had shown the invention to the Armour Company immediately after applying for a patent, and had not been informed by them that they were already supplied. No effort was made to contradict these statements.

Though not without some apprehension that Munster may have made the invention and reduced it to practice, we are constrained to affirm the decision of the Commissioner. We are not warranted in reversing his decision because of a mere doubt of its correctness. As before suggested, all doubt might have been removed, if the doors erected in the Armour plant were in fact successful reductions to practice of the invention of the issue, by the production of witnesses who could not be mistaken. The failure to do this was the fault of the appellant.

The decision awarding priority to Ashworth will therefore be affirmed. The clerk will certify this decision to the Commissioner of Patents as required by the law. *Affirmed.*

[Court of Appeals of the District of Columbia.]

MIEL *v.* YOUNG.

Decided May 7, 1907.

(128 O. G., 2532.)

1. INTERFERENCE—CONSTRUCTION OF CLAIM IN ISSUE.

A claim should be given the broadest interpretation which it will support, and limitations should not be imported into the claim from the specification to meet the exigencies of the particular situation in which the claim may stand at a given time.

2. SAME—SAME—LIMITATIONS NOT IMPORTED FROM PATENT SPECIFICATION.

Where in a stone-saw construction the claim calls for "removable means for reinforcing the lower ends of the blades during the initial part of a cutting operation" and it appears that the device of Miel, a patentee, was designed to prevent the blades from "chattering or wabbling" laterally, while Young's structure is for the purpose of enabling the blades of the saw "to stand the strain for their work" and to support the saw longitudinally, *Held* that there is no limitation in the claim, which refers broadly to reinforcing means, which necessitates the reading into the claim of structural features found only in the specification of the patent.

Mr. T. Walter Fowler and *Mr. R. C. Mitchell* for Miel.
Mr. Albert E. Dietrich for Young.

McCOMAS, *J.:*

In this case the Assistant Commissioner of Patents (*ante, 53;* 126 O. G., 2591,) awarded priority of invention to James S. Young in this interference, the subject-matter of which is a stone-saw, and the single issue is:

In a stone-saw, the combination of a saw-beam, a series of long bearing-blades carried thereby, and removable means for reinforcing the lower ends of the blades during the initial part of a cutting operation.

On December 31, 1904, Young, the appellee, filed his application for a patent for a stone-saw and while it was pending, on April 24, 1905, the appellant Miel filed his application for a patent for a stone-saw also and on November 14, 1905, obtained a patent therefor. The Examiner of Interferences awarded priority of invention to Young, the senior party, on the record, no testimony having been taken by either party to the interférence. Miel is the patentee and the single count of the issue is in terms the first claim of his patent. On November 20, 1905, Young filed an amendment containing his interfering claim. The Examiners-in-Chief concluded that the invention of the issue is an issue which Young had not disclosed in his application and that Miel is entitled to prevail on the question of priority because of the failure of Young to produce evidence showing that he was in possession of the invention of the issue prior to the filing date of Miel and, therefore, reversed the decision of the Examiner of Interferences in Young's favor.

Upon appeal the Assistant Commissioner of Patents reversed the decision of the Examiners-in-Chief and found for Young, and Miel appealed to this court.

The invention here relates to means for supporting the blades of stone-saws which consist of numerous strips of steel projecting perpendicularly from a beam. These blades are several feet in length and the ends of the blades, forcing an abrasive material against the stone, effect the sawing. Because of their length these blades tend to vibrate when sawing until having entered the stone, the sides of the kerf prevent them from vibrating laterally. To prevent vibration, Miel provided rigid blocks between the blades, the blocks being notched at the ends to receive the edges of the blades, the blocks being suspended from the beam by screw-threaded bars so adapted in position as to be shifted by means of nuts on the rods. When it becomes necessary to remove or raise the blocks, whose thickness is greater than the kerf formed by the saw, Miel's specification says he may taper the blades and thus draw the blocks up to the narrower portion of the space between the blades in order that they may press upon the edges of the blades and rigidly unite them.

Young unites the blades of his saw by thin strips of metal having hooked ends which pass through apertures in the blades, the apertures being perpendicular to the faces of the blades except as to a slight inclined portion at one end. The hooks on the supporting members of the end blades are threaded and provided with a nut by means of which all of the supporting members may be put under tension. The supporting-strips are thin and so arranged that they can enter the kerf. Young's specification states that the slots in the blade are slightly beveled to receive the upset or rivet-over portion of the inserted strip end. The drawing of Young's application shows that the strips are not riveted to the blades in the sense in which " rivet " is ordinarily used. The ends of the strips are not upset to form a head but the hooked end of the strip is sprung into the slot in the blade correspondingly shaped so that the Commissioner concludes, the resiliency of the metal would permit the springs to be forced into the slots and out again. Indeed Young specifically states that the strips can be moved from one position to another wherefore the Commissioner concludes that he has a right to make the claim in issue. That Young's reinforcing device may not be removable as readily as Miel's and that it is not designed to be removed after the initial stage of the cutting is completed is unimportant. If the device be removable, as the claim specifies, it suffices even though Young's device need not be removed during the entire sawing operation. We concur with the Commissioner that there is no limitation in the claim which refers broadly to reinforcing means which give weight to the claim that Miel's device was designed to prevent the blades from " chattering or wabbling " laterally, while Young's structure is for the purpose of enabling the blades of the saw " to stand the strain for their work," and to support the saw longitudinally.

This claim should be given the broadest interpretation which it will support and we should not strive to import limitations from the specification to meet the exigencies of the particular situation in which the claim may stand at a given time. Although Miel is a patentee, if the terms of his claim do not in their ordinary and natural meaning define his invention according to his intent he may apply for a reissue.

The reasonable presumption is that an inventor intends to protect his invention broadly, and consequently the courts have often said that the scope of a claim should not be restricted beyond the fair and ordinary meaning of the words, save for the purpose of saving it. * * * The senior party who has a patent may not be heard to ask that his claim be rewritten so that he may prevail in an interference. He would be in somewhat better position had his patent not been issued, or had he surrendered it for reissue. (*Andrews* v. *Nilson*, C. D., 1906, 717; 123 O. G., 1667; 27 App. D. C., 454. See *Podlesak* v. *McInnerney*, C. D., 1906, 558; 126 O. G., 2127; 26 App. D. C., 399.)

We concur with the Commissioner that upon this issue we should not read into it limitations not within it, limitations found only in the specification of the appellee's patent. Young has fully disclosed the invention defined by the terms of the interference.

The decision of the Commissioner of Patents *must be affirmed*, and the clerk of this court is directed to certify the proceedings in this court to the Commissioner of Patents according to law.

[Court of Appeals of the District of Columbia.]

RICHARDS *v.* BURKHOLDER.

Decided May 7, 1907.

(128 O. G., 2533.)

INTERFERENCE—PRIORITY—CONCEALMENT OF INVENTION.

If there be concealment or suppression of the invention, the field lies open to be occupied by a more diligent, though later, inventor, who when he has not only put the invention into public use, but has also obtained a patent for it, cannot be divested of his right to hold the field except upon proof beyond a reasonable doubt that the earlier and more negligent inventor has not gone back to an abandoned device or a device suppressed or concealed in order to establish a prior right.

Mr. John L. Jackson and *Mr. C. E. Pickard* for Richards.
Mr. C. C. Linthicum for Burkholder.

McCOMAS, *J.*:

This is an appeal by Richards from the decision of the Assistant Commissioner of Patents (*ante*, 166; 128 O. G., 2529) awarding priority of invention to Burkholder upon the following issues:

1. In a device of the class described, the combination with a hollow track opened in the rear for the reception of supporting-brackets, of supporting-brackets having spring-heads adapted to fit the inner contour of said hollow track, substantially as described.

2. In a device of the class described, the combination with a hollow track opened in the rear for the reception of supporting-brackets, of a supporting-bracket made of a single piece of metal and having a spring-head adapted to fit the inner contour of said hollow track, substantially as described.

3. The combination with a hollow track having a ·longitudinal opening in one side, of a supporting-bracket having portions doubled to form a head sprung into said hollow track and arms extending transversely through said opening in said track, substantially as described.

4. A supporting-bracket for a hollow slotted track, comprising spring-arms having attaching ends, and a connection between their opposite ends adapted to allow normal expansion of said arms, and forming a head to fit with the track, substantially as described.

The subject-matter of the issue is a supporting-bracket and track for door-hangers, the bracket being composed of a strip of plain metal, doubled to form a circular head, with arms extending transversely therefrom, and provided with attaching ends to be secured to a building, and the head being adapted to fit the inner surface of a pipe or tube, slotted in the rear, and affording a track for the wheel of the door-hanger.

A month after Burkholder had secured a patent on the invention, and a year after Burkholder had filed his application, Richards appeared and filed his application and alleged in his preliminary statement disclosure and reduction to practice July 10, 1902, which date would anticipate Burkholder, who claims conception of the invention in January, 1903, his patent having been granted October 4, 1904.

The three tribunals of the Patent Office concurred in awarding priority to Burkholder, all of them agreeing that the testimony on behalf of Richards fails to prove beyond a reasonable doubt that Richards conceived the invention and reduced it to practice prior to Burkholder's reduction to practice in 1903 and all of them base the decision upon the same ground, namely, that Richards failed to *sustain* the burden of proof resting up   to th   of reduction to practice. We concur in the reasoning and in the conclusion of the three tribunals. Therefore, we need not consider whether or not as a matter of law a bracket, which Richards claims to have made in 1902, was a reduction to practice, since it has not been proven beyond a reasonable doubt that such a bracket was made in that year.

As the Examiners-in-Chief well say:

Even if it be assumed that Richards conceived the invention in 1902, and then made some experiments his total abandonment of those experiments and neglect and loss of the physical things then made, together with the inaction of himself and assignee for two years justify us in concluding that he abandoned his efforts as unsatisfactory and that he did not in fact make a successful reduction to practice. (*Warner* v. *Smith*, C. D., 1898, 517; 84 O. G., 311; 13 App. D. C., 111.)

All the testimony tends to show that the device claimed to have been set up in the workroom of Richards and the device claimed to have been placed on the door of a shed were so placed in each instance for the purpose of testing the two devices on which the appellant relied to prove a reduction to practice.

If we assume that Richards satisfactorily proved the making of the bracket in question in July, 1902, we should not overrule the decision appealed from for Richards was not prevented by any compelling circumstance from giving his invention to the public by placing it on the market, or filing an application for a patent. If there be concealment or suppression of the invention, the field lies open to be occupied by a more diligent, though later inventor, who, when he has not only put the invention into public use but has also obtained a patent for it, cannot be divested of his right to hold the field except upon proof beyond a reasonable doubt that the earlier and more negligent inventor has not gone back to an abandoned device or a device suppressed or concealed in order to establish a prior right. We refrain from reviewing the voluminous testimony sufficiently reviewed in the three tribunals below but we also are impressed that the inactivity of Richards for two years during which period Burkholder entered the field, and ignorant of the claim of Richards independently produced the invention, put it upon the market, applied for and obtained the patent is fatal to the former claim.

Richards was in the employment of the Wilcox Manufacturing Company of Aurora, Ill., and claims to have produced this invention for that company. Although Richards claims he completed and tested his invention in the summer of 1902 and explained it to the officers of that company no steps were taken to ascertain whether it was patentable until the summer of 1903, nor was any attempt made to put it on the market until the summer of 1904 and the application was not filed until November 10, 1904, after the patent had issued to

Burkholder and after the Burkholder bracket had been advertised and a company had proceeded to take orders and ship it in quantities.

Burkholder's record date is October 21, 1903. Richards's record date is November 10, 1904. Apart from this priority of the appellee, the testimony of many witnesses and documentary evidence as well, show that Burkholder conceived the invention, disclosed it to others, promptly placed it on the market, and seasonably applied for the patent granted him.

It is true a number of witnesses support Richards's claim that he conceived the invention about July, 1902, and testify their knowledge of one or the other of the two devices of Richards and that his invention was made while he was in the room in the northwest corner of the second floor of the building of the Wilcox Manufacturing Company, but on behalf of Burkholder there is much testimony tending to show that Richards was moved from that room as early as April, 1902, and that he could not have made the invention in it after the first of July in that year as he claims. Credible witnesses testify that they saw the model made by Richards located in that room which others with opportunity to see it say it was not there. Again credible witnesses testify that they saw the device applied to the shed described by witnesses, while other witnesses with ample opportunity to observe testify that it was not there. Of course, in each instance this negative testimony is far less weighty than the positive testimony of witnesses in behalf of Richards, who claim to have seen the different devices in the two different places. It tends, however, to lessen the degree of conviction produced by Richards's whole case.

We have carefully examined the testimony and upon the issue of fact which is the only issue in this interference, we agree with all of the tribunals below that Richards has failed to prove his case beyond a reasonable doubt. As we have said in *Orcutt* v. *McDonald*, (C. D., 1906, 705; 123 O. G., 1287; 27 App. D. C., 228,) and in many other cases, where the tribunals of the Patent Office all agree in deciding the same way on questions of fact, this court will not reverse such a decision unless it clearly appears that the decision was against the weight of the evidence. In this case where we fully agree with them and where the only question raised upon this appeal which needs to be considered is the issue of fact, we refrain from reviewing the facts and content ourselves with concurring in the conclusion of the Commissioner of Patents, whose judgment therefore must be affirmed.

The decision of the Commissioner of Patents *must be affirmed*, and the clerk of this court is directed to certify the proceedings in this court to the Commissioner of Patents according to law.

[Court of Appeals of the District of Columbia.]

DUNBAR v. SCHELLENGER.

Decided February 5, 1907.

(128 O. G., 2837.)

1. INTERFERENCE—REOPENING FOR INTRODUCTION OF NEWLY-DISCOVERED EVIDENCE—REVIEW BY COURT OF APPEALS.

Where the tribunals of the Patent Office in the exercise of their discretion have refused to reopen a case for the introduction of newly-discovered evidence, their conclusions will be reviewed by the court of appeals only in case of an abuse of discretion.

2. SAME—PRIORITY—APPEAL TO COURT—CONSIDERATION OF PATENTABILITY.

"As regards the contention of the appellant that ' the structure in interference differs from the prior structure of Roberts in but two particulars,' * * * it is sufficient to say, that in so far as it appears to raise a question of patentability, that question has been settled by the allowance of the claims."

Mr. W. Clyde Jones, Mr. Robert L. Ames, and *Mr. Benjamin R. Johnson* for Dunbar.

Mr. C. A. Brown for Schellenger.

SHEPARD, *J.:*

This is an interference proceeding involving priority of invention of a means for operating the supervisory signals of a telephone system; and was declared between the application of Schellenger filed February 14, 1901, and that of Dunbar filed March 22, 1901.

The issue contains ten counts as follows:

1. The combination with a telephone-line, of a source of electricity and a pair of relays adapted to be bridged between the limbs of the talking-circuit thereof, a switch at the substation and a switch at the central station for controlling the circuit through said relays, and a signal adapted to be controlled by the conjoint action of said relays.

2. The combination with a pair of telephone-lines, of an inductive device through which the same are adapted to be united for conversation, a charging source of electricity and a pair of relays adapted to be bridged between the two limbs of each of said lines, one pair of relays being individual to one of said lines and the other pair being individual to the other line, switches at the substations and at the central station for controlling the circuit through said relays, and a signal controlled by the conjoint action of each pair of relays.

3. The combination with a metallic telephone-line free from permanent grounds outside the central office, of a charging-current source, a third conductor, a pair of relays at the central office, one of said relays being energized over the telephone-line and the other over a portion of the talking-circuit and the third conductor.

4. The combination with a metallic telephone-line, of a pair of relays and a charging-current source bridged across the line at the central station, a third conductor to which one pole of the current source is connected, both of said relays being adapted to be operated over the metallic telephone-line, and one of

said relays being adapted to be operated over a portion of said line and third conductor.

5. The combination with a metallic telephone-line, of an operator's plug and a cord-circuit, a source of current and a pair of relays bridged across said circuit, a third conductor connected with one pole of said source, one of said relays being adapted to be operated over the metallic line when the subscriber's telephone is in use, and the other to be operated over a part of the line and said third conductor when the subscriber's telephone is not in use and the operator's plug is connected with the line.

6. In a telephone system, the combination with a telephone-line, of a source of current and a relay bridged between the two limbs of the talking-circuit thereof, a second relay at the central office connected in a circuit including a portion of one side of the talking-circuit and means for energizing it, a switch at the substation and a switch at the central station for controlling the circuit through said relays, and a signal controlled by the conjoint action of said relays.

7. In a telephone system, the combination with a telephone-line, of a source of electricity at the central office, an operator's plug and a pair of relays associated therewith, one of said relays being energized from the said source of electricity as long as the said operator's plug is connected with the said line and over a path having a part coincident with the talking-circuit, and the other relay being energized as long as the said operator's plug is connected with the said line and when the subscriber's telephone is in use, and a signal associated with said pair of relays, the circuit of said signal being established by the operation of the first of said relays and said signal being rendered inoperative by the operation of the second of said relays.

8. The combination with telephone-lines extending from subscribers' stations to an exchange, of a cord-circuit at the exchange provided with two strands for forming connections between two telephone-lines, a pair of relays corresponding to each end of the cord-circuit and included in bridge thereof, a source of current for inclusion in circuit with each of said pairs of relays, a supervisory signal for each pair of relays and jointly controlled thereby, switching apparatus for controlling the operation of the relays, and a condenser included in each cord-strand between the connections of the relays therewith.

9. The combination with telephone-lines extending from substations to jacks at an exchange, of a cord-circuit at the exchange provided with two strands for forming connections between subscribers' lines, a pair of relays corresponding to each end of the cord-circuit and included in bridge thereof; a source of current for energizing the said relays, a supervisory signal for each pair of relays and jointly controlled thereby, switching mechanism at the substations for controlling the operation of one of each pair of relays, means including a jack and a cord-circuit plug inserted in the jack, whereby a closed circuit is established through the remaining relay of each pair which is independent of the operative position of the substation apparatus, and a condenser included in each cord-strand between the connections of the relays therewith.

10. In a telephone system, an operator's cord-circuit, a pair of relays each operated over circuits including portions of the talking-circuit and a supervisory signal having its circuit controlled by the contacts of both of said relays, one of said relays being adapted to normally close the circuit and to be energized over the telephone-line when the line is in use whereby the signal is at that time rendered inert, and the other relay being adapted to normally open the circuit whereby when the cord-circuit is not connected with the line the signal is inert and when connected with a line in use the signal is displayed.

The Examiner of Interferences held that Dunbar's evidence established September 17, 1900, as the date of conception of the invention of the issue; but being of the opinion that Schellenger's clearly showed conception and reduction to practice in August, 1900, priority was awarded to him. He expressed the opinion also, that even were the evidence of reduction to practice insufficient, Schellenger's diligence, nevertheless, entitled him to the benefit of his earlier conception.

The decision reviews the testimony at great length, and contains an elaborate description of the invention as disclosed in the applications of the respective parties. This description seems to be an accurate one, but its insertion would occupy unnecessary space.

After noting an appeal from this decision, Dunbar filed a motion to restore jurisdiction to the Examiner of Interferences in order that he might entertain a motion to reopen the case for the introduction of alleged newly-discovered evidence. The evidence consisted of the testimony of Schellenger as a witness, on July 5 and 18, 1905, on behalf of Clausen in an interference between Clausen and Dean, No. 23,797, relating to telephone circuits and signals. To the motion were attached, a transcript of said testimony, the affidavits of counsel, and the affidavit of an expert relating to the evidence in connection with the issues and the evidence in the present case. This affidavit does not recite the issue in *Clausen* v. *Dean*, but contains sketches made by the witness of Clausen's invention, and also undertakes an analysis of the claims of the present issue, and claims that they are readable upon the Clausen structure. The Commissioner transmitted the motion to the Examiner of Interferences for decision. The then Examiner of Interferences had succeeded the one who rendered the award of priority above mentioned. The decision denied the motion. As the admissibility and effect of the testimony recited in the motion have been earnestly contended for throughout the proceedings, and on the final hearing, we shall quote liberally from this decision. The Examiner said:

Dunbar's motion is based upon the allegation that certain testimony given by Schellenger when testifying in behalf of Clausen in another interference (*Clausen* v. *Dean*, No. 23,797) is to the effect that the invention at issue in this case was disclosed to him by Clausen at a date prior to the date of conception to which Schellenger testified in this interference. An examination of Schellenger's testimony given in the second interference indicates that the disclosure made to him by Clausen did in fact embody the subject-matter of several counts of the above-entitled interference.

Considerable stress has been laid upon the contention that the interference should be reopened on the ground that the proposed new evidence would affect Schellenger's credit as a witness. In view of the fact that Schellenger and Clausen appear to have worked together in making improvements along the same line, it seems more probable that the discrepancies in Schellenger's testimony in the two cases arose from failure of the attorneys for himself and

Clausen to properly limit the claims to their separate inventions. It is established, however, by the testimony of other witnesses, that Schellenger actually reduced the invention to practice before Dunbar. The possibility that Schellenger may not have been the originator of the invention in no way impairs the testimony of the other witnesses to the effect that Schellenger was in possession of the invention and reduced it to practice prior to Dunbar's established date of conception. These facts preclude the possibility of awarding priority of invention to Dunbar.

For these reasons Schellenger's deposition given in the second interference, even if introduced in the present case, could not affect the award of priority which has been rendered. Had such testimony as that contained in Schellenger's later deposition originally been in this case, it might have led the Examiner of Interferences to direct the attention of the Commissioner under Rule 126 to the fact that a statutory bar existed to the grant of a patent to Schellenger as to certain of his claims. Inasmuch, however, as the determination of the question as to whether or not such bar exists is an *ex parte* matter and not within the jurisdiction of the Examiner of Interferences, no good cause exists for reopening the interference for the purpose of introducing testimony relative to the existence of a statutory bar.

He then cites, and quotes from the opinions in *Foster* v. *Antisdel* (C. D., 1899, 413; 88 O. G., 1527; 14 App. D. C., 552) and *Prindle* v. *Brown*, (C. D., 1904, 680; 112 O. G., 957; 24 App. D. C., 114,) which hold that a junior applicant cannot overcome the prior date of his opponent by proving that a third party was the first inventor. The decision thereafter proceeds as follows:

The only possible grounds upon which the evidence in question could be admitted would be that it utterly destroyed the credibility not only of Schellenger but of all his corroborating witnesses as to his possession and reduction to practice of the invention prior to the date established by Dunbar. It does not appear that any reason exists for the inference that the variance between the testimony given by Schellenger in the two cases was due to any fraudulent intent on Schellenger's part. However this may be, there appears to be no reason for holding that the testimony given by the other witnesses for Schellenger is impaired by the state of facts brought to light in support of this motion.

It is also contended that the testimony of Schellenger in the other interference, which testimony it is now sought to introduce in evidence in this interference, should be accepted as an admission against interest, and would justify the holding that Schellenger is not an original inventor. For the reasons that have been stated above and clearly announced by the Commissioner in *Trufant* v. *Prindle* v. *Brown* (*supra*,) this question is not pertinent to the question of priority of invention as between Schellenger and Dunbar, since it is shown that Schellenger was the first in possession of the invention. This being true, Dunbar could not be adjudged the first inventor, even if it were admitted that Schellenger received his idea from some person other than Dunbar.

On appeal to him, the Commissioner affirmed this decision upon a full review of the question. He was clearly of the opinion that the testimony was inadmissable to show invention by another, not a party to the interference. His decision concludes as follows:

It does not appear that there was any abuse of discretion by the Examiner of Interferences in refusing to reopen the case. If it should appear upon consideration of the entire record upon appeal that the decision upon the question of priority would be changed by evidence that Schellenger's testimony is not entitled to full faith and credit, the case may be reopened for further testimony. The Examiner of Interferences, who has considered the entire record, is of the opinion that such reopening is not justified, and no good reason is seen for disturbing his decision upon interlocutory appeal. (C. D., 1906, 147; 121 O. G., 2663.)

The case was then referred to the Examiners-in-Chief to determine the appeal on the question of priority. These affirmed the award to Schellenger. On final appeal to the Commissioner this decision was affirmed. After a careful review of the evidence he said:

Not only is Schellenger entitled to the award of priority on the ground that he was the first to conceive and the first to reduce to practice, but also on the ground that he was exercising reasonable diligence at and before the time when Dunbar entered the field and up to the time of filing his application. (C. D., 1906, 428; 125 O. G., 348.)

Upon the question of admitting the evidence contained in the motion he said:

After the decision of the Examiner of Interferences on the question of priority and pending an appeal to the Examiners-in-Chief Dunbar brought a motion to reopen the interference for the purpose of introducing into the record a deposition given by Schellenger in a later interference between different parties, which, it was alleged, showed that Schellenger was not the inventor of certain counts of this interference and which also, it is alleged, discredited Schellenger, as it contained allegations contrary to those made in the present case. The Examiner of Interferences refused to reopen the case, and upon appeal from that decision, I held that the case would be reopened, if at all, only for the admission of evidence discrediting Schellenger's testimony, and that whether it should be so reopened would be determined when the case came before me for final hearing. Upon examination of the deposition in the later interference it is found that Schellenger testifies that one Henry P. Clausen, under whose direction Schellenger was working while in the employ of the American Electric Telephone Company, was the inventor of a certain circuit which Schellenger referred to as a "three-relay system." This circuit is specifically different from the "four-relay" system which forms the subject-matter of this interference. Assuming for the purpose of argument that some of the counts of this interference are broad enough to cover both of these structures, I am nevertheless convinced that such testimony does not materially lessen the weight to be given to Schellenger's testimony in this interference. It must be remembered that Schellenger was testifying in both instances with respect to specific constructions, in the first interference with respect to a "four-relay" system and in the later interference with respect to a "three-relay" system, whose circuits differed in many respects from the circuits of the "four-relay" system. In the earlier testimony Schellenger testified that he constructed a specific device upon a certain date. In his later deposition he testified that Clausen upon a certain date set up a different apparatus. There is no inconsistency in these statements. I am convinced that the deposition in the later interference furnishes no substantial basis for believing that the testimony first given was false. The only real effect of admitting this testimony would be to show, possibly, that some of the counts of this interference were first invented by a third party and not by Schellenger. As stated in a prior decision in this case, this question is to be considered, if at all, after the final determination of the question of priority. (Id.)

The appellee has moved to dismiss so much of the appeal as relates to the motion to reopen the case for the consideration of the newly-discovered evidence. Whether such an appeal can be entertained, at all, though the question has been raised and decided by the Commissioner along with the general question of priority, has never been expressly decided by this court. In *Richards* v. *Meissner* (C. D., 1905, 595; 114 O. G., 1831; 24 App. D. C., 305,) it was said by Mr. Justice Morris:

> The reopening of a cause for the introduction of newly-discovered evidence is always a matter for the trial court, and is in its discretion; and that discretion is not subject to review in a purely appellate tribunal, such as this court is.

The evidence was, however, incidentally discussed and it was said that there was no indication of the abuse of discretion. Reference was also made to the case of *Cross* v. *Phillips* (C. D., 1899, 342; 87 O. G., 1899; 14 App. D. C., 228,) in which one of the errors assigned was, the refusal of leave to amend a preliminary statement. There the Court said:

> In courts both of law and equity the right to amend is not an absolute one, but rests in the discretion of the court, and the exercise of this discretion is not reviewable unless it may be in case of its palpable abuse.

(See also, *Hammond* v. *Basch*, C. D., 1905, 615; 115 O. G., 804; 24 App. D. C., 469, 472.) In view of the character of these cases, we think, that the exercise of discretion in refusing to reopen a case for the introduction of newly-discovered evidence, might be the subject of review and correction when undoubtedly abused, and productive of palpable injustice. Clearly the Commissioner was right in his action in this instance on the ground that it is not admissible to show that a third person was, in fact, the first inventor. As regards the effect of the later deposition by way of discrediting the evidence of Schellenger in this case, it is sufficient to say, that, after a comparison of the two, with the aid of the elaborate and earnest argument on behalf of the appellant, we are not convinced of error in the final conclusion of the Commissioner.

The question of priority on the record, as submitted, remains to be considered. Each tribunal of the Patent Office, accepting the proof of conception by Dunbar on September 17, 1900, has agreed in holding that Schellenger conceived the invention of the issue and reduced it to practice in August, 1900. These concurrent conclusions, under the settled rule in such cases, impose the burden upon the appellant of showing error therein clearly. This he has failed to do. The several decisions contain fair and careful reviews of the testimony of Schellenger and his corroborating witnesses, and we do not think it important to add anything to the discussion. They appear to have given the proper weight to the evidence of each witness, carefully distinguishing between those fully competent to understand the nature and details of the invention when disclosed and tested, and those not well informed therein.

As regards the contention of the appellant that—

the structure in interference differs from the prior structure of Roberts in but two particulars, and all of the claims in issue are readable directly upon the Roberts structure, except for the limitations as to these two distinguishing features—

it is sufficient to say, that in so far as it appears to raise a question of patentability, that question has been settled by the allowance of the claims. (*Johnson* v. *Mueser*, present term.)

And in so far as it relates to the necessary elements of Schellenger's construction to answer the test of conception and reduction to practice, we think it is fairly met in the decision of the Examiners-in-Chief as follows:

The invention in controversy is so fully described in the decision of the Examiner of Interferences and in the briefs and applications of the respective parties, that we regard it as unnecessary to herein explain its details. In its general aspect said invention is a modification of or an improvement upon previously-existing means for operating the supervisory (or electric lamp) signals at the central station of a telephone system, by means of which signals the operator determines whether the called subscriber has responded, and whether either subscriber has concluded the conversation and placed his receiver upon the switch-hook of the telephone. A patent to one Roberts, No. 777,544 of December 13, 1904, mentioned in the record, illustrates the prior art. It discloses a telephone system in which the supervisory signals are controlled by four relays, two of said relays being disposed in each half of the apparatus at the exchange, and one of these two relays situated in a bridge across the cord or talking circuit, while the other relay is arranged in a local circuit connected with the bridge. In the apparatus here in controversy both relays are included in the bridge, and a portion of the cord or talking circuit is at certain times used as a part of the circuit for one of the relays. Although the issue does not call for any specific arrangement of the cord-circuits and does not require that the bridge shall be connected with these circuits in any unusual way, or that any particular supplementary devices shall be employed in connection with the system, it is contended on behalf of Dunbar that Schellenger has not carried his invention beyond the experimental stage when as alleged by him he set up and tested the apparatus upon which he relies for reduction to practice. It is pointed out that at that time he did not develop a satisfactory " busy test " and had not in contemplation any operative means for enabling the operator to automatically cut out the subscriber's bell-circuits when connections between the central station and the telephones at the substations are established.

The objection thus raised is in our opinion without weight for not only does the prior art reveal means which may be used for attaining both of the aforesaid objects, but the combinations covered by the issue possess their own ut ties irrespective of the presence or absence of calling and testing devices any kind. In other words, the issue is directed to a new and useful inven which although it is intended to be an element of a telephone-exchange, nevertheless possesses its own characteristic utility.

It may be remarked that had all of the expert tribunals of the Office denied the sufficiency of Schellenger's evidence of actual reduction to practice in August, 1900, on account of the character of the structure, and the failure to test it in a regular working telephone system, we would not, considering the nature and purpose of the invention, dissent from such a conclusion. (*Macdonald* v. *Edison*, C. D., 1903, 622; 105 O. G., 1263: 21 App. D. C., 527, 529; *Paul* v. *Hess*, C. D., 1905, 610; 115 O. G., 251; 24 App. D. C., 463, 467; *Gallagher* v. *Hein*, C. D., 1905, 624; 115 O. G., 1330; 25 App. D. C., 77, 82; *Ocumpaugh* v. *Norton*, C. D., 1905, 632; 115 O. G., 1850; 25 App. D. C., 90, 93.) But, as they are well informed in the art, and have concurred in holding the test sufficient, the conditions are not such as to satisfy us that they have erred in such finding.

The question is of no practical importance, however, because we fully agree with them that Schellenger, having shown his conception of the invention, was not lacking in diligence between the date of that conception and the presentation of his application. His delay was not great, and his financial condition, coupled with his necessary occupation during the period, furnishes a sufficient excuse for his failure to take speedier action.

It follows that the decision of the Commissioner will be affirmed. It is so ordered, and the clerk will certify this decision to the Commissioner of Patents as required by law. *Affirmed.*

[Court of Appeals of the District of Columbia.]

ROBINSON *v.* MCCORMICK.

Filed February 5, 1907.

(128 O. G., 3289.)

1. INTERFERENCE—PRIORITY—EMPLOYER AND EMPLOYEE.

Inventors are often compelled to have their conceptions embodied in construction by skilled mechanics and manufacturers, whose practical knowledge often enables them to suggest and make valuable improvements in simplifying and perfecting machines or devices, and the inventor is entitled to protection from their efforts to claim his invention. At the same time an employee is to be protected from the rapacity of his employer also, and if in doing the work assigned him the employee goes farther than mechanical skill enables him to do and makes an actual invention he is equally entitled to the benefit of his invention.

2. SAME—SAME—SAME—BURDEN ON EMPLOYEE TO SHOW INVENTION.

Where an employee claims protection for an improvement which he devised while working upon a general conception of his employer, the burden is generally upon him to show that he made an invention in fact.

3. SAME—SAME—SAME—EMPLOYER MUST DISCLOSE MORE THAN FINAL RESULT.

To claim the benefit of the employee's skill and achievement, it is not sufficient that the employer had in mind a desired result and employed one to devise means for its accomplishment. He must show that he had an idea of the means to accomplish the particular result, which he communicated to the employee, in such detail as to enable the latter to embody the same in some practical form.

4. SAME—SAME—REDUCTION TO PRACTICE BY AGENT.

The reduction to practice of an invention by an original inventor cannot be taken as a reduction to practice by another merely because the ownership of the claims of both may afterward become vested in the same person or persons. It is not enough to entitle an applicant to a patent that some one else, not his agent, has shown the practicability of the invention by reducing it to practice. (*Hunter* v. *Stikeman*, C. D., 1898, 564; 85 O. G., 610; 13 App. D. C., 214, 226.)

Mr. Melville Church for Robinson.
Mr. A. C. Paul for McCormick.

SHEPARD, *J.*:

This is an appeal from the decision of the Commissioner of Patents (C. D., 1906, 416; 124 O. G., 2903,) in an interference proceeding with the following issue:

1. A device for use in keeping accounts comprising a casing, a series of file-holders therein, each adapted to carry loose files, and an indicator for each file-holder normally in a position from which it must be moved in order to withdraw from or deposit a file within its holder, whereby the indicator is certainly changed from normal to indicating position whenever access is had to said file without having to remember to make such change, and whereby it may be certainly determined, after a certain period at a glance which file-holders have been used during said period.

2. A device for use in keeping accounts comprising a casing, a series of file-holders therein, each adapted to carry files, and indicators for the file-holders, each normally in a position from which it must be moved in order to withdraw from or deposit a file within its holder, whereby the movement of the indicator from normal position is not dependent on the memory of the operator, and whereby after a certain period it may be certainly determined at a glance which file-holders have had their indicators moved from normal to indicating position during said period.

As stated by the Examiner of Interferences:

The invention in issue is an indicator for duplicate-sales-slip files. In the use of a short account system a case or cabinet is provided wherein file-holders are kept each containing duplicate sales-slips whereon the customer's account and daily balances appear. It is customary to enter daily the totals of each individual's account in a book kept for that purpose. In order to obviate the necessity of handling all the file-holders in the cabinet every day an indicator was devised so that it could be ＿＿＿ at a glance which file-holders had been removed from the cabinet during ＿＿＿.

Robinson, whose applicati＿＿ ＿led January 12, 1904, alleged conception September 6, 190＿ ＿ November 6, 1903, and reduction to practice Nov＿＿

McCormick's application was filed February 16, 1905; he alleged conception, March 20, 1903, and reduction to practice December 22, 1903.

Each tribunal of the Patent Office substantially agreed that Robinson's evidence was not sufficient to show conception and reduction to practice prior to the date of filing his application. Apparently, he must at least have conceived the same some time in December, 1903, but under the conditions of the case it is unnecessary to determine the exact date of his conception. They all agreed in holding also that McCormick had a complete conception of the invention on or before December 1, 1903. All concurred in awarding priority to McCormick, on the ground that his invention had been reduced to practice by one Lumbard in December, 1903.

Assuming the correctness of the findings that McCormick was the first to conceive the invention, and that Robinson is only entitled to the benefit of his filed application as a constructive reduction to practice, we pass to the consideration of the finding that McCormick reduced the invention to actual practice in December, 1903. If the decision of the Commissioner on this point is without proper support, it must be reversed; otherwise affirmed.

It appears by recitals in the decision referred to, that one M. A. Lumbard had filed an application for a patent for a file-holder with automatic indicator, and had been placed in interference with Robinson. The Examiner of Interferences states that two of the counts of the issue of that interference were the same as the counts of the present issue; and counsel for McCormick state in their brief that Lumbard's application made claims on " one feature of the structure or combination constituting the issue." The record of that proceeding, however, is not incorporated in the record before us. In view of the evidence and the production, in connection therewith, of Lumbard's construction, the omission is not material. It is also stated that Lumbard took no evidence in the case, and the decision went against him on the record. The reason assigned for his abandonment of the controversy, by the counsel for McCormick, who represented Lumbard, is, the discovery by them, and the realization by Lumbard that McCormick, and not he, was the actual inventor of the broad issue of the interference.

The evidence shows that since some time prior to Lumbard's alleged conception, both he and McCormick were connected with the Complete Book-keeper Company of Des Moines, which had been organized as a corporation for the purpose of manufacturing a bookkeeping system devised by McCormick. Lumbard was its president and McCormick its general manager. Both were stockholders. The corporation appears to be owner of McCormick's rights as involved in *this inter*ference.

In testifying, McCormick explained the original sketch of the invention claimed to have been conceived by him early in 1903, as follows:

No. 1 is a perpendicular shaft running up and down on the left-hand side of the first row of files facing the cabinet. No. 2 is a small ratchet-wheel on the shaft No. 1 opposite each and every individual file. No. 3 is the indicator extending out over the individual file and attached to shaft No. 1 above and below the ratchet-wheel No. 2, said ratchet-wheel being fastened solid on the shaft No. 1 and said indicator No. 3 being loose on shaft No. 1 with a spring attached, when the indicator is pulled out, catches in said ratchet No. 2 and prevents it from being pushed back, said indicator also having a guard attached to it which goes clear around the ratchet-wheel with square or flat surface that locks it from being pulled out farther than at right angles with the cabinet or file. No. 4 is a lever attached to the top of shaft No. 1. No. 5 is a pin in the outer end of said lever. No. 6 is a horizontal bar put on the pins in lever on shafts No. 1, and which was designed to lock at one end so that when all balances were taken in the evening it could be unlocked and pushed so as to revolve shafts No. 1 until indicators that had been used during the day returned to place over the file. No. 7 is intended to mark the place where spring catches in ratchet. No. 8 indicates the individual customer's file and 9 the frame of the cabinet. This being the first rough pencil sketch when I first conceived the idea only gave the merest outlines so as to help me fix it in my mind and put it before my eyes.

He also testified that shortly after the formation of the company, early in December, 1903, he described the invention to Lumbard, as follows:

I described that my idea consisted of an indicator attached exclusively to the cabinet constructed by means of a perpendicular shaft commencing at the outside of the left end of rows in the cabinet when facing the cabinet putting one of these shafts between each row of files, having on these shafts a small ratchet-wheel opposite to each individual file, said ratchet-wheel fastened solid to the shaft; the attaching of an indicator for each file, said indicator being loose on the shaft with a spring attached which would work in the teeth on the ratchet-wheel; also attached to the indicator a yoke which would go clear around the ratchet-wheel outside, having at one point a flat surface which when the indicator was turned out at right angles with the cabinet to permit of the taking out of the book or file, said indicator could no go farther; that is, than to stand at right angles with the cabinet, said spring standing in the teeth of the ratchet would not permit of the indicator going back. The upper end of all of these horizontal shafts to be connected by cranks with a horizontal rod locked at one end so that indicators could only be thrown back at the close of the day by unlocking said rod and revolving said perpendicular shafts one-half circle so as to replace indicators that had been used over the ends of files.

Again, he said that he told Lumbard that it must be an " absolutely automatic device." Lumbard objected to it on the ground that it would be too expensive to construct, and said, from the ideas witness had given him, he thought he could make one to answer the purpose that would not be so expensive to construct.

The conversation was dropped at that point. I was going out of town for a few days, and when I returned Mr. Lumbard showed me a device which he had evolved, he said, from my idea.

What he meant by an " absolutely automatic device," is indicated in his statement of a previous disclosure to Long who also became an incorporator. He said that he told Long it would work—

automatically, that is, that when the indicator is set to get a book or file out of the cabinet, it would be impossible to throw it back to place over the file until the indicator device was unlocked and all indicators used that day thrown back at one time.

The actual working of the device as indicated in the foregoing descriptions was this: A person desiring to remove a file-holder from its pigeonhole would turn out the corresponding " flap " or " flipper " by hand; and when so turned out it remained an indicator until turned back with all other indicators by a movement of the rod which was under the control of the bookkeeper.

With this knowledge, Lumbard went to work and, without further disclosure, or any assistance by McCormick, constructed a file-holder with an automatic " flap " or " flipper " to serve as an indicator, that had been made an exhibit in the case. This device is simple, useful and of cheap construction. It is an ordinary file-holder with a small metal " flap " or " flipper " attached to the back of the book and lying flat on the cover when that book or file-holder is in place. It comes into view when the book or file-holder is withdrawn. It works loosely on the hinge of the cover, so that when the cover is opened or turned back for the deposit of a sales-slip or other memorandum in the files, it moves with it and stands straight out as an indicator when the cover is turned back and the file-holder returned to its pigeonhole or compartment. The file-holder may then be withdrawn and opened any number of times, without disturbing the indicator. When the bookkeeper has examined the file-holder, and made his entry, he turns the " flap " or " flipper " back to its normal position upon the cover and returns the file-holder to its place. The file-holder can be removed and returned without disturbing the " flap " or " flipper," which only turns back when the file-holder is opened by raising the cover to obtain access to the files underneath it. This arrangement is entirely independent of the cabinet-case. and the file-holder answers its particular purpose when laid upon a table or arranged with others upon a shelf. No matter where or how the file-holder is placed, the " flap " or " flipper " performs its functions as an indicator to the bookkeeper whenever the cover is opened to deposit a file. It is essentially different from the construction that McCormick, prior thereto, had in mind. That McCormick and Lumbard regarded it as patentably distinct is apparent from their action. Lumbard with the knowledge and approval of McCormick, immediately solicitor for the purpose of preparing the application of a patent therefor. It is this application which, after some amendments suggested in the Office, was later placed in interference with Robinson, with the result before mentioned. McCormick, as the holder of a previously-issued patent, was not altogether ignorant of the law that a patent can only be issued to the real inventor. The same solicitors were employed, subsequently, to make the present application for McCormick.

In the course of his cross-examination in relation to the abandonment of Lumbard's application, McCormick was asked this question:

When did you find out that Lumbard's application for patent would not give your company a monopoly of the indicator feature?

His reply was:

We found out when Mr. Robinson was put in interference with Lumbard that there was a question as to the priority of the conception of the idea between Mr. Lumbard and Mr. Robinson, and accepted as a fact, without any demand of proof, that Mr. Robinson stated the truth when he fixed the date of his conception as September, 1903, Mr. Lumbard frankly admitting that he did not conceive the idea of his until December, 1903.

After receiving a copy of Robinson's application and preliminary statement, he said that considerable time was spent in corresponding with their attorneys as to the advisability of contesting the interference between Robinson and Lumbard.

We shall not consume time with a review of the evidence explanatory of the prosecution of Lumbard's application, its final abandonment, and the presentation of McCormick's application, which, to say the least, is not completely satisfactory. In our view of the case, the question of McCormick's estoppel, or abandonment if his invention need not be considered.

The substantial question for determination is this: Does the benefit of the reduction to practice of Lumbard's construction in December, 1903, inure to McCormick? All three of the tribunals held that it did. The Examiner of Interferences said:

It is true the specific device made by Lumbard is different from that disclosed by McCormick and shown in his application, but it is no less a reduction to practice of the generic invention. (See *Slaughter* v. *Halle*, C. D., 1902, 210; 99 O. G., 2771; 21 App. D. C., 19; *Wyman* v. *Donnelly*, C. D., 1903, 556; 104 O. G., 310; 21 App. D. C., 81. * * * This reduction to practice is held to inure to the benefit of McCormick.

In support of this conclusion he cites, and quotes from, *Milton* v. *Kingsley*, (C. D., 1896, 420; 75 O. G., 2193; 7 App. D. C., 531.)

The Examiners-in-Chief briefly indorsed this conclusion, saying:

While this description does not comprehend every detail of the device shown in McCormick's application drawing, it is in our opinion sufficient to identify that construction as the one which McCormick had in contemplation in June, ... testimony, at least, shows that prior to the time when in December,

1903, McCormick made his alleged disclosure to Lumbard he was devising an indicator for file-holders which is substantially like that revealed by him to Lumbard.

The Commissioner, who agreed generally with the others, said:

In the device made by Lumbard as shown in Exhibit 4 the indicator is mounted upon the file-holder in such position that the opening of the file-holder will operate the indicator. This structure differs in detail from the disclosure by McCormick to him, which contemplated mounting the indicators on the casing in such position that the indicator must be operated to withdraw a file-holder from the casing.

After holding substantially that the work of Lumbard in improving upon McCormick's idea was no more than the work of a skilled mechanic in the execution of a general idea communicated to him for the purpose, he proceeds as follows:

Admitting that Lumbard is entitled to patent the specific structure invented by him in carrying out his own conception, it is not seen why this structure does not at the same time contain a reduction to practice of McCormick's invention which shall inure to McCormick as the sole conceiver thereof. The invention in issue is a broad one. Each count includes a casing, a series of file-holders, and an indicator for each holder. The specific form or location of the indicator is not stated. The only limitation is that it shall be normally in a position from which it must be moved to gain access to the file-holder. Many forms of indicators would answer this purpose. The counts of the issue read equally well upon a device including the indicator located as shown in Lumbard's Exhibit 4, McCormick's application drawings, or Figures 3, 4, 5, and 6 of the drawing of Robinson. Lumbard's device may be cheaper to make and an improvement upon the McCormick device; but there is no change in the operation of the system as a whole. It is well established where a different form of invention is made and tested from that disclosed by an applicant in his application and the claims are sufficiently broad to cover both forms that the form made and tested is a reduction to practice of the broad invention. (*Wyman v. Donnelly*, C. D., 1903, 536; 104 O. G., 310.) Similarly, the embodiment of the McCormick invention by Lumbard in structure, although of a different specific form, is a reduction to practice of the broad invention of McCormick.

It was urged by counsel for Robinson at the hearing that there was no proper combination between the casing and the file-holder in the device wherein the indicator was attached to the file-holder. It does not appear that this contention is entitled to any weight. The main object of the invention disclosed by the issue is to provide a device whereby it may be determined which of a number of holders employed in a system of keeping accounts have been open and used during the day. The casing becomes an essential element as a means for supporting the number of holders which it is necessary to use in the system. While it may be true that there is no direct coöperation between the indicator and the casing in this form of the invention, it is not necessary in a new combination of old elements that each element should modify or change the mode of operation of all the others, but only that the combination should produce a new and useful result as a product of the combination. (*National Cash Register Company et al. v. American Cash Register Company*, C. D., 1893, 160; 62 O. G., 449.)

We have stated the grounds of the concurring decisions at some *length to show* that the question under consideration is practically of law rather than fact.   In this consideration it must be borne in mind that the question of invention, as between McCormick and Lumbard, depends upon the thing disclosed by the former to the latter prior to the latter's construction, and not upon what is now shown in McCormick's application, in accordance with which the issue in controversy was framed.   This application not only includes the structure of Lumbard, but also improvements upon McCormick's original conception as disclosed by Lumbard.

Because of the relation between these two, who were officers and stockholders of the corporation, it is held that the benefit of Lumbard's work inures to McCormick because it merely carried out the idea given him by the latter.   Regarding the two as occupying substantially the relation of employer and employee at the time, the well-established principle is applied: that an inventor who employs another to embody his conception in practical form is entitled to any improvement thereon due to the mechanical skill of the employee. The latter must invent something, not merely improve, by the exercise of mechanical skill, upon a conception which he has been employed to work out.   (*Agawam* v. *Jordan*, 7 Wall., 583, 603; *Milton* v. *Kingsley*, C. D., 1896, 420; 75 O. G., 2193; 7 App. D. C., 531, 537; *Huebel* v. *Bernard*, C. D., 1900, 223; 90 O. G., 751; 15 App. D. C., 510, 514; *Gedge* v. *Cromwell*, C. D., 1902, 514; 98 O. G., 1486; 15 App. D. C., 192, 198; *Gallagher* v. *Hastings*, C. D., 1903, 531; 103 O. G., 1165; 21 App. D. C., 88, 89; *Flather* v. *Weber*, C. D., 1903, 70; 103 O. G., 223; 21 App. D. C., 179; *Sendelbach* v. *Gillette*, C. D., 1904, 597; 109 O. G., 276; 22 App. D. C., 168, 177.)   The reason of this rule is obvious.   Inventors are often compelled to have their conceptions embodied in construction by skilled mechanics or manufacturers, whose practical knowledge often enables them to suggest and make valuable improvements in simplifying and perfecting machines or devices.   These are things they are employed and paid to do.   The inventor is entitled to protection from their efforts to claim his invention.   At the same time, an employee is to be protected from the rapacity of his employer also; and if in doing the work assigned him, he goes farther than mechanical skill enables him to do, and makes an actual invention, he is equally entitled to the benefit of his invention.   Necessarily the relations between them generally impose upon him the burden of showing that he has made an invention in fact.

To claim the benefit of the employee's skill and achievement it is not sufficient that the employer had in mind a desired result, and employed one to devise means for its accomplishment.   He must show that he had an idea of the means to accomplish the particular result, which he communicated to the employee, in such detail as to enable the latter to embody the same in some practical form.   Tested by these principles we are of the opinion that the construction of Lumbard was more than a mechanical improvement upon the idea of means communicated to him by McCormick. It is admitted by all that the structure differs from that of McCormick; and the Commissioner admits that Lumbard would be entitled "to patent the specific structure invented by him in carrying out his own conception." He then rests his decision that McCormick is entitled to claim the benefit of the reduction to practice, upon the construction of the issue, the invention of which he said was a broad one:

Each count includes a casing, a series of file-holders, and an indicator for each holder. The specific form or location of the indicator is not stated.

As before suggested, the casing and the series of file-holders kept therein had been long in use and perform no new function in a book-keeping system of any kind. McCormick's communicated idea comprehended nothing more than the attachment of indicators to the casing through means of a rod, one opposite or adjacent to each pigeon-hole in the series of file-holders; and it seems quite clear that these indicators were intended to be moved out by hand, according to the original idea, before the corresponding file-holder could be withdrawn to deposit a slip in it. When out, they could not be turned back except by moving the rod. McCormick had no idea at that time of attaching the indicator to the file-holder itself. This was the conception of Lumbard. He rejected the complicated and expensive combination of McCormick and devised a simple "flap" or "flipper," for attachment to the file-holder itself, which was automatically operated whenever the cover of the file-holder was raised or turned back to deposit a slip. This had no necessary connection with a casing or a series of file-holders. It operated in the same way by itself, with others placed upon a shelf, or with an indefinite number of others arranged in series in a case of any size. Whether, then, Lumbard be regarded as the employee of McCormick, or his partner, or as a mere stockholder of the same corporation, which was the actual relation, we are of the opinion that he must be held to be the inventor of the automatic indicator attached to the file-holder, as shown in his construction.

If Lumbard had proceeded with his application, and been included in an interference with McCormick, he would be regarded as an independent inventor and not a mechanical developer and improver of an idea of means disclosed by the latter. In such case his reduction to practice would not, of course, be available by McCormick. That he was considered by himself, as well as by McCormick, an independent inventor, was shown by the first application for patent; and McCormick's conduct would have estopped him to thereafter claim the invention as against a continued claim by Lumbard. That they have, now, the same interest in establishing McCormick's present claim had a natural tendency to cause Lumbard, as a witness in this case, to minimize his own claim of invention as far as he could fairly do so. We think, too, that the substantial cause of abandoning the prosecution of Lumbard's application was the apprehension that Robinson might be able to go back several months behind the date to which Lumbard was necessarily confined, namely, December, 1903. Had Lumbard persisted in prosecuting the interference with Robinson, he would, under the view taken of the latter's evidence of conception by all of the tribunals of the Office, have obtained an award of priority. The reduction to practice of an invention by an original inventor cannot be taken as a reduction to practice by another merely because the ownership of the claims of both may afterward become vested in the same person or persons. It is not enough to entitle an applicant to a patent that some one else, not his agent, has shown the practicability of the invention by reducing it to practice. (*Hunter* v. *Stikeman*, C. D., 1898, 564; 85 O. G., 610; 13 App. D. C., 214, 226.)

Wyman v. *Donnelly* (C. D., 1903, 556; 104 O.G., 310; 21 App. D. C., 81, 85) is relied on to show that a machine first devised may be regarded as reduced to practice by the successful operation of another machine, with a change in a part of the complicated mechanism, which did not, however, change or affect the necessary elements of the issue. Without pausing to point out what may be other material differences between that case and this, it is only necessary to say that Donnelly was not only the conceiver of the invention, but the constructor, also, of both machines. There was no question of another inventor and constructor.

For the reasons given, we are constrained to reverse the decision appealed from. It is so ordered; and that this decision be certified to the Commissioner of Patents as the statute requires. *Reversed.*

[Court of Appeals of the District of Columbia.]

HANSEN v. DEAN.

Decided February 5, 1907.

(129 O. G., 483.)

1. INTERFERENCE—PRIORITY—PRESUMPTIONS ARISING FROM CONDUCT.
  Where an employee was assigned to the duty of producing a new telephone-transmitter and during the time he was experimenting on such devices constructed six or seven different transmitters, but did not construct any embodying the i̶n̶ in issue, the presumption is strong that he did not construct such ̶ ̶cause he was not possessed of the inventive idea.

2. SAME—SAME—SAME—FAILURE ... CLAIM TO INVENTION.
  Where an employe ... of producing a new telephone-transmitter, but aft ... ls to produce an acceptable

device and is assigned to the work of testing electrical instruments and while so employed he tests a transmitter invented by a coemployee containing the invention in issue and continues in his employment for several months thereafter without making claim to the one who had charge of the experimental work and who assigned him to such work that the invention was his, although the claim was made to others, and fails to construct a device or file an application until after he had left his employer and about seven months after he had tested the invention claimed by his coemployee, a claim that he invented the device during his experimental work can be given little weight.

Mr. Charles A. Brown, Mr. E. E. Clement, and *Mr. E. F. Colladay* for Hansen.

Mr. Curtis B. Camp and *Mr. Benjamin R. Johnson* for Dean.

ROBB, *J.:*

Appeal from a decision of the Commissioner of Patents in an interference proceeding awarding judgment of priority of invention to Dean, the senior party.

The issue is expressed in the following count:

In a telephone-transmitter, the combination with a diaphragm, a recess or chamber carried thereby, a supplemental diaphragm, a block secured to the supplemental diaphragm, a support for the block, and means to secure the block in its support in any position, whereby the block may be adjusted in its support by the vibration of the diaphragm and then secured in adjusted position.

Dean filed an application March 22, 1901, upon which a patent issued November 26, 1901. Inasmuch, however, as Hansen filed his application August 5, 1901, the applications were concurrently pending.

The first question, to which we address ourselves, is whether Hansen has overcome the filing date of Dean's application, for, if he has not, his appeal must fail.

This is the second interference between these parties. The first interference was between the same application of Hansen and a later application of Dean. That interference was dissolved by the Primary Examiner because the issues in his opinion were unpatentable. Hansen thereupon copied claim 15 of the Dean patent, and this interference was declared.

All the tribunals of the Patent Office concur in awarding priority to Dean. The Examiners-in-Chief and the Commissioner hold that Hansen has failed to overcome Dean's filing date, and they, therefore, confine their decision to a consideration of that question.

In view of the prior state of the art and the action of the Primary Examiner in dissolving the first interference for lack of patentability of its issues, it is apparent that the invention is a very narrow one and that the " means to secure the block in its support in any position " is of its very essence. This means consists of a set-screw, which is tightened after the block has become adjusted in the support by the vibration of the diaphragm.

During the winter or spring of 1899 Hansen commenced working for the Kellogg Switchboard and Supply Company, of Chicago, Ill., Dean's assignee, assembling and sometimes testing telephone-transmitters. Some time in June, 1899, Mr. Kempster B. Miller, who had charge of the manufacturing department of that company, authorized and directed Hansen " to work on the development of a new transmitter and to experiment on any ideas he evolved with a view to reducing the ideas to practical form." Mr. Miller graduated from Cornell University after a five years' course in electrical engineering. After his graduation he became an Assistant Examiner of the Patent Office and had charge of applications for patents relating to telephony. He resigned in 1896, and for a time was chief electrician of the Western Telephone Construction Company, of Chicago. Hansen was then also employed by that company, and worked under Miller's direction. In May, 1899, Miller engaged with the Kellogg Company. His testimony in this proceeding shows him to be a candid and intelligent witness, and highly skilled in the art. He testifies that the Kellogg Company was having considerable trouble with its transmitters, and that, being too busy himself to devote any time to experiments and knowing Hansen and having a friendly interest in him, he gave him an opportunity to work along original lines. Hansen immediately commenced experimental work, and, according to his own testimony, continued such work until fall, when he was put to work testing transmitters in which position he continued until June, 1901, when he severed his connection with the company. Thus far there is no conflict in the testimony, Hansen himself testifying that he was *"employed to design a transmitter."* Hansen claims he conceived and made a sketch of the invention in issue in June, 1899, and that he shortly thereafter disclosed his invention to others. He introduced in evidence the sketch he then made, but this sketch shows no means for securing the block in its support, and, therefore, falls short of showing the invention. The only witness, whose testimony even approaches corroboration of Hansen's claim, is the witness Meyer. Meyer testifies that on *one occasion* during the latter part of June, 1899, *four years before he testified* Hansen disclosed the invention to him. The witness reproduced on the witness-stand a sketch which not only contains all that Hansen's original sketch disclosed, but the means for securing the block as well. The witness admitted that he had discussed the matter with Hansen and his counsel before testifying, and that they had shown him sketches. The Examiners-in-Chief say of this witness:

This testimony, even if it were sufficient to disclose a device capable of mode of operation called for by this limited issue, is not convincing. Oral timony that on a single occasion a witness has seen a sketch which four years after he is able to reproduce, is evidence of a memory so remarkable that the statement is hardly credible.

The Commissioner, in commenting on the testimony of this witness, says:

When it is considered that Meyer testifies to a detail of the invention alleged to have been disclosed to him some four years before and then on a single occasion, that he identifies no sketches or exhibits in support of his oral testimony, that his memory of later events appears uncertain, and that he may have confused more recent disclosures of this detail of the invention with the date of the original disclosure, his testimony is by no means convincing as to the existence of the adjusting feature of the issue in the invention disclosed to him in 1899. Since this testimony is all the corroborating evidence Hansen is able to produce concerning his alleged conception of the complete invention of the issue in 1899, it is held insufficient to establish satisfactorily said conception.

The record discloses additional reasons for believing Hansen did not disclose this invention to Meyer or anybody else during 1899. While he constructed six or seven different transmitters during that period of experimentation, he did not construct any embodying this invention. He says the reason he did not was because he lacked mechanical skill, but we are forced to conclude that the real reason was because he did not possess the requisite inventive idea. He does not contend that he concealed his ideas from his superiors, but on the contrary complains that he was unable to interest them therein. He admits that Mr. Miller examined and discussed with him several of the transmitters he was attempting to develop, and that Mr. Miller was frequently in the room where he was conducting his experiments. Miller says:

I was, I may say, on a constant hunt for a good idea in transmitters. I remember distinctly when Mr. Dean first showed me such a transmitter as you have described; I at once saw the possibilities of it, and I believe I would have done so had Mr. Hansen shown it to me. * * * Mr. Hansen's statement that I would never take the time to listen to his ideas is absurd, and is untrue. * * * Mr. Hansen was assigned by me to the duty of producing a new transmitter, and in doing so was instructed to make up models of any ideas he evolved, which seemed practicable. The result was, after several weeks of very conscientious effort on his part, an absolute failure to produce what I, or any other of the engineers of the Kellogg Company at that time, considered to be a practical idea. * * * The result, as I have said, was failure, and it was with regret partly on Hansen's account, and partly because I wanted a good transmitter, that Hansen was taken off this work and put on the routine work of testing. * * * During the early employment of Mr. Hansen in the Chicago factory, that is during the summer and fall of '99, at which time he claims, I believe, to have produced the invention in controversy I was particularly careful to get to the bottom of Hansen's schemes. To have done otherwise would have certainly been poor management on my part, for I had assigned Mr. Hansen to a certain definite line of work, with the hope of his achieving a certain definite result.

Dean entered the employ of the Kellogg Company in October, 1900, and soon thereafter developed the invention in issue which previously conceived. This transmitter went through Hansen's hands to be tested, and he, therefore, had an opportunity to become perfectly familiar with its construction. He made no complaint to Miller that the invention was his, although he did make some complaint to others. He nevertheless continued in the employ of the Kellogg Company for several months. Soon after leaving the company he engaged with the American Electrical Telephone Company, and in July, 1901, four months after Dean's application was filed and about seven months after he had tested one of Dean's transmitters, he for the first time constructed a transmitter embodying this invention.

On this evidence, we think, the Commissioner was fully justified in reaching the conclusion that Hansen has not overcome Dean's record date. We are convinced that had Hansen conceived and disclosed this invention in 1899, it would have been adopted by the Kellogg Company. That Hansen may have had a certain definite result in mind is quite probable, but that he had devised any means for accomplishing that result is disproved by the surrounding facts and circumstances. His conduct from the time he says he conceived the invention in June, 1899, to June, 1901, when he left the Kellogg Company, was certainly inconsistent with his present contentions.

Without discussing the question of his lack of diligence from June, 1899, the date he says he conceived the invention, to a period subsequent to Dean's filing date, we hold that he has failed to show either conception or reduction to practice prior to March 22, 1901, Dean's record date, and, therefore, affirm the decision of the Commissioner, and it is so ordered.

The clerk of the court will certify this opinion and the proceedings of this court to the Commissioner of Patents, as required by law. *Affirmed.*

[Court of Appeals of the District of Columbia.]

WICKERS AND FURLONG *v.* McKEE.

Decided February 5, 1907.

(129 O. G., 869.)

1. INTERFERENCE—PRIORITY—REDUCTION TO PRACTICE—SUCCESSFUL TEST REQUIRED.

Where the invention consists of a plate graduated in such manner as to obviate the necessity for "make-ready." *Held* that to establish a successful reduction to practice requires a printing test under actual working conditions on a power-press and without the use of a "cut-overlay."

2. SAME—SAME—SAME—SAME.

Complete invention must ... ... ant to demonstration. The efforts of the inventor must have passed be... experiment, beyond the reach of possible or probable failure, must b... ed certainty by embodiment in the intended ... producing the desired result, tor where experiments have inspired hope of future achievement of the purpose for which they were designed, they still fall short of reduction to practice.

3. SAME—SAME—RIGHT TO MAKE CLAIM AN ANCILLARY QUESTION.

The question of the right of a party to make a claim may sometimes be an ancillary question to be considered in awarding priority of invention, and there are good reasons why the question of the right to make the claims may be considered a basis for an award of priority rather than a ground for a dissolution of an interference.

4. SAME—SAME—RIGHT TO MAKE CLAIMS.

The contention that a party has no right to make a claim for a process of producing a printing-surface because he describes a step of heating the plate which is not included in the issue cannot be admitted as well founded where his specification makes it clear that the step is not necessary in all cases.

Mr. J. H. Griffin for the appellants.
Mr. Walter F. Rogers and *Mr. Jacob Felbel* for the appellee.

McComas, J.:

The matter of this interference is improvement in manufacture of printing-blocks, and the issue is as follows:

1. A printing-block having an uneven printing face or surface, parts of said printing-surface being raised to correspond to the darkly-shaded parts of the subject to be printed, and other parts of its printing surface being depressed to correspond to the lighter-shaded parts of the subject to be printed, the whole surface-level of the block being a printing-surface but having uneven or facial differences in its plane.

2. A printing-surface having the sections thereof, which are designed to print the darker shades, permanently elevated above the levels of the sections adapted for the lighter shades.

3. A printing-surface having the sections thereof, which are designed to print the darker shades, permanently elevated above the levels of the sections adapted for the lighter shades, these levels being graded one into the other.

4. A printing-surface having sections thereof which are designed to print the darker shades permanently elevated above the levels of the sections adapted for the lighter shades, the levels being graded one into the other from the permanently-elevated parts to the lightest printing shade.

5. The herein-described process of producing printing-surfaces which consists first in forming a relief printing-surface in a yielding material and then producing a graded printing-surface by applying different degrees of pressure to various sections thereof and so as to produce permanent graded alterations in the surface in profile.

6. The herein-described process of producing printing-surfaces which consists in first forming a relief printing-surface in a thin plate, and then applying different degrees of pressure to various sections thereof, thereby producing permanent differences in profile in said plate, the levels of which are in correspondence with the darkness of the shades to be printed by the sections.

The four applicants in this interference are Wickers and Furlong, who filed their joint application. January 22, 1902, and on August 23d of the same year, filed a divisional application: Milton A. McKee, *who filed* December 21, 1901; Eugen Albert, who filed June 15, 1901;

and Burt F. Upham, who filed January 22, 1901. From the decision · of the Commissioner of Patents, (C. D., 1906, 326; 124 O. G., 905,) Wickers and Furlong appealed to this court.

The record in this case, which is interference No. 22,400 in the Patent Office, contains 2,000 pages and nearly two hundred exhibits. It is evident that the review of this case must be abridged so far as practicable. In succession, the three different tribunals of the Patent Office have agreed in their conclusions, and as we have so often announced, this court will not reverse the unanimous decisions except in a very clear case. We have found nothing in this matter of interference which makes the case before us an exception to this rule. This case is one of a series of related interferences in all of which the three tribunals of the Patent Office agreed in awarding priority to McKee. It was stipulated that the records and files of this case should be taken and considered to be parts of the transcripts of record in each of the other cases, respectively. The conclusion reached in the principal case before us enables us to make brief disposition of the interferences involved in the other cases.

The invention involved in these interferences relates to printing-plates and methods of producing the same and more particularly to such plates as are employed for printing illustrations, and the appellee argues the invention comprises a printing-plate which may be an original engraved plate, line or half-tone, or an electrotype, and processes for producing printing-plates.

In the prior art, the metal relief printing-plates were either " engraved plates," which were mechanically engraved, " half-tone plates," which were engraved by etching, and " electros," or electrotypes. The mechanically-engraved plates are made by transferring an illustration to the face of a metallic plate by one method or another and then cutting by use of a graver's tool the illustration in the plate. To produce half-tone plates, a negative of the chosen subject is made by photographing through a ruled screen, and a print or photographic transfer from such negative is made on the previously-sensitized front of the printing-plate. Because of the intervention of the screen in preparing the negative, this print has the " ruled " or " line " effect, the function of which effect is to cause the plate to take up ink. When the sensitized surface is developed, the plate is " etched " by immersing it in a chemical bath. Plates produced by either the mechanical or photo-engraving method are termed " engraved plates " or " original plates." The part of the plate which is to produce the imprint or picture sta[...]   lief, while the non-printing portion of the surfac[...]   ginal plate may be used for printing, but us[...]   [...] therefrom is employed. The " electro," th[...]   urt, is made by pressing the original [...]   [...] wax, thereby producing a mold or matrix in which the impression of the printing-surface is depressed, and the non-printing surface is in relief. This mold is dusted with graphite thus making its surface a conductor of electricity, a shell of copper is then deposited thereon electrolytically, thereby producing a copper replica of the original plate. By whichever of the methods described it may be produced, the engraved plate or the electro made therefrom is backed up with electrotype metal, thereby producing a printing-block suitable for use on a printing-press. Upon all plates and electrotypes it is essential that the pressure exerted by the printing-press at the moment of transferring ink to the surface of the paper, shall be applied strongly on the parts of the surface of the plates which correspond to the solids or shadows or darker shades of the picture and lightly upon those parts which correspond to the light or high lights of the picture.

In the prior art it has been the practice to take proofs from the plate in number corresponding with the printing-tones of the plate and then to make from these proofs a cut-overlay. This cut-overlay is made by first cutting out and discarding the lightest printing-tones from one of the proofs, and what remains is the base-sheet of the overlay, to which all other portions are attached. From the next proof, the lighter tones, and then the next lightest tones, are successively cut out and discarded and so on until in the last proof, all but the solids are cut out and discarded. These separate sheets are then pasted one upon the other so that the greatest number of thicknesses of the cut-overlay will correspond and register with the solids or shadows of the cut, while the lowest number, the thinnest portion, will correspond and register with the high lights of the cut. Indeed the extreme high light is often represented by openings through the whole cut-overlay. The cut-overlay so formed is so graded by the pasting together of the different cut-out proof-sheets that the thickest portions correspond with the more solid portions of the cut to be printed, and from these portions, the overlay tapers down to nothing where the high lights are to be printed. This cut-overlay is placed upon the cylinder of the printing-press so that in printing, the overlay and cut will register so that where the greatest amount of printing pressure is required, the thickest portion of the overlay will be opposite the solids of the cut, and so that where the least amount of pressure is required, opposite the high lights, the thinnest part will be in register.

The making and mounting of these cut-overlays upon the cylinder with accompanying necessary details consumes much time and requires the service of expert mechanics with artistic sense.

All of the parties to this interference proceeded upon the idea of *making* the printing side of the plate highest where the solids or shadows exist and gradually depressing the plate where the lighter tones are found, so that the varying pressures required may be accurately and aptly applied upon those parts of the plate which are to print darkest and upon those parts which are to print lightest and by apt graduation upon the intermediate portions. The means employed on the platen or impression-cylinder for pressing the paper at varying pressures against the flat printing-plate is termed an "overlay." The making of the overlay and placing it on this cylinder is called "making ready" and what results from the operation is called the "make-ready" of the press. By a "reverse overlay," is meant an overlay in which the thickest parts correspond to the high lights of the imprint and the thinnest part, to the darkest, the intermediate thicknesses being properly graded. A "reverse overlay" is never used on the back or reverse of the plate, but always on the face or obverse of the plate.

It is the object of the invention in issue, to produce a printing-plate, the printing-surface of which contains elevations and depressions corresponding with the tones of the imprint to be produced so as to dispense with the overlay on the impression-cylinder of the press so that instead of putting the "make-ready" on the impression-cylinder by means of the "overlay," such "make-ready" is put into the printing-surface of the plate itself. Such a plate has a graduated printed surface which produces an imprint whereby the several tones of the illustration are secured by these graduations whereas in the printing-plate of the prior art, with the flat printing-surface, the several tones were secured entirely by the overlay used on the impression-cylinder. The Commissioner of Patents holds accordingly that a graduated printed surface within the meaning of these interferences is a printing-surface containing all the "make-ready" in its face. The appellant, however, contends that the issues of the interferences are not limited to a plate having a portion only of the "make-ready" on its face. This contention of the appellants is quite material to their case on this appeal.

Wickers and Furlong, in their application filed on January 22, 1902, disclosed two processes for producing the invention in issue. One process was to place an ordinary overlay on the back of the plate to be treated so that the overlay registered with the face. The plate was then to be placed face downward upon wax or other semi-solid material and pressed, and the pressure of the overlay against the back of the plate would cause corresponding graduations in its face. This process was transferred to a divisional application upon a requirement of division by the   nd it was this application which was filed by Wickers and Fu   ust 23, 1902. The second process consists in etching the   ate so that the greatest amount of it is remov   rt of the face, the full thickness of the plate being left under the darkest tone and correspondingly graduating the various tones on other parts of the plate. The plate is then to be placed face downward on wax or other suitable material and pressure is to be exerted thereby transferring the graduations from the back of the plate to its face. By both processes, the printed surface of the plate is graduated, and simultaneously, the wax into which the plate has been pressed receives an intaglio of the printing-plate and of course becomes a matrix upon which an electrotype-shell may be deposited.

Both these applications are involved in this interference and Wickers and Furlong have their date of January 22, 1902, as the time of their constructive reduction to practice. The Examiner of Interferences decided that the testimony clearly established the fact that in 1897, Wickers and Furlong had a conception of the invention in issue and of a process for producing it, this process being substantially the same as the process disclosed in their application involved in the interference. The Examiners-in-Chief, however, concluded that Wickers and Furlong failed to prove prior conception, utterly failed to prove conception at any date in 1897, or at any time in fact prior to October, 1901. The Commissioner of Patents remarks that the Examiner of Interferences had found that Wickers and Furlong had a conception of the invention of all the interferences in August, 1897, while, as he observed, the Examiners-in-Chief had decided that in the present interference Wickers and Furlong had failed to prove their date of conception prior to October, 1901, and in the remaining interferences prior to their filing date, January 22, 1902. Therefore, the Commissioner concluded that in view of the fact that Wickers and Furlong in all of the interferences were the last to reduce to practice and were unquestionably lacking in diligence, it was unnecessary to determine their date of conception of the invention. We have examined, but it is impossible to here review, the voluminous testimony and numerous exhibits related to the question of conception, and early reduction to practice of this invention by Wickers and Furlong. Prior to 1897, and thereafter until 1902, Wickers had charge of the engraving department and Furlong was foreman of the electrotyping department in the establishment of the De Vinne Press, of New York city. Wickers says that in July, 1897, Furlong and he jointly conceived the invention in issue. Furlong says his employer De Vinne made a suggestion concerning rounding edges on vignetted cuts and while he was experimenting with this he consulted Wickers, who suggested that if it were possible to reduce the edges of vignetted cuts in electrotypes, it should also be possible to produce a graded surface over the entire face of the plate giving each shade its proper tone. This incident occurred early in that year and led to a series of experiments by Wickers who consulted with Furlong in the deavors to make such plates. Eighteen witnesses testified in behalf of Wickers and Furlong. Of these Foster, Boyer and Liecty, more fully speak concerning many exhibits as do Bloom and Hicks in less degree. Boyer was an electrotype-molder. Foster molded more than fifty original plates for Wickers and Furlong, and Liecty was an electrotype-finisher. The proof is quite convincing that Wickers and Furlong and especially Wickers, made experiments from time to time, and as some of the witnesses said, produced improved plates which were an aid to the pressman but did not do away entirely with the overlay. The press used in testing and experimental plates was a hand-press. Both Wickers and Furlong testify to experiments during 1897 and the two following years. Among the first was that of placing a copper overlay, exhibited, on the back of a plate, also exhibited, in register with the face and subjecting both to pressure, and the corresponding electrotype was in evidence and in some degree two witnesses corroborate the production of certain plates and Wickers claims to have disclosed the invention to various employees of the De Vinne Company. That all this testimony lacked definiteness and that in essential features the case of Wickers and Furlong fell short of that complete invention which must amount to demonstration is suggested by their attitude upon this appeal wherein they contend that it is not necessary that the make-ready be entirely dispensed with and that even a slight variation in the surface of the printing-plate is a sufficient compliance with the requirements of the issue. At least to be within the terms of the issue, we are convinced that they must have produced a plate by the process described, in making which, the make-ready was substantially dispensed with. These issues require as a reduction to practice of the invention a construction of printing-plates by the process claimed, having the characteristics described and we are inclined to agree that the demonstration by actual trial should be on power-presses and a clear showing that the proper graduation of tone on the imprint can be obtained without " making ready " or " overlaying " the impression-cylinder. Complete invention must amount to demonstration. The efforts of the inventor must have passed beyond experiment, beyond the reach of possible or probable failure, must have attained certainty by embodiment in the intended form, and must be capable of producing the desired result, for where experiments have inspired hope of future achievement of the purpose for which they were designed, they still fall short of reduction to practice; for the test of successful reduction to practice herein is the printing test under actual working conditions. (See *Hunter* v. *Stikeman*, C. D., 1898, 564; 85 O. G., 610; 13 App. D. C., 214; *McKenzie* v. *Cummings*, C. D., 1904, 683; 112 O. G., 1481; 24 App. D. C., 137; *Gilman* v. *Hinson*, C. D., 1906, 634; 122 O. G., 731; 26 App. D. C.,

409; *O'Connell* v. *Schmidt*, C. D., 1906, 662; 122 O. G., 2065; 27 App. D. C., 77.)

The witness Murray testifies that the various Wickers and Furlong's exhibit proofs produced by a hand-press are no fair test of the printing qualities of the plate, for such proof is produced at one given impression over the surface of the entire plate at one time and consequently a proof thus produced cannot be compared with the impression from a power printing-press, for the latter is extremely rigid on the impression and the point of contact is on a small portion of the printed surface at any given time, it is on a line with the length of the cylinder and is at no time over a quarter of an inch in width. Murray gives reasons why a hand-press proof shows up much better than one from the cylinder impression. We need not follow this and other witnesses who claim that an inventor who has confidence in anything he has done to a plate should not be satisfied until he has demonstrated that the plates are available in actual printing. This court has held that where invention belongs to a class requiring actual use or thorough tests to demonstrate its practicability, there can be no reduction to practice until one or the other thing happens and is proved. (*Gallagher* v. *Hein*, C. D., 1905, 624; 115 O. G., 1330; 25 App. D. C., 77.) We are not satisfied that the proofs produced by Wickers and Furlong are evidence of the printing qualities of the plates.

We concur with the Examiners-in-Chief and the Commissioner that it is only by subjecting the plate produced by the process claimed, to the printing test under the conditions of actual use that Wickers and Furlong can establish satisfactorily that such plate embodies the invention of this interference and therefore the plate must be printed from, without the use of " cut-overlays." A flat plate with an overlay may produce the same imprint as a graduated plate and to print from a plate with an overlay may make it uncertain that the plate itself has any graduation whatever. It is clear that some of the earlier plates of Wickers and Furlong lacked any perceptible graduation and in printing, the usual overlays were used on them. We concur too in the conclusion that of the numerous plates put in evidence by Wickers and Furlong, it is not clear that any were made or printed from, without overlays prior to the date of McKee's application, December 21, 1901. Late in 1901, an electro made from a plate was used in printing page 486 of the *Century Magazine* and there is a strong probability that the work was done without the use of an overlay on the impression-cylinder. The appellants' witnesses insist this incident happened in October of that year, but at that time McKee had already reduced the invention to practice and in December of that year filed his application.

There was remarkable lack of diligence on the part of Wickers and Furlong. Reckoning from the first experiment in August, 1897, there appear three intervals of about five or six months each, several intervals of three or four months each, and another still longer interval, until the spring of 1901, and another of six or seven months before the last of October, 1901. Wickers and Furlong with every convenience at hand for reducing the invention to practice, experimented only at intervals of time wide apart and the delay appeared to be due to business considerations and other distractions. As Justice Shepard has said in *Paul* v. *Hess*, (C. D., 1905, 610; 115 O. G., 251; 24 App. D. C., 462:)

Even if properly supported and covering the entire period of delay, this excuse would be insufficient as not of the character required. It involves mere business considerations, and not circumstances of a compelling nature. Diligence will not wait on business arrangements.

The appellants have failed to show that they were diligently engaged in reducing the invention to practice at the time their rivals entered the field. We are satisfied that in October, 1901, when Mc-Kee had reduced his invention to practice, and when Albert and Upham had filed their applications, there is not sufficient proof of Wickers and Furlong having done any serious work upon their problem for a long time prior to that date. Certain exhibits it is true were said to have been made in March and May, 1901, but the testimony is not convincing that these exhibits were made at that time. An original plate and an electrotype said by Wickers and Furlong to have been made at a prior date, lacked the necessary confirmation of a disinterested witness. While it appears that Wickers and Furlong did something with reference to the invention of the issue in February, 1900, there is a lack of corroborating testimony that the plates of 1900 and of the early part of 1901 were tested. Their conduct strongly indicates that they regarded these plates as unsuccessful experiments. They did nothing of consequence thereafter until October, 1901. We do not forget that they and their witnesses claim that intervals of delay never exceeded two months, but we are not convinced that the fact was so.

Both Wickers and Furlong held important places in the De Vinne printing establishment, where the *Century Magazine*, the *St. Nicholas Magazine* and the books of the Century Company were printed. Workmen were near by to prepare electrotypes and on presses fitted to print illustrations of every kind, they had ample facility for trying every phase of their ideas, for testing the feasibility of their invention. Beginning in 1897, we find their first substantial results clearly proved near the end of 1901. Appellants' counsel say that the only time they could devote to their experiments, was chance hours which they could spare from their responsible and absorbing duties. They say too that De Vinne paid little attention to their experiments and was absorbed in other experimental work not related to the appellant's invention. Still it is true Wickers and Furlong suffered intervals to elapse without renewed efforts, although the facilities near at hand were so valuable.

Wickers testifies that from the experiments in midsummer in 1897 to the production of plates in the spring of 1898, their experiments were carried on intermittently, and he denies there were any intervals so long as six months, though sometimes several months elapsed without renewed experiment. Furlong is quite indefinite, saying that Wickers and he endeavored to produce graded surfaces on printing-plates in the years just mentioned and did produce pronounced graded surfaces in each of the three succeeding years and he thinks also in 1902. Foster and Bloom say Wickers and Furlong worked at these plates at odd times and Boyer states the plates were taken up at leisure times and no interval exceeded two months.

In considering the proof of diligence, we have in mind the well-settled rule of the insufficiency of the uncorroborated testimony of sole or joint inventors. Since we agree with the Patent Office tribunals that they have failed to prove themselves to be the prior inventors, it is unimportant to consider whether, when they failed, they were or were not joint inventors. The Commissioner of Patents concludes that they have failed to establish that they actually reduced the invention to practice prior to their constructive reduction to practice by filing their application of January 22, 1902. Indeed, the Examiners-in-Chief hold that in the present interference, Wickers and Furlong have failed to prove a date of conception prior to October, 1901, and in the remaining interferences, prior to their filing date just mentioned.

In October, 1901, the activity of Wickers and Furlong is undisputed and the result of their subsequent work soon led to a constructive and actual reduction to practice of the invention by them. We think, however, their diligence was excited by the knowledge of McKee's entry into this field. The record of McKee is much clearer. He testifies that he conceived this invention early in August, 1900, and on the 10th of that month he disclosed it to his friend Cates, then foreman of the press-room of the "*Farm Journal.*" McKee then prepared a plate which was successfully used in printing the next regular edition of that journal. This plate was introduced in evidence and with it was exhibited a page of the *Farm Journal* which was printed from that plate, called the "Cate's plate." Cates fully corroborated McKee and testified that they printed from that plate without any make-ready on the impression-cylinder; that McKee's conception and *reduction to* practice in August, 1900, is fully established is too clear for argument and the fact is not controverted by any of his opponents. Even if McKee were not entitled to a date of conception earlier than his filing date of December 21, 1901, Wickers and Furlong must still fail because they failed to prove diligence.   But we agree with the Patent Office tribunals that in September and October, 1901, McKee made further reductions to practice.   His printing-plates made at this period were planed in the works of the De Vinne press and in the department wherein Furlong was the manager.   McKee's testimony is further corroborated by Greenway and the two Cottrells.   After McKee's plates had been planed in Furlong's department, McKee wrote a letter, which does not appear in evidence, and on October 15, 1901, Furlong wrote to McKee in the following terms:

Tuesday, p. m., Oct. 15, 1901.

MY DEAR MR. McKEE: Some days since I was pleased at receiving your letter announcing the success of the new method of shaving electrotypes and was delighted this a. m., on receiving convincing proofs from the plates.

You deserve much credit for the novel method which is new to me and in justice to you state I told Mr. Cottrell that I did not believe overlays on the plates while being shaved would produce the desired result because the electrotypes are not sufficiently yielding but am glad to know I was mistaken.

I am having some overlays—reverse overlays made here and will write you the result.

The delay in shipping last order of electrotypes was caused by carrying out the rules of this office which is "all outside electrotyping is subject to the convenience of *Century* work"—we are very busy here at present.

Hoping to see more samples of your printing by the new method and expecting a visit from you previous to returning to Philadelphia I remain yours

P. M. FURLONG.

Nor can it be doubted that the object of these inventions of McKee was in substance to do away with making ready.   McKee's specification thus states his method of producing a plate:

The main object of my invention is to dispense entirely with the work of "making ready" or of "underlaying" and "overlaying" and to make the necessary corrections (or cure the defects) in the plates themselves, and so, that after treatment of the plates they may be placed on the press and the printing directly proceeded with.

    *   *   *   *   *   *   *

So far as my knowledge extends, no printing-plate of this description has ever before been produced, and in consequence of my improvements in the plate it will be seen that all the objectionable, expensive and difficult work of "making ready" may now be entirely dispensed with, although I may add here that after the making of the plate—if the pressman should at any time during the course of the printing therefrom desire to change the character of impressions by further lightening or increasing the same he may for such purpose "underlay" or "overlay" in the usual manner, but ordinarily the plates may be made at the outset to conform exactly to what is required by the pressman or to what is demanded by the nature of the plate to be worked from.

In so far as certain features of my improvements in the art of treating or manipulating the plate are concerned, it will be understood that I do not wish to be limited to each and all of the steps of the complete process to which I prefer to subject the plate, for some of such steps may be used without others or in connection with still other steps or modes of treatment to produce certain of the results produced by me and to avoid either in whole or in part the work of "underlaying" and "overlaying."

The proof of McKee's reductions to practice show that he substantially dispensed with the make-ready and the demonstration of his success in actual trial on power-presses was immediate and beyond dispute.

In respect to the claim of Wickers and Furlong we concur with all the tribunals of the Patent Office that McKee was undoubtedly the prior inventor. Wickers and Furlong contend that McKee had no right to make certain claims forming counts of the issues of these interferences. The Examiners-in-Chief, however, refused to make the desired recommendation under Rule 126, for which appellants' counsel ask. In *Podlesak* v. *McInnerney* (C. D., 1906, 558; 120 O. G., 2127; 26 App. D. C., 399) this court has held that the question of the right of a party to make a claim may sometimes be an ancillary question to be considered in awarding priority of invention, and there are good reasons why the question of the right to make the claims may be considered a basis for an award of priority rather than a ground for a dissolution of an interference, and the Commissioner of Patents in his decision says that the right of McKee to make these certain claims question by Wickers and Furlong, will later be given consideration in the Office as ancillary to the question of priority.

The Commissioner further says that Wickers and Furlong's contention is that McKee is not entitled to make the claims 5 and 6 of the present interference " for the reason that his specification does not describe nor does his testimony show the steps of forming a relief printing-surface in a " yielding material" and the Commissioner holds for reasons well stated that there is no merit in this contention. The appellants further contend that McKee cannot make the process claims, forming counts of this or the companion interferences, because he heats his plate as a step in his treatment and these counts are silent as to the heating of the plate. Of course the purpose of the heat is to soften the plate and permit the work to be accomplished with less pressure. We agree with the Commissioner that heating is no more essential to McKee's process than to the process of Wickers and Furlong and that it may be omitted if greater pressure be applied. McKee himself does not consider his invention as limited to a process including heating, for his application as filed contained claims which omitted this step.

From the decision of the Examiner of Interferences Wickers and Furlong alone appealed. Upon the issue of this interference the Examiner of Interferences decided that Upham conceived the invention in 1899 but did not reduce the invention to practice prior to the filing of his application on January 22, 1901. He was not diligent at the time of McKee's conception and reduction to practice in August, 1900, and therefore was not entitled to prevail over McKee. The Examiner of Interferences also held that since Albert had taken no testimony he was restricted to his record date; that even if he were given the benefit of his alleged foreign patents, the earliest date to which he would be entitled for conception would be the date of his earliest foreign patent, which was April 16, 1901. This date would avail him no more than the date of his application involved in this interference, which was June 13, 1901. It was held, therefore, that Albert was not entitled to prevail over either Upham or McKee. At this stage Albert and Upham disappeared from further consideration upon this issue and as we concur with the three tribunals of the Patent Office that McKee is the prior inventor as to the issues of this interference, the decision of the Commissioner of Patents *is affirmed* and the clerk of this court will certify this opinion and decision to the Commissioner of Patents in accordance with law.

[Court of Appeals of the District of Columbia.]

WICKERS AND FURLONG *v.* ALBERT.

Decided February 5, 1907.

(129 O. G., 1268.)

INTERFERENCE—PRIORITY.

> The decision of the Commissioner of Patents awarding priority of invention to Albert affirmed, for the reasons stated in the case of *Wickers and Furlong* v. *McKee,* (*ante,* 587; 129 O. G., 869.)

Mr. J. H. Griffin for the appellants.
Mr. Eugen Albert pro se.

McCOMAS, *J.:*

A like stipulation with that made in No. 387 Patent Appeal Docket, respecting such parts of the record of the companion interference No. 22,400 (No. 386 Patent Appeal Docket), as are common to the two interferences, was entered into between the parties to this interference. The issue of this interference is as follows:

> The process of "making ready" the printing-surface of a printing-block, which consists in applying to the back of the printing-block a "relief" form having raised parts corresponding to the darkly-shaded parts of the subject to be printed, covering the printing-surface of the printing-block with yielding material, and then subjecting the printing-block and the "relief" form to pressure thereby raising the level of those parts of the printing-surface of the printing-block which correspond to the light-shaded parts of the subject to be

printed so as to obtain a correctly-shaded impression in a single printing operation.

In this case the three tribunals of the Patent Office concurred in awarding priority of invention in favor of Albert. The Examiner of Interferences held that Wickers and Furlong conceived this invention in 1897 but did not reduce to practice prior to their filing date, January 22, 1902, while Albert filed his application involved in this interference on June 15, 1901, at which time and for several months thereafter Wickers and Furlong were not exercising diligence, and he awarded priority of invention of the issue of this interference to Eugen Albert, the senior party. The Examiners-in-Chief and the Commissioner of Patents concurred in holding that Wickers and Furlong did not establish a date of conception prior to June 15, 1901, when Albert's application was filed, and that Albert was the first to conceive and the first to reduce to practice. The three tribunals, therefore, awarded priority to Albert and from such decision by the Commissioner of Patents Wickers and Furlong appealed to this court.

We have so fully stated our reason for concurring with the Commissioner of Patents and for concluding that Wickers and Furlong did not reduce to practice the invention of this issue until after the filing date of Albert's application, June 15, 1901, and that they were lacking in diligence at the time Albert entered the field, that we content ourselves by referring to the opinion of this court in the companion interference No. 386 Patent Appeal Docket, where we have discussed the matter which lead us to such conclusion.

The decision of the Commissioner of Patents *is affirmed* and the clerk of this court will certify this opinion and decision to the Commissioner of Patents in accordance with law.

[Court of Appeals of the District of Columbia.]

WICKERS AND FURLONG *v.* McKEE.

Decided February 5, 1907.

(129 O. G., 1269.)

INTERFERENCE—PRIORITY.

The decision of the Commissioner of Patents awarding priority of invention to McKee affirmed, for the reasons stated in the case of *Wickers and Furlong* v. *McKee,* (ante, 587; 129 O. G., 869.)

Mr. J. H. Griffin for the appellants.
Mr. Walter F. Rogers and *Mr. Jacob Felbel* for the appellee.

McCOMAS, *J.:*

A stipulation like that mentioned in our decision in No. 388 Patent *Appeal Docket*, making the record in No. 386 Patent Appeal Docket, the companion interference No. 22,400, as to such parts of that record as are common to the two interferences, part of this case, was entered into between the parties to this case. The issue of this interference is as follows:

1. That improvement in the art of treating manufactured relief printing-plates which consists in mechanically producing in the printing-face of such plate depressions and elevations at predetermined places where the printing is to be respectively light and heavy, and in also evening or leveling the back of the plate.

2. That improvement in the art of preparing printing-plates which consists in producing in the back of the plate depressions and elevations at predetermined places where the printing is to be respectively light and heavy, and then subsequently producing similar depressions and elevations in the face of the plate by pressing forward the elevations produced in the back of the plate.

3. That improvement in the art of preparing printing-plates which consists in first producing in the back of the plate a series of depressions and elevations and in then forcing the metal toward the face of the plate to produce therein a series of substantially similar depressions and elevations.

4. That improvement in the art of preparing printing-plates which consists in first producing in the back of the plates a series of depressions and elevations and in then forcing the metal toward the face of the plate to produce therein a series of substantially similar depressions and elevations and simultaneously smoothing or evening the back of the plate.

The three tribunals of the Patent Office concurred in awarding judgment of priority of invention of the issue of this interference to Milton A. McKee, the senior party, and for the reasons set forth in our decision in the companion interference No. 386 Patent Appeal Docket, *we affirm* the decision of the Commissioner of Patents in this case and the clerk of this court will certify this decision to the Commissioner of Patents in accordance with law.

[Court of Appeals of the District of Columbia.]

WICKERS AND FURLONG *v.* McKEE.

Decided February 5, 1907.

(129 O. G., 1269.)

INTERFERENCE—PRIORITY.

The decision of the Commissioner of Patents awarding priority of invention to McKee affirmed, for the reasons stated in the case of *Wickers and Furlong* v. *McKee*, (*ante*, 587; 129 O. G., 869.)

Mr. J. H. Griffin for the appellants.
Mr. Walter F. Rogers and *Mr. Jacob Felbel* for the appellee.

McCOMAS, *J.:*

By stipulation between the parties to this interference such parts of the record of the companion interference No. 22,400, (No. 386

Patent Appeal Docket) as are common to the two interferences are to be taken as part of the record in the case we are now considering. The issues of this interference are:

1. As a new article of manufacture, a relief printing-plate whose face constitutes the printing-surface and is formed with depressions and elevations at those portions where the impressions are to be respectively light and dark and whose back is even and level.

2. As a new article of manufacture, a relief printing-plate having an even and level back and a predetermined undulating face which constitutes the printing-surface of the plate and which is adapted to yield different predetermined heavy and light impressions, heavy impressions at the raised portions of the plate and light impressions at the depressed portions of the plate.

3. As a new article of manufacture, a relief printing-plate having an evenly-pressed back and a pressed-up printing-face composed of a series of printing projections and depressions formed at predetermined places where the printing pressures are to be respectively heavy and light.

The issue here deals with a printing-surface and method of producing the same and in this case, as in No. 386 of the Patent Appeal Docket, the three tribunals of the Patent Office concur in awarding priority of invention to McKee. The Examiner of Interferences, largely for the reasons we have stated in our opinion this day rendered in No. 386 on the Patent Appeal Docket, held that Wickers and Furlong conceived the invention of this issue in the summer of 1897 but did not make a reduction to practice prior to their filing date of January 22, 1902, and that although they were the first to conceive, they were last to reduce to practice, and owing to their lack of diligence, are not entitled to prevail over any of their rivals. He also held that Upham conceived this invention in 1899 but did not reduce to practice prior to the filing of his application on January 22, 1901; that he was not diligent at the time of McKee's conception and reduction to practice and, therefore, was not entitled to prevail over McKee. And he further decided that McKee conceived the invention and reduced it to practice in August, 1900, and because he was the first to reduce to practice, McKee was entitled to prevail over Upham and Wickers and Furlong on account of the lack of diligence of each of these applicants, and so he awarded judgment of priority of invention of the issue of this interference to Milton A. McKee, a junior party.

Wickers and Furlong, only, appealed to the Examiners-in-Chief from this decision of the Examiner of Interferences awarding priority to McKee, and the Examiners-in-Chief for the reasons stated by them in interference No. 22,400 (No. 386 Patent Appeal Docket) decided that Wickers and Furlong failed to show a conception of the invention prior to their application date and in all other particulars concurred with the Examiner of Interferences in holding that McKee was the prior inventor of the issue of this interference. They also declined to make certain recommendations under Rule 126 as specting the right of the party to make certain of the interfering claims. They affirmed the decision of the Examiner of Interferences.

Upon appeal to the Commissioner of Patents, that official affirmed the decision of the Examiners-in-Chief awarding priority to McKee. This court for the reasons stated in the companion interference No. 22,400 (No. 386 Patent Appeal Docket) *now affirms* the decision of the Commissioner of Patents in awarding priority of invention of the issue of this interference to Milton A. McKee, and the clerk of this court will certify to the Commissioner of Patents this opinion and decision in accordance with law.

[Court of Appeals of the District of Columbia.]

WICKERS AND FURLONG *v*. McKEE.

Decided February 5, 1907.

(129 O. G., 1270.)

INTERFERENCE—PRIORITY.

    The decision of the Commissioner of Patents awarding priority of invention to McKee affirmed, for the reasons stated in the case of *Wickers and Furlong* v. *McKee*, (*ante*, 587; 129 O. G., 869.)

Mr. J. H. Griffin for the appellants.
Mr. Walter F. Rogers and *Mr. Jacob Felbel* for the appellee.

McCOMAS, *J.*:

In this case by stipulation like that in No. 387, this day decided by this court, such parts of the record of the companion interference No. 22,400 (No. 386 Patent Appeal Docket,) between the same parties as are common to the two interferences, are to be taken as a part of the record in this case. The issue of this interference is:

    1. An engraved printing-plate reduced in thickness from the back and depressed from the front to correspond to the successive graduations of light and shade represented by the engraving on the face.

    2. That improvement in the art of preparing printing-plates which consists in preparing the back of the plate with depressions and elevations corresponding to those which are to appear in the face of the plate, and in then subjecting the plate to pressure and causing said depressions and elevations to appear in the face of the plate.

For reasons in the main agreeing with those given in the opinion of this court accompanying the decision this day rendered in No. 386 Patent Appeal Docket, the Examiner of Interferences held that McKee conceived the invention in issue and reduced it to practice in August, 1900; that Wickers and Furlong conceived the invention but did not reduce to practice prior to the filing of their application on January 22, 1902, and that because of their lack of diligence, Wickers and Furlóng were not entitled to prevail, and, therefore, he awarded priority of invention of the issue of this interference to Milton A. McKee, the senior party. Upon appeal to the Examiners-in-Chief, that tribunal affirmed the decision of the Examiner of Interferences and in so doing directed the attention of the Commissioner to the fact that McKee had no right to a claim corresponding to count one of the issue, it appearing that his application did not disclose an *engraved* printing-plate such as is called for by the first count. Upon appeal to the Commissioner of Patents that official affirmed the decision of the Examiners-in-Chief awarding priority of invention to McKee in respect of the second count and reversed it as to the first count of the issue of this interference. The Commissioner held that for the reasons stated in his decision in the companion interference No. 22,400 (No. 386 Patent Appeal Docket,) the question as to whether McKee's application does or does not disclose an engraved plate such as is called for by the first count, should be considered as ancillary to the question of priority of invention. The Commissioner added that McKee applied his process to the electrotype and no mention is made throughout his specification of treating an engraved plate, and in view of the well-known distinction in the art between an electrotype and engraved plate, held that McKee's specification will not support a claim corresponding to the first count of the issue of this interference.

The Commissioner, therefore, awarded priority of invention of count one of the issue to Wickers and Furlong because McKee had no right to make the claim corresponding to this count.

The Commissioner directed the Primary Examiner, when the applications are returned to him for *ex parte* action, to consider the question of the patentability of count one of this issue over count two of the issue and over the subject-matter of the companion interference in which McKee is held to be the prior inventor.

From this ruling of the Commissioner respecting count one of the issue, McKee's counsel dissents and insists that the term "an engraved plate" is not a misnomer when applied to an electrotype and that an electrotype is a duplicate of an original plate and, therefore, to all intents and purposes is an engraved printing-plate. McKee, however, did not disclose this species of printing-plate application and McKee's counsel urges that the final produc ... ors and ... long is an electrotype-plate and, therefore, by ... of the issue is likewise excluded by this ruling ... not appeal from this ruling and we concur will ... Patents in his decision that McKee is the prior ject-matter of the se ... this interfe ...

Therefore, the dec ... sioner of and the clerk of thi ... this opin ... *the Commissioner of* ... ce with la

[Court of Appeals of the District of Columbia.]

WICKERS AND FURLONG *v*. UPHAM.

Decided February 5, 1907.

(129 O. G., 1612.)

INTERFERENCE—PRIORITY—DILIGENCE.

The decision of the Commissioner of Patents holding that Wickers and Furlong were not exercising diligence when Upham filed his application and awarding priority to Upham on his record date affirmed. (See *Wickers and Furlong v. McKee, ante,* 587; 129 O. G., 860.)

Mr. J. H. Griffin for the appellants.

Mr. Walter F. Rogers and *Mr. Jacob Felbel* for the appellee.

McComas, J.:

This is another of the series of interferences which have been considered together, in which Wickers and Furlong, appellants here, were also appellants in the other cases of the series, and this case relates especially to the manufacture of printing-plates. The three tribunals of the Patent Office concur in awarding priority of invention of the issue of this interference to Burt F. Upham, the senior party, and the issue of this interference is as follows:

1. The herein-described process of producing printing-surfaces which consists in first forming a relief printing-surface in a thin metallic plate, supporting the same upon a yielding backing, and finally forcing into the face thereof a comparatively unyielding surface varying in profile in direct proportion to the lightness of the shades to be printed by the different sections of the printing-surface.

2. The process of "making ready" the printing-surface of a printing-block, which consists in applying to one side of the printing-block, a "relief" form having parts of its printing-surface raised, said raised parts corresponding with certain parts of the subject to be printed, covering the other side of the printing-block with yielding material, and then subjecting the printing-block and the said "relief" form while in contact with one another to pressure, thereby altering the level parts of the printing-surface of the printing-block so as to obtain a correctly-shaded impression in a single printing operation.

3. The process of making ready the printing-surface of a printing-block, which consists in applying to the face of the printing-block a "relief" form having raised parts corresponding to the light-shaded parts of the subject to be printed, covering the back of the printing-block with yielding material, and then subjecting the printing-block and said "relief" form to pressure, thereby setting back the level of those parts of the printing-surface of the block which correspond to the lightly-shaded parts of the subject to be printed below the level of those parts of the printing-surface of the printing-block which correspond to the darkly-shaded parts of the subject to be printed so as to obtain a correctly-shaded impression in a single printing operation.

We discussed the case of Wickers and Furlong in the companion interference in No. 386 Patent Appeal Docket so fully, that we repeat here the matters relevant to this issue discussed in that case. Mainly for the reasons there stated, the three tribunals of the Patent Office agree that Wickers and Furlong were not the prior inventors of the issue of this interference. The Examiner of Interferences decided in this case as in the others concerning related issues, that Wickers and Furlong conceived the invention defined in counts one and two of this issue in 1897 but did not reduce it to practice prior to their filing date, January 22, 1902, and, therefore, are not entitled to prevail in this interference.

We concur in his conclusion that Albert, who has taken no testimony, and who filed his application involved in this interference June 15, 1901, should be limited to his record date, but if he be given the benefit of certain of his foreign patents introduced here, the date of his conception and reduction to practice would be no earlier than April 16, 1901. This date would not benefit him nor entitle him to prevail over Upham who conceived this invention in 1899, and filed his application on January 22, 1901. Therefore, the Examiner held that Upham was entitled to prevail over Wickers and Furlong, who had a prior conception of the invention here involved, and who were not diligent in reducing it to practice after Upham's entry into the field. He also decided that Upham was entitled to prevail over Albert, whose date of conception and reduction to practice is subsequent to Upham's filing date.

The Examiners-in-Chief affirmed the decision of the Examiner of Interferences. They observed that the first and third counts of this issue are specific in that they require that the pressure by means of which the graduations in the printing-surface of the plate are produced, shall be applied to the face of the plate instead of to the back thereof as is required in other issues of the series of interferences to which this interference belongs. The Examiners-in-Chief also remarked that count two in this case covers broadly, subjecting one side of a printing-block supported upon a yielding body of material to the action of a "relief" form under pressure, thereby altering the level parts of the printing-surface, and they hold that even if Wickers and Furlong be entitled to a date of conception, which the Examiners say they are not, although their application of January 22, 1902, discloses the subject-matter of this count, they were not exercising diligence when Upham entered the field and therefore, if Upham were only entitled to the date of his interfering application, priority of invention had been properly awarded to Upham. Albert here disappears. Wickers and Furlong alone appeal to the Commissioner, who affirmed the decision of the Examiner-in-Chief and concurred with them upon the grounds stated and the Commissioner also determined that Upham conceived the invention in 1899, but did not reduce it to practice prior to the date of his application, January 22,   Commis that Upham was entitled to the award of priority whether he was the first or last to conceive the invention. From this third adverse decision in the Patent Office, Wickers and Furlong appealed to this court.

Upham alleged that he conceived the invention involved in the issue of this interference in March, 1899, and reduced it to practice about three months thereafter. He was then employed in the establishment of the *Youth's Companion* in Boston, when the idea came to him that he could treat a plate by putting an "overlay" or "make-ready" in the face of the plate.

Appellants' counsel contend that Upham's testimony that in the summer of 1899 he produced a satisfactory plate, having a graduated printed surface, and that he made the plate by using a reverse overlay upon the face of the plate with a thin piece of cardboard between the reverse overlay and the plate, and subjected it to pressure, and that the plate produced in this manner was printed from, without the use of any overlay upon the impression cylinder, is not sufficiently corroborated and that evidence is lacking because neither the plate nor the reverse overlay used nor an imprint from the plate was produced. It is insisted that his exhibits were all recently made. It is argued that his testimony of the conception of the invention and all he did prior to March, 1900, must be considered as abandoned experiments and that a memorandum prepared by Upham and signed by witnesses at the last-mentioned time shows his process is crude and that Upham is not entitled to priority over Wickers and Furlong in respect of the first and second counts of this issue. Appellants' counsel concede that as to the third count of this issue, Wickers and Furlong can claim no priority because there is no foundation for it in their application.

Upham testified that in October, 1900, he caused to be made for him by an electrotyper, a thin copper plate from which, in November following, he had made two original half-tones which he treated by his process and used on a printing-press. He described several other experiments in the same year of like character and used them on a printing-press without a make-ready on the impression-cylinder. In March, 1900, he wrote a description of one of his processes and of the object of the process which he signed and caused to be signed by two witnesses. He testified to a disclosure to his attorney late in 1899 and his application was filed on January 21, 1901, thereby becoming the senior party in the series of these interferences.

James Humphry, in charge of the press department of the *Youth's Companion*, testified that before Upham went to Texas late in 1899, he had experimented on cut   to do away with overlays and pressing a reverse overlay   of the plate. Humphry helped Upham proce   to and testifies that from it Upham produced a plate treated by his process and used it in printing the regular edition of the *Youth's Companion* for January 3, 1901. Malcolm and Anderson in material points corroborate Upham. Upham's attorney testifies that he, Upham, specifically disclosed the process of his invention to his attorney about a year before December 20, 1900, when the attorney was instructed to prepare Upham's application, and in the spring of 1900, his attorney says that Upham submitted to him an electrotype having a graduated surface as described in his application, and the witnesses to Upham's written memorandum, which strongly confirms Upham's testimony, testified that they affixed their signatures at the date named in that instrument. It would appear that Upham may be entitled to an earlier date than that of his application but as he was the senior party, it is not essential in this case to further consider this point. We do not hesitate to affirm the decision and *we do hereby affirm* the decision of the Commissioner of Patents and the clerk of this court will certify this opinion and decision to the Commissioner of Patents in accordance with law.

[Court of Appeals of the District of Columbia.]

IN RE WICKERS AND FURLONG.

Decided February 5, 1907.

(129 O. G., 2074.)

1. TWO APPLICATIONS FOR SAME INVENTION—EARLIER INVOLVED IN INTERFERENCE—REFUSAL OF PATENT ON LATER.

Where a party whose application is involved in interference proceedings presents another application based upon the invention involved in the interference, it is proper to refuse a patent upon the later application until the interference has been terminated. In such case it is just to suspend action on the later application.

2. PATENTABILITY—PROCESS OF MAKING-READY PRINTING-PLATES.

After the generic process of preparing printing-plates with projecting portions on the back thereof and pressing these to the face of the plates, giving a graduated surface, has been claimed and the specific mode of preparing the plates by the use of photolithographing and etching has also been claimed there is nothing left to claim in a separate application as a separate invention as a process of making-ready printing-plates. What remains would appear to be a mere carrying out of the purposes of the original invention, which ought to be obvious to skilled workers in the art.

Mr. J. H. Griffin for the appellant.
Mr. Fairfax Bayard for the Commissioner of Patents.

McCOMAS, J.:

In this case upon the application of Wickers and Furlong for a patent for an improvement in process of making printing-plates, filed March 1, 1905, these applicants appealed from the decision of the Principal Examiner, rejecting the claims of the application on the issues of three interferences in which certain applications of these appellants were involved. These interferences are *Wickers and Furlong* v. *Weinwurm*, No. 23,741; *Lammers* v. *Wickers and Furlong* v. *McKee*, No. 22,404, (No. 388 Patent Appeal Docket;) and *Wickers and Furlong* v. *McKee*, No. 22,405, (No. 389 Patent Appeal Docket.) The Examiner rejected certain claims on a British patent to Weinwurm, No. 14,508 of 1901. The Examiners-in-Chief affirmed the Examiner in refusing to allow the claims brought before them upon appeal, holding that the issues in the aforenamed interferences when considered together, substantially covered the real invention of this application of Wickers and Furlong, and suggesting doubt if these appellants can obtain a valid patent if the decisions in these interferences be adverse to them. Wickers and Furlong appealed to the Commissioner of Patents from this decision of the Examiners-in-Chief affirming the rejection by the Primary Examiner of the following claims:

1. The method of making printing-plates which consists in photographing the subject to be printed on the front end on the back of a metallic plate, such photographs being in register with each other; etching both surfaces of the plate; and deflecting the metal of the plate from the printing-face toward the back and producing a graduated printing-surface on the front of the plate.

2. The method of making printing-plates, which consists in photographing a subject to be printed on the respective faces of a sensitized plate; etching both faces of said plate, and subjecting the plate to pressure to cause elevations and depressions to appear in the printing-surface of the plate.

3. The method of making printing-plates which consists in sensitizing both faces of a metallic plate; producing photographic prints on the respective faces of said plate; and pressing the plate to cause elevations and depressions to appear in the printing-surface of said plate.

4. The method of making printing-plates, which consists in sensitizing both sides of a metallic plate; exposing said plate and a negative to the light and producing photographic prints in register with each other on the respective faces of said plate; etching both surfaces of the plate, and forcing the metal from the front toward the back of the plate to cause elevations and depressions to appear in the printing-surface of the plate.

5. The method of making printing-plates which consists in photographing a subject on the respective faces of a metallic plate; producing in the back of the plate elevations and depressions at predetermined places where the printing is to be respectively light and heavy, and subsequently producing similar depressions and elevations in the printing-surface of the plate by pressing forward the elevations produced in the back of the plate.

6. The method of making printing-plates which consists in photographing a subject on the respective faces of a metallic plate; etching both faces of the plate and producing on the back thereof elevations and depressions at predetermined places where the printing is to be respectively light and heavy, and pressing the plate to cause such elevations and depressions to appear in the etched front of the plate.

7. The method of making printing-plates which consists in photographing a subject on the respective faces of a metallic plate; etching the front of the plate; etching portions of the back of the plate deeper than the front thereof and producing elevations and depressions on the back; and deflecting the metal of the plate to cause the elevations and depressions of the back to appear on the etched front of the plate.

8. The improvement in the art of preparing printing-plates which consists in etching a picture of a subject on both sides of a metallic plate, and successively etching the back of the plate to produce thereon surfaces in different levels corresponding to the lights and shadows of the subject.

9. The improvement in the art of preparing printing-plates which consists in successively etching away various portions of a picture of a subject on the back of a metallic plate to various depths, thereby producing thereon surfaces in different levels corresponding to the lights and tones of a picture on the face.

10. The improvement in the art of preparing printing-plates which consists in producing on the back of a plate a picture of a subject to be printed; and then subjecting the back of the plate to successive etchings to produce thereon elevations and depressions at predetermined places opposite to the places on the face where the printing is to be respectively light and heavy.

11. The improvement in the art of preparing printing-plates which consists in photographing a subject to be printed on the back of a metallic plate; applying resist to said back; etching the exposed parts of the plate; and alternately removing parts of the resist and exposing the plate to an etching fluid to produce successive gradations in level of the back.

12. The method of making printing-plates which consists in etching depressions upon the rear side of a plate in register with a picture which has been produced on the front side of the plate, and subsequently subjecting the plate to pressure to produce gradations in the level of a printing-surface on the front of said plate.

13. The method of producing printing-plates which consists in protographing upon the face of the plate a picture to be printed, photographing upon the back of the plate a similar picture but reversely arranged with reference to the picture on the face of the plate and in register with it; etching both pictures on the plate the one on the back being etched below the surface in parts corresponding to lighter tones; and subsequently pressing the plate from the back to produce gradations in the level of a printing-surface on the etched face of the plate.

14. The method of producing printing-plates which consists in photographing upon the face of the plate a picture to be printed; photographing a similar but reversely-arranged picture on the back of the plate in register; etching both faces of the plate, and producing on the back of the plate elevations and depressions, and then pressing the elevated portions of the plate toward the face thereof.

15. The method of producing printing-plates which consists in photographing a picture to be printed upon the face of the plate; photographing a similar reversely-arranged picture on the back of the plate in register with the picture on the face; etching both faces of the plate and then further etching the back of the plate to produce elevations and depressions thereon, and then subjecting the back and face to pressures to produce gradations in the level of the etched printing-surface on the face of the plate.

16. The improvement in the art of making printing-plates which consists in etching a reversely-arranged photograph of the picture in a graduated manner so as to produce elevations and depressions on one face of the plate, then

forcing the elevated portions of the plate toward the face thereof, thereby graduating the levels in a printing-surface on such plate.

17. The process of making printing-plates which consists in producing on the back of the plate a reversely-arranged facsimile of the picture to be printed upon the face of the plate, then etching the back of the plate to successively greater depths from the dark to the high lights, and subsequently pressing the depressed portions of the plate toward the back so as to produce gradations in the level of a printing-surface on the face of the plate.

18. The method of making printing-plates which consists in producing on the face of the plate a photograph of the subject to be printed; photographing the subject to be printed on the back of the plate and in register with the photograph on the front; etching the face of the plate; etching the back of the plate to different depths in a graduated manner; and subjecting the plate to pressure to produce a graduated printing-surface on the front of the same.

19. The process of making printing-plates which consists in photographing reversely-arranged pictures in register with each other on the front and back of a metallic plate; etching a relief-surface on the back of the plate; and then applying pressure to the back and front of the plate, thereby producing permanent differences in profile in the printing-surface of the plate.

20. The process of making printing-plates which consists in photographing pictures on the front and back of a sensitized plate; etching the back of the plate to produce depressions and elevations corresponding, but arranged reversely to, those which are to appear in the face of the plate, and then pressing the plate to produce gradations in the level of a printing-surface on the face of the plate.

21. The method of preparing printing-plates which consists in producing an impression or picture in a metallic plate; etching the plate, and subjecting the plate to differential pressures whereby a graduated printing-surface is produced on a face of said plate.

22. The method of preparing printing-plates which consists in photographing a picture of a subject to be printed on a metallic plate; etching the plate; and in the thickness of said plate, and subjecting the plate to pressure to thereby displace the metal and produce a graduated printing-surface on the plate.

23. The method of preparing printing-plates which consists in photographing a picture of a subject to be printed on a metllic plate; etching the plate; and subjecting the plate to variable pressures whereby a graduated printing-surface is produced on a face of the plate.

24. That improvement in the art of preparing printing-plates which consists in sensitizing both faces of a metallic plate, and photographically printing from a single negative by exposing the sensitized surfaces successively to light through said negative.

The Commissioner also rejected all of these claims on the issues of three pending interferences and particularly upon the following counts:

8. The improvement in the art of preparing printing-plates which consists in etching a picture of a subject on both sides of a metallic plate, and successively etching the back of the plate to produce thereon surfaces in different levels corresponding to the lights and shadows of the subject.

9. The improvement in the art of preparing printing-plates which consists in successively etching away various portions of a picture of a subject on the back of a metallic plate to various depths, thereby producing thereon surfaces in different levels corresponding to the lights and tones of a picture on the face.

10. The improvement in the art of preparing printing-plates which consists in producing on the back of a plate a picture of a subject to be printed; and then subjecting the back of the plate to successive etchings to produce thereon elevations and depressions at predetermined places opposite to the places on the face where the printing is to be respectively light and heavy.

11. The improvement in the art of preparing printing-plates which consists in photographing a subject to be printed on the back of a metallic plate; applying resist to said back; etching the exposed parts of the plate; and alternately removing parts of the resist and exposing the plate to an etching fluid to produce successive gradations in level of the back.

24. That improvement in the art of preparing printing-plates which consists in sensitizing both faces of a metallic plate, and photographically printing from a single negative by exposing the sensitized surfaces successively to light through said negative.

Claims 8, 9, 10, 11, and 24 were also rejected on the British patent to Weinwurm No. 14,508 of 1902. The Commissioner held after a careful review that the issues of the interferences we have mentioned cover substantially the real invention of this application of Wickers and Furlong and that the appeal claims are not distinguishable from them. We will not here repeat his clear exposition in his opinion. He fully sustained the Examiner and Board of Examiners-in-Chief holding that the separate matters in all the claims brought up on appeal were involved in the issues in interference before mentioned. The Commissioner also regarded the decision of the Assistant Commissioner who had affirmed the rejection of the five claims mentioned on the British patent to Weinwurm and held that claims 8, 9, 10, 11, and 24 are not patentable over the British patent to Weinwurm. From this ruling, Wickers and Furlong have appealed to this court.

We have disposed of the series of interferences involving the questions sought to be raised by this appeal from the decision of the Commissioner of Patents refusing to grant a patent for a process of making printing-plates to these appellants upon their application filed March 1, 1905. The case of the interference of these appellants against Weinwurm is not before us. We are convinced that the claims of the application in which this appeal is taken, are for the same invention involved in the interferences named in the record in this case and we concur with the tribunals of the Patent Office that it would be improper to grant a patent under the circumstances to the appellants upon this application.

It is so well established that two valid patents may not be issued to a party based upon the same patentable invention that we need not cite authorities. It is the practice in the Patent Office where an application is allowed to a party to reject any other applications of the same party upon the allowed application unless such other applications claimed a clearly different invention from that claimed in the allowed application. In this way the Patent Office limits an *inventor* to a single patent based upon a single invention. It appears proper therefore in a case where a party whose application is involved in pending interference proceedings presents another application based upon the invention involved in an interference, to refuse a patent upon the later application until the interference has terminated. A different course would involve inextricable confusion. To suspend action upon such an application appears to us to be just. In the interference proceedings there is ample opportunity for the appellants to raise the question of the sufficiency of their opponent's application. We greatly doubt whether the affidavits in this record presented for the consideration of this court and controverting the sufficiency of disclosure found in the Weinwurm application in interference, could be profitably considered by this court. That question should come before us upon testimony taken in the interference proceeding. Since all the tribunals of the Patent Office concur in holding that all the appealed claims are for the same invention as claims of the appellants' earlier applications, involved in interference proceedings, we should hesitate to differ with these expert tribunals. The reasoning in several of these decisions is most persuasive that after the generic process of preparing printing-plates with projecting portions on the back thereof and pressing these to the face of the plates giving a graduated surface has been claimed, and the specific mode of preparing the plates by the use of photographing and etching has also been claimed, that there is nothing left to claim in a separate application as a separate invention as a process of making-ready printing-plates. What remains would appear to be a mere carrying out of the purposes of the original invention, matters which ought to be obvious to skilled workers in this art.

As we concur with the Commissioner upon this general ground for rejecting these claims, we need not discuss the rejection of five of these claims on the British patents to Weinwurm.

The decision of the Commissioner of Patents in refusing to issue a patent to the appellants upon their application in which this appeal comes before us *is affirmed* and the clerk of this court will certify this opinion and decision to the Commissioner of Patents in accordance with law.

[Court of Appeals of the District of Columbia.]

THE UNION DISTILLING COMPANY *v.* SCHNEIDER.

Decided February 5, 1907.

(129 O. G., 2503.)

1. INTERFERENCE—INTERLOCUTORY DECISION.

A decision of the Commissioner of Patents dissolving an interference is not a final order.

2. SAME—SAME—JURISDICTION OF COURT OF APPEALS OF DISTRICT OF COLUMBIA.
The court of appeals has no jurisdiction to consider an appeal from a
decision of the Commissioner of Patents which is not a final order, and
such an appeal will be dismissed.

Mr. A. E. Wallace for the appellant.
Mr. Fairfax Bayard for the Commissioner of Patents.

ROBB, *J.:*

This court has no jurisdiction to entertain the appeal herein. We
dismissed *Podlesak and Podlesak* v. *McInnerney*, November 21, 1906,
for want of jurisdiction. That was an appeal from an interlocutory
order of the Commissioner of Patents in an interference proceeding
dissolving the interference and remanding the case to the Primary
Examiner for further action not inconsistent with the views of the
Commissioner. It was urged that such an order was in effect a final
order, and, therefore, appealable to this court, but we entertained the
opposite view and dismissed the appeal. Exactly the same question
is involved here. An interference was declared in the Patent Office
between appellant, as an applicant for the registration of a trade-
mark, and John R. Schneider, a rival applicant here designated as
the appellee. Before the issue in that interference was determined
the Patent Office discovered evidence that another firm had used the
same mark in the same business prior to the date set up in the applications of the parties to the interference. The Examiner thereupon
dissolved the interference, from which ruling an appeal was taken to
the Commissioner whose opinion follows:

This is an appeal by The Union Distilling Co. from the decision of the Examiner of Trade-Marks dissolving the above-entitled interference on the ground
that the mark of the issue is a known trade-mark which was adopted and
used by another prior to the date of adoption alleged by the present applicants.

As evidence of such prior adoption and use the Examiner calls attention to
the mark registered by Mills, Johnson and Company on March 14, 1871.

The appellant calls attention to the fact that the registration cited was made
under the unconstitutional act of 1870 and to the further fact that the period of
thirty years for which the registration was granted has expired. It therefore
urges that such registration is not a valid reference, since it is not *prima facie*
evidence of ownership by the registrant. The question here raised was considered and decided in the case of the Star Distillery Company, (C. D., 1905, 493;
119 O. G., 964,) wherein it was held that registrations under the act of 1870 are
to be regarded as proper references until overcome in some way by the applicant.
The appellant asks that, if the ruling in the above-cited case is adhered to, it be
permitted to overcome the registration as a reference by an interference proceeding. It is clear, however, that there can be no interference, since interferences
can be declared only as to applications and existing registrations. The appellant's remedy would seem to be not at interference, but a showing in the form
of affidavits tending to overcome the presumption that the registrant under the
act of 1870 is still the owner of the mark. If such affidavits are filed a continuance of the present interference will necessarily follow.

The Examiner was right in dissolving the interference in the absence of a showing tending to overcome the reference cited, and therefore his decision *is affirmed.*

It is apparent that this appeal is not from a final order refusing registration, but from a mere interlocutory order from which no appeal lies to this court. Appellant's application has not yet been denied. It may be that, unless it satisfies the Patent Office that another firm had not previously adopted and used the trade-mark, or having previously adopted and used it subsequently abandoned it, its application will be denied and a final order to that effect entered. But such an order has not been made, and this appeal must, therefore, be dismissed for the want of jurisdiction, and it is so ordered.

The clerk of the court will certify this opinion and the proceedings in this court to the Commissioner of Patents, according to law. *Dismissed.*

[Court of Appeals of the District of Columbia.]

HORINE *v.* WENDE.

Decided April 10, 1907.

(129 O. G., 2858.)

1. INTERFERENCE—APPEAL TO COURT—AMENDMENT OF REASONS OF APPEAL.

Although neither the rules of the Court of Appeals of the District of Columbia nor of the Patent Office mention amendments to the reasons of appeal, when such amendment is made in due time to correct an assignment of error that may not be sufficiently specific or some inadvertence in its preparation and no possible injury could be done the opposing party, there appears to be no reason why it should not be permitted.

2. SAME—PRIORITY—SECOND INTERFERENCE—RES ADJUDICATA.

Where judgment is rendered in an interference proceeding in the Patent Office holding that the issue was limited to matters not found in certain exhibits upon which a party relies for an award of priority, although such party contends to the contrary, and no appeal is taken from such holding and the case is finally decided adversely to such party, *Held* that in a subsequent interference between the same parties on an issue which is the same as the prior issue, with the exception that in the second interference such limitations were omitted, the question of priority is *res adjudicata.*

Mr. C. E. Pickard for the appellant.
Mr. Chas. D. Davis and *Mr. Geo. E. Waldo* for the appellee.

SHEPARD, *J.:*

This is an interference proceeding involving priority of invention of a manifolding apparatus adapted to make, simultaneously, an original and two or three copies. The original is retained in a record-book while two of the copies in the form of slips connected in pairs are adapted to be removed. The invention is primarily designed for use by weigh-masters in stock-yards, the record of the number and weight of the animals, and the names of seller and buyer being entered in the record-book, and a duplicate slip given to the seller and buyer respectively.

The issue, as declared, contained six counts. The Examiner of Interferences awarded priority to Wende on counts 1, 2, 3, 5, and 6, and to Horine on count 4. ' Both parties appealed to the Examiners-in-Chief who affirmed the former decision as to counts 1, 2, 3, 4 and 5, and reversed it as to count 6. Horine, alone, appealed from this decision as to counts 1, 2, 3, and 5, to the Commissioner of Patents, who affirmed the same. Horine then prosecuted this appeal which involves said counts 1, 2, 3, and 5, reading as follows:

1. The combination of a record-book, a hinged support connected with said record-book and adapted to fold over upon a leaf thereof, an impression-sheet secured to said support at a point removed from the hinge thereof, said impression-sheet being adapted to fold over upon and present a prepared surface to the surface of said support which is uppermost when it rests upon a leaf of the record-book, and one or more copy-slips arranged to receive impressions from said impression-sheet when it is folded upon said support.

2. The combination of a record-book, a hinged support connected with said record-book and adapted to fold over upon a leaf thereof, an impression-sheet secured to a free edge of said support and adapted to fold over upon and present a prepared surface to the surface thereof which is uppermost when said support rests upon a leaf of the record-book, and one or more copy slips arranged to receive impressions from said impression-sheet when it is folded upon said support. ꞏ

3. The combination of a record-book, a hinged support connected with said record-book and adapted to fold over upon a leaf thereof, an impression-sheet secured to the edge of said support opposite the hinge thereof and adapted to fold over and present a prepared surface to the surface of said support which is uppermost when it rests upon a leaf of the record-book, and one or more copy-slips arranged to receive impressions from said impression-sheet when it is folded upon said support.

5. The combination of a record-book, a support swingingly connected with said record-book, parallel with the side edge thereof and adapted to fold over upon a leaf thereof, an impression-sheet secured to said support near a free edge thereof, and adapted to fold over upon and present a prepared surface to the surface thereof which is uppermost when said support rests upon a leaf of the record-book, and one or more copy-slips arranged to receive impressions from said impression-sheet when it is folded upon said support.

The record shows that Horine filed his application July 3, 1897, and that Wende filed December 21, 1898. On June 19, 1900, an interference was declared between the two in an issue of two counts, to which was subsequently added a third. These read as follows:

1. A manifolding-book comprising primary leaves secured together at one edge, a support hinged adjacent to the free edges of said primary leaves when the book is in position for writing, said support being adapted to be folded upon said primary leaves, secondary leaves secured to that side of said hinged support which is exposed when said support is folded upon said primary leaves, tertiary leaves attached to and adapted to fold over said secondary leaves, and transfer paper secured to the book and comprising prepared surfaces adapted to

be disposed in contact with the exposed secondary leaf and the tertiary leaf attached thereto, said transfer-paper being movable toward and from the primary leaves with the secondary leaves.

2. A manifolding-book comprising primary leaves secured together at one edge, a support hinged adjacent to the free edges of said primary leaves when the book is in position for writing, said support being adapted to be turned back upon said primary leaves, secondary leaves secured to that side of said hinged support which is exposed when said support is turned upon said primary leaves, tertiary leaves attached to and adapted to fold over said secondary leaves, quadruplicate leaves arranged one beneath each primary leaf and adapted to be turned therewith and transfer-paper secured to the book and comprising prepared surfaces adapted to be disposed in contact with the exposed secondary leaf and the tertiary leaf attached thereto and leaving a prepared surface exposed, said transfer-paper being movable toward and from the primary leaves with the secondary leaves.

3. The combination with a record-book, of a base or tablet adapted to be inserted between the leaves of the book, said base or tablet being pivotally mounted parallel with and near the edges of the leaves of the record-book, whereby it may be folded over upon and away from such leaves, one or more copy slips or sheets carried thereby and one or more carbon or impression sheets secured to the free edge of said base or tablet and adapted to fold over and upon the copy-slips carried by the base or tablet.

In the preliminary statement of Horine in this interference, it was alleged that he conceived the invention September 1, 1896, explained it to others on or about September 1, 1896, made sketches about September 1, 1896, and a model on or about the same day; that about November 1, 1896, he took steps to have a full-size device made embodying said invention, which was completed on or about November 15, 1896, and immediately tested and put to successful use. Wende's statement alleged conception about June 1, 1896, explanation to others on or about the same day, construction of a model on or about August 1, 1896, construction of a full-size manifolding-book embodying the invention on or about September 1, 1896, and the filling of Orders therefor made by the Stock-Yards Company during January, 1897.

Testimony was taken on the issue joined, and on May 26, 1903, the Examiner of Interferences decided in favor of Horine. This was in turn affirmed by the Examiners-in-Chief and the Commissioner; the final decision having been made January 2, 1904. On February 20, 1904, Horine filed amendments broadening the claims of the original application which were further amended from time to time until he succeeded in obtaining the final approval of the Office. Patent was finally issued to him covering some of these broader claims, on January 3, 1905. On February 7, 1905, Wende filed an amendment to the claims of his former application, canceling the former and substituting six new claims, copied in part from Horine's patent. In the letter accompanying this proposed amendment he referred to the fact that his former claims had been rejected under the decision in the interference, and stated that the new claims are designed to cover broadly a structure adapted to accomplish the objects of the invention as they relate to providing a book of the type shown in U. S. Patent No. 556,484—

so constructed and arranged that the leaves which receive original entries may be retained in the book as a permanent record, as set forth in the statement of the objects of the invention.

He then further stated:

In the interference in which this application was involved, attorney for appellant urged among other things, that Wende was entitled to an award of priority of invention of the issues for the reason that "Horine Exhibits Wende Books Nos. 1, 2 and 6 " were a reduction to practice of the issues and antedated Horine's date of conception. The Commissioner held that these exhibits were not reductions to practice of the issues of the invention, but that they had broad features in common with the invention in controversy and that it was possible that those broad features were patentable. Since the decision of said interference a patent has issued to Horine, the other party to said interference, containing claims which cover the invention broadly.

New claims have, therefore, been prepared covering these broad features, applicant being confident that he can establish to the satisfaction of the Patent Office officials that he was the prior inventor of the broad features referred to by the Commissioner.

In order to determine the question of priority as it relates to the invention of the broad issues, applicant has also included in his amendment claims copied from said patent to M. F. Horine, issued Jan. 3, 1903, No. 779,042.

To establish his claim of priority as regards the broad invention, applicant will rely largely upon the books or apparatus relied upon by him in the former interference and identified as " Horine Exhibits Wende Books Nos. 1, 2 and 6."

The application, with the amended claims, was allowed, and on February 28, 1905, the present interference was declared between the applicant and the patentee, Horine, the issue of which, and the proceedings thereon in the Patent Office, have been hereinabove recited.

The amendments of each party after the determination of the first interference related to the claims of each applicant, the description and specifications remain as originally made.

Horine moved to dissolve this second interference on the ground, among others:

That Wende is estopped by reason of the adverse final decision in a former interference between the same parties on the same applications from making the claims of the issues.

This motion was sustained by the Primary Examiner, but on appeal to the Commissioner his decision was reversed, and the motion to dissolve denied. (C. D., 1905, 376; 118 O. G., 1070.)

The parties entered into a stipulation making all of the depositions in the former case, and all exhibits in connection therewith, evidence in the pending case, and further providing that the record of each party in the present case shall consist of his record in the former case, together with all exhibits offered in connection therewith, and any additional depositions, exhibits or other evidence that may be offered. Wende took the depositions of several witnesses in addition to the evidence taken in the former trial case. Horine relied upon his former record.

Wende's second preliminay statement alleged conception " during the summer of 1896," explanation to others during the same summer, the making of full-size books, embodying the invention, during the latter part of August, 1896, and others about January 1, 1897, which were used by the Stock-Yards Company in January, 1897. This statement is substantially the same as the one in the first interference.

Before proceeding to consider the first question in order, which is the effect of the decision in the first interference, that the appellant contends was a final determination of the matters involved in the second, a preliminary question must be disposed of.

Before an appeal can be taken from an appealable decision of the Commissioner of Patents to the court, notice, and reasons of appeal must be filed in the Patent Office within forty days (exclusive of Sundays and legal holidays) from the date of the decision appealed from; and petition for appeal to this court, with a transcript of the record, must be filed within forty days (exclusive of Sundays and legal holidays,) from the time of giving the notice of appeal before mentioned. Notice of this appeal was given January 7, 1907, and reasons of appeal filed therewith. The ninth reason is:

That the Assistant Commissioner erred in not awarding priority of invention as to counts 1, 2, 3, and 5 to Horine, and in awarding priority as to such counts to Wende.

On February 1, 1907, notice was served on Wende's attorney of record, to the effect that under the ninth reason of appeal, aforesaid, appellant would ask a reversal of the decision on the ground that the decision in the former case was conclusive of the matters litigated in this interference. Pursuant to this notice of amendment the same was filed in the Patent Office, on February 14, 1907, and made a part of the transcript of the record filed in this court February 18, 1907. The petition for appeal filed in this court in accordance with its rules, specifically assigns this as one of the questions to be determined on appeal.

Without considering the point whether this court will take notice of a fundamental error, apparent upon the record, that may not have been specially assigned in the reasons of appeal which is in the nature of the ordinary assignment of error in actions at law or in equity,—or whether the particular error is embraced within the ninth reason of appeal, as broadly written, we are of the opinion that the amendment of the reasons of appeal should be entertained. Neither the rules of

. The difficulty in the application of the principle, that so frequently occurs in ordinary litigation, is often increased by the peculiar character of the proceedings in the Patent Office. The proceedings are *ex parte* during the process of amendment, under the suggestions of the Office, leading up to the allowance of the application; and it is only when the interference has been declared and the preliminary statements of the conflicting parties filed, that either has information of the proceedings of the other. The issue of the interference is prepared in the Patent Office. There are no formal pleadings. The applications which contain the descriptions of the invention, and the claims that relate to the matter of the issue, are the foundations of the case. The preliminary statements are required merely to give the respective dates of conception and reduction to practice of the invention described in the application, thereby fixing the boundaries of the evidence relied on for their establishment. To ascertain what facts have been finally adjudicated in an interference, resort must be had to the several applications, the preliminary statements, the claims in issue, the evidence produced, and the decisions of the tribunals of the Patent Office. These decisions, unlike the ordinary judgments of courts of law, are opinions reciting the grounds upon which the .award of priority is made, consisting of conclusions in respect of matters both of law and fact.

In this case we have before us the entire record of the former interference, including the applications and claims of the respective parties, their preliminary statements, the evidence and exhibits, as well as the decisions of the several tribunals of the. Patent Office which passed on the case in succession. But little additional evidence has been given in the present case and that wholly on behalf of the appellee. The determination of the second case depended in the main upon the evidence introduced in the former case.

The conditions recited are analogous to those presented in the recent case of *Blackford* v. *Wilder,* (*ante,* 491: 127 O. G., 1255: 28 App. D. C., 555,) in which it was held that the decision in the first interference between the same parties, was conclusive of matters litigated in the second. There are some differences between the two cases, it is true, but they do not materially affect the application of the governing principle. In *Blackford* v. *Wilder,* somewhat broader claims had been narrowed, pursuant to the requirements of the Office, in order to obtain allowance of patentability at all. After final award of priority to Blackford, by judgment of this court reversing the decision of the Commissioner, Wilder was permitted to amend his claims. His amendment broadened the former claims by omitting a specific feature of the issue of the former interference. This, if finally allowed, would have enabled him to obtain a patent dominating *that to* which Blackford had become entitled by reason of the final judgment before rendered in his favor. On the amended claims, another interference was declared between him and Blackford. Wilder's application had been drawn upon a construction called Exhibit E, on which he had chiefly relied in the former interference as evidence of his completion of the invention of the issue therein. He was permitted in the second case to introduce evidence to show that this exhibit had in it the necessary lighting member when produced in the first case. Of the construction of this exhibit there was no doubt, but the existence of the lighting member was one of the questions expressly decided against him. His amended claims broadened the invention into a claim for a burner, omitting the particular lighting member, but in other respects covering the invention described in his and Blackford's applications. The award of priority in the second case to Wilder, was reversed on the ground that the decision in the former case was conclusive of the matter in issue. It was said:

> The parties are the same. The applications are the same, and disclose the invention of each issue. The constructions relied on, respectively, as evidencing conception and reduction to practice of both issues are the same. The fundamental facts of both cases are the same.

Reference was made to the peculiar conditions of practice in the Patent Office permitting amendments after decisions in interference, and to rules thereof, devised to meet, by the application of the principle of estoppel by former decision, as far as possible, conditions that would necessarily call therefor. One of the early decisions of the Commissioner of Patents was also referred to in which the rule was declared that while a defeated party might be allowed to make additional patentable claims that could not be made by the prevailing party, none such should be allowed that could by any latitude of construction be held to embrace matter common to the structures of both parties. (C. D., 1891, 107; 56 O. G., 141.)

In *Corry and Barker* v. *Trout* v. *McDermott*, (C. D., 1904, 144; 110 O. G., 306) it was again said by the Commissioner:

> The declaration of a second interference between the same applications should be necessary only in rare cases and under very exceptional circumstances. It should not ordinarily be declared upon claims to the same device and differing from the first issue merely in scope. If a mere change in the scope of claims were considered good ground for a second interference, the number of successive interferences between the same parties would be practically unlimited, and the interference procedure would become an intolerable burden to applicants. The Office is justified in taking the decision as to priority of invention as *prima facie* evidence that the successful party was the first inventor not merely of the particular issue in controversy, but of the invention common to the two cases, whether more broadly or more specifically stated. The burden is upon the defeated party to show special circumstances of the particular case which make it improper to apply the decision to the other

claims presented. It is not sufficient that the claims differ, and that it is theoretically possible for one party to be the prior inventor as to the first and the other party prior inventor as to the second, for this would apply in all cases where the claims are not identical.

It was also said in *Blackford* v. *Wilder*, that the principle to be applied is the same declared in the case of two patents issued to the same party, where, to be valid, the second, if it covered matters described in the first, must be for something essentially distinct and separable from the invention covered by the first. (*Miller* v. *Eagle Mfg. Co.*, C. D., 1894, 147; 66 O. G., 845; 151 U. S., 186, 198.)

In the case at bar the amended claims were first presented by, and patented to Horine, and subsequently adopted by Wende; but it is not perceived that this makes any substantial difference between the two cases. The question nevertheless remains: What was determined in the first interference? It is unfortunate, perhaps, that the Patent Office practice permits amendment by the successful party to broaden the scope of his claims after a final decision in an interference upon claims for the same invention narrower in scope. That question, however, is not before us.

Assuming, for the purposes of this case, without so deciding at this time, that Wende would not be precluded by the decision in the first interference from making a new claim for a generic invention, separate and distinct from a mere specific form, (when not estopped by the conditions stated in *Bechman* v. *Wood*, (C. D., 1899, 453; 89 O. G., 2459; 15 App. D. C., 484, and cases therein cited,) we will inquire whether there is such a distinction between his new claims and those involved in the issue of the first interference.

The invention described is of a manifolding copying-book. the hinged support of which used in connection with the record-book and adapted to fold over so that one or more copy-slips may receive the impression, and be withdrawn for delivery to the buyer and seller, is the essential feature, as shown by its recurrence in the counts of each issue. That Wende considered, and urged that the counts of the first issue covered his entire invention. as described in his application, appears plainly in the decisions in the former case. His stock-yard's book represented the improved form of his invention, and it is said in the decisions in the present case, also embodied all of the counts of the present issue. This, however, was held, in the former case. to have been made subsequently to Horine's established date of reduction to practice. In addition thereto Wende relied upon said Exhibits 1, 2 and 6. In considering them the Commissioner said, in his then decision:

It may be admitted that Exhibits 1, 2 and 6 and the invention here in issue have certain features in common, and it is possible that those common features are patentable, but the issue contains limitations to features not present in both exhibits.

He then proceeded further to say:

One essential feature of this arrangement (that of the issue) is a support hinged adjacent to the free edges of the adjacent leaves. The support is adapted to be folded upon the primary leaves, and the secondary leaves are secured to it and carry the tertiary leaves. This hinged support is not present in Exhibits 1, 2 and 6, and consequently neither the leaves nor the carbon sheets are attached together and arranged in a way called for by the counts of the issue. If by a strained construction of the term it can be said that there is a support for the secondary leaves, it is not a support having the purpose and function of that in the present devices, and is, therefore, not the support called for by the issue.

The hinged support connected with the record-book and adapted to fold over for the making and removal of copy-slips, is clearly the controlling feature of the combination in both issues, and the only reason for holding in the first case that Exhibits 1, 2 and 6 did not embody the issue is on the specific ground, as stated by the Examiners-in-Chief, in their decision—

that they do not have these secondary and tertiary leaves secured to the hinged support or carried by such support.

It is the omission of these secondary and tertiary leaves that served, in their opinion, to distinguish the one issue from the other.

Wende may have been right in his view that Exhibits 1, 2 and 6 were sufficient to show conception, at least, of the invention of the first issue, as described in his application, without further broadening his claims so as to have a like broadening of the issue, in anticipation of technical objections. And the Commissioner may have been in error in his conclusion as regards this point; but whether so or not is not now an open question. Wende, satisfied with his own view, took his chances upon the issue as framed, and when defeated by the construction given to the issue and to his said exhibits, failed to appeal from the adverse decision. Whether that decision was right or wrong, cannot affect its operation as an estoppel. Having acquiesced in this decision, in that he failed to take a further appeal, he might, as above assumed, have made a new claim to a generic invention distinct from a purely specific one, if the former may be so regarded; but he could not by merely broadening the scope of the former claims to the invention described, bring the subject-matter into litigation again.

In our opinion, these broadened claims do not present the case of a generic invention separable and distinct from the matters covered by the former issue. As admitted in the decision of the Commissioner, before quoted, in which he declared that the exhibits did not show a necessary feature of the first issue, they and the invention in issue " have certain features in common." He declined, however, to give them what he called " a strained construction," that would bring them within that issue.   As before suggested, he may have been in error in refusing this construction.   Be that as it may, however, the most that we are able to say of the amended claims now is that they differ from those of the adjudicated issue in scope merely.   We are constrained to hold that this brings them under the rule as applied in *Blackford* v. *Wilder, supra,* and the Patent Office and other decisions recited therein with approval.

As this conclusion necessarily disposes of the appeal, there is no occasion to consider any other question in the case.

For the reasons given, the decision appealed from *will be reversed;* and it is so ordered.   The clerk will certify this decision to the Commissioner of Patents.   *Reversed.*

[Court of Appeals of the District of Columbia.]

KEMPSHALL *v.* ROYCE.

Decided March 5, 1907.

(129 O. G., 3162.)

1. INTERFERENCE—EVIDENCE—ADMISSIBILITY OF LETTER-PRESS COPIES.

   Where a party to an interference who is in possession of original copies of letters written in the regular course of business is asked to produce them, so that they may be used as evidence, but fails to do so, although he has ample time therefor, letter-press copies produced by the proper custodian of the same may be admitted with the same force and effect as the originals without throwing open the entire letter-press book to the inspection of the opposing party.

2. SAME—SAME—PRESUMPTION ARISING FROM FAILURE TO REBUT ADMISSIONS.

   Where the evidence indicated that the senior party derived the invention in controversy from the junior party and that prior to the junior party's application the senior party admitted that the invention was made by the junior party, *Held* that the election of the senior party to rely on his record date rather than to take the stand and explain such admission is significant evidence of their truth.

3. SAME—REFUSAL OF COMMISSIONER TO SUPPRESS EVIDENCE—NOT REVERSIBLE ERROR.

   The refusal of the Commissioner of Patents to suppress portions of a deposition because of the inclusion therein of alleged copies of letter-press copies of letters written by one party to the other is not reversible error.

Mr. W. W. Dodge for Kempshall.
Mr. C. P. Byrnes for Royce.

McCOMAS, *J.:*

This is an appeal by Kempshall from a decision of the Commissioner of Patents (C. D., 1906, 469; 125 O. G., 1347) awarding *priority* to Royce over Kempshall, patentee, upon an issue in interference stated in eleven counts relating to golf-balls. Less than half this number of counts should have sufficed. Three of the counts which follow contain all that is involved in this issue:

1. A playing-ball comprising a center piece built up of windings of elastic material, fibrous material interspersed in said windings, and held under pressure thereby, a layer of rubber thereon, and a suitable inclosing shell.

3. A playing-ball comprising a center piece built up of a continuous winding in miscellaneous directions of cured-rubber strip, fibrous material interspersed in said windings, said strip being continued into windings in miscellaneous directions to form a layer over said center piece, and a shell.

8. A playing-ball comprising a center piece built up of hair suitably compressed and intermingled in windings of cured rubber, and an inclosing shell.

Kempshall filed an application December 14, 1903, and a patent was granted to him May 31, 1904, for a golf-ball. Royce copied this patent in his application filed November 8, 1904. The Patent Office tribunals agree that there is invention in a center for a golf-ball of the peculiar construction we here consider. To form this center a cured-rubber strip, thin and flat, is wound while suitably compressed into a ball, and during the winding strands of hair are interspersed between the layers of rubber and intermingled in every direction so that the ball when wound is made up of hair and rubber. Before this invention it was old usage to wind a strip of rubber like that here used around a center in forming a golf-ball and the only invention found now by the Patent Office in the case before us was in substituting the hair interspersed in the winding in place of the separate center heretofore used in golf-balls.

Kempshall relied upon his filing date, December 14, 1903, and took no testimony. The testimony taken in behalf of Royce well supports his claim that he conceived this invention in October, 1903, and that disclosure and reduction to practice followed in November of that year. Kempshall and Royce are brothers-in-law and in the fall of 1903 Kempshall was president and Royce the secretary of the Kempshall Manufacturing Company which was engaged in making golf-balls. Royce was busy in the factory at Arlington, New Jersey; Kempshall was almost daily playing golf on the golf fields of certain clubs about Boston.

Royce claims to have disclosed the invention and to have sent golf-balls embodying the invention to Kempshall in November, 1903. It is conceded that the issue of this interference involves a question of originality rather than priority. This invention was made independently by one or the other of these two parties. The Examiner of Interferences concluded that the testimony in behalf of Royce did not satisfy him beyond a reasonable doubt that Royce originated this golf-ball center. The Examiners-in-Chief and the Commissioner of Patents found that Royce claimed to be the inventor and to have disclosed the invention to Kempshall prior to Kempshall's filing date, and that Royce was corroborated by Crane; that Kempshall does not claim to have disclosed the invention to Royce and does not deny his allegations and that there is no warrant for holding Kempshall, the patentee, to be the inventor.

There was a dispute respecting the admissibility in evidence of nine letters from Kempshall to Royce and of certain letters from Royce to Kempshall. The letters from Kempshall to Royce were fully proven and were properly admitted in evidence. Counsel for Royce on March 17, 1905, when testimony was first taken in behalf of Royce first secured a stipulation of record that letter-press copies of letters from Royce to Kempshall should be admitted and used in evidence as fully as if they were the original letters and when Royce, the secretary of the Kempshall Manufacturing Company was about to read from the letter-press copy-book of the company of which he was properly the custodian, Kempshall's counsel made frivolous objections. It appears from the record that Royce read from the letter-press book his own letter to Kempshall in Boston, dated November 2, 1903, despite objections from Kempshall's counsel, and thereupon counsel for Royce waived the stipulation just mentioned, and notified Kempshall's counsel to produce the original letters written by Royce in due course of business addressed to Mr. E. Kempshall, Westminster Hotel, Boston, and dated respectively upon certain dates in November and December specified. Kempshall's counsel did not offer to produce the letters, saying only that if in his opinion they were relevant and he could obtain them, he would produce them. The taking of the testimony continued during four different days and Kempshall's counsel made no effort to procure and produce any of these letters. Royce then proceeded to read from the letter-press book he had produced, his letter to Kempshall dated November 4, 1903, and then identified and introduced Kempshall's original letter to Royce purporting to be an answer to the last two letters just read from the letter-press book. And so the testimony proceeded, Royce reading from the letter-press book his letter to Kempshall, and next reading the original letter from Kempshall to him in response. In each instance counsel for Royce filed a copy of the letter which Royce read from the letter-press book produced in evidence. The examination of witnesses continued on March 17, 18, and 21st and was concluded on the 22d. In the beginning, the record shows that the parts of the letter-press book of the company containing letters of Royce to Kempshall was proffered in evidence after the stipulation had been entered into that letter-press copies of these letters should be used in evidence in lieu of the original and when Kempshall's counsel objected unless he should be permitted to examine the whole contents of the letter-press book containing the proffered letters and thereafter although notified to produce the originals on March 17th, he failed to produce the originals or give any account of them. Kempshall's counsel had time enough to produce the original letters and the letter-press copies of Royce's letters to Kempshall in the letter-press book were admissible, and from this book Royce read the letters which he swears were letter-press copies of his letters to Kempshall and Royce's counsel, who had liberty to examine these letter-press copies in the book, declined to examine them only because he was not permitted to examine all the other letters of the company's secretary or other agents contained in the same book. In every instance, the original letter from Kempshall to Royce admits of the receipt of Royce's letter read from the letter-press book or the receipt of golf-balls mentioned in Royce's letters to Kempshall. The record convinces us that during the days when Royce was being examined as a witness, Kempshall's counsel had ample time in which to produce the original letters and that the letter-press book containing the letters from Royce to Kempshall was introduced in evidence. The only irregularity that appears is the filing of copies of the letters contained in the letter-press book. Kempshall's counsel, we repeat, had an opportunity to inspect these letters and to cross-examine Royce respecting them. He did neither. His untenable objections and his conduct clearly show he was fully satisfied of the genuineness of these letters. Kempshall's counsel upon cross-examination asked Royce if all the statements contained in his letters were true and Royce swore that they were true and that he had produced all of the correspondence he had had with Kempshall relative to this matter, and we observe that many of the most material statements in the letters objected to, were affirmed by Royce upon his cross-examination.

The Commissioner of Patents overruled the motion of Kempshall's counsel to suppress the portions of Royce's deposition in which Royce's letters to Kempshall are included in the record. The Commissioner overruled this motion relying upon *McCormick* v. *Cleal*, (C. D., 1898, 492; 83 O. G., 1514; 12 App. D. C., 338.) We do not think the decision of the Commissioner constitutes reversible error in this case. We are satisfied that the oral testimony of Royce and of Crane and the letters of Kempshall fully support the conclusion reached by the Examiners-in-Chief and by the Commissioner, even if Royce's letters be not considered.

We will not in detail review the testimony which convinced the Examiners-in-Chief and the Commissioner that Royce first conceived and reduced to practice this invention.

Royce, in October, 1903, conceived the invention in the factory at Arlington, New Jersey, and then caused golf-balls to be made embodying it. He called them " Kempshall Flyer Click Balls." His statement of the mode of making these balls clearly brings them within the issue of this interference and Royce continued to manufacture these balls in large quantities from that time until he testified in this case. He was positive he had received no direction or suggestions from Kempshall, while Kempshall's original letters show that Royce had written him describing this new click-ball and that Kempshall was at first a severe critic of Royce's invention and dissuaded him from making them, and later Kempshall having tried the new click-balls sent by Royce to him was less hostile and finally became greatly impressed with their merits and in his letter to Royce dated December 15, 1903, says:

The click-ball is giving excellent satisfaction here and you deserve great credit. I think Mr. Chapman will see his way clear to continue your salary at $6,000 per year.

Soon thereafter Kempshall was so much pleased that he filed in his own name an application for a patent upon Royce's invention. Crane, vice-president and treasurer of the Kempshall Company, corroborates Royce, testifying that balls composed of hair and a continuous strip of rubber sheeting to form the core, were first brought to his attention by Royce in the fall of 1903, and that his company directed that these balls be tested to prove their utility with intent that a patent be applied for if the test was satisfactory. Crane also says that at a directors' meeting in May, 1904, when Kempshall was present, the merits of the new click-ball were being discussed, when Kempshall made the statement that he had applied for a patent, and Crane at once asked, and so did Royce, how was it possible for Kempshall to apply for a patent when the invention was not his, and Mr. Chapman remarked that he supposed, of course, Kempshall would protect the interests of the company, when Crane rejoined that it did not seem to him that it was a question of how Kempshall could protect the interests of the company but the question was how was it possible for Kempshall to swear to the originality of the invention which was not his own. Kempshall replied that he simply did it as a precautionary measure to protect the interests of the company, when Crane indignantly answered that Kempshall should not take out a patent for an invention to which he could not swear he was the original inventor. After this meeting adjourned, in walking up Broadway, Royce again asked Kempshall why he applied for a patent knowing this ball to be Royce's invention, and Kempshall repeated that he did it as a matter of precaution and added that at any time within two years from the date of his application for a patent, Royce could easily prove priority. The failure of Kempshall to testify to contradict Chapman, Crane, and Royce or to explain, if he could explain, these admissions, is significant. We are satisfied that on that date Kempshall admitted outright that he was not the inventor of this golf-ball, while Kempshall's own letters to Royce show that he all the while regarded Royce as the inventor of this golf-ball, which he had at first disparaged and later approved. The expressions of this court in a case in which Winslow relied upon the *prima facie* case made by the record in his favor apply here.

Instead of a resort to proof of the facts as they really existed .Winslow has elected to rest upon a technicality or the *prima facie* effect of a status acquired in the Office by virtue of seniority of application for his original patent. This may serve in some cases, but it is not always safe to rest exclusively upon it. A party by his conduct in doing acts or in omitting to act when circumstances would seem to require action may often furnish evidence more convincing in leading to a conclusion than even the sworn testimony of the party, and that would seem to be the case here. (*Winslow* v. *Austin*, C. D., 1899, 301; 86 O. G., 2171; 14 App. D. C., 143.)

It would be a denial of justice if the *prima facie* case of Kempshall reinforced by the considerable delay of Royce in making his application should outweigh the culpable attitude and conduct of Kempshall and his failure to testify in answer to the serious charges against him made by Royce and Crane. The delay of Royce was largely caused by Kempshall's failure to assign to his company this very patent, after he had assured the officials at the directors' meeting that his motive in obtaining the patent was to protect the interests of the company, and it appears that members of the company which had found Kempshall a very expensive president, temporized too long, in the hope that Kempshall would assign the patent and thus end all controversy.

We have no doubt that Royce is the inventor of the subject-matter of this interference and that in the fall of 1903 he disclosed this invention to Kempshall..

The decision of the Commissioner of Patents in this case must therefore *be affirmed* and the clerk of this court will certify this decision and opinion to the Commissioner of Patents in accordance with law.

[Court of Appeals of the District of Columbia.]

WM. A. ROGERS, LIMITED, *v.* INTERNATIONAL SILVER COMPANY.

Decided June 4, 1907.

(129 O. G., 3503.)

1. TRADE-MARKS—OPPOSITION—" WM. A. ROGERS " AND " WM. ROGERS MFG. CO."

The name " Wm. A. Rogers " *Held* entitled to registration under the last proviso of section 5 of the Trade-Mark Act approved February 20, 1905, notwithstanding the prior adoption and continuous use of the names " Wm. Rogers Mfg. Co" and " Wm. Rogers and Son," as a party is entitled to use his own name, actually or legally acquired, without regard to the confusion that may result from similarity.

2. SAME—SAME—SAME—SIMILARITY OF SURNAMES.

As an ordinary surname cannot be appropriated as a trade-mark to the exclusion of others of the same name, it follows that the rules of law relating to the similarity of technical trade-marks cannot be applied to the use of such surname as a mark, notwithstanding the confusion that may result from its legitimate use by such others. The law relating to unfair competition may apply under certain conditions, but not that of infringement.

3. SAME—SAME—SAME—PLEADING—EFFECT OF DEMURRER—SUBSEQUENTLY-FILED AFFIDAVIT.

A demurrer to an opposition to the registration of a trade-mark stands as an admission of the allegations of the opposition in so far as they state facts, and not conclusions of law and cannot be supported by an affidavit and subsequently filed by the applicant relating to facts set forth in the notice of opposition.

4. REGISTRATION—EFFECT OF.

The registration of a trade-mark is not conclusive of a right of property therein.

Mr. Chas. H. Duell, Mr. H. S. Duell, Mr. F. P. Warfield, and *Mr. William F. Bissing* for Wm. A. Rogers, Limited.

Mr. C. L. Sturtevant and *Mr. George H. Mitchell* for International Silver Company.

SHEPARD, *J.:*

The appeal is from a decision of the Commissioner of Patents (C. D., 1906, 301; 124 O. G., 318,) sustaining opposition to, and denying the registration of a trade-mark.

On May 25, 1905, Wm. A. Rogers, Limited, a corporation of the Province of Ontario, Dominion of Canada, applied for the registration of a trade-mark, consisting of the words " Wm. A. Rogers," used in the manufacture and sale of silver-plated flat ware, hollow ware, and tableware. It is displayed by stamping the ware, and by means of labels on packages and cases containing the same. Continuous use was claimed since the year 1894. Right to register is claimed under the proviso of the act of February 20, 1905, called the " ten-years clause."

After publication, opposition was filed by the International Silver Company, a corporation of the State of New Jersey. The allegations of the opposition are substantially:

1. That it is engaged at Meriden, State of Connecticut, and elsewhere in the manufacture of silver-plated tableware, and in its sale throughout the United States and in foreign countries.

2. That the Wm. Rogers Mfg. Co., a corporation organized in Connecticut in 1872, has been engaged since then in the manufacture and sale of silver-plated tableware.

3. That in May, 1899, the opposer became the successor to the business of said Wm. Rogers Mfg. Co., and became vested with its goo[...]

will, including trade-marks and trade-mark rights, and has continued said business since said date.

4. That said Wm. Rogers Mfg. Co., for the purpose of identifying its wares adopted and used from and after 1876 the trade-marks "Wm. Rogers Mfg. Co." and "Wm. Rogers and Son," with and without certain prefixes; and opposer as its successor has used the same throughout the United States and in foreign nations. The conspicuous and characteristic feature of both of said marks being the words "Wm. Rogers."

5. That by reason of the long-continued association of said trade-marks in the market with the products of opposer and its predecessor, and by reason of extensive advertisement, the same have become very widely known and valuable to opposer; and by reason thereof the goods bearing the same have come to be familiarly known in the market as "Wm. Rogers goods," and "Rogers goods," and the same are the essential part of the good-will of opposer's business, and are of great value, so that any injury thereto injures and destroys the value and profits of its said business.

6. That the trade-mark sought to be registered by applicant was adopted by William A. Rogers many years after the adoption by the Wm. Rogers Mfg. Co. of its trade-marks aforesaid, that were subsequently acquired by opposer. That it so clearly resembles the marks of opposer, that its registration will result in the confusion and deception of purchasers and the public generally. And the said applicant has not the exclusive right to use said mark, but others, including opposer, have prior rights either in the identical form, or in such near resemblance thereto as might be calculated to deceive. That the original William A. Rogers was permitted to use said mark as against the prior use of the marks of opposer, only because it was his name, and he never had the right to any exclusive use thereof, except as he was permitted to use it as his own name concurrently with the use by opposer and others of similar marks.

Demurrer was entered to this opposition on the following grounds:

1. It does not appear that the trade-mark so closely resembles opposer's marks as to result in confusion or deception of purchasers.

2. It does not appear that the opposer will be injured or damaged by the applicant's registration, in that it does not appear that said trade-mark was not in the actual and exclusive use of applicant or its predecessor, from whom it derived title, for ten years next preceding the passage of the act of February 20, 1905.

Subsequently an affidavit of William A. Rogers, general manager of applicant, was filed, alleging certain facts relating to the use of the several trade-marks by applicant, opposer, and others not in the combination of the latter. It is unnecessary to set this out, as it cannot be considered. The demurrer must stand as an admission of the allegations of the opposition, in so far as they state facts and not conclusions of law, and cannot be supported by the affidavit. The Examiner of Interferences, expressing the opinion that the similarity of the marks is so great as to produce confusion in the minds of the public, overruled the first ground of the demurrer. He sustained the second ground under his construction of the proviso of the act relating to ten years prior use. On appeal to the Commissioner the decision of the Examiner on the second ground was reversed. The applicant electing to stand on its demurrer, a final decision was made on the two grounds; that the similarity between the two marks is so close as to be likely to cause confusion and deceive the public; and that the trade-mark of the applicant has not been in actual and exclusive use for ten years prior to the passage of the act. For these reasons, registration was denied.

From the opinion of Judge Shipman in *R. W. Rogers Co. v. Wm. Rogers Mfg. Co.* (70 Fed., 1017) it appears that about fifty or more years ago, in the State of Connecticut, Rogers Bros., a firm composed of three brothers, first applied the art of electroplating to the manufacture of silver-plated ware in this country, and established and maintained a high reputation for the sterling quality of their wares. The name of Rogers Bros. stamped upon the back thereof obtained a widely-extended reputation. Since then, apparently, the surname Rogers has been used by many different persons, natural and artificial, in various collocations. The Wm. Rogers Mfg. Co.—predecessors of the opposer—as appears from the allegations of the opposition, was one of the early ones of these. William A. Rogers, a natural person, was another. Whether he is the same person who is the general manager of the appellant, Wm. A. Rogers, Limited, does not clearly appear; apparently he is. In 1894, he engaged a manufacturing firm to make silver-plated ware for him. This was stamped on the back, "Wm. A. Rogers," and put up in boxes of the ordinary size and shape for such ware, labeled "Wm. A. Rogers, N. Y." On a bill filed against him by the Wm. Rogers Mfg. Co., an injunction *pendente lite* was granted against his causing to be manufactured, or selling silver-plated ware stamped with the words, "Wm. A. Rogers." On appeal, the Circuit Court of Appeals, for the Second Circuit, reversed this order. It was said that while there were indicia of an unworthy purpose to gain advantage from a name well known to the purchasers of silver-plated ware, the facts were not sufficient to justify the conclusion that he was using his name unfairly and dishonestly in the business in which he was entitled to use it. (*Rogers v. Wm. Rogers Mfg. Co.*, 70 Fed. Rep., 1019.) In 1898, the Wm. Rogers Mfg. Co. filed another bill against William A. Rogers for alleged infringement of its trade-mark, and moved for a preliminary injunction, which was denied by Lacombe, circuit judge. In a brief opinion, he said that defendant's right to use the ordinary abbreviation of his name, " Wm. A. Rogers," had been settled in the former case. (70 Fed. Rep., 1019.) And that it did not appear that he had put up his goods, or offered them for sale, in any form of package describing them otherwise than as the goods of " Wm. A. Rogers." While he had, doubtless, availed himself of the similarity of name which naturally tends to confound his goods with those of the original Rogers, yet, so. far as the mere name produces such confusion, the plaintiff has no cause of complaint. After reciting some of the facts relating to defendant's probable motives, he said there was not enough to warrant the injunction—

so long as defendant's goods are packed and labeled with his own name, " Wm. A. Rogers," not collocated with other words in such manner as to induce any greater confusion in the minds of the public than would naturally be produced by the use of such name. (*Wm. Rogers Mfg. Co.* v. *Wm. A. Rogers*, 84 Fed. Rep., 639; [affirmed by C. C. A.;] 95 Id., 1007.)

The principle applied in those cases, between the predecessors of the parties to this opposition and involving the same trade-names, has been maintained by the Supreme Court of the United States. (*Howe Scale Co.* v. *Wyckoff, Seamans & Benedict*, C. D., 1905, 717; 116 O. G., 299; 198 U. S., 118, and cases cited.) That case involved the use of the name, " Remington." The conclusion of the Court was thus declared by Mr. Chief Justice Fuller:

We hold that, in the absence of contract, fraud, or estoppel, any man may use his own name, in all legitimate ways, and as the whole or a part of a corporate name.

As an ordinary surname cannot be appropriated as a trade-mark, to the exclusion of others of the same name, it follows that the rules of law relating to the similarity of technical trade-marks cannot be applied to the use of such surname as a mark, notwithstanding the confusion that may result from its legitimate use by such others. The law relating to unfair competition may apply, under certain conditions, but not that of infringement.

This brings us to the chief point of contention: Whether, under the last proviso of the fifth section of the Trade-Mark Act, approved February 20, 1905, the appellant is entitled to have registration of the name, " Wm. A. Rogers," by reason of its ten years previous use as a trade-mark. The provision reads as follows:

And provided further that nothing herein shall prevent the registration of any mark used by the applicant, or his predecessors, or by those from whom title to the mark is derived, in commerce with foreign nations or among the several States, or with Indian tribes, which was in actual and exclusive use as a trade-mark of the applicant or his predecessors from whom he derived title for ten years next preceding the passage of this act.

The intention of Congress in adopting this proviso was declared in the recent case of *in re Cahn, Belt & Co.*, (C. D., 1906, 627; 122 O. G., 354; 27 App. D. C., 173, 177.) Mr. Justice McComas, who delivered the opinion of the Court, said:

The last proviso of this section which was in the bill when it passed the House of Representatives, was amended in the Senate by twice substituting the word "mark" for the word "trade-mark" and in inserting in lieu of "and lawful" the word "exclusive." It is clear to us that these changes were made for the purpose of permitting the registration of marks which were not trade-marks but which had been actually used as trade-marks by the applicants or their predecessors, from whom they derived title, and in which the user had acquired property rights for more than ten years next preceding the passage of the act.

The last proviso of section 5, as amended and passed, was not intended to provide for the registration of technical trade-marks, for such marks had been cared for elsewhere in this act. This proviso permitted the registration of marks, not in either of the classes prohibited by this section, if such marks were in actual and exclusive use as a trade-mark for ten years next preceding the passage of the act. In respect of technical trade-marks, this proviso was absolutely useless. It was intended to save the right of registration to the marks described in the proviso.

The section had prohibited the registration of immoral or scandalous matter and public insignia as trade-marks, no matter how long the same had been before registered, and the proviso only extended the right of registration to marks not within either of the prohibited classes, if such marks had been in actual and exclusive use as a trade-mark during the ten years next preceding the passage of the act.

As the name of a person could not be appropriated as a technical trade-mark, but might, nevertheless, have been used by him as a mark to indicate the original of his goods, it is, under this interpretation of the proviso, entitled to be registered if in actual and exclusive use as such a mark for more than ten years next preceding February 20, 1905. That this name, "Wm. A. Rogers," was so used by him, and by the applicant under right derived from him, is not denied in the allegations of the opposition, but is practically admitted. The exclusive right to its use only is denied, and that on the ground that it so closely resembles the marks acquired by the opposer from its predecessor, namely, "Wm. Rogers Mfg. Co.," and "Wm. Rogers and Son," as to be calculated to confuse and deceive purchasers, and the public generally. This, of course, is a conclusion of law that is not admitted by the demurrer. As heretofore stated, this rule relating to similarity and simulation as applied in the case of recognized trade-marks, is not applicable to the names of persons legitimately used as marks for their goods. The Commissioner failed to recognize this distinction and held that the use of the name by the applicant had not been exclusive because it was a simulation of the marks of the opposer that had also been in use during the same period. As authority for his conclusion

he quoted the following extract from the opinion in the *Cahn, Belt &*
Co. case:

The application in this case admits that the mark we are now considering is a
simulation of the arms or seal of the State of Maryland, with variations it is
true, but still a simulation of the coat of arms of Maryland. The coat of arms
of Maryland was never in the exclusive use of the applicants during any period,
nor could the applicants ever acquire an exclusive use as a trade-mark of the
State coat of arms. In the sense of this proviso, the applicants had the actual
but never had the *exclusive* use of this simulation of the Maryland coat of arms,
and for this reason the appellants' trade-mark sought to be registered does not
come within the last proviso of the fifth section. The appellants never could
acquire such property right in the coat of arms of Maryland, or any simulation
thereof, against the State of Maryland.

What was there said had relation to a different state of facts from
those presented in this case. The mark was not the name of the
applicants or of any one of them, but a device claimed as a technical
trade-mark. It was, as said, nothing more than a simulation of the
arms and seal of the State of Maryland. As the applicants could not
register it for that reason, they claimed the right to do so under the
proviso because of its exclusive use by them as a trade-mark for more
than ten years before the enactment of the statute. But as it was of
the nature of a technical trade-mark, the exclusive right to the use of
which was in the State of Maryland, it was held that they could not
evade that exclusive right by using it in a slightly changed form.
Here, however, the applicant was lawfully entitled to use the name,
" Wm. A. Rogers," as a mark upon his goods, though any other person, of the identical name, might also have used it upon his own
goods. But it was not made to appear that there was another Wm.
A. Rogers making the same goods and using his name as a mark upon
them during that time. The sole use of his name for the time prescribed was enough, we think, to constitute an exclusive use of the
mark within the meaning of the proviso. The opposer did not show
any right to use the mark or name, " Wm. A. Rogers," but only those
of " Wm. Rogers Mfg. Co." and " Wm. Rogers and Son." In view
of what has been heretofore said, it is unnecessary to consider whether,
if these were all technical trade-marks, the applicant's mark so closely
resembles the others as to constitute an infringement. Each party
is entitled to use his own name, actually or legally acquired, without
regard to the confusion that may result from similarity. No right
of property will be concluded by the registration of appellant's mark.
All parties affected are free to maintain whatever rights they may
have in law or equity in the courts having jurisdiction therein.

The decision will, therefore, be reversed; and this decision will
be certified to the Commissioner of Patents as the law requires.
Reversed.

[Court of Appeals of the District of Columbia.]

LEWIS AND WILLIAMS *v.* CRONEMEYER.

Decided March 5, 1907.

(130 O. G., 300.)

1. INTERFERENCE—REDUCTION TO PRACTICE—TEST.

Where it appears that L. and W. constructed a machine embodying the tin-plate catcher set forth in the issue and secretly tested the same August 23, 1902, but it is not clear that freshly-tinned plates were used in the test, and the machine was at once dismantled, and that subsequently, in October, 1903, another machine was constructed which is said to have been operated until November 18, 1903, but was not again used until September, 1904, after L. and W. heard of C.'s patent, and no sheets which were run through this catcher are produced, and where another machine, which was made in February, 1905, in conformity with the first machine and tested in the presence of witnesses called in this case, required frequent adjustments of the catcher-disks to prevent the sheets from slipping and yet to place them far enough apart to avoid denting the sheets, *Held* that the experimental stage of the invention had not been passed and that such tests did not establish reduction to practice of the invention.

2. SAME—SAME—DILIGENCE.

Where L. and W. made and secretly tested a machine embodying the invention August 23, 1903, and at once dismantled the same, made and tested another machine October, 1903, but did not use the same again until September, 1904, and where L. and W. consulted their attorneys in November, 1903, and had the application papers prepared in January, 1904, but did nothing further toward filing their application until June, 1904, after they had heard of C.'s patent, *Held* that L. and W. were lacking in diligence and cannot prevail over C., who reduced the invention to practice and filed his application in September, 1903.

Mr. Harry Frease for Lewis and Williams.

Mr. C. P. Byrnes for Cronemeyer.

McCOMAS, *J.*:

The three tribunals of the Patent Office concurred in awarding priority of invention in this case to Cronemeyer and we must affirm the decision of the Commissioner of Patents appealed from. Such unanimity relieves us from a prolonged discussion of the case. The issues are:

1. A catcher for tinning-machines comprising a pair of positively-driven rollers having gripping portions provided with soft material to prevent marking of the plates.

2. A plate-catcher having positively-driven catch-rolls, said rolls having separated registering gripping portions of soft material.

3. A plate-catcher having a pair of driven rolls with soft gripping portions, a deflector above them, a raised support below the deflector, and an inclined chute for the sheets as they leave the deflector.

4. In a plate-catcher a pair of driven feed-rollers above the tinning-machine and having soft gripping portions, and means for yieldingly pressing at least one of said rollers toward the other.

It thus appears that the invention in issue is a catcher for tinning-machines. It is the office of this catcher to take hold of the tin-plate when it emerges from the rolls of the tinning-machine and discharge it from the machine. Cronemeyer is the senior party to whom was granted a patent six months before the application of Lewis and Williams, the appellants, was filed. In this interference, therefore, the burden of proof is upon them in an unusual degree. Mechanical catchers for tinning-machines were in use before Cronemeyer filed his application. In February, 1899, a patent was issued to Burson for a metal-plate catcher, which consisted of two steel rolls similar to the tinning-rolls, and as the tin-plate emerged from the tinning-rolls, Burson's machine caught it up by these steel rolls and discharged it from the machine.

In the invention in issue, instead of the rolls of Burson's patent, shafts are employed, having a series of pairs of disks between which the tin-plate sheet is caught when it emerges from the tinning-rolls. In Cronemeyer's patent these disks are formed of a number of linen disks clamped between sleeves on the shaft. In the application of Lewis and Williams it appears that the disks are made of tin and clamped in position on the shafts by threaded sleeves, or cast on the shaft. Burson's steel rolls mounted over a tinning-bath successfully seized and discharged freshly-tinned plates but in practice it was found that these steel rolls greatly marred the polished surface of the plates. It was the purpose of the invention of each of the parties to produce a catcher which would receive and discharge plates without marking or defacing their polished surfaces. Therefore, the important feature of the invention of this issue is the " gripping portions " on the feed-rollers " provided with soft material to prevent marking of the plate." Expedients for guiding the plates as they are discharged from the rollers are incidental, in the more limited counts of the issue.

Cronemeyer sought to avoid the defect in Burson's catcher by the use of the linen disks described. Lewis and Williams tried to avoid Burson's difficulty by the use of tin disks, which they claim are relatively soft and at least not hard enough to mark the freshly-tinned surfaces of the plates.

Lewis was the superintendent, and Williams was a foreman of the Morewood works of the American Tin Plate Company at Gas City, Indiana. They jointly conceived this invention before July 1, 1902, and about that date, they disclosed it to Smith and Hook, who under the instruction of Lewis and Williams, built a test machine which when completed was tested in the tin-house of the Morewood works on August 23, 1902, in the presence of four or five persons. Because they wished to keep secret their invention, after a few hours testing, Lewis and Williams had this machine broken up. Soon after, Williams departed from Gas City and became a superintendent for the Carnahan Tin Plate and Sheet Company at Canton, Ohio. Lewis joined him there in the same employment in July, 1903. Lewis and Williams discussed with Blecker, the secretary of the company, the merits of their tin-disk catcher, and soon completed and put into operation a catcher about the 1st of October, 1903. It remained in use until the middle of November following. Its use was discontinued for a long time and it was again in operation in September, 1904.

It is clear that Lewis and Williams were the first to conceive the invention in issue. All the tribunals of the Patent Office agree that the construction and testing of the machine at Gas City was not a reduction to practice of the invention in issue. As we have said, the Burson catcher with its steel rolls, successfully caught the plate but it marred them in so doing. Lewis and Williams testify, and they are corroborated by Smith and Hook, that a number of sheets were run through the machine at Gas City and there were no marks upon the plates. Thornburg says these plates had a little oil but no marks on them. Blackburn says the plates showed some abrasion but after they passed through the dusting and polishing machines, this abrasion was not noticeable.

At the time the appellants secretly tested their machine at Gas City, the plant was shut down and there is no satisfactory evidence that the particular tin-pot on which the new catcher was mounted contained molten tin. On the contrary, the evidence is most persuasive that tin plates no longer fresh were used in the experiment, and there is no evidence that the sheets used were retinned at the time. This experiment continued only for an hour or two and none of these sheets were preserved. The positive opinions of witnesses that these sheets showed no marks after passing through the cleaning and polishing machines would be more weighty had the test not occurred two days after the tin-house had shut down for the season, at which time the tin ordinarily would have been removed from the pot. Undue importance is given to the statement that the light in the tin-house was poor. It was the building in which tin plates were dipped and we infer there was light enough from the windows for the business therein conducted. This machine at Gas City was tested and dismantled on August 23, 1902. We are not satisfied beyond a reasonable doubt that this test was a successful reduction to practice.

The machine built in the Carnahan plant at Canton was installed on the 5th of October, 1903, and taken off on November 18, 1903. Williams says none of the sheets run through this catcher were marked and Thornburg says it worked well. No plates then produced appear among the exhibits. Lewis testifies that another *machine* was built and put in operation in the Carnahan works on

February 14, 1905, and this machine was later made to conform to the construction of the first machine tested at Gas City and he insists that the machine worked as well after this change as before. A series of plates caught up by this machine were exhibited and Lewis admits that some of them were marked but not marked to such an extent " that an assorter could turn them back as wasters or menders." When this machine was tested, before witnesses on both sides who appear in this case, it required frequent adjustment in order that the disks might be close enough together to prevent the sheets from slipping and yet far enough apart to avoid denting the sheets which often vary in thickness. Kimball, an intelligent witness for Cronemeyer, says the machine was adjusted every few minutes, which indicated that the machine did not successfully do its work. Lewis and Williams occupied important positions in the Carnahan plant and it is significant that after their second machine had been in operation for six or seven weeks in the fall of 1903 it was not used again until September, 1904. The applicants say it was taken off for repairs but the repairs necessary, Thornburg says, consumed only one day's work, and it is significant that it was not restored to use until after these applicants had heard that the patent had been granted Cronemeyer and that his invention was in use, and at no time does it appear that Lewis and Williams made use of more than one of their catchers at the same time upon tinning-pots in the Carnahan establishment. The Examiners-in-Chief fairly infer that the experimental stage of the invention had not been passed.

Nor were Lewis and Williams diligent in filing their application for a patent. Mr. Frease who so well presented appellants' case in this court says he was consulted about the 1st of November, 1903, and prepared the papers in January following; that Secretary Blecker, who had arranged to pay the fees, held back, and the matter was taken up in July, 1904, and the first application filed August 9, 1904. and though it is true the attorney says the appellants applied to him in June, 1904, to know why the application had not been filed, this interview did not occur until after they had heard of Cronemeyer's patent. We conclude that Lewis and Williams have failed to prove beyond a reasonable doubt that the tests of their catchers in 1902 and 1903 were so successful as to constitute a reduction to practice of the invention. They are the junior parties, and they were joint inventors, but they must in this case rely upon the success of the tests just mentioned to establish priority over Cronemeyer, the patentee, and these tests are not convincing. (*Guilbert* v. *Killinger*, C. D., 1898, 522; 84 O. G., 313; 13 App. D. C., 108; *Meyer* v. *Sarfert*, C. D., 1903, 529; 102 O. G., 1555; 21 App. D. C., 28; *Dashiell* v. *Tasker*, C. D., 1903, 551; 103 O. G., 2174; 21 App. D. C., 68; *Nielson* v. *Bradshaw*, C. D.,

1900, 274; 91 O. G., 648; 16 App. D. C., 96; *Kelly* v. *Fynn*, C. D., 1900, 339; 92 O. G., 1237; 16 App. D. C., 577.)

It was during this period that Cronemeyer appeared and reduced the invention to practice.

Cronemeyer testifies that in November, 1902, he conceived the idea of a catcher having gripping-rolls for use with a tin-plate machine. In December of 1903, he experimented with rolls having soft gripping portions; he tried rubber and asbestos, and by the first week in September of that year he used rolls, the gripping portions of which consisted of linen disks. Three witnesses testify that a catcher having linen or cotton disks was in use just before Cronemeyer took his vacation on September 5, 1903. The proof is satisfactory that Cronemeyer's catcher worked well until the disks were worn down, and his patent was applied for on September 21, 1903, and granted February 9, 1904. Lewis and Williams filed their application as we have stated, October 13, 1904, and when the testimony was taken Fraser stated that he had placed over fifty of the Cronemeyer catchers in the plants of the American Sheet and Tin Plate Company. It is unnecessary to review the ingenious argument of appellants' counsel that the Patent Office tribunals decided this case adversely to the appellants because their invention was not operative. We think the Commissioner appreciated that upon this interference priority of invention was the sole question to be determined and he rightly held that the appellants failed to prove beyond a reasonable doubt that they had reduced their conception of the invention to successful practice.

The decision of the Commissioner of Patents in this case must therefore be *affirmed* and the clerk of this court will certify this decision and opinion to the Commissioner of Patents in acordance with law.

[Court of Appeals of the District of Columbia.]

SHERWOOD *v.* DREWSEN.

Decided March 5, 1907.

(130 O. G., 657.)

1. INTERFERENCE—REDUCTION TO PRACTICE.

Reduction to practice must produce something of practical use, coupled with a knowledge, preferably by actual trial, that the thing will work practically for the intended purpose. The conception may give rational hopes of future fulfillment of the purpose at which it aims; but if as a matter of practice it falls short of success it is not a sufficient reduction to practice. Complete invention amounts to demonstration. When, as in this case, it had not quite passed beyond experiment not quite attained certainty and had fallen short of demonstration of the invention to produce the desired result, the inv inchoate. These parties sought certainty; but they had not attained certainty beyond all conjecture, which certainty the law requires. (See *McKenzie* v. *Cummings*, C. D., 1904, 683; 112 O. G., 1481; 24 App. D. C., 140; *Hunter* v. *Stikeman*, C. D., 1898, 564; 85 O. G., 610; 13 App. D. C., 219; *Coffin* v. *Ogden*, 5 O. G., 270; 18 Wall., 124.)

2. SAME—SAME—FILING OF APPLICATION.

Where neither the testimony presented by S. nor that offered in behalf of D. satisfactorily establishes conception of the invention in issue, *Held* that each party must be restricted to the date of filing of his application for conception and constructive reduction to practice, and since D. was the first to file, priority of invention must be awarded to him.

Mr. C. C. Linthicum for Sherwood.
Mr. J. E. H. Hyde for Drewsen.

McComas, *J.*, (Robb dissenting:)

In this appeal the issue of this interference is:

1. The process of preparing materials for paper-making from cornstalks, sugar-cane and analogous pithy stalks, which consists in: (1) cooking said stalks continuously in a single cooking liquor which contains the ordinary chemical reagents used to produce cellulose from vegetable fibers for a sufficient length of time to separate the fibers of the shell and the pith-cells from their incrustaceous matter; (2) separating the fibrous matter from the pith-cells by washing and screening; (3) collecting the fibrous materials and the pith-cells, substantially as described.

2. The process of preparing materials for paper-making from cornstalks, sugar-cane and analogous pithy stalks, which consists in: (1) cooking said stalks continuously in a single cooking liquor containing a caustic alkali for a sufficient length of time to separate the fibers of the shell and the pith-cells from their incrustaceous matter; (2) separating the fibrous matter from the pith-cells by washing and screening; (3) collecting fibrous material and the pith-cells, substantially as described.

3. The process of preparing materials for paper-making from cornstalks, sugar-cane and analogous pithy stalks which consists in: (1) cutting or otherwise dividing the stalks into pieces; (2) cooking said stalks continuously in a single cooking liquor which contains the ordinary chemical reagents used to produce cellulose from vegetable fibers for a sufficient length of time to separate the fibers of the shell and the pith-cells from their incrustaceous matter; (3) separating the fibrous matter from the pith-cells by washing and screening; (4) collecting the fibrous material and the pith-cells, substantially as described.

4. The process of preparing materials for paper-making from cornstalks, sugar-cane and analogous pith stalks which consists in: (1) cutting or otherwise dividing the stalks into pieces; (2) cooking said stalks continuously in a single cooking liquor containing a caustic alkali for a sufficient length of time to separate the fibers of the shell and the pith-cells from their incrustaceous matter; (3) separating the fibrous matter from the pith-cells by washing and screening; (4) collecting the fibrous material and the pith-cells, substantially as described.

The invention here involved is the disclosure that in a single cooking an entire cornstalk, sugar-cane, or other like pithy stem may be cooked, if the liquor be strong enough and the time be long enough, sufficiently to separate the fibers of the shell of the stalk and the pith-cells contained inside, also, from the other matter, without destroying the pith-cells, so that by washing and screening, the pith-cells may be separated from the fibrous material and the two kinds of cells may be separately collected. The claims, which are the counts of this issue, were first made by Drewsen and upon the suggestion of the Primary Examiner were adopted by Sherwood. The following extract from Drewsen's application explains these counts:

The difficulty in preparing fibrous material (cellulose,) or other products suitable for the manufacture of paper from these pithy stalks lies in the different character of the different parts of the stalk. A cornstalk proper, namely without leaves or husks, for instance, consists of two parts which can be used by paper manufacturers, to wit, the outside shell and the pith. The shell has a character similar to wood and contains a high percentage of fibers, while the pith is spongy and consists principally of oblong cells. This is also true of the sugar-cane.

The shell when treated with chemical substances, such as caustic soda, or sulfurous acid and lime, yields a large proportion of fibers which are adapted for paper-making and produce an opaque sheet of paper. The pith, on the other hand, when treated with the same substance disintegrates into cells and the sheet of paper derived therefrom is transparent and resembles imitation parchment-paper.

It has heretofore been supposed that this difference in character in the fibers of the shell and the cells of the pith required two separate cooking operations and that the former required a stronger solution and a longer time in cooking than the latter. It was also before thought that if the pith were cooked simultaneously with the shell in the same strength of the liquor and for the same length of time as are required for the disintegration of the fibers of the shell and their separation from the incrustaceous matter that the cells of the pith are practically destroyed and could not be utilized.

I have discovered, however, that this is not always the case, and that by the use of the proper means only a single operation of cooking is necessary for the entire stalk, shell, and pith, and that both can be used either separately or together in making the desired paper by using the following method.

The stalk is first cut up into pieces so as to expose the pith. These pieces are placed in a digester or rotary containing a solution of about fifteen per cent. of caustic soda; the stalks are then cooked for six hours under a steam-pressure of sixty pounds per square inch. The contents of the digester are run out into a vat and washed. The solids in the washed material, namely the cooked fibers and pith-cells, are thrown on a screen to separate such portions as are uncooked and are then run into a beating-engine provided with washers. The washers of this engine are covered either with perforated metal sheets or with wire meshes, having openings large enough to permit the pith-cells to pass through, yet small enough to retain the fibrous material. The separation of the cellulose fibers from the pith-cells is effected in the beater by continuous washing of the solid materials contained therein. The fibrous material is then ready to be placed upon the wet machine in a manner familiar to those acquainted with the prior art.

The water containing the pith-cells flowing from the washer is sometimes sufficiently thickened by the mass of pith-cells contained in it, to run directly onto the wet machine, and if it be not so thickened, the water containing the pith-cells is run off from the washer into settling-tanks where the pith-cells are allowed to settle. When they have settled in such tanks sufficiently to give the needed consistency, familiar to those skilled in the art, the clean water is run off from the tank and the pith-cells are carried to a wet machine to collect them for subsequent use either, alone, or together with the fibrous portion in a manner understood by persons skilled in this art. This process requires but a single cooking, which is effective to separate the fibers of the shell and the pith-cells, in the manner, and with the result just stated, and after this process the pith and shell fiber and the pith-cells, it is claimed, are in a condition ready for use in making paper without further treatment.

Sherwood in his specification states that:

This invention relates to an improved process of making fiber stock from cornstalks and analogous plants, and it has for its salient objects, to provide a process whereby two kinds of characteristically different fiber may be practically and effectively separated; to provide a process which may be carried on continuously, by the use of comparatively simple and inexpensive apparatus, and without chemically and physically changing the character of the fiber; to provide a process which is characterized by the absence of mechanical injury to the fiber-cells; and in general, to provide a simple and improved process of the character referred to.

I have discovered that these two kinds of fiber may be practically and effectually separated by first cooking the stalks in a reducing solution until the physical structure of the plant is broken down and the connective tissues disintegrated to such extent as to free the two fibers, and then subjecting the pulp thus produced to a screening operation in which the flowing action of a liquid is largely utilized for effecting the sorting out and separation of the two kinds of fiber.

Sherwood's lengthy specification does not particularly describe the reducing solution to which he refers nor the time required for the cooking, nor does he definitely describe the cooking process. His entire application treats of the process of mechanical separation of the two fibers after cooking and all of his original claims were concerned with the process of separation of the two classes of cells in the particular manner described in his specification. Some of his claims assume the prior cooking of the stalks; others speak of the art of making fiber from cornstalks " which consists in cooking the stalks in a reducing solution until reduced to a mass of pulp in which the connective tissue is broken down and the ultimate fiber freed."

In Sherwood's application and claims, the cooking is secondary, while the process of mechanical separation of the two varieties of cells from each other is primarily and particularly described. Drewsen in his application, from which we have quoted, primarily insists that he has discovered that only a single operation of cooking is necessary, instead of two as before supposed, for the disintegration of the fibers of the shell and th   s and that both varieties of cells can be preserved and utiliz   ately or together in making paper.

Both parties made prelim   filed proofs. Drewsen, the senior party, clai   invention, to have disclosed it to others and to have reduced it to practice during April, May and June, 1903, and his application was filed July 9, 1903. Sherwood claims conception, disclosure, and reduction to practice in September, 1902. He filed his application June 11, 1904. The Examiner of Interferences determined that Sherwood conceived the invention in September, 1902; that one Bonfield had obtained certain knowledge of it from Sherwood and had imparted his knowledge to Drewsen in June, 1903; that Drewsen failed to prove conception of the invention prior to that time and that Sherwood should prevail because he was the first and only inventor of the process in issue.

The Examiners-in-Chief and the Commissioner successively decided (C. D., 1906, 342; 124 O. G., 1205,) that neither party to this interference had reduced this invention to practice prior to the filing of their application in issue and, therefore, Bonfield had made no disclosure of the invention to Drewsen, the senior applicant, and that really Sherwood failed to prove a conception of the invention at any time before the date of his application.

The Commissioner and in effect the Examiners-in-Chief concur in the unusual conclusion that neither party proved conception or reduction to practice prior to the day that Drewsen filed his application, and that Sherwood, the junior party, is in like situation and only entitled to his filing date as the time of his conception and reduction to practice.

To make paper from cornstalks and like stalks was not novel but the paper produced was not so desirable commercially.

Everybody knew that a cornstalk was composed of a hard shell outside and a soft pith inside. It was learned that the shell by chemical cooking under pressure could be reduced to long cells suited to make soft and flexible paper, and that the pith could in like manner be reduced to short granular cells which would yield a hard brittle paper. All the parties interested in this interference, the principals and witnesses, knew these things.

Sherwood alleges that he conceived the invention in the middle of September, 1902, and in the same month reduced it to practice. During the four preceding years, Sherwood had been trying to utilize cornstalks and had invented a machine for mechanically separating the shell of the cornstalk from the pith. Mariner and Hoskin, chemists whom he had consulted, had advised him that paper-stock could not be economically produced from a cornstalk without first separating the pith and that paper-stock can be produced from the shell and that under proper treatment, the pith itself produces a substance of value in the preparation of paper.

It was then believed by these parties that the stalks could not be reduced in a single cooking operation without destroying the pith-cells by the action of the strong chemicals and by the long cooking required to reduce the hard shell of the stalk.

Near the end of the last-mentioned year, Sherwood by means of a company he had formed, established an experimental plant in Chicago in which was installed his depithing-machine and the experiments looking to the use of cornstalks in the manufacture of paperstock and of paper proceeded. These experiments were made with the depithed shell and the pith also, to discover the possibilities in the fiber and in the pith, of producing paper-stock. In addition to the depithing-machine, a rotary digester, a beating-machine, a screen, a stuff-chest, and a wet machine in conjunction with a boiler and a gas-engine were installed. In making experiments on the shell fiber to which the pith adhered, Sherwood observed that the pith-cells washed out with the wash-water and he proceeded so far as to allow the pith-cell to settle and from some of these, collected by means of a hand-screen, he made a rough sheet of paper. Sherwood regretted the waste of these pith-cells and endeavored to make use of them in the fall of 1902.

That Sherwood had observed the pith-cells were carried off with the waste water and that he collected these escaping pith-cells occasionally and made them into sheets of paper on a hand-screen is corroborated by Bonfield, Brand, and Miller, all fair and intelligent witnesses. This treatment of the subject-matter by Sherwood would appear to be almost the conception of the invention by him, but other considerations determine us to concur with the two higher tribunals of the Patent Office that neither Sherwood or any one else at the Chicago experiment plant at any time clearly appreciated the process, the disclosure of which in the application of Drewsen constitutes the invention of this issue.

On December 1, 1902, Sherwood filed an application which resulted in a patent. It is true that this application was a division of an application filed in October, 1901, but it was executed by Sherwood several months after he alleges he had conceived the invention and it related to the same subject-matter and he urged the importance of separating the pith from the fibrous portion of the stalk as far as practicable before subjecting either to chemical treatment or disintegration, and proceeded to show that the pith and fibrous parts of the stalk so separated may be treated separately in digesters or boilers and after such digestion, reunited if desired producing a product of value not to be obtained by dissolving both together in the first instance. This patent further stated that if less heat be used more time or a stronger solution would be required, and among other things, that the treatment of the pith must be gentler than that required for the proper digestion of the shell fiber. No stress is laid upon the collecting of pith-cells after the cooking of the stalk-shell. Emphasis is given only to the separation of the shell and pith by machine and the separate cooking of the pith.

Bonfield, working under Sherwood's direction, at the end of December, 1902, says that when the pith was treated, the shell fiber was screened away and recooked. It is significant that neither Sherwood nor his witnesses testify that they washed out the pith-cells from the shell fiber after a single cooking, yet Sherwood now claims that he then knew that more than one cooking was unnecessary to satisfactorily separate the pith-cells from the fiber-cells of the cornstalk and early in 1903, Sherwood's letters show that his main reliance was upon the use of the depithing-machine; that he sought a mechanical depithing of the stalks by the machine, instead of a chemical separation by cooking with chemical agents.

Sherwood had learned that the pith-cells must be removed for they caused the paper produced to be hard and stiff and unsuited for commercial use, and that if the pith-cells were eliminated, the fibrous material of the stalk would produce a paper white and soft. When it was found Sherwood's depithing-machine did not remove all of the pith, and that the remaining pith when cooked with the stalk, produced samples, even after the pulp was washed to remove the pith-cells, still unsatisfactory, experiments were continued. Wallace, an expert in paper-mill work as an engineer, was called in and being shown samples of paper made in October, 1902, dissuaded Sherwood and his companions from building mills until more satisfactory results had been obtained, and at his instance the company employed Drewsen whom Wallace recommended as his friend and as an expert in the chemistry of pulp and paper making. About November, 1902, Drewsen first met Sherwood in Chicago and thereafter Drewsen and Wallace coöperated with Sherwood in trying to raise capital to use the invention so far as it had advanced. These efforts did not succeed.

If Sherwood at this time had fully appreciated that the pith and shell of the cornstalk could have been separated by a single cooking operation and that the two varieties of cells could be separately collected and used either alone or together to produce paper-stock, it is exceeding strange that with the experiment plant and all needed apparatus at hand and while he was daily investigating in order to produce paper commercially, that he should have been content with now and then producing a single piece of paper upon a hand-mold and that while he was collecting small quantities of pith-cells, proceeding from the operation of the mechanical depithing, and the two separate cooking operations, upon which he relied in Chicago he still continued to rely upon the same process until after the filing of Drewsen's application.

Late in April, 1903, Drewsen, Sherwood, and Bonfield went to the Warren mills in Maine and industriously experimented until the end of May in that year when Sherwood and Drewsen went together to New York to interest capitalists in the scheme, leaving Bonfield to carry on further experiments at the Warren mills and to use up a quantity of raw material that remained on hand. The experiments at the Warren mills were carried on under Drewsen's directions, all three of these visitors directing their efforts to perfect the paper-making from the cornstalk. Before Drewsen went to Warren mills and in April, 1903, Drewsen had filed an application in which he had described a process requiring two cookings of a stalk.

This patent was afterward granted. In it Drewsen states that the shell when treated with caustic soda and sulfurous acid and lime, yields a large proportion of fibers which are adapted for paper-making, producing an opaque sheet of paper. The pith on the other hand when treated with the same substances disintegrates into cells and the sheet of paper produced is transparent resembling parchment-paper. He says the shell requires a stronger cooking liquor and a longer time than is required in cooking the pith. He proposes separating the shell from the pith mechanically and cooking them apart in caustic-soda solutions of different strength and thereafter uniting them in the proportions desired. The patent states that the split pieces of cornstalk were digested in a solution so weak that only the pith became disintegrated and the shell only partially so. The partly-cooked shells were then to be separated from the pith-cells and carried to a second digester to be cooked in a stronger solution so as to yield the fibrous material in the shell. This method was tried at Warren mills and the success was a qualified one. Bonfield submitted a report of all the experiments at Warren mills. Few of the experiments recorded throw light upon the controversy here. After Sherwood and Drewsen went away together, Bonfield in June, 1903, wrote two letters to Drewsen which the appellant insists disclosed this invention to Drewsen, which invention Bonfield sincerely believes Sherwood had imparted to him. In neither one of these letters, nor in the record of all the tests, do we find any definite information concerning the collection of the pith-cells. The paper produced by eliminating pith-cells steadily improved and in one of the later reports it is said that after washing twenty hours, they washed away as much pith as possible and it was remarked that "the pith settled quickly making it possible and practicable to save it." In none of these experiments is it recorded that the pith was actually saved or that it was proved that it was in condition for making paper, yet the issue we are considering requires that the pith-cell shall be collected and shall be in condition for making paper; therefore it is clear that none of these experiments can be held to constitute a reduction to practice of the process. We have said that Sherwood almost but not quite attained the conception of this invention. It is significant that while they were together seeking the same result and were most friendly, Sherwood did not disclose the invention to Drewsen. Before they departed from Warren mills. Drewsen appears, as an experienced chemist, to have lost faith in the mechanical separation of the two kinds of cells and to have gained increasing confidence in his power to separate them by chemical cooking, but we are convinced that Drewsen at that time also failed to conceive and reduce to practice this invention; that he narrowly missed it but still failed to achieve a " reduction to successful practice." All of the experiments in Chicago and in Maine are fully and fairly stated by intelligent and honest witnesses and after carefully examining the long record, we concur with the Commissioner of Patents that there is a want of satisfactory evidence that any one at any time conceived the invention and there is no evidence that either of the applicants had reduced it to practice when at the end of May. Sherwood and Drewsen left the Cumberland mill.

Counsel for appellant say that it was impossible that both parties in some way could be led to file applications for an invention which neither of them had conceived. We need not curiously inquire how Drewsen finally came upon the invention first disclosed by his application. We agree with the Commissioner that while the witnesses thought Sherwood disclosed the invention to them, he fell short of disclosure of that which he had nearly found. Not only what he said but all that he did fell short of this invention; apparently it eluded him while he still pursued mechanical devices for depithing and separating the two kinds of cells.

It happened that Bonfield remained to use up the material on hand. Both applicants contend that Bonfield reduced the invention to practice in June, 1903. Had he done so, it might be very difficult to say to whose advantage Bonfield's achievement accrued, but as we concur with the two highest tribunals of the Patent Office in saying that Bonfield's successors fell short of a reduction to successful practice, we quite end the discussion on this point. We cannot agree with the parties although upon this point they agree with each other. We must concur with the two tribunals just mentioned.

Reduction to practice must produce something of practical use coupled with a knowledge, preferably by actual trial, that the thing will work practically for the intended purpose. The conception may give rational hopes of future fulfilment of the purpose at which it aims, but if as a matter of practice it falls short of success, it is not a sufficient reduction to practice. Complete invention amounts to demonstration. When, as in this case, it had not quite passed beyond experiment and had not quite attained certainty and had fallen short of demonstrating the capacity of the invention to produce the desired result, the invention itself was still inchoate. These parties sought certainty but they had not attained certainty beyond all conjecture, which certainty the law requires. (See *McKenzie* v. *Cummings*, C. D., 1904, 683; 112 O. G., 1481; 24 App. D. C., 140; *Hunter* v. *Stikeman*, C. D., 1898, 564; 85 O. G., 610; 13 App. D. C., 219; *Coffin* v. *Ogden*, 5 O. G., 270; 18 Wall., 124.)

In Maine a great advance was made beyond the Chicago experiment for in the former place the escape of the pith-cells was more fully observed and the significant fact that they were not destroyed by the cooking and the idea that it was feasible to collect them for subsequent use was in the minds of all the persons engaged in these experiments. But the result of all the experiments was that by one cooking, the pith-cells and shell fibers could be so separated that pith-cells could be entirely washed away if it was desired to make soft sheets of paper. This court has often said that satisfactory evidence of reduction to practice must embrace all the elements of the issue and must leave nothing to inference, since no one of these elements can be determined to be subordinate and immaterial. (*Blackford* v. *Wilder*, C. D., 1903, 567; 104 O. G., 578; 21 App. D. C., 10; *Robinson* v. *Seelinger*, C. D., 1905, 640; 116 O. G., 1735; 25 App. D. C., 240.)

This process of preparing the materials for paper-making from cornstalks and the like, required the collecting of the fibrous materials and the pith-cells substantially as described. When it was that Drewsen attained a complete conception of the invention the record fails to show. The tribunals of the Patent Office all agree that the four claims in Drewsen's application, which Sherwood adopted. constitute invention and the filing of his application by a familiar rule constitutes a constructive reduction to practice of the invention and of every element of it and since Drewsen is the senior party we concur with the Commissioner that Drewsen is the prior inventor.

The decision of the Commissioner of Patents in this case must therefore be *affirmed* and the clerk of this court will certify this decision and opinion to the Commissioner of Patents in accordance with law.

[Court of Appeals of the District of Columbia.]

WOODS *v.* POOR.

Decided April 2, 1907.

(130 O. G., 1313.)

1. INTERFERENCE—PRIORITY—DILIGENCE—CIRCUMSTANCES TO BE CONSIDERED.
   There is no arbitrary rule or standard by which diligence may be measured. The sole object of the law being to mete out the fullest measure of justice, each case must be considered and decided in the light of

the circumstances of that case. The nature of the invention, the situation of the inventor, the length of time intervening between conception and reduction to practice, the character and reasonableness of the inventor's testimony and that of his witnesses are all important factors in determining the question of diligence

2. SAME—SAME—SAME.

Where on October 24, 1903, twenty-three days after his conception of the invention, Woods left the company by which he had been employed to embark in business on his own account, and during this period had made a blackboard drawing of the invention and frequently discussed with one Jacob, who was skilled in the art, the possibility of overcoming certain criticism, and where after establishing his own business he employed said Jacobs and resumed the consideration of these defects, and while he did not eventually modify his device, but filed his application January 27, 1904, *Held* he was not lacking in diligence, and priority was awarded to him over Poor, who reduced his invention to practice by filing his application December 17, 1903.

Mr. George W. Rea and *Mr. C. S. Pickard* for Woods.

Mr. Thomas F. Sheridan, Mr. Charles F. Fitts, and *Mr. Walter A. Scott* for *Poor*.

ROBB, *J.:*

This is an appeal in an interference case from the decision of the Commissioner of Patents. (*Ante*, 12; 126 O. G., 391.

The counts of the issue disclose the structure of the invention, and read as follows:

1. A side bearing for railway-cars comprising a casing or shell which has openings in its top and bottom and a roller in said shell adapted for rolling contact through said openings with bearing-surfaces; said casing or shell being provided with tracks located in position to support the roller when the latter is below and free from the upper bearing-surface and the said roller having free movement in the shell both endwise of the latter and vertically with respect to said tracks.

2. A side bearing for railway-cars comprising a casing or shell which has openings in its top and bottom and a roller in said shell adapted for rolling contact through said openings with bearing-surfaces and provided with trunnions at its ends; said casing or shell having inwardly-extending flanges forming tracks which are located in position to engage the said trunnions when the roller is below and free from the upward bearing-surface, and the said roller having free movement in the shell both endwise of the latter and vertically with respect to the said track.

3. In a device of the class described, the combination with a suitable roller, having oppositely-extending gudgeons, of a box open at the top to receive the roller and having a longitudinally-slotted bottom through which the roller projects, there being inwardly-extending side flanges on the box to limit the downward movement of the roller, and a cover for the box, separately formed and adapted to furnish an upper tread for the roller.

All the tribunals of the Patent Office concur in awarding priority of invention to Poor, the senior party, on the sole ground that Woods, *the junior* party, although first to conceive the invention, was lacking in diligence. The Commissioner, however, in his opinion states that the question " is not entirely free from doubt."

Counsel for appellee, with commendable fairness and conciseness, thus state the case:

Fortunately, there is no serious dispute as to most of the facts in the case, since the dates of invention of both parties are practically admitted. It is not disputed that Woods was the first to conceive the invention which forms the subject-matter of the interference, and this conception was on September 16, 1903, on which day Woods made the disclosure of his invention to others. It is not disputed that Woods reduced his invention to practice constructively by the filing of his application on January 27, 1904.

It is conclusively established by the record that Poor conceived the invention within a day or two of November 1, 1903, and this date is not seriously contested. Poor reduced his invention to practice on December 17, 1903, by the filing of his application.

The facts are, therefore, that Woods, though the first to conceive, was the last to reduce to practice; and that Poor conceived and reduced to practice in the interval between Woods's conception and reduction to practice.

Under these circumstances the burden of proof is placed upon Woods of showing either that at the time of Poor's conception he, Woods, was actively engaged in reduction to practice of his own conception and that this activity continued until his own reduction to practice, or of showing some sufficient excuse for his delay in reducing to practice.

It is apparent, therefore, that the only question here involved is whether Woods was using reasonable diligence in adapting and perfecting his invention just prior to November, 1903, the date his competitor entered the field, and continued such diligence to the time of filing his application January 27, 1904. It is perhaps not inappropriate at the outset to state what has many times been stated that there is no arbitrary rule or standard by which diligence may be measured. The sole object of the law being to mete out the fullest measure of justice, each case must be considered and decided in the light of the circumstances of that case. The nature of the invention, the situation of the inventor, the length of time intervening between conception and reduction to practice, the character and reasonableness of the inventor's testimony and that of his witnesses, are all important factors in determining the question of diligence. And, where the facts are admitted, and a mere question of law is involved, the court will not hesitate to reverse the judgment appealed from if convinced that an erroneous conclusion was reached. (*O'Connell v. Schmidt*, C. D., 1906, 662; 122 O. G., 2065; 27 App. D. C., 77.)

The record in this case discloses that the appellant, Woods, is by profession a mechanical engineer and something over thirty years of age; that he was vice-president and manager of the Kindl Car Truck Company of Chicago, Ill., from February, 1898, to October 24, 1903, at which time owing to differences arising between the president of that company, Samuel W. McMunn, and himself as to the division of profits arising from sales of roller-bearings embodied in Patent

No. 703,148, which was issued to said Woods and McMunn, he severed his connection with the company. During Woods's incumbency as vice-president the company had been manufacturing roller-bearings under said patent. Woods soon after leaving the company embarked in the railway supply business on his own account, in which business he continued during the remainder of the period covered by this controversy. On September 15, 1903, while at St. Louis, he conceived this invention and made a drawing of the same with a written explanation on the reverse side thereof. This drawing, even without the explanation, fully and completely discloses the device. He returned to Chicago that night, taking the drawing with him, and the next day showed it to J. M. McConahey, an attorney, and to John Jacob, who was the draftsman and superintendent of mechanical work for the Kindl Company, and skilled in the art. Each of these gentlemen signed their names as witnesses on the reverse side of the sketch. Immediately following this Woods discussed his discovery with Jacob, who was in his room daily. Large sketches were made upon a blackboard in Woods's office, and details of the idea were discussed. Jacob appears to have made certain objections and criticisms to the device as outlined, the result being, as Woods says, " that he endeavored to think of some means to overcome this criticism." The drawings remained upon the blackboard for several weeks, and frequent discussions continued to be had with Jacob concerning them. Woods had very limited capital in which to embark in business for himself, and appears to have been very busy with many matters immediately after leaving the Kindl Company. On October 24, 1903, Jacob severed his connection with the Kindl Company and engaged with Woods. Discussions as to the possibility of perfecting the device were again had. Woods, in his testimony, speaking of these discussions, said:

I had almost constantly in mind the question of overcoming the objections referred to before, made by Mr. Jacob. I myself and alone, as well as together with Mr. Jacob, frequently went over these matters in the endeavor to overcome Mr. Jacob's objections, but I was unable to do so.

On cross-examination he was asked:

Q. Then, between September 15, 1903, and January 27, 1904, all the physical work done by you toward developing this invention was limited to the black-board sketches which you have referred to in your direct examination; is not that true?

A. No, sir; Mr. Jacob and I, as well as myself alone, held numerous conversations which undoubtedly involved our making a number of sketches all looking to the overcoming of the objections of Mr. Jacob before referred to by me, and which objections I believed to be well founded.

Woods is fully corroborated by Jacob. In answer to a question as to what was done by Woods after he had exhibited the sketch of September 15, Jacob said:

We laid out details of this sketch on a blackboard with chalk. This blackboard was in Mr. Woods's office, and we looked his drawings on the blackboard over, with a view of more clearly finding the objections and remedies that could be made to overcome the weak construction to which I have referred.

He also testified that the drawings remained on the blackboard for two or three weeks, and that whenever he was in Woods's office they "discussed some points in reference to the drawings on the board;" and that the matter was discussed several times after he entered Woods's employ. In answer to the question, whether Woods ever succeeded in devising any means for overcoming the objections urged, witness said:

Mr. Woods advocated ribs and lugs to strengthen the sides, and we also discussed the possibilities of using different kinds of metal; that is, we looked into the merits of making the device either in steel or malleable iron, or cast-iron, and tried to arrive at a definite conclusion which of these different materials would make the best device, either from a mechanical or commercial standpoint.

The record discloses that Poor entered the employ of the Kindl Company October 24, 1903, and that, as heretofore stated, he conceived the invention in issue about November 1, 1903.

On this record we think Woods entitled to a judgment of priority. There is no doubt whatever that his date of conception antedates Poor's by a month and a half. There is no doubt that when he conceived the invention he fully realized and appreciated the value of his discovery, as he was highly skilled in the art, and, moreover, took immediate steps to fully explain his discovery to others to obtain indubitable evidence of having done so. Only twenty-three days intervened between the date of his return from St. Louis, where he conceived this invention, and the date of his leaving the Kindl Company. During that time he and Jacob had almost daily discussions as to the possibility of overcoming the criticisms which Jacob had made. Stress is laid on the fact that no models were made. We attach no importance to this fact, because, owing to the nature of the device, the blackboard drawings answered the same purpose. They enabled these two men highly skilled in the art as they were to consider and criticise and endeavor to perfect the device. That they did not succeed in further perfecting it should not redound to Woods's disadvantage, for the reason that the law does not require that the one, who first conceives a practical invention, shall perfect it thereafter to such an extent that it is better than the invention of others who subsequently enter the field. All the law requires is that the first to conceive shall be using reasonable diligence in endeavoring to perfect and adapt his invention when his rivals enter the field.

We have heretofore had occasion to remark that the law encourages such delay as is required to test the thoroughness and utility of supposed inventions, and to prevent the Patent Office from being overloaded with applications for patent for crude and incomplete devices. (*Griffin* v. *Swenson*, C. D., 1899, 440; 89 O. G., 919; 15 App. D. C., 135, 142.)

Soon after Woods severed his connection with the Kindl Company he secured the services of Jacob, and they both testified that Woods's invention again became the subject of discussion. Of course, we do not mean to say that mere casual discussion would alone be sufficient to show diligence, but we think the evidence in this case shows much more. It must be remembered also that only three weeks elapsed between the time Woods left the Kindl Company and the time Poor entered the field, and that Woods, just having embarked in business on his own account, was busy adjusting himself to new conditions. Nevertheless, this invention appears to have received consideration for he secured the services of the man who had pointed out its defects, and immediately resumed the discussion of those defects and the possibility of overcoming them. The delay in this case was less than the delay in *O'Connell* v. *Schmidt, supra,* and the facts in the two cases are quite similar. What was said in that case, therefore, applies to this.

Taking into consideration the nature of the invention, the circumstances surrounding him at the time, the comparatively short time between his date of conception and the date Poor entered the field, his promptness in filing his application thereafter, and the fact that reduction to practice was constructive and not actual in each case, we conclude that Woods has shown that degree of diligence which the law requires, and that he is justly entitled to the fruits of his discovery.

The decision of the Commissioner of Patents will, therefore, be reversed, with directions to the clerk of this court to certify this opinion to the Commissioner of Patents, according to law. *Reversed.*

[Court of Appeals of the District of Columbia.]

McCORMICK *v.* HALLWOOD.

Decided June 4, 1907.

(130 O. G., 1187.)

INTERFERENCE—PRIORITY—REDUCTION TO PRACTICE—LONG DELAY.

Where the evidence satisfactorily shows that Hallwood constructed a machine embodying the invention in issue and successfully operated it more than five years prior to the filing of his application and that several machines were afterward constructed and sent to various parts of the United States, *Held* that these acts should not be considered merely as evidence of an abandoned experiment, but as evidence of a reduction to practice, although other machines were built embodying an older form of device for performing the same function, where it appears that the old devices satisfactorily performed the desired function in ordinary use and that they were so made in order to dispose of old materials then on hand.

Mr. Frank Parker Davis and *Mr. J. B. Haywood* for the appellant.
Mr. Paul A. Staley for the appellee.

McCOMAS, *J.*:

The subject-matter of the issue involved in this appeal found in the counts of this interference from eight to sixteen, inclusive, and relates to means for preventing the overthrow of the adding-wheels in a cash-register. These counts are as follows:

8. The combination with a toothed wheel, a pivoted lever, a pawl on said lever for turning said wheel, an angular locking-lever also carried on the pivoted lever and normally engaging the pawl to lock the same into engagement with the wheel, and means movable into contact with said locking-lever after the pawl has come to rest to release the pawl from the wheel.

9. In a cash-register of the class described, the combination with a. registering mechanism, of operating-levers for the same, operating pawls mounted on said levers, locking bell-cranks mounted on said levers and each formed with an extended arm, movable tripping devices for said bell-cranks adapted to contact with the extended arms no matter what positions the operating-levers may have assumed.

10. In a cash-register, the combination with a register comprising a series of wheels, of a series of levers, pawls mounted on said levers, locking devices for said pawls also mounted on said levers, an independent rock-frame arranged to lock said pawls to the wheels, means connecting said frame to the movable parts of the machine and means for connecting the locking devices to said movable parts of the machine.

11. In a cash-register the combination with a register comprising a series of wheels, of operating-levers, pawls mounted on said levers and engaging said wheels, locking devices mounted on said levers and engaging said pawls and formed with operating extensions, and movable means independent of the levers and continuously in position for actuating said extension.

12. In a cash-register the combination with a register comprising a series of wheels, a series of levers, pawls mounted on said levers, locking devices for said pawls also mounted on said levers, an independent rock-frame arranged to lock said pawls to the wheels and operate the locking devices, and means connecting said frame to the movable parts of the machine.

13. In a cash-register the combination with a registering mechanism, a series of movable members, register-operating pawls mounted on said members, an operating member connected to the movable parts of the machine, a series of movable pawl-locking devices mounted on the movable members, and means for maintaining an operating connection between the operating member and the locking devices no matter what positions the movable members may take up.

14. In a cash-register the combination with a series of registering-wheels, of a series of pivoted levers, operating-pawls mounted on said levers, a series of locking-pawls mounted on said levers and having upwardly-projecting curved extensions, and a relatively stationary tripping device for said curved extensions arranged to operate the same, no matter what position the pivoted levers may have assumed.

15. In a cash-register, a registering-wheel, a pivoted lever, a pawl carried by said lever for turning the register-wheel, an angular locking-lever also carried

by said pivoted lever for engaging the pawl and locking it to the register-wheel, a key, and means released by the depression of said key for tripping the angular lever to free the pawl from its register-wheel, substantially as described.

16. In a cash-register, a register-wheel, a pivoted lever, a pawl carried by said lever for turning the register-wheel, an angular locking-lever also carried by said pivoted lever and having an extended arm, means for normally holding the locking lever in engagement with the pawl to lock the same to the register-wheel, and means engaging the extended arm of said angular lever to free the same from the wheel after the pawl has come to rest, substantially as described.

The adding-wheels are mounted on the main shaft of the machine on which the main and auxiliary yokes are mounted. Mounted on this shaft alternately with the adding-wheels are arms which carry pawls which are by springs pressed into engagement with the ratcheted peripheries of the adding-wheels and these pawls carrying arms, have legs which rest on the auxiliary yokes so that as the yokes drop, the arms follow them, the pawls tripping over the teeth of the adding-wheel. As the main yoke is swung upward, it carries auxiliary yokes and the arms with it, and the pawls engaging the teeth of the adding-wheels, the latter are turned so that the values of the pressed keys are added thereon.

The counts we here consider show devices to prevent the adding-wheel being carried by momentum beyond the pawls, thereby registering an amount greater than that indicated by the keys. The applications of McCormick, appellant, and of Hallwood, the appellee alike show means consisting of a bell-crank pivoted to the end of the pawl-carrying arm, the shorter arm being spring-pressed against the rear of the pawls; the longer arm of the bell-crank projects over a rocking frame-piece which is so arranged that when the main yoke moves downward it is rocked, throwing the bell-crank out of engagement with the pawls and allowing the latter to trip over the teeth of the adding-wheels but when the yoke moves upward it is rocked and allows the bell-crank to be thrown against the pawls, thereby locking the adding-wheels and pawl-carrying arms and preventing the adding-wheels from being overthrown. It is claimed that these means prevent the overthrow of the counting-wheels which register the amount of the purchase and add it to the amount registered from previous purchases. It was conceded in argument that without some such means such an overthrow could be produced by closing the cash-drawer violently or by pounding or hammering on it.

The tribunals below fully discussed the facts. The appellant, McCormick, took no testimony, relying on the date of the filing of his application as his dates of conception and reduction to practice and this date in respect of the counts we here consider is December 30, 1897. Hallwood is the junior party and upon him is the burden of proof in order to prevail in this interference. He has produced no testimony to support the dates of his conception and disclosure alleged in his preliminary statement. He produces much testimony tending to show that devices embodying the subject-matter of the issue were constructed and successfully tested during the summer of 1897. The Examiner of Interferences concluded that Hallwood proved a conception of the invention in issue at that time but that there was such delay in making use of the invention and in applying for a patent that the alleged reduction to practice was nothing more than an abandoned experiment. The Examiners-in-Chief concluded that Hallwood has fully proven a reduction to practice and reversed the decision of the Examiner of Interferences relating to the counts which we here consider and awarded priority of invention to Hallwood as to counts eight to sixteen, inclusive.

The Commissioner of Patents affirmed the decision of the Examiners-in-Chief, awarding priority of invention to McCormick as to counts one to seven, inclusive, and with these we are not here concerned, and awarding priority of invention to Hallwood as to counts eight to sixteen, inclusive. With the latter award we are concerned on this appeal.

We agree with the conclusion of the Examiners-in-Chief and of the Commissioner of Patents. It was satisfactorily shown that several machines embodying the subject-matter of the counts with which we are here concerned were made and tested by the Hallwood Company in 1897 before McCormick filed his application. It is true no one of these machines was in evidence but it was proved that they embodied the constructions in Hallwood's drawings number three and number four, number three disclosing the subject-matter of some, and number four disclosing the subject-matter of all of the counts we here consider.

The machine corresponding to drawing number three not proving satisfactory, the construction shown in drawing number four was substituted. The evidence of the witnesses Simpson, Vlerebome, Hill, Ward, Hildebrand, Hold, Squires, and Emory in connection with other facts and circumstances is convincing that a machine containing the devices corresponding to drawing number four and embodying the features of each count here in controversy was made, tested, and found satisfactory during the summer or early fall in 1892. Most of these witnesses were familiar with the machine to which the improvements were applied and identified the devices and speak intelligently of their operation. Hallwood testified that three machines, embodying the invention, were made and shipped to three cities he named. Although he produced none of them, the positive testimony of his witnesses satisfactorily supplies such omission. It is true that for some time after the successful reduction to practice Hallwood's company used an old form of interlock for the register, but it is also true that his company had on hand a stock of the old material and the ol interlock was sufficient for the ordinary use of the machines when not subjected to violent slamming. To say that the Hallwood Company adopted the tailpiece construction does not satisfy us that the company did not continue to use old material on hand. While the construction was not adopted commercially until some months later it was not discarded as unsatisfactory but quite the contrary. It is true that Spangler and Huckins, witnesses called by McCormick in rebuttal were employed by the Hallwood Company at the time and might have known of such a construction and both say they were ignorant of it. And it is notably true that Spangler's special employment and the experimental work in which he was engaged ought to have made it impossible for Hallwood's improved machine to have escaped Spangler's familiar acquaintance with it. The witnesses for Hallwood, however, so strongly confirm Hallwood that Spangler and Huckins are overborne. But on the other hand, Hill, Ward, and Emory during the same period tested these very devices and testified that they operated satisfactorily. We concur with the Examiners-in-Chief and the Commissioner of Patents in holding that Hallwood reduced to practice the construction of counts eight to sixteen, inclusive, before McCormick's application was filed, and that therefore Hallwood was properly awarded priority as the inventor in respect of these counts. All of the tribunals agreed that Hallwood was the first to conceive and it is clear he did not abandon his invention.

The decision of the Commissioner of Patents *is affirmed* and the clerk of this court will certify this opinion and decision to the Commissioner of Patents in the manner required by law.

[Court of Appeals of the District of Columbia.]

MACMULKIN *v.* BOLLÉE.

Decided June 4, 1907.

(130 O. G., 1691.)

INTERFERENCE—PRIORITY—APPEAL TO COURT—SUFFICIENCY OF DISCLOSURE CONSIDERED.

Whether or not an application involved in interference discloses the subject-matter in issue, and therefore whether or not the interference is properly declared, is a question to be ordinarily determined by the Patent Office, (*Ostergren* v. *Tripler*, C. D., 1901, 350; 95 O. G., 837; 17 App. D. C., 558; *Herman* v. *Fullman*, C. D., 1904, 625; 109 O. G., 1888; 23 App. D. C., 264, 265;) but in extreme cases where palpable error has been committed the court may review the decision of the Patent Office on this point. (*Podlesak and Podlesak* v. *McInnerney*, C. D., 1906, 558; 120 O. G., 2127; 26 App. D. C., 399.)

Mr. Hubert Howson for the appellant.
Mr. A. S. Pattison for the appellee.

McComas, J.:

MacMulkin, the appellant, filed his application on December 9, 1903, and Bollée, the appellee, filed on August 3, 1903, and is, therefore, the senior party, although a patent was issued to the appellant upon his subsequent application. MacMulkin took no testimony and conception and reduction to practice by him is therefore deemed to have happened at his filing date. Testimony taken by Bollée to show he had secured certain foreign patents was taken but need not be considered because his filing date is earlier than that of MacMulkin. The Examiner of Interferences awarded priority of invention to MacMulkin, holding that the original application of Bollée did not disclose the invention in controversy which was only disclosed by his subsequent drawings and specifications and so restricting Bollée to the date of filing them. Such date was subsequent to the filing of MacMulkin's application. The Examiners-in-Chief, who were affirmed by the Commissioner of Patents, (ante, 38; 126 O. G., 1356,) reversed the decision of the Examiner of Interferences and held that Bollée's original application did not disclose this invention and they therefore awarded priority to Bollée.

The three following issues show the matter in controversy:

1. A vaporizer for liquid hydrocarbons, comprising a number of hydrocarbon-inlets, a separate air-inlet to such hydrocarbon-inlet, a common outlet-pipe and means for cutting off one or more of the pairs of hydrocarbon-inlets and air-inlets simultaneously, as described.

2. A vaporizer for liquid hydrocarbons, comprising a number of inlets for hydrocarbons and means at all times to supply a constant flow to each inlet, an air-supply to each said inlet, an outlet for the vaporized mixture and a throttle-valve between the individual inlets and the outlet adapted to cut off or open more or fewer of the combined air and hydrocarbon inlets, substantially as described.

3. A vaporizer for liquid hydrocarbons, comprising an outlet-pipe, a throttle-valve opening thereto, a body part containing a plurality of chambers, a separate passage from each chamber to the throttle-valve and an air-supply and a hydrocarbon-supply to each chamber, the throttle-valve being adapted to cut off more or fewer of the chambers from the outlet-pipe, substantially as described.

Whether or not the application discloses the subject-matter of the interference and, therefore, whether or not the interference is properly declared, is a question to be ordinarily determined by the Patent Office. (See *Ostergren* v. *Tripler*, C. D., 1901, 350; 95 O. G., 837; 17 App. D. C., 558; *Herman* v. *Fullman*, C. D., 1904, 625; 109 O. G., 1888; 23 App. D. C., 264, 265.) However, this court has held that in extreme cases where palpable error has been committed, the decision of the Patent Office holding identity of invention between the devices of the parties to the interference may be reversed. (See *Podlesak and Podlesak* v. *McInnerney*, C. D., 1906, 558; 120 O. G., 2127; 26 App. D. C., 399.)

The case we are now considering is not such an exceptional case. .

The Primary Examiner first declared that because the specification did not explain what was meant by " carbureter " and by " sprayer " in Bollée's specifications, he could take no action on the merits. The Examiner of Interferences held that Bollée's application did not disclose any particular kind or form of carbureter and that such disclosure was only incorporated by amendment after MacMulkin's patent had issued and the inclusion of the added elements was new matter. The Commissioner, however, justly states that:

The Examiner's action in admitting the substitute specification and drawing was, in effect, a ruling on his part that the substitute specification and drawing did not contain new matter and that here was a foundation in Bollée's original application for the claims which he suggested to him.

The Examiners-in-Chief reversed the Examiner of Interferences and found that the invention was disclosed in Bollée's original application and, therefore, awarded to him priority of invention. They were affirmed by the Commissioner of Patents. We hold the finding of the Patent Office that the Bollée application as originally filed, disclosed the invention in controversy, is conclusive upon this court in this interference.

The only point at issue here is whether or not Bollée's original application discloses this invention and whether or not Bollée has the right to make the claims as based upon said application. If so, he is entitled to judgment of priority. The invention in issue is an improvement in carbureters for internal-combustion engines. It is intended to provide means for varying the quantity of explosive mixture supplied to the cylinder without altering the proportion of air to gas in the mixture; and this result is accomplished by providing a series of carbureters together with a valve by means of which one or more of the carbureters can be placed in communication with the cylinder. If Bollée's application of August 3, 1903, contained such a disclosure of this invention as to enable those skilled in the art to practice it, that date is to be deemed as the date of constructive reduction to practice by him and he is entitled to an award of priority in this case.

The Examiners-in-Chief concluded that taking the drawing and the specification together, Bollée's application shows a construction within the terms of the counts of this issue. They conclude that the first count requires that the vaporizer shall comprise a number of hydrocarbon-inlets, separate air-inlets for each of these, a common outlet-pipe, and means for cutting off one or more pairs of hydrocarbon-inlets and air-inlets simultaneously. In the second and third counts this last element is called a throttle-valve. The second count adds further means for a constant flow of hydrocarbon to each inlet, and the third count specifies further that the vaporizer has a body part with a series of chambers with a separate passage from each chamber to the throttle-valve, with an air and hydrocarbon supply for each chamber, and the Examiners-in-Chief very clearly argue that Bollée's original drawings and specifications disclose the exact invention of the counts of the issue.

In affirming this Board, the Acting Commissioner aptly said:

In the drawing of his original application Bollée showed a valve controlling communication between several chambers, which he termed "carbureters," and a passage leading to the cylinder of the engine. The primary purpose of a carbureter for an internal-combustion engine is to form a mixture of air with hydrocarbon. There can be no question, therefore, that the mere use of the term "carbureter" was a sufficient disclosure of the idea of providing "hydrocarbon-inlets," as specified in the issue. It is contended by MacMulkin that from all that appears in Bollée's application he might have intended to supply carbureted air from a reservoir, or if he intended to use an oil supply he might have used a common mixer leading to the various passages controlled by the valve. Bolée, however, in his original specification stated that he proposed to use a number of carbureters, and he referred to the several chambers controlled by the valve as "carbureters." He furthermore stated that practically perfect results could be secured by the use of two carbureters.

We agree with the Commissioner that it would be impossible for any one skilled in the art to read Bollee's original specification in connection with the drawings accompanying it without perceiving that air and hydrocarbon were to be supplied separately to each of the passages controlled by the valves. The specification refers to the use of " sprayers " and in effect states that the several chambers supply mixtures varying in the proportion of contained hydrocarbon, which result could only be secured by providing each of the chambers controlled by the valve with means for supplying both air and hydrocarbon, or, in other words, each chamber must be a carbureter, " a thing which was old and well known." Section 4888 Revised Statutes requires that the dscription shall be sufficiently full and clear—

to enable any person skilled in the art or science to which it appertains, or with which it is most nearly connected, to make, construct, compound, and use the same.

Bollée's specification and drawing meet this requirement. The exhaustive argument of appellant's counsel is met by the decision of the Patent Office that Bollée's original application was a constructive reduction to practice and that the amendment of his specification was in no wise an admission that his original application was an insufficient disclosure. It follows also that because his original application sufficed, no question of diligence in acquiring constructive reduction to practice arises here. The argument in behalf of the appellant that Bollée's application as amended does not disclose one essential element of the third issue and that the lack of a suction control leaves Bollée's disclosure an inoperative device, is not convincing. In respect to the point that count 3 requires three throttles it appears that the count called for only one throttle-valve namely the one which is adapted to cut off more or fewer of the chambers from the outlet-pipe as defined in that count. The new objection that Bollée's disclosure is not operative is in this instance a theoretical objection which need not here be discussed.

The decision of the Commissioner of Patents *is affirmed* and the clerk of this court will certify this opinion and decision to the Commissioner of Patents in the manner required by law.

[Court of Appeals of the District of Columbia.]

IN RE WILLIAMS.

Decided June 4, 1907.

(130 O. G., 1692.)

PATENTABILITY—MERE CHANGE IN DESIGN—NO INVENTION.

> Where the claim is distinguishable from the prior art by a mere arbitrary variation which amounts only to a change in mechanical design. *Held* that such a claim is unpatentable.

Mr. M. E. Robinson for the appellant.

Mr. Fairfax Bayard for the Commissioner of Patents.

SHEPARD, *J.*:

This is an appeal from the decision of the Commissioner of Patents (*ante*, 286; 130 O. G., 1688,) rejecting an application for a patent having the following claim:

> An outside burial-case consisting of a cement body of suitable form and size to receive a casket having an open top with a shoulder and an upwardly-standing flange outside of the shoulder around the upper edge of the wall, the flange having an inwardly-facing groove, a cement cover adapted to close the top of the case and rest on the shoulder and having around its edge an outwardly-facing groove, the groove of the cover and the groove of the flange together forming an upright elliptical space, and the cover and flange arranged to provide an open joint to receive in connection with said *elliptical space* a liquid cement, substantially as set forth.

Patent was denied on reference to a patent to Zarling—No. 712,030, issued October 28, 1902. The only difference between the two is in the shape of the space made to receive the liquid cement. In appellant's casket this space has around its edge an outwardly-facing groove, which makes it elliptical. In Zarling's patent this space is rectangular. The difference is one of design merely, and is clearly not patentable.

The decision is affirmed. This decision will be certified to the Commissioner of Patents as the law requires.

[Court of Appeals of the District of Columbia.]

BLUTHENTHAL AND BICKART *v.* BIGBIE BROTHERS & COMPANY.

Decided June 4, 1907.

(130 O. G., 2068.)

TRADE-MARKS—OWNERSHIP BY PARTNERS—RIGHTS UPON DISSOLUTION.

> Whatever interest in a trade-mark a retiring partner of a firm may have had ceases upon his withdrawal from the firm and remains with the surviving partner.

Mr. Joseph L. Atkins for the appellant.

Mr. E. T. Fenwick and *Mr. Smeltzer V. Kemp* for the appellee.

SHEPARD, *J.:*

This is an interference proceeding involving the right to the registration of the words " Old Velvet " as a trade-mark used in the manufacture and sale of whisky. Appellants filed April 4, and appellees April 19, 1905. The J. & G. Butler Company was also a party, but took no appeal from the final decision of the Commissioner.

The Examiner of Interferences decided in favor of Bigbie Brothers and Company, as against the other contestants, and his decision was affirmed by the Commissioner. (*Ante,* 22; 126 O. G., 1063.) There is no occasion to review the evidence, as that has been done with care, and at length, in both of the decisions referred to. Upon examination of the entire evidence, we are convinced of the soundness of the Commissioner's conclusions. As the appellees, being the last to make application, had the burden of showing prior adoption and use of the trade-mark, we deem it important only to make a brief statement of facts which we think their evidence clearly establishes. It appears that one Joseph Lawson was engaged in the sale of liquor in Lynchburg, Virginia, prior to 1861, and that he resumed said business in 1865 or 1866. During the time between then and February 19, 1887, the exact date of which is unimportant, he made or compounded an article of rye whisky which he labeled and sold as " Old Velvet." He went into partnership with one Kinnear, under the firm-name of Lawson and Kinnear. Kinnear retired and was succeeded by the son of Lawson, and the firm-name became Joseph Lawson and Son. The son retired or died before February 19, 1887. The several partnerships sold Old Velvet whisky at retail and wholesale, and the brand seems to have been well known. They used a stencil with which the brand was placed on the heads of barrels and kegs. On February 19, 1887, Joseph Lawson as surviving partner sold the entire stock of liquors to Bigbie Brothers Company, and leased the premises, which belonged to him alone, to them. He transferred the good-will and turned over to them, not only the stock on hand, but also the stencils, including Old Velvet, and the formula for making it. The purchasers continued the business, as successors to Joseph Lawson and Son. They used the stencil on barrels and kegs, and also procured a large number of labels, containing the words Old Velvet, which they applied to bottles containing whisky made after the formula therefor. Whisky, in barrels and bottles so branded and labeled, was sold continuously thereafter, and shipped to purchasers in Virginia and other States. Old Velvet was intended to be used as a trade-mark, and the brand was well known to customers. The earliest date of adoption and use claimed by appellants is February 8, 1888. Whether a date so early is established by the evidence it is immaterial to consider, as the one claimed is later than that established by the appellee.

The testimony rather indicates that the trade-mark was the separate property of Lawson. But the first retiring partner had an interest in it also, through its use during his membership of the firm, it ceased upon his withdrawal and remained with Lawson who continued to conduct the business at the same place and in the same way. (*Giles Remedy Co.* v. *Giles*, C. D., 1906, 552; 120 O. G., 1826; 26 App. D. C., 375, 382.) At any rate, the retiring partner does not appear to have asserted any interest thereafter. Assuming also that Joseph Lawson's son acquired an interest in the use of the trade-mark upon his accession to the partnership, whatever interest he may have taken passed by the sale and transfer made by the surviving partner to the appellees.

In our opinion the decision was right, and it will, therefore, *be affirmed*. This decision will be certified to the Commissioner of Patents as required by the law. *Affirmed.*

[Court of Appeals of the District of Columbia.]

McKNIGHT *v.* POHLE.

Decided June 4, 1907.

(130 O. G., 2069.)

INTERFERENCE—PRIORITY—FAILURE OF SENIOR PARTY TO DISCLOSE INVENTION.

Evidence considered and held to show that the application on which the patent involved in interference was granted did not, as originally filed, disclose the invention in issue, and priority therefore awarded to the junior party.

Mr. W. C. Pusey and *Mr. Joshua Pusey* for the appellant.
Mr. Augustus B. Stoughton for the appellee.

McCOMAS, *J.:*

In this case the three tribunals have substantially determined the issue against McKnight, appellant, and in favor of Pohle, appellee.

(C. D., 1905, 549; 119 O. G., 2519.) The following two counts disclose the issue:

1. The art of treating refractory ores containing precious metals and a refractory metalloid, which consists in pulverizing the ore, mixing with the pulverized ore a quantity of haloid salt of an alkaline metal, the relative proportions of the materials being substantially those quantitatively requisite to produce when heated in the presence of oxygen, a haloid salt of the precious metal, and an oxygen salt of the alkaline metal and the refractory metalloid, roasting the mixture with free access of air and agitation at a temperature sufficient to effect the reaction mentioned, but substantially shut off from the products of combustion, until the reactions above mentioned are accomplished, and volatilizing and recovering the precious metal values as haloids or oxyhaloids; substantially as described.

2. The art of treating refractory ores containing precious metals and a refractory metalloid, which consists in pulverizing the ore, mixing with the pulverized ore chlorid of sodium, the relative proportions of the materials being substantially those quantitatively requisite to produce when heated in the presence of oxygen, a chlorid of the precious metal and an oxygen salt of the sodium and the refractory metalloid, roasting the mixture with free access of air, but shut off from the products of combustion, and until a chlorid of the precious metal and an oxysalt of the refractory metalloid and the sodium is produced, and continuing the heating until the said chlorid is volatilized and carrying off and collecting the same separate and apart from the fumes of combustion of the furnace; substantially as described.

The operation described in Pohle's specification shows that the refractory ore is pulverized and mixed with common salt and sulfur and the mixture is heated and stirred in a current of air. Chlorids or oxychlorids of the valuable metals formed are carried off as vapors and these vapors condensing constitute the product of this process.

McKnight, having taken no testimony, the filing date of his application stands for his date of conception and constructive reduction to practice. McKnight's patent issued October 29, 1901, while Pohle did not file his application until February 26, 1902, and bears the burden of proving his case beyond reasonable doubt. The Examiner of Interferences found that Pohle conceived the invention in 1887 and that McKnight's application contained no basis for the claims in issue while the proof shows that McKnight derived portions of this process from Pohle and was not its inventor and that the invention was inserted in the McKnight application by amendments embodying Pohle's information. Without considering the question of actual reduction to practice by Pohle, the Examiner of Interferences awarded him priority.

The Examiners-in-Chief taking McKnight's application as affording proof of conception and as a constructive reduction to practice felt constrained by the doctri͟ ͟cata as applied to interference proceedings and ͟ ͟Knight had a right to make these claims i͟ ͟ntitled to a patent thereon, that his pa͟ ͟ohle's application. This tribunal, however, called the Commissioner's attention to their opinion that McKnight had never filed an application which can be regarded as one which is allowable to cover the counts of the issue or held to be a constructive reduction to practice thereof and that he had never obtained a patent valid to sustain the claims which are the counts of this issue; that lacking any constructive reduction to practice of those counts, and being without other evidence, he had no evidence of any reduction to practice of the issue of the application and that because of such failure to prove a reduction to practice, Pohle, who has proof of constructive reduction to practice, is the prior inventor of this issue. The Examiners-in-Chief concluded that the interference should be dissolved and the application of Pohle should be sent to patent. They agreed that the record of the application of McKnight's patent discloses that McKnight had no right to make in his application or in his patent the claims which are the issues of this interference. Hence *res adjudicata* does not apply.

The Commissioner concluded that Pohle failed to establish facts which would entitle him to prevail over McKnight if it be assumed that the latter's patent is grounded in his application as filed. The Commissioner then proceeds to review the testimony as the other tribunals had done. We, therefore, need not again summarize it. In *McKnight* v. *Pohle* (C. D., 1903, 619; 105 O. G., 977; 22 App. D. C., 219) many of the facts important here were involved and this court affirmed the Commissioner in sustaining a patent obtained by Pohle and Crosdale as joint inventors, which contains claims differing from the claims involved here only in the omission of the limitation to exclusion of products of combustion from the substances treated.

All of the tribunals observed that each count of the issue includes as part of the process which it defines, " roasting * * * with free access of air." McKnight's application for a patent, when filed, contained no suggestion of this step, while his drawing showed a closed vessel for heating the mixture of ground ore and salt. Pohle's caveat filed years before, showed an open-ended chamber. Not until April 16, 1901, did McKnight amend his case to include roasting the mixture with free access of air. The Commissioner and the other tribunals conclude from the testimony that McKnight and Collet, his attorney, before this amendment was filed, saw the specification and claims of an application of Pohle and Crosdale for the quite similar process to that in issue, to which we have referred, which included " roasting * * * with free access of air." We will not review the testimony which convinces us also that McKnight's amendments were obtained from Pohle in the way described by the witnesses, whose testimony is considered by all the Patent Office tribunals.

In *McKnight* v. *Pohle* (*supra*) in which McKnight was the junior party, this court referred to the omission of McKnight to mention the use of air in the application when filed for his patent here involved, and in that case affirmed the decision adverse to McKnight, which decision was based in part upon the conclusion that McKnight's application, when filed, did not include this feature of the invention. The opinion of Mr. Justice Shepard in that case is most pertinent here, especially so this conclusion:

In view of these circumstances, the testimony presented in behalf of McKnight as to his invention before January, 1900, is to be carefully scrutinized. It is significant, to say the least, that he did not disclose the invention in his application of January, 1900, if he was then in possession of the same. This omission coupled with the fact that he failed to disclose the same until it was admittedly disclosed to him by agents of another inventor, is almost sufficient of itself to warrant the conclusion that McKnight never independently invented the invention of the issue.

The Commissioner repeats his conclusion, therefore, that McKnight's original application did not disclose the invention now in issue and was not a proper foundation for the amendments by which it was made to include this invention, and further concludes that the patent granted upon this application is not to be accepted as proof of the invention of the issue at the date of the application and since the amendments were unwarranted the patent is not to be deemed evidence of this invention by McKnight at any time. We concur in this conclusion and in the decision that Pohle was entitled to a patent upon his application which fully disclosed the invention in issue. We see no reason to discuss here the other questions considered by the Commissioner of Patents. The conclusion that McKnight's patent does not support the invention in issue determines adversely his claim of priority of this invention.

The decision of the Commissioner of Patents *is affirmed* and this opinion and decision will be certified to the Commissioner of Patents in accordance with law.

[Court of Appeals of the District of Columbia.]

BURSON *v.* VOGEL.

Decided April 2, 1907.

(131 O. G., 942.)

1. INTERFERENCE — PRELIMINARY STATEMENT — ALLEGATIONS — RESTRICTION OF PROOF.

Where the preliminary statement of a party alleges that an "experimental" device was constructed in January, 1901, and no date of reduction to practice is given, such party will not be restricted to the date of his application for his reduction to practice where no objection was made to the statement on the ground that it was indefinite. (*Hammond* v. *Basch*, C. D., 1905, 615; 115 O. G., 804; 24 App. D. C., 469, distinguished.)

2. SAME—EVIDENCE—PRIVATE DIARY IN SHORTHAND.

An inventor after having testified in regard to his conception and the work done thereon produced a shorthand diary and read a number of entries from the diary showing dates and memoranda of work done. Of this evidence the court said: " Burson is a man over seventy years of age and appears to have kept a diary for fifty years in which he made a daily record of events. There is nothing in the appearance of this diary to excite suspicion. The dates follow consecutively. It is true that the record is in shorthand after the Pittman system; but it appears that interpretation thereof could be made with sufficient certainty by one skilled in that method. * * * We see no substantial difference between this and the ordinary use of memoranda by a witness to refresh his memory."

3. SAME—REDUCTION TO PRACTICE—REPRODUCTION OF ORIGINAL MACHINE.

A device which was experimented with and afterward laid aside and partly dismantled and which when produced in evidence did not have all of the original parts, some of the important parts being replacements, Held not to constitute a reduction to practice, the evidence tending to show the identity of the parts replaced and the original parts not being satisfactory.

4. SAME—SAME—CRUDE MACHINE—SUBSEQUENT IMPROVEMENTS.

A machine may be crude in construction, but if it contains all the essential elements of the invention of the issue and in its operation successfully demonstrates its practical efficacy and utility reduction to practice is accomplished. (*Coffee* v. *Guerant*, C. D. 1894, 384; 68 O. G., 279; 3 App. D. C., 497; *Norden* v. *Spaulding*, C. D. 1905, 588; 114 O. G., 1828; 24 App. D. C., 286; *Gallagher* v. *Hien*, C. D., 1905, 624; 115 O. G., 1830; 25 App. D. C. 77; *Lowrie* v. *Taylor*, C. D., 1906, 713; 123 O. G., 1665; 27 App. D. C., 522.) The mere fact that mechanical improvements may be suggested and made in the course of operation that tend to perfect the operation of the machine and increase its practical efficiency, while retaining the essential elements of the invention which it puts in practice, does not impair the effect of the original demonstration of utility, if established satisfactorily.

5. SAME—CONCEPTION OF INVENTION—IDEA OF MEANS NECESSARY.

The mere idea that there ought to be an arrangement to strip a stocking from a board or form on which it was mounted and return the board to the one who placed the stockings thereon and the illustration of this idea by the originator thereof by stripping a stocking from a form by the passage thereof between his hand and the edge of a table does not amount to a conception of an invention. No mechanism was described by which the desired result could be obtained. Invention consists of the conception of the idea and of means for putting it in practice and producing the desired result. Until the latter conception is complete and ready to be put in some practical form there is no available conception of the invention within the meaning of the patent law. (*Mergenthaler* v. *Scudder*, C. D., 1897, 724; 81 O. G., 1417; 11 App. D. C., 264.)

6. SAME—CONCEALMENT OR SUPPRESSION AFTER REDUCTION TO PRACTICE.

The failure to file an application for more than two years after reduction to practice where the machine was put into actual use in a factory the policy of the management of which was not to patent machines used for their own work is not such a concealment or suppression of the invention as will subordinate the inventor's rights to one who, claiming conception in July, 1900, reduced it to practice in April, 1901, but did not file an applica-

tion until May, 1902, and did not arrange to manufacture the same until June, 1903.

7. PUBLIC USE—QUESTION NOT CONSIDERED IN AN INTERFERENCE.

The question whether the invention in issue was placed in public use by one of the parties to an interference is not one which can be raised in an interference proceeding, but is one for the consideration of the Commissioner of Patents on the final allowance of the patent.

Mr. George W. Rea for the appellant.

Mr. Edgar M. Kitchin and *Mr. Edward T. Fenwick* for the appellee.

SHEPARD, *J.:*

This is an interference proceeding involving priority of invention of an improvement in singeing-machines.

The issue is embraced in twenty-two counts which show forth in a machine for singeing stockings, a combination of rollers, the ending-point of which is in proximity to the initial point, whereby the articles to be singed, mounted on stretching-boards, are continuously advanced from the starting-point to the ending-point, and in their journey pass between gas, or singeing jets; and a stripping device whereby the further motion of the board effects the withdrawal of the article stretched upon it, and returns the board to the point, where, having another article attached, it may be fed again to the machine for singeing and stripping.

For the sake of brevity, the following counts 1, 2, 11, 14, and 22, are extracted as fairly representing the issue:

1. A finishing-machine embodying stripping means, the articles to be treated being mounted on supports so as to be acted on by said means.

2. In combination with means for treating tubular fabrics supported from within upon suitable formers, of means for carrying the said formers with the articles to be treated through the said treating means, and means for stripping said articles from the formers.

11. In combination with singeing means, of means for carrying the supports holding the articles to be singed through the said singeing means, means for returning the supports and means for stripping the said articles from their supports on their return movement.

14. In combination with means for singeing stockings or like articles mounted upon supports, of means for carrying the supports with the articles thereon through said singeing means, means for changing the direction of movement of the supports after they have passed through the singeing means, and means for returning the supports.

22. In combination with means for singeing stockings or like articles mounted upon supports, of means for carrying the articles through the singeing means, an inclined belt located in the path of movement of the said supports for changing the direction of movement thereof, means for returning the supports to a point adjacent to the feed end of the machine, and means for stripping the articles from their supports.

The application of Vogel was filed May 28, 1902, and that of Burson April 17, 1903.

In his preliminary statement, Vogel alleged conception July 2, 1900, drawings made July 7, 1900, disclosure to others July 8, 1900; and that he embodied the invention in a full-sized machine which was completed about April 6, 1901, and operated successfully April 9, 1901. He also alleged the manufacture of machines for sale after September 22, 1903, under contract with manufacturers entered into April, 1903.

Burson alleged conception in August, 1899, sketches December, 1899, but no model; and disclosure to others December 27, 1899. He also alleged that he constructed one experimental machine in January, 1901, and has since had constructed two machines containing the invention in controversy.

The Examiner of Interferences awarded priority to Burson. On appeal to the Examiners-in-Chief, that decision was reversed; and they were affirmed by the Commissioner (C. D., 1906, 508; 125 O. G., 2361,) with final award to Vogel. From this decision Burson has appealed.

A preliminary question must be disposed of before passing to a consideration of the evidence relating to conception and reduction to practice of the invention of the issue.

The appellee contends that the allegation in the preliminary statement of Burson, to the effect that he constructed an experimental machine in January, 1901, does not amount to an allegation of a reduction to practice, and, hence, in respect of that machine and the two other machines thereafter constructed, to which no date is given, limits Burson to the date of his application as his first reduction to practice. We cannot concur in this view of the effect of the statement. It is not so precise as it might have been, and if exception had been taken to it on that ground, *in limine*, its amendment might possibly have been compelled; at any rate, if unamended, after exception, the limitation of its averments now insisted upon might reasonably be imposed. Neither of the two decisions adverse to Burson is rested upon such limitation.

We do not regard the case, under the circumstances, as falling under the rule applied in *Hammond* v. *Basch* (C. D., 1905, 615; 115 O. G., 804; 24 App. D. C., 469.) In that case the statement alleged the construction of a "model" in May, 1900, and this was followed by the specific allegation of actual reduction to practice in February, 1901, through the completion and use of a full-size, operative device. The invention was a simple one, and the evidence tended to show actual reduction to practice of the alleged model. But in view of the specific allegation of later reduction to practice in the statement, which remained unamended, it was held that the date thereof could not be carried back of the time alleged. In taking his testimony, the opposing party had the right to assume that the model was what it was alleged to be, and nothing more. Here the party, after-stating that he had made no model, alleged the construction of an experimental machine on a certain date, and did not follow it with an allegation of a later date of actual reduction to practice. An experimental machine—and the first construction of a complicated device usually is—may be, according to the evidence relating to its construction and use, a mere unsuccessful and, therefore, an abandoned experiment, or, though crude in its construction, may furnish a satisfactory demonstration of its utility. If, therefore, the evidence shall show that this experimental machine was successfully operated, Burson ought to have the benefit of it as of the date alleged. He cannot, of course, have the benefit of an earlier date than that alleged, no matter what his evidence may show. (*Lowrie* v. *Taylor*, C. D., 1906, 713; 123 O. G., 1665; 27 App. D. C., 522, and cases cited.)

Without reviewing the evidence at length, we think it sufficient to show that Burson had a conception of the invention and disclosed it to others as early as the first of July, 1900. His own testimony as to this is corroborated, and the entries in his diary, with this corroborating evidence, fix dates. As the recitals in this diary seem to have been rejected by the Commissioner, we think it proper to say that we cannot agree with his conclusions. Burson is a man over seventy years of age and appears to have kept a diary for fifty years in which he made a daily record of events. There is nothing in the appearance of this diary to excite suspicion. The dates follow consecutively. It is true that the record is in shorthand after the Pittman system; but it appears that interpretation thereof could be made with sufficient certainty by one skilled in that method. Having testified in regard to his conception and the work done therein, he read a number of entries from the diary showing dates and memoranda of work done. We see no substantial difference between this and the ordinary use of memoranda by a witness to refresh his memory. While such testimony, uncorroborated by other witnesses, is not sufficient proof of the conception of an invention, we think it has sufficient corroboration in the testimony of Ziock, the superintendent of the factory, and Westberg, a carpenter, who worked on all of the machines of Burson.

Under the ordinary burden of proof imposed upon a junior party, we do not think the evidence sufficient to show that the experimental machine was successfully reduced to practice. It was evidently experimented with, but was afterward laid aside and partly dismantled. When produced as an exhibit it had all of the necessary parts, but the important ones in this controversy were replacements. We are not satisfied with the evidence tending to show that the parts replaced were identical with those that had been removed. It was given some five years after the fact, and lacks certainty. The reduction to practice by the use of the experimental machine—No. 1—is, however, of no practical importance under the allegation of its construction in 1901. The proof shows, we think, that machines 2 and 3 were being constructed in December, 1900, and January, 1901, and were completed and tried during the latter month. This evidence, we think, shows a successful reduction to practice, at least during the early spring of 1901.

The Examiners-in-Chief held that the evidence relating to these two later machines was not sufficient to show reduction to practice, and held that Burson must be confined, therefore, to the date of filing his application. They base their conclusion upon the evidence of Burson, who said, with apparent candor, that machine 2 required—

considerable changing and bettering of different parts all of which changes, of course, stopped the operation of the machine while said changes were being made. The machine which is called No. 3 was better constructed and ran better but there were some changes and some interruptions in its work for some considerable time.

They say:

If these machines had in January, 1901, the construction which they now have, they were of course reduction to practice as defined in the issue, but the testimony does not satisfy us that they were in the condition which they now are, at that date, or that they were successful in operation at that time.

This conclusion ignores the further fact, testified to by Burson, that these changes were made in the line of better workmanship, and that substantially all the parts of the first construction were retained. The resemblance between the new machines, and their resemblance to the first experimental machine, indicate the presence in the former of the essential elements of the issue; and the evidence of the two witnesses before referred to is to the same effect.

A machine may be crude in construction, but if it contains all the essential elements of the invention of the issue, and in its operation successfully demonstrates its practical efficacy and utility, reduction to practice is accomplished. (*Coffee* v. *Guerant*, C. D., 1894, 384; 68 O. G., 279; 3 App. D. C., 497; *Norden* v. *Spaulding*, C. D., 1905, 588; 114 O. G., 1828; 24 App. D. C., 286; *Gallagher* v. *Hien*, C. D., 1905, 624; 115 O. G., 1330; 25 App. D. C., 77; *Lowrie* v. *Taylor*, C. D., 1906, 713; 123 O. G., 1665; 27 App. D. C., 522.) The mere fact that mechanical improvements may be suggested and made in the course of operation, that tend to perfect the operation of the machine and increase its practical efficiency, while retaining the essential elements of the invention which it puts in practice, does not impair the effect of the original demonstration of utility, if established satisfactorily. *Having* found that Burson's evidence sufficiently established his conception about July 1, 1900, and reduction to practice, as early at least as March 1, 1901, the burden was shifted to Vogel, the senior applicant.

The Examiner of Interferences awarded him July 8, 1900, as his date of conception. The Examiners-in-Chief held his evidence insufficient and restricted him, both in respect of conception and reductin to practice, to his filing date. The Commissioner, agreeing with them in their conclusions as regards Burson's claims to conception and reduction to practice, did not consider it necessary to pass upon Vogel's evidence, as his earlier filing date entitled him to the award of priority.

Vogel testified to his conception of the invention on July 8, 1900, and that he made a sketch showing the same on that date. No witness was produced who saw this sketch, and the only witness introduced to corroborate Vogel was one Loerding. His testimony was to the effect that a few days after July 4, 1900, Vogel came to witness who was at work on a machine singeing stockings, and said the machine was not complete; that there ought to be an arrangement to strip the stocking and return the board to the man who put them on. He then, by using his hands and the edge of the table removed a stocking and the board remained in his hand. No mechanism was described by which the desired result could be obtained. Invention consists of the conception of the idea and of means for putting it in practice and producing the desired result. Until the latter conception is complete and ready to be put in some practical form, there is no available conception of the invention within the meaning of the patent law. (*Mergenthaler* v. *Scudder*, C. D., 1897, 724; 81 O. G., 1417; 11 App. D. C., 264; *Funk* v. *Haines*, C. D., 1902, 559; 100 O. G., 1766.) Failing to establish the earlier date of conception, the next date is that of April, at which time also it would seem that Vogel embodied his completed idea in a machine and reduced it to practice. Whether it amounted to a complete reduction to practice is, however, immaterial because of the conclusion reached in respect of Burson's claim to earlier conception, which also antedates Vogel's alleged date, and to reduction to practice.

There was very great delay on the part of Burson in filing his application for a patent, but it does not appear that he suppressed or intended to conceal knowledge of his invention after its reduction to practice. The Burson Knitting Company was engaged in the manufacture of stockings and other knit goods on a large scale, and used the stripping-machines in the course thereof. Burson testified that it was the policy of the company not to patent machines used in work in its own factory. This is, perhaps, not an unusual practice on the part of manufacturers of products by the use of machines. Whether so or not it does not amount to such a concealment of the invention, after reduction to practice, as to subordinate his right to a later discoverer, under the rule governing in *Mason* v. *Hepburn*, (C. D., 1898, 510; 84 O. G., 147; 13 App. D. C., 86.)   (See *Trissell* v. *Thomas*, C. D., 1904, 616; 109 O. G., 809; 23 App. D. C., 219.)   Moreover, Vogel, claiming to have conceived the invention July 8, 1900, did not construct a machine for use until April, 1901.   Having constructed it and used it in manufacture in April, 1901, he delayed application for patent until May 28, 1902; and it was not until June, 1903, that he made an arrangement with a manufacturer to build machines and put them on the market.

Whether Burson's use of his machine in his factory for more than two years before applying for a patent, amounted to such public use within the meaning of section 4886, Revised Statutes, as to bar his right to a patent, is not a question which can be raised in this case which involves priority of invention as between him and Vogel.   The question is one for the consideration of the Commissioner on the final allowance of a patent.

Burson having been shown, as we view the evidence, to have been the first to conceive the invention, as well as to reduce it to practice, is entitled to the award of priority.   The decision of the Commissioner must therefore be reversed.   It is so ordered, and the clerk will certify this decision to the Commissioner of Patents as the law requires.   *Reversed.*

[Supreme Court of the District of Columbia.]

THE UNITED STATES OF AMERICA, *ex rel.* TUTTLE, *v.* ALLEN, COMMISSIONER OF PATENTS.

Decided December 21, 1906.

(126 O. G., 760.)

1. PRACTICE—MANDAMUS.
    The writ of mandamus cannot be used in the place of an appeal or writ of error to correct any erroneous decision made by the Primary Examiner in the course of his official duties.

2. SAME—SAME.
    The writ of mandamus cannot be used to control the exercise of judicial discretion.

3. DIVISION—SAME.
    Where division had been required between the claims of an application for patent and it was sought by mandamus to compel consideration of the claims upon their merits, *Held* that it is of no consequence to the court in rendering the decision upon mandamus whether the Office was right or wrong in requiring division.

4. ABANDONMENT OF APPLICATION.
    Where after final requirement of division numerous letters and petitions are filed in regard thereto, but no appeal is taken or compliance had within

the ensuing year, *Held* that it is not clear that the actions taken could prevent the operation of the statute as to abandonment.

5. SAME—APPEAL.

The action of the Office holding an application to be abandoned is, in effect, a rejection. If that action is erroneous, the applicant has his remedy by way of appeal.

Mr. Edward L. Gies for the petitioner.

Mr. John M. Coit for the respondent.

BARNARD, J.:

In this case the petitioner prays for a writ of mandamus to require the Commissioner of Patents to order a reconsideration of a requirement of the Examiner in charge, for a division of his application numbered 134,953, for a patent for an improvement in voting-machines, so far as relates to claim No. 11 in said application, which claim covers interlocking means between push-keys, both severally and in the aggregate, and a single whole-ticket key, for independent voting; and further, to require the respondent to cause an examination to be made of the relator's alleged new invention or discovery, as set forth and claimed in claim No. 1 of his said application; and also to cause an examination to be made of several other claims in his said application, not required to be separated from said claim No. 1 and presented in a separate application, with a view to the allowance or rejection of all said claims; and further to require the respondent to cancel an order heretofore made, holding that the relator had abandoned his said application.

The answer of the respondent, filed February 15, 1906, sets forth the history of the case, as shown by the record in the Patent Office, and attaches copies of orders, motions, petitions, etc., as exhibits.

On March 9, 1906, the relator filed an amendment to his petition in this court; and on the same day a stipulation of counsel was filed, which allowed certain additional facts to appear by way of answer, and allowed the petitioner time to file reply.

On March 20, 1906, the relator filed a reply; and on April 11, 1906, the respondent filed a demurrer thereto.

By a stipulation filed Nov. 23, 1906, the case thus made, was submitted to the court, on briefs, without oral argument.

The answer of the respondent, filed February 15, 1906, sets forth the history of the case, as shown by the record in the Patent Office, and attaches copies of orders, motions, petitions, etc., as exhibits.

On March 9, 1906, the relator filed an amendment to his petition in this court; and on the same day a stipulation of counsel was filed, which allowed certain additional facts to appear by way of answer, and allowed the petitioner time to file reply.

On March 20, 1906, the relator filed a reply; and on April 11, 1906, the respondent filed a demurrer thereto.

By a stipulation filed Nov. 23, 1906, the case thus made, was submitted to the court, on briefs, without oral argument.

It appears that relator's application for Letters Patent was filed Dec. 12, 1902, and the same contained a number of claims.

On Jan. 14, 1903, the Primary Examiner decided that there should be a division of the claims, under Rule 41 of the Patent Office. He specifically pointed out what claims were required to be grouped together, but by a clerical error, claim 11 was omitted from the group which defined an interlocking or key-arresting system, but was evidently intended to be grouped with claims 8, 9, 14, 15, and 21, relating to the same subject.

The relator asked a reconsideration of the first requirement for division, on Sept. 10, 1903, and again on Sept. 14, 1903; and the Examiner on Nov. 11, 1903, denied the petition for a reconsideration, and repeated his requirement, and made his action final, expressly requiring said claim 11 to be divided out.

On October 3, 1904, the relator appealed, by petition, from the action of the Examiner, to the Commissioner of Patents, from the several orders requiring a division, and asked that the Examiner be no longer allowed to insist upon said orders.

To this petition the Examiner filed his answer, Oct. 6, 1904; and Oct. 18, 1904, the Commissioner dismissed the petition, and stated that applicant's only remedy was by appeal to the Examiners-in-Chief.

On Oct. 24, 1904, the applicant filed an argument; and on Oct. 26, 1904, a petition, in which petition he asked that the Examiner waive his requirement of division for the present, and act upon the claims, in order that an appeal might be taken to the Examiners-in-Chief; and that the Examiner be directed to select such invention, and claims relating thereto, as might be retained in the original application.

On Oct. 28, 1904, the Commissioner denied the relator's petition of Oct. 26, 1904. (C. D., 1904, 537; 113 O. G., 1967.)

On Oct. 31, 1904, the applicant filed an amendatory petition, in which he requested that the Examiner be directed to retain claim 1, and all its pertinent claims, in the original application.

The Commissioner denied this petition, Nov. 2, 1904, and stated that when a division was required, it must be settled before the Office would examine the claims to determine their probable novelty and patentability; and also held, under the authority of the case of *U. S., ex rel. Steinmetz* v. *Allen* (C. D., 1904, 703; 109 O. G., 549) that the refusal to grant a patent because the application contained separate inventions, was in effect a rejection of the application, and entitled the applicant to an appeal to the Examiners-in-Chief.

On Nov. 1, 1904, relator filed another petition, dated Oct. 29, 1904, *gain urging* that the Examiner retain claim 1, and all its relative claims, in the original case, and act upon them, regardless of the orders of division.

On Nov. 3, 1904, the Commissioner denied the last petition, on the ground that the division must be settled before any action could be had on the merits; and again holding that the requirement for a division is deemed a rejection.

On Feb. 13, 1905, the Examiner informed the applicant that his case was held to have been abandoned on Nov. 11, 1904, for failure to prosecute within one year; that being one year from the time said claim 11 was expressly required to be divided out; and when the requirement for a division was confirmed, or made final.

The applicant thereupon wrote three letters under date of Feb. 17, Mar. 1, and Mar. 10, respectively, asking for prompt attention, and stating that the holding of abandonment was not understood, in that no action had been taken with reference to certain claims.

On April 11, 1905, the Commissioner repeated the holding of abandonment, and stated that applicant had forfeited his right to proceed, by his failure to specifically elect what claims were to be retained in his original application.

The applicant filed a petition on May 8, 1905, again asking a reconsideration of the case; and on May 11, 1905, the Examiner answered the petition, and repeated the holding of abandonment, because the applicant did not take proper action within a year from Nov. 11, 1903. Under date of June 5, 1905, the Commissioner denied this petition.   (C. D., 1905, 274; 117 O. G., 1796.)

It seems that the misunderstanding between the petitioner and the Patent Office began at the time the application for a patent was required to be divided, under Rules 41 and 42 of the Rules of Practice of the Patent Office. The Examiner in charge had decided that the applicant claimed in his application, independent inventions of such a nature that a single patent could not be issued to cover them.

In such case Rule 42 provides that the inventor will be required to limit the description, drawing, and claim of the pending application, to whichever invention he may elect. It also provides that if the independence of the inventions be clear, such limitation must be made before any action upon the merits; otherwise it may be made at any time before final action thereon, in the discretion of the Examiner.

The whole difficulty in which the applicant now finds himself, seems to have started by his persistence in trying to have the Examiner in charge reconsider the decision which required his application to be divided; and, notwithstanding the repeated decisions both of the Examiner and the Commissioner, confirming his first decision, he failed to take his appeal to the Examiners-in-Chief.

He seems to have continued, by appeals to the Commissioner on petition, and by applications to the Examiner in charge, to try to secure the reconsideration, or some modification of the order; and particularly to have the Examiner decide which inventions might be continued in connection with claim 1, as his pending application, instead of himself making the selection, as seems to be required by Rule 42.

The·original application containing a number of claims which could be divided into groups, the Examiner did not require a separate application for each claim, but did require a number of claims to be divided out of the original application, leaving certain claims therein for matters that did not constitute a distinct subject of invention, together with what are called combination claims.

If the applicant had deemed this action of the Examiner to be improper, he had his remedy by appeal, after the requirement for division had' been repeated and made final, which it was on Nov. 11, 1903, when the Examiner refused to reconsider the case on the applicant's petition and argument filed in September, 1903.

This remedy seems to have been established by the decision of the Supreme Court in the said case of the *United States ex rel. Steinmetz* v. *Allen*, (C. D., 1904, 703; 109 O. G., 549; 192 U. S., 543.)

Not having accepted the suggestion of the Examiner, that the application should be divided in the manner pointed out, and not having taken an appeal, the next difficulty in which the applicant found himself was, that at the expiration of one year from November 11, 1903, when the requirement was for a second time made and became final, his application was held to be abandoned under section 4894 of the Revised Statutes, (29th Statute-at-Large, 692.)

This statute requires that all applications for patents shall be completed and prepared for examination within one year after the filing of the application; and in default thereof, or upon failure to prosecute the same within one year after any action therein, of which notice shall have been given to the applicant, they shall be regarded as abandoned, unless it be shown to the satisfaction of the Commissioner, that such delay was unavoidable.

Rule 171, based on this statute, defines what shall be considered as an abandoned application.

Rules 31 and 77 are also based on the said statute, Rule 77 defining the time when the one year shall begin to run, namely, from the day when the last official notice of any action by the Office was mailed to the applicant.

Rule 171, after defining what an abandoned application is, defines what prosecution is necessary to save an application from abandonment, and says that such prosecution must include such proper action *as the condition* of the case may require.

The petitioner, having a right to appeal from the requirement to have his application divided, it is of no consequence in this court, in a mandamus proceeding, whether the Examiner was right or wrong in such decision.

If the applicant thought the Examiner was wrong, and he still insisted on the right to prosecute his application with the several claims therein joined, then he could have taken his appeal to the Examiners-in-Chief, and if their decision was adverse, a further appeal to the Commissioner of Patents.

The writ of mandamus cannot be used in the place of an appeal or writ of error, to correct any erroneous decision made by the Primary Examiner in the course of his official duties.

The applicant having his right of appeal, which must be presumed to be an adequate remedy, cannot rightfully ask the court to give him the same relief by the writ of mandamus. (*Ex parte Virginia Commissioners*, 112 U. S., 177; *Riverside Oil Company* v. *Hitchcock*, 21 App. D. C., 252.)

In the last-mentioned case, Mr. Justice Morris stated the established rule in these words:

> The writ of mandamus, it is well settled, cannot be used to serve the purpose of an appeal or writ of error; nor can it be used to control the exercise of judicial discretion.

Having this right of appeal, and having neglected to pursue it, within one year after the mailing of notice that the action of the Examiner in charge had been repeated and made final, can the petitioner escape the predicament in which he is placed by the express language of section 4894 of the Revised Statutes?

He took no action in the prosecution of his claim for patent, except the ineffectual action by way of repeated motions and petitions, in which he sought to have the Examiner reverse himself as to the requirement for division of his application, whereas Rule 171 requires that he should take such proper action as the condition of the case demands. That was, in this case, to file separate claims, and so divide his application, or to take his appeal from the order requiring such division, under section 4909 of the Revised Statutes.

It is not clear that such action on his part, as he did take, could prevent the operation of the statute as to abandonment, and I must therefore hold that he has no remedy by mandamus, to prevent the abandonment which the Office has declared.

If, however, the Office has declared that his application has been abandoned, and that decision should be erroneous, he has a remedy by appeal from that decision, which would bar him from any standing in this court in a proceeding for mandamus. On both of these points it seems to me that the respondent's contention must be sustained.

There is one other contention that the relator makes, namely, that he is entitled to the writ of mandamus to compel a consideration and decision as to his right to a patent under claim No. 1, of his application, and under such other claims as the Office may hold to be properly joined with said claim, No. 1. That is, without himself electing to abandon the claims required to be divided out, and electing what claims he wishes to prosecute in the pending application, he asks that the Office be required to proceed with its consideration of part of his application for a patent, on the merits. That is to say, that notwithstanding the Patent Office through its Examiner and Commissioner, holds that the relator's application has been abandoned; and notwithstanding the requirement that the application should be divided, before being examined on the merits, the court is asked to require, by mandamus, that the Examiner should proceed with the case, and proceed in a certain way.

The authorities have established the rule over and over again, that a mandamus will not lie to compel an officer having discretion to decide a question in a particular manner; and only where the petitioner has a clear legal right to the relief he claims, and it is a plain ministerial duty of the respondent to act in the premises, will the writ be issued.

In this case the action of the Patent Office is, in effect, a rejection of the plaintiff's application for a patent on two grounds, namely, because the requirement for division was not complied with; and because the application has been abandoned by failure to take the proper steps in its prosecution within one year.

Any order that the court might make to require the Office to proceed with the examination of claim No. 1, or any other claim, would operate as a reversal of the action taken by the Examiner and the Commissioner; and would be the substitution of the judgment of the court in place of that of the Patent Office, where jurisdiction has been vested by the statute, and where all the technical facilities have been provided for the examination and decision of questions pertaining to patents.

Many of the facts which are stated as appearing in this case, are admitted to be true by the stipulation filed herein on March 9th, 1906, and the petitioner has, by his reply to the answer to the respondent, admitted certain other of the facts assumed by the court in the foregoing statements.

In his said reply the relator repeats all the several allegations and averments contained in his petition, except such as are by the defendant's return fully admitted. He avers also that the several dates in the fourth paragraph of page 3 of defendant's first answer, should be 1904, and not 1903; and he admits that since the rule to show cause was issued herein, that he has filed in the Patent Office an appeal to the Examiners-in-Chief, from the action of the Primary Examiner, holding his application to have been abandoned.

It is insisted by the respondent that this appeal necessarily takes out of this case the right of the relator to insist upon an order of the court to require of the respondent a decision on the question of abandonment, and leaving only the other questions herein which have been above mentioned, and which contention I am inclined to think is correct.

Under section 1276 of the code of this District, the petitioner was allowed to plead or to traverse all or any of the material averments set forth in the respondent's answer, and the defendant was allowed to take issue or demur to said plea or traverse; and further proceedings were to be taken as in an action for a false return.

The proper practice under this section was pointed out by the court of appeals in the case of *West* v. *Hitchcock*, (19 App. D. C., 346.)

The demurrer to the reply seems to raise the question of the sufficiency of the petitioner's case; and, after considering all the facts which are admitted by the relator, or stated in his petition and reply; and after considering the matters claimed in his reply to be in avoidance of the facts contained in the answer of the respondent, I have reached the conclusion that the petitioner has failed in his reply and petition to state a plain right to the relief claimed by him; and that the court cannot properly grant him the writ of mandamus for any of the purposes asked for in the petition; and I will, therefore, sign an order sustaining the demurrer to the reply, and enter judgment for the defendant for costs, as appears to be proper under sections 1278 and 1279 of the code.

[Supreme Court of the District of Columbia.]

THE UNITED STATES OF AMERICA, *ex rel.* THE NEWCOMB MOTOR CO., *v.* ALLEN, (MOORE SUBSTITUTED.) COMMISSIONER OF PATENTS.

Decided June 21, 1907.

(130 O. G., 302.)

1. MANDAMUS NOT GRANTED—WHERE OTHER LEGAL REMEDIES EXIST.
   Where the relator is not without other complete and adequate remedies, a writ of mandamus will not lie.

2. SAME—MERELY TO EXPEDITE THE CASE.
   Although the writ of mandamus might serve as an inexpensive and summary conclusion of the whole matter, providing this court had jurisdiction to issue the writ, yet neither economy of time, nor expense can weigh anything as against the orderly procedure under the law of a given case.

3. SAME—WHERE COURT IS WITHOUT JURISDICTION.
   Where the Commissioner has in fact acted and rendered his decision touching the very matter here in controversy and has the clear legal right

to act and decide for himself, this court is without jurisdiction to review his action and above all to compel him by its writ to undo what he has done.

4. SAME—PRACTICE.

Where the Commissioner had the power to act and has acted, *Held* that it is wholly immaterial whether in the judgment of the court he was right or wrong in his determination and that in overruling the motion for a writ of mandamus no opinion will be expressed as to the merits of the relator's contentions.

Mr. Charles H. Duell, Mr. Robert N. Kenyon, and *Mr. Walter F. Rogers* for the petitioner.

Mr. Fairfax Bayard and *Mr. W. S. Ruckman* for the respondent.

Mr. Melville Church of counsel for the respondent and representing the General Electric Company.

ANDERSON, *J.:*

This case is before the court upon motion of the relator, based upon the petition and return herein, for a writ of mandamus against the respondent, Commissioner of Patents, directing him to vacate and set aside certain proceedings in the Patent Office bearing upon the subject-matter of certain interferences which had been declared and dissolved in that Office.

The interferences referred to involved, on the one side, two certain patents of the relator, and, on the other side, four certain pending applications for patents of parties named Thomson and Lemp.

The relator contends that upon the expiration of the limit of appeal fixed by the Examiner from his decision in the interferences that relator's opponents had no right to make the claims involved in the issues of interference and dissolving such interferences in consequence thereof, that such decision became final and *res judicata,* and that all further proceedings in the Patent Office respecting the right of the relator's opponents had no right to make the claims involved in the the jurisdiction of the Office.

It is by no means clear to the court, however, that the respondent has exceeded his jurisdiction in allowing these further proceedings. The determination of the question involved the construction of certain statutes prescribing the rights of parties before the Patent Office. and the respondent gave careful consideration to the whole question. and decided that the provision of the rules for interlocutory motions to dissolve interferences and appeals in connection therewith. was entirely independent of, and in no wise affected, the unconditional right given to applicants for patents by section 4909 Revised Statutes of the United States of appealing whenever their claims are. "twice rejected." by the Primary Examiner, and that it would be neither legal nor consistent with the statute to hold that a party's *failure* to exercise a right of appeal not given by the statute and resting solely upon, and being the creature of, the rules of the Patent Office, estops him from exercising a right of appeal *unconditionally* given to him by the statute.

If the respondent is right in his construction of section 4909 of the Revised Statutes of the United States, namely, that applicants for patents are thereby given the indisputable right of appeal whenever their claims are twice rejected by the Primary Examiner, and that Rules 122 and 124 have no application to such cases, but are limited to interlocutory motions to dissolve interferences and appeals in connection therewith, then clearly these rules cannot avail anything as against the statute, and cannot be invoked in support of the application for a writ of mandamus in this case. Whether the distinction thus pointed out by the respondent actually exists under a right interpretation of the law and the rules themselves is not for this court to decide, as the court is without jurisdiction so to do.

As was said by the United States Supreme Court in *Riverside Oil Co.* v. *Hitchcock*, (190 U. S., 324:)

Whether he decided right or wrong, is not the question. Having jurisdiction to decide at all, he had necessarily jurisdiction, and it was his duty to decide as he thought the law was, and the courts have no power whatever under those circumstances to review his determination by mandamus or injunction.

OTHER REMEDIES.

It seems to me that this is clearly not a case where the relator is without other legal remedy than that afforded by writ of mandamus, in order to rightly determine and enforce his rights in the premises, and thereby save himself harmless from any possible error in the decisions of which it complains. If the questions involved are in fact and in law *res judicata* as the relator contends, ample opportunity will be afforded it to fully and fairly press that contention for final determination upon appeal from the final decision in the interference proceedings between the relator and Thomson and Lemp, that must necessarily be prosecuted to a final conclusion before patents can issue to the latter for the inventions covered by the relator's patents. Moreover, if the Commissioner should decide against the relator's contentions, his right of appeal from such decision to the court of appeals would seem to be unquestionable, and, if the relator should prevail on such appeal, it necessarily follows that the court would reverse the Commissioner and enter an order of priority in its favor, as was done in *Blackford* v. *Wilder*, (*ante*, 491; 127 O. G., 1255.) While, on the other hand, if the court of appeals should decide against the relator, then its opponents would be entitled to their patents, with the right still reserved to the relator to avail himself of any error in the decisions leading to the granting of such patents in an interfering patent suit as provided under section 4918 Revised Statutes. Without undertaking to enumerate and define the specific statutory remedies available to the relator against the alleged errors in the decisions of which it complains; it is sufficient to say, in a word, that in the opinion of the court the relator is not without other complete and adequate legal remedies suited to the exact situation of this case.

While it is true that, if the questions here involved are *res judicata*, the writ of mandamus invoked by the relator would serve as an inexpensive and summary conclusion of the whole matter, providing this court had jurisdiction to issue the writ, yet neither economy of time or expense can weigh anything as against orderly procedure under the law of a given case.

As was said by the Supreme Court of the United States in *Bayard* v. *United States*, (127 U. S., 426, at p. 250:)

> The writ of mandamus is a remedy to compel the performance of a duty required by law, where the party seeking relief has no other legal remedy and the duty sought to be enforced is clear and indisputable.

The Commissioner has decided that the failure of Thomson and Lemp to prosecute their appeal from the decisions of the Primary Examiner dissolving the interferences, is not conclusive of the questions here involved; or, in other words, that these questions are not, by virtue of the decision of the Primary Examiner, *res judicata*. In so deciding, the Commissioner was necessarily required to study, compare and interpret, according to his own best judgment, aided presumably by the legal advisers of his Office; the various sections of the statutes relating thereto. And in so deciding he was acting clearly within his jurisdiction, as the head of the Office charged with the duty of exercising his judgment and discretion, as contradistinguished from the performance of a mere ministerial act or duty. It therefore follows, in the opinion of the court, that inasmuch as the Commissioner has in fact acted and rendered his decision touching the very matter here in controversy, and having the clear legal right to act and decide for himself, this court is without jurisdiction to review his action and above all to compel him by its writ to undo what he has done.

As was said by Mr. Justice Miller, in *Johnson* v. *Towsley*, (13 Wall., 72, 83:)

> When the law has confined to a specific tribunal, the authority to hear and determine such matters arising in the course of its duties, the decision of that tribunal, within the scope of its authority, is conclusive upon all others.

In the case of *Dunlap* v. *Black*, (128 U. S., 48,) it was also said by the Supreme Court of the United States:

> The Court will not interfere by mandamus with the executive officers of the Government in the exercise of their ordinary official duties, even where those duties require an interpretation of the law, the Court having no appellate

power for that purpose. Whether, if the law were properly before us for consideration, we should be of the same opinion or of a different opinion is of no consequence in the decision of the case.

In *Kirwin* v. *Murphy*, (189 U. S., 55,) the Court quoted with approval the following passage found in the case of *Litchfield* v. *The Register and Receiver*, (9 Wall., 577, 579:)

The principle has been so repeatedly decided in this Court, that the judiciary cannot interfere either by mandamus or injunction with executive officers such as the respondents here, in the discharge of their official duties, unless those duties are of a character purely ministerial, and involving no exercise of judgment or discretion, that it would be useless to repeat it here.

Having thus decided this court is without jurisdiction to require the respondent to undo what, in the exercise of his judgment and discretion and under his interpretation of the law and of the rules of his Office, he has done, it is wholly immaterial whether in the judgment of this court he is right or wrong in his determination of these questions; and I therefore express no opinion as to the merits of the relator's contentions in such connection, but content myself with thus briefly stating my reasons for overruling the relator's motion that the writ of mandamus issue notwithstanding the respondent's answer or return to the relator's petition.

The motion will therefore be *overruled*, the rule to show cause *discharged*, and the petition *dismissed*.

[Supreme Court of the United States.]

COMPUTING SCALE COMPANY OF AMERICA *v.* THE AUTOMATIC SCALE COMPANY.

Decided February 25, 1907.

(127 O. G., 849.)

1. PATENTABILITY—INVENTION—REARRANGEMENT OF ELEMENTS OF COMBINATION.
   Where a given combination of elements is old in an automatic computing-scale of the horizontal type and the prior art also shows a computing-scale arranged vertically, although it was not entirely automatic, a claim covering a rearrangement of the elements of the automatic horizontal scale to provide a vertical construction can be sustained only to a limited extent.

2. CONSTRUCTION OF CLAIMS—ACQUIESCENCE IN REJECTION OF PATENT OFFICE.
   Where an inventor seeking a broad claim which is rejected, in which rejection he acquiesces, substitutes therefor a narrower claim, he cannot be heard to insist that the construction of the claim allowed shall cover that which has been previously rejected. (*Corbin Cabinet Lock Company* v. *Eagle Lock Company*, C. D., 1893, 612; 65 O. G., 1066; 150 U. S., 38–40, and cases there cited.)

Mr. Melville Church for the appellant.
Mr. H. P. Doolittle for the appellee.

Mr. Justice DAY delivered the opinion of the Court.

This is an appeal from the Court of Appeals of the District of Columbia, (C. D., 1905, 704; 119 O. G., 1586;) affirming a decree of the Supreme Court of the District dismissing the bill of the Computing Scale Company of America, appellant, againt the Automatic Scale Company, based upon the alleged infringement of Letters Patent No. 700,919, granted to the complainant as the assignee of the inventor, Austin B. Hayden, said letters bearing date May 27, 1902, for an improvement in computing-scales.

The bill contained a prayer for an injunction and accounting. The answer denied the patentability of the alleged invention of the plain-

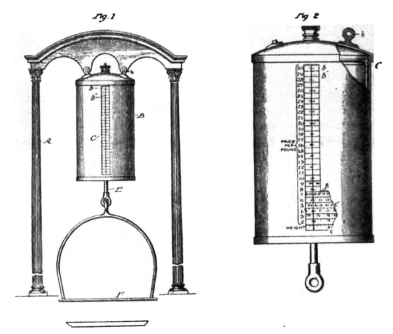

tiff, set up the alleged anticipating invention of one Christopher. and denied infringement.

The alleged improvement of Hayden is shown in the accompanying illustrations taken from the patent:

To understand these drawings they are to be viewed in the light of the description of the mechanism given by complainant's expert. which has the approval of the expert of the defendant, and was accepted as correct in the court of appeals. This description, somewhat abridged, is as follows:

The two principal parts of the mechanism are as follows: 1st, a vertically-arranged, non-rotating frame which comprises and includes a vertical cylin-

drical casing which incloses, conceals, and protects the major portion of the oper-'
ating portions of the scale, and upon which are marked the price indications
which indicate the price per pound at which the articles weighed are to be sold.
As clearly shown in the drawings, this external casing or frame is provided
with a vertically-disposed sight-opening through which the coacting mechanism
is observable, and along one vertical edge of the sight-opening are arranged the
numerals indicating the price per pound.

The second of these principal parts is a second cylinder located within the
casing, this cylinder constituting a computing-cylinder or chart-drum upon
which are placed indications indicating the weight in pounds of the article
weighed, and also having other indications indicating the price of an article
weighed· corresponding to the weight and to the price per pound. This chart-
drum or computing-cylinder extends vertically within the external casing and it
is arranged to rotate on a vertical axis within the external casing. This casing
is appropriately connected to the spring balancing mechanism and to the scale-

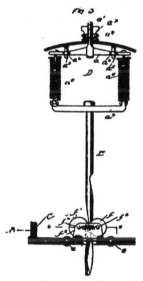

pan so that when the spring balancing mechanism moves up and down on the placing or removing of a load on the scale-pan, the chart-
drum will be rotated in one direction or the
other within the external casing or frame.

As shown in Fig. 2, the weight and value
indicating figures are placed in horizontal rows
on the external surface or periphery of the
rotatable chart-drum of the computing-cylinder,
the weight indications being shown in a horizontal row at the bottom, and the price indications in horizontal rows above, there being as
many of these horizontal rows of price-indica-
ting figures as there are "price-per-pound" indicating figures on the fixed external casing.
These value-indicating figures ·on the chart-
drum are computed at different rates corresponding to the "price-per-pound" figures on
the external casing. As indicated in figure 2
of the drawings of the patent, there is supposed
to be a weight on the scale-pan of five pounds,
this weight being indicated on the weight-scale,
and it will be seen that in such instance the
various value indications on the chart-drum
opposite the "price-per-pound" indications on the fixed casing, are in each illustrated instance, five times as great as the corresponding "price-per-pound"
indications. The drawings illustrate only a portion of the indicating-figures on
the chart-drum, but it will be understood in practice that this drum will be
entirely covered on its external surface with figures corresponding to the
weights multiplied by the figures indicating "price per pound" on the non-
rotatable external casing. Accordingly whenever the interior chart-drum is
turned a distance corresponding to the load placed on the scale-pan, the value
of the load can be read at once opposite the figures on the external casing which
correspond to the price per pound of the article weighed.

The various price indications on the chart-drum are visible through the sight-
opening in the external casing.

The mechanism whereby the chart-drum is rotated a distance corresponding to the weight of the load placed on the scale-pan is as follows: The balancing mechanism is a spring-balance comprising two springs which are suspended from a suitable portion of the non-rotating frame of the scale. To the lower ends of these springs is attached a cross-bar in the middle of which depends a rod this cross-bar and rod constituting the runner of the scale. (See Fig. 3.) The scale-pan is suspended from the lower end of this rod as illustrated in Figure 1. When a load is placed on the scale-pan the vertical runner moves vertically downward distending the spring to an extent proportional to the weight of the load. In order to indicate the weight this vertical movement of the spring-supported runner is converted or translated into a rotary movement of the chart-drum by suitable intervening mechanism. This intervening mechanism consists of a spiral groove of high pitch on the vertical rod and two rollers journaled in suitable bearings carried by the rotatable chart-drum, the bearings of one of these rollers being spring-pressed so that the rollers are held in yielding contact with the spiral groove on the rod. Consequently as the rod moves vertically the spiral groove thereof causes the chart-drum or computing-cylinder to rotate on its vertical axis.

Accordingly, the mechanism is such that the vertical movement of the runner is translated into rotary movement of the chart-drum and the chart-drum is rotated to an extent proportional to the vertical movement of the runner.

In his application, Hayden, having set forth a description of his invention, disclaiming any intention to limit his invention by the precise description of the specifications, except as appears from his claims, sets forth eleven (11) claims, which he alleges as new and desires to secure by Letters Patent.

The claims alleged to be infringed in this case are numbered 1, 2, 6, 7, and 8. Numbers 1 and 2 are practically alike, except that in No. 2 the spring-supported, load-bearing, and cylinder-revolving rod is described as non-rotatably suspended. Claims 6, 7, and 8 have some trifling variations, but, in the view we take of this case, they are sufficiently embodied in claim No. 6. We shall, therefore, consider, in arriving at a decision, claims 1 and 6. They are as follows:

1. In a spring-balance computing-scale, the combination of a suitably-supported vertical non-rotatable casing provided with a price-index, a vertical rotatable computing-cylinder journaled in said casing, provided with cost computations, a spring-supported load-bearing and cylinder-revolving rod suspended from said casing, and connecting means between rod and computing-cylinder, whereby by longitudinal movement of the rod rotary movement is imparted to said cylinder, substantially as and for the purpose set forth.

6. In a spring-balance, the combination of a non-rotating frame providing an external casing and having means for supporting it from above, weighing-springs secured at their upper ends to rigid parts of said frame, a vertically-movable runner which is suspended from the lower ends of said springs and is provided with depending means to support the load, a chart-drum rotatably mounted within said casing on a vertical axis and having external horizontal rows of value-indicating figures computed at different rates, said casing having a sight-opening through which portions of said value-indicating rows may be seen, and corresponding rate-indicating figures on the outer face of said frame adjacent to the value-indicating rows on the chart-drum, and mechanism for

translating the vertical movements of the runner into the rotary movements of the chart-drum.

Hayden did not assume to be a pioneer in this field of invention, but he claims to have made an improvement in computing-scales of the spring-balance type, and states his object to be specially to increase the computing capacity of scales of that type.

An examination of the record discloses that computing-scales have been the subject of prior inventions and were well known at the time of Hayden's application. It is true that the scales disclosed in the prior art were generally those having a horizontal axis, case, and cylinder, although it was not new to arrange a scale vertically.

If we are to read the claims as broadly as is contended for and omit for the present vertical construction shown by Hayden, we shall find in the patent of Phinney, No. 106,869, of August 30, 1870, a computing-scale having the general elements of a non-rotatable casing, provided with a price-index and rotatable cylinder journaled in the case and having computations thereon, a suspended, spring-supported, load-bearing, and cylinder-revolving rod, and connecting means between the rod and computing-cylinder, to impart rotary motion to the inner cylinder. This is perhaps more emphatically true in the invention of Smith, Patent No. 545,616, of September 3, 1895.

In the patent of Babcock, No. 421,805, February 18, 1890, a vertical construction is shown. It is true that Babcock's invention was not automatic in its operation, and required the intervention of the operator to complete the required process, but it serves to show that the idea of vertical construction was not new when Hayden entered the field. Taking the state of the art at that time, it is evident that there is little room to claim a broad construction of Hayden's improvement. It is well settled by numerous decisions of this Court that while a combination of old elements producing a new and useful result will be patentable, yet where the combination is merely the assembling of old elements producing no new and useful result, invention is not shown. (*Specialty Manufacturing Co.* v. *Fenton Metallic Manufacturing Co.*, 174 U. S., 492–498, and previous decisions of this Court there cited.)

It is true that many valuable inventions seem simple when accomplished, and yet are entitled to protection. The books abound in cases showing inventions involving only small departure from former means, yet making the differ   defective mechanism and a practical method of accom   In such cases a decision in favor of invention as di   mere mechanical improvement has not infrequ   w of the fact that the device has made the diff   ticable machine and a useful improvement displacing others occupying the field. (*Krementz* v. *The S. Cottle Co.*, C. D., 1894, 521; 69 O. G., 241; 148 U. S., 556; *Consolidated Brake Shoe Co.* v. *Detroit Steel & Spring Co.*, 47 Fed. Rep., 894; *Star Brass Works* v. *General Electric Co.*, 111 Fed. Rep., 398.)

In the present case it nowhere appears in the testimony, nor is it claimed in the specifications of Hayden's patent, that the prior mechanisms of horizontal construction were impracticable or insufficient. There is no suggestion that Hayden's invention has been the last step as between an inoperative machine and one practically operative and useful. There is no showing that it has been generally accepted in the trade and displaced the former machines used for the same purpose. Without resort to the record in the Patent Office, we think it is plain that the invention is but a small advance upon others already in use.

Broadly considered, the elements of Hayden's invention were in the horizontal machines, and the idea of vertical construction was old. Considering this invention in the light of what occurred in the Patent Office in connection with the other considerations already referred to, and the state of the art at the time, we think Hayden's invention can only be sustained to a limited extent.

Before taking up the record as disclosed in the file-wrapper and contents we may premise that it is perfectly well settled in this Court by frequent decisions that where an inventor, seeking a broad claim which is rejected, in which rejection he acquiesces, substitutes therefor a narrower claim, he cannot be heard to insist that the construction of the claim allowed shall cover that which has been previously rejected. (*Corbin Cabinet Lock Co.* v. *Eagle Lock Co.*, C. D., 1893, 612; 65 O. G., 1066; 150 U. S., 38–40, and cases there cited.)

A late statement of the rule, and one as favorable to the inventor as the previous cases would admit, is found in *Hubbell* v. *United States*, (C. D., 1900, 382,389; 93 O. G., 1124, 1126; 179 U. S., 77, 80,) as follows:

An examination of the history of the appellant's claim, as disclosed in the file-wrapper and contents, shows that in order to get his patent he was compelled to accept one with a narrower claim than that contained in his original application; and it is well settled that the claim as allowed must be read and interpreted with reference to the rejected claim and to the prior state of the art, and cannot be so construed as to cover either what was rejected by the Patent Office or disclosed by prior devices. (*Leggett* v. *Avery*, C. D., 1880, 283; 17 O. G., 445; 101 U. S., 256; *Shepard* v. *Carrigan*, C. D., 1886, 116; 34 O. G., 1157; 116 U. S., 593; *Knapp* v. *Morss*, C. D., 1893, 651; 65 O. G., 1593; 150 U. S., 221, 227.)

It is quite true that, where the differences between the claim as made and as allowed consist of the mere changes of expression, having substantially the same meaning, such changes, made to meet the views of the Examiners, ought not to be permitted to defeat a meritorious claimant. While not allowed to revive a rejected claim, by a broad construction of the claim allowed, yet the patentee is entitled to a fair construction of the terms of his claim as actually granted.

Looking to the record in the Patent Office, we find that claim 1, as originally presented, read as follows:

1. In a spring-balance computing-scale, the combination of a suitably-supported vertical non-rotatable casing provided with a price-index, a vertical rotatable computing-cylinder journaled in said casing, provided with cost computations, a spring-supported load-pan supported from said casing, and means connected with said pan and cylinder for rotating the cylinder as the pan is lowered under pressure, substantially as and for the purpose set forth.

The Examiner rejected this claim upon the patent of Smith, No. 545,616, price-scales, and in view of the patent of Turnbull, No. 378,382, spring-scales, saying, " It would not involve invention to arrange upon Turnbull's scales a vertical stationary casing having within it a revolvable computing-chart, the axis being connected with the index-carrying-shaft P shown in the Turnbull patent."

To this the applicant, through his attorneys, replied:

The first portion of the Examiner's letter is not understood, as there are no modifications referred to in lines 6 to 26 of page 3. A reconsideration of the claims is requested, for the reason that it is believed that the references cited do not anticipate any of the claims. In both of the references cited a rack-bar extending transversely of the center of rotation of the computing-chart serves, by means of engagement with a pinion at the axis of the computing-chart, to rotate the latter. This is entirely different from applicant's construction, and it is not seen that the references are pertinent to the issue. Certainly, the references neither singly nor taken together anticipate the structure set forth in the claims, and there can hardly be any question that the construction which applicant shows is a substantial improvement in the art. It is hoped that all the claims may be allowed.

But the Examiner again rejected claims 1, 8, and 9 upon the references of record, and held that it would not involve invention to arrange upon the vertical shaft of Turnbull's scale a computing-chart and inclosing case having the characteristics of Smith's scale. To this the attorneys for applicant answered:

These claims are canceled, not because considered unallowable, but because it is not desired to prosecute an appeal. In view of the fact that the allowed claims appear to cover the invention as it would be constructed in practice. The cancelation is made, therefore, without prejudice to the claims which remain.

The sixth claim was allowed upon the suggestion of the Examiner, as follows:

In a spring-balance, the combination of a non-rotating frame providing an external casing and having mear⸗ ᵗ⸗ from above, weighing-springs secured at their upper ⸗ ᵈ frame, a vertically-movable runner which is suspen⸗ ᵗ said springs and is provided with means to supp⸗ rotatably mounted within said casing on a ver⸗ ᵒⁿtal rows of value-indicating figures computed at different rates, said casing having a sight-opening through which portions of said value-indicating rows may be seen, and corresponding rate-indicating figures on the outer face of said frame adjacent to the value-indicating rows on the chart-drum, and mechanism for transmitting the vertical movement of the runner into the rotary movements of the chart-drum.

It was afterwards stated by the Examiner:

Upon consideration of claim 6 preparatory to the declaration of interference it is found that the claim does not clearly and patentably distinguish from the scale shown in the patent to Herr, No. 651,801, June 12, 1900, price-scales, and it is therefore necessary to reject the claim. It is believed, however, that the claim may be rendered allowable by inserting *depending* before "means" in line 6,

and, accordingly, the word "depending" was inserted in the claim, so as to make it in its present form. How this added anything to the patentability of the mechanism described it is difficult to perceive, in view of the presence of "depending means to support the load" in all scales of this class.

The general rule, as stated, as to the effect of a patentee striking out a broad claim and accepting a narrow one, is conceded by the learned counsel for appellant, but it is contended that if an inventor presents a broad claim and strikes it out and then presents and obtains an equally broad claim, he loses no right by such action, and may justly claim his allowed claim to be a broad one and have relief accordingly. But we think the action of the Department in this case cannot be thus eliminated. Claim 1, as presented, had contained the words "a spring-supported load-pan supported from said casing, and means connected with said pan and cylinder for rotating the cylinder as the pan is lowered under pressure," and as allowed there was inserted "a spring-supported load-bearing and cylinder-revolving rod suspended from said casing, and connecting means between rod and computing-cylinder, whereby by longitudinal movement of the rod rotary movement is imparted to said cylinder, substantially as and for the purpose set forth." This limitation to specific means is certainly a narrowing of the claim.

It was accepted, as the patentee said, "in view of the fact that the allowed claims appear to cover the invention as it would be constructed in practice."

We cannot think it was the intention of the Department, after requiring the insertion of "a spring-supported load-bearing and cylinder-revolving rod" and "connecting means between rod and computing-cylinder" to secure the rotary movement of the inner cylinder as a means of saving claim 1, to then permit the claim to be granted broadly in allowing other claims. And we believe it would be a more reasonable construction of the letter o ̶ ̶ ̶ ̶ cant to say that he recognized that his invention, "as cons ̶ ̶ ̶ ̶ ̶ read into it to sustain the claim the specific means shown for translating the vertical movement of the runner into the rotary movement of the chart-drum, rather than as saving a right to construe a claim broadly as including in one claim what had just been refused in another.

It is to be noted that Hayden, in his specifications, says:

> The spiral rod passing through the lower ends of the casing and serving, by means of its connection with the two cylinders, to rotate the computing-cylinder is regarded as the essence of this feature of the invention, however, regardless of the precise details of connection between cylinders and rod.

In view of the action of the Patent Office in this case and the acquiescence of the applicant, considered also in view of the state of the art, in our opinion it is necessary to have this novel element of the invention read into them in order to save the claims of Hayden's patent.

Conceding that this spiral rod and its connections with the cylinder in the manner and for the purposes stated is a novel feature in the combination and entitled to protection, it is of that narrow character of invention which does not entitle the patentee to any considerable range of equivalents, but must be practically limited to the means shown by the inventor. The distinction between pioneer inventions permitting a wide range of equivalents and those inventions of a narrow character, which are limited to the construction shown, has been frequently emphasized in the decisions of this Court. (*Cimiotti Unhairing Co.* v. *American Fur Refining Co.*, C. D., 1905, 729; 116 O. G., 1452; 198 U. S. 399, 406, and cases therein cited.)

Thus limiting the invention, we do not think the construction of the defendant amounts to an infringement. Its mechanism, by means of which the downward movement of the load accomplishes the rotary movement of the cylinder, consists of a bar which has a rod extended upward and carrying a rack which meshes with a pinion on a shaft journaled in bearings on a cross-bar of the frame of the machine. On this shaft is a gear meshing with the pinion, secured to an upright shaft journaled in bearings in the frame, and projecting above it so as to receive a light frame composed of cross-arms and a circular rim to which the chart-drum is secured. The downward movement of the load-supporting hook causes the rack to move in the same direction, rotating the horizontal shaft by means of the pinion, and this movement is communicated by means of the gearing to the upright shaft carrying the chart-drum. The cylinder-revolving rod with its connections, which, as we have seen, was made an essential element to accomplish invention in Hayden's device, is not found. The complainant's expert is of opinion that it is shown in the hook at the bottom of defendant's scale for holding the load-pan. We cannot agree to this conclusion; the hook is not the cylinder-revolving spiral rod and does not accomplish its function.

The court of appeals held the sixth claim void. We are of the opinion that it cannot be allowed for the broad claim "mechanism for translating the vertical movement of the runner into the rotary movement of the chart-drum," but must be limited to Hayden's suspended rod with its spiral, engaging with the rollers, or similar devices on the cylinder, practically in the manner and for the purposes shown by him. If the claim be thus limited, for the reasons we have already stated, the mechanism of the defendant does not infringe.

We find no error in the decree rendered by the court of appeals, and it is *affirmed*.

[Supreme Court of the United States.]

KESSLER *v.* ELDRED.

Decided May 13, 1907.

(128 O. G., 1690.)

1. PATENTS—DECREE OF NON-INFRINGEMENT—QUESTION RES ADJUDICATA THROUGHOUT THE UNITED STATES.

Held that a final decree for the defendant in one circuit in a suit upon a patent upon the ground of non-infringement entitled the defendant to continue the business of making and selling throughout the United States the article which he had theretofore been making and selling without molestation by the complainant through the patent in suit.

2. SAME—SAME—SUBSEQUENT SUIT AGAINST DEFENDANT'S CUSTOMERS—WRONGFUL.

Held that said decree makes a suit by the complainant against any of defendant's customers for alleged infringement of the patent sued upon a wrongful interference with defendant's business.

3. SAME—ASSUMPTION OF DEFENSE OF SUIT AGAINST CUSTOMER—NO ESTOPPEL FROM PROCEEDING DIRECTLY AGAINST COMPLAINANT.

Where a suit upon a patent terminates for the defendant and complainant thereafter sues a customer of the defendant upon the same patent and the aforesaid defendant assumes the defense of his customer's suit. *Held* that he is not thereby estopped from proceeding against the complainant for wrongfully interfering with his business.

4. SAME—SAME—SAME—MAY PROCEED IN EQUITY.

Held that the aforesaid defendant was entitled to proceed against the complainant in equity.

Mr. R. S. Taylor for Kessler.
Mr. C. C. Linthicum for Eldred.

This case comes to this Court from the Circuit Court of Appeals for the Seventh Circuit upon a certificate of that court of questions of law concerning which it desires instructions. Accompanying the certificates is a statement of facts. The statement of the facts and the certificate of the questions of law are as follows:

STATEMENT OF THE CASE.

Kessler, a citizen of Indiana, prior to 1898 had built up an extensive business in the manufacture and sale of electric cigar-lighters, and had customers throughout the United States. Eldred, a citizen of Illinois, and an inhabitant of the Northern District, was the owner of Patent No. 492,913, issued to Chambers on March 7, 1893, for an electric lamp-lighter. Eldred was a competitor of Kessler's and manufactured a similar form of lighter (entirely dissimilar from that described in the Chambers patent,) so that it was not a matter of much importance to customers which lighter they bought. In 1898 Eldred began a suit against Kessler in the District of Indiana for the infringement of the Chambers patent. The bill alleged that Kessler's manufacture and sale of the Kessler lighter infringed all the claims. The answer denied that Kessler's lighter infringed any of the Chambers claims. On final hearing the circuit court found for Kessler on the issue of non-infringement and dismissed the bill. That decree was affirmed in 1900 by the Circuit Court of Appeals for the Seventh Circuit. (*Eldred* v. *Kessler*, 106 Fed. Rep., 509.)

Subsequently, Eldred brought suit on the same patent in the Northern District of New York against Kirkland, who was selling a similar lighter, but not of Kessler's make. The circuit court found for Kirkland on the issue of non-infringement and dismissed the bill. The Circuit Court of Appeals for the Second Circuit reversed that decree and held the Kirkland lighter to be an infringement. (*Eldred* v. *Kirkland*, 130 Fed. Rep., 342.)

In June, 1904, Eldred filed a bill for infringement of the same patent in the Western District of New York against Breitwieser, user of Kessler lighters, which were identical with those held in *Eldred* v. *Kessler*, to be no infringement of the Chambers patent. Many of Kessler's customers were intimidated by the Breitwieser suit, so that they ceased to send in further orders for lighters and refused to pay their accounts for lighters already sold and delivered to them. Kessler assumed the defense of the Breitwieser suit, and will be compelled in the proper discharge of his duty to his customers to assume the burden and expense of all suits which may be brought by Eldred against other customers. In this state of affairs Kessler, a citizen of Indiana, in July, 1904, filed a bill against Eldred in the Circuit Court for the Northern District of Illinois, the State and district of Eldred's citizenship and residence, to en Eldred from prosecuting any suit in any court of the United St against any one for alleged infringement of the Chambers patent by purchase, use or sale of any electric cigar-lighter manufactured by Kessler and identical with the lighter in evidence before the Circuit Court for the District of Indiana and the Circuit Court of Appeals for the Seventh Circuit in the trial and adjudication of the suit of Eldred against Kessler. From an adverse decree by the circuit court Kessler perfected an appeal to this Court.

Upon the foregoing facts the questions of law concerning which this court desires the instruction and advice of the Supreme Court are these:

First. Did the decree in Kessler's favor, rendered by the Circuit Court for the District of Indiana in the suit of Eldred against Kessler, have the effect of entitling Kessler to continue the business of manufacturing and selling throughout the United States the same lighter he had theretofore been manufacturing and selling, without molestation by Eldred through the Chambers patent?

Second. Did the decree mentioned in the first question have the effect of making a suit by Eldred against any customer of Kessler's for alleged infringement of the Chambers patent by use or sale of Kessler's lighters a wrongful interference by Eldred with Kessler's business?

Third. Did Kessler's assumption of the defense of Eldred's suit against Breitwieser deprive Kessler of the right, if that right would otherwise exist, of proceeding against Eldred in the State and district of his citizenship and residence for wrongfully interfering with Kessler's business?

Fourth. If Eldred's acts were wrongful, had Kessler an adquate remedy at law?

Mr. JUSTICE MOODY delivered the opinion of the Court.

The industry of counsel has not discovered any decision on the exact questions presented by the certificate, and they agree that those questions are not settled by controlling authority. The decision of the case turns upon the effect of the judgment in the suit which Eldred brought against Kessler. Both manufactured and sold electric cigar-lighters. Eldred, being the owner of a patent issued to one Chambers for an electric lamp-lighter, brought a suit against Kessler, in which it was alleged by the plaintiff and denied by the defendant that the cigar-lighters manufactured by Kessler infringed each and all of the claims of the Chambers patent. On the issue thus joined there was final judgment for Kessler. This judgment. whether it proceeds upon good reasons or upon bad reasons. whether it was right or wrong, settled finally and everywhere, and so far as Eldred, by virtue of his ownership of the Chambers patent, was concerned, that Kessler had the right to manufacture, use and sell electric cigar-lighter before the court. The court, having before it the respective rights and duties on the matter in question of the parties to the litigation, conclusively decreed the right of Kessler to manufacture and sell his manufactures free from all interference from Eldred by virtue of the Chambers patent, and the corresponding duty of Eldred to recognize and yield to that right everywhere and always. After this conclusive determination of the respective rights and duties of the parties, Eldred filed a bill for an infringement of the same patent against Breitwieser, on account of his use of the same kind of Kessler cigar-lighter which had been passed on in the previous case, and Kessler has assumed the defense of that suit. Whether the judgment between Kessler and Eldred is a bar to the suit of *Eldred* v. *Breitwieser*, either because Breitwieser was a privy to the original judgment, or because the articles themselves were by that judgment freed from the control of that patent, we deem it unnecessary to inquire. We need not stop to consider whether the judgment in the case of *Eldred* v. *Kessler* had any other effect than to fix unalterably the rights and duties of the immediate parties to it, for the reason that only the rights and duties of those parties are necessarily in question here. It may be that the judgment in *Kessler* v. *Eldred* will not afford Breitwieser, a customer of Kessler, a defense to Eldred's suit against him. Upon that question we express no opinion. Neither it nor the case in which it is raised are before us. But the question here is whether, by bringing a suit against one of Kessler's customers, Eldred has violated the right of Kessler. The effect which may reasonably be anticipated of harassing the purchasers of Kessler's manufactures by claims for damages on account of the use of them, would be to diminish Kessler's opportunities for sale. No one wishes to buy anything, if with it he must buy a lawsuit. That the effect to be anticipated was the actual effect of the Breitwieser suit is shown by the statement of facts. Kessler's customers ceased to send orders for lighters, and even refused to pay for those which had already been delivered. Any action which has such results is manifestly in violation of the obligation of Eldred, and the corresponding right of Kessler, established by the judgment. Leaving entirely out of view any rights which Kessler's customers have or may have, it is Kessler's right that those customers should, in respect of the articles before the court in the previous judgment, be let alone by Eldred, and it is Eldred's duty to let them alone. The judgment in the previous case fails of the full effect which the law attaches to it if this is not so. If rights between litigants are once established by the final judgment of a court of competent jurisdiction those rights must be recognized in every way, and wherever the judgment is entitled to respect, by those who are bound by it. Having by virtue of the judgment the right to sell his wares freely without hindrance from Eldred, must Kessler stand by and see that right violated, and then bring an action at law for the resulting damage, or may he prevent the infliction of the unlawful injury by proceedings *in personam* in equity? If Eldred succeeds in his suit against one of Kessler's customers, he will naturally bring suits against others. He may bring suits against others, whether he succeeds in one suit or not. There may be and there is likely to be a multiplicity of suits. It is certain that such suits if unsuccessful would at the same time tend to diminish Kessler's sales and to impose upon him the expense of defending many suits in order to maintain the right which by a judgment has already been declared to exist. If the suits are successful the result will be practically to destroy Kessler's judgment right. Moreover, though the impairment or destruction of Kessler's right would certainly follow from the course of conduct which Eldred has begun, it would be difficult to prove in an action at law the extent of the damage inflicted. An action at law would be entirely inadequate to protect fully Kessler's unquestioned right, and under these circumstances, though there may be no exact precedent, we think that the jurisdiction in equity exists. Nor do we see any good reason why Kessler's interposition for the defense in the suit of *Eldred* v. *Breitwieser* debars him from his remedy in equity.

It follows from the foregoing reasoning that the first and second questions certified should be answered in the *affirmative,* and the third and fourth in the *negative,* and *it is so ordered.*

[Supreme Court of the United States]

MARY V. CORTELYOU AND JAMES G. CORTELYOU, ADMINISTRATORS OF THE ESTATE OF JOHN G. CORTELYOU, DECEASED; NEOSTYLE COMPANY, AND BRODRICK COPYGRAPH COMPANY OF NEW JERSEY, PETITIONERS. *c.* CHARLES ENEU JOHNSON & COMPANY.

Decided December 2, 1907.

(131 O. G., 2147.)

1. INFRINGEMENT—CONTRIBUTORY—SALE OF UNPATENTED SUPPLIES FOR USE WITH PATENTED MACHINE.

Where a machine is sold under the restriction that it was to be used only with supplies made by the vendor, a defendant who sells supplies which are used with such machine cannot be held liable as a contributory infringer of the patent for the machine where it does not appear that the defendant ever solicited an order for such supplies, or was ever notified by the plaintiffs of the rights which they claimed, or that the executive officers of defendant had knowledge of the special character of such machines or the restrictions on the purchase of supplies.

2. SAME—NOTICE—NOTICE TO SALESMAN NOT NOTICE TO COMPANY.
   Notice to a salesman of a company who was not an officer or general
   agent of the company is not such notice as will bind the principal with
   respect to all future transactions.

Mr. Edmund Wetmore and *Mr. S. O. Edmonds* for the petitioners.
Mr. Francis T. Chambers for the respondents.

Mr. JUSTICE BREWER delivered the opinion of the Court.

This is a suit to restrain an alleged infringement of a patent granted June 22, 1897, for the stencil-duplicating machine known as the rotary Neostyle. The plaintiffs below, petitioners here, represent the entire interest in the patent. There is no claim of any infringement by using or selling the patented machines, but of an indirect infringement in the following manner: For the last few years the rotary Neostyle has been sold subject to this license, which was plainly disclosed on the base-board of the machine:

License agreement. This machine is sold by the Neostyle Company with the license restriction that it can be used only with stencil paper, ink and other supplies made by the Neostyle Company, New York city.

The defendant company (which is engaged in the manufacture and sale of ink) is, it is contended, engaged in selling ink to the purchasers of these machines for use thereon; that it is thus inducing a breach of the license contracts and is responsible as indirectly infringing the patent rights of plaintiffs. The circuit court sustained the contention and entered an interlocutory decree for an injunction and an accounting. (138 Fed. Rep., 110.) On appeal the Circuit Court of Appeals for the Second Circuit reversed this decree and remanded the case to circuit court, with instructions to dismiss the bill (76 C. C. A. 455,) whereupon the case was brought here on certiorari.

The three judges of the circuit court of appeals concurred in reversing the decree of the circuit court on the ground that the evidence was not sufficient to show that the defendant had notice that the machines for which the ink was ordered had been sold under any restrictions, but they differed upon the question whether there was any liability in case sufficient notice of the license agreement had been brought home to the defendant. The majority were of the opinion that the doctrine of contributory infringement, which they conceded to exist, should not be extended beyond those articles which are either parts of a patented combination or device, or which are produced for the sole purpose of being so used, and should not be applied to the staple articles of commerce. In that view of the case the article supplied being ink, a thing of common use, its sale to a purchaser of the Neostyle machine would be no infringement.

While in *Bement* v. *National Harrow Company* (186 U. S., 70) this Court held, in respect to patent rights, that with few exceptions—

any conditions which are not in their very nature illegal with regard to this kind of property, imposed by the patentee and agreed to by the licensee for the right to manufacture or use or sell the article, will be upheld by the courts—

it is unnecessary to consider how far a stipulation in a contract between the owner of a patent right and the purchaser from him of a machine manufactured under that right, that it should be used only in a certain way, will sustain an action in favor of the vendor against the purchaser in case of a breach of that stipulation. So although—

if one maliciously interferes in a contract between two parties, and induces one of them to break that contract to the injury of the other party, the party injured can maintain an action against the wrongdoer—

Angle v. *Chicago, St. Paul &c. Railway*, (151 U. S. I, 13,) it is also unnecessary to determine whether this states the full measure of liability resting upon a party interfering and inducing the breaking of a contract, for we concur in the views expressed by all the judges of the court of appeals that there is no sufficient evidence of notice. True the defendant filled a few orders for ink to be used on a rotary Neostyle, but it does not appear that it ever solicited an order for ink to be so used, that it was ever notified by the plaintiffs of the rights which they claimed, or that anything which it did was considered by them an infringement upon those rights. Further, none of the chief executive officers of the company had knowledge of the special character of the rotary Neostyle machine or the restrictions on the purchase of supplies. The case of the plaintiffs in this respect rests mainly on the testimony of the witness, Gerber, who testified that at the instance of the manager of the Neostyle Company he wrote to the defendant for a one-pound can of black ink for use on the rotary Neostyle, saying—

I will be at my office Friday afternoon, between 1:30 and 3:30, and if convenient, have your representative call at that time.

A salesman of the defendant, named Randall, did call. The witness directed Randall's attention to the restrictions on the single machine he had in his office, and asked if he would have any trouble with the Neostyle Company if he used the defendant's ink. Randall replied in the negative, and added that—

the ink in question was not patented, that anybody could make or use it; that no trouble would come to me from the use of the ink which he sold.

The restriction on the machine shown to Randall was one formerly used by plaintiffs, but which had been discarded prior to this transaction and for it the present license agreement had been substituted.

The restriction shown to Randall stated that the machine was sold " with the express understanding that it is licensed to be used only with stencil paper and ink (both of which are patented) made by the Neostyle Company of New York city." Evidently from his reply Randall's attention was drawn to the question of a patent on the ink. Further he was not an officer or general agent of the defendant company, but simply a salesman and it cannot be that this talk with him is notice to and binding on his principal in respect to all future transactions.

After reviewing all the minor considerations to which our attention has been called by the plaintiffs, we see no sufficient reason for disagreeing with the unanimous opinion of the circuit court of appeals in respect to the matter of notice, and its decree *is affirmed.*

DIGEST OF DECISIONS.

[Decisions of the United States courts are indicated by an asterisk (*), of the Secretary of the Interior by a dagger (†), and the opinion of the Attorney-General by a double dagger (‡).]

ABANDONED APPLICATIONS. See *Access to Abandoned Applications; Copies of Abandoned Applications.*

ABANDONED EXPERIMENTS. See *Reduction to Practice*, 11, 15.

ABANDONMENT. See *Reissue Applications*, 6, 7.

ABANDONMENT OF APPLICATIONS. See *Trade-Marks*, 109.

1. DIVISION OF APPLICATIONS.—Where after final requirement of division numerous letters and petitions are filed in regard thereto, but no appeal is taken or compliance had within the ensuing year, *Held* that it is not clear that the actions taken could prevent the operation of the statute as to abandonment. *The United States of America, ex rel. Tuttle, v. Allen, Commissioner of Patents*, 676.

2. APPEAL.—The action of the Office holding an application to be abandoned is, in effect, a rejection. If that action is erroneous, the applicant has his remedy by way of appeal. *Id.*

3. SUFFICIENCY OF AMENDMENT.—Where the first amendment made by applicant five days before the expiration of the year from the Examiner's first action rejecting all the claims consisted of a few corrections to the specification, an argument as to the patentability of the claims, and the addition of a new claim, and the Examiner in admitting this amendment and rejecting the claims warned applicant that it was not such an action as the condition of the case required and that the added claim was so broad as to be met in nearly all selective signaling systems, and where, following this, applicant filed an amendment two days before the expiration of a year from the last action of the Examiner in which he amended all of the claims except the broad claim added by the previous amendment, which claim he neither canceled nor amended nor presented any reasons why he considered it allowable, *Held* that the latter amendment was not entirely responsive to the Examiner's rejection and was not sufficient to save the application from abandonment. *Ex parte Leich*, 31.

4. REPEATED DELAYS—RIGHTS STRICTLY CONSTRUED.—Where an applicant attempts to excuse the delay in the prosecution of his case on the ground that its subject-matter is dominated by certain claims in a copending application and that he considered it advisable to press the broad application to allowance before letting this application go to issue, *Held* that the conduct of applicant in the prosecution of his case has not been such as to entitle him to leniency in the application of the rule that amendments must be such as the condition of the case requires and that in electing to prosecute his application in this manner he must assume all risk as to the sufficiency of his actions. *Id.*

5. EXCUSE FOR DELAY.—Confusion upon the attorney's docket by reason of Office action suggesting claims for interference is not acceptable as a showing of unavoidable delay in responding to the prior Office action. *Ex parte Hess*, 58.

6. APPLICATION, JOINT—PROSECUTION OF BY ONE APPLICANT WHERE COAPPLICANT REFUSES TO ACT.—Where one of two joint inventors seeks to cause the abandonment of their application by preventing amendment thereof, claiming that he is a sole inventor, and also files a written abandonment of the application, *Held* that permission will be given to the coinventor to prosecute the application through an attorney of his own selection. *Ex parte Barrett and Alter*, 76.

7. ATTORNEYS—APPOINTMENT OF BY ONE OF TWO JOINT APPLICANTS.—Where the attorneys for joint applicants are prevented from amending the application by one of the joint inventors, who in order to cause the case to become abandoned also refuses to permit them to give an associate power of attorney to an attorney of the other joint applicant's selection, *Held* that an attorney appointed by the coinventor will be permitted to prosecute the application. *Id.*

8. MUST BE SIGNED BY ALL JOINT INVENTORS.—Where one coapplicant does not join in the written abandonment of an application, it can be given no effect. *Id.*

9. WITHDRAWAL FROM ISSUE—FAILURE TO TAKE ACTION.—Where an application is withdrawn from issue at the request of the applicant to await the allowance of a related application and no action is taken therein until after the expiration of the statutory period allowed for taking action, which dates from the notice of allowance, the application is abandoned in the absence of special circumstances excusing the delay. *Ex parte Brooks*, 77.

10. WHEN HOLDING IS PROPER.—Where 27 claims were rejected on August 9, 1905, and on June 9, 1906, the applicant amended two of the rejected claims and added two new claims, but made no allusion to the remaining 25 rejected claims, and the Examiner on August 14, 1906, on taking up the case in the regular course of his work, notified applicant that his case was abandoned, *Held* that the Examiner's action is entirely in accord with sound reason and well-established practice and is the only proper action which could have been given under the circumstances. *Ex parte Midgley*, 84.

11. UNRESPONSIVE ACTION NOT ENTITLED TO CONSIDERATION.—Petitioner's contention that his unresponsive amendment filed within the year is entitled to consideration and action upon its merits is clearly unfounded, since the statutes provide for no piecemeal consideration and the rules prohibit the same. *Id.*

12. APPLICANT RESPONSIBLE FOR FAILURE TO COMPLY WITH RULES.—The fact that the Examiner in the regular course of business did not reach applicant's case and give him notice of the insufficiency of his action until after the year allowed for action had expired does not relieve applicant of the necessity of taking responsive action within the year required by the rules or shift the responsibility for failure to comply with the rules to the Patent Office. *Id.*

13. WHERE DELAY WAS NOT UNAVOIDABLE.—Where the delay has not been terminated by the filing of an action fully responsive to the last rejection and where no good reason appears why such an action should not have been filed within the year allowed therefor, *Held* that the delay was not unavoidable and that the application is abandoned. *Id.*

14. **What is Responsive Action.**—On October 16, 1905, the Examiner finally rejected certain claims. The applicant on June 6, 1906, filed an amendment substituting new claims for those rejected, which amendment was refused entry by the Examiner in view of the final rejection. On September 24, 1906, applicant filed a request for reconsideration of the final rejection and refusal of his amendment, accompanied by a statement of reasons why he considered said actions improper. In reply he was notified by the Examiner on November 3, 1906, that his application was abandoned, and on November 6, 1906, he took this petition, *Held* that if the final rejection of October 16, 1905, was proper the condition of the case called for either a cancelation of the rejected claims or an appeal to the Examiners-in-Chief, and since such action was not taken within the year the case is abandoned; but in case the final rejection was irregular or premature, then the actions of June 6 and September 24 were such as the condition of the case required, and the application is not abandoned. *Ex parte Fowler, jr.,* 88.

15. **Failure of Applicant to Authorize Attorney to Take Action Does Not Excuse.**—The failure of the attorney to act within the statutory period is not excused by the allegation that he did not act earlier because not authorized by the applicant to do so, where it does not appear that he could not have been earlier authorized to proceed. *Ex parte Trebon,* 110.

16. **Unavoidable Delay.**—The delay of more than one year in responding to the Office action is not unavoidable in those cases where action might have been taken had reasonable efforts been exercised to that end at any time within the period following the Office action. *Id.*

17. **Same—Intention of Applicant.**—Applications are abandoned without regard to what the intention of the applicant may have been in case of delay for more than one year in responding to the Office action unless the delay was unavoidable. *Id.*

18. **Failure to Take Responsive Action.**—Where the action taken near the close of the year was not a proper action, *Held* that the applicant has a perfect right to delay action until the close of the year allowed by law therefor; but in doing so he assumes the risk of any mistake in the character of the action. *Ex parte Grant,* 131.

19. **Same.**—Since earlier action by applicant would have permitted correction of the mistake within the year and since it does not appear that earlier action could not have been taken, the failure to duly prosecute the application cannot be regarded as unavoidable, and it is therefore abandoned under the statute. *Id.*

20. **Delay Not Unavoidable.**—Where it is alleged that the case was inadvertently crossed off the attorney's docket, and therefore overlooked until after the period for action had expired, but it does not appear that there was any intention to respond to the last Office action until near the close of the year allowed therefor or that action could not have been taken in the earlier part of this period had it been so desired, *Held* that the delay was not unavoidable and the case is abandoned. *Ex parte Duryea,* 139.

21. **Claims Presented After Final Rejection Unaccompanied by Showing Does Not Avoid.**—Where after final rejection the applicant presents an amendment curing informalities and containing claims which differ substantially from those finally rejected, but does not make a showing of good and sufficient reasons why the amendment was not earlier presented, *Held* that the amendment is inadmissible, although it would

have been proper to cure the informalities by proper amendment, and that such action does not relieve the application from its condition as subject to appeal or save it from abandonment. *Ex parte Green*, 230.

22. REVIVAL—UNAVOIDABLE DELAY.—The fact that the Office did not suggest claims from a copending application does not render applicant's delay in prosecuting his case unavoidable. *Ex parte McKee*, 255.

23. FINAL ACTION ON FORM AND MERITS—APPEAL ON MERITS TOO LATE.— Where the Examiner finally rejected the claims of an application and also made final certain objections to such claims on July 3, 1906, and a petition upon the formal matters was taken on August 2, 1906, which was decided by the Commissioner on August 27, 1906, an appeal to the Examiners-in-Chief filed August 24, 1907, is filed without the period of one year allowed for prosecution, which dates from the final rejection and not from the decision of the Commissioner on the petition. *Ex parte Wentzel*, 352.

24. DELAY SLIGHT—UNAVOIDABLE.—Where delay beyond the year allowed for action is slight and the application prior to such delay had been prosecuted vigorously and in good faith and the applicant had reason to suppose that his action was filed in time, the delay may be regarded as unavoidable. *Id.*

25. SUFFICIENCY OF ACTION.—Where on December 29, 1905, an Examiner rejected certain claims and made a formal objection to another claim, to which the applicant made a sufficient response on January 27, 1906, with the exception that he failed to mention the informal claim, and the Examiner in his next action, on February 16, 1906, reiterated the formal objection, but did not state that the applicant's action by reason of failure to mention the informal claim was unresponsive and did not make such objection final, *Held* that an amendment curing the informality filed January 18, 1907, is filed in proper time, the renewal of the objection by the Examiner without objection to the insufficiency of the applicant's action of January 27, 1906, constituting a waiver of the question of incompleteness of such action. *Ex parte Westinghouse*, 372.

ABANDONMENT OF APPLICATIONS FOR REGISTRATION. See *Trade-Marks*, 75, 143.

ABANDONMENT OF INVENTION. See *Priority of Invention*, 18, 19.

ABANDONMENT OF TRADE-MARKS. See *Trade-Marks*, 82, 132.

ABBREVIATIONS. See *Name of Applicant*.

ACCESS TO ABANDONED APPLICATIONS. See *Copies of Abandoned Applications*.

1. NOTICE TO APPLICANT OR ASSIGNEE.—Where an application has been abandoned a long time, notice of the petition to inspect should be given to the owner of the invention, whether applicant or assignee.—*In re Commercial Mica Company*, 186.

2. ABANDONED APPLICATIONS—PETITION TO INSPECT.—A petition to inspect an abandoned application will be denied where the reference to the abandoned application in applicant's patent is not of such a nature as to indicate that it was relied upon for any purpose in the proceeding eventuating in the patent or to indicate a waiver by the patentee of the right of secrecy concerning said application. *In re The Bullock Electric Manufacturing Company*, 207.

3. SAME—SAME—PRACTICE.—Such petitions should be accompanied by a certificate of the court before whom a suit is pending. *Id.*

4. SAME—SAME—SERVICE.—Where an application has been abandoned a long time, service of petition to inspect upon the attorney of record is not sufficient, but service should be made upon the owner of the invention, whether applicant or assignee. *Id.*

ACCESS TO APPLICATIONS. See *Interference*, 9, 25.

ACCESS TO INTERFERENCE FILES. See *Interference*, 48, 67.

ACQUIESCENCE. See *Construction of Claims*, 3; *Interference*, 94.

ADOPTION AND USE. See *Trade-Marks*, 25, 27, 43, 58, 105.

ADMISSION OF EVIDENCE. See *Evidence*, 3, 4.

AFFIDAVITS. See *Interference*, 14, 42, 44; *Motion to dissolve Interference*, 2, 38; *Name of Applicant; Public Use and Sale*, 2, 3; *Trade-Marks*, 82, 84, 98.

INTERFERENCE—RIGHT TO MAKE CLAIM—TESTIMONY UNDER RULE 130—PRIMA FACIE SHOWING OF AGGREGATION—EXPERT AFFIDAVITS NOT ACCEPTED.—Where motion is made for leave to take testimony under the provisions of Rule 130 to establish that the claim as applied to one party's structure is a true combination, while as applied to the other party's structure is merely for an aggregation, affidavits in support of such motion which consist wholly of the opinion of expert patent lawyers as to the legal effect of the claims will not be received. *Pym* v. *Hadaway*, 189.

AFFIDAVIT UNDER RULE 75. See *Copies of Affidavit Filed Under Rule 75; Motion to Dissolve Interference*, 28.

AGENT. See *Infringement*, 6; *Reduction to Practice*, 4, 21.

AGGREGATION. See *Affidavits; Division of Applications*, 2.

ALLEGATIONS. See *Motion to Dissolve Interference*, 35, 40, 41, 43; *Preliminary Statement*, 4; *Trade-Marks*, 105, 142.

AMENDMENTS. See *Abandonment of Applications*, 3, 4, 10, 11, 14, 21, 25; *Appeal to the Commissioner of Patents*, 1; *Applications*, 1; *Claims*, 1; *Drawings*, 1; *Examination of Applications*, 6; *Interference*, 10, 12; *Motion to Dissolve Interference*, 12.

1. ENTRY AFTER REJECTION UNDER RULE 132.—Where following the termination of an interference and the rejection of the defeated party's claims he filed an amendment canceling the rejected claims and adding new claims, which amendment was refused admission by the Examiner on the ground that the prosecution before the Primary Examiner was closed by reason of the fact that the application had been appealed to the Examiners-in-Chief, allowed, and passed to issue prior to the declaration of the interference, *Held* that the rejection of the claims involved in the interference under Rule 132 is a new ground of rejection and that the rules and statute give applicant the right to amend in an endeavor to overcome said ground of rejection. *Ex parte Klepetko*, 1.

2. PETITION—RULE 78.—A petition for the entry of an amendment presented under Rule 78 after the allowance of the application will be denied where the amendment includes claims which the Examiner in his report upon the petition states are not patentable. *Ex parte Fleming*, 51.

3. RULE 78—DISCRETION OF EXAMINER.—The entry of claims under Rule 78 is not a matter of right, but a privilege allowed applicants where claims are found allowable by the Examiner upon such consideration of the case as he may deem proper. The Examiner will not be directed to consider the question of patentability of claims presented after his report upon petition. *Id.*

4. INTERFERENCE.—Where during the interference proceeding one of the parties filed an amendment canceling the claims rejected under Rule 124 and substituted a substitute specification and drawing, *Held* that the amendment is not of the character permitted under the rules during the interference proceeding and that the special circumstances are not such as to warrant its admission. *Harnisch* v. *Gueniffet, Benoit, and Nicault,* 127.

5. NEW MATTER—RIGHT TO MAKE CLAIMS.—Where the original specification of an application relating to combined type-writing and adding machines did not describe the adding machine, but stated that the invention was illustrated "in connection with an adding machine of the class known as 'registering accountants,'" and only the case and a few minor elements thereof were shown in the drawings, *Held* that an amendment of the application reciting a patent disclosing the construction referred to by the words "registering accountants" did not constitute a departure from the original disclosure in view of evidence showing that such term referred to a construction well known in the market embodying the construction of the patent and that such construction was the only one on the market which had the distinctive appearance illustrated in the original drawing, *Held,* further, that such party had a right to make claims to a combination including specific elements of such adding machine. *Hopkins* v. *Newman,* 356.

AMENDMENT TO OPPOSITION. See *Trade-Marks,* 15, 70.

AMENDMENT TO PRELIMINARY STATEMENT. See *Interference,* 76, 77, 83, 91; *Motion to Amend Preliminary Statement; Preliminary Statement,* 1, 2, 3.

ANCILLARY INVENTION. See *Employer and Employee,* 2.

ANCILLARY QUESTION. See *Priority of Invention,* 9, 10.

ANTICIPATION. See *Motion to Dissolve Interference,* 29; *Trade-Marks,* 38, 46, 47, 66, 67, 80, 110, 117, 118, 134.

PATENT—FAILURE OF SPECIFICATION TO STATE CHARACTER OF MATERIAL.—Where the specification of a patent cited as an anticipation does not state of what material the article is composed, it cannot ordinarily be assumed to be of any particular material. *Ex parte Walters,* 272.

APPEAL. See *Abandonment of Applications,* 1, 2, 23; *Appeal from the Examiner of Interferences; Appeal from the Examiners-in-Chief; Appeal to the Commissioner of Patents; Appeal to the Court of Appeals of the District of Columbia; Division of Applications,* 1; *Interference,* 6, 7, 8, 11, 12, 18, 19, 21, 23, 24, 31, 33, 61, 69, 70; *Mandamus,* 1; *Motion for Leave to Take Testimony; Motion for Rehearing,* 1, 2, 3, 6; *Motion to Dissolve Interference,* 38; *Motion to Take Testimony in Foreign Countries; Patentability,* 6; *Priority of Invention,* 4; *Rejection of Claims,* 1; *Trade-Marks,* 1, 136, 152, 154.

APPEAL FROM THE COMMISSIONER OF PATENTS. See *Appeal to the Court of Appeals of the District of Columbia,* 2.

APPEAL FROM THE EXAMINER OF INTERFERENCES. See *Interference,* 58; *Motion for Leave to Take Testimony; Trade-Marks,* 153.

NON-APPEALABLE QUESTION—DISMISSED.—Where a ruling is made that an appeal from the Examiner of Interferences will not be entertained by the Commissioner on a given question, an appeal on that question will not be considered, even though filed prior to the rendition of the decision. *Hanan and Gates* v. *Marshall,* 65.

APPEAL FROM THE EXAMINERS-IN-CHIEF. See *Appeal to the Commissioner of Patents*, 1; *Interference*, 64.

    INTERFERENCE—DISCLAIMER BY APPELLEE—DISMISSED.—Where appeal is taken from a decision of the Examiners-in-Chief on the question of priority and the appellee files a motion to dismiss the appeal, accompanied by a disclaimer of the invention in issue signed by the appellant, *Held* that the disclaimer will be considered a concurrence in the motion of the appellee to dismiss the appeal. *Wert v. Borst and Groscop*, 47.

APPEAL FROM FAVORABLE DECISION. See *Appeal to the Court of Appeals of the District of Columbia; Interference*, 17, 18, 19, 75; *Motion to Dissolve Interference*, 11.

APPEAL TO THE COMMISSIONER OF PATENTS. See *Appeal from the Examiner of Interferences; Interference* 21, 23.

    1. NEW REFERENCE DISCOVERED SUBSEQUENT TO.—Where a reference was discovered by the Office subsequent to a hearing by the Commissioner on an *ex parte* appeal from a decision of the Examiners-in-Chief affirming a rejection by the Primary Examiner, decision on the appeal was suspended for thirty days and applicant was notified that he might amend or take other action in view of the citation within the time stated, that a failure to amend within the time would amount to a waiver of the right to amend, and that upon failure to act a decision would be rendered upon consideration of the old and the new references. He was further notified that if he did not desire to amend a rehearing would be granted for argument upon the new reference upon request therefor. *Ex parte Fortuny*, 135.

    2. MOTION TO DISSOLVE—HEARING.—Where appeals are taken from the decision of the Examiner upon motions for dissolution both to the Commissioner and to the Examiners-in-Chief, action upon the appeal to the Commissioner will be suspended until after the decision of the Examiners-in-Chief is rendered, in order that all appeals upon the motions may be considered at the same time. Where the Examiner upon the rehearing entirely dissolves the interference, the question of irregularity in declaration of the interference becomes a moot question and will not be entertained unless the decision dissolving the interference is reversed on appeal. *O'Brien v. Gale, sr., v. Miller v. Zimmer v. Calderwood*, 184.

APPEAL TO THE COURT OF APPEALS OF THE DISTRICT OF COLUMBIA. See *Interference*, 56, 61, 69, 74; *Priority of Invention*, 5; *Reopening of Interference*, 1, 2, 3.

    1. CONSIDERATION OF PATENTABILITY BY COURT.—Where the Primary Examiner has held claims to be patentable and the Examiner of Interferences and the Examiners-in-Chief have omitted or declined to call the attention of the Commissioner to the unpatentability of the issue or where the Commissioner has declined to review the decision of the Primary Examiner after his attention has been called to the alleged unpatentability of the issue, the court of appeals of the District of Columbia should hold the question of patentability to be settled, except in an extraordinary case. The statute does not provide for an appeal to the court from a ruling by the Commissioner or of any subordinate tribunals affirming the patentability of a claimed invention. It is only from a decision adverse to the patentability of a claim that an appeal will lie. *Sobey v. Holsclaw*, 465.

    2. JURISDICTION OVER PROCEDURE BEFORE COMMISSIONER.—On an appeal from the Commissioner of Patents to the court of appeals of the District of Columbia on the question of priority of invention the court has no power

to hold that the Commissioner has committed an error for which a case should be reversed because of a claim that he refused to permit counsel to be heard in support of a given contention. The court cannot in such a proceeding control his action in a discretionary matter such as the extent of oral argument he will permit at a hearing of an interference. *Id.*

3. JURISDICTION OF COMMISSIONER AFTER APPEAL TO COURT ON PRIORITY.—After a decision of the court of appeals on the question of priority the Commissioner of Patents may refuse a patent to the successful interferant. *Id.*

APPEAL TO THE EXAMINERS-IN-CHIEF. See *Appeal to the Commissioner of Patents*, 2; *Decisions of the Examiners-in-Chief; Division of Applications*, 1; *Interference*, 7, 56, 57; *Motion to Dissolve Interference*, 12.

APPEAL TO THE SECRETARY OF THE INTERIOR. See *Interference*, 24.

APPLICANT. See *Access to Abandoned Applications*, 1, 3.

APPLICANT AND PATENTEE. See *Interference*, 16, 17.

APPLICANT AND REGISTRANT. See *Trade-Marks*, 79.

APPLICATIONS. See *Abandonment of Applications; Access to Abandoned Applications; Amendments; · Claims; Concealment of Invention; Construction of Claims; Construction of Statutes; Copies of Abandoned Applications; Designs, Drawings; Division of Applications; Examination of Applications; Foreign Executors or Administrators; Formal Objections; Interference*, 9, 10, 22, 24, 53; *Invention*, 7, 8; *Labels; Name of Applicant; Oath; Patentability: Priority of Invention*, 1, 2, 3; *Prosecution of Applications by Assignees; Public Use and Sale*, 1, 2; *Reduction to Practice*, 1, 2, 10; *Reissue Applications; Specifications; Trade-Marks; Withdrawal of Allowed Applications from Issue.*

1. AMENDMENT FROM DESIGN TO MECHANICAL CASE.—Where an applicant in presenting his own case requested in his petition the grant of a design patent upon a letter scale, but his specification, claim, and oath were of the form prescribed for mechanical application, and it appears from the actions by the applicant in the case that it was his intention to obtain protection for an article of manufacture, *Held* that he should be permitted to amend the case to accord with the form prescribed for *mechanical applications. Ex parte Saunders, jr.*, 363.

2. COMPLETION—DRAWINGS SIGNED BY ATTORNEY WITHOUT FULL POWER.—Where all papers necessary for a complete application are filed on October 30, 1902, but the drawings were signed by substitute attorneys who had not full power, and on November 28, 1902, full power is given to such attorneys, upon whose request the date of the application is changed to November 28, 1902, *Held* that the application is entitled to the date of October 30, 1902, as a constructive reduction to practice, the informality being one which could be cured, and was in fact cured, by subsequent ratification by the persons delegating the power. *Marconi v. Shoemaker*, 392.

3. SWORN TO IN BLANK—STRIKING FROM FILES—RULE 31.—Where an inventor assigns an invention and subsequently alleges that the application papers were executed in blank and petitions that the application be stricken from the files, *Held* that because of the assignment he is estopped from denying the validity of the executed papers, especially when the application has been on file nearly a year. *Ex parte Sharer*, 428.

APPLICATION EXECUTED IN BLANK. See *Applications*, 3.

ARBITRARY TERMS. See *Trade-Marks*, 25.

ASSIGNEES. See *Access to Abandoned Applications*, 1, 3; *Interference*, 37; *Prosecution of Applications by Assignees.*

ASSIGNMENTS. See *Applications*, 3.

ASSIGNMENT OF TRADE-MARKS. See *Trade-Marks*. 28, 143, 145.

ATTORNEYS. See *Abandonment of Applications*. 5, 6, 7, 15, 20; *Applications*, 2; *Motion to Dissolve Interference*, 29; *Priority of Invention*. 15; *Reissue Applications*, 1, 5, 7.

> UNITED STATES COMMISSIONERS INELIGIBLE TO ACT AS BEFORE THE PATENT OFFICE.—*Held* that under section 1782 of the Revised Statutes a person holding the office of United States commissioner is ineligible to practice as an attorney representing applicants for patents before the United States Patent Office. † *In re Bloch*, 432.

BAR TO PATENT. See *Interference*, 89; *Patentability*, 5.

BAR TO REGISTRATION. See *Trade-Marks*, 59, 79.

BILL IN EQUITY UNDER SECTION 4915, REVISED STATUTES. See *Copies of Affidavit Filed Under Rule 75; Reopening of Interference*, 4.

> FILING BY DEFEATED PARTY TO INTERFERENCE WILL NOT STAY ISSUE OF PATENT TO SUCCESSFUL PARTY.—The filing of a bill in equity under section 4915, Revised Statutes, by the defeated party to an interference will not operate to stay the issue of a patent to the successful party, nor will it justify the Commissioner of Patents in withholding it until the equity proceeding is terminated. (Citing case of *Sargent*, C. D., 1877, 125; 12 O. G., 475, and *Wells* v. *Boyle*, C. D., 1888, 36; 43 O. G., 753.) *Dunbar* v. *Schellenger*, 162.

BURDEN OF PROOF. See *Employer and Employee*, 4, 5.

CANCELATION OF FIGURES OF THE DRAWINGS. See *Drawings*, 2.

CANCELATION OF TRADE-MARK REGISTRATION. See *Trade-Marks*, 22, 23, 49, 50, 61, 62, 63, 82, 83, 84.

CERTIFICATE OF COURT. See *Access to Abandoned Applications*, 3; *Copies of Abandoned Applications*, 2; *Copies of Affidavit Under Rule 75; Foreign Executors or Administrators.*

CERTIFIED COPIES OF PARTS OF APPLICATIONS. See *Interference*, 25; *Motion to Amend Application*, 1.

CITIZENSHIP. See *Oath.*

CLAIMS. See *Affidavits; Amendments; Construction of Claims; Examination of Applications; Interference.* 10, 11, 12, 15, 16, 17, 19, 22, 30, 31, 78, 79, 80; *Motion to Dissolve Interference*. 9, 10, 11, 12, 13, 18, 19, 29, 33, 34; *Patentability*, 2, 5; *Priority of Invention*, 8, 9, 10; *Rejection of Claims.*

> 1. INDEPENDENT INVENTIONS—PRACTICE.—Where claims presented by amendment are held by the Examiner to be for an independent invention from that presented in the other claims, *Held* that the question of whether the claims are in fact for an independent invention must be settled before applicant can demand an action upon their merits. If for an independent invention, applicant is estopped from prosecuting said claims on their merits in this application, and they should be canceled. This question is the same as that ordinarily presented in a requirement for division, with the exception that in originally presenting and prosecuting claims to one invention only applicant has already made his election and has now no choice as to which set of claims he will cancel. (*Ex parte Selle*, C. D., 1904, 221; 110 O. G., 1728; *ex parte Tuttle*, C. D., 1904, 537; 113 O. G., 1907.) *Ex parte Bullock*, 88.

2. INDEFINITE AND FUNCTIONAL.—Where the claim is not for a combination of which the "means" for the purpose mentioned is an element, but is merely for means as an element and covers all possible means for accomplishing a certain function regardless of structure, *Held* that the claim is indefinite and functional. *Id.*

3. FUNCTIONAL—OPEN TO OBJECTION.—Claims which fail to include sufficient mechanical elements to effect the function expressed in the claims are open to objection, and ,from objection on such ground petition may be taken to the Commissioner. *Ex parte Plumb*, 367.

CLASS OF MERCHANDISE. See *Trade-Marks*, 89, 90, 92.

COLOR. See *Trade-Marks*, 9, 18, 29.

COMBINATION. See *Affidavits*.

COMMERCIAL SUCCESS. See *Designs*, 2; *Diligence*, 3.

COMMISSIONER OF PATENTS. See *Abandonment of Applications*, 23; *Appeal from the Examiner of Interferences; Appeal to the Commissioner of Patents; Appeal to the Court of Appeals of the District of Columbia; Bill in Equity Under Section 4915, Revised Statutes; Claims; Evidence.* 6; *Examination of Applications*, 7; *Interference*, 7, 19, 20, 21, 22, 24, 29, 30, 56, 57, 58, 59, 60, 75; *Mandamus*, 6, 7; *Motion to Amend Applications; Priority of Invention*, 11, 12, 13, 14; *Public Use and Sale*, 4; *Trade-Marks*, 11, 15, 30, 153.

CONCEALMENT OF INVENTION. See *Interference*, 10, 25, 45.

1. SUPPRESSION AFTER REDUCTION TO PRACTICE.—The failure to file an application for more than two years after reduction to practice where the machine was put into actual use in a factory the policy of the management of which was not to patent machines used for their own work is not such a concealment or suppression of the invention as will subordinate the inventor's rights to one who, claiming conception in July, 1900, reduced it to practice in April, 1901, but did not file an application until May, 1902, and did not arrange to manufacture the same until June, 1903. * *Burson v. Vogel*, 669.

2. SAME.—Where a party constructed a device in October, 1900, but allowed it to remain entirely within the knowledge of the inventor and his coemployees until knowledge was obtained of the invention of the opposing party, when the application in interference was filed showing a different form, apparently suggested by such knowledge, *Held* that such party's rights were forfeited by concealment. *Marconi v. Shoemaker*, 392.

CONCEPTION OF INVENTION. See *Interference*, 2, 3, 90. *Reduction to Practice*, 10.

IDEA OF MEANS NECESSARY.—The mere idea that there ought to be an arrangement to strip a stocking from a board or form on which it was mounted and return the board to the one who placed the stockings thereon, and the illustration of this idea by the originator thereof by stripping a stocking from a form by the passage thereof between his hand and the edge of a table does not amount to a conception of an invention. No mechanism was described by which the desired result could be obtained. Invention consists of the conception of the idea and of means for putting it in practice and producing the desired result. Until the latter conception is complete and ready to be put in some practical form there is no available conception of the invention within the meaning of the patent law. (*Mergenthaler v. Scudder* (C. D., 1897, 724; 81 O. G., 1417; 11 App. D. C., 264, 276.) * *Burson v. Vogel*, 669.

CONCESSION OF PRIORITY. See *Priority of Invention*, 6.

CONSTRUCTION OF CLAIMS. See *Interference*, 16, 17, 22, 79.

1. CLAIM—NEW MATTER—" MOUNTED UPON " CONSTRUED.—A claim for a latch mounted upon a mold-blade section of a type mold, *Held* to cover matter not within the original disclosure, the words " mounted upon " not being properly descriptive of a part which merely rides in or over another in a slot for the purpose. *In re Duncan, Prichard, and Macauley*, 460.

2. SAME—IMPLYING STRUCTURES NOT IN CLAIMS.—Where an applicant's claims to a trimmer for sewing-machines make no mention of a presserfoot, a difference in structure embodying a particular form of presserfoot which is not clearly pointed out in the record will not be assumed. *In re McNeil* v. *Sturtevant*, 478.

3. ACQUIESCENCE IN REJECTION BY PATENT OFFICE.—Where an inventor seeking a broad claim which is rejected, in which rejection he acquiesces, substitutes therefor a narrower claim, he cannot be heard to insist that the construction of the claim allowed shall cover that which had been previously rejected. (*Corbin Cabinet Lock Company* v. *Eagle Lock Company* C. D., 1893, 612; 65 O. G., 1066; 150 U. S., 38–40, and cases there cited.) *Computing Scale Company of America* v. *The Automatic Scale Company*, 687.

4. INTERFERENCE.—A claim should be given the broadest interpretation which it will support, and limitations should not be imported into the claim from the specification to meet the exigencies of the particular situation in which the claim may stand at a given time. *Miel* v. *Young*, 561.

5. SAME—LIMITATIONS NOT IMPORTED FROM PATENT SPECIFICATION.—Where in a stone-saw construction the claim calls for " removable means for reinforcing the lower ends of the blades during the initial part of a cutting operation " and it appears that the device of Miel, a patentee, was designed to prevent the blades from " chattering or wabbling " laterally, while Young's structure is for the purpose of enabling the blades of the saw " to stand the strain for their work " and to support the saw longitudinally, *Held* that there is no limitation in the claim, which refers broadly to reinforcing means, which necessitates the reading into the claim of structural features found only in the specification of the patent. *Id.*

CONSTRUCTION OF RULES. See *Amendments*, 1, 2, 3, 4 ; *Affidavits; Applications*, 3 ; *Construction of Statutes*, 1 ; *Decisions of the Examiner of Interferences*, 2 ; *Interference*, 11, 12, 19, 23, 25, 28, 31, 33, 34, 35, 39, 46, 51, 52, 81, 87 ; *Jurisdiction of the Examiners-in-Chief; Motion for Leave to Take Testimony*, 2 ; *Motion to Amend Applications*, 1, 2: *Motion to Dissolve Interference*, 5, 6, 13, 17, 36, 37, 39 ; *Prosecution of Applications by Assignees; Rejection of Claims*, 1, 5 ; *Testimony*, 1, 3 ; *Withdrawal of Allowed Applications from Issue*, 2.

CONSTRUCTION OF STATUTES. See *Appeal to the Court of Appeals of the District of Columbia*, 1 ; *Attorneys; Bill in Equity Under Section 4915, Revised Statutes; Decisions of the Examiner of Interferences*, 2 ; *Interference*, 18, 19, 20 ; *Labels*, 1 ; *Notary Public; Oath; Reissue Applications*, 4, 5, 6.

1. LIMITED TO QUESTION OF PRIORITY OF INVENTION.—The United States Supreme Court in the case of *ex rel. George A. Lowry* v. *Frederick I. Allen, Commissioner of Patents* (C. D. 1906, 765; 125 O. G., 2365), held that section 4904 of the Revised Statutes limits the declaration of inter-

ferences to the question of priority of invention. Should a party be
permitted to urge that the claims of the issue are patentable to neither
party in the interference, a decision that the issue is not patentable
would not result in a decision of priority of invention in favor of
either party or in the issue of a patent to one of the parties. In the
cases contemplated by Rule 130, however, a decision that the issue
is not patentable to one party would necessarily result in a decision
of priority in favor of the other party. *Dixon and Marsh v. Graves
and Whittemore*, 101.

2. APPLICATION DATE—FOREIGN APPLICATION—SECTION 4887, REVISED STAT-
UTES.—Under the second clause of section 4887 of the Revised Statutes
as amended March 3, 1903, an application for patent in the United
States is not entitled to the date of an application filed by the applicant in a foreign country prior to March 3, 1903, although the United
States application was filed after this date. *De Ferranti v. Lindmark*,
203.

8. APPLICATION—PERIOD OF ONE YEAR AFTER FILING OF APPLICATION IN
FOREIGN COUNTRY NOT EXTENDED.—Where the applicant filed an application in a foreign country on May 7, 1906, and a patent was granted
thereon, an application filed in this country after May 7, 1907, can not
be received. Applications which the law requires to be filed in this
Office within a certain time cannot be held to be so filed by reason
of the fact that they are in the hands of the postal authorities. *Ex
parte Ravelli*, 260.

4. SAME—SAME—REVISED STATUTES 4894 INAPPLICABLE.—Section 4894 of
the Revised Statutes only applies to applications which already have
a status in this Office and is not applicable to cases in which an application is filed in this Office more than one year from the date upon
which the applicant filed an application in a foreign country and upon
which he has received a patent. *Id.*

CONSTRUCTION OF TRADE-MARK STATUTES. See *Trade-Marks*, 14, 15,
16, 18, 19, 20, 22, 23, 28, 29, 36, 37, 50, 51, 52, 57, 58, 59, 61, 62, 67, 71, 81,
82, 85, 86, 87, 88, 89, 90, 96, 97, 113, 114, 118, 125, 142, 143.

CONTINUOUS APPLICATION. See *Reduction to Practice*, 2.

CONTINUOUS USE. See *Trade-Marks*, 27, 63, 78, 105, 107.

COPIES OF ABANDONED APPLICATIONS. See *Access to Abandoned Applications.*

1. APPLICATION REFERRED TO IN PATENT.—A reference in a patent to an
application is not sufficient to justify allowing copies of the application
to be made where the reference is not of such a nature as to indicate
that it was relied upon for any purpose in the proceeding eventuating
in the patent. *In re Commercial Mica Company*, 186.

2. SAME—CERTIFICATE OF COURT.—Petition to have such copies made denied
in the absence of a certificate of the court before whom the suit is
pending. *Id.*

COPIES OF AFFIDAVIT FILED UNDER RULE 75.

CERTIFICATE OF COURT REQUIRED.—The Patent Office will not, upon the request of the defeated party of an interference proceeding, furnish
copies of an affidavit filed *ex parte* by his opponent under Rule 75 to
overcome a reference against claims not involved in the interference
merely upon a showing that petitioner has brought a suit in equity
under section 4915, Revised Statutes, to determine priority of invention and desires a copy of such affidavit for use in such suit. Under

such circumstances a copy will be furnished only upon a certificate of the court that such affidavit would constitute material and proper evidence in such suit. *In re U. S. Standard Voting Machine Company,* 280.

COPIES OF INTERFERENCE PROCEEDINGS. See *Interference,* 48, 67.

COPIES OF INTERFERENCE RECORDS. See *Interference,* 9, 67.

CORPORATIONS. See *Trade-Marks,* 150.

CROSS-EXAMINATION. See *Interference,* 41, 42, 43, 44.

COURT OF APPEALS OF THE DISTRICT OF COLUMBIA. See *Appeal to the Court of Appeals of the District of Columbia; Priority of Invention,* 4; *Reopening of Interference,* 1, 2, 3, 4.

DATE OF FILING APPLICATIONS. See *Applications,* 2; *Concealment of Invention; Construction of Statutes,* 2, 3; *Preliminary Statement,* 4; *Reduction to Practice,* 2, 10.

DATE OF FILING MOTION. See *Motion for Rehearing,* 4.

DECEPTION. See *Trade-Marks,* 11, 12, 144, 147.

DECISIONS OF THE COMMISSIONER OF PATENTS. See *Interference,* 59, 60.

DECISIONS OF THE COMMISSIONER OF PATENTS AFFIRMED. See *Priority of Invention,* 11, 12, 13, 14.

DECISIONS OF THE EXAMINER. See *Formal Objections; Motion to Dissolve Interference,* 12, 17.

DECISIONS OF THE EXAMINERS-IN-CHIEF.

1. DECISION BY TWO MEMBERS.—A decision by two of the Examiners-in Chief is a decision of the Examiners-in-Chief. *Ex parte Helbig,* 385.

2. SAME—REHEARING.—A rehearing of an appeal to the Examiners-in-Chief is not necessary merely because one of the Examiners-in-Chief was not present. If the two members are present, the decision is valid. If they disagree, the case may be set for rehearing, as provided in Order No. 1664 (121 O. G., 1983.) *Id.*

DECISIONS OF THE EXAMINER OF INTERFERENCES. See *Interference,* 8, 19; *Motion for Leave to Take Testimony,* 2; *Motion to Take Testimony in Foreign Countries; Reopening of Interference,* 5.

1. INTERFERENCE—PRIORITY—BASED ON OPERATIVENESS OF DEVICE.—Where the Examiner of Interferences awarded priority of invention to one party on the ground that the application of his opponent fails to show an operative device, *Held* that the operativeness of an applicant's device affects his right to make the claim and that the action of the Examiner of Interferences was in accord with the rules and decisions. *Greenawalt* v. *Mark,* 21.

2. SAME—SAME.—The decision of the Examiner of Interferences is not a rejection of the claims under section 4903, Revised Statutes, although it may form a basis for such rejection by the Primary Examiner under Rule 132. *Id.*

DECISIONS OF THE PATENT OFFICE TRIBUNALS. See *Interference,* 21, 26, 40, 69; *Priority of Invention,* 4, 5; *Reopening of Interferences,* 1, 2.

DECLARATION OF INTERFERENCE. See *Appeal to the Commissioner of Patents,* 2; *Motion to Dissolve Interference,* 18, 19; *Trade-Marks,* 142.

DECREE. See *Infringement,* 1, 2.

DELAY IN APPLYING FOR REISSUE. See *Reissue Applications,* 1.

DELAY IN FILING APPLICATIONS. See *Interference* 37; *Priority of Invention,* 15.

DELAY IN FILING MOTIONS. See *Interference*, 49, 54, 72; *Motion to Amend Application*, 1, 2; *Motion to Dissolve Interference*, 20, 23, 29, 30, 32, 35; *Preliminary Statement*, 2; *Reopening of Interference*, 5.

DELAY IN FILING REISSUE APPLICATIONS. See *Reissue Applications*, 1, 2, 6, 7.

DELAY IN MAKING APPEAL. See *Abandonment of Applications*, 23; *Motion to Dissolve Interference*, 4.

DELAY IN PROSECUTING APPLICATIONS. See *Abandonment of Applications*, 4, 5, 9, 13, 15, 16, 17, 18, 19, 20, 22, 23, 24; *Public Use and Sale* 3.

DELAY IN REDUCTION TO PRACTICE. See *Interference*, 3, 4, 38.

DEMURRER. See *Trade-Marks*, 2, 98, 128, 129.

DEPOSITION. See *Interference*, 1, 41, 44.

DESCRIPTION. See *Specifications*.

DESCRIPTION OF GOODS. See *Trade-Marks*, 10, 67, 111, 130, 131, 137.

DESCRIPTIVE TERMS. See *Trade-Marks*, 24, 25, 39, 40, 42, 45, 55, 56, 59, 60, 64, 65, 71, 91, 100, 121, 122, 123, 126, 127, 134, 156, 157.

DESIGNS. See *Applications*, 1.

1. PATENTABILITY—NEW APPEARANCE MUST BE ORNAMENTAL.—A design patent for an article will be granted only when there can be found in such article a new appearance created by inventive process which serves the purpose of embellishment. It is not enough that the design should possess features of utilitarian attractiveness which would commend it to persons familiar with the art because of its functional value; it must possess an inherent beauty. *Ex parte Bettendorf*, 79.

2. SAME—FONT OF TYPE.—Where, as in the art of printing, the field of inventive design is limited to modifications of detail in predetermined forms of letters, and an inventor has succeeded in producing a new font having clearly distinguishing characteristics running through the whole, and the esthetic value of his production is confirmed by an extensive demand for the same, it is believed that he should be granted the right to a lawful monopoly of the results of his labor for the limited time provided by the design statutes. *Ex parte Smith*, 287.

DILIGENCE. See *Interference*, 2, 3, 38, 45; *Motion to Amend Preliminary Statement*, 2; *Priority of Invention*, 14, 15; *Reduction to Practice*, 8.

1. INTERFERENCE—PRIORITY—CIRCUMSTANCES TO BE CONSIDERED.—There is no arbitrary rule or standard by which diligence may be measured. The sole object of the law being to mete out the fullest measure of justice, each case must be considered and decided in the light of the circumstances of that case. The nature of the invention, the situation of the inventor, the length of time intervening between conception and reduction to practice, the character and reasonableness of the inventor's testimony and that of his witnesses, are all important factors in determining the question of diligence. *Woods* v. *Poor*, 651.

2. SAME—SAME—SAME.—Where on October 24, 1903, twenty-three days after his conception of the invention, Woods left the company by which he had been employed to embark in business on his own account, and during this period had made a blackboard drawing of the invention and frequently discussed with one Jacob, who was skilled in the art, the possibility of overcoming certain criticisms, and where after establishing his own business he employed said Jacob and resumed the consideration of these defects, and while he did not eventually modify his device, but filed his application January 27, 1904, *Held* he was not lacking in diligence, and priority was awarded to him over Poor, who

reduced his invention to practice by filing his application December 17, 1903. *Id.*

3. SAME—SAME—WORK ON AUXILIARY INVENTION.—Work on an auxiliary invention which the inventor regarded as necessary to the commercial success of his invention cannot be regarded as constituting diligence where the evidence does not satisfactorily show the nature of the experiments or when they were made. *Fordyce v. Stoetzel*, 306.

DISCLAIMER. See *Appeal from the Examiners-in-Chief; Interference*, 36.

DISCLOSURE OF INVENTION. See *Construction of Claims*, 1; *Drawings*, 1; *Interference*, 40, 69; *Preliminary Statement*, 1; *Priority of Invention*, 1, 2, 16, 17.

DISCRETION. See *Mandamus*, 2; *Preliminary Statement*, 3.

DISCRETION OF THE EXAMINER OF INTERFERENCES. See *Motion to Amend Preliminary Statement*, 3.

DISSOLUTION OF INTERFERENCE. See *Appeal to the Commissioner of Patents*, 2; *Motion to Dissolve Interference; Priority of Invention*, 7.

DIVISIONAL APPLICATIONS. See *Reduction to Practice*, 1, 2.

DIVISION OF APPLICATIONS. See *Abandonment of Applications*, 1; *Claims*, 1; *Mandamus*, 3; *Trade-Marks*, 89, 90.

1. SHOULD BE SETTLED BY APPEAL TO EXAMINERS-IN-CHIEF BEFORE ACTION ON PATENTABILITY OF CLAIMS.—Where the Examiner based his requirement for division upon proper grounds, the question of whether the Examiner is right in his requirement is a matter for consideration on appeal by the Examiners-in-Chief before action is made upon the patentability of the claims. *Ex parte Crain*, 18.

2. PRACTICE.—The fact that as an aid to applicant in electing how he will divide the Examiner cited patents showing the prior art and volunteered the opinion that the claims are for aggregations does not change the practice and does not warrant the assumption that the Examiner's action amounts to a refusal to examine the case on the ground that the claims cover aggregations. *Id.*

DOUBLE USE. See *Patentability*, 1.

DRAWINGS. See *Amendments*, 5; *Applications*, 2; *Priority of Invention*, 2; *Trade-Marks*, 19, 29, 31.

1. AMENDMENTS OF—SUFFICIENCY OF DISCLOSURE IN SPECIFICATION AND CLAIMS.—Where in the original specification one member is said to be secured to a part "by means of a bolt or pivot" and in an original claim the member is referred to as being "connected adjustably" with such part, but no means for permitting such adjustment is shown in the drawing, *Held* that amendment to the drawing should be permitted to show suitable means for performing the function claimed, if supported by a supplemental oath. *Ex parte Sylvestersen*, 228.

2. ELIMINATION OF UNNECESSARY ILLUSTRATIONS.—*Held* that the requirement by the Examiner that unnecessary figures be canceled and that the remaining figures be reduced to a reasonable scale and placed on a single sheet was right. *Ex parte Keil*, 408.

EARLIER APPLICATIONS. See *Interference*, 91.

EARLIER AND LATER APPLICATIONS, SAME INVENTOR. See *Interference*, 53.

EMPLOYEE. See *Priority of Invention*, 7, 8.

EMPLOYER AND EMPLOYEE. See *Interference*, 94.

1. ORIGINALITY—IMPROVEMENTS BY EMPLOYEE.—When one conceives the principle or plan of an invention and employs another to perfect the

details and realize his conception, though the latter may make valuable improvements therein, such improved result belongs to the employer. *Kreag v. Geen, 502.

2. SAME—ANCILLARY INVENTION.—Where a person has discovered an improved principle in a manufacture and employs others in assisting him to carry out that principle, and these in that employment make valuable additions to the preconceived design of the employer, such suggested improvements are in general to be regarded as the property of the party who discovered the original improved principle and may be embodied in his patent as part of his invention. (See *Agawam Co. v. Jordan*, 7 Wall., 583, 602; *Gedge v. Cromwell*, C. D., 1902, 514; 98 O. G., 1480; 19 App. D. C., 198; *Milton v. Kingsley*, C. D., 1896, 426; 75 O. G., 2195; 7 App. D. C., 537.) *Larkin v. Richardson*, 508.

3. INTERFERENCE—PRIORITY.—Inventors are often compelled to have their conceptions embodied in construction by skilled mechanics and manufacturers, whose practical knowledge often enables them to suggest and make valuable improvements in simplifying and perfecting machines or devices, and the inventor is entitled to protection from their efforts to claim his invention. At the same time an employee is to be protected from the rapacity of his employer also, and if in doing the work assigned him the employee goes farther than mechanical skill enables him to do and makes an actual invention he is equally entitled to the benefit of his invention. * *Robinson v. McCormick*, 574.

4. SAME—SAME—BURDEN ON EMPLOYEE TO SHOW INVENTION.—Where an employee claims protection for an improvement which he devised while working upon a general conception of his employer, the burden is generally upon him to show that he made an invention in fact. * *Id.*

5. SAME—SAME—EMPLOYER MUST DISCLOSE MORE THAN FINAL RESULT.— To claim the benefit of the employee's skill and achievement, it is not sufficient that the employer had in mind a desired result and employed one to devise means for its accomplishment. He must show that he had an idea of the means to accomplish the particular result, which he communicated to the employee in such detail as to enable the latter to embody the same in some practical form. * *Id.*

EQUITY. See *Infringement*, 4.

EQUIVALENTS. See *Interference*, 78, 90; *Invention*, 5; *Trade-Marks*, 137, 138.

ESTOPPEL. See *Applications*, 3; *Infringement*, 3; *Res. Adjudicata; Trade-Marks*, 94.

EVIDENCE. See *Copies of Affidavit Filed Under Rule 75; Diligence; Interference*, 4, 41, 43, 44, 84; *Priority of Invention*, 16; *Reduction to Practice*, 3, 11, 13, 14, 15; *Rejection of Claims*, 2; *Trade-Marks*, 12, 23, 117, 150.

1. INTERFERENCE—TESTIMONY—CONTROL OF WITNESSES.—The Patent Office has no power to compel the attendance of witnesses or to enforce the production of evidence of any kind. (*Lindstrom v. Lipschutz*, C. D., 1906; 120 O. G., 904; *Kelly et al. v. Park et al.*, C. D., 1897, 182; 81 O. G., 1931.) *Bay State Belting Company v. Kelton-Bruce Manufacturing Company*, 91.

2. SAME—SAME—BOOKS USED TO REFRESH MEMORY NEED NOT BE OFFERED IN EVIDENCE.—Books produced at the examination of a witness for the purpose of refreshing his memory need not be offered in evidence. (*Laas and Sponenburg v. Scott*, C. D., 1906, 621; 122 O. G., 352; *McCormick v. Cleal*, C. D., 1898, 492; 83 O. G., 1514.) *Id.*

3. SAME—SAME—SUPPRESSION—REFUSAL TO PLACE BOOKS IN EVIDENCE.— Where certain books were referred to by a witness for the purpose of refreshing his recollection, and opposing counsel, who was given an

opportunity to examine them, did not interpose any objection to the **books** or cross-examine the witness relative to the entries, *Held* that a subsequent refusal to produce the books for inspection or to offer them in evidence does not warrant the suppression of any part of the deposition of the witness who referred to said books. *Id.*

4. SAME—ADMISSIBILITY OF LETTER-PRESS COPIES.—Where a party to an interference who is in possession of original copies of letters written in the regular course of business is asked to produce them, so that they may be used as evidence, but fails to do so, although he has ample time therefor, letter-press copies produced by the proper custodian of the same may be admitted with the same force and effect as the originals without throwing open the entire letter-press book to the inspection of the opposing party. *Kempshall* v. *Royce*, 626.

5. SAME—PRESUMPTION ARISING FROM FAILURE TO REBUT ADMISSIONS.—Where the evidence indicated that the senior party derived the invention in controversy from the junior party and that prior to the junior party's application the senior party admitted that the invention was made by the junior party, *Held* that the election of the senior party to rely on his record date rather than to take the stand and explain such admissions is significant evidence of their truth. *Id.*

6. SAME—REFUSAL OF COMMISSIONER TO SUPPRESS EVIDENCE—NOT REVERSIBLE ERROR.—The refusal of the Commissioner of Patents to suppress portions of a deposition because of the inclusion therein of alleged copies of letter-press copies of letters written by one party to the other is not reversible error. *Id.*

EXAMINATION OF APPLICATIONS. See *Abandonment of Applications*, 3, 4, 14; *Claims; Division of Applications*, 2; *Motion to Dissolve Interference*, 7; *Rejection of Claims; Specifications.*

1. FINAL REJECTION—WHEN UNWARRANTED.—Where appellant's letter stated that the prior Office action was not understood, requested that the pertinency of the references be pointed out as a guide to applicant in the further prosecution of the case, and expressly stated that it was not intended as a request for reconsideration, *Held* that the action of the Examiner in treating this letter as calling for a reconsideration and in finally rejecting the claims was unwarranted. *Ex parte Fowler, Jr.*, 88.

2. SAME—WHEN PREMATURE.—Where in the Office action prior to the final rejection a claim was criticised, but its rejection was inadvertently omitted, *Held* that the final rejection was premature. *Id.*

3. CITATION OF REFERENCES.—Where several claims are rejected, it should appear in the Examiner's letter whether all the references are cited against each claim or whether they are cited distributively against the various claims. In the latter event it should be made clear in connection with each claim which references are relied upon in the rejection thereof. *Ex parte Lincoln*, 117.

4. COMBINATION OF REFERENCES.—Where references cited are to be taken jointly, the theory upon which they are combined must be pointed out. The Examiner need not, however, ordinarily apply the references to the claim element for element, the specification and drawings of the references being ordinarily sufficient to indicate their application to the claims. *Id.*

5. EXPLANATION OF REFERENCES.—If any doubt exists as to the interpretation placed by the Examiner upon a feature of the drawing or por-

tion of the specification, he will furnish an explanation in response to a specific request making clear the uncertainty existing in the mind of the applicant. *Id.*

6. AMENDMENT AFTER FINAL REJECTION—EXPLANATION BY EXAMINER PRIOR TO FINAL REJECTION.—Where after a rejection by the Primary Examiner an applicant requests a reconsideration and files an argument fully presenting the case upon the merits and the Examiner in view thereof finally rejects the claims, he cannot submit new claims and have them entered and considered thereafter upon the allegation that the letter asking for reconsideration was in fact a request for an explanation of the Examiner's position. *Ex parte Knapp and Cade,* 150.

7. RES ADJUDICATA—PRACTICE—REJECTION.—Where an application is filed the specification and claims of which the Examiner holds to be substantially the same as those of a prior application of the same party the claims of which have been declared unpatentable by the Commissioner and the courts, *Held* that the application should be examined and the claims rejected on the ground that the question of their patentability is *res adjudicata. Ex parte Millett and Reed,* 177.

8. SUFFICIENCY OF DISCLOSURE—PRACTICE.—Where no reason is given for the use of certain ingredients of the article of manufacture which are set forth in the specification and the Examiner is of the opinion that such ingredients have a deleterious effect or no effect at all, he should not refuse to act upon the merits of the case, but should reject the claim for this reason. *Ex parte Danford,* 356.

EXAMINER OF INTERFERENCES. See *Appeal from the Examiner of Interferences; Appeal to the Court of Appeals of the District of Columbia,* 1; *Decisions of the Examiner of Interferences; Interference,* 7, 8, 11, 19, 32, 49, 51, 58; *Motion for Leave to Take Testimony; Motion to Dissolve Interference.* 1, 2, 5, 6, 12; *Preliminary Statement,* 3; *Trade-Marks,* 1, 74, 82, 131, 153, 154.

EXAMINER OF TRADE-MARKS. See *Trade-Marks,* 89, 135.

EXCLUSIVE USE. See *Trade-Marks,* 50, 51, 52, 57, 58, 60, 61, 67, 87.

EXHIBITS. See *Trade-Marks,* 152.

EXPERIMENTAL DEVICES. See *Preliminary Statement,* 4.

EXPERIMENTAL MACHINES. See *Reduction to Practice,* 7.

EXPERIMENTS. See *Priority of Invention,* 6, 8; *Reduction to Practice,* 6.

FAILURE TO TAKE TESTIMONY. See *Interference,* 1.

FINAL FEE. See *Withdrawal of Allowed Applications from Issue,* 1.

FINAL HEARING. See *Motion to Amend Preliminary Statement,* 3; *Motion to Suppress Testimony; Reopening of Interference,* 6, 8.

FINAL REJECTION OF CLAIMS. See *Rejection of Claims.*

FIRST AND ORIGINAL INVENTOR. See *Employer and Employee,* 1, 2; *Interference,* 5, 36, 39, 54, 55, 93, 94; *Priority of Invention,* 17.

FOREIGN APPLICANT. See *Trade-Marks,* 30, 31.

FOREIGN APPLICATIONS. See *Construction of Statutes,* 2, 3, 4; *Trade-Marks,* 85, 118.

FOREIGN EXECUTORS OR ADMINISTRATORS.

FOREIGN INVENTORS—GERMANY—PROOF OF AUTHORIZATION.—Where it appears that the applicant, who was a subject of the Emperor of Germany and resided in Germany, is dead and application is made by Mrs. Niedenführ, his alleged administratrix, to prosecute the application, *Held* that in addition to a properly-authenticated certificate of inheritance there should be filed either a certificate of a German court of record that Mrs. Niedenführ is entitled to administer the estate, such certificate being properly proved by the certificate of a consular or diplomatic officer, or else a formal statement to that effect from the German embassy or the German consulate. *Ex parte Niedenführ*, 257.

FOREIGN INVENTOR. See *Interference*, 90.

FOREIGN PATENTS. See *Interference*, 89.

FOREIGN REGISTRATION OF TRADE-MARKS. See *Trade-Marks*, 30, 31.

FORMAL OBJECTIONS. See *Rejection of Claims*, 6.

DISCOVERED BY ISSUE AND GAZETTE DIVISION—DECISION OF EXAMINER CONTROLLING.—When in the revision of the application in the Issue and Gazette Division supposed formal objections are discovered, the Examiner's attention should be called thereto; but the Examiner's decision, indorsed upon the reference slip, that a supposed objection is not in fact one or that correction is not necessary should settle the matter for this Office. *Ex parte Faulkner*, 136.

FORMER DECISIONS CITED. See *Bill in Equity Under Section 4915, Revised Statutes; Claims*, 1; *Conception of Invention; Construction of Claims*, 3; *Construction of Statutes*, 1; *Employer and Employee*, 2; *Evidence*, 1, 2, *Interference*, 11, 17, 18, 40, 49, 57, 69, 73, 78; *Motion for Rehearing*, 5; *Motion to Dissolve Interference*, 4, 9, 19; *Patentability*, 1, 5; *Priority of Invention*, 11, 12, 13, 14, 19; *Reduction to Practice*, 4, 9, 17; *Reissue Applications*, 5, 6; *Res Adjudicata; Specifications; Trade-Marks*, 8, 9, 59, 65, 103, 109.

FORMER DECISIONS DISTINGUISHED. See *Interference*, 28; *Motion to Dissolve Interference*, 43; *Preliminary Statement*, 4; *Trade-Marks*, 140.

FORMER DECISIONS FOLLOWED. See *Trade-Marks*, 120.

FORMER DECISIONS MODIFIED. See *Motion for Leave to Take Testimony; Motion to Dissolve Interference*, 33.

FRAUDULENT INTENT. See *Reissue Applications*, 5.

FUNCTION. See *Interference*, 15.

FUNCTIONAL CLAIMS. See *Claims*, 2, 3.

GEOGRAPHICAL TERMS. See *Trade-Marks*, 32, 34, 44, 53, 54, 60, 64, 141.

HEARING. See *Interference*, 14, 30, 33, 34, 51, 52; *Trade-Marks*, 72, 73, 74.

IDENTICAL CLAIMS. See *Interference*, 33; *Motion to Dissolve Interference*, 10, 11; *Priority of Invention*, 6.

IDENTITY OF INVENTION. See *Interference*, 26, 53; *Testimony*.

INADVERTENCE OR MISTAKE. See *Reissue Applications*, 3, 4, 5.

INDEFINITENESS. See *Interference*, 88; *Motion to Dissolve Interference*, 14, 35, 41.

INFRINGEMENT. See *Trade-Marks*, 149.

1. PATENTS—DECREE OF NON-INFRINGEMENT—QUESTION RES ADJUDICATA THROUGHOUT THE UNITED STATES.—*Held* that a final decree for the defendant in one circuit in a suit upon a patent upon the ground of non-infringement entitled the defendant to continue the business of making and selling throughout the United States the article which he had theretofore been making and selling without molestation by the complainant through the patent in suit. *Kessler v. Eldred*, 696.

2. SAME—SAME—SUBSEQUENT SUIT AGAINST DEFENDANT'S CUSTOMERS WRONGFUL.—*Held* that said decree makes a suit by the complainant against any of the defendant's customers for alleged infringement of the patent sued upon a wrongful interference with defendant's business. *Id.*

3. SAME—ASSUMPTION OF DEFENSE OF SUIT AGAINST CUSTOMER—NO ESTOPPEL FROM PROCEEDING DIRECTLY AGAINST COMPLAINANT.—Where a suit upon a patent terminates for the defendant and complainant thereafter sues a customer of the defendant upon the same patent and the aforesaid defendant assumes the defense of his customer's suit, *Held* that he is not thereby estopped from proceeding against the complainant for wrongfully interfering with his business. **Id.*

4. SAME—SAME—SAME—MAY PROCEED IN EQUITY.—*Held* that the aforesaid defendant was entitled to proceed against the complainant in equity. **Id.*

5. CONTRIBUTORY—SALE OF UNPATENTED SUPPLIES FOR USE WITH PATENTED MACHINE.—Where a machine is sold under the restriction that it was to be used only with supplies made by the vendor, a defendant who sells supplies which are used with such machine cannot be held liable as a contributory infringer of the patent for the machine where it does not appear that the defendant ever solicited an order for such supplies, or was ever notified by the plaintiffs of the rights which they claimed, or that the executive officers of defendant had knowledge of the special character of such machines or the restrictions on the purchase of supplies **Cortelyou and Cortelyou, administrators, et al. v. Charles Enew Johnson & Company,* 700.

6. NOTICE TO SALESMAN NOT NOTICE TO COMPANY.—Notice to a salesman of a company who was not an officer or general agent of the company is not such notice as will bind the principal with respect to all future transactions. **Id.*

INOPERATIVENESS. See *Decisions of the Examiner of Interferences; Motion for Leave to Take Testimony,* 1; *Motion to Dissolve Interference,* 1, 2, 6; *Priority of Invention,* 4.

INTERFERENCE. See *Amendments,* 1, 4; *Affidavits; Appeal from the Examiner of Interferences; Appeal to the Examiners-in-Chief; Bill in Equity Under Section 4915, Revised Statutes; Concealment of Invention; Conception of Invention; Construction of Claims; Construction of Statutes,* 1; *Copies of Affidavit Filed Under Rule 75; Decisions of the Examiner of Interferences; Diligence; Employer and Employee; Evidence; Inter Partes Cases; Mandamus; Motion for Leave to Take Testimony; Motion for Rehearing; Motion to Amend Application; Motion to Amend Preliminary Statement; Motion to Dissolve Interference; Motion to Suppress Testimony; Motion to Take Testimony in Foreign Countries; Patentability; Preliminary Statement; Priority of Invention; Public Use and Sale; Reduction to Practice; Rejection of Claims; Reopening of Interference; Testimony; ᵗTrade-Marks,* 1, 3, 6, 13, 14, 21, 26, 35, 46, 47, 51, 52, 65, 76, 77, 79, 95, 107, 108, 109, 115, 116, 130, 131, 139, 140, 145, 146; *Withdrawal of Allowed Applications from Issue,* 3.

1. TRADE-MARK—FAILURE TO TAKE DEPOSITION IN ACCORDANCE WITH NOTICE—SUBSEQUENT DEPOSITION—SUPPRESSION.—Where a party to an interference gives notice to the opposing party of his intention to take testimony at a certain time and place, but fails to appear at the time and place stated, and no notice is given of his inability to take testimony in accordance with the notice, testimony taken under a subsequent notice will not be considered if proper objection is made by the opposing party unless it appears that the opposing party was not injured by the failure to act upon the original notice or that there were

good reasons for such failure to act then and for the failure to duly notify the opposing party of the postponement. *Densten* v. *Burnham*, 4.

2. PRIORITY—DILIGENCE.—Where P. conceived the invention in the early part of November, 1903, and filed his application December 11, 1903, and W. conceived the invention on September 16, 1903, but did not reduce it to practice prior to the filing of his application on January 27, 1904, *Held* that W. was lacking in diligence in the absence of a sufficient excuse for the delay. *Woods* v. *Poor*, 12.

3. SAME—SAME—ENDEAVOR TO IMPROVE DEVICE.—The claim of an inventor, advanced as an excuse for his delay in reducing to practice, that he was endeavoring to improve upon his conception is not supported by testimony showing merely that conversations were held looking to the improvement thereof where it does not appear that any changes were actually made or that any material changes were even suggested. *Id.*

4. SAME—SAME—CLAIM OF POVERTY NOT PROVED.—A claim of an inventor that he was financially unable to reduce his invention to practice after paying the necessary expenses of his business is not proved where the evidence does not show what the necessary expenses of the business were and where there is no evidence of the inventor's resources except his own statement that he had only a given amount of cash on hand. *Id.*

5. ORIGINALITY.—An allegation of derivation of an invention by one party from another is not proved by a mere showing that opportunity for such derivation existed. *Id.*

6. APPEAL AFTER EXPIRATION OF LIMIT OF APPEAL.—A motion to extend the limit of appeal to include an appeal filed about three weeks after the expiration of the limit of appeal, supported by affidavits tending to excuse the delay, granted, where it appeared that the granting of the motion was not opposed and that the appeal might be heard with an appeal filed by the opposing party, to whom no delay would therefore result. *Normand* v. *Krimmelbein*, 15.

7. SAME—MOTION CONSIDERED BY COMMISSIONER IN PERSON.—It is the practice for the Commissioner to consider in person a motion to extend the limit of appeal to include an appeal to the Examiners-in-Chief filed after the expiration of the limit of appeal rather than to restore jurisdiction to the Examiner of Interferences for this purpose. *Id.*

8. MOTION TO SUSPEND PROCEEDINGS—APPEAL.—The decision of the Examiner of Interferences refusing to suspend proceedings pending a determination of contempt proceedings brought in a United States circuit court for failure of witnesses to appear and testify in response to subpoena will not be disturbed where it does not appear that great hardship will otherwise ensue. *Outcault* v. *The New York Herald Company*, 17.

9. ACCESS TO APPLICATION OF FORMER OPPONENT.—Where the joint applicants H., G., and F. filed a concession in favor of the sole applicant H. and judgment was thereupon entered against the joint applicants, *Held* that the application of H., G., and F. is no longer involved in the interference proceeding, and the fact that it was formerly so involved is no reason for permitting D., another party to said interference, to obtain a copy of it at this time. *Herr* v. *Herr, Groves, and Foreman* v. *Dodds*, 20.

10. SHIFTING CLAIMS FROM ONE APPLICATION TO ANOTHER—TRANSMISSION AT REQUEST OF PRIMARY EXAMINER.—Where a party having two applications involved in companion interferences presents amendments canceling the interfering claims from one application and adding them to

the other for the purpose of withdrawing one application from interference and concealing its subject-matter, *Held* that the request of the
Primary Examiner that the interference be transmitted to him for the
purpose of considering these amendments should be granted, as the
other party will not be seriously inconvenienced by the slight delay
caused by taking the desired action. *Behrend* v. *Lamme*, 28.

11. CLAIMS PRESENTED UNDER RULE 109—PRACTICE.—The reasons which led
to the change in Rule 124, set forth in *Newcomb* v. *Thomson* (C. D.,
1906, 232; 122 O. G., 3012,) apply with nearly the same force to motions under Rule 109. The purpose of Rule 109 is to avoid a second
interference. If a party wishes to appeal from an adverse decision on
the merits of his claims presented under Rule 109, he should be permitted to do so to the full extent provided by law in order that the
necessity for a subsequent *ex parte* appeal and the possibility of a second interference may be avoided. *Townsend* v. *Copeland* v. *Robinson*, 35.

12. SAME—SAME.—The practice concerning motions to add claims under
Rule 109 should follow the procedure set forth in Rule 124 relative to
motions for dissolution. The amendment accompanying the motion
made under Rule 109 should be entered in the application, and if the
Examiner holds that the claims are not allowable to the party bringing the motion he will reject the claims. Following Rule 124, the Examiner will also set a time for reconsideration, and if after reconsideration he adheres to his original decision he will finally reject the
claims and fix a limit of appeal. *Id.*

13. MOTION TO TAKE TESTIMONY ON OPERATIVENESS—GOOD FAITH.—It must
appear from the showing accompanying a motion to take testimony on
the question of operativeness that the moving party is acting in good
faith and that the matters alleged in support of the motion are such
as to justify the setting of times for taking testimony. *Clement* v.
Browne v. *Stroud*, 48.

14. SAME—HEARING ON SUFFICIENCY OF SHOWING—COUNTER AFFIDAVITS.—
Motions to take testimony on the question of the operativeness of an
opposing party's device will generally be disposed of on the showing
made by the moving party, and when the moving party files affidavits
in support of his motion the Office will hear the opposing party on the
sufficiency of the showing; but counter affidavits should not be admitted. *Id.*

15. RIGHT TO MAKE CLAIM.—A party cannot be deprived of the right to
make a claim by reason of the fact that his structure performs some
function in addition to what is called for by the claim. *Miel* v. *Young*.
53.

16. SAME—LIMITATION OF CLAIM BY CONSTRUCTION CONDEMNED.—A claim
made by a patentee involved in interference with an applicant which
refers broadly to reinforcing means should not be limited by construction to reinforcing means operating in a specified way where
there is nothing in the record to show that such a limitation is necessary to render the claim patentable over the prior art and where it
is not clear that the reinforcing means disclosed by the applicant does
not operate in the same way as that disclosed by the patentee. *Id.*

17. SAME—ONE PARTY A PATENTEE—CONSTRUCTION OF CLAIM.—The fact
that one of the parties to an interference has obtained a patent should
have no bearing on the interpretation of a claim in issue in deter-

mining the right of an applicant to make such claim. If the terms of the claim do not in their ordinary meaning define the invention of the patentee as he wishes to have it defined, he may, as intimated in *Andrews* v. *Nilson* (C. D., 1906, 717; 123 O. G., 1667,) apply for a reissue. *Id.*

18. DISSOLUTION—APPEAL FROM AFFIRMATIVE DECISION ON PATENTABILITY.— Neither the rules of the Patent Office nor any section of the Revised Statutes provide for nor permit appeals from a decision rendered upon a motion for dissolution affirming the patentability of the issue. (*Allen* v. *Lowry*, C. D., 1905, 643; 116 O. G., 2253.) *Sobey* v. *Holsclaw*, 465.

19. APPEAL ON PRIORITY—PATENTABILITY OF ISSUE.—Where the patentability of the claims of an interference issue has been favorably passed upon by the Primary Examiner *ex parte* and also *inter partes* upon a motion to dissolve, from whose affirmative decision in the latter case no right of direct appeal is given either by the patent statutes or the rules of the Patent Office, and both the Examiner of Interferences and the Examiners-in-Chief have refused to direct the attention of the Commissioner, under Rule 126, to the fact that the claims were unpatentable, it cannot be successfully maintained that the Commissioner of Patents decided the question of priority without first determining and deciding that the subject-matter was patenable. *Id.*

20. SAME—REVIEW BY COMMISSIONER OF DECISION OF EXAMINER ON PATENTABILITY OR RIGHT TO MAKE CLAIMS.—The Primary Examiners, who are given statutory authority to decide questions of patentability, are under the supervision of the Commissioner, and it would seem to be not only his right but his duty to correct any manifest error committed by any of the Primary Examiners relative to the patentability of a supposed invention or of the right of an applicant to claim it whenever such error was called to his attention. To warrant any action on his part in such a case, the error must be so gross that it would be a wrong to the public to permit a patent to issue. It manifestly should not be based upon a mere difference of opinion. *Id.*

21. SAME—ADOPTION BY COMMISSIONER OF VIEWS OF SUBORDINATE TRIBUNALS.—Where the question of the patentability of the claims of the issue has been repeatedly raised before the subordinate tribunals of the Patent Office and is again raised upon appeal to the Commissioner on priority, the adoption by the Commissioner of the views of the subordinate tribunals is a sufficient determination by him of the question so far as it is necessary to be determined in an interference proceeding. *Id.*

22. ISSUES—CONSTRUED IN LIGHT OF APPLICATION FIRST CONTAINING THEM.— Since the claims of an interference issue are to be construed in the light of the application of the party first making them, it would be manifestly improper for the Commissioner of Patents to read into them for any purpose limitations not disclosed in the application of such party. *Id.*

23. MOTION TO DISSOLVE—NO APPEAL FROM HOLDING THAT COUNTS HAVE IDENTICAL MEANING.—From the decision of the Examiner holding that there is interference in fact or that the counts of the issue have the same meaning in the cases of the different parties no appeal is permitted under the provisions of Rule 124. *Dukesmith* v. *Corrington* v. *Turner*, 62.

24. DEFECTIVE APPLICATION OATH—APPEAL TO SECRETARY.—The decision of the Commissioner of Patents ruling that defects in the application oath of one of the parties, if there were such, might be corrected after the termination of the interference is judicial or quasi-judicial in character and subject only to review by the courts, and the Secretary of the Interior has no appellate or supervisory control of the matter. † *Dukesmith* v. *Corrington* v. *Turner*, 431.

25. ACCESS TO OPPONENT'S APPLICATION, PART OF WHICH IS CONCEALED UNDER RULE 105.—Where the interfering subject-matter of the application of one of the parties to an interference is disclosed to the other by means of a certified copy, as provided by Rule 105, an auxiliary invention which has been described and claimed by the former, but which might be omitted without destroying the operativeness of the invention in issue, will not be disclosed where the latter has presented no claim which includes this invention either broadly or specifically. *Kugele* v. *Blair*, 81.

26. PRIORITY—INTERFERENCE IN FACT—CONCLUSIONS BY PATENT OFFICE GENERALLY ACCEPTED BY COURT OF APPEALS.—Ordinarily where the point has been raised whether the application of one of the parties was broad enough in the terms of its specification and claims to embrace the invention of the other, and especially where the invention is one of elaborate and complicated mechanism, the decisions of the expert tribunals of the Patent Office in respect of identity have, for obvious reasons, been accepted as conclusive. * *Bechman* v. *Southgate*, 489.

27. SECOND INTERFERENCE—RES ADJUDICATA.—Where a second interference is declared between the same applications on an issue relating to the subject-matter of invention as that of a prior interference, of broader scope than the first issue, and the constructions relied on, respectively, as evidencing conception and reduction to practice of the invention of both issues are the same and the fundamental facts of both cases are the same, *Held* that the final decision in the first interference is conclusive and that the question of priority is *res adjudicata* unless it can be made to appear that the question upon which the determination of the second case rests is one that neither was nor could have been presented and determined in the first case. * *Blackford* v. *Wilder*, 491.

28. REFERENCE UNDER RULE 126—REJECTION OF CLAIMS.—Where the Examiners-in-Chief in their decision in an interference upon priority of invention call the attention of the Commissioner under Rule 126 to the fact that in their opinion the issue is not patentable and the decision becomes final by the expiration of the limit of appeal without appeal, the Examiner will be directed to reject in the application of the successful party the claim corresponding to the issue found by the Examiners-in-Chief to be unpatentable. (*Snider* v. *Bunnell*, C. D., 1903, 117; 103 O. G., 890, distinguished.) *Holz* v. *Hewitt*, 98.

29. SAME—SAME.—It is not to be presumed that the Examiners-in-Chief would form an opinion adverse to a party's interest and call attention to the same upon the record without careful consideration in those cases where the grounds of their opinion had already been considered by the Primary Examiner and held insufficient to warrant such adverse opinion. When they express an opinion under these circumstances, the same is clearly of sufficient force to bind the Primary Examiner and sustain his *pro forma* rejection of claims until the opinion is withdrawn by the Examiners-in-Chief themselves or over-

ruled by the Commissioner or court of appeals in the regular course of appeal. *Id.*

30. HEARING—RULES 126 AND 130 DISTINGUISHED.—Rule 126 does not provide for a hearing by the Commissioner, and no reason appears why a hearing should be given to an applicant whose claims are found to be unpatentable by the Board of Examiners-in-Chief in their consideration of the claim in connection with the question of priority of invention. *Id.*

31. APPEAL AFTER REJECTION OF CLAIM.—Where upon reference by the Examiners-in-Chief, under Rule 126, stating that in their opinion the issue of an interference is unpatentable, the Examiner is directed to reject the claims in the application of the successful party, the *pro forma* rejection of the Examiner puts the case at once in condition for a course of appeal which may be carried to the court of appeals if the application is otherwise in condition therefor. *Id.*

32. TESTIMONY TO SHOW ISSUE UNPATENTABLE TO EITHER PARTY IRRELEVANT TO QUESTION OF PRIORITY.—Where during the time assigned him for the purpose of taking testimony upon the question of priority of invention one party took merely the testimony of an expert for the purpose of showing that the issue is not patentable to either party over the prior art, *Held* that the decision of the Examiner of Interferences was proper in granting a motion to strike said testimony from the record on the ground that it is irrelevant to the question of priority. *Dixon and Marsh* v. *Graves and Whittemore*, 101.

33. UNPATENTABILITY OF ISSUE TO ALL PARTIES—PROPERLY RAISED BY MOTION TO DISSOLVE UNDER RULE 122.—Where it is contended that the non-patentability of the issue to either party to the interference may be urged at final hearing, *Held* that during the preliminary stages of the interference and before the parties have been put to the trouble and expense of taking testimony on the question of priority either party may raise the question of the patentability of the issue by motion to dissolve the interference under Rule 122. Contestants are thus given an opportunity to have determined the question of whether the Office was right in declaring the interference and whether the proceedings should continue before testimony as to priority is taken. It is essential to the orderly proceedings of the interference that the question of patentability be finally settled at this time, and for this purpose the rules provide for an appeal from the rejection of claims based on the decision on the motion to the full extent permitted by law. *Id.*

34. SAME—CANNOT BE RAISED UNDER RULE 130.—Where it is contended by one party to an interference that he has a right to urge the unpatentability of the issues to either party at the final hearing under Rule 130 and to take testimony in support thereof, *Held* that the contention is erroneous and that this rule permits a party to urge the non-patentability of a claim to his opponent as a basis for the decision upon priority of invention only when it is material to his own right to a patent. *Id.*

35. TESTIMONY—USE IN SUBSEQUENT INTERFERENCE.—Where the real parties in interest in a pending interference are the same as in a prior interference and the inventions involved are substantially the same, permission may be obtained, under the provisions of Rule 157, to use in the pending interference the testimony taken in the former interference. *Beall, jr.,* v. *Lyon*, 116.

36. ORIGINALITY—DISCLAIMER OF INVENTORSHIP.—A statement by applicant to his assignee that he does not regard himself as the inventor of the subject-matter claimed in such application is not sufficient to warrant an award of priority to an opponent where it appears that such statement was made during a controversy between the parties with regard to the amount of royalty which should be paid to the assignor. *Gibbons v. Peller, 529.

87. PRIORITY—DELAY AFTER ALLEGED CONCEPTION AND REDUCTION TO PRACTICE.—Where an inventor after an alleged reduction to practice of his invention lays it aside for five years, during which time he files several domestic and foreign applications and develops another system to accomplish the same purpose which he regards as superior, and fails to file an application until after the grant of a patent to another for the same invention who was proceeding in good faith, he is guilty of inexcusable laches. *Bliss v. McElroy, 537.

88. SAME—DILIGENCE.—F. conceived the invention in September, 1900, and disclosed it in September, 1903, but did nothing toward reducing it to practice until April, 1904. C. conceived the invention in January, 1904, and reduced it to practice in the following March. The excuse offered by F. for his delay was that he was too busy earning his living to attend to it, and, moreover, he did not have the means to reduce it to practice unless he borrowed the money, which he did not want to do, Held that F. was lacking in diligence, it being shown by the evidence that subsequent to his conception he borrowed $3,000 with which to engage in a venturesome undertaking, while a small amount of money would have enabled him to construct the invention. *Feinberg v. Cowan, 546.

39. TESTIMONY—RIGHT TO MAKE CLAIMS—PRIORITY.—In an interference proceeding where, in addition to the taking of testimony as to who was the first inventor, permission was obtained to take testimony concerning the right of one of the parties to make the claims for use at the first hearing on priority under Rule 130, Held that the rule contemplates but one contest, and that leading to an award of priority, and not two distinct contests and two separate proceedings. The taking of testimony on the question of priority should not therefore be suspended until the question of the right to make the claims has been determined. Hewitt v. Weintraub v. Hewitt and Rogers, 155.

40. PRIORITY—SUFFICIENCY OF DISCLOSURE—CONCLUSIVENESS OF PATENT OFFICE DECISIONS.—The decisions of the expert tribunals of the Patent Office on the question of the sufficiency of the disclosure of a party to an interference will be accepted by the court of appeals as conclusive, except in extreme cases where palpable error has been committed. (Seeberger v. Dodge C. D., 1905, 603: 114 O. G., 2382; 24 App. D. C., 481; Podlesak and Podlesak v. McInnerney, C. D., 1906, 558; 120 O. G., 2127; 26 App. D. C., 405.) *Kilbourn v. Hirner, 552.

41. EVIDENCE—CONSIDERATION OF DEPOSITION—FAILURE TO AFFORD OPPORTUNITY FOR CROSS-EXAMINATION.—Where the direct examination of a witness is completed and after answering certain questions upon cross-examination he is withdrawn from the stand on account of sickness and his counsel refuses to take any steps to produce him again in order that the cross-examination may be completed, on the ground that he had been sick for over a year, had undergone several operations, and that there was no probability that he would be able to testify

at any definite time in the future, if at all, *Held* that in so far as the answers given on direct examination were not tested by cross-examination the deposition should not be considered. *Munster v. Ashworth,* 156.

42. DEPOSITIONS—NOTICE OF TAKING—NOTICE WAIVED.—Where a record as made up by the officer before whom testimony is taken in an interference proceeding shows that counsel for one of the parties desired to examine certain witnesses as to whom no notice had been given by opposing counsel and the latter stated that while he had no objection to their direct examination he did not care to cross-examine and thereupon went away, *Held* that the depositions of such witnesses will not upon motion be stricken out because of lack of notice, notwithstanding an affidavit by counsel stating that he had refused to take the testimony of such witnesses. *Id.*

43. EVIDENCE—CONSIDERATION OF DEPOSITION—FAILURE TO AFFORD OPPORTUNITY FOR CROSS-EXAMINATION.—Where a witness after testifying on his own behalf and after answering a few questions on cross-examination states that he is unable to withstand the strain of cross-examination and leaves the stand and his counsel refuses to ask for an extension of time for taking testimony in order that the witness may be cross-examined at some time in the future, alleging that the witness is in such bad physical condition that there is no prospect of his being able to testify within a year, if at all, *Held* that counsel, knowing the condition of the witness, should either have refrained from offering him as a witness in his own behalf or, having done so, should have consented to some reasonable postponement. Under such circumstances the direct examination should have been excluded upon motion. **Munster v. Ashworth,* 556.

44. SAME—AFFIDAVIT ATTACHED TO DEPOSITION.—An affidavit of a physician attached to a deposition, setting forth the physical condition of a witness who has left the stand during cross-examination because of inability to stand the strain of cross-examination, forms no part of such deposition. The affiant should have been called and sworn to testify as a witness. **Id.*

45. PRIORITY—CONCEALMENT OF INVENTION.—If there be concealment or suppression of the invention, the field lies open to be occupied by a more diligent, though later, inventor, who when he has not only put the invention into public use, but has also obtained a patent for it, cannot be divested of his right to hold the field except upon proof beyond a reasonable doubt that the earlier and more negligent inventor has not gone back to an abandoned device or a device suppressed or concealed in order to establish a prior right. **Richards v. Burkholder,* 563.

46. SUGGESTION OF CLAIMS UNDER RULE 96—PRACTICE—INVENTOR AND ASSIGNEES PERSONALLY NOTIFIED.—In all cases where claims are suggested for the purpose of interference under the provisions of Rule 96, copies of the letter containing the suggested claims will be sent to the applicant and to the assignees, if the invention is assigned, as well as to the attorney of record. *Ex parte Doebler,* 183.

47. INTERVENTION BY EXCLUSIVE LICENSEE.—An exclusive licensee of an invention will not be permitted to intervene in the prosecution of an interference so long as the interference is being prosecuted in good faith by his licensor. *In re The National Railway Materials Company,* 193.

48. SAME—ACCESS TO RECORDS.—Where it appears that the inventor has entered the employment of a company which is the assignee of his opponent in an interference proceeding, the exclusive licensee of said inventor will, upon request, be furnished with copies of all notices in the interference and papers accompanying the same, including the preliminary statements, when approved, and the notices for taking testimony, and will also be permitted to be present at all proceedings in the interference. *Id.*

49. MOTION TO TRANSMIT MOTION TO AMEND—DELAY.—Where the Primary Examiner refused to dissolve an interference on the ground that the senior party had no right to make the claims, but the Examiner of Interferences under Rule 130 decided that he had no right to make the claims, *Held* that this state of facts was sufficient to excuse delay in bringing a motion to amend the issue under the practice announced in *Churchward* v. *Douglas* v. *Cutter* (C. D., 1903, 389; 106 O. G., 2016,) especially in view of the recent decisions of the court of appeals in *Blackford* v. *Wilder* (*ante*, 491; 127 O. G., 1255) and *Horine* v. *Wende* (*ante*, 615; 129 O. G., 2858.) *Becker* v. *Otis*, 197.

50. LIMIT OF APPEAL.—Where a judgment on the record is rendered and a limit of appeal set, the running thereof is not stayed by filing a petition to set the case down for hearing under Rule 130. *Pym* v. *Hadaway*, 209.

51. PRACTICE—RULE 130.—A refusal to reopen a case to permit Examiner of Interferences to consider a petition and set case down for hearing under Rule 130 proper where it appears from a consideration of the record that the question sought to be raised is not one of priority. *Id.*

52. SAME—SAME.—A party is deprived of no rights by a refusal to set for hearing under Rule 130 a case where the objections urged against one party's case apply equally well to that of the other. *Id.*

53. TWO APPLICATIONS FOR SAME INVENTION—EARLIER INVOLVED—REFUSAL OF PATENT ON LATER.—Where a party whose application is involved in interference proceedings presents another application based upon the invention involved in the interference, it is proper to refuse a patent upon the later application until the interference has been terminated. In such case it is just to suspend action on the later application. *In re Wickers and Furlong*, 608.

54. REOPENING—DELAY IN BRINGING MOTION—ORIGINALITY.—Where after judgment had been rendered against C., a junior party, for failure to take testimony, and later in another interference S. admitted a disclosure of the issue of this interference to him by C., but C. waited over a year after obtaining knowledge of this fact before bringing a motion to reopen, *Held* that the long delay indicates that the motion was not brought in good faith, but merely for the purpose of delay, and the motion to reopen denied. *Clausen* v. *Dunbar* v. *Schellenger*, 212.

55. SAME—EVIDENCE OF ORIGINALITY LONG AFTER FINAL JUDGMENT NOT RECEIVED.—Where judgment was rendered against C. by default and long afterward it appeared from testimony in a different interference that C. disclosed the invention to S., the successful party, *Held* that C., having failed to contest the question of originality or to move promptly to have the case reopened for the introduction of newly-discovered evidence as to this fact, has no greater right to contest the patentability of the issue to S. than any other member of the public and that right of S. to make the claim is not a matter for *inter partes* consideration. *Id.*

56. RECOMMENDATION OF EXAMINERS-IN-CHIEF UNDER RULE 126—NOT DE-
CIDED BY COMMISSIONER WITHOUT REMANDING TO PRIMARY EXAMINER.—
The recommendation of the Examiners-in-Chief that the issue is not
patentable is not a final decision of this question by them, and as the
statutes provide for appeals to the Court of Appeals of the District of
Columbia only after successive appeals have been taken to the Examiners-in-Chief and the Commissioner from a second rejection of the
Primary Examiner the question of patentability will not be reviewed
by the Commissioner until it has been finally passed upon by the lower
tribunals. *Serrell* v. *Donnelly*, 217.

57. SAME—ACTION BY PRIMARY EXAMINER—PRACTICE.—Where a case is
remanded to the Primary Examiner by the Commissioner upon reference by the Examiners-in-Chief under Rule 126, the Primary Examiner
will enter a *pro forma* rejection of the claims. (*Holz* v. *Hewitt, ante*,
98; 127 O. G., 1992.) He may, however, in such action include any
recommendation he may deem proper in order that the Examiners-in-
Chief may have the benefit of his expert knowledge of the art if the
case comes before them on appeal. *Id.*

58. EXTENSION OF TIME FOR TAKING TESTIMONY—PRACTICE.—It is well settled
that no appeal lies from the decision of the Examiner of Interferences
on motion to extend the time for taking testimony, and the sufficiency
of the showing made in support of the motion will not be considered by
the Commissioner on petition except in cases where it appears that
there has been a clear abuse of discretion operating to the injury of
one of the parties. *Wickers and Furlong* v. *Weinwurm*, 219.

59. INTERLOCUTORY DECISION.—A decision of the Commissioner of Patents
dissolving an interference is not a final order. **The Union Distilling
Company* v. *Schneider*, 613.

60. SAME—JURISDICTION OF COURT OF APPEALS OF DISTRICT OF COLUMBIA.—
The court of appeals has no jurisdiction to consider an appeal from a
decision of the Commissioner of Patents which is not a final order, and
such an appeal will be dismissed **Id.*

61. APPEAL TO COURT—AMENDMENT OF REASONS OF APPEAL.—Although neither
the rules of the court of appeals of the District of Columbia nor of the
Patent Office mention amendments to the reasons of appeal, when such
amendment is made in due time to correct an assignment of error that
may not be sufficiently specific or some inadvertence in its preparation
and no possible injury could be done the opposing party there appears
to be no reason why it should not be permitted. **Horine* v. *Wende*, 615.

62. PRIORITY—SECOND INTERFERENCE—RES ADJUDICATA.—Where judgment is
rendered in an interference proceeding in the Patent Office holding that
the issue was limited to matters not found in certain exhibits upon
which a party relies for an award of priority, although such party contends to the contrary, and no appeal is taken from such holding and the
case is finally decided adversely to such party, *Held* that in a subsequent interference between the same parties on an issue which is the
same as the prior issue, with the exception that in the second interference such limitations were omitted, the question of priority is *res adjudicata.* **Id.*

63. REOPENING.—An interference will not be reopened for the purpose of introducing newly-discovered evidence where it does not appear that the
evidence could not have been discovered at the time of taking testimony.
Latshaw v. *Duff* v. *Kaplan*, 254.

64. APPEAL—REHEARING.—An appeal from the Examiners-in-Chief will not be reheard for the purpose of considering a patent of one of the parties to the interference which is not in evidence. *Id.*

65. TESTIMONY—SURREBUTTAL.—Where an inventor testifying in rebuttal on behalf of his opponent denies that he is the inventor of a part of the invention in issue, his testimony constitutes such legal surprise as will entitle his assignee, who is prosecuting the invention, to take surrebuttal testimony. *Sandage v. Dean v. Wright v. McKenzie*, 250.

66. SAME—SAME.—Where the instances alleged to show that the inventor has testified falsely amount to no more than a difference of opinion between the witness and the affiant, a motion to take surrebuttal testimony should be denied. *Id.*

67. ACCESS TO RECORDS OF ANOTHER.—Where S. requested copies of the decision of the Examiner upon a motion for dissolution in another interference to which F. was a party and which is referred to in F.'s record, *Held* that since S. was not a party to the other interference and the claims forming the issue of that interference are not made by S. he should be denied access to the record of that interference, even though the issue thereof is based upon the same structure as that upon which the claims in the present interference are drawn. *Stone v. Fessenden*, 282.

68. SUSPENSION—POSTPONEMENT OF TIME FOR OPENING PRELIMINARY STATEMENTS.—An interference relating to a machine will not be suspended and the time for opening the preliminary statements postponed in order that one of the parties may take out a patent upon an application covering a closely related process not involved in the interference before the existence of such application is discovered by his opponent through access to the machine application which contains a cross-reference thereto. *Ex parte Field*, 284.

69. PRIORITY—APPEAL TO COURT—SUFFICIENCY OF DISCLOSURE CONSIDERED.—Whether or not an application involved in interference discloses the subject-matter in issue, and therefore whether or not the interference is properly declared, is a question to be ordinarily determined by the Patent Office (*Ostergren v. Tripler*, C. D., 1901, 350; 95 O. G., 837; 17 App. D. C., 558; *Herman v. Fullman*, C. D., 1904, 625,; 109 O. G., 1888; 23 App. D. C., 264, 265); but in extreme cases where palpable error has been committed the court may review the decision of the Patent Office on this point. (*Podlesak and Podlesak v. McInnerney*, C. D., 1906, 558; 120 O. G., 2127; 26 App. D. C., 399.) *MacMulkin v. Bollee*, 660.

70. CONSIDERATION OF PATENTABILITY ON APPEAL ON PRIORITY—SUPERVISORY AUTHORITY.—The question of the patentability of issue will be considered on appeal on priority only under the supervisory authority of the Commissioner for the purpose of correcting a manifest error. *Dixon and Marsh v. Graves and Whittemore*, 311.

71. JUDGMENT ON RECORD—ORDER TO SHOW CAUSE—SUFFICIENCY OF SHOWING.—Where in response to an order to the junior party to show cause why judgment of priority could not be rendered against him because his alleged date of conception was subsequent to the filing date of the senior party the junior party files a statement alleging that certain of the counts are specific to his structure and that the subject-matter covered thereby was not shown or described by the senior party, *Held* to be insufficient, as the question sought to be raised was one which

should have been raised by a motion to dissolve rather than by the mere filing of a statement. *Felbel* v. *Fox*, 312.

72. DELAY IN FILING MOTION—CHARACTER OF SHOWING REQUIRED.—A mere unverified statement accompanying a motion filed one day late stating that the motion should not be brought sooner on account of other work is insufficient. A showing in excuse for delay should be under oath, and it should state facts from which the Office may judge whether or not the delay was excusable. *Id.*

73. PRACTICE—ADHERENCE TO RULES NECCESSARY.—While it is not the desire of the Office to be too technical, it is better to insist upon a reasonable and just compliance with the rules of the Office, though it may work a hardship in an individual case, than to adopt a course that would result practically in abrogating the rules, with consequent confusion. (*Keller* v. *Wethey* v. *Roberts*, C. D., 1897, 157; 81 O. G., 331; *Estes* v. *Gause*, C. D., 1899, 164; 88 O. G., 1336.) *Id.*

74. FINAL JUDGMENT BY PATENT OFFICE—APPEAL TO COURT PENDING.—Judgment in an interference proceeding will not be made final by the Patent Office after the filing of a notice of appeal to the court of appeals of the District of Columbia and pending such appeal, on the ground that such notice was filed one day outside the forty-day period set by the rules of that court for filing notice of appeal, it being regarded as within the discretion of the court to waive a strict adherence to the rule and to entertain the appeal notwithstanding the delay in filing the notice. *Proutt* v. *Johnston and Johnston*, 318.

75. PRACTICE UNDER RULE 124—SUPERVISORY AUTHORITY OF COMMISSIONER.—No appeal lies from a favorable decision on the right to make the claims or the identity of meaning of the counts in the cases of different parties, and such a decision will be reviewed on petition in the exercise of the Commissioner's supervisory authority only to correct some palpable error in the decision which is clear and evident on its face. *Lipschutz* v. *Floyd*, 319.

76. PRELIMINARY STATEMENT—SECOND PROPOSED AMENDMENT—SHOWING REQUIRED.—Where after decision upon a motion for dissolution a party moves to amend his preliminary statement and it is held that the showing in support thereof is insufficient to warrant such amendment, a second motion to amend will not be granted where no good reason appears why the showing then made could not have been presented in connection with the first motion. Parties cannot be permitted to try their cases piecemeal and experimentally. *Borg* v. *Strauss*, 320.

77. SAME—SAME—SAME.—Amendments to preliminary statements are to be permitted after a party has had an opportunity to inspect his opponent's case only in cases where *bona fide* mistakes of fact have been made and a full and clear showing is made that there was no negligence in discovering the true facts. *Id.*

78. CONSTRUCTION OF ISSUE—EQUIVALENTS.—Where the claim in issue calls for a "plurality of blast nozzles," a device which has an "oscillating blast nozzle" cannot be considered as a reduction to practice on the ground that it is an equivalent. In the consideration of an interference the Patent Office is no more competent than the courts to say that an element which an applicant has placed in his claims is an immaterial one. (*Streat* v. *Freckleton*, C. D., 1899, 85; 87 O. G., 695.) *Collom* v. *Thurman*, 330.

the other for the purpose of withdrawing one application from interference and concealing its subject-matter, *Held* that the request of the
Primary Examiner that the interference be transmitted to him for the
purpose of considering these amendments should be granted, as the
other party will not be seriously inconvenienced by the slight delay
caused by taking the desired action. *Behrend* v. *Lomme*, 28.

11. CLAIMS PRESENTED UNDER RULE 109—PRACTICE.—The reasons which led
to the change in Rule 124, set forth in *Newcomb* v. *Thomson* (C. D.,
1906, 282; 122 O. G., 3012,) apply with nearly the same force to motions under Rule 109. The purpose of Rule 109 is to avoid a second
interference. If a party wishes to appeal from an adverse decision on
the merits of his claims presented under Rule 109, he should be permitted to do so to the full extent provided by law in order that the
necessity for a subsequent *ex parte* appeal and the possibility of a second interference may be avoided. *Townsend* v. *Copeland* v. *Robinson*, 35.

12. SAME—SAME.—The practice concerning motions to add claims under
Rule 109 should follow the procedure set forth in Rule 124 relative to
motions for dissolution. The amendment accompanying the motion
made under Rule 109 should be entered in the application, and if the
Examiner holds that the claims are not allowable to the party bringing the motion he will reject the claims. Following Rule 124, the Examiner will also set a time for reconsideration, and if after reconsideration he adheres to his original decision he will finally reject the
claims and fix a limit of appeal. *Id.*

13. MOTION TO TAKE TESTIMONY ON OPERATIVENESS—GOOD FAITH.—It must
appear from the showing accompanying a motion to take testimony on
the question of operativeness that the moving party is acting in good
faith and that the matters alleged in support of the motion are such
as to justify the setting of times for taking testimony. *Clement* v.
Browne v. *Stroud*, 48.

14. SAME—HEARING ON SUFFICIENCY OF SHOWING—COUNTER AFFIDAVITS.—
Motions to take testimony on the question of the operativeness of an
opposing party's device will generally be disposed of on the showing
made by the moving party, and when the moving party files affidavits
in support of his motion the Office will hear the opposing party on the
sufficiency of the showing; but counter affidavits should not be admitted. *Id.*

15. RIGHT TO MAKE CLAIM.—A party cannot be deprived of the right to
make a claim by reason of the fact that his structure performs some
function in addition to what is called for by the claim. *Miel* v. *Young*,
53.

16. SAME—LIMITATION OF CLAIM BY CONSTRUCTION CONDEMNED.—A claim
made by a patentee involved in interference with an applicant which
refers broadly to reinforcing means should not be limited by construction to reinforcing means operating in a specified way where
there is nothing in the record to show that such a limitation is necessary to render the claim patentable over the prior art and where it
is not clear that the reinforcing means disclosed by the applicant does
not operate in the same way as that disclosed by the patentee. *Id.*

17. SAME—ONE PARTY A PATENTEE—CONSTRUCTION OF CLAIM.—The fact
that one of the parties to an interference has obtained a patent should
have no bearing on the interpretation of a claim in issue in deter-

mining the right of an applicant to make such claim. If the terms
of the claim do not in their ordinary meaning define the invention of
the patentee as he wishes to have it defined, he may, as intimated
in *Andrews* v. *Nilson* (C. D., 1906, 717; 123 O. G., 1667,) apply for a
reissue. *Id.*

18. DISSOLUTION—APPEAL FROM AFFIRMATIVE DECISION ON PATENTABILITY.—
Neither the rules of the Patent Office nor any section of the Revised
Statutes provide for nor permit appeals from a decision rendered upon
a motion for dissolution affirming the patentability of the issue. (*Allen*
v. *Lowry*, C. D., 1905, 643; 116 O. G., 2253.) *Sobey* v. *Holsclaw*, 465.

19. APPEAL ON PRIORITY—PATENTABILITY OF ISSUE.—Where the patentability of the claims of an interference issue has been favorably passed
upon by the Primary Examiner *ex parte* and also *inter partes* upon a
motion to dissolve, from whose affirmative decision in the latter case
no right of direct appeal is given either by the patent statutes or the
rules of the Patent Office, and both the Examiner of Interferences and
the Examiners-in-Chief have refused to direct the attention of the
Commissioner, under Rule 126, to the fact that the claims were unpatentable, it cannot be successfully maintained that the Commissioner
of Patents decided the question of priority without first determining
and deciding that the subject-matter was patenable. *Id.*

20. SAME—REVIEW BY COMMISSIONER OF DECISION OF EXAMINER ON PAT
ENTABILITY OR RIGHT TO MAKE CLAIMS.—The Primary Examiners, who
are given statutory authority to decide questions of patentability, are
under the supervision of the Commissioner, and it would seem to be
not only his right but his duty to correct any manifest error committed
by any of the Primary Examiners relative to the patentability of a
supposed invention or of the right of an applicant to claim it whenever
such error was called to his attention. To warrant any action
on his part in such a case, the error must be so gross that it would
be a wrong to the public to permit a patent to issue. It manifestly
should not be based upon a mere difference of opinion. *Id.*

21. SAME—ADOPTION BY COMMISSIONER OF VIEWS OF SUBORDINATE TRIBU
NALS.—Where the question of the patentability of the claims of the
issue has been repeatedly raised before the subordinate tribunals of
the Patent Office and is again raised upon appeal to the Commissioner
on priority, the adoption by the Commissioner of the views of the
subordinate tribunals is a sufficient determination by him of the
question so far as it is necessary to be determined in an interference
proceeding. *Id.*

22. ISSUES—CONSTRUED IN LIGHT OF APPLICATION FIRST CONTAINING THEM.—
Since the claims of an interference issue are to be construed in the
light of the application of the party first making them, it would be
manifestly improper for the Commissioner of Patents to read into
them for any purpose limitations not disclosed in the application of
such party. *Id.*

23. MOTION TO DISSOLVE—NO APPEAL FROM HOLDING THAT COUNTS HAVE
IDENTICAL MEANING.—From the decision of the Examiner holding that
there is interference in fact or that the counts of the issue have the
same meaning in the cases of the different parties no appeal is permitted under the provisions of Rule 124. *Dukesmith* v. *Corrington* r
Turner, 62.

24. **DEFECTIVE APPLICATION OATH—APPEAL TO SECRETARY.**—The decision of the Commissioner of Patents ruling that defects in the application oath of one of the parties, if there were such, might be corrected after the termination of the interference is judicial or quasi-judicial in character and subject only to review by the courts, and the Secretary of the Interior has no appellate or supervisory control of the matter. † *Dukesmith* v. *Corrington* v. *Turner,* 431.

25. **ACCESS TO OPPONENT'S APPLICATION, PART OF WHICH IS CONCEALED UNDER RULE 105.**—Where the interfering subject-matter of the application of one of the parties to an interference is disclosed to the other by means of a certified copy, as provided by Rule 105, an auxiliary invention which has been described and claimed by the former, but which might be omitted without destroying the operativeness of the invention in issue, will not be disclosed where the latter has presented no claim which includes this invention either broadly or specifically. *Kugele* v. *Blair,* 81.

26. **PRIORITY—INTERFERENCE IN FACT—CONCLUSIONS BY PATENT OFFICE GENERALLY ACCEPTED BY COURT OF APPEALS.**—Ordinarily where the point has been raised whether the application of one of the parties was broad enough in the terms of its specification and claims to embrace the invention of the other, and especially where the invention is one of elaborate and complicated mechanism, the decisions of the expert tribunals of the Patent Office in respect of identity have, for obvious reasons, been accepted as conclusive. * *Bechman* v. *Southgate,* 489.

27. **SECOND INTERFERENCE—RES ADJUDICATA.**—Where a second interference is declared between the same applications on an issue relating to the subject-matter of invention as that of a prior interference, of broader scope than the first issue, and the constructions relied on, respectively, as evidencing conception and reduction to practice of the invention of both issues are the same and the fundamental facts of both cases are the same, *Held* that the final decision in the first interference is conclusive and that the question of priority is *res adjudicata* unless it can be made to appear that the question upon which the determination of the second case rests is one that neither was nor could have been presented and determined in the first case. * *Blackford* v. *Wilder,* 491.

28. **REFERENCE UNDER RULE 126—REJECTION OF CLAIMS.**—Where the Examiners-in-Chief in their decision in an interference upon priority of invention call the attention of the Commissioner under Rule 126 to the fact that in their opinion the issue is not patentable and the decision becomes final by the expiration of the limit of appeal without appeal, the Examiner will be directed to reject in the application of the successful party the claim corresponding to the issue found by the Examiners-in-Chief to be unpatentable. (*Snider* v. *Bunnell,* C. D., 1903, 117; 103 O. G., 890, distinguished.) *Holz* v. *Hewitt,* 98.

29. **SAME—SAME.**—It is not to be presumed that the Examiners-in-Chief would form an opinion adverse to a party's interest and call attention to the same upon the record without careful consideration in those cases where the grounds of their opinion had already been considered by the Primary Examiner and held insufficient to warrant such adverse opinion. When they express an opinion under these circumstances, the same is clearly of sufficient force to bind the Primary Examiner and sustain his *pro forma* rejection of claims until the opinion is withdrawn by the Examiners-in-Chief themselves or over-

ruled by the Commissioner or court of appeals in the regular course of appeal. *Id.*

30. HEARING—RULES 126 AND 139 DISTINGUISHED.—Rule 126 does not provide for a hearing by the Commissioner, and no reason appears why a hearing should be given to an applicant whose claims are found to be unpatentable by the Board of Examiners-in-Chief in their consideration of the claim in connection with the question of priority of invention. *Id.*

31. APPEAL AFTER REJECTION OF CLAIM.—Where upon reference by the Examiners-in-Chief, under Rule 126, stating that in their opinion the issue of an interference is unpatentable, the Examiner is directed to reject the claims in the application of the successful party, the *pro forma* rejection of the Examiner puts the case at once in condition for a course of appeal which may be carried to the court of appeals if the application is otherwise in condition therefor. *Id.*

32. TESTIMONY TO SHOW ISSUE UNPATENTABLE TO EITHER PARTY IRRELEVANT TO QUESTION OF PRIORITY.—Where during the time assigned him for the purpose of taking testimony upon the question of priority of invention one party took merely the testimony of an expert for the purpose of showing that the issue is not patentable to either party over the prior art, *Held* that the decision of the Examiner of Interferences was proper in granting a motion to strike said testimony from the record on the ground that it is irrelevant to the question of priority. *Dixon and Marsh v. Graves and Whittemore,* 101.

33. UNPATENTABILITY OF ISSUE TO ALL PARTIES—PROPERLY RAISED BY MOTION TO DISSOLVE UNDER RULE 122.—Where it is contended that the non-patentability of the issue to either party to the interference may be urged at final hearing, *Held* that during the preliminary stages of the interference and before the parties have been put to the trouble and expense of taking testimony on the question of priority either party may raise the question of the patentability of the issue by motion to dissolve the interference under Rule 122. Contestants are thus given an opportunity to have determined the question of whether the Office was right in declaring the interference and whether the proceedings should continue before testimony as to priority is taken. It is essential to the orderly proceedings of the interference that the question of patentability be finally settled at this time, and for this purpose the rules provide for an appeal from the rejection of claims based on the decision on the motion to the full extent permitted by law. *Id.*

34. SAME—CANNOT BE RAISED UNDER RULE 130.—Where it is contended by one party to an interference that he has a right to urge the unpatentability of the issues to either party at the final hearing under Rule 130 and to take testimony in support thereof, *Held* that the contention is erroneous and that this rule permits a party to urge the non-patentability of a claim to his opponent as a basis for the decision upon priority of invention only when it is material to his own right to a patent. *Id.*

35. TESTIMONY—USE IN SUBSEQUENT INTERFERENCE.—Where the real parties in interest in a pending interference are the same as in a prior interference and the inventions involved are substantially the same, permission may be obtained, under the provisions of Rule 157, to use in the pending interference the testimony taken in the former interference. *Beall, jr., v. Lyon,* 116.

79. Same.—While applications are pending in this Office the claims thereof will be construed as broadly as the ordinary meaning of the language employed will permit *Junge* v. *Harrington*, 340.

.80. Same.—The party who first presents claims should not later be heard to urge limitations upon the terms thereof which might readily have been expressed therein had it been intended that they should be so restricted. *Id.*

81. Rule 130.—Rule 130 does not confer upon a party the absolute right to contest his opponent's right to a claim, but allows him to do so only when the objections urged against his opponent's right to make the claim do not apply with equal force to his own case. *Pym* v. *Hadaway*, 344.

82. Limit of Appeal from Decision on Priority.—The bringing of motions or the taking of petitions to the Commissioner will not stay the running of the limit of appeal from a decision on priority. *Id.*

83. Preliminary Statement—Amendment—Carrying Back Date of Reduction to Practice.—The junior party to an interference permitted to amend his preliminary statement by carrying the date of the production of two full-sized devices from a date subsequent to the opponent's filing date, on which the opponent alone relies for reduction to practice, to a date prior thereto, where the motion to amend was brought only thirteen days after the filing of the original statement and before any testimony was taken and where it appears from affidavits filed that prior to the execution of his first preliminary statement he examined such records and consulted with such persons as would in his opinion enable him to secure all the necessary facts. *Davis* v. *Kennard*, 350.

84. Evidence—Private Diary in Shorthand.—An inventor after having testified in regard to his conception and the work done thereon produced a shorthand diary and read a number of entries from the diary showing dates and memoranda of work done. Of this evidence the court said: "Burson is a man over seventy years of age and appears to have kept a diary for fifty years in which he made a daily record of events. There is nothing in the appearance of this diary to excite suspicion. The dates follow consecutively. It is true that the record is in shorthand after the Pittman system; but it appears that interpretation thereof could be made with sufficient certainty by one skilled in that method. * * * We see no substantial difference between this and the ordinary use of memoranda by a witness to refresh his memory." * *Burson* v. *Vogel*, 669.

85. Right to Make Claims—Res Adjudicata.—Where the Examiner, on a motion to dissolve, holds that a party has a right to make the claims in issue and upon petition to the Commissioner by the opposing party asking him, under his supervisory authority, to review the favorable decision of the Examiner the Commissioner refuses to pass upon the question, it cannot be successfully urged that the question of the right of such party to make the claims is *res adjudicata*. *Hopkins* v. *Newman*, 356.

86. Priority—Second Interference—Res Adjudicata.—As to claims involved in a second interference between the same parties which could have been made in the first interference, *Held* that a final decision in the first interference on the question of priority renders that question *res adjudicatd*. *Id.*

87. PRINTING TESTIMONY.—The fact that the senior party took no testimony is not a sufficient reason for waiving the requirements of Rule 162. *Albers Bros. Milling Company* v. *Forrest*, 368.

88. INDEFINITE MOTION—AMENDED MOTION—TRANSMISSION.—It is well settled that piecemeal action cannot be permitted; but where a party acting in good faith files a motion which is held to be indefinite and an amended motion curing the informalities is promptly filed within the limit of appeal set from the previous decision the amended motion' should be transmitted. *Gold* v. *Gold*, 377.

89. PRIORITY—FOREIGN PATENT AS BAR NOT CONSIDERED.—Where the proofs of the junior party to an interference are insufficient to overcome the date of a foreign patent granted to the senior party, the question whether a foreign patent granted to such senior party stands as a bar to the allowance of his United States application will be left for *ex parte* consideration after the termination of the interference. *Gueniffet, Benoit, and Nicault* v. *Wictorsohn*, 379.

90. SAME—CONCEPTION—KNOWLEDGE IN THIS COUNTRY BY FOREIGN INVENTOR.—Mere knowledge of an invention in this country by a foreign inventor or his agent, *Held* not equivalent to a conception of the invention in this country. *Id.*

91. PRELIMINARY STATEMENT—AMENDMENT—MISTAKE OF LAW.—An amendment to a preliminary statement will not be permitted upon the allegation of the moving party that at the time of the declaration of the interference he supposed that the issue was restricted to the machine shown in the application, but that he later learned that the Examiner construed it so broadly as to read on a prior application, where it did not appear that the Examiner had construed the issue except by declaring the interference, and that the Examiner had held, on a motion to shift the burden of proof, that the issue was not readable upon the earlier· application. In any event the mistake was one of law and affords no ground for amendment. *Miller* v. *Wallace*, 391.

92. PRIORITY—CONSTRUCTIVE REDUCTION TO PRACTICE OVERCOME BY PUBLICATION.—A published description of an invention by the inventor describing the invention in such full and intelligible manner as to enable persons skilled in the art to understand the operation of the invention and to carry it into practical use is sufficient to overcome the filing date of the application of the opposing party. *Marconi* v. *Shoemaker*, 392.

93. ORIGINALITY—FAILURE TO ASSERT CLAIM TO INVENTION.—Where W. stated in the presence of K. and a witness that he proposed to file an application for patent for an invention which each now claims to have made and K. at that time made no protest, but a few days later went to W. and asked to have his name in the patent, *Held* that as it appeared that W. was at the head of the business and was a man of violent temper and that K. made it a practice not to dispute W. in the presence of others, and in view of the fact that K. was an intelligent man at the head of a large department his request to have his name in the patent indicated that he regarded himself at that time to be the inventor of the process in issue. *Weidmann* v. *Knup*, 404.

94. SAME—SILENCE AFTER FILING APPLICATION.—A failure to assert the origination of an invention by a subordinate officer against the claims of his superior cannot be regarded as acquiescence in the superior officer's claims to the invention where prior to that time the subordinate officer had filed an application for such invention. *Id.*

INTERFERENCE PROCEEDINGS. See *Amendments*, 4; *Interference*, 21, 39, 42; *Motion to Dissolve Interference*, 15.

INTERLOCUTORY DECISION. See *Interference*, 59.

INTER PARTES CASES.

  SERVICE—PETITIONS AND MOTIONS.—All petitions and motions in *inter partes* cases must be accompanied by proof of service or by copies to be forwarded by the Office. *Browne v. Stroud*, 57.

INTERSTATE COMMERCE. See *Trade-Marks*, 78.

INTERVENING RIGHTS. See *Reissue Applications*, 3, 5.

INVALID REGISTRATION. See *Trade-Marks*, 48.

INVENTION. See *Concealment of Invention; Conception of Invention; Designs*, 2; *Patentability; Priority of Invention; Reduction to Practice*, 6, 9.

  1. PATENTABILITY—CARRYING FORWARD AN OLD IDEA.—Where the prior art disclosed a train of gearing positively connecting the hour, minute, and second hands of a time mechanism, whereby the rotation of one would cause the proper relative movement of the others, and it also disclosed a winding and setting mechanism controlling the proper relative rotation of the minute and hour hands, it did not amount to invention to insert an additional gear and pinion in the latter mechanism to secure the proper position of the second-hand with relation to the minute and hour hands upon operation of the setting mechanism. *In re Volkmann and Traux*, 462.

  2. SAME—REARRANGEMENT OF ELEMENTS OF COMBINATION.—Where a given combination of elements is old in an automatic computing-scale of the horizontal type and the prior art also shows a computing-scale arranged vertically, although it was not entirely automatic, a claim covering a rearrangement of the elements of the automatic horizontal scale to provide a vertical construction can be sustained only to a limited extent. *Computing Scale Company of America v. The Automatic Scale Company*, 687.

  3. SAME.—CHANGE OF LOCATION.—The change of location of projections on the seat portion of a bed couch, *Held* to relate to mechanical skill. *Ex parte Hoey*, 108.

  4. SAME—SAME.—The change in location of projections on the seat portion of a bed couch from the upper to the lower side of the seat does not amount to invention. It is possible, but not apparent, that a better balance of the seat and back is secured by changing these projections. It is possible that a more attractive exterior is thereby presented. It is possible that a more salable article is thereby secured; but all this does not prove originality of invention. While courts deal liberally with inventors in sustaining patents having but slight distinctions over prior structures, they do not and ought not to permit the real inventor to be deprived of the fruits of his genius and labor by a mere copyist. *In re Hoey*, 516.

  5. SAME—SUBSTITUTION OF EQUIVALENTS.—Where it is old to heat exhaust air as it passes from the high-pressure to the low-pressure cylinder of a compound air engine by means of a liquid substance, and it is also old to use atmospheric air to impart heat to air within a receptacle, it does not amount to invention to substitute the latter heating medium for the former. *In re Hodges*, 543.

  6. SAME—PROCESS OF MAKING-READY PRINTING PLATES.—After the generic process of preparing printing plates with projecting portions on the

back thereof and pressing these to the face of the plates, giving a graduated surface, has been claimed, and the specific mode of preparing the plates by the use of photolithographing and etching has also been claimed, there is nothing left to claim in a separate application as a separate invention as a process of making-ready printing plates. What remains would appear to be a mere carrying out of the purposes of the original invention, which ought to be obvious to skilled workers in the art.—*In re Wickers and Furlong, 608.

7. SAME—CHANGES INVOLVING MECHANICAL SKILL ONLY—NO INVENTION.— Where the device shown in the application differs from that of a prior patent merely in the shape of the grooves in which a sealing mixture is to be placed, Held that it would be a mere matter of mechanical skill to adapt the shape of the groove to the nature of the sealing material to be used. Ex parte Williams, 286.

8. SAME—SAME.—Where the claim is distinguishable from the prior art by a mere arbitrary variation which amounts only to a change in mechanical design. Held that such a claim is unpatentable. *In re Williams, 664.

IRREGULARITY IN DECLARATION OF INTERFERENCE. See Motion to Dissolve Interference, 27, 41, 42, 43.

JOINT AND SOLE APPLICANTS. See Interference, 9.

JOINT APPLICATIONS. See Abandonment of Applications, 6, 7, 8.

JOINT INVENTORS. See Abandonment of Applications, 6, 7, 8.

JUDGMENT OF THE PATENT OFFICE IN INTERFERENCE PROCEEDINGS. See Interference, 74.

JUDGMENT ON THE RECORD. See Interference, 50, 71; Motion to Dissolve Interference, 37, 39.

JURISDICTION OF THE COMMISSIONER OF PATENTS. See Appeal to the Court of Appeals of the District of Columbia, 3; Interference, 24.

JURISDICTION OF THE COURT OF APPEALS OF THE DISTRICT OF COLUMBIA. Appeal to the Court of Appeals of the District of Columbia, 2; See Interference, 60.

JURISDICTION OF THE EXAMINER. See Motion for Rehearing, 1, 2, 3, 6.

JURISDICTION OF THE EXAMINERS-IN-CHIEF.

CASES "PENDING" BEFORE.—Cases are considered to be "pending before" the Examiners-in-Chief for the purpose of entertaining a motion for rehearing (Rule 142) until the expiration of the statutory period or specified limit of appeal or until such appeal shall have been taken. Ex parte Floyd, 195.

JURISDICTION OF THE SUPREME COURT OF THE DISTRICT OF COLUMBIA. See Mandamus, 5, 6.

LABELS. See Trade-Marks, 90, 144.

1. THE WORDS "RED CROSS" REFUSED REGISTRATION IN VIEW OF THE ACT OF JANUARY 5, 1905.—The words "Red Cross," whether construed as "the sign of the Red Cross" expressed in language or as the alternative of the sign "Red Cross," clearly come within the spirit and intent of the provisions of section 4 of the act entitled "An act to incorporate the American National Red Cross," approved January 5, 1905, prohibiting the use of "such sign or any insignia colored in imitation thereof for the purposes of trade or as an advertisement to induce the sale of any article whatsoever. Ex parte Strauss, 133.

2. REGISTRABILITY.—The use of a paraph under certain words of a label which is otherwise devoid of artistic merit is not sufficient to render the label registrable. Ex parte The Samuel Winslow Skate Mfg. Co., 343.

LACHES. See *Interference*, 37; *Reissue Applications*, 1; *Trade-Marks*, 58.

LICENSES. See *Interference*, 48.

LIMITATION OF CLAIMS. See *Construction of Claims*, 4, 5; *Interference*, 16, 17, 22, 79, 80; *Invention*, 2; *Reissue Applications*, 3, 4, 6, 7.

LIMITATION OF TRADE-MARK. See *Trade-Marks*, 103.

LIMIT OF APPEAL. See *Abandonment of Applications*, 23; *Interference*, 6, 12, 28, 50, 82, 88; *Jurisdiction of Examiners-in-Chief*; *Motion for Rehearing*, 1, 2, 4; *Motion to Dissolve Interference*, 3, 4, 17; *Trade-Marks*, 153.

LIMIT OF TIME. See *Abandonment of Applications*, 9; *Construction of Statutes*, 3; *Motion to Dissolve Interference*, 29; *Trade-Marks*, 16, 17, 70; *Withdrawal of Allowed Applications from Issue*, 1, 2.

MACHINES. See *Infringement*, 5; *Patentability*, 1, 2; *Reduction to Practice*, 7, 8, 12, 13, 14, 15, 16, 17; *Trade-Marks*, 155.

MANDAMUS.

1. PRACTICE.—The writ of mandamus cannot be used in the place of an appeal or writ of error to correct any erroneous decision made by the Primary Examiner in the course of his official duties. *The United States of America, ex rel. Tuttle,* v. *Allen, Commissioner of Patents,* 676.

2. SAME.—The writ of mandamus cannot be used to control the exercise of judicial discretion. *Id.*

3. DIVISION.—Where division had been required between the claims of an application for patent and it was sought by mandamus to compel consideration of the claims upon their merits, *Held* that it is of no consequence to the court in rendering the decision upon mandamus whether the Office was right or wrong in requiring division. *Id.*

4. NOT GRANTED—WHERE OTHER LEGAL REMEDIES EXIST.—Where the relator is not without other complete and adequate remedies, a writ of mandamus will not lie. *The United States of America, ex rel. The Newcomb Motor Co.,* v. *Allen (Moore substituted,) Commissioner of Patents,* 683.

5. SAME—MERELY TO EXPEDITE THE CASE.—Although the writ of mandamus might serve as an inexpensive and summary conclusion of the whole matter, providing this court had jurisdiction to issue the writ, yet neither economy of time nor expense can weigh anything as against the orderly procedure under the law of a given case. *Id.*

6. SAME—WHERE COURT IS WITHOUT JURISDICTION.—Where the Commissioner has, in fact, acted and rendered his decision touching the very matter here in controversy and has the clear legal right to act and decide for himself, this court is without jurisdiction to review his action and above all to compel him by its writ to undo what he has done. *Id.*

7. PRACTICE.—Where the Commissioner had the power to act and has acted. *Held* that it is wholly immaterial whether in the judgment of the court he was right or wrong in his determination and that in overruling the motion for a writ of mandamus no opinion will be expressed as to the merits of the relator's contentions. *Id.*

MECHANICAL SKILL. See *Employer and Employee*, 3, 4, 5; *Invention*, 3, 4, 6, 7, 8.

MERITS OF THE CASE. See *Motion to Dissolve Interference*, 17.

MISTAKE. See *Abandonment of Applications*, 18, 19; *Interference*, 91; *Motion to Amend Preliminary Statement*, 1, 2.

MODEL. See *Motion to Dissolve Interference*, 29.

MOTION FOR LEAVE TO TAKE TESTIMONY. See *Affidavits; Interference,* 13, 14; *Motion to Dissolve Interference,* 1, 2.

1. INTERFERENCE—TESTIMONY TO SHOW INOPERATIVENESS.—Where a motion for permission to take testimony for the purpose of showing that the opponent's device is inoperative, pending the determination of a motion to dissolve the interference, was denied by the Examiner of Interferences on the ground that the rules do not provide for the taking of testimony in interference cases prior to the determination of a motion to dissolve, *Held* that no appeal lies from the decision of the Examiner of Interferences on the question of taking testimony to show inoperativeness and that no occasion is presented for the exercise of the supervisory authority of the Commissioner. *Barber* v. *Wood,* 96.

2. SAME—APPEAL.—Where a motion for permission to take testimony in opposition to an opponent's right to make the claims in issue for use at final hearing under the provisions of Rule 130 is denied by the Examiner of Interferences, *Held* that an appeal will be permitted from his adverse decision. (Practice announced in *Lowry and Cowley* v. *Spoon,* C. D., 1906, 381; 124 O. G., 1846, and *Hanan and Gates* v. *Marshall, ante,* 65; 126 O. G., 3423 modified.) *Pym* v. *Hadaway,* 131.

MOTION FOR REHEARING. See *Jurisdiction of the Examiners-in-Chief.*

1. INTERFERENCE—JURISDICTION TO DETERMINE AFTER LIMIT OF APPEAL.—The question of the Examiner's retaining jurisdiction to determine, after the expiration of the limit of appeal, a motion for rehearing brought before the expiration of the limit of appeal is a different matter from that of the termination of the limit of appeal. No good reason appears for holding that a tribunal may not properly render a decision on a motion for rehearing brought before the expiration of the limit of appeal, even though the date of the decision is after the ⋅ limit of appeal has expired. *Naulty* v. *Cutler,* 8.

2. SAME—DOES NOT EXTEND LIMIT OF APPEAL.—The filing of the motion for rehearing does not extend the limit of appeal, and in case the motion is denied the moving party will have lost his right of appeal unless he has taken the precaution to file his appeal within the limit originally set or has obtained an extension of the limit of appeal. *Id.*

3. SAME—QUESTION OF APPEAL.—The rule that there is no appeal from a decision denying a rehearing does not cover the case where the holding is want of jurisdiction to entertain the motion. *Id.*

4. SAME—DATE OF FILING.—Where a motion was filed by N. on the last day of the limit of appeal and on the same day notice by registered letter was mailed to C.'s attorney and C. makes no contention that said notice was not received in ample time to prepare for the hearing, *Held* that N. is entitled to the date of the receipt of his motion in this Office as its date of filing. *Id.*

5. SAME—PRACTICE.—It is not the practice to require service of requests or motions for rehearing upon the opposite party (*Townsend* v. *Copeland* v. *Robinson,* C. D., 1906, 379; 124 O. G., 1845,) or to set such motions for hearing, unless examination of the motion and of the record shows that a rehearing ought to be granted. (*Adams* v. *Murphy,* C. D., 1900, 100; 91 O. G., 2373.) *Id.*

6. SAME—JURISDICTION NOT AFFECTED BY APPEAL.—Where a motion is filed for rehearing of the Examiner's decision and also an appeal from said decision, *Held* that the filing of the appeal does not oust the Examiner of jurisdiction to entertain the motion. *Id.*

sideration by the Primary Examiner under the head of irregularity in declaring the interference of the facts he has already considered under the right to make the claims. *Adkins and Lewis* v. *Seeberger*, 87.

4. SAME.—A long and unexcused delay in filing an appeal constitutes a sufficient reason for denying an extension of the limit of appeal. (*Hewitt* v. *Steinmetz*, C. D., 1906, 174; 122 O. G., 1395.) *Id.*

5. EXERCISE OF SUPERVISORY AUTHORITY OF COMMISSIONER.—Where the question presented upon a motion for dissolution can be raised, under Rule 130, at final hearing before the Examiner of Interferences and upon appeals from such decision, there is no occasion for the exercise of the supervisory authority of the Commissioner. *Id.*

6. INOPERATIVENESS OF OPPONENT'S DEVICE—PRACTICE.—Under Rule 130 where the operativeness of an opponent's device or his right to make the claim is material to the right of a party to a patent said party may urge the matter at final hearing before the Examiner of Interferences as a basis for his award of priority; but as a condition precedent to such right the party must first present the matter upon a motion for dissolution or show good reason why such motion was not made and prosecuted. *Barber* v. *Wood*, 96.

7. REJECTION OF CLAIMS—REQUEST FOR FURTHER EXPLANATION.—Where in acting upon a motion to dissolve the interference the Primary Examiner held the counts of the issue unpatentable and upon reconsideration finally rejected the claims, *Held* that if petitioner did not understand the position of the Examiner or desired a more specific statement of his position concerning the references he should have made his request before the dates set for reconsideration and closing of the case before the Examiner. While the Examiner should indicate the grounds for his rejection as fully as in the ordinary *ex parte* consideration of a case, the applicant can request as a matter of right a more complete explanation only while the case is still pending before the Examiner. *Bastian* v. *Champ*, 111.

8. DENIAL BY A PARTY OF HIS OWN RIGHT TO MAKE CLAIM—TRANSMISSION.—A motion for dissolution based upon the ground that the moving party has no right to make the claim to the subject-matter in issue should not be transmitted to the Primary Examiner. *Martin* v. *Mullin*, 119.

9. INTERFERENCE IN FACT.—If there is no interference in fact, it is either because one of the parties has no right to make the claims or because the claims have different meanings in the applications of the different parties. The parties will not be heard to deny their own right to make the claims. (*Miller* v. *Perham*, C. D., 1906, 157; 121 O. G., 2667.) *Daggett* v. *Kaufmann*, 121.

10. APPEAL—RIGHT OF OPPONENT TO MAKE CLAIM.—There is no appeal from the decision of the Primary Examiner affirming the opponent's right to make the claims or the identity of meaning of the claims in their respective applications. *Id.*

11. EXERCISE OF SUPERVISORY AUTHORITY OF COMMISSIONER.—Where at the hearing upon a motion for dissolution attention is directed to a patent which is in a remote art and it appears that the Examiner has held the claims in issue patentable thereover, no such unusual circumstances as will justify the exercise of supervisory authority exist. *Id.*

12. TRANSMISSION.—Where on appeal from the decision of the Primary Examiner dissolving an interference the Examiners-in-Chief affirmed the decision of the Examiner as to claims 2, 3, and 4 and reversed it as

claim 1, and thereupon one party filed an amendment to his case, while ·the other party brought a motion to dissolve, *Held* that the decision of the Examiner of Interferences refusing to transmit the motion to dissolve to the Primary Examiner is correct, since the motion is based on the proposed amendment and presupposes its entry. *Harnisch* v. *Gueniffet, Benoit, and Nicault*, 127.

13. DIFFERENCE IN MEANING OF CLAIMS.—The provision in Rule 122 for dissolution upon the ground of difference in the meaning of claims was placed there to cover a clean-cut class of cases which theoretical considerations show may arise, but which, in fact, are of very rare occurrence. To justify transmission of a motion brought upon this ground, facts must be alleged indicating something more than a possible lack of right upon the part of one or the other of the parties to use the language of the claim in issue. *Cushman* v. *Edwards*, 129.

14. DEFINITENESS.—A motion to dissolve on the ground of non-patentability, which states that a given count " does not involve patentable invention over each of the following Letters·Patent," after which certain patents are specified, is not open to the objection of indefiniteness. *McCanna* v. *Morris*, 141.

15. TRANSMISSION—GROUND OF PUBLIC USE.—Public use is considered in the practice of this Office as a separate question requiring an investigation independent of the question of priority of invention involved in an interference proceeding. A motion for dissolution based upon the ground of public use should not therefore be transmitted. *Barber* v. *Wood*, 174.

16. BASED UPON CONTINGENCY—NOT TRANSMITTED.—A motion by one party to an interference to dissolve the interference as to certain counts in case certain other counts are found to be unpatentable in view of the same references upon a motion to dissolve brought by his opponent should not be transmitted. *Turner* v. *Macloskie*, 176.

17. SETTING LIMIT OF APPEAL—PRACTICE.—Where the decision of the Examiner upon motions for dissolution includes an adverse decision upon the merits of a party's case which is subject to reconsideration under the provisions of Rule 124, no limit of appeal should be set in any of the motions until the decision is rendered upon the rehearing. *O'Brien* v. *Gale, sr.,* v. *Miller* v. *Zimmer* v. *Calderwood*, 184.

18. CLAIMS MADE UNDER PROTEST—INFORMALITY OF DECLARATION.—Where suggested claims were made by the joint applicants under protest, with a statement that they did not think they had a right to make the same, giving their reasons therefor, *Held* that the declaration of interference did not constitute informality within the contemplation of the rules and that the transmission of a motion for dissolution based upon this ground was properly refused. *Eichelberger and Hibner* v. *Dillon*, 230.

19. SAME—MOVING PARTY'S RIGHT TO MAKE CLAIMS.—Where claims have been suggested to an applicant and he made the same under protest, with a statement that he does not believe he has a right to make them, and where after inspecting the other party's application he still contends that he has no right to make these claims, *Held* that he should be permitted to argue the question before the Primary Examiner, and the motion to dissolve should therefore be transmited. (*Miller* v. *Perham*, C. D., 1906, 157; 121 O. G., 2667, modified.) *Id.*

20. MOTION TO TRANSMIT—DELAY IN BRINGING.—Where the reasons which are alleged to excuse delay in bringing a motion appear clearly from the record, it is only necessary for the moving party to call attention thereto. *Cutler* v. *Carichoff*, 126.

21. SAME—SAME.—The fact that similar motions have been brought in companion interferences constitute no sufficient excuse for delay in bringing a motion to dissolve. *Id.*

22. SAME—SAME—APPLICATION OF REFERENCES.—Where a motion for dissolution refers to the prior art cited in the records of the applications and gives no information as to what patents are to be urged against the respective counts or how they are to be used or combined to anticipate invention stated in said counts, *Held* that the motion is too indefinite and transmission of the same was properly refused. *Brown v. Inwood and Lavenberg,* 249.

23. SAME—SAME.—Where the hearing on a motion to transmit a motion to dissolve is extended by stipulation of the parties and before the hearing an amended motion is filed stating the grounds of the first motion more specifically, *Held* that the motion, if in proper form, should have been transmitted even if the first motion was not sufficiently specific. *Smith v. Fox,* 269.

24. SAME—SAME.—Where the opposing party is not given sufficient notice of the hearing on the motion to transmit a motion to dissolve, the motion should not be refused transmission on that ground, but the hearing should be continued. *Phillips v. Scott,* 270.

25. SAME—SAME.—Where it is moved to dissolve an interference on the ground that the issue is not patentable in view of certain references cited, but it is not stated how these references are to be applied, the motion to transmit should be denied. *Id.*

26. SAME—SAME—NON-PATENTABILITY—APPLICATION OF REFERENCES.—The allegation in a motion for dissolution that the issue is unpatentable in view of eight references, of which it is said that " each of the counts is also met in each of the above patents, singly or in combination," is vague and indefinite, and the transmission of the motion for dissolution was properly refused. *Thullen v. Townsend,* 271.

27. SAME—SAME.—A motion to dissolve on the ground of irregularity in the declaration of the interference properly refused transmission where the alleged irregularity is that the issue of the present interference is substantially the same as that of a former interference which the Primary Examiner dissolved. *Sugden and Pidgin v. Laganke and Smith v. Marshall,* 276.

28. NON-PATENTABILITY—REFERENCE FAILING TO ANTEDATE ALLEGATIONS OF PRELIMINARY STATEMENT—TRANSMISSION.—Although the date of a reference relied upon in a motion to dissolve alleging anticipation of the issue is later than the date of conception set up in the preliminary statement of the opposing party, the motion may nevertheless be transmitted in order that the Primary Examiner may consider the pertinency of the reference and permit the filing of an affidavit alleging the facts required by Rule 75 outside of those contained in such preliminary statement. *Martin v. Goodrum et al.,* 279.

29. DELAY IN BRINGING—RIGHT TO MAKE CLAIM.—Where a motion to dissolve, on the ground that the adverse party had no right to make the claims and that his application did not show an operative device, was brought nearly two months after the expiration of the thirty days, *Held* that the fact that attorneys were busy with other matters and that it was necessary to make certain models constitutes no sufficient excuse for the delay, especially as no showing was made why it was necessary to make so many models or to take so long a time to complete them. *Josleyn v. Hulse,* 290.

30. SAME.—The pendency of a motion under Rule 109 is no excuse for the delay in bringing a motion to dissolve. *Id.*

31. OATH TO REISSUE APPLICATION INSUFFICIENT.—A motion to dissolve an interference involving a reissue application, alleging that the oath accompanying the application was insufficient to warrant the grant of a reissue patent, should be transmitted to the Primary Examiner. *Emmet* v. *Fullagar*, 322.

32. DELAY IN BRINGING—EXCUSE.—The fact that numerous appeals and petitions have ·been taken to have transmitted a motion to dissolve which was not in proper form constitutes no excuse for the delay in bringing the motion in proper form. *Brantingham* v. *Draver and Draver*, 324.

33. SAME—TRANSMISSION—RIGHT TO MAKE CLAIM AND DIFFERENCE IN MEANING OF CLAIMS.—Where in a motion for dissolution the right of the adverse party to make the claims in issue is denied and it is also alleged that the claims when read upon the structures disclosed by the respective parties have different meanings, reasons relied upon in support of such contentions being clearly pointed out, *Held* that the motion to dissolve should be transmitted as to both grounds. (*Cushman* v. *Edwards, ante,* 129; 128 O.G., 456, modified.) *Eilerman et al.* v. *McElroy,* 326.

34. SAME—CLAIMS HAVING DIFFERENT MEANINGS IN OPPOSING PARTIES' APPLICATIONS—PRACTICE.—Where it is found upon motion for dissolution that the claims in issue have different meanings in the cases of the respective parties, the Examiner should require one or both of the applicants to so modify the claims as to avoid a conflict in the terms employed to define the respective inventions. *Id.*

35. DELAY IN BRINGING—EXCUSE.—A delay of seven days in filing an amended motion to dissolve, curing objections relating to indefiniteness of the allegations of a prior motion, may be excused where it appears that the first motion attempted in good faith to comply with the practice of the Office. *Auxer* v. *Peirce, jr.,* 328.

36. GROUND OF NON-PATENTABILITY BASED ON ART TO BE SUBSEQUENTLY CITED—TRANSMISSION.—*Held* that a motion to dissolve an interference on the ground that the claims in issue are not patentable in view of certain patents and others which "will be cited more than five days before the hearing" should not be transmitted. Rule 122 requires that the motion for dissolution must "contain a full statement of grounds relied upon." *Papendell* v. *Bunnell et al.,* 336.

37. BROUGHT IN ANSWER TO ORDER TO SHOW CAUSE UNDER RULE 114 MAY BE TRANSMITTED.—The fact that a record judgment may be rendered against a junior party under the provisions of Rule 114 does not preclude him from presenting motions for dissolution. *Id.*

38. AFFIDAVITS.—When a party may not appeal from a decision on a motion to dissolve, he may not appeal from a determination upon the admissibility of affidavits filed with that motion. *Brown* v. *Inwood and Lavenberg,* 378.

39. PROPER ANSWER TO ORDER TO SHOW CAUSE UNDER RULE 114.—A motion to dissolve on the ground of non-patentability of the issue is a proper answer to an order under Rule 114 to show cause why judgment of priority should not be rendered on the record. *Field* v. *Colman,* 382.

40. MOTION TO SHIFT BURDEN OF PROOF—ORDER OF CONSIDERATION.—The consideration of a motion to dissolve alleging non-patentability of the issue should not be postponed until after the determination of a motion to shift the burden of proof, as such practice would result in piecemeal prosecution of the motion to dissolve. *Id.*

41. INDEFINITENESS OF ISSUE—HOW RAISED.—Vagueness and indefiniteness of the issue are proper questions to raise under allegations of informality or irregularity in the declaration of the interference. *Id.*

42. INFORMALITY OF DECLARATION,—A motion to dissolve on the ground of informality in declaring the interference was properly refused transmission where it appears that the alleged informality relates to the right of the parties to make the claim. *Danquard v. Courville*, 427.

43. MOVING PARTY'S RIGHT TO MAKE THE CLAIM.—Where both parties are applicants and under the head of informality in declaring the interference it is alleged in a motion to dissolve that the claims do not apply to the structures of either party, *Held* that this is not such an admission as to justify a decision on priority adverse to the moving party. (The case of *Lipe v. Miller*, C. D., 1904, 114; 109 O. G., 1608, distinguished.) *Id.*

MOTION TO EXTEND LIMIT OF APPEAL. See *Interference*, 6, 7.

MOTION TO EXTEND TIME FOR TAKING TESTIMONY. *See Interference*, 58.

MOTION TO REOPEN INTERFERENCE. See *Reopening of Interference*, 2, 5.

MOTION TO SHIFT BURDEN OF PROOF. See *Motion to Dissolve Interference*, 40.

MOTION TO SUPPRESS TESTIMONY. See *Interference*, 32, 42, 43; *Trade-Marks*, 119, 120, 151, 154.

1. INTERFERENCE—CONSIDERATION POSTPONED UNTIL FINAL HEARING.—Where a consideration of a motion to suppress testimony would involve a consideration of a large portion of the record, a decision upon the motion will be postponed until final hearing. *Dyson v. Land v. Dunbar v. Browne*, 292.

2. SAME—QUESTION OF RIGHT TO TAKE SURREBUTTAL TESTIMONY.—The right to take surrebuttal testimony is not merely dependent upon the propriety of opponent's testimony and is therefore not affected by a 'refusal to consider a motion to suppress prior to final hearing. *Id.*

MOTION TO SUSPEND INTERFERENCE. See *Interference*, 8; *Trade-Marks*, 1.

MOTION TO TAKE TESTIMONY IN FOREIGN COUNTRIES.

INTERFERENCE—SUFFICIENCY OF SHOWING—APPEAL.—The sufficiency of a showing in support of a motion to take testimony abroad is a matter which should be left largely to the discretion of the Examiner of Interferences, and his decision granting such a motion should not be reviewed except where clear error is made to appear. *Keith, Erickson, and Erickson v. Lundquist*, 175.

NAME OF APPLICANT.

"RAY" FULL CHRISTIAN NAME—No AFFIDAVIT NECESSARY.—The name "Ray" is commonly used as a full Christian name, and no affidavit should be required in connection therewith. *Ex parte Faulkner*, 136.

NEW CLAIMS. See *Examination of Applications*, 6.

NEWLY-DISCOVERED EVIDENCE. See *Interference*, 55, 63, 65; *Reopening of Interference*.

NEW MATTER. See *Amendments*, 5; *Constitution of Claims*, 1; *Motion to Amend Application*, 3; *Priority of Invention*, 3; *Reissue Applications*, 2.

NEW REFERENCE. See *Appeal to the Commissioner of Patents*, 1.

NOTARY PUBLIC.

    1. OATH—BEFORE NOTARIES PUBLIC—APPLICATION OF ACT OF JUNE 29, 1906.—The act of June 29, 1906, amending section 558 of the code of the District of Columbia relative to the powers of notaries public, is of local application only. *Ex parte Hipp*, 41.

    2. AMENDED SECTION 558 OF THE CODE OF THE DISTRICT OF COLUMBIA CONSTRUED.—*Held* that the " proviso "—"And provided further, That no notary public shall be authorized to take acknowledgments, administer oaths, certify papers, or perform any official acts in connection with matters in which he is employed as counsel, attorney, or agent in which he may be in any way interested before any of the Departments aforesaid "—in the recent act of Congress amending section 558 of the code of the District of Columbia applies to all notaries who may practice before the Departments and not merely to notaries of the District of Columbia. ‡ *Opinion of the Attorney-General*, 437.

NOTICE. See *Access to Abandoned Applications*, 1; *Infringement*, 6.

NOTICE OF HEARING. See *Motion to Dissolve Interference*, 24, 25.

NOTICE OF SUGGESTED CLAIMS. See *Interference*, 46.

NOTICE OF TAKING TESTIMONY. See *Interference*, 1, 42.

OATH. See *Interference*, 24, 72; *Motion to Dissolve Interference*, 31; *Notary Public*, 1.

    APPLICATIONS—SECTION 4892, REVISED STATUTES, CONSTRUED.—Where an applicant is not a citizen of any country and so alleges in his oath, *Held* to be a proper compliance with the requirements of section 4892, Revised Statutes, and that this section should not be construed as requiring citizenship of some country as a condition precedent to the grant of a patent. *Ex parte Benecke*, 66.

OLD DEVICES. See *Reduction to Practice*, 11.

OPERATIVENESS. See *Decisions of the Examiner of Interferences*, 1; *Reduction to Practice*, 18, 19, 20, 21.

OPINION OF THE ATTORNEY-GENERAL. See *Notary Public*, 2.

OPPOSITION. See *Trade-Marks*, 2, 15, 16, 57, 58, 62, 69, 70, 71, 72, 73, 74, 75, 86 87, 88, 96, 97, 98, 101, 102, 104, 105, 106, 119, 125, 126, 128, 129.

ORAL ARGUMENT. See *Appeal to the Court of Appeals of the District of Columbia*, 2.

OWNERSHIP. See *Reduction to Practice* 4; *Trade-Marks*, 3, 8, 25, 34, 105, 124, 125.

PARTNERSHIP. See *Trade-Marks*, 124.

PATENTABILITY. See *Amendments*, 2, 3; *Appeal to the Court of Appeals of the District of Columbia*, 1; *Designs; Examination of Applications*, 7; *Interference*, 16, 18, 19, 20, 21, 28, 29, 30, 31, 32, 33, 34, 56, 70; *Invention; Motion to Dissolve Interference*, 14, 16, 25, 26, 35, 36, 37, 39; *Priority of Invention*, 5; *Reopening of Interference*, 2.

    1. DOUBLE USE.—A patent will not be granted upon the discovery of a new and analogous function for an old machine. (*Roberts* v. *Ryer*, C. D., 1876, 439; 10 O. G., 204; 91 U. S., 150; *Ansonia Co.* v. *Electrical Supply Co.*, C. D., 1892, 313; 58 O. G., 1692; 144 U. S., 11; *Potts* v. *Creager*, C. D., 1895, 143; 70 O. G., 494; 155 U. S. 597.) *In re McNeil* v. *Sturtevant*, 478.

    2. REVERSAL OF PARTS.—Claims which comprise merely a reversal of parts disclosed in a prior machine are not patentable. *Id.

    3. SYSTEM FOR SPACING FREE-HAND LETTERS—NOT AN ART, MACHINE, MANUFACTURE, OR COMPOSITION OF MATTER.—A " system " which consists in the adoption of a certain scale for the height of letters and then de-

termining in terms of this scale the proper width of the letters and the spaces between consecutive letters, *Held*, to be neither an art, machine, manufacture, or composition of matter, and therefore not patentable, although the system as such is apparently new and useful. *Ex parte Meinhardt*, 237.

4. SAME—REHEARING.—While it is conceivable that some person after long and arduous study might discover a new method for solving certain mathematical problems which was much simpler and shorter than any known method, such method would not be a proper subject for patent. So, in the present case, applicant's plan for spacing free-hand letters, no matter what its merits, does not come within the classes for which protection can be secured under the patent laws. *Ex parte Meinhardt*, 238.

5. PRIOR PATENT OF APPLICANT DISCLOSING BUT NOT CLAIMING INVENTION.— A patent disclosing a process and apparatus and claiming only the process is no bar to the allowance of an application covering the apparatus filed by the same party within two years after the grant of the patent. (*Ex parte Mullen & Mullen*, C. D., 1890, 9; 50 O. G., 837.) *Ex parte Isaacs & Speed*, 316.

6. APPEAL ON PRIORITY.—The question of the patentability of the issue will not be considered on appeal on priority under such special circumstances as would warrant the exercise of the supervisory authority of the Commissioner. *Hess* v. *Joerissen* v. *Felbel*, 369.

PATENTEE AND APPLICANT. See *Interference*, 45.

PENDING APPLICATIONS. See *Trade-Marks*, 20.

PETITION TO THE COMMISSIONER OF PATENTS. See *Abandonment of Applications*, 23; *Claims*, 3; *Interference*, 58, 82, 85.

POVERTY. See *Interference*, 4, 38.

POWER OF ATTORNEY. See *Applications*, 2.

PRACTICE IN THE PATENT OFFICE. See *Interference*, 58, 73, 75; *Mandamus*, 7; *Motion to Dissolve Interference*, 34; *Rejection of Claims*, 1; *Reopening of Interference*, 3, 4, 6; *Trade-Marks*, 29, 77, 104.

PRELIMINARY STATEMENT. See *Interference*, 68, 76, 77, 83, 91; *Motion to Amend Preliminary Statement; Motion to Dissolve Interference*, 28; *Priority of Invention*, 5.

1. INTERFERENCE—AMENDMENT—CARRYING BACK OF OPPONENT'S DATE.—A party will not be permitted to amend his preliminary statement to carry back his date of disclosure to cover the date proved by his opponent in a prior interference with a third party where the amended date is earlier than that set up in a preliminary statement filed three years before in an interference between him and said third party and where the affidavit in support of the motion indicates an uncertainty whether the alleged disclosure took place prior to the date originally given. *Beall, jr.,* v. *Lyon*, 5.

2. SAME—SAME.—Where D. was notified that his preliminary statement was indefinite and should be amended, but no amendment was made, and the present motion was not brought until eight months later and after testimony had been taken by D., and was inspired by a statement placed on the record by his opponent, *Held* that the motion was properly denied in the absence of a showing in excuse for the long delay in bringing the motion or the failure to respond to the requirement for a more definite statement or of a satisfactory showing of accident or mistake or of newly-discovered evidence. *Dixon* v. *McElroy*, 105.

3. SAME—SAME.—The question of amending the preliminary statement is a matter largely within the discretion of the Examiner of Interferences. Unless it be shown that such discretion has been abused his decision will not be disturbed. *Karpenstein v. Hertzberg*, 106.

4. SAME—ALLEGATIONS—RESTRICTION OF PROOF.—Where the preliminary statement of a party alleges that an "experimental" device was constructed in January, 1901, and no date of reduction to practice is given, such party will not be restricted to the date of his application for his reduction to practice where no objection was made to the statement on the ground that it was indefinite. (*Hammond v. Basch*, C. D., 1905, 615; 115 O. G., 804; 24 App. D. C., 469, distinguished.) *Burson v. Vogel*, 669.

PRIMA FACIE CASE. See *Public Use and Sale*, 2, 3; *Trade-Marks*, 83, 84.

PRINTED RECORD. See *Trade-Marks*, 120.

PRIORITY OF ADOPTION AND USE. See *Trade-Marks*, 3, 10, 21, 26, 60, 96.

PRIORITY OF INVENTION. See *Appeal from the Examiners-in-Chief; Appeal to the Court of Appeals of the District of Columbia*, 2, 3; *Construction of Statutes*, 1; *Decisions of the Examiner of Interferences*, 1; *Diligence*, 1, 2; *Employer and Employee*, 3, 4, 5; *Interference*, 2, 3, 19, 21, 26, 27, 28, 30, 32, 33, 34, 36, 37, 38, 39, 40, 45, 62, 69, 71, 82, 86, 89, 90, 92; *Motion to Dissolve Interference*, 15, 43; *Reduction to Practice*, 5, 10; *Rejection of Claims*, 2; *Reopening of Interference*, 2.

1. INTERFERENCE—INSUFFICIENCY OF DISCLOSURE IN APPLICATION.—Where M., a patentee, who is junior party in an interference, did not take testimony, but relied upon the insufficiency of the disclosure of B.'s application, which was pending at the time M.'s application was filed, and his patent issued, and it subsequently appears that B.'s original application did, in fact, disclose the invention in issue, *Held* that priority of invention should be awarded to B., the senior party. *MacMulkin v. Bollée*, 38.

2. SAME—SAME.—Where in his original drawing B. showed a valve controlling communication between several chambers and a passage leading to the cylinder of an engine and in his specification referred to the chambers as "carbureters" supplying sprayers with mixtures varying in proportion of hydrocarbon contained in the several chambers, *Held* that the use of the word "carbureter" was a sufficient disclosure of the idea of providing "hydrocarbon inlets" in which air and hydrocarbon were to be supplied separately to each of the passages controlled by the valve, as called for by the issue. *Id.*

3. SAME—DECLARATION—SUGGESTION OF CLAIMS NEGATIVES PRESUMPTION OF NEW MATTER IN SUBSTITUTE SPECIFICATION.—Where the Examiner stated in a letter to B. suggesting the claims in interference that the interference was not declared during the pendency of M.'s application for the reason that B.'s original specification so obscurely presented his invention that it could not be understood at that time, *Held* that the Examiner's action in admitting a substitute specification and drawing was, in effect, a ruling on his part that the substitute specification and drawing did not contain new matter. *Id.*

4. SAME—APPEAL TO COURT—OPERATIVENESS.—The court of appeals of the District of Columbia will not consider the operativeness of a device disclosed by one of the interfering parties as incident to the main question of priority where that question has been settled in favor of such party by the Patent Office in accordance with the practice of that Office. *Duryea and White v. Rice, jr.*, 443.

5. SAME—APPEAL—CONSIDERATION OF PATENTABILITY.—Where the junior party to an interference concedes that his preliminary statement fails to overcome the filing date of the senior party and the patentability of the issue has been favorably passed upon by the tribunals of the Patent Office, before whom the question was brought in accordance with the practice of that Office, on appeal to the court of appeals from a judgment on priority the question of patentability will not be considered where it is raised merely for the purpose of preventing the grant of a patent to the senior party, except in an extraordinary case. *Potter* v. *McIntosh*, 505.

6. SAME—CONCESSION OF NOT NECESSARILY ACQUIESCENCE IN IDENTITY OF CLAIMS.—An award of priority may mean either that one of two inventors of the same thing is subsequent in date to another or that one party is the only inventor of the issue, because the other never invented the same at all, and there seems to be no reason why this should not be as true where the award is based upon concession as where it is based upon testimony. *Martin* v. *Mullin*, 119.

7. SAME—PRESUMPTIONS ARISING FROM CONDUCT.—Where an employee was assigned to the duty of producing a new telephone transmitter and during the time he was experimenting on such devices constructed six or seven different transmitters, but did not construct any embodying the invention in issue, the presumption is strong that he did not construct such device, because he was not possessed of the inventive idea. *Hansen* v. *Dean*, 583.

8. SAME—SAME—FAILURE TO ASSERT CLAIM TO INVENTION.—Where an employee is assigned to the duty of producing a new telephone transmitter, but after experiments to this end fails to produce an acceptable device and is assigned to the work of testing electrical instruments and while so employed he tests a transmitter invented by a coemployee containing the invention in issue and continues in his employment for several months thereafter without making claim to the one who had charge of the experimental work and who assigned him to such work that the invention was his, although the claim was made to others, and fails to construct a device or file an application until after he had left his employer and about seven months after he had tested the invention claimed by his coemployee, a claim that he invented the device during his experimental work can be given little weight. *Id.*

9. SAME—RIGHT TO MAKE CLAIM AN ANCILLARY QUESTION.—The question of the right of a party to make a claim may sometimes be an ancillary question to be considered in awarding priority of invention, and there are good reasons why the question of the right to make the claims may be considered a basis for an award of priority rather than a ground for a dissolution of an interference. *Wickers and Furlong*, v. *McKee*, 587.

10. SAME—RIGHT TO MAKE CLAIMS.—The contention that a party has no right to make a claim for a process of producing a printing surface because he describes a step of heating the plate which is not included in the issue cannot be admitted as well founded where his specification makes it clear that the step is not necessary in all cases. *Id.*

11. SAME.—The decision of the Commissioner of Patents awarding priority of invention to Albert affirmed, for the reasons stated in the case of *Wickers and Furlong* v. *McKee* (*ante*, 587; 129 O. G., 869.) *Wickers and Furlong* v. *Albert*, 599.

12. SAME.—The decision of the Commissioner of Patents awarding priority of invention to McKee affirmed, for the reasons stated in the case of *Wickers and Furlong* v. *McKee* (*ante*, 587; 129 O. G., 869.) **Wickers and Furlong* v. *McKee*, 600, 601.

13. SAME.—The decision of the Commissioner of Patents awarding priority of invention to McKee affirmed, for the reasons stated in the case of *Wickers and Furlong* v. *McKee* (*ante*, 587; 129 O. G., 869.) **Wickers and Furlong* v. *McKee*, 603.

14. SAME—DILIGENCE.—The decision of the Commissioner of Patents holding that Wickers and Furlong were not exercising diligence when Upham filed his application and awarding priority to Upham on his record date affirmed. (See *Wickers and Furlong* v. *McKee*, *ante*, 587; 129 O. G., 869.) **Wickers and Furlong* v. *Upham*, 605.

15. SAME—SAME.—Where Poe, who was the first to conceive, but the last to constructively reduce to practice, was diligent at the time Scharf entered the field and the delay of three months between this time and the filing of his application was due to no inaction on the part of Poe, but to the fact that the attorney for his assignee, who was particularly skilled in the art and prepared all its patent applications, was delayed by other work which had accumulated because of his sickness, and the testimony shows that there was no intentional delay upon his part in the preparation of Poe's application, *Held* that Poe was not lacking in diligence. *Poe* v. *Scharf*, 261.

16. SAME—FAILURE OF SENIOR PARTY TO DISCLOSE INVENTION.—Evidence considered and held to show that the application on which the patent involved in interference was granted did not as originally filed disclose the invention in issue, and priority therefore awarded to the junior party. *McKnight v. *Pohle*, 666.

17. SAME—ORIGINALITY.—Where an invention is reduced to practice by B. while working as an assistant of H. and in pursuance of a general plan arranged by H. and his associate officers with a view to the attainment of the result actually accomplished by such invention, the presumption is that the reduction to practice is a result of H.'s disclosures to B., and in order for the latter to prevail on the question of priority he must affirmatively show that he was an independent inventor. *Braunstein* v. *Holmes*, 303.

18. SAME—SECOND INTERFERENCE—RES ADJUDICATA.—Where in the first interference between the same parties C. formally abandoned the invention specifically stated in the issue, *Held* that in a second interference the issue of which is based upon the same disclosure as that upon which the issue of the first interference was based judgment must be rendered against C. upon the ground that the matter is *res adjudicata*. *Hallwood* v. *Carroll*, 416.

19. SAME—SAME—SAME.—The fact that no testimony was taken in the first interference does not avoid the application of the doctrine of *res adjudicata* to the second interference, even though the issue of the latter includes details not expressly recited in the first interference (citing *Blackford* v. *Wilder*, *ante*, 491; 127 O. G., 1255, and *Wende* v. *Horine*, *ante*, 615; 129 O. G., 2858.) *Id.*

PROCESS AND APPARATUS. See *Patentability*, 5; *Reissue Applications*, 3, 4.
PROCESS AND MACHINE. See *Interference*, 68.
PROOF. See *Trade-Marks*, 106, 126, 127.
PROOF OF AUTHORIZATION OF FOREIGN EXECUTORS OR ADMINISTRATORS. See *Foreign Executors or Administrators*.

PROPERTY RIGHTS. See *Trade-Marks*, 60, 93, 94, 99, 124, 132.

PROSECUTION OF APPLICATIONS. See *Abandonment of Applications*, 6, 7, 8.

PROSECUTION OF APPLICATIONS BY ASSIGNEES.

ASSIGNEE OF ENTIRE INTEREST—RIGHT TO PROSECUTE APPLICATION TO EX-CLUSION OF INVENTOR.—Rules 5 and 20, which provide that the assignee of the entire interest of an invention may prosecute the application for patent to the exclusion of the inventor, *Held* to be valid. †*In re Adams*, 434.

PROSECUTION OF INTERFERENCE BY LICENSE. See *Interference*, 47, 48.

PROTEST. See *Motion to Dissolve Interference*, 19, 20.

PUBLICATION. See *Interference*, 92.

PUBLICATION IN THE OFFICIAL GAZETTE. See *Trade-Marks*, 17.

PUBLIC POLICY. See *Trade-Marks*, 147, 148.

PUBLIC USE AND SALE. See *Motion to Dissolve Interference*, 15.

1. PROCEEDINGS INSTITUTED WHERE APPLICANT CLAIMS ISSUE OF INTERFER-ENCE IN WHICH HE IS NOT AT PRESENT INVOLVED.—Where in response to an order to show cause why public use proceedings should not be instituted against his application an applicant states that an interference is in progress involving the same subject-matter and it appears that his application was not added to the interference by reason of the progress in that interference already made when his application was filed, *Held* that public use proceedings should be instituted, as a finding of public use applicable to this application would cause all proceedings upon the applications in interference and this application to terminate with the interference now pending. *In re Setter*, 61.

2. PRIMA FACIE CASE—SHOWING REQUIRED.—Where the single affidavit upon which the protest rests sets forth the conclusions of the affiant that the machine alleged to have been in public use corresponded to a certain claim of the application instead of giving a description of the machine itself, *Held* that the showing made is entirely insufficient to justify the institution of a public use proceeding. *In re Booth Brothers*, 140.

3. SAME—SAME.—In a public use protest the facts should be set forth as fully as possible, so that the Office may pass upon the identity of the machine used with that claimed by the applicant and upon the success of its operation in determining whether proceedings shall be instituted. Corroborating affidavits should also be filed if other witnesses are to be relied upon. Altogether, the protestants should present their *prima facie* case as well as may be done by affidavits, so as to give the applicant opportunity to intelligently oppose the institution of the proceeding and the consequent delay in the prosecution of his application. *Id.*

4. QUESTION NOT CONSIDERED IN AN INTERFERENCE.—The question whether the invention in issue was placed in public use by one of the parties to an interference is not one which can be raised in an interference proceeding, but is one for the consideration of the Commissioner of Patents on the final allowance of the patent. *Burson v. Vogel*, 669.

PUBLIC USE PROCEEDINGS. See *Public Use and Sale*.

REBUTTAL TESTIMONY. See *Reduction to Practice*, 21; *Trade-Marks*, 119.

RECONSIDERATION. See *Examination of Applications*, 1, 2, 6; *Interference*, 12; *Motion to Dissolve Interference*, 3, 7; *Rejection of Claims*, 3.

REDUCTION TO PRACTICE. See *Applications*, 2; *Concealment of Invention*; *Interference*, 2, 3, 37, 38, 78, 92; *Preliminary Statement*, 4; *Priority of Invention*, 15, 17.

1. CONSTRUCTIVE—DIVISIONAL APPLICATION ENTITLED TO DATE OF ORIGINAL.— An application was filed on June 8, 1895, covering an igniter and an engine. The claims to the engine were erroneously rejected, were canceled, the application was allowed, and subsequently became forfeited. On July 16, 1898, the application was renewed, and additional claims to the engine were included. Division was required between the claims to the igniter and the engine. On March 28, 1899, applicant canceled the claims to the engine, and on April 25, 1899, the Office acted on the remaining claims to the igniter. Subsequently applicant reinstated the claims to the engine, and the Office again permitted him to elect which of the inventions he would prosecute in the application, but afterwards informed him that he was bound by the previous cancelation of the claims to the engine, and applicant thereupon, on October 30, 1900, canceled the engine claims, and after several communications between the Office and applicant the application matured into a patent, dated January 12, 1904. On April 16, 1903, applicant filed a divisional application covering the engine, *Held* that the divisional application is entitled to the date of the original application of June 8, 1895, as a constructive reduction to practice. *Duryea and White v. Rice, jr.*, 443.

2. CONTINUING APPLICATION—DIVISIONAL APPLICATION COPENDING WITH ORIGINAL.—A divisional application filed while the original application is pending in the Office covering matter carved out of the original is a continuation of the latter and is entitled to its date as a constructive reduction to practice, even though such divisional application was filed more than two years after an action by the Office on claims which applicant elected to retain in response to a requirement of division. *Id.*

3. INTERFERENCE—SIMPLE DEVICE—ORIGINAL DEVICE NOT PRODUCED.—Where the device in issue is said to belong to that class of simple devices the mere production of which without test is regarded as an actual reduction to practice, but the device originally made was not produced in evidence, and the testimony tending to establish the identity of a later device, which was introduced in evidence, with the original device is so general as to leave it uncertain whether this later device is of the same strength, size, shape, and proportion as the original, *Held* that actual reduction to practice is not proved. *Richards v. Burkholder*, 166.

4. SAME—BY AGENT.—The reduction to practice of an invention by an original inventor cannot be taken as a reduction to practice by another merely because the ownership of the claims of both may afterward become vested in the same person or persons. It is not enough to entitle an applicant to a patent that some one else, not his agent, has shown the practicability of the invention by reducing it to practice. (*Hunter v. Stikeman*, C. D., 1898, 564; 85 O. G., 610; 13 App. D. C., 214, 226.) *Robinson v. McCormick*, 574.

5. SAME—PRIORITY—SUCCESSFUL TEST REQUIRED.—Where the invention consists of a plate graduated in such manner as to obviate the necessity for "make-ready," *Held* that to establish a successful reduction to practice requires a printing test under actual working conditions on a power-press and without the use of a "cut-overlay." *Wickers and Furlong v. McKee*, 587.

6. SAME—SAME—SAME.—Complete invention must amount to demonstration. The efforts of the inventor must have passed beyond experiment, beyond the reach of possible or probable failure, must have attained certainty by embodiment in the intended form, and must be capable of

producing the desired result, for where experiments have inspired hope of future achievement of the purpose for which they were designed they still fall short of reduction to practice. * *Id.*

7. SAME—TEST.—Where it appears that L. and W. constructed a machine embodying the tin-plate catcher set forth in the issue and secretly tested the same August 23, 1902, but it is not clear that freshly-tinned plates were used in the test, and the machine was at once dismantled, and that subsequently, in October, 1903, another machine was constructed which is said to have been operated until November 18, 1903, but was not again used until September, 1904, after L. and W. heard of C.'s patent, and no sheets which ·were run through this catcher are produced, and where another machine, which was made in February, 1905, in conformity with the first machine and tested in the presence of witnesses called in this case, required frequent adjustments of the catcher-disks to prevent the sheets from slipping and yet to place them far enough apart to avoid denting the sheets, *Held* that the experimental stage of the invention had not been.passed and that such tests did not establish reduction to practice of the invention. * *Lewis and Williams* v. *Cronemeyer*, 638.

8. SAME—DILIGENCE.—Where L. and W. made and secretly tested a machine embodying the invention August 23, 1903, and at once dismantled the same, made and tested another machine October, 1903, but did not use the same again until September, 1904, and where L. and W. consulted their attorneys in November, 1903, and had the application papers prepared in January, 1904, but did nothing further toward filing their application until June, 1904, after they had heard of C.'s patent, *Held*, that L. and W. were lacking in diligence and cannot prevail over C., who reduced the invention to practice and filed his application in September, 1903. * *Id.*

9. SAME—INVENTION.—Reduction to practice must produce something of practical use, coupled with a knowledge, preferably by actual trial, that the thing will work practically for the intended purpose. The conception may give rational hopes of future fulfilment of the purpose at which it aims; but if as a matter of practice it falls short of success it is not a sufficient reduction to practice. Complete invention amounts to demonstration. When, as in this case, it had not quite passed beyond experiment and had not quite attained certainty and had fallen short of demonstrating the capacity of the invention to produce the desired result, the invention itself was still inchoate. These parties sought certainty; but they had not attained certainty beyond all conjecture, which certainty the law requires. (See *McKenzie* v. *Cummings*, C. D., 1904, 683; 112 O. G., 1481; 24 App. D. C., 140; *Hunter* v. *Stikeman*, C. D., 1898, 564; 85 O. G., 610; 13 App. D. C., 219; *Coffin* v. *Ogden*, 5 O. G., 270; 18 Wall., 124.) (* *Sherwood* v. *Drewsen*, 642.)

10. SAME—FILING OF APPLICATION.—Where neither the testimony presented by S. nor that offered in behalf of D. satisfactorily establishes conception of the invention in issue, *Held* that each party must be restricted to the date of filing of his application for conception and constructive reduction to practice, and since D. was the first to file, priority of invention must be awarded to him. * *Id.*

11. SAME—PRIORITY—LONG DELAY.—Where the evidence satisfactorily shows that Hallwood constructed a machine embodying the invention in issue and successfully operated it more than five years prior to the filing of

his application and that several machines were afterward constructed and sent to various parts of the United States, *Held* that these acts should not be considered merely as evidence of an abandoned experiment, but as evidence of a reduction to practice, although other machines were built embodying an older form of device for performing the same function, where it appears that the old devices satisfactorily performed the desired function in ordinary use and that they were so made in order to dispose of old materials then on hand. * *McCormick* v. *Hallwood*, 656.

12. SAME—SAME—TEST.—As a general rule, before a machine can be considered as a reduction to practice it must be subjected to a test, and the test must demonstrate the fitness of the machine for a useful purpose. *Gordon* v. *Wentworth*, 295.

13. SAME—SAME—EVIDENCE OF SUCCESSFUL TEST.—The mere general statements of witnesses that a device operated successfully, unsupported by the production of the articles upon which the machine operated at the time, must be regarded as meager evidence of a successful test. *Id.*

14. SAME—SAME—SAME—SUCCESSFUL OPERATION OF DEVICE AT TRIAL.—If a machine may be successfully operated at the time testimony is taken, this fact, taken in connection with statements of witnesses that it operated successfully when first constructed, may be considered sufficient evidence of a successful test where it appears that the device has not been changed in the meantime. *Id.*

15. SAME—SAME—EVIDENCE THAT DEVICE WAS UNSUCCESSFUL.—Where after an alleged successful test a device is thrown aside and apparently forgotten until knowledge is gained of a rival's successful invention, notwithstanding an apparent demand for such a device, *Held* that such conduct carries a strong presumption that the device was regarded only as an unsuccessful experiment. *Id.*

16. REPRODUCTION OF ORIGINAL MACHINE.—A device which was experimented with and afterwards laid aside and partly dismantled and which when produced in evidence did not have all of the original parts, some of the important parts being replacements, *Held* not to constitute a reduction to practice, the evidence tending to show the identity of the parts replaced and the original parts not being satisfactory. *Burson* v. *Vogel*, 669.

17. CRUDE MACHINE—SUBSEQUENT IMPROVEMENTS.—A machine may be crude in construction, but if it contains all the essential elements of the invention of the issue and in its operation successfully demonstrates its practical efficacy and utility reduction to practice is accomplished. (*Coffee* v. *Guerant*, C. D., 1894, 384; 68 O. G., 279; 3 App. D. C., 497, 499; *Norden* v. *Spaulding*, C. D., 1905, 588; 114 O. G., 1828; 24 App. D. C., 286, 290; *Gallagher* v. *Hien*, C. D., 1905, 624; 115 O. G., 1330; 25 App. D. C., 77, 82; *Lowrie* v. *Taylor*, C. D., 1906, 713; 123 O. G., 1695; 27 App. D. C., 522, 526.) The mere fact that mechanical improvements may be suggested and made in the course of operation that tend to perfect the operation of the machine and increase its practical efficiency, while retaining the essential elements of the invention which it puts in practice, does not impair the effect of the orignal demonstraton of utility if established satisfactorily. *Id.*

18. EVIDENCE OF SUCCESS OF TESTS.—In view of the failure of the inventor to testify as to the character or results of tests of a magneto-receiver for wireless telegraphy and the testimony of a witness who assisted in the tests that the signals were faint, the unsupported statement of an

electrical engineer who tested the device that his operator received intelligible messages is not sufficient to establish the operativeness of the device, especially where it does not appear with what certainty or rapidity the signals or messages were received. *Marconi v. Shoemaker*, 392.

19. SAME—CONSTRUCTION OF ANOTHER DEVICE.—The construction of another device to obviate defects in a prior device tends to show that the first device was unsatisfactory. *Id.*

20. SAME—SAME.—Where it is claimed that the form of device described and illustrated in the application produced the most satisfactory results, and it appears that a device of this construction was built and tested and afterwards several modifications of such device were made and tried without success, and that a prior construction was finally reverted to, and that a number of devices of the latter construction were built for use in preference to the former, the presumption is warranted, in the absence of testimony establishing a satisfactory test, that such device was not successful. *Id.*

21. SAME—EX PARTE TEST DURING REBUTTAL TESTIMONY.—A test by a party during the taking of rebuttal testimony out of the presence of the opposing party or his agent is entitled to no consideration as proof of the operativeness of the device several years previous under different conditions. *Id.*

REFERENCES. See *Examination of Applications*, 1, 3, 4, 5; *Motion to Dissolve Interference*, 25, 26, 28, 33; *Rejection of Claims*, 3, 4, 7, 8.

REGISTRABILITY. See *Labels; Trade-Marks*, 33, 36, 37, 39, 40, 41, 44, 45, 46, 47, 53, 54, 55, 56, 57, 58, 62, 64 67, 68, 69, 71, 86, 87, 88, 92, 93, 94, 100, 112, 113, 123, 154, 155, 156.

REGISTRATION. See *Trade-Marks*, 8, 9, 48, 49, 50, 51, 52, 57, 58, 61, 62, 63, 78, 79, 81, 85, 99, 103, 115, 117, 118, 121, 135, 136, 138, 142, 144.

REHEARING. See *Appeal to the Commissioner of Patents; Decisions of the Examiners-in-Chief*, 2; *Interference*, 64; *Motion for Rehearing; Motion to Dissolve Interference*, 17.

REISSUE APPLICATIONS. See *Interference*, 17; *Motion to Dissolve Interference*, 31.

1. LONG DELAY IN FILING APPLICATION EXCUSED.—H. filed an application on September 16, 1896, upon which a patent was granted on April 20, 1897. In 1898 H. instructed his attorneys to prepare a reissue application, but before such application was filed F. obtained a patent dated July 4, 1899, on an application filed May 31, 1898, covering mechanism of the character covered by H.'s patent. In looking over the record of the F. patent H. found an affidavit filed to overcome the rejection of his claims, the oath stating that the invention had been made "many months prior to September 16, 1896," the filing date of H.'s application. In view of this affidavit H. considered it useless to apply for a reissue. In a suit brought in 1904 by the assignee of the F. patent against the assignee of the H. patent it was brought out that the machine to which the affidavit referred as having been made "many months" before H. filed his application had, in fact, been made in 1889 or 1890, and the court held that said machine was either inoperative and impracticable or abandoned by laches. *Held* that under the circumstances a reissue applied for promptly after the decision of the court should not be refused on the ground of delay in applying therefor. *Ex parte Hiett*, 33.

2. NEW MATTER.—Where a patent describes certain parts of a device as having a specified function, a claim in an application for the reissue

of such patent which refers to such parts as "means" for performing a different function, requiring a relative location of the parts which was not originally disclosed, relates to new matter. The facts that the reissue application was not filed for about two years after the grant of the patent and that the claim was not made for about nine months after the filing of such application strongly indicate that the claim was not suggested by the original disclosure. *In re Hoey, 516.

8. SAME INVENTION—PROCESS AND APPARATUS.—Where an application clearly discloses a process and an apparatus and through inadvertence, accident, or mistake the applicant accepts a patent with a limited claim to the apparatus, although the process is the dominant part of his invention, Held that the patent may be reissued to include the process in the absence of intervening rights. *In re Heroult, 521.

4. SAME—INADVERTENCE, ACCIDENT, OR MISTAKE.—Where a patentee clearly discloses a process and an apparatus for carrying out the process and claims only the apparatus, the failure to claim the process was either intentional or the result of inadvertence, accident, or mistake, for which section 4916, Revised Statutes, furnishes a remedy. *Id.

5. SAME—ACTS OF ATTORNEYS.—Applicants usually act through solicitors or attorneys, and their inadvertence, accidents, and mistakes, if such in fact, are remediable under the statute permitting reissue when it is clear that there is no fraudulent or deceptive intent or attempt to destroy an intervening right. (In re Briede, C. D., 1906, 677; 123 O. G., 322; 27 App. D. C., 298,301.) *Id.

6. DELAY OF TWO YEARS—PRESUMPTION OF ABANDONMENT.—Delay of two years in filing an application for a reissue of a patent with broader claims will usually be treated as an abandonment to the public of everything not claimed in the original. This rule is based upon the analogy between a reissue application and the case of an inventor who fails to apply for a patent of his invention within two years from the date of its public use or sale, which the statute ordains is conclusive evidence of its abandonment. (See in re Starkey, C. D., 1903, 607; 104 O. G., 2150; 21 App. D. C., 519, and cases cited therein.) *In re Ams. 532.

7. LONG DELAY—FAILURE OF ATTORNEYS TO UNDERSTAND INVENTION.—Where the invention covered by a patent is simple and the patent clearly and definitely describes it, and the patentee immediately upon the issue thereof discovers that the single claim allowed is too narrow and does not properly cover his invention, and upon calling his attorney's attention to this fact they advised him that the claim was as broad as could be obtained, and it does not appear that they acted in bad faith, Held that a delay of five years in seeking a reissue cannot be excused upon the plea that the original attorneys did not understand the invention. since under the circumstances it was the duty of the patentee to consult other counsel without delay. *Id.

REJECTION OF CLAIMS. See Amendments, 1, 4; Construction of Claims, 3; Examination of Applications; Interference, 12, 28, 29, 31, 33; Motion to Dissolve Interference, 7.

1. INTERFERENCE—MOTION TO DISSOLVE—REQUEST FOR FURTHER EXPLANATION—PRACTICE.—Where the Examiner rejected the claims constituting the issue in his decision dissolving the interference and not in the application files, Held the proper practice under Rule 124 is for the Examiner to indicate his findings regarding the claims in his decision on the motion in the interference file and at the same time to make the rejection of the claims affected in the application files. In making such

rejection, if desired, reference may be made as a basis therefor to the findings in the decision on the motion. The purpose of this practice is to enable applicants to appeal to the full extent provided by statute and, if an appeal is desired, to require the appeal to be taken at once. *Bastian* v. *Champ*, 111.

2. CANNOT BE BASED UPON EVIDENCE TAKEN IN SECOND INTERFERENCE WHICH HAS BEEN HELD TO BE RES ADJUDICATA.—Where in a second interference the question of priority was held to be *res adjudicata* and a decision rendered in favor of Blackford, Blackford's claims corresponding to the issue of the interference cannot be rejected upon the ground that they are anticipated by an exhibit introduced into the second interference by Wilder. Inasmuch as the second interference should not have been declared, the testimony taken therein is of no force and is to be given no effect for any purpose whatever. *In re Wilder*, 126.

3. FINAL REJECTION—PREMATURE.—In response to an action by an applicant canceling two rejected claims and substituting claims therefor, accompanied by an argument setting forth how the substitute claims distinguished from the references, the Examiner rejected the substitute claims, stating that "there is no invention in applicant's device over the art cited." Thereupon the applicant asked for an·explanation of the grounds of rejection, distinctly stating that he was not asking for a reconsideration, in response to which the Examiner explained the references and finally rejected the claims. *Held* that the final rejection was premature. While the Examiner contended that the substitute claims were substantially the same as previous claims with respect to which the references had been explained, the Examiner did not finally reject the claims on the first action nor did he refuse the request for explanation on the ground that the pertinency of the references had been previously explained. *Ex parte Walker*, 191.

4. SAME—SAME.—Where after a rejection in which reasons are given why references cited anticipate the claims applicant amends the claims and files an argument that one of the patents cited belongs to a different art and requests that the Examiner explain why the patent cited was analogous to the invention in issue, *Held* that a final rejection was premature and that the Examiner should have given the explanation requested. *Ex parte Burge*, 208.

5. RECOMMENDATIONS UNDER RULE 139—ACTION OF PRIMARY EXAMINER—PRACTICE.—The recommendation of the Examiners-in-Chief under Rule 139 that in their opinion claims are not patentable is binding upon the Primary Examiner, and he should enter a *pro forma* rejection of such claims upon the grounds stated by the Examiners-in-Chief. If the Examiner is of the opinion that the claims should be rejected for any other reasons, they should also be stated in his letter of rejection. *Ex parte Shaw*, 222.

6. FORMAL OBJECTION DOES NOT RENDER PREMATURE.—Where the Examiner points out certain formal objections in his letter finally rejecting the claims of an application, *Held* that the final rejection is not thereby rendered premature. *Ex parte Green*, 239.

7. EXPLANATION OF GROUNDS OF, BY EXAMINERS.—Where in answer to a rejection by the Examiner giving a fair statement of his reasons for rejection the applicant responds by fully stating what he considered to be disclosed in the references, what he considered to be covered by the rejected claims, and why such claims were not anticipated and requests

a further statement from the Examiner as to the bearing of the references upon the broadest claim presented, the Examiner should not finally reject merely upon the reasons formerly stated, but he should make a further statement of the reasons of rejection in the light of applicant's argument. *Ex parte Herbst*, 335.

8. FINAL—WHEN WARRANTED.—Where substitute claims were rejected upon the same references as the prior claims and it was stated that the "claims are substantially like those previously rejected on the same references, being, if anything, a little broader," *Held* that a final rejection was proper. *Ex parte Lasance*, 374.

REOPENING OF INTERFERENCE. See *Interference*, 51, 52, 54, 55, 63.

1. FOR INTRODUCTION OF NEWLY-DISCOVERED EVIDENCE—REVIEW BY COURT OF APPEALS.—Where the tribunals of the Patent Office in the exercise of their discretion have refused to reopen a case for the introduction of newly-discovered evidence, their conclusions will be reviewed by the court of appeals only in case of an abuse of discretion. *Dunbar* v. *Schellenger*, 567.

2. PRIORITY—APPEAL TO COURT—CONSIDERATION OF PATENTABILITY.—"As regards the contention of the appellant that 'the structure in interference differs from the prior structure of Roberts in but two particulars,' * * * it is sufficient to say, that in so far as it appears to raise a question of patentability, that question has been settled by the allowance of the claims." *Id.*

3. PRACTICE.—The court of appeals of the District of Columbia having held that a second interference involving claims differing merely in scope from those involved in the first interference should not have been declared, the latter will not be reopened for the purpose of allowing the issue of the second interference to be contested therein. *Wende* v. *Horine*, 266.

4. SAME.—The fact that a proceeding by bill in equity under section 4915, Revised Statutes, might prove slow and expensive should not outweigh the necessity for proper and orderly procedure in an interference. *Id.*

5. DELAY IN BRINGING MOTION.—A motion to reopen a case for the purpose of allowing a party to print testimony taken by his opponent will be denied where such motion was brought after the decision of the Examiner of Interferences was rendered and no satisfactory reason for such delay is given. *Parker* v. *Corkhill*, 301.

6. PIECEMEAL CONDUCT OF CASE.—A piecemeal conduct of a case cannot be allowed. Where a contestant elects to stand upon the record as presented at final hearing, he is bound by the decision rendered thereon. *Id.*

7. TO TAKE TESTIMONY TO STRENGTHEN CASE.—A practice which would allow a contestant to experimentally conduct his case to a probable failure and then permit him after consultation and with competent assistance to make further endeavors to show what he could and should have earlier shown with such assistance would be contrary to all well-established rules and legal principles. *Standard Import Co., Ltd.*, v. *New Orleans Import Co., Ltd.*, 365.

8. SAME—MOTION BROUGHT BEFORE FINAL HEARING.—The fact that a motion to reopen an interference to take additional evidence was brought before final hearing is no reason why it should be granted. *Id.*

RES ADJUDICATA. See *Examination of Applications*, 7; *Infringement*, 1, 2, 3, 4; *Interference*, 27, 62, 85, 86; *Priority of Invention*, 18, 19; *Rejection of Claims*, 2; *Trade-Marks*, 13, 62.

DOCTRINE STATED BY THE SUPREME COURT.—The doctrine of *res adjudicata*, or estoppel by former judgment, has been thus declared by the Supreme Court of the United States: "When the second suit is upon the same cause of action and between the same parties as the first, the judgment in the former is conclusive in the latter as to every question which was or might have been presented and determined in the first action; but when the second suit is upon a different cause of action, though between the same parties, the judgment in the former action operates as an estoppel only as to the point or question actually litigated and determined, and not as to other matters which might have been litigated and determined." (*Nesbit* v. *Riverside Independent District*, 144 U. S., 610, 618; *New Orleans* v. *Citizen's Bank*, 167 U. S., 371, 386; *S. P. R. R.* v. *U. S.*, 168 U. S., 1, 48)—and the doctrine as thus laid down is applicable to adjudications made in the Patent Office. *Blackford* v. *Wilder*, 491.

RESPONSIVE ACTION BY APPLICANT. See *Abandonment of Applications; Rejection of Claims*, 3, 7, 8.

RIGHT TO MAKE CLAIMS. See *Amendment*, 5; *Interference*, 15, 16, 20, 39, 81, 85; *Motion to Dissolve Interference*, 8, 10, 19, 29, 33, 43; *Testimony*, 1, 2.

RIGHT TO MARK. See *Trade-Marks*, 4, 5, 14, 15, 58, 61, 149.

SECOND INTERFERENCE. See *Interference*, 11, 27, 35, 62, 86; *Priority of Invention*, 18, 19; *Rejection of Claims*, 2; *Reopening of Interference*, 3; *Testimony*, 3.

SERVICE UPON OWNER OF PATENT OF PETITION TO INSPECT. See *Access to Abandoned Applications*, 1, 3, 4.

SIMILARITY OF MARKS. See *Trade-Marks*, 2, 35, 38, 65, 66, 67, 81, 86, 87, 88, 96, 97, 101, 103, 106, 116, 126, 127, 128, 129, 132, 133, 134, 137, 138, 139, 140.

SPECIFICATIONS. See *Amendments*, 4, 5; *Anticipation; Construction of Claims*, 4, 5; *Drawings*, 1; *Examination of Applications*, 8; *Priority of Invention*, 2, 3.

    APPLICATION—DESCRIPTION—LAUDATORY STATEMENTS.—An applicant should under no circumstances be allowed in his specification to make derogatory statements as to the inventions of others; but within reasonable limits he may in pointing out the advantages of his invention indicate also what he regards as the defects or deficiencies common to structures representing the unimproved art, and the fact that in making this distinction he states that his device is superior to preceding forms in certain respects wherein it differs from them is not a matter of importance. (Citing *ex parte Shaw*, C. D., 1890, 31; 50 O. G., 1129; *ex parte Schoshusen*, C. D., 1905, 214, 116 O. G., 2008,) *Ex parte Heylman*, 29.

SUFFICIENCY OF EVIDENCE. See *Public Use and Sale*, 2, 3.

SUGGESTED CLAIMS. See *Abandonment of Application*, 5, 22; *Interference*, 46; *Priority of Invention*, 3.

SUITS FOR INFRINGEMENT. See *Infringement*.

SUPERVISORY AUTHORITY OF THE COMMISSIONER OF PATENTS. See *Interference*, 20, 70, 75, 85; *Motion for Leave to Take Testimony*, 1; *Motion to Dissolve Interference*, 5, 11; *Patentability*, 6.

SUPERVISORY AUTHORITY OF THE SECRETARY OF THE INTERIOR. See *Interference*, 24.

SUPPLEMENTAL OATH. See *Drawings*, 1.

SUPPRESSION OF EVIDENCE. See *Evidence*, 3, 6.

SUPPRESSION OF TESTIMONY. See *Interference*, 1, 39; *Trade-Marks*, 107. 120.

SUPREME COURT OF THE UNITED STATES. See *Construction of Statutes*, 1; *Res Adjudicata*.

SURREBUTTAL TESTIMONY. See *Interference*, 65, 66; *Motiont to Suppress Testimony*.

SUSPENSION OF INTERFERENCE. See *Interference*, 68.

SUSPENSION OF PROCEEDINGS. See *Appeal to the Commissioner of Patents*, 1.

TECHNICAL TERMS. See *Priority of Invention*, 2.

TEN-YEARS' CLAUSE. See *Trade-Marks*, 36, 37, 51, 52, 57, 58, 59, 67, 85, 86, 87, 88, 142.

TESTIMONY. See *Evidence*, 1, 2, 3; *Interference*, 1, 3, 32, 35, 39, 42, 43, 63, 80, 82, 83, 87; *Motion for Leave to Take Testimony; Motion to Suppress Testimony; Preliminary Statement*, 2; *Priority of Invention*, 1, 6; *Reduction to Practice*, 3; *Rejection of Claims*, 2; *Reopening of Interference*, 5, 7, 8; *Trade-Marks*, 21, 26, 119, 120, 152.

1. UNDER RULE 130—RIGHT TO MAKE CLAIMS.—The question whether certain elements of the issue are not present in one party's structure, but can only be read into such issue by applying limitations which do not operate in the manner defined in the claims, is one of fact, upon which the opposing party may be permitted to present testimony. *Weintraub v. Hewitt and Rogers*, 49.

2. SAME—IDENTITY OF INVENTION.—There appears to be no warrant for the taking of testimony relative to the identity of the inventions of the parties to an interference. If the inventions are not identical, it must follow either that one of the parties has no right to make the claims in issue or that the claims are indefinite and ambiguous and do not with sufficient exactness define the invention of either party. This is not a question of priority of invention. *Id.*

3. USE IN SECOND INTERFERENCE—RULE 157.—Where C. was denied the privilege of introducing testimony taken in his behalf in a prior interference between the same parties in view of the opposition of E. and M. on the ground that they were not represented at the taking of C.'s testimony, a motion by E. and M. to introduce testimony taken in their behalf in the same interference should not be granted merely because C. was represented at the examination of their witnesses. *Corey v. Eiseman and Misar*, 59.

4. INTERFERENCE—PRINTING.—The fact that only one party has taken testimony constitutes no sufficient reason for excusing him from printing the same. *Peak v. Brush*, 200.

TESTS. See *Priority of Invention*, 8; *Reduction to Practice*, 3, 4, 5, 7, 8, 11, 12, 13, 14, 15, 18, 19, 20, 21.

TRADE-MARKS. See *Interference*, 1.

1. INTERFERENCE—MOTION TO SUSPEND PROCEEDINGS—APPEAL.—The decision of the Examiner of Interferences refusing to suspend proceedings pending a determination of contempt proceedings brought in a United States circuit court for failure of witnesses to appear and testify in response to subpœna will not be disturbed where it does not appear that great hardship will otherwise ensue. *Outcault v. The New York Herald Company*, 17.

2. OPPOSITION—DISSIMILARITY OF MARKS—DEMURRER.—*Held* that trademarks consisting of the words " Zodenta " and " Sozodont " are quite

dissimilar and that "Zodenta" is not calculated to mislead or deceive the average purchaser who may seek to buy "Sozodont." The resemblance is not such as to preclude a proper determination of the question upon demurrer. *Hall and Ruckel v. Ingram, 441.

3. INTERFERENCE—PRIORITY—OWNERSHIP.—Where the claim of Bigbie Brothers & Co. to ownership of the mark of the issue through transfer from Joseph Lawson & Son in 1887 is questioned, but neither of the other parties to the interference claims title from the Lawsons, Held that said other parties' claims to registration are defeated by the use of the mark in issue by Bigbie Brothers & Co. in 1887 and subsequently, irrespective of whether Bigbie Brothers & Co.'s use was based upon ownership, and that Lawson's right to the mark after the transfer in 1887 is only of consequence, therefore, in determining whether Bigbie Brothers & Co. shall be denied registration, notwithstanding their position as the first to adopt and use the mark among those before the Office seeking registration. Bigbie Brothers & Co. v. Bluthenthal & Bickart v. The J. & H. Butler Company, 22.

4. TO ACQUIRE RIGHTS NAME MUST BE PHYSICALLY APPLIED TO GOODS.—The mere adoption of a name for its goods does not vest in the company trade-mark rights. To acquire such rights, the name must be physically applied to the goods in trade, as by brands or labels on the packages sold. Id.

5. RIGHTS ACQUIRED ONLY BY PRESENCE OF MARK UPON GOODS AFTER PASSING FROM HANDS OF ORIGINATOR.—There is no liability to confusion of the origin of goods which are sold only on the premises of the originator. The utility of a trade-mark does not come into existence until the goods have passed from the hands of the originator, and it is only by the presence of the mark upon the goods after they have so passed that rights to the same as a trade-mark are believed to become established. Id.

6. INTERFERENCE—MARK USED TO INDICATE GRADE INSTEAD OF ORIGIN OF GOODS NOT A TRADE-MARK.—The price lists and sample pack of cards indicate that the company adopted the mark to designate a certain grade or style of cards which they offered for sale at a specified price and to distinguish this variety of cards from numerous other styles made and sold by said company. There is no evidence that the mark was used to indicate the origin or manufacture of the cards; but, on the contrary, a fanciful figure labeled "Trade Mark" appears to be for the purpose of indicating the origin of the goods and to constitute properly the trade-mark of the company, Held that the mark in controversy was used by said company as a grade, quality, or style mark, and not as a technical trade-mark. The United States Playing Card Company v. C. M. Clark Publishing Company, 44.

7. GRADE-MARK NOT A VALID TRADE-MARK.—Where a mark is adopted and used primarily to indicate style, grade, or quality of goods, and not for the purpose of indicating origin or manufacture of the goods, Held that it does not constitute a valid trade-mark. Id.

8. REGISTRATION—SYMBOLS INDICATING MERELY QUALITY NOT REGISTRABLE.— A trade-mark consisting of "flakes of mica impressed or otherwise applied to the external surface of an insulating tube or tubular coverings for electric wires" was properly refused registration, for the reason that the registration would operate, so far as it could have any effect, to give the applicant a monopoly of conduits or tubular coverings of flake-mica composition. The office of a trade-mark in a legal sense is

ary 20, 1905," and the opponent desires to amend by adding that the mark is not registrable because it is a geographical name or term, *Held* that the broad reference to clause (*b*) of section 5 of the act merely conveys the idea that in this part of the act is to be found the prohibition against the registration of names of individuals, that the proposed amendment is based on new ground, and is not proper subject-matter for an amendment filed after the expiration of the thirty days prescribed in the statute. *The Albert Dickinson Company* v. *Conklin*, 63.

16. SAME—GENERAL REFERENCE NOT SUFFICIENT.—It is not a sufficient ground for a notice of opposition to make a general reference to the Trade-Mark Act or to some part thereof. *Id.*

17. PUBLICATION IN OFFICIAL GAZETTE.—A trade-mark will not be republished merely for the purpose of extending the period of thirty days provided by statute for the filing of oppositions. *In re J. G. B. Siegert & Hijos*, 64.

18. ACT OF MAY 4, 1906, CONSTRUED.—Section 1 of the act of May 4, 1906, amending section 1 of the Trade-Mark Act of February 20, 1905, by inserting after the words " a description of the trade-mark itself " the words " only when needed to express colors not shown in the drawing," is construed to mean that the drawing should be relied upon to disclose the mark and that a description of the mark should be permitted " only when needed to express colors not shown in the drawing." *Ex parte E. C. Atkins & Company*, 67.

19. SAME.—The purpose of the amendment contained in section 1 of the act of May 4, 1906, is to make the registration definite by limiting it to the disclosure in the drawing, leaving the question of what is an immaterial variation in the mark to the courts. *Id.*

20. SAME—APPLIES TO APPLICATIONS PENDING AT DATE IT BECAME EFFECTIVE.— The fact that the application was filed under the former statutes does not excuse the applicant from complying with the amended statute, since the latter makes no exception of applications pending at the date it became effective. *Id.*

21. INTERFERENCE—PRIORITY—CREDIBILITY OF TESTIMONY.—Where the testimony presented in behalf of both the opposing parties is sbuject to uncertainty, the testimony of Rosenbush concerning the adoption of the mark in 1895 or 1896, which is supported by the testimony of his former partner, Levie, is entitled to as great weight as the testimony of a single disinterested witness testifying from his unaided memory concerning the adoption of the mark by The Rose Shoe Manufacturing Company nearly eight years after the event. *A. A. Rosenbush & Company* v. *The Rose Shoe Manufacturing Company*, 69.

22. CANCELATION OF REGISTRATION—SECTION 13 OF ACT OF 1905 CONSTRUED.— Section 13 of the act of 1905, providing for the cancelation of trade-mark registrations, applies only to those registrations made under that act. *Funke* v. *Baldwin*, 73.

23. SAME—SAME—NOT APPLICABLE TO REGISTRATIONS UNDER ACTS OF 1881 AND 1882.—By section 30 of the act of 1905 all legislation inconsistent with the provisions of the act of 1905 is repealed except the Trade-Mark acts of 1881 and 1882 in their application to registrations made thereunder. The acts of 1881 and 1882 are to stand, so far as registrations made thereunder are concerned, whether consistent with the act of 1905 or otherwise. *Id.*

30. REGISTRATION BY FOREIGNERS—MUST CORRESPOND WITH FOREIGN REGISTRA
TION.—The only mark which a foreign applicant is entitled to register
in this country is the mark which he has registered in the country in
which he is located. Such mark is presumably that set forth and
shown in the foreign registration, and the Office must so assume until
furnished with proofs to the contrary. *Ex parte Pietro*, 107.

31. SAME—SAME—DRAWING.—Where a foreigner applies for registration in
this country, his registration in the country in which he is located will
be presumed to set forth and show his trade-mark, and in the absence
of proof to the contrary the drawing of his application for registration
in this country will be required to conform to such foreign registration.
Id.

32. GEOGRAPHICAL—"CONTINENTAL."—The word "Continental" as applied to
dump, flat, logging, and ballast push and mine cars is primarily geographical and not registrable. *Ex parte Continental Car and Equipment Company*, 113.

33. REGISTRABILITY DEPENDS UPON PREDOMINANCE OF ARBITRARY FEATURE.—
The registrability of a trade-mark depends upon the predominance of
the arbitrary features to give character to the mark. It cannot be
based upon features incapable of exclusive appropriation merely because they are embellished by arbitrary features which are in themselves insignificant. *Id.*

34. SAME—"CONTINENTAL" NOT MADE REGISTRABLE BY SURROUNDING SAME
WITH DIAMOND-SHAPED FIGURE.—The geographical word "Continental"
being the predominant feature of the mark by which the goods would
become known, a diamond-shaped figure surrounding the same instead
of being a further distinguishing feature of the mark serves merely as
a frame to give prominence to the inclosed symbol of ownership. *Id.*

35. INTERFERENCE—MOTION TO DISSOLVE—INTERFERENCE IN FACT.—The marks
of the parties consist, respectively, of the words "Raven" and "Crow"
accompanied in each case by a representation of a black bird perched
on a branch of a tree, *Held* there is no interference between the words
"Raven" and "Crow," and although there is a certain similarity in
the representations of the birds, taking the marks as a whole there is
no such resemblance as would be likely to cause confusion or mistake
in the mind of the public or deceive purchasers. *The United States
Graphite Company v. Bomhard*, 115.

36. NAME OF PATENTED ARTICLE—REGISTRABLE UNDER TEN-YEAR PROVISO OF
SECTION 5 OF ACT OF 1905—"YALE" FOR LOCKS AND LATCHES.—*Held* that
the word "Yale" is registrable as a trade-mark for locks and latches
under the ten-year proviso of section 5 of the act of 1905, although it is
the name of a patented article. *Ex parte The Yale & Towne Manufacturing Company*, 122.

37. SAME—SAME—EXCLUSIVE USE.—The function of the name of a patented
article is twofold: (1) It designates or identifies the thing patented,
and (2) it indicates the original source of manufacture of the article.
Where a word or name which has been applied to a patented article has
in addition to its descriptive significance also become indicative of the
origin of that article, a limited right remains in the original maker
after the expiration of the patent to exclude others from such unqualified use of the word or name as would deceive a careful public
into the belief that their articles are those of the original maker. This
right to exclude, it is believed, satisfies the requirement of "exclusive
use" stated in the ten-year proviso of the act of February 20, 1905. *Id.*

nently thereon and having in addition thereto the inscription "Elk Grove Creamery. Manufacturers of finest pasteurized Elgin Butter" presented in various styles of lettering and set off in circles and scrolls with other minor ornamentation, should be refused. *Id.*

48. REGISTRATION FOR CARTONS—INVALID.—Where a mark is registered for cartons, but the actual trade which the mark represents is in merchandise contained in the cartons, *Held* that the registration is invalid. *Pioneer Suspender Company* v. *Lewis Oppenheimer's Sons*, 144.

49. NOT USED ON GOODS—CANCELATION.—Where certain words were registered as a trade-mark for merchandise of certain characteristics and the words as used by the registrant in trade represented goods of different characteristics, *Held* that the registration should be canceled. *Id.*

50. SAME—SAME—SECTION 13 ACT OF 1905 CONSTRUED.—*Held* that the right to use referred to in the first ground of cancelation set forth in section 13 of the trade-mark act means a right of exclusive use and that the use referred to in the second ground is a use of the mark as a trade-mark for the goods mentioned in the registration. *Id.*

51. "TEN-YEAR" PROVISO—EXCLUSIVE USE BUT NOT NECESSARILY SOLE USE REQUIRED.—The word "exclusive" in the ten-year proviso of section 5 of the trade-mark act is believed to necessarily imply the right to exclude. Provided there is a clear right to exclude, however, it is not thought that there must necessarily have been sole use, otherwise, use by another, no matter how fraudulent or trivial, would defeat the right to registration under this provision of the statute. *Beech Hill Distilling Company* v. *Brown-Forman Company*, 146.

52. SAME—SAME.—Where it appears that each party to this interference independently originated the mark and neither party had knowledge of the use of the mark by the other party until nearly two years after the Beech Hill Distilling Company began using the mark and that then the Brown-Forman Company made no objection, but acquiesced in the use of the mark by the former company, *Held* that these circumstances do not show such exclusive use on the part of the Brown-Forman Company as to entitle it to register the mark in issue under the ten-year proviso of section 5 of the trade-mark act. *Id.*

53. GEOGRAPHICAL—"ORIENT."—The word "Orient" as applied to ink-ribbons and carbon-paper is primarily geographical in significance, and therefore not registrable. *Ex parte Crescent Typewriter Supply Company*, 149.

54. SAME—ASSOCIATION WITH ARBITRARY SYMBOL—"ORIENT" WITHIN A WREATH.—The fact that the geographical word "orient" is printed in a certain manner and inclosed within a wreath does not make the word registrable as a trade-mark. *Id.*

55. "STANDARD" DESCRIPTIVE—NOT REGISTRABLE.—*Held* that the word "Standard" as applied to phonographs is descriptive, and therefore not registrable. *In re National Phonograph Company*, 550.

56. SAME—IMMATERIAL WHETHER TRULY OR FALSELY DESCRIPTIVE.—The applicant's claim to the use of "Standard" as a trade-mark is in no wise strengthened, because the word is applied only to machines of inferior design which are not in any sense standard. The word cannot be appropriated as a trade-mark whether it is truly descriptive or falsely descriptive. *Id.*

57. TEN-YEAR PROVISO—EXCLUSIVE USE DOES NOT NECESSARILY REQUIRE SOLE USE.—The word "exclusive" in the ten-year proviso is believed

as "bull" whisky interference in fact existed. (*Coleman* v. *Crump,* 70 N. Y., 573, 580, cited.) *The Ellison-Harvey Co.* v. *Monarch,* 170.

66. "Spring Hill" Anticipated by "Spring Valley."—*Held* that the words "Spring Hill" as a trade-mark for whisky so nearly resembles a prior registered mark, which is described as a "crescent" or "new moon" and the words "Spring Valley" as to cause confusion in trade. *Ex parte L. & A. Scharff,* 172.

67. Anticipation of "Ten-Year" Marks.—The allegation of ten years' exclusive use next preceding the passage of the act of February 20, 1905, does not confer registrability upon the mark if it so nearly resembles a registered or known trade-mark owned and in use by another upon merchandise of the same descriptive properties as to be likely to cause confusion in trade. *Id.*

68. Representation of Merchandise with Mere Name of an Individual Appearing Thereon—Not Registrable.—When the trade-mark shown in the drawing comprises the representation of an ingot of bearing metal of a particular form with the name "Dodge" cast thereon and similar bars of metal are shown in prior registrations, *Held* that since the applicant can have no trade-mark in the form or appearance of the merchandise or in the mere name of an individual appearing thereon the mark is not registrable. *Ex parte Dodge Manufacturing Company,* 173.

69. Opposition—Allegation of Use of Mark.—An alleged use of the mark sought to be registered by the opposer as a part of its name and in its advertising is not a trade-mark use, and therefore forms no basis for refusing registration to the applicant. *In re Battle Creek Sanitarium Company, Limited,* 180.

70. Same—Amendment.—Amendment to an opposition subsequent to the expiration of thirty days after publication will not be permitted where it would result in presenting a new ground in an opposition which is otherwise invalid. *Id.*

71. Same—"Self Loading" as Applied to Cartridges a Descriptive Term.—Where an applicant desires to register the words "Self Loading" as a trade-mark for cartridges adopted for use on a rifle placed upon the market by applicant and called a "self-loading" rifle from the fact that the gun reloads itself. *Held* that the words as applied to the cartridges state the purpose for which they are made and sold that the reasons for the prohibition of the statute to the registration of marks which consist merely of descriptive matters are applicable to this case, and that the mark is in fact, nothing more than a descriptive term. *The Peters Cartridge Company* v. *The Winchester Repeating Arms Company,* 181.

72. Same—Hearings—Motion to Postpone.—A hearing will not be postponed because hearings before two tribunals of the Office were set for the same hour. The hearing before one tribunal can be easily arranged to follow the termination of the hearing before the other. *Bomhard* v. *United States Graphite Company,* 187.

73. Same—Issuing Order to Show Cause—Practice.—Order to show cause properly issued without setting the case down for a hearing. *Id.*

74. Same—Same—Refused to Extend Time for.—A decision of the Examiner of Interferences denying a motion to extend time to show cause will not be reversed in the absence of a clear showing of abuse of discretion. *Id.*

84. SAME—SAME.—Where the application for cancelation is in the form of an
affidavit sworn to by the president of the company filing the application
and contains positive allegations of facts which, if true, constitute
proper ground for cancelation of the registration under the statute,
Held that a *prima facie* case is made out, such as will warrant instituting the cancelation proceeding and requiring the registrant to file
its plea, answer, or demurrer. *Id.*

85. FOREIGN APPLICANT—REQUIREMENTS FOR REGISTRATION BY "TEN-YEAR"
PROVISO.—The requirement that a foreigner who applies for registration
shall show either that the mark has been registered in the country
where he resides or is located or that he has a manufacturing establishment within the territory of the United States is applicable to
those cases where registration is sought under the "ten-year" proviso
as well as where the mark is a technical trade-mark. *Ex parte Actien-
Gesellschaft für Anilin-Fabrikation*, 223.

86. OPPOSITION—IDENTITY OF MARKS.—*Held* that the mark "Alizarine Black
4 B" of the applicant so nearly resembles the mark "Alizarine Black
4" of the opposer and the words "Alizarine Black 3 B" used by the
Farbenfabriken of Elberfeld Company as to cause confusion in trade
and is therefore not registrable under the ten-year proviso of section 5
of the act of 1905. *Kuttroff* v. *Cassella Color Company*, 225.

87. SAME—TESTIMONY SHOWING USE BY THIRD PARTIES CONSIDERED.—The
stipulated use of the mark "Alizarine Black 3 B" by parties other than
those directly involved in this proceeding is admissible to show that
the applicant did not have exclusive use of the mark for ten years
next preceding the passage of the act of February 20, 1905. *Id.*

88. SAME—DESCRIPTIVE USE OF MARK BY OTHER PARTIES.—Where the use by
others of the mark sought to be registered has been as a descriptive use
rather than a continued trade-mark use, but it appears that the mark
was "used in the usual and regular order of business on the tins or
kegs or whatever containers contained the colors," *Held* that such use
was similar to a trade-mark use and would render the users liable
under section 16 of the trade act to be held as infringers if the applicant's mark should be registered, and that since such use if subsequent
to applicant's would infringe, when prior thereto it is good cause for
refusing registration. *Id.*

89. CLASSIFICATION—DIVISION.—The scope of the classes of merchandise
established under section 2 of the act of May 4, 1906, is peculiarly
within the knowledge of the Examiner of Trade-Marks, and his conclusions upon questions of classification will not be disturbed except in
cases of obvious error. *Ex parte Nestlé and Anglo-Swiss Condensed
Milk Company.* 227.

90. SAME—SAME.—Where it appears from the labels submitted as specimens
that "coffee with milk" is intended for use in making beverages only
and that "cocoa with milk" and "chocolate with milk" are adapted to
be used in making "chocolate creams," "blanc-mange," and for "other
culinary purposes," *Held* that the requirement that the former be
classified in Class 46, Coffee, tea, and substitutes, and the latter in
Class 47, Confectionery, in order to preserve the established lines of
classes is well founded. *Id.*

91. "INFALLIBLE"—DESCRIPTIVE—NOT REGISTRABLE.—*Held* that the word
"Infallible" as applied to flour is descriptive or indicative of the
quality of the flour, and therefore not registrable. *Ex parte The Sauers
Milling Company.* 231.

a cross having rays radiating from its upper portion, associated with the title-phrase " Liqueur de St. Dominic," and the name " Charles Jacquin et Cie " appearing above and below the title-phrase, the whole inclosed in a circular border of dots and crosses arranged alternately, does not so nearly resemble the mark of the opponent, which comprises the words " Veritable Benedictine," " D. O. M.," and the representation of a " cross," as to cause confusion in the mind of the public, where crosses of various types have been used upon liqueurs and cordials by many other dealers. *Gourd* v. *Charles Jacquin et Cie., Inc.*, 242.

102. SAME—UNFAIR COMPETITION IN TRADE NOT CONSIDERED.—The question of unfair competition in trade cannot be considered in an opposition proceeding. *Id.*

103. LIMITATION BY REGISTRATION.—Where it is stated in the certificate of registration that the essential features of the trade-mark are the words " Veritable Benedictine," " D. O. M.," and a " cross," *Held* that the registrant having limited himself in the registration to a mark containing these features is not entitled broadly to the use of a cross so as to exclude others from the use of the same regardless of the similarity of the marks. (citing *Richter* v. *Reynolds et al.*, C. D., 1894, 260; 67 O. G., 404; 59 Fed. Rep., 577.) *Id.*

104. SAME—PRACTICE.—Where no pleading was filed in response to a notice of opposition and no action taken in response to an order to show cause why the opposition should not be sustained, *Held* that a judgment sustaining such notice of opposition was proper. *The Drevet Manufacturing Company* v. *The Liquozone Company*, 247.

105. SAME—ALLEGATION OF ADOPTION AND USE.—An allegation in a notice of opposition that the opposer adopted " Glycozone " as a trade-mark for a remedy for the treatment of germicidal diseases and that its use was begun prior to the use of the trade-mark " Liquozone" and that it is still sold to a large extent is a sufficient allegation of ownership and continuous use. *Id.*

106. SAME—SIMILARITY OF MARKS.—Where two marks which are not identical in appearance are similar in sound and it is alleged that such similarity has caused confusion in trade and the applicant does not see fit to put the opposer to proof of the allegation, the contention as to similarity should be sustained. *Id.*

107. INTERFERENCE—USE OF MARK.—A mere casual use of a mark is insufficient to establish a right to protection in the use thereof. *Luthy & Company* v. *Peoria Drill & Seeder Company*, 250.

108. SAME—SAME.—Slight and immaterial changes in an article to which a trade-mark is applied do not render the use of said mark fraudulent. *Id.*

109. SAME—ABANDONMENT.—A declaration of abandonment filed for the purpose of terminating an interference must be unconditional and unequivocal. (*Gabrielson* v. *Felbel*, C. D., 1906, 108; 121 O. G., 691.) *The Thomson Wood Finishing Company* v. *Rinald Brothers*, 256.

110. ANTICIPATION.—" La Camille " for corsets, *Held* to be anticipated by " Camille Royal Combination " for feminine apparel. *Ex parte International Corset Company*, 265.

111. IDENTITY OF MERCHANDISE—FEMININE APPAREL—CORSETS.—*Held* that the term " feminine apparel " stated as the particular description of the goods to which the registrant's mark is applied is comprehensive enough to include " corsets." *Id.*

123. DESCRIPTIVE WORDS ARRANGED IN AN ARBITRARY MANNER.—Combining descriptive words in an arbitrary manner does not render a mark registrable. *Id.*

124. OWNERSHIP BY PARTNERS—RIGHTS UPON DISSOLUTION.—Whatever interest in a trade-mark a retiring partner of a firm may have had ceases upon his withdrawal from the firm and remains with the surviving partner. * *Bluthenthal and Bickart v. Bigbie Brothers & Company,* 665.

125. OPPOSITION—REGISTRATION OF A NON-TECHNICAL MARK MAY BE OPPOSED BY OWNER OF A SIMILAR NON-TECHNICAL MARK.—Where an applicant seeks to register a mark under the ten-year proviso of section 5 of the act of 1905 and the registration of that mark is opposed by a party who claims ownership of a mark consisting of a surname or a geographical term which resembles the applicant's mark, *Held* that the notice of opposition will not be dismissed upon the ground that the opposer's mark is not a proper trade-mark. *Kentucky Distilleries and Warehouse Company* v. *P. Dempsey & Company,* 309.

126. SAME—PROOF OF CONFUSION IN TRADE.—Where the opposer alleged in his notice of opposition that confusion in trade had occurred, but introduced no testimony that such confusion had taken place, and where the marks are not so nearly alike that in the absence of proof as to actual confusion it can be held that confusion would be likely to occur, the applicant's mark will not be refused. *Id.*

127. SAME—DOUBTFUL SIMILARITY—"MAYFIELD," "MAYFAIR."—*Held* that the marks "Mayfield" and "Mayfair" are not so nearly alike that in the absence of proof as to actual confusion it can be held that confusion would be so likely to occur as to justify refusing to register the applicant's mark. *Id.*

128. SAME—DISSIMILARITY OF MARKS—DEMURRER.—*Held* that trade-marks for electric-wiring purpose consisting of the words "Wirelets" and "Condulets" are not so similar in appearance as to deceive a purchaser using reasonable care and diligence in the selection of the goods and that a demurrer to the notice of opposition was properly sustained. *Crouse-Hinds Company* v. *Appleton Electric Company,* 333.

129. SAME—SAME—UNFAIR COMPETITION IN TRADE NOT CONSIDERED.—The question of unfair competition in trade cannot be considered in an opposition proceeding. *Id.*

130. INTERFERENCE—RE-FORMATION OF ISSUE.—Where the issue of a trade-mark interference is declared to be for "mixed paints," it should not be re-formed so as to read "ready-mixed paints" when one of the parties does not use the words "ready-mixed paints" to define the goods upon which the mark is used. *Lewis and Bros. Company* v. *Phoenix Paint and Varnish Company,* 334.

131. SAME—SAME CLASS OF GOODS—CONSIDERED AT FINAL HEARING.—The question whether the goods to which a mark forming the issue of an interference has been applied by the respective parties are of the same descriptive properties is a question which may be decided by the Examiner of Interferences at final hearing. *Id.*

132. ABANDONMENT—SUBSEQUENT RIGHTS OF OTHERS.—If the word "Star" or the representation of a star as a trade-mark for beer has become public property, an applicant is not entitled to the registration of a mark for the same class of goods consisting of two superimposed equilateral triangles forming a six-pointed star, with a monogram of the letters "G. E." in the center thereof, unless his mark differs from a

mere star to such an extent that the simultaneous use of the same would not be likely to cause confusion in the mind of the public. *Ehret* v. *Star Brewery Company*, 346.

133. IDENTITY.—A mark consisting of a six-pointed star having in the center thereof a monogram of the letters " G. E.," *Held* to so nearly resemble a mark in prior use by another, consisting of a six-pointed star surrounded by two concentric circles, between which are the words " The Celebrated Star Lager Beer," as to be likely to cause confusion in the mind of the public. *Id.*

134. ANTICIPATION.—*Held* that the trade-mark " Royal Blend " for coffee is anticipated by a registered mark comprising a Maltese cross surmounted by a crown and bearing the word " Royal." *Held* also that the word " Blend " for coffee is merely descriptive of the merchandise, and its presence as part of the mark does not confer any arbitrary or distinguishing significance upon the mark sought to be registered. *Ex parte Granger & Company*, 349.

135. ACTION OF THE EXAMINER—POINTING OUT DISTINCTIONS BETWEEN APPLICANT'S MARK AND PREVIOUSLY REGISTERED MARKS.—While it is proper for an applicant to cite previous registration for the purpose of showing that his mark should be registered, it is not necessary for the Examiner of Trade-Marks to explain why these marks were registered. *Ex parte Vance Shoe Company*, 354.

136. REQUIREMENT THAT CLASS OF MERCHANDISE BE LIMITED IS IN EFFECT A REJECTION.—Where the Examiner required that the particular description of his merchandise stated by the applicant as falling in Class 23 be limited to " Pliers without a cutting edge " or that the class stated be changed to Class 20 and the particular description of goods made to read " Nippers and pliers provided with a cutting edge." *Held* that this action is in effect a refusal to register the mark, and the applicant's remedy is by appeal and not by petition. *Ex parte Utica Drop Forge and Tool Co.*, 365.

137. THE WORDS " SPOT CORD " AND A CORD HAVING SPOTS THEREON NOT ALTERNATIVES.—The words " Spot Cord " as a trade-mark for braided sash-cord, *Held* not in conflict with the use of spots on a cord, the latter being a mere symbol which may be translated into words other than the words " spot cord." Spots on a cord and the words " Spot Cord " are not true alternatives. *Silver Lake Company* v. *Samson Cordage Works*, 370.

138. THE WORDS " SPOT CORD " NOT INDEFINITE.—The words " Spot Cord " not being the mere equivalent or alternative, in a trade-mark sense, of a cord having spots thereon, such words will not be refused registration on the ground that a mark consisting of spots on a cord is too indefinite to form trade-mark subject-matter. *Id.*

139. INTERFERENCE IN FACT—ARROW PIERCING LETTER " B " AND LETTERS " X L C R " PIERCED BY ARROW INCLOSED IN DIAMOND-SHAPED BORDER.—*Held* that a trade-mark comprising the letters " X L C R " pierced by an arrow, the whole being inclosed in a diamond-shaped figure, does not so nearly resemble a trade-mark for the same merchandise which comprises the letter " B " pierced by an arrow as to cause confusion in the mind of the public. *The W. Bingham Company* v. *G. W. Bradley's Sons*, 375.

140. SAME—EX PARTE SMITH & HEMENWAY DISTINGUISHED.—Where the words are alike in appearance or where the common features of a mark are of sufficient prominence as to cause the merchandise

of both parties to become known by a common name, the interference should be continued in order that the Office may have the benefit of testimony showing whether confusion in trade has actually occurred; but where there is so marked a difference in appearance and significance of the marks when considered as a whole that no likelihood of confusion in trade is apparent the interference should be dissolved. *Id.*

141. "BROOKWOOD"—NOT GEOGRAPHICAL.—The mark "Brookwood" for whisky *Held* not geographical. *L. W. Levy & Co.* v. *Uri*, 386.

142. APPLICATION—ALLEGATION UNDER TEN-YEAR PROVISO—TECHNICAL MARK—Where the declaration of an application for the registration of a trade-mark contains the allegations requisite to obtain registration of the mark as a technical mark, it may be registered as such, notwithstanding the fact that other allegations are made sufficient to obtain registration under the ten-year proviso of the trade-mark act, such additional allegations being in the nature of mere surplusage. *Id.*

143. ASSIGNMENT OF BUSINESS AND TRADE-MARK FILING OF APPLICATION.— The assignment of the business with which a trade-mark is used, together with the trade-mark and good-will of the business after the filing of an application for the registration of such mark, does not work an adandonment of the application, but necessitates suitable action under section 10 of the trade-mark act in order that registration may be issued to the assignee. *Id.*

144. MISREPRESENTATION ON LABELS—REGISTRATION NOT REFUSED.—The use of the words "Pure Old Rye Whisky" on labels containing the trademark "Brookwood" adopted and used for whisky composed of rye and other whiskies *Held* not such deception as would warrant the refusal of registration, there apparently being no actual intent to deceive. *Id.*

145. INTERFERENCE—SUBSTITUTION OF ASSIGNEE.—Where an application for registration of a trade-mark which is involved in an interference has been assigned and the assignment recorded in the Patent Office contains a request that the certificate of registration be issued to the assignee, *Held* that the assignee may be substituted for the nominal applicant in the interference proceedings. *L. W. Levy & Company* v. *Uri*, 389.

146. SAME—SAME.—*Held* that the technical relation of plaintiff and defendant does not exist in trade-mark interference proceedings and that the substitute for the applicant of the party to whom the certificate of registration may be issued if the final decision in the interference should be adverse to the opposing party should not be refused even if the courts do not allow the substitution by a defendant of a party defendant. *Id.*

147. DECEPTIVE.—A mark containing the legend "Guaranteed under the Food and Drugs Act of June 30, 1906," *Held* deceptive, since the registration of such a mark would lead the public to believe that the Government had guaranteed the purity of the article upon which the mark was used. *Ex parte Alart and McGuire*, 409.

148. PUBLIC POLICY.—It is believed to be against public policy to register a mark which indicates or suggests that the Government has given its official approval of the character or quality of the merchandise to which such mark is affixed. *Id.*

149. MARK MUST BE AFFIXED TO THE GOODS.—In order that a party may acquire a trade-mark right, it must be shown that he affixed the mark to

Lightning Source UK Ltd.
Milton Keynes UK
UKHW011833031218
333382UK00008B/540/P